Criminology

Criminology

LARRY J. SIEGEL
University of Massachusetts—Lowell

Fifth Edition

WEST PUBLISHING COMPANY

Minneapolis/St. Paul   New York   Los Angeles   San Francisco

Copyediting: Marilynn Taylor
Text Design: Lois Stanfield, LightSource Images
Proofreading: Lynn Reichel
Indexing: E. Virginia Hobbs
Composition: Parkwood Composition Services, Inc.
Cover Image: Georgia O'Keeffe (American, 1889–1988),
　　"Radiator Building" Night—New York, 1927

Production, Prepress, Printing and Binding by West Publishing Company.

WEST'S COMMITMENT TO THE ENVIRONMENT

In 1906, West Publishing Company began recycling materials left over from the production of books. This began a tradition of efficient and responsible use of resources. Today, up to 95 percent of our legal books and 70 percent of our college and school texts are printed on recycled, acid-free stock. West also recycles nearly 22 million pounds of scrap paper annually—the equivalent of 181,717 trees. Since the 1960s, West has devised ways to capture and recycle waste inks, solvents, oils, and vapors created in the printing process. We also recycle plastics of all kinds, wood, glass, corrugated cardboard, and batteries, and have eliminated the use of Styrofoam book packaging. We at West are proud of the longevity and the scope of our commitment to the environment.

 TEXT IS PRINTED ON 10% POST CONSUMER RECYCLED PAPER　PRINTED WITH SOY INK　

British Library Cataloguing-in-Publication Data. A catalogue record for this book is available from the British Library.

Library of Congress Cataloging-in-Publication Data

Siegel, Larry J.
　Criminology / Larry J. Siegel. —5th ed.
　　p.　cm.
　Includes bibliographical references and indexes.
　ISBN 0-314-04560-0
　1. Criminology.　2. Crime—United States.　I. Title.
HV6025.S48　1995
364—dc20
　　　　　　　　　　　　　　　　94-34057
　　　　　　　　　　　　　　　　CIP

Photo Credits
2 ©Daniel Brody/Stock, Boston; 3 AP/Wide World Photos; 4 AP Photo/Pool, Ken Lubas, Los Angeles Times; 10 AP/Wide World Photos; 17 ©1990 Jeffrey D. Scott/Impact Visuals; 19 AP/Wide World Photos; 26 ©L. Waters/Palm Beach Post/Sygma; 31 The Bettmann Archive; 36 The Bettmann Archive; 38 ©1994 James Carroll/ Stock, Boston; 44 Bill Biggart/Impact Visuals; 47 Jean-Louis Atlan/Sygma; 54 ©1993 Michael Dwyer/Stock, Boston; 58 AP/Wide World Photos; 63 AP/Wide World Photos; 66 ©Gale Zucker/Stock, Boston; 81 UPI/Bettmann; 84 ©1991 Andrew Lichtensten/Impact Visuals; 92 AP/Wide World Photos; 94 ©1992 Brian Palmer/Impact Visuals; 95 Marcus Felson; 95 Lawrence E. Cohen; 101 ©1991 Harvey Finkle/Impact Visuals; 108 The Bettmann Archive; 110 The Bettmann Archive; 117 ©1992 Spencer Grant/ Stock, Boston; 119 ©1991 Fredrik Bodin/Stock, Boston; 122 AP/ Wide World Photos; 137 ©L. P. Laffont/Sygma; 138 AP/Wide World Photos; 139 The Bettmann Archive; 141 Alexander Tsiaras/Stock, Boston; 144 Terrie Moffitt; 155 AP/Wide World Photos; 159 ©Gale Zucker/Stock, Boston; 173 ©1990 Fredrik Bodin/Stock, Boston; 175 AP/Wide World Photos; 179 William Julius Wilson; 190 ©1984 John Maher/Stock, Boston; 197 ©1992 Ted Soqui/ Impact Visuals; 205 AP/Wide World Photos; 209 ©1983 Jim Anderson/Stock, Boston; 216 ©1993 Andrew Lichtenstein/ Impact Visuals; 219 ©1986 Terry Lee/Black Star; 221 ©1991 Thor Swift/ Impact Visuals; 235 AP/Wide World Photos; 238 AP/Wide World Photos; 242 AP/Wide World Photos; 255 Meda Chesney-Lind; 257 ©1993 Marilyn Humphries/Impact Visuals; 263 UPI/Bettmann; 265 ©1993 Andrew Lichtenstein, Impact Visuals; 271 ©1994 Charles Kennard/Stock, Boston; 273 Travis Hirschi; 276 Fay Photo Service, 1949, Courtesy of Harvard Law School Art Collection; 283 ©1993 Jeffry D. Scott/Impact Visuals; 284 Lloyd DeGrane, University of Chicago News Office; 284 J. D. Levine, Northeastern University; 292 ©1984 George Cohen/Impact Visuals; 296 ©1990 Ted Soqui/ Impact Visuals; 310 J. D. Levine, Northeastern University; 315 AP/ Wide World Photos; 316 ©Bill Nation/Sygma; 331 ©1977 David A. Krathwohl/Stock, Boston; 340 ©1990 Akos Szilvasi/Stock, Boston; 344 AP/Wide World Photos; 346 Tom Ebenhoh; 350 AP/ Wide World Photos; 356 AP/Wide World Photos; 361 AP/Wide World Photos; 369 ©1991 Kirk Condyles/ Impact Visuals; 379 AP/ Wide World Photos; 382 UPI/ Bettmann; 385 AP/Wide World Photos; 394 Tannenbaum/ Sygma; 396 AP/Wide World Photos; 402 The Bettmann Archive; 405 ©1992 Rob Nelson/Black Star; 427 AP/ Wide World Photos; 431 ©1990 Bill Burke/Impact Visuals; 442 AP/ Wide World Photos; 443 ©1994 Jan Underwood/Sygma; 444 The Bettmann Archive; 446 ©Rhoda Sidney/Stock, Boston; 453 AP/ Wide World Photos; 464 ©1989 Spencer Grant/Stock, Boston; 472 ©1989 Dorothy Littell Greco/Stock, Boston; 480 AP/Wide World Photos; 491 ©1992 Tom McKitterick/Impact Visuals; 493 ©1992 Clark Jones/Impact Visuals; 495 AP/Wide World Photos; 497 TENPRINTER® photo courtesy of Digital Biometrics, Inc.; 507 AP/Wide World Photos; 511 ©1992 Ken Martin/Impact Visuals; 516 The Bettmann Archive; 529 AP/Wide World Photos; 540 AP/ Wide World Photos; 547 AP/Wide World Photos; 552 The Bettmann Archive; 563 ©1993 Linda Rosier/ Impact Visuals; 569 ©1990 Mark Ludak/Impact Visuals; 572 ©Andrew Lichtenstein/ Impact Visuals; **Color Timeline Insert:** (upper left) ©Cary Wolinsky/ Stock, Boston; (upper right) ©J. P. Laffont/Sygma; (lower left) AP/Wide World Photos; (lower right) ©Hazel Hankin/Stock, Boston; **Synopsis Insert:** (from left to right) Library of Congress; Library of Congress; Stock Montage, Inc.; Library of Congress; The Bettman Archive.

This book is dedicated to the memory of two great and inspiring teachers, taken from us much too soon, who set an example of scholarship that I have tried to follow:

Michael J. Hindelang (1945–1982)
Donald J. Newman (1924–1990)

Contents

☰ Section 3

CRIME TYPOLOGIES **291**

11 Violent Crime **292**

12 Economic Crimes: Street Crimes **331**

13 Organizational Criminality: White-Collar and Organized Crime **350**

Close-Ups

Preface

Events of the past few years remind us of the great impact crime, law, and justice have on the American psyche. The already famous, such as Leona Helmsley, Mike Tyson, O. J. Simpson, and Tonya Harding, made headlines for months when they became involved in crime. Some who were formerly unknown, such as John and Lorena Bobbitt and Lyle and Erik Menendez, became familiar names when they were involved in criminal acts that captivated public attention; one boy, Michael Fay, made headlines for his punishment—being flogged in Singapore. The media seems incapable of ever losing interest in notorious killers, serial murderers, drug lords, and sex criminals. It is not surprising then that many Americans are more concerned about crime than almost any other social problem. Most of us are worried about becoming the victims of violent crime, having our houses broken into or our cars stolen. We alter our behavior to limit the risk of victimization and question whether legal punishment alone can control criminal offenders. We watch movies about law firms, clients, fugitives, and stone-cold killers. We are shocked at graphic accounts of drive-by shootings, police brutality, and prison riots.

I, too, have had a life-long interest in crime, law, and justice. Why do people behave the way they do? What causes one person to become violent and antisocial, while another channels his or her energy into work, school, and family? How can the behavior of the "good boy in the high-crime neighborhood"—the "at-risk" kid who successfully resists the "temptation of the streets"—be explained? Conversely, what accounts for the behavior of the multimillionaire who cheats on his or her taxes or engages in fraudulent schemes? The former has nothing yet is able to resist crime; the latter has everything and falls prey to its lure.

I have been able to channel this interest into a career as a teacher of criminology. My goal in writing this text is to help students generate the same interest in criminology that has sustained me during my twenty-four years in college teaching. What could be more important or fascinating than a field of study that deals with such wide-ranging topics as the motivation for mass murder, the association between media violence and interpersonal aggression, the family's influence on drug abuse, and the history of organized crime? Criminology is a dynamic field, changing constantly with the release of major research studies, Supreme Court rulings, and governmental policy. Its dynamism and diversity make it an important and engrossing area of study.

One reason that the study of criminology is so important is that debates continue over the nature and extent of crime and the causes and prevention of criminality. Some view criminals as society's victims who are forced to violate the law because of poverty and the lack of opportunity. Others view aggressive, antisocial behavior as a product of mental and physical abnormalities, present at birth or soon after, which are stable over the life course. Still another view is that crime is a function of the rational choice of greedy, selfish people who can only be deterred though the threat of harsh punishments.

There is also concern about the treatment of known criminals: should they be punished? Helped? Locked up? Given a second chance? Should crime control policy focus on punishment or rehabilitation? When Michael Fay was flogged in Singapore, some commentators openly praised that country's government for its tough stance on crime; a few even voiced the opinion that corporal punishment might work well in this country. Would you like to see a whipping post set up in your town?

Because interest in crime and justice is so great and so timely, this text is designed to review these ongoing issues and cover the field of criminology in an organized and comprehensive manner. It is meant as a broad overview of the field, designed to whet the reader's appetite and encourage further and more in-depth exploration.

Topic Areas

Criminology is divided into four main sections or topic areas.

Section 1 provides a framework for studying criminology. The first chapter defines the field and discusses its most basic concepts: the definition of crime, the component areas of criminology, the history of criminology, criminological research methods, and the ethical issues that confront the field. The second chapter covers the criminal law and its functions, processes, defenses, and reform. Chapter 3 covers the nature, extent, and patterns of crime. Chapter 4 is devoted to the concept of victimization, including the nature of victims, theories of victimization, and programs designed to help crime victims.

Section 2 contains six chapters that cover criminological theory: why do people behave the way they do? These views include rational choice and deterrence theories (Chapter 5); biological and psychological views (Chapter 6); structural, cultural, and ecological theories (Chapter 7); social process theories that focus on socialization and include learning and control (Chapter 8); and social conflict and radical criminology (Chapter 9). Chapter 10 is new and covers the attempts by criminologists to integrate different theories into a unified whole.

Section 3 is devoted to the major forms of criminal behavior. Four chapters cover violent crime, common theft offenses, white-collar and organized crimes, and public order crimes, including sex offenses and substance abuse.

Section 4 focuses on the criminal justice system. The opening chapter provides an overview of the entire justice process, legal concepts, and justice perspectives. The following chapters cover police, court, and the correctional systems in greater depth.

The text has been carefully structured to cover relevant material in a comprehensive, balanced, and objective fashion.

What's New in This Edition

The fifth edition retains many of the same organizational features of the fourth edition with some notable differences. The material on the history of criminological theory and thought has been condensed and is now included in Chapter 1. Chapter 10 is new and is a detailed account of multifactor, latent trait, and life course theories. In addi-

tion to this new chapter, each of the preexisting chapters has undergone considerable revision and reworking.

Chapter 1, "Crime and Criminology," has been updated with a new section on the history of criminology. The time line tracing the history of criminological thought has been expanded.

Chapter 2, "The Criminal Law and Its Processes," contains new material on the development of the law, the association between crimes and torts, and revisions in the insanity plea.

Chapter 3, "The Nature and Extent of Crime," covers crime trends and patterns. New material is presented on gun control, including a discussion of the Brady Bill.

Chapter 4, "Victims and Victimization," focuses on the nature and extent of victimization, theories of victimization, and the government's response to victimization. New material is included on the costs of victimization and victimization within families.

Chapter 5, "Choice Theories," offers more material on the rational criminal, including the decision to choose crime, situational crime prevention, and routine activities theory. Braithwaite's concept of reintegrative shaming is discussed.

Chapter 6, "Biological and Psychological Theories of Crime Causation," includes expanded sections on the neuropsychology of conduct disorder and on the media and violence.

In Chapter 7, "Social Structure Theories," the discussion of teenage gangs has been updated. Two new versions of strain theory are discussed, including Agnew's general strain theory and Messner and Rosenfeld's institutional anomie theory.

Chapter 8, "Social Process Theories," updates material on control and learning theory, and discusses two new labeling-type theories: Kaplan's general theory of deviance and Hiemer and Matsueda's social control theory.

Chapter 9, "Social Conflict Theories," contains new material on radical feminist theory, left realism, peacemaking, and deconstructionism.

Chapter 10, "Integrated Theories: Multifactor, Latent Trait, and Life Course," a new chapter, contains detailed discussions of Sampson and Laub's crime in the making theory and Farrington's integrated approach to the study of delinquent careers, along with material on violent female career criminals.

Chapter 11, "Violent Crime," offers new material on mass murder, hate crimes, spouse abuse, and the causes of violence.

Chapter 12, "Economic Crimes: Street Crimes," now contains sections on juvenile fire starters and female burglars.

Chapter 13, "Economic Crimes: Organizational Criminality: White-Collar and Organized Crime," includes new material on controlling white-collar crime, the BCCI case, the Russian Mafia, and international white-collar crime.

Chapter 14, "Public Order Crime; Sex and Substance Abuse," contains new material on paraphilia, controlling prostitution, and drug legalization.

Chapter 15, "Overview of the Criminal Justice System," has new sections covering the analysis of justice goals and philosophies.

Chapter 16, "The Police," offers new material on problem-oriented, community, and private policing.

Chapter 17, "The Judicatory Process," presents new material on sentencing practices and the judicial process.

Chapter 18, "Corrections," includes updated sections on alternative sanctions, including fines, forfeiture, house arrest, electronic monitoring, and intensive probation supervision.

Alternative Versions

Once again, there are two versions of *Criminology*. Both have fourteen identical chapters covering crime, law, criminological theory, and crime typologies. One version, entitled *Criminology*, contains an additional four chapters covering the criminal justice system, while the other, entitled *Criminology: Theories, Patterns, and Typologies*, omits these chapters. The eighteen-chapter book is designed for instructors who wish to cover criminal justice institutions and practices within a criminology course, while the fourteen-chapter version is aimed at programs in which material on criminal justice is taught in a separate course or where time constraints limit the amount of textual material that can be covered.

Every attempt has been made to make the presentation of material interesting, balanced, and objective. No single political or theoretical position dominates the text; instead, the many diverse views that are contained within criminology and characterize its interdisciplinary nature are presented. The text includes analysis of the most important scholarly works and scientific research reports, while at the same time, it presents topical information on recent cases and events, such as the Bobbitt case and the Heidi Fleiss prostitution ring. To enliven the presentation, boxed inserts focus on important criminological issues and topics, such as the female burglars and whether crime pays.

Acknowledgments

Many people helped make this book possible. Those who reviewed the fourth edition and made suggestions that I attempted to follow to the best of my ability include: Thomas Arvanites, Jim Ruiz, Kevin Thompson, Agnes Baro, John Martin, Mae Conley, Mary Dietz, and Ed Wells.

Others who helped with material or advice include: Patricia Atchison, Joseph Blake, Thomas Courtless, Julia Hall, Linda O'Daniel, Nikos Passas, Kip Schlegel, Joseph Vielbig, Daniel Georges-Abeyie, Bonnie Berry, James Black, Stephen Brodt, Edward Green, Dennis Hoffman, Alan Lincoln, Gerrold Hotaling, Joseph Jacoby, James McKenna, Paul Tracy, Charles Vedder, Sam Walker, David Friedrichs, Chris Eskridge, William Wakefield, Frank Cullen, Mary Schwartz, Chuck Fenwick, John Laub, Spencer Rathus, Bob Regoli, Marvin Zalman, James Fyfe, Lee Ellis, Lorne Yeudall, Darrell Steffensmeier, M. Douglas Anglin, Bob Langworthy, Jim Inciardi, Alphonse Sallett, James A. Fox, Jack Levin, Charles Faupel, Graeme Newman, Meda Chesney-Lind, and Colin McCauley. Special thanks must also go to Kathleen Maguire, editor of the *Sourcebook of Criminal Justice;* the staffs at the Hindelang Research Center in Albany, New York, and the Institute for Social Research at the Unviersity of Michigan; James Byrne at the Criminal Justice Research Center at the University of Massachusetts-Lowell; and Kristina Rose and Janet Rosenbaum of the National Criminal Justice Reference Service.

The form and content of this new edition were directed by my editor, Mary Schiller. Without her guidance, I would not have been able to publish this book. Beth Olson, my production editor, must be given a lot of credit for putting together a beautiful design and going out of her way to be patient, kind, and sensitive.

Larry Siegel
Bedford, New Hampshire

Concepts
of Crime,
Law, and
Criminology

How is crime defined? How much crime is there, and what are the trends and patterns in the crime rate? How many people fall victim to crime, and who is likely to become a crime victim? How did our system of criminal law develop, and what are the basic elements of crimes? What is the science of criminology all about? These are some of the core issues that will be addressed in the first four chapters of this text. Chapter 1 introduces students to the field of criminology: its nature, area of study, methodologies, and historical development. Concern about crime and justice has been an important part of the human condition for more than 5,000 years, since the first criminal codes were set down in the Mideast. And while the scientific study of crime, criminology, is considered a modern science, it has existed for more than 200 years.

Chapter 2 introduces students to one of the key components of criminology—the development of criminal law. It discusses the social history of law, the purpose of law, and how law defines crime. Criminal defenses and the reform of the law are briefly examined. The final two chapters of this section review the various sources of crime data to derive a picture of crime in the United States. Chapter 3 focuses on the nature and extent of crime, while Chapter 4 is devoted to victims and victimization. There are important and stable patterns in the rates of crime and victimization that indicate that these are not random events. The way crime and victimization is organized and patterned profoundly influences how criminologists view the causes of crime.

Crime and Criminology

☰ Introduction

In August 1990, residents of Gainesville, Florida, were shocked when five young students were brutally murdered. Newspaper accounts told how the victims, four female University of Florida students and one male Santa Fe Community College student, had been stabbed dozens of times and raped, and their mutilated bodies posed in sexually suggestive positions; one had been beheaded.[1] Soon after the murders took place, a 35-year-old drifter named Danny Harold Rolling was arrested for a grocery store robbery. Rolling quickly became the prime suspect in the murder case, but it was not until nearly four years later that he was found guilty of killing the students.

Under Florida law, the jury in a capital case decides on the penalty in a separate hearing after guilt has been determined. On March 24, 1994, after 13 days of testimony, the jury recommended Rolling be sentenced to death.[2] During the jury phase of the sentencing, Rolling pleaded for mercy and claimed that his behavior was a result of the emotional and physical abuse he had suffered at the hands of his father. His mother, Claudia, a native of Shreveport, Louisiana, submitted a videotape backing his claim of abuse and ended it by stating, "Take me, I'm the one that had to have failed him somewhere." The recommendation next is considered by the trial judge who makes the final sentencing decision in the case. Rolling said that he wished he could turn back the clock to before the murders took place, but he told the judge, "alas, I am not the keeper of time,

Serial killer Danny Rolling after his arrest by police in Gainesville, Florida. Rolling was convicted and sentenced to death for killing five college students. Rolling claimed that his killing spree was a result of the childhood abuse he suffered at the hands of his father. Should a prior history of abuse be considered when punishing killers such as Rolling?

only a small part of history and mankind's fall from grace. I'm sorry, your honor."[3] The trial judge accepted the jury's recommendation and sentenced Rolling to death on April 20, 1994.

The Gainesville murders illustrate why crime and criminal behavior are topics that have long fascinated people. Crime touches all segments of society. Both the poor and desperate as well as the affluent engage in criminal activity. Crime occurs across racial, class, and gender lines. It involves some acts that shock the conscience and others that may seem to be relatively harmless human foibles.

As the Gainesville killings show, criminal acts may be the work of strangers who prey on people they have never met. Or they can involve friends and family members in **intimate violence.**[4] Regardless of whether crime is shocking or pardonable, there is still little consensus about its cause or what can be done to prevent it. What sets someone like Danny Rolling off? Can such behavior be excused, even if it is the product of a dysfunctional home and a diseased mind? Could someone who was really "normal" ever commit such horrible crimes? What can be done to avoid a Danny Rolling? Is it possible that his execution can deter other serial killers? Because these questions are difficult to answer, many people fear crime, and about half report being afraid to walk alone in their own neighborhood at night.[5] The public's fear may be justified because, as the

Former football star and Hollywood personality O. J. Simpson appears in criminal court with his attorney, Robert Shapiro, on June 20, 1994. Such high-profile cases have generated significant interest in the study of crime and justice. Can a well-known person such as Simpson receive a fair trial when the media focuses so much attention on the case?

Close-Up "Is the United States Crime-Prone?" indicates, the United States may be more crime-prone than most other nations.

Concern about crime and the need to develop effective measures to control criminal behavior have spurred the development of the study of **criminology.** This academic discipline is devoted to the development of valid and reliable information about the causes of crime as well as crime patterns and trends. **Criminologists** use scientific methods to study the nature, extent, cause, and control of criminal behavior. Unlike media commentators, whose opinions about crime can be colored by personal experiences, biases, and values, criminologists bring objectivity and the scientific method to the study of crime and its consequences. Because of the threat of crime and the social problems it represents, the field of criminology has gained prominence as an academic area of study.

This text reviews criminology and analyzes its major areas of inquiry. It focuses on the nature and extent of crime, the cause of crime, crime patterns, and crime control. This chapter introduces criminology: How is it defined? What are its goals? Its history? How do criminologists define crime? How do they conduct research? What ethical issues face those wishing to conduct criminological research?

What Is Criminology?

Criminology is the scientific approach to the study of criminal behavior. In their classic definition, criminologists Edwin Sutherland and Donald Cressey state:

> Criminology is the body of knowledge regarding crime as a social phenomenon. It includes within its scope the processes of making laws, of breaking laws, and of reacting toward the breaking of laws. . . . The objective of criminology is the development of a body of general and verified principles and of other types of knowledge regarding this process of law, crime, and treatment.[6]

Sutherland and Cressey's definition includes the most important areas of interest to criminologists: the development of criminal law and its use to define crime, the cause of law violations, and the methods used to control criminal behavior. Also important is their use of the term *verified principles* to signify the use of the scientific method in criminology. Criminologists use objective research methods to pose research questions (hypotheses), gather data, create theories, and test their validity.

They use every method of established social science inquiry: analysis of existing records, experimental designs, surveys, historical analysis, and content analysis.

An essential part of criminology is the fact that it is an **interdisciplinary** science. Relatively few academic centers grant graduate degrees in criminology. Many criminologists have also been trained in diverse fields, most commonly sociology, but also criminal justice, political science, psychology, economics, and the natural sciences. While for most of the twentieth century, criminology's primary orientation has been sociological, today, it can be viewed as an integrated approach to the study of criminal behavior. Though it combines elements of many other fields, the primary interest of its practitioners is understanding the true nature of law, crime, and justice.

Criminology and Criminal Justice

In the late 1960s, interest in the so-called crime problem gave rise to the development of research projects, such as those conducted by the American Bar Foundation, that were aimed at understanding the way police, courts, and correctional agencies actually operated.[7] Eventually, academic programs devoted to studying the **criminal justice system** were opened.

Although the terms *criminology* and *criminal justice* may seem similar, and people often confuse the two, there are major differences between these fields of study. Criminology explains the etiology (origin), extent, and nature of crime in society, whereas criminal justice refers to the agencies of social control that handle criminal offenders. While criminologists are mainly concerned with crime and its consequences, criminal justice scholars are engaged in describing, analyzing, and explaining the behavior of the agencies of justice—police departments, courts, and correctional facilities.[8]

Since both fields are crime-related, they do overlap. Criminologists must be aware of how the agencies of justice operate and how they influence crime and criminals. Criminal justice experts cannot begin to design programs of crime prevention or rehabilitation without understanding something of the nature of crime. It is common, therefore, for criminal justice programs to feature courses on criminology and for criminology courses to evaluate the agencies of justice. The tremendous interest in criminal justice has led to the creation of more than a thousand justice-related academic programs; not

CLOSE-UP

Is the United States Crime-Prone?

People in the United States are justifiably concerned about crime; most people view it as a major social problem. Public opinion polls indicate that about 40 percent of Americans feel it is not safe to walk at night in their own neighborhood! There are grounds for this concern, considering that the United States is more crime-prone than other industrialized countries. According to a report of the Sentencing Project, a private, non-profit agency devoted to improving the justice system, the crime rate in the United States exceeds that of most other nations. The report indicates that the United States led the world with its murder, rape, and robbery rates. The U.S. murder rate is four times as great as Italy's, nine times England's, and 11 times Japan's—even twice that of war-torn Northern Ireland. Violence directed against women is, comparatively, even more shocking: the rape rate in the United States is eight times higher than in France, 15 times higher than England's, 20 times that of Portugal, 23 times Italy's, 26 times greater than that of Japan, and 46 times higher than in Greece. The robbery rate in the United States was 150 times greater than in Japan, 47 times higher than in Ireland, and over 100 times greater than in Greece. Put another way, if the United States had the same murder rate as England's, it would experience 2,500 homicides a year instead of 24,000; if it had Japan's robbery rate, 4,500 robberies would occur anually instead

of the actual number of more than 600,000!

Considering these statistics, it is not surprising that the United States puts far more people in prison than other countries. As Table A and Figure A show, the percentage of the population sent to prison and jail in the United States exceeds that of such notoriously punitive countries as Singapore, Romania, and South Africa.

Despite this, some question exists of whether the United States is actually more punitive. Recent cross-national research by James Lynch shows that the United States is more punitive than some but not all other nations. Germany, for example, punishes both violent and

TABLE A Incarceration Rates for Selected Nations

1989		1992–1993	
Nation	**Rate of Incarceration per 100,000 Population**	**Nation**	**Rate of Incarceration per 100,000 Population**
United States	426	Russia	558
South Africa	333	United States	519
Soviet Union	268	South Africa	368
Hungary	196	Singapore	229
Malaysia	126	Romania	193
Northern Ireland	120	Hong Kong	179
Hong Kong	118	Poland	160
Poland	106	Thailand	159
New Zealand	100	New Zealand	135
United Kingdom	97	Canada	116
Turkey	96	Mexico	97
Portugal	83	Portugal	93
France	81	Spain	90
Austria	77	France	84
Spain	76	Germany	80
Switzerland	73	Greece	60
Australia	72		
Denmark	68		
Italy	60		
Japan	45		
Netherlands	40		
Philippines	22		

(Note: Data taken from Marc Mauer, *Americans Behind Bars: A Comparison of International Rates of Incarceration* [Washington, D.C.: The Sentencing Project, 1991]; idem, *Americans Behind Bars: The International Use of Incarceration* [Washington, D.C.: The Sentencing Project, 1994]. Incarceration rates for 1992/1993 are for either 1992 or 1993, depending on the availability of data for each nation.)

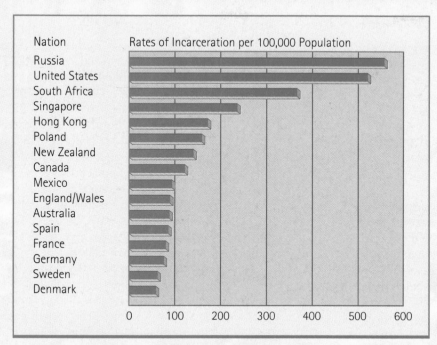

FIGURE A **Incarceration Rates for Selected Nations, 1992/1993**

property crimes more harshly than does the United States; our sentencing practices are quite similar to those used in Canada.

It is difficult to understand why the United States seems so much more crime-prone than other developed countries. Cultural dynamics may be operating here that make U.S. society more dangerous. Among the suspected reasons are: a large underclass; urban areas in which the poorest and wealthiest citizens reside in close proximity; racism and discrimination; the failure of the educational system; the troubled American family; easy access to handguns; and a culture that defines success in terms of material wealth.

Each of these factors may explain the disproportionate amount of crime in the United States.

Is Change in Sight?

These findings must be interpreted with some caution. International crime rate differences may be a function of the way crime data is gathered and processed: U.S. crime data may be more (or less) accurate than the statistics collected in other developed nations.

And, while the United States is still the "world leader" in violence, there is evidence of a disturbing upswing in violent crime abroad. Between 1989 and 1992, the murder rate in England rose 9 percent,

Germany's rose 37 percent, and Sweden's 16 percent. Racial assaults increased dramatically in Germany (up 400 percent) and England (up 107 percent) during the same period. Russia and the former Soviet republics have seen the rise of large-scale organized crime gangs that commonly use violence and intimidation.

Fueling the rise in European violence has been a dramatic growth in the number of illegal guns smuggled in from the former Soviet republics. Unrestrictive immigration has brought newcomers who face cultural differences, lack of job prospects, and racism. Social and economic pressures, including unemployment and cutbacks in the social welfare system, add pressure.

European crime rates are still comparably low. There were more homicides in New York City than in all of Germany in 1992. Yet international crime rates may yet converge.

Discussion Questions

1. Will countries such as Japan experience growth in their crime rates as they become more economically dominant?

2. What factors do you think contribute to the high U.S. crime rate?

SOURCE: James Lynch, "A Cross-National Comparison of the Length of Custodial Sentences for Serious Crimes," *Justice Quarterly* 10 (1993): 639–60; Committee on the Judiciary, U.S. Senate, *Fighting Crime in America: An Agenda for the 1990s* (1991); Marc Mauer, *Americans Behind Bars: The International Use of Incarceration* (Washington, D.C.: Sentencing Project, 1994); Elizabeth Neuffer, "Violent Crime Rise Fueling Fears in a Changing Europe," *Boston Globe*, 10 April 1994, p. 1.

surprisingly, these programs are often staffed by criminologists. These two fields not only coexist but help each other grow and develop.

Criminology and Deviance

Criminology is also sometimes confused with the study of **deviant behavior.** However, significant distinctions can be made between these areas of scholarship.

Deviant behavior is behavior that departs from social norms.[9] Included within the broad spectrum of deviant acts are behaviors ranging from violent crimes to joining a nudist colony.

Crime and deviance are often confused because not all crimes are deviant and not all deviant acts are crimes. For example, using recreational drugs, such as marijuana, may be illegal, but is it deviant? A significant percentage of U.S. youth have used or are using drugs. Therefore, to argue that all crimes are behaviors that depart from the norms of society is probably erroneous. Similarly, many deviant acts are not criminal. For example, suppose a passerby observes a person drowning and makes no effort to save that person. Though the general public would probably condemn the person's behavior as callous, immoral, and deviant, no legal action could be taken since citizens are not required by law to effect rescues. In sum, many criminal acts, but not all, fall within the concept of deviance. Similarly, some deviant acts, but not all, are considered crimes.

Two issues that involve deviance are of particular interest to criminologists. How do deviant behaviors become crimes? When should crimes be **legalized**—considered socially deviant behaviors immune to state sanction and legal punishment? The first issue involves the historical development of law. Many acts that are legally forbidden today were once considered merely unusual or deviant behavior. For example, the sale and possession of marijuana was legal in this country until 1937, when it was prohibited under federal law. To understand the nature and purpose of law, criminologists study the process by which crimes are created from deviance. Marijuana use was banned because of an extensive lobbying effort by Harry Anslinger, head of the Federal Bureau of Narcotics, who used magazine articles, public appearances, and public testimony to sway public opinion against marijuana use.[10] In one famous article, which appeared in 1937, Anslinger told how "an entire family was murdered by a youthful [marijuana] addict in Florida . . . [who] with an axe had killed his father, mother, two brothers, and a sister."[11] As a result of these efforts, a deviant behavior, marijuana use, became a criminal behavior, and previously law-abiding citizens were now defined as criminal offenders.

Criminologists also consider whether outlawed behaviors have evolved into social norms and, if so, whether they should either be legalized or have their penalties reduced **(decriminalized).** For example, there was much debate over the legalization of abortion and gambling, and there is frequent discussion about legalizing the use of recreational drugs and the creation of pornography today. If an illegal act becomes a norm, should society reevaluate its criminal status and let it become merely an unusual or deviant act? Conversely, if scientists show that a normative act, such as smoking or drinking, poses a serious health hazard, should it be made illegal? Many recent efforts have been made to control morally questionable behavior and restrict the rights of citizens to freedom of their actions.

In sum, criminologists are concerned with the concept of deviance and its relationship to criminality. The shifting definition of deviant behavior is closely associated with our concepts of crime. The relationship between criminology, criminal justice, and deviance is illustrated in Figure 1.1.

A Brief History of Criminology

The scientific study of crime and criminality is a relatively recent development. Although written criminal codes have existed for thousands of years, these were restricted to defining crime and setting punishments (see Chapter 2). What motivated people to violate the law remained a matter of conjecture.

During the Middle Ages, superstition and fear of satanic possession dominated thinking. People who violated social norms or religious practices were believed to be witches or possessed by demons. The prescribed method for dealing with the possessed was burning at the stake, a practice that survived into the seventeenth century. For example, between 1575 and 1590, Nicholas Remy, head of the Inquisition in the French province of Lorraine, ordered 900 sorcerers and witches burned to death; a contemporary, Peter Binsfield, the bishop of the German city of Trier, ordered the death of 6,500 people. An estimated 100,000 people were prosecuted throughout Europe for witchcraft during the sixteenth and sev-

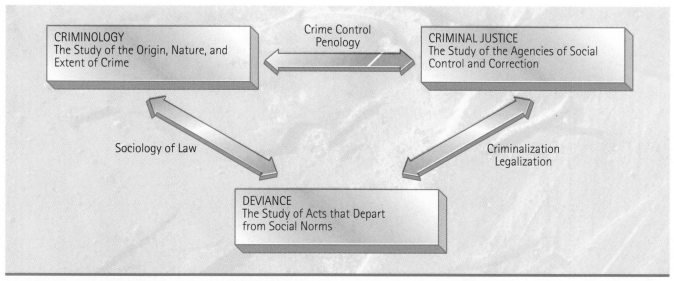

FIGURE 1.1   Relationship between Criminology, Criminal Justice, and Deviance

enteenth centuries. It was also commonly believed that some families produced offspring who were unsound or unstable and that social misfits were inherently damaged by reason of their "inferior blood."[12] Even those who questioned demonic possession advocated extremely harsh penalties as a means of punishing criminals and setting an example for others. Both violent and property crimes were often punished with execution.

Classical Criminology

By mid-eighteenth century, social philosophers began to call for rethinking the prevailing concepts of law and justice. They argued for a more rational approach to punishment, stressing that the relationship between crimes and their punishment should be balanced and fair. This view was based on the prevailing philosophy of the time called **utilitarianism,** which emphasized that behavior must be useful, purposeful, and reasonable. Rather than cruel public executions designed to frighten people into obedience or punish those the law failed to deter, reformers called for a more moderate and just approach to penal sanctions. The most famous of these was Cesare Beccaria (1738–1794), whose writings described both a motive for committing crime and methods for its control.

Beccaria believed that people want to achieve pleasure and avoid pain. Crimes must therefore provide some pleasure to the criminal. It follows that to deter crime, one must administer pain in an appropriate amount to counterbalance the pleasure obtained from crime. Beccaria's famous theorem was that

> In order for punishment not to be in every instance, an act of violence of one or many against a private citizen, it must be essentially public, prompt, necessary, the least possible in the given circumstances, proportionate to the crimes, and dictated by the laws.[13]

Crime then is a **rational choice** that can be controlled by the judicious application of criminal punishments.

The writings of Beccaria and his followers form the core of what today is referred to as **classical criminology.** As originally conceived in the eighteenth century, classical criminology theory had several basic elements: (1) people in society have free will to choose criminal or conventional solutions to meet their needs or settle their problems; (2) criminal solutions may be more attractive than conventional ones because they usually require less work for a greater payoff; (3) a person's choice of criminal solutions may be controlled by fear of society's reaction to such acts; (4) the more severe, certain, and swift the reaction, the better it can control criminal behavior; and (5) the most efficient crime prevention device is punishment sufficient to make crime an unattractive choice.

Criminalizing popular vices can have widespread consequences. During the 1920s the Volstead Act made it illegal to buy or sell alcohol. Prohibition-era bootleggers became rich supplying alcohol to the people who still wanted to drink. No bootlegger was more powerful than Chicago's Al Capone (wearing white hat), seen here in police custody in 1931.

The classical perspective influenced judicial philosophy during much of the late eighteenth and nineteenth centuries. Prisons began to be used as a form of punishment, and sentences were geared proportionately to the seriousness of the crime. Capital punishment was still widely used but slowly began to be employed for only the most serious crimes. The byword was "let the punishment fit the crime." Classical concepts have remained a central part of criminological thought and are the forerunners of the more recent rational choice theories of crime discussed in Chapter 5.

During the nineteenth century, a new vision of the world challenged the validity of classical theory and presented an innovative way of looking at the causes of crime.

Nineteenth-Century Positivism

While the classical position held sway as a guide to crime, law, and justice for almost 100 years, during the late nineteenth century, a new movement began that would challenge its dominance. The **positivist** tradition developed as the scientific method began to take hold in Europe. This movement was inspired by new discoveries in biology, astronomy, and chemistry. If the scientific method could be applied to the study of nature, then why not use it to study human behavior? Auguste Comte (1798–1857), considered the founder of sociology, applied scientific methods to the study of society. According to Comte, societies pass through stages that can be grouped on the basis of how people try to understand the world in which they live. People in primitive societies consider inanimate objects as having life (for example, the sun is a god); in later social stages, people embrace a rational, scientific view of the world. Comte called this final stage the positive stage, and those who followed his writings became known as positivists.

As we understand it today, the positivist tradition has two main elements. The first is the belief that human behavior is a function of external forces that are beyond individual control. Some of these forces are social, such as the effect of wealth and class, while others are political and historical, such as war and famine. Other forces are more personal and psychological, such as an individual's brain structure and his or her biological make-up or mental ability. Each of these forces operates to influence human behavior.

The second aspect of positivism is the embrace of the scientific method to solve problems. Positivists rely on the strict use of empirical methods to test hypotheses. That is, they believe in the factual, first-hand observation and measurement of conditions and events. Positivists would agree that an abstract concept such as "intelligence" exists because it can be measured by an IQ test. They would challenge a concept such as the "soul" because it is a condition that cannot be verified by the scientific method. The positivist tradition was spurred on by Charles Darwin (1809–1882), whose work on the evolution of man encouraged a nineteenth-century "cult of science" that mandated that all human activity could be verified by scientific principles.

Positivist Criminology

If the scientific method could be used to explain all behavior, then it was to be expected that by the mid-nineteenth century, "scientific" methods were applied to understanding criminality. The earliest of these "scientific" studies were biologically oriented. Physiognomists, such as J. K. Lavater (1741–1801), studied the facial features of criminals to determine whether the shape of ears, nose, and eyes and the distance between them were associated with antisocial behavior. Phrenologists, such as Franz Joseph Gall (1758–1828) and Johann K. Spurzheim (1776–1832), studied the shape of the skull and bumps on the head to determine whether these physical attributes were linked to criminal behavior. Phrenologists believed that external cranial characteristics dictate which areas of the brain control physical activity. Though their primitive techniques and quasi-scientific methods have been thoroughly discredited, these efforts were an early attempt to use a "scientific" method to study crime.

Cesare Lombroso and the Criminal Man

In Italy, Cesare Lombroso was studying the cadavers of executed criminals in an effort to scientifically determine whether law violators were physically different from people of conventional values and behavior. Lombroso (1835–1909), known as the "father of criminology," was a physician who served much of his career in the Italian army. That experience gave him ample opportunity to study the physical characteristics of soldiers convicted and executed for criminal offenses. Later, he studied inmates at institutes for the criminally insane at Pavia, Pesaro, and Reggio Emilia.[14]

Lombrosian theory can be outlined in a few simple statements.[15] First, Lombroso believed that serious offenders, those who engaged in repeated assault- or theft-related activities, inherited criminal traits. These "born criminals" inherited physical problems that impel them into a life of crime. This view helped spur interest in a **criminal anthropology.**[16] Second, born criminals suffer from **atavistic anomalies**—physically, they are throwbacks to more primitive times when people were savages. For example, criminals were believed to have the enormous jaws and strong canine teeth common to carnivores and savages who devour raw flesh. In addition, Lombroso compared criminals' behavior to that of the mentally ill and those suffering some forms of epilepsy. According to Lombrosian theory, criminogenic traits can be acquired through indirect heredity, from a "degenerate family with frequent cases of insanity, deafness, syphilis, epilepsy, and alcoholism among its members." Direct heredity—being related to a family of criminals—is the second primary cause of crime.

Lombroso's version of criminal anthropology was brought to the United States via articles and textbooks that adopted his ideas. He attracted a circle of followers who expanded upon his vision of biological determinism. His work was actually more popular in the United States than it was in Europe. By the turn of the century, American authors were discussing "the science of penology" and "the science of criminology."[17] The theories of criminology that have their roots in Lombroso's biological determinism and view individual characteristics as the cause of crime will be discussed in Chapter 6.

The Development of Sociological Criminology

At the same time that biological views were dominating criminology, another group of thinkers was developing the field of sociology to scientifically study the major social changes that were then taking place in nineteenth-century society.

Sociology seemed an ideal perspective from which to study society. After thousands of years of stability, the world was undergoing a population explosion: the population estimated at 600 million in 1700 had risen to 900 million by 1800. People were flocking to cities in ever-increasing numbers. Manchester, England, had 12,000 inhabitants in 1760 and 400,000 in 1850; during the same period, the population of Glasgow, Scotland, rose from 30,000 to 300,000. The development of such machinery as power looms had doomed cottage industries and given rise to a factory system in which large numbers of people toiled for extremely low wages. The spread of agricultural machines increased the food supply while reducing the need for a large rural work force; the excess laborers further swelled the cities' populations. At the same time, political, religious, and social traditions continued to be challenged by the scientific method.

Foundations of Sociological Criminology

The foundations of sociological criminology can be traced to the works of L. A. J. (Adolphe) Quetelet (1796–1874) and Emile Durkheim (1858–1917). Quetelet was a Belgian mathematician who began (along with a Frenchman, Andre-Michel Guerry) what is known as the cartographic school of criminology.[18] Quetelet, who made use of social statistics developed in France in the early nineteenth century (called the *Comptes generaux de l'administration de la justice*), was one of the first social scientists to use objective mathematical techniques to investigate the influence of social factors, such as season, climate, sex, and age, on the propensity to commit crime. Quetelet's most important finding was that social forces were significantly correlated with crime rates. In addition to finding a strong influence of age and sex on crime, Quetelet also uncovered evidence that season, climate, population composition, and poverty also were related to criminality. More specifically, he found that crime rates were greatest in the summer, in southern areas, among heterogenous populations, and among the poor and uneducated and were influenced by drinking habits.[19] Quetelet was a pioneer of sociologically oriented criminology. He identified many of the relationships between crime and social phenomena that still serve as a basis for criminology today.

Emile Durkheim

(David) Emile Durkheim (1858–1917) was one of the founders of sociology and a significant contributor to criminology.[20] His definition of crime as a normal and necessary social event has been more influential on modern criminology than any other.

Durkheim was a positivist who had a sociological rather than a biological orientation. According to his vision of social positivism, crime is seen as part of human nature because it has existed in every age, in both poverty and prosperity.[21] Crime is normal because it is virtually impossible to imagine a society in which criminal behavior is totally absent. Such a society would almost demand that all people be and act exactly alike. The inevitability of crime is linked to the differences (heterogeneity) within society. Since people are so different from one another and employ such a variety of methods and forms of behavior to meet their needs, it is not surprising that some will resort to criminality. Even if "real" crimes were eliminated, human weaknesses and petty vices would be elevated to the status of crimes. As long as human differences exist, then, crime is inevitable and one of the fundamental conditions of social life.

Crime, argued Durkheim, can also be useful and on occasion even healthy for a society to experience. The existence of crime implies that a way is open for social change and that the social structure is not rigid or inflexible. Put another way, if crime did not exist, it would mean that everyone behaved the same way and agreed totally on what is right and wrong. Such universal conformity would stifle creativity and independent thinking. To illustrate this concept, Durkheim offered the example of the Greek philosopher Socrates, who was considered a criminal and put to death for corrupting the morals of youth. In addition, Durkheim argued that crime is beneficial because it calls attention to social ills. A rising crime rate can signal the need for social change and promote a variety of programs designed to relieve the human suffering that may have caused crime in the first place.

In *The Division of Labor in Society,* Durkheim described the consequences of the shift from a small, rural society, which he labeled mechanical, to the more modern "organic" society with a large urban population, division of labor, and personal isolation. From this shift flowed **anomie,** or norm and role confusion, a powerful sociological concept that helps describe the chaos and disarray accompanying the loss of traditional values in modern society. Durkheim's research on suicide indicated that anomic societies maintain high suicide rates; by implication, anomie might cause other forms of deviance to develop.

Durkheim's writing and research has had a profound effect on criminology and will be discussed further in Chapter 7.

The Chicago School and Beyond

The primacy of sociological positivism was secured by research begun in the early twentieth century by Robert Ezra Park (1864–1944), Ernest W. Burgess (1886–1966), Louis Wirth (1897–1952), and their colleagues in the Sociology Department at the University of Chicago. Known as the **Chicago School,** these sociologists pioneered research on the social ecology of the city and inspired a generation of scholars to conclude that social forces operating in urban areas create criminal interactions; some neighborhoods become "natural areas" for crime.[22] These urban neighborhoods maintain such a high level of poverty that critical social institutions, such as the school and the family, break down. The resulting social disorganization reduces the ability of social institutions to control behavior, and the outcome is a high crime rate.

The Chicago School sociologists and their contemporaries focused on the functions of social institutions and how their breakdown influences behavior. They pioneered the ecological study of crime: crime was a function of where one lived.

During the 1930s, another group of sociologists, influenced by psychology, began to add a social-psychological component to criminological theory. They concluded that the individual's relationship to important social processes, such as education, family life, and peer relations, was the key to understanding human behavior. In any social milieu, children who grow up in a home wracked by conflict, attend an inadequate school, and associate with deviant peers become exposed to pro-crime forces. One position was that people *learn* criminal attitudes from older, more experienced law violators; another view was that crime occurs when families fail to *control* adolescent misbehavior. Each of these views linked criminality to the failure of socialization.

By mid-century, most criminologists had embraced either the ecological or the socialization view of crime. However, these were not the only views of how social institutions influence human behavior. In Europe, the writings of another social thinker, Karl Marx (1818–1883), had pushed the understanding of social interaction in another direction and sowed the seeds for a new approach in criminology.[23]

Conflict Criminology

Oppressive labor conditions prevalent during the rise of industrial capitalism convinced Marx that the character of every civilization is determined by its mode of production—the way its people develop and produce material goods (materialism). The most important relationship in industrial culture is between the owners of the means of production, the capitalist **bourgeoisie,** and the people who do the actual labor, the **proletariat.** The economic system controls all facets of human life; consequently, people's lives revolve around the means of production. The exploitation of the working class, he believed, would eventually lead to class conflict and the end of the capitalist system.

While Marx did not attempt to develop a theory of crime and justice, his writings were applied to legal studies by a few social thinkers, including Ralf Dahrendorf, George Vold, and Willem Bonger.[24] Their attempts to mold a Marxist/conflict criminology will be discussed in some detail in Chapter 10.

Though these writings laid the foundation for a Marxist criminology, decades passed before Marxist theory had an important impact on criminology. In the United States during the 1960s, social and political upheaval was fueled by the Vietnam War, the development of an antiestablishment counterculture movement, the civil rights movement, and the women's movement. Young sociologists who became interested in applying Marxist principles to the study of crime began to analyze the social conditions in the United States that promoted class conflict and crime. What emerged from this intellectual ferment was a Marxist-based radical criminology that indicted the economic system as producing the conditions that support a high crime rate. The radical tradition has played a significant role in criminology ever since.

Criminology Today

The various schools of criminology developed over 200 years. Though they have undergone great change and innovation, each continues to have an impact on the field. For example, classical theory has evolved into rational choice and deterrence theories, which will be discussed in

Chapter 5. Choice theorists argue that criminals are rational and use available information to decide if crime is a worthwhile undertaking; deterrence theory holds that this choice is structured by the fear of punishment.

Criminal anthropology has also evolved considerably. While criminologists no longer believe that a single trait or inherited characteristic can explain crime, some are convinced that biological and mental traits interact with environmental factors to influence all human behavior, including criminality. Biological and psychological theorists study the association between criminal behavior and such traits as diet, hormonal makeup, personality, and intelligence. This view will be discussed in Chapter 6.

Sociological theories, tracing back to Quetelet and Durkheim, maintain that individuals' life-styles and living conditions directly control their criminal behavior. Those at the bottom of the social structure cannot achieve success and thus experience anomie, strain, failure, and frustration. These views will be discussed in Chapter 7.

Some sociologists who have added a social-psychological dimension to their views of crime causation find that individuals' learning experiences and socialization directly control their behavior. In some cases, children learn to commit crime by interacting with and modeling their behavior after others they admire, while other criminal offenders are people whose life experiences have shattered their social bonds to society. This social process view will be discussed in Chapter 8.

The writings of Marx and his followers continue to be influential. Many criminologists still view social and political conflict as the root cause of crime. The inherently unfair economic structure of the United States and other advanced capitalist countries is the engine that drives the high crime rate; this view is analyzed in Chapter 9.

Recently, criminologists have been combining elements of each of these views into integrated theories of crime causation; these theoretical models will be discussed in Chapter 10.

Criminology, then, has had a rich history that still exerts an important influence on the thinking of its current practitioners. Each of the major perspectives is summarized in Figure 1.2.

☰ What Criminologists Do: The Criminological Enterprise

Regardless of their background or training, criminologists are primarily interested in studying crime and crim-

inal behavior. As Marvin Wolfgang and Franco Ferracutti put it:

> A criminologist is one whose professional training, occupational role, and pecuniary reward are primarily concentrated on a scientific approach to, and study and analysis of, the phenomenon of crime and criminal behavior.[25]

Within the broader arena of criminology are several subareas that, taken together, make up the **criminological enterprise.** Criminologists may specialize in a subarea, in the same way that psychologists might specialize in a subfield of psychology, such as child development, perception, personality, psychopathology, or sexuality. Some of the more important criminological specialties are described below and summarized in Figure 1.3.

Criminal Statistics

The subarea of criminal statistics involves measuring the amount and trends of criminal activity. How much crime occurs annually? Who commits it? When and where does it occur? Which crimes are the most serious? Criminologists interested in criminal statistics try to create valid and reliable measurements of criminal behavior. For example, they create techniques to access the records of police and court agencies. They develop paper-and-pencil survey instruments and then employ them with large samples of citizens to determine the percentage of people who actually commit crime and the number of law violators who escape detection by the justice system. They also develop techniques to identify the victims of crime to establish more accurate indicators of the "true" number of criminal acts: how many people are victims of crime and what percentage report crime to police. The study of criminal statistics is one of the most crucial aspects of the criminological enterprise because without valid and reliable data sources, efforts to conduct research on crime and create criminological theories would be futile.

Sociology of Law

The sociology of law is a subarea of criminology concerned with the role social forces play in shaping criminal law and, concomitantly, the role of criminal law in shaping society. Criminologists study the history of legal thought in an effort to understand how criminal acts, such as theft, rape, and murder, evolved into their present form. Criminologists also may be asked to join in the debate when a new law is proposed to banish or control behavior. For example, across the United States, a

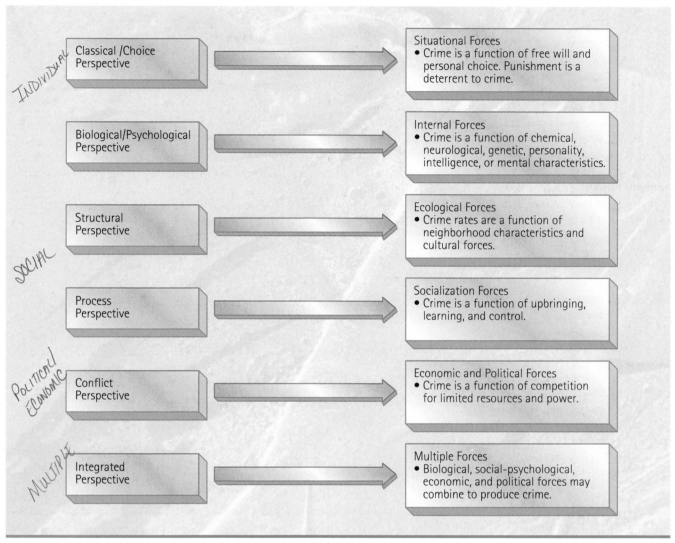

FIGURE 1.2   **The Major Perspectives of Criminology**

The major perspectives focus on *individual* (biological, psychological, and choice theories), *social* (structural and process theories), *political* and *economic* (conflict), and *multiple* (integrated) factors.

debate has been raging over the legality of art works, films, photographs, and even rock albums that some people find offensive and lewd and others consider harmless. What role should the law take in curbing the public's access to media and culture? Should society curb actions that some people consider immoral but by which no one is actually harmed? And how is harm defined: is a child who reads a pornographic magazine "harmed"? Criminologists also partake in updating the content of the criminal law. The law must be flexible to respond to changing times and conditions. Computer fraud, airplane hijacking, theft from automatic teller machines, and illegally tapping into TV cable lines are acts that obviously did not exist when the criminal law was originally formed. Sometimes, the law must respond to new versions of traditional or common acts. For example, Dr. Jack Kevorkian has made headlines for helping people to kill themselves by using his "suicide machine." While some felt that Kevorkian's device, which allows the user to self-inject a fatal overdose of drugs, was immoral and socially harmful, there was no law banning second-party help in suicides. In response, Michigan has passed legislation making it a felony to help anyone commit suicide.[26] Are Kevorkian's activities

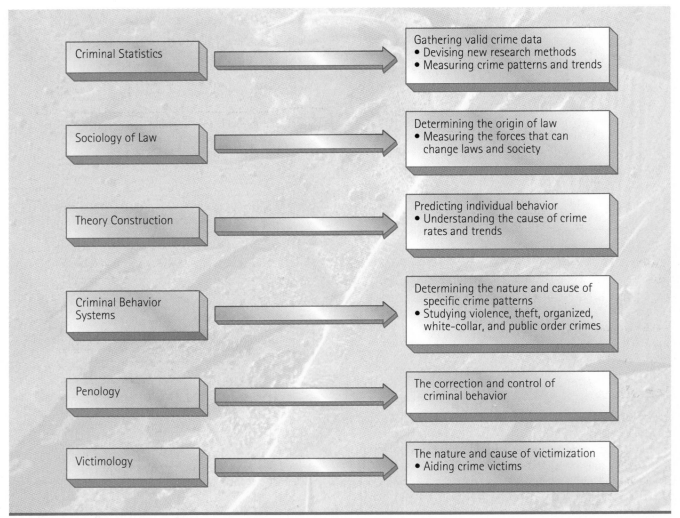

FIGURE 1.3   **The Criminological Enterprise**

the product of a care and concern for human suffering or a callous criminal act?

Theory Construction

A question that has tormented criminologists from the first is, why do people engage in criminal acts? Why, when they know their actions can bring harsh punishment and social disapproval, do they steal, rape, and murder? In short, why do people behave the way they do? Does crime have a social or an individual basis? Is it a psychological, biological, social, political, or economic phenomenon? Since criminologists bring their personal beliefs and backgrounds to bear when they study criminal behavior, there are diverse theories of crime

causation. Psychocriminologists view crime as a function of personality, development, social learning, or cognition. Biocriminologists study the biochemical, genetic, and neurological linkages to crime. Sociologists look at the social forces producing criminal behavior. Understanding the true cause of crime remains a difficult problem. Criminologists are still unsure why, given similar conditions, one person elects criminal solutions to his or her problems, while another conforms to accepted social rules of behavior. Further, understanding crime rates and trends has proven difficult: Why do rates rise and fall? Why are crime rates higher in some areas or regions than in others? Why are some groups more crime-prone than others?

Criminal Behavior Systems

The criminal behavior systems subarea of criminology involves research on specific criminal types and patterns: violent crime, theft crime, public order crime, and organized crime. Numerous attempts have been made to describe and understand particular crime types. For example, Marvin Wolfgang's famous study, *Patterns in Criminal Homicide,* is considered a landmark analysis of the nature of homicide and the relationship between victim and offender.[27] Edwin Sutherland's analysis of business-related offenses helped coin a new phrase—**white-collar crime**—to describe economic crime activities.

The study of criminal behavior also involves research on the links between different types of crime and criminals. This is known as crime typology. Unfortunately, typologies often disagree, so no standard exists within the field. Some typologies focus on the criminal, suggesting the existence of offender groups, such as professional criminals, psychotic criminals, occasional criminals, and so on. Others focus on the crimes, clustering them into such categories as property crimes, sex crimes, and so on.

Penology

The study of penology involves the correction and control of known criminal offenders. Penologists formulate strategies for crime control and then help implement these policies in "the real world." While the field of criminal justice overlaps this area, criminologists have continued their efforts to develop new crime-control programs and policies. Some criminologists view penology as involving rehabilitation and treatment. Their efforts are directed at providing behavior alternatives for would-be criminals and treatment for individuals convicted of law violations. This view portrays the criminal as someone society has failed; someone under social, psychological, or economic stress; someone who can be helped if society is willing to pay the price. Others argue that crime can only be prevented through a strict policy of social control. They advocate such strict penological measures as capital punishment and mandatory prison sentences. Future penological research efforts seem warranted, since most criminal offenders continue to commit crime after their release from prison (recidivate).

Victimology

Victimology focuses on the victims of crime. The popularity of victimology can be traced to the early work of Hans von Hentig and later work by Stephen Schafer.[28]

These authors were among the first to suggest that victims play an important role in the criminal process, that their actions may actually precipitate crime, and that the study of crime is not complete unless the victim's role is considered. In recent years, criminologists have devoted ever increasing attention to the victim's role in the criminal process. The areas of particular interest include: using victim surveys to measure the nature and extent of criminal behavior, calculating the actual costs of crime to victims, creating probabilities of victimization risk, studying victim culpability or precipitation of crime, and designing services for the victims of crime. Victimology has taken on greater importance as more criminologists focus their attention on the victim's role in the criminal event.

After his arrest for breaking and entering, AIDS sufferer Patrick McGuire was forced to spend his final months in jail after local hospitals refused to treat him because of his past behavior. Penologists must be able to find more effective methods for dealing with special-needs inmates such as McGuire.

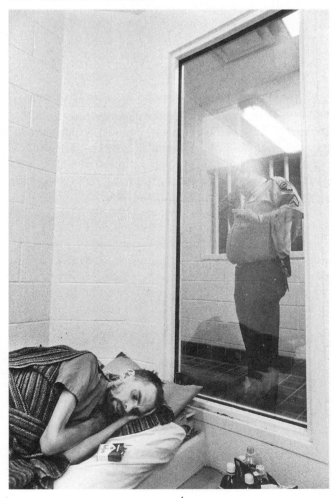

≡ How Do Criminologists View Crime?

Professional criminologists usually align themselves with one of several schools of thought or perspectives in their field. Each perspective maintains its own view of what constitutes criminal behavior and what causes people to engage in criminality. This diversity of thought is not unique to criminology; biologists, psychologists, sociologists, historians, economists, and natural scientists disagree among themselves about critical issues in their fields. It is not surprising that conflicting views exist within criminology, considering the multidisciplinary nature of the field. It is common for criminologists to disagree on the nature and definition of crime itself. A criminologist's choice of orientation or perspective depends in part on his or her definition of crime: the beliefs and research orientations of most criminologists are related to their conceptualization of crime. This section discusses the three most common concepts of crime used by criminologists.

The Consensus View of Crime

According to the consensus view, crimes are behaviors believed to be repugnant to all elements of society. The substantive criminal law, which sets out the definition of crimes and their punishments, reflects the values, beliefs, and opinions of society's mainstream. The term *consensus* is used because it implies that there is general agreement among a majority of citizens on what behaviors should be outlawed by the criminal law and henceforth viewed as crimes.

Several attempts have been made to create a concise, yet thorough and encompassing, consensus definition of crime. The eminent criminologists Edwin Sutherland and Donald Cressey have taken the popular stance of linking crime with the criminal law:

> Criminal behavior is behavior in violation of the criminal law . . . [I]t is not a crime unless it is prohibited by the criminal law [which] is defined conventionally as a body of specific rules regarding human conduct which have been promulgated by political authority, which apply uniformly to all members of the classes to which the rules refer, and which are enforced by punishment administered by the state.[29]

This approach to crime implies that its definition is a function of the beliefs, morality, and direction of the existing legal power structure. Note also Sutherland and Cressey's statement that the criminal law is applied "uniformly to all members of the classes to which the rules refer." This statement reveals the authors' faith in the concept of an ideal legal system that can deal adequately with all classes and types of people. While laws banning burglary and robbery are directed at controlling the neediest members of society, laws banning insider trading, embezzlement, and corporate price-fixing are aimed at controlling the wealthiest. The reach of the criminal law is not restricted to any single element of society.

The consensus model of crime is probably accepted by a majority of practicing criminologists and is the one most often used in criminology texts. Nonetheless, various issues confuse it, especially the relationship of crime to morality. Let us now examine that issue in more depth.

The Conflict View of Crime

In opposition to the consensus view, the conflict view depicts society as a collection of diverse groups—owners, workers, professionals, students—who are in constant and continuing conflict. Groups able to assert their political power use the law and the criminal justice system to advance their economic and social position. Criminal laws, therefore, are viewed as acts created to protect the haves from the have-nots. Conflict criminologists often compare and contrast the harsh penalties exacted on the poor for their "street crimes" (burglary, robbery, and larceny) with the minor penalties the wealthy receive for their white-collar crimes (securities violations and other illegal business practices). While the poor go to prison for minor law violations, the wealthy are given lenient sentences for even the most serious breaches of law.

According to the conflict view, the definition of crime is controlled by wealth, power, and position and not by moral consensus or the fear of social disruption.[30] Crime, according to this definition, is a political concept designed to protect the power and position of the upper classes at the expense of the poor. Even crimes prohibiting violent acts, such as rape and murder, may have political undertones: Banning violent acts ensures domestic tranquility and guarantees that the anger of the poor and disenfranchised classes will not be directed at their wealthy capitalist exploiters. The conflict view of crime then would include in a list of "real" crimes: violations of human rights due to racism, sexism, and imperialism; unsafe working conditions, inadequate child care, inadequate opportunities for employment and education, and substandard housing and medical care; crimes of economic and political domination; pollution of the environment; price-fixing; police brutality; assassinations and war-making; violations of human dignity, denial of physical needs and necessities, and impediments to self-determination; deprivation of adequate food and blocked opportunities to participate in political decision making.[31] While this list might be criticized as containing vague and subjectively chosen acts, an advocate of the conflict view would counter that consensus law also contains crimes that reflect opinion and taste, for example, obscenity, substance abuse, and gambling.

The Interactionist View of Crime

The interactionist view of crime traces its antecedents to the symbolic interaction school of sociology, first popularized by George Herman Mead, Charles Horton Cooley, and W. I. Thomas.[32] This position holds that: (1) people act according to their own interpretations of reality, according to the meaning things have for them; (2) they learn the meaning of a thing from the way others react to it, either positively or negatively; and (3) they reevaluate and interpret their own behavior according to the meaning and symbols they have learned from others.

According to the interactionist view of crime, the law reflects the preferences of people who hold social power and who use their influence to impose their definition of right and wrong on the rest of the population. The women depicted here are being publicly punished by order of Chinese dictator Chiang Kai Shek, who, in 1935, passed a law requiring women to show more courtesy, keep cleaner kitchens, and have a more frugal life. Can a small but powerful minority ever produce such ridiculous laws and punishments in this country?

According to this perspective, the definition of crime reflects the preferences and opinions of people who hold social power in a particular legal jurisdiction and who use their influence to impose their definition of right and wrong on the rest of the population. Criminals are individuals whom society chooses to label as outcasts or deviants because they have violated social rules. In a classic statement, sociologist Howard Becker argued, "The deviant is one to whom that label has successfully been applied; deviant behavior is behavior people so label."[33] Crimes are outlawed behaviors because society defines them that way and not because they are inherently evil or immoral acts.

The interactionist view of crime is similar to the conflict perspective because they both suggest that behavior is outlawed when it offends people who maintain the social, economic, and political power necessary to have the law conform to their interests or needs. However, unlike the conflict view, the interactionist perspective does not attribute capitalist economic and political motives to the process of defining crime. Instead, interactionists see the criminal law as conforming to the beliefs of "moral crusaders" or **moral entrepreneurs** who use their influence to shape the legal process in the way they see fit.[34] Laws against pornography, prostitution, and drugs are believed to be motivated more by moral crusades than by capitalist sensibilities. Consequently, interactionists are concerned with shifting moral and legal standards. To the interactionist, crime has no meaning unless people react to it, labeling perpetrators as deviant and setting them on a course of sustained criminal activity. The one-time criminal, if not caught or labeled, can simply return to a "normal" way of life with little permanent damage—the college student who tries marijuana does not view himself, nor do others view him, as a criminal or a drug addict. Only when prohibited acts are recognized and sanctioned do they become important, life-transforming events. Because of the damage it does, interactionists believe that society should intervene as little as possible in the lives of law violators lest they be labeled and stigmatized.

Defining Crime

The consensus view of crime dominated criminological thought until the late 1960s. Criminologists devoted themselves to learning why lawbreakers violated the rules of society. The criminal was viewed as an outlaw who, for one reason or another, flaunted the rules defin-

ing acceptable conduct and behavior. In the 1960s, the interactionist perspective gained prominence. The rapid change U.S. society was experiencing made traditional law and values questionable. Many criminologists were swept along in the social revolution of the 1960s and likewise embraced an ideology that suggested that crimes reflected rules imposed by a conservative majority on nonconforming members of society. At the same time, more radical scholars gravitated toward conflict explanations.

Today, each position still has many followers. This is important because criminologists' personal definitions of crime dominate their thinking, research, and attitudes toward their profession. Because they view crime differently, criminologists have taken a variety of approaches in explaining its causes and suggesting methods for its control. Considering these differences, it is possible to take elements from each school of thought to formulate an integrated definition of crime:

> Crime is a violation of societal rules of behavior as interpreted and expressed by a criminal legal code created by people holding social and political power. Individuals who violate these rules are subject to sanctions by state authority, social stigma, and loss of status.

This definition combines the consensus view's position that the criminal law defines crimes with the conflict perspective's emphasis on political power and control and the interactionist view's concepts of stigma. Thus, crime as defined here is a political, social, and economic function of modern life.

Doing Criminology

Criminologists have used a wide variety of research techniques to measure the nature and extent of criminal behavior. To understand and evaluate theories and patterns of criminal behavior, it is important to develop some knowledge of how these data are collected. It is also important to understand the methods used in criminology because this understanding provides insight into how professional criminologists approach various problems and questions in their field.

Survey Research

A great deal of crime measurement is based on analysis of survey data. Surveys include interviewing or questioning a group of subjects about research topics under consideration. This method is also referred to as **cross-sectional research,** since it involves the simultaneous measurement of subjects in a sample who come from different backgrounds and groups (that is, a cross-section of the community). Most surveys involve *sampling*—selecting for study a limited number of subjects who are representative of entire groups sharing similar characteristics, called *populations.* For example, a criminologist might interview a sample of 3,000 prison inmates drawn from the population of more than 950,000 inmates in the United States; in this case, the sample represents the entire population of U.S. inmates. Or a sample of burglary incidents could be taken from Miami; here, the sample would represent the population of Miami burglaries. It is assumed that the characteristics of people or events in a carefully selected sample will be quite similar to those of the population at large. Survey research can be designed to measure the attitudes, beliefs, values, personality traits, and behavior of participants. Self-report surveys ask participants to describe in detail their recent and lifetime criminal activity; victimization surveys seek information from people who have been victims of crime; attitude surveys may measure the attitudes, beliefs, and values of different groups, such as prostitutes, students, drug addicts, police officers, judges, or juvenile delinquents.

Surveys in Practice

Survey or cross-sectional research is among the most widely used methods of criminological study. It is an excellent and cost-effective technique for measuring the characteristics of large numbers of people. Because questions and methods are standardized for all subjects, uniformity is unaffected by the perceptions or biases of the person gathering the data. The statistical analysis of data from carefully drawn samples enables researchers to generalize their findings from small groups to large populations. Though surveys measure subjects at a single point in their lifespan, questions can elicit information on subjects' prior behavior as well as their future goals and aspirations.[35]

Despite their utility, surveys are not without their problems. Since they typically involve a single measurement, they are of limited value in showing how subjects change over time. In addition, surveys have been criticized because they assume that subjects will be honest and forthright. Though efforts are usually made to ensure the validity of questionnaire items, it is difficult to guard against people who either deliberately lie and misrepresent information or are unsure of answers and give mistaken responses. Surveys of delinquents and criminals are especially suspect since they rely on the willingness of a group of people not known for their candor about intimate and personal matters. Surveys are also limited when the area to be studied involves the way people interact with one another or other topics an individual may not be able to judge personally, such as how he or she is perceived by significant others. Despite these drawbacks, surveys continue to be an extremely popular method of gathering criminological data.

Longitudinal Research

Longitudinal research involves the observation of a group of people who share a like characteristic **(cohort)** over time. For example, researchers might select all girls born in Albany, New York, in 1970 and then follow their behavior patterns for 20 years. The research data might include their school experiences, arrests, hospitalizations, and information about their family life (divorces, parental relations). The subjects might be given repeated intelligence and physical exams; their diets could be monitored. Data could be collected directly from the subjects or without their knowledge from schools, police, and other sources. If the research were carefully conducted, it might be possible to determine which life experiences, such as growing up in an intact home or failing at school, typically preceded the onset of crime and delinquency.

Since it is extremely difficult, expensive, and time-consuming to follow a cohort over time and since most of the sample do not become serious criminals, another approach is to take an intact group of known offenders and look back into their early life experiences by checking their educational, family, police, and hospital records; this format is known as a retrospective cohort study.[36]

To carry out cohort studies, criminologists frequently use records of social organizations, such as hospitals, schools, welfare departments, courts, police departments, and prisons. School records contain data on a student's academic performance, attendance, intelligence, disciplinary problems, and teacher ratings. Hospitals record incidents of drug use and suspicious wounds indicative of child abuse. Police files contain reports of criminal activity, arrest data, personal information on suspects, victim reports, and actions taken by police officers. Court records allow researchers to compare the personal characteristics of offenders with the outcomes of their court appearances—conviction rates and types of sentence. Prison records contain information on inmates' personal characteristics, adjustment problems, disciplinary records, rehabilitation efforts, and length of sentence served.

Aggregate Data Research

Criminologists also make use of large data bases gathered by government agencies and research foundations. U.S. Census Bureau data, Labor Department employment data, reports of state correctional departments, and so on have all been used by criminologists in their research. The most important of these sources is the Uniform Crime Report (UCR), compiled by the Federal Bureau of Investigation (FBI).[37] The UCR is an annual report that reflects the number of crimes reported by citizens to local police departments and the number of arrests made by police agencies in a given year. The UCR is probably the most important source of official crime statistics and will be discussed more completely in Chapter 4.

Aggregate data can be used to focus on the social forces that effect crime. For example, to study the relationship between crime and poverty, criminologists make use of data collected by the Census Bureau on income and the number of people on welfare and single-parent families in an urban area and then cross-reference this information with official crime statistics from the same locality. Aggregate data can tell us about the effect of overall social trends and patterns on the crime rate.

Experimental Research

To conduct experimental research, criminologists manipulate or intervene in the lives of their subjects to see the outcome or effect the intervention has. True experiments usually have three elements: (1) random selection of subjects; (2) a control or comparison group; and (3) an experimental condition. For example, experimental research might involve a sample of convicted felons who have been sentenced to prison. Some of the sample, chosen at random, would be asked to participate in a community-based treatment program. A follow-up could then determine whether those placed in the community program were less likely to recidivate (repeat their offenses) than those who served time in the correctional institution.

An intact-group or quasi-experiment is undertaken when it is impossible to randomly select subjects or manipulate conditions. For example, a criminologist may want to measure the change in driving fatalities and drunk driving arrests brought about by a new state law creating mandatory jail sentences for persons convicted of driving while intoxicated (DWI). Since they cannot ask police to randomly arrest drunk drivers, they can compare the state's DWI arrest and fatality trends with those of nearby states that have more lenient DWI statutes. While not a true experiment, this approach would give an indication of the effectiveness of mandatory sentences since the states are comparable except for their drunk driving legislation.

Another approach, referred to as a time-series design, would be to record statewide DWI arrest and fatality data for the months and years preceding and following passage of the mandatory jail statute. The effectiveness of mandatory jail terms as a deterrent to DWI would be supported if a drop in the arrest and fatality rates coincided with the bill's adoption.

Criminological experiments are relatively rare because they are difficult and expensive to conduct; they involve the manipulation of subjects' lives, which can cause ethical and legal roadblocks; and they require long follow-up periods to verify results. Nonetheless, they have been an important source of criminological data.

Observational Research

Another common criminological method is the first-hand observation of criminals to gain insight into their motives and activities. This may involve going into the field and participating in group activities, such as was done in William Whyte's famous study of a Boston gang, *Street Corner Society*.[38] Other observers conduct field studies but remain in the background, observing but not being part of the ongoing activity.[39]

Still another type of observation involves bringing subjects into a structured laboratory setting and observing how they react to a predetermined condition or stimulus. This approach is common in studies testing the effect of observational learning on aggressive behavior; for example, exposing subjects to violent films and then observing their subsequent behavioral changes.[40]

Criminology then relies on many of the basic research methods common to other fields, including sociology, psychology, and political science. Multiple methods are needed to ensure that the goals of criminological inquiry can be achieved.

≡ Ethical Issues in Criminology

A critical issue facing students of criminology involves recognizing the field's political and social consequences.

All too often, criminologists forget the social responsibility they bear as experts in the area of crime and justice. When acted on by government agencies, their pronouncements and opinions become the basis for sweeping social policy. The lives of millions of people can be influenced by criminological research data. We have witnessed many debates over gun control, capital punishment, and mandatory sentences. While some criminologists have successfully argued for massive social service programs to reduce the crime rate, others consider them a waste of time. By holding themselves up to be experts on law-violating behavior, criminologists place themselves in a position of power; the potential consequences of their actions are enormous. Therefore, they must be aware of the ethics of their profession and prepared to defend their work in the light of public scrutiny. Major ethical issues include: what is to be studied, who is to be studied, and how studies are to be conducted.

Under ideal circumstances, when criminologists choose a subject for study, they are guided by their own scholarly interests, pressing social needs, the availability of accurate data, and other, similar concerns. Nonetheless, in recent years, a great influx of government and institutional funding has influenced the direction of criminological inquiry. Major sources of monetary support include the Justice Department's National Institute of Justice and the Office of Juvenile Justice and Delinquency Prevention. Both the National Science Foundation and the National Institute of Mental Health have been prominent sources of government funding. Private foundations, such as the Ford Foundation, have also played an important role in supporting criminological research.

Though the availability of research money has spurred criminological inquiry, it has also influenced the directions research has taken. Since state and federal governments provide a significant percentage of available research funds, they may also dictate the areas that can be studied. A potential conflict of interest arises when the institution funding research is itself one of the principal subjects of the research project. For example, governments may be reluctant to fund research on fraud and abuse of power by government officials. They may also exert a not-so-subtle influence on the criminologists seeking research funding: if criminologists are too critical of the government's efforts to reduce or counteract crime, perhaps they will be barred from receiving further financial help. This situation is even more acute when we consider that criminologists typically work for universities or public agencies and are under pressure to bring in a steady flow of research funds or to maintain the continued viability of their agency. Even when criminologists maintain discretion of choice, the direction of their efforts may not be truly objective.

A second major ethical issue in criminology concerns who is to be the subject of inquiries and study. Too often, criminologists have focused their attention on the poor and minorities while ignoring the middle-class criminal, white-collar crime, organized crime, and government crime. Critics have charged that by "unmasking" the poor and desperate, criminologists have justified any harsh measures taken against them. For example, social scientists have suggested that criminals have lower intelligence quotients than the average citizen and that minority status is the single greatest predictor of criminality.[41] Though such research is often methodologically unsound and admittedly tentative, it can focus attention on the criminality of one element of the community while ignoring others. Also, subjects are often misled about the purpose of the research. When white and African-American youngsters are asked to participate in a survey of their behavior, they are rarely told in advance that the data they provide may later be used to prove the existence of significant racial differences in their self-reported crime rates. Should subjects be told what the true purpose of a survey is? Would such disclosures make meaningful research impossible? How far should criminologists go when collecting data? Is it ever permissible to deceive subjects to collect data?

≡ Summary

Criminology is the scientific approach to the study of criminal behavior and society's reaction to law violations and violators. It is essentially an interdisciplinary field; many of its practitioners were originally trained as sociologists, psychologists, economists, political scientists, historians, and natural scientists. Criminology has a rich history with roots in the utilitarian philosophy of Becarria, the biological positivism of Lombroso, the social theory of Durkheim, and the political philosophy of Marx.

A number of fields are related to criminology. In the late 1960s, criminal justice programs were created to examine and improve the U.S. system of justice. Today, many criminologists work in criminal justice educational programs. Criminology and criminal justice are mutually dedicated to understanding the nature and control of criminal behavior. The study of deviant behavior also overlaps with criminology because many "deviant" acts, but not all, are violations of the criminal law.

Included among the various subareas that make up the criminological enterprise are criminal statistics, the sociology of law, theory construction, criminal behavior systems, penology, and victimology.

In viewing crime, criminologists use one of three perspectives: the consensus view, the conflict view, and the interactionist view. The consensus view is that crime is illegal behavior defined by the existing criminal law, which reflects the values and morals of a majority of citizens. The conflict view is that crime is behavior created so that economically powerful individuals can retain their control over society. The interactionist view portrays criminal behavior as a relativistic, constantly changing concept that reflects society's current moral values. According to the interactionist view, criminal behavior is behavior so labeled by those in power; criminals are people society chooses to label as outsiders or deviants.

Criminologists use a variety of research methods. These include surveys, longitudinal studies, record studies, experiments, and observations. In doing research, criminologists must be concerned about ethical standards because their findings can have a significant impact on individuals and groups.

≡ KEY TERMS

intimate violence	criminal anthropology
criminology	atavistic anomalies
criminologists	anomie
interdisciplinary	Chicago School
criminal justice system	bourgeoisie
deviant behavior	proletariat
legalized	criminological enterprise
decriminalized	white-collar crime
utilitarianism	moral entrepreneurs
rational choice	cross-sectional research
classical criminology	cohort
positivist	

≡ NOTES

1. "Jury Recommends Death for Florida Killer of Five," *New York Times,* 25 March 1994, p. A14.
2. Ibid.
3. Reuters, "Serial Murderer Asks Florida Judge for Mercy," *Boston Globe,* 30 March 1994, p. 13.
4. See, generally, Joel Milner, ed., Special Issue: Physical Child Abuse, *Criminal Justice and Behavior* 18 (1991); Russell Dobash, R. Emerson Dobash, Margo Wilson, and Martin Daly, "The Myth of Sexual Symmetry in Marital Violence," *Social Problems* 39 (1992): 71–86; Martin Schwartz and Walter DeKeseredy, "The Return of the 'Battered Husband Syndrome': Typification of Women as Violent," *Crime, Law and Social Change* 4 (1993, in press).
5. George Gallup, Gallup Poll, March 1992, in Kathleen Maguire, Ann Pastore, and Timothy Flanagan, *Sourcebook of Criminal Justice Statistics 1992* (Washington, D.C.: U.S. Government Printing Office, 1993), p. 189.
6. Edwin Sutherland and Donald Cressey, *Principles of Criminology,* 6th ed. (Philadelphia: J. B. Lippincott, 1960), p. 3.
7. For a review of the development of criminal justice as a field of study, see Frank Remington, "Development of Criminal Justice as an Academic Field," *Journal of Criminal Justice Education* 1 (1990): 9–20.
8. Marvin Zalman, *A Heuristic Model of Criminology and Criminal Justice* (Chicago: Joint Commission on Criminology Education and Standards, University of Illinois, Chicago Circle, 1981), pp. 9–11.
9. Charles McCaghy, *Deviant Behavior* (New York: MacMillan, 1976), pp. 2–3.
10. Edward Brecher, *Licit and Illicit Drugs* (Boston: Little, Brown, 1972), pp. 413–16.
11. Ibid., p. 414.
12. Eugen Weber, *A Modern History of Europe* (New York: W. W. Norton, 1971), p. 398.
13. Marvin Wolfgang, *Patterns in Criminal Homicide* (Philadelphia: University of Pennsylvania Press, 1958).
14. Howard Becker, *Outsiders: Studies in the Sociology of Deviance* (New York: Free Press, 1963), p. 21.
15. Ibid., p. 9.
16. Nicole Hahn Rafter, "Criminal Anthropology in the United States," *Criminology* 30 (1992): 525–47.
17. Ibid., p. 535.
18. L. A. J. Quetelet, *A Treatise on Man and the Development of His Faculties* (Gainesville, Fla.: Scholars' Facsimiles and Reprints, 1969), pp. 82–96.
19. Ibid., p. 85.
20. See, generally, Robert Nisbet, *The Sociology of Emile Durkheim* (New York: Oxford University Press, 1974), p. 209.
21. Emile Durkheim, *Rules of the Sociological Method,* trans. S. A. Solvay and J. H. Mueller, ed. G. Catlin (New York: Free Press, 1966), pp. 65–73; Emile Durkheim, *De la Division de Travail Social: Étude sur L'organisation des Societies Superieures* (Paris: Felix Alcan, 1893); idem, *The Division of Labor in Society* (New York: Free Press, 1964); idem, *Suicide: A Study in Sociology* (Glencoe, Ill.: Free Press, 1951).
22. Robert Park and Ernest Burgess, *The City* (Chicago: University of Chicago Press, 1925).
23. Karl Marx and Friedrich Engels, *Capital: A Critique of Political Economy,* trans. E. Aveling (Chicago: Charles Kern, 1906); Karl Marx, *Selected Writings in Sociology and Social Philosophy,* trans. P. B. Bottomore (New York: McGraw Hill, 1956). For a general discussion of Marxist

thought, see Michael Lynch and W. Byron Groves, *A Primer in Radical Criminology* (New York: Harrow and Heston, 1986), pp. 6–26.

24. Willem Bonger, *Criminality and Economic Conditions* (1916, abridged ed., Bloomington: Indiana University Press, 1969); Ralf Dahrendorf, *Class and Class Conflict in Industrial Society* (Palo Alto, Calif.: Stanford University Press, 1959).

25. Marvin Wolfgang and Franco Ferracuti, *The Subculture of Violence* (London: Social Science Paperbacks, 1967), p. 20.

26. Associated Press, "Michigan Senate Acts to Outlaw Aiding Suicides," *Boston Globe,* 20 March 1994, p. 22.

27. Wolfgang, *Patterns in Criminal Homicide.*

28. Hans von Hentig, *The Criminal and His Victim* (New Haven: Yale University Press, 1948); Stephen Schafer, *The Victim and His Criminal* (New York: Random House, 1968).

29. Edwin Sutherland and Donald Cressey, *Criminology,* 8th ed. (Philadelphia: J. B. Lippincott, 1960), p. 8.

30. Eugene Doleschal and Nora Klapmuts, "Toward a New Criminology," *Crime and Delinquency* 5 (1973): 607.

31. Michael Lynch and W. Byron Groves, *A Primer in Radical Criminology* (Albany, N.Y.: Harrow and Heston, 1989), p. 32.

32. See Herbert Blumer, *Symbolic Interactionism* (Englewood Cliffs, N.J.: Prentice-Hall, 1969).

33. Becker, *Outsiders,* p. 9.

34. Ibid.

35. Michael Gottfredson and Travis Hirschi, "The Methodological Adequacy of Longitudinal Research on Crime," *Criminology* 25 (1987): 581–614.

36. See, generally, David Farrington, Lloyd Ohlin, and James Q. Wilson, *Understanding and Controlling Crime* (New York: Springer-Verlag, 1986), pp. 11–18.

37. Federal Bureau of Investigation, *Crime in the United States, 1992* (Washington, D.C.: U.S. Government Printing Office, 1993).

38. William F. Whyte, *Street Corner Society* (Chicago: University of Chicago Press, 1955).

39. Herman Schwendinger and Julia Schwendinger, *Adolescent Subcultures and Delinquency* (New York: Praeger, 1985).

40. For a review of these studies, see L. Rowell Huesmann and Neil Malamuth, eds., "Media Violence and Antisocial Behavior," *Journal of Social Issues* 42 (1986): 31–53.

41. See, for example, Michael Hindelang and Travis Hirschi, "Intelligence and Delinquency: A Revisionist Review," *American Sociological Review* 42 (1977): 471–86.

2

The Criminal Law and Its Processes

Introduction

Despite the fact that criminologists hold different views about the concept of crime, most agree that the existing criminal law controls the definition and content of crime. The criminal code, developed over many generations, incorporates historical traditions, moral beliefs, and social values, as well as political and economic developments and conditions. The criminal law is a living concept, constantly evolving to keep pace with society. It governs the form and direction of almost all human interaction. Business practices, family life, education, property transfer, inheritance, and other common forms of social relations must conform to the rules set out by the legal code. Most important for our purposes, the law defines behaviors society labels as criminal. As noted in Chapter 1, most criminologists have adopted the legal definition of crime in their research and writing. Consequently, it is important for students of criminology to have a basic understanding of the law and its relationship to crime and deviance. This chapter will review the nature and purpose of the law, chart its history, and discuss its elements.

The Origin of Law

We know that crimes and criminal behavior were recognized in many early societies.[1] In preliterate societies, common custom and tradition (**mores** and **folkways**) were the equivalents of law. Each group had its own set of customs, which were created to deal with situations that arose in daily living. These customs would often be followed long after the reason for their origin was forgotten. Many customs had the force of law and eventually some developed into formal or written law.

The concept of crime was recognized in the earliest surviving legal codes. One of the first was developed in about 2000 B.C. by King Dungi of Sumer (an area that is part of present-day Iraq). Its content is known today because it was later adopted by Hammurabi (1792–1750 B.C.), the sixth king of Babylon, in his famous set of written laws that is today known as the **Code of Hammurabi.** Preserved on basalt rock columns, the code sets out crimes and their correction. Punishment was based on physical retaliation or **lex talionis** ("an eye for an eye"). The severity of punishment depended on class standing: for assault, slaves would be put to death; freemen might lose a limb.

Babylonian laws were strictly enforced by judges who were themselves controlled by advisers to the king. Such crimes as burglary and theft were common in ancient Babylon, and officials had to take their duties seriously. Local officials were expected to apprehend criminals. If they failed in their duties, they had to personally replace lost property; if murderers were not caught, the responsible official paid a fine to the deceased's relatives.

Another of the ancient legal codes still surviving is the Mosaic Code of the Israelites (1200 B.C.). According to tradition, God entered into a covenant or contract with the tribes of Israel in which they agreed to obey his law, as presented to them by Moses, in return for God's special care and protection. The Mosaic Code is not only the foundation of Judeo-Christian moral teachings, but it also is a basis for the U.S. legal system: prohibitions against murder, theft, perjury, and adultery precede by several thousand years the same laws found in the U.S. legal system.

Also surviving is the Roman law contained in the **Twelve Tables** (451 B.C.). The Twelve Tables were formulated by a special commission of ten men in response to pressure from the lower classes **(plebeians).** The plebeians believed that an unwritten code gave arbitrary and unlimited power to the wealthy classes **(patricians)** who served as magistrates. The original code was written on bronze plaques, which have been lost, but records of sections, which were memorized by every Roman male, survive. The remaining laws deal with debt, family relations, property, and other daily matters. A sample section of this code is set out in Table 2.1.

TABLE 2.1 Table VIII: Torts or Delicts

If any person has sung or composed against another person a song such as was causing slander or insult to another, he shall be clubbed to death. If a person has maimed another's limb, let there be retaliation in kind unless he makes agreement for settlement with him. Any person who destroys by burning any building or heap of corn deposited alongside a house shall be bound, scourged, and put to death by burning at the stake, provided that he has committed the said misdeed with malice aforethought; but if he shall have committed it by accident, that is, by negligence, it is ordained that he repair the damage, or, if he be too poor to be competent for such punishment, he shall receive a lighter chastisement.

The Dark Ages

The early formal legal codes were lost during the Dark Ages, which lasted for hundreds of years after the fall of Rome. During this period, superstition and fear of magic and satanic black arts dominated thinking.

Some attempts were made at regulating the definition and punishments of crime during the early feudal period. Those that still exist feature monetary payments as punishments for crimes. Some early German and Anglo-Saxon societies developed legal systems featuring compensation (**wergild**) for criminal violations. For example, under the legal code of the Salic Franks, killing a freewoman of childbearing age was punished by wergild in the amount of 24,000 denars; if the woman was past childbearing age, the wergild was reduced to 8,000 denars.

Guilt was determined by ordeals, such as having the accused place his or her hand in boiling water or hold a hot iron to see if God would intervene and heal the wounds. It was also possible to challenge one's accuser to a duel, the outcome determining the legitimacy of the accusation (trial by combat). Guilt could be disputed with the help of **oath-helpers,** groups of 12 to 25 people who would support the accused's innocence.

Despite such "reforms," up until the eighteenth century, the systems of crime, punishment, law, and justice were chaotic. The law was controlled by the lords of the great manors, who tried cases according to local custom and rule. Although there was general agreement that such acts as theft, assault, treason, and blasphemy constituted crimes, the penalties on law violators were often arbitrary, discretionary, and cruel. Punishments included public flogging, branding, beheading, and burning. Peasants who violated the rule of their masters were violently put down. According to a fourteenth-century Norman chronicle, disobedient peasants or those who stole from their masters were treated harshly:

> Some had their teeth pulled out, others [were] impaled, eyes torn out, hands cut off, ankles charred, others burnt alive or plunged in boiling lead.[2]

Even simple wanderers and vagabonds were viewed as dangerous and subject to these extreme penalties.

Origins of Common Law

Because the ancient legal codes had been lost during the Middle Ages, the concept of law and crime was chaotic, guided by superstition and local custom. Slowly, in England, a common law developed that helped standardize law and justice. The foundation of law in the United States is the English common law.

Before the Norman Conquest in 1066, the legal system among the early English (Anglo-Saxons), like elsewhere in Europe, was very decentralized. Each county (**shire**) was divided into units called **hundreds,** which were groups of one hundred families. The hundred was further divided into groups of ten called **tithings.** The tithings were responsible for maintaining order among themselves and dealing with disturbances, fires, wild animals, and so on.

Petty cases were tried by courts of the hundred group, the **hundred-gemot.** More serious and important cases could be heard by an assemblage of local landholders, or the **shire-gemot,** or by the local nobleman, the **hali-gemot;** if the act concerned in any way spiritual matters, it could be judged by clergymen and church officials in courts known as holy-motes or ecclesiastics. Therefore, the law varied in substance from county to county, hundred to hundred, and tithing to tithing.

Crime and Custom

Crimes during this period were viewed as personal wrongs, and compensation therefore was often paid to the victims. If payment was not made, the victims' families would attempt to forcibly collect damages or seek revenge. The result could be a blood feud between two families. The recognized crimes included treason, homicide, rape, property theft, assault (putting another in fear), and battery (wounding another). For treasonous acts, the punishment was death. Theft during the Anglo-Saxon era could result in slavery for the thieves and their families. If caught in the act of fleeing with the stolen goods, the thief could be killed.

For many other acts, including both theft and violence, compensation could be paid to the victim. For example, even a homicide could be settled by paying wergild to the deceased's family, unless the crime was carried out by poison or ambush—in which case, it was punished by death. Eventually, wergild was divided so that of the sum (**bot**) paid, part (**wer**) went to the king, and the remainder (**wite**) went to the victim or, in the case of death, the deceased's kin.

A scale of compensation existed for lesser injuries, such as the loss of an arm or an eye. Important persons, churchmen, and nuns received greater restitution than the general population and paid more if they were the criminal defendant (*wer* means worth and refers to what the person, and therefore the crime, was worth). The nobility began to see the value in the wer, and it became the predominant portion of the bot; it is the precursor of the modern-day criminal fine. To a great degree, criminal law was designed to provide an equitable solution to what was considered a private dispute.

The Norman Conquest

After the Norman Conquest in 1066, William the Conqueror, the Norman leader, did not immediately change the substance of Anglo-Saxon law. At the outset of William's reign, justice was administered as it had been in previous centuries. The church courts handled acts that might be considered sin, and the local hundred or manor courts (referred to as court-leet) dealt with most secular violations. However, to secure control of the countryside and to ensure military supremacy over his newly won lands, William replaced the local tribunals with royal administrators who dealt with the most serious breaches of the peace.

Since the royal administrators could not constantly be present in each community, a system was developed in which they traveled in a circuit throughout the land, holding court in each county several times a year. When court was in session, the royal administrator, or judge, would summon a number of citizens who would, on their oath, tell of the crimes and serious breaches of the peace that had occurred since the judge's last visit. The royal judge then would decide what to do in each case, using local custom and rules of conduct as his guide. If, for example, a local freeholder was convicted of theft, he might be executed if those before him had suffered that fate for a similar offense. However, if in previous cases the thief had been forced to make restitution to the victim, then that judgment would be rendered in the present case. This system, known as **stare decisis** (Latin for "to stand by decided cases"), was used by the early courts to determine the outcome of future cases; courts were bound to follow the law established in previously decided cases unless the law was overruled by a higher authority, such as the king or the pope.

≡ The Common Law

The present English system of law came into existence during the reign of Henry II (1154–1189). Henry also used traveling judges, better known as circuit judges. These judges followed a specific route known as a circuit and heard cases that previously had been under the jurisdiction of local courts. Juries, which began to develop about this time, were groups of local landholders whom the judges called not only to decide the facts of cases but also to investigate the crimes, accuse suspected offenders, and even give testimony at trials (see the Close-Up "Origin of the Jury Trial"). Gradually, royal prosecutors came into being. These representatives of the Crown submitted evidence and brought witnesses to testify before the jury. But not until much later was the accused in a criminal action allowed to bring forth witnesses to rebut charges; and not until the eighteenth century were witnesses required to take oaths. Few formal procedures existed, and both the judge and the prosecutor felt free to intimidate witnesses and jurors when they considered it necessary. The development of these routine judicial processes heralded the beginnings of the common law.

As it is used today, the term *common law* refers to a law applied to all subjects of the land, without regard for geographic or social differences. As best they could, Henry's judges began to apply a national law instead of the law that held sway in local jurisdictions. This attempt was somewhat confused at first, from having to take into account both local custom and the Norman conquerors' feudal law. However, as new situations arose, judges took advantage of legal uncertainty by either inventing new solutions or borrowing from the laws of European countries. During formal and informal gatherings, the circuit judges shared these incidents, talked about unique cases, and discussed their decisions, thus developing an oral tradition of law; later, as cases began to be written about, more concrete examples of common-law decisions began to emerge. Together, these cases and decisions filtered through the national court system and eventually produced a fixed body of legal rule and principles. Thus, common law is judge-made law, or case law. It is the law found in previously decided cases. Crimes such as murder, burglary, arson, and rape are common-law crimes—they were initially defined and created by judges.

Common Law and Statutory Law

The common law was and still is the law of the land in England. In most instances, the common law retained traditional Anglo-Saxon concepts. For example, the common law originally defined murder as the unlawful killing of another human being with malice aforethought.[3] By this definition, for offenders to be found guilty of murder, they must (1) have planned the crime and (2) have intentionally killed the victim out of spite or hatred. However, this general definition proved inadequate to deal with the many situations in which one person took another's life. Over time, to bring the law closer to the realities of human behavior, English judges added other forms of murder: killing someone in the heat of passion, killing someone out of negligence, and killing someone in the course of committing another crime, such as during a robbery. Each form of murder was given a different title (that is, manslaughter, felony murder) and provided with a different degree of punishment. Thus, the common law was a constantly evolving legal code.

In some instances, the creation of a new common-law crime can be traced back to a particular case. For example, an unsuccessful attempt to commit an illegal act was not considered a crime under early common law. The modern doctrine that criminal attempt can be punished under law can be traced directly back to 1784 and the case of *Rex v. Scofield*. In that case, Scofield was charged with having put a lit candle and combustible material in a house he was renting with the intention of burning it down; however, the house did not burn. He defended himself by arguing that an attempt to commit a misdemeanor was not actually a misdemeanor. In rejecting this argument, the court stated: "The intent may make an act, innocent in itself, criminal; nor is the completion of an act, criminal in itself, necessary to constitute criminality."[4] After *Scofield*, attempt became a common-law crime, and today, most U.S. jurisdictions have enacted some form of criminal attempt law **(inchoate crimes).**

CLOSE-UP

Origin of the Jury Trial

In early medieval Europe and England, disputed criminal charges were often decided by an ordeal. In a trial by fire, the accused would have a hot iron placed in their hand, and if the wound did not heal properly, it was considered proof of their guilt. In a trial by combat, the defendant could challenge his accuser to a duel; the accuser had the option of finding an alternate to fight in his place.

Settling trials by ordeal fell out of favor when the Catholic Church, at the Fourth Lateran Council (1215), decreed that priests could no longer participate in trials by ordeal. Without the use of the ordeal in "disputed" criminal cases, courts both in England and in the rest of Europe were not sure how to proceed.

In England, the Church ban on ordeal meant a new method of deciding criminal trials needed to be developed. To fill the gap, British justices adapted a method that had long been used to determine real estate taxes. Since the time of William the Conqueror, 12 knights in each district were called before an "inquest" of the king's justices to give local tax information. Instead of the slow determination of feudal taxes by judges, these "twelve free and lawful men of the neighbourhood" would view the land and testify as to who last had peaceful possession so that an accurate accounting could be made. Since they were available when the king's justices were present on circuit, the Writ of Novel Disseisin, first established in 1166 under Henry II, also required them to settle "claim jumping" disputes over land.

By 1219, the jury (from the Latin term *jurati,* to be sworn) called to decide land cases also began to hear criminal cases. At first, jurors were like witnesses, telling the judge what they knew about the case; these courts were known as assise or assize (from the Latin *assideo,* to sit together). By the fourteenth century, jurors became the deciders of fact. Over the centuries, the English jury came to be seen as a check on the government. The great case that established the principle of jury independence, *Bushell's Case* (1670), arose when a London jury acquitted William Penn, a leading Quaker and later the founder of Pennsylvania, of unlawful assembly in connection with his preaching in the street after a Quaker church was padlocked. The jurors were imprisoned by an angry royalist judge. They were freed when British Chief Judge Vaughn held that unless a jury were corrupt, they were free to reach a verdict based on the evidence, or else the jury would be nothing but a rubber stamp and useless.

Discussion Questions

1. Do you think that the common-law development of a jury trial is relevant in today's world?
2. Should a jury of one's peers be replaced by professionals who are schooled in the law?

SOURCE: Marvin Zalman and Larry Siegel, *Criminal Procedure, Constitution and Society* (St. Paul: West Publishing, 1991).

When the situation required it, the English Parliament enacted legislation to supplement the judge-made common law. Violations of these laws are referred to as *statutory crimes.* For example, in 1723, the Waltham Black Act punished with death offenses against rural property, from the poaching of small game to arson, if the criminal was armed or disguised.[5] Moreover, the act eroded the rights of the accused; it allowed the death sentence to be carried out without a trial if the accused failed to surrender when ordered to do so. The underlying purpose of the act was Parliament's desire to control the behavior of peasants whose poverty forced them to poach on royal lands. In the Black Act, then, the British ruling class created a mechanism for protecting its property and position of social power. Statutory laws usually reflect existing social conditions. They deal with issues of morality, such as gambling, sexual activity, and drug-related offenses. For example, a whole series of statutory laws, such as those concerning embezzlement and fraud, were created to protect the well-being of British, and later U.S., business enterprise.[6]

The English common law was created by judges in hearings in courts such as the Old Bailey in London. Courts do not seem to have changed much; they are open to the public, crowded, and the scene of human drama.

Common Law in America

Before the American Revolution, the colonies, then under British rule, were subject to the law handed down by English judges. After the colonies acquired their independence, they adapted and changed the English law to fit their needs. In many states, legislatures standardized such common-law crimes as murder, burglary, arson, and rape by putting them into statutory form. In other states, comprehensive penal codes were passed, thus abolishing the common-law crimes. An example of this process of modifying the common law can be found in the Massachusetts statute defining arson. The common-law definition of *arson* is "the malicious burning of the dwelling of another." Massachusetts has expanded this definition by passing legislation defining *arson* as "the willful and malicious setting fire to, or burning of, *any building or contents thereof even if they were burned by the owner.*"[7] (Emphasis added.) As in England, whenever the common law proved inadequate to deal with changing social and moral issues, the states and Congress supplemented it with legislative statutes, creating new elements in the various state and federal legal codes. As noted before, early in the nation's history, it was both legal and relatively easy to obtain narcotics, such as heroin, opium, and cocaine.[8] Their use became habits of the middle class. However, public and governmental concern arose over the use of narcotics by immigrants, such as the Chinese, who had come to the United States to build railroads and work in mines. Eventually, changes in public sentiment resulted in the 1914 passage of the Harrison Act, which outlawed trade in opium and its derivatives. Later, in 1937, pressure from federal law enforcement officials led to passage of the Marijuana Tax Act, which outlawed the sale or possession of that drug. We can see in the case of marijuana how the statutory law is subject to change. When use of "pot" became widespread among the middle class in the 1960s, several states revised their laws and effectively decriminalized the possession of marijuana. The statutory law began to reflect the views of individual states' legislatures on the use of soft drugs by their citizens. In some states, marijuana possession is still punished by many years in prison; in others, by a small fine.

Common Law in Other Cultures

The British common-law tradition was imposed not only on the American colonies but also on its other overseas possessions, including its African colonies. In some instances, this has created a dual legal system divided between traditional tribal law and British common law. For example, Edna Erez and Bankole Thompson have described the conflict between traditional tribal and British common law in the African country of Sierra Leone.[9] According to Erez and Thompson, women in Sierra Leone are still considered the property of their fathers and later their husbands or heads of families. If a woman is raped, the case is usually brought to the customary courts, which handle complaints according to traditional tribal customs. If the accused is found to be guilty of sexual assault, referred to as "woman-damage," he will be forced to pay compensation to the victim's family. Since this is a property issue, consent of the victim is not important; the "damage" involves a trespass or misuse of "someone's property." The victim's story is usually accepted because the tribal custom is that a woman should confess a wrongful sexual act or else suffer divinely inspired ill fate and misfortune. After admitting guilt, the accused typically agrees to compensate either the victim's parents or husband for the damage he caused. If the defendant refuses to admit guilt or pay damages, the case can be brought under the jurisdiction of the General Courts, which use British common law; the maximum penalty can be life in prison. Threat of complaint to the formal justice system is used as an incentive to settle the case according to tribal law and pay monetary penalties rather than face trial, conviction, and imprisonment. In Sierra Leone, British common law and the traditional tribal customs are often at cross-purposes. Yet the two systems can function together because each serves to maintain group norms.

≡ Classification of Law

Law can be classified in a number of different ways that can help us understand its nature and purpose. Three of the most important classifications are discussed next.

Crimes and Torts: Similarities

Law can be divided into two broad categories—criminal law and civil law. Civil law is all law other than criminal law and includes such legal areas as property law (the law governing transfer and ownership of property) and contract law (the law of personal agreements). Of all areas of the civil law, **tort law** (the law of personal wrongs and damage) is most similar in intent and form to the criminal law.

A tort is a civil action in which an individual asks to be compensated for personal harm. The harm may be either physical or mental and includes such acts as trespass, assault and battery, invasion of privacy, libel (false and injurious writings), and slander (false and injurious statements). A tort can occur when someone is injured by the actions of another. It may also occur when a behavior is an indirect cause of injury, that is, when it sets off a chain of events that leads to injury or death. In 1990, for example, the families of two youths who had attempted suicide sued the heavy metal rock group Judas Priest and CBS Records because they claimed the group had put the subliminal message "do it" in its albums to effect "mind control" over the band's fans. Though the group was vindicated, the judge ruled that its recordings were not protected by the First Amendment right to free speech if indeed they had employed privacy-invading mind-control messages.[10]

Because some torts are similar to some criminal acts, a person can possibly be held both criminally and civilly liable for one action. For example, if one man punches another, it is possible for the assailant to be charged by the state with assault and battery—and imprisoned if found guilty—and be sued by the victim in a tort action of assault in which he could be required to pay monetary damages. In a 1993 Massachussets case, Jennifer Hoult received an award of $500,000 from her father, David, after a federal court accepted her claim that he had raped her at least 3,000 times from the time she was a child of four until she reached age 16. The case is a milestone because the statute of limitations for bringing a tort action in a rape case was three years. However, in the *Hoult* case, the jury found that because the plaintiff had repressed her memory of the rapes, the statute of limitations did not start running until she had regained her memory through psychological therapy.[11]

Perhaps the most important similarity is that criminal law and civil law have a common purpose. Both attempt to control people's behavior by setting limits on what acts are permissible; both accomplish this through state-imposed sanctions.

Crimes and Torts: Differences

There are also several differences between criminal law and civil law. First, the main purpose of criminal law is to give the state the power to protect the public from harm by punishing individuals whose actions threaten the social order. In tort law, the harm or injury is considered a private wrong, and the main concern is to compensate individuals for harm done to them by others.

In a criminal action, the state initiates the legal proceedings by bringing charges and prosecuting the violator. If it is determined that the criminal law has been broken, the state can impose punishment, such as imprisonment, probation (community supervision by the court), or a fine payable to the state. In a civil action, however, the injured person must initiate proceedings. In a successful action, the injured individual usually receives financial compensation for the harm done.

Another major difference is the burden of proof required to establish the defendant's liability. In criminal matters, the defendant's guilt must be proven beyond a reasonable doubt. This standard, while less than absolute certainty, means that the deciders of guilt, after considering the evidence presented to them, are entirely satisfied that the party is guilty as charged; if there is any doubt, they must find for the defendant. In a civil case, the defendant is required to pay damages if by a *preponderance of the evidence,* the trier of fact finds that he or she committed the wrong. According to this doctrine, while both parties may share some blame, the defendant is at fault if he or she contributed more than 50 percent to the cause of the dispute. Establishing guilt by a preponderance of the evidence is easier than establishing it beyond a reasonable doubt.[12] Table 2.2 summarizes the differences and similarities between crimes and torts.

Felony and Misdemeanor

In addition to being divided from civil law, criminal laws can be further classified as either felonies or misdemeanors. The distinction is based on seriousness: A **felony** (from the term *felonia,* an act by which a vassal forfeited his fee) is a serious offense; a **misdemeanor** is a minor or petty crime. Such crimes as murder, rape, and burglary are felonies; such crimes as unarmed assault and battery, petty larceny, and disturbing the peace are misdemeanors. Most states distinguish between a felony and a misdemeanor on the basis of time sentenced and place of imprisonment. Under this model of classification, a felony is usually defined as a crime punishable by death or imprisonment for more than one year in a state prison; a misdemeanor is defined as a crime punished by less than a year in a local county jail or house of correction. Some common felonies and misdemeanors are defined in the Close-Up "Common-Law Crimes."

Mala in Se and Mala Prohibitum

It is also possible to classify crimes as **mala in se** and **mala prohibitum.**

Some illegal acts, referred to as mala in se crimes, are rooted in the core values inherent in Western civilization. These "natural laws" are designed to control such behaviors as inflicting physical harm on others (assault, rape, murder), taking possessions that rightfully belong to another (larceny, burglary, robbery), or harming another person's property (malicious damage, trespass) that have traditionally been considered a violation of the morals of Western civilization.

Another type of crime, sometimes called statutory crime or mala prohibitum crime, involves violations of laws that reflect current public opinion and social values. In essence, statutory crimes are acts that conflict with contemporary standards of morality. Crimes are periodically created to control behaviors that conflict with the functioning of society. Mala prohibitum offenses include drug use and possession of unlicensed handguns. While it is relatively easy to link mala in se crimes to a basic concept of morality, it is much more difficult to do so if the acts are mala prohibitum.

TABLE 2.2 A Comparison of Criminal and Tort Law

Similarities
Both criminal and tort law seek to control behavior. Both laws impose sanctions. Similar areas of legal action exist; for example, personal assault and control of white-collar offenses, such as environmental pollution.

Differences	
Criminal Law	**Tort Law**
Crime is a public offense.	Tort is a civil or private wrong.
The sanction associated with criminal law is incarceration or death.	The sanction associated with a tort is monetary damages.
The right of enforcement belongs to the state.	The individual brings the action.
The government ordinarily does not appeal.	Both parties can appeal.
Fines go to the state.	The individual receives compensation for harm done.
The standard of proof is "beyond a reasonable doubt."	Guilt is established by a preponderance of the evidence.

CLOSE-UP

Common-Law Crimes

• *The substantive law defines crimes and prescribes the punishments that can be imposed on people engaging in criminal activity. Though each state uses its own definitions, enough similarity exists among them to suggest a general formula for defining most common criminal activities. Below, some familiar illegal acts are set out and an example of each is given.*

Crimes against the Person

First-degree murder—unlawful killing of another human being with malice aforethought and with premeditation and deliberation.

Second-degree murder—unlawful killing of another human being with malice aforethought but without premeditation and deliberation.

Voluntary manslaughter—intentional killing committed under extenuating circumstances that mitigate the killing, such as killing in the heat of passion after being provoked.

Involuntary manslaughter—unintentional killing, without malice, that is neither excused nor justified, such as homicide resulting from criminal negligence.

Battery—unlawful touching of another with intent to cause injury.

Assault—intentional placing of another in fear of receiving an immediate battery.

Rape—unlawful sexual intercourse with a female by a male without her consent.

Sexual assault—forcible sexual relations with a person by another.

Statutory rape—sexual intercourse with a person who is under the age of consent.

Examples

A person buys some poison and pours it into a cup of coffee another person will be drinking, intending to kill that person. The motive: to get the insurance benefits of the victim.

A person intending to greatly harm another after a disagreement in a bar hits that person in the head with a baseball bat, and the victim dies as a result of the injury. Hitting someone hard with a bat is known to cause serious injury. Because the act was committed in spite of this fact, it is second-degree murder.

A husband coming home early from work finds his wife in bed with another man. The husband goes into a rage and shoots and kills both lovers with a gun he keeps by his bedside.

After becoming drunk, a woman drives a car at high speed down a crowded street and kills a pedestrian.

A person seeing someone sitting in his favorite seat in the cafeteria goes up to that person and pushes him out of the seat.

A person aims an unloaded gun at someone and says she is going to shoot that person, who believes the gun is loaded.

After a party, a man offers to drive a young female acquaintance home. He takes her to a wooded area and, despite her protests, forces her to have sexual relations with him.

An older man forces a young boy to have sexual relations with him.

A boy, aged 18, and his girlfriend, aged 15, have sexual relations. Though the victim voluntarily participates, her age makes her incapable of legally consenting to have sexual relations.

Crimes against the Person (continued)

Robbery—wrongful taking and carrying away of personal property from a person by violence or intimidation.

Inchoate (Incomplete) Offenses

Attempt—an intentional act for the purpose of committing a crime that is more than mere preparation or planning of the crime. However, the crime is not completed.

Conspiracy—voluntary agreement between two or more persons to achieve an unlawful object or to achieve a lawful object using means forbidden by law.

Solicitation—efforts by one person to encourage another person to commit or attempt to commit a crime by means of advising, enticing, inciting, ordering, or otherwise soliciting their aid.

Crimes against Property

Burglary—breaking and entering of a dwelling house of another with the intent to commit a felony.

Arson—intentional burning of a dwelling of another.

Larceny—taking and carrying away the personal property of another with the intent to steal the property.

Embezzlement—fraudulent appropriation of another's property by one already in lawful possession.

Receiving stolen goods—receiving of stolen property with the knowledge that the property is stolen and with the intent to deprive the owner of the property.

Discussion Questions

1. Do you know the definitions used for such crimes as burglary, murder, or rape in your jurisdiction?
2. Why is robbery considered a violent crime and not a property crime?

Examples (continued)

A man armed with a loaded gun approaches another man on a deserted street and demands his wallet.

Examples

A person intending to kill another places a bomb in the second person's car so that it will detonate when the ignition key is turned. The bomb is discovered before the car is started. Attempted murder has been committed.

A drug company official sells larger-than-normal quantities of drugs to a doctor, knowing that the doctor is distributing the drugs illegally. The drug company official is guilty of conspiracy.

A person offers another $100 to set fire to a third person's house. The person requesting that the fire be set is guilty of solicitation, whether the fire is set or not.

Examples

Intending to steal some jewelry and silver, a person breaks a window and enters another's house at ten o'clock at night.

A person, angry that her boss did not give her a raise, goes to her boss's house and sets fire to it.

While a woman is shopping, she sees a diamond ring displayed at the jewelry counter. When no one is looking, the woman takes the ring and walks out of the store.

A bank teller receives a cash deposit from a customer and places it in the cash drawer with other deposits. A few minutes later, he takes the deposit out of the cash drawer and keeps it by placing it in his pocket.

A fence accepts some television sets from a thief with the intention of selling them, knowing that the sets have been stolen.

3. Should statutory rape be considered as serious as forcible rape?
4. What is the difference between *malice aforethought* and *premeditation?*

SOURCE: Developed by Therese J. Libby, J.D.

☰ Functions of the Criminal Law

The substantive criminal law today is a written code defining crimes and their punishments. In the United States, state and federal governments have developed their own unique criminal codes. Though all the codes have their differences, most use comparable terms, and the behaviors they are designed to control are often quite similar. Regardless of which culture or jurisdiction created them or when, criminal codes have several distinct functions. The most important of these are described below.

Social Control

The primary purpose of the criminal law is to control the behavior of people within its jurisdiction. The criminal law is a written statement of rules to which people must conform their behavior. Every society also maintains unwritten rules of conduct—ordinary customs and conventions referred to as *folkways* and universally followed behavior called norms and morals, or *mores.* However, it is the criminal law that formally prohibits behaviors believed by those in political power to threaten societal well-being and which may challenge their own authority. For example, in U.S. society, the criminal law incorporates centuries-old prohibitions against the following behaviors harmful to others: taking the possessions of another person, physically harming another person, damaging another person's property, and cheating another person out of his or her possessions. Similarly, the law prevents actions that challenge the legitimacy of the government, such as planning its overthrow, collaborating with its enemies, and so on. Whereas violations of mores and folkways may be informally punished by any person, control of the criminal law is given to those in political power.

Banishes Personal Retribution

By delegating enforcement to others, the criminal law controls an individual's need to seek retribution, or vengeance, against those who violate his or her rights. By punishing people who infringe on the rights, property, and freedom of others, the law shifts the burden of revenge from the individual to the state. As Oliver Wendell Holmes stated, this prevents "the greater evil of private retribution."[13] Though state retaliation may offend the sensibilities of many citizens, it is greatly preferable to a system in which people would have to seek justice for themselves.

One purpose of the criminal law is to eliminate personal retribution and revenge. Here, a woman in ancient Montenegro is being stoned to death after being accused of adultery. The criminal law prevents such barbaric customs by turning social control over to objective state authorities.

Expresses Public Opinion and Morality

The criminal law also reflects constantly changing public opinions and moral values. Mala in se crimes, such as murder and forcible rape, are almost universally prohibited, but the prohibition of legislatively created mala prohibitum crimes, such as traffic law and gambling violations, changes according to shifting social conditions and attitudes. The criminal law is used to codify these changes. For example, if a state government decides to legalize certain outlawed behaviors, such as gambling or marijuana possession, it will amend the state's criminal code. The criminal law then has the power to define the boundaries of moral and immoral behavior. Nonetheless, it has proven difficult to legally control public morality because of the problems associated with (1) gauging the will of the majority, (2) respecting the rights of the minority, and (3) enforcing laws that many people consider trivial or self-serving.

The power of the law to express norms and values can be viewed in the development of the crime of **vagrancy** (the going about from place to place by a person without visible means of support and who, though able to work for his or her maintenance, refuses to do so). In a famous treatise, criminologist William Chambliss linked the historical development of the law of vagrancy to the prevailing economic interests of the ruling class. He argued that the original vagrancy laws were formulated in the fourteenth century after the bubonic plague had killed significant numbers of English peasants, threatening the labor-intensive feudal economy. The first vagrancy laws were aimed at preventing workers from leaving their estates to secure higher wages elsewhere. They punished migration and permissionless travel, thereby mooring peasants to their manors and aiding wealthy landowners.[14]

In an opposing view of the social conditions that influenced the creation of vagrancy laws, Jeffrey Adler argues that early English vagrancy laws were less concerned with maintaining capitalism than with controlling beggars and relieving the overburdened public relief and welfare systems.[15] Adler suggests that early American vagrancy laws provided town officials with a mechanism to repel the moral threat to the community posed by vagrants, "sabbath breakers," paupers, and the wandering poor; economic demands had little to do with the content of the law.

Deters Criminal Behavior

The criminal law's social control function is realized through its ability to deter potential law violators. The threat of punishment associated with violating the law is designed to prevent crimes before they occur. During the Middle Ages, public executions were held to drive this point home. Today, the criminal law's impact is felt through news accounts of long prison sentences and an occasional execution.

The deterrent power of the criminal law is tied to the power it gives the state to sanction offenders. While violations of folkways and mores are controlled informally, breaches of the criminal law are left to the jurisdiction of political agencies. Those violating mores and folkways can be subject to social disapproval, whereas criminal law violators alone are subject to physical coercion and punishment. Today, the most common punishments are fines, community supervision or probation, incarceration in jails or prison, and, in rare instances, execution.

Maintains the Social Order

All legal systems are designed to support and maintain the boundaries of the social system they serve. In medieval England, the law protected the feudal system by defining an orderly system of property transfer and ownership. Laws in some socialist nations protect the primacy of the state by strictly curtailing profiteering and individual enterprise. Our own capitalist system is also supported and sustained by the criminal law. In a sense, the content of the criminal law is more of a reflection of the needs of those who control the existing economic and political system than a representation of some idealized moral code. In U.S. society, by meting out punishment to those who damage or steal property, the law promotes the activities needed to sustain an economy based on the accumulation of wealth. It would be impossible to conduct business through the use of contracts, promissory notes, credit, banking, and so on unless the law protected private capital.

The criminal law has not always protected commercial enterprise; if one merchant cheated another, it was considered a private matter. Then in 1473, in the *Carrier's Case,* an English court ruled that a merchant who held and transported merchandise for another was guilty of theft if he kept the goods for his own purposes.[16] Before the *Carrier's Case,* the law did not consider it a crime for people to keep something that was already in their possession. Breaking with legal precedent, the British court recognized that the new English mercantile trade system could not be sustained if property rights had to be individually enforced. To this day, the substantive criminal law prohibits such business-related acts as larceny, fraud, embezzlement, and commercial theft. Without the law to protect it, the free enterprise system could not exist.

≡ The Legal Definition of a Crime

The media often tell us about people who admit at trial that they committed the act they are accused of but are not found guilty of the crime. In most instances, this occurs because state or federal prosecutors have not proven that the defendants' behavior falls within the legal definition of a crime. To fulfill the legal definition, all elements of the crime must be proven. For example, in Massachusetts, the common-law crime of burglary in the first degree is defined as:

> Whoever breaks and enters a dwelling house in the nighttime, with intent to commit a felony, or whoever, after having entered with such intent, breaks into such dwelling house in the nighttime, any person being lawfully therein,

and the offender being armed with a dangerous weapon at the time of such breaking or entry, or so arriving himself in such house or making an actual assault on a person lawfully therein, commits the crime of burglary.[17]

Note that burglary has the following elements:

- It happens at night.

- It involves breaking or entering or both.

- It happens at a dwelling house.

- The accused is armed or arms himself or herself after entering the house or commits an actual assault on a person lawfully in the house.

- The accused intends to commit a felony.

For the state to prove a crime occurred and the defendant committed it, the prosecutor must show that the accused engaged in the guilty act or *actus reus* and had the *mens rea* or intent to commit the act. The actus reus can be either an aggressive act, such as taking someone's money, burning a building, or shooting someone, or it can be a failure to act when there is a legal duty to do so, such as a parent's neglecting to seek medical attention for a sick child. The mens rea (guilty mind) refers to an individual's state of mind at the time of the act or, more specifically, the person's intent to commit the crime. For most crimes, both the actus reus and the mens rea must be present for the act to be considered a crime. For example, if George decides to kill Bob and then takes a gun and shoots Bob, George can be convicted of the crime of murder, because both elements are present. George's shooting of Bob is the actus reus; his decision to kill Bob is the mens rea. However, if George only thinks about shooting Bob but does nothing about it, the element of actus reus is absent, and no crime has been committed. Thoughts of committing an act do not alone constitute a crime. Let us now look more closely at these issues.

Actus Reus

As mentioned, the **actus reus** is the criminal act itself. For an act to be considered illegal, the action must be voluntary. For example, if one person shoots another, that certainly could be considered a voluntary act. However, if the shooting occurs while the person holding the gun is having an epileptic seizure or a heart attack or sleepwalking, he or she will not be held criminally liable, because the act was not voluntary. But if the individual knew he or she had such a condition and did not take precautions to prevent the act from occur-

People face legal liability due to their occupation. While a sunbather does not have a duty to save a drowning person, lifeguards must be vigilant since they can be legally responsible if someone is injured or killed while the lifeguard is on duty.

ring, then the person could be held responsible for the criminal act. For instance, if Tom has an epileptic seizure while he is hunting and his gun goes off and kills Victor, Tom will not be held responsible for Victor's death. But if Tom knew of his condition and further knew that a seizure could occur at any time, he could be convicted of the crime because it was possible for him to foresee the danger of handling a gun, yet he did nothing about it. The central issue concerning voluntariness is whether the individual has control over his or her actions.

A second type of actus reus is the failure to act when there is a legal duty to do so. A legal duty arises in three common situations:

1. *Relationship of parties based on status.* These relationships include parent and child and husband and wife. If a husband finds his wife unconscious because she took an overdose of sleeping pills,

he has a duty to try to save her life by seeking medical aid. If he fails to do so and she dies, he can be held responsible for her death.

2. *Imposition by statute.* For example, some states have passed laws that require a person who observes an automobile accident to stop and help the other parties involved.
3. *Contractual relationship.* These relationships include lifeguard and swimmer, doctor and patient, and baby-sitter and child. Because lifeguards have been hired to ensure the safety of swimmers, they have a legal duty to come to the aid of drowning persons. If a lifeguard knows a swimmer is in danger and does nothing about it and the swimmer drowns, the lifeguard is legally responsible for the swimmer's death.

The duty to act is a legal and not a moral duty. The obligation arises from the relationship between the parties or from explicit legal requirements. For example, a private citizen who sees a person drowning is under no legal obligation to save that person. Although we may find it morally reprehensible, the private citizen could walk away and let the swimmer drown without facing legal sanctions. In any discussion of the actus reus of a crime, it should be mentioned that in some circumstances, words are considered acts. In the crime of sedition, the words of disloyalty constitute the actus reus. Further, if a person falsely yells "fire" in a crowded theater and people are injured in the rush to exit, that person is held responsible for the injuries, because his or her word constitutes an illegal act.

Mens Rea

In most situations, for an act to constitute a crime, it must be done with criminal intent—otherwise known as **mens rea.** *Intent* in the legal sense can mean carrying out an act intentionally, knowingly, and willingly. However, the definition also encompasses situations in which recklessness or negligence establishes the required criminal intent. Some crimes require specific intent, and others require general intent. The type of intent needed to establish criminal liability varies depending on how the crime is defined. Most crimes require a general intent, or an intent to commit the crime. Thus, when Ann picks Bill's pocket and takes his wallet, her intent is to steal. Specific intent, on the other hand, is an intent to accomplish a specific purpose as an element of the crime. It involves an intent in addition to the intent to commit the crime. For example, burglary is the breaking and entering of a dwelling house with the intent to commit a felony. The breaking and entering aspect requires a general intent; the intent to commit a felony is a specific intent. If Dan breaks into and enters Emily's house because he intends to steal Emily's diamonds, he is guilty of burglary. However, if Dan merely breaks into and enters Emily's house but has no intent to commit a crime once inside, he cannot be convicted of burglary because he lacked specific intent.

Criminal intent also exists if the results of an action, though originally unintended, are substantially certain to occur. For example, Kim, out for revenge against her former boyfriend John, poisons the punch bowl at John's party. Before John has a drink himself, several of his guests die as a result of drinking the punch. Kim could be said to have intentionally killed the guests even though that was not the original purpose of her action. The law would hold that Kim or any other person should be substantially certain that the others at the party would drink the punch and be poisoned along with John.

The concept of mens rea also encompasses the situation in which a person intends to commit a crime against one person but injures another party instead. For instance, if Sam, intending to kill Larry, shoots at Larry but misses and kills John, Sam is guilty of murdering John, even though he did not intend to do so. Under the doctrine of **transferred intent,** the original criminal intent is transferred to the unintended victim.

Mens rea is also found in situations in which harm has resulted because a person has acted negligently or recklessly. Negligence involves a person's acting unreasonably under the circumstances. Criminal negligence is often found in situations involving drunken driving. If a drunken driver speeding and zigzagging across lanes hits and kills another person, criminal negligence exists. In the case of drunken driving, the law maintains that a reasonable person would not drive a car when drunk and thus unable to control the vehicle. The intent that underlies the finding of criminal liability for an unintentional act is known as **constructive intent.**

Both the actus reus and the mens rea must be present before a person can be convicted of a crime. However, several crimes defined by statute do not require mens rea. The actor is guilty simply by doing what the statute prohibits; mental intent does not enter the picture. These offenses are known as **strict-liability crimes,** or public welfare offenses. Health and safety regulations, traffic laws, and narcotic control laws are strict-liability statutes. The underlying purpose of these laws is to protect the public, and therefore, intent is not required.[18]

≡ Criminal Defenses

When people defend themselves against criminal charges, they must refute one or more of the elements of the crime of which they have been accused. A number of different approaches can be taken to criminal defense. First, defendants may deny the actus reus by arguing that they were falsely accused and the real culprit has yet to be identified. Defendants may also claim that while they did engage in the criminal act they are accused of, they lacked the mens rea, or mental intent needed to be found guilty of the crime. If a person whose mental state is impaired commits a criminal act, it is possible for the person to excuse his or her law-violating actions by claiming he or she lacked the capacity to form sufficient intent to be held criminally responsible for the actions. Insanity, intoxication, and ignorance are among the types of excuse defenses. Another type of defense is that of justification. Here, the individual usually admits committing the criminal act but maintains that the act was justified and that he or she therefore should not be held criminally liable. Among the justification defenses are necessity, duress, self-defense, and entrapment. Persons standing trial for criminal offenses may defend themselves by claiming either that their actions were justified under the circumstances or that their behavior can be excused by their lack of mens rea. If either the physical or mental elements of a crime cannot be proven, then the defendant cannot be convicted. We will now examine some of these defenses and justifications in greater detail.

Ignorance or Mistake

As a general rule, ignorance of the law is no excuse. However, courts have recognized that ignorance can be an excuse if the government fails to make enactment of a new law public or if the offender relied on an official statement of the law that was later deemed incorrect. Ignorance or mistake can be an excuse if it negates an element of a crime. For example, if Andrew purchases stolen merchandise from Eric but is unaware that the material was illegally obtained, he cannot be convicted of receiving stolen merchandise because he had no intent to do so. But if Rachel attempts to purchase marijuana from a drug dealer and mistakenly buys hashish, she can be convicted of a drug charge because she intended to purchase illegal goods; ignorance does not excuse evil intent.[19]

While ignorance or mistake does not excuse crime when there is evil intent, there is conflict when the evil was purely of moral and not legal consequence. For example, some cases of statutory rape (sexual relations with minor females) have been defended on the grounds that the perpetrators were ignorant of their victim's true age. This defense has been allowed in states where sex between consenting adults is legal under the rationale that if a reasonable mistake had not been made, no crime would have occurred. Nonetheless, if the mistake seems unreasonable (for example, if the victim was a preteen), the original charge will stand.[20]

Insanity

Insanity is a defense to criminal prosecution in which the defendant's state of mind negates his or her criminal responsibility. A successful insanity defense results in a verdict of "not guilty by reason of insanity." Insanity here is a legal category. As used in U.S. courts, it does not necessarily mean that persons using the defense are mentally ill or unbalanced, only that their state of mind at the time the crime was committed made it impossible for them to have the necessary intent to satisfy the legal definition of a crime. Thus, a person can be diagnosed as a psychopath or psychotic but still be judged legally sane. However, it is usually left to psychiatric testimony in court to prove a defendant legally sane.

A person found to be legally insane at the time of trial is placed in the custody of state mental health authorities until diagnosed as sane. Sometimes, a person who was sane when he or she committed a crime becomes insane soon afterward. In that instance, the person receives psychiatric care until capable of standing trial and is then tried on the criminal charge, since the person actually had mens rea at the time the crime was committed. On rare occasions, persons who were legally insane at the time they committed a crime become rational soon afterward. In that instance, the state can neither try them for the criminal offense nor have them committed to a mental health facility.

The test used to determine whether a person is legally insane varies between jurisdictions. U.S. courts generally use either the M'Naghten Rule or the Substantial Capacity Test.

The M'Naghten Rule.
In 1843, an English court established the M'Naghten Rule, also known as the right-wrong test. Daniel M'Naghten, believing Edward Drummond to be Sir Robert Peel, the prime minister of Great Britain, shot and killed Drummond (Peel's secretary). At his trial for murder, M'Naghten claimed that he could not be held responsible for the murder because his delusions had caused him to act. The jury

agreed with M'Naghten and found him not guilty by reason of insanity.

Because of the importance of the people involved in the case, the verdict was not well received. The British House of Lords reviewed the decision and requested the court to clarify the law with respect to insane delusions. The court's response became known as the **M'Naghten Rule:**

> To establish a defense on the ground of insanity, it must be proved that at the time of the committing of the act the party accused was labouring under such a defect of reason from disease of the mind, as not to know the nature and quality of the act he was doing; or, if he did know, that he did not know he was doing what was wrong.[21]

Essentially, the M'Naghten Rule maintains that an individual is insane if he or she is unable to tell the difference between right and wrong because of some mental disability.

The M'Naghten Rule is a widely used test for legal insanity in the United States. In about half of the states, this rule is the legal test when an issue of insanity is presented. However, over the years, much criticism has arisen concerning M'Naghten. First, great confusion has surfaced over such terms as *disease of the mind* and *know the nature and quality of the act.* These terms have never been properly clarified. Second, critiques, mainly from the mental health profession, have pointed out that the rule is unrealistic and narrow in that it does not cover situations in which people know right from wrong but cannot control their actions.

Irresistible Impulse.

Because of questions about M'Naghten, approximately 15 states have supplemented the rule with another test, known as the Irresistible Impulse Test.[22] This test allows the defense of insanity to be used for situations in which defendants were unable to control their behavior because of a mental disease. Thus, the defendants do not have to prove that they did not know the difference between right and wrong, only that they could not control themselves at the time of the crime.

The Substantial Capacity Test.

The Substantial Capacity Test, originally a section of the American Law Institute's Model Penal Code, states:

> A person is not responsible for criminal conduct if at the time of such conduct as a result of mental disease or defect he lacks substantial capacity either to appreciate the criminality [wrongfulness] of his conduct or to conform his conduct to the requirement of the law.[23]

The Substantial Capacity Test is essentially a combination of the M'Naghten Rule and the Irresistible Impulse Test. It is, however, broader in its interpretation of insanity, for it requires only a lack of substantial capacity instead of complete impairment, as in M'Naghten and the Irresistible Impulse Test. This test also differs in that it uses the term *appreciate,* instead of *know,* the term used in M'Naghten. About half the states now use variations of the Substantial Capacity Test.

The Insanity Controversy.

The insanity defense has been the source of debate and controversy. Many critics of the defense maintain that inquiry into a defendant's psychological makeup is inappropriate at the trial stage; they would prefer that the issue be raised at the sentencing stage, after guilt has been determined. Opponents also charge that criminal responsibility is separate from mental illness and that the two should not be equated. It is a serious mistake, they argue, to consider criminal responsibility as a trait or quality that can be detected by a psychiatric evaluation. Moreover, some criminals avoid punishment because they are erroneously judged by psychiatrists to be mentally ill. Conversely, some people who are found not guilty by reason of insanity because they suffer from a mild personality disturbance are incarcerated as mental patients far longer than they would have been imprisoned if they had been convicted of a criminal offense.

Advocates of the insanity defense say that it serves a unique purpose. Most successful insanity verdicts result in the defendant's being committed to a mental institution until he or she has recovered. The general assumption, according to two legal authorities, Wayne LaFave and Austin Scott, is that the insanity defense makes it possible to single out for special treatment certain persons who would otherwise be subjected to further penal sanctions following conviction. LaFave and Scott further point out that the "real function of the insanity defense is to authorize the state to hold those who must be found not to possess the guilty mind, even though the criminal law demands that no person be held criminally responsible if doubt is cast on any material element of the offense charged."[24]

The insanity plea was thrust into the spotlight when John Hinckley's unsuccessful attempt to kill President Ronald Reagan was captured by news cameras. Hinckley was found not guilty by reason of insanity. Public outcry against this seeming miscarriage of justice prompted some states to revise their insanity statutes. New Mexico, Georgia, Alaska, Delaware, Michigan, Illinois, and Indiana, among other states, have created the plea of guilty but insane, in which the defendant is required to serve the first part of his or her sentence in a hospital and, once "cured," to be then sent to prison. In 1984, the federal government revised its criminal code to restrict insanity as a defense solely to individuals who are unable to understand the nature and wrongfulness of their acts; a defendant's irresistible impulse will no longer be considered. The burden of proof has made an important shift from the prosecutor's need to prove sanity to the defendant's need to prove insanity.[25]

About 11 states have followed the federal government's lead and made significant changes in their insanity defenses, such as shifting the burden of proof from prosecution to defense; three states (Idaho, Montana, and Utah) no longer use evidence of mental illness as a defense in court, though psychological factors can influence sentencing. On March 28, 1994, the U.S. Supreme Court failed to overturn the Montana law (*Cowan v. Montana*, 93-1264) thereby giving the states the right to abolish the insanity defense if they so choose.

Although such backlash against the insanity plea is intended to close supposed legal loopholes allowing dangerous criminals to go free, the public's fear may be misplaced. It is estimated the insanity plea is used in fewer than 1 percent of all cases.[26] Moreover, evidence shows that relatively few insanity defense pleas are successful. Even if the defense is successful, the offender must be placed in a secure psychiatric hospital or the psychiatric ward of a state prison. Since many defendants who successfully plead insanity are nonviolent offenders, it is certainly possible that their hospital stay will be longer than the prison term they would have received if they had been convicted of the crimes of which they were originally accused.[27] Despite efforts to ban its use, the insanity plea is probably here to stay. Most crimes require mens rea, and unless we are willing to forgo that standard of law, we will be forced to find not guilty those people whose mental state makes it impossible for them to rationally control their behavior.

Intoxication

Intoxication, which includes the taking of alcohol or drugs, is generally not considered a defense. However, there are two exceptions to this rule. First, an individual who becomes intoxicated either by mistake, through force, or under duress can use involuntary intoxication as a defense. Second, voluntary intoxication is a defense when specific intent is needed and the person could not have formed the intent because of his or her intoxicated condition. For example, if a person breaks into and enters another's house but is so drunk that he or she cannot form the intent to commit a felony, the intoxication is a defense against burglary but not against the breaking and entering.

Duress

Duress is a defense to a crime when the defendant commits an illegal act because the defendant or a third person has been threatened by another with death or serious bodily harm if the act is not performed. For example, if Pete, holding a gun on Jerry, threatens to kill Jerry unless he breaks into and enters Bill's house, Jerry has a defense of duress for the crime of breaking and entering. This defense, however, does not cover the situation in which defendants commit a serious crime, such as murder, to save themselves or others. The reason for this exception is that the defense is based on the social policy that, when faced with two evils (harm to oneself or violating the criminal law), it is better to commit the lesser evil to avoid the threatened harm. In the situation of murder versus threatened harm, however, the taking of another's life is considered the greater of the two evils.

Necessity

The defense of necessity is applied in situations in which a person must break the law to avoid a greater evil caused by natural physical forces (storms, earthquakes, illness). This defense is only available when committing the crime is the lesser of two evils. For example, a person lacking a driver's license is justified in driving a car to escape a fire. However, as the famous English case *Regina v. Dudley and Stephens* indicates, necessity does not justify the intentional killing of another.[28] In that case, three sailors and a cabin boy had been shipwrecked and floating in the open seas in a lifeboat. After nine days without food and seven without water, two of the sailors, Dudley and Stephens, killed the cabin boy, and the three sailors ate his body and drank his blood. Four days later, the sailors were rescued. The court acknowledged that the cabin boy most likely would have died naturally because he was in the weakest condition but nevertheless judged the killing unjustified.

Self-Defense

Self-defense involves a claim that the defendant's actions were a justified response to the provocative behavior of the victim. Self-defense can be used to protect one's person or one's property.

An individual is justified in using force against another to protect himself or herself. When that happens, the person claims to have acted in self-defense and is therefore not guilty of the harm done. If the defendant was justified in using force, self-defense excuses such crimes as murder, manslaughter, and assault and battery. The law, however, has set limits as to what is reasonable and necessary self-defense. First, defendants must have a reasonable belief that they are in danger of death or great harm and that it is necessary for them to use force to prevent harm to themselves. For example, if Mary threatens to kill Jan but it is obvious that Mary is unarmed, Jan is not justified in pulling her gun and shooting Mary. However, if Mary, after threatening Jan, reaches into her pocket as if to get a gun and Jan then pulls her gun and shoots Mary, Jan could claim self-defense, even if it is discovered that Mary was unarmed. In this situation, Jan had a reasonable belief that harm was imminent and that it was necessary to shoot first to avoid injury to herself.

Second, the amount of force used must be no greater than that necessary to prevent personal harm. For instance, if Steve punches Ben, Ben could not justifiably hit Steve with an iron rod. Ben could, however, punch Steve back if he believed Steve was going to continue punching. Another issue arises concerning self-defense in situations in which deadly force may be necessary: Does a person have a duty to avoid using deadly force against an attacker by retreating if possible? U.S. courts are split on this issue. The majority of states maintain that the person attacked does not have to retreat, even if he or she can do so safely. This position is based on the policy that a person should not be forced to act in a humiliating or cowardly manner. However, many states do require that a person try to retreat, if it is possible to do so safely, before using deadly force. Even in most of these jurisdictions, however, people are not required to retreat if attacked in their homes or offices. The rules concerning self-defense also apply to situations involving the defense of a third person. Thus, if a person reasonably believes that another is in danger of unlawful bodily harm from an assailant, the person may use the force necessary to prevent the danger.

Using force to defend one's property from trespass or theft is allowable if the force is reasonable. This means that the use of force should be a last resort after requests to stop interfering with the property or legal action has failed. Also, the use of deadly force is not considered reasonable when only protection of property is concerned. This is based on the social policy that human life is more important than property.

The Goetz Case. The self-defense concept received national publicity when, on December 22, 1984, Bernhard Goetz shot four would-be robbers on a subway in New York. Despite some concern over the racial nature of the incident (Goetz is white and his assailants African-American), public support seemed overwhelmingly on the side of self-defense. The four youths admitted that they were on their way to steal money from video games and that they had demanded money from Goetz in a threatening manner. However, the prosecution charged that Goetz was only approached by two of the youths, who were panhandling, and that Goetz not only overreacted to the instant provocation but used an illegal handgun to shoot the youths. The most powerful evidence for the prosecution was the taped interviews Goetz made after he had surrendered to police in Concord, New Hampshire. He said on the videotape, "I wanted to kill those guys. I wanted to maim those guys. I wanted to make them suffer in every way I could." On the tape, Goetz claimed to have approached one of the boys he shot and, leaning over him, said, "You look all right, here's another." The tapes were used by the prosecutor to show Goetz as an obsessed, paranoid person who lived by his own rules.

In his defense, Goetz argued that his videotaped statements should be discounted as the unreliable perceptions of a traumatized crime victim. He also brought in psychological testimony that indicated that the extreme fear he felt may have caused his body to go on "automatic pilot." The prosecution's case was not helped when two of the boys were convicted for violent offenses, including the rape of a pregnant woman, before the trial began. Nor was it helped by the fact that the jury foreman had been the victim of a subway robbery in 1981. In the end, the case hinged on the judge's instructions to the jury that under New York law, the use of force is justified if the defendant had a reasonable belief that he or she was under the threat of deadly force himself or herself or that the defendant was to become the victim of a violent felony, such as robbery. The jury believed Goetz acted reasonably under the circumstances and acquitted him of all charges, except the relatively minor one of possessing an illegal handgun.[29]

Entrapment

Entrapment is another defense that excuses a defendant from criminal liability. The entrapment defense is raised when the defendant maintains that law enforcement officers induced him or her to commit a crime. The defendant would not have committed the crime had it

Bernhard Goetz, shown here reading a paper on a New York subway, was acquitted after a jury believed he acted in self-defense when he shot four youths who had attacked him while on a similar ride.

not been for trickery, persuasion, or fraud on the officers' part. In other words, if law enforcement officers plan a crime, implant the criminal idea in a person's mind, and pressure that person into doing the act, the person may plead entrapment. This situation is different from that in which an officer simply provides an opportunity for the crime to be committed and the defendant is willing and ready to do the act. For example, if a plainclothes police officer poses as a potential customer and is approached by a prostitute, no entrapment has occurred. However, if the same officer approaches a woman and persuades her to commit an act of prostitution, the defense of entrapment is appropriate.

In the famous ABSCAM case, federal agents posing as Arab businessmen recorded efforts by high-ranking government officials to solicit bribes as payment for using their influence in Congress. Though the federal agents were disguised and seemed to encourage the bribe attempts, courts ruled that their actions did not involve entrapment, since the agents were merely pro-viding an opportunity for the bribe attempts to be made and not planting the criminal idea in the minds of the government officials. However, in the equally famous DeLorean case involving cocaine smuggling, the jury believed John DeLorean was entrapped by the FBI since an informer acting on the agency's behalf originally suggested the idea of importing cocaine. Though DeLorean was a willing participant in the $24 million deal, the idea started with an agent of the government, and DeLorean was therefore found not guilty.

Reforming the Criminal Law

In recent years, many states and the federal government have been examining their substantive criminal law. Since the law, in part, reflects public opinion regarding various forms of behavior, what was a crime 40 years ago may not be considered so today. In some states, crimes such as possession of marijuana have been decriminalized—given reduced penalties. Such crimes may be punishable by a fine instead of a prison sentence. Other former criminal offenses, such as vagrancy, have been legalized—all criminal penalties have been removed. And, in some jurisdictions, penalties have been toughened, especially for violent crimes, such as rape and spousal assault.

The future direction of the criminal law in the United States remains unclear; both expansions and contractions can be expected. Certain actions will be adopted as criminal and given more attention, such as crimes by corporations and political corruption. Other offenses, such as recreational drug use, may be reduced in importance or removed entirely from the criminal law system. In addition, changing technology will require modification in the criminal law. For example, such technologies as automatic teller machines and cellular phones have already spawned a new generation of criminal acts involving "theft" of access numbers and cards. As the "information highway" is laid down, the nation's computer network advances, and biotechnology produces new substances, the criminal law will be forced to address threats to the public safety that are today unknown.

≡ Summary

The substantive criminal law is a set of rules that specifies the behavior society has outlawed. The criminal law can be distinguished from the civil law on the basis that the former involves powers given to the state to enforce social rules, while the latter controls interactions between private citizens. The criminal law serves several important purposes: it represents public opinion and moral values, it enforces social controls, it deters criminal behavior and wrongdoing, it punishes transgressors, and it banishes private retribution. The criminal law used in U.S. jurisdictions traces its origin to the English common law. Common law was formulated during the Middle Ages when King Henry II's judges began to use precedents set in one case to guide actions in another; this system is called stare decisis.

In the U.S. legal system, common-law crimes have been codified by lawmakers into state and federal penal codes. Today, most crimes fall into the category of felony or misdemeanor. Felonies are serious crimes usually punished by a prison term, whereas misdemeanors are minor crimes that carry a fine or a light jail sentence. Common felonies include murder, rape, assault with a deadly weapon, and robbery; misdemeanors include larceny, simple assault, and possession of small amounts of drugs.

Every crime has specific elements. In most instances, these elements include the actus reus (guilty act), which is the actual physical part of the crime; for example, taking money or burning a building. In addition, most crimes also contain a second element, the mens rea (guilty mind), which refers to the state of mind of the individual who commits a crime—more specifically, the person's intent to do the act.

At trial, the accused can defend themselves by claiming to have lacked mens rea and, therefore, not to be responsible for the criminal actions. One type of defense is excuse for mental reasons, such as insanity, intoxication, necessity, or duress. Another defense is justification by reason of self-defense or entrapment. Of all defenses, insanity is perhaps the most controversial. In most states, persons using an insanity defense claim that they did not know what they were doing when they committed a crime or that their mental state did not allow them to tell the difference between right and wrong (the M'Naghten Rule). Insanity defenses can also include the claims that the offender was motivated by an irresistible impulse or lacked the substantial capacity to conform his or her conduct to the criminal law. Regardless of the insanity defense used, critics charge that mental illness is separate from legal responsibility and that the two should not be equated. Supporters counter that the insanity defense allows mentally ill people to avoid penal sanctions.

The criminal law is undergoing constant reform. Some acts are being decriminalized—their penalties are being reduced—while laws are being revised to make penalties for some acts more severe. The law must confront social and technological change.

≡ KEY TERMS

more	wer
folkways	wite
Code of Hammurabi	stare decisis
lex talionis	inchoate crimes
Twelve Tables	tort law
plebeians	felony
patricians	misdemeanor
wergild	mala in se
oath-helpers	mala prohibitum
shire	vagrancy
hundreds	actus reus
tithings	mens rea
hundred-gemot	transferred intent
shire-gemot	constructive intent
hali-gemot	strict-liability crimes
bot	M'Naghten Rule

☰ NOTES

1. The historical material in the following sections was derived from a number of sources. The most important include: Rene Wormser, *The Story of Law,* rev. ed. (New York: Simon and Schuster, 1962); Jackson Spielvogel, *Western Civilization* (St. Paul: West Publishing, 1991); Eugen Weber, *A Modern History of Europe* (New York: W. W. Norton, 1971); James Heath, *Eighteenth-Century Penal Theory* (New York: Oxford University Press, 1963); David Jones, *History of Criminology* (Westport, Conn.: Greenwood Press, 1986); Fred Inbau, James Thompson, and James Zagel, *Criminal Law and Its Administration* (Mineola, N.Y.: Foundation Press, 1974); Wayne LaFave and Austin Scott, *Criminal Law,* 2d ed. (St. Paul: West Publishing, 1986); and Sanford Kadish and Monrad Paulsen, *Criminal Law and Its Processes* (Boston: Little, Brown, 1975).

2. Weber, *A Modern History of Europe,* p. 9.

3. LaFave and Scott, *Handbook on Criminal Law* (St. Paul, Minn.: West Publishing, 1982), pp. 528–29.

4. Caldwell 397 (1784), cited in LaFave and Scott, *Handbook on Criminal Law,* p. 422.

5. 9 George I, C. 22, 1723, cited in Douglas Hay, "Crime and Justice in Eighteenth and Nineteenth Century England," in *Crime and Justice,* vol. 2, ed. Norval Norris and Michael Tonrey (Chicago: University of Chicago Press, 1980), p. 51.

6. Jerome Hall, *Theft, Law, and Society* (Indianapolis: Bobbs-Merrill, 1952); Chapter 1 is generally considered the best source for the history of common-law theft crimes.

7. Mass. Gen. Laws Ann. (West 1982) ch. 266, pp. 1–2.

8. See, generally, Alfred Lindesmith, *The Addict and the Law* (New York: Vintage Books, 1965), chap. 1.

9. Edna Erez and Bankole Thompson, "Rape in Sierra Leone: Conflict between the Sexes and Conflict of Laws," *International Journal of Comparative and Applied Criminal Justice* 14 (1990): 201–10.

10. William Henry, "Did the Music Say 'Do It'?" *Time,* 30 July 1990, p. 65.

11. Mathew Brelis, "Man Must Pay $500,000 for Raping Daughter," *Boston Globe,* 2 July 1993, p. 1.

12. For example, see *Brinegar v. United States,* 388 U.S. 160 (1949); *Speiser v. Randall,* 357 U.S. 513 (1958); *In re Winship,* 397 U.S. 358 (1970).

13. Oliver Wendell Holmes, *The Common Law,* ed. Mark De Wolf (Boston: Little, Brown, 1881), p. 36.

14. William Chambliss, "A Sociological Analysis of the Law of Vagrancy," *Social Problems* 12 (1964): 67–77; idem, "On Trashing Marxist Criminology," *Criminology* 27 (1989): 231–39.

15. Jeffrey Adler, "A Historical Analysis of the Law of Vagrancy," *Criminology* 27 (1989): 209–30; Adler, "Vagging the Demons and Scoundrels: Vagrancy and the Growth of St. Louis, 1830–1861," *Journal of Urban History* 13 (1986): 3–30.

16. *Carrier's Case,* Y.B. 13 Edw. 4, f. 9, pl. 5 (Star Chamber and Exchequer Chamber, 1473), discussed at length in Jerome Hall, *Theft, Law and Society* (Indianapolis: Bobbs-Merrill, 1952), chap. 1.

17. Mass. Gen. Laws Ann. (West 1983) ch. 266, p. 14.

18. 320 U.S. 277 (1943).

19. LaFave and Scott, *Handbook on Criminal Law,* p. 356.

20. Ibid., p. 361.

21. 8 Eng. Rep. 718 (1843).

22. Kadish and Paulsen, *Criminal Law and Its Processes,* pp. 215–16.

23. *Model Penal Code* 401 (1952).

24. LaFave and Scott, *Handbook on Criminal Law,* p. 516.

25. Comprehensive Crime Control Act of 1984—Pub. L. No. 98-473, 403. 23.

26. Rita Simon and David Aaronson, *The Insanity Defense: A Critical Assessment of Law and Policy in the Post-Hinckley Era* (New York: Praeger, 1988).

27. Samuel Walker, *Sense and Nonsense about Crime* (Monterey, Calif.: Brooks Cole, 1985), p. 120.

28. *Regina v. Dudley and Stephens,* 14 Q.B. 273 (1884).

29. John Kennedy, "Goetz Acquitted of Major Charges in Subway Shooting," *Boston Globe,* 17 June 1987, p. 1.

Chapter

3

The Nature and Extent of Crime

☰ Introduction

How much crime is there? What are the patterns and trends in crime? Who commits crime? What is the nature of criminality? These are some of the most important questions in the study of criminology. Without such information, it would be possible neither to formulate theories that explain the onset of crime nor to devise social policies that facilitate its control or elimination.

In this chapter, data collected on criminal offenders will be reviewed in some detail. They will be used to provide a summary of crime patterns and trends. A number of questions will be addressed: Are crime rates increasing? Where and when does crime take place? What are the social and individual patterns that affect the crime rate? What effect do age, race, gender, and social class have on the crime rate? Finally, we review the concept of criminal careers and discover what available crime data can tell us about the onset, continuation, and termination of criminality.

☰ The Uniform Crime Report

The Federal Bureau of Investigation's Uniform Crime Report (UCR) is the best known and most widely cited source of aggregate criminal statistics.[1] The FBI receives and compiles records from over 16,000 police departments serving a majority of the U.S. population. Its major unit of analysis involves the **index crimes,** or **Type I crimes:** murder and nonnegligent manslaughter, forcible rape, robbery, aggravated assault, burglary, larceny, arson, and motor vehicle theft. Table 3.1 defines these crimes. The FBI tallies and annually publishes the number of reported offenses by city, county, standard metropolitan statistical area, and geographical divisions of the United States. In addition to these statistics, the UCR provides information on the number and characteristics (age, race, gender) of individuals who have been arrested for these and all other crimes, except traffic violations **(Type II crimes).**

The methods used to compile the UCR are quite complex. Each month, law enforcement agencies report

TABLE 3.1 Type I Offenses

Criminal homicide—(a) Murder and nonnegligent manslaughter: the willful (nonnegligent) killing of one human being by another. Deaths caused by negligence, attempts to kill, assaults to kill, suicides, accidental deaths, and justifiable homicides are excluded. Justifiable homicides are limited to: (1) the killing of a felon by a law enforcement officer in the line of duty; and (2) the killing of a felon by a private citizen. (b) Manslaughter by negligence: the killing of another person through gross negligence. Traffic fatalities are excluded. While manslaughter by negligence is a Type I crime, it is not included in the crime index.

Forcible rape—The carnal knowledge of a female forcibly and against her will. Included are rapes by force and attempts or assaults to rape. Statutory offenses (no force used—victim under age of consent) are excluded.

Robbery—The taking or attempting to take anything of value from the care, custody, or control of a person or persons by force or threat of force or violence and/or by putting the victim in fear.

Aggravated assault—An unlawful attack by one person upon another for the purpose of inflicting severe or aggravated bodily injury. This type of assault usually is accompanied by the use of a weapon or by means likely to produce death or great bodily harm. Simple assaults are excluded.

Burglary–breaking or entering—The unlawful entry of a structure to commit a felony or a theft. Attempted forcible entry is included.

Larceny–theft (except motor vehicle theft)—The unlawful taking, carrying, leading, or riding away of property from the possession or constructive possession of another. Examples are thefts of bicycles or automobile accessories, shoplifting, pocket-picking, or the stealing of any property or article which is not taken by force and violence or by fraud. Attempted larcenies are included. Embezzlement, con games, forgery, worthless checks, and so on, are excluded.

Motor vehicle theft—The theft or attempted theft of a motor vehicle. A motor vehicle is self-propelled and runs on the surface and not on rails. Specifically excluded from this category are motorboats, construction equipment, airplanes, and farming equipment.

the number of index crimes known to them. A count of these crimes is taken from records of all complaints of crime these agencies received from victims, officers who discovered the infractions, or other sources.

Whenever complaints of crime are determined through investigation to be unfounded or false, they are eliminated from the actual count. The number of "actual offenses known" is reported to the FBI whether or not anyone is arrested for the crime, the stolen property is recovered, or prosecution is undertaken.

In addition, law enforcement agencies each month report the total crimes that were cleared. Crimes are cleared in two ways: (1) when at least one person is arrested, charged, and turned over to the court for prosecution, or (2) by exceptional means, when some element beyond police control precludes the physical arrest of an offender (for example, the offender leaves the country). Traditionally, about 20 percent of all reported index crimes are cleared by arrest. Violent crimes are more likely to be solved than property crimes, probably because police devote more resources to these more serious acts, because witnesses (including the victim) are available to identify offenders, and because, in many instances, the victim and offender were previously acquainted.

Data on the number of clearances involving only the arrest of offenders under the age of 18, data on the value of property stolen and recovered in connection with Type I offenses, and detailed information pertaining to criminal homicide are also reported.

The UCR employs three methods to express crime data. First, the number of crimes reported to the police and arrests made are expressed as raw figures (for example, 23,760 murders occurred in 1992). In addition, the percent changes in the amount of crime between years are computed (for example, murder decreased 3.8 percent between 1991 and 1992). Finally, crime rates per 100,000 people are computed. That is, when the UCR indicates that the murder rate was 9.3 in 1992, it means that about 9.3 people in every 100,000 were murdered between January 1 and December 31 of 1992. The equation used is:

$$\frac{\text{Number of reported crimes}}{\text{Total U.S. population}} \times 100{,}000 = \frac{\text{Rate per}}{100{,}000}$$

Critique of the Uniform Crime Report

Despite its importance and wide use by criminologists, the accuracy of the UCR has been heavily criticized. The three greatest areas of concern—reporting practices, law enforcement practices, and methodological problems—are discussed below.

Reporting Practices. One major concern of criminologists is that many serious crimes are not reported by victims to police and therefore do not become part of the UCR. The reasons for not reporting vary. Some people do not have property insurance and therefore believe it is useless to report theft-related crimes. In other cases, the victim may fear reprisals from the offender's friends or family.

Surveys of the victims of crime indicate that fewer than half of all criminal incidents are reported to the police, chiefly because the victim believed the incident was "a private matter," that "nothing could be done," or that the "victimization was not important enough."[2] These findings indicate that the UCR data may significantly underrepresent the total number of annual criminal events. (See Figure 3.1.)

Law Enforcement Practices. The way police departments record and report criminal and delinquent activity also affects the validity of UCR statistics. This effect was recognized more than 40 years ago, when between 1948 and 1952, the number of burglaries in New York City rose from 2,726 to 42,491, and larcenies increased from 7,713 to 70,949.[3] These increases were found to be related to the change from a precinct to a centralized reporting system for crime statistics. A central reporting system instituted in Philadelphia in 1952 resulted in a sharp rise in index crimes—from 16,773 in 1951 to 28,560 in 1953.[4]

How police interpret the definitions of index crimes may also affect reporting practices. One study found that the Boston police reported only completed rapes to the FBI, while the Los Angeles police reported completed rapes, attempted rapes, and sexual assaults; these reporting practices helped account for the fact that Los Angeles's rape rate was far higher than Boston's.[5] Similarly, Patrick Jackson found that arson may be seriously underreported because many fire departments do not report to the FBI and those that do exclude many fires that are probably set by arsonists.[6]

Lawrence Sherman and Barry Glick have also found that local police departments make systematic errors in UCR reporting.[7] All 196 departments they surveyed counted an arrest only after a formal booking procedure, although the UCR requires arrests to be counted if the suspect is released without a formal charge. In addition, 29 percent did not include citations, and 57 percent did

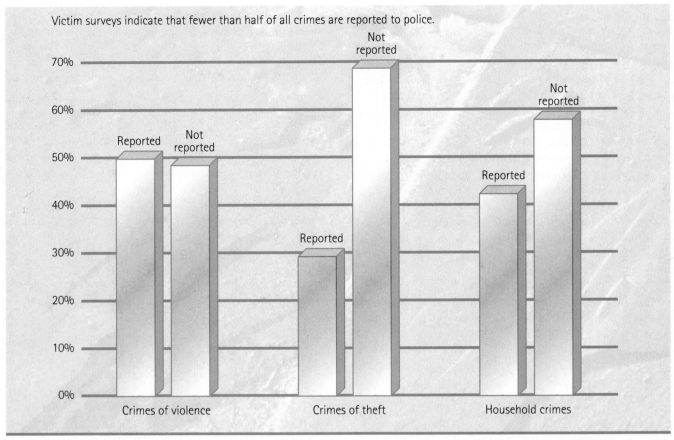

FIGURE 3.1   **Percent of Victimizations, by Type of Crime and Whether or Not Reported to the Police**

SOURCE: Lisa Bastian and Marshall DeBerry, *Criminal Victimization in the United States* (Washington, D.C.: Bureau of Justice Statistics, 1994).

not include summonses, though the UCR requires it. An audit of arrests found an error rate of about 10 percent in every Type I offense category.

Of a more serious nature are allegations that police officials may deliberately alter reported crimes to improve their department's public image. Police administrators interested in lowering the crime rate may falsify crime reports; for example, by classifying a burglary as a nonreportable trespass.[8]

Finally, increased police efficiency and professionalism may actually help *increase* crime rates. As more sophisticated, computer-aided technology is developed for police work and as the education and training of law enforcement employees increases, so too might their ability to record and report crimes, thereby producing higher crime rates.

Methodological Problems. Methodological issues also add to the problems of the UCR's validity. Leonard Savitz has collected a list of 20 such issues, including:

1. No federal crimes are reported.
2. Reports are voluntary and vary in accuracy and completeness.
3. Not all police departments submit reports.
4. The FBI uses estimates in its total crime projections.
5. If multiple crimes are committed by an offender, only the most serious is recorded. Thus, if a narcotics addict rapes, robs, and murders a victim, only the murder is recorded as a crime.
6. Each act is listed as a single offense for some crimes but not others. If a man robbed six people in a bar, the offense is listed as one robbery; but if he assaulted them, it would be listed as six assaults.
7. Incomplete acts are lumped together with completed ones.
8. Important differences exist between the FBI's definition of a crime and those used in a number of states.[9]

Future of the Uniform Crime Report. What does the future hold for the UCR? The FBI is preparing to implement some important changes in the Uniform Crime Reports. First, the definitions of many crimes will be revised. For example, rape will be defined in sexually neutral terms: *the carnal knowledge of a person, forcibly and/or against that person's will; or not forcibly or against the person's will where the victim is incapable of giving consent because of his or her temporary or permanent mental incapacity.*

An attempt also will be made to provide more detailed information on individual criminal incidents through the National Incident-Based Reporting System. Instead of submitting statements of the kinds of crime that individual citizens reported to the police and summary statements of resulting arrests, it is planned that local police agencies would provide at least a brief account of each incident and arrest within 22 crime patterns, including incident, victim, and offender information. These expanded crime categories would include numerous additional crimes, such as blackmail, embezzlement, drug offenses, and bribery. This would allow a national data base on the nature of crime, victims, and criminals to be developed.[10] Other information to be collected would be statistics gathered by federal law enforcement agencies, as well as data on hate or bias crimes. These changes were initiated in 1989, and the first reports reflecting them should be out in the near future. If it is implemented on schedule, this new UCR program may bring about greater uniformity in cross-jurisdictional reporting and improve the accuracy of official crime data.

≡ Self-Report Surveys

The problems associated with official statistics have led many criminologists to seek alternative sources of information in assessing the true extent of crime patterns. In addition, official statistics do not say much about the personality, attitudes, and behavior of individual criminals. They also are of little value in charting the extent of substance abuse in the population because relatively few abusers are arrested. Criminologists have therefore sought additional sources to supplement and expand official data.

One frequently employed alternative to official statistics is the **self-report survey.** Self-report studies are designed to allow participants to reveal information about their violations of the law. The studies have many different formats. For example, the criminologist can approach people who have been arrested by police, or even prison inmates, and interview them about their illegal activities. Subjects can also be first telephoned at home and then mailed a survey form. Most often, self-report surveys are administered to large groups through a mass distribution of questionnaires. The names of subjects can be requested, but more commonly, they remain anonymous. The basic assumption of self-report studies is that the anonymity of the respondents and the promise of confidentiality backed by the academic credentials of the survey administrator will encourage people to accurately describe their illegal activities. Self-reports are viewed as a mechanism to get at the "dark figures of crime," the figures missed by official statistics. Table 3.2 shows some typical self-report items.

Most self-report studies have focused on juvenile delinquency and youth crime, for two reasons.[11] First, the school setting makes it convenient to test thousands of subjects simultaneously, all of them with the means to respond to a research questionnaire at their disposal (pens, desks, time). Second, since attendance is universal, a school-based self-report survey is an estimate of the activities of a cross-section of the community.

Self-reports, though, are not restricted to youth crime and have been used to examine the offense histories of prison inmates, drug users, and other subsets of the population.

Self-reports make it possible to assess the number of people in the population who have committed illegal acts and the frequency of their law violations. They are particularly useful for assessing the extent of the national substance abuse problem because most drug use goes undetected by police. And, because most self-report instruments also contain items measuring subjects' attitudes, values, personal characteristics, and behaviors, the data obtained from them can be used for various purposes, such as testing theories, measuring attitudes toward crime, and computing the association between crime and important social variables, such as family relations, educational attainment, and income.

Self-reports provide a broader picture of the distribution of criminality than official data because they do not depend on the offender being apprehended. They can be used to estimate the number of criminal offenders unknown to the police and who never figure in the official crime statistics, some of whom may even be serious or chronic offenders.[12] Since many criminologists believe that class, gender, and racial bias exists in the criminal justice system, self-reports allow evaluation of the distribution of criminal behavior across racial, class, and gender lines. Their use enables criminologists to

TABLE 3.2 Self-Report Survey Questions

Please indicate how often in the past 12 months you did each act. (Check the best answer.)					
	Never Did Act	One Time	2–5 Times	6–9 Times	10+ Times
Stole something worth less than $50	_____	_____	_____	_____	_____
Stole something worth more than $50	_____	_____	_____	_____	_____
Used cocaine	_____	_____	_____	_____	_____
Been in a fistfight	_____	_____	_____	_____	_____
Carried a weapon such as a gun or knife	_____	_____	_____	_____	_____
Fought someone using a weapon	_____	_____	_____	_____	_____
Stole a car	_____	_____	_____	_____	_____
Used force to steal	_____	_____	_____	_____	_____
(For boys) Forced a girl to have sexual relations against her will	_____	_____	_____	_____	_____

determine if the official arrest data is truly representative of the offender population or reflects bias, discrimination, and selective enforcement. For example, racial bias may be present if self-reports indicate that black and white respondents report equal amounts of crime, but the official data indicate that minorities are *arrested* more often than whites. In sum, self-reports can provide a significant amount of information about offenders that cannot be found in the official statistics.

Evaluating Self-Report Studies

Though self-report data have had a profound effect on criminological inquiry, some important methodological issues have been raised about their accuracy. Critics of self-report studies frequently suggest that it is unreasonable to expect people to candidly admit illegal acts. They have nothing to gain, and the ones taking the greatest risk are the ones with official records who may be engaging in the most criminality. On the other hand, some people may exaggerate their criminal acts, forget some of them, or be confused about what is being asked. Most surveys contain an overabundance of trivial offenses—skipping school, running away, using a false identification (ID)—often lumped together with serious crimes to form a "total crime index." Consequently, comparisons between groups can be highly misleading. Nor can we be certain how valid self-report studies are, because we have nothing reliable to measure them

against. Correlation with official reports is expected to be low, because the inadequacies of such reports were largely responsible for the development of self-reports in the first place.

Various techniques have been used to verify self-report data.[13] The "known group" method compares incarcerated youths with "normal" groups to see whether the former report more delinquency. Another approach is to use peer informants who can verify the honesty of a subject's answers. Subjects are tested twice to see if their answers remain stable. Sometimes questions are designed to reveal respondents who are lying on the survey; for example, an item might say: "I have never done anything wrong in my life." It is also possible to compare the answers youths give with their official police records. A typical approach is to ask youths if they have ever been arrested for or convicted of a delinquent act and then check their official records against their self-reported responses. A number of studies using this method have found a remarkable uniformity between self-reported answers and official records[14] In a classic study, John Clark and Larry Tifft used a polygraph to verify the responses given on a self-report survey; they reported that the "lie detector" results validated survey data.[15] In what is probably the most thorough analysis of self-report methodologies, Michael Hindelang, Travis Hirschi, and Joseph Weis closely reviewed the literature concerning the reliability and validity of self-reports and conducted their own independent analysis using data gathered in Seattle, Washington, and other sites.[16] They concluded that the problems of accuracy in self-reports are surmountable, that self-reports are more accurate than most criminologists believe, and that self-reports and official statistics are quite compatible.[17]

Are Self-Reports Valid?

While these findings are encouraging, nagging questions still remain about the validity of self-reports. Even if 90 percent of a school population voluntarily participates in a self-report study, researchers can never know for sure whether or not the few who refuse to participate or are absent that day comprise a significant portion of the school's population of persistent high-rate offenders. School surveys also miss incarcerated youth and dropouts whose numbers may include some of the most serious offenders. Recent research by Terence Thornberry and his associates implies that the "missing cases" in self-reports may be more crime-prone than the general population.[18]

It is also possible that self-reports are weakest in the one area they are most heavily relied on: measuring substance abuse.[19] Thomas Gray and Eric Wish have found that drug users may significantly underreport the frequency of their substance abuse. Gray and Wish surveyed a group of juvenile detainees and also tested them with urinalysis. They found that *less than one-third* of the kids who tested positively for marijuana also reported using it; only 15 percent of those testing positive for cocaine admitted using it during the prior month. While this research involves a sample of incarcerated youth who might be expected to underreport drug use, the findings undercut the validity of self-report surveys.[20] Wish and Christina Polsenberg conducted similar research with adult pretrial detainees in Washington, D.C., and again found that self-reports significantly undercounted drug abuse.[21]

So while the consensus of opinion is that self-reports are both a valid and reliable measure of most delinquent and criminal behaviors, their accuracy in determining the behavior of two critical elements of the offending population, chronic offenders and persistent drug abusers, may be limited.

≡ Victim Surveys

A third source of crime data are surveys that ask the victims of crime about their encounters with criminals. Since many victims do not report their experiences to the police, victim surveys are considered a method of getting at the dark figures of crime.

The first national survey of 10,000 households was conducted in 1966 as part of the President's Commission on Law Enforcement and the Administration of Justice. The commission was a ground-breaking attempt that brought many of the nation's leading law enforcement and academic experts together to develop a picture of the crime problem in the United States and how the criminal justice system responds to criminal behavior. The national survey indicated that the number of criminal victimizations in the United States was far higher than previously believed because many victims failed to report crime to the police, fearing retaliation or official indifference.

This early research encouraged development of the most widely used and most extensive victim survey to date, the **National Crime Victimization Survey** (NCVS).[22]

The National Crime Victimization Survey

The National Crime Victimization Survey is conducted by the U.S. Bureau of the Census in cooperation with the Bureau of Justice Statistics of the U.S. Department of Justice. In the national surveys, samples of housing units are selected using a complex, multistage sampling technique.

The total annual sample size for the most recent national survey is about 66,000 households, containing about 110,000 individuals over 12 years of age. The total sample is composed of six independently selected subsamples interviewed twice a year about victimizations suffered in the preceding six months. The crimes they are asked about include personal and household larcenies, burglary, motor vehicle theft, assaults, robberies, and any other violent acts.

Households remain in the sample for about three years, and new homes rotate into the sample on an ongoing basis. The NCVS reports that the interview completion rate in the national sample is about 96 percent of those selected to be interviewed in any given period. Considering the care with which the samples are drawn and the high completion rate, NCVS data are considered a relatively unbiased and valid estimate of all victimizations for the target crimes included in the survey.

Critique of the NCVS

Like the UCR and self-report surveys, the NCVS may also suffer from some methodological problems, so its findings must be interpreted with caution. Among the potential problems are:

1. Overreporting due to victims' misinterpretation of events. For example, a lost wallet is reported as stolen, or an open door is viewed as a burglary attempt.
2. Underreporting due to embarrassment of reporting crime to interviewers, fear of getting in trouble, or simply forgetting an incident.
3. Inability to record the personal criminal activity of those interviewed, such as drug use or gambling; murder is also not included, for obvious reasons.

Are Crime Statistics Sources Compatible?

Are the various sources of criminal statistics compatible? Each has its own strengths and weaknesses. The FBI survey is carefully tallied and contains data on the number of murders and people arrested, information that the other data sources lack; yet it omits the many crimes victims choose not to report to the police and is subject to the reporting caprices of individual police departments. The NCVS does contain unreported crime and important information on the personal characteristics of victims, but the data consists of estimates made from relatively limited samples of the total U.S. population, so that even narrow fluctuations in the rates of some crimes can have a major impact on findings; it also relies on personal recollections that may be inaccurate. The NCVS does not include data on important crime patterns, including murder and drug abuse. Self-report surveys can provide information on the personal characteristics of offenders, their attitudes, values, beliefs, and psychological profile that is unavailable from any other source. Yet, at their core, self-reports rely on the honesty of criminal offenders and drug abusers, a population not generally known for accuracy and integrity.

There may be an upward trend in violence rates because it has proven so easy to purchase high-powered weapons such as the AK47 shown here for sale in a local gun shop. Will the ban on the sale of such weapons help lower crime rates?

Despite these differences, a number of prominent criminologists have concluded that the data sources are more compatible than was first believed possible. While their tallies of crimes are certainly not in synch, the **crime patterns and trends** they record are often quite similar.[23] For example, all three sources are in general agreement about the personal characteristics of serious criminals (such as age and gender) and where and when crime occurs (such as urban areas, nighttime, and summer months).

While this may be persuasive, some criminologists still question the compatibility between the data sources and imply that they measure separate concepts (for example, reported crimes, actual crimes, and victimization rates).[24] This ongoing academic debate punctuates the fact that interpreting crime data is often problematic. Because each source of crime data uses a different method to obtain results, differences inevitably will occur between them. These differences must be carefully considered when interpreting the data on the nature and trends in crime that follow.[25]

Official Crime Trends in the United States

Studies using official statistics have indicated that a gradual increase in the crime rate, especially in violent crime, occurred from 1830 to 1860. Following the Civil War, this rate increased significantly for about 15 years. Then, from 1880 to the time of World War I, with the possible exception of the years immediately preceding and following the war, the number of reported crimes decreased. After a period of readjustment, the overall crime rate steadily declined until the Depression (about 1930), whereupon another general increase, or crime wave, was recorded.[26] Crime rates increased gradually following the 1930s until the 1960s, when they grew much faster. The homicide rate, which had declined from the 1930s to the 1970s, began a period of sharp increase.

As Figure 3.2 indicates, the crime rate began to increase sharply in 1960 and continued to do so through

FIGURE 3.2 **Crime Rate Trends 1960–1993**

SOURCE: Lisa Bastian and Marshall DeBerry, *Criminal Victimization in the United State 1992* (Washington, D.C.: Bureau of Justice Statistics, 1994).

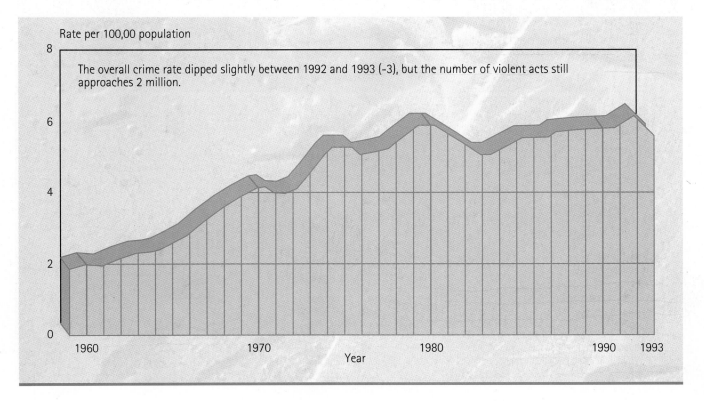

Rate per 100,00 population

The overall crime rate dipped slightly between 1992 and 1993 (-3), but the number of violent acts still approaches 2 million.

the 1970s until 1981, when more than 13.4 million index crimes were reported—a rate of 5,950 per 100,000 people. After a decline in the mid-1980s to 11.1 million crimes, the number of crimes increased to about 14 million, or about 5,700 crimes per 100,000 population, in 1993. While the property crime rate has remained rather stable, the more serious violent crimes show a significant increase in both number and rate. Between 1983 and 1993, the violent crime rate increased about 40 percent.

Self-Report Trends

In general, self-reports indicate that the number of people who break the law is far greater than the number projected by the official statistics. In fact, when truancy, alcohol consumption, petty theft, and recreational drug use are included in self-report scales, almost everyone tested is found to have violated some law.[27] Furthermore, self-reports dispute the notion that criminals and delinquents specialize in one type of crime or another; offenders seem to engage in a "mixed bag" of crime and deviance.[28]

Self-report studies indicate that the most common offenses are truancy, alcohol abuse, use of a false ID, shoplifting or larceny under fifty dollars, fighting, marijuana use, and damage to the property of others. It is not unusual for self-reports to find combined substance abuse, theft, violence, and damage rates of more than 50 percent among suburban, rural, and urban high school youths. What is surprising is the consistency of these findings in samples taken from southern, eastern, midwestern, and western states.

When the results of recent self-report surveys are compared with various studies conducted over a 20-year period, a uniform pattern emerges. The use of drugs and alcohol increased markedly in the 1970s, leveled off in the 1980s, and declined in the early 1990s; theft, violence, and damage-related crimes seem more stable. Although a self-reported crime wave has not occurred, neither has there been any visible reduction in self-reported criminality.[29]

Table 3.3 contains data from an annual self-report study conducted by researchers at the University of Michigan Institute for Social Research (ISR). This national survey of over 2,500 high school seniors, one of the most important sources of self-report data, also finds a widespread yet stable pattern of youth crime since 1978.[30] The ISR survey does show that young people commit a great deal of crime: about one-third of high school seniors now report stealing in the last 12 months, 13 percent injured someone so badly that the victim had to see a doctor, 32 percent admitted shoplifting, and 26 percent engaged in breaking and entering. The fact that at least one-third of all U.S. high school students

TABLE 3.3 **Self-Reported Delinquent Acts, High School Class of 1993***

	Percent Who Committed Act				
Delinquent Act	Never	Once	Twice	3 or 4 Times	5 or more Times
Serious flight	82	10	4	3	1
Gang or group fight	78	11	6	3	2
Hurt someone badly	87	7	3	2	2
Used a weapon	95	2	1	1	1
Stealing less than $50	68	14	7	5	7
Stealing more than $50	89	5	2	2	3
Shoplifting	60	13	6	5	7
Car theft	94	3	1	1	1
Larceny from car	93	3	2	1	1
Breaking and entering	74	12	7	3	3
Arson	97	2	1	1	1
Damaged school property	85	6	4	2	2
Damaged work property	94	3	2	1	1

*2,627 students completed survey; percentages are rounded.
SOURCE: Jerald Bachman, Lloyd Johnston, and Patrick O'Malley, *Monitoring the Future, 1993* (Ann Arbor, Mich.: University of Michigan, Institute for Social Research, 1994).

engaged in theft and at least 19 percent committed a serious violent act during the past year shows that criminal activity is widespread and not restricted to a few "bad apples."

Victim Data Trends

According to the most recently available NCVS data (1992), about 33 million personal crimes occur each year. As Figure 3.3 indicates, there was a stable but steady increase in the total number of crimes between 1973 and 1981, when more than 41 million were recorded. Since then, the number of estimated criminal incidents began five years of decline to a 1986 low of 34.1 million events and has continued to hover around that number. However, the decline in the overall victimization rate masks a slight upturn in violent crime, which reflects trends reported in the UCR.

It is quite apparent that the number of crimes accounted for by the NCVS is considerably larger than the number of crimes reported to the FBI. For example, while the UCR recorded 672,000 robberies in 1992, the NCVS estimates that about 1.2 million actually occurred. The reason for such discrepancies is that fewer than half the violent crimes, less than one-third the personal theft crimes (such as pocket-picking), and fewer than half of the household thefts are reported to police. The reasons

most often given by victims for not reporting crime include believing that "nothing can be done about it," that it was a "private matter," or that they did not want to "get involved." Victims seem to report to the police only crimes that involve considerable loss or injury. If we are to believe NCVS findings, the official statistics do not provide an accurate picture of the crime problem since many crimes go unreported to the police.

☰ Explaining Crime Trends

How can the recent trends in the reported crime rate be explained? Criminologists view change in the age distribution of the population as having the greatest influence on recent violent crime trends: as a general rule, the crime rate follows the proportion of young males in the population. The postwar baby-boom generation reached their teenage years in the 1960s, just as the crime rate began a sharp increase. Since both the victims and perpetrators of crime tend to fall in the 18-to-25 age category, the rise in crime reflected the age structure of society. With the "graying" of society in the 1980s and a decline in the birth rate, it was not surprising that the overall crime rate stabilized.

FIGURE 3.3   **Victimization Trends, 1973–1992**

SOURCE: Lisa Bastian, *Criminal Victimization, 1992* (Washington, D.C.: Bureau of Justice Statistics, 1993), p. 1.

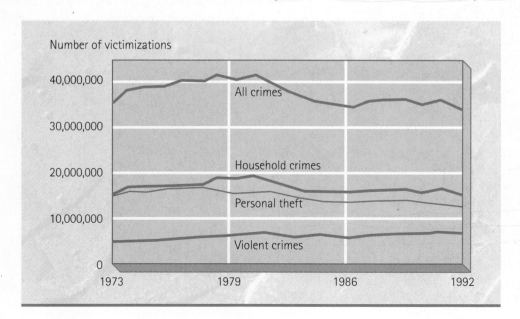

How can the recent crime patterns be explained? Why has the violence rate trended upward?

One reason may be that the baby boomers' children are now growing up, increasing the size of the "at risk" population. While the percentage of the population aged 17 to 25 is no higher than a decade ago, this new set of adolescents and young adults are more "criminally precocious" than their parents: they start committing violent crimes earlier, at a greater frequency, and they are better armed. Between 1970 and 1992, the rate of adolescents arrested for homicide *more than doubled,* while homicide arrest rates for adults actually *declined.* Official data shows that adolescent participation in more serious felonies, such as murder and rape, have increased significantly.[31]

Economic recession and the restructuring of the economy may have produced a climate of hopelessness in the nation's largest cities, which encourages criminal violence. Teenage unemployment rates have drifted upward and are especially high in urban areas that contain large at-risk populations. Increases in other social ills, including the number of single-parent families, divorce and dropout rates, nonrecreational drug use, and teen pregnancies may also influence crime rates. For example, cross-national research indicates that child homicide rates are greatest in those nations, including the United States, that have the highest rates of illegitimacy and teenage mothers.[32] As illegitimacy rates rise and social spending is cut, the rate of violent crime might trend upward.

Some experts tie increases in the violent crime rate to drug-trafficking gangs in the nation's largest cities. Well-armed drug-dealing gangs do not hesitate to use violence to control territories, intimidate rivals, and increase "market share." Washington, D.C., provides a dramatic example of the drug-crime relationship: In 1985, 21 percent of the homicides there were reported as drug-related; by 1988, 80 percent of the homicides were drug-related.[33] The use of addicting drugs seems epidemic in the largest and poorest urban areas; these areas are also the locale of violent crime. Drug-crime arrests increased almost 60 percent between 1983 and 1993, indicating that police are giving greater attention to substance abuse cases.[34]

It is also possible that the violence rate has not changed at all but that police agencies are doing a better job of collecting and reporting criminal incidents to the FBI. However, the UCR is thought to be at least a reliable indicator of the most serious violent crime—murder—and the official data show that the murder rate has increased significantly in the last five years. While property crime levels have been stable, the nation has experienced an upswing in the most violent crimes.

☰ What the Future Holds

It is always risky to speculate about the future of crime trends since current conditions can change rapidly. But some criminologists have gone "out on a limb" to predict future patterns. Darrell Steffensmeier and Miles Harer suggest that violent crime will drop during the remainder of the 1990s as the baby boomers pass into middle and old age; they speculate that the property crime rate will at first decline, then level off and begin rising toward the end of the decade as the baby-boomlet kids born in the early 1980s begin to hit their "peak" crime years. After the year 2000, both property and vio-

A contingent of female police officers in Tokyo. Does the Japanese cultural emphasis on honor, duty, and loyalty help explain Japan's relatively low crime rate? (See the Close-Up "Crime and Shame.")

lent crimes are predicted to increase.[35] Steffensmeier and Harer find that the age structure of society is the single most powerful influence on the crime rate.

Of course, such predictions are based on population trends and can be thrown off by changes in the structure of the population and even cultural forces. For example, it is possible that current national outrage over violent crime will help make violence so shameful that local residents will be willing to take drastic actions to reduce crime, cooperate with the police, and pressure families to control the young. Research by Rosemary Gartner and Robert Nash Parker shows that murder rates in Japan and Scotland are unaffected by population trends because in these nations, violence is considered shameful and a disgrace.[36] Can changing moral values influence crime rates? The Close-Up "Crime and Shame: Crime Rates in the United States and Japan" takes a look at this question.

Crime Patterns

What do the various sources of criminological statistics tell us about crime in the United States? What is known about the nature of crime and criminals? What trends or patterns exist in the crime rate that can help us understand the causes of crime?

Criminologists look for stable patterns in the crime rate to gain insight into the nature of crime. If crime rates are consistently higher at certain times, in certain areas, and among certain groups, this knowledge might be used to explain the onset or cause of crime. For example, if criminal statistics show that crime rates are consistently higher in poor neighborhoods in large urban areas, then crime may be a function of poverty and neighborhood decline. If, in contrast, crime rates are spread evenly across the social structure, then there would be little evidence that crime has an economic basis; crime might then be linked to socialization, personality, intelligence, or some other trait *unrelated* to class position or income. What then are the traits and patterns in the crime rate?

The Ecology of Crime

There seem to be patterns in the crime rate that are linked to temporal and ecological factors. Some of the most important of these are discussed below.

Season and Climate. Most reported crimes occur during the warm summer months of July and August. During the summer, teenagers, who usually have the highest crime levels, are out of school and have greater opportunity to commit crime. During warm weather, people spend more time outdoors, making themselves easier targets. Similarly, homes are left vacant more often during the summer, making them more vulnerable to property crimes. Two exceptions to this trend are murders and robberies, which occur frequently in December and January (though rates are also high during the summer).

Population Density. Areas with low per-capita crime rates tend to be rural. Large urban areas have by far the highest violence rates. These findings are also supported by victim data. Exceptions to this trend are low-population resort areas with large transient or seasonal populations—such as Atlantic City, New Jersey, and Nantucket, Massachusetts.

Region. Definite differences are apparent in regional crime rates. For many years, southern states had significantly higher rates in almost all crime categories than were found in other regions of the country; this data convinced some criminologists that there was a *southern subculture of violence.* However, the western states now have the dubious *distinction* of having the highest crime and violence rates.

Use of Firearms

There is little question that firearms play a major role in the commission of crime. According to the NCVS, firearms were involved in 20 percent of robberies, 10 percent of assaults, and 6 percent of rapes. In 1992, the UCR reported that 68 percent of all murders involved firearms; most of these weapons (80 percent) were handguns.

The relationship between crime and firearms is not surprising, considering the widespread availability and use of handguns. Recent self-report surveys of 835 serious juvenile offenders incarcerated in four different states and 758 male students in ten inner-city high schools located near the juvenile incarceration facilities indicate that gun possession is commonplace.[37] The major findings of these studies are contained in Figure 3.4.

Despite these grim statistics, gun control remains a hotly debated issue. The Close-Up titled "Gun Control" discusses this topic.

Crime and Shame: Crime Rates in the United States and Japan

While the official crime rate in the United States has steadily increased, crime trends in Japan remain extremely low. This is despite the fact that Japan is a large industrialized country whose population is jammed into overcrowded urban areas. As Figure A shows, the Japanese felony crime rate has dropped significantly since reaching an all-time high during the post-World War II period, while the crime rate in the United States has increased dramatically. It is not surprising that the fear of crime is also relatively low in Japan, even though—like their American counterparts—the Japanese news media tend to focus a lot of attention on the few lurid and violent incidents that do occur. How can this difference be explained?

Cultural differences may play an important role in controlling crime in Japan. In the United States, individualism and self-gratification are emphasized, and success is defined in terms of material goods and possessions. To achieve an upper-class life-style, people are willing to engage in confrontations, increasing the likelihood of violence.

In Japan, honor is the most important personal trait. Japan's homogeneous society has a written history that spans 14 centuries. The Japanese are deeply loyal to historic traditions, which provide a sense of moral order. They belong to a network of social groups that provide a sense of place and of self, which creates a strong commitment to social norms. In contrast, America's polyglot society has not allowed the same sort of moral order or tradition to develop. The most important cultural norms in Japan are extraordinary patience when seeking change, a cooperative approach to decision making, extreme respect for seniority and age, and concern for society at the expense of the individual. Japanese customs that subordinate personal feelings for the good of the group produce fewer violent confrontations than the U.S. stress on individualism.

Nowhere are obedience and respect more important in Japan than in the relationships with family members and friends. Children owe parents total respect; younger siblings must obey older brothers and sisters; younger friends show reverence toward older acquaintances; and all show respect to the emperor. Bowing, a familiar Japanese custom, symbolizes this respect. The Japanese then are deterred from criminal behavior not only because of moral principles of right and wrong but also to avoid embarrassment to self, family, or acquaintances. John Braitwaite notes that this fear of shame is the key to the crime rate differences in the United States and Japan. While law breakers are shunned in the United States, the Japanese confront shameful acts in an effort to reintegrate offenders into society (Braithwaite's concept of reintegrative shaming will be discussed further in Chapter 5).

Though Japanese crime rates are low, what crime there is tends to involve organized criminal gangs. Youth in the *bosozoku* (hot-rodder) and "yankee" gangs flaunt conventional dress and speech codes so important in Japan. Members embrace an overtly macho behavioral code, featuring violence, reckless driving, and drug use. They may "graduate" into **yakuza gangs,** the huge orga-

Social Class and Crime

A still unresolved issue in the criminological literature is the relationship between social class and crime. Traditionally, crime has been thought to be a lower-class phenomenon. After all, people at the lowest rungs of the social structure have the greatest incentive to commit crimes. Those unable to obtain desired goods and services through conventional means may consequently resort to theft and other illegal activities—such as the sale of narcotics—to obtain them; these activities are referred to as **instrumental crimes.** Those living in poverty areas are also believed to engage in disproportionate amounts of violent crime as a means of expressing their rage, frustration, and anger against society. Rates of these **expressive crimes,** such as rape and assault, may also be higher in poverty areas because those engaging in violence can develop an alternative source of positive self-image by viewing themselves as tough, strong, or "bad."

Official statistics indicate that crime rates in inner-city, high-poverty areas are generally higher than those in suburban or wealthier areas. Studies using aggregate police statistics (arrest records) have consistently shown that crime rates in lower-class areas are higher than in

nized crime groups that are responsible for a significant portion of all crimes in Japan. *Yakuzas* engage in drug trafficking, extortion, gambling, and other criminal conspiracies similar to American organized crime activities. They are often hired by legitimate enterprises to "settle" labor disputes, close business deals, and collect debts. While membership in traditional organized crime families is on the wane in the United States, the number of *yakuza* members has increased sharply to an estimated 88,000, four times as many as their American "colleagues." Interestingly, the *yakuzas* demand the same sense of loyalty and respect given legitimate social institutions; honor in Japan has no bounds.

Discussion Questions

1. Considering all things, what aspects of Japanese society do you think are responsible for its low crime rate?
2. What can we do to bring the crime rate down in the United States?

SOURCE: Ted Westermann and James Burfeind, *Crime and Justice in Two Societies, Japan and the United States* (Pacific Grove, Calif.: Brooks/Cole, 1991); Joachim Kersten, "Street Youths, *Bosozoku,* and *Yakuza:* Subculture Formation and Social Reactions in Japan," *Crime and Delinquency* 39 (1993): 277–95; Koichiro Ito, "Research on the Fear of Crime: Perceptions and Realities of Crime in Japan," *Crime and Delinquency* 39 (1993): 392–95; Michael Vaughn and Nobuho Tomita, "A Longitudinal Analysis of Japanese Crime from 1926–1987: The Pre-War, War and Post-War Eras," *International Journal of Comparative and Applied Criminal Justice* 14 (1990): 145–60; John Braithwaite, *Crime, Shame and Reintegration* (Cambridge: Cambridge University Press, 1989).

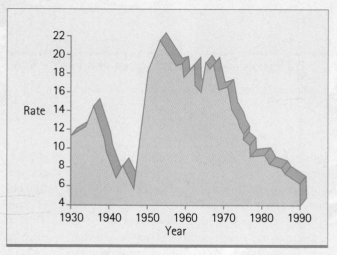

FIGURE A   Felony rates per 100,00 in Japan from 1926 to 1990.

wealthier neighborhoods. Another "official" indicator of a class-crime relationship can be obtained through surveys of prison inmates, which consistently show that prisoners were members of the lower class and unemployed or underemployed in the years before their incarceration.

An alternate explanation for these findings is that the relationship between official crime and social class is a function of law enforcement practices and not actual criminal behavior patterns. Police may devote more resources to poverty areas, and consequently, apprehension rates may be higher there. Similarly, police may be more likely to formally arrest and prosecute lower-class citizens than those in the middle and upper classes, which may account for the lower class's overrepresentation in the official statistics and the prison population.

Class and Self-Reports.   Because of these factors, self-report data have been used extensively to test the class-crime relationship. If people in all social classes self-report similar crime patterns but only those in the lower class are formally arrested, that would explain the higher crime rates in lower-class neighborhoods. However, if lower-class people report greater criminal activity than their middle- and upper-class peers, it would indicate that

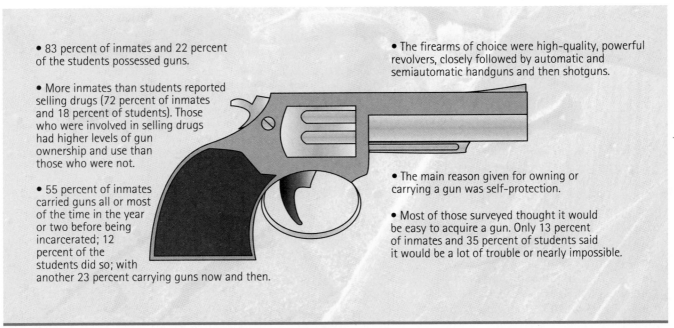

- 83 percent of inmates and 22 percent of the students possessed guns.

- More inmates than students reported selling drugs (72 percent of inmates and 18 percent of students). Those who were involved in selling drugs had higher levels of gun ownership and use than those who were not.

- 55 percent of inmates carried guns all or most of the time in the year or two before being incarcerated; 12 percent of the students did so; with another 23 percent carrying guns now and then.

- The firearms of choice were high-quality, powerful revolvers, closely followed by automatic and semiautomatic handguns and then shotguns.

- The main reason given for owning or carrying a gun was self-protection.

- Most of those surveyed thought it would be easy to acquire a gun. Only 13 percent of inmates and 35 percent of students said it would be a lot of trouble or nearly impossible.

FIGURE 3.4   Possession of Handguns: School and Inmate Surveys

SOURCE: Joseph Sheley and James Wright, *Gun Acquisition and Possession in Selected Juvenile Samples* (Washington, D.C.: National Institute of Justice, 1993), p. 1.

the official statistics are an accurate representation of the crime problem.

Surprisingly, early self-report studies conducted in the 1950s, specifically those conducted by James Short and F. Ivan Nye, did not find a direct relationship between social class and youth crime.[38] They found that socioeconomic class was related to official processing by police, court, and correctional agencies but not to the actual commission of crimes. In other words, while lower- and middle-class youth self-reported equal amounts of crime, the lower-class youth had a greater chance of getting arrested, convicted, and incarcerated and becoming official delinquents. In addition, factors generally associated with lower-class membership, such as broken homes, were found to be related to institutionalization but not to admissions of delinquency. Other studies of this period reached similar conclusions.[39]

For more than 20 years after the use of self-reports became widespread, a majority of self-report studies agreed that a class-crime relationship did not exist: if the poor possessed more extensive criminal records than the wealthy, it was because of differential law enforcement and not class-based behavior differences. In what is considered to be the definitive work on this subject, Charles Tittle, Wayne Villemez, and Douglas Smith reviewed 35 studies containing 363 separate estimates concerning the relationship between class and crime.[40] They concluded that little if any support exists for the contention that crime is primarily a lower-class phenomenon. Consequently, Tittle and his associates argued that official statistics probably reflect class bias in the processing of lower-class offenders. The Tittle review is usually cited by criminologists as the strongest statement refuting the claim that the lower class is disproportionately criminal. In 1990, writing with Robert Meier, Tittle once again reviewed existing data (published between 1978 and 1990) on the class-crime relationship and again found little evidence that a consistent association could be found between class and crime.[41]

Evidence for a Class–Crime Relationship. While convincing, this research has sparked significant debate over the validity of studies assessing the class-crime relationship. Many self-report instruments include trivial offenses, such as using a false ID or drinking alcohol. Their inclusion may obscure the true class-crime relationship because affluent youth frequently engage in trivial offenses, such as petty larceny, using drugs, and simple assault. If only serious felony offenses are considered, a true class-crime relationship could be determined.

The most widely cited evidence that a class-crime relationship does in fact exist can be found in the work of Delbert Elliott and his colleagues Suzanne Ageton and David Huizinga. Using a carefully drawn national sample of 1,726 youths ages 11 to 17 and a sophisticated self-report instrument, Elliott and Ageton found lower-class youths to be much more likely than middle-class youths to engage in serious delinquent acts, such as burglary, assault, robbery, sexual assault, and vandalism.[42] Lower-class youths were much more likely than middle-class youths to be chronic offenders, committing numerous personal and property crimes (more than 200 per youth).

Elliott and Ageton conclude that self-report data give findings about class and crime that are actually similar to those of official data. Those studies showing middle- and lower-class youths to be equally delinquent rely on measures weighted toward minor crimes (for example, using a false ID or skipping school). When serious crimes, such as burglary and assault, are used in the comparison, lower-class youths are significantly more delinquent.[43]

The Class–Crime Controversy. The relationship between class and crime is an important one for criminological theory. If crime is related to class

James Brady was severely wounded by John Hinckley when Hinckley attempted to assassinate President Ronald Reagan. James and Mary Brady's efforts helped spur the passage of the "Brady Bill" which requires a waiting period before the purchase of a handgun. Should gun sales and possession be outlawed outright? See the following Close-Up on Gun Control.

CLOSE-UP

Gun Control

In December 1993, Colin Ferguson opened fire on a railroad car in Long Island, New York, killing six people and wounding more than a dozen more before he was subdued by passengers. Ferguson used Black Talon shells in his Ruger automatic, a hollow-point bullet designed to burst on impact and cause maximum damage to the target. The incident was a shocking reminder of the deadly effect of an automatic pistol, in this case in the hands of an enraged killer. The incident renewed the resolve of some reformers to reduce the incidence of violent crime by banning handguns.

Considering the estimated more than 50 million illegal handguns in the United States today, it should come as no surprise that handguns are linked to many violent crimes, including 20 percent of all injury deaths (second to autos) and 60 percent of all homicides and suicides: Handguns are the cause of death of about two-thirds of all police killed in the line of duty.

Despite their danger, carrying handguns has become commonplace. National surveys of adolescents, including one conducted in 1993 for the Harvard University School of Public Health, have found that up to 15 percent of all students report carrying a gun to school and 13 percent had been threatened with gun violence. Carrying a handgun is not gender-specific. A survey of inner-city female students by M. Dwayne Smith found that 11 percent carried a gun at least "now and then."

While these data have been disputed by gun advocates, it has spurred many Americans to advocate control of the sale of handguns and a ban on cheap "Saturday night specials." In contrast, most conservatives view gun control as a threat to personal liberty and call for severe punishment of criminals, rather than control of handguns. What is more, they argue, the Second Amendment of the U.S. Constitution protects the "right to bear arms."

Control Methods

Efforts to control handguns have many different sources. Each state and many local jurisdictions have laws banning or restricting sales or possession of guns. Others regulate dealers who sell guns. For example, the Federal Gun Control Act of 1968 prohibits dealers from selling guns to minors, ex-felons, and drug users. In addition, each dealer must keep detailed records of who purchases guns. Unfortunately, the resources available to enforce this law are meager.

Another method is to create a waiting period before a purchaser can obtain a handgun so that authorities can check the buyer's background. In 1993, Congress passed the *Brady Bill*, which requires a week-long waiting period (to do a background check) before a gun can be sold to an applicant. The bill was named after former Press Secretary James Brady, who was severely wounded in the attempted assassination of President Ronald Reagan by John Hinckley.

While the legislation is a good step, there is still question whether such measures can control gun violence. A methodologically sophisticated analysis by David McDowall and his colleagues of jurisdictions that have already increased waiting periods indicates that such measures have little effect on gun violence.

Another approach is to punish severely people caught with unregistered handguns. The most famous attempt to regulate handguns is the Massachusetts Bartley-Fox Law, which provides a mandatory one-year prison term for possession of a handgun (outside the home) without a permit. A detailed analysis of violent crime in Boston in the years after the law's passage found that the use of handguns in robberies and murders did decline substantially (in robberies by 35 percent and murders by 55 percent in a two-year period). However, these optimistic results must be tempered by two facts: rates for similar crimes dropped significantly in comparable cities that did not have gun control laws, and the use of other weapons, such as knives, increased in Boston.

Some jurisdictions have attempted to reduce gun violence by adding an extra punishment, such as a mandatory prison sentence, for any crime involving a handgun. So far, evaluations of this method show mixed results. David McDowall, Colin Loftin, and Brian Wiersma found that mandatory sentencing laws for gun crimes significantly reduced homicide rates in six different jurisdictions; assault and robbery rates however, were not affected by the gun crime laws.

Even when positive results from gun control laws have been found, gun advocates have tried to refute the findings. When Loftin and his associates showed that a handgun control law was an effective instrument for reducing the homicide rate in Washington, D.C., Gary Kleck, Chester Britt, and David Bordua reanalyzed the data and claimed that positive findings may be an artifact of faulty methodology. By adjusting the years in which comparisons are made, the Kleck research found that gun homicides *increased* rather than *decreased* in the Washington area after the passage of the gun control law. In a study evaluating the handgun laws of all 50 states, David Lester found scant evidence that strict handgun laws influence homicide rates. So while there is some evidence that gun control laws can reduce violence rates, the issue is far from settled.

The Difficulty of Gun Control
Why is it difficult to show that gun control efforts have a significant effect on the level of violence? Most guns used in crime are obtained illegally. Even if legitimate gun stores were more strictly regulated, it would not inhibit private citizens from selling, bartering, or trading handguns. Unregulated gun fairs and auctions are common throughout the United States. So many guns are in use that controlling their ownership or banning their manufacture would have a negligible impact for years to come. Sophisticated automatic weapons, some of which are laser-aimed,

have become armament for juvenile gangs and criminal groups. Some police departments, feeling "outgunned," have switched from the traditional .38-caliber police special revolver to 9 mm pistols that have 15 rounds.

If handguns are banned or outlawed, they would become more valuable; illegal importation of guns might increase, as it has for another controlled substance—narcotics. Increasing penalties for gun-related crimes has also met with limited success, since judges may be reluctant to alter their sentencing policies to accommodate legislators. Regulating dealers is difficult and tighter controls on them would only encourage private sales and bartering. Many gun deals are made at gun shows with few questions asked. Even if purchased by a legitimate gun enthusiast, these weapons can fall into the wrong hands as a result of burglaries and break-ins.

Despite the difficulty of effective control, some combination of oversight and penalty seems imperative, and efforts should be made to discover, if at all possible, whether handgun control could, indeed, reduce violent crime rates.

Discussion Questions
1. Should the sale and possession of handguns be banned?
2. What are some of the possible negative consequences of a strict handgun control law?

SOURCE: David McDowall, Colin Loftin, and Brian Wiersma, "A Comparative Study of the Preventive Effects of Mandatory Sentencing Laws for Gun

Crimes," *Journal of Criminal Law and Criminology* 83 (1992): 378–91; M. Dwayne Smith, "Possession and Carrying of Firearms among a Sample of Inner-City High School Females" (Paper presented at the annual meeting of the American Society of Criminology, Phoenix, Arizona, November 1993); Colin Loftin, David McDowall, Brian Wiersma, and Talbert Cottey, "Effects of Restrictive Licensing of Handguns on Homicide and Suicide in the District of Columbia," *New England Journal of Medicine* 325 (1991): 1615–20; Gary Kleck, Chester Britt, and David Bordua, "The Emperor Has No Clothes: Using Interrupted Time Series Designs to Evaluate Social Policy" (Paper presented at the annual meeting of the American Society of Criminology, Phoenix, Arizona, November 1993); Gary Kleck, "The Incidence of Gun Violence among Young People," *Public Perspective* 4 (1993): 3–6; Samuel Walker, *Sense and Nonsense about Crime and Drugs* (Monterey, Calif.: Brooks/Cole, 1985); Glenn Pierce and William Bowers, "The Bartley-Fox Gun Law's Short-Term Impact on Crime," *Annals* 455 (1981): 120–37; Colin Loftin, Milton Heumann, and David McDowall, "Mandatory Sentencing and Firearms Violence: Evaluating an Alternative to Gun Control," *Law and Society Review* 17 (1983): 287–319; David Lester, *Gun Control* (Springfield, Ill.: Charles Thomas, 1984); James Wright, Peter Rossi, and Kathleen Daly, *Under the Gun: Weapons, Crime and Violence in America* (New York: Aldine, 1983).

position, then it follows that structural factors, such as poverty and neighborhood disorganization, are the cause of criminal behavior. However, if class and crime are unrelated, then it is evident that the causes of crime must be related to factors experienced by members of all social classes—psychological impairment, family conflict, peer pressure, school failure, and so on.

One reason that a true measure of the class-crime relationship has so far eluded criminologists is that the methods now employed to measure "class" vary widely. So many different indicators are used that findings are ambiguous. For example, David Brownfield found that some widely used measures of social class, such as father's occupation and education, are only weakly related to self-reported crime, while others, such as unemployment or membership on the welfare roles, are much stronger correlates of criminality.[44]

It is also possible that the association between class and crime may be more complex than a simple linear relationship (the poorer you are, the more crime you commit). Age, race, and gender may all influence the connection between class and crime.[45] For example, conservative, lower-class parents may control their daughters closely while giving sons greater freedom to commit crime. In contrast, liberal, upper-class parents may allow their daughters as much freedom as their sons have. The result is that upper-class girls are actually more criminal than their lower-class sisters, confounding the class-crime relationship.[46] Similarly, Miles Harer and Darrell Steffensmeier found that race also mediates the class-crime relationship: poor whites were more violent than affluent whites; the effect of income has little influence on black crime rates.[47] Considering these findings, it is not surprising that the true relationship between class and crime is difficult to determine: the effect may be obscured because its impact varies within and between groups.

Like so many other criminological controversies, the debate over the true relationship between class and crime will most likely persist. The weight of recent evidence seems to suggest that serious and official crime is more prevalent among the lower classes, while less-serious and self-reported crime is spread more evenly throughout the social structure.[48] Income inequality, poverty, and resource deprivation are all associated with the most serious violent crimes, including homicide and assault.[49] Nonetheless, while crime rates may be higher in lower-class areas, *poverty* alone cannot explain why a *particular* individual becomes a chronic violent criminal; if it *could,* the crime problem would be much worse than it is now.[50]

Age and Crime

There is general agreement that age is inversely related to criminality. Criminologists Travis Hirschi and Michael Gottfredson state, "Age is everywhere correlated with crime. Its effects on crime do not depend on other demographic correlates of crime."[51] Regardless of economic status, marital status, race, sex, and so on, younger people commit crime more often than their older peers; research indicates this relationship is stable across time periods ranging from 1935 to the present.[52]

Official statistics tell us that young people are arrested at a disproportionate rate to their numbers in the population; victim surveys generate similar findings for crimes in which the age of the assailant can be determined.

A disproportionate number of all criminal acts are committed by teenagers aged 16 to 19. The crime rate begins to drop sharply at age 30 because younger criminals have "aged out of crime."

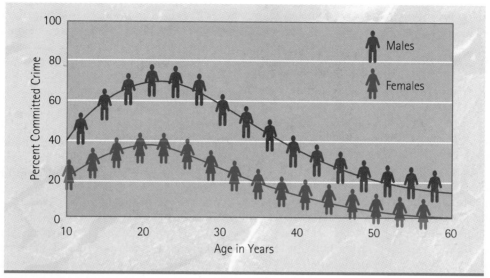

FIGURE 3.5   **Gender and Crime over the Life Span**

Research also shows that the age distribution of crime is remarkably stable. That is, the proportion of teenagers committing crime today is about the same as it has been for 40 years (though young people are today committing greater numbers of the most violent crimes).[53]

While youths aged 15 to 19 collectively make up about 7 percent of the total U.S. population, they account for about 30 percent of the index crime arrests and 16 percent of the arrests for all crimes. As a general rule, the peak age for property crime is believed to be 16 and for violence, 18. In contrast, adults 45 and over, who make up 30 percent of the population, account for only 8 percent of the index crime arrests. The elderly are particularly resistant to the temptations of crime; they make up 12 percent of the population and less than 1 percent of the arrests. Elderly males 65 and over are predominantly arrested for alcohol-related matters (public drunkenness, drunk driving) and elderly females for larceny theft (shoplifting); the crime rate of both groups has remained stable for the past 20 years.[54]

It is also possible to derive some estimates of rates of offending by age for the violent personal crimes measured by the National Crime Victim Survey because victims had the opportunity to view their attackers and estimate their ages. Research shows that the estimated rates of offending for youths aged 18 to 20 is about three times greater than the estimated rate of adults 21 and over; youths aged 12 to 17 offended at a rate twice that of adults. For some specific crimes,

such as robbery and personal larceny, the youthful offending rate is perceived to be almost six times the adult rate.[55]

Age and Crime I: Age Does Not Matter. The relationship between age and crime is of major theoretical importance because many existing criminological theories fail to adequately explain why the crime rate drops with age, which is referred to as **aging out** or the **desistance phenomenon.** This theoretical failure has been the subject of considerable academic debate. One position, championed by respected criminologists Travis Hirschi and Michael Gottfredson, is that the relationship between age and crime is constant, and therefore, the age variable is actually irrelevant to the study of crime. Because all people, regardless of their demographic characteristics (race, gender, class, family structure, domicile, work status, and so on), commit less crime as they age, it is not important to consider age as a factor in explaining crime.[56] Even hard-core chronic offenders will commit less crime as they age.[57] Hirschi and Gottfredson find that differences in offending rates for groups (for example, between males and females or between the rich and poor) that exist at any point in their respective life cycles will be maintained throughout their lives. As Figure 3.5 illustrates, if 15-year-old boys are four times as likely to commit crime as 15-year-old girls, then 50-year-old men will be four times as likely to commit crime as 50-year-old women, though the actual number of crimes committed by both males and females will constantly be declining.

Age and Crime II: Age Matters.

Those who oppose the Hirschi and Gottfredson view of the age-crime relationship suggest that social factors directly associated with a person's age, such as life-style, economic situation, or peer relations, explain desistance and the aging-out process.[58] People begin to specialize in crime as they age, and the frequency or type of an offender's criminal behavior is not constant. Evolving patterns or cycles of criminal behavior may be keyed to personal characteristics and life-style, including gender, race, and class.[59] For example, the female homicide rate peaks at age 20 and then continues at a *stable* but low rate through adulthood; in contrast, the male homicide rate is much higher but begins to drop after age 30.[60]

The likelihood of a long-term criminal career may be determined by the age at which offending commences.[61] People who get involved in criminality at a very early age (**early onset**) and who gain official records will be the ones most likely to become chronic offenders.[62] Research shows that preschoolers (under age 5) who are labeled as "troublesome" or "difficult" by parents are the ones most likely to become persistent offenders through their adolescence.[63] Their criminal behavior is resistant to the aging-out process.

The population then may contain different sets of criminal offenders, one group whose criminality declines with age (as predicted by Hirschi and Gottfredson) and another whose criminal behavior re-mains constant through their maturity.[64] In addition, the rates of individual crime types peak at different ages and follow different trajectories. Crimes that provide significant economic gain, such as gambling, embezzlement, and fraud, are less likely to decline with maturity than high-risk, low-profit offenses, such as assault.[65] The age-crime pattern may also undergo change; it has been noted that a greater proportion of violent criminal be-havior is concentrated among youthful offenders than it was 40 years ago.

In sum, some criminologists view the relationship between crime and age as constant, while others believe that it varies according to offense and offender. This difference has important implications for criminological research and theory. If age is a constant, then the criminality of any group can be accurately measured at any single point in time. If, on the other hand, the relationship between age and crime varies, it would be necessary to conduct longitudinal studies that follow criminals over their life cycle to fully understand how their age influences their offending patterns.[66] Crime would then be conceived of as a type of social event that takes on different meanings at different times in a person's life.[67]

Disagreements over this critical issue have produced some of the most spirited debates in the recent criminological literature.[68] Right now, efforts are being undertaken to examine this issue in the United States and in other nations (using cohorts drawn in Sweden and Britain). Early results from the Scandinavian study find many general similarities with U.S. research.[69] Clearly, more research is required on this important topic.

Why Does Aging Out Occur?

Despite the debate raging over the relationship between age and crime, there is little question that the overall crime rate declines with age. Why does this phenomenon take place? One view is that there is a direct relationship between aging and desistance. As they mature, troubled youths are able to develop a long-term life view and resist the need for immediate gratification.[70] Gordon Trasler found that kids view teenage crime as "fun." Youths view their petty but risky and exciting crimes as a social activity that provides adventure in an otherwise boring and unsympathetic world. As they grow older, Trasler finds, their life patterns are inconsistent with criminality; delinquents literally grow out of crime.[71]

James Q. Wilson and Richard Herrnstein argue that the aging-out process is a function of the natural history of the human life cycle.[72] Deviance in adolescence is fueled by the need for conventionally unobtainable money and sex and reinforced by close relationships with peers who defy conventional morality. At the same time, teenagers are becoming independent from parents and other adults who enforce conventional standards. They have a new sense of energy and strength and are involved with peers who are similarly vigorous and frustrated. Adulthood brings increasingly powerful ties to conventional society, not the least of which is the acquisition of a family. Adults also develop the ability to delay gratification and forgo the immediate gains that law violations bring; crime rates consequently decline with age.

Another view is that the influence of age on crime is mediated by life experiences. For example, Barry Glassner, Margaret Ksander, Bruce Berg, and Bruce Johnson find that desistance is linked to the fear of punishment.[73] According to Glassner and his associates, youths are well aware that once they reach their legal majority, punishment takes a decidedly more sinister turn. They are no longer protected by the kindly arms of the juvenile justice system. As one teenage boy told them:

"When you're a teenager, you're rowdy. Nowadays, you aren't rowdy. You know, you want to settle down because you can go to jail now. [When] you are a boy, you can be put into a detention home. But you can go to jail now. Jail ain't no place to go."[74]

Aging out of crime may also be influenced by the success or failure of interpersonal relationships. Charles Tittle suggests that children who are labeled antisocial by teachers, police, parents, and neighbors find they may then have little choice but to remain committed to their criminal careers.[75] If, however, offenders believe that they have little chance of achieving success, money, and happiness through crimes, then they are more likely to desist.[76]

While most people age out of crime, some may find a criminal career a reasonable alternative. Yet even people who actively remain in a criminal career will eventually slow down as they age. Crime is too dangerous, physically taxing, and unrewarding, and punishments too harsh and long-lasting, to become a long-term way of life for most people. The uniformity of maturational changes in the crime rate suggests that it must be part of a biological "evolutionary process."[77] By middle age, even the most chronic offenders terminate criminal behavior.

Gender and Crime

The three major forms of criminal statistics generally agree that male crime rates are considerably higher than those of females; victims report that their assailant was a male in more than 80 percent of all violent personal crimes. The Uniform Crime Report arrest statistics indicate that the overall male-female arrest ratio is usually about four male offenders to one female offender; for violent crimes, the ratio is closer to seven males to one female. NCVS data indicate that the male-female ratio for violent crimes in which the victim could identify the gender of their attacker was about the same as recorded in UCR arrest data.

Recent self-report data collected by the Institute for Social Research at the University of Michigan also show that males commit more serious crimes, such as robbery, assault, and burglary, than females. However, while the patterns in self-reports are parallel to official data, the ratios seem smaller. In other words, males self-report more criminal behavior than females but not to the degree suggested by official data.

Explaining Gender Differences: Early Views.
Because of gender differences in the crime rate, the focus of criminology has been on male crime patterns.

Criticism has been leveled at the field's inattention to the role of females in crime.[78]

The early criminological literature paid scant attention to female criminals. Because of their relatively few numbers, female criminals were portrayed in some early writings as emotional, physical, or psychological aberrations. The most widely cited evidence was contained in Cesare Lombroso's 1895 book, *The Female Offender*.[79] Lombroso argued that whereas women generally were more passive and less criminal than men, there was a small group of female criminals who lacked "typical" female traits of "piety, maternity, undeveloped intelligence, and weakness."[80] In physical appearance as well as in emotionality, delinquent females appeared closer to both criminal and noncriminal men than to other women. Lombroso's theory became known as the **masculinity hypothesis;** in essence, a few "masculine" females were responsible for the handful of crimes women commit.

Another early view of female crime focused on the supposed dynamics of sexual relationships. Female criminals were viewed as either sexually controlling or sexually naive, either manipulating men for profit or being manipulated by them. The female's criminality was often masked because criminal justice authorities were reluctant to take action against a woman.[81] Referred to as the **chivalry hypothesis,** this view holds that much of the criminality of females is hidden because of the generally protective and benevolent attitudes toward them in our culture.[82] In other words, police are less likely to arrest, juries less likely to convict, and judges less likely to incarcerate female offenders.

While popular 50 years ago, such views have since been discredited.

Recent Views of Female Criminality.
By midcentury, it was common for criminologists to portray gender differences in the crime rate as a function of socialization. Textbooks explained the relatively low female crime rate by citing the fact that in contrast to boys, girls were supervised more closely and protected from competition.[83] The few female criminals were described as troubled individuals, alienated at home, who pursued crime as a means of compensating for their disrupted personal lives.[84] The streets became a "second home" to girls whose physical and emotional adjustment was hampered by a strained home life, marked by such conditions as absent fathers, overly competitive mothers, and so on.

In the 1970s, several influential works, most notably Freda Adler's *Sisters in Crime*[85] and Rita James Simon's *The Contemporary Woman and Crime,* revolutionized the thinking on the cause of gender differences in the crime rate.[86] Their research, which today is referred to as **liberal feminist theory,** focused attention on the social and economic role of women in society and its relationship to female crime rates. Both Adler and Simon believed that the traditionally lower crime rate for women could be explained by their "second-class" economic and social position. They further contended that as women's social roles changed and their life-styles became more like those of males, their crime rates would converge.

Criminologists, responding to this research, began to refer to the "new female criminal." The rapid increase in the female crime rate during the 1960s and 1970s, especially in what had traditionally been male-oriented crimes (burglary, larceny), gave support to the convergence model presented by Adler and Simon. In addition, self-report studies seemed to indicate that the pattern of female criminality, if not its frequency, was quite similar to that of male criminality.[87]

The New Female Criminal Reconsidered. Increases in the female crime rate were not sustained in the 1980s, causing some scholars to reassess the concept of the "new female criminal."[88] Some criminologists, most notably Darrell Steffensmeier and Renee Steffensmeier, concluded that the emancipation of women has had relatively little influence on female crime rates.[89] They dispute that increases in the female arrest rate reflect economic or social change brought about by the women's movement. For one thing, many female criminals come from the socioeconomic class least affected by the women's movement; their crimes seem more a function of economic inequality than women's rights. For another, the offense patterns of women are still quite different from those of men, who are still committing a disproportionate share of serious crimes, such as robbery, burglary, murder, and assault.[90] Writing with Cathy Streifel, Darrell Steffensmeier found that the gender ratio in the crime rate was essentially stable between 1935 and 1985; the gender-crime association seemed unaffected by cultural changes during this half century.[91]

Steffensmeier and his associates have also conducted cross-national research that fails to find an association between economic development and female crime rates.[92] There is little evidence that nations undergoing economic development also experience increases in the female violence rate.[93]

Another view is that female arrest rates rose in the 1960s and 1970s because police, angry over affirmative action programs, were willing to formally arrest and process female offenders; female liberation brought an end to the *chivalry hypothesis.* Women, the argument went, were not becoming more criminal, but the men who judge them were becoming less tolerant.[94] While persuasive, this view is not supported by existing data. Though most research efforts conclude that the differences in processing female and male offenders have declined, some research shows that the justice system is still more apt to punish males more severely than females. For example, Cassia Spohn and her associates found that prosecutors were more likely to dismiss charges against female defendants and prosecute males to the fullest extent of the law.[95]

Is Convergence Possible? Will the gender differences in the crime rate eventually dissolve? Are gender differences permanent and unchanging? Not all criminologists have abandoned the convergence argument. Criminologist Roy Austin has recently reexamined official and self-report data and claims that a long-term convergence trend is clearly established.[96] In a similar vein, Beth Bjerregaard and Carolyn Smith's study of youth gangs in Rochester, New York, shows that females have increased gang membership and that for both males and females, gang activity is associated with increased levels of crime and drug abuse.[97]

Perhaps it was too soon for criminologists to write off "the new female criminal." It is possible, as Austin claims, that crime convergence has been delayed by a slower-than-expected change in gender roles; the women's movement has not yet achieved its full impact on social life.[98] One reason is that while expanding their economic role, women have not abandoned their conventional role as family caretaker and home provider; women today are being forced to cope with added financial and social burdens. If gender roles were truly equivalent, then crime rates may eventually converge; these changes are now taking place.

Race and Crime

Official crime data indicate that minority-group members are involved in a disproportionate share of criminal activity. The UCR tells us that although African-Americans make up about 12 percent of the general population, they account for about 45 percent of Type I violent crime arrests and 32 percent of the property crime arrests, as well as a disproportionate number of Type II arrests (except for alcohol-related arrests, which primarily are of white offenders).

Since the UCR statistics represent arrest data, racial differences in the crime rate may be more of a reflection of police practices than a true picture of criminal participation. Consequently, criminologists have sought to verify the UCR findings through analysis of NCVS and self-report data.

The NCVS supplies racial data on crimes in which victims were able to observe their attackers—rape, assault, and robbery. Analysis of this data shows that the results are consistent with the official crime statistics.[99] Though African-Americans are identified as committing a disproportionate share of personal violent crime, the proportions are somewhat less than reported in the UCR arrest statistics, especially for the crime of rape. This could mean that police are more likely to arrest black suspects for that crime or that women attacked by black offenders are more likely to report the crime to police. Also, rape tends to be an intraracial crime, and black women are more likely to report rapes to police than are white women.

Self-Report Differences. Another way to examine this issue is to compare the racial differences in self-reported data with those found in the official delinquency records. Charges of racial discrimination in the arrest process would be supported if racial difference in self-report data is insignificant.

Early efforts by Leroy Gould in Seattle, Harwin Voss in Honolulu, and Ronald Akers in seven midwestern states found the relationship between race and self-reported delinquency was virtually nonexistent.[100]

Two recent self-report studies that make use of large national samples of youth have also found little evidence of racial disparity in offending. The first, conducted by the Institute for Social Research at the University of Michigan, found that if anything, black youth self-report less delinquent behavior and substance abuse than whites.[101] The second, a nationwide study of youth by social scientists at the Behavioral Science Institute at Boulder, Colorado, found few interracial differences in crime rates, though black youths maintained a much greater chance of being arrested and taken into custody.[102]

These and other self-report studies seem to indicate that the delinquent behavior rates of black and white teenagers are generally similar and that differences in arrest statistics may indicate a differential selection policy by police.[103]

Causes of Racial Disparity in Crime. Racial differences in the crime rate remain an extremely sensitive issue. While there are still questions about the validity of UCR data, the fact remains that African-Americans are arrested for a disproportionate amount of violent crime, such as robbery and murder. While it is possible that the UCR is merely a reflection of dis-criminatory arrest practices, as self-report studies would have us believe, it is improbable that police discretion alone could account for these proportions: it is doubtful that police routinely ignore white killers, robbers, and rapists while arresting violent black offenders. Also, the NCVS indicates that a disproportionate number of violent crimes are committed by racial minorities.

Today, many criminologists concede that recorded differences in the black-white violent crime arrest rate cannot be explained away solely by racism or differential treatment within the criminal justice system.[104] To do so would be to ignore the social problems that exist in the nation's inner cities. How then can racial patterns be explained?

Most theories put forward to explain black-white crime differentials focus on economic deprivation, social disorganization, subcultural adaptations, and the legacy of racism and discrimination on personality and behavior.[105] The fact that U.S. culture influences African-American crime rates is underscored by the fact that black violence rates are much lower in other nations—both those that are predominantly white, such as Canada, and those that are predominantly black, such as Nigeria.[106]

One approach has been to trace the black experience in the United States. Some criminologists view black crime as a function of socialization in a society where the black family was torn apart and black culture destroyed in such a way that recovery has proven impossible. James P. Comer argues that the early slave experiences left a wound that has been deepened by racism and lack of opportunity.[107] Children of the slave society were thrust into a system of forced dependency and negative self-feelings. Comer writes that it was a system that promoted powerful forces for identification with an aggressor (slave master and other whites) and ambivalence and antagonism toward one's self and group. After emancipation, blacks were shut out of the social and political mainstream. Frustrated and angry, they were isolated in segregated communities, turning within for support. Their entire American experience provided for negative self-images, anger, and rage. Comer states:

> In reaction to failure, the most vibrant and reactive often become disrupted and violent in and out of schools, both individually and in groups or gangs. Neighborhoods and communities of adequately functioning families are then overwhelmed by the reactive and most troubled individuals and families. Models of violence and other troublesome behavior for children abound in relatives, friends, and neighbors unsuccessful in previous generations.[108]

According to Comer, the intraracial nature of black violence is in reaction to an "inability to cope with the larger society or to identify with black and white leaders and institutional achievements. Frustration and anger is taken out on people most like self."[109]

Comer's view fits well with the criminological concept that a subculture of violence has developed in inner-city ghetto areas that condones the use of physical force as solutions for everyday encounters.[110]

In his influential book, *Criminal Violence, Criminal Justice,* Charles Silberman also views the problem as a function of the black experience in this country—"an experience that differs from that of other ethnic groups." Silberman's provocative argument is that black citizens have learned to be violent because of their treatment in U.S. society. First, they were violently uprooted from their African homelands. Then their slavery was maintained by violence. After emancipation, their lower-class position was enforced by violent means, such as intimidation by the Ku Klux Klan. To strike back meant harsh retaliation by the white-controlled law. Moving to northern cities, blacks suffered two burdens unknown to other migrants: their color and their heritage of slavery. After all, the color black in U.S. culture connotes sinister, dirty, evil, or bad things, while white stands for goodness and purity (the good guys always wear white hats; social outcasts are blacklisted; brides wear white, and witches wear black). Consequently, to survive and reach cultural and personal fulfillment, African-Americans have developed their own set of norms, values, and traditions. In the 1960s, many blacks began to adopt the image, first developed in southern folklore and myth, of being "bad" in their personal lives. After 350 years of fearing whites, Silberman writes,

> black Americans have discovered that the fear runs the other way, that whites are intimidated by their very presence; it would be hard to overestimate what an extraordinarily liberating force this discovery is. . . . 350 years of festering hatred has come spilling out.[111]

Is Convergence Possible? Considering these overwhelming social problems, is it possible that racial differences in the crime rate will soon converge? One argument is that if economic conditions improve in the minority community, then the differences in black and white crime rates will eventually disappear.[112] A trend toward residential integration, which has been underway since 1980, may also help reduce crime rate differentials.[113]

There is also data that shows that improvement in the nation's overall economic condition and increased integration may *not* be enough to produce convergence. African-Americans have been shut out of the economic mainstream even during periods of relative prosperity. Between the economic boom years of 1960 to 1988, white crime rates tended to *decrease*. Economic expansion had the opposite effect on African-American crime rates; they actually *increased* during periods of national economic growth.[114] This seemingly inexplicable finding may be a result of a two-tiered African-American culture, one desperately poor and the other relatively affluent. Both lower- and middle-class whites and middle-class African-Americans are able to prosper during periods of economic growth. In contrast, lower-class African-Americans, left out of the economic mainstream, experience a growing sense of frustration and failure. It should come as no surprise that an element of the population that is shut out of educational and economic opportunities enjoyed by the rest of society may be prone to the lure of illegitimate gain and criminality. Gary LaFree and his associates find that young African-American males in the inner city believe they have a lack of social and economic opportunity. While the economic data says they are doing better, news accounts of "protests, riots and acts of civil disobedience" tell them otherwise.[115]

In sum, the weight of the evidence shows that while there is little difference in the self-reported crime rates of racial groups, African-Americans are more likely to be arrested for serious violent crimes. The causes of black crime have been linked to poverty, racism, hopelessness, lack of opportunity, and urban problems experienced by all too many black citizens.

Criminal Careers

The crime data show that most offenders commit a single criminal act and upon arrest discontinue their antisocial activity. Others commit a few crimes of less serious nature. It is a small group of highly criminal offenders, however, who account for a majority of all criminal offenses. These persistent offenders are referred to as **career criminals** or **chronic offenders.**

A 1972 cohort study conducted by Marvin Wolfgang and his associates at the University of Pennsylvania created the current interest in careers in crime. This landmark study suggested that there were great differences in the offender population and developed methods for testing the escalation and termination of criminal careers. Let us now turn to a more detailed analysis of this ground-breaking work.

Delinquency in a Birth Cohort

The concept of the chronic or career offender is most closely associated with the research efforts of Wolfgang and his associates.[116] In 1972, Wolfgang, Robert Figlio, and Thorsten Sellin published a landmark study, *Delinquency in a Birth Cohort,* that has profoundly influenced the very concept of the criminal offender. Wolfgang, Figlio, and Sellin used official records to follow the criminal careers of a cohort of 9,945 boys born in Philadelphia in 1945 from the time of their birth until they reached 18 years of age in 1963. Official police records were used to identify delinquents. About one-third of the boys (3,475) had some police contact. The remaining two-thirds (6,470) had none. Each delinquent's actions were given a seriousness weight score for every delinquent act.[117] The weighting of delinquent acts allowed the researchers to differentiate, for example, between a simple assault requiring no medical attention for the victim and a serious assault in which the victim needed hospitalization.

Wolfgang and his colleagues obtained data from school records, including subject IQ scores and measures of academic performance and conduct. Socioeconomic status was determined by locating the residence of each member of the cohort and assigning him the median family income for that area.

The most well-known discovery of Wolfgang and his associates was that of the so-called chronic offender. The cohort data indicated that 54 percent (1,862) of the sample's delinquent youths were repeat offenders, while the remaining 46 percent (1,613) were one-time offenders. However, the repeaters could be further categorized as nonchronic recidivists and chronic recidivists. The former consisted of 1,235 youths who had been arrested more than once but less than five times and who made up 35.6 percent of all delinquents. The latter were a group of 627 boys arrested five times or more who accounted for 18 percent of the delinquents and 6 percent of the total sample of 9,945.

It was the chronic offenders (known today as "the chronic 6 percent") who were involved in the most dramatic amounts of delinquent behavior; they were responsible for 5,305 offenses, or 51.9 percent of all offenses. Even more striking was the involvement of chronic offenders in serious criminal acts. Of the entire sample, they committed 71 percent of the homicides, 73 percent of the rapes, 82 percent of the robberies, and 69 percent of the aggravated assaults.

Wolfgang and his associates found that arrest and court experience did little to deter the chronic offender. In fact, punishment was *inversely* related to chronic offending: the more stringent the sanction chronic offenders received, the more likely they would be to engage in repeated criminal behavior.

Birth Cohort II

The subjects who made up Wolfgang's original birth cohort were born in 1945. How have behavior patterns changed in subsequent years? To answer this question, Wolfgang and his associates selected a new, larger birth cohort, born in Philadelphia in 1958, and followed them until their maturity.[118] The 1958 cohort is larger than the original. It has 28,338 subjects—13,811 males and 14,527 females.

Although the proportion of delinquent youths is about the same as that in the 1945 cohort, those in the larger sample were involved in 20,089 delinquent arrests. Chronic offenders (five or more arrests as juveniles) made up 7.5 percent of the 1958 sample (compared with 6.3 percent in 1945) and 23 percent of all delinquent offenders (compared with 18 percent in 1945). Chronic female delinquency was relatively rare—only 1 percent of the females in the survey were chronic offenders.

Chronic male delinquents continued to commit more than their share of criminal behavior. They accounted for 61 percent of the total offenses and a disproportionate amount of the most serious crimes: 61 percent of the homicides, 76 percent of the rapes, 73 percent of the robberies, and 65 percent of the aggravated assaults. The chronic female offender was less likely to be involved in serious crimes.

It is interesting that the 1958 cohort, as a group, was involved in significantly more serious crime than the 1945 group. For example, their violent offense rate (149 per 1,000 in the sample) was three times higher than the rate for the 1945 cohort (47 per 1,000 subjects).

The 1945 cohort study found that chronic offenders dominate the total crime rate and continue their law-violating careers as adults. The newer cohort study is showing that the chronic offender syndrome is being maintained in a group of subjects who were born 13 years later than the original cohort and, if anything, are more violent than their older brothers. Finally, the efforts of the justice system seem to have little preventive effect on the behavior of chronic offenders: the more often a person was arrested, the more likely he or she was to be arrested again. For males, 26 percent of the entire group had one violent-offense arrest; of that 26 percent, 34 percent went on to commit a second violent offense, while 43 percent of the three-time losers went on to a fourth arrest, and so on.

Chronic Offender Research

Wolfgang's pioneering effort to identify the chronic career offender has been replicated by a number of other important research studies. Lyle Shannon also used the cohort approach to investigate career delinquency patterns.[119] He employed three cohorts totaling 6,127 youths born in 1942, 1949, and 1955 in Racine, Wisconsin. Shannon also encountered the phenomenon of the chronic career offender who engages in a disproportionate amount of delinquent behavior and later becomes involved in adult criminality. He found that less than 25 percent of each cohort's male subjects had five or more nontraffic offenses but accounted for 77 percent to 83 percent of all police contacts (by males) in their cohort. Similarly, from 8 percent to 14 percent of the persons in each cohort were responsible for all the serious felony offenses. According to Shannon, if one wished to identify the persons responsible for about 75 percent of the felonies and much of the other crimes— then approximately 5 percent of each cohort—the persons with two or three felony contacts would be the target population. It is important to note that involvement of juveniles with the justice system did little to inhibit their adult criminality. Though most youths discontinued their criminal behavior after their teenage years, the few who continued are those who became well known to the police when they were teenagers.

A number of other cohort studies have accumulated data supportive of the Wolfgang research. D. J. West and D. P. Farrington's ongoing study of youths born in London from 1951 to 1954 has also shown that a small number of recidivists continue their behavior as adults and that arrest and conviction had little influence on their behavior other than to amplify the probability of their law violations: youths who had multiple convictions as juveniles tended to have multiple convictions as adults.[120] The most important childhood risk factors associated with chronic offending include a history of troublesomeness, a personality that reveres daring behavior, a delinquent sibling, and a convicted parent. Farrington finds that the most chronic offenders could be identified by age ten on the basis of personality and background features.[121]

Stability in Crime: From Delinquent to Criminal

Another important research project utilizing the cohort data was the birth cohort follow-up, a longitudinal analysis that followed a 10 percent sample of the original cohort (974 subjects) through their adulthood to age 30.[122] The researchers divided the sample into three groups: those who had been juvenile offenders only, those who were adult offenders only, and persistent offenders (those who had offenses in both time periods). Those classified as chronic juvenile offenders in the original birth cohort made up 70 percent of the "persistent" group. They had an 80 percent chance of becoming adult offenders and a 50 percent chance of being arrested four or more times as adults. In comparison, subjects with no juvenile arrests had only an 18 percent chance of being arrested as an adult. The chronic offenders also continued to engage in the most serious crimes. Though they accounted for only 15 percent of the follow-up sample, the former chronic delinquents were involved in 74 percent of all arrests and 82 percent of all serious crimes, such as homicide, rape, and robbery. The cohort follow-up clearly showed that chronic juvenile offenders continue their law-violating careers as adults.

The cohort follow-up helped create a picture of the criminal as someone who had a troubled life reaching early into childhood and who has measurable behavior problems in such areas as learning and motor skills, cognitive abilities, family relations, and other areas of social, psychological, and physical functioning.[123] Additional research has supported the concept of the continuity of crime. Kids who are found to be disruptive and antisocial as early as age five or six years are the ones most likely to exhibit stable, long-term patterns of disruptive behavior through adolescence.[124] Recent research by John Laub and Robert Sampson shows that youthful offenders are more than four times as likely to continue offending as adults and exhibit similar patterns of general deviant behavior: as adults, former delinquents are more likely to abuse alcohol, get into trouble while in military service, become economically dependent, have lower aspirations, get divorced or separated, and have a weak employment record.[125]

Criminal Career Development in Other Cultures

While developmental research has been ongoing in the United States, there have also been European efforts to corroborate findings. The Stockholm cohort project (Project Metropolitan) contains 15,117 male and female subjects. Recent analysis of data from this project indicates that criminal career development in Sweden follows many of the same patterns found in U.S. cohorts.[126]

Similarly, David Farrington and J. David Hawkins used data from a sample of 411 males born in London to chart the life courses of delinquent offenders. Farrington and Hawkins found that the frequency of offending was predicted by early onset of antisocial behavior, associating with deviant peers, certain personality traits (such as a low level of anxiety), poor school achievement, and dysfunctional family relations; this finding is not dissimilar from data gathered in the United States. Those delinquents who persisted into adulthood (ages 21 to 32) exhibited low IQs, substance abuse, chronic unemployment, and a low degree of commitment to school.[127]

In sum, research in both the United States and Europe shows that a small group of offenders are responsible for a great deal of all crime. These youths begin their offending career at an extremely young age and persist into their adulthood. Punishment does little to deter their behavior and, if anything, prompts escalation of their criminal activity.

Despite these efforts, understanding the forces that control the direction of a criminal career and predicting its onset and termination, escalation and decline, remain a goal of future research efforts.

Policy Implications of the Chronic Offender Concept

The chronic offender concept has a great deal of import for the study of criminology. If relatively few offenders become chronic, persistent criminals, then it is possible that they possess some individual trait that is responsible for their criminality. Most people exposed to troublesome social conditions, such as poverty, do not become chronic offenders; it is unlikely that social conditions alone then can cause chronic offending. If not, what does?

Another question that intrigues criminologists is, "If we can identify chronic offenders, what should we do about them? How can chronic offenders be controlled if punishment actually escalates the frequency of their criminal activity?"

The chronic offender has become a central focus of criminal justice system policy. Concern about repeat offenders has been translated into programs at various stages of the justice process. For example, police departments and district attorney's offices around the nation have set up programs to focus their resources on capturing and prosecuting dangerous or repeat offenders.[128]

Even more important has been the effect of the chronic offender on sentencing policy. Around the country, legal jurisdictions are developing sentencing policies designed to incapacitate serious offenders for long periods of time without hope of probation or parole. Among the policies spurred by the chronic offender concept is mandatory sentences for violent or drug-related crimes in more than 30 states, commonly known as a "three strikes and you're out" policy.

≡ Summary

There are three primary sources of crime statistics: the Uniform Crime Reports based on police data accumulated by the FBI, self-report of criminal behavior surveys, and victim surveys. They tell us that there is quite a bit of crime in the United States and that the amount of violent crime is increasing. Each data source has its strengths and weaknesses, and though quite different from one another, they actually agree on the nature of criminal behavior.

The data sources show that there are stable patterns in the crime rate. Ecological patterns show that some areas of the country are more crime-prone than others, that there are seasons and times for crime, and that these patterns are quite stable. There is also evidence of a gender and age gap in the crime rate: men usually commit more crime than women; young people commit more crime than the elderly. The crime data show that people commit less crime as they age, but the significance and cause of this pattern is still not completely understood.

Similarly, there appear to be racial and class patterns in the crime rate. However, it is still unclear whether these are true differences or a function of discriminatory law enforcement.

One of the most important findings in the crime statistics is the existence of the chronic offender, a repeat criminal responsible for a significant amount of all law violations. Chronic offenders begin their career early in life and, rather than aging out of crime, persist into their adulthood. The discovery of the chronic offender has led to the study of developmental criminology—why people persist, desist, terminate, or escalate their deviant behavior.

≡ KEY TERMS

index crimes	expressive crimes
Type I crimes	aging out
Type II crimes	desistance phenomenon
self-report survey	early onset
National Crime	masculinity hypothesis
Victimization Survey	chivalry hypothesis
crime patterns and trends	liberal feminist theory
yakuza gangs	career criminals
instrumental crimes	chronic offenders

☰ NOTES

1. Federal Bureau of Investigation, *Crime in the United States, 1992* (Washington, D.C.: U.S. Government Printing Office, 1993). Herein cited as FBI, *Uniform Crime Report* in footnotes and referred to in text as Uniform Crime Report, or UCR. Uniform Crime Report data are supplemented with preliminary data from the 1993 FBI crime survey.

2. Lisa Bastian, *Criminal Victimization, 1992* (Washington, D.C.: Bureau of Justice Statistics, 1993), p. 5. Hereinafter cited as NCVS, 1992.

3. Paul Tappan, *Crime, Justice and Corrections* (New York: McGraw-Hill, 1960).

4. Daniel Bell, *The End of Ideology* (New York: Free Press, 1967), p. 152.

5. Duncan Chappell, Gilbert Geis, Stephen Schafer, and Larry Siegel, "Forcible Rape: A Comparative Study of Offenses Known to the Police in Boston and Los Angeles," in *Studies in the Sociology of Sex,* ed. James Henslin (New York: Appleton Century Crofts, 1971), pp. 169–93.

6. Patrick Jackson, "Assessing the Validity of Official Data on Arson," *Criminology* 26 (1988): 181–95.

7. Lawrence Sherman and Barry Glick, "The Quality of Arrest Statistics," *Police Foundation Reports* 2 (1984): 1–8.

8. David Seidman and Michael Couzens, "Getting the Crime Rate Down: Political Pressure and Crime Reporting," *Law and Society Review* 8 (1974): 457.

9. Leonard Savitz, "Official Statistics," in *Contemporary Criminology,* ed. Leonard Savitz and Norman Johnston (New York: John Wiley, 1982), pp. 3–15.

10. Roger Hood and Richard Sparks, *Key Issues in Criminology* (New York: McGraw-Hill, 1970), p. 72.

11. A pioneering effort in self-report research is A. L. Porterfield, *Youth in Trouble* (Fort Worth, Texas: Leo Potishman Foundation, 1946); for a review, see Robert Hardt and George Bodine, *Development of Self-Report Instruments in Delinquency Research: A Conference Report* (Syracuse, N.Y.: Syracuse University Youth Development Center, 1965). See also Fred Murphy, Mary Shirley, and Helen Witner, "The Incidence of Hidden Delinquency," *American Journal of Orthopsychology* 16 (1946): 686–96.

12. Franklyn Dunford and Delbert Elliott, "Identifying Career Criminals Using Self-Reported Data," *Journal of Research in Crime and Delinquency* 21 (1983): 57–86.

13. See, for example, Spencer Rathus and Larry Siegel, "Crime and Personality Revisited: Effects of MMPI Sets on Self-Report Studies," *Criminology* 18 (1980): 245–51; John Clark and Larry Tifft, "Polygraph and Interview Validation of Self-Reported Deviant Behavior," *American Sociological Review* 31 (1966): 516–23.

14. See, for example, Harwin Voss, "Ethnic Differences in Delinquency in Honolulu," *Journal of Criminal Law, Criminology and Police Science* 54 (1963): 322–27; Maynard Erickson and LaMar Empey, "Court Records, Undetected Delinquency and Decision Making," *Journal of Criminal Law, Criminology and Police Science* 54 (1963): 456–59; H. B. Gibson, Sylvia Morrison, and D. J. West, "The Confession of Known Offenses in Response to a Self-Reported Delinquency Schedule," *British Journal of Criminology* 10 (1970): 277–80; John Blackmore, "The Relationship between Self-Reported Delinquency and Official Convictions amongst Adolescent Boys," *British Journal of Criminology* 14 (1974): 172–76.

15. Clark and Tifft, "Polygraph and Interview Validation of Self-Reported Deviant Behavior."

16. Michael Hindelang, Travis Hirschi, and Joseph Weis, *Measuring Delinquency* (Beverly Hills: Sage, 1981).

17. Ibid., p. 196.

18. Terence Thornberry, Beth Bjerregaard, and William Miles, "The Consequences of Respondent Attrition in Panel Studies: A Simulation Based on the Rochester Youth Development Study," *Journal of Quantitative Criminology* 9 (1993): 127–58.

19. Minu Mathur, Richard Dodder, and Harjit Sandhu, "Inmate Self-Report Data: A Study of Reliability," *Criminal Justice Review* 17 (1992): 258–67.

20. Thomas Gray and Eric Wish, *Maryland Youth at Risk: A Study of Drug Use in Juvenile Detainees* (College Park, Md.: Center for Substance Abuse Research, 1993).

21. Eric Wish and Christina Polsenberg, "Arrestee Urine Tests and Self-Reports of Drug Use: Which Is More Related to Rearrest?" (Paper presented at the annual meeting of the American Society of Criminology, Phoenix, Arizona, November 1993).

22. NCVS, 1992, p. 2.

23. Alfred Blumstein, Jacqueline Cohen, and Richard Rosenfeld, "Trend and Deviation in Crime Rates: A Comparison of UCR and NCVS data for Burglary and Robbery," *Criminology* 29 (1991): 237–48. See also Hindelang, Hirschi, and Weis, *Measuring Delinquency*.

24. For a critique, see Scott Menard, "Residual Gains, Reliability, and the UCR-NCVS Relationship: A Comment on Blumstein, Cohen and Rosenfield (1991)," *Criminology* 30 (1992): 105–15.

25. David McDowall and Colin Loftin, "Comparing the UCR and NCVS over Time," *Criminology* 30 (1992): 125–33.

26. Clarence Schrag, *Crime and Justice: American Style* (Washington, D.C.: U.S. Government Printing Office, 1971).

27. For example, the following studies have noted the great discrepancy between official statistics and self-report studies: Erickson and Empey, "Court Records"; Martin Gold, "Undetected Delinquent Behavior," *Journal of Research in Crime and Delinquency* 3 (1966): 27–46; James Short and F. Ivan Nye, "Extent of Undetected Delinquency, Tentative Conclusions," *Journal of Criminal Law, Criminology and Police Science* 49 (1958): 296–302; Michael Hindelang, "Causes of Delinquency: A Partial Replication and Extension," *Social Problems* 20 (1973): 471–87.

28. D. Wayne Osgood, Lloyd Johnston, Patrick O'Malley, and Jerald Bachman, "The Generality of Deviance in Late

Adolescence and Early Adulthood," *American Sociological Review* 53 (1988): 81–93.

29. D. Wayne Osgood, Patrick O'Malley, Jerald Bachman, and Lloyd Johnston, "Time Trends and Age Trends in Arrests and Self-Reported Illegal Behavior," *Criminology* 27 (1989): 389–417.

30. Lloyd Johnston, Patrick O'Malley, and Jerald Bachman, *Monitoring the Future, 1990* (Ann Arbor, Mich.: Institute for Social Research, 1991); Timothy Flanagan and Kathleen Maguire, *Sourcebook of Criminal Justice Statistics, 1989* (Washington, D.C.: U.S. Government Printing Office, 1990), pp. 290–91.

31. Glenn Pierce and James Alan Fox, *Recent Trends in Violent Crime: A Closer Look* (Boston: National Crime Analysis Program, Northeastern University, 1992).

32. Rosemary Gartner, "Family Structure, Welfare Spending, and Child Homicide in Developed Democracies," *Journal of Marriage and the Family* 53 (1991): 231–40.

33. Steven Dillingham, *Violent Crime in the United States* (Washington, D.C.: Bureau of Justice Statistics, 1991), p. 17.

34. FBI, *Uniform Crime Report,* 1992, p. 221.

35. Darrell Steffensmeier and Miles Harer, "Did Crime Rise or Fall during the Reagan Presidency? The Effects of an 'Aging' U.S. Population on the Nation's Crime Rate," *Journal of Research in Crime and Delinquency* 28 (1991): 330–39.

36. Rosemary Gartner and Robert Nash Parker, "Cross-National Evidence on Homicide and the Age Structure of the Population," *Social Forces* 69 (1990): 351–71.

37. Joseph Sheley and James Wright, *Gun Acquisition and Possession in Selected Juvenile Samples* (Washington, D.C.: National Institute of Justice, 1993).

38. Short and Nye, "Extent of Undetected Delinquency."

39. Ivan Nye, James Short, and Virgil Olsen, "Socio-economic Status and Delinquent Behavior," *American Journal of Sociology* 63 (1958): 381–89; Robert Dentler and Lawrence Monroe, "Social Correlates of Early Adolescent Theft," *American Sociological Review* 63 (1961): 733–43. See also Terence Thornberry and Margaret Farnworth, "Social Correlates of Criminal Involvement: Further Evidence of the Relationship between Social Status and Criminal Behavior," *American Sociological Review* 47 (1982): 505–18.

40. Charles Tittle, Wayne Villemez, and Douglas Smith, "The Myth of Social Class and Criminality: An Empirical Assessment of the Empirical Evidence," *American Sociological Review* 43 (1978): 643–56.

41. Charles Tittle and Robert Meier, "Specifying the SES/Delinquency Relationship," *Criminology* 28 (1990): 271–301.

42. Delbert Elliott and Suzanne Ageton, "Reconciling Race and Class Differences in Self-Reported and Official Estimates of Delinquency," *American Sociological Review* 45 (1980): 95–110.

43. See also Delbert Elliott and David Huizinga, "Social Class and Delinquent Behavior in a National Youth Panel: 1976–1980," *Criminology* 21 (1983): 149–77. For a similar view, see John Braithwaite, "The Myth of Social Class and Criminality Reconsidered," *American Sociological Review* 46 (1981): 35–58; Hindelang, Hirschi, and Weis, *Measuring Delinquency,* p. 196.

44. David Brownfield, "Social Class and Violent Behavior," *Criminology* 24 (1986): 421–39.

45. Douglas Smith and Laura Davidson, "Interfacing Indicators and Constructs in Criminological Research: A Note on the Comparability of Self-Report Violence Data for Race and Sex Groups," *Criminology* 24 (1986): 473–88.

46. See Gary Jensen, "Unraveling the Mystery of Social Class and Juvenile Crime: A Study of Mediating Causal Mechanisms" (Paper presented at the annual meeting of the American Society of Criminology, Phoenix, Arizona, November 1993).

47. Miles Harer and Darrell Steffensmeier, "The Differing Effects of Economic Inequality on Black and White Rates of Violence," *Social Forces* 70 (1992): 1035–54.

48. Judith Blau and Peter Blau, "The Cost of Inequality: Metropolitan Structure and Violent Crime," *American Sociological Review* 147 (1982): 114–29; Richard Block, "Community Environment and Violent Crime," *Criminology* 17 (1979): 46–57; Robert Sampson, "Structural Sources of Variation in Race-Age-Specific Rates of Offending across Major U.S. Cities," *Criminology* 23 (1985): 647–73.

49. Chin-Chi Hsieh and M. D. Pugh, "Poverty, Income Inequality, and Violent Crime: A Meta-Analysis of Recent Aggregate Data Studies," *Criminal Justice Review* 18 (1993): 182–99.

50. Alan Lizotte, Terence Thornberry, Marvin Krohn, Deborah Chard-Wierschem, and David McDowall, "Neighborhood Context and Delinquency: A Longitudinal Analysis," in *Cross National Longitudinal Research on Human Development and Criminal Behavior,* ed., E. M. Weitekamp and H. J. Kerner (Stavernstr, Netherlands: Kluwer, 1994), pp. 217–27.

51. Travis Hirschi and Michael Gottfredson, "Age and Explanation of Crime," *American Journal of Sociology* 89 (1983): 552–84, at 581.

52. Darrell Steffensmeier and Cathy Streifel, "Age, Gender, and Crime across Three Historical Periods: 1935, 1960 and 1985," *Social Forces* 69 (1991): 869–94.

53. Chester Britt, "Constancy and Change in the U.S. Age Distribution of Crime, 1952–1987" (Paper presented at the annual meeting of the American Society of Criminology, Baltimore, Maryland, November 1990).

54. For a comprehensive review of crime and the elderly, see Kyle Kercher, "Causes and Correlates of Crime Committed by the Elderly," in *Critical Issues in Aging Policy,* ed. E. Borgatta and R. Montgomery (Beverly Hills: Sage, 1987), pp. 254–306; Darrell Steffensmeier, "The Invention of the 'New' Senior Citizen Criminal," *Research on Aging* 9 (1987): 281–311.

55. John Laub, David Clark, Leslie Siegel, and James Garofolo, *Trends in Juvenile Crime in the United States: 1973–1983* (Albany, N.Y.: Hindelang Research Center,

1987).

56. Hirschi and Gottfredson, "Age and the Explanation of Crime."

57. Michael Gottfredson and Travis Hirschi, "The True Value of Lambda Would Appear to Be Zero: An Essay on Career Criminals, Criminal Careers, Selective Incapacitation, Cohort Studies and Related Topics," *Criminology* 24 (1986): 213–34; further support for their position can be found in Lawrence Cohen and Kenneth Land, "Age Structure and Crime," *American Sociological Review* 52 (1987): 170–83.

58. Kyle Kercher, "Explaining the Relationship between Age and Crime: The Biological versus Sociological Model" (Paper presented at the American Society of Criminology meeting, Montreal, Canada, November 1987).

59. Alfred Blumstein, Jacqueline Cohen, and David Farrington, "Criminal Career Research: Its Value for Criminology," *Criminology* 26 (1988): 1–37.

60. Candace Kruttschnitt, "Violence by and against Women: A Comparative and Cross-National Analysis," *Violence and Victims* 8 (1994): in press.

61. David Greenberg, "Age, Crime, and Social Explanation," *American Journal of Sociology* 91 (1985): 1–21.

62. Marvin Wolfgang, Robert Figlio, and Thorsten Sellin, *Delinquency in a Birth Cohort* (Chicago: University of Chicago Press, 1972); Lyle Shannon, *Assessing the Relationship of Adult Criminal Careers to Juvenile Careers: A Summary* (Washington, D.C.: U.S. Department of Justice, 1982); D. J. West and David P. Farrington, *The Delinquent Way of Life* (London: Hienemann, 1977); Donna Hamparian, Richard Schuster, Simon Dinitz, and John Conrad, *The Violent Few* (Lexington, Mass.: Lexington Books, 1978).

63. Rolf Loeber, Magda Stouthamer-Loeber, and Stephanie Green, "Age at Onset of Problem Behaviour in Boys and Later Disruptive and Delinquent Behaviours," *Criminal Behaviour and Mental Health* 1 (1991): 229–46.

64. Arnold Barnett, Alfred Blumstein, and David Farrington, "Probabilistic Models of Youthful Criminal Careers," *Criminology* 25 (1987): 83–107.

65. Darrell Steffensmeier, Emilie Andersen Allan, Miles Harer, and Cathy Streifel, "Age and the Distribution of Crime: Variant or Invariant?" (Paper presented at the American Society of Criminology meeting, Montreal, Canada, November 1987).

66. Peter Greenwood, "Differences in Criminal Behavior and Court Responses among Juvenile and Young Adult Defendants," in *Crime and Justice, an Annual Review of Research,* ed. Michael Tonry and Norval Morris (Chicago: University of Chicago Press, 1986), pp. 151–89.

67. John Hagan and Alberto Palloni, "Crimes as Social Events in the Life Course: Reconceiving a Criminological Controversy," *Criminology* 26 (1988): 87–101.

68. Travis Hirschi and Michael Gottfredson, "Age and Crime, Logic and Scholarship: Comment on Greenberg," *American Journal of Sociology* 91 (1985): 22–27; idem,

"All Wise after the Fact Learning Theory, Again: Reply to Baldwin," *American Journal of Sociology* 90 (1985): 1330–33; John Baldwin, "Thrill and Adventure Seeking and the Age Distribution of Crime: Comment on Hirschi and Gottfredson," *American Journal of Sociology* 90 (1985): 1326–29.

69. Per-Olof Wikstrom, "Age and Crime in a Stockholm Cohort," *Journal of Quantitative Criminology* 6 (1990): 61–82.

70. Edward Mulvey and John LaRosa, "Delinquency Cessation and Adolescent Development: Preliminary Data," *American Journal of Orthopsychiatry* 56 (1986): 212–24.

71. Gordon Trasler, "Cautions for a Biological Approach to Crime," in *The Causes of Crime, New Biological Approaches, ed.* Sarnoff Mednick, Terrie Moffitt, and Susan Stack (Cambridge: Cambridge University Press, 1987), pp. 7–25.

72. James Q. Wilson and Richard Herrnstein, *Crime and Human Nature* (New York: Simon and Schuster, 1985), pp. 126–47.

73. Barry Glassner, Margaret Ksander, Bruce Berg, and Bruce Johnson, "A Note on the Deterrent Effect of Juvenile versus Adult Jurisdiction," *Social Problem* 31 (1983): 219–21.

74. Ibid., p. 219.

75. Charles Tittle, "Two Empirical Regularities (Maybe) in Search of an Explanation: Commentary on the Age/Crime Debate," *Criminology* 26 (1988): 75–85.

76. Neal Shover and Carol Thompson, "Age, Differential Expectations and Crime Desistance," *Criminology* 30 (1992): 89–105.

77. Walter Gove, "The Effect of Age and Gender on Deviant Behavior: A Biopsychosocial Perspective," in *Gender and the Life Course,* ed. A. Ross: (Chicago: Aldine, 1985), p. 131.

78. Imogene Moyer, "Academic Criminology: A Need for Change," *American Journal of Criminal Justice* 9 (1985): 197–212.

79. Cesare Lombroso, *The Female Offender* (New York: Appleton Publishers, 1920).

80. Ibid., p. 122.

81. Otto Pollack, *The Criminality of Women* (Philadelphia: University of Pennsylvania, 1950).

82. For a review of this issue, see Darrell Steffensmeier, "Assessing the Impact of the Women's Movement on Sex-Based Differences in the Handling of Adult Criminal Defendants," *Crime and Delinquency* 26 (1980): 344–57.

83. Darrell Steffensmeier and Robert Clark, "Sociocultural versus Biological/Sexist Explanations of Sex Differences in Crime: A Survey of American Criminology Textbooks, 1918–1965," *American Sociologist* 15 (1980): 246–55.

84. Gisela Konopka, *The Adolescent Girl in Conflict* (Englewood Cliffs, N.J.: Prentice-Hall, 1966); Clyde Vedder and Dora Somerville, *The Delinquent Girl* (Springfield, Ill.: Charles C. Thomas, 1970).

85. Freda Adler, *Sisters in Crime* (New York: McGraw-Hill, 1975).

86. Rita James Simons, *The Contemporary Woman and Crime* (Washington, D.C.: U.S. Government Printing Office, 1975).

87. Michael Hindelang, "Age, Sex, and the Versatility of Delinquency Involvements," *Social Forces* 14 (1971): 525–34; Martin Gold, *Delinquent Behavior in an American City* (Belmont, Calif.: Brooks/Cole, 1970); Gary Jensen and Raymond Eve, "Sex Differences in Delinquency: An Examination of Popular Sociological Explanations," *Criminology* 13 (1976): 427–48.

88. Meda Chesney-Lind, "Female Offenders: Paternalism Reexamined," in *Women, the Courts and Equality,* ed. Laura Crites and Winifred Hepperle (Newberry Park, Calif.: Sage, 1987), pp. 114–39.

89. Darrel Steffensmeier and Renee Hoffman Steffensmeier, "Trends in Female Delinquency," *Criminology* 18 (1980): 62–85; see also idem, "Crime and the Contemporary Woman: An Analysis of Changing Levels of Female Property Crime, 1960–1975," *Social Forces* 57 (1978): 566–84; Joseph Weis, "Liberation and Crime: The Invention of the New Female Criminal," *Crime and Social Justice* 1 (1976): 17–27; Carol Smart, "The New Female Offender: Reality or Myth," *British Journal of Criminology* 19 (1979): 50–59; Steven Box and Chris Hale, "Liberation/Emancipation, Economic Marginalization or Less Chivalry," *Criminology* 22 (1984): 473–78.

90. Chesney-Lind, "Female Offenders: Paternalism Reexamined," p. 115.

91. Steffensmeier and Streifel, "Age, Gender, and Crime across Three Historical Periods."

92. Darrell Steffensmeier, Emilie Allan, and Cathy Streifel, "Development and Female Crime: A Cross-National Test of Alternative Explanations," *Social Forces* 68 (1989): 262–83.

93. Kruttschnitt, "Violence by and against Women."

94. Meda Chesney-Lind, "Women and Crime: The Female Offender," *Sigma: Journal of Women in Culture and Society* 12 (1986): 78–96.

95. Cassia Spohn, John Gruhl, and Susan Welch, "The Impact of the Ethnicity and Gender of Defendants on the Decision to Reject or Dismiss Felony Charges," *Criminology* 25 (1987): 175–91.

96. Roy Austin, "Recent Trends in Official Male and Female Crime Rates: The Convergence Controversy," *Journal of Criminal Justice* 21 (1993): 447–66.

97. Beth Bjerregaard and Carolyn Smith, "Gender Differences in Gang Participation, Delinquency, and Substance Abuse," *Journal of Quantitative Criminology* 9 (1993): 329–55.

98. Austin "Recent Trends in the Male and Female Crime Rate," p. 464.

99. John Laub, David Clark, Leslie Siegel, and James Garofolo, *Trends in Juvenile Crime in the United States: 1973–1983* (Albany, N.Y.: Hindelang Research Center, 1987).

100. Leroy Gould, "Who Defines Delinquency: A Comparison of Self-Report and Officially Reported Indices of Delinquency for Three Racial Groups," *Social Problems* 16 (1969): 325–36; Voss, "Ethnic Differentials in Delinquency in Honolulu"; Ronald Akers, Marvin Krohn, Marcia Radosevich, and Lonn Lanza-Kaduce, "Social Characteristics and Self-Reported Delinquency," *Sociology of Delinquency,* ed. Gary Jensen (Beverly Hills: Sage, 1981), pp. 48–62.

101. Institute for Social Research, *Monitoring the Future* (Ann Arbor, Mich.: ISR, 1992), pp. 102–4.

102. David Huizinga and Delbert Elliott, "Juvenile Offenders: Prevalence, Offender Incidence, and Arrest Rates by Race," *Crime and Delinquency* 33 (1987): 206–23. See also Dale Dannefer and Russell Schutt, "Race and Juvenile Justice Processing in Court and Police Agencies," *American Journal of Sociology* 87 (1982): 1113–32.

103. Paul Tracy, "Race and Class Differences in Official and Self-Reported Delinquency," in *From Boy to Man, from Delinquency to Crime,* ed. Marvin Wolfgang, Terence Thornberry, and Robert Figlio (Chicago: University of Chicago Press, 1987), p. 120.

104. Daniel Georges-Abeyie, "Definitional Issues: Race, Ethnicity and Official Crime/Victimization Rates," in *The Criminal Justice System and Blacks,* ed. D. Georges-Abeyie (New York: Clark Boardman, 1984), p. 12; Robert Sampson, "Race and Criminal Violence: A Demographically Disaggregated Analysis of Urban Homicide," *Crime and Delinquency* 31 (1985): 47–82.

105. Barry Sample and Michael Philip, "Perspectives on Race and Crime in Research and Planning," in *The Criminal Justice System and Blacks,* ed. D. Georges-Abeyie (New York: Clark Boardman, 1984), pp. 21–36.

106. Kruttschnitt, "Violence by and against Women," p. 4.

107. James Comer, "Black Violence and Public Policy," in *American Violence and Public Policy,* ed. Lynn Curtis (New Haven: Yale University Press, 1985), pp. 63–86.

108. Ibid., p. 80.

109. Ibid., p. 81.

110. Marvin Wolfgang and Franco Ferracuti, *The Subculture of Violence* (London: Tavistock, 1967).

111. Charles Silberman, *Criminal Violence, Criminal Justice* (New York: Random House, 1979), pp. 153–65.

112. Roy Austin, "Progress toward Racial Equality and Reduction of Black Criminal Violence," *Journal of Criminal Justice* 15 (1987): 437–59.

113. Reynolds Farley and William Frey, "Changes in the Segregation of Whites from Blacks During the 1980's: Small Steps toward a More Integrated Society," *American Sociological Review* 59 (1994): 23–45.

114. Melvin Thomas, "Race, Class and Personal Income: An Empirical Test of the Declining Significance of Race Thesis, 1968–1988," *Social Problems* 40 (1993): 328–39.

115. Gary LaFree, Kriss Drass, and Patrick O'Day, "Race and Crime in Postwar America: Determinants of African-American and White Rates, 1957–1988," *Criminology* 30 (1992): 157–88.

116. Marvin Wolfgang, Robert Figlio, and Thorsten Sellin, *Delinquency in a Birth Cohort* (Chicago: University of Chicago Press, 1972).

117. See Thorsten Sellin and Marvin Wolfgang, *The Measurement of Delinquency* (New York: Wiley, 1964), p. 120.

118. Paul Tracy and Robert Figlio, "Chronic Recidivism in the 1950 Birth Cohort" (Paper presented at the American Society of Criminology meeting, Toronto, October 1982); Marvin Wolfgang, "Delinquency in Two Birth Cohorts," in *Perspective Studies of Crime and Delinquency,* ed. Katherine Teilmann Van Dusen and Sarnoff Mednick (Boston: Kluwer-Nijhoff, 1983), pp. 7–17. The following sections rely heavily on these sources.

119. Lyle Shannon, *Criminal Career Opportunity* (New York: Human Sciences Press, 1988); idem, *Assessing the Relationship of Adult Criminal Careers to Juvenile Careers.*

120. D. J. West and David P. Farrington, *The Delinquent Way of Life* (London: Hienemann, 1977).

121. David Farrington and Donald West, "Criminal, Penal and Life Histories of Chronic Offenders: Risk and Protective Factors and Early Identification," *Criminal Behavior and Mental Health* in press (1994).

122. See, generally, Marvin Wolfgang, Terence Thornberry, and Robert Figlio, eds. *From Boy to Man, from Delinquency to Crime* (Chicago: University of Chicago Press, 1987).

123. Jennifer White, Terrie Moffitt, Felton Earls, Lee Robins, and Phil Silva, "How Early Can We Tell? Predictors of Childhood Conduct Disorder and Adolescent Delinquency," *Criminology* 28 (1990): 507–35.

124. R. Tremblay, R. Loeber, C. Gagnon, P. Charlebois, S. Larivee, and M. LeBlanc, "Disruptive Boys with Stable and Unstable High Fighting Behavior Patterns during Junior Elementary School," *Journal of Abnormal Child Psychology* 19 (1991): 285–300.

125. John Laub and Robert Sampson, "Unemployment, Marital Discord, and Deviant Behavior: The Long-Term Correlates of Childhood Misbehavior" (Paper presented at the annual meeting of the American Society of Criminology, Baltimore, November 1990; rev. version).

126. Wikstrom, "Age and Crime in a Stockholm Cohort."

127. David Farrington and J. David Hawkins, "Predicting Participation, Early Onset, and Later Persistence in Officially Recorded Offending," *Criminal Behavior and Mental Health* 1 (1991): 1–33.

128. Susan Martin, "Policing Career Criminals: An Examination of an Innovative Crime Control Program," *Journal of Criminal Law and Criminology* 77 (1986): 1159–82.

ShIP

nd
tion

Introduction

For many years, crime victims were not considered an important topic for criminological study. Victims were viewed as the passive receptors of a criminal's anger, greed, or frustration; they were people considered to be in the "wrong place at the wrong time." In the late 1960s, a number of pioneering studies found that, contrary to popular belief, the victim's function is an important one in the crime process. Victims can influence the direction of criminal behavior by playing an active role in the criminal incident, such as when an assault victim initially insults and provokes his eventual attacker. Research efforts found that victims can also play an indirect role in the criminal incident, such as when a woman adopts a life-style that continually brings her into high-crime areas.

The discovery that the victim plays an important role in the crime process has prompted the scientific study of the victim, or **victimology;** those criminologists who focus their attention on the crime victim refer to themselves as **victimologists.** Victim studies have also taken on great importance because of concern for those injured in violent crimes or who suffer loss due to economic crimes. The National Crime Victimization Survey indicates that the annual number of victimizations in the United States approaches 34 million incidents. More than 1 million victims are injured seriously enough each year to require medical care.[1] The Centers for Disease Control now ranks homicide as the seventh leading cause of premature mortality in the United States (the leaders are unintentional injuries, cancer, and heart disease); the chances of dying prematurely as a homicide victim have almost doubled since 1968.[2]

In this chapter, the focus is on victims and their relationship to the criminal process. First, using available victim data, the nature and extent of victimization is analyzed. We then turn to a discussion of the relationship between victims and criminal offenders. The various theories of victimization are covered: What is the victim's role in the crime problem? How has society responded to the needs of victims, and what special problems do they still face?

Problems of Crime Victims: Loss

Being the target or a victim of rape, robbery, or assault is a terrible burden that can have considerable long-term consequences.[3] Based on estimates of property taken during larcenies, burglaries, and other reported crimes, the FBI estimates victims lost about $15.4 billion in property in 1992.[4] The NCVS estimates victim losses of about $17.6 billion during the same period, as shown in Table 4.1.[5] As Table 4.2. shows, the average loss per crime ranged from about $4,000 per motor vehicle theft to $124 per assault. About 71 percent of personal crime and 91 percent of household crime involved some form of economic loss, which included cash losses, property damage, medical expenses, and lost pay. These losses are immediate and some costs, such as medical expenses and psychological counseling fees, may accumulate for years after.

Economic loss is only one small part of the cost of being victimized. In an important analysis, Mark Cohen used jury awards in civil injury cases to estimate the "real cost" of crime to victims.[6] As Table 4.3 shows, a crime such as rape costs its victim an average of $51,058, including $4,617 in direct losses, $43,651 for pain and suffering, and $2,880 for the risk of death. In other words, Cohen estimates that if a rape victim sued her attacker for damages, the jury award would amount to about $51,000. In contrast to the FBI statistics, Cohen estimates that the cost of crime to victims is a staggering $92.6 billion annually.

In addition to the direct cost to the targets of crime, there are also indirect costs to the rest of society; in a sense, we are all crime victims. A survey by *Business*

TABLE 4.1 **Total Economic Loss to Victims of Crime, 1992**

All crime victims	$17,646,000,000
Victims with Losses	
Personal crimes	**$4,110,000,000**
Crimes of violence	1,362,000,000
Rape	33,000,000
Robbery	680,000,000
Assault	649,000,000
Crimes of personal theft	2,748,000,000
Larceny with contact	76,000,000
Larceny without contact	2,672,000,000
Household crimes	**$13,536,000,000**
Burglary	3,970,000,000
Household larceny	1,750,000,000
Motor vehicle theft	7,816,000,000

SOURCE: Patsy Klaus, *The Costs of Crime to Victims* (Washington, D.C.: Bureau of Justice Statistics, 1994), p. 2.

TABLE 4.2 Average Loss per Crime, 1992

Mean loss, all crimes*	$524
Personal crimes	**$218**
Crimes of violence	206
Rape	234
Robbery	555
Assault	124
Household crimes	**$914**
Personal and household theft	221
Burglary	834
Motor vehicle theft	3,990

*Data includes all forms of economic loss, medical expenses, and time lost from work because of the crime.
SOURCE: Patsy Klaus, *The Costs of Crime to Victims* (Washington, D.C.: Bureau of Justice Statistics, 1994), p. 1.

Week magazine came up with the astounding figure of $450 billion dollars annually as an appropriate figure for losses due to crime:

- Criminal justice $90 billion
- Private protection and security $65 billion
- Urban decay $50 billion
- Property loss $45 billion
- Medical care $5 billion
- Shattered lives $170 billion

While the magazine's editors failed to disclose how they arrived at these estimates, and some figures certainly may be overstated, the point they are making should not be taken lightly: crime is an extremely expensive drain on the nation's well-being and resources.[7]

≡ Problems of Crime Victims: Suffering

The problems associated with crime are not restricted to its costs. Victims are likely to suffer serious physical injury, often requiring medical treatment. The suffering endured by crime victims does not end when their attacker leaves the scene of the crime. They may suffer more "victimization" at the hands of the justice system. Victims may find that questioning by police may be

insensitive, including innuendos or suspicion that they were somehow at fault. They may have difficulty learning what is happening in the case. Property is often kept for a long time as evidence and may never be returned. Wages may be lost for time spent testifying in court. Time may be wasted when victims appear in court only to have the case postponed or dismissed. They may find that the authorities are indifferent to their fear of retaliation if they cooperate in the offender's prosecution. They may be fearful of testifying in court and being embarrassed by defense attorneys.[8]

After the incident is over, victims may suffer stress and anxiety, even after physical traumas and financial losses and the justice process have been forgotten. For example, the long-term emotional trauma suffered by women in the aftermath of sexual and physical assault is well documented.[9] A recent review of the aftermath of spousal assaults indicated an extremely high prevalence of depression, post-traumatic stress disorder, anxiety disorder, and obsessive compulsive disorder.[10]

Women are not the only ones who suffer in the aftermath of violence. In a study conducted in England, Elizabeth Stanko and Kathy Hobdell found that male victims of violent attacks also suffer post-crime stress disorders. Viewing themselves from a "male frame" of reference, victims expressed feelings of being "weak and helpless." Because victimization threatened their sense of masculinity, they had trouble expressing their feelings and asking for support. Stanko and Hobdell encountered an important gender difference: while female victims tend to internalize and place the blame for their victimization on themselves, males externalize blame, expressing anger toward their attackers. Coping with these feelings of anger becomes a problem for supporters who want to offer male victims care and comfort.[11]

Victimization, then, presents financial, physical, and emotional strains that are difficult to overcome.

TABLE 4.3 Average Cost of Crime to Victim

Kidnapping	$110,469	Assault	$12,028
Bombing	$77,123	Motor vehicle theft	$3,127
Rape	$51,058	Burglary	$1,372
Arson	$33,549	Larceny	
Bank robbery	$18,810	Personal	$181
Robbery	$12,594	Household	$173

SOURCE: Adapted from Mark Cohen, "Pain, Suffering, and Cost Jury Awards: A Study of Cost of Crime to Victims," *Law and Society Review* 22 (1988): 547.

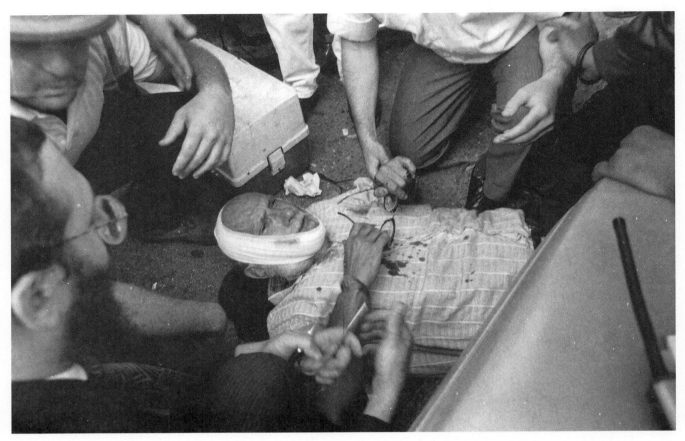

More than 33 million become crime victims each year. The plight of the victim: loss, pain, suffering, injury, and death.

Nature of Victimization

How many crime victims are there in the United States, and what are the trends and patterns in victimization? The National Victimization Crime Survey is the leading source of information today about the nature and extent of victimization. As you may recall from Chapter 3, the NCVS employs a highly sophisticated and complex sampling methodology to annually collect data from thousands of citizens. Statistical estimation techniques are then employed on the sample data to make estimates of victimization rates, trends, and patterns that occur in the entire U.S. population. At last count, an estimated 33.6 million criminal events occurred during 1992, as Figure 4.1 shows. As was the case for crime data, there are patterns in the victimization survey findings that are stable and repetitive. These patterns are critical social facts because they indicate that victimization is not a random event but a function of personal and ecological factors. The stability of these patterns allows judgments to be made about the nature of victimization, and policies can

then be created that might eventually reduce the victimization rate. Who are victims? Where does victimization take place? What is the relationship between victims and criminals? Answers to these questions can come from the National Crime Vicitimization Survey data. In the following sections, some of the most important patterns and trends in victimization are discussed.

The Social Ecology of Victimization

The NCVS data can tell us a lot about the ecology of victimization—where, when, and how it occurs. Of offenses included in the survey, most occurred in the evening hours (6 P.M. to 6 A.M.); only personal larcenies with contact, such as purse-snatching and pocket-pickings, predominated during daytime hours. Crimes of violence occurred more often at night. Generally, the more serious forms of these crimes were more likely to take place after 6 P.M.; the less serious, before then. For

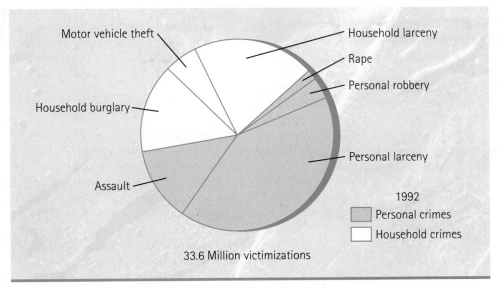

FIGURE 4.1 **Percent Distribution of Victimizations by Sector and Type of Crime, 1992**

SOURCE: Adapted from Lisa Bastian and Marshall DeBerry, Jr., *Criminal Victimization in the United States, 1992* (Washington, D.C.: U.S. Government Printing Office, 1994), p. 15.

example, the greatest proportion of aggravated assaults occurred at night, while unarmed robberies happened during the day.

The most likely site for each crime category was an open, public area, such as a street, a park, or a field. Only the crimes of rape and simple assault with injury were likely to occur in the home. Nonetheless, a significant number of rapes, robberies, and aggravated assaults occurred in public places.

Neighborhood characteristics influence the chances of victimization. Those living in the central city had significantly higher rates of theft and violence than suburbanites; people living in nonmetropolitan, rural areas had a victimization rate almost half that of city dwellers. The risk for murder victimization, for both men and women, is significantly higher in disorganized, inner-city areas, where gangs flourish and drug trafficking is commonplace.[12]

≡ The Victim's Household

Another way to look at the social ecology of victimization patterns is to examine the type of household or dwelling unit most likely to contain victims or to be victimized. According to the NCVS statistics, about 23

percent of the 96 million U.S. households contain at least one individual who experienced victimization of some sort during the past 12 months.[13] While household victimization rates have remained rather stable since 1986, they have actually declined from the late 1970s, when about 31 percent of U.S. households reported victimization.

What factors are associated with households that contain crime victims? The NCVS tells us that larger, higher-income, African-American, western, and urban areas are the most vulnerable to crime. In contrast, poor, rural white homes in the northeast were the least likely to contain crime victims or be the target of theft offenses, such as burglary or larceny. People who own their own home are less vulnerable than renters.

NCVS data indicate that recent population movements and changes may be accounting for current patterns in household victimization patterns. U.S. society has become extremely mobile, moving from urban to suburban and rural areas. In addition, family size has been reduced; more people than ever before are living in single-person homes (about 25 percent of households). It is possible that the decline in household victimization rates during the past 15 years can be explained by the fact that smaller households in less-populated areas have a lower victimization risk.

Because of this high incidence of crime, Americans maintain a significant chance of becoming a victim sometime during their lifetime. The probability of the average 12-year-old being the victim of violent crime sometime in his or her life is about 83 percent; 25 percent of all U.S. citizens will experience violence three or more times. Even more startling is the fact that 99 percent of the U.S. population will experience personal theft, and 87 percent will become a theft victim three or more times.[14] As Table 4.4 shows, vulnerability to criminal victimization is extremely high. Your chances of being a crime victim are greater than being injured in a car accident or having a heart attack.

≡ Victim Characteristics

Social and demographic characteristics distinguish victims and nonvictims. The most important of these involve gender, race, age, and social status.

Gender

The NCVS provides information on the background characteristics of the victims of crime. As Table 4.5 shows, gender affects victimization risk. Males are about twice as likely as females to be victims of robbery and three times as likely to be assaulted; they are more likely to experience theft, but the differences from females are less pronounced.

When males are the victim of violent crime, the perpetrator is described as a stranger; females are much more likely to be attacked by a relative than males; about two-thirds of all attacks against females were committed by a husband, boyfriend, family member, or

TABLE 4.4 Likelihood of Victimization

Events	Rate per 1,000 per Year
Violent victimization	31
Assault (aggravated and simple)	25
Injury in motor vehicle accident	22
Victimization with injury	11
Serious (aggravated) assault	8
Robbery	6
Heart disease death	5
Rape (women only)	1
Motor vehicle accident death	.2
Carjacking	.2
Homicide/legal intervention	.1

SOURCE: Michael Rand, *Carjacking* (Washington, D.C.: Bureau of Justice Statistics, 1994), p. 1.

acquaintance. And, although crimes against males have actually decreased during the past 20 years, the female victimization rate has remained stable.[15] Figure 4.2 illustrates the risk of violent crime faced by females in America.

Age

Young people face a much greater risk of becoming a victim than do older persons. As Table 4.5 shows, victimization risk diminishes rapidly after age 25. The elderly, who are thought of as being the helpless targets of predatory criminals, are actually much safer than their grandchildren.

The association between age and victimization may be bound up in the life-style shared by young people. Adolescents often stay out late at night, go to public places, and hang out with other kids who have a high risk of criminal involvement. About two-thirds of adolescents aged 12 to 19 are attacked by offenders in the same age category, while a great majority of adults are victimized by adult criminals. Teens face a high victimization risk because of their exposure to the most criminal element in the population—other teenagers.

Adolescents also face a high victimization risk because they spend a great deal of time in one of the most dangerous places in the community: the public school. Each year, about 9 percent of all male and female students become crime victims. About 2 million crimes take place in school buildings or on school grounds, including about 400,000 violent crimes and 1.5 million property offenses.[16]

Violence in the Home. Young people may also experience a disproportionate share of violence because U.S. homes have become very dangerous places. A national survey conducted by sociologists Richard Gelles and Murray Straus found that in a given year, between 1.4 and 1.9 million children in the United States are subject to physical abuse by their parents.[17] The survey showed that physical abuse was rarely a one-time act; the average number of assaults per year was 10.5, and the median was 4.5. In addition to parent-child abuse, Gelles and Straus found that 16 percent of the couples in their sample reported a violent act toward a spouse (husband or wife); 50 percent of multichild families reported attacks between siblings; and 20 percent had incidents where children attacked parents. In another national survey conducted in 1985, Gelles and Straus found that the incidence of very severe violence toward children may be on the decline.[18] Nonetheless, they still estimate that approximately 1.5 million children are annually subjected to severe violence. Other studies and national surveys have confirmed that more than 1 million kids are abused each year.[19]

While the focus usually falls on parents who injure children, family violence can also involve children who injure or kill parents; about 300 people are killed by their children each year.[20] This issue of parental victimization is discussed in the Close-Up on parricide, or the killing of a close relative.

An extremely disturbing trend has been the meteoric rise in the number of reported sexual abuse cases.

In 1976, less than one in 10,000 children was reported to be the victim of sexual abuse, while today, the figure stands at more than 100 in 10,000.[21] While this increase in reported abuse could be caused by a dramatic increase in the actual sexual abuse of children, it is more likely the result of greater public awareness of the problem, state efforts to encourage reporting, the proliferation of programs to prevent sexual maltreatment, and expansion of the definition of sexual abuse. These findings underscore the reason adolescents have a much greater victimization risk than adults.

TABLE 4.5 **Victimization Rates per 1,000 Persons, 1992**

| | Crimes of Violence | | | | | | |
	Total	Total*	Robbery	Total	Assault Aggravated	Simple	Crimes of theft
Sex							
Male	101.4	38.8	8.1	30.1	12.0	18.1	62.6
Female	81.8	25.9	3.9	21.1	6.1	15.0	55.9
Age							
12–15	171.0	75.7	9.8	64.8	20.1	44.7	95.3
16–19	172.7	77.9	15.4	60.9	26.3	34.5	94.8
20–24	177.0	70.1	11.4	56.0	18.1	38.0	106.9
25–34	111.1	37.6	7.7	29.4	9.3	20.1	73.4
35–49	75.1	21.2	3.8	17.1	6.8	10.2	53.9
50–64	43.3	10.0	2.8	7.1	2.3	4.8	33.3
65 or older	21.1	4.8	1.5	3.1	1.3	1.8	16.3
Race							
White	88.7	29.9	4.7	24.6	7.8	16.8	58.8
Black	110.8	50.4	15.6	33.5	18.3	15.2	60.4
Other	88.3	23.7	5.1	18.6	5.3	13.3	64.6
Ethnicity							
Hispanic	100.1	38.1	10.6	26.9	10.0	16.8	61.9
Non-Hispanic	90.3	31.4	5.4	25.3	8.9	16.4	58.9
Family Income							
Less than $7,500	136.7	64.4	11.1	52.0	23.1	28.8	72.3
$7,500–$9,999	94.4	40.3	11.5	28.8	9.3	19.5	54.1
$10,000–$14,999	85.9	34.3	7.1	26.6	9.0	17.6	51.6
$15,000–$24,999	88.1	34.1	5.4	27.8	9.7	18.1	54.0
$25,000–$29,999	93.3	35.6	6.3	29.3	6.3	23.0	57.6
$30,000–$49,999	83.3	26.6	4.8	20.9	6.6	14.3	56.6
$50,000 or more	92.2	21.2	3.7	16.9	5.5	11.4	71.0
Residence							
Central city	116.5	43.2	10.8	31.5	12.1	19.4	73.3
Suburban	84.8	28.2	4.4	23.1	7.3	15.8	56.5
Nonmetropolitan areas	72.4	25.2	2.7	22.1	7.8	14.3	47.2

*Includes data on rape not shown separately.

SOURCE: Lisa Bastian, *Criminal Victimization in the United States, 1992* (Washington, D.C.: Bureau of Justice Statistics, 1993), p. 6.

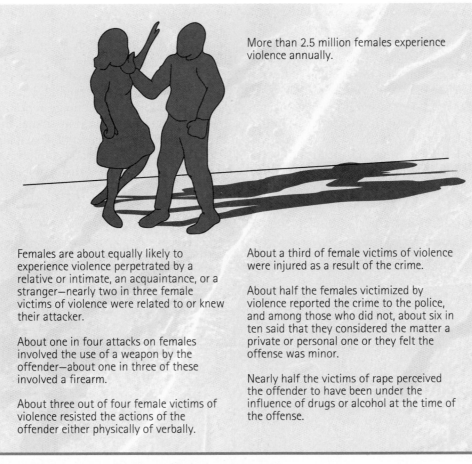

More than 2.5 million females experience violence annually.

Females are about equally likely to experience violence perpetrated by a relative or intimate, an acquaintance, or a stranger—nearly two in three female victims of violence were related to or knew their attacker.

About one in four attacks on females involved the use of a weapon by the offender—about one in three of these involved a firearm.

About three out of four female victims of violence resisted the actions of the offender either physically of verbally.

About a third of female victims of violence were injured as a result of the crime.

About half the females victimized by violence reported the crime to the police, and among those who did not, about six in ten said that they considered the matter a private or personal one or they felt the offense was minor.

Nearly half the victims of rape perceived the offender to have been under the influence of drugs or alcohol at the time of the offense.

FIGURE 4.2   Females' Risk of Violent Crime

SOURCE: Ronet Bachman, *Violence against Women* (Washington, D.C.: Bureau of Justice Statistics, 1994).

Social Status

The poorest Americans might be expected to be the most likely victims of crime, since they live in areas that are crime-prone: inner-city, urban neighborhoods. NCVS data in Table 4.5 do in fact show that the least affluent (annual incomes of less than $7,500) were by far the most likely to be victims of violent crimes, and this association occurs across all gender, racial, and age groups. Theft victimization takes on a different pattern. Members of the highest-income group face approximately the same risk as the poorest; people whose annual household income exceeds $50,000 were the most frequent target of property crimes

Victim data suggest that thieves choose their targets carefully, selecting those who seem best able to provide them with a substantial haul. In contrast, the targets of violence, an expressive crime, are among the nation's poorest people. And while the wealthy face a higher rate of personal theft, the poorest are the most likely to be the victim of burglaries.

Marital Status

Marital status also influences victimization risk. The unmarried or never married are victimized more often than married people or widows and widowers. These relationships are probably influenced by age, gender, and life-style: since young males have the greatest victimization risk, it stands to reason that widows, who are older females, will suffer much lower victimization rates. Because they go out in public more often and interact with high-risk peers, it comes as no surprise to find that unmarried males have a violent crime victimization rate more than ten times that of widowed females. These data are further evidence of the relationship between life-style and victimization risk.

Race

One of the most important distinctions found in the NCVS data is the racial differences in the victim rate. African-Americans experience violent crimes at a higher rate than other groups. NCVS data in Table 4.5 show that African-American citizens had strikingly higher rates of violent personal crimes than whites; the race-specific risk of theft victimization was more similar. Black males maintained a rate of 63 victimizations per 1,000 persons; in contrast, white males had a victimization rate of 36 per 1,000, black females 40, and white females 24.

Crimes committed against African-Americans tended to be more serious than those committed against whites.[22] African-Americans experience higher rates of rape, robbery, and aggravated assault, while whites were more often the victims of simple assault and personal theft. The most striking difference recorded by the NCVS between racial groups was in the incidence of robberies: African-Americans were more than three times as likely to be robbery victims as whites.

Black victims also faced other threats from predatory criminals. Offenders were more likely to have weapons in violent crimes committed against African-Americans than in those against whites. In fact, black victims faced gun-toting criminals almost twice as often as whites. Black victims were also more likely than white victims to be physically attacked during a violent crime and were four times more likely to sustain serious injuries.

Young African-American males are also at great risk for being homicide victims. They face a murder risk four or five times greater than that of young African-American females, five to eight times higher than that of young white males, and 16 to 22 times higher than that of young white females. A longitudinal analysis conducted by the Centers for Disease Control indicates that the murder victimization rate of African-American males is increasing at a much faster pace than that of these other groups.[23]

Why do these discrepancies exist? Young black males tend to live in the nation's largest cities in areas beset by alcohol and drug abuse, poverty, racial discrimination, and violence. Forced to live in the nation's most dangerous areas, their life-style places them in the highest "at risk" population group.

☰ The Victims and Their Criminals

The NCVS data can be used to tell us something about the characteristics of people who commit crime. Of course, this information is available only on criminals who actually came in contact with the victim through such crimes as rape, assault, or robbery.

Though most violent crimes were committed by strangers (60 percent), a surprising number of violent crime victims (2.6 million) were either related to or acquainted with their attackers. In all, about 40 percent of all violent crimes are committed by people who were described as at least well known to the victim. About 10 percent of the multiple-offender and 20 percent of the single-offender crimes involved family members, including parents, children, siblings, spouses, or ex-spouses. Included in the overall number were about 200,000 robberies, an instrumental crime usually not considered to involve people who were acquainted with one another (about 85 percent of all robberies do, however, involve strangers).

Victims reported that a majority of crimes were committed by a single offender over age 20. About one-quarter of the victims indicated their assailant was a young person under 30 years of age, a pattern that may reflect the criminal activities of youth gangs and groups in the United States. Whites were the offenders in a majority of single-offender rapes and assault, but a majority of multiple-offender crimes involved black criminals.

Crime tends to be intraracial: blacks victimize blacks (84 percent) and whites victimize whites (73 percent). However, most crimes by white offenders were committed against other whites (98 percent), while only half of all crimes by African-American offenders victimized African-Americans (48 percent). These findings are supported by surveys of prison inmates: while 4.7 percent of white inmates report attacking black victims, black inmates report that 43 percent of their victims were white.[24] The racial pattern recorded here reflects the nation's population makeup: Because the country's population is predominantly white, it stands to reason that, regardless of the offender's racial characteristics, the victim will also most likely be white. Nonetheless, most crimes do seem to involve people who share the same racial characteristics as the offender.

The NCVS also asks victims if their assailants were under the influence of drugs or alcohol. Victims reported that substance abuse was involved in about

CLOSE-UP

Parents Who Get Killed and the Children Who Kill Them

The nation was fascinated in 1993 and 1994 by the sensational case of Eric and Lyle Menendez, two wealthy California brothers who killed their parents. The brothers claimed that they acted in self-defense after years of physical and sexual abuse at their father's hands. Their acts are referred to as **parricide,** or the killing of a close relative. Most often, this crime involves **patricide,** the killing of a father, or **matricide,** the killing of a mother.

Criminologist Kathleen Heide has conducted extensive research on the nature and extent of family homicides. She finds that the killing of a parent is almost a daily event in the United States, averaging about

300 incidents per year. While the killing of parents is typically committed by adults, about 15 percent of mothers and 25 percent of fathers were killed by juvenile offspring. In addition, about 30 percent of stepmothers and 34 percent of stepfathers were killed by adolescents. These numbers are quite startling when we consider that only 10 percent of all homicide arrests involve juveniles.

Heide finds five conditions that foreshadow parricide. Children who will one day kill their parents are raised in a dysfunctional family of substance-abusing parents; they are severely abused verbally, physically, and/or sexually; violence in the family escalates throughout their life; they become increasingly vulnerable to stressors in the home environment; and firearms are readily available.

Heide finds that parricide is typically committed by one of three types of offenders:

The Severely Abused Child—An estimated 90 percent of parricide cases involve children who were severely abused by parents. These kids were psychologically abused and then witnessed and/or suffered physical, sexual, and verbal abuse. Their parricide represented an act of desperation—the only way out of a situation they could no longer endure. This type of crime made national headlines in 1983, when 16-year-old Richard Jahnke and his 17-year-old sister, Deborah, killed their father, an Internal Revenue Service agent, after years of sexual and physical abuse at his hands.

The Severely Mentally Ill Child—A few children who kill are suffering from severe psychosis. Their personalities are disorganized, perceptions distorted, and communication disjointed. They expe-

---

30 percent of violent crime incidents, including about 40 percent of the rapes, 25 percent of the robberies, and 30 percent of the assaults.[25] These numbers, though startling, may underestimate the association between substance abuse and crime. Surveys of prison inmates find that over half (54 percent) of violent inmates report being under the influence of either drugs or alcohol at the time they committed the crime for which they were incarcerated.[26]

Intimate Violence

Though most victims did not know their attackers, there has been a disturbing trend of people being victimized by an intimate acquaintance: family member, ex-spouse, boyfriend, or ex-boyfriend.[27] Since 1979, more than 25 million Americans have been victimized by someone whom they may have loved and trusted.[28]

A gender gap exists in intimate violence. Women were victims of intimate violence at a rate three and a half times that of men (6.3 per 1,000 compared to 1.8 per 1,000); they were also six times more likely to be victimized by a spouse, boyfriend, ex-spouse, or ex-boyfriend. An estimated 625,000 females are victimized each year by intimates, and more than 6 million have been attacked since 1979.

Theories of Victimization

For many years, criminological theory focused on the actions of the criminal offender; the role of the victim was virtually ignored. Then a number of scholars found that the victim was not a passive target in crime but someone whose behavior can influence his or her own fate. One of the first criminologists who discovered that victims were an important part of the crime process was Hans von Hentig. In the 1940s, his writings portrayed the crime victim as someone who "shapes and molds

rience hallucinations and bizarre delusions. Heide tells of the case of Jonathan Cantero, who stabbed his mother 40 times and tried to cut off her left hand to "demonstrate his allegiance to Satan."

The Dangerously Antisocial Child— Some parricidal youth maintain an antisocial or psychopathic personality. They kill their parents for purely selfish ends, such as obtaining an inheritance or getting money for drugs. Heide relates the case of Michelle White, 14, and her 17-year-old brother, John, Jr., who hired a neighbor to kill their father and then used his credit cards to buy $1,000 worth of video games, televisions, and other merchandise; their father's corpse lay decaying in the kitchen as they cooked their meals.

Heide finds that the typical parent/stepparent slain was a white, non-Hispanic male. The slayer, a son who was an adult at the time the crime occurred, used a handgun to kill the parent. Slayings involving multiple offenders and multiple victims were quite rare.

Mothers, more so than fathers, tended to be killed by older offspring. Perhaps the mother-child bond is stronger and more enduring, protecting the mother while the child is young. The strength of this bond may tie them together for a longer time, making violence more likely as the child becomes an adult. The number of stepparents being killed has trended upwards, a pattern of concern considering the changing face of American families. Heide finds that public attitudes toward parricidal youth are changing from horror to sympathy now that it is recognized that most kids who kill are responding to life-threatening physical abuse.

Discussion Questions

1. Should abuse be considered a defense to parricide?
2. If you were a prosecuting attorney, how would you handle the case of a ten-year-old who kills his father after an argument?

SOURCE: Kathleen Heide, *Why Kids Kill Parents: Child Abuse and Adolescent Homicide* (Columbus: Ohio State University Press, 1992); idem, "Parents Who Get Killed and the Children Who Kill Them," *Journal of Interpersonal Violence* 8 (1993): 531–44; idem, "Juvenile Involvement in Multiple Offender and Multiple Victim Parricides," *Journal of Police and Criminal Psychology* 9 (1993): 53–64; idem, "A Typology of Adolescent Parricide Offenders" (Paper presented at the annual meeting of the American Society of Criminology, Baltimore, November 1990).

---

the criminal."[29] The criminal might have been a predator, but the victim may have helped the offender by becoming a willing prey. Another pioneering victimologist, Stephen Schafer, focused on the victim's responsibility in the "genesis of crime."[30] Schafer found that some victims may have provoked or encouraged the criminal. These early works helped focus attention on the role of the victim in the crime problem and led to further research efforts that have sharpened the image of the crime victim. Today, a number of different theories attempt to explain the cause of victimization, the most important of which are discussed below.

Victim Precipitation Theory: Active and Passive

Is it possible that people cause their own victimization? According to the **victim precipitation** view, some people may actually initiate the confrontation that eventual-ly leads to their injury or death. Victim precipitation can be active or passive.

Active precipitation occurs when victims act provocatively, use threats or "fighting words," or even attack first. This model of victim-precipitated crime was first popularized by Marvin Wolfgang in his 1958 study of criminal homicide. He defined the term *victim precipitation* as follows:

> The term "victim-precipitated" is applied to those criminal homicides in which the victim is a direct, positive precipitator in the crime. The role of the victim is characterized by his having been the first in the homicide drama to use physical force against his subsequent slayer. The victim-precipitated cases are those in which the victim was the first to show and use a deadly weapon, to strike a blow in an altercation—in short, the first to commence the interplay or resort to physical violence.[31]

Examples of a victim-precipitated homicide include the death of an aggressor in a barroom brawl or a wife who kills her husband after he attacks and threatens to kill her. Wolfgang found that 150, or 26 percent, of the 588 homicides in his sample could be classified as victim-precipitated.[32]

Passive precipitation occurs when the victim unknowingly threatens the attacker. The relationship can occur because of personal conflict, for example, when two people are in competition over a job, promotion, love interest, or some other scarce and coveted commodity. Though the victims may never have met their attacker or even knew of their existence, the killer feels menaced and acts accordingly.[33]

In another scenario, the victim may belong to a group whose mere presence threatens the attacker's reputation, status, or economic well-being. For example, hate crime violence may be precipitated by immigrant group members arriving in the community to compete for jobs and housing; women in the work force may threaten insecure and emotionally unstable men and prompt sexual violence.

Research indicates that passive precipitation is related to power; if the target group can establish themselves economically or gain political power in the community, their vulnerability will diminish. While they are still a potential threat, they are now too formidable a target to attack; they are no longer passive precipitators. For example, research conducted in Canada by Rosemary Gartner and Bill McCarthy shows that women employed in the work force were underrepresented as homicide victims; unemployed women suffered higher homicide victimization rates.[34] By implication, economic power reduced victimization risk.

Whether active or passive, the concept of victim precipitation implies that in some but not all crimes, the victim's actions in some way caused the crime: the crime could not have taken place if the victim had not acted.

Victim Precipitation and Rape.

Nowhere is the concept of victim precipitation more controversial than in the crime of rape. In 1971, Menachim Amir suggested female victims often contributed to their attacks through a relationship with the rapist.[35] While Amir's findings seem outrageous, courts have continued to return "not guilty" verdicts in rape cases if a victim's actions can in any way be construed as consenting to sexual intimacy. Date rapes, which may start out as romantic though not intimate relationships and then deteriorate into rape, are rarely treated with the same degree of punitiveness as stranger rapes.[36] Some state laws still require victims to prove they fought off the attacker. As law professor Susan Estrich claims in her book *Real Rape*:

> . . . the force standard continues to protect, as "seduction," conduct which should be considered criminal. It ensures broad male freedom to "seduce" women who feel themselves to be powerless, vulnerable, and afraid. It effectively guarantees men freedom to intimidate women and exploit their weakness and passivity, so long as they don't "fight" with them, and it makes clear that the responsibility should be placed squarely on the women.[37]

While this "legal victimization" is publicly condemned, defendants are still found not guilty many times because judges or juries believe that a sexual assault was victim-precipitated. In one nationally publicized 1989 case, a Florida defendant was acquitted after jury members concluded his victim "asked for it the way she was dressed." Steven Lord, the 26-year-old defendant, was freed after the jury was told his victim was wearing a lace miniskirt with nothing on underneath

A young man injured during a protest march is led away by police. Do people who engage in political and social protests precipitate victimization and injury?

and "was advertising for sex." The acquittal came despite the fact that other women testified that they had been raped by Lord.[38]

Efforts to disassociate the casualties of rape from the concept of victim precipitation have resulted in modification of rape laws; these will be discussed further in Chapter 11.

Life-Style Theory

Some criminologists believe that people may become crime victims because they have a **life-style** that increases their exposure to criminal offenders. Both NCVS and UCR data sources show that victimization risk is increased by such behaviors as staying single, associating with young men, going out in public places late at night, and living in an urban area. Conversely, one's chances of victimization can be reduced by staying home at night, moving to a rural area, staying out of public places, earning more money, and getting married. The important point is that crime is not a random occurrence, but rather a function of the behavior and actions of its targets.

Crime and victim seem bound then in an association in which the probability of the former is dependent on the activities of the latter.[39] Crime occurs because potential victims' life-styles place them in jeopardy: one's chances of being attacked are much greater at 2 A.M. in an unguarded New York City park than in a locked farmhouse in rural North Dakota.

High-Risk Life-Styles. **Victimization risk** is greatest among groups that have high-risk life-styles. For ex-ample, teens may have the greatest risk of victimization because their life-style places them in an "at-risk" location—the neighborhood high school. Here, the most criminal element of the population, teenage males, congregate; each year, millions of crimes occur on school grounds.[40]

Adolescents' life-styles continue to place them at risk once they leave school grounds. Gary Jensen and David Brownfield found that kids who "hang out" with their friends and get involved in the "recreational pursuit of fun" face an elevated risk for victimization. For example, their friends may give them a false ID so they can go drinking in the neighborhood bar; hanging out in taverns at night places them at risk because many fights and assaults occur in places that serve liquor.[41]

Adolescents are not the only ones with high-risk life-styles. A number of research studies find that the homeless population is extremely vulnerable to physical harm because they are constantly exposed to the criminal population in large urban areas.[42] Recent research by Kevin Fitzpatrick, Mark La Gory, and Ferris Ritchey found that not only did the homeless have a considerably higher victimization risk than the general population, but homeless victims tended to be more vulnerable than the general homeless population; they had a history of mental hospitalization, depression, and physical problems, including fainting and blackout spells.[43]

EQUIVALENT GROUP HYPOTHESIS. A variation of the life-style view is that victims and criminals share similar characteristics because they are not actually separate groups.

The equivalent group hypothesis is supported by research showing that crime victims also self-report significant amounts of criminal behavior. A number of studies have shown that adolescents who engage in delinquent behavior or join gangs also face the greatest risk of victimization. For example, Joan McDermott found that the young victims of school crime were likely to strike back at other students to regain lost possessions or recover their self-respect.[44] In another study, Simon Singer employed data from the Philadelphia cohort (see Chapter 3) and found that the victims of violent assault were those most likely to become offenders themselves.[45] Similarly, Janet Lauritsen, Robert Sampson, and John Laub found a significant association between participation in self-reported delinquent behavior and personal victimization in such crimes as robbery and assault.[46] Gary Jensen and David Brownfield conclude:

> . . . for personal victimizations, those most likely to be the victims of crime are those who have been most involved in crime; and the similarity of victims and offenders reflects that association.[47]

The criminal-victim connection may exist because the conditions that create criminality also predispose people to victimization. Both criminal and victim share similar life-style and residence characteristics. Some former criminals may later become targets because they are perceived as vulnerable: criminal offenders are unlikely to call the police, and if they do, who will believe them? Some victims may commit crime out of frustration; others may use violence as a means of revenge, self-defense, or social control. Some may have learned antisocial behavior as a consequence of their own victimization experiences, as in the case of abused children.[48] Recent research by Elise Lake shows that over *85 percent* of female offenders had experienced physical and sexual violence both inside and outside the home at the hands of parents, intimate partners, and strangers.[49]

Routine Activities Theory

An important attempt to describe the conditions that produce victimization risk is contained in a series of papers by Lawrence Cohen and Marcus Felson. Their view is referred to as **routine activities theory.**[50]

Cohen and Felson assume that both the motivation to commit crime and the supply of offenders are constant.[51] In every society, there will always be some people who are willing to break the law for gain, revenge, greed, or some other motive. Consequently, Cohen and Felson believe that the volume and distribution of **predatory crime** (violent crimes against the person and crimes in which an offender attempts to steal an object directly) are closely related to the interaction of three variables that reflect the routine activities of the typical American life-style: the availability of **suitable targets** (such as homes containing easily transportable and salable goods); the absence of **capable guardians** (such as police, homeowners, neighbors, friends, and relatives); and the presence of **motivated offenders** (such as a large number of unemployed teenagers). The presence of these components increases the likelihood that a predatory crime will take place: Targets are more likely to be victimized if they are poorly guarded and exposed to a large group of motivated offenders.

Cohen and Felson have used the routine activities approach, illustrated in Figure 4.3, to explain the rise in the crime rate since 1960. They argue that the number of adult caretakers at home during the day (guardians) decreased because of increased female participation in the work force; while mothers are at work and children in day care, homes are left unguarded. Similarly, with the growth of suburbia and the decline of the traditional neighborhood, the number of such familiar guardians as family, neighbors, and friends has diminished. At the same time, the volume of easily transportable wealth increased, creating a greater number of available targets. In one study, Cohen and his associates linked burglary rates to the purchase of a commodity easily stolen and disposed of: television sets.[52] Finally, with the baby-boom generation coming of age during 1960 to 1980, there was an excess of motivated offenders, and the crime rate increased as predicted.

Routine activities theory is similar to the life-style approach because it shows how a person's routine living arrangements can effect victimization risk: People who live in unguarded areas are going to be at the mercy of motivated offenders. The Close-Up "Crime and Everyday Life" shows how these relationships can be influenced by cultural and structural change.

According to routine activities theory, frequenting hazardous establishments such as bars and taverns increases victimization risk.

Testing Routine Activities Theory. Numerous attempts have been made to substantiate the principles of routine activities theory.[53] For example, Cohen and Felson maintain some personal characteristics increase the likelihood that one's routine activities will place one at a great risk for victimization: being a young minority-group member, having a low socioeconomic status, living in an urban area, and being a single parent. Supporting this view, Michael Maxfield found that victimization was most common in homes composed of a single parent and multiple children. Single parents may be less able to protect their families and themselves from the most common predatory criminals: other family members and former loved ones.[54]

Homes that are well guarded are the least likely to be burglarized.[55] Similarly, David Maume shows that rape rates are highest in areas where socioeconomic distress results in divorce, unemployment, and overcrowded living conditions, factors that reduce the number of guardians and increase the number of potential offenders.[56]

The routine activities view also suggests that lifestyle plays an important role in victimization risk. Those who maintain a high-risk life-style by staying out late at night and having frequent activity outside the home also run increased chances of victimization.[57] Steven Messner and Kenneth Tardiff studied patterns of urban homicide and found that life-styles significantly influenced victimization: people who tended to stay at home were the ones most likely to be killed by family or friends.[58] James Lasley found that youth in Britain who stay out late at night and use excessive amounts of alcohol stand the greatest risk of becoming crime victims.[59]

Because of the uniformity of this supporting research, routine activities theory has become "the most popular theory of victimization."[60]

Critique of Routine Activities. Not all criminologists support the routine activites model. In a recent review, Christopher Birkbeck and Gary LaFree argue that empirical tests of routine activities are often based on false and ambiguous assumptions.[61] For example, according to routine activities theory, the affluent should have a lower victimization risk than the poor because they have the means to purchase security. Yet affluence allows people to increase their activity outside the home, and wealth makes a tempting target, factors that also are associated with greater risk. According to Birkbeck and LaFree, routine activities theory may explain why some people become victims, but it fails to explain if others were first considered and then discarded, and if so, why that decision was made.[62]

Some empirical efforts have not found the relationships predicted by routine activities theory. For example, when James Massey and his associates examined data on property victimization in Atlanta, they found that the risk of property crime victimization was not dependent on or affected by "guardianship"; their conclusion was that "support for routine activities is weak at best."[63]

Lawrence Cohen, with Marcus Felson, developed routine activities theory.

Marcus Felson demonstrates the hanger strategy for preventing shoplifting in a university bookstore by reversing the direction of every other hanger. See the Close-Up "Crime and Everyday Life."

CLOSE-UP

Crime and Everyday Life

A core premise of routine activities theory is that all things being equal, the greater the *opportunity* to commit crime, the *higher* the crime and victimization rates.

This thesis is cogently presented in a new work by Marcus Felson, *Crime and Everyday Life*. Using a routine activities perspective, Felson tries to show why crime rates are so high in America and why its citizens suffer so much victimization.

According to Felson, crime in the United States grew as the country changed from a nation of small villages and towns to large urban environments. In a village, not only could a thief be easily recognized, but the commodities stolen could be identified long after the crime occurred. Cities provided the critical population mass that allowed predatory criminals to hide and evade apprehension. After the crime, criminals could blend in the crowd and disperse their loot; public transportation systems provided quick exits for escape.

The recent trend toward modernization and suburbanization has created new everyday opportunities for crime. The modern-day equivalent of the urban center is the suburban shopping mall. Here, strangers converge in large numbers and youths hang out. The interior is filled with people so drug deals can be concealed in the pedestrian flow. Stores have attractively displayed goods that encourage shoplifting and employee pilferage. Substantial numbers of cars are parked in areas that make larceny and car theft virtually undetectable. Carrying away stolen merchandise in a car is easy: who notices people placing items in a car in a shopping mall lot? Shoppers can be attacked in parking lots as they go in isolation to and from their cars.

As American suburbs have grown, labor and family life have dispersed from the household, decreasing guardianship. The microwave, freezer, and automatic dishwashers have freed adolescents from common household chores. Rather than help prepare the family dinner and wash dishes afterward, suburban adolescents have the freedom to meet with their peers and avoid parental controls. As car ownership has increased, teens have greater access to transportation outside of parental control. Greater mobility makes it impossible for neighbors to know whether a teen belongs in an area or is an intruder planning to commit a crime.

Change in the educational system has also created criminal opportunity. Schools have become larger and more complex, providing ideal sites for crime. The many hallways and corridors prevent teachers from knowing who belongs where; spacious school grounds reduce teacher supervision.

Felson finds that these changes in the structure and function of society have helped increase and sustain crime rates. Rather than change people, crime prevention strategies must reduce the opportunity to commit crime.

Discussion Questions

1. What recent technological changes influence crime rates? Video games? Paging systems? Fax machines?
2. Would increased family contact decrease adolescent crime rates, or would it increase the opportunity for child abuse?

SOURCE: Marcus Felson, *Crime and Everyday Life: Insights and Implications for Society* (Thousand Oaks, Calif.: Pine Forge Press, 1994).

It has also been suggested that routine activities theory places too much emphasis on the victim and overlooks offender differences. Why do offenders choose to commit crime? It is unlikely that all offenders perceive criminal opportunity or apprehension risk the same way. Leslie Kennedy and Stephen Baron suggest that peer group pressure and cultural norms exert pressure on potential offenders, guide their motivation, and influence their choices; routine activities theory, they conclude, neglects to account for the factors that shape criminal choice.[64]

The Proximity Hypothesis

Some criminologists challenge the finding of an association between victim life-style and offending.[65] An alternative view is that both criminals and victims live in close physical proximity to one another and criminals tend to select victims who share similar backgrounds and circumstances.[66] The **proximity hypothesis** is based on the logical assumption that people who reside in socially disorganized, high-crime areas have the greatest risk of coming into contact with criminal offenders, irrespective of their own behavior or life-style. Victims do not encourage crime; they are simply in the wrong place at the wrong time.[67] By implication, there is little reason for victims in lower-class areas to alter their life-style or take safety precautions since routine activities do not in fact influence the likelihood of victimization.[68]

This view then is that the probability of victimization depends more on where one lives than how one lives. People who risk exposure to criminals because they live in close proximity to them are at much greater risk of victimization than people who reside in less risky areas but have attractive, unguarded homes.[69] Neighborhood crime levels are more important for determining the chances of victimization than individual characteristics. Even those people who exhibit high-risk traits, such as unmarried males, will decrease their chances of victimization if they reside in a low-crime area.[70]

Deviant Places. The proximity hypothesis suggests that there may be **deviant places** in which crime flourishes. Rodney Stark has described these areas as poor, densely populated, highly transient neighborhoods in which commercial and residential property exist side by side.[71] The commercial property provides criminals with easy access to targets for theft crimes, such as shoplifting and larceny. Successful people stay out of these stigmatized areas; they are homes for "demoralized kinds of people" who are easy targets for crime: the homeless, the addicted, the retarded, and the elderly poor.[72] By implication, criminal victimization can be avoided by moving to an area with greater law enforcement and fewer deviant residents.

≡ Crime and Victimization

Which has the greatest influence on victimization risk, place of residence or life-style? Perhaps both. A recent study by Pamela Wilcox Rountree, Kenneth Land, and Terance Miethe of crime and victimization rates across Seattle neighborhoods indicates that both victim life-style and domicile interact to produce crime and victimization rates. People who live in more affluent areas and take safety precautions significantly lower their chances of becoming a crime victim; the effect was less pronounced in poor areas. Residents of poor areas have a much greater risk of becoming victims because they live in areas with many motivated offenders; to protect themselves, they have to "try harder" to be safe than the more affluent.[73]

The Rountree research shows that both a victim's behavior and habitat are linked to criminality: people who take chances, who live in high-risk neighborhoods,

FIGURE 4.3 **Routine Activities Theory**

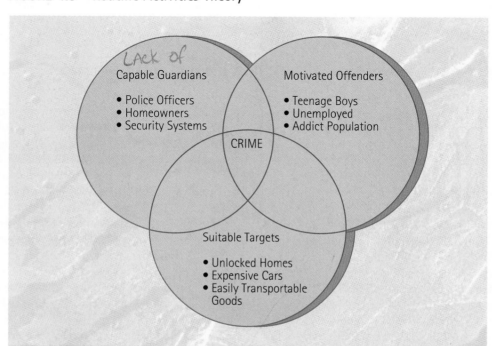

Lack of

Capable Guardians
- Police Officers
- Homeowners
- Security Systems

Motivated Offenders
- Teenage Boys
- Unemployed
- Addict Population

CRIME

Suitable Targets
- Unlocked Homes
- Expensive Cars
- Easily Transportable Goods

and who are law violators themselves share the greatest risk of victimization.[74] While victim behavior cannot, of course, explain the onset of *criminality*, it can influence the *occasion* of crime. Though criminal motivation may be acquired very early in the life cycle, the decision to commit a particular crime may depend on the actions and reactions of potential victims.

☰ Caring for the Victim

National victim surveys indicate that almost every American age 12 and over will one day become the victim of common-law crimes, such as larceny and burglary, and in the aftermath suffer financial problems, mental stress, and physical hardship.[75] When Dean Kilpatrick and his associates interviewed 391 adult females in a southern city they found that 75 percent had been victimized by crime at least once in their lives, including being raped (25 percent) and sexually molested (18 percent). Disturbingly, 25 percent of the victims developed post-trauma stress syndrome, and their psychological symptoms lasted for more than a decade after the crime occurred.[76] The long-term effect of sexual victimization can include years of problem avoidance, social withdrawal, and self-criticism.[77]

Helping the victim to cope is the responsibility of all of society. Law enforcement agencies, courts, and correctional and human service systems have come to realize that due process and human rights exist for both the defendant and the victim of criminal behavior.

The Government's Response

Because of public concern over violent personal crime, President Ronald Reagan created a Task Force on Victims of Crime in 1982.[78] This group undertook an extensive study on crime victimization in the United States to determine how victims of crime could be assisted. It found that crime victims had been transformed into a group of citizens burdened by a justice system that had been designed for their protection. Their participation as both victims and witnesses was often overlooked, and concern for the defendant's rights was given greater emphasis. The task force suggested that a balance be achieved between recognizing the rights of the victim and providing due process for the defendant. Its most significant recommendation was that the Sixth Amendment to the U.S. Constitution be augmented by a statement saying: "In every criminal prosecution, the victim shall have the right to be present and to be heard at all

critical stages of the judicial proceedings."[79] Other recommendations included providing for the protection of witnesses and victims from intimidation, requiring restitution in criminal cases, developing guidelines for fair treatment of crime victims and witnesses, and expanding programs of victim compensation.[80] Consequently, the Justice Department provided research funds to create and expand victim-witness programs, which identify the needs of victims and witnesses who were involved in a criminal incident. In addition, the Omnibus Victim and Witness and Protection Act required the use of victim impact statements at sentencing in federal criminal cases, greater protection for witnesses, more stringent bail laws, and the use of restitution in criminal cases. In 1984, the Comprehensive Crime Control Act and the Victims of Crime Act authorized federal funding for state victim compensation and assistance projects.[81] With these acts, the federal government began to respond to the plight of the victim and make victim assistance an even greater concern of the public and the justice system.

Victim Service Programs

As a result of these efforts, an estimated 2,000 victim-witness assistance programs have been developed around the United States.[82] Victim-witness programs are organized on a variety of governmental levels and serve a range of clients. A national survey by Albert Roberts has collected information on victim services in operation in the United States. Some of the most important and common victim assistance programs are discussed below.[83]

Victim Compensation

One of the primary agendas of victim advocates has been to lobby for legislation creating crime victim compensation programs.[84] As a result of such legislation, the victim ordinarily receives compensation from the state to pay for damages associated with the crime. Rarely are two compensation schemes alike, however, and many state programs suffer from lack of adequate funding and proper organization within the criminal justice system. Victim assistance projects seek to help the victim learn about **victim compensation** services and related programs. Today, victim compensation programs exist in 45 states and the federal government. Compensation may be made for medical bills, loss of wages, loss of future earnings, and counseling. In the case of death, the victim's survivors can receive burial expenses and compensation for loss of support.[85] Awards typically range from $100 to $15,000, though

Alaska provides aid up to $40,000. An important service of most victim service programs is to familiarize clients with compensation programs and help them apply for aid. On occasion, programs will provide emergency assistance to indigent victims until compensation is available. Emergency assistance may come in the form of food vouchers or re-placement of prescription medicines.

Court Services

A common victim program service is to help victims deal with the criminal justice system. One approach is to prepare victims and witnesses by explaining court procedures: how to be a witness; how bail works; what to do if the defendant makes a threat. Lack of such knowledge can cause confusion, making some victims reluctant to testify. Many victim programs also provide transportation to and from court and counselors who remain in the courtroom during hearings to explain procedures and provide support. Court escorts are particularly important for elderly victims, the handicapped, victims of child abuse and assault, and those who have been intimidated by friends or relatives of the defendant.

Public Education

More than half of all victim programs engage in public education efforts to help familiarize the general public with their services and with other agencies that help crime victims. In some instances, these are primary education programs that teach methods of dealing with conflict without resorting to violence. For example, school-based programs present information on spouse and dating abuse followed by a discussion of how to reduce violent incidents.[86]

Sometimes the educational aspect of victim services can be more immediate and personal. Most programs will help employers to understand the plight of their employee victims. Because victims may miss work or suffer post-crime emotional trauma, they may need to be absent from work for extended periods of time. If employers are unwilling to give them leave, victims may refuse to participate in the criminal justice process. Being an advocate with employers and explaining the needs of victims is a service provided by more than half of all victim programs.

Crisis Intervention

Most victim programs make referrals for services to help victims recover from their ordeal. It is common to refer clients to the local network of public and private social service agencies that can provide emergency and long-term assistance with transportation, medical care, shelter, food, and clothing. In addition, more than half of the victim programs provide **crisis intervention** to victims, many of whom are feeling isolated, vulnerable, and in need of immediate services. Some do their counseling at the program's office, while others do outreach in victims' homes, at the crime scene, or in a hospital. No crime requires more crisis intervention efforts than rape and sexual assault. After years of rape being ignored by the justice system, increased sensitivity to rape and its victims has spurred the opening of crisis centers around the country. These centers typically feature 24-hour-a-day emergency phone lines and information on police, medical, and court procedures. Some provide volunteers to assist the victim as her case is processed through the justice system. The growth of such programs—which began with the Washington, D.C., Rape Crisis Center's phone line in 1972—has been so explosive that services are available in more than 1,000 centers located in almost all major cities and college communities.[87]

Most rape programs provide the following services to victims:

1. *Emergency assistance:* including information, referral, and some support, usually provided over the telephone, and available 24 hours a day;
2. *Face-to-face crisis intervention or accompaniment:* usually provided in the hospital, police station, courts, or other public location, also available 24 hours a day; and
3. *Counseling:* either one-on-one or in groups, a varying number of sessions, often provided at the center, usually scheduled, and limited to business hours and evenings.[88]

While crisis intervention has become widespread, child care for victims is less common. According to the national survey of crime victim programs, about one-third are able to provide some form of child care, most often short-term, while the victim is in counseling or in court.

Victim's Rights

In an important article, Frank Carrington suggested that crime victims have legal rights that should ensure them basic services from the government. According to Carrington, just as society has guranteed the offender the right to counsel and a fair trial, it also has the obligation to ensure basic rights for law-abiding citizens. These rights range from adequate protection under the law from violent crimes to victim compensation and assistance from the criminal justice system. Among suggested changes that might enhance the relationship between the victim and the criminal justice system are:

Liberally using preventive detention (pretrial jailing without the right to bail) for dangerous criminals who are awaiting trial.

Eliminating delays between the arrest and the initial hearing and between the hearing and the trial, which would limit the opportunity an offender has to intimidate victims or witnesses.

Eliminating plea bargaining, or if that proves impossible, allowing victims to participate in the plea negotiations.

Controlling defense attorney's cross-examination of victims.

Allowing hearsay testimony of police at the preliminary hearing, instead of requiring the victim to appear.

Abolishing the exclusionary rule, which allows the guilty to go free on technicalities.

Allowing victims to participate in sentencing.

Creating minimum sentences for crimes that convicted offenders must serve.

Prohibiting murderers given life sentences from being freed on furlough or parole.

Making criminals serve time on each crime they are convicted of and reducing the use of concurrent sentences, which allow them to serve time simultaneously for multiple crimes.

Tightening the granting of parole and allowing victims to participate in parole hearings.

Providing full restitution and/or compensation to victims in all crimes.[89]

Some of these suggestions seem reasonable policy alternatives, while others, such as repudiating the exclusionary rule, may be impossible to achieve since they violate offenders' due process protections. However, some jurisdictions have actually incorporated similar language within their legal codes. For example, California has adopted a Victim's Bill of Rights that has a provision stating that "restitution shall be ordered . . . in every case, regardless of the sentence of disposition imposed . . . unless compelling and extraordinary reasons exist to the contrary."[90] The rights of victims in the criminal process received a boost on June 27, 1991, when the U.S.

Supreme Court decided in *Payne v. Tennessee* (No. 90-5721) that juries would be permitted to consider the emotional impact of a victim's murder on surviving family members. Pervis Payne was sentenced to death for killing a woman and her young daughter. In arguing for the death penalty, the prosecutor told the jury how the victim's three-year-old son, Nicholas, who survived the attack "cries for his mom . . . . He doesn't seem to understand why she doesn't come home . . . . Somewhere down the road Nicholas is going to grow up . . . he is going to want to know what type of justice was done. He is going to want to know what happened. With your verdict, you will provide the answer." The Court reasoned that since defense attorneys may bring forth unlimited evidence in support of the defendant's good character, it is only fair that the prosecution be given the opportunity to rebut the defense's claims. The Court in Payne overruled the standing prohibition against victim statements in death penalty cases, and the decision may signal greater judicial sensitivity to the rights of victims.

≡ Self-Protection

While the general public generally approves of the police, fear of crime and concern about community safety has prompted many people to become their own "police force" and take an active role in community protection and citizen crime-control groups.[91] Research indicates that a significant number of crimes may not be reported to police simply because victims prefer to take matters into their own hands.[92] One way this trend has manifested is in the concept of **target hardening**, or making one's home and business crime-proof through locks, bars, alarms, and other devices.[93] A national victimization risk survey found that substantial numbers of people have taken specific steps to secure their homes or place of employment.[94] One-third of the households reported taking one or more crime prevention measures, including installing a burglar alarm (7 percent), participating in a neighborhood watch program (7 percent), or engraving valuables with an identification number (25 percent). Other commonly used crime prevention techniques include a fence or barricade at the entrance; a doorkeeper, guard, or receptionist in an apartment building; an intercom or phone to gain access to the building; surveillance cameras; window bars; warning signs; and dogs chosen for their ability to guard the house. The use of these measures was inversely proportional to perception of neighborhood safety: people who feared crime were more likely to use crime-prevention techniques.

Though the true relationship is still unclear, there is mounting evidence that people who engage in household protection are less likely to become victims of property crimes.[95] One recent study conducted in the Philadelphia area found that people who install burglar alarms are less likely to become the victims of burglary than those who forgo similar preventive measures.[96]

Fighting Back

In addition to target hardening, citizens are arming themselves and taking courses in firearm training in record numbers.[97] Research by Douglas Smith and Craig Uchida indicates that gun ownership is highest among people who have already been the victims of crime, who perceive police protection as inadequate, who believe the crime rate is increasing in their neighborhood, and who take a dim view of their chances for avoiding additional victimization.[98] Those using firearms for protection report little confidence in police and the courts.[99]

Does fighting back prevent crimes? Gary Kleck found that victims are ready and willing to use their guns against offenders. Each year, victims use guns about 1 million times, killing between 1,500 to 2,800 potential felons and wounding between 8,700 and 16,000. Kleck's research shows, ironically, that by fighting back, victims kill far more criminals than the estimated 250 to 1,000 killed annually by police.[100]

Should citizens be encouraged to possess handguns, and do such extreme measures of self-protection really work? How successful are victims when they fight back? Research indicates that victims who fight back often frustrate their attackers but also face increased odds of being physically harmed during the attack.[101] For example, Polly Marchbanks and her associates found that fighting back did in fact decrease the odds of a rape being completed but increased the victim's chances of

Community members band together to drive the drug dealers out of their neighborhood. Can such self-help efforts lower the crime rate?

injury.[102] Marchbanks speculates that while resistance may draw the attention of bystanders and make the rape physically difficult to complete, it can also cause offenders to escalate their violence. Similar results were derived in a federal survey that found that victims who fought back during a robbery were less likely to experience completed crimes than passive victims, but they also were more likely to be injured. The victims who escaped both serious injury and property loss were the ones who used the most violent responses to crime, such as a weapon, or the least violent, such as reasoning with their attackers. Those who fought back with their fists or who tried to get help were the most likely to experience both injury and theft.[103]

Is the risk of further injury worth the trade-off of reducing the incidence of completed crimes? Gary Kleck's research finds that the risk of collateral injury is relatively rare and that potential victims should be encouraged to fight back.[104] In contrast, Gary Green argues that firearm ownership brings with it many other social problems, including accidental deaths and the use of stolen guns in other crimes. According to Green, the use of violent self-protection methods may have some benefits that are counterbalanced by their drawbacks.[105] So fighting back had its benefits but also its drawbacks, and sometimes nonviolence may work just as well.

Community Organization

Not everyone is capable of buying a handgun or semi-automatic weapon and doing battle with predatory criminals. Another approach has been for communities to organize on the neighborhood level against crime. Citizens have been working independently and in cooperation with local police agencies in neighborhood patrol and block watch programs. These programs organize local citizens in urban areas to patrol neighborhoods, watch for suspicious people, help secure the neighborhood, lobby for improvements (such as increased lighting), report crime to police, put out community newsletters, conduct home security surveys, and serve as a source for crime prevention information or tips.[106] While such programs are welcome additions to police services, little evidence exists that they have an appreciable effect on the crime rate. There is also concern that their effectiveness is spottier in low-income, high-crime areas, which are in the most need of crime prevention assistance.[107] Block watches and neighborhood patrols seem more successful when they are part of general-purpose or multi-issue community groups rather than

when they focus directly on crime problems.[108] In sum, community crime prevention programs, target hardening, and self-defense measures are flourishing around the United States. They are a response to the fear of crime and the perceived shortcomings of police agencies to ensure community safety. Along with private security, they represent attempts to supplement municipal police agencies and expand the "war on crime" to become a personal, neighborhood, and community concern.

☰ Summary

Criminologists now consider victims and victimization a major focus of study. More than 30 million U.S. citizens suffer from crime each year, and the social and economic costs of crime are in the billions of dollars. Like crime, victimization has stable patterns and trends. Violent crime victims tend to be young, poor, single males living in large cities. Most crime takes place at night in open public places. Many victimizations occur in the home, and many victims are the target of relatives and loved ones. Sometimes parents are the victims of their children, a crime known as parricide. There are a number of theories of victimization. One view, called victim precipitation, is that victims provoke criminals. More common are life-style theories that suggest that victims put themselves in danger by engaging in high-risk activities, such as going out late at night, living in a high-crime area, and associating with high-risk peers. The routine activities theory maintains that a pool of motivated offenders exists and that they will take advantage of unguarded, suitable targets. Numerous programs help victims by providing court services, economic compensation, public education, and crisis intervention. Some have gone so far as to suggest that the U.S. Constitution be amended to include protection of victims' rights. Rather than depend on the justice system, some victims have attempted to help themselves. In some instances, this self-help means community organization for self-protection. In other instances, victims have armed themselves and fought back against their attackers. Evidence exists that fighting back reduces the number of completed crimes but is also related to victim injury.

☰ KEY TERMS

victimology	patricide
victimologists	matricide
parricide	victim precipitation

active precipitation

passive precipitation

life-style

victimization risk

routine activities theory

predatory crime

suitable targets

capable guardians

motivated offenders

proximity hypothesis

deviant places

victim compensation

crisis intervention

target hardening

≡ NOTES

1. Lisa Bastian and Marshall DeBerry, *Criminal Victimization in the United States, 1992* (Washington, D.C.: Bureau of Justice Statistics, 1993), p. 68. Hereinafter cited as NCVS, 1992.

2. Beverly Martinez-Schnell and Richard Waxweiler, "Increases in Premature Mortality Due to Homicide—United States, 1968–1985," *Violence and Victims* 4 (1989): 287–93.

3. Arthur Lurigio, "Are All Victims Alike? The Adverse, Generalized, and Differential Impact of Crime," *Crime and Delinquency* 33 (1987): 452–67.

4. FBI, *Crime in the United States, 1992* (Washington, D.C.: U.S. Government Printing Office, 1993), p. 160. Hereinafter cited as FBI, *Uniform Crime Report, 1992.*

5. Patsy Klaus, *The Costs of Crime to Victims* (Washington, D.C.: Bureau of Justice Statistics, 1994).

6. Mark Cohen, "Pain, Suffering, and Cost Jury Awards: A Study of the Cost of Crime to Victims," *Law and Society Review* 22 (1988): 537–55.

7. Michael Mandel and Paul Magnusson, "The Economics of Crime," *Business Week,* 13 December 1993, pp. 72–85.

8. Peter Finn, *Victims* (Washington, D.C.: Bureau of Justice Statistics, 1988), p. 1.

9. See generally, M.D. Pagelow, *Woman Battering: Victims and Their Experiences* (Beverly Hills: Sage, 1981).

10. Walter Gleason, "Mental Disorders in Battered Women," *Violence and Victims* 8 (1993): 53–66.

11. Elizabeth Stanko and Kathy Hobdell, "Assault on Men, Masculinity and Male Victimization," *British Journal of Criminology* 33 (1993): 400–15.

12. M. Dwayne Smith and Victoria Brewer, "A Sex-Specific Analysis of Correlates of Homicide Victimization in United States Cities," *Violence and Victims* 7 (1992): 279–87.

13. Michael Rand, *Crime and the Nation's Households, 1992* (Washington, D.C.: Bureau of Justice Statistics, 1993).

14. Herbert Koppel, *Lifetime Likelihood of Victimization* (Washington, D.C.: Bureau of Justice Statistics Technical Report, 1987).

15. Ronet Bachman, *Violence against Women* (Washington, D.C.: Bureau of Justice Statistics, 1994).

16. Linda Bastian and Bruce Taylor, *School Crime* (Washington, D.C.: Bureau of Justice Statistics, 1991).

17. Murray Straus, Richard Gelles, and Suzanne Steinmentz, *Behind Closed Doors: Violence in the American Family* (Garden City, N.Y.: Anchor Books, 1980); Richard Gelles and Murray Straus, "Violence in the American Family," *Journal of Social Issues* 35 (1979): 15–39.

18. Richard Gelles and Murray Straus, *Is Violence toward Children Increasing? A Comparison of 1975 and 1985 National Survey Rates* (Durham, N.H.: Family Violence Research Program, 1985).

19. Personal communication, February 1994; *Study Findings, National Incidence and Prevalence of Child Abuse and Neglect* (Washington, D.C.: U.S. Department of Health and Human Services, 1988).

20. FBI, *Uniform Crime Report, 1992,* p. 19.

21. Data provided by the American Humane Society, Denver, Colorado, February 1994.

22. Catherine Whitaker, *Black Victims* (Washington, D.C.: Bureau of Justice Statistics, 1990).

23. U.S. Centers for Disease Control, "Homicide among Young Black Males—United States, 1978–1987," *Morbidity and Mortality Weekly Report* 39 (7 December 1990): 869–73.

24. Christopher Innes and Lawrence Greenfeld, *Violent State Prisoners and Their Victims* (Washington, D.C.: Bureau of Justice Statistics, 1990), p. 4.

25. NCVS, 1992, p. 58.

26. Innes and Greenfeld, *Violent State Prisoners and Their Victims.*

27. Caroline Wolf Harlow, *Female Victims of Violent Crime* (Washington, D.C.: Bureau of Justice Statistics, 1991).

28. Estimate based on data in Ibid., p. 1.

29. Hans von Hentig, *The Criminal and His Victim: Studies in the Sociobiology of Crime* (New Haven: Yale University Press, 1948), p. 384.

30. Stephen Schafer, *The Victim and His Criminal* (New York: Random House, 1968), p. 152.

31. Marvin Wolfgang, *Patterns of Criminal Homicide* (Philadelphia: University of Pennsylvania Press, 1958).

32. Ibid., p. 252.

33. Martin Daly and Margo Wilson, *Homicide* (New York: Aldine de Gruyter, 1988).

34. Rosemary Gartner and Bill McCarthy, "The Social Distribution of Femicide in Urban Canada, 1921–1988," *Law and Society Review* 25 (1991): 287–311.

35. Menachim Amir, *Patterns in Forcible Rape* (Chicago: University of Chicago Press, 1971).

36. Susan Estrich, *Real Rape* (Cambridge: Harvard University Press, 1987).

37. Ibid., p. 69.

38. Associated Press, "Jury Stirs Furor by Citing Dress in Rape Acquittal," *Boston Globe,* 6 October 1989, p. 12.

39. Lawrence Cohen and Marcus Felson, "Social Change and Crime Rate Trends: A Routine Activities Approach," *American Sociological Review* 44 (1979): 588–608; L. Cohen, James Kleugel, and Kenneth Land, "Social Inequality and Predatory Criminal Victimization: An Exposition and Test of a Formal Theory," *American*

Sociological Review 46 (1981): 505–24; Steven Messner and Kenneth Tardiff, "The Social Ecology of Urban Homicide: An Application of the Routine Activities Approach," *Criminology* 23 (1985): 241–67.

40. See, generally, Gary Gottfredson and Denise Gottfredson, *Victimization in Schools* (New York: Plenum Press, 1985).

41. Gary Jensen and David Brownfield, "Gender, Lifestyles, and Victimization: Beyond Routine Activity Theory," *Violence and Victims* 1 (1986): 85–99.

42. Les Whitbeck and Ronald Simons, "A Comparison of Adpative Strategies and Patterns of Victimization among Homeless Adolescents and Adults," *Violence and Victims* 8 (1993): 135–51.

43. Kevin Fitzpatrick, Mark La Gory, and Ferris Ritchey, "Criminal Victimization among the Homeless," *Justice Quarterly* 10 (1993): 353–68.

44. Joan McDermott, "Crime in the School and in the Community: Offenders, Victims and Fearful Youth," *Crime and Delinquency* 29 (1983): 270–83.

45. Simon Singer, "Homogeneous Victim-Offender Populations: A Review and Some Research Implications," *Journal of Criminal Law and Criminology* 72 (1981): 779–99.

46. Janet Lauritsen, John Laub, and Robert Sampson, "Conventional and Delinquent Activities: Implications for the Prevention of Violent Victimization among Adolescents," *Violence and Victims* 7 (1992): 91–102.

47. Gary Jensen and David Brownfield, "Gender, Lifestyles and Victimization: Beyond Routine Activities," *Violence and Victims* (1986): 85–101.

48. Ross Vasta, "Physical Child Abuse: A Dual Component Analysis," *Developmental Review* 2 (1982): 128–35.

49. Elise Lake, "An Exploration of the Violent Victim Experiences of Female Offenders," *Violence and Victims* 8 (1993): 41–50.

50. Lawrence Cohen and Marcus Felson, "Social Change and Crime Rate Trends: A Routine Activities Approach," *American Sociological Review* 44 (1979): 588–608. .

51. For a review, see James LeBeau and Thomas Castellano, "The Routine Activities Approach: An Inventory and Critique" (Unpublished manuscript, Center for the Studies of Crime, Delinquency and Corrections, Southern Illinois University–Carbondale, 1987).

52. Lawrence Cohen, Marcus Felson, and Kenneth Land, "Property Crime Rates in the United States: A Macrodynamic Analysis, 1947–1977, with Ex-ante Forecasts for the Mid-1980s," *American Journal of Sociology* 86 (1980): 90–118.

53. See also, Messner and Tardiff, "The Social Ecology of Urban Homicide"; Philip Cook, "The Demand and Supply of Criminal Opportunities," in *Crime and Justice,* vol. 7, ed. Michael Tonry and Norval Morris (Chicago: University of Chicago Press, 1986), pp. 1–28; Ronald Clarke and Derek Cornish, "Modeling Offender's Decisions: A Framework for Research and Policy," in *Crime and Justice,* vol. 6, ed. Michael Tonry and Norval Morris

(Chicago: University of Chicago Press, 1985), pp. 147–87.

54. Michael Maxfield, "Household Composition, Routine Activity, and Victimization: A Comparative Analysis," *Journal of Quantitative Criminology* 3 (1987): 301–20.

55. James Lynch and David Cantor, "Ecological and Behavioral Influences on Property Victimization at Home: Implications for Opportunity Theory," *Journal of Research in Crime and Delinquency* 29 (1992): 335–62.

56. David Maume, "Inequality and Metropolitan Rape Rates: A Routine Activity Approach," *Justice Quarterly* 6 (1989): 513–27.

57. Terance Miethe, Mark Stafford, and Douglas Stone, "Lifestyle Changes and Risks of Criminal Victimization," *Journal of Quantitative Criminology* 6 (1990): 357–75.

58. Messner and Tardiff, "The Social Ecology of Urban Homicide."

59. James Lasley, "Drinking Routines, Lifestyles and Predatory Victimization: A Causal Analysis," *Justice Quarterly* 6 (1989): 529–42.

60. Christopher Birkbeck and Gary LaFree, "The Situational Analsysis of Crime and Deviance," *Annual Review of Sociology* 19 (1993): 113–37.

61. Ibid., pp. 127–28.

62. Ibid., p. 128.

63. James Massey, Marvin Krohn, and Lisa Bonati, "Property Crime and the Routine Activities of Individuals," *Journal of Research in Crime and Delinquency* 26 (1989): 378–400 at 396.

64. Leslie Kennedy and Stephen Baron, "Routine Activities and a Subculture of Violence: A Study of Violence on the Street," *Journal of Research in Crime and Delinquency* 30 (1993): 88–112.

65. Jeffrey Fagan, Elizabeth Piper, and Yu-Teh Cheng, "Contributions of Victimization to Delinquency in Inner Cities," *Journal of Criminal Law and Criminology* 78 (1987): 586–613.

66. Ibid.

67. James Garofalo, "Reassessing the Lifestyle Model of Criminal Victimization," in *Positive Criminology,* ed. Michael Gottfredson and Travis Hirschi (Newbury Park, Calif.: Sage, 1987), pp. 23–42.

68. Terance Miethe and David McDowall, "Contextual Effects in Models of Criminal Victimization," *Social Forces* 71 (1993): 741–59.

69. Terance Miethe and Robert Meier, "Opportunity, Choice, and Criminal Victimization: A Test of a Theoretical Model," *Journal of Research in Crime and Delinquency* 27 (1990): 243–66.

70. Robert Sampson and Janet Lauritsen, "Deviant Lifestyles, Proximity to Crime and the Offender-Deviant Link in Personal Violence," *Journal of Research in Crime and Delinquency* 27 (1990): 110–39.

71. Rodney Stark, "Deviant Places: A Theory of the Ecology of Crime," *Criminology* 25 (1987): 893–911.

72. Ibid., p. 902.

73. Pamela Wilcox Rountree, Kenneth Land, and Terance

Miethe, "Macro-Micro Integration in the Study of Victimization: A Hierarchical Logistic Model Analysis across Settle Neighborhoods" (Paper presented at the annual meeting of the American Society of Criminology, Phoenix, Arizona, November 1993).

74. Sampson and Lauritsen, "Deviant Lifestyles."

75. Patricia Resnick, "Psychological Effects of Victimization: Implications for the Criminal Justice System," *Crime and Delinquency* 33 (1987): 468–78.

76. Dean Kilpatrick, Benjamin Saunders, Lois Veronen, Connie Best, and Judith Von, "Criminal Victimization: Lifetime Prevalence, Reporting to Police, and Psychological Impact," *Crime and Delinquency* 33 (1987): 479–89.

77. Mark Santello and Harold Leitenberg, "Sexual Aggression by an Acquaintance: Methods of Coping and Later Psychological Adjustment," *Violence and Victims* 8 (1993): 91–103.

78. U.S. Department of Justice, *Report of the President's Task Force on Victims of Crime* (Washington, D.C.: U.S. Government Printing Office, 1983).

79. Ibid., p. 115.

80. Ibid., pp. 2–10; and "Review on Victims—Witnesses of Crime," *Massachusetts Lawyers Weekly,* 25 April 1983, p. 26.

81. Robert Davis, *Crime Victims: Learning How to Help Them* (Washington, D.C.: National Institute of Justice, 1987).

82. Peter Finn and Beverly Lee, *Establishing a Victim-Witness Assistance Program* (Washington, D.C.: U.S. Government Printing Office, 1988).

83. This section leans heavily on Albert Roberts, "Delivery of Services to Crime Victims: A National Survey," *American Journal of Orthopsychiatry* 6 (1991): 128–37; see also idem, *Helping Crime Victims: Research, Policy and Practice* (Newbury Park, Calif.: Sage, 1990).

84. Randall Schmidt, "Crime Victim Compensation Legislation: A Comparative Study," *Victimology* 5 (1980): 428–37.

85. Roberts, "Delivery of Services to Crime Victims," p. 133.

86. Pater Jaffe, Marlies Sudermann, Deborah Reitzel, and Steve Killip, "An Evaluation of a Secondary School Primary Prevention Program on Violence in Intimate Relationships," *Violence and Victims* 7 (1992): 129–45.

87. Vicki McNickle Rose, "Rape as a Social Problem: A Byproduct of the Feminist Movement," *Social Problems* 25 (1977): 75–89.

88. Janet Gornick, Martha Burt, and Karen Pittman, "Structure and Activities of Rape Crises Centers in the Early 1980s," *Crime and Delinquency* 31 (1985): 247–68.

89. See Frank Carrington, "Victim's Rights Litigation: A Wave of the Future," in *Perspectives on Crime Victims,* ed. Burt Galaway and Joe Hudson (St. Louis: C.V. Mosby, 1981); victim's rights adapted from Emilio Viano, "Victim's Rights and the Constitution: Reflections on a Bicentennial," *Crime and Delinquency* 33 (1987): 438–51.

90. *California Penal Code,* section 1191.1, (St. Paul: West Publishing, 1985).

91. This section relies on an excellent review of this topic in Dennis Rosenbaum, "Community Crime Prevention: A Review and Synthesis of the Literature," *Justice Quarterly* 5 (1988): 323–95.

92. Leslie Kennedy, "Going It Alone: Unreported Crime and Individual Self-Help," *Journal of Criminal Justice* 16 (1988): 403–13.

93. Ronald Clarke, "Situational Crime Prevention: Its Theoretical Basis and Practical Scope," in *Annual Review of Criminal Justice Research*, ed. Michael Tonry and Norval Morris (Chicago: University of Chicago Press, 1983).

94. Catherine Whitaker, *Crime Prevention Measures* (Washington, D.C.: Bureau of Justice Statistics, 1986).

95. Rosenbaum, "Community Crime Protection," p. 347.

96. Andrew Buck, Simon Hakim, and George Rengert, "Burglar Alarms and the Choice Behavior of Burglars," *Journal of Criminal Justice* 21 (1993): 497–507; for an opposing view, see Lynch and Cantor, "Ecological and Behavioral Influences on Property Victimization at Home."

97. Gary Kleck and David Bordua, "The Factual Foundation for Certain Key Assumptions of Gun Control," *Law and Policy Quarterly* 5 (1983): 271–98.

98. Douglas Smith and Craig Uchida, "The Social Organization of Self-Help: A Study of Defensive Weapon Ownership," *American Sociological Review* 53 (1988): 94–102.

99. Robert Young, David McDowall, and Colin Loftin, "Collective Security and Ownership of Firearms for Protection," *Criminology* 25 (1987): 47–62.

100. James Fyfe, "Police Use of Deadly Force: Research and Reform," *Justice Quarterly* 5 (1988): 157–76.

101. Alan Lizotte, "Determinants of Completing Rape and Assault," *Journal of Quantitative Criminology* 2 (1986): 203–17.

102. Polly Marchbanks, Kung-Jong Lui, and James Mercy, "Risk of Injury from Resisting Rape," *American Journal of Epidemiology* 132 (1990): 540–49.

103. Caroline Wolf Harlow, *Robbery Victims* (Washington, D.C.: Bureau of Justice Statistics, 1987).

104. Gary Kleck, "Rape and Resistance," *Social Problems* 37 (1990): 149–62.

105. Gary Green, "Citizen Gun Ownership and Criminal Deterrence: Theory, Research and Policy," *Criminology* 25 (1987): 63–81.

106. James Garofalo and Maureen McLeod, *Improving the Use and Effectiveness of Neighborhood Watch Programs* (Washington, D.C.: National Institute of Justice, 1988).

107. Peter Finn, *Block Watches Help Crime Victims in Philadelphia* (Washington, D.C.: National Institute of Justice, 1986).

108. Ibid.

Theories

of Crime

Causation

An important goal of the criminological enterprise is to create valid and accurate theories of crime causation. Social scientists have defined theory as sets of statements that say why and how several concepts are related. For a set of statements to qualify as a theory, it must also be possible to deduce some conclusions from it that are subject to empirical verification; that is, theories must predict or prohibit certain observable events or conditions.*

Criminologists have sought to collect vital facts about crime and interpret them in a scientifically meaningful fashion. By developing empirically verifiable statements, or hypotheses, and organizing them into theories of crime causation, they hope to identify the root causes of crime.

Since the late nineteenth century, criminological theory has pointed to various underlying causes of crime. The earliest theories generally attributed crime to a single underlying cause: atypical body build, genetic abnormality, insanity, physical anomalies, and poverty. Later theories attributed crime causation to multiple factors: poverty, peer influence, school problems, and family dysfunction.

In this section, theories of crime causation are grouped into five chapters. Chapters 4 and 5 focus on theories based on individual traits. They hold that crime is either a free-will choice made by an individual, a function of personal psychological or biological abnormality, or both. Chapters 6 through 9 investigate theories based in sociology and political economy. These theories portray crime as a function of the structure, process, and conflicts of social living. Chapter 10 is devoted to theories that combine or integrate these various concepts into a cohesive, complex view of crime.

* Rodney Stark, *Sociology,* 2d ed. (Belmont, Calif.: Wadsworth, 1987), p. 618.

5 Choice Theories

THE CATO'NINE-TAILS.

≡ Introduction

Why do people violate the law and risk apprehension, trial, and punishment? To many criminologists, the decision to commit a crime is a function of personal choice. The decision to violate the law—commit a robbery, sell drugs, attack a rival, fill out a false tax return—is made for a variety of reasons, including greed, revenge, need, anger, lust, jealousy, thrill-seeking, or vanity. The central issue is that the illegal act is a matter of personal decision making, a *rational choice,* made after weighing the potential benefits and consequences of crime: the jealous suitor concludes that the risk of punishment is worth the satisfaction of punching out a rival; the greedy shopper considers the chance of apprehension by store detectives so small that she takes a "five-finger discount" on a new sweater; the drug dealer concludes that the huge profits that he can earn from a single shipment of cocaine far outweigh the possible costs of apprehension.

The view that crime, in all its different forms, is a matter of reasoned choice originated in **classical theory** and has since evolved into what is known as **rational choice** or **choice theory**.

This chapter will review the philosophical underpinnings of choice theory, which first appeared as the classical school of criminology. Discussion will then turn to theoretical models that flow from the concept of choice and hold that because criminals are rational, their behavior can be controlled or deterred by the fear of punishment. These views include general deterrence theory, specific deterrence theory and incapacitation theory. Finally, the chapter will briefly review how choice theory has influenced policy-making in the area of criminal justice.

≡ The Development of Classical Theory

Theories of crime that have at their core the rational decision making of motivated criminals can trace their roots to the classical school of criminology. As you may recall from Chapter 1, classical criminology was based on the works of Cesare Beccaria and other utilitarian philosophers. It has as its core the concept that (a) people choose all behavior, including criminal behavior, (b) their choices can be controlled by the fear of punishment, and (c) the more severe, certain, and swift the punishment, the greater its ability to control criminal behavior.[1]

In keeping with his utilitarian views, Beccaria called for fair and certain punishment to deter crime. He stated: "The fundamental principle that should govern the creation and maintenance of laws is 'the greatest happiness to be shared by the greatest number of people.'"[2] He viewed law and justice as conditions similar to those that the French philosopher Jean Jacques Rousseau described in his concept of the social contract: a set of rules that guarantee life, liberty, and happiness to all people. Beccaria stated: "Weary of living in a continual state of war, and of enjoying a liberty rendered useless by the uncertainty of preserving it, [people] sacrificed a part so that they might enjoy the rest of it in peace and safety."[3] Yet he did not suggest that people obey laws freely, sacrificing a portion of their personal liberty merely to promote the common good. Since people are egotistical and self-centered, they must be goaded by the fear of punishment, which provides a tangible motive for them to obey the law and suppress the despotic spirit that resides in every person.

Crime and Punishment. Rather than stress the cruelty of punishment to control criminality, Beccaria believed it would be more effective to closely link crime with its consequences in the minds of would-be criminals. Of greatest importance to Beccaria was establishing the proper proportions between crimes and punishments. There are several reasons for this approach. Most important, if two crimes that do not equally injure society are punished equally, then people will not be deterred from committing the greater of the two crimes. For example, if both bank robbery and murder were punished by death, a bank robber would have little reason to refrain from killing any witnesses to the robbery. To be effective, the punishment for a crime must be justified by the harm done.

Though some have questioned Beccaria's principles and motives, even his harshest critics recognize that he is one of the rare reformers to have an enduring influence on justice policy and a true criminological success story.[4] Beccaria's ideas and writings inspire criminologists who believe that criminals choose to commit crime and that crime can be controlled by the judicious application of criminal punishments.

The Rise and Fall of Classical Theory

Beccaria's vision had a powerful influence over events in the criminal justice system.[5] The belief that punishment should fit the crime and that people should be punished proportionately for what they did and not to satisfy the whim of a capricious judge or ruler was widely accepted throughout Europe and the United States. In Britain, philosopher Jeremy Bentham (1748–1833) helped popularize Beccaria's views in his writings on **utilitarianism.** According to this view, actions are evaluated by their tendency to produce advantage, pleasure, and happiness and to avoid or prevent mischief, pain, evil, or unhappiness.[6] Bentham believed that the purpose of all law is to produce and support the total happiness of the community it serves. Since punishment is in itself harmful, its existence is only justified if it promises to prevent greater evil than it creates. Punishment, therefore, has four main objectives:

1. to prevent all criminal offenses;
2. when it cannot prevent a crime, to convince the offender to commit a less serious one;
3. to ensure that a criminal uses no more force than is necessary; and
4. to prevent crime as cheaply as possible.[7]

The most stunning example of how the classical philosophy of Beccaria and Bentham was embraced in Europe occurred in 1789, when France's post-revolutionary Constituent Assembly adopted these ideas in the *Declaration of the Rights of Man:*

> the law has the right to prohibit only actions harmful to society. . . . The law shall inflict only such punishments as are strictly and clearly necessary . . . no person shall be punished except by virtue of a law enacted and promulgated previous to the crime and applicable to its terms.

Similarly, a prohibition against "cruel and unusual punishments" was incorporated in the Eighth Amendment to the U.S. Constitution. The use of torture and severe punishments was largely abandoned in the nineteenth century. The practice of incarcerating criminals and structuring prison sentences to fit the severity of crime was a reflection of classical criminology. While the proportionality demanded by Beccaria was often ignored by the legal system, the general theme of gearing punishment to deter crime was widely accepted.

Though a predominant criminological view for over 100 years, by the end of the nineteenth century, the popularity of the classical approach began to decline, and by mid-twentieth century, the perspective was neglected by mainstream criminologists. During this period, positivist criminologists focused on the internal and external factors—poverty, IQ, education, home life—that were believed to be the true causes of criminality. Since these conditions could not be easily controlled, the concept of punishing people because of life situations seemed foolish and cruel. Progress in psycho-

Jeremy Bentham's (1748–1833) utilitarian theory was a cornerstone of classical criminology. Bentham believed that the purpose of all law is to produce and support the total happiness of the community it serves. Do you agree?

logical treatment and counseling led to a mood in U.S. and European correctional circles that stressed the rehabilitation of known criminals and the prevention of crime by treatment rather than punishment. Criminologists who continued to advocate punishment as a means of crime control were considered conservative, reactionary, and vengeful. Though classical principles still controlled the way police, courts, and correctional agencies operated and though some political candidates, such as Richard Nixon, ran on "law and order" planks, most criminologists rejected classical criminology.

≡ Choice Theory Emerges

Beginning in the mid-1970s, the classical approach began to enjoy a resurgence of popularity. The rehabilitation of known criminals, considered a cornerstone of positivist policy, came under attack. According to positivist criminology, if crime was caused by some social or psychological problem, such as poverty, then crime rates could be reduced by providing good jobs and economic opportunities. A number of national surveys (the most well-known being Robert Martinson's *What Works?*) failed to uncover examples of rehabilitation programs that prevented future criminal activity.[8] A well-publicized book, *Beyond Probation* by Charles Murray and Louis Cox, went as far as suggesting that punishment-oriented programs could suppress future criminality much more effectively than those that relied on rehabilitation and treatment efforts.[9]

A significant increase in the reported crime rate, as well as serious disturbances in the nation's prisons, frightened the general public. To many criminologists, reviving the classical concepts of social control and punishment made more sense than futilely trying to improve entrenched social conditions or rehabilitate criminals using ineffectual methodologies.[10]

Thinking about Crime

Beginning in the late 1970s, a number of criminologists began producing books and monographs that expounded the theme that criminals are rational actors who plan their crimes, fear punishment, and deserve to be penalized for their misdeeds. In a 1975 book that came to symbolize renewed interest in classical views, *Thinking about Crime,* political scientist James Q. Wilson debunked the positivist view that crime was a function of external forces, such as poverty, that could be altered by government programs. Instead, he argued, efforts should be made to reduce criminal opportunity by deterring would-be offenders and incarcerating known criminals.

Persons who are likely to commit crime, he maintained, lack inhibition against misconduct, value the excitement and thrills of breaking the law, have a low stake in conformity, and are willing to take greater chances than the average person. If they could be convinced that their actions will bring severe punishment, only the totally irrational would be willing to engage in crime.[11] While incapacitating criminals should not be the sole goal of the justice system, such a policy does have the advantage of *restraining* offenders and preventing their future criminality without having to figure out how to change their attitudes or nature, a goal that

has proven difficult to accomplish. He made this famous observation:

> Wicked people exist. Nothing avails except to set them apart from innocent people. And many people, neither wicked nor innocent, but watchful, dissembling, and calculating of their chances, ponder our reaction to wickedness as a clue to what they might profitably do.[12]

Here Wilson seems to be saying that unless we react forcefully to crime, those "sitting on the fence" will get a clear message: crime pays. The Close-Up "Does Crime Pay?" considers the true rewards of crime.

Coinciding with the publication of Wilson's book was a conservative shift in U.S. public policy which resulted in the election of Ronald Reagan to the presidency in 1980. Political decision makers embraced ideas suggested by Wilson as a means to bring the crime rate down. These views have helped shape criminal justice policy for the past two decades.

From these roots, a more contemporary version of classical theory evolved that is based on intelligent thought processes and criminal decision making; it is today referred to as the *rational choice* approach to crime causation.[13]

The Concept of Rational Choice

According to rational choice theory, law-violating behavior is an event that occurs when an offender decides to risk transgressing after considering both personal (such as need for money, revenge, thrills and entertainment) and situational factors (how well a target is protected, the efficiency of the local police force). Before choosing to commit a crime, the **reasoning criminal** evaluates the risk of apprehension, the seriousness of expected punishment, the potential value of the criminal enterprise, and his or her immediate need for criminal gain. The decision to commit a specific type of crime then is a matter of personal decision making based on a weighing of available information. Conversely, the decision to forgo crime may be based on the criminal's perception that the economic benefits are no longer there or the risk of apprehension is too great. For example, studies of residential burglary indicate that criminals will forgo activity if they believe a neighborhood is well patrolled by police.[14] In fact, evidence exists that when police begin to concentrate patrols in a particular area of the city, crime rates tend to

CLOSE-UP

Does Crime Pay?

Rational offenders might be induced to commit crime if they perceive that crime pays more than they could possibly earn from a legitimate job. Crime pays if, taking into account the probability of arrest and the cost of punishment, the benefits of employment are lower than the expected benefits of theft. Does crime, in fact, pay?

To answer this question, James Q. Wilson and Allan Abrahamse used a sample of incarcerated inmates to determine their perceived and actual "take" from crime. Wilson and Abrahamse divided the group into mid- and high-rate offenders in one of six crime categories: burglary, theft, swindling, auto theft, robbery and mixed offenses predominantly involving drug sales.

Using crime loss estimates derived from the NCVS survey, Wilson and Abrahamse find that mid-rate burglars on average earn about $2,368 per year from crime, far less than the $7,391 (after taxes) they could have earned in a legitimate job. High-rate burglars, who commit an average of 193 crimes per year, take home $5,711, roughly the same they would have earned from a job (the potential earnings of high-rate burglars is reduced because they spend more time behind bars). Even if free for the entire year, high-rate burglars would have earned about the same as they would if they had held a job for the same period—a little less than $10,000.

Crime profits are reduced by the costs of a criminal career: legal fees, bail bonds, loss of family income, and the psychic cost of a prison sentence. Given these costs, most criminals actually earn little from crime. Would you, query Wilson and Abrahamse, be willing to become a high-rate robber if you knew that you would be spending half your life in prison for an annual salary of under $15,000?

Why Do People Do It?

If crime pays so little, why are there so many criminals? There are a number of reasons criminals choose crime despite its relatively low payoff.

One reason is that criminals tend to overestimate the money they can earn from crime. In some cases, their estimates were more than 12 times higher than a realistic assessment of their earning potential. For example, burglars estimated that they could earn $2,674 per month from crime, while a more realistic figure is only $230!

Some criminals believe that they have no choice but to commit crime because legitimate work is unavailable. This may be a false assumption. About two-thirds of the inmates reported having been employed before they were imprisoned. Rather than being excluded from the job market, criminals seem to be relatively unsuccessful participants within it; they are under-, not unemployed.

Criminals are realistic about their long-term careers, believing that eventually everyone is caught and punished. However, they are overly *optimistic* about getting away with each individual crime. They believe that the odds of getting caught for a particular crime are rather small, and being impulsive, they take the short-term view that each particular crime *is worth the risk*: they may eventually get caught, *but not this time.*

Crime could be deterred if would-be criminals understood the true costs of committing crime and the relatively small payoff of a criminal career, but that does not usually occur, nor is there an easy way to make it happen.

Discussion Questions

1. What crimes, if any, do pay?
2. How would you design an effective crime control policy considering the misunderstanding criminals have about their own vocation?

SOURCE: James Q. Wilson and Allan Abrahamse, "Does Crime Pay?" *Justice Quarterly* 9 (1992): 359–77.

increase in adjacent areas that may be perceived by criminals as "safer" (referred to as "crime displacement").[15]

Criminals may be deterred by the perception that the risks of crime are too great for their current life-style. In one study, Neal Shover found that older criminals may turn from a life of crime when they develop a belief that the risk of crime is greater than its potential profit.[16] In this sense, making a rational choice is a function of experience and learning. The veteran criminal has discovered the limitations of his or her powers and knows when to take a chance and when to be cautious. Learning and experience then are important elements of the rational choice perspective.[17]

Offense and Offender Specifications

Rational choice theorists view crime as both **offense- and offender-specific.**[18] That crime is "offense-specific" refers to the fact that offenders will react selectively to the characteristics of particular offenses. For example, theft involves evaluation of the target's likely cash yield; the availability of resources, such as a getaway car, and the probability of capture by police.[19] That crime is "offender-specific" refers to the fact that criminals are not simply driven people who for one reason or another engage in random acts of antisocial behavior. Before deciding to partake in crime, they analyze whether they have the prerequisites for committing a criminal act, including their skills, motives, needs, and fears. Criminal acts might be ruled out if the potential offenders perceive that they can reach a desired personal goal through legitimate means or if they are too afraid of getting caught.[20] Note the distinction made here between crime and criminality.[21] Crime is an event; criminality is a personal trait. Criminals do not commit crime all the time; noncriminals may on occasion violate the law. Some high-risk people lacking opportunity may never commit crime; given enough provocation or opportunity, a low-risk, law-abiding person may commit crime.

≡ Rational Choice and Routine Activities

Rational choice theory dovetails with routine activities theory. As you may recall from Chapter 4, routine activities theory maintains that along with a supply of motivated offenders, the absence of capable guardians and the presence of **suitable targets** determines crime and victimization rate trends. This view coincides with the rational choice approach to crime because both imply that crime rates are a product of criminal *opportunity*: increase the number of guardians, decrease the suitability of targets, or reduce the offender population, and crime rates should likewise decline; increase opportunity and crime rates will likewise increase.

Suitable Targets

Research indicates that criminal choice is influenced by the perception of target vulnerability. As they go about their daily activities, traveling to school or work, potential criminals may encounter targets of illegal opportunity: an empty carport, an open door, an unlocked car, or a bike left on the street. Paul Cromwell and his associates found that corner homes, usually near traffic lights or stop signs, are the ones most likely to be burglarized: stop signs give criminals a legitimate reason to stop their cars and look for an attractive target.[22] Burglars say they prefer secluded homes, such as those at the end of a cul-de-sac, surrounded by wooded areas.[23] Thieves also report being concerned about the convenience of their target. They are more apt to choose sites for burglaries and robberies that are familiar to them and that are located in easily accessible and open areas.[24]

Because criminals often go on foot or use public transportation, they are unlikely to travel long distances to commit crimes and are more likely to drift toward the center of a city than move toward outlying areas.[25] Garland White found that *permeable* neighborhoods, those with a greater than usual number of access streets from traffic arteries into the neighborhood, are the ones most likely to have high crime rates.[26] It is possible criminals choose these neighborhoods for burglaries because they are familiar and well traveled, they appear more open and vulnerable, and they offer more potential escape routes.[27] Here, we can see the influence of a routine activity on criminal choice: the more suitable and accessible the target, the more likely that crime will occur.[28]

Capable Guardians

Routine activity also implies that the presence of **capable guardians** may deter crime. Criminals tend to shy away from victims who are perceived to be armed and potentially dangerous. In a series of interviews conducted with career property offenders, Kenneth Tunnell found that burglars will avoid targets if they feel there are police in the area or if "nosy neighbors" might be suspicious and cause trouble.[29] And evidence is accumulating that predatory criminals are aware of an area's law enforcement capability: those with the reputation of employing aggressive "crime-fighting" cops are less likely to attract potential offenders than areas perceived to have passive law enforcers.[30]

Guardianship can also involve passive or mechanical devices, such as security fences or burglar alarms. Research indicates that physical security measures can improve guardianship and limit offender access to targets.[31]

Motivated Criminals

Routine activities theory predicts that crime rates correspond to the number of **motivated criminals** in the population. Rational offenders may be less likely to commit crime if they believe that they can achieve personal goals through legitimate means; job availability reduces crime. In contrast, criminal motivation increases when there is a need to accumulate wealth; a rising cost of living has been associated with increasing criminal motivation.[32]

If crime is rational, criminal motivation may be reduced if potential offenders perceive *alternatives* to crime. Tunnell's career criminals said they committed crimes because they considered legitimate opportunities unavailable to people with their limited education and background. As one offender told him:

> I tried to stay away from crime. . . . Nobody would hire me. I was an ex-con and I tried, I really tried to get gainful employment. There was nobody looking to hire me with my record. I went in as a juvenile and came out as an adult and didn't have any legitimate employment résumé to submit. Employment was impossible. So, I started robbing.[33]

Note how crime became the choice when legitimate alternatives were absent. In contrast, potential offenders who perceive legitimate alternatives, such as high-paying jobs, are less likely to choose crime.[34]

Criminal motivation may also be altered by the opportunity and need to commit crime. Kids who are attached to their parents and spend their weekends at home find their criminal motivation reduced.[35] Those whose parental relations are strained are more likely to become attached to peers who increase criminal motivation.[36]

≡ Is Crime Rational?

Is crime rational? It is relatively easy to show that some crimes are the product of rational and objective thought,

especially when they involve an ongoing criminal conspiracy centered on economic gain. When prominent bankers in the savings and loan industry were indicted for criminal fraud, their elaborate financial schemes not only showed signs of rationality but exhibited brilliant, though flawed, financial expertise. Charles Keating, imprisoned for his role in the $2 billion collapse of the Lincoln Savings and Loan, bolstered his activities by making more than $1.3 million in political contributions to influential government officials, including five U.S. senators who became known as the **Keating Five.**[37] The stock market manipulations of Wall Street insiders, such as Ivan Boesky and Michael Milken, and the drug dealings of organized crime bosses demonstrate a reasoned analysis of market conditions, interests, and risks.

While it is not surprising that ongoing criminal conspiracies involving organized and white-collar crime exhibit evidence of rationality, what about common-law crimes such as burglary and larceny? These would seem more likely to be random acts of criminal opportunity than well-thought-out and planned conspiracies. However, there is evidence that these "street crimes" may also be the product of careful analysis of risk assessment, including environmental, social, and structural factors. Ronald Clarke and Patricia Harris find that auto thieves are very selective in their choice of targets. If they want to strip cars for their parts, they are most likely to choose Volkswagons; if they want to sell the cars or keep them permanently, they choose Mercedes; for temporary use, Buick Riveras and Toyota Supras are top-ranked.[38] Vehicle selection seems to be based on their attractiveness and suitability for a particular purpose: German cars are selected for stripping because they usually have high-quality audio equipment that has good value on the second-hand market; target selection seems highly rational.

Rational choice may also be present when criminals choose the legal jurisdiction for their crimes on the basis of the punishments they could face. Evidence exists that jurisdictions with relatively low incarceration rates also experience the highest crime rates.[39] Perhaps "street smart" offenders know which areas offer the least threat and plan their crimes accordingly.

Choosing Targets

Evidence of rational choice may also be found in the way criminals locate their targets. Victimization data obtained by the NCVS indicates that high-income households ($25,000 or more annually) are the most likely targets of property crimes; in contrast, the wealthy are rarely the victims of violent crimes.[40] It is unlikely that these patterns could result from random events.

Studies of both professional and occasional criminals also yield evidence that choosing targets is a rational event. Burglars seem to be making prudent choices when they check to make sure that no one is home before they enter a residence. Some call ahead, while others ring the doorbell, preparing to claim they had the wrong address if someone answers. Some check to find out which families have star high school athletes, since those that do are sure to be at the game, leaving their houses unguarded.[41] Others seek the unlocked door and avoid the one with a dead bolt; houses with dogs are usually considered off limits.[42]

Burglars indicate that they carefully choose their targets. Some avoid freestanding buildings because they can more easily be surrounded by police; others select targets that are known to do a primarily cash business, such as bars, supermarkets, and restaurants.[43] Burglars also report being sensitive to the activities of their victims. They note that homemakers often develop predictable behavior patterns, which helps them plan their crimes.[44] Burglars seem to prefer "working" between 9 A.M. and 11 A.M. and in midafternoon, when parents are either working or dropping off or picking up kids at school. Burglars avoid Saturdays because most families are at home; Sunday morning during church hours is considered a prime time for weekend burglaries.[45]

Can Violence Be Rational?

While there is evidence that instrumental crimes, such as burglaries are rational, can expressive, violent acts in which the offender gains little material benefit and risks significant punishment also be the product of a reasoned decision-making process?

Evidence exists that even violent criminals are selective in their choice of suitable targets. In their interview survey of violent felons, James Wright and Peter Rossi found that violent offenders avoid victims who may be armed and dangerous. About three-fifths of all felons surveyed were more afraid of armed victims than police, about 40 percent had avoided a victim because they believed the victim was armed, and almost one-third reported that they had been scared off, wounded, or captured by armed victims.[46]

Not only do violent criminals avoid "dangerous" armed victims, they may be attracted to particular types of targets. Research indicates that rapists attack victims of approximately the same age; such targeting indicates an attempt at rational decision making.[47] Even serial murderers, outwardly the most irrational of all offenders, tend to pick their targets with care. Most choose victims who are either defenseless or cannot count on police protection: prostitutes, gay men, hitchhikers, children, hospital patients, the elderly, the homeless. Rarely do serial killers target weightlifters, martial arts experts, or any other potentially powerful group.[48] So while violent acts appear to be irrational, they also involve calculation of risk and reward.

The Situation of Crime

The focus of rational choice theory is on the opportunity to commit crime and not the criminal. Motivated criminals are assumed; there are always people willing and able to bypass the law, given the proper conditions and opportunity. Some irrational or mentally disturbed people may commit crime without thought to potential hazard, but it seems likely that immediate or situational variables will determine and guide most criminal behavior: people commit crime when they view its outcome as beneficial.[49] People who consider themselves "bad" or "criminal" may simply need fewer **situational inducements** to commit crime than those who consider themselves "good" or "law-abiding."

Sociologist Jack Katz argues that there are in fact immediate benefits to criminality, which he labels the **"seductions of crime."**[50] These situational inducements directly precede the commission of a crime and draw offenders into law violations: someone challenges their authority or moral position and they vanquish their opponent with a beating; they want to maximize their pleasure by doing something exciting, so they break into and vandalize a school building.

According to Katz, choosing crime can help satisfy personal needs. For some people, shoplifting and vandalism are attractive because getting away with it is a thrilling (Katz calls this "sneaky thrills") demonstration of personal competence; monetary gain is not their prime motive. Even murder can have an emotional payoff. Killers behave like the avenging gods of mythology, choosing to have life-or-death control over their victims.

Katz finds that situational inducements created from emotional upheaval can also structure the decision to commit crime. When an individual is faced with humiliation, righteousness, arrogance, or ridicule, violent reactions seem a natural response. When someone is rebuked at a party because he or she is disturbing people, the person responds, "So, I'm acting like a fool, am I?" and goes on the attack. Public embarrassment leads to action: the person must "sacrifice" or injure the body of the victim to maintain his or her "honor."

≡ Eliminating Crime

It follows that if crime is rational and people choose to commit crime, then crime can be controlled or eradicated by convincing potential offenders that the choice of crime is a poor one, that it will not bring them reward but instead pain, hardship, and deprivation. A number of potential strategies flow from this premise:

1. Situational crime prevention is aimed at convincing would-be criminals to avoid specific targets. It relies on the doctrine that crime can be avoided if motivated offenders are denied access to suitable targets. When people install security systems in their home or hire security guards, they are broadcasting the message: guardianship is great here, stay away, the potential reward is not worth the risk of apprehension.
2. General deterrence strategies are aimed at making potential criminals fear the consequences of crime. The threat of punishment is aimed at convincing rational criminals that crime does not pay.
3. Specific deterrence refers to punishing known criminals severely so that they will never be tempted to repeat their offenses. If crime is rational, then painful punishments should reduce its future allure.
4. Incapacitation strategies attempt to reduce crime rates by denying motivated offenders the opportunity to commit crime. If, despite the threat of law and punishment, some people still find crime attractive, then the only way to control their behavior is to take them out of society.

In the following sections, each of these crime reduction or control strategies based on the rationality of criminal behavior will be discussed in some detail.

Situational Crime Prevention

Rational choice theory recognizes that people choose crime for a variety of reasons, including mental, physical, familial, social, and economic factors. Unfortunately, these factors are not easily subject to treatment or change: it is not realistic to expect society to heal broken families, raise IQs, cure the mentally unsound, or make every poor person rich. Since criminal activity is offense-specific, crime prevention, or at least crime reduction, should be achieved through policies that convince potential criminals to desist from criminal activities, delay their actions, or avoid a particular target. As routine activity theory holds, criminal acts will be avoided if potential targets are carefully guarded. Desperate people may contemplate crime, but only the truly irrational would attack a well-defended, inaccessible target. Some might choose to forgo criminal activity; others may seek out a more vulnerable objective. Crime prevention can be achieved then by reducing the opportunities people have to commit particular crimes, a practice known as **situational crime prevention**.

Situational crime prevention was first popularized in the United States in the early 1970s by Oscar Newman, who coined the term **defensible space** to signify that crime could be prevented or displaced through the use of residential architectural designs that reduce criminal opportunity, such as well-lit housing projects that maximize surveillance.[51] In a similar vein, C. Ray Jeffery wrote *Crime Prevention through Environmental Design,* which extended Newman's concepts and applied them to nonresidential areas, such as schools and factories.[52] According to this view, such mechanisms as security systems, dead-bolt locks, high-intensity street lighting, and neighborhood watch patrols should be able to reduce criminal opportunity.[53]

Situational Crime Prevention: Strategies

Today, choice theorists maintain that situational crime prevention may be achieved by creating a strategy or overall plan to reduce crime and then developing specific tactics to achieve that goal.[54]

Situational crime reduction strategies typically focus on the routine activities that produce crime: limiting the number of motivated offenders; increasing guardianship; reducing access to suitable targets. Marcus Felson suggests that such "total community" strategy might include some or all of the following elements:

1. Uniform school release schedules so that there is no doubt when kids belong in school and when they are truant.
2. Truancy control efforts.
3. After-school activities to keep kids under adult supervision.
4. Organized weekend activities with adult supervision.
5. School lunch programs designed to keep kids in school and away from shopping areas.
6. No-cash policies in schools to reduce kids' opportunity to either be a target or engage in the consumption of drugs or alcohol.
7. Keep shopping areas and schools separate.

Situational crime prevention suggests that crimes may be prevented by taking such steps as decreasing the access to targets through effective security systems.

8. Construct housing to maximize guardianship and minimize illegal behavior.
9. Encourage neighborhood stability so that residents will be acquainted with one another.
10. Encourage privatization of parks and recreation facilities so that people will be responsible for their area's security.

Felson's approach is designed to reduce the overall crime rate by limiting the access a highly motivated offender group (high school kids) have to tempting targets. Notice that it is not designed to eliminate a specific crime but to reduce the overall crime rate.

Situational Crime Prevention: Tactics

Crime prevention tactics involve a plan of action to reduce or eliminate a specific crime problem. In an important work, *Situational Crime Prevention*, Ronald

Clarke sets out the three main types of crime prevention tactics in use today: increase the effort needed to commit the crime, increase the risks of committing the crime, and reduce the rewards for committing the crime. These three basic techniques and some methods that can be used to achieve them are illustrated in Table 5.1.

Some of the tactics of situational crime prevention include target-hardening techniques, such as placing steering locks on cars; empirical evidence indicates that the placement of steering locks has helped reduce car theft in the United States, Britain, and Germany.[55] Another approach has been to make targets less accessible, for example, by putting unbreakable glass on storefronts, locking gates, and fencing yards; having the owner's photo on credit cards should reduce the use of stolen cards.

It is also possible to increase the risks of crime by improving surveillance lighting, creating neighborhood watch programs, controlling building entrances and exits, installing burglar alarms and security systems, and

TABLE 5.1 **The 12 Techniques of Situational Prevention**

Increasing the Effort	Increasing the Risks	Reducing the Rewards
Target Hardening	*Entry/Exit Screening*	*Target Removal*
Steering locks	Border searches	Removable car
Bandit screens	Baggage	radio
Slug rejector	screening	Exact change
device	Automatic ticket	fares
Vandal-proofing	gates	Cash reduction
Toughened glass	Merchandise tags	Remove coin
Tamper-proof	Library tags	meters
seals	Electronic point	Phonecard
	of sale	Pay by check
Access Control	*Formal Surveillance*	*Identifying Property*
Locked gates	Police patrols	Cattle branding
Fenced yards	Security guards	Property marking
Parking lot	Informant	Vehicle licensing
barriers	hotlines	Vehicle parts
Entry phones	Burglar alarms	marking
ID badges	Red light	PIN for car radios
PIN numbers	cameras	LOJACK
	Curfew decals	
Deflecting Offenders	*Surveillance by Employees*	*Removing Inducements*
Bus stop	Bus conductors	"Weapons effect"
placement	Park attendants	Graffiti cleaning
Tavern location	Concierges	Rapid repair
Street closures	Pay phone	Plywood road
Graffiti board	location	signs
Litter bins	Incentive	Gender-neutral
Spittoons	schemes	phone listing
	Closed-circuit TV	Park Camarro off
	systems	street
Controlling Facilitators	*Natural Surveillance*	*Rule Setting*
Spray-can sales	Pruning hedges	Drug-free school
Gun control	"Eyes on the	zone
Credit card photo	street"	Public park
Ignition interlock	Lighting bank	regulations
Server	interiors	Customs
intervention	Street lighting	delaration
Caller ID	Defensible space	Income tax
	Neighborhood	returns
	Watch	Hotel registration
		Library checkout

SOURCE: R. Clarke, *Situational Crime Prevention* (Albany, N.Y.: Harrow & Heston, 1992), p. 13.

increasing the number of private security officers and police patrols. Target reduction strategies include making car radios removable so they can be kept at home at night, marking property so that it is more difficult to sell when stolen, and having gender-neutral phone listings to discourage obscene phone calls. Tracking systems, such as those made by the LOJACK Corporation, help police locate and return stolen vehicles.

At their core, situational crime prevention efforts seek clearly defined solutions to specific crime problems. For example, Clarke shows how caller-ID in New Jersey resulted in significant reductions in the number of obscene phone calls. Caller-ID displays the telephone number of the party *placing* the call. The threat of exposure had a deterrent effect on the number of obscene calls reported to police.[56] In another such study, Barbara Morse and Delbert Elliott found that installing a locking device on cars that prevents inebriated drivers from starting the vehicle significantly reduced drunk-driving rates.[57] And in her analysis of gasoline "drive-offs" from convenience stores, Nancy LaVigne found that removing signs from store windows, installing brighter lights, and instituting a pay-first policy can reduce the number of incidents of people filling their tanks and driving off without paying.[58]

Displacement, Extinction, Discouragement, and Diffusion

While situational crime prevention seems plausible, it can also produce unforeseen and unwanted consequences. Preventing crime from occurring in one locale does little to deter criminal motivation. People who desire the benefits of crime may choose alternative targets. Crime, then, is not prevented but deflected or displaced.[59] For example, beefed-up police patrols in one area may shift crimes to a more vulnerable neighborhood.[60] While **crime displacement** cannot be a solution to the general problem of crime, some evidence exists that deflection efforts can partially reduce the frequency of crime or produce less serious offense patterns.[61]

There is also the problem of **extinction**: Crime reduction programs may produce a short-term positive effect, but benefits dissipate as criminals adjust to new conditions. They learn to dismantle alarms or avoid patrols; they may become motivated to try new offenses they had previously avoided. For example, if every residence in a neighborhood were provided with a foolproof burglar alarm system, motivated offenders might then turn to armed robbery, a riskier and more violent crime.

While displacement and extinction may be a problem, Ronald Clarke and David Weisburd note a hidden benefit of situational crime prevention, **diffusion of benefits**.[62] Diffusion occurs when efforts to prevent one crime cause the unintended prevention of another. Diffusion may be produced by two independent effects. Crime control efforts may *deter* criminals by causing them to fear apprehension. For example, video cameras set up in a mall to reduce shoplifting can also reduce property damage because would-be vandals fear they are being caught on camera.

Another type of diffusion effect is called **discouragement.** By limiting one type of target, would-be lawbreakers may forgo criminal activity because crime no longer pays. For example, an electronic scanning device set up to reduce the theft of books from libraries may also reduce the theft of compact discs and videocassettes: If books are off limits, then thieves may not consider it worth the trip to the library to take the limited supply of CDs and videocassettes, even though the latter are *not* marked for scanning.

According to the situational crime prevention model, if the opportunity to commit crime can be reduced, crime rates will fall. Changing offender behavior is difficult to achieve; changing criminal opportunity is a more realistic solution.

General Deterrence

According to the rational choice view, motivated, rational people will violate the law if left free and unrestricted. Rational offenders want the goods and services crime provides without having to work for them; they will commit crime if they do not fear apprehension and punishment. The concept of general deterrence holds that crime rates will be influenced and controlled by the threat of criminal punishment. If people fear apprehension and punishment, they will not risk breaking the law. An inverse relationship should exist then between crime rates and the severity, certainty, and celerity (speed) of legal sanctions. If, for example, the punishment for a crime is increased and if the effectiveness and efficiency of the justice system in enforcing the law prohibiting that act is improved, then the number of people engaging in that act should decline.

The factors of severity, certainty, and celerity may also influence one another. For example, if a crime—say, robbery—is punished very severely, but few robbers are ever caught or punished, it is likely that the severity of punishment for robbery will not deter people from robbing. On the other hand, if the certainty of apprehension and conviction is increased by modern technology, more efficient police work, or some other factor, then even minor punishments might deter the potential robber.

Research on General Deterrence

Much research has been carried out to determine whether deterrent measures, such as arrest and punishment, affect people's behavior. Some studies make use of aggregate data sources, such as the Uniform Crime Reports or prison statistics, to evaluate the deterrent effect of objective efforts by the justice system, while others use self-report surveys to determine if the perception of punishment deters crime. Still others use experimental data to evaluate deterrent measures. Because of their importance and independence, these three methods referred to as objective, perceptual, and experimental research, will be discussed separately.

Can the threat of punishment deter illegal acts? The creators of this sign obviously believe that it can!

Objective Measures

According to deterrence theory, if the probability of arrest, conviction, and sanctioning increases, crime rates should decline (that is, because rational offenders realize that the likelihood of punishment outweighs the benefits of crime).

Some research efforts do in fact show an inverse relationship between crime rates and the objective certainty of punishment; as the chance of arrest, conviction, and imprisonment increases, the crime rate declines.[63] In one often-cited study of arrest probability in Florida, Charles Tittle and Alan Rowe concluded that if police could make an arrest in at least 30 percent of all reported crimes, the crime rate would significantly decline.[64]

More recent research by Jiang Wu and Allen Liska is supportive but notes that this effect is race-specific: African-American arrest probability influences African-American offense rates alone, while white arrest probabilities affect white offending patterns. Wu and Liska conclude that in large cities, the threat of arrest is communicated within neighborhoods and has an independent effect on residents of each racial grouping.[65]

The relationship between objective measures of punishment and crime rates is far from settled. A number of studies have found little relationship between the likelihood of being arrested or imprisoned and corresponding crime rates.[66] Some research efforts that have found a deterrent effect show that the threat of punishment seems to work better for some crimes than others. For example, Edwin Zedlewski found that police involvement could lower the burglary rate, while larceny rates remained unaffected by law enforcement efforts.[67]

Measurement Problems. One reason for the inconclusive evidence generated by objective measures research is that findings are highly susceptible to measurement error.[68] It has proven difficult to obtain accurate measures of key variables, such as arrest rates, incarceration rates, and indicators of deterrence. Research studies have used different or inconsistent indicators, which makes findings difficult to compare or interpret. For example, police departments that inflate crime clearance rates to improve their image will generate data showing that law enforcement efforts can deter crime; in contrast, a deterrent effect is negated by departments that report fewer crime clearances.[69]

It is also possible that what appears to be a deterrent effect may actually reflect the effect of some other legal phenomenon and not real fear of punishment. For example, deterrence is supported if the crime rate falls as the number of people in prison increases; by implication, fear of being sent to prison is deterring would-be criminals. However, what appears to be a deterrent effect may actually be an effect of incapacitation: the fear of prison does not reduce crime; rather, taking the most serious criminals off the street is what reduces the crime rate.

In sum, measurement and other methodological problems have made it extremely difficult to assess whether the criminal justice system's efforts to control crime have a deterrent influence on potential criminals.[70]

Experimental Research

Another approach to testing deterrence theory is to set up experiments to see if subjects respond to the threat of legal sanctions. In these experimental models, levels of criminal behavior are determined, a threat is introduced, and a second measurement is taken. In some instances, a control group that has not experienced the threat is used for comparison.

A number of experimental studies have attempted to determine whether perceived threats can be used to control deviant behaviors and common criminal behaviors. The most well-known research of this sort is H. Laurence Ross's analysis of the deterrent effects of antidrunk driving laws on motor vehicular violations. Ross found that when laws are toughened, there is a short-term deterrent effect. However, because the likelihood of getting caught is relatively low, the impact of deterrent measures on alcohol-impaired driving is negligible over the long term.[71] In a later study, Ross, along with Richard McCleary and Gary LaFree, evaluated the effect of a new law in Arizona that mandated jail sentences for drunk driving convictions; time series analysis indicated that the new law had little deterrent effect.[72]

Some research efforts have found that deterrent strategies may work. Gary Green has shown that they have an effect for at least one crime, using an illegal, unauthorized descrambler to obtain pay cable television programs.[73] Green first determined how many people out of a sample of 3,500 in a western town were using a descrambler and avoiding payments to the local cable company. Threatening letters were sent to the 67 violators, conveying the general message that illegal theft of cable signals would be criminally prosecuted; the letter did not indicate that the subject's personal violation had been discovered. Green found that about two-thirds of the 67 violators reacted to the threat by desisting and trying to hide their crime by removing the illegal device; a six-month follow-up showed that the intervention effect had a long-lasting effect. Green's positive results indicate the need for future experimental research on deterrence.

Police Experiments. If crime can be controlled through deterrence, then it follows that increasing police presence and activity should be able to reduce the crime rate. Perhaps the most famous experiment to evaluate the general deterrent effect of the threat of legal sanctions was conducted by the Kansas City, Missouri, police department.[74] To evaluate the effectiveness of police patrols, 15 independent police beats or districts were divided into three groups: the first retained a normal police patrol; the second (proactive) was supplied with two to three times the normal amount of patrol forces; the third (reactive) eliminated its preventive patrol entirely, and police officers responded only when summoned by citizens to the scene of a crime. Surprisingly, data from the Kansas City study indicated that these variations in patrol techniques had little effect on the crime patterns in the 15 locales. The presence or absence of patrol forces did not seem to affect residential or business burglaries, auto thefts, larcenies involving auto accessories, robberies, vandalism, or other criminal behavior. Variations in police patrol techniques appeared to have little effect on citizens' attitudes toward the police, their satisfaction with police, or their fear of future criminal behavior.

Other police departments have instituted **crackdowns,** sudden changes in police activity designed to increase the communicated threat or actual certainty of punishment, to lower crime rates. For example, a police task force targets street-level narcotics dealers by using undercover agents and surveillance cameras in known drug-dealing locales. An analysis of 18 police crackdowns by Lawrence Sherman indicates that they may have an initial deterrent effect on controlling crime that suffers diffusion over time. Table 5.2 describes various police crackdowns.[75]

TABLE 5.2 **Examples of Police Crackdowns**

Police crackdowns can target specific neighborhoods or specific offenses, and their duration can range from a few weeks to several years. The following illustrate this range. Initial and residual deterrent effects varied, sometimes based on factors outside the scope of the crackdowns themselves.

Drug crackdown, Washington, D.C. A massive police presence—60 police officers per day and a parked police trailer—in the Hanover Place neighborhood open-air drug market provided an effective initial deterrent.

Lynn, Masachusetts, open-air heroin market. A four-year crackdown using four to six police officers led to 140 drug arrests in the first ten months and increased demand for drug treatment.

Operation Clean Sweep, Washington, D.C. The city allocated 100 to 200 officers—many on overtime—to 59 drug markets, making 60 arrests a day. Tactics included roadblocks, observation of open-air markets, and "reverse-buy" sell-and-bust by undercover officers, and seizure of cars.

Repeat Call Address Policing (RECAP) Experiment, Minneapolis. A special unit of five police officers attempted to reduce calls for service from 125 residential addresses by increasing their presence with landlords and tenants. This short-term targeting of resources led to a 15-percent drop in calls from these addresses, compared to 125 control addresses.

Nashville, Tennessee, patrol experiment. A sharp increase in moving patrol at speeds under 20 miles per hour in four four high-crime neighborhoods netted a measurable

high-crime neighborhoods netted a measurable decrease in Type 1 index crime during two short crackdowns (11 days and 15 days).

Disorder crackdown in Washington, D.C. Massive publicity accompanied a crackdown in illegal parking and disorder that was attracting street crime to the Georgetown area of the city. Police raised their weekend manpower 30 percent and installed a trailer at a key intersection to book arrestees.

New York City subway crackdown. This massive crackdown involved increasing the number of police officers from 1,200 to 3,100, virtually guaranteeing an officer for every train and every station. Crime fell during the first two years of the crackdown but rose again during the following six years.

Cheshire, England, drunk driving crackdowns. During two short-term crackdowns, one accompanied by continuing publicity, police increased breathalyzer tests up to sixfold between 10 P.M. and 2 A.M. Significant deterrent effects continued up to six months after the crackdowns ceased.

London prostitution crackdown. Stepped up arrests of prostitutes, pimps, and brothel keepers—combined with cautions of their customers—succeeded in reducing "curb-crawling," with no displacement.

New Zealand drunk driving crackdowns. Deterrent effects of two short-term crackdowns were felt even before they began, because of intensive publicity about the impending crackdowns and stepped up administration of breathalyzer tests.

SOURCE: Lawrence Sherman, "Police Crackdowns," *NIJ Reports,* March/April 1990, p. 3.

The Special Case of Capital Punishment

It stands to reason that if deterrent measures truly have an impact on behavior, then fear of the death penalty, the ultimate legal deterrent, should reduce murder rates. A failure of the death penalty to deter violent crime jeopardizes the validity of the entire deterrence concept. Various studies have tested the assumption that capital punishment deters violent crime. The research can be divided into three types: immediate impact studies, comparative research, and time series analysis.

Immediate Impact. One type of study looks at the immediate effect of an execution on the murder rate. If

This electric chair was used in Texas to execute 361 convicted felons between 1924 and 1964. Though there is little evidence that capital punishment can deter murder, can the death penalty be justified on other grounds, for example, because convicted killers *deserve* to be executed for their crimes?

capital punishment does have a deterrent effect, the reasoning goes, then it should occur immediately after a well-publicized execution has taken place. One of the first noteworthy studies of this type was conducted in Philadelphia in 1935 by Robert Dann.[76] He chose five highly publicized executions of convicted murderers in different years and determined the number of homicides in the 60 days before and after each execution. Each 120-day period had approximately the same number of homicides, as well as the same number of days on which homicides occurred. Dann's study revealed that an average of 4.4 more homicides occurred during the 60 days following an execution than during those preceding it, suggesting that the overall impact of executions might actually *increase* the incidence of homicide.

That executions may actually increase the likelihood of murder was labeled by William Bowers and Glenn Pierce as the **brutalization effect.** This effect occurs when potential criminals model their behavior after state authorities: If the government can kill its enemies, so can they.[77] Recent research by John Cochran, Mitchell Chamlin, and Mark Seth found that a well-publicized execution in Oklahoma had little immediate deterrent impact on murder rates, though for some crimes (stranger homicides), a brutalization effect was observed; post-execution (stranger) murder rates increased by one per month.[78]

While this evidence does not support deterrence, other research efforts have found an immediate impact. David Phillips studied the immediate effect of executions in Britain from 1858 to 1914 and found a temporary deterrent effect based on the publicity following the execution.[79] A more contemporary (1950 to 1980) evaluation of executions in the United States by Steven Stack concluded that capital punishment does indeed have an immediate impact and that 16 well-publicized executions may have saved 480 lives.[80]

In sum, a number of criminologists find that executions actually increase murder rates, while others argue that their immediate impact can lower murder rates.

Comparative Research. Another type of research compares the murder rates in jurisdictions that have abolished the death penalty with the rates of those that employ the death penalty. Using this approach, Karl Schuessler analyzed 11 states' murder rates for the years 1930 to 1949 while considering their "execution risk" (the numbers of executions for murder per 1,000 homicides per year). His conclusion: homicide rates and execution risks move independently of each other.[81]

Two pioneering studies, one by Thorsten Sellin (1959) and the other by Walter Reckless (1969), also showed little difference in the murder rates of adjacent states, regardless of their use of the death penalty; capital punishment did not appear to influence the reported rate of homicide.[82]

More recent updates of research of this method have also shown little reason to believe that executions deter homicide.[83] In one sophisticated study, Derral Cheatwood identified 293 pairs of counties in the United States and compared their murder rates while considering whether they were located in a state having a death penalty statute, the number of people on death row, and the number of people executed since 1976. His conclusion: having and using a death penalty has no deterrent effect on violent crime rates.[84]

The failure to show a deterrent effect of the death penalty is not limited to cross-state comparisons. Research by Dane Archer, Rosemary Gartner, and Marc Beittel in 14 nations around the world found little evidence that countries with a death penalty have lower violence rates than those without; homicide rates actually *decline* after capital punishment is abolished, a direct contradiction to its supposed deterrent effect.[85]

Time Series. Advanced econometric statistical analysis has been used to conduct time series analysis, a complex statistical technique that tells researchers how the murder rate changes when death penalty statutes are created or eliminated. The most widely cited study is Isaac Ehrlich's 1975 work, which made use of national crime and execution data.[86] According to Ehrlich, the perception of execution risk is an important determinant of whether one individual will murder another. As a result of his analysis, Ehrlich concluded that each individual execution per year in the United States would save seven or eight people from being victims of murder.

Ehrlich's research has been widely cited by advocates of the death penalty as empirical proof of the deterrent effect of capital punishment. However, subsequent research that attempted to replicate Ehrlich's analysis showed that his approach was flawed and capital punishment is no more effective as a deterrent than life imprisonment.[87]

In sum, studies that have attempted to show the deterrent effect of capital punishment on the murder rate indicate that the execution of convicted criminals has relatively little influence on behavior.[88] While it is still uncertain why the threat of capital punishment has failed as a deterrent, the cause may lie in the nature of homicide itself: murder is often an expressive "crime of passion" involving people who knew each other and who may be under the influence of drugs and alcohol; murder is also found to be a by-product of the criminal activity of people who suffer from the burdens of poverty and income inequality.[89] These factors may either prevent or inhibit rational evaluation of the long-term consequences of an immediate violent act.

The failure of the "ultimate deterrent" to deter the "ultimate crime" has been used by critics to question the validity of general deterrence. As a whole, experimental research that evaluates the effects of legal deterrents—arrest, sentencing, imprisonment, capital punishment—has failed to show a consistent and significant ability to control crime with these measures.

Perceptual Research

Deterrence theory is also supported if people who *perceive* that they will be caught and punished if they engage in some crime are deterred and refrain from engaging in that act. Deterrence is contradicted if perceptions of punishment have little or no effect on behavior.[90]

Several attempts have been made to measure the association between perceptions of punishment and behavior, and in general, they indicate that the certainty and not the severity of punishment may have a deterrent effect on behavior.[91] In one such study, Harold Grasmick and Robert Bursik found that people who expected to be sanctioned for such crimes as tax cheating, theft, and drunk driving reported that they were unlikely to commit these crimes in the future.[92] A cross-sectional survey by Steven Klepper and Daniel Nagin found that people who believe they will be caught and subjected to criminal prosecution will be less likely to engage in tax evasion than those who fear neither apprehension nor prosecution.[93]

One criticism of **perceptual deterrence** research is that it usually involves samples of noncriminals, such as college students, and crimes of minor seriousness, such as smoking marijuana. Experienced offenders, who are more criminally motivated and less committed to moral values, may be less likely to be deterred by the fear of punishment.[94] A number of recent research efforts have attempted to confront this oversight by using samples of active or known criminals. In one such study, Julie Horney and Ineke Haen Marshall found that criminal's perceptions of arrest risk were inversely related to offense participation; the greater the perceived risk of apprehension, the less likely criminals would be willing to risk crime.[95] In another, Scott Decker and his associates found that the perceived risk of getting caught influenced active burglars more so than the threat of severe punishments.[96]

The effects of perceptual deterrence seem to be the greatest on people who believe they are certain to be arrested for a crime and certain to be punished if arrested. Put another way, those people who believe apprehension will almost always result in harsh punishments will be the most likely to avoid the risk of criminal behavior.[97]

Panel Studies

A major problem of perceptual research is the causal ordering of the data. It is actually not surprising that people who have *already* committed criminal acts report that they do not feel threatened by legal sanctions and that law-abiding citizens perceive more legal danger. It is also difficult to determine whether people who say they will not commit crimes in the future because they fear punishment actually remain law-abiding. To verify that the threat of legal punishment inhibits behavior, a researcher must prove that lawbreakers perceived little threat *before* they engaged in criminal acts.

A number of researchers have attempted to accomplish this goal by measuring an intact group, or panel, of subjects over time. The deterrence concept would be supported if people's perceptions of sanctions can be shown to remain stable between measurements and if those who at first feared the deterrent effect of the law later refrained from engaging in criminal behaviors. Several studies have explored this issue. In one, Donna Bishop surveyed 2,147 high school students at a nine-month interval.[98] Although her data indicate that perceptions of "deterrence are often unstable," Bishop did find a significant deterrent effect. Kids who *admitted* criminal behavior during the first survey also believed they were *unlikely* to be caught and punished; this perception that crime was a low-risk behavior resulted in their continued law violations.

While persuasive, Bishop's findings have been challenged by similar panel studies that found little evidence that perceptions of punishment actually deter crime.[99]

Beyond these ambiguous findings, panel studies have also been criticized because of their methodological problems. The most telling criticism is that perceptions change over time and that any measure of deterrence may be influenced by fluctuations in the way people perceive punishment.[100]

Involvement with the Law. Both single-measure and panel studies do not give unqualified support to the hypothesis that fear of crime reduces criminal violations.

One reason may be that many offenders repeat their criminal acts *(recidivate) after* they have been caught and punished, so there is little reason to expect that prior experience with the law will increase perceptions of deterrence or reduce crime.

There are indications that experienced offenders are in fact the ones least threatened by the threat of future punishment.[101] Research by Eleni Apospori, Geoffrey Alpert, and Raymond Paternoster found that people who have been caught and sanctioned subsequently *lower* their estimates of the risk involved in law violations. The researchers also found that the more experienced the offender, the bigger the drop in fear of legal sanctions; criminal convictions actually help *lower* the perceived risk of legal sanctions.[102] Not only do criminals overestimate the payoff of crime, but they underestimate the risk. This finding runs counter to deterrence theory. However, subsequent analysis by Apospori and Alpert found that criminals who receive the most *severe* punishments are the ones most likely to be deterred from future criminality.[103] The Apospori research indicates that unless the justice system is prepared to hand down harsh and punitive sanctions, the process of arrest, prosecution, and punishment may be a counterdeterrent and actually help increase criminal activity.

Informal Sanctions

While the ability to deter crime through the actual or perceived threat of legal sanctions has been difficult to assess, there is now evidence that fear of **informal sanctions** may have a crime-reducing impact.

Informal sanctions occur when significant others, such as parents, peers, neighbors, and teachers, direct their disapproval, stigma, anger, and indignation toward an offender. If this happens, law violators run the risk of feeling shame, being embarrassed, and suffering a loss of respect.[104] Can the fear of public humiliation deter crime?

Research efforts have in fact established the influence of informal sanctions. In a national survey of almost 2,000 subjects, Charles Tittle found that perception of informal sanctions was a more effective determinant of deterrence than perception of formal sanctions.[105] Tittle concluded that social control seems to be rooted almost entirely in how people perceive negative reactions from interpersonal acquaintances (family, friends), while formal sanctions (arrest, prison) are irrelevant to the general public. Tittle found that legal sanctions do no more than supplement informal control processes by influencing a small segment of "criminally inclined" persons.[106]

Other studies have also found that people who are committed to conventional moral values and believe crime to be "sinful" are unlikely to violate the law.[107] Evidence from Britain shows that efforts to control drunk driving by shaming offenders produced a moral climate that helped reduce its incidence.[108] Perhaps the same moral effect can help reduce drug use in the United States.

Shame and Humiliation.

Those fearful of being rejected by family and peers are also reluctant to engage in deviant behavior.[109] Two factors seem to stand out: personal shame over violating the law and the fear of public humiliation if the deviant behavior becomes public knowledge. In a series of studies, Harold Grasmick and Robert Bursik find that people who say that involvement in crime will cause them to feel ashamed are less likely to commit theft, fraud, and motor vehicular offenses than those people who report not feeling ashamed about crime.[110] Their research has also shown that people are more likely to respond to antilittering drives (with Karyl Kinsey) and antidrunk-driving campaigns (with Bruce Arneklev) if the thought of being accused of littering or driving drunk makes them feel ashamed or embarrassed.[111] There is also evidence that women are much more likely to fear shame and embarrassment than men, a finding that may help explain gender differences in the crime rate.[112]

Other research efforts have also found that fear of shame and embarrassment can be a powerful deterrent to crime.[113] In one study, Kirk Williams and Richard Hawkins find that fear of getting arrested can deter spouse abuse but that potential abusers were more afraid of social costs (for example, loss of friends and family disapproval) than they were of legal punishments (such as going to jail). William and Hawkins found that the potential for self-stigma and personal humiliation was the greatest deterrent to crime.[114]

The effect of informal sanctions may vary according to the cohesiveness of community structure and type of crime. Informal sanctions may be most effective in highly unified areas where everyone knows one another and the crime cannot be hidden from public view. The threat of informal sanctions may also have the greatest influence on instrumental crimes, which involve planning, and not on impulsive or expressive criminal behaviors or those associated with substance abuse.[115]

This research seems to indicate that public education on the social cost of crime that stresses the risk of shame and humiliation may be a more effective crime-prevention tool than the creation and distribution of legal punishments; potential offenders may be deterred if they can be convinced that crime is sinful or immoral.[116]

General Deterrence in Review

Some experts, such as Ernest Van Den Haag, believe that the purpose of the law and justice system is to create a "threat system."[117] That is, the threat of legal punishment should, on the face of it, deter lawbreakers through fear. Who among us can claim that they never had an urge to commit crime but were deterred by fear of discovery and its consequences? Nonetheless, few studies show that perceptions of deterrence or objective deterrent measures actually reduce the propensity to commit crime or lower the crime rate. The relationship between crime rates and deterrent measures is far less than choice theorists might expect. How can this discrepancy be explained?

First, deterrence theory assumes a rational offender who weighs the costs and benefits of a criminal act before deciding on a course of action. There is reason to believe that in many instances, criminals are desperate people acting under the influence of drugs and alcohol or suffering from personality disorders. Surveys show a significant portion of all offenders, approximately 70 percent, are substance abusers.[118] It is likely that the threat of future punishment has little influence on these people.

Second, many offenders are members of what is referred to as the underclass—people cut off from society, lacking the education and skills they need to be in demand in the modern economy.[119] It may be unlikely that such desperate people will be deterred from crime by fear of punishment because, in reality, they perceive few other options for success.

Third, as Beccaria's famous equation tells us, the threat of punishment involves not only its severity but its certainty and speed. Our legal system is not very effective. Only 10 percent of all serious offenses result in apprehension and arrest (since half go unreported and police make arrests in about 20 percent of reported crimes). As apprehended offenders are processed through all the stages of the criminal justice system, the odds of their receiving serious punishment diminishes. Some offenders then may believe that they will not be severely punished for their acts and consequently have little regard for the law's deterrent power.

As you may recall, offenders who suffer the most lenient sanctions are the ones least likely to fear future legal punishments. Raymond Paternoster found that adolescents, a group responsible for a disproportionate amount of crime, may be well aware that the juvenile court "is generally lenient in the imposition of meaningful sanctions on even the most serious offenders."[120] Research by James Williams and Daniel Rodeheaver shows that even those accused of murder, the most serious of crimes, are often convicted of lesser offenses and spend relatively short amounts of time behind bars.[121] In making their "rational choice," offenders may be aware that the deterrent effect of the law is minimal.

Specific Deterrence

The general deterrence model focuses on future or potential criminals. In contrast, the theory of specific (also called special or particular) deterrence holds that criminal sanctions should be so powerful that known criminals will never repeat their criminal acts. For example, the drunk driver whose sentence is a large fine and a week in the county jail will, it is hoped, be convinced that the price to be paid for drinking and driving is too great to consider future violations; burglars who spend five years in a tough, maximum-security prison should find their enthusiasm for theft dampened.[122] In principle, punishment works if a connection can be established between the planned action and memories of its consequence; if these recollections are adequately intense, the action will be prevented or reduced in frequency.[123]

Research on Specific Deterrence

At first glance, specific deterrence does not seem to work because a majority of known criminals are not deterred by their punishment. Most prison inmates had prior records of arrest and conviction before their current offense.[124] About two-thirds of all convicted felons are re-arrested within three years of their release from prison, and those who have been *punished* in the *past* are the most *likely* to recidivate.[125]

There does exist empirical research indicating that in some instances, offenders who receive harsher punishments than their peers will be less likely to recidivate or if they do commit crimes again, do so less frequently.[126] Using data acquired in Scandinavian countries, Perry Shapiro and Harold Votey found that an arrest for drunk driving can actually reduce the probability of offender recidivism. It seems that an arrest increases a person's belief that he or she will be re-arrested if he or she drinks and drives and heightens the person's perception of the unpleasantness associated with an arrest.[127] Similarly, Douglas Smith and Patrick Gartin's

research shows that getting arrested reduces the likelihood that novice offenders will repeat their criminal activity and that experienced offenders will reduce future offending rates after an arrest.[128]

These research studies indicate that under some circumstances, specific deterrence measures, such as arrest or a prison term, may reduce the probability of future criminality. However, the association between crime and specific deterrent measures remains uncertain at best.

The Domestic Violence Studies

Efforts to reduce the incidence of spouse abuse and domestic violence through mandatory arrest policies showcase the specific deterrent effect of legal punishment. The ground-breaking research was conducted in Minneapolis, Minnesota, by Larry Sherman and Richard Berk.[129] Sherman and Berk examined the effect of police action on domestic dispute cases. They had police officers randomly assign treatments to the domestic assault cases they encountered on their beat. One approach was to give some sort of advice and mediation, another was to send the assailant from the home for a period of eight hours, and the third was to arrest the assailant. They found that where police took formal action (arrest), the chance of recidivism was substantially less than when they took less punitive measures, such as warning the offenders or ordering them out of the house for a cooling-off period. A six-month follow-up found that only 10 percent of the arrested group repeated their violent behavior, compared to 19 percent of the advised group and 24 percent of the sent-away group. Sherman and Berk concluded that a formal arrest, the most punitive alternative, was the most effective means of controlling domestic violence, regardless of what happened to the offender in court.

While the findings of the Minneapolis experiment seemed to affirm the effectiveness of specific deterrence, efforts to replicate the experimental design in other locales, including Omaha; Milwaukee; Atlanta; Colorado Springs; Dade County, Florida; and Charlotte, North Carolina, have so far failed to duplicate the original findings.[130] In these locales, formal arrest was not a greater deterrent to spouse abuse than warning or advising the assailant; in some cases, the frequency of domestic assaults increased after arrest.[131] There are also indications that police officers in the original Minneapolis experiment failed to assign cases in a random fashion, which altered the experimental findings.[132]

Despite these setbacks, there are indications that specific deterrence policies can under some circumstances deter domestic abuse. One study showed that a period of short-term custody lasting about three hours may reduce recidivism; unfortunately, deterrent effects decayed over time.[133] Evidence also exists that one subset of offenders—those with a greater stake in conformity—are more deterrable than those with little social commitment; deterrence seems to work with those who have more to lose, such as a high-paying job.[134]

It is difficult to explain why the specific deterrent effect of arrest is either absent, decays over time, or only affects a subset of offenders (those married and employed).[135] It is possible that offenders who suffer arrest are initially fearful of punishment but eventually replace fear with anger and violent intent toward their mate when their case does not result in severe punishment. However, research on the effectiveness of prosecution of spousal abusers indicates that little specific deterrence occurs even when an abuse case is brought before the criminal court.[136] In one experiment initiated in Indianapolis to evaluate the effect of prosecuting domestic violence cases in the criminal courts, the only policy that proved to be a successful deterrent was one that permitted victims to drop charges after their abusers had been arrested.[137] Perhaps the empowerment of victims, letting them take control of the situation, by giving them the choice of prosecution if they decide it is in their best interests, can produce a more powerful specific deterrent effect.[138]

Pain versus Shame

If current efforts at specific deterrence are less than successful, should new approaches be attempted? In their two widely discussed works on specific deterrence, criminologists Graeme Newman and John Braithwaite take opposing approaches to reforming criminals.

Newman embraces traditional concepts of specific deterrence in his book, *Just and Painful*.[139] However, he adds a new wrinkle in his provocative suggestion that society should return to the use of corporal punishment. He advocates the use of electric shocks to punish offenders because they are over with quickly, they have no lasting effect, and they can easily be adjusted to fit the severity of a crime.

According to Newman, corporal punishment could be used as an alternative sanction to fill the gap between the severe punishment of prison and the nonpunishment of probation. Electric shocks can be controlled and calibrated to fit the crime. For violent crimes in which the victim was terrified and humiliated and for which a local community does not wish to incarcerate, a violent corporal punishment should be considered, such as whipping. In these cases, humiliation of the offender is

seen as justifiably deserved. In sum, Newman embraces specific deterrence strategies if they can be relatively inexpensive, immediate, individualized, and leave no lasting disabilities. His ideas received national attention in 1994 when a young American boy was flogged in Singapore after he plead guilty to vandalizing property. The Singapore incident produced a nationwide debate over the value of corporal punishment.

Reintegrative Shaming. Braithwaite's *Crime, Shame and Reintegration,* takes a radically different approach from Newman.[140] Braithwaite notes that countries, such as Japan, in which conviction for crimes brings an inordinate amount of shame, have extremely low crime rates. In Japan, prosecution of the criminal only proceeds when the normal process of public apology, compensation, and forgiveness by the victim breaks down.

Shame is a powerful tool of informal social control. Citizens in cultures in which crime is not shameful do not internalize an abhorrence for crime because when they are punished, they view themselves as merely "victims" of the justice system; their punishment comes at the hands of neutral strangers being paid to act. In contrast, shaming relies on the participation of victims.[141]

Braithwaite divides the concept of shame into two distinct types. The most common form of shaming typically involves **stigmatization.** This form of shaming involves an ongoing process of degradation in which the offender is branded as an evil person and cast out of society. Shaming can occur at a school disciplinary hearing or a criminal court trial. Bestowing stigma and degradations may have a general deterrent effect: it makes people afraid of social rejection and public humiliation. As a specific deterrent, stigma is doomed to failure: people who suffer humiliation at the hands of the justice system "reject their rejectors" by joining a deviant subculture of like-minded people who, collectively, resist social control.

Braithwaite argues that crime control can be better achieved through a policy of **reintegrative shaming.** Here, disapproval is extended to the offenders' evil deed, while at the same time they are cast as respected people who can be reaccepted by society. A critical element of reintegrative shaming occurs when the offenders begin to understand and recognize their wrongdoing and shame themselves. To be reintegrative, shaming must be brief and controlled and then followed by "ceremonies" of forgiveness, apology, and repentance.

To prevent crime, Braithwaite charges, society must encourage reintegrative shaming. For example, the women's movement can reduce domestic violence by mounting a crusade to shame spouse abusers.[142] In addition, an effort must be made to create pride in solving problems nonviolently, in caring for others, and in respecting the rights of women.

As you may recall, there is evidence that the fear of personal shame can have a general deterrent effect. It may also be applied to produce specific deterrence. Braithwaite and Stephen Mugford report on attempts to apply reintegrative shaming techniques with juvenile offenders in Australia. One program brings offenders together with victims (so that they can experience shame) and with close family members and peers (who help with reintegration).[143] Efforts like these can humanize a system of justice that today relies on repression and not forgiveness as the basis of specific deterrence.

Incapacitation

It stands to reason that if more criminals were sent to prison, the crime rate should go down. Because most people age out of crime, the duration of a criminal career is limited. Placing offenders behind bars during their "prime crime" years should lessen their lifetime opportunity to commit crime. The shorter the span of opportunity, the fewer the number of offenses they can commit over their life course; hence, crime is reduced.

Seems logical, but does it work? For the past 20 years, there has been significant growth in the number and percentage of the population held in prison and jails; today, more than 1.4 million Americans are incarcerated in prison and jails. Despite this massive effort to restrict criminal opportunity, there has been little reduction in the overall crime rate. Violence rates and incarceration trends have shared a similar trajectory: as the prison population swells, so too has the rate of violent crime![144]

Research on Incapacitation

Research on the benefits of incapacitation has not shown that increasing the number of people behind bars or the length of their stay can effectively reduce crime. A number of studies have set out to measure the precise effect of incarceration rates on crime rates, and the results have not supported a strict incarceration policy.[145] In an often-cited study, David Greenberg employed prison and FBI index crime data to estimate the effect of imprisonment on crime rates. He found that

if the prison population were cut in half, the crime rate would most likely go up only 4 percent; if prisons were entirely eliminated, crime might increase 8 percent.[146] Looking at this relationship from another perspective, if the average prison sentence were increased 50 percent, the crime rate might be reduced only 4 percent. Greenberg concludes: Prisons may be terribly unpleasant, psychologically destructive, and at times dangerous to life and limb, but there is no compelling evidence that imprisonment substantially increases (or decreases) the likelihood of criminal involvement.[147]

Isaac Ehrlich obtained similar results in a study of prison rates and incapacitation; he estimated that a 50-percent reduction in average time served would result in a 4.6-percent increase in property crime and a 2.5-percent increase in violent crime.[148] Lee Bowker found that an increase in incarceration rates may actually lead to an increase in crime rates.[149]

A few studies have found an inverse relationship between incarceration rates and crime rates. Shlomo Shinnar and Reuel Shinnar's research on incapacitation in New York led them to conclude that a policy of mandatory prison sentences of five years for violent crime and three for property offenses could reduce the reported crime rate by a factor of four or five.[150] Similarly, a study by Stephan Van Dine, Simon Dinitz, and John Conrad estimated that a mandatory prison sentence of five years for any felony offense could reduce the murder, rape, robbery, and serious assault rates by 17 percent. A similar sentence limited to repeat felons would reduce the rate of these crimes by 6 percent.[151]

With these few exceptions, existing research indicates that the crime control effects of a strict incapacitation policy are modest at best.[152]

The Logic of Incarceration

Why hasn't an incarceration strategy worked? There is little evidence that incapacitating criminals will deter them from future criminality and even more reason to believe that they may be more inclined to commit crimes upon release. As you may recall, prison has few specific deterrent effects: the more prior incarceration experiences inmates had, the more likely they were to recidivate (and return to prison) within 12 months of their release.[153] Whatever reason they had to commit crime before their incarceration, there is little to suggest that a prison sentence will reduce criminogenic forces. The criminal label precludes their entry into many legitimate occupations and solidifies their attachment to criminal careers.

The economics of crime suggest that if money can be made from criminal activity, there will always be someone to take the place of the incarcerated offender. New criminals will be recruited and trained, offsetting any benefit accrued by incarceration. Incarcerating established offenders may open new opportunities for competitors who were suppressed by the more experienced criminals. For example, the incarceration of organized crime members helped open drug markets to new gangs; the flow of narcotics into the country increased after organized crime leaders were imprisoned.

Incarceration may not work because the majority of criminal offenses are committed by teens and very young adult offenders who are unlikely to be sent to prison for a single felony conviction. Incarcerated criminals, aging behind bars, are already past the age where they are "at risk" to commit crime. A strict incarceration policy may result in people being kept in prison beyond the time they are a threat to society while a new cohort of high-rate adolescents are on the street.

It is also terribly expensive to maintain an incapacitation strategy. The prison system costs more than $10 billion annually. Even if incarceration could reduce the crime rate, the costs would be enormous. At a time of deficits and fiscal austerity, would U.S. taxpayers be willing to spend billions more on new prison construction and annual maintenance fees?

Selective Incapacitation: Three Strikes and You're Out

A more efficient incapacitation model is suggested by the "discovery" of the chronic career criminal. If in fact a relatively small number of people account for a relatively large percentage of the nation's crime rates, then an effort to incapacitate these few troublemakers might have a significant payoff. In an often-cited work, Peter Greenwood of the Rand Corporation suggests that a policy of **selective incapacitation** could be an effective crime-reduction strategy.[154] In his study of over 2,000 inmates serving time for theft offenses in California, Michigan, and Texas, he found that the selective incapacitation of chronic offenders could both reduce the rate of robbery offenses 15 percent and the inmate population by 5 percent.

According to Greenwood's model, chronic offenders can be distinguished on the basis of their offending patterns and life-style (for example, their employment record and history of substance abuse). Once identified, high-risk offenders would be eligible for sentencing enhancements that would substantially increase the time they serve in prison.

Another concept receiving widespread attention is the **"three strikes and you're out"** policy of giving people convicted of three violent offenses a mandatory life term without parole. Many states already employ habitual offender laws that provide long (or life) sentences for repeat offenders. Criminologist Marc Mauer argues that such strategies, though compelling, will not work because most "three-time losers" are at the verge of aging out of crime anyway; that current sentences for violent crimes are already severe; that an expanding prison population will drive up already high prison costs; that there would be racial disparity in sentencing; and that the police would be in danger because two-time offenders would violently resist a third arrest, knowing they face a life sentence.[155]

Policy Implications of Choice Theory

From the origins of classical theory to the development of modern rational choice views, the belief that criminals choose to commit crime has had an important influence on the relationship between law, punishment, and crime. When police patrol in well-marked cars, it is assumed that their presence will deter would-be criminals. When the harsh realities of prison life are portrayed in movies and TV shows, the lesson is not lost on potential criminals. Nowhere is the idea that the threat of punishment can control crime more evident than in the implementation of tough mandatory criminal sentences to control violent crime and drug trafficking.

Despite its questionable deterrent effect, the death penalty is also viewed as an effective means of restricting criminal choice: at the least, it ensures that convicted criminals never get the opportunity to kill again. Many observers are dismayed because people who are convicted of murder sometimes kill again when released on parole. One study of 52,000 incarcerated murderers found that 810 had been previously convicted of murder and had killed 821 people following their previous release from prison.[156] About 9 percent of all inmates on death row have had prior convictions for homicide; if they had been executed for their first offense, hundreds of people would be alive today.[157]

So while research on the core principles of choice theory and deterrence theories produces mixed results, there is little doubt that these models have had an important impact on crime-prevention strategies.

Just Dessert

The concept of criminal choice has also prompted the creation of justice policies referred to as **just dessert.** The just dessert position has been most clearly spelled out by criminologist Andrew Von Hirsch in his book *Doing Justice.*[158]

Von Hirsch suggests the concept of dessert as a theoretical model to guide justice policy.[159] Von Hirsch's views can be summarized in these three statements:

1. Those who violate others' rights deserve to be punished.
2. We should not deliberately add to human suffering; punishment makes those punished suffer.
3. However, punishment may prevent more misery than it inflicts; this conclusion reestablishes the need for dessert-based punishment.[160]

This utilitarian view is the key to the dessert approach: Punishment is needed to preserve the social equity disturbed by crime; nonetheless, the severity of the punishment should be commensurate with the seriousness of the crime.

Dessert theory is also concerned with the rights of the accused. It alleges that the rights of the person being punished should not be unduly sacrificed for the good of others (as with deterrence). The offender should not be treated as more (or less) **blameworthy** than is warranted by the character of his or her offense. For example, Von Hirsch asks the following question: If two crimes, A and B, are equally serious, but if severe penalties are shown to have a deterrent effect only with respect to A, would it be fair to punish the person who has committed crime A more harshly simply to deter others from committing the crime? Conversely, imposing a light sentence for a serious crime would be unfair, because it would treat the offender as being less blameworthy than he or she is. In sum, the just dessert model suggests that retribution justifies punishment because people deserve what they get for past deeds. Punishment based on deterrence or incapacitation is wrong because it involves an offender's future actions, which cannot accurately be predicted. Punishment should be the same for all people who commit the same crime. Criminal sentences based on individual needs or characteristics are inherently unfair since all people are equally blameworthy for their misdeeds.

The influence of Von Hirsch's views can be seen in sentencing models which give the same punishments to all people who commit the same type of crime.

≡ Summary

Choice theory assumes that criminals carefully choose whether to commit criminal acts. These theories are summarized in Table 5.3. However, people are influenced by their fear of the criminal penalties associated with being caught and convicted for law violations. The more severe, certain, and swift the punishment, the more likely it is to control crime. The choice approach is rooted in the classical criminology of Cesare Beccaria and Jeremy Bentham. These eighteenth-century social philosophers argued that punishment should be certain, swift, and severe enough to deter crime.

The growth of positivist criminology, which stressed external causes of crime and rehabilitation of known offenders, reduced the popularity of the classical approach in the twentieth century. However, in the late 1970s, the concept of criminal choice once again became an important perspective of criminologists. Today, choice theorists view crime as offense- and offender-specific. Research shows that offenders consider their targets carefully before deciding on a course of action. By implication, crime can be prevented or displaced by convincing potential criminals that the risks of violating the law exceed the benefits.

Deterrence theory holds that if criminals are indeed rational, an inverse relationship should exist between punishment and crime. However, a number of factors confound the relationship. For example, if people do not believe they will be caught, even harsh punishment may not deter crime. Deterrence theory has been criticized on the grounds that it wrongfully assumes that criminals make a rational choice before committing crimes, ignores the intricacies of the criminal justice system, and does not take into account the social and psychological factors that may influence criminality. Research designed to test the validity of the deterrence concept has not indicated that deterrent measures actually reduce the crime rate.

Specific deterrence theory holds that the crime rate can be reduced if known offenders are punished so severely that they never commit crimes again. There is little evidence that harsh punishments actually reduce the crime rate. Incapacitation theory maintains that if deterrence does not work, the best course of action is to incarcerate known offenders for long periods of time so that they lack criminal opportunity. Research efforts have not provided clear-cut proof that increasing the number of people in prison—and increasing prison sentences—will reduce crime rates.

TABLE 5.3 **Choice Theories**

Theory	Major Premise	Strengths
Choice Theories		
rational choice	Law-violating behavior is an event that occurs after offenders weigh information on their personal needs and the situational factors involved in the difficulty and risk of committing a crime.	Explains why high-risk youth do not constantly engage in delinquency acts. Relates theory to delinquency control policy. It is not limited by class or other social variables.
routine activities	Crime and delinquency is a function of the presence of motivated offenders, the availability of suitable targets, and the absence of capable guardians.	Can explain fluctuations in crime and delinquency rates. Shows how victim behavior influences criminal choice.
general deterrence	People will commit crime and delinquency if they perceive that the benefits outweigh the risks. Crime is a function of the severity, certainty, and speed of punishment.	Shows the relationship between crime and punishment. Suggests a real solution to crime.
specific deterrence	If punishment is severe enough, criminals will not repeat their illegal acts.	Provides a strategy to reduce crime.
incapacitation	Keeping known criminals out of circulation will reduce crime rates.	Recognizes the role opportunity plays in criminal behavior. Provides solution to chronic offending.

Choice theory has been influential in shaping public policy. The criminal law is designed to deter potential criminals and fairly punish those who have been caught engaging in illegal acts. Some courts have changed sentencing policies to adapt to classical principles, and the U.S. correctional system seems geared toward incapacitation and special deterrence. The renewed use of the death penalty is testimony to the importance of classical theory.

≡ KEY TERMS

classical theory
rational choice
choice theory
utilitarianism
reasoning criminal
offense- and offender-
  specific
suitable targets
capable guardians
motivated criminals
Keating Five
situational inducements
seductions of crime

situational crime
  prevention
defensible space
crime displacement
extinction
diffusion of benefits
discouragement
crackdowns
brutalization effect
perceptual deterrence
informal sanctions
stigmatization
reintegrative shaming

selective incapacitation
"three strikes and you're out"

just dessert
blameworthy

≡ NOTES

1. Francis Edward Devine, "Cesare Beccaria and the Theoretical Foundations of Modern Penal Jurisprudence," *New England Journal on Prison Law* 7 (1982): 8–21.
2. Ibid.
3. Ibid.
4. Graeme Newman and Pietro Marongiu, "Penological Reform and the Myth of Beccaria," *Criminology* 28 (1990): 325–46.
5. Bob Roshier, *Controlling Crime* (Chicago: Lyceum Books, 1989), p. 10.
6. Jeremy Bentham, *A Fragment on Government and an Introduction to the Principle of Morals and Legislation*, ed. Wilfred Harrison (Oxford: Basil Blackwell, 1967).
7. Ibid., p. xi.
8. Robert Martinson, "What Works?—Questions and Answers about Prison Reform," *Public Interest* 35 (1974): 22–54.
9. Charles Murray and Louis Cox, *Beyond Probation* (Beverly Hills: Sage, 1979).
10. Ronald Bayer, "Crime, Punishment and the Decline of

Liberal Optimism," *Crime and Delinquency* 27 (1981): 190.

11. James Q. Wilson, *Thinking about Crime,* rev. ed. (New York: Vintage Books, 1983), p. 260.

12. Ibid. p. 128.

13. See, generally, Derek Cornish and Ronald Clarke, eds. *The Reasoning Criminal: Rational Choice Perspectives on Offending* (New York: Springer Verlag, 1986); Philip Cook, "The Demand and Supply of Criminal Opportunities," in *Crime and Justice,* vol. 7, ed. Michael Tonry and Norval Morris (Chicago: University of Chicago Press, 1986), pp. 1–28; Ronald Clarke and Derek Cornish, "Modeling Offender's Decisions: A Framework for Research and Policy," in *Crime and Justice,* vol. 6, ed. Michael Tonry and Norval Morris (Chicago: University of Chicago Press, 1985), pp. 147–87; Morgan Reynolds, *Crime by Choice: An Economic Analysis* (Dallas: Fisher Institute, 1985).

14. George Rengert and John Wasilchick, *Suburban Burglary: A Time and Place for Everything* (Springfield, Ill.: Charles Thomas, 1985).

15. John McIver, "Criminal Mobility: A Review of Empirical Studies," in *Crime Spillover,* ed. Simon Hakim and George Rengert (Beverly Hills: Sage, 1981), pp. 110–21. Carol Kohfeld and John Sprague, "Demography, Police Behavior, and Deterrence," *Criminology* 28 (1990): 111–36.

16. Neal Shover, *Aging Criminals* (Beverly Hills, Sage, 1985).

17. Ronald Akers, "Rational Choice, Deterrence and Social Learning Theory in Criminology: The Path Not Taken," *Journal of Criminal Law and Criminology* 81 (1990): 653–76.

18. Derek Cornish and Ronald Clarke, "Understanding Crime Displacement: An Application of Rational Choice Theory," *Criminology* 25 (1987): 933–47.

19. Lloyd Phillips and Harold Votey, "The Influence of Police Interventions and Alternative Income Sources on the Dynamic Process of Choosing Crime as a Career," *Journal of Quantitative Criminology* 3 (1987): 251–74.

20. Ibid.

21. Michael Gottfredson and Travis Hirschi, *A General Theory of Crime* (Stanford, Calif.: Stanford University Press, 1990).

22. Paul Cromwell, James Olson, and D'Aunn Wester Avery, *Breaking and Entering, An Ethnographic Analysis of Burglary* (Newbury Park, Calif.: Sage, 1989).

23. Andrew Buck, Simon Hakim, and George Rengert, "Burglar Alarms and the Choice Behavior of Burglars: A Suburban Phenomenon," *Journal of Criminal Justice* 21 (1993): 497–507.

24. Ralph Taylor and Stephen Gottfredson, "Environmental Design, Crime, and Prevention: An Examination of Community Dynamics," in *Communities and Crime,* ed. Albert Reiss and Michael Tonry (Chicago: University of Chicago Press, 1986), pp. 387–416.

25. Michael Costanzo, William Halperin, and Nathan Gale, "Criminal Mobility and the Directional Component in Journeys to Crime," in *Metropolitan Crime Patterns,* ed.

Robert Figlio, Simon Hakim, and George Rengert (Monsey, N.Y.: Criminal Justice Press, 1986), pp. 73–95.

26. Garland White, "Neighborhood Permeability and Burglary Rates," *Justice Quarterly* 7 (1990): 57–67.

27. Ibid., p. 65.

28. James Massey, Marvin Krohn, and Lisa Bonati, "Property Crime and the Routine Activities of Individuals," *Journal of Research in Crime and Delinquency* 26 (1989): 378–400; note, however, that the findings here generally disagree with the routine activities theory.

29. Kenneth Tunnell, *Choosing Crime* (Chicago: Nelson-Hall, 1992), p. 105.

30. Robert Sampson and Jacqueline Cohen, "Deterrent Effects of the Police on Crime: A Replication and Theoretical Extension," *Law and Society Review* 22 (1988): 163–88.

31. Marcus Felson et al. "Preventing Crime at Newark Subway Stations," *Security Journal* 1 (1990): 137–40.

32. Simha Landau and Daniel Fridman, "The Seasonality of Violent Crime: The Case of Robbery and Homicide in Israel," *Journal of Research in Crime and Delinquency* 30 (1993): 163–91.

33. Tunnell, *Choosing Crime,* p. 67.

34. Angela Browne and Kirk Williams, "Exploring the Effect of Resource Availability and the Likelihood of Female-Perpetrated Homicides," *Law and Society Review* 23 (1989): 89–93.

35. Mark Warr, "Parents, Peers, and Delinquency," *Social Forces* 72 (1993): 247–64.

36. John Hagan, "Destiny and Drift: Subcultural Preferences, Status Attainments, and the Risks and Rewards of Youth," *American Sociological Review* 56 (1991): 567–82.

37. Associated Press, "Thrift Hearings Resume Today in Senate," *Boston Globe,* 2 January 1991, p. 10.

38. Ronald Clarke and Patricia Harris, "Auto Theft and Its Prevention," in Michael Tonry and Norval Morris, eds.: *Crime and Justice: An Annual Edition.* (Chicago: University of Chicago Press, 1992), pp. 1–54, at 20–21.

39. George Rengert, "Spatial Justice and Criminal Victimization," *Justice Quarterly* 6 (1989): 543–64.

40. Michael Rand, *Crime and the Nation's Households, 1989* (Washington, D.C.: Bureau of Justice Statistics, 1990), p. 4.

41. Cromwell, Olson, and Avery, *Breaking and Entering,* p. 24.

42. Ibid., pp. 30–32.

43. John Gibbs and Peggy Shelly, "Life in the Fast Lane: A Retrospective View by Commercial Thieves," *Journal of Research in Crime and Delinquency* 19 (1982): 229–30.

44. George Rengert and John Wasilchick, *Space, Time and Crime: Ethnographic Insights into Residential Burglary* (Washington, D.C.: National Institute of Justice, 1989); see also idem, *Suburban Burglary.*

45. Cromwell, Olson, and Avery, *Breaking and Entering.*

46. James Wright and Peter Rossi, *Armed and Considered Dangerous: A Survey of Felons and Their Firearms* (Hawthorne, N.Y.: Aldine De Guyer, 1983), pp. 141–59.

47. Richard Felson and Marvin Krohn, "Motives for Rape,"

Journal of Research in Crime and Delinquency 27 (1990): 222–42.

48. Eric Hickey, *Serial Murderers and Their Victims* (Pacific Grove, Calif.: Brooks/Cole, 1991), p. 84.

49. Christopher Birkbeck and Gary LaFree, "The Situational Analysis of Crime and Deviance," *American Review of Sociology* 19 (1993): 113–37; Karen Heimer and Ross Matsueda, "Role-Taking, Role Commitment, and Delinquency: A Theory of Differential Social Control," *American Sociological Review* (in press, 1994).

50. Jack Katz, *Seductions of Crime* (New York: Basic Books, 1988).

51. Oscar Newman, *Defensible Space: Crime Prevention through Urban Design* (New York: Macmillan, 1973).

52. C. Ray Jeffery, *Crime Prevention through Environmental Design* (Beverly Hills, Sage, 1971).

53. See also Pochara Theerathorn, "Architectural Style, Aesthetic Landscaping, Home Value, and Crime Prevention," *International Journal of Comparative and Applied Criminal Justice* 12 (1988): 269–77.

54. Marcus Felson, "Routine Activities and Crime Prevention, in National Council for Crime Prevention, *Studies on Crime and Crime Prevention, Annual Review,* vol. 1 (Stockholm: Scandinavian University Press, 1992), pp. 30–34.

55. Barry Webb, "Steering Column Locks and Motor Vehicle Theft: Evaluations for Three Countries," in *Crime Prevention Studies,* ed. Ronald Clarke (Monsey, N.Y.: Criminal Justice Press, 1994), pp. 71–89.

56. Ronald Clark, "Deterring Obscene Phone Callers: The New Jersey Experience," *Situational Crime Prevention,* ed. Ronald Clark (Albany, N.Y.: Harrow and Heston, 1992) pp. 124–32.

57. Barbara Morse and Delbert Elliott, "Effects of Ignition Interlock Devices on DUI Recidivism: Findings from a Longitudinal Study in Hamilton County, Ohio," *Crime and Delinquency* 38 (1992): 131–57.

58. Nancy LaVigne, "Gasoline Drive-Offs: Designing a Less Convenient Environment," in *Crime Prevention Studies* Vol. 2, ed. Ronald Clarke (New York: Criminal Justice Press, 1994) pp. 91–114.

59. Robert Barr and Ken Pease, "Crime Placement, Displacement, and Deflection," in *Crime and Justice, A Review of Research,* vol. 12, ed. Michael Tonry and Norval Morris (Chicago: University of Chicago Press, 1990), pp. 277–319.

60. Clarke, *Situational Crime Prevention,* p. 27.

61. Ibid., p. 35.

62. Ronald Clarke and David Weisburd, "Diffusion of Crime Control Benefits: Observations of the Reverse of Displacement," in *Crime Prevention Studies,* vol. 2, ed. Ronald Clarke, (New York: Criminal Justice Press, in press).

63. See, generally, Jack Gibbs, "Crime Punishment and Deterrence," *Social Science Quarterly* 48 (1968): 515–30; Solomon Kobrin, E. W. Hansen, S. G. Lubeck, and R. Yeaman, *The Deterrent Effectiveness of Criminal Justice Sanction Strategies: Summary Report* (Washington, D.C.: U.S. Government Printing Office, 1972).

64. Charles Tittle and Alan Rowe, "Certainty of Arrest and Crime Rates: A Further Test of the Deterrence Hypothesis," *Social Forces* 52 (1974): 455–62.

65. Jiang Wu and Allen Liska "The Certainty of Punishment: A Reference Group Effect and Its Functional Form," *Criminology* 31 (1993): 447–64.

66. Robert Bursik, Harold Grasmick, and Mitchell Chamlin, "The Effect of Longitudinal Arrest Patterns on the Development of Robbery Trends at the Neighborhood Level," *Criminology* 28 (1990): 431–50; Theodore Chiricos and Gordon Waldo, "Punishment and Crime: An Examination of Some Empirical Evidence," *Social Problems* 18 (1970): 200–17.

67. Edwin Zedlewski, "Deterrence Findings and Data Sources: A Comparison of the Uniform Crime Rates and the National Crime Surveys," *Journal of Research in Crime and Delinquency* 20 (1983): 262–76.

68. Jack Gibbs and Glenn Firebaugh, "The Artifact Issue in Deterrence Research," *Criminology* 28 (1990): 347–67.

69. Alfred Blumstein, Jacqueline Cohen, and Daniel Nagin, *Deterrence and Incapacitation: Estimating the Effects of Criminal Sanctions on Crime Rates* (Washington, D.C.: National Academy of Science, 1978), pp. 3–4.

70. See, generally, Raymond Paternoster, "Absolute and Restrictive Deterrence in a Panel of Youth: Explaining the Onset, Persistence/Desistance, and Frequency of Delinquent Offending," *Social Problems* 36 (1989): 289–307; idem, "The Deterrent Effect of Perceived Severity of Punishment: A Review of the Evidence and Issues," *Justice Quarterly* 42 (1987): 173–217.

71. H. Laurence Ross, "Implications of Drinking-and-Driving Law Studies for Deterrence Research," in *Critique and Explanation, Essays in Honor of Gwynne Nettler,* ed. Timothy Hartnagel and Robert Silverman (New Brunswick, N.J.: Transaction Books, 1986), pp. 159–71.

72. H. Laurence Ross, Richard McCleary, and Gary LaFree, "Can Mandatory Jail Laws Deter Drunk Driving? The Arizona Case," *Journal of Criminal Law and Criminology* 81 (1990): 156–67.

73. Gary Green, "General Deterrence and Television Cable Crime: A Field Experiment in Social Crime," *Criminology* 23 (1986): 629–45.

74. George Kelling, Tony Pate, Duane Dieckman, and Charles Brown, *The Kansas City Preventive Patrol Experiment: A Summary Report* (Washington, D.C.: Police Foundation, 1974).

75. Lawrence Sherman, "Police Crackdowns," *NIJ Reports,* March/April 1990, pp. 2–6 at 2.

76. Robert Dann, "The Deterrent Effect of Capital Punishment," *Friends Social Service Series* 29, 1935.

77. William Bowers and Glenn Pierce, "Deterrence or Brutalization: What Is the Effect of Executions?" *Crime and Delinquency* 26 (1980): 453–84.

78. John Cochran, Mitchell Chamlin, and Mark Seth, "Deterrence or Brutalization? An Impact Assessment of Oklahoma's Return to Capital Punishment," *Criminology* 32 (1994): 107–34.

79. David Phillips, "The Deterrent Effect of Capital Punishment," *American Journal of Sociology* 86 (1980): 139–48; Hans Zeisel, "A Comment on the 'Deterrent Effect of Capital Punishment' by Phillips," *American Journal of Sociology* 88 (1982): 167–69; see also Sam McFarland, "Is Capital Punishment a Short-Term Deterrent to Homicide? A Study of the Effects of Four Recent American Executions," *Journal of Criminal Law and Criminology* 74 (1984): 1014–32.

80. Steven Stack, "Publicized Executions and Homicide, 1950–1980," *American Sociological Review* 52 (1987): 532–40; for a study challenging Stack's methods, see William Bailey and Ruth Peterson, "Murder and Capital Punishment: A Monthly Time-Series Analysis of Execution Publicity," *American Sociological Review* 54 (1989): 722–43.

81. Karl Schuessler, "The Deterrent Influence of the Death Penalty," *Annals of the Academy of Political and Social Sciences* 284 (1952): 54–62.

82. Thorsten Sellin, *The Death Penalty* (Philadelphia: American Law Institute, 1959); Walter Reckless, "Use of the Death Penalty," *Crime and Delinquency* 15 (1969): 43–51.

83. Richard Lempert, "The Effect of Executions on Homicides: A New Look in an Old Light," *Crime and Delinquency* 29 (1983): 88–115.

84. Derral Cheatwood, "Capital Punishment and the Deterrence of Violent Crime in Comparable Counties," *Criminal Justice Review* 18 (1993): 165–81.

85. Dane Archer, Rosemary Gartner, and Marc Beittel, "Homicide and the Death Penalty: A Cross-National Test of a Deterrence Hypothesis," *Journal of Criminal Law and Criminology* 74 (1983): 991–1014.

86. Isaac Ehrlich, "The Deterrent Effect on Capital Punishment: A Question of Life and Death," *American Economic Review* 65 (1975): 397–417.

87. James Fox and Michael Radelet, "Persistent Flaws in Econometric Studies of the Deterrent Effect of the Death Penalty," *Loyola of Los Angeles Law Review* 23 (1987): 29–44; William B. Bowers and Glenn Pierce, "The Illusion of Deterrence in Isaac Ehrlich's Research on Capital Punishment," *Yale Law Journal* 85 (1975): 187–208.

88. William Bailey, "Disaggregation in Deterrence and Death Penalty Research: The Case of Murder in Chicago," *Journal of Criminal Law and Criminology* 74 (1986): 827–59.

89. Steven Messner and Kenneth Tardiff, "Economic Inequality and Level of Homicide: An Analysis of Urban Neighborhoods," *Criminology* 24 (1986): 297–317.

90. Donald Green, "Past Behavior as a Measure of Actual Future Behavior: An Unresolved Issue in Perceptual Deterrence Research," *Journal of Criminal Law and Criminology* 80 (1989): 781–804.

91. Paternoster, "The Deterrent Effect of the Perceived Severity of Punishment: A Review of the Evidence and Issues."

92. Harold Grasmick and Robert Bursik, "Conscience, Significant Others, and Rational Choice: Extending the Deterrence Model," *Law and Society Review* 24 (1990): 837–61.

93. Steven Klepper and Daniel Nagin, "The Deterrent Effect of Perceived Certainty and Severity of Punishment Revisited," *Criminology* 27 (1989): 721–46.

94. Irving Piliavin, Rosemary Gartner, Craig Thornton, and Ross Matsueda, "Crime, Deterrence, and Rational Choice," *American Sociological Review* 51 (1986): 101–19.

95. Julie Horney and Ineke Haen Marshall, "Risk Perceptions among Serious Offenders: The Role of Crime and Punishment," *Criminology* 30 (1992): 575–94.

96. Scott Decker, Richard Wright, and Robert Logie, "Perceptual Deterrence among Active Residential Burglars: A Research Note," *Criminology* 31 (1993): 135–47.

97. Harold Grasnick and George Bryjak, "The Deterrent Effect of Perceived Severity of Punishment," *Social Forces* 59 (1980): 471–91.

98. Donna Bishop, "Deterrence: A Panel Analysis," *Justice Quarterly* 1 (1984): 311–28.

99. Raymond Paternoster, "Decisions to Participate in and Desist from Four Types of Common Delinquency: Deterrence and the Rational Choice Perspective," *Law and Society Review* 23 (1989): 7–29; idem, "Examining Three-Wave Deterrence Models: A Question of Temporal Order and Specification," *Journal of Criminal Law and Criminology* 79 (1988): 135–63; Raymond Paternoster, Linda Saltzman, Gordon Waldo, and Theodore Chiricos, "Estimating Perceptual Stability and Deterrent Effects: The Role of Perceived Legal Punishment in the Inhibition of Criminal Involvement," *Journal of Criminal Law and Criminology* 74 (1983): 270–97; M. William Minor and Joseph Harry, "Deterrent and Experiential Effects in Perceptual Deterrence Research: A Replication and Extension," *Journal of Research in Crime and Delinquency* 19 (1982): 190–203; Lonn Lanza-Kaduce, "Perceptual Deterrence and Drinking and Driving among College Students," *Criminology* 26 (1988): 321–41.

100. Kirk Williams and Richard Hawkins, "Perceptual Research on General Deterrence: A Critical Overview," *Law and Society Review* 20 (1986): 545–72.

101. Eleni Apospori, Geoffrey Alpert, and Raymond Paternoster, "The Effect of Involvement with the Criminal Justice System: A Neglected Dimension of the Relationship Between Experience and Perceptions," *Justice Quarterly* 9 (1992): 379–92.

102. Ibid., p. 390.

103. Eleni Apospori and Geoffrey Alpert, "Research Note: The Role of Differential Experience with the Criminal Justice System in Changes in Perceptions of Severity of Legal

Sanctions over Time," *Crime and Delinquency* 39 (1993): 184–94.

104. Harold Grasmick, Robert Bursik, and Karyl Kinsey, "Shame and Embarrassment as Deterrents to Noncompliance with the Law: The Case of an Anti-Littering Campaign" (Paper presented at the annual meeting of the American Society of Criminology, Baltimore, November 1990), p. 3.

105. Charles Tittle, *Sanctions and Social Deviance* (New York: Praeger, 1980).

106. For an opposite view, see Steven Burkett and David Ward, "A Note on Perceptual Deterrence, Religiously Based Moral Condemnation, and Social Control," *Criminology* 31 (1993): 119–34.

107. Ibid.

108. John Snortum, "Drinking-Driving Compliance in Great Britain: The Role of Law as a 'Threat' and as a 'Moral Eye-Opener,' " *Journal of Criminal Justice* 18 (1990): 479–99.

109. Green, "Past Behavior as a Measure of Actual Future Behavior," p. 803; Matthew Silberman, "Toward a Theory of Criminal Deterrence," *American Sociological Review* 41 (1976): 442–61; Linda Anderson, Theodore Chiricos, and Gordon Waldo, "Formal and Informal Sanctions: A Comparison of Deterrent Effects," *Social Problems* 25 (1977): 103–14. See also Maynard Erickson and Jack Gibbs, "Objective and Perceptual Properties of Legal Punishment and Deterrence Doctrine," *Social Problems* 25 (1978): 253–64.

110. Grasmick and Bursik, "Conscience, Significant Others, and Rational Choices," p. 854.

111. Grasmick, Bursik, and Kinsey, "Shame and Embarrassment as Deterrents to Noncompliance with the Law"; Harold Grasmick, Robert Bursik, and Bruce Arneklev, "Reduction in Drunk Driving as a Response to Increased Threats of Shame, Embarrassment, and Legal Sanctions," *Criminology* 31 (1993): 41–69.

112. Harold Grasmick, Brenda Sims Blackwell, and Robert Bursik, "Changes in the Sex Patterning of Perceived Threats of Sanctions," *Law and Society Review* 27 (1993): 679–99.

113. Daniel Nagin and Raymond Paternoster, "Enduring Individual Differences and Rational Choice Theories of Crime," *Law and Society Review* 27 (1993): 467–85.

114. Kirk Williams and Richard Hawkins, "The Meaning of Arrest for Wife Assault," *Criminology* 27 (1989): 163–81.

115. Thomas Peete, Trudie Milner, and Michael Welch, "Levels of Social Integration in Group Contexts and the Effects of Informal Sanction Threat on Deviance," *Criminology* 32 (1994): 85–105.

116. Ronet Bachman, Raymond Paternoster, and Sally Ward, "The Rationality of Sexual Offending: Testing a Deterrence/Rational Choice Conception of Sexual Assault," *Law and Society Review* 26 (1992): 343–58.

117. Ernest Van Den Haag, "The Criminal Law as a Threat System," *Journal of Criminal Law and Criminology* 73 (1982): 709–85.

118. Joyce Ann O'Neil, Eric Wish, and Christy Visher, *Drugs and Crime 1989* (Washington, D.C.: National Institute of Justice, 1990).

119. Ken Auletta, *The Under Class* (New York: Random House, 1982).

120. Paternoster, "Decisions to Participate in and Desist from Four Types of Common Delinquency."

121. James Williams and Daniel Rodeheaver, "Processing of Criminal Homicide Cases in a Large Southern City," *Sociology and Social Research* 75 (1991): 80–88.

122. James Q. Wilson, *Thinking about Crime* (New York: Basic Books, 1975).

123. James Q. Wilson and Richard Herrnstein, *Crime and Human Nature* (New York: Simon and Schuster, 1985), p. 494.

124. Lawrence Greenfeld, *Examining Recidivism* (Washington, D.C.: U.S. Government Printing Office, 1985).

125. Allen Beck and Bernard Shipley, *Recidivism of Prisoners Released in 1983* (Washington, D.C.: Bureau of Justice Statistics, 1989).

126. Charles Murray and Louis Cox, *Beyond Probation* (Beverly Hills: Sage, 1979).

127. Perry Shapiro and Harold Votey, "Deterrence and Subjective Probabilities of Arrest: Modeling Individual Decisions to Drink and Drive in Sweden," *Law and Society Review* 18 (1984): 111–49.

128. Douglas Smith and Patrick Gartin, "Specifying Specific Deterrence: The Influence of Arrest on Future Criminal Activity," *American Sociological Review* 54 (1989): 94–105.

129. Lawrence Sherman and Richard Berk, "The Specific Deterrent Effects of Arrest for Domestic Assault," *American Sociological Review* 49 (1984): 261–72; see also Richard Berk and Phyllis J. Newman, "Does Arrest Really Deter Wife Battery? An Effort to Replicate the Findings of the Minneapolis Spouse Abuse Experiment," *American Sociological Review* 50 (1985): 253–62.

130. See, generally, Franklyn Dunford, "The Measurement of Recidivism in Cases of Spouse Assault," *Journal of Criminal Law and Criminology* 83 (1992): 120–36.

131. J. David Hirschel, Ira Hutchison, and Charles Dean, "The Failure of Arrest to Deter Spouse Abuse," *Journal of Research in Crime and Delinquency* 29 (1992): 7–33; J. David Hirschel and Ira Hutchinson, "Female Spouse Abuse and the Police Response: The Charlotte, North Carolina Experiment," *Journal of Criminal Law and Criminology* 83 (1992): 73–119; David Huizinga and Delbert Elliott, "The Role of Arrest in Domestic Assault: The Omaha Experiment," *Criminology* 28 (1990): 183–206; David Hirschel, Ira Hutchinson, Charles Dean, Joseph Kelley, and Carolyn Pesackis, *Charlotte Spouse Abuse Replication Project: Final Report* (Washington, D.C.: National Institute of Justice, 1990).

132. Richard Berk, Gordon Smyth, and Lawrence Sherman, "When Random Assignment Fails: Some Lessons from the Minneapolis Spouse Abuse Experiment," *Journal of Quantitative Criminology* 4 (1989): 209–23.

133. Lawrence Sherman, Janell Schmidt, Dennis Rogan, Patrick

Gartin, Ellen Cohn, Dean Collins, and Anthony Bacich, "From Initial Deterrence to Long-Term Escalation: Short-Custody Arrest for Poverty Ghetto Domestic Violence," *Criminology* 29 (1991): 821–50.

134. Anthony Pate and Edwin Hamilton, "Formal and Informal Deterrents to Domestic Violence: The Dade County Spouse Assault Experiment," *American Sociological Review* 57 (1992): 691–97.

135. Richard Berk, Alec Campbell, Ruth Klap, and Bruce Western, "The Deterrent Effect of Arrest in Incidents of Domestic Violence: A Bayesian Analysis of Four Field Experiments," *American Sociological Review* 57 (1992): 698–708.

136. Jeffrey Fagan, "Cessation of Family Violence: Deterrence and Dissuasion," in *Family Violence,* ed. Lloyd Ohlin and Michael Tonry (Chicago: University of Chicago Press, 1989), pp. 377–426.

137. David Ford with Mary Jean Regoli, *The Indianapolis Domestic Violence Prosecution Experiment* (Washington, D.C.: National Institute of Justice, 1993).

138. David Ford and Mary Jean Regoli, "The Criminal Prosecution of Wife Assaulters," in *Legal Responses to Wife Assault*, ed. N. Zoe Hilton (Newbury Park, Calif.: Sage, 1993), pp. 127–64.

139. Graeme Newman, *Just and Painful* (New York: Macmillan, 1983), pp. 139–43.

140. John Braithwaite, *Crime, Shame and Reintegration* (Melbourne, Australia: Cambridge University Press, 1989).

141. Ibid., p. 81.

142. For more on this approach, see Jane Mugford and Stephen Mugford, "Shame and Reintegration in the Punishment and Deterrence of Spouse Assault" (Paper presented at the annual meeting of the American Society of Criminology, San Francisco, 1991).

143. John Braithwaite and Stephen Mugford, "Conditions of Successful Reintegration Ceremonies: Dealing with Juvenile Offenders," *British Journal of Criminology*, in press.

144. Darrell Steffensmeier and Miles Harer, "Bulging Prison, an Aging U.S. Population, and the Nation's Crime Rate," *Federal Probation* 57 (1993): 3–10.

145. Steven S. Clarke, "Getting 'Em Out of Circulation: Does Incarceration of Juvenile Offenders Reduce Crime?" *Journal of Criminal Law and Criminology* 65 (1974): 528–35.

146. David Greenberg, "The Incapacitative Effects of Imprisonment: Some Estimates," *Law and Society Review* 9 (1975): 541–80.

147. Ibid., p. 558.

148. Isaac Ehrlich, "Participation in Illegitimate Activities: An Economic Analysis," *Journal of Political Economy* 81 (1973): 521–67.

149. Lee Bowker, "Crime and the Use of Prisons in the United States: A Time Series Analysis," *Crime and Delinquency* 27 (1981): 206–12.

150. Reuel Shinnar and Shlomo Shinnar, "The Effects of the Criminal Justice System on the Control of Crime: A Quantitative Approach," *Law and Society Review* 9 (1975): 581–611.

151. Stephan Van Dine, Simon Dinitz, and John Conrad, *Restraining the Wicked: The Dangerous Offender Project* (Lexington, Mass.: Lexington Books, 1979).

152. For review of this issue, see James Austin and John Irwin, *Does Imprisonment Reduce Crime? A Critique of "Voodoo" Criminology* (San Francisco: National Council of Crime and Delinquency, 1993).

153. John Wallerstedt, *Returning to Prison,* Bureau of Justice Statistics Special Report (Washington, D.C.: U.S. Department of Justice, 1984).

154. Peter Greenwood, *Selective Incapacitation* (Santa Monica, Calif.: Rand Corp., 1982).

155. Marc Mauer, Testimony before the U.S. Congress, House Judiciary Committee on "Three Strikes and You're Out," 1 March, 1994.

156. Stephen Markman and Paul Cassell, "Protecting the Innocent: A Response to the Bedeau-Radelet Study," *Stanford Law Review* 41(1988): 121–70 at 153.

157. Lawrence Greenfeld and James Stephan, *Capital Punishment,* 1992 (Washington, D.C.: Bureau of Justice Statistics, 1993), p. 8.

158. Andrew Von Hirsch, *Doing Justice* (New York: Hill and Wang, 1976).

159. Ibid., pp. 15–16.

160. Ibid.

Chapter

6

Biosocial and Psychological Theories of Crime Causation

☰ Introduction

A generation of Americans has grown up on films and TV shows that portray violent criminals as mentally deranged and physically abnormal. Beginning with Alfred Hitchcock's film *Psycho,* producers have made millions, depicting the ghoulish acts of crazed baby-sitters *(Hand That Rocks the Cradle),* deranged room-mates *(Single, White Female),* psychotic tenants *(Pacific Heights),* demented secretaries *(The Temp),* unhinged police *(Maniac Cop),* irrational literary fans *(Misery),* abnormal girlfriends *(Fatal Attraction),* and unstable husbands *(Sleeping with the Enemy);* even child star McCauley Caulkin has played an abnormal, violent child *(The Good Son).* Is it any wonder that we respond to a particularly horrible crime by saying of the perpetrator, "That guy must be crazy" or "She is a monster!"?

The view that criminals are somehow physically and/or mentally different is not restricted to the moviegoing public. Since the nineteenth century, criminologists have suggested that physical and psychological traits may influence behavior. It is believed that some personal trait must separate the deviant members of society from the nondeviant. These personal differences explain why, when faced with the same life situations, one person commits crime and becomes a chronic offender, while another attends school, church, and neighborhood functions and obeys the laws of society. All people may be aware of and even fear the sanctioning power of the law, but some are unable to control their urges and passions. These people commit crimes of violence and destruction.

As a rule, no single biological or psychological concept is thought to adequately explain all criminality. Rather, as common sense would suggest, each offender is considered unique, physically and mentally; consequently, there must be different explanations for each person's behavior. Some may have learned to be violent by being personally exposed to violence during their

Violent themes abound in movies such as *Friday the Thirteenth* "starring" the slasher in the hockey mask, Jason Voorhees. Do such films contribute to the public's view that criminals are mentally or physically abnormal?

adolescence. Others may be suffering from nervous system (**neurological**) problems, while still others may have a blood chemistry disorder that heightens their antisocial activity.

Criminologists who focus on the individual see many explanations for crime, because, in fact, there are many differences among criminal offenders. Biological and psychological theorists are not overly concerned with legal definitions of crime. Their studies focus on basic human behavior and drives—aggression, violence, and impulsivity. Most recognize that human traits alone do not produce criminality and that crime-producing interactions involve both personal traits—such as intelligence, personality, and chemical and genetic makeup—and environmental factors—such as family life, educational attainment, and neighborhood conditions. While some people may have a predisposition toward aggression, environmental stimuli are needed to either trigger antisocial acts or help contain them; this is referred to as **biosocial theory.** Physical or mental traits are, therefore, but one part of a large pool of environmental, social, and personal factors that account for criminality.

The biosocial and psychological views of crime take on greater importance in light of recent findings about chronic recidivism and the development of criminal careers. If only a small percentage of all offenders go on to become persistent repeaters, then it is possible that what sets them apart from the criminal population is an abnormal biochemical makeup, brain structure, or genetic makeup.[1] Even if criminals do "choose crime," the fact that some repeatedly make that choice could well be linked to their physical and mental makeup. This chapter then will review the various components of biosocial and psychological theories of crime.

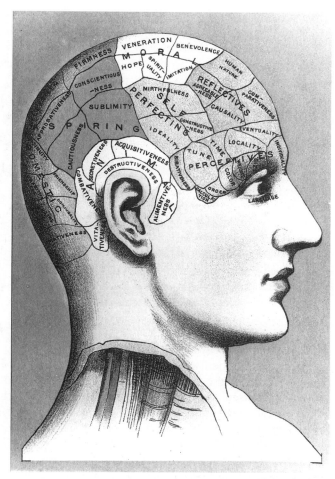

Before positivists applied the scientific method to the study of human behavior, phrenologists argued that behavior and thought were controlled by different sectors of the skull. People's behavior was believed to correspond to the size, shape, and contours of their heads.

≡ Foundations of Biological Theory

As you may recall, biological explanations of criminal behavior first became popular during the middle part of the nineteenth century with the introduction of positivism—the use of the scientific method and empirical analysis to study behavior. Cesare Lombroso's work on the "born criminal" was a direct offshoot of the application of the scientific method to the study of crime. His identification of primitive **atavistic anomalies** was based on what he believed was sound empirical research using established scientific methods.

Lombroso was not alone in the early development of biological theory. A contemporary of Lombroso,

Raffaele Garofalo (1852–1934) shared his belief that certain physical characteristics indicate a criminal nature. For example, Garofalo stated that among criminals, "a lower degree of sensibility to physical pain seems to be demonstrated by the readiness with which prisoners submit to the operation of tattooing."[2] Enrico Ferri (1856–1929), another student of Lombroso, believed that a number of biological, social, and organic factors caused delinquency and crime.[3] Ferri added a social dimension to Lombroso's work and was a pioneer in the view that criminals should not be held personally or morally responsible for their actions because forces outside their control caused criminality.

Advocates of the inheritance school traced the activities of several generations of families believed to have an especially large number of criminal members. The most famous of these studies involved the Jukes and the Kallikaks. Richard Dugdale's *The Jukes: A Study in Crime, Pauperism, Disease, and Heredity* (1875) and Arthur Estabrook's later work *The Jukes in 1915* traced the history of the Jukes, a family responsible for a disproportionate amount of crime.[4]

A later attempt at criminal anthropology, the body-build or **somatotype** school developed by William Sheldon, held that criminals manifest distinct physiques that make them susceptible to particular types of delinquent behavior. *Mesomorphs* have well-developed muscles and an athletic appearance. They are active, aggressive, sometimes violent, and the most likely to become criminals. *Endomorphs* have heavy builds and are slow-moving. They are known for lethargic behavior. *Ectomorphs* are tall and thin and less social and more intellectual than the other types.[5]

The work of Lombroso and his contemporaries is regarded today as a historical curiosity, not scientific fact. Their research methodology has been discredited. They did not use control groups from the general population to compare results. Many of the traits they assumed to be inherited are not really genetically determined. Many of the biological features they identified could be caused by deprivation in surroundings and diet. Even if most criminals shared some biological traits, they might be products not of heredity but of some environmental condition, such as poor nutrition or health care. It is equally likely that only criminals who suffer from biological abnormality are caught and punished by the justice system. In his later writings, even Lombroso admitted that the born criminal was just one of many criminal types. Because of these deficiencies, the validity of individual-oriented explanations of criminality became questionable and for a time passed from the criminological mainstream.

Impact of Sociobiology

> What seems no longer tenable at this juncture is any theory of human behavior which ignores biology and relies exclusively on socio-cultural learning. . . . Most social scientists have been wrong in their dogmatic rejection and blissful ignorance of the biological parameters of our behavior.[6]

Biological explanations of crime fell out of favor in the early twentieth century. During this period, criminologists became concerned about the social influences on crime, such as the neighborhood, peer group, family life, and social class status. The work of biocriminologists was viewed as methodologically unsound and gen-

erally invalid. Then, in the early 1970s, spurred by the publication of *Sociobiology* by Edmund O. Wilson, the biological basis for crime once again emerged into the limelight.[7]

Sociobiology differs from earlier theories of behavior in that it stresses that biological and genetic conditions affect the perception and learning of social behaviors, which in turn are linked to existing environmental structures. Sociobiologists view the gene as the ultimate unit of life that controls all human destiny. While the environment and experience do have an impact on behavior, most actions are controlled by a person's "biological machine." Most important, people are controlled by the innate need to have their genetic material survive and dominate others. Consequently, they do everything in their power to ensure their own survival and that of others who share their gene pool (relatives, fellow citizens, and so forth). Even when they come to the aid of others **(reciprocal altruism),** people are motivated by the belief that their actions will be reciprocated and that their gene survival capability will be enhanced.

Sociobiologists view biology, environment, and learning as mutually interdependent factors. Problems in one area can be altered by efforts in another. For example, people suffering from learning disorders can be given special tutoring to improve their reading skills. In this view then, people are biosocial organisms whose personalities and behaviors are influenced by physical as well as environmental conditions. Although sociobiology has been criticized as methodologically unsound and socially dangerous, it has had a tremendous effect on reviving interest in finding a basis for crime and delinquency, because if biological (genetic) makeup controls human behavior, it follows that it should also be responsible for determining whether a person chooses law-violating or conventional behavior.

≡ Biosocial Theory

The influence of sociobiology helped revive interest in the biological basis of crime. Rather than view the criminal as controlled by biological conditions determined at birth, modern biocriminologists believe that biological, environmental, and social conditions work in concert to produce human behavior; they usually refer to themselves as biosocial theorists. Biosocial theory has several core principles.[8] First, it assumes that genetic makeup contributes significantly to human behavior. Biosocial theorists do not assume that all humans are born with

Biosocial theorists use experimental measurements to determine the physical and mental factors associated with violence and aggression.

environment interact to either limit or enhance an organism's capacity for learning. People learn through a process involving the brain and central nervous system. Learning is not controlled by social interactions but by biochemistry and cellular interaction. Learning can take place only when physical changes occur in the brain. There is a significant link, therefore, between behavior patterns and physical or chemical changes that occur in the brain, autonomic nervous system, and central nervous system.[9]

Some, but not all, biosocial theorists also believe that behavior is influenced by instinctual drives. Developed over the course of human history, instincts are inherited, natural, and unlearned dispositions that activate specific behavior patterns designed to reach certain goals. For example, people are believed to have a drive to "possess and control" other people and things. Some theft offenses may be motivated by the instinctual need to possess goods and commodities. Rape and other sex crimes may be linked to the primitive instinctual drive males have to "possess and control" females.[10]

The following subsections will examine some of the more important issues in biosocial theory.[11] First, we will look at how biochemical factors are believed to affect the learning of proper behavior patterns. Then, we will turn to the relationship of brain function and crime. Finally, we will briefly consider current ideas about genetic and evolutionary factors and crime.

Biochemical Factors

Some theorists believe that biochemical factors, such as those produced by diet, environmental conditions, and allergies, control and influence violent behavior. This view of crime received national attention when Dan White, the confessed killer of San Francisco Mayor George Moscone and city Councilman Harvey Milk, claimed his behavior was precipitated by an addiction to sugar-laden junk foods.[12] White's "Twinky defense" prompted a California jury to find him guilty of the lesser offense of diminished capacity manslaughter rather than first-degree murder (White committed suicide after serving his prison sentence). Some of the more important biochemical factors that have been linked to criminality are set out in detail below.

Chemical and Mineral Influences

Biocriminologists maintain that minimum levels of minerals and chemicals are needed for normal brain

equal potential to learn and achieve **(equipotentiality)** and that thereafter their behavior is controlled by social forces. Whereas traditional criminologists suggest, either explicitly or implicitly, that all people are born equal and that their parents, schools, neighborhoods, and friends control their subsequent development, biosocial theorists argue that no two people are alike (with rare exceptions, such as identical twins) and that the combination of human genetic traits and the environment produces individual behavior patterns.

Learning Potential

Another critical focus of biosocial theory is the importance of brain functioning, mental processes, and learning. Social behavior, including criminal behavior, is learned. Each individual organism is believed to have a unique potential for learning. The physical and social

functioning and growth, especially in the early years of life. If people with normal needs do not receive the appropriate nutrition, they will suffer from vitamin deficiency. If people have genetic conditions that cause greater-than-normal needs for certain chemicals and minerals, they are said to suffer from vitamin dependency. People with vitamin deficiency or dependency can manifest many physical, mental, and behavioral problems. For example, alcoholics often suffer from thiamine deficiency because of their poor diets and consequently are susceptible to the serious, often fatal Wernicke-Korsakoff disease.[13] Research conducted over the past decade shows that the dietary inadequacy of certain chemicals and minerals, including sodium, potassium, calcium, amino acids, monoamines, and peptides, can lead to depression, mania, cognitive problems, memory loss, and abnormal sexual activity.[14] Research studies examining the relationship between crime and vitamin deficiency and dependency have seemed to find a close link between antisocial behavior and insufficient quantities of some B vitamins—B3 and B6—and vitamin C. In addition, studies have purported to show that a major proportion of all schizophrenics and children with learning and behavior disorders are dependent on vitamins B3 and B6.[15]

Another suspected nutritional influence on behavior is a diet especially high in carbohydrates and sugar.[16] For example, some recent research found that the way the brain processed glucose was related to scores on tests measuring reasoning power.[17] In addition, sugar intake levels have been associated with attention span deficiencies.[18] Diets high in sugar and carbohydrates also have been linked to violence and aggression. Stephen Schoenthaler conducted an experiment with 276 incarcerated youths to determine whether a change in the amount of sugar in their diet would have a corresponding influence on their behavior within the institutional setting.[19] In the experiment, several dietary changes were made: sweet drinks were replaced with fruit juices; table sugar was replaced with honey; breakfast cereals high in sugar were eliminated; molasses was substituted for sugar in cooking; and so on. Schoenthaler found that these changes produced a significant reduction in disciplinary actions within the institution: the number of assaults, thefts, fights, and disobedience within the institution declined about 45 percent. It is important to note that these results were consistent when such factors as age, previous offense record, and race of the offender were considered.

These are but a few of the research efforts linking sugar intake to emotional, cognitive, and behavioral performance.[20] As a group, they suggest that in every segment of society, there are violent, aggressive, and amoral people whose improper food, vitamin, and mineral intake may be responsible for their antisocial behavior. If diet could be improved, then the frequency of violent behavior would be reduced.

While these results are impressive, a number of biologists have questioned this association, and some recent research efforts have failed to find a link between sugar consumption and violence.[21] Many people who maintain diets high in sugar and carbohydrates are not violent or crime-prone; it is difficult, therefore, to suggest that antisocial behavior is a function of diet alone.[22]

Hypoglycemia

Hypoglycemia occurs when glucose (sugar) in the blood falls below levels necessary for normal and efficient brain functioning. The brain is sensitive to the lack of blood sugar because it is the only organ that obtains its energy solely from the combustion of carbohydrates. Thus, when the brain is deprived of blood sugar, it has no alternate food supply to call upon, and its metabolism slows down, impairing its function. Symptoms of hypoglycemia include irritability, anxiety, depression, crying spells, headaches, and confusion.

Research studies have linked hypoglycemia to outbursts of antisocial behavior and violence. As early as 1943, D. Hill and W. Sargent linked murder to hypoglycemia.[23] Several studies have related assaults and fatal sexual offenses to hypoglycemic reactions.[24] Hypoglycemia has also been connected with a syndrome characterized by aggressive and assaultive behavior, glucose disturbance, and brain dysfunction. Some attempts have been made to measure hypoglycemia using subjects with a known history of criminal activity. Studies of jail and prison inmate populations have found a higher than normal level of hypoglycemia.[25] The presence of high levels of reactive hypoglycemia has been found in groups of habitually violent and impulsive offenders.[26]

Hormonal Influences

Criminologist James Q. Wilson writing in his 1993 book, *The Moral Sense,* concludes that hormones, enzymes, and neurotransmitters may be the key to understanding human behavior. They help explain gender differences in the crime rate. Males, he writes, are biologically and naturally more aggressive than females, while women are more nurturing of the young and important for survival of the species.[27] Hormone levels also help explain the aging-out process. Levels of testosterone, the principal male steroid hormone, decline during the life cycle and may explain why violence rates diminish over time.[28]

A number of biosocial theorists are now evaluating the association between violent behavior episodes and hormone levels, and the findings suggest that abnormal levels of male sex hormones **(androgens)** do in fact produce aggressive behavior. [29] In their review of the literature, Christy Miller Buchanan, Jacquelynne Eccles, and Jill Becker found evidence that hormonal changes are related to mood and behavior and, concomitantly, that adolescents experience more intense mood swings, anxiety, and restlessness than their elders.[30] An association between hormonal activity and antisocial behavior is suggested because rates of both factors peak in adolescence.

One area of concern has been **testosterone,** the most abundant androgen, which controls secondary sex characteristics, such as facial hair and voice timbre.[31] Research conducted on both human and animal subjects has found that prenatal exposure to unnaturally high levels of androgens permanently alters behavior. Girls who were unintentionally exposed to elevated amounts of androgens during their fetal development display an unusually high long-term tendency toward aggression; boys prenatally exposed to steroids that decrease androgen levels displayed decreased aggressiveness.[32] In contrast, samples of inmates indicate that testosterone levels were higher in men who committed violent crimes than in the other prisoners.[33]

Hormones and Violence.

How do hormone levels influence violent behaviors? According to Lee Ellis, hormones cause areas of the brain to become less sensitive to environmental stimuli. Males, who possess high androgen levels, are more likely than females to need excess stimulation and to be willing to tolerate pain in their quest for thrills. Androgens are linked to brain seizures that, under stressful conditions, can result in emotional volatility. Ellis also believes that androgens affect the brain structure itself. They influence the left hemisphere of the neocortex, the part of the brain that controls sympathetic feelings toward others.[34]

Writing with Phyllis Coontz, Ellis summarizes the physical reactions produced by hormones that influence violence:

1. A lowering of average resting arousal under normal environmental conditions to a point that individuals are motivated to seek unusually high levels of environmental stimulation and are less sensitive to any harmful aftereffects resulting from this stimulation

2. A lowering of seizuring thresholds in and around the limbic system, increasing the likelihood that strong and impulsive emotional responses will be made to stressful environmental encounters.

3. A rightward shift in neocortical functioning, resulting in an increased reliance on the brain hemisphere that is most closely integrated with the limbic system and is least prone to reason in logical-linguistic forms or to respond to linguistic commands.[35]

According to Ellis and Coontz, these effects promote violence and other serious crimes by causing people to seek greater levels of environmental stimulation and to tolerate more punishment, increasing impulsivity, emotional volatility, and antisocial emotions.[36]

While some research studies have been unable to demonstrate hormonal differences in samples of violent and nonviolent offenders, drugs that decrease testosterone levels are now being used to treat male sex offenders.[37] The female hormones **estrogen** and **progesterone** have been administered to sex offenders to decrease their sexual potency.[38] The long-term side effects of this treatment and their potential danger are still unknown.[39]

Premenstrual Syndrome.

Hormonal research has not been limited to male offenders. The suspicion has long existed that the onset of the menstrual cycle triggers excessive amounts of the female sex hormones, which affects antisocial, aggressive behavior. This condition is commonly referred to as **premenstrual syndrome,** or PMS. The link between PMS and delinquency was first popularized by Katharina Dalton, whose studies of English women indicated that females are more likely to commit suicide and be aggressive and otherwise antisocial just before or during menstruation.[40] While the Dalton research is often cited as evidence of the link between PMS and crime, methodological problems make it impossible to accept her findings at face value. Criminologist Julie Horney impressively reviewed the literature on PMS and crime and found alternative explanations for a PMS-violence link. She finds it is possible that the psychological and physical stress of aggression brings on menstruation and not vice versa.[41]

Allergies

Allergies are defined as unusual or excessive reactions of the body to foreign substances.[42] For example, hay fever is an allergic reaction caused when pollen cells enter the body and are fought or neutralized by the body's natural defenses. The result of the battle is itching, red eyes and active sinuses.

Cerebral allergies cause an excessive reaction of the brain, whereas neuroallergies affect the nervous system. Neuroallergies and cerebral allergies are believed to cause the allergic person to produce enzymes that attack wholesome foods as if they were dangerous to the body.[43] They may also cause swelling of the brain and produce sensitivity in the central nervous system, conditions linked to mental, emotional, and behavioral problems. Research indicates a connection between allergies and hyperemotionality, depression, aggressiveness, and violent behavior.[44]

Neuroallergy and cerebral allergy problems have also been linked to hyperactivity in children, which may portend antisocial behavior and the labeling of children as potential delinquents. The foods most commonly involved in producing such allergies are cow's milk, wheat, corn, chocolate, citrus, and eggs; however, about 300 other foods have been identified as allergens. The potential seriousness of the problem has been raised by studies linking the average consumption of one suspected cerebral allergen—corn—to cross-national homicide rates.[45]

Environmental Contaminants

Dangerous amounts of lead, copper, cadmium, mercury, and inorganic gases, such as chlorine and nitrogen dioxide, can now be found in the ecosystem. Research indicates that these environmental contaminants can influence behavior. At high levels, these substances can cause severe illness or death; at more moderate levels, they have been linked to emotional and behavioral disorders.[46] Some studies have linked the ingestion of food dyes and artificial colors and flavors to hostile, impulsive, and otherwise antisocial behavior in youths.[47] Other research efforts have been directed at measuring the influence of metals, such as lead, on behavior. Ingestion of lead may help explain why hyperactive children manifest conduct problems and antisocial behavior.[48] Lighting may be another important environmental influence on antisocial behavior. Research projects have suggested that radiation from artificial light sources, such as fluorescent tubes and television sets, may produce antisocial, aggressive behavior.[49]

≡ Neurophysiological Studies

Some researchers, such as Terrie Moffitt, focus their attention on **neurophysiology,** or the study of brain

activity.[50] They believe that neurological and physical abnormalities are acquired as early as the fetal or perinatal stage or through birth delivery trauma and then control behavior through the life span.[51]

The relationship between neurological dysfunction and crime first received a great deal of attention in 1968, when Charles Whitman, after killing his wife and his mother, barricaded himself in a tower at the University of Texas with a high-powered rifle and proceeded to kill 14 people and wound 24 others before he was killed by police. An autopsy revealed that Whitman suffered from a malignant infiltrating brain tumor. Whitman had previously experienced uncontrollable urges to kill and had gone to a psychiatrist seeking help for his problems. He kept careful notes documenting his feelings and his inability to control his homicidal urges, and he left instructions for his estate to be given to a mental health foundation so it could study mental problems such as his.[52]

The following sections discuss various brain function patterns that have been related to criminality.

Terrie Moffitt has conducted significant research on the neuropsychology of crime, studying, in particular, juvenile delinquents in New Zealand.

Measuring Neurological Impairments

There are numerous ways to measure neurological functioning, including memorization and visual awareness tests, short-term auditory memory tests, and verbal IQ tests. These tests have been found to distinguish delinquent offenders from a nondelinquent control group.[53]

Probably the most important measure of neurophysiological functioning is the **electroencephalograph** (EEG). An EEG records the electrical impulses given off by the brain.[54] It represents a signal composed of various rhythms and transient electrical discharges, commonly called brain waves, which can be recorded by electrodes placed on the scalp. The frequency is given in cycles per second, measured in hertz (Hz), and usually ranges from 0.5 to 30 Hz. Measurements of the EEG reflect the activity of neurons located in the cerebral cortex. The rhythmic nature of this brain activity is determined by mechanisms that involve subcortical structures, primarily the thalamus portion of the brain. In what is considered the most significant investigation of EEG abnormality and crime, a randomly selected group of 335 violent delinquents was divided into those who were habitually violent and those who had committed a single violent act. While 65 percent of the habitually aggressive had abnormal EEG recordings, only 24 percent of the one-time offenders had recordings that deviated from the norm. When the records of individuals who had brain damage, were mentally retarded, or were epileptic were removed from the sample, the percentage of abnormality among boys who had committed a solitary violent crime was the same as that of the general population, about 12 percent. However, the habitually aggressive subjects still showed a 57 percent abnormality.[46]

Other research efforts have linked abnormal EEG recordings to antisocial behavior in children. Although about 5 to 15 percent of the general population has abnormal EEG readings, about 50 to 60 percent of adolescents with known behavior disorders display abnormal recordings.[55] Behaviors highly correlated with abnormal EEG included poor impulse control, inadequate social adaptation, hostility, temper tantrums, and destructiveness.[56] Studies of adults have associated slow and bilateral brain waves with hostile, hypercritical, irritable, nonconforming, and impulsive behavior.[57] Psychiatric patients with EEG abnormalities have been reported to be highly combative and to suffer episodes of rage. Studies of murderers have shown that a disproportionate number manifest abnormal EEG recordings.[58] In an important analysis of existing research, Diana Fishbein and Robert Thatcher have found that EEG analysis can detect a variety of organic problems linked to antisocial behavior and that the EEG is a valuable tool for detecting crime-producing physical conditions.[59]

Minimal Brain Dysfunction

Minimal brain dysfunction (MBD) is related to an abnormality in cerebral structure. It has been defined as abruptly appearing, maladaptive behavior that interrupts the life-style and life flow of an individual. In its most serious form, MBD has been linked to serious antisocial acts, an imbalance in the urge-control mechanisms of the brain, and chemical abnormality. Included in the category of minimal brain dysfunction are several abnormal behavior patterns, including dyslexia, visual perception problems, hyperactivity, poor attention span, temper tantrums, and aggressiveness. One type of minimal brain dysfunction is manifested through episodic periods of explosive rage. This form of the disorder is considered an important cause of such behavior as spouse beating, child abuse, suicide, aggressiveness, and motiveless homicide. One perplexing feature of this syndrome is that people who are afflicted with it often maintain warm and pleasant personalities between episodes of violence.

Some studies measuring the presence of minimal brain dysfunction in offender populations have found that up to 60 percent exhibit brain dysfunction on psychological tests.[60] Lorne Yeudall studied 60 criminal patients and found that they were characterized by lateral brain dysfunction of the dominant hemisphere of the brain.[61] Yeudall was able to predict with 95 percent accuracy the recidivism of violent criminals.[62] Of interest to both educators and criminologists is the relationship between MBD and the so-called learning-disabled child. Research has shown that although learning-disabled (LD) children violate the law at the same rate as non-LD children, they are overrepresented in official arrest and juvenile court statistics.[63]

Attention Deficit Disorder

Many parents have noticed that their children do not pay attention to them—they run around and do things in their own way. Sometimes this inattention is a function of age; in other instances, it is a symptom of attention deficit disorder (ADD), in which a child shows a developmentally inappropriate lack of attention, impulsivity, and hyperactivity. The various symptoms of ADD are described in Table 6.1. About 3 percent of U.S. children, most often boys, are believed to suffer from this disorder, and it is the most common reason children are

TABLE 6.1 **Symptoms of Attention Deficit Disorder**

Lack of Attention

Frequently fails to finish projects
Does not seem to pay attention
Does not sustain interest in play activities
Cannot sustain concentration on schoolwork or related tasks
Is easily distracted

Impulsivity

Frequently acts without thinking
Often "calls out" in class
Does not want to wait his or her turn in lines or games
Shifts from activity to activity
Cannot organize tasks or work
Requires constant supervision

Hyperactivity

Constantly runs around and climbs on things
Shows excessive motor activity while asleep
Cannot sit still; is constantly fidgeting
Does not remain in his or her seat in class
Is constantly on the go like a "motor"

SOURCE: Adapted from American Psychiatric Association, *Diagnostic and Statistical Manual of the Mental Disorders*, 3d ed. (Washington, D.C.: American Psychiatric Press, 1987), pp. 50–53.

referred to mental health clinics. The condition, especially when combined with hyperactive disorder, has been associated with poor school performance, grade retention, placement in special needs classes, bullying, stubbornness, and lack of response to discipline.[64] While the origin of ADD is still unknown, suspected causes include neurological damage, prenatal stress, and even food additives and chemical allergies; recent research has suggested a genetic link.[65]

A series of research studies now link ADD, minimal brain dysfunctions (MBD) (such as poor motor function), hyperactivity, and below-average written and verbal cognitive ability to the onset and sustenance of a delinquent career. Research by Terrie Moffitt and Phil Silva suggests that youths who suffer *both* ADD and MBD and grow up in a dysfunctional family are the ones most vulnerable to chronic and persistent delinquency.[66] Eugene Maguin and his associates have found that the relationship between chronic delinquency and attention disorders may be mediated by school failure: Kids who are poor readers are the most prone to antisocial behavior; many poor readers also have attention problems.[67]

This ADD-crime association is important because symptoms of ADD seem stable through adolescence into adulthood.[68] Early diagnosis and treatment of children suffering ADD may enhance their life chances. Today, the most typical treatment is doses of stimulants, such as Ritalin and Dexedrine, which ironically help control emotional and behavioral outbursts.

Other Brain Dysfunctions.   Other brain dysfunctions have been related to violent crime. Persistent criminality has been linked to dysfunction in the frontal and temporal regions of the brain since they are believed to play an important role in the regulation and inhibition of human behavior, including the formation of plans and intentions, and in the regulation of complex behaviors.[69] Research by Lorne Yeudall and his associates found that brain lesions that occur at specific points of the neurological system, such as the auditory system, can have permanent effects on behavior.[70] Clinical evaluation of depressed and aggressive psychopathic subjects showed a significant number (more than 75 percent) had dysfunction of the temporal and frontal regions of the brain. The researchers conclude:

> Evidence from our research over the past 13 years, as well as the findings of others, is consistent with the hypothesis of a high incidence of disturbed functioning of the central nervous system in the persistent offender.[71]

The presence of brain tumors has also been linked to a wide variety of psychological problems, including personality changes, hallucinations, and psychotic episodes.[72] There is evidence that people with tumors are prone to depression, irritability, temper outbursts, and even homicidal attacks (for example, the Whitman case). Clinical case studies of patients suffering from brain tumors indicate that previously docile people may undergo behavior changes so great that they attempt to seriously harm their families and friends; when the tumor is removed, their behavior returns to normal.[73] In addition to brain tumors, head injuries caused by accidents, such as falls or auto crashes, have been linked to personality reversals marked by outbursts of antisocial and violent behavior.[74]

A variety of central nervous system diseases, including cerebral arteriosclerosis, epilepsy, senile dementia, Korsakoff's syndrome, and Huntington's chorea, have also been associated with memory deficiency, orientation loss, and affective (emotional) disturbances dominated by rage, anger, and increased irritability.[75]

Brain Chemistry

Neurotransmitters are chemical compounds that influence or activate brain functions. Those studied in relation to aggression include androgens, dopamine, norepinephrine, serotonin, monoamine oxidase, and GABA.[76] Evidence exists that abnormal levels of these chemicals are associated with aggression. For example, several researchers have reported inverse correlations between serotonin concentrates in the blood and impulsive and/or suicidal behavior.[77] Conversely, violence-prone people have been successfully treated with antipsychotic drugs that help control levels of neurotransmitters; these are sometimes referred to as "chemical restraints" or "chemical straightjackets."

Lee Ellis has found that prenatal exposure of the brain to high levels of androgens can result in a brain structure that is less sensitive to environmental inputs. Affected individuals seek more intense and varied stimulation and are willing to tolerate more adverse consequences than individuals not so affected.[78] Such exposure also results in a *rightward shift* in (brain) hemispheric functioning and a concomitant diminution of cognitive and emotional tendencies. It should not be surprising then that left-handers are disproportionately represented in the criminal population since the movement of each hand tends to be controlled by the hemisphere of the brain on the opposite side of the body.

In another analysis, Ellis found that individuals with a low supply of the enzyme monoamine oxidase (MAO) engage in behaviors linked with violence and property crime, including defiance of punishment, impulsivity, hyperactivity, poor academic performance, sensation-seeking and risk-taking, and recreational drug use. Abnormal levels of MAO may explain both individual and group differences in the crime rate. For example, Ellis finds that females have higher levels of MAO than males, a condition that may explain gender differences in the crime rate.[79]

Brain Chemistry and "Thrills."

Recent research has suggested that the brain and neurological system can produce natural or endogenous opiates, which are chemically similar to the narcotics opium and morphine. It has been suggested that the risk and thrills involved in crime cause the neurosystem to produce increased amounts of these natural narcotics. The result is an elevated mood state, perceived as an exciting and rewarding experience that acts as a positive reinforcer to crime.[80] The brain then produces its own natural "high" as a reward for risk-taking behavior. While some people achieve this high by rock climbing and skydiving, others engage in crimes of violence.

It has long been suspected that obtaining "thrills" is a motivator of crime. Adolescents may engage in such crimes as shoplifting and vandalism simply because they offer the attraction of "getting away with it"; delinquency is a thrilling demonstration of personal competence.[81] Violent criminals may find that having life-and-death control over their victims is a source of thrills and excitement. The stimulation of violence is electrifying, helping to explain why some people engage in otherwise "senseless crimes."

Genetic Influences

Early biological theorists believed that criminality ran in families. Though research on deviant families, such as the Jukes and Kallikaks, is not taken seriously today, modern biosocial theorists are still interested in genetics. If some human behaviors are influenced by heredity, why not antisocial tendencies? Evidence exists that animals can be bred to have aggressive traits: pit bulldogs, fighting bulls, and fighting cocks have been selectively mated to produce superior predators. Of course, no similar data are available for people, but a growing body of research is focusing on the genetic factors associated with human behavior.[82] This line of reasoning was cast in the spotlight when Richard Speck, the convicted killer of eight nurses in Chicago, was said to have inherited an abnormal XYY chromosomal structure (XY is normal in males). There was much public concern that all XYYs were potential killers and should be closely controlled. Civil libertarians expressed fear that all XYYs could be labeled dangerous and violent regardless of whether they had engaged in violent activities.[83] When it was disclosed that neither Speck nor most violent offenders actually had an extra Y chromosome, interest in the XYY theory dissipated.[84] However, the Speck case drew researchers' attention to looking for a genetic basis of crime. Is it possible that the tendency for crime and aggression is inherited?

Twin Studies

If, in fact, inherited traits cause criminal behaviors, it should be expected that twins would be quite similar in their antisocial activities. However, since twins are usually brought up in the same household and exposed to the same set of social conditions, determining whether their behavior was a result of biological, sociological, or psychological conditions would be difficult. Biocriminologists have tried to overcome this dilemma by comparing identical, monozygotic (MZ) twins with fraternal, dizygotic (DZ) twins of the same sex.[85] MZ twins are genetically identical, while DZ twins have only half their genes in common. If heredity does determine criminal behavior, we should expect that MZ twins would be much more similar in their antisocial activities than DZ twins.

The earliest studies conducted on the behavior of twins detected a significant relationship between the criminal activities of MZ twins and a much lower association between those of DZ twins. A review of relevant studies conducted between 1929 and 1961 found that 60 percent of MZ twins shared criminal behavior patterns (if one twin was criminal, so was the other), while only 30 percent of DZ twins were similarly related.[86] These findings may be viewed as powerful evidence that a genetic basis for criminality exists.

Recent studies have supported these findings, though the level of association is more moderate than previously thought. Karl Christiansen studied 3,586 male twin pairs and found a 52 percent concordance for MZ pairs and a 22 percent concordance for DZ pairs. This result suggests that the identical MZ twins may share a genetic characteristic that increases the risk of their engaging in criminality.[87] Similarly, David Rowe and D. Wayne Osgood have analyzed the factors that influence self-reported delinquency in a sample of twin pairs and concluded that genetic influences actually have significant explanatory power.[88] While persuasive, this evidence is certainly not conclusive proof that crime is genetically predetermined. Not all research efforts have found that MZ twin pairs are more closely related in their criminal behavior than DZ or ordinary sibling pairs, and some that have found an association note that it is at best "modest."[89]

Adoption Studies

It seems logical that if the behavior of adopted children is more similar to that of their biological parents than to that of their adoptive parents, then the idea of a genetic basis for criminality would be supported. If, on the other hand, adoptees are more similar to their adoptive parents than their biological parents, an environmental basis for crime would seem more valid.

Several studies indicate that some relationship may exist between biological parents' behavior and the behavior of their children, even when their contact has been infrequent.[90] In one major study, Barry Hutchings

and Sarnoff Mednick analyzed 1,145 male adoptees born in Copenhagen, Denmark, between 1927 and 1941; of these, 185 had criminal records.[91] After following up on 143 of the criminal adoptees and matching them with a control group of 143 noncriminal adoptees, Hutchings and Mednick found that the criminality of the biological father was a strong predictor of the child's criminal behavior. When both the biological and the adoptive fathers were criminal, the probability that the youth would engage in criminal behavior greatly expanded: 24.5 percent of the boys whose adoptive and biological fathers were criminals had been convicted of a criminal law violation; only 13.5 percent of those whose biological and adoptive fathers were not criminals had similar conviction records.[92]

Evaluating Genetic Research

While findings from twin and adoption studies are not conclusive, they have not refuted the hypothesis that there is some genetic basis to criminality. After all, research now suggests that a number of human behaviors, including sexual orientation, may be determined by genetic makeup.[93] There is also a significant association between sibling behavior patterns.[94] According to this view then, child-rearing practices and family environments may influence personality development and intellectual capability, but so too does genetic makeup. Children are programmed genetically to learn and are thereafter influenced by many environmental factors; genetic makeup is the key determinant of how social forces influence behavior.

Even if violence and aggression is not an inherited trait per se, the research supports genetic control of important human traits that are at the least *associated* with criminality.[95] While people may not inherit a gene that directly causes violence, personality conditions linked to aggression, such as psychopathy, impulsivity, and neuroticism, and psychopathology, such as schizophrenia (see below), may be heritable.[96]

Those who oppose the genes-crime relationship point to the inadequate research designs and weak methodologies of supporting research. Even when a general relationship can be detected, the newer, better designed research studies provide *less support* than earlier, less methodically sound studies.[97]

The genes-crime relationship is quite controversial since it implies that the propensity to commit crime is present at birth and cannot be altered. It raises moral dilemmas. If in utero genetic testing could detect a gene for violence, should a fetus be aborted? Should those holding a particular genetic makeup be followed and watched as a precautionary measure?

Evolutionary Factors

A recent biosocial emphasis has been on evolutionary factors in criminality. As civilization has evolved, certain traits and characteristics have become ingrained and instinctual. These biosocial characteristics may be responsible for some crime patterns.

Gender differences in the violence rate have been explained by the evolution of mammalian mating patterns. Hypothetically, to ensure survival of the gene pool (and the species), it is beneficial for a male of any species to mate with as many suitable females as possible since each can bear its offspring. In contrast, because of the long period of gestation, females require a secure home and a single, stable nurturing partner to ensure their survival. Because of these differences in mating patterns, the most aggressive males mate most often and have the greatest number of offspring. Over the history of the human species, aggressive males have also had the greatest impact on the gene pool. The descendants of these aggressive males now account for the disproportionate amount of male aggression and violence.[98]

Ellis finds that males today continue to show evidence that they "lean" toward *r-selection,* a process that emphasizes producing large numbers of offspring; in contrast, females are *k-selected,* which emphasizes fewer offspring but more care and devotion. Persons who commit violent crimes seem to exhibit r-selection traits, such as a premature birth, early and frequent sexual activity, neglect as a child, and a short life expectancy.[99]

The relationship between evolutionary factors and crime has just begun to be studied. Criminologists are now exploring how social organizations and institutions interact with evolutionary biological traits to influence personal decision making, including criminal strategies.[100]

Evaluation of the Biosocial Perspective

Biosocial perspectives on crime raise some challenging questions for criminology. They have in turn been challenged by critics, who suggest they are racist and dysfunctional. If biology can explain the cause of street crimes, such as assault, murder, or rape, the argument goes, and if, as the official crime statistics suggest, the poor and minority-group members commit a disproportionate number of such acts, then by implication, biological theory says that members of these groups are biologically different, flawed, or inferior.

Biosocial theory is challenged because it seems less concerned with the effect of a crime-producing social environment than with flawed human traits and characteristics. The theory focuses on the violent crimes of the lower classes while ignoring the white-collar crimes of the upper and middle classes. It gives short shrift to the geographic, social, and temporal patterns in the crime rate uncovered by the FBI and victimization data sources. Furthermore, biological theory seems to divide people into criminals and noncriminals on the basis of their physical makeup and ignores that self-reports indicate that almost everyone has engaged in some type of illegal activity during his or her lifetime.

Biosocial theorists counter that their views should not be confused with Lombrosian, deterministic biology. Rather than suggest that there are born criminals and noncriminals, they maintain that some people carry the potential to be violent or antisocial and that environmental conditions can sometimes trigger antisocial responses.[101] This would explain why some otherwise law-abiding citizens engage in a single, seemingly unexplainable antisocial act and, conversely, why some people with long criminal careers often engage in conventional behavior.

As Israel Naschshon and Deborah Denno point out, no biological factor, normal or abnormal, predetermines behavior, because behavior is a product of interacting biological and environmental events.[102] For example, recent research by Avshalom Caspi and his associates indicates that girls who reach physical maturity at an early age are the ones most likely to engage in delinquent acts. This finding might suggest a relationship between biological traits (hormonal activity) and crime. However, the Caspi research found that the association may also have an environmental basis. Physically mature girls are the ones most likely to have prolonged contact with a crime-prone group: older adolescent boys.[103] Here, the combination of biological change, social relationships, and routine opportunities predicts crime rates.

The most significant criticism of biosocial theory has been the lack of adequate empirical testing. In most research efforts, sample sizes are relatively small and nonrepresentative. A great deal of biosocial research is conducted with samples of adjudicated offenders who have been placed in clinical treatment settings. Methodological problems make it impossible to determine whether findings apply only to offenders who have been convicted of crimes and placed in treatment or to the population of criminals as a whole.[104] A great deal of research is needed to clarify the relationships proposed by biosocial researchers and to silence critics.

Psychological Theories of Crime

Another branch of positivist criminology focuses on the mental aspects of crime, including the association between intelligence, personality, learning, and criminal behavior.

The earliest "psychological" view was that criminals were possessed by evil spirits or demons. Later theories suggested that mental illness and insanity were inherited and that deviants were inherently mentally damaged by reason of their inferior genetic makeup. An early pioneer of the concept of insanity was the English physician Henry Maudsley (1835–1918). Maudsley believed that insanity and criminal behavior were strongly linked: "Crime is a sort of outlet in which their unsound tendencies are discharged; they would go mad if they were not criminals, and they do not go mad because they are criminals."[105]

In *The English Convict*, Charles Goring (1870–1919) used his "biometric method" to study the characteristics of 3,000 English convicts.[106] He found little difference in the physical characteristics of criminals and noncriminals but instead uncovered a significant relationship between crime and a condition he referred to as "defective intelligence." Goring believed that criminal behavior was inherited and could therefore best be controlled by regulating the reproduction of families exhibiting such traits as "feeblemindedness, epilepsy, insanity, and defective social instinct."[107]

Theory of Imitation

Gabriel Tarde (1843–1904) used a somewhat different psychological approach in his early research: he is the forerunner of modern-day learning theorists.[108] Unlike Maudsley and Goring, who viewed criminals as mentally impaired, Tarde believed people learn from one another through a process of imitation. Tarde proposed three laws of imitation to describe why people engaged in crime: First, individuals in close and intimate contact with one another imitate each other's behavior. Second,

imitation spreads from the top down; consequently, youngsters imitate older individuals, paupers imitate the rich, peasants imitate royalty, and so on. Crime among young, poor, or low-status people is really their effort to imitate wealthy, older, high-status people (for example, through gambling, drunkenness, accumulation of wealth).

Tarde's third law is the law of insertion. New acts and behaviors are superimposed on old ones and subsequently act either to reinforce or discourage previous customs. For example, drug taking may be a popular fad among college students who previously used alcohol. However, students may find that a combination of both substances provides even greater stimulation, causing the use of both drugs and alcohol to increase. Or a new criminal custom can develop that eliminates an older one—for example, train robbing has been replaced by truck hijacking. Tarde's ideas are quite similar to modern social learning theorists who believe that both interpersonal and observed behavior, such as a movie or television, can influence criminality.

Since the pioneering work of Maudsley, Tarde, and Goring, psychologists, psychiatrists, and other mental health professionals have long played an active role in formulating criminological theory. In their quest to understand and treat all varieties of abnormal mental conditions, psychologists have encountered clients whose behavior falls within categories society has labeled as criminal, deviant, violent, and antisocial.

This section is organized along the lines of the predominant psychological views most closely associated with the cause of criminal behavior; these perspectives are outlined in Figure 6.1. Some psychologists view antisocial behavior from a psychoanalytic perspective: their focus is on early childhood experience and its effect on personality. In contrast, behaviorists stress social learning and behavior modeling as the keys to criminality. Cognitive theorists analyze human perception and how it effects behavior. There is also a biological branch of psychology that holds that behavior is controlled by the effect of biochemical, neurological, and genetic influences on the brain. This latter viewpoint is quite similar to the biosocial views previously discussed, and much biosocial theory is conducted by psychologists.

Psychodynamic Perspective

Psychodynamic or psychoanalytic psychology was originated by Viennese doctor Sigmund Freud (1856–1939) and has since remained a prominent segment of psychological theory.[109]

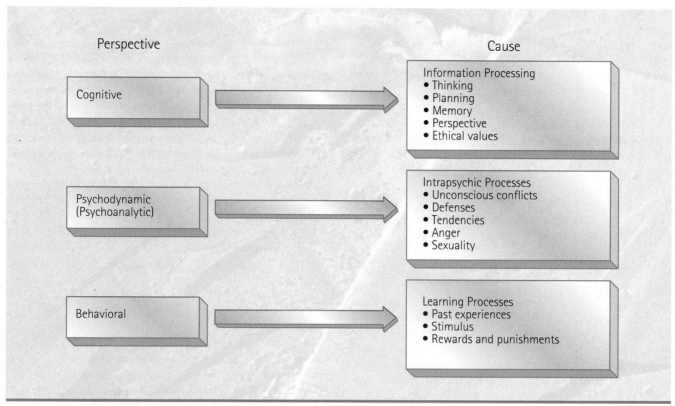

FIGURE 6.1   **Psychological Perspectives of Criminality**

According to psychodynamic theory, the human mind performs three separate functions. The *conscious* mind is the aspect of the mind that people are most aware of—hunger, pain, thirst, desire. The *preconscious* mind contains elements of experiences that are out of awareness but can be brought back to consciousness at any time—memories, experiences. The *unconscious* part of the mind contains biological desires and urges that cannot readily be experienced as thoughts. Part of the unconscious contains feelings about sex and hostility, which people keep below the surface of consciousness by a process called **repression.**

Psychodynamic theory also holds that the human personality contains a three-part structure. The *id,* the primitive part of people's mental makeup present at birth, represents unconscious biological drives for sex, food, and other life-sustaining necessities. The id follows the *pleasure principle*: it requires instant gratification without concern for the rights of others.

The *ego* develops early in life, when a child begins to learn that its wishes cannot be instantly gratified. The ego is that part of the personality that compensates for the demands of the id by helping the individual guide his or her actions to remain within the boundaries of social convention. The ego is guided by the *reality principle*: it takes into account what is practical and conventional by societal standards.

The *superego* develops as a result of incorporating within the personality the moral standards and values of parents, community, and significant others. It is the moral aspect of people's personalities; it passes judgments on their behavior.

Human Development.   The most basic human drive present at birth is *eros,* the instinct to preserve and create life. Eros is expressed sexually. Consequently, very early in their development, humans experience sexuality, which is expressed in the seeking of pleasure through various parts of the body. During the first year of life, a child attains pleasure by sucking and biting; Freud called this the oral stage. During the second and third years of life, the focus of sexual attention is on the elimination of bodily wastes—the anal stage. The phallic stage occurs during the third year of life; children now focus their attention on their genitals. Males begin to have sexual feelings for their mother (the *Oedipus* complex) and girls for their fathers (the *Electra complex*). Latency begins at age six; during this period, feelings of sexuality are repressed until the genital stage begins at puberty; this marks the beginning of adult sexuality.

If conflicts are encountered during any of the psychosexual stages of development, a person can become fixated at that point. The person will as an adult exhibit behavior traits characteristic of those encountered during infantile sexual development. For example, an infant who does not receive enough oral gratification during the first year of life is likely as an adult to engage in such oral behavior as smoking, drinking, or drug abuse or to be clinging and dependent in personal relationships. Thus, the root of adult behavior problems can be traced to problems developed in the earliest years of life.

Psychodynamics of Abnormal Behavior

According to the psychodynamic perspective, people who experience feelings of mental anguish and are afraid that they are losing control of their personalities are said to be suffering from a form of **neuroses** and are referred to as **neurotics.** Those people who have lost total control and who are dominated by their primitive id are known as **psychotics.** Their behavior may be marked by bizarre episodes, hallucinations, and inappropriate responses. According to the psychodynamic view, the most serious types of antisocial behavior, such as murder, might be motivated by psychosis, while neurotic feelings would be responsible for less serious delinquent acts and status offenses, such as petty theft and truancy.

Psychosis takes many forms, the most common labeled **schizophrenia.** Schizophrenics exhibit illogical and incoherent thought processes and a lack of insight into their behavior. They may experience delusions and hallucinate. For example, they may see themselves as agents of the devil, avenging angels, or the recipients of messages from animals and plants. David Berkowitz, the "Son of Sam" or the "44-calibre killer," exhibited these traits when he claimed that his killing spree began when he received messages from a neighbor's dog. Paranoid schizophrenics suffer complex behavior delusions involving wrongdoing or persecution—they think everyone is out to get them.

Psychosis and Crime.

Freud did not spend much time theorizing about crime. He did link criminality to an unconscious sense of guilt a person retains because of his childhood Oedipus complex or her Electra complex. He believed that in many criminals, especially youthful

ones, it is possible to detect a very powerful sense of guilt that existed before the crime and is therefore not its result but its motive. It is as if it was a relief to the person to be able to fasten the unconscious sense of guilt onto something real and immediate.[110]

Other psychologists have used psychoanalytic concepts to link criminality to abnormal mental states produced by early childhood trauma. For example, Alfred Adler (1870–1937), the founder of individual psychology, coined the term **inferiority complex** to describe people who have feelings of inferiority and compensate for them with a drive for superiority; controlling others may help reduce personal inadequacies. Erik Erikson (1902–1984) identified the **identity crisis**—a period of serious personal questioning people undertake in an effort to determine their own values and sense of direction. Adolescents undergoing an identity crisis might exhibit out-of-control behavior and experiment with drugs and other forms of deviance.

The psychoanalyst whose work is most closely associated with criminality is August Aichorn.[111] After examining many delinquent youths, Aichorn concluded that societal stress, though damaging, could not alone result in a life of crime unless a predisposition existed that prepared youths psychologically for antisocial acts. This mental state, which he labeled **latent delinquency,** is found in youngsters whose personality requires them (1) to seek immediate gratification (to act impulsively), (2) to consider satisfaction of their personal needs more important than relating to others, and (3) to satisfy instinctive urges without consideration of right and wrong (that is, they lack guilt).

Psychodynamics of Criminal Behavior

Since this early work, psychoanalysts have continued to view the criminal as an id-dominated person who suffers from the inability to control impulsive, pleasure-seeking drives.[112] Perhaps because they suffered unhappy experiences in childhood or had families that could not provide proper love and care, criminals suffer from weak or damaged egos that make them unable to cope with conventional society. Weak egos are associated with immaturity, poor social skills, and excessive dependence on others; people with weak egos may be easily led by antisocial peers into crime and drug abuse. Some offenders have undeveloped superegos and consequently lack internalized representations of those behaviors that are punished in conventional society; they commit crimes because they have difficulty understanding the wrongfulness of their actions.[113]

Personality conflict or underdevelopment may result in neurotic or psychotic behavior patterns. Offenders classified as neurotics are driven by an unconscious desire to be punished for prior sins, either real or imaginary; they may violate the law to gain attention or punish their parents. In its most extreme form, criminality may be viewed as a form of psychosis that prevents offenders from appreciating the feelings of their victims or controlling their own impulsive needs for gratification.

Crime then is a manifestation of feelings of oppression and the inability of people to develop the proper defense mechanisms to keep these feelings under control. Criminality actually allows troubled people to survive by producing positive psychic results: it helps them to feel free and independent, it gives them the possibility of excitement and the chance to use their skills and imagination, it provides them with the promise of positive gain, it allows them to blame others for their predicament (for example, the police), and it gives them a chance to rationalize their sense of failure ("If I hadn't gotten into trouble, I could have been a success").[114]

The psychodynamic model of the criminal offender depicts an aggressive, frustrated person dominated by events that occurred early in childhood.

≡ Behavioral Theories

Behavior theory maintains that human actions are developed through learning experiences. Rather than focus on unconscious personality traits or cognitive development patterns produced early in childhood, behavior theorists are concerned with the actual behaviors people engage in during the course of their daily lives. The major premise of behavior theory is that people alter their behavior according to the reactions it receives from others. Behavior is supported by rewards and extinguished by negative reactions or punishments. Behavior is constantly being shaped by life experiences.

Behaviorist theory is quite complex with many different subareas. With respect to criminal activity, the behaviorist views crimes, especially violent acts, as learned responses to life situations that do not necessarily represent abnormal or morally immature responses.

Social Learning Theory

Social learning is the branch of behavior theory most relevant to criminology.[115] Social learning theorists, most notably Albert Bandura, argue that people are not actually born with the ability to act violently but that they learn to be aggressive through their life experiences.

These experiences include personally observing others acting aggressively to achieve some goal or watching people being rewarded for violent acts on television or in movies. People learn to act aggressively when, as children, they model their behavior after the violent acts of adults. Later in life, these violent behavior patterns persist in social relationships. The boy who sees his father repeatedly strike his mother with impunity is the one most likely to grow up to become a battering parent and husband. Though social learning theorists agree that mental or physical traits may predispose a person toward violence, they believe that the activation of a person's violent tendencies is achieved by factors in the environment. The specific forms that aggressive behavior takes, the frequency with which it is expressed, the situations in which it is displayed, and the specific targets selected for attack are largely determined by social learning. However, people are self-aware and engage in purposeful learning. Their interpretations of behavior outcomes and situations influence the way they learn from experiences. One adolescent who spends a weekend in jail for drunk driving may find it the most awful experience of her life, one that teaches her to never drink and drive; another finds it an exciting experience about which he can brag to his friends.

Social Learning and Violence.   Social learning theorists view violence as something learned through a process called **behavior modeling.** In modern society, aggressive acts are usually modeled after three principal sources. Most prominent is the behavior model reinforced by family members. Bandura reports that studies of family life show that children who use aggressive tactics have parents who use similar behaviors when dealing with others.

A second influence on the social learning of violence is provided by environmental experiences. People who reside in areas in which violence is a daily occurrence are more likely to act violently than those who dwell in low-crime areas whose norms stress conventional behavior.

A third source of behavior modeling is provided by the mass media. Films and television shows commonly depict violence graphically. Moreover, violence is often portrayed as an acceptable behavior, especially for heroes who never have to face legal consequences for their actions. For example, David Phillips found the homicide rate increases significantly immediately after a heavyweight championship prize fight.[116] (See the Close-Up entitled "The Media and Violence.")

What triggers violent acts? Various sources have been investigated by social learning theorists. One position is that a direct, pain-producing physical assault will

CLOSE-UP

The Media and Violence

In October 1993, a five-year-old Ohio boy set a fire that caused the death of his two-year-old sister. The boy's mother charged that the youth was influenced by the MTV show "Beavis and Butthead," whose cartoon heroes regularly start fires and chant "fire is good." MTV responded to the public outcry over the incident by moving the show's broadcast time from 7 P.M. to 10:30 P.M. A national survey conducted in the wake of the controversy found that almost 80 percent of the general public believes that violence on TV can cause violence "in real life."

Does the media influence behavior? Does broadcast violence cause aggressive behavior in viewers? This has become a hot topic because of the persistent theme of violence on television and in films. Critics have called for drastic measures ranging from the banning of TV violence to putting warning labels on heavy metal albums because of a fear that listening to hard-rock lyrics produces delinquency.

If there is in fact a TV-violence link, the problem is indeed alarming. Systematic viewing of TV begins at two-and-a-half years of age and continues at a high level during the preschool and early school years; it has been estimated that children aged 2 to 5 watch TV for 27.8 hours each week; children aged 6 to 11, 24.3 hours per week; and teens, 23 hours per week. Marketing research indicates that adolescents aged 11 to 14 rent violent horror movies at a higher rate than any other age group; kids this age use older peers and siblings and apathetic parents to gain access to R-rated films. More than 40 percent of U.S. households now have cable TV, which features violent films and shows. Even children's programming is saturated with violence. A 1992 University of Pennsylvania study found that children's programming contained an average of 32 violent acts per hour, that 56 percent had violent characters, and that 74 percent had characters who became the victims of violence (though "only 3.3 percent had characters who were actually killed"). The average child views 8,000 TV murders before finishing elementary school.

There have been numerous anecdotal cases of violence linked to TV and films. In 1974, a nine-year-old California girl was raped with a bottle by four other girls who said they had watched a similar act in the television movie *Born Innocent,* which depicted life in a reformatory for girls; her parents' lawsuit against NBC, the network that broadcast the film, was dismissed in court. In 1977, Ronald Zamora killed an elderly woman and then plead guilty by reason of insanity. His attorney claimed Zamora was addicted to TV violence and could no longer differentiate between reality and fantasy; the jury did not buy the defense, and Zamora was found guilty as charged. At least 43 deaths have been linked to the movie *The Deer Hunter,* which featured a scene in which a main character kills himself while playing Russian roulette for money. In a famous incident, John Hinckley shot President Ronald Reagan due to his obsession with actress Jodie Foster, which developed after he watched her play a prostitute in the film *Taxi Driver.* Hinckley viewed the film at least 15 times. More recently, well-publicized violent episodes in which a number of theater patrons were killed have been linked to the gang-related movies *Colors* and *New Jack City.*

Psychologists believe that media violence does not in itself *cause* violent behavior because if it did, there would be millions of daily incidents in which viewers imitated the aggression they watched on TV or movies. But most psychologists agree that media violence *contributes* to aggression. There are several explanations for the effects of television and film violence on behavior:

- Media violence can provide aggressive "scripts" that children store in memory. Repeated exposure to these scripts can increase their retention and lead to changes in attitudes. Exposure to violent displays of any type could provide cues leading to the retrieval of these and other scripts and to the emission of aggressive behavior.
- Observational learning occurs when the violence seen on television is copied by the child viewer. Children learn to be violent from television in the same way that they learn cognitive and social skills from their parents and friends.
- Television violence increases the arousal levels of viewers and makes them more prone to act aggressively. Studies measuring the galvanic skin response of subjects—a physical indication of arousal based on the amount of electricity conducted across the palm of the hand—show that viewing

Critics demand that TV shows limit their violent content. Yet a great deal of the violence shown on TV occurs during news and sports shows. Should these events, such as films of the beating of Rodney King shown during the trial of the police officers involved, not be allowed on TV?

violent television shows led to increased arousal levels in young children.

- Television violence promotes attitude changes, which can then result in behavior changes. Watching television violence promotes such negative attitudes as suspiciousness and the expectation that the viewer will become involved in violence. Attitudes of frequent television viewers toward aggression

become positive when they see violence as a common and socially acceptable behavior.

- Television violence helps already aggressive youths justify their behavior. It is possible that, instead of causing violence, television helps violent youths rationalize their behavior as a socially acceptable and common activity.

- Television violence may disinhibit aggressive behavior, which

is normally controlled by other learning processes. Disinhibition takes place when adults are viewed as being rewarded for violence and when violence is seen as socially acceptable. This contradicts previous learning experiences in which violent behavior was viewed as wrong.

Such august bodies as the American Psychological Association, the National Institute of Mental Health, and the National Research Council support the TV-violence link. They base their conclusion on research efforts that indicate that watching violence on TV leads to increased levels of violence in the laboratory as well as in natural settings.

A number of experimental approaches have been tried. Groups of subjects have been exposed to violent TV shows in a laboratory setting and their behavior afterward compared to control groups who viewed nonviolent programming; observations have also been made in playgrounds, athletic fields, and residences. Other experiments require subjects to answer attitude surveys after watching violent TV shows. Still another approach is to use aggregate measures of TV viewing; for example, the number of violent TV shows on the air during a given time period is compared to crime rates during the same period.

Most evaluations of experimental data indicate that watching violence on TV is correlated to aggressive behaviors. In an important review of the literature, Wendy Wood, Frank Wong, and J. Gregory Chachere concluded that violent media has at least a short-term impact on behavior. Subjects who view violent TV shows are likely to commence aggressive behavior almost immediately.

Though this evidence is persuasive, the relationship between media and violence is still unproven. A number of critics argue that the evidence simply does not support the claim that watching TV or movies and listening to heavy metal music is related to antisocial behavior. Simon Singer found that teen-aged heavy metal fans were no more delinquent than nonlisteners. Candace Kruttschnitt and her associates found that an individual's exposure to violent TV shows is only weakly related to subsequent violent behavior. There is also little evidence that areas that experience the highest levels of violent TV viewing also have rates of violent crime that are above the norm.

Millions of children watch violence every night yet fail to become violent criminals. If violent TV shows caused interpersonal violence, then there should be few ecological and regional patterns in the crime rate, of which there are many. Put another way, how can regional differences in the violence rate be explained considering the fact that people all across the nation watch the same TV shows and films?

Critics also assert that experimental results are inconclusive and short-lived. People may have an immediate reaction to viewing violence on TV, but aggression is quickly extinguished once the viewing ends. Experiments that show a correlation between aggression and TV fail to link the association with actual criminal behaviors, such as rape or assault. The weight of the experimental results does indicate that violent media has an immediate impact on people with a preexisting tendency toward crime and violence. But do kids who act more aggressively after watching violent TV later grow up to become rapists and killers?

Considering the evidence, should the viewing of violent TV shows be

usually trigger a violent response. Yet the relationship between painful attacks and aggressive responses has been found to be inconsistent; whether people counterattack in the face of physical attack depends in part on their skill in fighting and their perception of the strength of their attackers. Verbal taunts and insults have also been linked to aggressive responses. People who are predisposed to aggression by their learning experiences are likely to view insults from others as a challenge to their social status and to react with violence. Still another violence-triggering mechanism is a perceived reduction in one's life conditions. Prime examples of this phenomenon are riots and demonstrations in poverty-stricken ghetto areas. Studies have shown that discontent also produces aggression in the more successful members of lower-class groups who have been led to believe they can succeed but have been thwarted in their aspirations. While it is still uncertain how this relationship is constructed, it is apparently complex. No matter how deprived some individuals are, they will not resort to violence. It seems evident that people's perceptions of their relative deprivation have differing effects on their aggressive responses.

In summary, social learning theorists have said that the following four factors help produce violence and aggression:

curtailed or controlled? One answer would be to have government regulators limit the content of programs or restrict times that violent shows may be aired (presumably, as in the "Beavis and Butthead" case, after adolescent bedtimes). Critics charge that such policies run afoul of First Amendment guarantees of free speech; who is to say when a TV show is too violent? The TV industry has volunteered to broadcast advisories warning parents that shows contain violent themes and advertise these warnings in local newspaper listings.

While such practices may help guide some parents, they do little to restrict TV watching when children are home alone (though it may soon be possible to equip television sets with computer chips that prevent the reception of shows designated as having violent themes). Controlling the media may also be difficult because many violent events are part of the local news or sporting events. For example, Garland White, Janet Katz, and Kathryn Scarborough found that when the local football team *wins*, violent assaults on women increase; sports dominance may trigger feelings of power and control, which results in sexual aggression in males. This research received nationwide attention and prompted antibattering public service announcements during the Super Bowl. If such findings are valid, it is unlikely that those concerned with media violence can engineer a ban of pro football games on television.

The most reasonable option may simply to be to reduce the number of TV shows with violent themes, an unlikely event considering that the amount of TV violence tripled during the past decade.

Discussion Questions

1. Should the government control the content of TV shows and limit the amount of weekly violence?
2. How can we explain the fact that millions of kids watch violent TV shows and remain nonviolent?

SOURCE: Garland White, Janet Katz, and Kathryn Scarborough, "The Impact of Professional Football Games upon Violent Assaults on Women," *Violence and Victims* 7 (1992): 157–71; Simon Singer, "Rethinking Subcultural Theories of Delinquency and the Cultural Resources of Youth" (Paper presented at the annual meeting of the American Society of Criminology, Phoenix, Arizona, November 1993); Albert Reiss and Jeffrey Roth, eds., *Understanding and Preventing Violence* (Washington, D.C.: National Academy Press, 1993); Reuters, Seventy-nine Percent in Survey Link Violence on TV and Crime," *Boston Globe,* 19 December 1993, p. 17; Scott Snyder, "Movies and Juvenile Delinquency: An Overview," *Adolescence* 26 (1991): 121–31; Steven Messner, "Television Violence and Violent Crime: An Aggregate Analysis," *Social Problems* 33 (1986): 218–35; Candace Kruttschnitt, Linda Heath, and David Ward, "Family Violence, Television Viewing Habits, and Other Adolescent Experiences Related to Violent Criminal Behavior," *Criminology* 243 (1986): 235–67; Jonathan Freedman, "Television Violence and Aggression: A Rejoinder," *Psychological Bulletin* 100 (1986): 372–78; Wendy Wood, Frank Wong, and J. Gregory Chachere, "Effects of Media Violence on Viewers' Aggression in Unconstrained Social Interaction," *Psychological Bulletin* 109 (1991): 371–83.

---

1. *An event that heightens arousal*—such as a person's frustrating or provoking another through physical assault or verbal abuse.
2. *Aggressive skills*—learned aggressive responses picked up from observing others, either personally or through the media.
3. *Expected outcomes*—the belief that aggression will somehow be rewarded. Rewards can come in the form of reducing tension or anger, gaining some financial reward, building self-esteem, or gaining the praise of others.
4. *Consistency of behavior with values*—the belief, gained from observing others, that aggression is justified and appropriate, given the circumstances of the current situation.

≡ Cognitive Theory

One area of psychology that has received increasing recognition in recent years has been the **cognitive school.** Psychologists with a cognitive perspective focus on mental processes and how people perceive and mentally represent the world around them and solve problems. The pioneers of this school were Wilhelm Wundt

(1832–1920), Edward Titchener (1867–1927), and William James (1842–1920). Today, there are several subdisciplines within the cognitive area. The moral development branch is concerned about the way people morally represent and reason about the world. Humanistic psychology stresses self-awareness and "getting in touch with feelings." The information processing branch focuses on the way people process, store, encode, retrieve, and manipulate information to make decisions and solve problems.

Moral and Intellectual Development Theory

The moral and intellectual development branch of cognitive psychology is perhaps the most important for criminological theory. Jean Piaget (1896–1980), the founder of this approach, hypothesized that people's reasoning processes develop in an orderly fashion, beginning at birth and continuing until they are 12 years old and older.[117] At first, during the sensorimotor stage, children respond to the environment in a simple manner, seeking interesting objects and developing their reflexes. By the fourth and final stage, the formal operations stage, they have developed into mature adults who can use logic and abstract thought.

Lawrence Kohlberg first applied the concept of moral development to issues in criminology.[118] He found that people travel through stages of moral development, during which their decisions and judgments on issues of right and wrong are made for different reasons. It is possible that serious offenders have a moral orientation that differs from that of law-abiding citizens. Kohlberg's stages of development are:

STAGE 1—Right is obedience to power and avoidance of punishment.

STAGE 2—Right is taking responsibility for oneself, meeting one's own needs, and leaving to others the responsibility for themselves.

STAGE 3—Right is being good in the sense of having good motives, having concern for others, and "putting yourself in the other person's shoes."

STAGE 4—Right is maintaining the rules of a society and serving the welfare of the group or society.

STAGE 5—Right is based on recognized individual rights within a society with agreed-upon rules—a social contract.

STAGE 6—Right is an assumed obligation to principles applying to all humankind—principles of justice, equality, and respect for human life.

Kohlberg classified people according to the stage on this continuum at which their moral development ceased to grow.

In studies conducted by Kohlberg and his associates, criminals were found to be significantly lower in their moral judgment development than noncriminals of the same social background.[119] Since his pioneering efforts, researchers have continued to show that criminal offenders are more likely to be classified in the lowest levels of moral reasoning (stages 1 and 2), while noncriminals have reached a higher stage of moral development.[120]

Recent research indicates that the decision not to commit crimes may be influenced by one's stage of moral development. People at the lowest levels report that they are deterred from crime because of their fear of sanctions; those in the middle consider the reactions of family and friends; those at the highest stages refrain from crime because they believe in duty to others and universal rights.[121] The deterrent effect of informal sanctions and feelings of shame then (Chapter 5) may hinge on the level of a person's moral development.

Moral development theory suggests that people who obey the law simply to avoid punishment or who have outlooks mainly characterized by self-interest are more likely to commit crimes than those who view the law as something that benefits all of society and who sympathize with the rights of others; higher stages of moral reasoning are associated with conventional behaviors, such as honesty, generosity, and nonviolence.

Information Processing

When cognitive theorists who study information processing try to explain antisocial behavior, they do so in terms of perception and analysis of data. When people make decisions, they engage in a sequence of cognitive thought processes. They first *encode* information so that it can be interpreted. They then search for a proper response and decide upon the most appropriate action; finally, they act on their decision.[122]

According to this cognitive approach, violence-prone people may be using information incorrectly when they make decisions. One reason is that they may be relying on mental "scripts" learned in childhood that tell them how to interpret events, what to expect, how they should react, and what the outcome of the interaction should be.[123] Hostile children may have learned improper scripts by observing how others react to events; their own parents' aggressive and inappropriate behavior would have considerable impact. Violence becomes a stable behavior because the scripts that emphasize aggressive responses are repeatedly rehearsed as the child matures.

To violence-prone kids, people seem more aggressive than they actually are and intend them ill when there is no reason for alarm. As these children mature, they use fewer cues than most people to process information. Some use violence in a calculating fashion as a means of getting what they want; others react in an overly volatile fashion to the slightest provocation. Aggressors are more likely to be vigilant, on edge, or suspicious. When they attack victims, they may believe they are defending themselves, even though they are misreading the situation.[124]

Information processing theory has been used to explain the occurrence of date rape. Sexually violent males believe that when their dates say no to sexual advances, the women are really "playing games" and actually want to be taken forcefully.[125]

Treatment based on information processing acknowledges that people are more likely to respond aggressively to a provocation when thoughts intensify the insult or otherwise stir feelings of anger. Cognitive therapists attempt to teach explosive people to control aggressive impulses by viewing social provocations as problems demanding a solution rather than as insults requiring retaliation. Programs are aimed at teaching problem-solving skills that may include listening, following instructions, joining in, and using self-control. Treatment interventions based on learning social skills are relatively new, but there are some indications that this approach can have long-term benefits for reducing criminal behavior.[126]

Crime and Mental Illness

Each of the schools of psychology has a unique approach to the concept of mental abnormality. Psychoanalysts view mental illness as a retreat from unbearable stress and conflict; cognitive psychologists link it to thought disorders and overstimulation; behaviorists might look to environmental influences, such as early family experiences and social rejection. Regardless of the cause of mental illness, is there a link between it and crime?

A great deal of research indicates that many offenders who engage in serious, violent crimes suffer from some sort of mental disturbance. James Sorrells's well-known study of juvenile murderers, "Kids Who Kill," found that many homicidal youths could be described in such terms as "overtly hostile," "explosive or volatile," "anxious," and "depressed."[127] Likewise, in a study of 45 males accused of murder, Richard Rosner and his associates found that 75 percent could be classified as having some mental illness, including schizophrenia.[128] Abusive mothers have been found to have mood and personality disorders and a history of psychiatric diagnoses.[129]

There is also a significant body of literature indicating that those who are diagnosed as mentally ill are more likely to violate the law than the mentally sound. The reported substance abuse among the mentally ill is significantly higher than that of the general population.[130] Two recent research reports, one by Bruce Link and his associates and another by Ellen Steury, found that the diagnosed mentally ill appear in arrest and court statistics at a rate disproportionate to their presence in the population.[131]

Despite this evidence, some question remains whether as a group the mentally ill are any more criminal

A schizophrenic prisoner and guard in a high security prison in Warwick, Rhode Island: the association between crime and mental illness is still being debated.

than the mentally sound. The mentally ill may be more likely to withdraw or harm themselves than to act aggressively toward others.[132] Research conducted in New York shows that upon release, prisoners who had prior histories of hospitalization for mental disorders were *less* likely to be rearrested than those had never been hospitalized.[133] And both the Link and the Steury research, which did find a mental illness-crime association, report that the great majority of known criminals are not mentally ill and that the relationship is at best "modest."

While these research efforts give only tentative support to the proposition that mental disturbance or illness can be an underlying cause of violent crime, it is still possible that some link exists. Some but not all mentally ill people also manifest personality disorders, including psychopathy and neuroticism (see below). It is possible that these deeply troubled people are the ones most at risk to chronic criminal behavior.[134]

Personality and Crime

Personality can be defined as the reasonably stable patterns of behavior, including thoughts and emotions, that distinguish one person from another.[135] One's personality reflects a characteristic way of adapting to life's demands and problems. The way we behave is a function of how our personality enables us to interpret life events and make appropriate behavioral choices. Can the cause of crime be linked to personality? This issue has always caused significant debate.[136] In their early work, Sheldon Glueck and Eleanor Glueck identified a number of personality traits that they believed characterized antisocial youth:

self-assertiveness	sadism
defiance	lack of concern for others
extroversion	feeling unappreciated
ambivalence	distrust of authority
impulsiveness	poor personal skills
narcissism	mental instability
suspicion	hostility
destructiveness	resentment[137]

The Glueck research is representative of the view that antisocial people maintain a distinct set of personality traits and that their actions will involve them with agents of social control.

Several other research efforts have attempted to identify criminal personality traits.[138] For example, Hans Eysenck identified two personality traits that he associated with antisocial behavior: extraversion-introversion and stability-instability. Extreme introverts are overaroused and avoid sources of stimulation, while in contrast, extreme extraverts are unaroused and seek sensation. Introverts are slow to learn and be conditioned; extraverts are impulsive individuals who lack the ability to examine their own motives and behaviors. Those who are unstable, a condition that Eysenck calls **neuroticism,** are anxious, tense, and emotionally unstable.[139] People who are both neurotic and extraverted lack self-insight and are impulsive and emotionally unstable; they are unlikely to have reasoned judgments of life events. While extravert neurotics may act self-destructively, for example by abusing drugs, more stable people will be able to reason that such behavior is ultimately harmful and life-threatening. Eysenck believes that the direction of the personality is controlled by genetic factors and is heritable.

A number of other personality deficits have been identified in the criminal population. A common theme is that criminals are hyperactive, impulsive individuals with short attention spans (attention deficit disorder), conduct disorders, anxiety disorders, and depression.[140] These traits make them prone to problems ranging from psychopathology to drug abuse, sexual promiscuity, and violence.[141] As a group, people who share these traits are believed to have a character defect referred to interchangeably as the antisocial, sociopathic, or psychopathic personality, which is discussed in the Close-Up entitled "The Antisocial Personality."

Research on Personality

Since maintaining a deviant personality has been related to crime and delinquency, numerous attempts have been made to devise accurate measures of personality and determine whether they can predict antisocial behavior. Two types of standardized personality tests have been constructed. The first are projective techniques that require a subject to react to an ambiguous picture or shape by describing what it represents or by telling a story about it. The Rorschach Inkblot Test and the Thematic Apperception Test are examples of two widely used projective tests. Such tests are given by clinicians trained to interpret responses and categorize them according to established behavioral patterns. While these were not used extensively, some early research found that delinquents and nondelinquents could be separated on the basis of their personality profiles.[142] The second frequently used method of psychological testing is the personality inventory. These tests require subjects to agree or disagree with groups of questions in a self-administered survey. The most widely used psychological test is the Minnesota Multiphasic Personality Inventory, commonly called the MMPI. Developed by R. Starke Hathaway and J. Charnley McKinley, the MMPI has subscales that purport to measure many different personality traits, including psychopathic deviation (Pd scale), schizophrenia (Sc), and hypomania (Ma).[143]

Elio Monachesi and Hathaway pioneered the use of the MMPI to predict criminal behavior. They concluded that scores on some of the MMPI scales, especially the Pd scale, predicted delinquency. In one major effort, they administered the MMPI to a sample of ninth-grade boys and girls in Minneapolis and found that Pd scores had a significant relationship to later delinquent involvement. Other research studies have detected an association between scores on the Pd scale and criminal involvement.[144] Another frequently administered personality test, the California Personality Inventory (CPI), has also been used to distinguish deviants from nondeviant groups.[145]

Despite the time and energy put into using the MMPI and other scales to predict crime and delinquency, the results have proved inconclusive. Three surveys of the literature of personality testing—one by Karl Schuessler and Donald Cressey (covering the pre-1950 period), another by Gordon Waldo and Simon Dinitz (covering the period 1950 to 1965), and another, more recent survey by David Tennenbaum—found inconclusive evidence that personality traits could consistently predict criminal involvement.[146] While some law violators may suffer from an abnormal personality structure, there are also many more whose personalities are indistinguishable from the norm. Efforts to improve the MMPI have resulted in the MMPI-2, a new scale with, it is hoped, improved validity; current research efforts should determine whether this version can successfully identify the potential for crime and violence.[147]

Are Some People Crime-Prone? Interest in the personality characteristics of criminals has been increasing. Because the most commonly used scales, such as the CPI and MMPI, have not been uniformly successful in predicting criminality, psychologists have turned to other measures, including the Multidimensional Personality Questionnaire (MPQ), to assess such personality traits as control, aggression, alienation, and well-being. Research by Avshalom Caspi and his associates finds that scales of the MPQ can produce "robust personality correlates of delinquency" and that these measures are valid across genders, races, and cultures.[148] The Caspi research indicates that adolescent offenders who are "crime-prone" respond to frustrating events with strong negative emotions, feel stressed and harassed, and are adversarial in their interpersonal relationships. Crime-prone people maintain "negative emotionality," a tendency to experience aversive affective states, such as anger, anxiety, and irritability. They also are predisposed to weak personal contraints; they have difficulty controlling impulsive behavior urges. Because they are both impulsive and aggressive, crime-prone people are quick to take action against perceived threats.

Evidence that personality traits predict crime and violence is important because it suggests that the root cause of crime can be found in the forces that influence human development at an early stage in the life course. If these results were valid, rather than focus on job creation and neighborhood improvement, crime control efforts might be better focused on helping families raise children who are reasoned and reflective and enjoy a safe environment.

☰ Intelligence and Crime

Some criminologists have maintained that many delinquents and criminals have a below-average intelligence quotient and that low IQ is a cause of their criminality. Early criminologists believed that low intelligence was a major cause of crime and delinquency. Criminals were believed to be inherently substandard in intelligence and thus naturally inclined to commit more crimes than more intelligent persons. Furthermore, it was thought that if authorities could determine which individuals had low IQs, they might identify potential criminals before they committed socially harmful acts. Since social scientists had a captive group of subjects in training schools and penal institutions, they began to measure the correlation between IQ and crime by testing adjudicated offenders. Thus, inmates of penal institutions were used as a test group around which numerous theories about intelligence were built, leading ultimately to the nature-versus-nurture controversy that is still going on today. These concepts are discussed in some detail in the following sections.

CLOSE-UP

The Antisocial Personality

Some but not all serious violent offenders may have a disturbed character structure commonly called **psychopathy, sociopathy, or antisocial personality.**

Psychopaths exhibit a low level of guilt and anxiety and persistently violate the rights of others. Although they may exhibit superficial charm and above-average intelligence, this often masks a disturbed personality that makes them incapable of forming enduring relationships with others and continually involves them in such deviant behaviors as violence, risk-taking, substance abuse, and impulsivity.

From an early age, the psychopath's home life was filled with frustrations, bitterness, and quarreling. Consequently, throughout life, he or she is unreliable, unstable, demanding, and egocentric. Hervey Cleckley, a leading authority on psychopathy, described them as follows:

[Psychopaths are] chronically antisocial individuals who are always in trouble, profiting neither from experience nor punishment, and maintaining no real loyalties to any person, group, or code. They are frequently callous and hedonistic, showing marked emotional immaturity, with lack of responsibility, lack of judgment and an ability to rationalize their behavior so that it appears warranted, reasonable and justified.

Considering these personality traits, it is not surprising that research studies show that people evaluated as psychopaths are significantly more criminal and violence-prone when compared to nonpsychopathic control groups and that psychopaths continue their criminal careers long after other offenders burn out or age out of crime. Psychopaths are continually in trouble with the law and therefore are likely to wind up in penal institutions. It has been estimated that up to 30 percent of all inmates can be classified as psychopaths or sociopaths, but a more realistic figure is probably 10 percent; not all psychopaths become criminals, and, conversely, most criminals are not psychopaths.

What Causes Psychopathy?
Though psychologists are still not certain of psychopathy's cause, a number of factors are believed to contribute to the development of a psychopathic or sociopathic personality. They include having a psychopathic parent, parental rejection and a lack of love during childhood, and inconsistent discipline. The early relationship between mother and child is also quite significant. Children who lack the opportunity to form an attachment to a mother figure in the first three years of life, who suffer sudden separation from the mother figure, or who see changes in the mother figure are most likely to develop psychopathic personalities. According to biologically oriented psychologists, psychopathy has its basis in a measurable physical condi-

Nature Theory

Nature theory argues that intelligence is largely determined genetically, that ancestry determines IQ, and that low intelligence as demonstrated by low IQ is linked to behavior, including criminal behavior. When the newly developed IQ tests were administered to inmates of prisons and juvenile training schools in the first decades of the century, the nature position gained support because a very large proportion of the inmates scored low on the tests. Henry Goddard found during his studies in 1920 that many institutionalized persons were what he considered "feebleminded"; he concluded that at least half of all juvenile delinquents were mental defectives.[149] Goddard's results were challenged in 1931, when Edwin Sutherland evaluated IQ studies of criminals and delinquents and noted significant variation in the findings.[150] The discrepancies were believed to reflect refinements in testing methods and scoring rather than differences in the mental ability of criminals. In 1926, William Healy and Augusta Bronner tested groups of delinquent boys in Chicago and Boston and found that 37 percent were subnormal in intelligence. They concluded that delinquents were five to ten times more likely to be mentally deficient than normal boys.[151] These and other early studies were embraced as proof that low IQ scores indicated potentially delinquent children and that a correlation existed between innate low intelligence and deviant behavior. IQ tests were believed to measure the inborn genetic makeup of individuals, and many criminologists accepted

tion—psychopaths suffer from levels of arousal that are lower than normal. Research studies have also found that psychopaths have lower skin conductance levels and fewer spontaneous responses than normal subjects. This view links psychopathy to autonomic nervous system (ANS) dysfunction. The ANS mediates physiological activities associated with emotions and is manifested in such measurements as heartbeat rate, blood pressure, respiration, muscle tension, papillary size, and electrical activity of the skin (called galvanic skin resistance). Another view is that psychopathy is caused by a dysfunction of the limbic inhibitory system manifested through damage to the frontal and temporal lobes of the brain. Consequently, psychopaths may need greater-than-average stimulation to bring them up to comfortable levels. People diagnosed as psychopaths are believed to be thrill seekers who engage in violent, destructive behavior; research shows that antisocial individuals are often

sensation seekers who desire a hedonistic pursuit of pleasure, an extraverted life-style, partying, drinking, and a variety of sexual partners. The desire for this stimulation may originate in their physical differences. Psychologists James Ogloff and Stephen Wong found that psychopaths may possess ineffective coping mechanisms in the presence of aversive or negative stimuli. Psychopaths may be less capable of regulating their activities than other people. While nonpsychopaths may become anxious and afraid when facing the prospect of committing a criminal act, psychopaths in the same circumstances feel no such fear. Ogloff and Wong conclude that their reduced anxiety levels result in behaviors that are more impulsive and inappropriate and in deviant behavior, apprehension, and incarceration. Psychologists have attempted to treat patients diagnosed as psychopaths by giving them adrenaline, which increases their arousal levels.

Discussion Questions

1. Should people diagnosed as psychopaths be separated and treated even if they have not yet committed a crime?

2. Should psychopathic murderers be spared the death penalty because they lack the capacity to control their behavior?

SOURCE: James Ogloff and Stephen Wong, "Electrodermal and Cardiovascular Evidence of a Coping Response in Psychopaths," *Criminal Justice and Behavior* 17 (1990): 231–45; Laurie Frost, Terrie Moffitt, and Rob McGee, "Neuropsychological Correlates of Psychopathology in an Unselected Cohort of Young Adolescents," *Journal of Abnormal Psychology* 98 (1989): 307–13; Hervey Cleckley, "Psychopathic States," in *American Handbook of Psychiatry*, ed. S. Aneti (New York: Basic Books, 1959), pp. 567–69; Spencer Rathus and Jeffrey Nevid, *Abnormal Psychology* (Englewood Cliffs, N.J.: Prentice-Hall, 1991), pp. 310–16; Helene Raskin White, Erich Labouvie, and Marsha Bates, "The Relationship between Sensation Seeking and Delinquency: A Longitudinal Analysis," *Journal of Research in Crime and Delinquency* 22 (1985): 197–211.

the idea that individuals with substandard IQs were predisposed toward delinquency and adult criminality.

Nurture Theory

The rise of culturally sensitive explanations of human behavior in the 1930s led to the nurture school of intelligence. This theory states that intelligence must be viewed as partly biological but primarily sociological. Nurture theorists discredited the notion that persons commit crimes because they have low IQs. Instead, they postulated that environmental stimulation from parents, relatives, social contacts, schools, peer groups, and innumerable others create a child's IQ level and that low IQs result from an environment that also encourages

delinquent and criminal behavior. Thus, if low IQ scores are recorded among criminals, these scores may reflect the criminals' cultural background, not their mental ability.

Studies challenging the assumption that people automatically committed criminal acts because they had below-average IQs began to appear as early as the 1920s. John Slawson studied 1,543 delinquent boys in New York institutions and compared them with a control group of New York City boys in 1926.[152] Slawson found that although 80 percent of the delinquents achieved lower scores in abstract verbal intelligence, delinquents were about normal in mechanical aptitude and nonverbal intelligence. These results indicated the possibility of cultural bias in portions of the IQ tests. He also found that there was no relationship between the number of arrests, the types of offenses, and IQ. Kenneth Eels and his associates found that tests used in the 1950s systematically underestimated the abilities of children of the working class. They argued that traditional intelligence tests predict who will succeed in a school system that makes use of abstract ideas and experiences that only middle-class children are likely to have: "There are reasoning abilities in the lower class that schooling could capitalize on if it were redesigned to be less verbal and culture-laden."[153] Robert Rosenthal and Lenore Jacobsen further debunked the notion that academic success and IQ scores were linked.[154]

IQ and Criminality

While the alleged IQ-crime link was dismissed by mainstream criminologists during much of the 1960s and '70s, it once again became an important area of study when respected criminologists Travis Hirschi and Michael Hindelang published a widely read 1977 paper linking the two variables.[155] After reexamining existing research data, Hirschi and Hindelang concluded that "the weight of evidence is that IQ is more important than race and social class" for predicting criminal and delinquent involvement. Rejecting the notion that IQ tests are race- and class-biased, they concluded that major differences exist between criminals and noncriminals within similar racial and socioeconomic class categories. Their position is that low IQ increases the likelihood of criminal behavior through its effect on school performance. That is, youths with low IQs do poorly in school, and school failure and academic incompetence are highly related to delinquency and later to adult criminality.

Hirschi and Hindelang's inferences have been supported by research conducted by both U.S. and international scholars.[156] In one recent analysis, Donald Lynam, Terrie Moffitt, and Magda Stouthamer-Loeber found a direct IQ-delinquency link among a sample of adolescent boys while controlling for race, class, and motivation. School performance helped explain the relationship between race and IQ only among African-American youth (that is, low IQ led to school failure and delinquency); among white youth, the IQ-delinquency association was constant regardless of school performance.[157] Other scientists have found that criminality is related to indicators of limited mental ability.[158]

The IQ-crime relationship has also been found in cross-national studies. Terrie Moffitt, William Gabrielli, Sarnoff Mednick, and Fini Schulsinger found a significant relationship between low IQ and delinquency among samples of Danish youth.[159] They conclude that

children with a low IQ may be likely to engage in delinquent behavior because their poor verbal ability is a handicap in the school environment.[160] Research by Canadian neural-psychologist Lorne Yeudall and his associates found samples of delinquents possessed IQs about 20 points less than nondelinquent control groups on the Wechsler Adult Intelligence Scale.[161] An IQ-crime link was found by Hakan Stattin and Ingrid Klackenberg-Larsson in a longitudinal study of Swedish youth. The Stattin research is important because it shows that low IQ measures taken at age three are significant predictors of later criminality over the life course.[162]

The case for an IQ-delinquency link is also made by James Q. Wilson and Richard Herrnstein in their 1985 book, *Crime and Human Nature*.[163] Wilson and Herrnstein, however, argue that the link is an indirect one: being in possession of a low IQ alone is not enough to cause a person to engage in antisocial behavior. Rather, the relationship is the product of a third intervening factor—poor school performance. As Wilson and Herrnstein conclude, "A child who chronically loses standing in the competition of the classroom may feel justified in settling the score outside, by violence, theft, and other forms of defiant illegality."[164] This conclusion is supported by another study conducted by Deborah Denno, which found that school environment is related to delinquency and that IQ level can be used to predict school achievement.[165]

IQ and Crime Reconsidered

While this evidence points to an association between IQ and crime, the issue is far from settled. A number of studies, such as that conducted by Scott Menard and Barbara Morse, find that IQ level has negligible influence on criminal behavior.[166] Deborah Denno failed to substantiate any direct relationship between mental ability and delinquency among a sample of 800 youths in Philadelphia.[167]

By their very nature, research efforts attempting to show a causal relationship between IQ and crime are beset by methodological difficulties. Aside from the well-documented criticisms suggesting that IQ tests are race- and class-biased, there is also the problem of sampling. Research using known criminals runs the risk of measuring the intelligence of only those people who have been apprehended, convicted, and sentenced. This group is unrepresentative of the criminal population, since it excludes offenders who escape detection (and who may have higher IQs). And, even if it can be shown that known offenders have lower IQs than the general population, this relationship could be more of a result of criminal justice system policy than the propensity of people with low IQs to commit crime.

If self-reports of both measures are used to overcome the selectivity problem, results may still be invalid because of the inherent risks of self-report data, such as the absence of persistent or chronic offenders. Self-report research also may be confounded by the problem of causal ordering since both criminality and IQ are measured simultaneously. Consequently, an IQ-crime link is subject to multiple interpretations: kids with low IQs are prone to commit crime; or, delinquents maintain a life-style that lowers their achievement on IQ tests.

Social Policy Implications

For most of the twentieth century, biological and psychological views of criminality have had an important influence on crime control and prevention policy. These views can be seen in front-end or primary prevention programs that seek to treat personal problems before they manifest themselves as crime. Thousands of family therapy organizations, substance abuse clinics, mental health associations, and so on are operating around the United States. Referrals to these are made by teachers, employers, courts, welfare agencies, and others. It is assumed that if a person's problems can be treated before they become overwhelming, some future crimes will be prevented. Secondary prevention programs provide such treatment as psychological counseling to youths and adults after they have violated the law. Attendance in such programs may be a mandatory requirement of a probation order, part of a diversionary sentence, or aftercare at the end of a prison sentence.

Biologically oriented therapy is also being used in the criminal justice system. Programs have altered diet, changed lighting, compensated for learning disabilities, treated allergies, and so on.[168] What is more controversial has been the use of mood-altering chemicals, such as lithium, pemoline, imipramine, phenytoin, and benzodiazepines, to control the behavior of antisocial people. Another practice that has elicited outcries of concern is the use of psychosurgery (brain surgery) to control antisocial behavior; surgical procedures have been used to alter the brain structure of convicted sex offenders in an effort to eliminate or control their sex drives. Results are still in the preliminary stage, but some critics have argued these procedures are without scientific merit.[169]

Some criminologists view biologically oriented treatments as a key to solving the problem of the chronic offender. Sarnoff Mednick and his associates have suggested that the biological analysis of criminal traits could pave the way for the development of preventive measures, regardless of whether the trait is inherited or acquired. They argue that a number of inherited physical traits that cause disease have been successfully treated with medication after their genetic code had been broken; why not, then, a genetic solution to crime?[170]

While such biological treatment is a relatively new phenomenon, it has become commonplace since the 1920s to offer psychological treatment to offenders before, during, and after a criminal conviction. For example, beginning in the 1970s, pretrial programs have sought to divert offenders into nonpunitive rehabilitative programs designed to treat rather than punish them. Based on some type of counseling regime, diversion programs are commonly used with first offenders, nonviolent offenders, and so on. At the trial stage, judges often order psychological profiles of convicted offenders for planning a treatment program. Should they be kept in the community? Do they need a more secure confinement to deal with their problems? If correctional confinement is called for, inmates are commonly evaluated at a correctional center to measure their personality traits or disorders. Correctional facilities almost universally require inmates to partake in some form of psychological therapy: group therapy, individual analysis, transactional analysis, and so on. Parole decisions may be influenced by the prison psychologist's evaluation of the offender's adjustment.

Beyond these efforts, the law recognizes the psychological aspects of crime when it permits the insanity plea as an excuse for criminal liability or when it allows trial delay because of mental incompetency.

Summary

The earliest positivist criminologists were biologists. Led by Cesare Lombroso, these early researchers believed some people manifested primitive traits that made them born criminals. Today, their research is debunked because of poor methodology, testing, and logic. Biological views fell out of favor in the early twentieth century. In the 1970s, spurred by the publication of Edmund O. Wilson's *Sociobiology,* several criminologists again turned to study of the biological basis of criminality. For the most part, the effort has focused on the cause of violent crime. Interest has centered on several areas: (1) biochemical factors, such as diet, allergies, hormonal imbalances, and environmental contaminants (such as lead); (2) neurophysiological factors, such as brain disorders, EEG abnormalities, tumors, and head injuries; and (3) genetic factors, such as the XYY syndrome and inherited traits. Biocriminology is in its infancy, and no definite studies have been undertaken.

Psychological attempts to explain criminal behavior have their historical roots in the concept that all criminals are insane or mentally damaged. This position is no longer accepted. Today, there are three main psychological perspectives. The psychodynamic view, the creation of Sigmund Freud, links aggressive behavior to personality conflicts developed in childhood. According to some psychoanalysts, psychotics are aggressive, unstable people who can easily become involved in crime. Cognitive psychology is concerned with human development and how people perceive the world. Criminality is viewed as a function of improper information processing and/or moral development. In contrast, behavioral and social learning theorists see criminality as a learned behavior. Children who are exposed to violence and see it rewarded may become violent as adults.

Psychological traits, such as personality and intelligence, have been linked to criminality. One important area of study has been the psychopath, a person who lacks emotion and concern for others. The controversial issue of the relationship of IQ to criminality has been resurrected once again with the publication of research studies purporting to show that criminals have lower IQs than noncriminals. Psychologists have developed standardized tests with which to measure personality traits. One avenue of research has been to determine whether criminals and noncriminals manifest any differences in their responses to test items.

Table 6.2 reviews the biological and psychological theories.

TABLE 6.2 Biological and Psychological Theories

Theory	Major Premise	Strengths
Biosocial		
Biochemical	Crime, especially violence, is a function of diet, vitamin intake, hormonal imbalance, or food allergies.	Explains irrational violence. Shows how the environment interacts with personal traits to influence behavior.
Neurological	Criminals and delinquents often suffer brain impairment, as measured by the EEG. Attention deficit disorder and minimum brain dysfunction are related to antisocial behavior.	Explains irrational violence. Shows how the environment interacts with personal traits to influence behavior.
Genetic	Criminal traits and predispositions are inherited. The criminality of parents can predict the delinquency of children.	Explains why only a small percentage of youth in a high-crime area become chronic offenders.
Evolutionary	As the human race evolved, traits and characteristics have become ingrained. Some of these traits make people aggressive and predisposed to commit crime.	Explains high violence rates and aggregate gender differences in the crime rate.
Psychological		
Psychodynamic	The development of the unconscious personality early in childhood influences behavior for the rest of a person's life. Criminals have weak egos and damaged personalities.	Explains the onset of crime and why crime and drug abuse cut across class lines.
Behavioral	People commit crime when they model their behavior after others they see being rewarded for the same acts. Behavior is enforced by rewards and extinguished by punishment.	Explains the role of significant others in the crime process. Shows how family life and media can influence crime and violence.
Cognitive	Individual reasoning processes influence behavior. Reasoning is influenced by the way people perceive their environment and by their moral and intellectual development.	Shows why criminal behavior patterns change over time as people mature and develop their moral reasoning. May explain aging-out process.

≡ KEY TERMS

neurological
biosocial theory
atavistic anomalies
somatotype
reciprocal altruism
equipotentiality
hypoglycemia
androgens
testosterone
estrogen
progesterone
premenstrual syndrome
 (PMS)
neurophysiology
electroencephalograph
 (EEG)
minimal brain dysfunction
 (MBD)

psychodynamic
repression
neuroses
neurotics
psychotics
schizophrenia
inferiority complex
identity crisis
latent delinquency
social learning
behavior modeling
cognitive school
psychopathy
sociopathy
antisocial personality
neuroticism

≡ NOTES

1. Israel Nachshon, "Neurological Bases of Crime, Psychopathy and Aggression," in *Crime in Biological, Social and Moral Contexts*, ed. Lee Ellis and Harry Hoffman (New York: Praeger, 1990), p. 199. Herein cited as *Crime in Biological Contexts*.

2. Raffaele Garofalo, *Criminology*, trans. Robert Miller (Boston: Little, Brown, 1914), p. 92.

3. Enrico Ferri, *Criminal Sociology* (New York: D. Appleton, 1909).

4. See Richard Dugdale, *The Jukes* (New York: Putnam, 1910); Arthur Estabrook, *The Jukes in 1915* (Washington, D.C.: Carnegie Institute of Washington, 1916).

5. William Sheldon, *Varieties of Delinquent Youth* (New York: Harper Bros., 1949).

6. Pierre van den Bergle, "Bringing The Beast Back in: Toward a Biosocial Theory of Aggression," *American Sociological Review* 39 (1974): 779.

7. Edmund O. Wilson, *Sociobiology* (Cambridge: Harvard University Press, 1975).

8. See, generally, Lee Ellis, "Introduction: The Nature of the Biosocial Perspective," *Crime in Biological Contexts,* pp. 3–18.

9. See, for example, Tracy Bennett Herbert and Sheldon Cohen, "Depression and Immunity: A Meta-Analytic Review," *Psychological Bulletin* 113 (1993): 472–86.

10. See, generally, Lee Ellis, *Theories of Rape* (New York: Hemisphere Publications, 1989).

11. Leonard Hippchen, "Some Possible Biochemical Aspects of Criminal Behavior," *Journal of Behavioral Ecology* 2 (1981): 1–6; Sarnoff Mednick and Jan Volavka, "Biology and Crime," in *Crime and Justice*, ed. Norval Morris and Michael Tonry (Chicago: University of Chicago Press, 1980), pp. 85–159; Saleem Shah and Loren Roth, "Biological and Psychophysiological Factors in Criminality," in *Handbook of Criminology*, ed. Daniel Glazer (Chicago: Rand McNally, 1974), pp. 125–40.

12. *Time*, 28 May 1979, p. 57.

13. Leonard Hippchen, ed., *Ecologic-Biochemical Approaches to Treatment of Delinquents and Criminals* (New York: Von Nostrand Reinhold, 1978), p. 14.

14. Michael Krassner, "Diet and Brain Function," *Nutrition Reviews* 44 (1986): 12–15.

15. Hippchen, *Ecologic-Biochemical Approaches to Treatment of Delinquents and Criminals.*

16. J. Kershner and W. Hawke, "Megavitamins and Learning Disorders: A Controlled Double-Blind Experiment," *Journal of Nutrition* 109 (1979): 819–26.

17. Richard Knox, "Test Shows Smart People's Brains Use Nutrients Better," *Boston Globe,* 16 February 1988, p. 9.

18. Ronald Prinz and David Riddle, "Associations between Nutrition and Behavior in 5-Year-Old Children," *Nutrition Reviews Supplement* 44 (1986): 151–58.

19. Stephen Schoenthaler and Walter Doraz, "Types of Offenses Which Can Be Reduced in an Institutional Setting Using Nutritional Intervention," *International Journal of Biosocial Research* 4 (1983): 74–84; and idem, "Diet and Crime," *International Journal of Biosocial Research* 4 (1983): 74–84. See also A. G. Schauss, "Differential Outcomes among Probationers Comparing Orthomolecular Approaches to Conventional Casework Counseling" (Paper presented at the annual meeting of the American Society of Criminology, Dallas, 9 November 1978); A. Schauss and C. Simonsen, "A Critical Analysis of the Diets of Chronic Juvenile Offenders, Part I," *Journal of Orthomolecular Psychiatry* 8 (1979): 222–26; A. Hoffer, "Children with Learning and Behavioral Disorders," *Journal of Orthomolecular Psychiatry* 5 (1976): 229.

20. Prinz and Riddle, "Associations between Nutrition and Behavior in 5-Year-Old Children."

21. H. Bruce Ferguson, Clare Stoddart, and Jovan Simeon, "Double-Blind Challenge Studies of Behavioral and Cognitive Effects of Sucrose-Aspartame Ingestion in Normal Children," *Nutrition Reviews Supplement* 44 (1986): 144–58; Gregory Gray, "Diet, Crime and Delinquency: A Critique," *Nutrition Reviews Supplement* 44 (1986): 89–94.

22. Dian Gans, "Sucrose and Unusual Childhood Behavior," *Nutrition Today* 26 (1991): 8–14.

23. D. Hill and W. Sargent, "A Case of Matricide," *Lancet* 244 (1943): 526–27.

24. E. Podolsky, "The Chemistry of Murder," *Pakistan Medical Journal* 15 (1964): 9–14.

25. J. A. Yaryura-Tobias and F. Neziroglu, "Violent Behavior, Brain Dysrhythmia and Glucose Dysfunction: A New Syndrome," *Journal of Orthopsychiatry* 4 (1975): 182–88.

26. Matti Virkkunen, "Reactive Hypoglycemic Tendency among Habitually Violent Offenders," *Nutrition Reviews*

Supplement 44 (1986): 94–103.

27. James Q. Wilson, *The Moral Sense* (New York: Free Press, 1993).

28. Walter Gove, "The Effect of Age and Gender on Deviant Behavior: A Biopsychosocial Perspective," in *Gender and the Life Course*, ed. A. S. Rossi (New York: Aldine, 1985), pp. 115–44.

29. Alan Booth and D. Wayne Osgood, "The Influence of Testosterone on Deviance in Adulthood: Assessing and Explaining the Relationship," *Criminology* 31 (1993): 93–118.

30. Christy Miller Buchanan, Jacquelynne Eccles, and Jill Becker, "Are Adolescents the Victims of Raging Hormones? Evidence for Activational Effects of Hormones on Moods and Behavior at Adolescence," *Psychological Bulletin* 111 (1992): 62–107.

31. Booth and Osgood, "The Influence of Testosterone on Deviance in Adulthood."

32. Albert Reiss and Jeffrey Roth, eds. *Understanding and Preventing Violence* (Washington, D.C.: National Academy Press, 1993), p. 118. This report by the National Research Council Panel on the Understanding and Control of Violent Behavior is hereafter cited as *Understanding Violence*.

33. L. E. Kreuz and R. M. Rose, "Assessment of Aggressive Behavior and Plasma Testosterone in a Young Criminal Population," *Psychosomatic Medicine* 34 (1972): 321–32.

34. Lee Ellis, "Evolutionary and Neurochemical Causes of Sex Differences in Victimizing Behavior: Toward a Unified Theory of Criminal Behavior and Social Stratification," *Social Science Information* 28 (1989): 605–36.

35. For a general review, see Lee Ellis and Phyllis Coontz, "Androgens, Brain Functioning, and Criminality: The Neurohormonal Foundations of Antisociality," in *Crime in Biological Contexts*, pp. 162–93.

36. Ibid., p. 181.

37. Robert Rubin, "The Neuroendocrinology and Neurochemistry of Antisocial Behavior," in *The Causes of Crime, New Biological Appoaches*, ed. Sarnoff Mednick, Terrie Moffitt, and Susan Stack (Cambridge: Cambridge University Press, 1987), pp. 239–62.

38. J. Money, "Influence of Hormones on Psychosexual Differentiation," *Medical Aspects of Nutrition* 30 (1976): 165.

39. Mednick and Volavka, "Biology and Crime."

40. Katharina Dalton, *The Premenstrual Syndrome* (Springfield, Ill.: Charles C. Thomas, 1971).

41. Julie Horney, "Menstrual Cycles and Criminal Responsibility," *Law and Human Nature* 2 (1978): 25–36.

42. H. E. Amos and J. J. P. Drake, "Problems Posed by Food Additives," *Journal of Human Nutrition* 30 (1976): 165.

43. Ray Wunderlich, "Neuroallergy as a Contributing Factor to Social Misfits: Diagnosis and Treatment," in *Ecologic-Biochemical Approaches to Treatment of Delinquents and Criminals*, ed. Leonard Hippchen (New York: Von Nostrand Reinhold, 1978), pp. 229–53.

44. See, for example, Paul Marshall, "Allergy and Depression: A Neurochemical Threshold Model of the Relation between the Illnesses," *Psychological Bulletin* 113 (1993): 23–39.

45. A. R. Mawson and K. J. Jacobs, "Corn Consumption, Tryptophan, and Cross-National Homicide Rates," *Journal of Orthomolecular Psychiatry* 7 (1978): 227–30.

46. Alexander Schauss, *Diet, Crime and Delinquency* (Berkeley, Calif.: Parker House, 1980).

47. C. Hawley and R. E. Buckley, "Food Dyes and Hyperkinetic Children," *Academy Therapy* 10 (1974): 27–32.

48. Oliver David, Stanley Hoffman, Jeffrey Sverd, Julian Clark, and Kytja Voeller, "Lead and Hyperactivity, Behavior Response to Chelation: A Pilot Study," *American Journal of Psychiatry* 133 (1976): 1155–58.

49. John Ott, "The Effects of Light and Radiation on Human Health and Behavior," in *Ecologic-Biochemical Approaches to Treatment of Delinquents and Criminals*, ed. Leonard Hippchen (New York: Von Nostrand Reinhold, 1978), pp. 105–83. See also A. Kreuger and S. Sigel, "Ions in the Air," *Human Nature* (July 1978): 46–47; Harry Wohlfarth, "The Effect of Color Psychodynamic Environmental Modification on Discipline Incidents in Elementary Schools over One School Year: A Controlled Study," *International Journal of Biosocial Research* 6 (1984): 44–53.

50. Terrie Moffitt, "The Neuropsychology of Juvenile Delinquency: A Critical Review, in *Crime and Justice, An Annual Review*, vol. 12, ed. Norval Morris and Michael Tonry (Chicago: University of Chicago Press, 1990), pp. 99–169.

51. Terrie Moffitt, Donald Lyman, and Phil Silva, "Neuropsychological Tests Predicting Persistent Male Delinquency," *Criminology* 32 (1994): 277–300; Elizabeth Kandel and Sarnoff Mednick, "Perinatal Complications Predict Violent Offending," *Criminology* 29 (1991): 519–29; Sarnoff Mednick, Ricardo Machon, Matti Virkunen, and Douglas Bonett, "Adult Schizophrenia Following Prenatal Exposure to an Influenza Epidemic," *Archives of General Psychiatry* 44 (1987): 35–46; C. A. Fogel, S. A. Mednick, and N. Michelson, "Hyperactive Behavior and Minor Physical Anomalies," *Acta Psychiatrica Scandinavia* 72 (1985): 551–56.

52. R. Johnson, *Aggression in Man and Animals* (Philadelphia: Saunders, 1972), p. 79.

53. Deborah Denno, *Biology, Crime and Violence: New Evidence* (Cambridge: Cambridge University Press, 1989).

54. Diana Fishbein and Robert Thatcher, "New Diagnostic Methods in Criminology: Assessing Organic Sources of Behavioral Disorders," *Journal of Research in Crime and Delinquency* 23 (1986): 240–67.

55. Lorne Yeudall, "A Neuropsychosocial Perspective of Persistent Juvenile Delinquency and Criminal Behavior" (Paper presented at the New York Academy of Sciences, 26 September 1979).

56. R. W. Aind and T. Yamamoto, "Behavior Disorders of Childhood," *Electroencephalography and Clinical*

Neurophysiology 21 (1966): 148–56.

57. See, generally, Jan Volavka, "Electroencephalogram among Criminals," in *The Causes of Crime, New Biological Approaches,* ed. Sarnoff Mednick, Terrie Moffitt, and Susan Stack (Cambridge: Cambridge University Press, 1987), pp. 137–45.

58. Z. A. Zayed, S. A. Lewis, and R. P. Britain, "An Encephalographic and Psychiatric Study of 32 Insane Murderers," *British Journal of Psychiatry* 115 (1969): 1115–24.

59. Fishbein and Thatcher, "New Diagnostic Methods in Criminology."

60. D. R. Robin, R. M. Starles, T. J. Kenney, B. J. Reynolds, and F. P. Heald, "Adolescents Who Attempt Suicide," *Journal of Pediatrics* 90 (1977): 636–38.

61. R. R. Monroe, *Brain Dysfunction in Aggressive Criminals* (Lexington, Mass.: D.C. Heath, 1978).

62. L. T. Yeudall, *Childhood Experiences as Causes of Criminal Behavior* (Senate of Canada, Issue no. 1, Thirteenth Parliament, Ottawa, 1977).

63. Charles Murray, *The Link between Learning Disabilities and Juvenile Delinquency* (Washington, D.C.: U.S. Government Printing Office, 1976), p. 65; see also B. Claire McCullough, Barbara Zaremba, and William Rich, "The Role of the Juvenile System in the Link between Learning Disabilities and Delinquency," *State Court Journal* 3 (1979): 45; Hill and Sargent, "A Case of Matricide."

64. Stephen Faraone, et al., "Intellectual Performance and School Failure in Children with Attention Deficit Hyperactivity Disorder and in Their Siblings," *Journal of Abnormal Psychology* 102 (1993): 616–23.

65. Ibid.

66. Terrie Moffitt and Phil Silva, "Self-Reported Delinquency, Neuropsychological Deficit, and History of Attention Deficit Disorder," *Journal of Abnormal Child Psychology* 16 (1988): 553–69.

67. Eugene Maguin, Rolf Loeber, and Paul LeMahieu, "Does the Relationshp between Poor Reading and Delinquency Hold for Males of Different Ages and Ethnic Groups?" *Journal of Emotional and Behavioral Disorders* 1 (1993): 88–100.

68. Elizabeth Hart, et al., "Developmental Change in Attention-Deficit Hyperactivity Disorder in Boys: A Four-Year Longitudinal Study," *Journal of Consulting and Clinical Psychology* (in press, 1994).

69. Yeudall, "A Neuropsychosocial Perspective of Persistent Juvenile Delinquency and Criminal Behavior," p. 4; F. A. Elliott, "Neurological Aspects of Antisocial Behavior," in *The Psychopath: A Comprehensive Study of Antisocial Disorders and Behaviors,* ed. W. H. Reid (New York: Brunner/Mazel, 1978), pp. 146–89.

70. Lorne Yeudall, Orestes Fedora, and Delee Fromm, "A Neuropsychosocial Theory of Persistent Criminality: Implications for Assessment and Treatment," in *Advances in Forensic Psychology and Psychiatry,* ed. Robert Rieber (Norwood, N.J.: Ablex Publishing, 1987), pp. 119–91.

71. Ibid., p. 177.

72. Ibid., pp. 24–25.

73. H. K. Kletschka, "Violent Behavior Associated with Brain Tumor," *Minnesota Medicine* 49 (1966): 1853–55.

74. V. E. Krynicki, "Cerebral Dysfunction in Repetitively Assaultive Adolescents," *Journal of Nervous and Mental Disease* 166 (1978): 59–67.

75. C. E. Lyght, ed., *The Merck Manual of Diagnosis and Therapy* (West Point, Fla.: Merck, 1966).

76. *Understanding Violence*, p. 119.

77. M. Virkkunen, M. J. DeJong, J. Bartko, and M. Linnoila "Psychobiological Concomitants of History of Suicide Attempts among Violent Offenders and Impulsive Fire Starters," *Archives of General Psychiatry* 46 (1989): 604–06.

78. Lee Ellis, "Left- and Mixed-Handedness and Criminality: Explanations for a Probable Relationship," in *Left-handedness, Behavioral Implications and Anomalies,* ed. S. Coren (Amsterdam: Elsevier, 1990): 485–507.

79. Lee Ellis, "Monoamine Oxidase and Criminality: Identifying an Apparent Biological Marker for Antisocial Behavior," *Journal of Research in Crime and Delinquency* 28 (1991): 227–51.

80. Walter Gove and Charles Wilmoth, "Risk, Crime and Neurophysiologic Highs: A Consideration of Brain Processes That May Reinforce Delinquent and Criminal Behavior," in *Crime in Biological Contexts*, pp. 261–93.

81. Jack Katz, *Seduction of Crime: Moral and Sensual Attractions of Doing Evil* (New York: Basic Books, 1988), pp. 12–15.

82. For a general view, see Richard Lerner and Terryl Foch, *Biological-Psychosocial Interactions in Early Adolescence* (Hilldale, N.J.: Lawrence Erlbaum Associates, 1987).

83. T. R. Sarbin and L. E. Miller, "Demonism Revisited: The XYY Chromosome Anomaly," *Issues in Criminology* 5 (1970): 195–207.

84. Mednick and Volavka, "Biology and Crime," p. 93.

85. Ibid., p. 94.

86. Ibid., p. 95.

87. See Sarnoff A. Mednick and Karl O. Christiansen, eds. *Biosocial Bases in Criminal Behavior* (New York: Gardner Press, 1977).

88. David Rowe, "Genetic and Environmental Components of Antisocial Behavior: A Study of 265 Twin Pairs," *Criminology* 24 (1986): 513–32; David Rowe and D. Wayne Osgood, "Heredity and Sociological Theories of Delinquency: A Reconsideration," *American Sociological Review* 49 (1984): 526-40.

89. Gregory Carey, "Twin Imitation for Antisocial Behavior: Implications for Genetic and Family Environment Research," *Journal of Abnormal Psychology* 101 (1992): 18–25; David Rowe and Joseph Rodgers, "The Ohio Twin Project and ADSEX Studies: Behavior Genetic Approaches to Understanding Antisocial Behavior" (Paper presented at the American Society of Criminology Meeting,

Montreal, Canada, November 1987).

90. R. J. Cadoret, C. Cain, and R. R. Crowe, "Evidence for a Gene-Environment Interaction in the Development of Adolescent Antisocial Behavior," *Behavior Genetics* 13 (1983): 301–10.

91. Barry Hutchings and Sarnoff A. Mednick, "Criminality in Adoptees and Their Adoptive and Biological Parents: A Pilot Study," in *Biological Bases in Criminal Behavior*, ed. S. A. Mednick and K. O. Christiansen (New York: Gardner Press, 1977).

92. For similar results, see Sarnoff Mednick, Terrie Moffitt, William Gabrielli, and Barry Hutchings, "Genetic Factors in Criminal Behavior: A Review," *Development of Antisocial and Prosocial Behavior* (New York: Academic Press, 1986), pp. 3–50; Sarnoff Mednick, William Gabrielli, and Barry Hutchings, "Genetic Influences in Criminal Behavior: Evidence from an Adoption Cohort," in *Perspective Studies of Crime and Delinquency,* ed. Katherine Teilmann Van Dusen and Sarnoff Mednick (Boston: Kluver-Nijhoff, 1983), pp. 39–57.

93. Sharon Begley, "Does DNA Make Some Men Gay?" *Newsweek,* 26 July 1993, p. 59.

94. Janet Lauritsen, "Sibling Resemblance in Juvenile Delinquency: Findings from the National Youth Survey," *Criminology* 31 (1993): 387–411.

95. David Rowe, "As the Twig Is Bent: The Myth of Child-Rearing Influences on Personality Development," *Journal of Counseling and Development* 68 (1990): 606–11; David Rowe, Joseph Rogers, and Sylvia Meseck-Bushey, "Sibling Delinquency and the Family Environment: Shared and Unshared Influences," *Child Development* 63 (1992): 59–67.

96. Gregory Carey and David DiLalla, "Personality and Psychopathology: Genetic Perspectives," *Journal of Abnormal Psychology* 103 (1994): 32–43.

97. Glenn Walters, "A Meta-Analysis of the Gene-Crime Relationship," *Criminology* 30 (1992): 595–613.

98. Lee Ellis, "The Evolution of Violent Criminal Behavior and Its Nonlegal Equivalent," *Crime in Biological Contexts,* pp. 63–65.

99. Lee Ellis, "Sex Differences in Crimiality: An Explanation Based on the Concept of r/K Selection," *Mankind Quarterly* 30 (1990): 17–37.

100. Lawrence Cohen and Richard Machalek, "A General Theory of Expropriative Crime: An Evolutionary Ecological Approach," *American Journal of Sociology* 94 (1988): 465–501.

101. Deborah Denno, "Sociological and Human Developmental Explanations of Crime: Conflict or Consensus," *Criminology* 23 (1985): 711–41.

102. Israel Nachshon and Deborah Denno, "Violence and Cerebral Function," in *The Causes of Crime, New Biological Approaches,* ed. Sarnoff Mednick, Terrie Moffitt, and Susan Stack (Cambridge: Cambridge University Press, 1987), pp. 185–217.

103. Avshalom Caspi, Donald Lyman, Terrie Moffitt, and Phil Silva, "Unraveling Girl's Delinquency: Biological, Dispositional, and Contextual Contributions to Adolescent Misbehavior," *Developmental Psychology* (in press, 1993).

104. Glenn Walters and Thomas White, "Heredity and Crime: Bad Genes or Bad Research," *Criminology* 27 (1989): 455–86 at 478.

105. See Peter Scott, "Henry Maudsley," in *Pioneers in Criminology,* ed. Hermann Mannheim (Montclair, N.J.: Prentice-Hall, 1981).

106. Charles Goring, *The English Convict: A Statistical Study, 1913* (Montclair, N.J.: Patterson Smith, 1972).

107. Edwin Driver, "Charles Buckman Goring," in *Pioneers in Criminology,* ed. Hermann Mannheim (Montclair, N.J.: Patterson Smith, 1970), p. 440.

108. Gabriel Tarde, *Penal Philosophy*, trans. R. Howell (Boston: Little, Brown, 1912).

109. See, generally, Donn Byrne and Kathryn Kelly, An *Introduction to Personality* (Englewood Cliffs, N.J.: Prentice-Hall, 1981).

110. Sigmund Freud, "The Ego and the Id," in *Complete Psychological Works of Sigmund Freud*, vol. 19 (London: Hogarth, 1948), p. 52.

111. August Aichorn, *Wayward Youth* (New York: Viking Press, 1935).

112. David Abrahamsen, *Crime and the Human Mind* (New York: Columbia University Press, 1944), p. 137; see, generally, Fritz Redl and Hans Toch, "The Psychoanalytic Perspective," in *Psychology of Crime and Criminal Justice,* ed. Hans Toch (New York: Holt, Rinehart and Winston, 1979), pp. 193–95.

113. See, generally, D. A. Andrews and James Bonta, *The Psychology of Criminal Conduct* (Cincinnati, Ohio: Anderson, 1994), pp. 72–75.

114. Seymour Halleck, *Psychiatry and the Dilemmas of Crime* (Berkeley: University of California Press, 1971).

115. This discussion is based on three works by Albert Bandura: *Aggression: A Social Learning Analysis* (Englewood Cliffs, N.J.: Prentice-Hall, 1973); *Social Learning Theory* (Englewood Cliffs, N.J.: Prentice-Hall, 1977); and "The Social Learning Perspective: Mechanisms of Aggression," in *Psychology of Crime and Criminal Justice,* ed. Hans Toch (New York: Holt, Rinehart and Winston, 1979), pp. 198–236.

116. David Phillips, "The Impact of Mass Media Violence on U.S. Homicides," *American Sociological Review* 48 (1983): 560–68.

117. See, generally, Jean Piaget, *The Moral Judgment of the Child* (London: Kegan Paul, 1932).

118. Lawrence Kohlberg, *Stages in the Development of Moral Thought and Action* (New York: Holt, Rinehart and Winston, 1969).

119. L. Kohlberg, K. Kauffman, P. Scharf, and J. Hickey, *The Just Community Approach in Corrections: A Manual* (Niantic: Connecticut Department of Corrections, 1973).

120. Scott Henggeler, *Delinquency in Adolescence* (Newbury

Park, Calif.: Sage, 1989), p. 26.

121. Carol Veneziano and Louis Veneziano, "The Relationship between Deterrence and Moral Reasoning," *Criminal Justice Review* 17 (1992): 209–16.

122. K. A. Dodge, "A Social Information Processing Model of Social Competence in Children," in *Minnesota Symposium in Child Psychology,* vol. 18, ed. M. Perlmutter (Hillsdale, N.J.: Erlbaum, 1986), pp. 77–125.

123. L. Huesman and L. Eron, "Individual Differences and the Trait of Aggression," *European Journal of Personality* 3 (1989): 95–106.

124. J. E. Lochman, "Self and Peer Perceptions and Attributional Biases of Aggressive and Nonaggressive Boys in Dyadic Interactions," *Journal of Consulting and Clinical Psychology* 55 (1987): 404–10.

125. D. Lipton, E. C. McDonel, and R. McFall, "Heterosocial Perception in Rapists," *Journal of Consulting and Clinical Psychology* 55 (1987): 17–21.

126. *Understanding Violence*, p. 389.

127. James Sorrells, "Kids Who Kill," *Crime and Delinquency* 23 (1977): 312–20.

128. Richard Rosner, "Adolescents Accused of Murder and Manslaughter: A Five-Year Descriptive Study," *Bulletin of the American Academy of Psychiatry and the Law* 7 (1979): 342–51.

129. Richard Famularo, Robert Kinscherff, and Terence Fenton, "Psychiatric Diagnoses of Abusive Mothers, A Preliminary Report," *Journal of Nervous and Mental Disease* 180 (1992): 658–60.

130. Richard Wagner, Dawn Taylor, Joy Wright, Alison Sloat, Gwynneth Springett, Sandy Arnold, and Heather Weinberg, "Substance Abuse among the Mentally Ill," *American Journal of Orthopsychiatry* 64 (1994): 30–38.

131. Bruce Link, Howard Andrews, and Francis Cullen, "The Violent and Illegal Behavior of Mental Patients Reconsidered," *American Sociological Review* 57 (1992): 275–92; Ellen Hochstedler Steury, "Criminal Defendants with Psychiatric Impairment: Prevalence, Probabilities and Rates," *Journal of Criminal Law and Criminology* 84 (1993): 354–74.

132. Marc Hillbrand, John Krystal, Kimberly Sharpe, and Hilliard Foster, "Clinical Predictors of Self-Mutilation in Hospitalized Patients," *Journal of Nervous and Mental Disease* 182 (1994): 9–13.

133. Carmen Cirincione, Henry Steadman, Pamela Clark Robbins, and John Monahan, *Mental Illness as a Factor in Criminality: A Study of Prisoners and Mental Patients* (Delmar, N.Y.: Policy Research Associates, 1991). See also idem, *Schizophrenia as a Contingent Risk Factor for Criminal Violence* (Delmar, N.Y.: Policy Research Associates, 1991).

134. Howard Berenbaum and Frank Fujita, "Schizophrenia and Personality: Exploring the Boundaries and Connections between Vulnerability and Outcome," *Journal of Abnormal Psychology* 103 (1994): 148–58.

135. See, generally, Walter Mischel, *Introduction to Personality,* 4th ed. (New York: Holt, Rinehart and Winston, 1986).

136. D. A. Andrews and J. Stephen Wormith, "Personality and Crime: Knowledge and Construction in Criminology," *Justice Quarterly* 6 (1989): 289–310; Donald Gibbons, "Comment—Personality and Crime: Non-Issues, Real Issues, and a Theory and Research Agenda," *Justice Quarterly* (1989): 311–24.

137. Sheldon Glueck and Eleanor Glueck, *Unraveling Juvenile Delinquency* (Cambridge: Harvard University Press, 1950).

138. See, generally, Hans Eysenck, *Personality and Crime* (London: Routledge and Kegan Paul, 1977).

139. Hans Eysenck and M. W. Eysenck, *Personality and Individual Differences* (New York: Plenum, 1985).

140. David Farrington, "Psychobiological Factors in the Explanation and Reduction of Delinquency," *Today's Delinquent* (1988): 37–51.

141. Laurie Frost, Terrie Moffitt, and Rob McGee, "Neuropsychological Correlates of Psychopathology in an Unselected Cohort of Young Adolescents," *Journal of Abnormal Psychology* 98 (1989): 307–13.

142. Sheldon Glueck and Eleanor Glueck, *Delinquents and Nondelinquents in Perspective* (Cambridge: Harvard University Press, 1968).

143. See, generally, R. Starke Hathaway and Elio Monachesi, *Analyzing and Predicting Juvenile Delinquency with the MMPI* (Minneapolis: University of Minnesota Press, 1953).

144. R. Starke Hathaway, Elio Monachesi, and Lawrence Young, "Delinquency Rates and Personality," *Journal of Criminal Law, Criminology, and Police Science* 51 (1960): 443–60; Michael Hindelang and Joseph Weis, "Personality and Self-Reported Delinquency: An Application of Cluster Analysis," *Criminology* 10 (1972): 268; Spencer Rathus and Larry Siegel, "Crime and Personality Revisited," *Criminology* 18 (1980): 245–51.

145. See, generally, Edward Megargee, *The California Psychological Inventory Handbook* (San Francisco: Josey-Bass, 1972).

146. Karl Schuessler and Donald Cressey, "Personality Characteristics of Criminals," *American Journal of Sociology* 55 (1950): 476–84; Gordon Waldo and Simon Dinitz, "Personality Attributes of the Criminal: An Analysis of Research Studies 1950–1965," *Journal of Research in Crime and Delinquency* 4 (1967): 185–201; David Tennenbaum, "Research Studies of Personality and Criminality," *Journal of Criminal Justice* 5 (1977): 1–19.

147. Edward Helmes and John Reddon, "A Perspective on Developments in Assessing Psychopathology: A Critical Review of the MMPI and MMPI-2," *Psychological Bulletin* 113 (1993): 453–71.

148. Avshalom Caspi, Terrie Moffitt, Phil Silva, Magda Stouthamer-Loeber, Robert Krueger, and Pamela Schmutte, "Are Some People Crime-Prone? Replications of the Personality-Crime Relationship across Countries, Genders, Races and Methods," *Criminology* 32 (1994):

163–95.

149. Henry Goddard, *Efficiency and Levels of Intelligence* (Princeton, N.J.: Princeton University Press, 1920); Edwin Sutherland, "Mental Deficiency and Crime," in *Social Attitudes*, ed. Kimball Young (New York: Henry Holt, 1931), chap. 15.

150. Sutherland, "Mental Deficiency and Crime."

151. William Healy and Augusta Bronner, *Delinquency and Criminals: Their Making and Unmaking* (New York: McMillan, 1926).

152. John Slawson, *The Delinquent Boys* (Boston: Budget Press, 1926).

153. Kenneth Eels, et al., *Intelligence and Cultural Differences* (Chicago: University of Chicago Press, 1951), p. 181.

154. Robert Rosenthal and Lenore Jacobsen, *Pygmalion in the Classroom* (New York: Holt, 1968).

155. Travis Hirschi and Michael Hindelang, "Intelligence and Delinquency: A Revisionist Review," *American Sociological Review* 42 (1977): 471–586.

156. Robert Gordon, "IQ Commensurability of Black-White Differences in Crime and Delinquency" (Paper presented at the annual meeting of the American Psychological Association, Washington, D.C., August 1986); idem, "Two Illustrations of the IQ-Surrogate Hypothesis: IQ versus Parental Education and Occupational Status in the Race-IQ-Delinquency Model" (Paper presented at the annual meeting of the American Society of Criminology, Montreal, Canada, November 1987).

157. Donald Lynam, Terrie Moffitt, and Magda Stouthamer-Loeber, "Explaining the Relation between IQ and Delinquency: Class, Race, Test Motivation, School Failure or Self-Control," *Journal of Abnormal Psychology* 102 (1993): 187–96.

158. Christine Ward and Richard McFall, "Further Validation of the Problem Inventory for Adolescent Girls: Comparing Caucasian and Black Delinquents and Nondelinquents," *Journal of Consulting and Clinical Psychology* 54 (1986): 732–33; L. Hubble and M. Groff, "Magnitude and Direction of WISC-R Verbal Performance IQ Discrepancies among Adjudicated Male Delinquents," *Journal of Youth and Adolescence* 10 (1981): 179–83.

159. Terrie Moffitt, William Gabrielli, Sarnoff Mednick, and Fini Schulsinger, "Socioeconomic Status, IQ, and Delinquency," *Journal of Abnormal Psychology* 90 (1981): 152–56.

160. Ibid., p. 155. For a similar finding, see Hubble and Groff, "Magnitude and Direction of WISC-R Verbal Performance IQ Discrepancies among Adjudicated Male Delinquents."

161. Lorne Yeudall, Delee Fromm-Auch, and Priscilla Davies, "Neuropsychological Impairment of Persistent Delinquency," *Journal of Nervous and Mental Diseases* 170 (1982): 257–65.

162. Hakan Stattin and Ingrid Klackenberg-Larsson, "Early Language and Intelligence Development and Their Relationship to Future Criminal Behavior," *Journal of Abnormal Psychology* 102 (1993): 369–78.

163. James Q. Wilson and Richard Herrnstein, Crime and Human Nature (New York: Simon and Schuster, 1985), p. 148.

164. Ibid., p. 171.

165. Deborah Denno, "Sociological and Human Developmental Explanations of Crime: Conflict or Consensus," *Criminology* 23 (1985): 711–41.

166. Scott Menard and Barbara Morse, "A Structuralist Critique of the IQ-Delinquency Hypothesis: Theory and Evidence," *American Journal of Sociology* 89 (1984): 1347–78.

167. Denno, "Sociological and Human Developmental Explanations of Crime."

168. Susan Pease and Craig T. Love, "Optimal Methods and Issues in Nutrition Research in the Correctional Setting," *Nutrition Reviews Supplement* 44 (1986): 122–31.

169. Mark O'Callaghan and Douglas Carroll, "The Role of Psychosurgical Studies in the Control of Antisocial Behavior," in *The Causes of Crime, New Biological Approaches*, ed. Sarnoff Mednick, Terrie Moffitt, and Susan Stack (Cambridge: Cambridge University Press, 1987), pp. 312–28.

170. Mednick, Moffitt, Gabrielli, and Hutchings, "Genetic Factors in Criminal Behavior: A Review," pp. 47–48.

7 Social Structure Theories

Introduction

> . . . motivations for crime do not result simply from the flaws, failures, or free choices of individuals. A complete explanation of crime ultimately must consider the sociocultural environments in which people are located.[1]

Sociology has been the primary focus of criminology since early in the twentieth century. As you may recall from Chapter 1, sociological positivism can be traced to the works of Quetelet, Comte, and Durkheim.

In the United States, the primacy of sociological criminology was secured by research begun in the early twentieth century by Robert Ezra Park (1864–1944), Ernest W. Burgess (1886–1966), Louis Wirth (1897–1952), and their colleagues in the Sociology Department at the University of Chicago. Known as the **Chicago School,** these sociologists pioneered research work on the social ecology of the city and inspired a generation of scholars to conclude that social forces operating in urban areas create criminal interactions; some neighborhoods become "natural areas" for crime.

In 1915, University of Chicago sociologist **Robert Ezra Park** called for anthropological methods of description and observation to be applied to urban life.[2] He was concerned about how neighborhood structure developed, how isolated pockets of poverty formed, and what social policies could be used to alleviate urban problems. Later, Park, with Ernest Burgess, studied the social ecology of the city and found that some neighborhoods form **natural areas** of wealth and affluence, while others suffered poverty and disintegration.[3] Regardless of their race, religion, or ethnicity, the everyday behavior of people living in these areas was controlled by the social and ecological climate.

Over the next 20 years, Chicago School sociologists carried out an ambitious program of research and scholarship on urban topics, including criminal behavior patterns. Such works as Harvey Zorbaugh's *The Gold Coast and the Slum,*[4] Frederick Thrasher's *The Gang,*[5] and Louis Wirth's *The Ghetto*[6] are classic examples of objective, highly descriptive accounts of urban life. Their influence was such that most criminologists have been trained in sociology, and criminology courses are routinely taught in departments of sociology.

Sociological Criminology

There are many reasons why sociology has remained the predominant approach of U.S. criminologists during this century. First, it has long been evident that varying patterns of criminal behavior exist within the social structure. Some geographic areas are more prone to violence and serious theft-related crimes than others. Criminologists have attempted to discover why such patterns exist and how they can be eliminated. Explanations of crime as an individual-level phenomenon fail to account for these consistent patterns in the crime rate. If violence, as some criminologists suggest, is related to chemical or chromosome abnormality, then how can ecological differences in the crime rate be explained? It is unlikely that all people with physical anomalies live in one section of town. There has been a heated national debate over the effects of violent TV shows on adolescent aggression. Yet adolescents in cities and towns with widely disparate crime rates, ranging from Los Angeles to Bedford, New Hampshire, all watch the same shows and movies; how can crime rate differences in these areas be explained? If violence had a biological and/or psychological origin, should it not be distributed more evenly throughout the social structure?

Sociology is concerned with social change and the dynamic aspects of human behavior. It follows transformations in norms, values, institutions, and their subsequent effect on individual and group behavior. These concepts are useful today because the changing structure of modern postindustrial society continues to have a tremendous effect on intergroup and interpersonal relationships.[7] There has been a reduction in the influence of the family and an increased emphasis on individuality, independence, and isolation. Weakened family ties have been linked to crime and delinquency.[8]

Another important social change has been the rapid changes in technology and its influence on the social system. People who lack the requisite social and educational training have found that the road to success through upward occupational mobility has become almost impassible. Lack of upward mobility may make drug dealing and other crimes an attractive solution to socially deprived but economically enterprising people. Recent evidence shows that adults who are only marginally employed are the ones most likely to commit crime; the quality of employment and not merely unemployment influences criminality (see the Close-Up on crime and unemployment).[9]

Sociology's stress on intergroup and interpersonal transactions also promotes it as a source for criminological study. Criminologists believe that understanding the dynamics of interactions between individuals and important social institutions, such as their families, their peers, their schools, their jobs, criminal justice agencies, and the like, is important for understanding the cause of

It is estimated that 37 million Americans may live in poverty. Here one, Phyllis Dillingham, a deaf mute, hangs up laundry to dry outside her trailer in West Sumner, Maine, with the help of her daughter, Christine. Dillingham is among 56,000 Maine residents who receive Aid to Families with Dependent Children. Dillingham wanted to go back to work but couldn't afford a baby-sitter.

crime.[10] The relationship of one social class or group to another or to the existing power structure that controls the nation's legal and economic system may also be closely related to criminality. Sociology is concerned with the benefits of positive human interactions and the costs of negative ones. Crime is itself an interaction and therefore should not be studied without considering the interactions of all participants in a criminal act—the law violator, the victim, the law enforcers, the lawmakers, and social institutions.

To summarize, concern about the ecological distribution of crime, the effect of social change, and the interactive nature of crime itself has made sociology the foundation of modern criminology. This chapter reviews sociological theories that emphasize the relationship between social status and criminal behavior. In Chapter 8, the focus will shift to theories that emphasize socialization and its influence on crime and deviance; Chapter 9 covers theories based on the concept of social conflict.

Economic Structure

People in the United States live in a **stratified** society. Social strata are created by the unequal distribution of wealth, power, and prestige. Social classes are segments of the population whose members have a relatively similar portion of desirable things and who share attitudes, values, norms, and an identifiable life-style. In U.S. society, it is common to identify people as upper-, middle-, and lower-class citizens, with a broad range of economic variations existing within each group. The upper-upper class is reserved for a small number of exceptionally well-to-do families who maintain enormous financial and social resources. The lower class consists of an estimated 37 million people who live in poverty (defined officially as a family of four making under $14,335 per year); almost 15 percent of the total U.S. population now lives in poverty.[11] As Figure 7.1 shows, the number of Americans living in poverty and the percentage of the population living below the **poverty line**

CLOSE-UP

Crime and Unemployment

The social structure approach links crime to the economic deprivation experienced in ghetto areas. It follows that rates of unemployment are related to crime rates: if people do not hold jobs, they will be more likely to turn to crime as a means of support. Is this assumption valid? Is there a relationship between crime and unemployment?

Despite the logic of this proposition, little clear-cut evidence exists linking unemployment and crime rates. For example, even during the economic prosperity of the 1960s, the crime rate rose dramatically. Richard Freeman reviewed the literature on the subject and found that crime and unemployment are only weakly related. Though Freeman found evidence that criminals have poorer work records than noncriminals, there was little indication that changing market conditions would cause them to choose legitimate earning opportunities. Though crime rates in cities and states are slightly linked to labor market conditions, the relationship between them is tenuous.

One possible reason for the weaker-than-expected relationship between crime and unemployment rates is that while joblessness increases the motivation to commit crime, it simultaneously decreases the opportunity to gain from criminal enterprise. During periods of economic hardship, potential victims will have fewer valuable items in their possession and will guard those valuables more closely. Parents who are unemployed can be at home to supervise their children, reducing their opportunity to commit crime; teenagers have higher crime rates than any other age group. David Cantor and Kenneth Land explain that these two factors—supply and demand—cancel each other out, resulting in an insignificant relationship between crime and unemployment rates. Their findings jibe with the routine activities view that crime rates will vary not only with the presence of motivated offenders but also with the presence of available, lightly protected targets.

These results should not be unexpected. It seems unlikely that hard-working people will turn to crime because they lost their job. Crime rates are highest among adolescents who are not yet part of the work force and are unlikely to be directly affected by employment rates.

While the link between crime and unemployment may be weaker than expected on an aggregate or macro-level, individual or micro-level data indicates that the two variables may be related. Surveys of adult inmates show that many were unemployed and underemployed before their incarceration; median income of both male and female inmates was below the poverty level. These data must be interpreted with caution, since they may reflect the relationship between economic status and criminal sentencing, rather than the one between crime and work force participation: unemployed offenders may stand a greater chance of being incarcerated than the employed, who often are offered probation. Nonetheless, the fact that known offenders are under- or unemployed is generally supportive of a crime-unemployment relationship.

Research by Gary Kleck, Theodore Chiricos, and their associates indicates that the relationship between crime and unemployment is more complex than previously believed. Unemployment may have effects on the crime rate that are specific to offense, time period, gender, and age. Unemployment seems to have

---

are actually greater today than they were 20 years ago (though somewhat less than in 1960 before the "War on Poverty" of the Johnson administration). The government's definition of the poverty line seems quite low. A more realistic figure of an $18,000 annual income per family of four would mean that more than 50 million U.S. citizens live in poverty.[12]

Lower-Class Culture

Lower-class slum areas are scenes of inadequate housing and health care, disrupted family lives, underem-

ployment, and despair. Members of the lower class also suffer in other ways. They are more prone to depression, less likely to have achievement motivation, and less likely to put off immediate gratification for future gain. Some are driven to desperate measures to cope with their economic plight: it is estimated that about 22,000 newborn babies are abandoned each year in hospitals by mothers who are poverty stricken, drug-addicted, or homeless.[13]

Members of the lower class are constantly bombarded by the media with a flood of advertisements linking material possessions to self-worth, but they are often

the greatest influence on opportunistic property crimes, such as burglary, and the least on violent assaultive crimes. This new research indicates that the relationship between crime and unemployment is not simply one in which limited income causes people to commit crime for the sake of economic gain. It is possible, Kleck and Chiricos conclude, that on an individual level, *unemployment* increases crime because it reduces people's stakes in conformity. By severing attachments to co-workers and reducing parents' ability to be breadwinners, unemployment reduces the attachment people have to conventional institutions and their ability to exert authority over their children.

It is also possible that the crime-unemployment relationship travels a different path than expected: rather than joblessness motivating people to commit crime, it is possible that criminal behavior excludes offenders from the workplace. Put another way, an early experience with delinquent behavior and drug abuse is likely to result in protracted unemployment as an adult.

John Hagan explains this relationship as a function of *social embeddedness*. This term refers to the fact that early behavior patterns become stable, lifelong habits and tendencies; past and current behaviors make future events more likely. Using longitudinal data from an English cohort, Hagan found that kids with early criminal experiences, whose friends are delinquent, and whose parents are convicted criminals become *embedded* in behaviors that result in later adult unemployment. The chain of events runs from having criminal friends and parents, engaging in delinquency, and gaining police and court contacts to losing the opportunity for meaningful employment as adults. Embeddedness in a deviant life-style is contrasted with the establishment of roots in a conventional one: youths who get early work experience, who make contacts, and learn the ropes of the job market establish the groundwork for a successful career. Hagan concludes: "Criminal youths are embedded in contexts that isolate them from the likelihood of legitimate adult employment."

Is there an association between crime and unemployment? The data suggests these two variables are interrelated but that it is just as likely that crime *causes* unemployment and not that the *unemployed* become *criminals*.

Discussion Questions

1. To prevent crime, should all people be guaranteed the right to work?

2. Would a job at the minimum wage be a realistic crime-reducing alternative to unemployment?

SOURCES: John Hagan, "The Social Embeddedness of Crime and Unemployment," *Criminology* 31 (1993): 465–92; Theodore Chiricos, "Rates of Crime and Unemployment: An Analysis of Aggregate Research Evidence," *Social Problems* 34 (1987): 187–212; Gary Kleck, Theodore Chiricos, Michael Hayes, and Laura Myers, "Unemployment, Crime, and Opportunity: A Target-Specific Crime Rate Analysis" (Paper presented at the American Society of Criminology meeting, Montreal, Canada, November 1987); David Cantor and Kenneth Land, "Unemployment and Crime Rates in the Post-World War II United States: A Theoretical and Empirical Analysis," *American Sociological Review* 50 (1985): 317–32; Richard Freeman, "Crime and Unemployment," in *Crime and Public Policy*, ed. James Q. Wilson (San Francisco: Institute for Contemporary Studies, 1983), pp. 89–106.

unable to attain desired goods and services through conventional means. Though they are members of a society that extols material success above any other, they are unable to satisfactorily compete for such success with members of the upper classes.

The social problems found in lower-class slum areas have been described as an "epidemic" that spreads like a contagious disease, destroying the inner workings that enable neighborhoods to survive; they become "hollowed out."[14] As neighborhood quality decreases, the probability that residents will develop problems sharply increases. Adolescents in the worst neighborhoods share the greatest risk of dropping out of school and becoming teenage parents.

Racial Disparity

The disabilities suffered by the lower-class citizen are particularly acute for racial minorities. African-Americans have a mean income level significantly lower than that of whites and an unemployment rate markedly higher. Though it is estimated that two-thirds to three-quarters of the urban poor are white, minorities are overrepresented

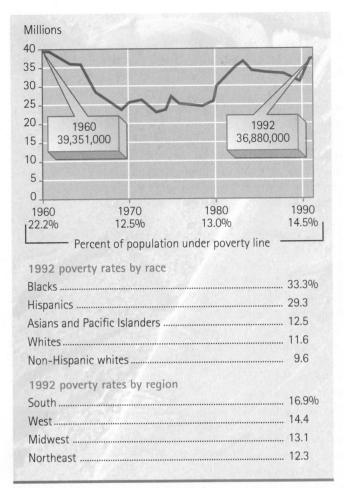

FIGURE 7.1 Americans Living in Poverty
The number of Americans living in poverty jumped to 36.9 million in 1992. The poverty line in 1992 was $14,335 for a family of four and $7,143 for an individual.

SOURCE: U.S. Census Bureau, 1994.

within the poverty classes. The poverty rate for African-American families is *three times* that of the white population. More than half of African-American families are fatherless and husbandless, headed by a female who is the sole breadwinner and who is often aided by welfare and Aid to Dependent Children (ADC). About 56 percent of never-married African-American women have children, compared to 15 percent of white women and 33 percent of Hispanic women.[15]

Research conducted for the Joint Center for Political and Economic Studies found that more than 85 percent of African-American children under three years of age living in families headed by women who had never married were today living in poverty. Even more disturbing is the fact that the number and percentage of African-American children living in poverty in urban areas out-

side the South has increased substantially since 1970 (African-American poverty has actually declined in the South).[16]

Economic problems are not the only ones faced by racial minorities. Research also shows that African-American men in the United States have a much shorter life span than white men, who can expect to live an average six years longer (69.4 years versus 75.4 years).[17] In fact, life-styles among the urban African-American underclass are so disturbed that their life span is considerably shorter than that of the poorest Third World countries. One study by doctors in New York found that while only 40 percent of the male residents of Harlem live to age 65, 55 percent of the males in Bangladesh, one of the world's poorest countries, reach this age.[18]

The problems faced by minority-group members may soon increase because poverty is on the increase. Racial segregation and isolation of poor African-Americans and Hispanics in urban areas is similarly increasing.[19] A recent report by the Harvard University Project of School Desegregation shows that the percentage of minority students attending schools with more than a 50 percent minority student population has risen since 1970, reversing gains made during the civil rights movement in the 1960s. About one-third of all African-American children attend schools in which more than 90 percent of the students are minorities; these schools often face insufficient funding and a high level of poverty.[20] Clearly, the problems of racial segregation continue and may even be growing.

The Underclass

In 1966, sociologist Oscar Lewis argued that the crushing life-style of slum areas produces a culture of poverty passed from one generation to the next.[21] The **culture of poverty** is marked by apathy, cynicism, helplessness, and mistrust of social institutions, such as schools, government agencies, and the police. This mistrust prevents slum dwellers from taking advantage of the meager opportunities available to them. Lewis's work was the first of a group that described the plight of **at-risk** children and adults. In 1970, Gunnar Myrdal described a worldwide **underclass** cut off from society, its members lacking the education and skills needed to be effectively in demand in modern society[22]; in 1983, Ken Auletta described a U.S. underclass in much the same terms.[23]

The Truly Disadvantaged

In 1987, William Julius Wilson provided a description of the plight of the lowest levels of the underclass, which he labeled the **truly disadvantaged.**[24] Wilson portrayed members of this group as socially isolated people

Sociologist William Julius Wilson is the author of *The Truly Disadvantaged*.

Are the Poor "Undeserving"?

Despite all our technological success, the fact that a significant percentage of U.S. citizens either are homeless or live in areas of concentrated poverty is an important social problem. The media frequently focuses on the distress suffered by homeless and poverty-stricken families. Yet, some view impoverished people as somehow responsible for their own fate, the so-called *undeserving poor;* if they tried, the argument goes, they could "improve themselves."[27]

This conclusion is baseless. It is a sad fact that poverty is becoming evermore concentrated among minority groups who are forced to live in physically deteriorated, inner-city neighborhoods that have high crime, poor schools, and excessive mortality.[28] A study by the National Research Council on inner-city poverty in the United States concludes that poor people living in areas of extreme poverty are more likely to suffer social ills than poor people living in more affluent communities.[29] People living in urban ghettos suffer higher rates of unemployment, are more dependent on welfare, and are more likely to live in single-parent households than *equally indigent people who reside in more affluent areas*. The burden of living in these high-poverty areas, then, goes beyond merely "being poor"; under these conditions, self-help and upward mobility is highly problematic.

Community effects may be particularly damaging on children. Adolescents residing in areas of concentrated poverty are more likely to suffer in their cognitive development, sexual and family formation, practices, school attendance habits, and transition to employment.[30] Lack of education and family stability make them poor candidates for employment.

These findings suggest that the poor of inner-city ghettos confront obstacles far greater than the mere lack of financial resources. The National Research Council's review indicates that the social problems faced by many ghetto residents render them unprepared to take advantage of employment opportunities even in tight labor markets.[31] The fact that many of the underclass are African-American children who can expect to spend all their life in poverty is probably the single most important problem facing the nation today.[32]

who dwell in urban inner cities, occupy the bottom rung of the social ladder, and are the victims of discrimination. They live in areas in which the basic institutions of society—family, school, housing—have long since declined. Their decline triggers similar breakdowns in the strengths of inner-city areas, including the loss of community cohesion and the application of informal sanctions against illicit behavior. These effects magnify the isolation of the underclass from mainstream society and promote a ghetto culture and behavior.[25]

Since the "truly disadvantaged" rarely come into contact with the actual source of their oppression, they direct their anger and aggression at those with whom they are in close and intimate contact. Members of this group, plagued by under- or unemployment, begin to lose self-confidence, a feeling supported by the plight of kin and friendship groups who also experience extreme economic marginality. Self-doubt is a neighborhood norm, overwhelming those forced to live in areas of concentrated poverty.[26]

Social Structure Theories

Considering the deprivations suffered by the lower class, it is not surprising that a disadvantaged economic class position has been viewed by many criminologists as a primary cause of crime. This view is referred to here as **social structure theory.** As a group, social structure theories suggest that forces operating in deteriorated lower-class areas push many of their residents into criminal behavior patterns. These theories consider the existence of unsupervised teenage gangs, high crime rates, and social disorder in slum areas as major social problems.

Lower-class crime is often the violent, destructive product of youth gangs and marginally employed young adults. Although members of the middle and upper classes also engage in crime, social structure theorists view middle-class crime as being of relatively lower frequency, seriousness, and danger to the general public. The "real crime problem" is essentially a lower-class phenomenon, beginning in youth and continuing into young adulthood.

Most social structure theories focus on the law-violating behavior of youth. They suggest that the social forces that cause crime begin to affect people while they are relatively young and continue to influence them throughout their life. Though not all youthful offenders become adult criminals, many begin their training and learn criminal values as members of youth gangs and groups. Social structure theorists challenge those who would suggest that crime is an expression of psychological imbalance, biological traits, insensitivity to social controls, personal choice, or any other individual-level factor. They argue that people living in equivalent social environments seem to behave in a similar, predictable fashion. If the environment did not influence human behavior, then crime rates would be distributed equally across the social structure, which they are not.[33] Since

crime rates are higher in lower-class urban centers than middle-class suburbs, social forces must be operating in urban slums that influence or control behavior.[34] Let us now turn to a discussion of the most important social structure theories of crime.

Branches of Social Structure Theory

There are three independent yet overlapping branches within the social structure perspective—**social disorganization, strain theory,** and **cultural deviance theory,** as outlined in Figure 7.2. Social disorganization theory focuses on the conditions within the urban environment that affect crime rates. A disorganized area is one in which institutions of social control, such as the family, commercial establishments, and schools, have broken down and can no longer carry out their expected or stated functions. Indicators of social disorganization include high unemployment and school dropout rates, deteriorated housing, low income levels, and large numbers of single-parent households. Residents in these areas experience conflict and despair, and antisocial behavior flourishes.

Strain theory, the second branch of social structure theory, holds that crime is a function of the conflict between the goals people have and the means they can use to legally obtain them. Strain theorists argue that while social and economic goals are common to people

FIGURE 7.2   **Branches of Social Structure Theory**

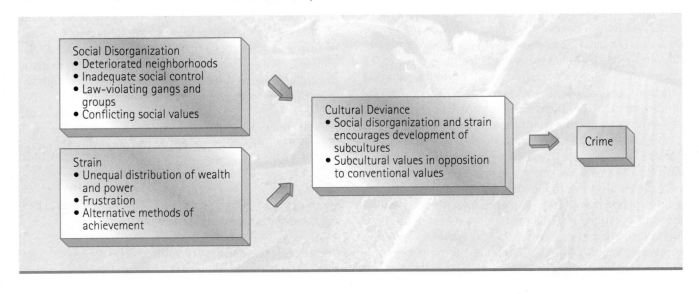

in all economic strata, the ability to obtain them is class-dependent. Most people in the United States desire wealth, material possessions, power, prestige, and other life comforts. Members of the lower class are unable to achieve these symbols of success through the conventional means. Consequently, they feel anger, frustration, and resentment, which is referred to as *strain*. Lower-class citizens can either accept their condition and live out their days as socially responsible, if unrewarded, citizens, or they can choose an alternative means of achieving success, such as theft, violence or drug trafficking.

Cultural deviance theory, the third variation of structural theory, combines elements of both strain and social disorganization. According to this view, because of strain and social isolation, a unique lower-class culture develops in disorganized neighborhoods. These independent **subcultures** maintain a unique set of values and beliefs that are in conflict with conventional social norms. Criminal behavior is an expression of conformity to lower-class subcultural values and traditions and not a rebellion from conventional society. Subcultural values are handed down from one generation to the next in a process called **cultural transmission.**

While distinct in critical aspects, each of these three approaches has at its core the view that socially isolated people, living in disorganized neighborhoods, are the ones most likely to experience crime-producing social forces. Each branch of social structure theory will now be discussed in some detail.

≡ Social Disorganization Theory

Social disorganization theory links crime rates to neighborhood ecological characteristics. Crime rates are high in highly transient "changing neighborhoods" in which the fabric of social life has become frayed. These localities are unable to provide essential services, such as education, health care, and proper housing, and experience significant levels of unemployment, single-parent families, and families on welfare and ADC.

Social disorganization theory views crime-ridden neighborhoods as ones in which residents are trying to leave at the earliest opportunity. Since residents are uninterested in community matters, the common sources of control—the family, school, business community, social service agencies—are weak and disorganized. Personal relationships are strained because neighbors are constantly moving and leaving. Constant resident turnover weakens communications and blocks attempts at solving neighborhood problems or establishing common goals.[35]

The Work of Shaw and McKay

Social disorganization theory was popularized by the work of two Chicago sociologists, Henry McKay and Clifford R. Shaw, who linked life in transitional slum areas to the inclination to commit crime. Shaw and McKay began their pioneering work on crime in Chicago during the early 1920s while working as researchers for a state-supported social service agency.[36] They were heavily influenced by the thoughts of the Chicago School sociologists Ernest Burgess and Robert Park, who had pioneered the ecological analysis of urban life (see Chapter 1).

Shaw and McKay began their analysis during a period in the city's history that was not atypical of the transition taking place in many other urban areas. Chicago had experienced a mid-nineteenth-century population expansion, fueled by a dramatic influx of foreign-born immigrants and, later, migrating southern families. Congregating in the central city, the newcomers occupied the oldest housing and therefore faced numerous health and environmental hazards.

Physically deteriorating sections of the city soon developed. This condition prompted the city's wealthy, established citizens to become concerned about the moral fabric of Chicago society. The belief was widespread that immigrants from Europe and the rural South were crime-prone and morally dissolute. In fact, local groups were created with the very purpose of "saving" the children of poor families from moral decadence.[37] It was popular to view crime as the property of inferior racial and ethnic groups.

Transitional Neighborhoods

Shaw and McKay explained crime and delinquency within the context of the changing urban environment and ecological development of the city. They saw that Chicago had developed into distinct neighborhoods (*natural areas*), some affluent and others wracked by extreme poverty. These **transitional neighborhoods** suffered high rates of population turnover and were incapable of inducing residents to remain and defend the neighborhood against criminal groups.

Newly arrived immigrants from Europe and the South congregated in these transitional neighborhoods. Their children were torn between assimilation into a new culture and abiding by the traditional values of their parents. Informal social control mechanisms that had restrained behavior in the "old country" or rural areas were disrupted. These slum areas were believed to be the spawning grounds of young criminals.

In transitional slum areas, successive changes in the composition of population, the disintegration of the alien cultures, the diffusion of divergent cultural standards, and the gradual industrialization of the area result in dissolution of neighborhood culture and organization. The continuity of conventional neighborhood traditions and institutions is broken. The effectiveness of the neighborhood as a unit of control and as a medium for the transmission of the moral standards of society is greatly diminished. Children growing up in these areas have little access to the cultural heritages of conventional society. For the most part, the organization of their behavior takes place through participation in the spontaneous play groups and organized gangs that develop in these areas. The values they develop are then passed down through succeeding generations in a process of *cultural transmission.*

Concentric Zones

Shaw and McKay identified the areas in Chicago that had excessive crime rates. Using a model of analysis pioneered by Ernest Burgess, they noted that distinct ecological areas had developed in the city, comprising a series of five concentric circles, or zones, and that there were stable and significant differences in interzone crime rates (see Figure 7.3). The areas of heaviest concentration of crime appeared to be the transitional inner-city zones, where large numbers of foreign-born citizens had recently settled.[38] The zones farthest from the city's center had correspondingly lower crime rates. Analysis of these data indicated a surprisingly stable pattern of criminal activity in the five ecological zones over a 65-year period.

Shaw and McKay concluded that in the transitional neighborhoods, deviant and conventional values compete side by side with each other. Kids growing up in the street culture often find that adults who have adopted a deviant life-style are the most financially successful people in the neighborhood; for example, the gambler, pimp, or drug dealer. Required to choose between conventional and deviant life-styles, many slum kids opt for the latter. They join with like-minded youths and form law-violating gangs and cliques. The development of teenage law-violating groups is an essential element of youthful misbehavior in slum areas. Because of their deviant values, slum youths often come into conflict with existing middle-class norms, which demand strict obedience to the legal code. Consequently, a **value**

conflict occurs that sets the delinquent youth and his or her peer group even farther apart from conventional society. The result is a fuller acceptance of deviant goals and behavior. Shut out of conventional society, neighborhood street gangs become fixed institutions, recruiting new members and passing on delinquent traditions from one generation to the next.

Shaw and McKay's statistical analysis confirmed their theoretical suspicions. They found that even though crime rates changed, the highest rates were always in zones I and II (central city and transitional area). The areas with the highest crime rates retained high rates even when their ethnic composition changed (in this case, from German and Irish to Italian and Polish).[39]

The Legacy of Shaw and McKay

Social disorganization concepts articulated by Shaw and McKay have remained prominent within criminology for more than 70 years. Most important of Shaw and McKay's findings was that crime rates corresponded to neighborhood structure. Crime was a creature of the destructive ecological conditions in urban slums. Criminals were not, as some criminologists of the time believed, biologically inferior, intellectually impaired, or psychologically damaged. Crime was a constant fixture in a slum area regardless of the racial or ethnic identity of its residents.

Since the basis of their theory was that neighborhood disintegration and slum conditions are the primary causes of criminal behavior, Shaw and McKay paved the way for the many community action and treatment programs developed in the last half-century. Shaw was the founder of one very influential community-based treatment program, the Chicago Area Project, which will be discussed later in this chapter.

Another important feature of Shaw and McKay's work is that it depicted both adult criminality and delinquent gang memberships as a normal response to the adverse social conditions in urban slum areas. Their findings mirror Durkheim's concept that crime can be normal and useful.

Despite these noteworthy achievements, the validity of Shaw and McKay's findings has been subject to challenge. Some have faulted their assumption that neighborhoods are essentially stable, while others have found their definition of social disorganization confusing.[40] The most important criticism, however, concerns their use of police records to calculate neighborhood crime rates. A zone's high crime rate may be a function of the level of local police surveillance and therefore obscure interzone crime rate differences. Numerous studies indicate that police use extensive discretion

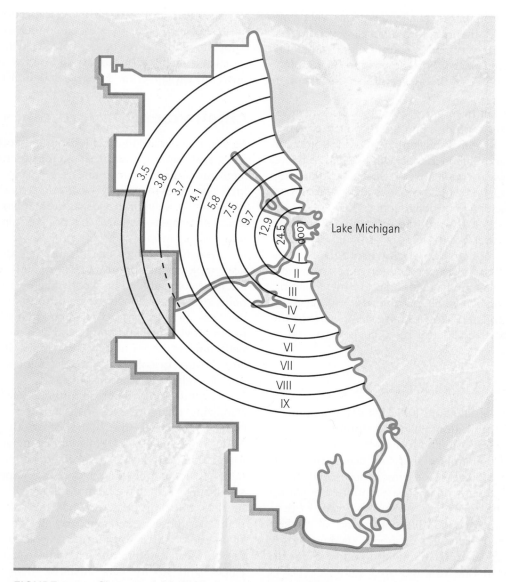

FIGURE 7.3   **Shaw and McKay's Concentric Zones Map of Chicago**

NOTE: Arabic numerals represent the rate of male delinquency.
SOURCE: Clifford R. Shaw, et al., *Delinquency Areas* (Chicago: University of Chicago Press, 1929), p. 99.
Reprinted with permission. Copyright 1929 by the University of Chicago. All rights reserved.

when arresting people and that social status is one factor that influences their decisions.[41] It is likely that people in middle-class neighborhoods commit many criminal acts that never show up in official statistics, while people in lower-class areas face a far greater chance of arrest and court adjudication.[42] The relationship between ecology and crime rates may be a reflection of police behavior and not criminal behavior.

These criticisms aside, the Shaw-McKay theory provides a valuable contribution to our understanding of the causes of criminal behavior. By introducing a new variable—the ecology of the city—into the study of crime, the authors paved the way for a whole generation of criminologists to focus on the social influences on criminal and delinquent behavior.

The Social Ecology School

During the 1970s, criminologists were influenced by several critical analyses of social disorganization theory that presented well-thought-out challenges to its validity.[43] During this period, theories with a social psychological orientation, stressing offender socialization within the family, school, and peer group, dominated the criminological literature (these theories will be discussed in Chapter 9).

Despite its "fall from grace," the social disorganization tradition was kept alive by "area studies" conducted by Bernard Lander in Baltimore, David Bordua in Detroit, and Roland Chilton in Indianapolis. These showed that such ecological conditions as substandard housing, low income, and unrelated people living together predicted a high incidence of delinquency.[44]

Then in the 1980s, a group of criminologists began to revive concern about the effects of social disorganization.[45] These modern-day **social ecologists** developed a "purer" form of structural theory that stresses the association of community deterioration and economic decline to criminality while placing less emphasis on value conflict. In the following sections, some of the more recent social ecological research is discussed in some detail.

Community Deterioration

A growing body of literature indicates that community-level social disorganization, including disorder, poverty, alienation, disassociation, and fear of crime, can explain crime rates.[46] Communities that are deteriorated and have a high percentage of deserted houses and apartments experience high crime rates; abandoned buildings serve as a "magnet for crime."[47] The percentage of people living in poverty and the percentage of broken homes are strongly related to neighborhood crime rates.[48] Gangs flourish in deteriorated neighborhoods, adding to the crime rate. In one Chicago area study, G. David Curry and Irving Spergel found that gang homicide rates were associated with such variables as the percentage of the neighborhood living below the poverty line, the lack of mortgage investment in a neighborhood, the unemployment rate, and the influx of new immigrant groups; these factors are usually found in disorganized areas.[49]

The relationship between community deterioration and crime is not unique to the United States. Cross-national research by Scandinavian criminologists Per-Olof Wikstrom and Lars Dolmen found a clear link between crime and measures of social disorganization in a number of European countries.[50] Robert Sampson and W. Byron Groves established that socially disorganized neighborhoods in Great Britain experienced the highest amounts of crime and victimization. Communities characterized by sparse friendship networks, unsupervised teenage peer groups, and low organizational participation also had the greatest amounts of criminality. Sampson and Groves were able to demonstrate that social disorganization theory is robust and has the power to explain crime rates outside the United States.[51]

Employment Opportunities

As you may recall, the relationship between unemployment and crime is unsettled: aggregate crime rates and aggregate unemployment rates seem weakly related. Yet high unemployment may have crime-producing effects in particular neighborhoods or areas. Shaw and McKay found that areas wracked by poverty also experience social disorganization.[52]

Research indicates that neighborhoods that provide few employment opportunities for youth and adults are the most vulnerable to predatory crime.[53] Unemployment helps destabilize households, and unstable families are the ones most likely to contain children who put a premium on violence and aggression as a means of dealing with limited opportunity. Crime rates increase when large groups or cohorts of people of the same age compete for relatively scant resources.[54]

Limited employment opportunities also reduce the stabilizing influence of parents and other adults, who once counteracted the allure of youth gangs. Elijah Anderson's analysis of Philadelphia neighborhood life found that "old heads" (respected neighborhood residents) who at one time played an important role in socializing youth, have been displaced by younger street hustlers and drug dealers. While the "old heads" complain that these newcomers may not have "earned" or "worked for" their fortune in the "old-fashioned way," the old heads admire and envy these kids whose gold chains and luxury cars advertise their wealth amid poverty.[55]

Even the most deteriorated neighborhoods have a surprising degree of familial and kinship strength. Yet the consistent pattern of crime and neighborhood disorganization that follows periods of high unemployment can neutralize their social control capability.

Community Fear

Disorganized neighborhoods suffer social and physical *incivilities*—rowdy youth, trash and litter, graffiti, abandoned storefronts, burned-out buildings, littered lots, strangers, drunks, vagabonds, loiterers, prostitutes, noise, congestion, angry words, dirt, and stench. The presence of such incivilities helps convince residents of disorganized areas that their neighborhood is dangerous and they face a considerable chance of becoming crime victims. Perceptions of crime and victimization produce neighborhood fear.[56]

Fear becomes most pronounced in areas undergoing rapid and unexpected racial and age-composition changes, especially when they are out of proportion to the rest of the city.[57] Fear can become contagious. People tell others of their personal involvement with victimization, spreading the word that the neighborhood is getting dangerous and that the chances of future victimization is high.[58] People dread leaving their homes at night and withdraw from community life. Not surprisingly, people who have already been victimized are more fearful of the future than those who have escaped crime.[59]

When fear grips a neighborhood, business conditions begin to deteriorate, population mobility increases, and a "criminal element" begins to drift into the area.[60] Fear helps produce more crime, increasing the chances of victimization, producing even more fear, in a never-ending loop.[61]

Siege Mentality

One unique aspect of community fear is the development of a **siege mentality,** in which the outside world is considered the enemy out to destroy the neighborhood. Elijah Anderson found that residents in the African-American neighborhoods he studied believed in the existence of a secret plan to eradicate the population by such strategies as permanent unemployment, police brutality, imprisonment, drug distribution, and AIDS.[62] Evidence of this conspiracy hatched by white officials and political leaders could be clearly viewed in the lax law enforcement efforts in poor areas. Police cared little about black-on-black crime because it helped reduce the population.

The siege mentality results in mistrust of critical social institutions, including business, government, and schools. Government officials seem arrogant and haughty. Residents become self-conscious, worried about respect, and attuned to anyone who disrespects or "disses" them. When police ignore crime in poor areas or, conversely, when they are violent and corrupt, anger flares, and people take to the streets and react in violent ways.

Population Turnover

In our postmodern society, urban areas undergoing rapid structural changes in racial and economic composition also seem to experience the greatest change in crime rates.

Recent studies recognize that change and not stability is the hallmark of inner-city areas. A neighborhood's residents, wealth, density, and purpose are constantly evolving. Even disorganized neighborhoods acquire new identifying features. Some may become multiracial, while others become racially homogeneous; some areas become stable and family-oriented, while in others, mobile, never-married people predominate.[63]

As areas decline, residents flee to safer, more stable localities. Those who can't move find themselves surrounded by a constant influx of new residents. High population turnover can have a devastating affect on community culture because it interrupts communication and information flow.[64] A culture may develop that dictates standards of dress, language, and behavior to neighborhood youth that are in opposition to those of conventional society. All these factors are likely to produce increasing crime rates.

Community Change

Social ecologists have attempted to chart the change that undermines urban areas. Robert Bursik and Harold Grasmick found that urban areas may have life cycles, which begin with the building of residential dwellings, followed by a period of decline with marked decreases in socioeconomic status and increases in population density.[65] Later stages in this life cycle include changing racial or ethnic makeup, population thinning, and finally a renewal stage in which obsolete housing is replaced and upgraded *(gentrification)*. There are indications that areas undergoing such change experience increases in their crime rates.[66]

In an often-cited study, sociologists Leo Scheurman and Solomon Kobrin also find that communities go through cycles in which neighborhood deterioration precedes increasing rates of crime and delinquency.[67] Those communities most likely to experience a rapid increase in antisocial behavior contain large numbers of single-parent families and unrelated people living together, have gone from having owner-occupied to renter-occupied units, and have an economic base that has lost semiskilled and unskilled jobs (indicating a growing residue of discouraged workers who are no longer seeking employment).[68] These ecological disruptions strain existing social control mechanisms and inhibit their ability to control crime and delinquency.

A large body of research developed by Robert Bursik and his associates shows that changing life-styles in Chicago neighborhoods, including declining economic status, increasing population, and racial shifts, are associated with increased neighborhood crime rates.[69]

Writing with Janet Heitgerd, Bursik found that areas adjoining neighborhoods undergoing racial change will experience corresponding increases in their own crime rates.[70] This phenomenon may reflect community reaction to perceived racial conflict. In changing neighborhoods, adults support the law-violating behavior of youths and encourage them to protect their property and way of life by violently resisting newcomers.

Poverty Concentration

One aspect of community change may be the concentration of poverty in deteriorated neighborhoods. William Julius Wilson describes how working and middle-class families flee inner-city poverty areas, resulting in a **concentration effect** in which elements of the most disadvantaged population are consolidated in urban ghettos. As the working and middle classes move out, they take with them their financial and institutional resources and support. Businesses are disinclined to locate in poverty areas; banks become reluctant to lend money for new housing or businesses.[71]

Areas marked by concentrated poverty become isolated and insulated from the social mainstream and more prone to criminal activity. Gangs also concentrate in these areas, bringing with them a significant increase in criminal activity. Carolyn Block and Richard Block studied the ecology of gang activity in Chicago and found that the two most dangerous areas (Garfield Park and Humboldt Park) had 76 times more gang-related street crime than the two least dangerous areas (Mount Greenwood and Edison Park).[72]

The concentration effect contradicts, in some measure, Shaw and McKay's assumption that crime rates increase in transitional neighborhoods. Today the areas that may be the most crime-prone may be stable, homogenous areas whose residents are "trapped" in public housing and urban ghettos. Ethnically and racially isolated areas maintain the highest crime rates.[73]

Weak Social Controls

Most neighborhood residents share the common goal of living in a crime-free area. Some communities have the power to regulate the behavior of their residents through the influence of community institutions, such as the family and school. Other neighborhoods, experiencing social disorganization, find that efforts at social control are weak and attenuated. When community social control efforts are blunted, crime rates increase, further weakening neighborhood cohesiveness in a never-ending cycle.

Neighborhoods maintain a variety of agencies and institutions of social control. Some operate on the primary or private level and involve peers, families, and relatives. These sources exert informal control by either awarding or withholding approval, respect, and admiration. Informal control mechanisms include direct criticism, ridicule, ostracism, desertion, or physical punishment.[74]

Communities also use internal networks and local institutions to control crime. Sources of institutional social control include businesses, stores, schools, churches, and social service and volunteer organizations.[75]

Stable neighborhoods are also able to arrange for external sources of social control. For example, community organizations and local leaders may have sufficient political clout to get funding for additional law enforcement personnel. The presence of police sends a message that the area will not tolerate deviant behavior. Criminals and drug dealers avoid such areas and relocate to easier and more appealing "targets."[76]

Neighborhoods that are disorganized cannot mount an effective social control effort. Since the population is transient, interpersonal relationships remain superficial; social institutions such as schools and churches cannot work effectively in a climate of alienation and mistrust. In these areas, the absence of political power brokers limits access to external funding and police protection. Without money from the outside, the neighborhood lacks the ability to "get back on its feet."[77]

Social control is also weakened because unsupervised peer groups and gangs, which flourish in disorganized areas, disrupt the influence of neighborhood control agents.[78] Children who reside in disorganized neighborhoods find that involvement with conventional social institutions, such as schools and afternoon programs, is blocked; they are instead at risk for recruitment into gangs and law violating groups.[79]

Taken in sum, the writings of the social ecology school show that a) social disorganization produces criminality and b) the quality of community life, including levels of change, fear, incivility, poverty, and deterioration, has a direct influence on an area's crime rate.

Social disorganization theory is concerned with aggregate crime rates and not the toll urban decay takes on any particular individual. Yet living in a disorganized area should impact the lives of individuals. How does neighborhood disorganization affect the feelings, attitudes, and behavior of community residents? How do people cope with perceptions of isolation and deprivation? What effect do these feelings have on criminal activities? Criminologists who ask these questions are referred to as strain theorists, and it is to their views we now turn.

Strain Theories

Strain theories constitute the second branch of social structure theory. Strain theorists view crime as a direct result of the frustration and anger people experience over their inability to achieve the social and financial success they desire. While most people share similar values and goals, the ability to achieve them is stratified by socioeconomic class. Strain is limited in affluent areas because educational and vocational opportunities are available. In disorganized slum areas, strain occurs because legitimate avenues for success are all but closed. To relieve strain, indigents may be *forced* to either use deviant methods to achieve their goals, such as theft or drug trafficking, or reject socially accepted goals outright and substitute other, more deviant goals, such as being tough and aggressive.

Anomie

The concept of strain is derived from Emile Durkheim's notion of *anomie* (from the Greek *a nomos*, without norms). According to Durkheim, an anomic society is one in which rules of behavior—norms—have broken down or become inoperative during periods of rapid social change, war, conflict, or unrest. Anomie undermines society's social control function. Every society works to limit people's goals and desires. If a society becomes anomic, it can no longer establish and maintain control over its population's wants and desires. Since people find it difficult to control their appetites, their demands become unlimited.

As originally conceived, anomie resulted from disruption in the social world arising from natural or human-made catastrophes, such as economic depression, war, famine, and so on. Durkheim also recognized an anomie of prosperity, which occurred when sudden good fortune disrupted a person's concept of norms, rules, and behavior. Anomie may also occur when there are so many conflicting social rules that it is impossible to choose among them. As a society becomes increasingly complex, its rules and law become increasingly abundant, making appropriate behavior difficult, if not impossible. Under these circumstances, obedience to

legal codes may be strained and alternative behavior choices, such as crimes, inevitable.

Theory of Anomie

The most important criminological application of Durkheim's scholarship was Robert Merton's **theory of anomie**.[80]

Merton adapted Durkheim's abstract concept to fit the condition of U.S. society.[81] He found that two elements of all modern cultures interact to produce potentially anomic conditions: culturally defined goals and socially approved means for obtaining them. For example, U.S. society stresses the goals of acquiring wealth, success, and power. Socially permissible means include hard work, education, and thrift. Merton argues that every social system maintains a unique combination of goals and means. Merton's position is that the legitimate means to acquire wealth are stratified across class and status lines. Those with little formal education and few economic resources soon find that they are denied the ability to legally acquire money and other success symbols. When socially mandated goals are uniform throughout society and access to legitimate means is bound by class and status, the resulting strain produces an anomic condition among those who are locked out of the legitimate opportunity structure. Consequently, they may develop criminal or delinquent solutions to the problem of attaining goals.

TABLE 7.1 **Typology of Individual Modes of Adaptation**

Modes of Adaptation	Cultural Goals	Institutionalized Means
I. Conformity	+	+
I. Innovation	+	−
II. Ritualism	−	+
V. Retreatism	−	−
V. Rebellion	±	±

SOURCE: Robert Merton, "Social Structure and Anomie," in *Social Theory and Social Structure* (Glencoe Ill.: Free Press, 1957).

Social Adaptations

Merton argues that each person has his or her own concept of the goals of society and the means at his or her disposal to attain them. Whereas some people have inadequate means of attaining success, others who do have the means reject societal goals as being unsuited to them. Table 7.1 shows Merton's diagram of the hypothetical relationship between social goals, the means for getting them, and the individual actor.

Conformity.
Conformity occurs when individuals both embrace conventional social goals and also have the means at their disposal to attain them. In a balanced, stable society, this is the most common social adaptation. If a majority of its people did not practice conformity, the society would cease to exist.

Innovation.
Innovation occurs when an individual accepts the goals of society but rejects or is incapable of attaining them through legitimate means. Many people desire material goods and luxuries but lack the financial ability to attain them. The resulting conflict forces them to adopt innovative solutions to their dilemma: they steal, sell drugs, or extort money. Of the five adaptations, innovation is most closely associated with criminal behavior.

If successful, innovation can have serious, long-term social consequences. Criminal success helps convince otherwise law-abiding people that innovative means work better and faster than conventional ones. The prosperous drug dealer's expensive car and flashy clothes give out the message that "crime pays." "The process thus enlarges the extent of anomie within the system," claims Merton, "so that others, who did not respond in the form of deviant behavior to the relatively slight anomie which they first obtained, come to do so as anomie is spread and is intensified."[82] This explains why crime is created and sustained in certain low-income ecological areas.

Ritualism.
Ritualism occurs when social goals are lowered in importance and means are elevated. Ritualists gain pleasure from the practice of traditional ceremonies that have neither a real purpose nor a goal. The strict set of manners and customs in religious orders, feudal societies, clubs, and college fraternities encourage and appeal to ritualists.

Retreatism.
Retreatists reject *both* the goals and the means of society. Merton suggests that people who adjust in this fashion are "in the society but not of it."

Included in this category are "psychotics, psychoneurotics, chronic autists, pariahs, outcasts, vagrants, vagabonds, tramps, chronic drunkards, and drug addicts." Because such people are morally or otherwise incapable of using *both* legitimate and illegitimate means, they attempt to escape their lack of success by withdrawing—either mentally or physically.

Rebellion.
Rebellion involves the substitution of an alternative set of goals and means for conventional ones. Revolutionaries who wish to promote radical change in the existing social structure and who call for alternative life-styles, goals, and beliefs are engaging in rebellion. Rebellion may be a reaction against a corrupt and hated government or an effort to create alternate opportunities and life-styles within the existing system.

Evaluation of Anomie Theory

According to anomie theory, social inequality leads to perceptions of anomie. To resolve the goals-means conflict and relieve their sense of strain, some people innovate by stealing or extorting money, others retreat into drugs and alcohol, others rebel by joining revolutionary groups, while still others get involved into ritualistic behavior by joining a religious cult.

Merton's view of anomie has been one of the most enduring and influential sociological theories of criminality. By linking deviant behavior to the success goals that control social behavior, anomie theory attempts to pinpoint the cause of the conflict that produces personal frustration and consequent criminality. By acknowledging that society unfairly distributes the legitimate means to achieving success, anomie theory helps explain the existence of high-crime areas and the apparent predominance of delinquent and criminal behavior among the lower class. By suggesting that social conditions, not individual personalities, produce crime, Merton greatly influenced the directions taken to reduce and control criminality during the latter half of the twentieth century.

A number of questions are left unanswered by anomie theory.[83] Merton does not explain why people differ in their choice of criminal behavior. Why does one anomic person become a mugger, while another deals drugs? Anomie may be used to explain differences in crime rates, but it cannot explain why most young criminals desist from crime as adults. Does this mean that perceptions of anomie dwindle with age? Is anomie short-lived?

Critics have also suggested that people pursue a number of different goals, including educational, athletic, and social success. Juveniles may be more interested in immediate goals, like having an active social life or being a good athlete, than long-term "ideal" achievements, such as monetary success. Achieving these goals is not a matter of social class alone; other factors, including athletic ability, intelligence, personality, and family life, can either hinder or assist goal attainment.[84] Anomie theory also assumes that all people share the same goals and values, which is false.[85] Because of these and other criticisms, the theory of anomie, along with other structural theories, fell into a period of decline for almost 20 years.

Institutional Anomie Theory

Anomie and other strain-type theories were neglected when criminologists turned their attention to social psychological views of criminality (see Chapter 9). However, in the 1990s, there has been a resurgence of interest in this view, and a number of prominent criminologists have produced works that have built upon strain concepts. Some of the more prominent are discussed in detail below.

A recent addition to the strain literature has been the publication of *Crime and the American Dream* by Steven Messner and Richard Rosenfeld.[86] Their version of anomie theory views antisocial behavior as a function of *cultural* and *institutional* influences in American society.

Messner and Rosenfeld agree with Merton's view that the success goal is pervasive in American culture. They refer to this as the **"American Dream,"** a term that they employ as both a goal and a process. As a goal, the American Dream involves the accumulation of material goods and wealth under conditions of open individual competition. As a process, it involves both socialization to the pursuit of material success and the belief that prosperity is an achievable goal in the American culture. Anomic conditions occur because the desire to succeed at any cost drives people apart, weakens the collective sense of community, fosters ambition, and restricts the desirability of other kinds of achievement, such as a "good name" and respected reputation.

That Americans are conditioned to succeed "at all costs" should come as no surprise because our capitalist system encourages innovation in the pursuit of monetary rewards. Businesspeople such as Ross Perot and Lee Iaccocca are considered national heroes and leaders. What is distinct about American society, according to Messner and Rosenfeld, and what most likely determines the exceedingly high national crime rate, is that

anomic conditions have been allowed to "develop to such an extraordinary degree."[87]

Why does anomie pervade American culture? According to Messner and Rosenfeld, it is because institutions that might otherwise control the exaggerated emphasis on financial success have been rendered powerless or obsolete. There are three reasons social institutions have been undermined:

1. Noneconomic functions and roles have been *devalued*. Performance in other institutional settings—the family, school, or community—is assigned a lower priority than the goal of financial success.
2. When conflicts emerge, noneconomic roles become subordinate to and must *accommodate* economic roles. The schedules, routines, and demands of the workplace take priority over those of the home, the school, the community, and other aspects of social life.
3. Economic standards and norms *penetrate* into noneconomic realms. Economic terms become part of the common language: people want you to get to the "bottom line"; spouses view themselves as "partners" who "manage" the household. Business leaders run for public office promising to "run the country like a corporation."

According to Messner and Rosenfeld, the relatively high American crime rates can be explained by the interrelationship between culture and institutions. At the cultural level, the dominance of the American Dream mythology ensures that many people will develop wishes and desires for material goods that cannot be satisfied by legitimate means; anomie becomes a norm. At the institutional level, the dominance of economic concerns weakens the informal social control exerted by the family and school. These conditions reinforce each other in a never-ending loop: culture determines institutions and institutional change influences culture.

The Messner-Rosenfeld version of anomie builds upon Merton's views by trying to explain why the success goal has reached such a place of prominence in the American culture. The message "to succeed by any means necessary" has become a national icon.

Relative Deprivation Theory

Criminologists have long assumed that **income inequality** increases both perceptions of strain and crime rates. Sharp divisions between the rich and poor

According to relative deprivation theory, crime rates are highest in areas in which poor and affluent areas are in close proximity.

create an atmosphere of envy and mistrust. According to John Braithwaite, those societies in which income inequality flourishes, *inegalitarian societies*, are especially demeaning to the poor. Criminal motivation is fueled both by perceived humiliation and the *right* to humiliate a victim in return.[88]

If income inequality causes strain, then it stands to reason that crime rates will be highest in areas where the affluent and indigent live in close proximity to one another. This is referred to as **relative deprivation.** This view is most closely associated with sociologists Judith Blau and Peter Blau.[89] Their relative deprivation theory combines concepts specified in anomie with those also found in social disorganization models.

According to the Blaus' research, lower-class people who feel deprived because of their race or class and who reside in urban areas that also house the affluent eventually develop a sense of injustice and discontent.

The poor learn to distrust a society that has nurtured social inequality and blocked any chance of their legitimate advancement. Constant frustration produces pent-up aggression, hostility, and, eventually, violence and crime.[90] The Blaus maintain that a collective sense of **social injustice,** directly related to income inequality, develops in communities in which the poor and wealthy live in close proximity to one another. This perception leads to a state of disorganization and anger. The relatively deprived justifiably feel enraged and vent their hostility in criminal behavior.

Adolescents raised in inner-city poverty areas, such as those in Boston, New York, Chicago, and Los Angeles, will experience this crime-producing frustration, since their neighborhoods are usually located in the same metropolitan area as some of the most affluent neighborhoods in the United States: Beacon Hill, Park Avenue, Lake Shore Drive, and Bel Aire. Relative deprivation is felt most acutely by African-American youths because they consistently suffer racial and economic deprivations that place them in a lower status than other urban residents.[91]

Research evaluating the relative deprivation model shows that crime rates do in fact increase when contiguous neighborhoods become polarized along class lines.[92] Income inequality seems to predict both property and violent crime rates.[93] Research also indicates that residing in an economically integrated neighborhood also harms the children of the more *affluent families,* producing greater dropout rates and more out-of-wedlock births.[94]

While the weight of the evidence supports relative deprivation, a few efforts have failed to show that racial inequality, a central element of the Blaus' theory, is a strong predictor of crime rates.[95]

The theory of relative deprivation, then, holds that people living in deteriorated urban areas, who lack basic human needs, including proper health care, clothing, and shelter (resource deprivation), and who reside in close proximity to those who enjoy the benefits of higher social position will inevitably resort to such crimes as homicide, robbery, and aggravated assault.[96]

Is Relative Deprivation "Relative"?

Is relative deprivation restricted to the lower classes, or can it also be responsible for crimes of the affluent? In other words, is relative deprivation "relative"?

It is possible that even the most affluent Americans will feel strain when they fail to achieve "unlimited goals."[97] That is, no matter their level of affluence, people may perceive strain because the goals they set for themselves are so lofty that they can never be achieved; for example, the millionaire is disappointed because she is not a multimillionaire.

Some affluent people may feel relatively deprived when they compare themselves to the accomplishments of their more socially successful peers. The relatively affluent may then use illegal means to satisfy their own "unrealistic" success goals. Nikos Passas has described this phenomenon:

> Upper-class individuals . . . are by no means shielded against frustrations, relative deprivation and anomia created by a discrepancy between cultural ends and available means, especially in the context of industrial societies, where the ends are renewed as soon as they are reached.[98]

Perhaps some of the individuals involved in the savings and loan scandals or Wall Street insider trading cases felt "relatively deprived" and socially frustrated when they compared the paltry few millions they had already accumulated with the hundreds of millions held by the "truly wealthy," whom they envied.

Roy Austin and Chris Hebert's research also indicates that relative deprivation is "relative."[99] They found that perceptions of relative deprivation may have little to do with economic and social reality. Austin and Hebert find that as economic inequality between blacks and whites *decreased,* white crime rates *increased.* Though whites maintained a distinct advantage in power and resources, Austin and Hebert speculate, they perceived economic progress made by African-Americans as a step backward for themselves. Feelings of relative deprivation resulted in the rise of white power groups, antibusing movements, and higher crime rates. Crime rates rose when lower-class whites began to feel relatively less privileged than lower-class African-Americans.

These research efforts support the relative deprivation model and indicate it may be more complex than originally thought.

≡ General Strain Theory

Sociologist Robert Agnew has reformulated strain concepts into a **general strain theory** (GST) in an effort to broaden its focus and make it a more general explanation of criminal activity among all elements of society.[100] He agrees with the criticism that in its original form (Merton's anomie theory), strain theory neglected to consider that there were multiple forms of strain and multiple paths for achieving success.

Agnew finds that the failure to achieve material success may not be the only cause of crime. Criminality can also be a result of **negative affective states**—the anger, frustration, and adverse emotions—which come in the wake of negative and destructive social relationships. Negative affective states are produced by a variety of sources of strain:

Strain caused by the failure to achieve positively valued goals: This category of strain, similar to what Merton speaks of in his theory of anomie, is a result of the disjunction between aspirations and expectations. This type of strain will occur when a youth aspires for wealth and fame but, lacking financial and educational resources, assumes that such goals are impossible to achieve.

Strain caused by the disjunction of expectations and achievements: Strain can also be produced when there is a disjunction between *expectations* and achievements. When people compare themselves to peers who seem to be doing a lot better financially or socially (such as making more money or getting better grades), even those doing relatively well feel strain. For example, they get into college but not into a prestige school, like some of their friends. Perhaps they are not being treated fairly because the "playing field" is tilted against them; "Other kids have connections," they say. Perceptions of inequity may result in many adverse reactions, ranging from running away from its source to lowering the benefits of others through physical attacks or vandalism of their property.

Strain as the removal of positively valued stimuli from the individual: Strain may occur because of the actual or anticipated removal or loss of a positively valued stimuli from the individual.[101] For example, the loss of a girl- or boyfriend can produce strain, as can the death of a loved one, moving to a new neighborhood or school, and the divorce or separation of parents. The loss of positive stimuli may lead to delinquency as the adolescent tries to prevent the loss, retrieve what has been lost, obtain substitutes, or seek revenge against those responsible for the loss.

Strain as the presentation of negative stimuli: Strain may also be caused by the presence of negative or noxious stimuli. Included within this category are such pain-inducing social interactions as child abuse and neglect, crime victimization, physical punishment, family and peer conflict, school failure, and interaction with stressful life events ranging from verbal threats to air pollution.

While these sources of strain are independent from one another, they may overlap and be cumulative in practice. For example, insults from a teacher may be viewed as an unfair application of negative stimuli, which interferes with academic aspirations. The greater the intensity and frequency of strain experiences, the greater their impact and the more likely they are to cause delinquency.

According to Agnew, each type of strain will increase the likelihood of experiencing such negative emotions as disappointment, depression, fear, and, most important, anger. Anger increases perceptions of injury and of being wronged. It produces a desire for revenge, energizes individuals to take action, and lowers inhibitions; violence and aggression seem justified if you have been wronged and are righteously angry.

Because it produces these emotions, strain can be considered a predisposing factor for delinquency when it is chronic and repetitive and creates a hostile, suspicious, and aggressive attitude. Individual strain episodes may serve as a situational event or trigger that produces delinquency, such as when a particularly stressful event ignites a violent reaction.

Coping with Strain

Agnew recognizes that not all people who experience strain eventually become criminals. Some are able to marshal their emotional, mental, and behavioral resources to cope with the anger and frustration produced by strain. Some defenses are cognitive; individuals may be able to rationalize frustrating circumstances. Not getting the career they desire is "just not that important"; they may be poor, but the "next guy is worse off," and if things didn't work out, then they "got what they deserved." Others seek behavioral solutions: they run away from adverse conditions or seek revenge against those who caused the strain. Others will try to regain emotional equilibrium with techniques ranging from physical exercise to drug abuse.

The general strain theory acknowledges that the ability to cope with strain varies with personal experiences over the life course. Kids who lack economic means are less likely to cope than those who have at their command sufficient financial resources. Personal temperament, prior learning of delinquent attitudes and behaviors, and association with delinquent peers who reinforce anger are among other factors effecting the ability to cope with strain.

Strain and Criminal Careers

As you may recall, the cohort studies show that criminal behavior begins early in life, then remains stable over the life course. Considering that strain-producing interactions are not constant, how can GST explain both chronic offending and the stability of crime?

GST recognizes that certain people have traits that may expose them to strain. These include a difficult temperament, being overly sensitive or emotional, low tolerance for adversity, and poor problem-solving skills. These traits, linked to aggressive and antisocial behavior, seem to be stable over a person's life cycle.[102]

Aggressive people who have these traits are likely to have poor interpersonal skills and are more likely to be treated negatively by others; their combative personalities make them feared and disliked. They are likely to live in families whose caretakers share similar personality traits. They are also more likely to reject conventional peers and join deviant groups. Such individuals are more likely to be subject to a high degree of strain over the course of their lives.

Crime peaks during late adolescence because this is a period of social stress caused by the weakening of parental supervision and the development of relationships with a diverse peer group. Expectations may increase, and some kids are unable to meet academic and social expectations. Adolescents are very concerned about their standing with peers. Those deficient in these areas may find they are social outcasts, another source of strain. In adulthood, crime rates drop because these sources of strain are reduced. New sources of self-esteem emerge, and adults seem more likely to bring their goals in line with reality.

Agnew's work is quite important because it both clarifies the concept of strain and directs future research agendas. It also adds to the body of literature that describes how events over the life cycle influence delinquency patterns. Because sources of strain vary over time, so too should crime rates. In a recent empirical analysis of his theory using longitudinal survey data, Agnew, with Helene Raskin White, found that adolescents who score high on scales measuring perceptions of strain labeled "life hassles" (for example, "my classmates do not like me," adults and friends "don't respect my opinions") and "negative life events" (experiencing crime victimization, the death of a close friend, or a serious illness) are also the ones most likely to engage in delinquency.[103] This research indicates that as adolescents travel through life, events and relationships they encounter shape the direction and frequency of their behavior.

≡ Cultural Deviance Theory

The third branch of social structure theory combines the effects of social disorganization and strain to explain how people living in deteriorated neighborhoods react to social isolation and economic deprivation. Because their life-style is draining, frustrating, and dispiriting, members of the lower class create an independent *sub-culture* with its own set of rules and values. While middle-class culture stresses hard work, delayed gratification, formal education, and being cautious, the lower-class subculture stresses excitement, toughness, risk-taking, fearlessness, immediate gratification, and "street smarts." The lower-class subculture is an attractive alternative because the urban poor find that it is impossible to meet the behavioral demands of middle-class society. Unfortunately, subcultural norms often clash with conventional values. Slum dwellers are forced to violate the law because they obey the rules of the deviant culture with which they are in close and immediate contact.

Conduct Norms

The concept that the lower class develops a unique culture in response to strain can be traced to Thorsten Sellin's classic 1938 work, *Culture Conflict and Crime*, a theoretical attempt to link cultural adaptation to criminality.[104] Sellin's main premise is that criminal law is an expression of the rules of the dominant culture. The content of the law, therefore, may create a clash between conventional, middle-class rules and splinter groups, such as ethnic and racial minorities who are excluded from the social mainstream. These groups maintain their own set of conduct norms—rules governing the day-to-day living conditions within these subcultures.[105] Complicating matters is the fact that most of us belong to several social groups. In a complex society, the number of groups people belong to—family, peer, occupational, and religious—is quite large. "A conflict of norms is said to exist when more or less divergent rules of conduct govern the specific life situation in which a person may find himself."[106] According to Sellin, **culture conflict** occurs when the rules expressed in the criminal law clash with the demands of group **conduct norms.** To make his point, Sellin cited the case of a Sicilian father in New Jersey who killed the 16-year-old seducer of his daughter and then expressed surprise at being arrested; he had "merely defended his family honor in a traditional way."[107] Conduct norms are universal; they are not the product of one group, culture, or political structure.

Focal Concerns

In his classic 1958 paper, "Lower Class Culture as a Generating Milieu of Gang Delinquency," Walter Miller identified the unique value system that defines lower-class culture.[108] Obedience to these **focal concerns** dominates life among the lower class. Focal concerns do not necessarily represent a rebellion against middle-class values; rather, these values have evolved specifically to fit conditions in slum areas. The major lower-class focal concerns are set out in more detail below.[109]

Trouble. Getting into trouble includes such behavior as fighting, drinking, and sexual misconduct. In lower-class communities, people are evaluated by their actual or potential involvement in trouble-making activity. Dealing with trouble can confer prestige—for example, when a man gets a reputation for being able to handle himself well in a fight. Not being able to handle trouble, and having to pay the consequences, can make a person look foolish and incompetent.

Toughness. Lower-class males want local recognition of their physical and spiritual toughness. They refuse to be sentimental or soft and instead value physical strength, fighting ability, and athletic skill. Those who cannot meet these standards risk getting a reputation for being weak, inept, and effeminate.

Smartness. Members of the lower-class culture want to maintain an image of being "street-wise" and savvy, using their "street smarts," and having the ability to outfox and outcon the opponent. Though formal education is not admired, knowing essential survival techniques, such as gambling, conning, and outsmarting the law, is a requirement.

Excitement. Another important feature of the lower-class life-style is the search for fun and excitement to enliven an otherwise drab existence. The search for excitement may lead to gambling, fighting, getting drunk, and sexual adventures. In between, the lower-class citizen may simply "hang out" and "be cool."

Fate.   Lower-class citizens believe their lives are in the hands of strong spiritual forces that guide their destinies. Getting lucky, finding good fortune, and hitting the jackpot are all slum dwellers' daily dreams.

Autonomy.   A general concern exists in lower-class cultures about personal freedom and autonomy. Being independent of authority figures, such as the police, teachers, and parents, is required; losing control is an unacceptable weakness, incompatible with toughness.

According to Miller, clinging to lower-class focal concerns will in turn promote behavior that often runs afoul of the law. Toughness may mean displaying fighting prowess; street smarts lead to drug deals; excitement may result in drinking, gambling, or drug abuse. It is this obedience to the prevailing cultural demands of lower-class society, and not alienation from conventional society, that causes urban crime.

These views of a lower-class subculture formed by strain inspired a number of formal theories that predicted the onset of gang delinquency in lower-class areas. The two best known are described below.

Theory of Delinquent Subcultures

Albert Cohen first articulated the theory of delinquent subculture in his classic 1955 book, *Delinquent Boys.*[110]

Cohen's central position was that delinquent behavior of lower-class youths is actually a protest against the norms and values of the middle-class U.S. culture. Because social conditions make them incapable of achieving success legitimately, lower-class youths experience a form of culture conflict that Cohen labels **status frustration.**[111] As a result, many of them join together in gangs and engage in behavior that is "nonutilitarian, malicious, and negativistic."[112]

Cohen viewed the delinquent gang as a separate subculture, possessing a value system directly opposed to that of the larger society. He describes the subculture as one that takes "its norms from the larger culture but turns them upside down. The delinquent's conduct is right by the standards of his subculture precisely because it is wrong by the norms of the larger cultures."[113]

According to Cohen, the development of the delinquent subculture is a consequence of socialization practices found in the ghetto or slum environment. Deficient socialization renders lower-class kids unable to achieve conventional success. Cohen suggests that lower-class parents are incapable of teaching children the necessary techniques for entering the dominant middle-class culture. Developmental handicaps suffered by lower-class kids include lack of education, poor speech and communication skills, and inability to delay gratification. These children lack the basic skills necessary to achieve social and economic success in the demanding U.S. society.

Middle-Class Measuring Rods

One significant handicap that lower-class children face is the inability to positively impress authority figures, such as teachers, employers, or supervisors. In U.S. society, these positions tend to be held by members of the middle class who have difficulty relating to the lower-class youngster. Cohen calls the standards set by these authority figures **middle-class measuring rods.** The conflict and frustration lower-class youths experience when they fail to meet these standards is a primary cause of delinquency.

Lower-class youths who have difficulty adjusting to the middle-class measuring rods of one institution may find themselves prejudged by others. The ratings are reviewed and magnified by the periodic updating of records and the informal exchanges of information that commonly occur among the leaders of institutions, who frequently are also the pillars and decision makers of the community. A school record may be reviewed by juvenile court authorities, a juvenile court record may be opened by the military, and a military record can influence the securing of a job. A person's status and esteem in the community is largely determined by the judgments that most often reflect the traditional values of American society.[114] Negative evaluations become part of a permanent file that follows an individual for the rest of his or her life. When he or she wants to improve, evidence of prior failures are used to discourage advancement.

The Formation of Deviant Subcultures

Cohen believes lower-class boys who suffer rejection by middle-class decision makers usually elect to join one of three existing subcultures: the corner boy, the college boy, or the delinquent boy.

The *corner boy* role is the most common response to middle-class rejection. The corner boy is not a chronic delinquent but may be a truant who engages in petty or status offenses, such as precocious sex and recreational drug abuse. His main loyalty is to his peer group, on which he depends for support, motivation, and interest. His values, therefore, are those of the group with which he is in close personal contact. The corner boy, well aware of his failure to achieve the standards of the American dream, retreats into the comforting world of his lower-class peers and eventually becomes a stable member of his neighborhood, holding a menial job, marrying, and remaining in the community.

The *college boy* embraces the cultural and social values of the middle class. Rather than scorning middle-class measuring rods, he actively strives to be successful by those standards. Cohen views this type of youth as one who is embarking on an almost hopeless path, since he is ill-equipped academically, socially, and linguistically to achieve the rewards of middle-class life.

The *delinquent boy* adopts a set of norms and principles in direct opposition to middle-class values. He engages in **short-run hedonism,** living for today and letting "tomorrow take care of itself."[115] Delinquent boys strive for **group autonomy.** They resist efforts by family, school, or other sources of authority to control their behavior. They may join a gang because it is perceived as autonomous, independent, and the focus of "attraction, loyalty, and solidarity."[116] Frustrated by their inability to succeed, these boys resort to a process Cohen calls **reaction formation.** Symptoms of reaction formation include overly intense responses that seem disproportionate to the stimuli that trigger them. For the delinquent boy, this takes the form of irrational, malicious, and unaccountable hostility to the enemy, "the norms of respectable middle-class society."[117] Reaction formation causes delinquent boys to overreact to any perceived threat or slight. They sneer at the college boy's attempts at assimilation and scorn the corner boy's passivity. The delinquent boy is willing to take risks, violate the law, and flaunt middle-class conventions.

Cohen's work helps explain the factors that promote and sustain a delinquent subculture. By introducing the concepts of status frustration and middle-class measuring rods, Cohen makes it clear that social forces and not individual traits promote and sustain a delinquent career. By introducing the corner boy-college boy-delinquent boy triad, he helps explain why many lower-class youths fail to become chronic offenders: there is more than one social path open to indigent youth.[118] His work is a skillful integration of strain and social disorganization theories and has become an enduring element of the criminological literature.

≡ Theory of Differential Opportunity

In their well-known work *Delinquency and Opportunity*, Richard Cloward and Lloyd Ohlin also combine strain and social disorganization principles into a portrayal of a gang-sustaining criminal subculture.[119]

Cloward and Ohlin, agreeing with Cohen, find that independent delinquent subcultures exist within society:

> A delinquent subculture is one in which certain forms of delinquent activity are essential requirements for the performance of the dominant roles supported by the subculture.[120]

Youth gangs are an important part of the delinquent subculture. While not all illegal acts are committed by gang youth, they are the source of the most serious, sustained, and costly criminal behaviors. Delinquent gangs spring up in disorganized areas where youths lack the opportunity to gain success through conventional means. True to strain theory principles, Cloward and Ohlin portray slum kids as individuals who want to conform to middle-class values but lack the means to do so: "Reaching out for socially approved goals under conditions that preclude their legitimate achievement may become a prelude to deviance."[121]

Differential Opportunities

The centerpiece of the Cloward and Ohlin theory is the concept of **differential opportunity.** According to this concept, people in all strata of society share the same success goals; however, those in the lower class have limited means of achievement. People who perceive themselves as failures within conventional society will seek alternative or innovative ways to gain success. People who conclude that there is little hope for advancement by legitimate means may join with like-minded peers to form a gang. Gang members provide the emotional support to handle the shame, fear, or guilt they may develop while engaging in illegal acts. Delinquent subcultures reward them in a way that conventional society cannot hope to duplicate. The youth who is considered a failure at school and is only qualified for a menial job at a minimum wage can earn thousands of dollars plus the respect of his or her peers by joining a gang and engaging in drug deals or armed robberies.

Cloward and Ohlin recognize that the opportunity for both successful conventional and criminal careers is limited. In stable areas, adolescents may be recruited by professional criminals, drug traffickers, or organized crime groups. Unstable areas cannot support flourishing criminal opportunities. In these socially disorganized neighborhoods, adult role models are absent and young criminals have few opportunities to join established gangs or learn the fine points of professional crime. Their most important finding, then, is that all opportunities for success, *both illegal and conventional*, are closed for the most "truly disadvantaged" youth.

Because of differential opportunity, kids are likely to join one of three types of gangs.

Criminal Gangs. Criminal gangs exist in stable slum areas in which close connections among adolescent, young adult, and adult offenders create an environment for successful criminal enterprise.[122] Youths are recruited into established criminal gangs that provide a training ground for a successful criminal career. Gang membership provides a learning experience in which the knowledge and skills needed for success in crime are acquired. During this "apprenticeship stage," older, more experienced members of the criminal subculture hold youthful "trainees" on tight reins, limiting activities that might jeopardize the gang's profits (for example, engaging in nonfunctional, irrational violence). Over time, new recruits learn the techniques and attitudes of the criminal world and how to "cooperate successfully with others in criminal enterprises."[123] To become a fully accepted member of the criminal gang, novices must prove themselves reliable and dependable in their contacts with their criminal associates and be "right guys." They are introduced to the middlemen of the crime business—drug importers, fences, pawn shop operators—and also to legal connections—crooked police officers and shady lawyers—who can help them gain their freedom in the rare instances when they are apprehended.

Conflict Gangs. Conflict gangs develop in communities unable to provide either legitimate or illegitimate opportunities. These highly disorganized areas are marked by transient residents and physical deterioration. Crime in this area is "individualistic, unorganized, petty, poorly paid, and unprotected."[124] There are no successful adult criminal role models from whom youths can learn criminal skills. When such severe limitations on both criminal and conventional opportunity intensify frustrations of the young, violence is used as a means of gaining status. The stereotype of the conflict gang member is the swaggering gang tough who fights with weapons to win respect from rivals and engages in unpredictable and destructive assaults on people and property. Conflict gang members must be ready to fight to protect their own and their gang's integrity and honor. By doing so, they acquire a "rep," which provides them with a means for gaining admiration from their peers and consequently helps them develop their own self-image. Conflict gangs "represent a way of securing access to the scarce resources for adolescent pleasure and opportunity in underprivileged areas."[125]

Retreatist Gangs. Retreatists are double failures, unable to gain success through legitimate means and unwilling to do so through illegal ones. Some retreatists have tried crime or violence but are either too clumsy, weak, or scared to be accepted in criminal or violent gangs. They then "retreat" into a role on the fringe of society. Members of the retreatist subculture constantly search for ways of getting high—alcohol, pot, heroin, unusual sexual experiences, music. They are always "cool," detached from relationships with the conventional world. To feed their habits, retreatists develop a "hustle"—pimping, conning, selling drugs, and committing petty crimes. Personal status in the retreatist subculture is derived from peer approval.

Analysis of Differential Opportunity Theory

Cloward and Ohlin's theory is important both because of its integration of cultural deviance and social disorganization variables and its recognition of different modes of criminal adaptation. The fact that criminal cultures can be supportive, rational, and profitable seems to be a more realistic reflection of the actual world of the delinquent than Cohen's original view of purely negativistic, destructive delinquent youths who oppose all social values. Cloward and Ohlin's tripartite model of urban delinquency also relates directly to the treatment and rehabilitation of delinquents. While other social structure theorists portray delinquent youths as having values and attitudes in opposition to middle-class culture, Cloward and Ohlin suggest that many delinquents share the goals and values of the general society but lack the means to obtain success. This position suggests that delinquency prevention can be achieved by providing youths with the means for obtaining the success they truly desire without the need to change their basic attitudes and beliefs.

The Gang Problem

The validity of opportunity theory is underscored by the gang activity recorded in the nation's cities. As opportunity theory predicts, gang activity today flourishes in the inner-city ghetto areas of Detroit, New York, Los Angeles, and Chicago. In addition, smaller cities, such as Cleveland and Columbus, Ohio, and Milwaukee, Wisconsin, for the first time are experiencing serious gang problems with the development of local gangs and the migration of gang members from larger communities. A national survey of gang migration by Cheryl Maxson and Malcolm Klein describes the levels of movement from one city to another as "astounding." A decade ago, about 200 of the 1,100 cities they studied had gangs;

Gang symbols and graffiti are part of the alternative subculture that the gang provides for alienated inner-city youth. Cultural deviance theories are supported by the recent increase in gang membership and activity in the nation's inner cities.

local police force: Chicago estimates 29,000 gang members, while Los Angeles contains an estimated 55,000. Other cities reporting large gang populations (in excess of 5,000 members) include Minneapolis, Milwaukee, Denver, Las Vegas, Albuquerque, Santa Ana and Long Beach, California. The figure of a quarter of a million gang members cited above does not include members in New York City and Philadelphia, cities with potentially large numbers of gangs but from which data was unavailable.

Why has gang activity increased? One compelling reason may be the involvement of youth gangs in the distribution and sales of illegal drugs. In some areas, gangs have replaced traditional organized crime families as the dominant supplier of illegal substances. The introduction of the relatively cheap cocaine derivative "crack," which provides a powerful, albeit short-term "high," helped open new markets in the drug trade.[128]

Gang formation may be the natural consequence of the evolution of the American industrial base from a manufacturing economy with a surplus of relatively high-paying jobs to a low-wage service economy.[129] The American city, which traditionally required a large population base for its manufacturing plants, now faces incredible economic stress as these plants shut down. In this uneasy economic climate, gangs form and flourish in areas where the moderating influence of successful adult role models and stable families declines and where adolescents face constrained choices and weak social controls.[130] Gang activity provides members with a stable income stream in an otherwise unproductive urban marketplace. From this perspective, youth gangs are a response to the glooming of the American economy.

The rise of gang memberships in a declining industrial market and the development of drug profits as an alternative or innovative method of financial success are social conditions predicted by opportunity theory. The prevalence of gang activity in urban America provides staunch support for the social structure approach.

Evaluation of Social Structure Theories

The social structure approach has significantly influenced both criminological theory and crime prevention strategies. Its core concepts seem to be valid in view of the high crime and delinquency rates and gang activity occurring in the deteriorated inner-city slum areas of the

today, the number is 700. Of the 150 cities in the United States with populations of more than 100,000, 82 percent had experienced gang migration from larger cities.[126]

Another survey of gangs, the National Assessment of Gang Activity sponsored by the National Institute of Justice, found that 91 percent of the nation's 79 largest cities report the presence of youth gangs involved in criminal activity. Data from these larger cities indicate that there are at least 3,876 gangs containing 202,981 members. Additional data collected from 29 smaller cities and 11 county jurisdictions increase these numbers to 4,881 gangs with 249,324 members.[127]

Some of the reporting cities indicate that the number of gang members far exceeds the personnel on the

nation's largest cities. The public's image of the slum includes roaming bands of violent teenage gangs, drug users, prostitutes, muggers, and similar frightening examples of criminality. All of these are present today in urban ghetto areas.

Despite such images, we cannot be sure that it is lower-class culture itself that promotes crime and not some other force operating in society. Critics of this approach deny that residence in urban areas is alone sufficient to cause people to violate the law.[131] They counter with the charge that lower-class crime rates may be an artifact of bias in the criminal justice system. Lower-class areas seem to have higher crime rates because residents are arrested and prosecuted by agents of the justice system who, as members of the middle class, exhibit class bias.[132] Class bias is often coupled with discrimination against minority-group members, who have long suffered at the hands of the justice system.

Even if the higher crime rates recorded in lower-class areas are valid, it is still true that most members of the lower class are not criminals. The discovery of the chronic offender indicates that a significant majority of people living in lower-class environments are not criminals and that a relatively small proportion of the population commits most crimes. If social forces alone could be used to explain crime, how can we account for the vast number of urban poor who remain honest and law-abiding? Given these circumstances, law violators must be motivated by some individual mental, physical, or social process or trait.[133]

It is also questionable whether a distinct lower-class culture actually exists. Several researchers have found that gang members and other delinquent youths seem to value middle-class concepts, such as sharing, earning money, and respecting the law, as highly as middle-class youths. Criminologists contend that lower-class youths value education as highly as middle-class students.[134] Opinion polls can also be used as evidence that a majority of lower-class citizens maintain middle-class values. National surveys find that people in the lowest income brackets want tougher drug laws, more police protection, and greater control over criminal offenders.[135] These opinions seem similar to conventional middle-class values rather than representative of an independent, deviant subculture. While this evidence contradicts some of the central ideas of social structure theory, the discovery of stable patterns of lower-class crime, the high crime rates found in disorganized inner-city areas, and the rise of teenage gangs and groups support a close association between crime rates and social class position.

Social Structure Theory and Social Policy

Social structure theory has had a significant influence on social policy. If the cause of criminality is viewed as a separation between lower-class individuals and conventional goals, norms, and rules, it seems logical that alternatives to criminal behavior can be provided by giving slum dwellers opportunities to share in the rewards of conventional society. Crime prevention efforts based on social structure precepts can be traced back to the **Chicago Area Project,** supervised by Clifford R. Shaw. This program attempted to organize existing community structures to develop social stability in otherwise disorganized slums. The project sponsored recreation programs for children in the neighborhoods, including summer camping. It campaigned for community improvements in such areas as education, sanitation, traffic safety, physical conservation, and law enforcement. Project members also worked with police and court agencies to supervise and treat gang youth and adult offenders. In a 25-year assessment of the project, Solomon Kobrin found that it was successful in demonstrating the feasibility of creating youth welfare organizations in high-delinquency areas.[136] Kobrin also discovered that the project made a distinct contribution to ending the isolation of urban males from the mainstream of society.

Social structure concepts, especially the views of Cloward and Ohlin, were a critical ingredient in the Kennedy and Johnson administrations' "War on Poverty," begun in the early 1960s. Rather than organizing existing community structures, as Shaw's Chicago Area Project had done, this later effort called for an all-out attack on the crime-producing structures of slum areas. The cornerstone of the War on Poverty's crime prevention effort was called Mobilization for Youth (MFY). This New York City-based program was funded for over $12 million. It was designed to serve multiple purposes: it provided teacher training and education to help educators deal with the problem youth, created work opportunities through a youth job center, organized neighborhood councils and associations, provided street workers to deal with teen gangs, and set up counseling services and assistance to neighborhood families. Subsequent War on Poverty programs included the Job Corps; VISTA (the urban Peace Corps); Head Start and Upward Bound (educational enrichment programs); Neighborhood Legal Services; and the largest community organizing effort, the Community Action Program. War on Poverty programs, such as MFY, were sweeping efforts to change the social structure of the slum area. They sought to reduce crime by developing a sense of community pride and solidarity in poverty areas and providing educational and job opportunities for crime-prone youths. As history tells us, the programs failed. Federal and state funding often fell into the hands of middle-class managers and community developers and not the people it was designed to help. Managers were accused of graft and corruption. Some community organizers engineered rent strikes, lawsuits, protests, and the like, which angered government officials and convinced them that financial backing of such programs should be ended. Rather than appeal to the political power structure, program administrators alienated it. Still later, the mood of the country began to change. The more conservative political climate under the Nixon, Ford, Reagan, and Bush administrations did not favor federal sponsorship of radical change in U.S. cities. Instead of a total community approach to solve the crime problem, a more selective crime prevention policy was adopted. Some War on Poverty programs—Head Start, Neighborhood Legal Services, and the Community Action Program—have continued to help people; nonetheless, this attempt to change the very structure of society must be judged a noble failure (Head Start will be discussed further in Chapter 8).

☰ Summary

Sociology has been the main orientation of criminologists because they know that crime rates vary among elements of the social structure, that society goes through changes that affect crime, and that social interaction relates to criminality. Social structure theories suggest that people's places in the socioeconomic structure of society influence their chances of becoming a criminal. Poor people are more likely to commit crimes because they are unable to achieve monetary or social success in any other way. Social structure theory has three schools of thought: social disorganization, strain, and cultural deviance theory (summarized in Table 7.2).

Social disorganization theory suggests that slum dwellers violate the law because they live in areas in which social control has broken down. The origin of social disorganization theory can be traced to the work of Clifford R. Shaw and Henry D. McKay. Shaw and McKay concluded that disorganized areas marked by divergent values and transitional populations produced criminality. Modern social ecology theory looks at such issues as community fear, unemployment, seige mentality, and deterioration.

Strain theories comprise the second branch of the social structure approach. They view crime as a result of the anger people experience over their inability to achieve legitimate social and economic success. Strain theories hold that most people share common values and beliefs, but the ability to achieve them is differentiated throughout the social structure. The best-known strain theory is Robert Merton's theory of anomie, which describes what happens when the means people have at their disposal are not adequate to satisfy their goals. Steven Messner, Richard Rosenfeld, and Robert Agnew have extended this theory by showing that strain has multiple sources.

Cultural deviance theories hold that a unique value system develops in lower-class areas. Lower-class values approve of such behaviors as being tough, never showing fear, and defying authority. People perceiving strain will bond together in their own groups or subcultures for support and recognition. Albert Cohen links the formation of subcultures to the failure of lower-class citizens to achieve recognition from middle-class decision makers, such as teachers, employers, and police officers. Richard Cloward and Lloyd Ohlin have argued that crime results from lower-class people's perception that their opportunity for success is limited. Consequently, youths in low-income areas may join criminal, conflict, or retreatist gangs.

☰ KEY TERMS

Chicago School	value conflict
Robert Ezra Park	social ecologists
natural areas	siege mentality
stratified	concentration effect
poverty line	theory of anomie
culture of poverty	American Dream
at-risk	income inequality
underclass	relative deprivation
truly disadvantaged	social injustice
social structure theory	general strain theory
social disorganization	negative affective states
theory	culture conflict
strain theory	conduct norms
cultural deviance theory	focal concerns
subcultures	status frustration
cultural transmission	middle-class measuring rods
transitional neighborhoods	short-run hedonism

TABLE 7.2 **Social Structure Theories**

Theory	Major Premise	Strengths
Social Disorganization Theory		
Shaw and McKay's concentric zone theory	Crime is a product of transitional neighborhoods that manifest social disorganization and value conflict.	Identifies why crime rates are highest in slum areas. Points out the factors that produce crime. Suggests programs to help reduce crime.
social ecology theory	The conflicts and problems of urban social life and communities, including fear, unemployment, deterioration and siege mentality, influence crime rates.	Accounts for urban crime rates and trends.
Strain Theory anomie theory	People who adopt the goals of society but lack the means to attain them seek alternatives, such as crime.	Points out how competition for success creates conflict and crime. Suggests that social conditions and not personality can account for crime. Can explain middle- and upper-class crime.
general strain theory	Strain has a variety of sources. Strain causes crime in the absence of adequate coping mechanisms.	Identifies the complexities of strain in modern society. Expands on anomie theory. Shows the influences of social events on behavior over the life course.
institutional anomie theory	Material goals pervade all aspects of American life.	Explains why crime rates are so high in American culture.
relative deprivation	Crime occurs when the wealthy and poor live in close proximity to one another.	Explains high crime rates in deteriorated inner-city areas located near more affluent neighborhoods.
Cultural Deviance Theory Sellin's culture conflict theory	Obedience to the norms of their lower-class culture puts people in conflict with the norms of the dominant culture.	Identifies the aspects of lower-class life that produce street crime. Adds to Shaw and McKay's analysis. Creates the concept of culture conflict.
Miller's focal concern theory	Citizens who obey the street rules of lower-class life (focal concerns) find themselves in conflict with the dominant culture.	Identifies the core values of lower-class culture and shows their association to crime.
Cohen's theory of delinquent gangs	Status frustration of lower-class boys, created by their failure to achieve middle-class success, causes them to join gangs.	Shows how the conditions of lower-class life produce crime. Explains violence and destructive acts. Identifies conflict of lower class with middle class.
Cloward and Ohlin's theory of opportunity	Blockage of conventional opportunities causes lower-class youths to join criminal, conflict, or retreatist gangs.	Shows that even illegal opportunities are structured in society. Indicates why people become involved in a particular type of criminal activity. Presents a way of preventing crime.

group autonomy
reaction formation

differential opportunity
Chicago Area Project

≡ **NOTES**

1. Steven Messner and Richard Rosenfeld, *Crime and the American Dream* (Belmont, Calif.: Wadsworth, 1994), p. 11.
2. Robert E. Park, "The City: Suggestions for the Investigation of Behavior in the City Environment," *American Journal of Sociology* 20 (1915): 579–83.
3. Robert Park, Ernest Burgess, and Roderic McKenzie, *The City* (Chicago: University of Chicago Press, 1925).
4. Harvey Zorbaugh, *The Gold Coast and the Slum* (Chicago: University of Chicago Press, 1929).
5. Frederick Thrasher, *The Gang* (Chicago: University of Chicago Press, 1927).
6. Louis Wirth, *The Ghetto* (Chicago: University of Chicago Press, 1928).
7. Daniel Bell, *The Coming of Post-Industrial Society* (New

York: Basic Books, 1973).

8. See, generally, Stephen Cernkovich and Peggy Giordano, "Family Relationships and Delinquency," *Criminology* 25 (1987): 295–321; Paul Howes and Howard Markman, "Marital Quality and Child Functioning: A Longitudinal Investigation," *Child Development* 60 (1989): 1044–51.

9. Emilie Andersen Allan and Darrell Steffensmeier, "Youth, Underemployment, and Property Crime: Differential Effects of Job Availability and Job Quality on Juvenile and Young Adult Arrest Rates," *American Sociological Review* 54 (1989): 107–23.

10. Edwin Lemert, *Human Deviance, Social Problems and Social Control* (Englewood Cliffs, N.J.: Prentice-Hall, 1967).

11. U.S. Department of Commerce, Bureau of the Census, Census Data 1992 (Washington, D.C.: U.S. Government Printing Office, 1994).

12. Based on William Julius Wilson, "Studying Inner-City Social Dislocations: The Challenge of Public Agenda Research," *American Sociological Review* 56 (1991): 1–14 at 3.

13. Jennifer Dixon, "Thousands of Infants Left in Hospitals in '91," *Boston Globe*, 9 November 1993, p. 5.

14. Jonathan Crane, "The Epidemic Theory of Ghettos and Neighborhood Effects on Dropping Out and Teenage Childbearing," *American Journal of Sociology* 96 (1991): 1226–59; see also Rodrick Wallace, "Expanding Coupled Shock Fronts of Urban Decay and Criminal Behavior: How U.S. Cities Are Becoming 'Hollowed Out,'" *Journal of Quantitative Criminology* 7 (1991): 333–55.

15. Cynthia Rexroat, *Declining Economic Status of Black Children, Examining the Change* (Washington, D.C.: Joint Center for Political and Economic Studies, 1990).

16. Ibid.

17. Dolores Kong, "Social, Economic Factors Seen in Black Death Rates," *Boston Globe*, 8 December 1989, p. 1.

18. Associated Press, "Harlem More Deadly Than Bangladesh," *Boston Globe*, 18 January 1990, p. 18.

19. Douglas Massey and Mitchell Eggers, "The Ecology of Inequality: Minorities and the Concentration of Poverty, 1970–1980," *American Journal of Sociology* 95 (1990): 1153–88; Melvin Thomas, "Race, Class and Personal Income: An Empirical Test of the Declining Significance of Race Thesis, 1968–1988," *Social Problems* 40 (1993): 328–39.

20. Personal communication, Harvard Project on School Desegregation, Harvard University, Cambridge, 15 December 1993.

21. Oscar Lewis, "The Culture of Poverty," *Scientific American* 215 (1966): 19–25.

22. Gunnar Myrdal, *The Challenge of World Poverty* (New York: Vintage Books, 1970).

23. Ken Auletta, *The Under Class* (New York: Random House, 1982).

24. William Julius Wilson, *The Truly Disadvantaged* (Chicago: University of Chicago Press, 1987).

25. Ibid., p. 138.

26. Wilson, "Studying Inner-City Social Dislocations."

27. Herbert Gans, "Deconstructing the Underclass: The Term's Danger as a Planning Concept," *Journal of the American Planning Association* 56 (1990): 271–77.

28. Massey and Eggers, "The Ecology of Inequality."

29. Laurence Lynn and Michael G. H. McGeary, eds., *Inner-City Poverty in the United States* (Washington, D.C.: National Academy Press, 1990), p. 3.

30. Ibid.

31. Wilson, *The Truly Disadvantaged*.

32. Rexroat, *Declining Economic Status of Black Children*, p. 1.

33. David Brownfield, "Social Class and Violent Behavior," *Criminology* 24 (1986): 421–38.

34. See Charles Tittle and Robert Meier, "Specifying the SES/Delinquency Relationship," *Criminology* 28 (1990): 271–95, at 293.

35. See Ruth Kornhauser, *Social Sources of Delinquency* (Chicago: University of Chicago Press, 1978), p. 75.

36. Clifford R. Shaw and Henry D. McKay, *Juvenile Delinquency and Urban Areas*, rev. ed. (Chicago: University of Chicago Press, 1972).

37. Anthony Platt, *The Child Savers: The Invention of Delinquency* (Chicago: University of Chicago Press, 1968).

38. Shaw and McKay, *Juvenile Delinquency and Urban Areas*, p. 52.

39. Ibid., p. 171.

40. For a discussion of these issues, see Robert Bursik, "Social Disorganization and Theories of Crime and Delinquency: Problems and Prospects," *Criminology* 26 (1988): 521–39.

41. Robert Sampson, "Effects of Socioeconomic Context of Official Reaction to Juvenile Delinquency," *American Sociological Review* 51 (1986): 876–85.

42. Jeffrey Fagan, Ellen Slaughter, and Eliot Hartstone, "Blind Justice? The Impact of Race on the Juvenile Justice Process," *Crime and Delinquency* 33 (1987): 224–58; Merry Morash, "Establishment of a Juvenile Police Record," *Criminology* 22 (1984): 97–113.

43. The most well-known of these critiques is Kornhauser, *Social Sources of Delinquency*.

44. Bernard Lander, *Towards an Understanding of Juvenile Delinquency* (New York: Columbia University Press, 1954); David Bordua, "Juvenile Delinquency and 'Anomie': An Attempt at Replication," *Social Problems* 6 (1958): 230–38; Roland Chilton, "Continuities in Delinquency Area Research: A Comparison of Studies in Baltimore, Detroit, and Indianapolis," *American Sociological Review* 29 (1964): 71–73.

45. For a general review, see James Byrne and Robert Sampson, eds., *The Social Ecology of Crime* (New York: Springer Verlag, 1985).

46. See, generally, Bursik, "Social Disorganization and Theories of Crime and Delinquency," pp. 519–51.

47. William Spelman, "Abandoned Buildings: Magnets for

Crime?" *Journal of Criminal Justice* 21 (1993): 481–93.

48. Steven Messner and Kenneth Tardiff, "Economic Inequality and Levels of Homicide: An Analysis of Urban Neighborhoods," *Criminology* 24 (1986): 297–317.

49. G. David Curry and Irving Spergel, "Gang Homicide, Delinquency, and Community," *Criminology* 26 (1988): 381–407.

50. Per-Olof Wikstrom and Lars Dolmen, "Crime and Crime Trends in Different Urban Environments," *Journal of Quantitative Criminology* 6 (1990): 7–28.

51. Robert Sampson and W. Byron Groves, "Community Structure and Crime: Testing Social Disorganization Theory," *American Journal of Sociology* 94 (1989): 774–802.

52. Bursik, "Social Disorganization and Theories of Crime and Delinquency," p. 520.

53. Richard McGahey, "Economic Conditions, Organization, and Urban Crime," in *Communities and Crime*, ed. Albert Reiss and Michael Tonry (Chicago: University of Chicago Press, 1986), pp. 231–70.

54. Scott Menard and Delbert Elliott, "Self-Reported Offending, Maturational Reform, and the Easterlin Hypothesis," *Journal of Quantitative Criminology* 6 (1990): 237–68.

55. Elijah Anderson, *Streetwise: Race, Class and Change in an Urban Community* (Chicago: University of Chicago Press, 1990), pp. 243–44.

56. Randy LaGrange, Kenneth Ferraro, Michael Supancic, "Perceived Risk and Fear of Crime: Role of Social and Physical Incivilities," *Journal of Research in Crime and Delinquency* 29 (1992): 311–334.

57. Ralph Taylor and Jeanette Covington, "Community Structural Change and Fear of Crime," *Social Problems* 40 (1993): 374–92.

58. Wesley Skogan, "Fear of Crime and Neighborhood Change," in *Communities and Crime*, ed. Albert Reiss and Michael Tonry (Chicago: University of Chicago Press, 1986), pp. 191–232.

59. Stephanie Greenberg, "Fear and Its Relationship to Crime, Neighborhood Deterioration and Informal Social Control," in *The Social Ecology of Crime*, ed. James Byrne and Robert Sampson (New York: Springer Verlag, 1985), pp. 47–62.

60. Skogan, "Fear of Crime and Neighborhood Change."

61. Ibid.

62. Anderson, *Streetwise: Race, Class and Change in an Urban Community*, p. 245.

63. Finn Aage-Esbensen and David Huizinga, "Community Structure and Drug Use: From a Social Disorganization Perspective," *Justice Quarterly* 7 (1990): 691–709.

64. Wesley Skogan, *Disorder and Decline: Crime and the Spiral of Decay in American Neighborhoods* (New York: Free Press, 1990), pp. 15–35.

65. Robert Bursik and Harold Grasmick, "Decomposing Trends in Community Careers in Crime" (Paper presented at the annual meeting of the American Society of

Criminology, Baltimore, November 1990).

66. Ralph Taylor and Jeanette Covington, "Neighborhood Changes in Ecology and Violence," *Criminology* 26 (1988): 553–89.

67. Leo Scheurman and Solomon Kobrin, "Community Careers in Crime," in *Communities and Crime*, ed. Albert Reiss and Michael Tonry (Chicago: University of Chicago Press, 1986), pp. 67–100.

68. Ibid.

69. See, generally, Robert Bursik, "Delinquency Rates as Sources of Ecological Change," in *The Social Ecology of Crime*, ed. James Byrne and Robert Sampson (New York: Springer Verlag, 1985), pp. 63–77.

70. Janet Heitgerd and Robert Bursik, "Extracommunity Dynamics and the Ecology of Delinquency," *American Journal of Sociology* 92 (1987): 775–87.

71. Wilson, *The Truly Disadvantaged*.

72. Carolyn Rebecca Block and Richard Block, *Street Gang Crime in Chicago* (Washington, D.C.: National Institute of Justice, 1993), p. 7.

73. Barbara Warner and Glenn Pierce, "Reexamining Social Disorganization Theory Using Calls to the Police as a Measure of Crime," *Criminology* 31 (1993): 493–519.

74. Donald Black, "Social Control as a Dependent Variable," in *Toward a General Theory of Social Control*, ed. D. Black (Orlando: Academic Press, 1990).

75. Bursik and Grasmick, "The Multiple Layers of Social Disorganization" (Paper presented at the annual meeting of the American Society of Criminology, New Orleans, November 1992).

76. Rodney Stark, "Deviant Places: A Theory of the Ecology of Crime," *Criminology* 25 (1987): 893–911.

77. Robert Bursik and Harold Grasmick, "Economic Deprivation and Neighborhood Crime Rates, 1960–1980," *Law and Society Review* 27 (1993): 263–78.

78. Skogan, *Disorder and Decline*.

79. Robert Sampson and W. Byron Groves, "Community Structure and Crime: Testing Social Disorganization Theory," *American Journal of Sociology* 94 (1989): 774–802; Denise Gottfredson, Richard McNeill, and Gary Gottfredson, "Social Area Influences on Delinquency: A Multilevel Analysis," *Journal of Research in Crime and Delinquency* 28 (1991): 197–206.

80. Robert Merton, *Social Theory and Social Structure*, enlarged ed. (New York: Free Press, 1968).

81. For an analysis, see Richard Hilbert, "Durkheim and Merton on Anomie: An Unexplored Contrast in Its Derivatives," *Social Problems* 36 (1989): 242–56.

82. Ibid., p. 243.

83. Albert Cohen, "The Sociology of the Deviant Act: Anomie Theory and Beyond," *American Sociological Review* 30 (1965): 5–14.

84. Robert Agnew, "The Contribution of Social Psychological Strain Theory to the Explanation of Crime and Delinquency," in *Advances in Criminological Theory*, 6 (1994): in press.

85. These criticisms are articulated in Messner and Rosenfeld, *Crime and the American Dream,* p. 60.

86. Ibid.

87. Steven Messner and Richard Rosenfeld, "An Institutional-Anomie Theory of the Social Distribution of Crime" (Paper presented at the annual meeting of the American Society of Criminology, Phoenix, Arizona, November 1993).

88. John Braithwaite, "Poverty Power, White-Collar Crime and the Paradoxes of Criminological Theory," *Australian and New Zealand Journal of Criminology* 24 (1991): 40–58.

89. Judith Blau and Peter Blau, "The Cost of Inequality: Metropolitan Structure and Violent Crime," *American Sociological Review* 147 (1982): 114–29.

90. Peter Blau and Joseph Schwartz, *Crosscutting Social Circles* (New York: Academic Press, 1984).

91. Scott South and Steven Messner, "Structural Determinants of Intergroup Association," *American Journal of Sociology* 91 (1986): 1409–30; Steven Messner and Scott South, "Economic Deprivation, Opportunity Structure and Robbery Victimization," *Social Forces* 64 (1986): 975–91.

92. Taylor and Covington, "Neighborhood Changes in Ecology and Violence," p. 582; Richard Block, "Community Environment and Violent Crime," *Criminology* 17 (1979): 46–57; Robert Sampson, "Structural Sources of Variation in Race-Age-Specific Rates of Offending across Major U.S. Cities," *Criminology* 23 (1985): 647–73; Richard Rosenfeld, "Urban Crime Rates: Effects of Inequality, Welfare Dependency, Region and Race," in *The Social Ecology of Crime,* ed. James Byrne and Robert Sampson (New York: Springer Verlag, 1985), pp. 116–30.

93. Ruth Peterson and William Bailey, "Rape and Dimensions of Gender Socioeconomic Inequality in U.S. Metropolitan Areas," *Journal of Research in Crime and Delinquency* 29 (1992): 162–77.

94. Jeanne Brooks-Gunn, Greg Duncan, Pamela Klato Klebanov, and Naomi Sealand, "Do Neighborhoods Influence Child and Adolescent Development?" *American Journal of Sociology* 99 (1993): 353–95.

95. Steven Messner and Reid Golden, "Racial Inequality and Racially Disaggregated Homicide Rates: An Assessment of Alternative Theoretical Explanations" (Paper presented at the annual meeting of the American Society of Criminology, Baltimore, November 1990); see also Miles Harer and Darrell Steffensmeier, "The Different Effects of Economic Inequality on Black and White Rates of Violence" (Paper presented at the annual meeting of the American Society of Criminology, Chicago, November 1988).

96. Kenneth Land, Patricia McCall, and Lawrence Cohen, "Structural Covariates of Homicide Rates: Are There Any Invariances across Time and Social Space?" *American Journal of Sociology* 95 (1990): 922–63; Robert Bursik and James Webb, "Community Change and Patterns of Delinquency," *American Journal of Sociology* 88 (1982): 24–42.

97. Robert Agnew, "A Durkheimian Strain Theory of Delinquency" (Paper presented at the annual meeting of the American Society of Criminology, Baltimore, November 1990).

98. Nikos Passas, "Anomie and Relative Deprivation" (Paper presented at the annual meeting of the Eastern Sociological Society, Boston, 1987).

99. Roy Austin and Chris Hebert, "Black Powerlessness and Crime" (Paper presented at the annual meeting of the American Society of Criminology, Phoenix, November 1993).

100. Robert Agnew, "Foundation for a General Strain Theory of Crime and Delinquency," *Criminology* 30 (1992): 47–87.

101. Ibid., p. 57.

102. Robert Agnew, "Stability and Change in Crime over the Life Course: A Strain Theory Explanation," in *Advances in Criminological Theory,* vol. 7, *Developmental Theories of Crime and Delinquency,* ed. Terence Thornberry (New Brunswick, N.J.: Transaction Books, in press).

103. Robert Agnew and Helene Raskin White, "An Empirical Test of General Strain Theory," *Criminology* 30 (1992): 475–99.

104. Thorsten Sellin, *Culture Conflict and Crime,* bulletin no. 41 (New York: Social Science Research Council, 1938).

105. Ibid., p. 22.

106. Ibid., p. 29.

107. Ibid., p. 68.

108. Walter Miller, "Lower-Class Culture as a Generating Milieu of Gang Delinquency," *Journal of Social Issues* 14 (1958): 5–19.

109. Ibid., pp. 14–17.

110. Albert Cohen, *Delinquent Boys* (New York: Free Press, 1955).

111. Ibid., p. 25.

112. Ibid., p. 28.

113. Ibid.

114. Clarence Schrag, *Crime and Justice American Style* (Washington, D.C.: U.S. Government Printing Office, 1971), p. 74.

115. Cohen, *Delinquent Boys,* p. 30.

116. Ibid., p. 31.

117. Ibid., p. 133.

118. J. Johnstone, "Social Class, Social Areas, and Delinquency," *Sociology and Social Research* 63 (1978): 49–72; Joseph Harry, "Social Class and Delinquency: One More Time," *Sociological Quarterly* 15 (1974): 294–301.

119. Richard Cloward and Lloyd Ohlin, *Delinquency and Opportunity* (New York: Free Press, 1960).

120. Ibid., p. 7.

121. Ibid., p. 85.

122. Ibid., p. 171.

123. Ibid., p. 23.

124. Ibid., p. 73.

125. Ibid., p. 24.

126. See Barry Krisberg and James Austin, *Children of Ishmael* (Palo Alto, Calif.: Mayfield Publishing, 1978); Agnew, "Foundation for a General Strain Theory of Crime and Delinquency."

127. G. David Curry, Robert J. Fox, Richard Ball, and Daryl Stone, *National Assessment of Law Enforcement Anti-Gang Information Resources, Final Report* (Morgantown, W.Va.: National Assessment Survey, 1992); Cheryl Maxson and Malcolm Klein, "The Scope of Street Gang Migration in the U.S.: An Interim Report to Survey Participants (University of Southern California, February 1993, Unpublished mimeograph).

128. Finn-Aage Esbensen and David Huizinga, "Gangs, Drugs, and Delinquency in a Survey of Urban Youth," *Criminology* 31 (1993): 565–91; Malcom Klein, Cheryl Maxson, and Lea Cunningham, "Crack, Street Gangs, and Violence," *Criminology* 29 (1991): 623–50; see also Irving Spergel, "Youth Gangs: Continuity and Change," in *Crime and Justice,* vol. 12, ed. Michael Tonry and Norval Morris (Chicago: University of Chicago Press, 1990), pp. 171–277.

129. Felix Padilla, *The Gang as an American Enterprise* (New Brunswick, N.J.: Rutgers University Press, 1992); see also Jeffery Fagan, "The Political Economy of Drug Dealing among Urban Gangs," in *Drugs and the Community*, ed. Robert Davis, Arthur Lurigio, and Dennis Rosenbaum (Springfield, Ill.: Charles Thomas, 1993), pp. 19–54.

130. Pamela Irving Jackson, "Crime, Youth Gangs, and Urban Transition: The Social Dislocations of Postindustrial Economic Development," *Justice Quarterly* 8 (1991): 379–97.

131. For a general criticism, see Kornhauser, *Social Sources of Delinquency.*

132. Charles Tittle, "Social Class and Criminal Behavior: A Critique of the Theoretical Foundations," *Social Forces* 62 (1983): 334–58.

133. James Q. Wilson and Richard Herrnstein, *Crime and Human Nature* (New York: Simon and Schuster, 1985).

134. Kenneth Polk and F. Lynn Richmond, "Those Who Fail," in *Schools and Delinquency*, ed. Kenneth Polk and Walter Schafer (Englewood Cliffs, N.J.: Prentice-Hall, 1974), p. 67.

135. Timothy Flanagan and Kathleen Maguire, *Sourcebook of Criminal Justice Statistics* (Washington, D.C.: U.S. Government Printing Office, 1990), pp. 125–218.

136. Solomon Kobrin, "The Chicago Area Project—25-Year Assessment," *Annals of the American Academy of Political and Social Science* 322 (1959): 20–29.

8

Social Process Theories

Introduction

Many criminologists question whether a person's place in the social structure *alone* can control the onset of criminality. After all, the majority of people residing in the nation's most deteriorated urban areas are law-abiding citizens who hold conventional values and compensate for their lack of social standing and financial problems by hard work, frugal living, and keeping an eye to the future. Conversely, self-report studies tell us that many members of the privileged classes engage in theft, drug use, and other crimes.

It is also unlikely that neighborhood deterioration and disorganization alone cannot explain why a particular individual embarks on a criminal career.[1] Relatively few delinquent offenders living in the most deteriorated areas remain persistent, chronic offenders. Most desist despite the continuing pressure of social decay.

To explain these contradictory findings, attention has been focused on **social-psychological processes** common to people at all junctures of the social structure. Social process theories hold that criminality is a function of individual **socialization.** They draw attention to the interactions people have with the various organizations, institutions, and processes of society. As they pass through the life cycle, most people are influenced by the direction of their familial relationships, peer group associations, educational experiences, and interactions with authority figures, including teachers, employers, and agents of the justice system. If these relationships are positive and supportive, they will be able to succeed within the rules of society; if these relationships are dysfunctional and destructive, conventional success may be impossible and criminal solutions may become a feasible alternative.

Social process theories share one basic concept: All people, regardless of their race, class, or gender, have the potential to become delinquents or criminals. Although members of the lower class may have the added burdens of poverty, racism, poor schools, and disrupted family lives, even middle- or upper-class people may turn to crime if their life experiences are intolerable or destructive. Consequently, social process theorists focus their attention on the socialization of youth and attempt to identify the developmental factors—family relationships, peer influences, educational difficulties, self-image development—that lead first to delinquent behavior and then to adult criminality.

The influence of social process theories has endured because the relationship between social class and crime is still uncertain. Following a thorough review of the most recent research, Charles Tittle and Robert Meier still found the association between economic status and crime "problematic"; class position alone cannot explain crime rates.[2] A number of research studies show that even in the most deteriorated areas, it is the quality of interpersonal interactions with parents, peers, and schools that control criminality; environment alone cannot determine behavior.[3] If this research is valid, then socialization and not structure may be the key to understanding crime.

Social Processes and Crime

Criminologists have long studied the critical elements of socialization to determine how they contribute to the development of a criminal career. Prominent among these elements are the family, the peer group, and school.

Family Relations

> Evidence that parenting factors may play a critical role in determining whether or not people misbehave as children and even later as adults is one of the most replicated findings in the deviance literature.[4]

Family relationships have for some time been considered a major determinant of behavior.[5] Youths who grow up in a household characterized by conflict and tension, where parents are absent or separated, or where there is a lack of familial love and support will be susceptible to the crime-promoting forces in the environment.[6] Even those children living in so-called high-crime areas will be better able to resist the temptations of the streets if they receive fair discipline, care, and support from parents who provide them with strong, positive role models.[7] The relationship between family structure and crime is critical when the high rates of divorce and single parents are considered. In 1960, there were 35 divorced people for every 1,000 in an intact marriage; today, there are 131 per 1,000.[8] Similarly, the U.S. Census Bureau reports that 28 percent of the 35 million families with children were headed by a single parent; in 1970, 13 percent of families with children were headed by a single parent.[9] The number of never-married women with at least one child has increased 60 percent in the past decade.[10]

At one time, growing up in a **broken home** was considered a primary cause of criminal behavior. However, many criminologists today discount the association between family structure and the onset of criminality, claiming that family conflict and discord is a more important determinant of behavior than family structure.[11] Not all experts, though, discount the effects of family structure on crime. James Q. Wilson and Richard Herrnstein claim that even if single mothers (or fathers) can make up for the loss of a second parent, it is simply *more* difficult to do so and the chances of failure increase.[12] Single parents may find it difficult to provide adequate supervision. There is evidence that children who live with single parents receive less encouragement and less help with school work. They may be more prone to rebellious acts, such as running away and truancy.[13] Children in two-parent households are more likely to want to go on to college than kids in single-parent homes; poor school achievement and limited educational aspirations have been associated with delinquent behavior.[14]

Because their incomes are reduced in the aftermath of marital breakup, many divorced mothers are forced to move to residences in deteriorated neighborhoods; disorganized neighborhoods place children at risk to crime and drug abuse.[15] Nor does remarriage seem to mitigate the effects of divorce on youth: children living with a stepparent exhibit as many problems as youths in divorce situations and considerably more problems than those who are living with both biological parents.[16] There is also little evidence that children of divorce improve over time; family disruption has unmistakable long-term effects.

Other family factors considered to have predictive value include inconsistent discipline, poor supervision, and the lack of a warm, loving, supportive parent-child relationship.[17] Parental deviance has also been linked to a child's criminal behavior. John Laub and Robert Sampson have found evidence that the children of parents who engage in criminality and substance abuse are more likely to engage in law-violating behavior than the offspring of conventional parents.[18]

There is also a suspected link between child abuse, neglect, sexual abuse, and crime.[19] A growing number of studies are finding that the victims of child abuse grow up to be abusing and violent adults.[20] Child abuse is most prevalent among families living in socially disorganized neighborhoods, explaining in part the association between poverty and violence.[21]

Educational Experience

Adolescent achievement in the school and educational process has also been linked to criminality. Studies show that children who do poorly in school, lack educational motivation, and feel alienated are the most likely to engage in criminal acts.[22] Schools help contribute to criminality when they set problem youths apart from conventional society by creating a track system that identifies some students as college-bound and others as academic underachievers or potential dropouts.[23] Recent research indicates that many school dropouts, especially those who have been expelled, face a significant chance of entering a criminal career.[24] In contrast, doing well in school and developing feelings of attachment to teachers have been linked to resistance to crime.[25]

It is not surprising that the U.S. school system has been the subject of recent criticism concerning its methods, goals, and objectives.[26] The nation's educational system is underfunded, understaffed, and in crisis; reading and math ability levels have been in decline. These trends do not bode well for the crime rate. Most important, surveys indicate that an extraordinary amount of serious criminal behavior occurs within the schools themselves.[27]

Peer Relations

Psychologists have long recognized that the peer group has a powerful effect on human conduct and can have a dramatic influence on decision making and behavior choices.[28] Early in children's lives, parents are the primary source of influence and attention. Between the ages of eight and 14, children begin to seek out a stable peer group; both the number and variety of friendships increase as children go through adolescence. Soon, friends begin having a greater influence over decision making than parents.[29] By their early teens, children report that their friends give them emotional support when they are feeling bad and that they can confide intimate feelings to peers without worrying about their confidences being betrayed. As they go through adolescence, children form **cliques,** small groups of friends who share activities and confidences. They also belong to **crowds,** loosely organized groups of children who share interests and activities. While clique members share intimate knowledge, crowds are brought together by mutually shared activities, such as sports, religion, or hobbies. Popular youths can be members of a variety of cliques and crowds. In later adolescence, peer approval has a major impact on socialization.

The most popular youths do well in school and are socially astute. In contrast, children who are rejected by their peers are more likely to display aggressive behavior and disrupt group activities through bickering or other antisocial behavior.[30] Peer relations, then, are a significant aspect of maturation.

Peers exert a powerful influence on youth and pressure them to conform to group values. Peers guide children and help them learn to share and cooperate, cope with aggressive impulses, and discuss feelings they would not dare bring up at home. With peers, youths can compare their own experiences and learn that others have similar concerns and problems; they realize they are not alone. It should come as no surprise, then, that much adolescent criminal activity begins as a group process.[31]

Delinquent peers can exert tremendous influence on behavior, attitudes, and beliefs.[32] In every level of the social structure, youths who fall in with a "bad crowd" become more susceptible to criminal behavior patterns.[33] Deviant peers help provide friendship networks that support delinquency and drug use.[34] And because delinquent friends tend to be "sticky" (once acquired, they are not easily lost), peer influence may continue through the life span.[35]

Social Process Theories

To many criminologists, the elements of socialization described above are the chief determinants of criminal behavior. According to this view, people living in even the most deteriorated urban areas can successfully resist inducements to crime if they have a good self-image, have learned moral values, and have the support of their parents, peers, teachers, and neighbors. The girl with a positive self-image who is chosen for a college scholarship, has the warm, loving support of her parents, and is viewed as someone "going places" by friends and neighbors is less likely to adopt a criminal way of life than another adolescent who is abused at home, lives with criminal parents, and whose bond to the school and peer group is shattered because she is labeled a "troublemaker." [36]

Like social structure theories, the social process approach has several independent branches (see Figure 8.1). The first branch, **social learning theory,** suggests that people learn the techniques and attitudes of crime from close and intimate relationships with criminal peers; crime is a learned behavior. The second, **social control theory,** maintains that everyone has the potential to become a criminal but that most people are controlled by their bond to society; crime occurs when the forces that bind people to society are weakened or broken. The third branch, **labeling theory,** says people become criminals when significant members of society label them as such and they accept those labels as a personal identity.

Put another way, social learning theories assume people are born "good" and learn to be "bad"; social control theory assumes people are born "bad" and must be controlled in order to be "good"; labeling theory assumes that whether "good" or "bad," people are controlled by the reactions of others. Each of these independent branches will be discussed separately.

FIGURE 8.1   **The Branches of Social Process Theory**

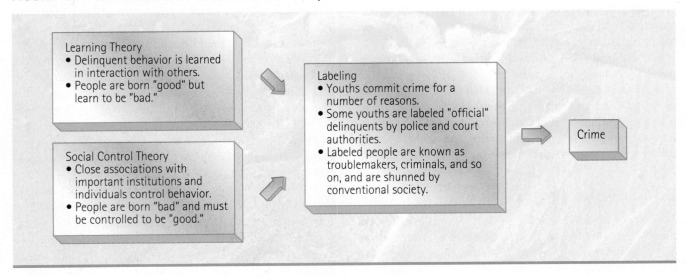

≡ Social Learning Theory

As you may recall, in the late nineteenth century, Gabriel Tarde's theory of imitation held that criminals imitate "superiors" they admire and respect.[37] Today, social learning theorists find that crime is a product of learning the norms, values, and behaviors associated with criminal activity. Social learning can involve the actual techniques of crime—how to hot-wire a car or roll a joint—as well as the psychological aspects of criminality—how to deal with the guilt or shame associated with illegal activities. This section briefly reviews the three most prominent forms of social learning theory—differential association theory, differential reinforcement theory, and neutralization theory.

≡ Differential Association Theory

Edwin H. Sutherland (1883–1950), often considered the preeminent U.S. criminologist, first put forth the theory of **differential association** (DA) in 1939 in his text *Principles of Criminology.*[38] The final form of the theory appeared in 1947. When Sutherland died in 1950, his work was continued by his long-time associate Donald Cressey. Cressey was so successful in explaining and popularizing his mentor's efforts that DA remains one of the most enduring explanations of criminal behavior. Sutherland's research on white-collar crime, professional theft, and intelligence led him to dispute the notion that crime was a function of the inadequacy of people in the lower classes.[39]

To Sutherland, criminality stemmed neither from individual traits nor socioeconomic position; instead, he believed it to be a function of a learning process that could affect any individual in any culture. A few ideas are basic to the theory of differential association:[40] Crime is a politically defined construct. It is defined by government authorities who are in political control of a particular jurisdiction. In societies wracked by culture conflict, the definition of crime may be inconsistent and consequently rejected by some groups of people. Put another way, people may vary in their relative attachments to criminal and noncriminal definitions. The acquisition of behavior is a social learning process, not a political or legal process. Skills and motives conducive to crime are learned as a result of contacts with procrime values, attitudes, and definitions and other patterns of criminal behavior.

Principles of Differential Association

The basic principles of differential association are explained in the statements below:[41]

- Criminal behavior is learned. This statement differentiates Sutherland's theory from prior attempts to classify criminal behavior as an inherent characteristic of criminals. By suggesting that delinquent and criminal behavior is actually learned, Sutherland implied that it can be classified in the same manner as any other learned behavior, such as writing, painting, or reading.

- Criminal behavior is learned in interaction with other persons in a process of communication. Sutherland believed that illegal behavior is learned actively. An individual does not become a law violator simply by living in a criminogenic environment or by manifesting personal characteristics, such as low IQ or family problems, associated with criminality. Instead, criminal and other deviant behavior patterns are learned. People actively participate in the process with other individuals who serve as teachers and guides to crime. Thus, criminality cannot occur without the aid of others.

Differential Association theory suggests that deviant behavior is learned in intimate associations with significant others.

- The principal part of the learning of criminal behavior occurs within intimate personal groups. People's contacts with their most intimate social companions—family, friends, peers—have the greatest influence on their learning of deviant behavior and attitudes. Relationships with these individuals color and control the interpretation of everyday events. For example, research shows that children who grow up in homes where parents abuse alcohol are more likely to view drinking as being socially and physically beneficial.[42] Social support for deviance helps people to overcome social controls so that they can embrace criminal values and behaviors. The intimacy of these associations far outweighs the importance of any other form of communication—for example, movies or television. Even on those rare occasions when violent motion pictures seem to provoke mass criminal episodes, these outbreaks can be more readily explained as a reaction to peer group pressure than as a reaction to the films themselves.

- Learning criminal behavior includes learning the techniques of committing the crime, which are sometimes very complicated and sometimes very simple, and learning the specific direction of motives, drives, rationalizations, and attitudes. Since criminal behavior is similar to other learned behavior, it follows that the actual techniques of criminality must be acquired and learned. Young delinquents learn from their associates the proper way to pick a lock, shoplift, and obtain and use narcotics. In addition, novice criminals must learn to use the proper terminology for their acts and then acquire "proper" reactions to law violations. For example, getting high on marijuana and learning the proper way to smoke a joint are behavior patterns usually acquired from more experienced companions. Moreover, criminals must learn how to react properly to their illegal acts—when to defend them, rationalize them, show remorse for them.

- The specific direction of motives and drives is learned from perceptions of various aspects of the legal code as being favorable or unfavorable. Since the reaction to social rules and laws is not uniform across society, people constantly come into contact with others who maintain different views on the utility of obeying the legal code. When definitions of right and wrong are extremely varied, people experience what Sutherland calls culture conflict. The attitudes toward criminal behavior of the important people in an individual's life influence the attitudes that an individual develops. The conflict of social attitudes is the basis for the concept of differential association.

- A person becomes a criminal when he or she perceives more favorable than unfavorable consequences to violating the law (see Figure 8.2). According to Sutherland's theory, individuals become law violators when they are in contact with persons, groups, or events that produce an excess of definitions favorable toward criminality and are isolated from counteracting forces. A definition favorable toward criminality occurs, for example, when a person is exposed to friends sneaking into a theater to avoid paying for a ticket or talking about the virtues of getting high on drugs. A definition unfavorable toward crime occurs when friends or parents demonstrate their disapproval of crime. Of course, neutral behavior, such as reading a book, exists. It is neither positive nor negative with respect to law violation. Cressey argues that this behavior is important, "especially as an occupier of the time of a child so that he is not in contact with criminal behaviors during the time he is so engaged in the neutral behavior."[43]

- Differential associations may vary in frequency, duration, priority, and intensity. Whether a person learns to obey the law or to disregard it is influenced by the quality of social interactions. Those of lasting duration have greater influence than those that are more brief. Similarly, frequent contacts have greater effect than rare and haphazard contacts. Sutherland did not specify what he meant by *priority,* but Cressey and others have interpreted the term to mean the age of children when they first encounter definitions of criminality. Contacts made early in life probably have a greater and more far-reaching influence than those developed later on. Finally, *intensity* is generally interpreted to mean the importance and prestige attributed to the individual or groups from whom the definitions are learned. For example, the influence of a father, mother, or trusted friend far outweighs the effect of more socially distant figures.

- The process of learning criminal behavior by association with criminal and anticriminal patterns involves all of the mechanisms that are involved in any other learning. This statement suggests that

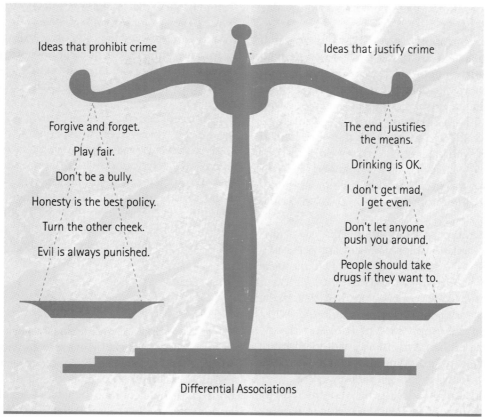

Ideas that prohibit crime

Ideas that justify crime

Forgive and forget.

Play fair.

Don't be a bully.

Honesty is the best policy.

Turn the other cheek.

Evil is always punished.

The end justifies
the means.

Drinking is OK.

I don't get mad,
I get even.

Don't let anyone
push you around.

People should take
drugs if they want to.

Differential Associations

FIGURE 8.2   Differential Association Theory

Differential association theory assumes that criminal behavior will occur when the definitions for crime
outweigh the definitions against crime.

the learning of criminal behavior patterns is similar to the learning of nearly all other patterns and
is not a matter of mere imitation.

• While criminal behavior is an expression of general needs and values, it is not excused by those
general needs and values, since noncriminal
behavior is also an expression of the same needs
and values. This principle suggests that the
motives for criminal behavior cannot logically be
the same as those for conventional behavior.
Sutherland rules out such motives as desire to
accumulate money or social status, personal frustration, or low self-concept as causes of crime,
since they are just as likely to produce noncriminal behavior, such as getting a better education
or working harder on a job. It is only the learning of deviant norms through contact with an
excess of definitions favorable toward criminality
that produces illegal behavior.

In sum, DA theory holds that people learn criminal
attitudes and behavior while in their adolescence from
close and trusted relatives and companions. A criminal
career develops if learned antisocial values and behaviors are not at least matched or exceeded by conventional attitudes and behaviors. Criminal behavior is
learned in a process similar to the learning of any other
human behavior.

Testing Differential Association

Despite the importance of DA theory, research devoted
to testing its assumptions has been relatively sparse. It
has proven difficult to conceptualize the principles of
the theory so that they can be empirically tested. For
example, social scientists find it difficult to evaluate such
vague concepts as "definition toward criminality." It is also
difficult to follow people over time, establish precisely
when definitions toward criminality begin to outweigh

prosocial definitions, and determine if this imbalance produces criminal behavior.

Despite these limitations, several notable research efforts have been aimed at testing hypotheses derived from DA theory. One important area of research is on the friendship patterns of delinquent youth. DA implies that criminals maintain close and intimate relations with deviant peers.[44] In a classic work, James Short surveyed institutionalized youth and found that they maintained close associations with delinquent youths prior to their law-violating acts.[45] Similarly, Albert Reiss and A. Lewis Rhodes found an association between delinquent friendship patterns and the probability that a youth would commit a criminal act.[46]

More recent studies have also found that law violators maintain close relationships with deviant peers in a fashion predicted by DA. Mark Warr found that antisocial kids who maintain delinquent friends over a long duration are much more likely to persist in their delinquent behavior than those without such peer support.[47] While his research is generally supportive of DA, Warr discovered that *recent* rather than *early* friends had the greatest influence on criminality, a finding that contradicts DA's emphasis on the priority of criminal influences.

A survey of 1,563 adolescents conducted by Douglas Smith, Christy Visher, and G. Roger Jarjoura also found that exposure to delinquent peers was able to explain the onset, frequency, and persistence of delinquent behavior.[48] And, when interviewing adults arrested for illegal hunting (poaching), Gary Green found that almost all had been socialized at an early age with definitions favorable toward this offense by friends and family members.[49]

DA principles seem especially relevant as an explanation of the onset of substance abuse and a career in the drug trade; learning proper techniques and attitudes from an experienced user or dealer appears to be a requirement. Denise Kandel and Mark Davies discovered that drug users maintain even closer ties to their friends than nonusers.[50] In his interview study of low-level drug dealers, Kenneth Tunnell found that many novices were tutored by a more criminal dealer who helped them make connections with buyers and sellers:

> I had a friend of mine who was an older guy and he introduced me to selling marijuana to make a few dollars. I started selling a little and made a few dollars. For a young guy to be making a hundred dollars or so, it was a lot of money. So I got kind of tied up in that aspect of selling drugs.[51]

Tunnell found that making connections is an important part of the dealer's world. It does not seem surprising that research shows that adolescent drug users are likely to have intimate relationships with a peer friendship network that supports their substance abuse.[52]

DA theory also assumes that people who have assimilated procrime attitudes are also the ones most likely to engage in criminal activity.[53] These findings have been observed in cross-cultural research. In one study conducted in Hong Kong, Yuet-Wah Cheung and Agnes M. C. Ng found that DA items were the most significant predictor of delinquent behavior in a sample of 1,139 secondary school students. Cheung and Ng conclude that in Hong Kong, deviant youth may be imitating friends' behavior or attempting to "keep up appearances" by yielding to group pressure.[54]

The Future of Differential Association

While these findings are persuasive, self-report research in support of DA must be interpreted with caution. Since subjects are usually asked about their peer relations, learning experiences, perceptions of differential associations, and their criminal behaviors simultaneously, it is impossible to determine whether differential associations were the *cause* or the *result* of criminal behavior. While it is possible that youths learn about crime and then commit criminal acts, it is also possible that experienced delinquents and criminals seek out like-minded peers after they engage in antisocial acts and that the internalization of deviant attitudes follows, rather than precedes, criminality.[55]

To answer critics, researchers must develop more valid measures of differential associations.[56] One possibility is that longitudinal analysis might be used to measure subjects repeatedly over time to determine if those exposed to excess definitions toward deviance eventually become deviant themselves.

Despite measurement and validity problems, DA theory maintains an important place in the study of delinquent behavior. For one thing, it provides a consistent explanation of all types of delinquent and criminal behavior. Unlike the social structure theories discussed previously, it is not limited to the explanation of a single facet of antisocial activity, for example, lower-class gang activity. The theory can also account for the extensive delinquent behavior among the affluent, who may be exposed to such crime-producing definitions as "get ahead at all costs" and "only the weak and stupid are poor."

Differential Reinforcement Theory

Differential reinforcement (DR) theory (also called social learning theory) is another attempt to explain crime as a type of learned behavior. It is a revision of Sutherland's work that incorporates elements of psychological learning theory popularized by B. F. Skinner and Albert Bandura (see Chapter 6).[57]

The description of the theory is summarized by Ronald Akers in his 1977 work, *Deviant Behavior: A Social Learning Approach*.[58] According to Akers, people learn social behavior by operant conditioning, behavior controlled by stimuli that follows the behavior. Social behavior is acquired through direct conditioning and modeling of others' behavior. Behavior is reinforced when positive rewards are gained or punishment is avoided (negative reinforcement). It is weakened by negative stimuli (punishment) and loss of reward (negative punishment). Whether deviant or criminal behavior is begun or persists depends on the degree to which it has been rewarded or punished and the rewards or punishments attached to its alternatives. This is the theory of differential reinforcement.

According to Akers, people learn to evaluate their own behavior through interaction with significant others and groups in their lives. This process makes use of such devices as norms, attitudes, and orientations. The more individuals learn to define their behavior as good or at least as justified, rather than as undesirable, the more likely they are to engage in it. Akers's theory posits that the principal influence on behavior comes from "those groups which control individuals' major sources of reinforcement and punishment and expose them to behavioral models and normative definitions."[59] The important groups are the ones with which a person is in differential association—peer and friendship groups, schools, churches, and similar institutions. Behavior results when an individual perceives an excess of reinforcements over punishments for certain acts or their alternatives. Definitions conducive to deviant behavior occur when positive or neutralizing definitions of that behavior offset negative definitions of it. Subsequently, "deviant behavior can be expected to the extent that it has been differentially reinforced over alternative behavior . . . and is defined as desirable or justified."[60] Once people are initiated into crime, their behavior can be reinforced by exposure to deviant behavior models, association with deviant peers, and lack of negative sanctions from parents or peers. The deviant behavior, originated by imitation, is sustained by social support. It is possible that differential reinforcements help establish criminal careers and are a key factor in explaining persistent criminality.

Analyzing Differential Reinforcement Theory

The principles of differential reinforcement have been subject to empirical review. In a test of his theory, Akers and his associates surveyed 3,065 male and female adolescents on drug- and alcohol-related activities and their perception of variables related to social learning and DR. Items in the scale included the respondents' perception of esteemed peers' attitudes toward drug and alcohol abuse, the number of people they admired who actually used controlled substances, and whether people they admired would reward or punish them for substance abuse. Akers found a strong association between drug and alcohol abuse and social learning variables: kids who believed they would be rewarded for deviance by those they respect were the ones most likely to engage in deviant behavior.[61]

Other research efforts have supported Akers's work. For example, using longitudinal data, Marvin Krohn and his associates found that social learning principles could predict the incidence of cigarette smoking in a sample of junior and senior high school boys.[62] These researchers found that reinforcement of smoking by parents and friends contributed to adolescent misbehavior and that differential associations by themselves were insufficient to predict deviance.

Differential reinforcement theory is an important view of the cause of criminal activity. It considers how both the *effectiveness* and *content* of socialization condition crime. Because not all socialization is positive, it accounts for the fact that negative reinforcements can produce criminal results. This jibes with research showing that parental deviance is related to adolescent antisocial behavior.[63] Akers's work also fits well with the rational choice theory because they both suggest that people learn the techniques and attitudes necessary to commit crime. Criminal knowledge is gained through experience. After considering the outcome of their past experiences, potential offenders decide which criminal acts will be profitable and which are dangerous and should be avoided.[64] Why do people make rational choices about crime? Because they have learned to balance risks against the potential for criminal gain.

Neutralization Theory

Neutralization theory is identified with the writings of David Matza and his associate Gresham Sykes.[65] Sykes and Matza view the process of becoming a criminal as a learning experience. However, while other learning theorists, such as Sutherland and Akers, dwell on the learning of techniques, values, and attitudes necessary for performing criminal acts, Sykes and Matza maintain that most delinquents and criminals hold conventional values and attitudes but master techniques that enable them to **neutralize** these values and drift back and forth between illegitimate and conventional behavior. Matza argues that even the most committed criminals and delinquents are not involved in criminality all the time; they also attend schools, family functions, and religious services. Their behavior can be conceived as falling along a continuum between total freedom and total restraint. This process, which he calls **drift,** refers to the movement from one extreme of behavior to another, resulting in behavior that is sometimes unconventional, free, or deviant and at other times constrained and sober.[66] Learning techniques of neutralization allows a person to temporarily "drift away" from conventional behavior and get involved in deviance.[67]

Techniques of Neutralization

Sykes and Matza suggest that people develop a distinct set of justifications for their law-violating behavior. These neutralization techniques allow them to temporarily drift away from the rules of the normative society and participate in **subterranean behaviors.**

Sykes and Matza base their theoretical model on several observations.[68] First, criminals sometimes voice a sense of guilt over their illegal acts. If a stable criminal value system existed in opposition to generally held values and rules, it would be unlikely that criminals would exhibit any remorse for their acts, other than regret at being apprehended. Second, offenders frequently respect and admire honest, law-abiding persons. Really honest persons are often revered; and if for some reason such persons are accused of misbehavior, the criminal is quick to defend their integrity. Those admired may include sports figures, priests and other clergy, parents, teachers, and neighbors. Third, criminals draw a line between those whom they can victimize and those whom they cannot. Members of similar ethnic groups, churches, or neighborhoods are often off limits. This practice implies that criminals are aware of the wrong-fulness of their acts. Why else limit them? Finally, criminals are not immune to the demands of conformity. Most criminals frequently participate in many of the same social functions as law-abiding people—for example, in school, church, and family activities. Because of these factors, Sykes and Matza conclude that criminality is the result of the neutralization of accepted social values through the learning of a standard set of techniques that allow people to counteract the moral dilemmas posed by illegal behavior.[69] Their research helped Sykes and Matza identify the following **techniques of neutralization:**

- *Denial of responsibility*—Young offenders sometimes claim their unlawful acts were simply not their fault. Criminals' acts resulted from forces beyond their control or were accidents.

- *Denial of injury*—By denying the wrongfulness of an act, criminals are able to neutralize illegal behavior. For example, stealing is viewed as borrowing; vandalism is considered mischief that has gotten out of hand. Society often agrees with the criminal's point of view, labeling their illegal behavior as pranks and thereby affirming the criminal's view that crime can be socially acceptable.

- *Denial of victim*—Criminals sometimes neutralize wrongdoing by maintaining that the victim of crime "had it coming." Vandalism may be directed against a disliked teacher or neighbor; or homosexuals may be beaten up by a gang because their behavior is considered offensive. Denying the victim may also take the form of ignoring the rights of an absent or unknown victim—for example, the unseen owner of a department store. It becomes morally acceptable for the criminal to commit such crimes as vandalism when the victims, because of their absence, cannot be sympathized with or respected.

- *Condemnation of the condemners*—An offender views the world as a corrupt place with a dog-eat-dog code. Since police and judges are on the take, teachers show favoritism, and parents take out their frustrations on their kids, it is ironic and unfair for these authorities to condemn his misconduct. By shifting the blame to others, criminals are able to repress the feeling that their own acts are wrong.

- *Appeal to higher loyalties*—Novice criminals often argue that they are caught in the dilemma of being loyal to their own peer group while at the same time attempting to abide by the rules of the larger society. The needs of the group take precedence over the rules of society because the demands of the former are immediate and localized.

In sum, the theory of neutralization presupposes a condition in which such slogans as "I didn't mean to do it," "I didn't really hurt anybody," "They had it coming to them," "Everybody's picking on me," and "I didn't do it for myself" are used by people to neutralize unconventional norms and values so they can drift into criminal modes of behavior.

Empirical Research

A valid test of neutralization theory would have to be able to show that a person first neutralized his or her moral beliefs and then drifted into criminality. Otherwise, any data that showed an association between crime and neutralization could be interpreted as suggesting that people who commit crime later make an attempt at rationalizing their behavior. It is also possible that criminals and noncriminals have different moral values, and therefore, neutralizing them is unnecessary.[70] The validity of the Sykes-Matza model depends on showing that all people share similar more values and must neutralize them first to engage in criminal behavior; so far, such data are unavailable.

Despite this limitation, several attempts have been made to empirically verify the assumptions of neutralization theory.[71] There are indications, for example, that institutionalized youths excuse deviant behaviors to a significantly greater degree than the general population; this finding indicates that people who commit criminal acts also have learned to rationalize their guilt.[72] Another study by Mark Pogrebin and his associates found that psychotherapists accused of sexually exploiting their clients express neutralizations for their behavior reminiscent of those identified by Sykes and Matza. Some blamed the victim for "seducing them"; others claimed there was little injury caused by the sexual encounter; others sought scapegoats to blame for their actions.[73]

≡ Evaluation of Learning Theories

Learning theories make a significant contribution to our understanding of the onset of criminal behavior. Nonetheless, the general learning model has been subject to some criticism. One complaint is that learning theorists fail to account for the origin of criminal definitions. How did the first "teacher" learn criminal techniques and definitions? Who came up with the original neutralization technique?

Learning theories also imply that people systematically learn techniques that allow them to be active and successful criminals, but they fail to adequately explain spontaneous and wanton acts of violence and damage and other expressive crimes that appear to have little utility or purpose. It is estimated that about 70 percent of all arrestees were under the influence of drugs and alcohol when they committed their crime: Do "crack heads" pause to neutralize their moral inhibitions before mugging a victim? Do drug-involved kids stop to consider what they have "learned" about moral values?[74]

Little evidence exists that people *learn* the techniques that enable them to become criminals *before* they actually commit criminal acts. It is equally plausible that people who are already deviant seek out others with similar life-styles. Early onset of deviant behavior is now considered a key determinant of criminal careers. It is difficult to see how young adolescents had the opportunity to learn criminal behavior and attitudes.

Despite these criticisms, learning theories maintain an important place in the study of delinquent and criminal behavior. Unlike social structure theories, they are not limited to the explanation of a single facet of antisocial activity—for example, lower-class gang activity; they may be used to explain criminality across class structures. Even corporate executives may be exposed to a variety of procriminal definitions and learn to neutralize moral constraints. Learning theories can be applied to a wide assortment of criminal activity.

≡ Social Control Theories

Social control theories maintain that all people have the potential to violate the law and that modern society presents many opportunities for illegal activity. Criminal activities, such as drug abuse and car theft, are often exciting pastimes that hold the promise of immediate reward and gratification. Considering the attractions of crime, the question control theorists pose is, "Why then do people obey the rules of society?" To a choice theorist, the answer would be fear of punishment; to a structural theorist, obedience is a function of having access to legitimate opportunities; to a learning theorist, obedience is acquired through contact with law-abiding parents and peers. In contrast, control theorists argue that people obey the law because they have a **commitment to**

conformity—a real, present, and logical reason to obey the rules of society.[75] Perhaps they believe that getting caught at criminal activity will hurt a dearly loved parent or jeopardize their chance at a college scholarship, or perhaps they feel that their job will be forfeited if they get in trouble with the law. In other words, people's behavior, including their criminal activity, is controlled by their attachment and commitment to conventional institutions, individuals, and processes. If that commitment is absent, they are free to violate the law and engage in deviant behavior; the "uncommitted" are not deterred by the threat of legal punishments.[76]

Self-Concept and Crime

Early versions of control theory speculated that low self-control was a product of weak self-concept and poor self-esteem. Youths who felt good about themselves and maintained a positive attitude were able to resist the temptations of the streets; a positive self-esteem helped kids *control* temptations toward delinquency. As early as 1951, Albert Reiss described how delinquents had weak "ego ideals" and lacked the "personal controls" to produce conforming behavior.[77] Scott Briar and Irving Piliavin noted that youths who believe criminal activity will damage their self-image and their relationships with others will be most likely to conform to social rules; they have a "commitment to conformity." In contrast, those less concerned about their social standing are free to violate the law.[78]

Empirical research indicates that an important association between self-image and delinquency may in fact exist.[79] Howard Kaplan found that youths with poor self-concepts are the ones most likely to engage in delinquent behavior and that successful participation in criminality actually helped raise their self-esteem.[80] For

According to control theory, people whose commitment to society is weak are the ones most likely to engage in criminal and delinquent behaviors. These young "squatter punks" spend the night begging for spare change and drinking forty-ounce deli beer.

example, kids who are having problems in school realize that they will feel much better if they can escape teachers' critical judgments by dropping out and joining a gang whose members value their cunning and fighting ability. Youths who maintain both the lowest self-image and the greatest need for approval are the ones most likely to seek self-enhancement from delinquency.[81]

≡ Containment Theory

In an early effort to describe how self-image controls criminal tendencies, Walter Reckless and his associates argued that youths growing up in even the most criminogenic areas can insulate themselves from crime if they have sufficiently positive **self-esteem.** Reckless called an individual's ability to resist criminal inducements "containments," the most important of which are a positive self-image and "ego strength."[82] Kids who have these traits can resist crime-producing "pushes and pulls." Among the crime-producing forces that a strong self-image counteracted were:

- *Internal pushes.* Internal pushes involve such personal factors as restlessness, discontent, hostility, rebellion, mental conflict, anxieties, and need for immediate gratification.

- *External pressures.* External pressures are adverse living conditions that influence deviant behavior. They include relative deprivation, poverty, unemployment, insecurity, minority status, limited opportunities, and inequalities.

- *External pulls.* External pulls are represented by deviant companions, membership in criminal subcultures or other deviant groups, and such influences as mass media and pornography.

Reckless and his associates made an extensive effort to validate the principles of containment theory. In a series of studies analyzing containment principles within the school setting, Reckless and his colleagues concluded that the ability of nondelinquents to resist crime depends on their maintaining a positive self-image in the face of environmental pressures toward delinquency. Despite the success Reckless and his associates had in verifying their containment approach, their efforts have been criticized for lack of methodological rigor, and the validity of containment theory has been disputed.

Reckless's version of control theory was a pioneering effort that set the stage for subsequent theoretical developments. These too follow his central premise that

people are "controlled" by their feelings about themselves and others they are in contact with. In general then, control theory maintains that while all people perceive inducements to crime, some are better able to resist them than others.

≡ Social Control Theory

Social control theory, originally articulated by Travis Hirschi in his influential 1969 book, *Causes of Delinquency,* replaced containment theory as the dominant version of control theory.[83]

Hirschi links the onset of criminality to the weakening of the ties that bind people to society. Hirschi assumes that all individuals are potential law violators but are kept under control because they fear that illegal behavior will damage their relationships with friends, parents, neighbors, teachers, and employers. Without these social ties or bonds, and in the absence of sensitivity to and interest in others, a person is free to commit criminal acts. Hirschi does not view society as containing competing subcultures with unique value systems. Most people are aware of the prevailing moral and legal code. He suggests, however, that in all elements of society, there is variation in the way people respond to conventional social rules and values. Among all ethnic, religious, racial, and social groups, people whose bond to society is weak may fall prey to criminogenic behavior patterns.

Elements of the Social Bond

Hirschi argues that the social bond a person maintains with society is divided into four main elements: attachment, commitment, involvement, and belief (see Figure 8.3).

Attachment. Attachment refers to a person's sensitivity to and interest in others.[84] Psychologists believe that without a sense of attachment, a person becomes a psychopath and loses the ability to relate coherently to the world. The acceptance of social norms and the development of a social conscience depend on attachment to and caring for other human beings. Hirschi views parents, peers, and schools as the important social institutions with which a person should maintain ties. Attachment to parents is the most important. Even if a family is shattered by divorce and separation, a child must retain a strong attachment to one or both parents. Without attachment to family, it is

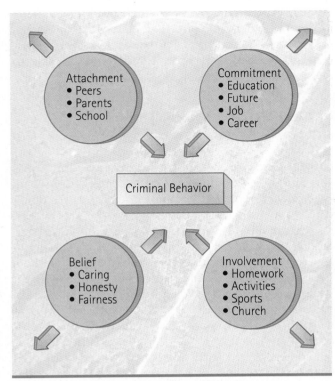

FIGURE 8.3   Elements of the Social Bond

unlikely that feelings of respect for others in authority will develop.

Commitment.   Commitment involves the time, energy, and effort expended in conventional lines of action. It embraces such activities as getting an education and saving money for the future. Social control theory holds that if people build up a strong involvement in life, property, and reputation, they will be less likely to engage in acts that will jeopardize their positions. Conversely, lack of commitment to conventional values may foreshadow a condition in which risk-taking behavior, such as crime, becomes a reasonable behavior alternative.

Involvement.   Heavy involvement in conventional activities leaves little time for illegal behavior. Hirschi believes that involvement—in school, recreation, and family—insulates a person from the potential lure of criminal behavior, while idleness enhances it.

Belief.   People who live in the same social setting often share common moral beliefs; they may adhere to such values as sharing, sensitivity to the rights of others, and admiration for the legal code. If these beliefs are

absent or weakened, individuals are more likely to participate in antisocial acts. Hirschi further suggests that the interrelationship of elements of the social bond controls subsequent behavior. For example, people who feel kinship and sensitivity to parents and friends should be more likely to adopt and work toward legitimate goals. On the other hand, a person who rejects social relationships probably lacks commitment to conventional goals. Similarly, people who are highly committed to conventional acts and beliefs are more likely to be involved in conventional activities.

Empirical Research

One of Hirschi's most significant contributions was his attempt to test the principal hypotheses of social control theory. He administered a detailed self-report survey to a sample of over 4,000 junior and senior high school students in Contra Costa County, California.[85] In a detailed analysis of the data, Hirschi found considerable evidence to support the control theory model. Among Hirschi's more important findings are the following:

- Youths who were strongly attached to their parents were less likely to commit criminal acts.

- Commitment to conventional values, such as striving to get a good education and refusing to drink and "cruise around," was also related to conventional behavior.

- Youths involved in conventional activity, such as homework, were less likely to engage in criminal behavior. Youths involved in unconventional behavior, such as smoking and drinking, were more delinquency-prone.

- Delinquent youths maintained weak and distant relationships with people. Nondelinquents were attached to their peers.

- Delinquents and nondelinquents shared similar beliefs about society.

Hirschi's data lent important support to the validity of control theory. Even when the statistical significance of his findings was less than he expected, the direction of his research data was extremely consistent. Only in very rare instances did his findings contradict the theory's most critical assumptions.

Supporting Research

Because of its importance and influence on criminology, control theory has been the focus of numerous efforts to corroborate Hirschi's original findings. Associations between indicators of attachment, belief, commitment, and involvement with measures of delinquency have tended to be positive and significant.[86] Research indicates that evidence of family detachment, including intrafamily conflict, abuse of children, and lack of affection, supervision, and family pride, are predictive of delinquent conduct.[87] Youths who are detached from the educational experience are at risk to criminality.[88] Lack of attachment to family, peers, and school has been found to predict delinquency in cross-cultural samples of youth.[89]

Other research efforts have shown that positive beliefs are related to criminality. Children who are involved in religious activities and hold conventional religious beliefs are less likely to become involved in substance abuse.[90] Similarly, youths who are involved in conventional leisure activities, such as supervised social activities and noncompetitive sports, are less likely to engage in delinquency than those who are involved in unconventional leisure activities and unsupervised, peer-oriented social pursuits.[91]

Opposing Views

There is also research that disputes some or all of the elements of control theory. For example, one issue has been whether the theory can explain all modes of criminality (as Hirschi maintains) or is restricted to particular groups or forms of criminality. Marvin Krohn and James Massey surveyed 3,065 junior and senior high school students and found that control variables were better able to explain female delinquency than male delinquency and minor delinquency (such as alcohol and

According to Hirschi, an attachment to a close-knit family, in which parents encourage conventional behaviors and beliefs, helps control youthful misbehavior.

marijuana abuse) than more serious criminal acts.[92] Similar gender differences were uncovered in school-based research by Jill Leslie Rosenbaum and James Lasley; they also found control variables were more predictive of female than male behavior.[93] Perhaps girls, more so than boys, are more deeply influenced by the quality of their bond to society.

Other research efforts have disputed Hirschi's view that delinquents are lone wolves whose only personal relationships are exploitive; a delinquent's friendship patterns may be closer to those of conventional youth than predicted by Hirschi.[94] In addition, Hirschi's conclusion that any form of social attachment is beneficial, even to deviant peers and parents, has been disputed by a number of research studies. Though his classic study supported the basic principles of control theory, Michael Hindelang did find that attachment to delinquent peers *escalated* rather than *restricted* criminality.[95] Gary Jensen and David Brownfield found that youths attached to drug-abusing parents are *more* likely to become drug users themselves.[96] And Mark Warr's research indicates that attachment to delinquent friends is a powerful predictor of delinquency, strong enough to overcome the controlling effect of positive family relationships.[97]

Does Crime Break Social Bonds?

The most severe criticism of control theory has been leveled by sociologist Robert Agnew, who claims that Hirschi has miscalculated the direction of the relationship between criminality and a weakened social bond.[98] While Hirschi's theory projects that a weakened bond *leads* to delinquency, Agnew suggests that the chain of events may flow in the *opposite* direction: kids who break the law find that their bond to parents, schools, and society eventually becomes weak and attenuated.

Other studies have also found that criminal behavior weakens social bonds and not vice versa.[99] It is possible that these findings reflect changes in the direction of the social bond over the life course. Using samples of 12-, 15-, and 18-year-old boys, Randy LaGrange and Helene Raskin White found that there was indeed age differences in the perceptions of the social bond: Mid-teens are surprisingly likely to be influenced by their parents and teachers; boys in the other two age groups are more deeply influenced by their deviant peers.[100] LaGrange and White attribute this finding to the problems of mid-adolescence, where there is a great need to develop "psychological anchors" to conformity. It is possible then that at one age level, weak bonds (to parents) lead to delinquency, while at another, strong bonds (to peers) lead to delinquency.

These criticisms aside, the weight of the existing empirical evidence is supportive of control theory, and it has emerged as one of the preeminent theories in criminology.[101] For many criminologists, it is perhaps the most important way of understanding the onset of youthful misbehavior.[102]

Though his work has achieved a prominent place in the criminological literature, Hirschi, along with Michael Gottfredson, has restructured his concept of control by *integrating* biosocial, psychological, and rational choice theory ideas into a *General Theory of Crime*. Because this theory is essentially integrated, it will be discussed more fully in Chapter 10.

☰ Labeling Theory

Labeling theory explains criminal career formation in terms of destructive social **interactions** and encounters. Its roots are found in the **symbolic interaction** theory of sociologists Charles Horton Cooley and George Herman Mead.[103] Mead believed that people communicate via symbols—a symbol being anything that stands for or represents something else. People interpret symbolic gestures from others and incorporate them in their self-image. How people view reality then depends on the content of the messages and situations they encounter, the subjective interpretation of these interactions, and how they shape future behavior.

Labeling theory picks up on these concepts of interaction and interpretation.[104] Throughout their lives, people are given a variety of symbolic labels during interactions with others. These labels imply a variety of behavior and attitude characteristics. For example, people labeled "insane" are assumed to be dangerous, dishonest, unstable, and otherwise unsound. Valued labels, including "smart," "honest," and "hard worker," can improve self-image and social standing. Negative labels, including "troublemaker," "mentally ill,", and "stupid," help stigmatize their targets and reduce their self-image. Both positive and negative labels involve subjective interpretation of behavior: a "troublemaker" is merely someone whom people label as "troublesome." There need not be any objective proof or measure indicating that the person is actually a troublemaker. Though a label may be a function of rumor, innuendo, or unfounded suspicion, its adverse impact can be immense.

If a devalued status is conferred by a significant other—teacher, police officer, elder, parent, or valued peer—the negative label may cause permanent harm to the target. The degree to which a person is perceived as a **social deviant** may affect his or her treatment at home, at work, at school, and in other social situations. Kids may find that their parents consider them a "bad influence" on younger brothers and sisters. School officials may limit them to classes reserved for people with behavior problems. Adults labeled "criminal," "ex-con," or "drug addict" may find their eligibility for employment severely restricted. And, of course, if the label is bestowed as the result of conviction for a criminal offense, the labeled person may be subject to official sanctions ranging from a mild reprimand to incarceration.

Beyond these immediate results, labeling advocates maintain that, depending on the visibility of the label and the manner and severity with which it is applied, a person will have an increasing commitment to a deviant career. "Thereafter he may be watched; he may be suspect . . . he may be excluded more and more from legitimate opportunities."[105] Labeled persons may find themselves turning to others similarly stigmatized for support and companionship. Isolated from conventional society, they may identify themselves as members of an outcast group and become locked into a deviant career.

Because the process of acquiring **stigma** is essentially interactive, labeling theorists blame criminal career formation on the social agencies originally designed for its control. Often mistrustful of institutions, such as police, courts, and correctional agencies, labeling advocates find it logical that these institutions produce the stigma that is so harmful to the very people they are trying to help, treat, or correct. Rather than reduce deviant behavior, for which they were designed, such label-bestowing institutions actually help maintain and amplify criminal behavior.

Crime and Labeling Theory

Labeling theorists use an interactionist definition of crime. "Deviance is not a property inherent in certain forms of behavior," argues sociologist Kai Erickson, "it is a property conferred upon those forms by the audience which directly or indirectly witnesses them."[106] This definition has been amplified by Edwin Schur, who states:

> Human behavior is deviant to the extent that it comes to be viewed as involving a personally discreditable departure from a group's normative expectation, and it elicits interpersonal and collective reactions that serve to "isolate," "treat," "correct" or "punish" individuals engaged in such behavior.[107]

"Ugly Mike" and his girlfriend are bouncers at rock concerts and are paid in beer for their efforts. Describe their personality, lifestyle, and behavior. Does your answer include negative labels?

Crime and deviance, therefore, are defined by the social audience's reaction to people and their behavior and the subsequent effects of that reaction; they are not defined by the moral content of the illegal act itself. In its purest form, labeling theory argues that such crimes as murder, rape, and assault are only bad or evil because people label them as such. After all, the difference between an excusable act and a criminal one is often a matter of legal definition, which changes from place to place and from year to year. Labeling theorists would argue that such acts as abortion, marijuana use, possession of a handgun, and gambling have been legal at some points and places in history and illegal at others. Howard Becker refers to people who create rules as **moral entrepreneurs.** He sums up their effect as follows:

> Social groups create deviance by making rules whose infractions constitute deviance, and by applying those rules to particular people and labeling them as outsiders. From this point of view, deviance is not a quality of the act a person commits, but rather a consequence of the application by others of rules and sanctions to an "offender." The deviant is one to whom the label has successfully

been applied; deviant behavior is behavior that people so label.[108]

Differential Enforcement

An important principle of labeling theory is that the law is differentially applied, benefiting those who hold economic and social power and penalizing the powerless. Labeling theorists argue that the probability of being brought under the control of legal authority is a function of a person's race, wealth, gender, and social standing. They point to studies indicating that police officers are more likely to formally arrest males, minority-group members, and those in the lower class and to use their discretionary powers to give beneficial treatment to more favored groups.[109] Similarly, labeling advocates cite evidence that minorities and the poor are more likely to be prosecuted for criminal offenses and receive harsher punishments when convicted.[110] This evidence is used to support the labeling concept that personal characteristics and social interactions are actually more important variables in the criminal career formation process than the mere violation of the criminal law. Labeling theorists also argue that the content of the law reflects power relationships in society. They point to the evidence that white-collar crimes are most often punished by a relatively small fine and rarely result in prison sentences, and they contrast this treatment with the long prison sentences given to those convicted of "street crimes," such as burglary or car theft.[111] In sum, a major premise of labeling theory is that the law is differentially constructed and applied. It favors the powerful members of society who direct its content and penalizes people whose actions represent a threat to those in control.[112]

Becoming Labeled

Labeling theorists are not especially concerned with explaining why people originally engage in acts that result in their being labeled.[113] Labeling theorists would not dispute any of the previously discussed theories of the onset of criminality: crime may be a result of greed, personality, social structure, learning, or control. Labeling theorists' concern is with criminal career formation and not the origin of criminal acts.

It is, however, consistent with the labeling approach to suggest that the less personal power and fewer resources a person has, the greater the chance he or she will become labeled. In the labeling view, a person is labeled deviant primarily as a consequence of the **social**

distance between the labeler and the person labeled. Race, class, and ethnic differences between those in power and those without influence the likelihood of labeling. For example, the poor or minority-group teenager may run a greater chance of being officially processed for criminal acts by police, courts, and correctional agencies than the wealthy white youth.

Of course, not all labeled people have chosen to engage in label-producing activities, such as crime. Some labels are bestowed on people for behaviors over which they have little control. Negative labels of this sort include "homosexual," "mentally ill," and "mentally deficient." In these categories, too, the probability of being labeled may depend on the visibility of the person in the community, the tolerance of the community for unusual behavior, and the person's own power to combat labels.

Consequences of Labeling

Criminologists are most concerned with two effects of labeling: the creation of stigma and the effect on self-image. Labels are believed to produce stigma. The labeled deviant becomes a social outcast who may be prevented from enjoying higher education, well-paying jobs, and other social benefits. Labeling theorists consider public condemnation an important part of the label-producing process. It may be accomplished in such "ceremonies" as a hearing in which a person is found to be mentally ill or a trial in which an individual is convicted of crime. A public record of the deviant acts causes the denounced person to be ritually separated from a place in the legitimate order and placed outside the world occupied by citizens of good standing. Harold Garfinkle has called transactions that produce irreversible, permanent labels "successful degradation ceremonies."[114]

Beyond these immediate results, the label tends to redefine the whole person. For example, the label "ex-con" may create in people's imaginations a whole series of behavior descriptions—tough, mean, dangerous, aggressive, dishonest, sneaky—that a person who has been in prison may or may not possess. People begin to react to the content of the label and what the label signifies and not to the actual behavior of the person who bears it. This is referred to as retrospective reading, a process in which the past of the labeled person is reviewed and reevaluated to fit his or her current outcast status. For example, boyhood friends of an assassin or killer are interviewed by the media and report that the suspect was withdrawn, suspicious, and negativistic as a youth. Now we can understand what prompted his current behavior; the label must certainly be accurate.[115]

Labels become the basis of personal identity. As the negative feedback of law enforcement agencies, parents, friends, teachers, and other figures amplifies the force of the original label, stigmatized offenders may begin to reevaluate their own identities. If they are not really evil or bad, they may ask themselves, why is everyone making such a fuss about them? Frank Tannenbaum referred to this process as the *dramatization of evil*. With respect to the consequences of labeling delinquent behavior, Tannenbaum states:

> The process of making the criminal, therefore, is a process of tagging, defining, identifying, making conscious and self-conscious; it becomes a way of stimulating, suggesting and evoking the very traits that are complained of. If the theory of relation of response to stimulus has any meaning, the entire process of dealing with the young delinquent is mischievous insofar as it identifies him to himself or to the environment as a delinquent person. The person becomes the thing he is described as being.[116]

Primary and Secondary Deviance

One of the more well-known views of the labeling process is Edwin Lemert's concept of **primary and secondary deviance.**[117]

According to Lemert, *primary deviance* involves norm violations or crimes that have very little influence on the actor and can be quickly forgotten. For example, a college student takes a "five-finger discount" at the campus bookstore. He successfully steals a textbook, uses it to get an A grade in a course, goes on to graduate, is admitted into law school, and later becomes a famous judge. Because his shoplifting goes unnoticed, it is a relatively unimportant event that has little bearing on his future life.

In contrast, *secondary deviance* occurs when a deviant event comes to the attention of significant others or social control agents who apply a negative label. The newly labeled offender then reorganizes his or her behavior and personality around the consequences of the deviant act. The shoplifting student is caught by a security guard and expelled from college. With his law school dreams dashed and future cloudy, his options are limited; people who know him say he "lacks character," and he begins to share their opinion. He eventually becomes a drug dealer and winds up in prison (see Figure 8.4).

Secondary deviance involves resocialization into a deviant role. The labeled person is transformed into one who "employs his behavior or a role based upon it as a means of defense, attack, or adjustment to the overt and covert problems created by the consequent social reaction to him."[118] Secondary deviance produces a deviance amplification effect. Offenders feel isolated from the mainstream of society and become firmly locked within their deviant role. They may seek out others similarly labeled to form deviant subcultures or groups. Ever more firmly enmeshed in their deviant role, they are locked into an escalating cycle of deviance, apprehension, more powerful labels, and identity transformation. Lemert's concept of secondary deviance expresses the core of labeling theory: deviance is a process in which one's identity is transformed. Efforts to control the offenders, whether by treatment or punishment, simply help lock them in their deviant role.

A number of attempts have been made to formulate theories of deviant career formation that have a labeling

FIGURE 8.4   The Cycle of Secondary Deviance

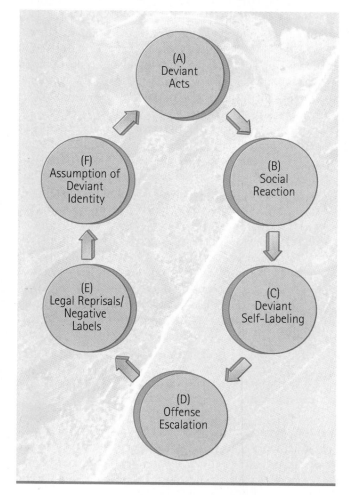

perspective. The sections below describe two such efforts.

General Theory of Deviance

Another theoretical model that draws upon labeling theory concepts is Howard Kaplan's *General Theory of Deviance*. A concise analysis of Kaplan's work begins with the assumption that people who cannot conform to social group standards face negative sanctions. Sanctions are brought against those who are considered failures either because they lack desirable physical, social, or psychological traits or because they fail to behave according to group expectations.

Those exposed to negative social sanctions experience **self-rejection** and a lower self-image. The experience of self-rejecting attitudes ("At times, I think I am no good at all") results in both a weakened commitment to conventional values and behaviors and the acquisition of motives to deviate from social norms. Facilitating this attitude and value transformation is the bond social outcasts form with similarly labeled peers.[119] Membership in a deviant subculture often involves conforming to group norms that conflict with those of conventional society. Deviant group membership then encourages criminality and drug abuse.

Deviant behaviors that defy conventional values can serve a number of different purposes. Some acts are defiant, designed to show contempt for the source of the negative labels, while others are planned to distance the target from further contact with the source of criticism (for example, an adolescent runs away from critical parents).[120]

Kaplan has tested his theoretical model using surveys of adolescents. His research findings support a model in which social sanctions lead to self-rejection, deviant peer associations, and eventual deviance amplification.[121] This model is important because it accounts for the creation of labels, their impact on self-image, and the long-term effect they have on criminal careers.

Differential Social Control

Karen Heimer and Ross Matsueda propose a version of labeling theory that also leans on control theory concepts; they call this the theory of *differential social control*.[122]

Agreeing with the labeling perspective, Heimer and Matsueda find that self-evaluations reflect actual or perceived appraisals made by others. Kids who view themselves as delinquents are giving an inner voice to their perceptions of how parents, teachers, peers, and neighbors feel about them. Kids who believe that others view them as antisocial or troublemakers take on attitudes and *roles* that *reflect* this assumption; they expect to be suspected and then rejected. Labeled youth may then join up with similarly outcast delinquent peers who facilitate their behavior. Eventually, antisocial behavior becomes habitual and automatic.

Tempering or enhancing the effect of this **reflective role-taking** are informal and institutional *social control* processes. Families, schools, peers, and the social system can either help control kids and dissuade them from crime or encourage and sustain deviance. When these groups are dysfunctional, such as when parents use drugs, they encourage, rather than control, antisocial behavior.

Heimer and Matsueda have conducted empirical research that supports the core of their model. They found that **reflected appraisal** as a rule violator has a significant effect on delinquency: Kids who believe that their parents and friends consider them deviants and troublemakers are the ones most likely to engage in delinquency. In another analysis, Heimer found that kids with "damaged" self-images are the ones most likely to engage in risk-taking behaviors, such as delinquency; *self-image,* influenced and directed by social interaction and approval, controls the content of behavior.[123]

This work by Heimer and Matsueda is important because it is an alternative to "traditional" labeling theory that incorporates concepts of social control and symbolic interaction. Further research on this model may revive interest in the labeling perspective.

Research on Labeling Theory

Research on labeling theory can be classified into two distinct categories. The first focuses on the characteristics of offenders who are chosen for labels. Labeling theory maintains that these offenders should be relatively powerless people who are unable to defend themselves against the negative labeling. The second type of research attempts to discover the effects of being labeled. Labeling theorists predict that people who are labeled should view themselves as deviant and commit increasing amounts of criminal behavior.

Who Gets Labeled?   It is widely believed that poor and powerless people are victimized by the law and justice system and that labels are not equally distributed across class and racial lines. For example, a report of the

National Minority Advisory Council on Criminal Justice argues that although substantive and procedural laws govern almost every aspect of the American criminal justice system, discretionary decision making controls its operation at every level. From the police officer's decision on whom to arrest, to the prosecutor's decisions on whom to charge and for how many and what kind of charges, to the court's decision on whom to release or on whom to permit bail, to the grand jury's decision on indictment, to the judge's decision on the length of the sentence, discretion works to the detriment of minorities, including African-Americans, Hispanics, Asian-Americans, and Native Americans.[124] This allegation is supported by data accumulated by Carl Pope and William Feyerherm, who reviewed more than 30 years of research on minorities in the juvenile justice system and found that race bias adversely influences decision making.[125]

There is also evidence that those in power try to streamline the labeling process by discounting or ignoring the "protestations of innocence" made by suspects accused of socially undesirable acts, such as child abuse. Leslie Margolin found that people accused of child abuse were routinely defined as "non-credible" when they denied accusations of abuse and were only believed when they confessed their guilt. In contrast, victims were believed when they made accusations but were considered "non-credible" when they claimed the suspect was innocent.[126]

While these arguments are persuasive, little definitive evidence exists that the justice system is inherently unfair and biased. Procedures such as arrest, prosecution, and sentencing seem to be more often based on legal factors, such as prior record and crime seriousness, than personal characteristics, such as class and race.[127] These findings do little to support labeling theory.

The Effects of Labeling.

There is empirical evidence that negative labels actually have a dramatic influence on the self-image of offenders. Considerable empirical evidence indicates that social sanctions lead to self-labeling and deviance amplification.[128]

Parents do in fact negatively label their children who suffer a variety of problems, including antisocial behavior and school failure.[129] This process is important because once they are labeled as a troublemaker, adolescents begin to reassess their self-image. Ross Matsueda found that parents who label their kids as troublemakers promote deviance amplification: labeling causes parents to become alienated from their child; negative labels reduce a child's self-image and increase delinquency.[130]

There are also research studies showing that official or institutional stigma does in fact produce self-labeling and damaged identities.[131] For example, kids labeled troublemakers in school are the ones most likely to drop out; dropping out has been linked to delinquent behavior.[132] Another study found that male drug users labeled as addicts by social control agencies eventually become self-labeled and increased their drug use.[133] And Lawrence Sherman and his associates found a limited labeling effect for people arrested in domestic violence cases: people with a low "stake in conformity," that is, who are jobless and unmarried, increased offending after being given official labels.[134]

While this evidence is supportive, other research studies find that labeling has an insignificant effect on criminal career formation.[135] In an in-depth analysis of research on the crime-producing effects of labels, Charles Tittle found little evidence that stigma produces crime.[136] Tittle claims that many criminal careers occur without labeling, that labeling often comes after, rather than before, chronic offending, and that criminal careers may not follow even when labeling takes place. There is growing evidence that the onset of criminal careers occurs early in life and that those who go on to a "life of crime" are burdened with so many social, physical, and psychological problems that negative labeling may be a relatively insignificant event.[137]

In sum, while there is considerable evidence that people who are labeled by parents, schools, and the criminal justice system stand a good chance of getting involved in deviance, it is still unclear whether this outcome is actually a labeling effect or the product of some other personal and social factors that also caused the labeling to occur.

Criticisms of Labeling Theory

Labeling theory has been the subject of significant academic debate. Those who criticize it point to its inability to specify the conditions that must exist before an act or individual is labeled deviant; that is, why some people are labeled while others remain "secret deviants."[138] Critics also charge that labeling theory fails to explain differences in crime rates; if crime is a function of stigma and labels, why are crime rates higher in some parts of the country at particular times of the year?[139] Labeling theory also ignores the onset of deviant behavior (that is, it fails to ask why people commit the initial deviant act) and does not deal with the reasons delinquents and criminals decide to forgo a deviant career.[140]

One sociologist, Charles Wellford, questions the validity of several premises essential to the labeling approach. He takes particular issue with the labeling assumption that no act is intrinsically criminal. Wellford points to the fact that some crimes, such as rape and homicide, are almost universally sanctioned. He says: "Serious violations of the law are universally understood and are, therefore, in that sense, intrinsically criminal."[141] Furthermore, he suggests, the labeling theory proposition that almost all law enforcement is biased against the poor and minorities is equally spurious: "I contend that the overwhelming evidence is in the direction of minimal differential law enforcement, determination of guilt and application of sanction." According to Wellford, this means that law enforcement officials most often base their arrest decisions on such factors as the seriousness of the offense and pay less attention to such issues as the race, class, and demeanor of the offender—factors that labeling theorists often link to the labeling decision. Finally, Wellford questions the concept of self-labeling. Though labeling may indeed affect offenders' attitudes about themselves, there is little evidence that attitude changes are related to actual behavior changes. Wellford believes instead that criminal behavior is situationally motivated and depends on ecological and personal conditions.[142] Because of these criticisms, a number of criminologists who once valued its premise now reject labeling theory. Some charge that it all too often focuses on "nuts, sluts, and perverts" and ignores the root causes of crime.[143]

Labeling Reexamined. While criticisms of labeling theory have reduced its importance in the criminological literature, its utility as an explanation of crime and deviance should not be dismissed. It has, for example, special value as an explanation of chronic offending. It seems logical that negative labeling is connected to the onset of persistent offending; after all, the chronic offender is defined as someone who has been repeatedly labeled by the justice system.[144]

Raymond Paternoster and Leeann Iovanni have identified some other features of the labeling perspective that are important contributions to the study of criminality:[145]

1. The labeling perspective identifies the role played by social control agents in the process of crime causation. Criminal behavior cannot be fully understood if the agencies and individuals empowered to control and treat it are neglected.

2. Labeling theory recognizes that criminality is not a disease or pathological behavior. It focuses attention on the social interactions and reactions that shape individuals and their behavior.

3. It distinguishes between criminal acts (primary deviance) and criminal careers (secondary deviance) and shows that these concepts must be interpreted and treated differently.

Labeling theory is also important because of its focus on interaction and the situation of crime. Rather than view the criminal as a robot-like creature whose actions are predetermined, it recognizes that crime is often the result of complex interactions and processes. The decision to commit crime involves actions of a variety of people including peers, the victim, the police, and other key characters. Labels may expedite crime because they guide the actions of all parties in criminal interactions. Actions deemed innocent when performed by one person are considered provocative when engaged in by another labeled as a deviant. Similarly, labeled people may be quick to judge, take offense, or misinterpret behavior because of past experience. They experienced conflict in the past, so why not now?

An Evaluation of Social Process Theory

The branches of social process theory—social learning, social control, and labeling—are compatible because they suggest that criminal behavior is part of the socialization process. Criminals are people whose interactions with critically important social institutions and processes—the family, schools, justice system, peer groups, employers, and neighbors—are troubled and disturbed. Though there is some disagreement about the relative importance of those influences and the form they take, there seems to be little question that social interactions shape the behavior, beliefs, values, and self-image of the offender. People who have learned deviant social values, find themselves detached from conventional social relationships, or are the subject of stigma and labels from significant others will be the most likely to fall prey to the attractions of criminal behavior. These negative influences can influence people in all walks of life, beginning in their youth and continuing through their majority. The major strength of the social process view is the vast body of empirical data showing that delinquents and criminals are indeed people who grew up in dysfunctional families, who had troubled childhoods, and who failed at school, at work, and in marriage. Prison data show that these characteristics are typical of inmates.

While persuasive, these theories have trouble accounting for some of the patterns and fluctuations in the crime rate. If social process theories are correct, for example, people in the West and South must be socialized differently than those in the Midwest and New England, since these latter regions have much lower crime rates. How can the fact that crime rates are lower in October than in July be explained if crime is a function of learning or control? Criminologists who have attempted to integrate theoretical models have helped answer these questions. These integrated theories are discussed in Chapter 10.

≡ Social Process Theory and Social Policy

Social process theories have had a major influence on social policy-making since the 1950s. Learning theories have greatly influenced concepts of treatment of the criminal offender. Their effect has mainly been felt by young offenders, who are viewed as being more salvageable than "hardened" criminals. Advocates of the social learning approach argue that if people become criminal by learning definitions and attitudes toward criminality, they can "unlearn" them by being exposed to definitions toward conventional behavior. This philosophy was used in numerous treatment facilities throughout the United States, the most famous being the Highfields Project in New Jersey and the Silverlake Program in Los Angeles. These residential treatment programs for young male offenders used group interaction sessions to attack the criminal behavior orientations held by residents (being tough, using alcohol and drugs, believing that school was for "sissies"), while promoting conventional lines of behavior (going straight, saving money, giving up drugs). It is common today for residential and nonresidential programs to offer similar treatment programs. They teach kids to say no to drugs, to forgo delinquent behavior, or to stay in school. It is even common for celebrities to return to their old neighborhood to tell kids to stay in school or off of drugs. If learning did not affect behavior, such exercises would be futile.

Control theories have also influenced criminal justice and other social policy-making. Programs have been developed to improve people's commitments to conventional lines of action. Some work at creating and strengthening bonds early in life before the onset of criminality. The educational system has been the scene of numerous programs designed to improve basic skills and create an atmosphere in which youths will develop a bond to their schools. The Close-Up on the Head Start program discusses perhaps the largest and most successful attempt to solidify social bonds.

Control theories' focus on the family has been put into operation in programs designed to strengthen the bond between parent and child. Others attempt to "repair" bonds that have been broken and frayed. Examples of this approach are the career, work furlough, and educational opportunity programs being developed in the nation's prisons. These programs are designed to help inmates maintain a stake in society so they will be less willing to resort to criminal activity on their release.

Labeling theorists caution against too much intervention. Rather than ask social agencies to attempt to rehabilitate people having problems with the law, they argue, "less is better." Put another way, the more institutions try to "help" people, the more these people will be stigmatized and labeled. For example, a special education program designed to help problem readers may cause them to be labeled by themselves and others as slow or stupid; a mental health rehabilitation program created with the best intentions may cause clients to be labeled as crazy or dangerous.

The influence of labeling theory can be viewed in the development of diversion and restitution programs. Diversion programs are designed to remove both juvenile and adult offenders from the normal channels of the criminal justice process by placing them in programs designed for rehabilitation. For example, a college student whose drunken driving causes injury to a pedestrian may, before a trial occurs, be placed for six months in an alcohol treatment program. If he successfully completes the program, charges against him will be dismissed. Thus, he avoids the stigma of a criminal label. Such programs are common throughout the nation. Often, they offer counseling; vocational, educational, and family services; and medical advice. Another label-avoiding innovation that has gained popularity is restitution. Rather than face the stigma of a formal trial, an offender is asked to either pay back the victim of the crime for any loss incurred or do some useful work in the community in lieu of receiving a court-ordered sentence.

Despite their good intentions, stigma-reducing programs have not met with great success. Critics charge that they substitute one kind of stigma for another—for instance, attending a mental health program in lieu of a criminal trial. In addition, diversion and restitution programs usually screen out violent offenders and repeat offenders. Finally, there is little hard evidence that the

CLOSE-UP

Head Start

Head Start is probably the best-known effort to help lower-class youths achieve proper socialization and, in so doing, reduce their potential for future criminality.

Head Start programs were instituted in the 1960s as part of the Johnson administration's War on Poverty. In the beginning, Head Start was a two-month summer program for children about to enter school that was aimed at embracing the "whole child." Comprehensive programming helped improve physical health, enhance mental processes, and improve social and emotional development, self-image, and interpersonal relationships.

Preschoolers were provided with an enriched educational environment to develop their learning and cognitive skills. They were given the opportunity to use pegs and pegboards, puzzles, toy animals, dolls, letters and numbers, and other materials that middle-class children take for granted and that give them a leg up in the educational process.

Today, there are over 1,300 centers around the nation containing 36,000 classrooms servicing 700,000 children and their families, on a budget of almost $3 billion annually. Services have been expanded beyond the two-month summer program; thirteen million children have been served by Head Start since it began.

Considerable controversy has surrounded the success of the Head Start program. In 1970, the Westinghouse Learning Corporation issued a definitive evaluation of the Head Start effort and concluded that there was no evidence of lasting cognitive gains on the part of the participating children. Initial gains seemed to evaporate during the elementary school years, and by the third grade, the performance of the Head Start children was no different than their peers.

While disappointing, this evaluation focused on IQ levels and gave short shrift to improvement in social competence and other survival skills. More recent research has produced dramatically different results. One report found that by age five, children who experienced the enriched day care offered by Head Start averaged more than ten points higher on their IQ scores than their peers who did not participate in the program. Other research that carefully compared Head Start children to similar youths who did not attend the program found that the former made significant intellectual gains: Head Start children were less likely to have been retained in a grade or placed in classes for slow learners; they outperformed peers on achievement tests; and they were more likely to graduate from high school. Head Start kids also make strides in nonacademic areas: they have better health, immunization rates, nutrition, and enhanced emotional characteristics after leaving the program. Research also shows that the Head Start program can have important psychological benefits for the mothers of participants, such as decreasing depression and anxiety and increasing feelings of life satisfaction. While findings in some areas may be tentative, they are all in the same direction: Head Start enhances school readiness and has enduring effects on social competence.

If, as many experts believe, there is a close link between school performance, family life, and crime, programs such as Head Start can help some potentially criminal youths avoid problems with the law. By implication, their success indicates that programs that help socialize youngsters can be used to combat urban criminality. While some problems have been identified in individual centers, the government has shown its faith in Head Start as a socialization agent by planning to expand services in the coming years; by 1998, total funding could be $8 billion.

Discussion Questions

1. Does a program like Head Start substitute one type of negative label (special-needs kid) for another (slow starter)?
2. If Head Start works, shouldn't every child have the benefit of the program?

SOURCES: Edward Zigler and Sally Styfco, "Head Start, Criticisms in a Constructive Context," *American Psychologist* 49 (1994): 127–32; Nancy Kassebaum, "Head Start, Only the Best for America's Children," *American Psychologist* 49 (1994): 123–26; Faith Lamb Parker, Chaya Piorkowski, and Lenore Peay, "Head Start as Social Support for Mothers: The Psychological Benefits of Involvement," *American Journal of Orthopsychiatry* 57 (1987): 220–33; Seymour Sarason and Michael Klaber, "The School as a Social Situation," *Annual Review of Psychology* 36 (1985): 115–40.

recidivism rate of people who have attended alternative programs represents an improvement over the rate of people who have been involved in the traditional criminal justice process.

☰ Summary

Social process theories view criminality as a function of people's interaction with various organizations, institutions, and processes in society. People in all walks of life have the potential to become criminals if they maintain destructive social relationships. Social process theory has three main branches: social learning theory stresses that people learn how to commit crimes; social control theory analyzes the failure of society to control criminal tendencies; and labeling theory maintains that negative labels produce criminal careers. These theories are summarized in Table 8.1. The social learning branch of social process theory suggests that people learn criminal behaviors much as they learn conventional behavior. Differential association theory, formulated by Edwin Sutherland, holds that criminality is a result of a person's

TABLE 8.1 Social Process Theories

Theory	Major Premise	Strengths
Social Learning Theories		
differential association theory	People learn to commit crime from exposure to antisocial definitions.	Explains onset of criminality. Explains the presence of crime in all elements of social structure. Explains why some people in high-crime areas refrain from criminality. Can apply to adults and juveniles.
differential reinforcement theory	Criminal behavior depends on the person's experiences with rewards for conventional behaviors and punishment for deviant ones. Being rewarded for deviance leads to crime.	Adds learning theory principles to differential association. Links sociological and psychological principles.
neutralization theory	Youths learn ways of neutralizing moral restraints and periodically drift in and out of criminal behavior patterns.	Explains why many delinquents do not beome adult criminals. Explains why youthful law violators can participate in conventional behavior.
Social Control Theories		
containment theory	Society produces pushes and pulls toward crime. In some people, they are counteracted by internal and external containments, such as a good self-concept and group cohesiveness.	Brings together psychological and sociological principles. Can explain why some people are able to resist the strongest social pressure to commit crime.
control theory	A person's bond to society prevents him or her from violating social rules. If the bond weakens, the person is free to commit crime.	Explains the onset of crime; can apply to both middle- and lower-class crime. Explains its theoretical constructs adequately so they can be measured. Has been empirically tested.
Labeling Theory		
labeling theory	People enter into law-violating careers when they are labeled for their acts and organize their personalities around the labels.	Explains the role of society in creating deviance. Explains why some juvenile offenders do not become adult criminals. Develops concepts of criminal careers.
general theory of deviance	People exposed to negative labels experience self-rejection which causes them to bond with social outcasts.	Considers the relationship between negative labels, self-image, and personal relations.
differential social control	Social rejection leads to self-fulfilling prophecy. Weak social controls encourage deviance.	Considers the role of social control in the labeling process.

perceiving an excess of definitions in favor of crime over definitions that uphold conventional values. Ronald Akers has reformulated Sutherland's work using psychological learning theory. He calls his approach differential reinforcement theory. Sykes and Matza's theory of neutralization stresses youths' learning of behavior rationalizations that enable them to overcome societal values and norms and engage in illegal behavior. Control theory is the second branch of the social process approach.

Control theories maintain that all people have the potential to become criminals but that their bonds to conventional society prevent them from violating the law. Walter Reckless's containment theory suggests that a person's self-concept aids his or her commitment to conventional action. Travis Hirschi describes the social bond as containing elements of belief, commitment, attachment, and involvement. Weakened bonds allow youths to become active in antisocial behavior.

Labeling theory holds that criminality is promoted by becoming negatively labeled by significant others. Such labels as "criminal," "ex-con," and "junkie" serve to isolate people from society and lock them into lives of crime. Labels create expectations that the labeled person will act in a certain way; so-labeled people are always watched and suspected. Eventually, these people begin to accept their labels as personal identities, locking them further into lives of crime and deviance. Edwin Lemert has said that people who accept labels are involved in secondary deviance. Unfortunately, research on labeling has not supported its major premises. Consequently, critics have charged that it lacks credibility as a description of crime causation. Social process theories have had a great influence on social policy. They have controlled treatment orientations as well as community action policies.

≡ KEY TERMS

social-psychological processes
socialization
broken home
cliques
crowds
social learning theory
social control theory
labeling theory
differential association
differential reinforcement
neutralize
drift
subterranean behaviors

techniques of neutralization
commitment to conformity
self-esteem
interactions
symbolic interaction
social deviant
stigma
moral entrepreneurs
social distance
primary and secondary deviance
self-rejection
reflective role-taking
reflected appraisal

≡ NOTES

1. Alan Lizotte, Terence Thornberry, Marvin Krohn, Deborah Chard-Wierschem, and David McDowall, "Neighborhood Context and Delinquency: A Longitudinal Analysis," in *Cross-National Longitudinal Research on Human Development and Criminal Behavior,* ed. E. M. Weitekamp and H. J. Kerner (Netherlands: Kluwer, 1994), pp. 217–27.

2. Charles Tittle and Robert Meier, "Specifying the SES/Delinquency Relationship," *Criminology* 28 (1990): 271–99 at 274.

3. Lizotte, Thornberry, Krohn, Chard-Wierschem, and McDowall, "Neighborhood Context and Delinquency."

4. Ann Goetting, "The Parenting Crime Connection," *Journal of Primary Prevention* 14 (1994): 167–84.

5. Sheldon Glueck and Eleanor Glueck, *Unraveling Juvenile Delinquency* (Cambridge: Harvard University Press, 1950); Ashley Weeks, "Predicting Juvenile Delinquency," *American Sociological Review* 8 (1943): 40–46.

6. For general reviews of the relationship between families and delinquency, see Alan Jay Lincoln and Murray Straus, *Crime and the Family* (Springfield, Ill.: Charles C. Thomas, 1985); Rolf Loeber and Magda Stouthamer-Loeber, "Family Factors as Correlates and Predictors of Juvenile Conduct Problems and Delinquency," in *Crime and Justice, An Annual Review of Research,* vol. 7, ed. Michael Tonry and Norval Morris (Chicago: University of Chicago Press, 1986), pp. 29–151; Goetting, "The Parenting Crime Connection."

7. Joseph Weis, Katherine Worsley, and Carol Zeiss, "The Family and Delinquency: Organizing the Conceptual Chaos" (Center for Law and Justice, University of Washington, 1982, Monograph).

8. United Press International, "U.S. One in Four Children Had Single Parent," *Boston Globe,* 21 January 1988, p. 11.

9. "Two-Parent Households with Children Declining," *Wall Street Journal,* 30 January 1991, p. A2.

10. U.S. Department of the Census, *Fertility of American Women, June 1992* (Washington, D.C.: U.S. Government Printing Office, 1993), p. 34.

11. Lawrence Rosen and Kathleen Neilson, "Broken Homes," in *Contemporary Criminology,* ed. Leonard Savitz and Norman Johnston (New York: Wiley, 1982), pp. 126–35.

12. James Q. Wilson and Richard Herrnstein, *Crime and Human Nature* (New York: Simon and Schuster, 1985), p. 249.

13. L. Edward Wells and Joseph Rankin, "Families and Delinquency: A Meta-Analysis of the Impact of Broken Homes," *Social Problems* 38 (1991): 71–90.

14. Nan Marie Astone and Sara McLanahan, "Family Structure, Parental Practices and High School Completion," *American Sociological Review* 56 (1991): 309–20.

15. Mary Pat Traxler, "The Influence of the Father and Alternative Male Role Models on African-American Boys' Involvement in Antisocial Behavior" (Paper presented at

the annual meeting of the American Society of Criminology, New Orleans, November 1992).

16. Paul Amato and Bruce Keith, "Parental Divorce and the Well-Being of Children: A Meta-Analysis," *Psychological Bulletin* 110 (1991): 26–46.

17. Joseph Rankin and L. Edward Wells, "The Effect of Parental Attachments and Direct Controls on Delinquency," *Journal of Research in Crime and Delinquency* 27 (1990): 140–65.

18. John Laub and Robert Sampson, "Unraveling Families and Delinquency: A Reanalysis of the Glueck's Data," *Criminology* 26 (1988): 355–80.

19. Richard Famularo, Karen Stone, Richard Barnum, and Robert Wharton, "Alcoholism and Severe Child Maltreatment," *American Journal of Orthopsychiatry* 56 (1987): 481–85; Richard Gelles, "Child Abuse and Violence in Single-Parent Families: Parent Absence and Economic Deprivation," *American Journal of Orthopsychiatry* 59 (1989): 492–501; Cecil Willis and Richard Wells, "The Police and Child Abuse: An Analysis of Police Decisions to Report Illegal Behavior," *Criminology* 26 (1988): 695–716; Carolyn Webster-Stratton, "Comparison of Abusive and Nonabusive Families with Conduct-Disordered Children," *American Journal of Orthopsychiatry* 55 (1985): 59–69.

20. Herman Daldin, "The Fate of the Sexually Abused Child," *Clinical Social Work Journal* 16 (1988): 20–26; Gerald Ellenson, "Horror, Rage and Defenses in the Symptoms of Female Sexual Abuse Survivors," *Social Casework: The Journal of Contemporary Social Work* 70 (1989): 589–96.

21. Susan Zuravin, "The Ecology of Child Abuse and Neglect: Review of the Literature and Presentation of Data," *Violence and Victims* 4 (1989): 101–20.

22. *The Forgotten Half: Pathways to Success for America's Youth and Young Families* (Washington, D.C.: William T. Grant Foundation, 1988); Lee Jussim, "Teacher Expectations: Self-Fulfilling Prophecies, Perceptual Biases, and Accuracy," *Journal of Personality and Social Psychology* 57 (1989): 469–80.

23. Jeannie Oakes, *Keeping Track, How Schools Structure Inequality* (New Haven: Yale University Press, 1985); Marc LeBlanc, Evelyne Valliere, and Pierre McDuff, "Adolescent's School Experience and Self-Reported Offending: A Longitudinal Test of Social Control Theory" (Paper presented at the annual meeting of the American Society of Criminology, Baltimore, November 1990).

24. G. Roger Jarjoura, "Does Dropping Out of School Enhance Delinquent Involvement? Results from a Large-Scale National Probability Sample," *Criminology* 31 (1993): 149–72; Terence Thornberry, Melaine Moore, and R. L. Christenson, "The Effect of Dropping Out of High School on Subsequent Criminal Behavior," *Criminology* 23 (1985): 3–18.

25. Carolyn Smith, Alan Lizotte, Terence Thornberry, and Marvin Krohn, *Resilient Youth: Identifying Factors That Prevent High-Risk Youth from Engaging in Delinquency and Drug Use* (Albany, N.Y: Rochester Youth Development Study, 1994), pp. 19–21.

26. National Commission on Excellence in Education, *A Nation at Risk* (Washington, D.C.: U.S. Government Printing Office, 1982).

27. *Weapons in Schools* (Washington, D.C.: Office of Juvenile Justice and Delinquency Prevention, 1989); U.S. Department of Justice, *Disorder in Our Public Schools* (Washington, D.C.: U.S. Government Printing Office, 1984).

28. Irving Janis, *Groupthink: Psychological Studies of Policy Decisions and Fiascoes* (Boston: Houghton Mifflin, 1982).

29. Thomas Berndt, "The Features and Effects of Friendships in Early Adolescence," *Child Development* 53 (1982): 1447–69; Thomas Berndt and T. B. Perry, "Children's Perceptions of Friendships as Supportive Relationships," *Developmental Psychology* 22 (1986): 640–48; Spencer Rathus, *Understanding Child Development* (New York: Holt, Rinehart and Winston, 1988), p. 462.

30. Delbert Elliott, David Huizinga, and Suzanne Ageton, *Explaining Delinquency and Drug Use* (Beverly Hills: Sage, 1985); Helene Raskin White, Robert Padina, and Randy LaGrange, "Longitudinal Predictors of Serious Substance Use and Delinquency," *Criminology* 6 (1987): 715–40.

31. See, generally, John Hagedorn, *People and Folks: Gangs, Crime and the Underclass in a Rustbelt City* (Chicago: Lakeview Press, 1988).

32. Scott Menard, "Demographic and Theoretical Variables in the Age-Period Cohort Analysis of Illegal Behavior," *Journal of Research in Crime and Delinquency* 29 (1992): 178–99.

33. For a general review, see Patrick Jackson, "Theories and Findings about Youth Gangs," *Criminal Justice Abstracts,* June 1989, pp. 313–27.

34. Marvin Krohn and Terence Thornberry, "Network Theory: A Model for Understanding Drug Abuse among African-American and Hispanic Youth," in *Drug Abuse among Minority Youth: Advances in Research and Methodology,* ed. Mario De La Rosa and Juan-Luis Recio Adrados (Washington, D.C.: U. S. Department of Health and Human Services, 1993).

35. Mark Warr, "Age, Peers, and Delinquency," *Criminology* 31 (1993): 17–40.

36. Walter Miller, *Violence by Youth Gangs and Youth Groups as a Crime Problem in Major American Cities* (Washington, D.C.: U.S. Government Printing Office, 1975).

37. Gabriel Tarde, *The Laws of Imitation* (1903; reprint, Gloucester, Mass.: Peter Smith, 1962); Piers Beirne, "Between Classicism and Positivism: Crime and Penalty in the Writings of Gabriel Tarde," *Criminology* 25 (1987): 785–819.

38. Edwin H. Sutherland, *Principles of Criminology* (Philadelphia: Lippincott, 1939).

39. See, for example, Edwin Sutherland, "White-Collar Criminality," *American Sociological Review* 5 (1940): 2–10.

40. This section is adapted from Clarence Schrag, *Crime and Justice: American Style* (Washington, D.C.: U.S.

Government Printing Office, 1971), p. 46.

41. See Edwin Sutherland and Donald Cressey, *Criminology,* 8th ed. (Philadelphia: Lippincott, 1970), pp. 77–79.

42. Sandra Brown, Vicki Creamer, and Barbara Stetson, "Adolescent Alcohol Expectancies in Relation to Personal and Parental Drinking Patterns," *Journal of Abnormal Psychology* 96 (1987): 117–21.

43. Ibid.

44. Ross Matsueda and Karen Heimer, "Race, Family Structure and Delinquency: A Test of Differential Association and Social Control Theories," *American Sociological Review* 52 (1987): 826–40.

45. James Short, "Differential Association as a Hypothesis: Problems of Empirical Testing," *Social Problems* 8 (1960): 14–25.

46. Albert Reiss and A. Lewis Rhodes, "The Distribution of Delinquency in the Social Class Structure," *American Sociological Review* 26 (1961): 732.

47. Mark Warr, "Age, Peers, and Delinquency," *Criminology* 31 (1993): 17–40.

48. Douglas Smith, Christy Visher, and G. Roger Jarjoura, "Dimensions of Delinquency: Exploring the Correlates of Participation, Frequency, and Persistence of Delinquent Behavior," *Journal of Research in Crime and Delinquency* 28 (1991): 6–32.

49. Gary Green, "Resurrecting Polygraph Validation on Self-Reported Crime Data: A Note on Research Method and Ethics Using the Deer Poacher," *Deviant Behavior* 11 (1990): 131–37.

50. Denise Kandel and Mark Davies, "Friendship Networks, Intimacy, and Illicit Drug Use in Young Adulthood: A Comparison of Two Competing Theories," *Criminology* 29 (1991): 441–67.

51. Kenneth Tunnell, "Inside the Drug Trade: Trafficking from the Dealer's Perspective," *Qualitative Sociology* 16 (1993): 361–81 at 367.

52. Krohn and Thornberry, "Network Theory," pp. 123–24.

53. Charles Tittle, *Sanctions and Social Deviance* (New York: Praeger, 1980).

54. Yuet-Wah Cheung and Agnes M. C. Ng, "Social Factors in Adolescent Deviant Behavior in Hong Kong: An Integrated Theoretical Approach," *International Journal of Comparative and Applied Criminal Justice* 12 (1988): 27–44.

55. Robert Burgess and Ronald Akers, "A Differential Association—Reinforcement Theory of Criminal Behavior," *Social Problems* 14 (1966): 128–47.

56. Ross Matsueda, "The Current State of Differential Association Theory," *Crime and Delinquency* 34 (1988): 277–306.

57. See, for example, Albert Bandura, *Social Learning and Personality Development* (New York: Holt, Rinehart and Winston, 1963).

58. Ronald Akers, *Deviant Behavior: A Social Learning Approach,* 2d ed. (Belmont, Mass.: Wadsworth, 1977).

59. Ronald Akers, Marvin Krohn, Lonn Lonza-Kaduce, and

Marcia Radosevich, "Social Learning and Deviant Behavior: A Specific Test of a General Theory," *American Sociological Review* 44 (1979): 638.

60. Ibid.

61. Ibid., pp. 636–55.

62. Marvin Krohn, William Skinner, James Massey, and Ronald Akers, "Social Learning Theory and Adolescent Cigarette Smoking: A Longitudinal Study," *Social Problems* 32 (1985): 455–71.

63. Gary Jensen and David Brownfield, "Parents and Drugs," *Criminology* 21 (1983): 543–54.

64. Ronald Akers, "Rational Choice, Deterrence and Social Learning Theory in Criminology: The Path Not Taken," *Journal of Criminal Law and Criminology* 81 (1990): 653–76.

65. Gresham Sykes and David Matza, "Techniques of Neutralization: A Theory of Delinquency," *American Sociological Review* 22 (1957): 664–70; David Matza, *Delinquency and Drift* (New York: John Wiley, 1964).

66. Matza, *Delinquency and Drift,* p. 51.

67. Sykes and Matza, "Techniques of Neutralization," pp. 664–70; see also David Matza, "Subterranean Traditions of Youths," *Annals of the American Academy of Political and Social Science* 378 (1961): 116.

68. Sykes and Matza, "Techniques of Neutralization," pp. 664–70.

69. Ibid.

70. Michael Hindelang, "The Commitment of Delinquents to Their Misdeeds: Do Delinquents Drift?" *Social Problems* 17 (1970): 509.

71. Robert Regoli and Eric Poole, "The Commitment of Delinquents to Their Misdeeds: A Reexamination," *Journal of Criminal Justice* 6 (1978): 261–69.

72. Robert Ball, "An Empirical Exploration of Neutralization Theory," *Criminologica* 4 (1966): 22–32. For a similar view, see M. William Minor, "The Neutralization of Criminal Offense," *Criminology* 18 (1980): 103–20.

73. Mark Pogrebin, Eric Poole, and Amos Martinez, "Accounts of Professional Misdeeds: The Sexual Exploitation of Clients by Psychotherapists," *Deviant Behavior* 13 (1992): 229–52.

74. Eric Wish, *Drug Use Forecasting 1990* (Washington, D.C.: National Institute of Justice, 1991).

75. Scott Briar and Irvin Piliavin, "Delinquency: Situational Inducements and Commitment to Conformity," *Social Problems* 13 (1965–1966): 35–45.

76. Lawrence Sherman and Douglas Smith, with Janell Schmidt and Dennis Rogan, "Crime, Punishment, and Stake in Conformity: Legal and Informal Control of Domestic Violence," *American Sociological Review* 57 (1992): 680–90.

77. Albert Reiss, "Delinquency as the Failure of Personal and Social Controls," *American Sociological Review* 16 (1951): 196–207.

78. Briar and Piliavin, "Delinquency: Situational Inducements and Commitment to Conformity."

79. John McCarthy and Dean Hoge, "The Dynamics of Self-Esteem and Delinquency," *American Journal of Sociology* 90 (1984): 396–410; Edward Wells and Joseph Rankin, "Self-Concept as a Mediating Concept in Delinquency," *Social Psychology Quarterly* 46 (1983): 11–22.

80. Howard Kaplan, *Deviant Behavior in Defense of Self* (New York: Academic Press, 1980); idem, "Self-Attitudes and Deviant Response," *Social Forces* 54 (1978): 788–801.

81. L. Edward Wells, "Self-Enhancement through Delinquency: A Conditional Test of Self-Derogation Theory," *Journal of Research in Crime and Delinquency* 26 (1989): 226–52.

82. See, generally, Walter Reckless, *The Crime Problem* (New York: Appleton Century Crofts, 1967). Among the many research reports by Walter Reckless and his colleagues are: Walter Reckless, Simon Dinitz, and Ellen Murray, "Self-Concept as an Insulator against Delinquency," *American Sociological Review* 21 (1956): 744–46; Reckless, Dinitz, and Murray, "The Good Boy in a High Delinquency Area," *Journal of Criminal Law, Criminology, and Police Science* 48 (1957): 1826; Walter Reckless, Simon Dinitz, and Barbara Kay, "The Self-Component in Potential Delinquency and Potential Non-delinquency," *American Sociological Review* 22 (1957): 566–70; Walter Reckless and Simon Dinitz, "Pioneering with Self-Concept as a Vulnerability Factor in Delinquency," *Journal of Criminal Law, Criminology, and Police Science* 58 (1967): 515–23.

83. Travis Hirschi, *Causes of Delinquency* (Berkeley: University of California Press, 1969).

84. Ibid., p. 231.

85. Ibid., pp. 66–74.

86. Marc LeBlanc, "Family Dynamics, Adolescent Delinquency, and Adult Criminality" (Paper presented at the Society for Life History Research Conference, Keystone, Colorado, October 1990), p. 6.

87. Patricia Van Voorhis, Francis Cullen, Richard Mathers, and Connie Chenoweth Garner, "The Impact of Family Structure and Quality on Delinquency: A Comparative Assessment of Structural and Functional Factors," *Criminology* 26 (1988): 235–61.

88. LeBlanc, Valliere, and McDuff, "Adolescent's School Experience and Self-Reported Offending."

89. Marianne Junger and Wim Polder, "Some Explanations of Crime among Four Ethnic Groups in the Netherlands," *Journal of Quantitative Criminology* 8 (1992): 51–78.

90. John Cochran and Ronald Akers, "An Exploration of the Variable Effects of Religiosity on Adolescent Marijuana and Alcohol Use," *Journal of Research in Crime and Delinquency* 26 (1989): 198–225.

91. Robert Agnew and David Peterson, "Leisure and Delinquency," *Social Problems* 36 (1989): 332–48.

92. Marvin Krohn and James Massey, "Social Control and Delinquent Behavior: An Examination of the Elements of the Social Bond," *Sociological Quarterly* 21 (1980): 529–43.

93. Jill Leslie Rosenbaum and James Lasley, "School, Community Context, and Delinquency: Rethinking the Gender Gap," *Justice Quarterly* 7 (1990): 493–513.

94. Peggy Giordano, Stephen Cernkovich, and M. D. Pugh, "Friendships and Delinquency," *American Journal of Sociology* 91 (1986): 1170–1202.

95. Michael Hindelang, "Causes of Delinquency: A Partial Replication and Extension," *Social Problems* 21 (1973): 471–87.

96. Gary Jensen and David Brownfield, "Parents and Drugs," *Criminology* 21 (1983): 543–54. See also M. Wiatrowski, D. Griswold, and M. Roberts, "Social Control Theory and Delinquency," *American Sociological Review* 46 (1981): 525–41.

97. Mark Warr, "Parents, Peers, and Delinquency," *Social Forces* 72 (1993): 247–64.

98. Robert Agnew, "Social Control Theory and Delinquency: A Longitudinal Test," *Criminology* 23 (1985): 47–61.

99. Alan E. Liska and M. D. Reed, "Ties to Conventional Institutions and Delinquency: Estimating Reciprocal Effects," *American Sociological Review* 50 (1985): 547–60.

100. Randy LaGrange and Helene Raskin White, "Age Differences in Delinquency: A Test of Theory," *Criminology* 23 (1985): 19–45.

101. Michael Wiatrowski, David Griswold, and Mary K. Roberts, "Social Control Theory and Delinquency," *American Sociological Review* 46 (1981): 525–41.

102. Ibid.

103. George Herman Mead, *Mind, Self and Society* (Chicago: University of Chicago Press, 1934); idem, *The Philosophy of the Act* (Chicago: University of Chicago Press, 1938).

104. Bruce Link, Elmer Streuning, Francis Cullen, Patrick Shrout, and Bruce Dohrenwend, "A Modified Labeling Theory Approach to Mental Disorders: An Empirical Assessment," *American Sociological Review* 54 (1989): 400–423.

105. President's Commission on Law Enforcement and the Administration of Youth Crime, *Task Force Report: Juvenile Delinquency and Youth* (Washington, D.C.: U.S. Government Printing Office, 1967), p. 43.

106. Kai Erickson, "Notes on the Sociology of Deviance," *Social Problems* 9 (1962): 397–414.

107. Edwin Schur, *Labeling Deviant Behavior* (New York: Harper & Row, 1972), p. 21.

108. Howard Becker, *Outsiders, Studies in the Sociology of Deviance* (New York: Macmillan, 1963), p. 9.

109. Christy Visher, "Gender, Police Arrest Decision, and Notions of Chivalry," *Criminology* 21 (1983): 5–28.

110. Marjorie Zatz, "Race, Ethnicity and Determinate Sentencing," *Criminology* 22 (1984): 147–71.

111. Roland Chilton and Jim Galvin, "Race, Crime and Criminal Justice," *Crime and Delinquency* 31 (1985): 3–14.

112. Joan Petersilia, "Racial Disparities in the Criminal Justice System: A Summary," *Crime and Delinquency* 31 (1985): 15–34.

113. Walter Gove, *The Labeling of Deviance: Evaluating a*

Perspective (New York: John Wiley, 1975), p. 5.

114. Harold Garfinkle, "Conditions of Successful Degradation Ceremonies," *American Journal of Sociology* 61 (1956): 420–24.

115. John Lofland, *Deviance and Identity* (Englewood Cliffs, N.J.: Prentice-Hall, 1969).

116. Frank Tannenbaum, *Crime and the Community* (New York: Columbia University Press, 1938), pp. 19–20.

117. Edwin Lemert, *Social Pathology* (New York: McGraw-Hill, 1951).

118. Ibid., p. 75.

119. See, for example, Howard Kaplan and Hiroshi Fukurai, "Negative Social Sanctions, Self-Rejection, and Drug Use," *Youth and Society* 23 (1992): 275–98.

120. Howard Kaplan, *Toward a General Theory of Deviance: Contributions from Perspectives on Deviance and Criminality* (College Station, Texas: Texas A&M University, n.d.).

121. Howard Kaplan, Robert Johnson, and Carol Bailey, "Deviant Peers and Deviant Behavior: Further Elaboration of a Model," *Social Psychology Quarterly* 30 (1987): 277–84.

122. Karen Heimer and Ross Matsueda, "Role-Taking, Role-Commitment and Delinquency: A Theory of Differential Social Control," *American Sociological Review* (in press, 1994).

123. Karen Heimer, "Gender, Race, and the Pathways to Delinquency: An Interactionist Explanation," in *Crime and Inequality,* ed. John Hagan and Ruth Peterson (Stanford, Calif.: Stanford University Press, in press).

124. National Minority Council on Criminal Justice, *The Inequality of Justice* (Washington, D.C.: National Minority Advisory Council on Criminal Justice, 1981), p. 200.

125. Carl Pope and William Feyerherm, "Minority Status and Juvenile Justice Processing," *Criminal Justice Abstracts* 22 (1990): 327–36; see also Carl Pope, "Race and Crime Revisited," *Crime and Delinquency* 25 (1979): 347–57.

126. Leslie Margolin, "Deviance on Record: Techniques for Labeling Child Abusers in Official Documents," *Social Problems* 39 (1992): 58–68.

127. Charles Corley, Stephen Cernkovich, and Peggy Giordano, "Sex and the Likelihood of Sanction," *Journal of Criminal Law and Criminology* 80 (1989): 540–53.

128. Howard Kaplan and Robert Johnson, "Negative Social Sanctions and Juvenile Delinquency: Effects of Labeling in a Model of Deviant Behavior," *Social Science Quarterly* 72 (1991): 98–122.

129. Ruth Triplett, "The Conflict Perspective, Symbolic Interactionism, and the Status Characteristics Hypothesis," *Justice Quarterly* 10 (1993): 540–58.

130. Ross Matsueda, "Reflected Appraisals: Parental Labeling, and Delinquency: Specifying a Symbolic Interactionist Theory," *American Journal of Sociology* 97 (1992): 1577–1611.

131. Suzanne Ageton and Delbert Elliott, *The Effect of Legal Processing on Self-Concept* (Boulder, Colo.: Institute of Behavioral Science, 1973).

132. Christine Bowditch, "Getting Rid of Troublemakers: High School Disciplinary Procedures and the Production of Dropouts," *Social Problems* 40 (1993): 493–507.

133. Melvin Ray and William Downs, "An Empirical Test of Labeling Theory Using Longitudinal Data," *Journal of Research in Crime and Delinquency* 23 (1986): 169–94.

134. Sherman and Smith, with Schmidt and Rogan, "Crime, Punishment, and Stake in Conformity."

135. Paul Lipsett, "The Juvenile Offender's Perception," *Crime and Delinquency* 14 (1968): 49; Jack Foster, Simon Dinitz, and Walter Reckless, "Perception of Stigma following Public Intervention for Delinquent Behavior," *Social Problems* 20 (1972): 202.

136. Charles Tittle, "Labeling and Crime: An Empirical Evaluation," in *The Labeling of Deviance: Evaluating a Perspective,* ed. Walter Gove (New York: John Wiley, 1975), pp. 157–79.

137. David Farrington, "Early Predictors of Adolescent Aggression and Adult Violence," *Violence and Victims* 4 (1989): 79–100.

138. Jack Gibbs, "Conceptions of Deviant Behavior: The Old and the New," *Pacific Sociological Review* 9 (1966): 11–13.

139. Schur, *Labeling Deviant Behavior,* p. 14.

140. Ronald Akers, "Problems in the Sociology of Deviance," *Social Problems* 46 (1968): 463.

141. Charles Wellford, "Labeling Theory and Criminology: An Assessment," *Social Problems* 22 (1975): 335–47.

142. Ibid., p. 337.

143. Alexander Liazos, "The Poverty of the Sociology of Deviance: Nuts, Sluts, and Perverts," *Social Problems* 20 (1971): 103–20.

144. Charles Tittle, "Two Empirical Regularities (Maybe) in Search of an Explanation: Commentary on the Age/Crime Debate," *Criminology* 26 (1988): 75–85.

145. Raymond Paternoster and Leeann Iovanni, "The Labeling Perspective and Delinquency: An Elaboration of the Theory and an Assessment of the Evidence," *Justice Quarterly* 6 (1989): 358–94.

9

Social Conflict Theories

☰ Introduction

It would be unusual to pick up the morning paper and not see headlines loudly proclaiming renewed strife between the United States and its overseas adversaries, between union negotiators and management attorneys, between citizens and police authorities, or between feminists and reactionary males protecting their turf. The world is filled with conflict. Conflict can be destructive when it leads to war, violence, and death; it can be functional when it results in positive social change. Criminologists who view crime as a function of social conflict and economic rivalry are aligned with a number of schools of thought, referred to as conflict, critical, Marxist, or radical schools of criminology, or one of

their affiliated branches, including but not limited to peacemaking, left realism, radical feminism, and deconstructionism (see Figure 9.1).

The goal of social conflict theorists is to explain crime within economic and social contexts and to express the connection between the nature of social class, crime, and social control.[1] Conflict theorists are concerned with such issues as the role government plays in creating a criminogenic environment; the relationship of personal or group power in controlling and shaping the criminal law; the role of bias in the operations of the justice system; and the relationship between a capitalist free-enterprise economy and crime rates.

Conflict theorists view crime as the outcome of class struggle. Conflict works to promote crime by creating a social atmosphere in which the law is a mechanism for

FIGURE 9.1 The Branches of Social Conflict Theory

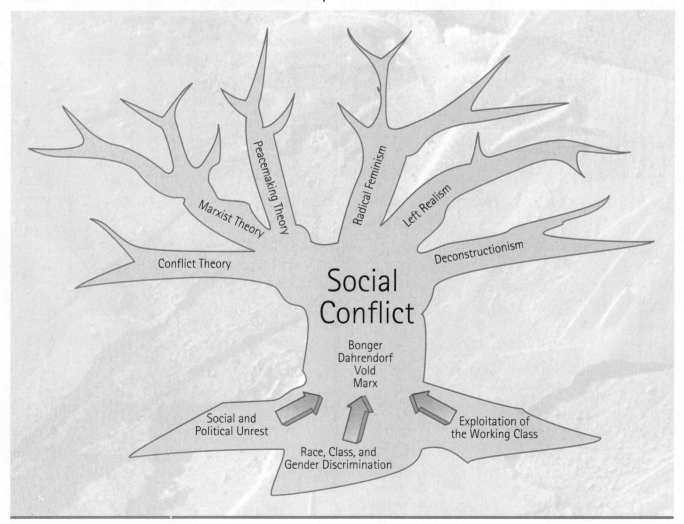

controlling dissatisfied, have-not members of society, while maintaining the position of the powerful. That is why crimes that are the province of the wealthy, such as illegal corporate activities, are sanctioned much more leniently than those, such as burglary, that are considered lower-class activities.

As you may recall from Chapter 1, the philosophical and economic analysis of Karl Marx forms the historical roots of the conflict perspective of criminology. Marx identified the economic structures in society that controlled all human relations. Theorists who use Marxian analysis reject the notion that law is designed to maintain a tranquil and fair society and that criminals are malevolent people who wish to trample the rights of others. Conflict theorists consider such acts as racism, sexism, imperialism, unsafe working conditions, inadequate child care, substandard housing, pollution of the environment, and war making as a tool of foreign policy as "true crimes"; the crimes of the helpless—burglary, robbery, and assault—are more expressions of rage over unjust conditions than actual crimes.[2] By focusing on the state's role in producing crime, Marxist thought serves as the basis for all conflict theory.

This chapter will review criminological theories that allege that criminal behavior is a function of conflict, a reaction to the unfair distribution of wealth and power in society. The social conflict perspective has several independent branches. One, generally referred to as **conflict theory,** assumes that crime is caused by the intergroup conflict and rivalry that exists in every society. A second branch focuses more directly on the crime-producing traits of capitalist society; the various schools of thought in this area of scholarship include *critical, radical, and Marxist* criminology.[3] Other sections are devoted to *feminist, new realist, peacemaking,* and *deconstructionist* thought. Hereafter, the terms *radical* or *Marxist criminology* will be used interchangeably, and where appropriate, distinctions will be made between the various schools of thought they contain.

≡ Marxist Thought

Karl Marx lived in an era of unrestrained capitalist expansion.[4] The tools of the Industrial Revolution had become regular features of society by 1850. Mechanized factories, the use of coal to drive steam engines, and modern transportation all inspired economic development. Production had shifted from cottage industries to large factories. Industrialists could hire workers on their own terms, and conditions in their factories were atrocious. Trade unions that promised workers salvation from these atrocities were ruthlessly suppressed by owners and government agents.

Marx had found his early career as a journalist interrupted by government suppression of the newspaper where he worked because of its liberal editorial policy. He then moved to Paris, where he met Friedrich Engels (1820–1895), who would become his friend and economic patron. By 1847, Marx and Engels had joined with a group of primarily German socialist revolutionaries known as the Communist League.

Productive Forces and Productive Relations

In 1848, Marx issued his famous manifesto—a statement of his ideas. Marx focused his attention on the economic conditions of the capitalist system. He believed its development had turned workers into a dehumanized mass who lived an existence that was at the mercy of their capitalist employers. Young children were sent to work in mines and factories from dawn to dusk. People were being beaten down by a system that demanded obedience and cooperation and offered little in return. These oppressive conditions led Marx to conclude that the character of every civilization is determined by its mode of production—the way its people develop and produce material goods (materialism).

Production has two components: (1) productive forces, which include such things as technology, energy sources, and material resources; and (2) productive relations, which are the relationships that exist among the people producing goods and services. The most important relationship in industrial culture is between the owners of the means of production, the capitalist bourgeoisie, and the people who do the actual labor, the proletariat. Throughout history, society has been organized this way—master-slave, lord-serf, and now capitalist-proletarian. According to Marx and Engels, capitalist society is subject to the development of a rigid class structure. At the top is the capitalist bourgeoisie. Next come the working proletariat who actually produce goods and services. At the bottom of society are the fringe members who produce nothing and live, parasitically, off the work of others—the *lumpen proletariat.*

In Marxist theory, the term *class* does not refer to an attribute or characteristic of a person or a group; rather, it denotes position in relation to others. Thus, it is not necessary to have a particular amount of wealth or prestige to be a member of the capitalist class; it is more

These boys were used as laborers in a West Virginia coal mine in 1908. Marx believed such exploitation of the working classes would one day provoke revolution and the downfall of the capitalist system.

important to have the power to exploit others economically, legally, and socially. The political and economic philosophy of the dominant class influences all aspects of life. Consciously or unconsciously, artists, writers, and teachers bend their work to the whims of the capitalist system. Thus, the economic system controls all facets of human life; and consequently, people's lives revolve around the means of production. As Marx said:

> In all forms of society, there is one specific kind of production which predominates over the rest, whose relations thus assign rank and influence to the others. It is a general illumination which bathes all the other colours and modifies their particularity. It is a particular ether which determines the specific gravity of every being which has materialized within it.[5]

Marx believed that societies and their structures were not stable but could change through slow evolu-

tion or sudden violence. Historically, such change occurs because of contradictions present in a society. These contradictions are antagonism or conflicts between elements in the existing social arrangement that in the long run are incompatible with one another. If these social conflicts are not resolved, they tend to destabilize society, leading to social change.

Surplus Value

How could social change occur in capitalist society? Marx held that the laboring class produces goods that exceed wages in value (the theory of *surplus value*). The excess value goes into the hands of the capitalists as profit; they then use most of it to acquire an ever-expanding capitalist base that relies on advanced technology for efficiency. Since capitalists are in constant competition with each other, they must find ways of producing goods more efficiently and cheaply. One way is to pay workers the lowest possible wages or to replace them with labor-saving machinery (see figure 9.2). Soon the supply of efficiently made goods outstrips the ability of the laboring classes to purchase them, a condition that precipitates an economic crisis. During this period, weaker enterprises go under and are consequently incorporated into ever-expanding, monopolistic mega-corporations strong enough to further exploit the workers. Marx believed that in the ebb and flow of the business cycle, the capitalist system contained the seeds of its own destruction and that from its ashes would grow a socialist state in which the workers themselves would own the means of production.

In his analysis, Marx used the dialectic method, based on the analysis developed by the philosopher Georg Hegel (1770–1831). Hegel argued that for every idea, or thesis, there exists an opposing argument, or antithesis. Since neither position can ever be truly accepted, the result is a merger of the two ideas, a synthesis. Marx adapted this analytic method for his study of class struggle. History, argued Marx, is replete with examples of two opposing forces whose conflict promotes social change. When conditions are bad enough, the oppressed will rise up to fight the owners and eventually replace them. Thus, in the end, the capitalist system will destroy itself.

Marx on Crime

Marx did not write a great deal on the subject of crime, but he mentioned it in a variety of passages scattered throughout his writing. He viewed crime as the product

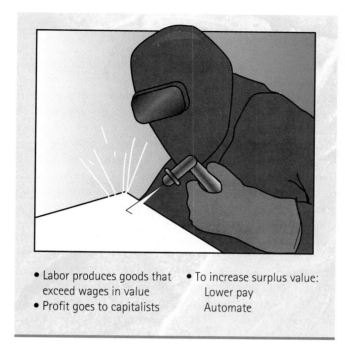

- Labor produces goods that exceed wages in value
- Profit goes to capitalists
- To increase surplus value: Lower pay Automate

FIGURE 9.2 **Surplus Value**

of law enforcement policies akin to a labeling process theory.[6] He also saw a connection between criminality and the inequities found in the capitalist system. He states:

> there must be something rotten in the very core of a social system which increases in wealth without diminishing its misery, and increases in crime even more rapidly than in numbers.[7]

His collaborator, Friedrich Engels, however, did spend some time on the subject in his work *The Condition of the Working Class in England in 1844*.[8] Engels portrayed crime as a function of social demoralization—a collapse of people's humanity reflecting a decline in society. Workers, demoralized by capitalist society, are caught up in a process that leads to crime and violence. Workers were social outcasts, ignored by the structure of capitalist society and treated as brutes.[9] Left to their own devices, working people committed crime because their choice was a slow death of starvation or a speedy one at the hands of the law. The brutality of the capitalist system turns workers into animal-like creatures without a will of their own.

Developing a Conflict Theory of Crime

The writings of Karl Marx and Friedrich Engels greatly influenced the development of social conflict thinking. While Marx himself did not write much on the topic of crime, his views on the relationship between the economic structure and social behavior deeply influenced other thinkers. Conflict theory was first applied to criminology by three distinguished scholars, Willem Bonger, Ralf Dahrendorf, and George Vold. In some instances, their works share the Marxist view that industrial society is wracked by conflict between the proletariat and the bourgeoisie; in other instances, their writings diverge from Marxist dogma. The writing of each of these pioneers is briefly discussed below.

The Contribution of Willem Bonger

Willem Bonger was born in 1876 in Holland and committed suicide in 1940, rather than submit to Nazi rule. He is famous for his Marxist socialist concepts of crime causation, which were first published in 1916.[10]

Bonger believed that crime is of social and not biological origin and that, with the exception of a few special cases, crime lies within the boundaries of normal human behavior. The response to crime is punishment—the application of penalties considered more severe than spontaneous moral condemnation. It is administered by those in political control—that is, by the state. No act is naturally immoral or criminal. Crimes are antisocial acts that reflect current morality. Since the social structure is changing continually, ideas of what is moral and what is not change continually. The tension between rapidly changing morality, which is common in modern society, and a comparatively static, predominantly bourgeois criminal law can become very great.

Bonger believed that society is divided into have and have-not groups, not on the basis of people's innate ability but because of the system of production that is in force. In every society that is divided into a ruling class and an inferior class, penal law serves the will of the former. Even though criminal laws may appear to protect members of both classes, hardly any act is punished that does not injure the interests of the dominant class. Crimes then are considered to be antisocial acts because they are harmful to those who have the power at their command to control society.

Bonger argued that attempts to control law violations through force are a sign of a weak society. The capitalist system, characterized by extreme competition, is held together by force rather than consensus. The social order is maintained for the benefit of the capitalists at the expense of the population as a whole. Bonger argued that all people desire wealth and happiness. Unfortunately, in a capitalist society, people can enjoy luxuries and advantages only if they possess large amounts of capital. People are encouraged by capitalist society to be egotistical, caring only for their own lives and pleasures and ignoring the plight of the disadvantaged. As a consequence of the present environment, Bonger claimed, people have become very egotistic and more capable of crime than if the system had developed under a socialist philosophy.

Though the capitalist system makes both the proletariat and the bourgeoisie crime-prone, only the former are likely to become officially recognized criminals. The key to this problem is that the legal system discriminates against the poor by legalizing the egoistic actions of the wealthy. Upper-class individuals, the bourgeoisie, will commit crime if (a) they have an opportunity to gain an illegal advantage and (b) their lack of moral sense enables them to violate social rules. It is the drive toward success at any price that pushes wealthier individuals toward criminality. Recognized, official crimes are a function of poverty. The relationship can be direct, as when a person steals to survive, or indirect, as when poverty kills the social sentiments in each person and between people.

It is not the absolute amount of wealth that affects crime but its distribution. If wealth is distributed unequally through the social structure and people are taught to equate economic advantage with superiority, then those who are poor and therefore inferior will be crime-prone. The economic system will intensify any personal disadvantage people have—for example, psychological problems—and increase their propensity to commit crime.

Bonger concluded that almost all crime will disappear if society progresses from competitive capitalism, to monopoly capitalism, to having the means of production held in common, to the ultimate state of society—the redistribution of property according to the maxim "each according to his needs." If this stage of society cannot be reached, a residue of crime will always remain. If socialism can be achieved, then remaining crimes will be of the irrational psychopathic type caused by individual mental problems. Bonger's writing continues to be one of the most often-cited sources of Marxist thought.

The Contribution of Ralf Dahrendorf

In formulating their views, today's conflict theorists also rely heavily on the writings of pioneering social thinker **Ralf Dahrendorf.**[11] Dahrendorf believed that modern society is organized into what he called imperatively coordinated associations. These associations comprise two groups: those who possess authority and use it for social domination and those who lack authority and are dominated. Since the domination of one segment of society—for example, industry—does not mean dominating another—such as government, society is a plurality of competing interest groups.

In his classic work, *Class and Class Conflict in Industrial Society*, Dahrendorf attempted to show how society has changed since Marx formulated his concepts of class, state, and conflict. Dahrendorf argued that Marx did not foresee the changes that have occurred in the laboring classes. "The working class of today," Dahrendorf stated, "far from being a homogeneous group of equally unskilled and impoverished people, is in fact a stratum differentiated by numerous subtle and not so subtle distinctions."[12] Workers are divided into the unskilled, semiskilled, and skilled; the interests of one group may not match the needs of the others: Marx's concept of a cohesive proletarian class has proved inaccurate. Consequently, Dahrendorf embraced a non-Marxist conflict orientation. Dahrendorf proposed a unified conflict theory of human behavior, which can be summarized in the following statements:

- Every society is at every point subject to processes of change; social change is everywhere.

- Every society displays at every point dissent and conflict; social conflict is everywhere.

- Every element in a society renders a contribution to its disintegration and change.

- Every society is based on the coercion of some of its members by others.

Dahrendorf did not speak directly to the issue of crime, but his model of conflict serves as a pillar of modern conflict criminology.

The Contribution of George Vold

Though Dahrendorf contributed its theoretical underpinnings, conflict theory was actually adapted to criminology by **George Vold.**[13] Vold argued that crime can also be explained by social conflict. Laws are created by politically oriented groups who seek the assistance of the government to help them defend their rights and protect their interests. If a group can marshal enough support, a law will be created to hamper and curb the interests of some opposition group. As Vold said, "The whole political process of law making, law breaking and law enforcement becomes a direct reflection of deep-seated and fundamental conflicts between interest groups and their more general struggles for the control of the police power of the state." Every stage of the process—from the passage of the law, to the prosecution of the case, to the relationships between inmate and guard, parole agent and parolee—is marked by conflict.

Vold found that criminal acts are a consequence of direct contact between forces struggling to control society. Though their criminal content may mask their political meaning, closer examination of even the most basic violent acts often reveals political undertones.

Vold's model cannot be used to explain all types of crime. It is limited to situations in which rival group loyalties collide. It cannot explain impulsive, irrational acts unrelated to any group's interest. Despite this limitation, Vold found that a great deal of criminal activity results from intergroup clashes.

≡ Conflict Theory

Conflict theory came into criminological prominence during the 1960s. Vold and Dahrendorf had published their influential works in the late 1950s. At the same time, self-report studies were yielding data suggesting that crime and delinquency were much more evenly distributed through the social structure than had been indicated by the official statistics.[14] If this were true, then middle-class participation in crime was going unrecorded, while the lower class was the subject of discriminatory law enforcement practices by the criminal justice system.

Criminologists began to view the justice system as a mechanism to control the lower class and maintain the status quo, rather than as the means of dispensing fair and evenhanded justice.[15] The publication of important labeling perspective works, such as Lemert's *Social Pathology* and Becker's *Outsiders,* also contributed to the development of the conflict model.[16] Labeling theorists rejected the notion that crime is morally wrong and called for the analysis of the interaction among crime, criminal, victim, and social control agencies. Some crim-

inologists charged that labeling theory did not go far enough in analyzing the important relationships in society, charging that labeling theorists were content with studying "nuts, sluts and perverts."[17]

Because they felt the labeling perspective was apolitical, a group of criminologists began to produce scholarship and research directed at (1) identifying "real" crimes in U.S. society, such as profiteering, sexism, and racism; (2) evaluating how the criminal law is used as a mechanism of social control; and (3) turning the attention of citizens to the inequities in U.S. society.[18] One of these sociologists, David Greenberg, comments on the scholarship that was produced:

> The theme that dominated much of the work in this area was the contention that criminal legislation was determined not by moral consensus or the common interests of the entire society, but by relative power of groups determined to use the criminal law to advance their own special interests or to impose their moral preferences on others.[19]

Adding impetus to this movement was the general and widespread social and political upheaval of the late 1960s and early '70s. These forces included anti-Vietnam War demonstrations, counterculture movements, and various forms of political protest. Conflict theory flourished within this framework, since it provided a systematic basis for challenging the legitimacy of the government's creation and application of law. The crackdown on political dissidents by agents of the federal government, the prosecution of draft resisters, and the like all seemed designed to maintain control in the hands of political power brokers.

Conflict Criminology

In the early 1970s, conflict theory began to have a significant influence on criminological study. Several influential scholars, inspired by the writings of Dahrendorf and Vold, abandoned the criminological mainstream and adapted a conflict orientation. William Chambliss and Robert Seidman wrote the well-respected treatise *Law, Order and Power,* which documented how the justice system operates to protect the rich and powerful. After closely observing its operations, Chambliss and Seidman drew this conclusion:

> In America it is frequently argued that to have "freedom" is to have a system which allows one group to make a profit over another. To maintain the existing legal system requires a choice. That choice is between maintaining a legal system that serves to support the existing economic

system with its power structure and developing an equitable legal system accompanied by the loss of "personal freedom." But the old question comes back to plague us: Freedom for whom? Is the black man who provides such a ready source of cases for the welfare workers, the mental hospitals, and the prisons "free"? Are the slum dwellers who are arrested night after night for "loitering," "drunkenness," or being "suspicious" free? The freedom protected by the system of law is the freedom of those who can afford it. The law serves their interests, but they are not "society"; they are one element of society. They may in some complex societies even be a majority (though this is very rare), but the myth that the law serves the interests of "society" misrepresents the facts.[20]

We can observe in Chambliss and Seidman's writing some of the common objectives of conflict criminology: to describe how the control of the political and economic system affects the administration of criminal justice; to show how the definitions of crime favor those who control the justice system; to analyze the role of conflict in contemporary society. Their scholarship also reflects another major objective of conflict theory: to show how justice in U.S. society is skewed so that those who deserve to be punished the most (wealthy white-collar criminals whose crimes cost society millions of dollars) are actually punished the least, while those whose crimes are relatively minor and committed out of economic necessity (petty, underclass thieves) receive the stricter sanctions.[21]

Power Relations

Another motive of conflict theory is to describe the criminogenic influence of social and economic power—the ability of persons and groups to determine and control the behavior of others. The unequal distribution of power produces conflict; conflict is rooted in the competition for power. Power is the means by which people shape public opinion to meet their personal interests. According to the conflict view, crime is defined by those in power; laws are culturally relative and not bound by any absolute standard of right and wrong.[22] The ability of the powerful to control people is exemplified by the relationship between the justice system and African-Americans.

In an insightful paper, criminologist Daniel Georges-Abeyie has documented the subtle and not-so-subtle ways the justice system victimizes blacks.[23] Poor ghetto youths are driven to commit crimes that get them processed by the system "early and often." Discretionary decisions by law enforcement officers brand them felons and not misdemeanants; they are shunted into the criminal courts and not diversion programs. Busy public defenders "too often short shift their clients into plea bargains that assure early criminal records." Health care workers and teachers are quick to report suspected violent acts to the police; this results in frequent and early arrests of minority adults and youths. Police departments routinely employ "petit-apartheid" policies of searching, questioning, and detaining all black males in an area if a violent criminal has been described as looking or sounding black. By creating the image of pervasive black criminality and coupling it with unfair treatment, those in power further alienated poor blacks from the mainstream, perpetuating a class- and race-divided society.

The Social Reality of Crime

Richard Quinney was one of the most influential conflict theorists. He integrated his beliefs about power, society,

Political conflict may often result in violence. Here, survivors of the World Trade Center bombing on February 26, 1993, are aided by rescuers. The bomb was set as an act of political sabotage against the United States.

and criminality into a theory he referred to as the **social reality of crime.** The theory's six propositions are contained in Table 9.1.[24] According to Quinney, criminal definitions (law) represent the interests of those who hold power in society. Where there is conflict between social groups—for example, the wealthy and the poor—those who hold power will create laws to benefit themselves and hold rivals in check. So the rather harsh punishments for property crime in the United States are designed to help those who already have wealth keep it in their possession; in contrast, the lenient sanctions attached to corporate crimes are designed to give the already powerful a free hand at economic exploitation. Quinney wrote that the formulation of criminal definitions is based on such factors as (1) changing social conditions; (2) emerging interests; (3) increasing demands that political, economic, and religious interests be protected; and (4) changing conceptions of public interest. In the sixth statement on the social reality of crime, Quinney pulls together the ideas he developed in the preceding five: concepts of crime are controlled by the powerful, and the criminal justice

system works to secure the needs of the powerful. When people develop behavior patterns that conflict with these needs, the agents of the rich—the justice system—define them as criminals. Because of their reliance on power relations, criminal definitions are a constantly changing set of concepts that mirror the political organization of society. Law is not an abstract body of rules that represents an absolute moral code. Law is an integral part of society, a force that represents a way of life and a method of doing things. Crime is a function of power relations and an inevitable result of social conflict. Criminals are not simply social misfits but people who have come up short in the struggle for success and are seeking alternative means of achieving wealth, status, or even survival.[25] Consequently, law violations can be viewed as political or even quasi-revolutionary acts.[26]

Research on Conflict Theory

Research efforts designed to test conflict theory seem quite different from those evaluating consensus models. Similar methodologies are often used, but conflict-centered research places less emphasis on testing hypotheses of a particular theory and instead attempts to show that conflict principles hold up under empirical scrutiny. Topics of interest include such issues as comparing the crime rates of members of powerless groups with those of members of the elite classes. Conflict researchers examine the operation of the justice system to uncover bias and discrimination. They also attempt to chart the historical development of criminal law and to identify laws created with the intent of preserving the power of the elite classes at the expense of the poor. Conflict theorists maintain that social inequality creates the need for people to commit some crimes, such as burglary and larceny, as a means of social and economic survival, while others, such as assault, homicide, and drug use, are a means of expressing rage, frustration, and anger. Conflict theorists point to data showing that crime rates vary according to indicators of poverty and need. For example, David McDowall compared homicide rates in Detroit, Baltimore, Cleveland, and Memphis with infant mortality rates over a 50-year period (since the latter variable is an efficient measure of poverty) and found that they were significantly interrelated.[27] Other data collected by ecologists show that crime is strongly related to measures of social inequality, such as income level, deteriorated living conditions, and relative economic deprivation.[28]

Another area of conflict-oriented research involves the operations of the criminal justice system: Does it operate as an instrument of class oppression or as a fair

TABLE 9.1 The Social Reality of Crime

1. *Definition of Crime:* Crime is a definition of human conduct that is created by authorized agents in a politically organized society.
2. *Formulation of Criminal Definition:* Criminal definitions describe behaviors that conflict with the interests of the segments of society that have the power to shape public policy.
3. *Application of Criminal Definitions:* Criminal definitions are applied by the segments of society that have the power to shape the enforcement and administration of criminal law.
4. *Development of Behavior Patterns in Relation to Criminal Definitions:* Behavior patterns are structured in segmentally organized society in relation to criminal definitions, and within this context, persons engage in actions that have relative probabilities of being defined as criminal.
5. *Construction of Criminal Conceptions:* Conceptions of crime are constructed and diffused in the segments of society by various means of communication.
6. *The Social Reality of Crime:* The social reality of crime is constructed by the formulation and applications of criminal definitions, the development of behavior patterns to criminal definitions, and the construction of criminal conceptions.

SOURCE: Richard Quinney, *The Social Reality of Crime* (Boston: Little, Brown, 1970), pp. 15–23.

and even-handed social control agency? Some conflict researchers have found evidence of class bias. For example, criminologists David Jacobs and David Britt found that state jurisdictions with significant levels of economic disparity were also the most likely to have the largest number of police shooting fatalities. Their data suggests that police act more forcefully in areas where class conflicts create the perception that extreme forms of social control are needed to maintain order.[29] Similarly, Alan Lizotte examined 816 criminal cases processed by the Chicago criminal courts during a one-year period and found that members of powerless, disenfranchised groups are the most likely to receive prejudicial sentences in criminal courts.[30] Other research efforts have shown that both white and black offenders are more likely to receive stricter sentences in criminal courts if their personal characteristics (single, young, urban, male) give them the appearance of being a member of the **"dangerous classes."**[31] Conflict theorists also point to studies that show that the criminal justice system is quick to take action when the victim of crime is wealthy, white, and male but disinterested when the victim is poor, black, and female as evidence of the how power positions affect justice.[32] It is not surprising then that Thomas Arvanites's analysis of national population trends and imprisonment rates shows that as the percentage of minority-group members increases, the imprisonment rate does likewise.[33] This outcome, suggests Arvanites, may be a function of society becoming "less tolerant of nonwhite populations and/or feeling more threatened by them." Data showing racial discrimination by the justice systems supports conflict theory.

Analysis of Conflict Theory

Conflict theorists attempt to identify the power relations in society and draw attention to their role in promoting criminal behavior. The aim is to describe how class differentials produce an ecology of human behavior that favors the wealthy and powerful over the poor and weak. To believe their view, we must reject the consensus view of crime, which states that law represents the values of the majority, that legal codes are designed to create a just society, and that by breaking the law, criminals are predators who violate the rights of others. To a conflict theorist, the criminal law is a weapon employed by the affluent to maintain their dominance in the class struggle. This view is not without its critics. Some criminologists consider the conflict view "naive," suggesting instead that crime is a matter of rational choice made by offenders motivated more by greed and selfishness than poverty and hopelessness.[34]

Critics also point to data indicating only a weak relationship between indicators of economic factors and crime rates; such data indicates that crime is less likely to be a function of poverty and class conflict than a product of personal needs, socialization, or some other related factor.[35] For example, while Arvanites's research, cited above, found that race influenced imprisonment, there was little clear-cut evidence that economic factors, such as unemployment rates or poverty levels, influenced crime rates.[36]

Similarly, studies of the criminal justice process, including police discretion, criminal court sentencing, and correctional policy, have not all found indicators of class or race bias, an outcome predicted by conflict theory.[37] Theodore Chiricos and Gordon Waldo examined the prison sentences of 10,488 inmates in three southeastern states and concluded that socioeconomic status is unrelated to the length of prison terms assigned by the courts.[38] Stephen Klein, Joan Petersilia, and Susan Turner evaluated sentencing decisions in California and found little evidence of race bias; African-Americans were neither more likely to be sent to prison than white offenders nor to receive longer prison terms.[39] Evidence that the justice system is not class- and race-biased refutes conflict theory and supports consensus, traditional criminology.

There is also cross-cultural research indicating that crime rates are not reduced when a free-market system is replaced by a less-competitive economic model. One analysis of crime in the African country of Tanzania found that when the free enterprise system was replaced by a socialist system, the crime rate actually increased. New crimes, such as theft by public servants and corruption, appear to increase in response to government policies establishing socialism.[40]

Despite these critiques, conflict theory has had an important niche in the criminological literature. However, more radical versions of the general conflict model have become predominant, and attention is now turned to these more critical versions of social conflict theory.

Marxist Criminology

Above all, Marxism is a critique of capitalism.[41]

Marxist criminologists view crime as a function of the capitalist mode of production—capitalism produces haves and have-nots, each engaging in a particular branch of criminality.[42] In a capitalist society, those in political power also control the definition of crime and the emphasis of the criminal justice system.[43] Consequently, the only crimes available to the poor, or proletariat, are the severely sanctioned "street crimes": rape, murder, theft, and mugging. Members of the middle class, or petit bourgeoisie, cheat on their taxes and engage in petty corporate crime (employee theft), acts that generate social disapproval but are rarely punished severely. The wealthy bourgeoisie are involved in acts that should be described as crimes but are not—racism, sexism, and profiteering. Though there are regulatory laws to control business activities, these are rarely enforced, and violations are lightly punished. Laws regulating corporate crime are really window dressing designed to impress the working class with how fair the justice system really is. In reality, the justice system is the equivalent of an army that defends the owners of property in their ongoing struggle against the workers.[44]

The Development of Radical Criminology

The development of radical theory can be traced to the National Deviancy Conference (NDC), formed in 1968 by a group of British sociologists. With about 300 members, this organization sponsored several national symposiums and dialogues. Members came from all walks of life, but at its core was a group of academics who were critical of the positivist criminology being taught in English and U.S. universities. More specifically, they rejected the conservative stance of criminologists and their close financial relationship with government funding agencies. Originally, the NDC was not a Marxist-oriented group but rather investigated the concept of deviance from a labeling perspective. It called attention to ways in which social control might actually be a cause of deviance rather than a response to antisocial behavior. Many conference members became concerned about the political nature of social control. A schism developed within the NDC, with one group clinging to the now-conservative interactionist/labeling perspective, while the second embraced Marxist thought. Then, in 1973, radical theory was given a powerful academic boost when British scholars Ian Taylor, Paul Walton, and Jock Young published *The New Criminology*.[45] This brilliant work was a thorough and well-constructed critique of existing concepts in criminology and a call for development of new criminological methods. *The New Criminology* became the standard resource for scholars critical of both the field of criminology and the existing legal process.

While these events were transpiring in Britain, a small group of scholars in the United States began to follow a new radical approach to criminology. The locus of the radical school was the criminology program at the University of California at Berkeley. The most noted Marxist scholars at that institution were Anthony Platt, Paul Takagi, Herman Schwendinger, and Julia Schwendinger. Marxist scholars at other U.S. academic institutions included Richard Quinney (originally a conflict theorist), William Chambliss, Steven Spitzer, and Barry Krisberg. The U.S. radicals were influenced by the widespread social ferment during the late 1960s and early 1970s. The war in Vietnam, prison struggles, and the civil rights and feminist movements produced a climate in which criticism of the ruling class seemed a natural by-product. Mainstream, positivist criminology was criticized as being overtly conservative, progovernment, and antihuman. Critical criminologists scoffed when their fellow scholars used statistical analysis of computerized data to describe criminal and delinquent behavior. As Barry Krisberg has written:

> Many of our scientific heroes of the past, upon rereading, turned out to be racists or, more generally, apologists for social injustice. In response to the widespread protests on campuses and throughout society, many of the contemporary giants of social science emerged as defenders of the status quo and vocally dismissed the claims of the oppressed for social justice.[46]

Many of the new Marxist criminologists had enjoyed distinguished careers as positivist criminologists. Some, such as Chambliss and Quinney, were moved by career interests from positivism to social conflict theory to a radical-Marxist approach to crime. Marxists did not meet with widespread approval at major universities. Rumors of purges were common during the 1970s, and the criminology school at Berkeley was eventually closed for what many believe were political reasons. Even today, conflict exists between critical thinkers and mainstream academics. Prestigious Harvard Law School and other law centers have been the scenes of conflict and charges of purges and tenure denials because some professors held critical views of law and society. While some isolated radicals are tolerated if "they could not cause much trouble," the majority have been heavily victimized by what David Friedrichs refers to as "academic McCarthyism."[47]

In the following years, new branches of a radical criminology were developing in the United States and abroad. In the early 1980s, the left realism school was started by scholars affiliated with the Middlesex Polytechnic and the University of Edinburgh in Great Britain. In the United States, scholars influenced in part by the pioneering work of Dennis Sullivan and Larry Tifft, created the peacemaking movement.[48] And at the same time, feminist scholars began to apply critical analysis to the relationship between gender, power, and criminality. These movements have coalesced into a rich and complex criminological tradition.

Fundamentals of Marxist Criminology

As a general rule, Marxist criminologists ignore formal theory construction with its heavy emphasis on empirical testing. They scoff at the objective "value-free" stance of mainstream criminologists and instead argue that there should be a political, ideological basis for criminological scholarship.[49] Crime and criminal justice must be viewed in a historical, social, and economic context. Radicals use the conflict definition of crime. Crime is a political concept designed to protect the power and position of the upper classes at the expense of the poor. As you may recall, some but not all radicals would include in a list of "real" crimes such acts as violations of human rights due to racism, sexism, and imperialism and other violations of human dignity and physical needs and necessities. Part of the radical agenda then, argues criminologist Robert Bohm, is to make the public aware that these behaviors "are crimes just as much as burglary and robbery."[50]

The nature of a society controls the direction of its criminality; criminals are not social misfits but rather a product of the society and its economic system in which they reside. "Capitalism," claims Bohm, "as a mode of production, has always produced a relatively high level of crime and violence."[51] According to Michael Lynch and W. Byron Groves, three implications follow from this view:

1. Each society will produce its own types and amounts of crime;
2. Each society will have its own distinctive ways of dealing with criminal behavior; and
3. Each society gets the amount and type of crime that it deserves.[52]

This analysis tells us that criminals are not a group of outsiders who can be controlled by an increased law enforcement presence. Criminality is a function of the social and economic organization of society. To control crime and reduce criminality is to end the social conditions that promote crime.

Economic Structure and Surplus Value

While no single view or theory defines Marxist criminology today, its general theme is the relationship between crime and the ownership and control of private property in a capitalist society.[53] That ownership and control, according to sociologist Gregg Barak, is the principal basis of power in U.S. society.[54] Social conflict is fundamentally related to the historical and social distribution of productive private property. Destructive social conflicts inherent within the capitalist system cannot be resolved unless that system is destroyed or ended.

One important aspect of the capitalist economic system is the effect of **surplus value.** As you may recall, Marx used this term to refer to the value resulting from production when the cost of labor is less than the cost of the goods it produces. The excess value or profit can either be reinvested or used to enrich the owners. To increase the rate of surplus value, workers can be made to work harder for less pay, be made more efficient, or be replaced by "labor-saving" machines or technology. Therefore, economic growth does not have the same benefits for all elements of the population and in the long run may produce the same effect as a depression or recession!

According to Michael Lynch and his associates, as the rate of surplus value increases, more people are displaced from productive relationships and the size of the "marginal" population swells. As corporations "downsize" to increase profits, high-paying labor and managerial jobs are lost to computer-driven machinery. Displaced workers are forced into service jobs at minimum wage. Many become temporary employees without benefits or a secure position.

As more people are thrust outside the economic mainstream (*marginalization*), a larger portion of the population is forced to live in areas (structural locations) conducive to crime. Once people are marginalized, commitment to the system declines, producing another criminogenic force: a weakened bond to society.[55]

The effect of surplus value is not unique to the United States. Crime and violence has escalated in former socialist republics that have converted to free-market economies. As you may recall, some scholars have criticized conflict theory with the argument that crime rates *increase* as countries change from capitalism to socialism. Yet there is evidence that an opposite change, from socialism to capitalism, drives crime rates even higher. Both China and the former Soviet Union have experienced an upsurge in gang activity as they embrace market economies; Russia may now have a murder rate higher than that of the United States.[56]

While some form of these themes can be found throughout Marxist writing, there are actually a number of schools of thought within the radical literature. Some of these different approaches are discussed below in some detail.

Instrumental Marxism

One group of Marxists are referred to as **instrumentalists.** They view the criminal law and criminal justice system solely as an instrument for controlling the poor, have-not members of society; the state is the "tool" of the capitalists.

According to the instrumental view, capitalist justice serves the powerful and rich and enables them to impose their morality and standards of behavior on the entire society. Under capitalism, economic power enables its holders to extend their self-serving definition of illegal or criminal behavior to encompass those who might threaten the status quo or interfere with their quest for ever-increasing profits.[57] For example, David Jacobs's research shows how the concentration of monetary assets in the nation's largest firms is translated into the political power needed to control the tax laws and limit the firms' tax liabilities.[58]

The poor, according to this branch of Marxist theory, may or may not commit more crimes than the rich, but they certainly are arrested and punished more often. Under the capitalist system, the poor are driven to crime because a natural frustration exists in a society in which affluence is well publicized but unattainable. When class conflict becomes unbearable, frustration can spill out in riots, such as the one that occurred in Los Angeles on April 29, 1992, and was described as a "class rebellion of the under-privileged against the privileged."[59]

Because of class conflict, a deep-rooted hostility is generated among members of the lower class toward a social order they are not allowed to shape or participate in.[60] Instrumental Marxists consider it essential to **demystify** law and justice, that is, to unmask its true purpose. They charge that conventional criminology is devoted to identifying the social conditions that cause crime. Those criminological theories that focus upon family structure, intelligence, peer relations, and school performance serve to keep the lower classes servile by showing why they are more criminal, less intelligent, and more prone to school failure and family problems than the middle class. Demystification involves the identification of the destructive intent of capitalist-inspired and -funded criminology. The goal of criminology should be to explicate the rule of law in capitalist society and show how it works to preserve ruling-class power. The essence of instrumental Marxist theory can be summarized in the following statements:

- U.S. society is based on an advanced capitalist economy.

- The state is organized to serve the interests of the dominant economic class, the capitalist ruling class.

- Criminal law is an instrument of the state and ruling class to maintain and perpetuate the existing social and economic order.

- Crime control in capitalist society is accomplished through a variety of institutions and agencies established and administered by a governmental elite, representing ruling-class interests for the purpose of establishing domestic order.

- The contradictions of advanced capitalism—the disjunction between existence and essence—require that the subordinate classes remain oppressed by whatever means necessary, especially through the coercion and violence of the legal system.

- Only with the collapse of capitalist society and the creation of a new society, based on socialist principles, will there be a solution to the crime problem.[61]

Concepts of Instrumental Marxism.   The writings of a number of other influential instrumental Marxist theorists have helped shape this field of inquiry. According to Herman Schwendinger and Julia Siegel Schwendinger, legal relations in the United States secure an economic infrastructure that centers around a capitalist mode of production. The legal system is designed to guard the position of the owners (bourgeoisie) at the expense of the workers (proletariat). Legal relations maintain the family and school structure so as to secure the labor force. Even common-law crimes, such as murder and rape, are implemented to protect capitalism. According to the Schwendingers, the basic laws of the land (such as constitutional laws) are based on the conditions that reproduce the class system as a whole. Laws are aimed at securing the domination of the capitalist system. Though the system may at times secure the interests of the working class, for example, when laws are created that protect collective bargaining, due to the inherent antagonisms built into the capitalist system, all laws generally contradict their stated purpose of producing justice. Legal relations maintain patterns of individualism and selfishness and, in so doing, perpetuate a class system characterized by anarchy, oppression, and crime.[62]

Barry Krisberg has linked crime to the differentials in privilege that exist in capitalist society. According to Krisberg, crime is a function of **privilege.** Crimes are created by the powerful to further their domination. They deflect attention from the violence and social injustice the rich inflict upon the masses to keep them subordinate and oppressed. Krisberg is concerned with how privilege influences criminality. He defines privilege as the possession of that which is valued by a particular social group in a given historical period. Privilege includes such rights as life, liberty, and happiness; such traits as intelligence, sensitivity, and humanity; and such material goods as monetary wealth, luxuries, land, and the like. The privilege system is also concerned with the distribution and preservation of privilege. Krisberg argues that force—the effective use of violence and coercion—is the major factor in determining which social group ascends to the position of defining and holding privilege.[63]

Other Marxist scholars have called for a review of the role of the professional criminologist. For example, Anthony Platt has charged that criminologists have helped support state repression with their focus on poor and minority-group criminals:

> We are just beginning to realize that criminology has serviced domestic repression in the same way that economics, political science, and anthropology have greased the wheels and even manufactured some of the important parts of modern imperialism. Given the ways in which this system has been used to repress and maintain the powerlessness of poor people, people of color, and young people, it is not too farfetched to characterize many criminologists as domestic war criminals.[64]

Platt goes on to suggest that criminology must redefine its goals and definitions:

> In the past, we have been constrained by a legal definition of crime which restricts us to studying and ultimately helping to control only legally defined "criminals." We need a more humanistic definition of crime, one which reflects the reality of a legal system based on power and privilege. To accept the legal definition of crime is to accept the fiction of neutral law. A human rights definition of crime frees us to examine imperialism, racism, sexism, capitalism, exploitation, and other political or economic systems which contribute to human misery and deprive people of their potentialities.[65]

Michael Lynch observes that instrumental Marxist theory may be limited because it is based on assumptions that are incorrect: the law and justice always operate in the interests of the ruling class; members of the ruling class "conspire" to control society; what benefits one member of the ruling class benefits them all. In reality, charges Lynch, some laws benefit the lower classes, and capitalists compete with one another rather than conspire.[66] Because of these deficiencies, some radicals have turned from instrumental theory and embraced structural Marxism.

Structural Marxism

Structural Marxists disagree with the view that the relationship between law and capitalism is unidimensional, always working for the rich and against the poor.[67] Law is not the exclusive domain of the rich, but it is used to maintain the long-term interests of the capitalist system and control members of any class who pose a threat to its existence. If law and justice were purely instruments of the capitalist class, why would laws controlling corporate crimes, such as price-fixing, false advertising, and illegal restraint of trade, have been created and enforced? To a structuralist, the law is designed to keep the capitalist system operating in an efficient manner, and anyone, capitalist or proletarian, who "rocks the boat" is targeted to be sanctioned. For example, antitrust legislation is designed to prevent any single capitalist from dominating the system and preventing others from "playing the game." One person cannot get too powerful at the expense of the economic system as a whole.

One of the most highly regarded structural Marxist works is Stephen Spitzer's Marxian theory of deviance.[68] He finds that law in the capitalist system defines as deviant (or criminal) any person who disturbs, hinders, or calls into question any of the following:

- Capitalist modes of appropriating the product of human labor (for example, when the poor steal from the rich).

- The social conditions under which capitalist production takes place (for example, when some people refuse or are unable to perform wage labor).

- Patterns of distribution and consumption in capitalist society (for example, when people use drugs for escape and transcendence, rather than sociability and adjustment).

- The process of socialization for productive and nonproductive roles (for example, when youths refuse to be schooled or deny the validity of family life).

- The ideology that supports the functioning of capitalist society (for example, when people become proponents of alternative forms of social organization).

Among the many important points Spitzer makes is that capitalist societies have special ways of dealing with those who oppose its operation. One mechanism is to normalize formerly deviant or illegal acts by absorbing them into the mainstream of society—for example, through legalizing abortions. Conversion involves co-opting deviants by making them part of the system—for example, a gang leader may be recruited to work with younger delinquents. Containment involves segregating deviants into isolated geographic areas so that they can easily be controlled—for example, by creating a ghetto. Finally, Spitzer believes that capitalist society actively supports some criminal enterprises, such as organized crime, so that they can provide a means of support for groups who might otherwise become a burden on the state.

Research on Marxist Criminology

Marxist criminologists rarely use standard social science methodologies to test their views because many believe the traditional approach of measuring research subjects is antihuman and insensitive.[69] Marxists believe that the research conducted by mainstream liberal/positivist criminologists is designed to unmask the weak and powerless members of society so they can be better dealt with by the legal system—a process called **correctionalism.** They are particularly offended by purely empirical studies, such as those showing that minority-group members have lower IQs than the white majority or that the inner city is the site of the most serious crime while middle-class areas are relatively crime-free. While uncommon, empirical research is not considered totally incompatible with Marxist criminology, and there have been some important efforts to quantitatively test its fundamental assumptions.[70] For example, Alan Lizotte and his associates have shown that the property crime rate reflects a change in the level of surplus value; the capitalist system's emphasis on excessive profits accounts for

the need of the working class to commit property crime.[71] Despite these few exceptions, Marxist research tends to be historical and analytical and not quantitative and empirical. Social trends are interpreted to understand how capitalism has affected human interaction. Marxists investigate both macrolevel issues, such as how the accumulation of wealth affects crime rates, and microlevel issues, such as the effect of criminal interactions on the lives of individuals living in a capitalist society. Of particular importance to Marxist critical thinkers is the analysis of the historical development of capitalist social-control institutions, such as criminal law, police agencies, courts, and prison systems.

Crime, the Individual, and the State

Marxists devote considerable attention to the study of the relationships between crime, victims, the criminal, and the state. Two common themes emerge: (1) crime and its control are a function of capitalism, and (2) the justice system is biased against the working class and favors upper-class interests. Marxian analysis of the criminal justice system is designed to identify the often-hidden processes that exert control over people's lives. It seeks an understanding of how conditions, processes, and structures became as they are today. For example, William Chambliss analyzed the process by which deviant behavior is defined as criminal or delinquent in U.S. society.[72] In a similar vein, Timothy Carter and Donald Clelland used a Marxist approach to show that dispositions in a juvenile court were a function of social class.[73] David Greenberg also studied the association between social class and sentencing and later, with Drew Humphries, evaluated how power relationships help undermine any benefit the lower class gets from sentencing reforms.[74] In general, Marxist research efforts have yielded evidence linking operations of the justice system to class bias.[75] In addition to conducting studies showing the relationship between crime and the state, some critical researchers have attempted to show how capitalism intervenes throughout the entire spectrum of crime-related phenomena. Research by Herman Schwendinger and Julia Schwendinger attempts to show how capitalist social expectations affect women in the aftermath of a rape experience. Described in the Close-Up on capitalism's influence on rape, the Schwendingers' effort is a good example of Marxist analytical research.[76] Critical research of this sort is designed to reinterpret commonly held beliefs about society within the framework of Marxist social and economic ideas.[77] The goal is not to prove statistically that capitalism causes crime but rather to show that it creates an

CLOSE-UP

How Capitalism Influences Rape

Herman Schwendinger's and Julia Schwendinger's study of rape provides an excellent example of Marxian critical analysis. The Schwendingers' goal is to find out why women who are raped often feel guilty about their role in the rape experience. The Schwendingers believe that a rape victim frequently experiences guilt because she has been raised in a sexist society and has internalized discriminatory norms. Women have traditionally been viewed as the weaker sex, dependent on persons in authority, such as parents or husbands.

The Schwendingers postulate that dependency originates historically in socioeconomic conditions that are often directly related to family life in capitalist society. During the early stages of capitalism, families underwent strain when industry demanded a labor force of men, only infrequently supplemented by single women. The role of father was strained as men were separated from their households. The woman's role became more narrowly defined as childbearer and child raiser. The limited economic role of women helped to define them as dependents. Married women, especially, were viewed as nonproductive, since they did not participate in commodity markets, where people earn money.

In reality, women's household productivity must be viewed as an essential contribution to working-class life; yet theirs is an unpaid contribution that often goes unappreciated by husbands and the rest of society. Since the housewife only produces for family use, her labor is necessarily unpayable; and while her needs are partly supported by the husband's wage, she is totally dependent on that wage for access to the commodities necessary for the family's existence. Because she has been socialized into dependency by the capitalist system, a woman's sense of self-worth may be more responsive to the evaluations of other persons. Furthermore, negative evaluations, such as those created by a rape experience, are likely to be turned inward by the woman, creating unwarranted self-recrimination and remorse.

The family is not the only culprit in this transaction. Schools and the mass media further reinforce dependency by teaching boys and girls in school to "look down on women." Textbooks stereotype the woman's role; girls are depicted as helpless and frightened. Vocational tests provide fewer opportunities for girls. In media presentations, women are usually depicted as housewives and mothers. When women are portrayed on television commercials, they seem "concerned mainly with clean floors and clean hair—housework and their personal appearance."

Though women have made strides in the job market, their labor is often in low-paid, low-mobility occupations, such as secretary or piece worker. Consequently, their appearance in the labor force often does little to improve their economic dependency. It is for these reasons that women often blame themselves for being raped. The Schwendingers imply that women feel they have "let down" the people they depend on when they are trapped in a rape encounter. A woman's own sense of inadequacy leads to self-blame for the attack and prevents her from focusing on the true culprits: the rapist and the capitalist system whose economic structure results in a rape-producing climate. The Schwendingers' research approach illustrates the Marxian stress on analysis and interpretation of social process and their disdain for quantitative statistical evidence.

Discussion Questions

1. What can society do to help women who are the victims of rape?
2. Does the Schwendingers' portrayal of a rape victim seem accurate?

SOURCE: Herman Schwendinger and Julia Schwendinger, "Rape Victims and the False Sense of Guilt," *Crime and Social Justice* 13 (1980): 4–17.

environment in which crime is inevitable. Marxist research is humanistic, situational, descriptive, and analytical rather than statistical, rigid, and methodological.

Historical Analyses

A second type of Marxist research focuses on the historical background of commonly held institutional beliefs and practices. One aim is to show how changes in the criminal law corresponded to the development of capitalist economy. For example, Michael Rustigan analyzed historical records to show that law reform in nineteenth-century England was largely a response to pressure from the business community to make the punishment for property law violations more acceptable.[78] In a similar vein, Rosalind Petchesky has explained how the relationship between prison industries and capitalism evolved during the nineteenth century, while Paul Takagi has described the rise of state prisons as an element of centralized state control over deviants.[79] Another topic of importance to Marxist critical thinkers is the development of modern police agencies. Since police often play an active role in putting down labor disputes and controlling the activities of political dissidents, their interrelationships with capitalist economics is of particular importance to Marxists. Prominent examples of research in this area include Stephen Spitzer and A. T. Scull's discussion of the history of private police and Dennis Hoffman's historical analysis of police excesses in the repression of an early union, the International Workers of the World (popularly known as the Wobblies).[80] Sidney Harring has provided one of the more important analyses of the development of modern policing, showing how police developed as an antilabor force that provided muscle for industrialists at the turn of the century.[81] In the Close-Up on private policing, a Marxist analysis is used to describe the growth of private police and security.

Critique of Marxist Criminology

Marxist criminology has met with a great deal of criticism from some members of the criminological mainstream who charge that its contribution has "been hot air, heat, but no real light."[82] In turn, radicals have accused mainstream criminologists of being culprits in the development of state control over individual lives and "selling out" their ideals for the chance to receive government funding. In making these charges, these theorists have caused disturbances in the halls of academia. Rumors of purges of Marxist theorists have cropped up; lawsuits involving the denial of academic tenure to Marxists have not been uncommon.

Mainstream criminologists have also attacked the substance of Marxist thought. For example, Jackson Toby argues that Marxist theory is a simple rehash of the old tradition of helping the underdog. He likens the ideas behind Marxist criminology to the ideas in such traditional and literary works as *Robin Hood* and Victor Hugo's *Les Miserables,* in which the poor steal from the rich to survive.[83] In reality, Toby claims, most theft is for luxury, not survival. Moreover, he disputes the idea that the crimes of the rich are more reprehensible and less understandable than those who live in poverty. Criminality and immoral behavior occur at every social level, but Toby believes that the relatively disadvantaged contribute disproportionately to crime and delinquency rates.[84]

Another critic, Carl Klockars charges that Marxists ignore all the varied prestige and interest groups that exist in a pluralistic society and focus almost unilaterally on class differentials.[85] Klockars scoffs, for example, at critical thinkers who charge that efforts by the government to create social reforms are disguised attempts to control the underclass. Is it logical to believe that giving people more rights is a trick to allow greater control to be exerted over them? "People are more powerful with the right to a jury than without it. . . . The rights of free speech, free press, free association, public trial, habeas corpus, and governmental petition extended substantial power to colonials . . . who had previously been denied them."[86] Klockars's views of the problems of Marxist theory are summarized in the following statements:

- Marxist criminology as a social movement is untrustworthy. Marxists refuse to confront the problems and conflicts of socialist countries, such as the gulags and purges of the Soviet Union under Stalin.

- Marxist criminology is predictable. Capitalism is blamed for every human vice. "After class explains everything, after the whole legal order is critiqued, after all predatory and personal crime is attributed to the conditions and reproduction of capitalism, there is nothing more to say—except more of the same."[87]

- Marxist criminology does little to explain the criminality existing in states that have abolished private ownership of the means of production (Cuba, China).

- Marxists ignore objective reality. For example, they overlook empirical evidence of distinctions

CLOSE-UP

Private Policing and the Legitimation of Strikebreaking

Private policing and private security firms are particularly well suited to take advantage of the contradictions of crime in a capitalist society. The term *contradictions* implies that crime, an element commonly assumed to have only negative consequences, also creates a large profit for a certain segment of society. In fact, crime creates "a way of life" not only for criminals, but also for those who own private security firms and for private security guards (members of the working class) who protect private property. By looking at crime as a result of structural problems inherent in capitalist economies, we see that criminals' profits and profit in the private security industry emanate from the same source—capitalism. As an industry in modern America, private policing nets tremendous profits.

Private policing, like early fee-for-service constable systems or current civil court procedures, is a class-based institution. It enables the rich to buy additional protection while the lower classes, who need protection the most since they are victimized more often by crime, remain without adequate police services. This class bias of private policing can be traced back to the origins of this industry. Private policing was born during the same period as modern policing, the mid-1800s. While public police concentrated on maintaining public order and controlling the "dangerous classes," the "protection of private property and the detection of crime were left to private police agencies." Public police concentrated their efforts on maintaining "order" in the city, while private police served the needs of the capitalist class directly.

In the early 1850s, Allan Pinkerton founded the first private police agency in Chicago. The impetus behind Pinkerton's private police force was, first, to provide additional police services to those who could afford it and, second, to supplement the services provided by Chicago's police force. Those who required and could afford additional police protection often had industrial interests to protect, and from this early class alliance, the Pinkerton agency quickly evolved into an antilabor organization. Its antilabor practices began with spying on employees, and by the depression of 1877, the Pinkertons specialized in strikebreaking. By 1892, the Pinkerton agency had participated in the repression of more than 77 strikes nationwide. Pinkerton's agency used many strong-arm tactics to break strikes, and its reliance on violence led many to denounce the agency's methods.

In response to these overtly repressive and unacceptable tactics, several states attempted to legitimate the repression of striking workers by establishing police forces designed to suppress riots and strikes in less forceful ways. This led Pennsylvania's legislature in 1866 to form the "Coal and Iron Police" to deal with striking coal miners and iron workers. However, these institutions also responded directly to the needs of capital. They did not produce a significant reduction in the use of violence to break strikes.

The creation of the State Police in Pennsylvania in 1905 was another attempt to reduce the use of Pinkertons and legitimize strikebreaking activities. "With their creation, capital gained an efficient tax-supported military force invested with public authority." Through the use of Pinkerton-style strikebreaking methods, the Pennsylvania State Police quickly dashed any hopes of being regarded as a more humane strikebreaking force. American labor leaders described the State Police as "legalized state strikebreakers" who used methods similar to "cossacks" to break strikes.

Discussion Questions

1. Should corporations be allowed to have private police forces?
2. Do you believe that law enforcement agencies, both public and private, are instruments of government oppression?

SOURCE: Michael Lynch and Byron Groves, *A Primer in Radical Criminology* (Albany, N.Y.: Harrow & Heston, 1989), pp. 90–91.

that exist between people in different classes. Such tactics will eventually destroy the foundation for a new postrevolutionary social science, should one be needed.

- Marxists attempt to explicate issues that, for most people, need no explanation. The revelation that politicians are corrupt and businesspeople greedy comes as a shock to no one.

- The evil that Marxists consistently discover and dramatize is seen from a moral ground set so high that it loses meaning and perspective. Every aspect of capitalist society is suspect, including practices and freedoms that most people cherish as the cornerstones of democracy (right to trial, free press, religion, and so on).

- By presenting itself as a mystical, religionlike entity, Marxist criminology is relieved of the responsibility for the exploitation, corruption, crime, and human abuse that has been and continues to be perpetrated in socialist countries.

In response, Marxist scholars charge that critics rely on "traditional" variables, such as "class" and "poverty," in their analysis of radical thought. While important, these do not reflect the key issues in the structural and economic process. In fact, like crime, they too may be the *outcome* of the capitalist system.[88]

Though radical criminologists dispute criticisms, they have also reponded by creating new theoretical models that incorporate Marxist ideas in an innovative manner. In the sections below, some recent forms of radical theory are discussed in some detail.

Left Realism

Some radical scholars, such as Anthony Platt, have addressed the need for the left to respond to the increasing power of the right wing and at the same time address such problems as street crime and violence.[89] One new approach has been the development of the **left realism** school.[90] According to sociologists Martin Schwartz and Walter DeKeseredy, the core premise of left realism is that radical crimiologists have ignored the victimization of the working class to focus on upper-class crime.[91] Left realism recognizes that street crime is "real"; the fear of violence among the lower classes has allowed the right wing to seize "law and order" as a political issue. Street crime is not the work of Robin

Hoods or revolutionaries who steal from the rich. Most street criminals prey upon members of their own race and class and are happy to keep the proceeds for themselves. According to Schwartz and DeKeseredy, street criminals may be the "ultimate capitalists," hustling their way to obtain the coveted symbols of success.[92] While the implementation of a socialist economy would help eliminate the crime problem, left realists recognize that something must be done in the meantime to control crime under the existing capitalist system. To create crime control policy, left realists welcome not only radical ideas but build upon the work of strain theorists, social ecologists, and other "mainstream" views. Community-based efforts seem to hold the most promise as crime-control techniques.

Origins of Left Realism

Left realism is most often connected to the writings of British scholars John Lea and Jock Young. In their well-respected 1984 work, *What Is to Be Done about Law and Order?*, they reject the utopian views of "idealistic" Marxists who portray street criminals as revolutionaries.[93] They take the "realistic" approach that street criminals prey on the poor and disenfranchised, thus making them doubly abused, first by the capitalist system and then by members of their own class.

Lea and Young's view of crime causation borrows from conventional sociological theory and closely resembles the relative deprivation approach: Experiencing poverty in the midst of plenty creates discontent; discontent without legitimate opportunity breeds crime. As they put it, "The equation is simple: relative deprivation equals discontent; discontent plus lack of political solution equals crime."[94]

The left realism approach seems to be an important compromise between the historic idealism of the left and traditional sociological theory, which portrays crime as a violation of legal rules that reflect the consensus of society. Left realists also realize that crime victims in all classes need and deserve protection and have suggested that crime control reflect community needs. They do not view police and the courts as inherently evil tools of capitalism whose tough tactics alienate the lower classes. These institutions are instead viewed as potentially life-saving public services if their use of force could be reduced and their sensitivity to the public increased.[95]

Left realism has been critiqued by radical thinkers as legitimizing the existing power structure: by supporting the existing definitions of law and justice, it suggests that the "deviant" and not the capitalist system is the root cause of society's problems. Is it not advocating the very institutions that "currently imprison us and our patterns of thought and action"?[96] In rebuttal, a left realist would charge that it is unrealistic to speak of a socialist state lacking a police force or system of laws and justice; the criminal code does in fact repesent public opinion.

Radical Feminist Theory

Like so many theories in criminology, most of the efforts of radical theorists have been devoted to explaining male criminality.[97] To remedy this theoretical lapse, a number of feminist writers have attempted to explain the cause of crime, gender differences in the crime rate, and the exploitation of female victims from a radical feminist perspective. Scholars in this area usually can be described as holding one of two related philosophical orientations: Marxist feminism or radical feminism.

Marxist Feminism

The first group of writers can be described as **Marxist feminists,** who view gender inequality as stemming from the unequal power of men and women in a capitalist society. They view gender inequality as a function of the exploitation of females by fathers and husbands; women are considered a "commodity" worth possessing, like land or money.[98] The origin of gender differences can be traced to the development of private property and male domination over the laws of inheritance.[99]

An example of this approach can be found in *Capitalism, Patriarchy, and Crime* by Marxist James Messerschmidt. According to Messerschmidt, capitalist society is marked by both patriarchy and class conflict. Capitalists control the labor of workers, while men control women both economically and biologically.[100] This "double marginality" explains why females in a capitalist society commit fewer crimes than males: they are isolated in the family and have fewer opportunities to engage in elite deviance (white-collar and economic crimes); they are also denied access to male-dominated street crimes. For example, powerful males will commit white-collar crimes, as will powerful females. However, the female crime rate is restricted because of the patriarchial nature of the capitalist system.[101] Since capitalism renders women powerless, they are forced to commit less serious, nonviolent, self-destructive crimes, such as abusing drugs.

Powerlessness also increases the likelihood that women will become the target of violent acts.[102] Lower-class males are shut out of the economic opportunity structure. One way to improve their self-image is through acts of machismo that may involve violence or abuse of women. It is not surprising to find that a significant percentage of female victims are attacked by a spouse or intimate partner.

Radical Feminism

In contrast, **radical feminists** view the cause of female crime as originating with the onset of male supremacy **(patriarchy),** the subsequent subordination of women, male aggression, and the efforts of men to control females sexually.[103] They focus on the social forces that shape women's lives and experiences to explain female criminality.[104] For example, they attempt to show how the sexual victimization of girls is a function of male socialization because so many young males learn to be aggressive and exploitive of women. Males seek out same-sex peer groups for social support and find within them encouragement for the exploitation and sexual abuse of women. On college campuses, peers encourage sexual violence against women defined as "teasers," "bar pickups," or "loose women"; a code of secrecy then protects the aggressors from retribution.[105] Sexual and physical exploitation triggers a reaction among young girls. They may run away or abuse substances, which is labeled deviant or delinquent behavior.[106] In a sense, the female criminal is a victim herself.

The radical perspective is supported by a 1993 national survey conducted by the Center for Research on Women at Wellesley College that found that 90 percent of adolescent girls are sexually harassed in school, almost 30 percent report having been pressured to "do something sexual," and 10 percent were forced to do something sexual.[107]

According to the radical feminist view, exploitation acts as a trigger for the onset of delinquent and deviant behavior. When female victims run away and abuse substances, they may be reacting to abuse at home and at school. Their attempts at survival are then labeled deviant or delinquent; victim blaming is not uncommon. The Wellesley survey of sexual harassment found that teachers and school officials ignore about 45 percent of complaints made by female students. They found that some school officials responded to reports of sexual harassment by asking the young victim, "Do you like it?" and saying, "They must be doing it for a reason." Because agents of social control often choose to ignore reports of abuse and harassment, young girls may feel trapped and desperate.

How the Justice System Penalizes Women.
Radical feminists have also indicted the justice system and its patriarchal hierarchy as contributing to the onset of female delinquency.

From its inception, the juvenile justice system has viewed the great majority of female delinquents as sexually precocious girls who have to be brought under control. One study of the early Los Angeles Juvenile Court by Mary Odem and Steven Schlossman found that in 1920, so-called delinquency experts identified young female "sex delinquents" as a major social problem that required a forceful public response. Civic leaders who were concerned about immorality mounted a eugenics and social hygiene campaign that identified the "sex delinquent" as a moral and sexual threat to American society and advocated a policy of *eugenics* or sterilization to prevent these inferior individuals from having children. Los Angeles responded by hiring the first female police officers in the nation to deal with girls under arrest and female judges to hear girls' cases in juvenile court; it also established a female detention center and a girl's reformatory. When Odem and Schlossman evaluated the juvenile court records of delinquent girls who entered the Los Angeles Juvenile Court in 1920, they found that the majority were petitioned for either suspected sexual activity or behavior that placed them at risk of sexual relations. Despite the limited seriousness of these charges, the majority of girls were detained before their trials, and while in Juvenile Hall, all were given a compulsory pelvic exam. Girls adjudged sexually delinquent on the basis of the exam were segregated from the merely incorrigible girls to prevent moral corruption. Those testing positive for venereal disease were confined in Juvenile Hall Hospital for usually from one to three months. More than *29 percent* of these female adolescents were eventually committed to custodial institutions.[108]

The judicial victimization of female delinquents has continued. A well-known feminist writer, Meda Chesney-Lind, has written extensively on the victimization of female delinquents by agents of the juvenile justice system.[109] She found that police in Honolulu, Hawaii, were likely to arrest female adolescents for sexual activity and to ignore the same behavior among male delinquents. Some 74 percent of the females in her sample were charged with sexual activity or incorrigibility, but only 27 percent of the boys faced the same charges. Moreover, the court ordered physical examinations in over 70 percent of the female cases, but only about 15 percent of the males were forced to undergo this embarrassing procedure. Girls were also more likely to be sent to a detention facility before trial, and the length of their detention averaged three times that of the boys. Finally, a higher percentage of females than males were institutionalized for similar delinquent acts. Chesney-Lind explains her data by suggesting that because female adolescents have a much narrower range of acceptable behavior than male adolescents, any sign of misbehavior in girls is seen as a substantial challenge to authority and to the viability of the double standard of sexual inequality. Female delinquency is viewed as relatively more serious than male delinquency and therefore is more likely to be severely sanctioned.

Meda Chesney-Lind, a prominent feminist scholar, has conducted extensive research on the victimization of young female offenders by the juvenile justice system.

Power-Control Theory

John Hagan and his associates have created a radical-feminist model that uses gender differences to explain the onset of criminality. The most significant statements of these views are contained in a series of scholarly articles and expanded in Hagan's 1989 book, *Structural Criminology*.[110] Hagan's view is that crime and delinquency rates are a function of two factors: (1) class position (power) and (2) family functions (control).[111] The link between these two variables is that within the family, parents reproduce the power relationships they hold in the workplace. The class position and work experiences of parents influence the criminality of children. A position of dominance at work is equated with control in the household. In families that are **paternalistic,** fathers assume the traditional role of breadwinners, while mothers have menial jobs or remain at home to supervise domestic matters. Within the paternalistic home, mothers are expected to control the behavior of their daughters while granting greater freedom to sons. In such a home, the parent-daughter relationship can be viewed as a preparation for the "cult of domesticity," which makes girls' involvement in delinquency unlikely, while boys are freer to deviate because they are not subject to maternal control. Consequently, male siblings exhibit a higher degree of delinquent behavior than their sisters. On the other hand, in egalitarian families—those in which the husband and the wife share similar positions of power at home and in the workplace—daughters gain a kind of freedom that reflects reduced parental control. These families produce daughters whose law-violating behavior mirrors their brothers'. Ironically, these kind of relationships also occur in female-headed households with absent fathers. Similarly, Hagan and his associates found that when both fathers and mothers hold equally valued managerial positions, the similarity between the rates of their daughters' and sons' delinquency is greatest. By implication, middle-class girls are the most likely to violate the law because they are less closely controlled than their lower-class counterparts. And in homes in which both parents hold positions of power, girls are more likely to have the same expectations of career success as their brothers. Consequently, siblings of both sexes will be socialized to take risks and engage in other behavior related to delinquency. Power-control theory, then, implies that middle-class youth of both sexes will have higher overall crime rates than their lower-class peers (though lower-class males may commit the more serious crimes).

Testing Power-Control Theory.

Power-control theory has received a great deal of attention in the criminological community because it encourages a new approach to the study of criminality, one that includes gender differences, class position, and the structure of the family. While its basic premises have not yet been thoroughly tested, some critics have questioned its core assumption that power and control variables can explain crime.[112] More specifically, critics fail to replicate the finding that upper-class kids are more likely to deviate than their lower-class peers or that class and power interact to produce delinquency.[113] In response, Hagan and his colleagues suggest that these views are incorrect and power-control theory retains its power to significantly add to our knowledge of the causes of crime.[114] Despite their assurances, empirical testing may produce further refinement of the theory. For example, Kevin Thompson found few gender-based supervision and behavior differences in worker-, manager,- or owner-dominated households.[115] However, parental supervision practices were quite different in families headed by the chronically unemployed, and these conformed to the power-control model. The Thompson research indicates that the concept of class employed by Hagan may have to be reconsidered: power-control theory may actually explain criminality among the truly disadvantaged and not the working class.

Deconstructionism

A number of radical thinkers have embraced semiotics and deconstructionist analysis. While difficult to articulate concisely, these perspectives focus on the critical analysis of communication and language in legal codes.[116] Rules and regulations are analyzed to determine whether they contain language and content that forces racism or sexism to become institutionalized.

Deconstructionists believe that language is value-laden and contains the same sort of inequities that are present in the rest of the social structure. Concerns with materialism and social inequality appear in the content of the law and control its direction. Capitalism puts a price tag on all merchandise. Law, legal skill, and justice are "commodities" that can be bought and sold like any other.[117]

Peacemaking Criminology

Suffering has risen out of disunity and separation from the embracing totality, and it can be ended only with the return of all sentient beings to a condition of wholeness.[118]

These demonstrators are taking action against hate crime in order to promote cooperation and understanding. Peacemaking criminologists believe that such efforts must be made to reduce the level of hatred and violence in our society.

One of the newer movements in radical theory is **peacemaking criminology.** To members of the peacemaking movement, the main purpose of criminology is to promote a peaceful and just society. Rather than standing on empirical analysis of data sets, peacemaking draws its inspiration from religious and philosophical teachings ranging from Quakerism to Zen.

Peacemakers view the efforts of the state to punish and control as crime-encouraging rather than crime-discouraging. These views were first articulated in a series of books with an anarchist theme written by Larry Tifft and Dennis Sullivan more than 15 years ago.[119] In his forward to Sullivan's *The Mask of Love*, Larry Tifft writes:

> The violent punishing acts of the state and its controlling professions are of the same genre as the violent acts of individuals. In each instance these acts reflect an attempt to monopolize human interaction.[120]

Sullivan recognizes the futility of correcting and punishing criminals in the context of our conflict-ridden society:

> The reality we must grasp is that we live in a culture of severed relationships, where every available institution provides a form of banishment but no place or means for people to become connected, to be responsible to and for each other.[121]

The writings imply that mutual aid rather than coercive punishment is the key to a harmonious society. Today, advocates of the peacemaking movement, such as Harold Pepinsky and Richard Quinney (who has shifted from conflict theorist, to Marxist and now to peacemaker), try to find humanist solutions to crime and other social problems.[122] Rather than punishment and prison, they advocate such policies as mediation and conflict resolution.

Summary

Social conflict theorists view crime as a function of the conflict that exists in society. Social conflict has its theoretical basis in the works of Karl Marx, as interpreted by Willem Bonger, Ralf Dahrendorf, and George Vold. Conflict theorists suggest that crime in any society is caused by class conflict. Laws are created by those in power to protect their rights and interests. All criminal acts have political undertones. Richard Quinney has called this concept the social reality of crime. Unfortunately, research efforts to validate the conflict approach have not produced significant findings. One of conflict theory's most important premises is that the justice system is biased and designed to protect the wealthy. Research has not been unanimous in supporting this point.

Marxist criminology views the competitive nature of the capitalist system as a major cause of crime. The poor commit crimes because of their frustration, anger, and need. The wealthy engage in illegal acts because they are used to competition and because they must do so to keep their positions in society. Marxist scholars, such as Quinney, Platt, and Krisberg, have attempted to show that the law is designed to protect the wealthy and powerful and to control the poor, have-not members of society. There are a number of branches of radical theory referred to as instrumental Marxism and structural Marxism (see Table 9.2 for a summary of these theories). Research on Marxist theory focuses on how the system of justice was designed and how it operates to further class interests. Quite often, this research uses historical analysis to show how the capitalist classes have exerted their control over the police, courts, and correctional agencies. Both Marxist and conflict criminology have been heavily criticized by consensus criminologists. Jackson Toby sees Marxists as being sentimental and unwilling to face reality. Carl Klockar's criticism suggests Marxists make fundamental errors in their concepts of ownership and class interest.

During the 1990s, new forms of conflict theory are emerging. Feminist writiers draw attention to the influence of patriarchical society on crime; left realism takes a centrist position on crime by showing its rational and destructive nature; peacemaking criminology brings a call for humanism to criminology; deconstructionism looks at the symbolic meaning of law and culture.

TABLE 9.2 Social Conflict Theories

Theory	Major Premise	Strengths
conflict theory	Crime is a function of class conflict. The definition of the law is controlled by people who hold social and political power.	Accounts for class differentials in the crime rate. Shows how class conflict influences behavior.
Marxist theory	The capitalist means of production creates class conflict. Crime is a rebellion of the lower class. The criminal justice system is an agent of class warfare.	Accounts for the associations between economic structure and crime rates.
instrumental Marxist theory	Criminals are revolutionaries. The real crime is sexism, racism, and profiteering.	Broadens the definition of crime and demystifies or explains the historical development of law.
structural Marxist theory	The law is designed to sustain the capitalist economic system.	Explains the existence of white-collar crime and business-control laws.
radical feminist theory	The capital system creates patriarchy, which oppresses women.	Explains gender bias, violence against women, and repression.
left realism	Crime is a function of relative deprivation; criminals prey on the poor.	Represents a compromise between conflict and traditional criminology.
deconstructionism	Language controls the meaning and use of the law.	Provides a critical analysis of meaning.
peacemaking	Peace and humanism can reduce crime; conflict resolution strategies can work.	Offers a new approach to crime control through mediation.

≡ KEY TERMS

conflict theory	privilege
Karl Marx	structural Marxists
Willem Bonger	correctionalism
Ralf Dahrendorf	left realism
George Vold	Marxist feminists
social reality of crime	radical feminist
dangerous classes	patriarchy
surplus value	paternalistic
instrumentalists	peacemaking criminology
demystify	

≡ NOTES

1. Michael Lynch, "Rediscovering Criminology: Lessons from the Marxist Tradition," in *Marxist Sociology: Surveys of Contemporary Theory and Research,* ed. Donald McQuarie and Patrick McGuire (New York: General Hall Press, 1994).

2. Michael Lynch and W. Byron Groves, *A Primer in Radical Criminology,* 2d ed. (Albany, N.Y.: Harrow and Heston, 1989), pp. 32–33.

3. Ibid., p. 4.

4. See, generally, Karl Marx and Friedrich Engels, *Capital: A Critique of Political Economy,* trans. E. Aveling (Chicago: Charles Kern, 1906); Karl Marx, *Selected Writings in Sociology and Social Philosophy,* trans. P. B. Bottomore (New York: McGraw-Hill, 1956). For a general discussion of Marxist thought, see Michael Lynch and W. Byron Groves, *A Primer in Radical Criminology* (New York: Harrow and Heston, 1986), pp. 6–26.

5. Karl Marx, *Grundrisse: Introduction to the Critique of Political Economy,* trans. Martin Nicolaus (New York: Vintage, 1973), pp. 106–107.

6. Lynch, "Rediscovering Criminology."

7. Karl Marx, "Population, Crime and Pauperism," in Karl Marx and Friedrich Engels, *Ireland and the Irish Question* (Moscow: Progress, 1859, reprinted 1971), p. 92.

8. Friedrich Engels, *The Condition of the Working Class in England in 1844* (London: Allen and Unwin, 1950).

9. Lynch, "Rediscovering Criminology," p. 5.

10. Willem Bonger, *Criminality and Economic Conditions* (1916, abridged ed., Bloomington: Indiana University Press, 1969).

11. Ralf Dahrendorf, *Class and Class Conflict in Industrial Society* (Palo Alto, Calif.: Stanford University Press, 1959).

12. Ibid., p. 48.

13. George Vold, *Theoretical Criminology* (New York: Oxford University Press, 1958).

14. James Short and F. Ivan Nye, "Extent of Undetected Delinquency: Tentative Conclusions," *Journal of Criminal Law, Criminology, and Police Science* 49 (1958): 296–302.

15. For a general view, see David Friedrichs, "Crime, Deviance and Criminal Justice: In Search of a Radical Humanistic Perspective," *Humanity and Society* 6 (1982): 200–26.

16. Edwin Lemert, *Social Pathology* (New York: McGraw-Hill, 1951); Howard Becker, *Outsiders: Studies in the Sociology of Deviance* (New York: MacMillan, 1963).

17. Alexander Liazos, "The Poverty of the Sociology of Deviance: Nuts, Sluts and Perverts," *Social Problems* 20 (1972): 103–20.

18. See, generally, Robert Meier, "The New Criminology: Continuity in Criminological Theory," *Journal of Criminal Law and Criminology* 67 (1977): 461–69.

19. David Greenberg, ed., *Crime and Capitalism* (Palo Alto, Calif.: Mayfield Publishing, 1981), p. 3.

20. William Chambliss and Robert Seidman, *Law, Order and Power* (Reading, Mass.: Addison-Wesley, 1971), p. 503.

21. John Braithwaite, "Retributivism, Punishment and Privilege," in *Punishment and Privilege,* ed. W. Byron Groves and Graeme Newman (Albany, N.Y.: Harrow and Heston, 1986), pp. 55–66.

22. Austin Turk, "Class, Conflict and Criminology," *Sociological Focus* 10 (1977): 209–20.

23. Daniel Georges-Abeyie, "Race, Ethnicity, and the Spatial Dynamic: Toward a Realistic Study of Black Crime, Crime Victimization, and Criminal Justice Processing of Blacks," *Social Justice* 16 (1989): 35–54.

24. Richard Quinney, *The Social Reality of Crime* (Boston: Little, Brown, 1970), pp. 15–23.

25. Austin Turk, *Criminality and Legal Order* (Chicago: Rand McNally, 1969), p. 58.

26. Lynch and Groves, *A Primer in Radical Criminology,* 2d ed., p. 38.

27. David McDowall, "Poverty and Homicide in Detroit, 1926–1978," *Victims and Violence* 1 (1986): 23–34; David McDowall and Sandra Norris, "Poverty and Homicide in Baltimore, Cleveland, and Memphis, 1937–1980" (Paper presented at the annual meeting of the American Society of Criminology, Montreal, November 1987).

28. Judith Blau and Peter Blau, "The Cost of Inequality: Metropolitan Structure and Violent Crime," *American Sociological Review* 147 (1982): 114–29; Richard Block, "Community Environment and Violent Crime," *Criminology* 17 (1979): 46–57; Robert Sampson, "Structural Sources of Variation in Race-Age-Specific Rates of Offending across Major U.S. Cities," *Criminology* 23 (1985): 647–73.

29. David Jacobs and David Britt, "Inequality and Police Use of Deadly Force: An Empirical Assessment of a Conflict Hypothesis," *Social Problems* 26 (1979): 403–12.

30. Alan Lizotte, "Extra-Legal Factors in Chicago's Criminal Courts: Testing the Conflict Model of Criminal Justice," *Social Problems* 25 (1978): 564–80.

31. Terance Miethe and Charles Moore, "Racial Differences in Criminal Processing: The Consequences of Model Selection on Conclusions about Differential Treatment," *Sociological Quarterly* 27 (1987): 217–37.

32. Douglas Smith, Christy Visher, and Laura Davidson,

"Equity and Discretionary Justice: The Influence of Race on Police Arrest Decisions," *Journal of Criminal Law and Criminology* 75 (1984): 234–49.

33. Thomas Arvanites, "Increasing Imprisonment: A Function of Crime or Socio-economic Factors?" *American Journal of Criminal Justice* 17 (1992): 19–38.

34. Jackson Toby, "The New Criminology Is the Old Sentimentality," *Criminology* 16 (1979): 513–26.

35. Kenneth Land and Marcus Felson, "A General Framework for Building Dynamic Macro Social Indicator Models: An Analysis of Changes in Crime Rates and Police Expenditures," *American Journal of Sociology* 82 (1976): 565–604.

36. Arvanites, "Increasing Imprisonment," p. 34.

37. See generally, William Wilbanks, *The Myth of a Racist Criminal Justice System* (Monterey, Calif.: Brooks/Cole, 1987).

38. Theodore Chiricos and Gordon Waldo, "Socioeconomic Status and Criminal Sentencing: An Empirical Assessment of a Conflict Proposition," *American Sociological Review* 40 (1975): 753–72.

39. Stephen Klein, Joan Petersilia, and Susan Turner, "Race and Imprisonment Decisions in California," *Science* 247 (1990): 812–16.

40. Basil Owomero, "Crime in Tanzania: Contradictions of a Socialist Experiment," *International Journal of Comparative and Applied Criminal Justice* 12 (1988): 177–89.

41. Lynch and Groves, *A Primer in Radical Criminology*, 2d ed., p. 6.

42. This section borrows heavily from Richard Sparks, "A Critique of Marxist Criminology," in *Crime and Justice,* vol. 2, ed. Norval Morris and Michael Tonry (Chicago: University of Chicago Press, 1980), pp. 159–208.

43. Jeffery Reiman, *The Rich Get Richer and the Poor Get Prison* (New York: Wiley, 1984), pp. 43–44.

44. For a general review of Marxist criminology, see Lynch and Groves, *A Primer in Radical Criminology,* 2d ed.

45. Ian Taylor, Paul Walton, and Jock Young, *The New Criminology: For a Social Theory of Deviance* (London: Routledge and Kegan Paul, 1973).

46. Barry Krisberg, *Crime and Privilege: Toward a New Criminology* (Engelwood Cliffs, N.J.: Prentice-Hall, 1975), p. 167.

47. David Friedrichs, "Critical Criminology and Critical Legal Studies," *Critical Criminologist* 1 (1989): 7.

48. See, for example, Larry Tifft and Dennis Sullivan, *The Struggle to Be Human: Crime, Criminology and Anarchism* (Orkney Islands, Over-the Water-Sanday: Cienfuegos Press, 1979); Dennis Sullivan, *The Mask of Love* (Port Washington, N.Y.: Kennikat Press, 1980).

49. R. M. Bohm, "Radical Criminology: An Explication," *Criminology* 19 (1982): 565–89.

50. Robert Bohm, "Radical Criminology: Back to the Basics" (Paper presented at the annual meeting of the American Society of Criminology, Phoenix, Arizona, November 1993), p. 2.

51. Ibid., p. 4.

52. Lynch and Groves, *A Primer in Radical Criminology*, 2d ed., p. 7.

53. W. Byron Groves and Robert Sampson, "Critical Theory and Criminology," *Social Problems* 33 (1986): 58–80.

54. Gregg Barak, "'Crimes of the Homeless' or the 'Crime of Homelessness': A Self-Reflexive, New-Marxist Analysis of Crime and Social Control" (Paper presented at the annual meeting of the American Society of Criminology, Montreal, November 1987).

55. Michael Lynch, "Assessing the State of Radical Criminology: Toward the Year 2000" (Paper presented at the annual meeting of the American Society of Criminology, Phoenix, Arizona, November 1993).

56. Bohm, "Radical Criminology," p. 5.

57. Gresham Sykes, "The Rise of Critical Criminology," *Journal of Criminal Law and Criminology* 65 (1974): 211.

58. David Jacobs, "Corporate Economic Power and the State: A Longitudinal Assessment of Two Explanations," *American Journal of Sociology* 93 (1988): 852–81.

59. Deanna Alexander, "Victims of the L.A. Riots: A Theoretical Consideration" (Paper presented at the annual meeting of the American Society of Criminology, Phoenix, Arizona, November 1993).

60. Ibid., p. 2.

61. Richard Quinney, "Crime Control in Capitalist Society," in *Critical Criminology*, ed. Ian Taylor, Paul Walton, and Jock Young (London: Routledge and Kegan Paul, 1975), p. 199.

62. Herman Schwendinger and Julia Schwendinger, "Delinquency and Social Reform: A Radical Perspective," in *Juvenile Justice,* ed. Lamar Empey (Charlottesville: University of Virginia Press, 1979), pp. 246–90.

63. Krisberg, *Crime and Privilege.*

64. Elliott Currie, "A Dialogue with Anthony M. Platt," *Issues in Criminology* 8 (1973): 28.

65. Ibid., p. 29.

66. Lynch, "Rediscovering Criminology," p. 14.

67. John Hagan, *Structural Criminology* (New Brunswick, N.J.: Rutgers University Press, 1989), pp. 110–19.

68. Stephen Spitzer, "Toward a Marxian Theory of Deviance," *Social Problems* 22 (1975): 638–51.

69. Roy Bhaskar, "Empiricism," in *A Dictionary of Marxist Thought,* ed. T. Bottomore (Cambridge: Harvard University Press, 1983), pp. 149–50.

70. Byron Groves, "Marxism and Positivism," *Crime and Social Justice* 23 (1985): 129–50; Michael Lynch, "Quantitative Analysis and Marxist Criminology: Some Old Answers to a Dilemma in Marxist Criminology," *Crime and Social Justice* 29 (1987): 110–17.

71. Alan Lizotte, James Mercy, and Eric Monkkonen, "Crime and Police Strength in an Urban Setting: Chicago, 1947–1970," in *Quantitative Criminology,* ed. John Hagan (Beverly Hills: Sage, 1982), pp. 129–48.

72. William Chambliss, "The State, the Law and the Definition

of Behavior as Criminal or Delinquent," in *Handbook of Criminology,* ed. D. Glazer (Chicago: Rand McNally, 1974), pp. 7–44.

73. Timothy Carter and Donald Clelland, "A Neo-Marxian Critique, Formulation and Test of Juvenile Dispositions as a Function of Social Class," *Social Problems* 27 (1979): 96–108.

74. David Greenberg, "Socio-Economic Status and Criminal Sentences: Is There an Association?" *American Sociological Review* 42 (1977): 174–75; David Greenberg and Drew Humphries, "The Co-optation of Fixed Sentencing Reform," *Crime and Delinquency* 26 (1980): 206–25.

75. Steven Box, *Power, Crime and Mystification* (London: Tavistock, 1984); Gregg Barak, *In Defense of Whom? A Critique of Criminal Justice Reform* (Cincinnati: Anderson Publishing, 1980); for an opposing view, see Franklin Williams, "Conflict Theory and Differential Processing: An Analysis of the Research Literature," in *Radical Criminology: The Coming Crisis,* ed. J. Inciardi (Beverly Hills: Sage, 1980), pp. 213–31.

76. Herman Schwendinger and Julia Schwendinger, "Rape Victims and the False Sense of Guilt," *Crime and Social Justice* 13 (1980): 4–17.

77. For more of their work, see Herman Schwendinger and Julia Schwendinger, *Adolescent Subcultures and Delinquency* (New York: Praeger, 1985); idem, "The Paradigmatic Crisis in Delinquency Theory," *Crime and Social Justice* 18: 70–78 (1982); idem, "The Collective Varieties of Youth," *Crime and Social Justice* 5 (1976): 7–25; idem, "Marginal Youth and Social Policy," *Social Problems* 24 (1976): 184–91.

78. Michael Rustigan, "A Reinterpretation of Criminal Law Reform in Nineteenth-Century England," in *Crime and Capitalism,* ed. D. Greenberg (Palo Alto, Calif.: Mayfield Publishing, 1981), pp. 255–78.

79. Rosalind Petchesky, "At Hard Labor: Penal Confinement and Production in Nineteenth-Century America," in *Crime and Capitalism,* ed. D. Greenberg (Palo Alto, Calif.: Mayfield Publishing, 1981), pp. 341–57; Paul Takagi, "The Walnut Street Jail: A Penal Reform to Centralize the Powers of the State," *Federal Probation* 49 (1975): 18–26.

80. Steven Spitzer and Andrew Scull, "Privatization and Capitalist Development: The Case of the Private Police," *Social Problems* 25 (1977): 18–29; Dennis Hoffman, "Cops and Wobblies" (Ph.D. diss., Portland State University, 1977).

81. Sidney Harring, "Policing a Class Society: The Expansion of the Urban Police in the Late Nineteenth and Early Twentieth Centuries," in *Crime and Capitalism,* ed. D. Greenberg (Palo Alto, Calif.: Mayfield Publishing, 1981), pp. 292–313.

82. Jack Gibbs, "An Incorrigible Positivist," *Criminologist* 12 (1987): 2–3.

83. Toby, "The New Criminology Is the Old Sentimentality."

84. Sparks, "A Critique of Marxist Criminology," pp. 198–99.

85. Carl Klockars, "The Contemporary Crises of Marxist Criminology," in *Radical Criminology: The Coming Crisis,* ed. J. Inciardi (Beverly Hills: Sage, 1980), pp. 92–123.

86. Ibid., pp. 112–14.

87. Ibid.

88. Michael Lynch, W. Byron Groves, and Alan Lizotte, "The Rate of Surplus Value and Crime: A Theoretical and Empirical Examination of Marxian Economic Theory and Criminology," *Crime, Law and Social Change* 1 (in press, 1994).

89. Anthony Platt, "Criminology in the 1980s: Progressive Alternatives to 'Law and Order,'" *Crime and Social Justice* 21–22 (1985): 191–99.

90. See, generally, Roger Matthews and Jock Young, eds. *Confronting Crime* (London: Sage, 1986); for a thorough review of left realism, see Martin Schwartz and Walter DeKeseredy, "Left Realist Criminology: Strengths, Weaknesses and the Feminist Critique," *Crime, Law and Social Change* 15 (1991): 51–72.

91. Martin Schwartz and Walter DeKeseredy, "Left Realist Criminology: Strengths, Weaknesses and the Feminist Critique," *Crime, Law and Social Change* 15 (1991): 51–72.

92. Ibid., p. 54.

93. John Lea and Jock Young, *What Is to Be Done about Law and Order?* (Harmondsworth, England: Penguin, 1984).

94. Ibid., p. 88.

95. Richard Kinsey, John Lea, and Jock Young, *Losing the Fight against Crime* (London: Blackwell, 1986).

96. Schwartz and DeKeseredy, "Left Realist Criminology," p. 58.

97. For a general review of this issue, see Kathleen Daly and Meda Chesney-Lind, "Feminism and Criminology," *Justice Quarterly* 5 (1988): 497–538; Douglas Smith and Raymond Paternoster, "The Gender Gap in Theories of Deviance: Issues and Evidence," *Journal of Research in Crime and Delinquency* 24 (1987): 140–72; Pat Carlen, "Women, Crime, Feminism, and Realism," *Social Justice* 17 (1990): 106–23.

98. Julia Schwendinger and Herman Schwendinger, *Rape and Inequality* (Beverly Hills: Sage, 1983).

99. Daly and Chesney-Lind, "Feminism and Criminology," p. 536.

100. James Messerschmidt, *Capitalism, Patriarchy and Crime* (Totowa, N.J.: Rowman and Littlefield, 1986); for a critique of this work, see Herman Schwendinger and Julia Schwendinger, "The World according to James Messerschmidt," *Social Justice* 15 (1988): 123–45.

101. Kathleen Daly, "Gender and Varieties of White Collar Crime," *Criminology* 27 (1989): 769–93.

102. Jane Roberts Chapman, "Violence against Women as a Violation of Human Rights," *Social Justice* 17 (1990): 54–71.

103. For a review of feminist theory, see Sally Simpson, "Feminist Theory, Crime and Justice," *Criminology* 27 (1989): 605–32.

104. Suzie Dod Thomas and Nancy Stein, "Criminality, Imprisonment, and Women's Rights in the 1990's," *Social Justice* 17 (1990): 1–5.

105. Walter DeKeseredy and Martin Schwartz, "Male Peer Support and Woman Abuse: An Expansion of DeKeseredy's Model," *Sociological Spectrum* 13 (1993): 393–413.

106. Daly and Chesney-Lind, "Feminism and Criminology." See also Drew Humphries and Susan Caringella-MacDonald, "Murdered Mothers, Missing Wives: Reconsidering Female Victimization," *Social Justice* 17 (1990): 71–78.

107. Center for Research on Women, *Secrets in Public: Sexual Harassment in Our Schools* (Wellesley, Mass.: Wellesley College, 1993).

108. Mary Odem and Steven Schlossman, "Guardians of Virtue: The Juvenile Court and Female Delinquency in Early 20th-Century Los Angeles," *Crime and Delinquency* 37 (1991): 186–203.

109. Meda Chesney-Lind, "Judicial Enforcement of the Female Sex Role: The Family Court and the Female Delinquent," *Issues in Criminology* 8 (1973): 51–69; see also idem, "Women and Crime: The Female Offender," *Signs: Journal of Women in Culture and Society* 12 (1986): 78–96; idem, "Female Offenders: Paternalism Reexamined," in *Women, the Courts, and Equality,* ed. Laura L. Crites and Winifred L. Hepperle (Newbury Park, Calif.: Sage, 1987): 114–39; idem, "Girls' Crime and a Woman's Place: Toward a Feminist Model of Female Delinquency" (Paper presented at a meeting of the American Society of Criminology, Montreal, 1987).

110. Hagan, *Structural Criminology.*

111. John Hagan, A. R. Gillis, and John Simpson, "The Class Structure and Delinquency: Toward a Power-Control Theory of Common Delinquent Behavior," *American Journal of Sociology* 90 (1985): 1151–78; John Hagan, John Simpson, and A. R. Gillis, "Class in the Household: A Power-Control Theory of Gender and Delinquency," *American Journal of Sociology* 92 (1987): 788–816.

112. Gary Jensen, "Power-Control versus Social-Control Theory: Identifying Crucial Differences for Future Research" (Paper presented at the annual meeting of the American Society of Criminology, Baltimore, November 1990).

113. Gary Jensen and Kevin Thompson, "What's Class Got to Do with It? A Further Examination of Power-Control Theory," *American Journal of Sociology* 95 (1990): 1009–23. For some critical research, see Simon Singer and Murray Levine, "Power Control Theory, Gender and Delinquency: A Partial Replication with Additional Evidence on the Effects of Peers," *Criminology* 26 (1988): 627–48.

114. For a lengthy review, see Hagan, *Structural Criminology.*

115. Kevin Thompson, "Gender and Adolescent Drinking Problems: The Effects of Occupational Structure," *Social Problems* 36 (1989): 30–38.

116. See, generally, Lynch, "Rediscovering Criminology," pp. 27–28.

117. Dragan Milovanovic, *A Primer in the Sociology of Law* (New York: Harrow and Heston, 1988) pp. 127–28.

118. Richard Quinney, "The Way of Peace: On Crime, Suffering and Service," in *Criminology as Peacemaking,* ed. Harold Pepinsky and Richard Quinney (Bloomington: Indiana Univerity Press, 1991), pp. 8–9.

119. See, for example, Tifft and Sullivan, *The Struggle to Be Human;* and Sullivan, *The Mask of Love.*

120. Larry Tifft, Forward, to Dennis Sullivan, *The Mask of Love,* (Port Washington, N.Y.: Kennikat Press, 1980), p. 6.

121. Ibid., p. 141.

122. Pepinsky and Quinney, *Criminology as Peacemaking.*

10 Integrated Theories: Multifactor, Latent Trait, and Life Course

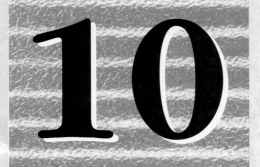

WANTED BY THE FBI

INTERSTATE FLIGHT - MURDER

THEODORE ROBERT BUNDY

☰ Introduction

While early criminologists readily embraced the theoretical work of their colleagues, modern criminologists have tended to be more specialized; they classify themselves as choice, conflict, labeling, control, or some other kind of theorist.[1] As a result, criminological theory today ranges from the most radical (Marxist, conflict, and peacemaking theory) to the most conservative (rational choice and biosocial theory) views. The ideological differences between these positions creates a gulf that sometimes seems impossible to bridge, especially when advocates are dismissive of competing viewpoints. Recently, to derive more powerful and robust explanations of crime, some criminologists have begun *integrating* these individual factors into complex, **multifactor theories** that attempt to blend seemingly independent concepts into coherent explanations of criminality.

A number of reasons account for the recent popularity of **integrated theory.** One is practical: the development of large, computerized data bases and software that facilitates statistical analysis now makes theory integration practical. Criminologists of an earlier era simply did not have the tools to conduct the sophisticated computations necessary for theory integration.

The other reason is substantive. Single-factor theories focus on the onset of crime; they tend to divide the world simply into criminals and noncriminals, those who have a crime-producing condition and those who do not. For example, people who feel anomie become deviant, those who do not, remain law-abiding; people with high testosterone levels are violent, people with low levels are not.

The view that people can be classified as either criminals or noncriminals and this status is stable over the course of one's life is now being challenged. Criminologists today are concerned not only with the onset of criminality but its termination: why do people age out or desist from crime? If, for example, criminality is a function of intelligence, as some criminologists claim, why do most delinquents fail to become adult criminals? It seems unlikely that intelligence level increases as young offenders mature. If the *onset* of criminality can be explained by intelligence level, then some other factor must explain its *termination*.

It has also become important to chart the natural history of a criminal career. Why do some offenders escalate their criminal activities, while others decrease or limit their law violations? Why do some offenders specialize in a particular crime, while others become generalists? Why do some criminals reduce criminal activity and then resume it once again? This approach is sometimes referred to as **developmental criminology**.

Integrated theories have also helped focus on the chronic or persistent offender (see Chapter 3). As you may recall, the Philadelphia cohort studies conducted by Wolfgang and his associates identified the existence of a relatively small group of chronic offenders who committed a significant amount of all serious crimes and persisted in criminal careers into their adulthood. Single-factor theories have trouble explaining why only a relatively few of the many individuals exposed to criminogenic influences in the environment actually become chronic offenders. For example, structural theories make a convincing case for a link between crime and social variables, such as neighborhood disorganization and cultural deviance. It is more difficult for these theories to explain why only a few adolescents in the most disorganized areas mature into chronic offenders. Why do so many underprivileged youths resist crime despite their exposure to social disorganization and cultural deviance? There may be more than a single reason one person engages in criminal behavior and another, living under similar circumstances, can avoid a criminal career.

By integrating a variety of ecological, socialization, psychological, biological, and economic factors into a coherent structure, criminologists are attempting to answer these complex questions. The following chapter provides an overview of these integrated theories.

☰ Integrated Theories

It is possible to divide integrated theories into three groups on the basis of their view of human development and change: multifactor theories, latent trait theories, and life course theories.

Multifactor Theories

The earliest integrated theories are referred to as multifactor theories. These suggest that social, personal, and economic factors each exert influence on criminal behavior. *Multifactor* theories combine the influences of structural, socialization, conflict, and individual level variables. At an individual level, the propensity to commit crime varies because each person maintains a unique set of life conditions and influences. On a macro level, aggregate crime rates change because economic and social conditions vary.

According to multifactor theories, kids who come from the lowest economic strata, make deviant friends, and learn deviant values are the ones most likely to engage in crime. The kids pictured above travel across the country by hopping freight trains. Are they "at risk" to crime?

The multifactor approach helps criminologists explain both criminal career formation and desistance from crime: While many youths are at risk to crime, relatively few face the complete set of hazards that result in a criminal career, including an impulsive personality, dysfunctional family, disorganized neighborhood, deviant friends, and school failure.

Latent Trait Theories

In a critical article, David Rowe, D. Wayne Osgood, and W. Alan Nicewander proposed the concept of **latent trait theory** to explain the flow of crime over the life cycle. This model assumes a distribution across the population of a personal characteristic that controls the propensity to offend.[2] This disposition or *latent trait* may be present at birth or established early in life and *remains stable over time*. Suspected latent traits include defective intelligence, impulsive personality, and genetic makeup.

The positive association between past and future criminality detected in the cohort studies of career criminals (Chapter 3) may reflect the presence of this underlying criminogenic trait. That is, if low IQ causes delinquency in childhood, it should also cause the same people to offend as adults, since intelligence is usually stable over the life span. Because latent traits are stable, people who are antisocial during their adolescence are the ones most likely to be persistent criminals throughout their life span.

Because latent traits are stable, fluctuations in offending over time reflect criminal *opportunities* and not the propensity to commit crime. For example, assume that a stable latent trait such as low IQ causes some people to commit crime. Teenagers have more *opportunity* to commit crime than adults of *equal intelligence;* therefore, adolescent crime rates are higher. While the *propensity* to commit crime is *stable*, the *opportunity* to commit crime fluctuates over time.

Life Course Theories

Another approach that has emerged is **life course theory.** In contrast to the latent trait view, life course theories holds that the *propensity* to commit crimes is not stable and *changes* over time; it is a developmental process. Some career criminals may desist from crime only to resume their activities at a later date. Some commit offenses at a steady pace, while others escalate the rate of their criminal involvement. Offenders may specialize in one type of crime or become generalists who commit a variety of illegal acts. Criminals may be influenced by family matters, financial needs, and changes in life-style and interests. While latent traits may be important, they alone do not influence the direction of criminal careers.

Life course theories also recognize that as people mature, the factors that influence their behavior also change.[3] At first, family relations may be most influential; in later adolescence, school and peer relations predominate; in adulthood, marital relations may be the most critical influence. Some antisocial kids who are "in trouble" throughout their adolescence may manage to find stable work and maintain intact marriages as adults; these life events help them desist from crime. In contrast, the less fortunate who develop arrest records and get involved with the "wrong crowd" later can only find menial jobs and are at risk for criminal careers. Social forces that are critical at one stage of life may have little meaning or influence at another.

Commonalities and Distinctions

While these three views seem irreconcilable, they in fact share some common ground. They indicate that a criminal career must be understood as a passage along which people travel, that it has a beginning and an end, and that events and life circumstances influence the journey. The factors that affect a criminal career may include structural factors, such as income and status; socialization factors, such as family and peer relations; biological factors, such as size and strength; psychological factors, including intelligence and personality; and opportunity factors, such as inadequate police protection and a supply of easily stolen merchandise. Life course and multifactor theories tend to stress the influence of changing interpersonal and structural factors; latent trait theories assume that it is not people but criminal opportunities that change.

These perspectives differ in their view of human development: Do people change, as life course theories suggest, or are they stable, constant, and changeless, as the latent trait view indicates? Is there a dominant key that controls human destiny, or are there multiple influences on human behavior? Are the social and personal factors that influence people stable, or do they change as a person matures?

In the sections below, some of the most important integrated theories that address the development and sustenance of a criminal career are discussed in some detail.

Multifactor Theories

Multifactor theories integrate a variety of variables into a cohesive explanation of criminality. Unlike the latent trait view, these theories recognize that factors that appear later in life, such as peer relations, exert an important influence on people.

Efforts to create multifactor theories are not new. Over a decade ago, Daniel Glazer combined elements of differential association with classical criminology and control theory in his differential anticipation theory.[4] Glazer's version asserts: "A person's crime or restraint from crime is determined by the consequences he anticipates from it."[5] According to Glazer, people commit crimes whenever and wherever the expectations of gain from them exceed the expectations of losses (rational choice). This decision is tempered by the quality of their social bonds and their relationships with others (control theory), as well as their prior learning experiences (learning theory).

Since Glazer's pioneering efforts, significant attempts have been made to integrate such social process concepts as learning, labeling, and control with structural and other variables. A few prominent examples of integrated theory are briefly discussed below.

Social Development Theory

Joseph Weis and his associates have attempted to integrate the social control approach with the social structure models discussed earlier.[6] Weis recognizes that factors related to a person's place in the social structure—sex, race, and economic status—exert powerful forces on the individual's behavioral choices. At the same time, socialization also contributes to the likelihood that an individual will engage in criminal or conventional behavior.

Weis, working with J. David Hawkins and John Sederstrom, developed the model of criminality illustrated in Figure 10.1.

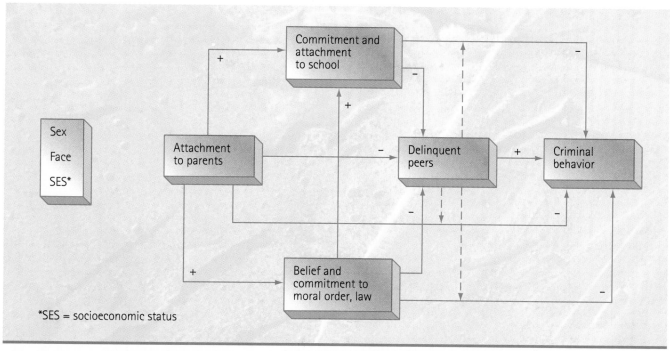

FIGURE 10.1 **Social Development: An Integration of Control and Cultural Deviance Theories**

SOURCE: Joseph Weis and John Sederstrom, *Reports of the National Juvenile Justice Assessment Centers, The Prevention of Serious Delinquency: What to Do* (Washington, D.C.: U.S. Department of Justice, 1981), p. 35.

Weis's model uses elements of both control and social structure theories. In a low-income, disorganized community, the influences of front-line socializing institutions are weak. Families are under great stress; educational facilities are inadequate; there are fewer material goods; and respect for the law is weak. Because crime rates are high, there are greater opportunities for law violation, putting even greater strain on the agencies of social control.

Within this context of weak social control and community disorganization, legitimate social institutions are incapable of combating the lure of criminal groups and gangs. The family remains the front-line defense to a criminal career. Positive familial relationships are related to developing a commitment and attachment to school and the educational process. Concomitantly, youths whose educational experience is a meaningful one marked by academic success and commitment to educational achievement will be more likely to develop conventional beliefs and values, become committed to conventional activities, and seek out and be influenced by noncriminal peers. But if youths do not find participation in school and family activities rewarding, they will be likely to seek associations with others who are

equally disillusioned and consequently engage in deviant activities that hold the promise of alternative rewards.

Weis's model can account for both the high crime rates found in lower-class areas as well as the influence of critical agents of the social order on criminal behavior.

Elliott's Integrated Theory

Another attempt at theory integration has been proposed by Delbert Elliott and his colleagues David Huizinga and Suzanne Ageton of the Behavioral Research Institute in Boulder, Colorado.[7] Their view combines the features of strain (Chapter 7), social learning, and control theories into a single theoretical model.

According to the Elliott view, illustrated in Figure 10.2, perceptions of strain (the condition that occurs when people begin to believe they cannot achieve success through conventional means, such as education or job), inadequate socialization, and living in socially disorganized areas lead youths to develop weak bonds with conventional groups, activities, and norms. Weak conventional bonds and continued high levels of perceived strain lead some youth to seek out and become

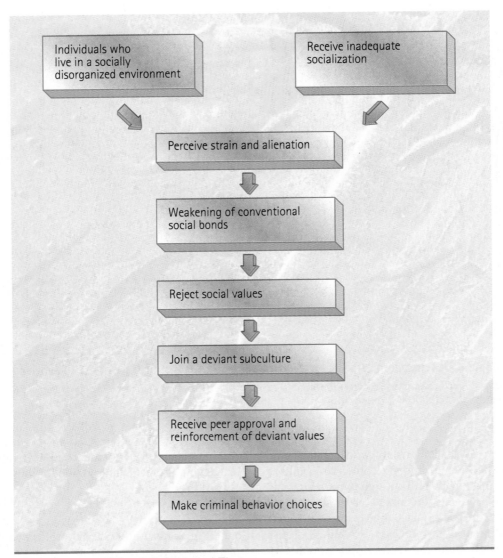

FIGURE 10.2   Elliott's Integrated Theory

bonded to like-minded peer groups. From these delinquent associations come positive reinforcements for delinquent behaviors; delinquent peers help provide role models for antisocial behavior. Bonding to delinquent groups when combined with alienation from conventional groups and norms leads to a high probability of involvement in delinquent behavior.

Elliott and his colleagues tested their theoretical model with data taken from a national youth survey of approximately 1,800 youths who were interviewed annually over a three-year period. With only a few minor exceptions, the results supported their integrated theory. One difference was that some subjects reported developing strong bonds to delinquent peers even if they did not reject the values of conventional society.

Elliott and his colleagues interpret this finding as suggesting that youths living in disorganized areas may have little choice but to join with law-violating youth groups since conventional groups simply do not exist. Elliott also found that initial experimentation with drugs and delinquency predicted both joining a teenage law-violating peer group and becoming involved with additional delinquency.

The picture Elliott draws of the teenage delinquent is not dissimilar to Weis's social development model: Living in a disorganized neighborhood, feeling hopeless and unable to get ahead, and becoming involved in petty crimes eventually leads to a condition where conventional social values become weak and attenuated. Concern for education, family relations, and respect for the social order are weakened. A deviant peer group becomes an acceptable substitute, and consequently the attitudes and skills that support delinquent tendencies are amplified. The result: early experimentation with drugs and delinquency becomes a way of life.

Integrated Structural Marxist Theory

Not all multifactor views of crime rely solely on mainstream concepts. In one important work, conflict theorists Mark Colvin and John Pauly have created a theory that integrates conflict concepts with structural and process factors in a theory of crime that they label **integrated structural theory,** illustrated in Figure 10.3.[8]

According to Colvin and Pauly, crime is a result of socialization within the family. Coercive family relationships marked by conflict and despair are the forerunner of criminal careers. Family relations and therefore criminality are actually controlled by the marketplace.

The quality of one's work experience is shaped by the historical interaction between competition among capitalists and the level of class struggle.[9] Wage earners who occupy an inferior position in the economic hierarchy will experience coercive relationships with their supervisors and employers. Negative experiences in the workplace create strain and alienation within the family setting, which in turn relates to inconsistent and overly punitive discipline at home. Juveniles who live in such an environment will become alienated from their parents and at the same time experience adjustment problems in social institutions, especially school. For example, youths growing up in a family headed by parents who are at the bottom of workplace control structures are also the ones most likely to go to under-funded schools, do poorly on standardized tests, and be placed in slow learning tracks; each of these factors has been correlated with delinquent behavior.

Negative social relations at home and at school result in feelings of alienation and strain. These are reinforced by associations with groups of similarly alienated peers. In some cases, the peer groups will be oriented toward patterns of violent behavior, while in other instances, the groups will enable their members to benefit economically from criminal behavior.

According to integrated structural theory, it is naive to believe that a crime control policy can be formulated without regard for its basic root causes. Coercive punishments or misguided treatments cannot be effective unless the core relationships with regard to material production are changed. Those who produce goods must be given a greater opportunity to control the forms of production and, in so doing, be given the power to shape their lives and the lives of their families. While integrated structural Marxist theory has not yet been subject to numerous empirical tests, recent research by Steven Messner and Marvin Krohn was generally supportive of its core principles.[10]

≡ The Latent Trait Approach

Latent trait type theories assume that some latent trait(s) or condition(s), in most cases present at birth or soon after, can account for the onset of criminality. Thereafter, the propensity for crime remains stable throughout a person's life. Social forces and opportunity can then influence the likelihood of crime. People age out of crime because as they mature there are simply fewer opportunities to commit crime and greater inducement to remain "straight."

What are some of the suspected traits linked to crime? As you may recall, offending patterns have been linked to such biosocial factors as attention deficit disorders and such psychological traits as impulsivity. Individual-level factors seem ideally suited for a role in

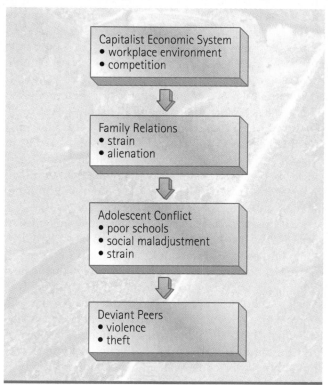

FIGURE 10.3   Integrated Structural Theory

Capitalist Economic System
• workplace environment
• competition

⬇

Family Relations
• strain
• alienation

⬇

Adolescent Conflict
• poor schools
• social maladjustment
• strain

⬇

Deviant Peers
• violence
• theft

theory integration because, as noted earlier in Chapter 6, it is evident that alone, they cannot explain crime rate patterns and changes. Almost all biosocial and psychological advocates recognize the multidimensionality of crime. As biosocial theorist Lee Ellis maintains, (1) the physical-chemical functioning of the brain is responsible for all human behavior, (2) brain function is controlled by genetic and environmental factors, and (3) environmental influences on brain function encompass both physical (drugs, chemicals, and injuries) and experiential (social) factors. Ellis finds that all three components of modern biocriminology (biochemistry, genetics, and neurology) work in concert with social and experiential factors to control crime.[11]

Two integrated theories that assume that crime is a function of a latent trait are discussed below in some detail.

Crime and Human Nature

One of the most widely read and analyzed works in the criminological literature is James Q. Wilson and Richard Herrnstein's book *Crime and Human Nature*.[12] These two prominent social scientists make a convincing argument that personal traits, such as genetic makeup, intelligence, and body build, may outweigh the importance of social variables as predictors of the crime rate. Wilson and Herrnstein, therefore, propose an integrated theory of criminality that includes elements of biosocial makeup, personality, rational choice, and structure and social process.

According to Wilson and Herrnstein, all human behavior, including criminality, is determined by its perceived consequences. A criminal incident occurs when an individual chooses criminal over conventional behavior (referred to as "noncrime") after weighing the potential gains and losses of each; crime then is a function of *rational choice*. According to Wilson and Herrnstein, "the larger the ratio of net rewards of crime to the net rewards of noncrime, the greater the tendency to commit the crime."[13]

The rewards for crime can include material gain, sexual gratification, revenge, and peer approval. The consequences can include pangs of conscience, victim reprisals, social disapproval, and the threat of legal punishment. While crime's consequences may deter some would-be criminals, their impact may be neutralized by the fact that they are typically distant threats, while in contrast, the *rewards* of crime are immediate and current. The rewards for choosing noncrime are also gained in the future: if you "stay clean," someday people will learn to respect you, your self-image and reputation will improve, and you may achieve happiness and freedom.

Of course, one can never be quite sure of the rewards of either crime or noncrime. The burglar may hope for the "big score" but instead experience arrest, conviction, and incarceration; people who "play it straight" may find that their sacrifice does not get them to the place in society they desire.

Choosing Crime or Noncrime

The choice between crime and noncrime is quite often a difficult one. Criminal choices are reinforced by the desire to obtain basic rewards—food, clothing, shelter, sex—or learned goals—wealth, power, status—without having to work and save for them. Even if an individual has been socialized to choose noncrime, crime can be an attractive alternative, especially if any potential negative consequences are uncertain and delayed far into the future. By analogy, cigarette smoking is common because its potentially fatal consequences are distant and uncertain; taking cyanide or arsenic is rare because the effects are immediate and certain (though in some other ways, not too different).

Wilson and Herrnstein's model is integrative because it assumes that biological and psychological traits influence the crime-noncrime choice. They find that a close link exists between a person's decision to choose crime and such biosocial factors as low intelligence, mesomorphic body type, genetic influences (parental criminality), and possessing an autonomic nervous system that responds too quickly to stimuli. Psychological traits, including an impulsive or extraverted personality and low intelligence, also determine the potential to commit crime; one of their more controversial assertions is that the relationship between crime and intelligence is "robust and significant."[14] Being in possession of these traits will not by themselves guarantee that a person will become a criminal; however, all things being equal, those who have them will be more likely to choose crime over noncrime.

Wilson and Herrnstein do not ignore the influence of social factors on criminality. They believe that a turbulent family life, school failure, and membership in a deviant teenage subculture also have a powerful influence on criminality. According to Wilson and Herrnstein, biosocial, psychological, and social conditions, working in concert, can influence thought patterns and, eventually, individual behavior patterns. For example, intelligence level is considered to be an important determinant of criminal behavior choice. Its influence is mediated by a social variable, school performance: A child who chron-

Latent trait theories suggest that some condition present at birth or soon after controls behavior throughout the lifespan. Are these skinheads a product of their environment? Or, is it possible that they possess some latent trait, such as an impulsive personality, which explains their persistent antisocial behavior?

ically loses standing in the competition of the classroom may feel justified in settling the score outside by violence, theft, and other forms of defiant illegality. School failure enhances the rewards for crime by engendering feelings of unfairness. In addition, failure in school predicts, to a substantial degree, failure in the marketplace. For someone who stands to gain little from legitimate work, the rewards of noncrime are relatively weak. Failure in school, therefore, not only enhances the rewards for crime, but it predicts weak rewards for noncrime.[15]

Somewhat surprisingly, Wilson and Herrnstein do not view harsh punishment as the answer to the crime problem. They argue that the solution can be achieved by strengthening the besieged U.S. family and helping it to orient children toward noncrime solutions to their problems. The family, regardless of its composition, can help a child cultivate character, conscience, and respect for the moral order. Similarly, schools can help by teaching the benefits of accepting personal responsibility and, within limits, helping students understand what constitutes "right conduct."

Wilson and Herrnstein have assembled an impressive array of supportive research in *Crime and Human Nature*. Critics of their work have focused on the fact that much of the evidence that they use to support their view suffers from sampling inadequacy, questionable measurement techniques, observer bias, and neglect of sociological dimensions.[16] These criticisms aside, their work presents a dramatic attempt to integrate two of the most prominent theoretical movements in the study of criminality.

General Theory of Crime

In an important work, *A General Theory of Crime,* Travis Hirschi, writing with Michael Gottfredson, has modified and redefined some of the principals articulated in his social control theory (see Chapter 8) by integrating the concepts of control with those of biosocial, psychological, routine activities, and rational choice theories.[17] While in his original version of control theory, Hirschi focused on the social controls that attach people to conventional society, in this new work, he concentrates on **self-control** as a stabilizing force. The two views are connected, however, because both social control (or social bonds) and self-control are acquired through early experiences with effective parenting.

The Act and the Offender

In their general theory, Gottfredson and Hirschi consider the *criminal offender* and the *criminal act* as separate concepts (see Figure 10.4). On the one hand, criminal acts, such as robberies or burglaries, are illegal events or deeds that people engage in when they perceive them to be advantageous. For example, burglaries are typically committed by young males looking for cash, liquor, and entertainment; the crime provides "easy, short-term gratification."[18] Even if the number of offenders remains constant, crime rates may fluctuate because of the presence or absence of criminal opportunities. This aspect of the theory relies on concepts similar to rational choice and routine activities theories.

On the other hand, criminal offenders are people predisposed to commit crimes. They are not robots who commit crime without restraint; their days are also filled with conventional behaviors, such as going to school, parties, concerts, and church. But given the same set of criminal opportunities, criminogenic people have a much higher probability of violating the law than do noncriminals.

By recognizing that there are stable differences in people's propensity to commit crime, the general theory adds a *biosocial* element to the concept of social control: individual differences are stable over the life course and so is the propensity to commit crime; it is only opportunity that changes.

What Makes People Crime-Prone?

What, then, causes people to become excessively crime-prone? To Gottfredson and Hirschi, the explanation for

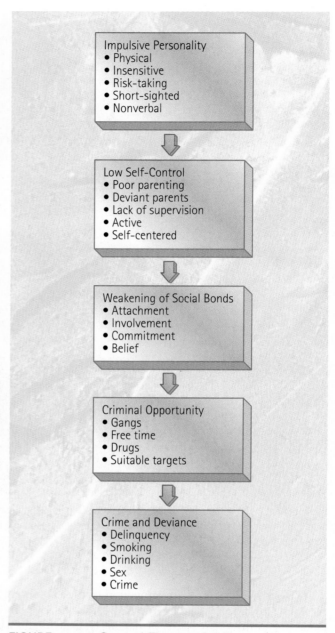

FIGURE 10.4   **General Theory of Crime**

individual differences in the tendency to commit criminal acts can be found in a person's level of *self-control.* People with limited self-control tend to be **impulsive;** they are insensitive, physical (rather than mental), risk-taking, short-sighted, and nonverbal.[19] They have a "here and now" orientation and refuse to work for distant goals; they lack diligence, tenacity, and persistence in a course of action. People lacking self-control tend to be adventuresome, active, physical, and self-centered.

As they mature, they have unstable marriages, jobs, and friendships.[20] Criminal acts are attractive to them because they provide easy and immediate gratification, or, as Gottfredson and Hirschi put it, "money without work, sex without courtship, revenge without court delays."[21] Since those with low self-control enjoy risky, exciting, or thrilling behaviors with immediate benefits, they are more likely to enjoy criminal acts that require stealth, danger, agility, speed, and power, than conventional acts, which demand long-term study and cognitive and verbal skills. Table 10.1 lists the elements of self-control.

Considering their desire for easy pleasures, it should come as no surprise that people lacking self-control will also engage in noncriminal behaviors that provide them with immediate and short-term gratifica-tion, such as smoking, drinking, gambling, and illicit sexuality.[22]

What causes people to lack self-control? Gottfredson and Hirschi trace the root cause of poor self-control to inadequate child-rearing practices. Parents who refuse or are unable to monitor a child's behavior, to recognize deviant behavior when it occurs, and to punish that behavior will produce children who lack self-control. Kids who are not attached to their parents, who are poorly supervised, and whose parents are criminal or deviant themselves are the most likely to develop poor self-control.

Low self-control develops early in life and remains stable into and through adulthood.[23] Considering the continuity of criminal motivation, Hirschi and Gottfredson have questioned the utility of the juvenile justice system

Michael Gottfredson (right) and Travis Hirschi (left), authors of *A General Theory of Crime*, link criminality to an impulsive personality and lack of self-control.

TABLE 10.1 **The Six Elements of Self-Control**

1. Ability to delay gratification
2. Tendency to be diligent, tenacious, and persistent
3. Inclination to be cautious, cognitive, and verbal
4. Tendency to engage in long-term pursuits and relationships
5. Possession of cognitive or academic skills
6. The ability to be concerned and sensitive to the needs and suffering of others

and of giving special, and presumably more lenient, treatment to delinquent offenders: Why separate youthful and adult offenders legally, when the source of their criminality (for example, impulsivity), is essentially the same?[24]

Self-Control and Crime

Gottfredson and Hirschi claim that the principles of self-control theory can be used to explain all varieties of criminal behavior and all the social and behavioral correlates of crime. That is, such widely disparate crimes as burglary, robbery, embezzlement, drug dealing, murder, rape, and insider trading all stem from a deficiency of self-control. Likewise, gender, racial, and ecological differences in the crime rate can be explained by discrepancies in self-control. Put another way, if the male crime rate is higher than the female crime rate (which it is), the discrepancy can be explained by the fact that males have lower levels of self-control.

Unlike other theoretical models that are limited to explaining narrow segments of criminal behavior (such as theories of teenage gang formation), Gottfredson and Hirschi argue that self-control applies equally to all crimes, ranging from murder to corporate theft. For example, Gottfredson and Hirschi maintain that rates of white-collar crime remain quite low because people lacking in self-control rarely attain the position necessary to commit those crimes. However, the relatively few white-collar criminals lack self-control in the manner rapists and burglars lack self-control. Gottfredson and Hirschi recognize that all people become less crime-prone as they age. While the criminal activity of low self-control individuals also declines, they maintain an offense rate that remains consistently higher than those with strong self-control.

Supporting Evidence. Following the publication of the *General Theory of Crime*, several research efforts

have been conducted that support the theoretical views of Gottfredson and Hirschi. One approach is to identify indicators of impulsiveness and self-control and determine whether scales measuring these factors correlate with measures of criminal activity; a number of studies have had success in showing this type of association.[25] For example, both male and female drunk drivers were found to be impulsive individuals who manifest low self-control.[26] Research on violent recidivists indicate that they can be distinguished from other offenders on the basis of their impulsive personality structure.[27]

Two recent studies, one by Daniel Nagin and Raymond Paternoster and the other by Harold Grasmick and his associates, have also found general support for the self-control concept.[28] Both efforts found that low-self control alone cannot explain a majority of criminal acts and that other forces, including the evaluation of criminal opportunity, may be involved in the production of criminality. It is possible that the causal chain flows from an (1) impulsive personality to (2) lack of self-control to (3) the withering of social bonds to (4) the opportunity to commit crime and delinquency to (5) deviant behavior.[29]

An Analysis of the General Theory of Crime

Gottfredson and Hirschi's general theory provides answers to many of the questions left unresolved by Hirschi's original control model. By separating the concepts of criminality and crime, Gottfredson and Hirschi help explain why some people who lack self-control can escape criminality: they lack criminal opportunity. Kids who are at risk because they have an impulsive personality may forgo criminal careers because they lack criminal opportunity: they are enrolled in tennis lessons; they go to church; they join the Boy Scouts; they enter the military; they have great athletic ability and make the team.

If the opportunity is strong enough, even those people with relatively strong self-control may be tempted to violate the law; the incentives to commit crime may overwhelm self-control. Opportunity can explain why the so-called "good kid," who has a strong school record and positive parental relationships, gets involved in drugs or vandalism or why the corporate executive with a spotless record gets caught up in business fraud. Even a successful executive may find his or her self-control inadequate if the potential for illegal gain runs into the tens of millions. It is also possible, as Michael Benson and Elizabeth Moore contend, that in some cases, the fear of failure, and not the desire for criminal opportunity, overwhelms self-control. During tough economic times, the manager who fears dismissal may be tempted to circumvent the law to improve the bottom line.[30]

Though the general theory seems persuasive, several questions remain unanswered.[31] Saying someone lacks self-control implies that he or she suffers from a personality defect that makes him or her impulsive and rash. The view that criminals maintain a deviant personality is not new; psychologists have long sought evidence of a "criminal personality."[32] Yet the search for the criminal personality has proven elusive, and there is still no conclusive proof that criminals can be distinguished from noncriminals on the basis of personality alone.

The theory also fails to address social ecological patterns in the crime rate. For example, if crime rates are higher in Los Angeles than Albany, New York, can it be assumed that Angelinos are more impulsive than Albanians? Or that they have more criminal opportunities? Gottfredson and Hirschi explain racial differences in the crime as a failure of child-rearing practices in the African-American community.[33] In so doing, they overlook issues of institutional racism, poverty, and relative deprivation, which have been shown to have a significant impact on crime rate differentials.

The general theory also ignores the moral concept of right and wrong, or "belief," which Hirschi considered a cornerstone in his earlier writings on the social bond.[34] Does this mean that the learning and assimilation of moral values has little effect on criminality? Because it omits the concept of belief, the general theory of crime can be distinguished from control theories that assume that people are controlled by their sense of right and wrong.

Finally, the general theory assumes that people do not change; it is opportunity that changes. Is it possible that human personality and behavior patterns remain little altered over the life course? Research by Scott Menard, Delbert Elliott, and Sharon Wofford indicate that factors that help control criminal behavior, such as peer relations and school performance, *vary over time.* Factors that have a controlling effect in early adolescence may fade and be replaced by others.[35] For example, Elliott and Menard found that having delinquent peers precedes and encourages future criminality; this finding contradicts self-control theory, which assumes that criminality is both a constant and independent of personal relationships.[36]

While these questions remain, the strength of the general theory lies in its scope and breadth; it attempts to explain all forms of crime and deviance, from lower-class gang delinquency to sexual harassment in the business community.[37] By integrating concepts of criminal choice, criminal opportunity, socialization, and personality, Gottfredson and Hirschi make a plausible argument that all deviant behaviors may originate at the same source.

Life Course Theories

As you may recall from Chapter 4, a great deal of research has been conducted on the relationship of age and crime and the activities of chronic offenders. This body of scholarship has prompted interest in the **life cycle** of crime: what causes the onset of criminality? What sustains a criminal career over a person's life course? A number of themes are now emerging. One is that the seeds of a criminal career are planted early in life: **early onset** of deviance is a strong predictor of later criminality. Research shows that kids who will become delinquent in adolescence begin their deviant careers by experiencing adjustment problems as early as the preschool years.[38] Studies of narcotics addicts show that the earlier the onset of substance abuse, the more frequent, varied, and sustained the addict's criminal career.[39]

Another theme is the **continuity of crime:** the best predictor of future criminality is past criminality. Kids who are repeatedly in trouble during adolescence are the ones who will still be antisocial as adults. Criminal activity beginning early in the life course is likely to be sustained because these offenders seem to lack the "social survival skills" necessary to find work or develop the interpersonal relationships needed to allow them to "drop out" of crime.[40]

Life course theorists conclude that multiple social, personal, and economic factors can influence criminality and that as these factors change over time, so too does criminal involvement.[41] A number of factors that encourage delinquency during the life course have been identified, including educational failure and family relations. Criminality, according to this view, cannot be attributed to a single cause, nor does it represent a single underlying tendency.[42]

The Glueck Research

One of the cornerstones of the recent life course research lies in renewed interest in the research efforts of Sheldon Glueck and Eleanor Glueck. While at Harvard

The cornerstone of life course research lies in the scholarly efforts of Sheldon Glueck and Eleanor Glueck.

University in the 1930s, the Gluecks popularized research on the life cycle of delinquent careers. In a series of longitudinal research studies, they followed the careers of known delinquents to determine the factors that predicted persistent offending.[43] The Gluecks made extensive use of interviews and records in their elaborate comparisons of delinquents and nondelinquents.[44]

The Gluecks' research was a precursor of the life course school. They focused on early onset of delinquency as a harbinger of a criminal career: "the deeper the roots of childhood maladjustment, the smaller the chance of adult adjustment." They also noted the stability of offending careers: children who are antisocial early in life are the ones most likely to continue their offending careers into adulthood.

The Gluecks identified a number of personal and social factors related to persistent offending, the most important of which, family relations, included the quality of discipline and emotional ties with parents. The adolescent raised in a large, single-parent family of limited economic means and educational achievement was the one most vulnerable to delinquency.

The Gluecks did not restrict their analysis to social variables. When they measured such biological and psychological traits as body type, intelligence, and personality, they found that physical and mental factors also played a role in determining behavior. Children with low intelligence, who have a background of mental disease, and who maintain a powerful physique (mesomorphs) were the ones most likely to become persistent offenders.

The Gluecks' research was virtually ignored for nearly 30 years as the study of crime and delinquency shifted almost exclusively to social and social-psychological factors (poverty, neighborhood deterioration, socialization) that formed the nucleus of structural and process theories. The Gluecks' methodology and their integration of biological, psychological, and social factors was heavily criticized by the mainstream sociologists who dominated the field. For many years, their work was ignored in criminology texts and overlooked in the academic curriculum.

Life Course Emerges

During the past decade, the Glueck "legacy" was "rediscovered" in a series of papers by criminologists John Laub and Robert Sampson. These scholars argued that the careful empirical measurements made by the Gluecks, which had been cast aside by the criminological community, were actually an ideal platform for studying criminal careers.[45] Laub and Sampson have reanalyzed the Glueck data and employed it in a series of articles that have gained wide readership. Their work will be discussed in greater detail later in the chapter.

A 1990 review paper by Rolf Loeber and Marc LeBlanc was another important event in the development of life course theory.[46] In this critical work, Loeber and LeBlanc proposed that criminologists devote time and effort to understanding some basic questions about the evolution of criminal careers: Why do people begin committing antisocial acts? Why do some stop or desist, while others continue or persist? Why do some escalate the severity of their criminality, that is, go from shoplifting to drug dealing to armed robbery, while others deescalate and commit less serious crime as they mature? If some terminate their criminal activity, what, if anything, causes them to begin again? Why do some criminals specialize in certain types of crime, while others are generalists engaging in a garden variety of antisocial behavior? According to Loeber and LeBlanc's **developmental view,** criminologists must devote their attention to the way a criminal career unfolds over a person's life cycle.

A number of key research efforts also found that criminogenic influences change and develop. In their studies on delinquency prevention, Gerald Patterson and his colleagues at the Oregon Social Learning Center found that poor parental discipline and monitoring was a key to the onset of criminality in early childhood. Then, in middle childhood, social rejection by conventional peers and academic failure sustained antisocial behavior; in later adolescence, commitment to a deviant peer group created a "training ground" for crime. Kids who are improperly socialized by unskilled parents are the ones most likely to rebel by wandering the streets with their deviant peers.[47] While the *onset* of a criminal career is a function of poor parenting skills, its maintenance and support is connected to social relations that emerge later in life.[48]

Similar results have been obtained from the Pittsburgh Youth Study, a longitudinal analysis of elementary school-age boys that indicates that early onset is correlated with social withdrawal, depression, deviant peers, and family problems, while later onset (at ages 13 or 14) was geared toward low educational motivation.[49]

From these and similar efforts has emerged a view of crime that incorporates personal change and growth. The factors that produce crime and delinquency at one point in the life cycle may not be relevant at another; as people mature, the social, physical, and environmental influences on their behavior are transformed.

In the sections below, some of the more important concepts associated with the life course perspective are reviewed, and some prominent life course theories are set out in detail.

Is There a Problem Behavior Syndrome?

Most criminological theories portray crime as the *result* of social problems rather than their *cause*. Learning theorists view a troubled home life and deviant friends as precursors of criminality; structural theorists maintain that acquiring deviant cultural values leads to criminality.

In contrast, the life course view is that criminality may best be understood as one of many social problems faced by at-risk youth. Criminality may be part of a **problem behavior syndrome (PBS),** a group of antisocial behaviors that cluster together and typically involve substance abuse, smoking, precocious sexuality and early pregnancy, educational underachievement, suicide attempts, sensation seeking, and unemployment.[50] Research efforts have found that the early onset of criminality is correlated with a garden variety of these antisocial behaviors.[51] For example, a recent survey of Minnesota students in grades six, nine, and 12 shows that children who experienced physical and sexual abuse at the hands of parents or other adults were also likely to have eating disorders (binge eating, purging, anorexia) and increased levels of cigarette smoking, alcohol consumption, stress, anxiety, hard-drug use, and suicidal thoughts; they are likely to have families with histories of alcohol abuse and drug addiction.[52] Multisite research has shown that PBS is not unique to any single area of the country and that kids are getting involved in elements of PBS, including drug use, delinquency, and precocious sexuality, at a very early age.[53]

PBS may be a more complex problem than was initially believed. Richard Jessor has identified a number of factors that lead to what he labels "health/life compromising outcomes." Some of these are biological or environmental, while others rest on personality traits. These factors may act alone or in concert to effect risk-taking behaviors, including delinquency and substance abuse, which eventually lead to a destructive adult life-style characterized by low self-esteem, disease, unemployment, and suicide.[54] Jessor's inclusion of health and illness risk has been confirmed by research showing that kids who suffer elements of PBS are more likely to be accident-prone and require more health care and hospitalization than the general population.[55]

Helene Raskin White studied a sample of 400 youth measured repeatedly over a six-year cycle and found that behaviors that clustered together included delinquency, substance abuse, school misconduct and underachievement, precocious sexual behavior, violence, suicide, and mental health problems.[56] White found problem behaviors to be stable: subjects who experienced multiple problems at age 15 continued to experience them at age 21. Nonetheless, she also found gender differences in the way behaviors clustered and that the associations among specific problem behaviors were unstable over time. In a subsequent research analysis conducted with Erich Labouvie, White found that delinquents and drug abusers actually could fall into one of several behaviorally defined groups: some were involved in delinquency but not drug abuse; others used drugs but were crime-free; some were generalists who engaged in both delinquency and drug abuse. This latter group could be differentiated from the others as being more intelligent but also displaying higher levels of psychological problems, lack of control, and lower emotional stability.[57]

So problem behaviors may cluster in a number of different ways, affecting people as they mature from adolescence into adulthood.[58] The interconnection of problem behaviors should increase the risk of teenage pregnancy, AIDS, and other sources of social distress that require a combination of behaviors (sex, drug use, violence).

Pathways to Crime

Are there different pathways to crime? Life course theorists recognize that there may be more than a single road traveled by career criminals: some may specialize in violence and extortion; some may be involved in theft and fraud; others may engage in a variety of criminal acts.

Using data taken from a longitudinal cohort study conducted in Pittsburgh, Rolf Loeber and his associates are now mapping the **pathways** to crime traveled by at-risk youth.[59] Loeber and his associates have so far identified three distinct paths to a criminal career:

The **authority conflict pathway** begins at an early age with stubborn behavior and defiance of parents. This leads to defiance (doing things one's own way, refusing to do things, disobedience) and then to authority avoidance (staying out late, truancy, and running away).

The **covert pathway** begins with minor underhanded behavior (lying, shoplifting) that leads to property damage (setting fires, damaging property) and eventually escalates to more serious forms of criminality ranging from joyriding, pocket-picking, larceny, and fencing to passing bad checks, using bad credit cards, car theft, drug dealing, and breaking and entering.

The **overt pathway** consists of an escalation of aggressive acts beginning with aggression (annoying others, bullying) leading to physical (and gang) fighting to violence (attacking someone, strong arming, forced theft).

The Loeber research indicates that each of these paths may lead to a sustained deviant career. Some enter two and even three paths simultaneously: they are stubborn, lie to teachers and parents, are bullies, and commit petty thefts; these adolescents are the ones most likely to become persistent offenders as they mature.

So while some persistent offenders may specialize in one type of behavior, others engage in a variety of criminal acts and antisocial behaviors as they mature. For example, they cheat on tests, bully kids in the school yard, take drugs, commit a burglary, go on to steal a car, and then shoplift from a store. In the Close-Up on violent female criminals, the life course of one such offender group is discussed in detail.

Theories of the Criminal Life Course

An ongoing effort has been made to track persistent offenders over their life course.[60] The early data seems to support what is already known about delinquent-criminal career patterns: early onset predicts later offending, there is continuity in crime (juvenile offenders are the ones most likely to become adult criminals), and chronic offenders commit a significant portion of all crimes.[61]

Based on these findings, a number of systematic theories that account for the onset, continuance, and desistance from crime have been formulated. In the following sections, three life course theories are discussed in some detail.

Farrington's Theory of Delinquent Development

One of the most important of the longitudinal studies tracking persistent offenders is the *Cambridge Study in Delinquent Development*. This effort has followed the offending careers of 411 London boys born in 1953.[62] This cohort study, directed since 1982 by David Farrington, is one of the most serious attempts to isolate the factors that predict the continuity of criminal behavior through the life course. The study uses self-report data as well as in-depth interviews and psychological testing. The boys were interviewed eight times over a period of 24 years, beginning at age eight and continuing to age 32.[63]

The results of the Cambridge study have been quite important because they show that many of the same patterns found in the United States are repeated in a cross-national sample: the existence of chronic offenders, the continuity of offending, and early onset leading to persistent criminality.

Farrington found that the traits present in persistent offenders can be observed as early as age eight (see Table 10.2). The chronic criminal, typically a male, begins as a property offender, and is born into a low-income, large family headed by parents who have criminal records and with delinquent older siblings. The future criminal receives poor parental supervision, including the use of harsh or erratic punishment and child-rearing techniques; his parents are likely to divorce or separate.

CLOSE-UP

Violent Female Street Criminals

While considerable research interest is now being devoted to female offenders, very little has been done to chart the life course of one subset of this group: violent female street criminals. To correct this oversight, Deborah Baskin and Ira Sommers interviewed a sample of known violent female felons in New York City. Their data provides considerable insight into formation and maintenance of a criminal career.

Baskin and Sommers found that about 60 percent of violent female offenders begin their criminal career at a very early age; about half reported regular fighting as early as ten years old, and about 40 percent reported that they regularly left home carrying a weapon. In contrast, the other 40 percent reported that they did not engage in fighting until much later, not until they had left school. Because of the clear time differential when these females began their criminal careers, Basken and Sommers conducted an independent analysis of the early- and late-onset offenders.

The women in both groups suffered from severe social and emotional problems. All were likely to have been raised in single-parent families and have received little parental supervision. Both groups experienced physical and sexual abuse at the hand of a parent or guardian and were likely to have witnessed abuse between their guardians. Almost half were raised in households that relied on public welfare. More than half had a parent who was either a substance abuser or had been incarcerated sometime during his or her childhood.

Women in the early onset group could be distinguished by the severity of their childhood problems. They were the ones most likely to reside in areas with high concentrations of poverty and to have family histories of psychiatric problems requiring hospitalization. They were more likely to be truant, leave school early, and associate with delinquent peers while in school. They also were more likely to be placed in a juvenile detention center.

The major distinction between the groups, however, could be found in the scale and direction of their offending careers. While both groups were drug users, early-onset women began abusing substances two years ahead of the late-onset group. The early-onset group were involved in a variety of crimes, including serious robberies, assaults, and burglaries, even before they became involved with drug use. In contrast, the later-onset group were involved mostly in nonviolent crimes, such as shoplifting and prostitution, *up until* they began taking drugs. The violent offending of the latter group then is clearly part of a drug-crime connection. In contrast, the violent behavior of the early-onset women was part of a generalized PBS.

The Baskin-Sommers research is supportive of the life course view: events in these women's lives shaped the direction of their offending careers. The researchers found that there are in fact different pathways to a crime. In contrast to latent trait theory, they found that events that occur later in life, for example, drug addiction, influence criminality. Baskin and Sommers also show that environment influences offending, a finding in contrast with the latent trait approach.

As Baskin and Sommers suggest, further research with larger and more diverse samples is needed to validate their initial findings.

Discussion Questions

1. What are some of the pathways to chronic offending among violent females?
2. Do you believe that some conditions present at birth can control future criminal behavior?

SOURCE: Deborah Baskin and Ira Sommers, "Females' Initiation into Violent Street Crime," *Justice Quarterly* 10 (1993): 559–81.

The chronic offender tends to associate with friends who are also future criminals. By age eight, he is already exhibiting antisocial behavior, including dishonesty and aggressiveness. At school, he tends to have low educational achievement and is restless, troublesome, hyperactive, impulsive, and often truant.

After leaving school at age 18, the persistent criminal tends to maintain a relatively well paid but low-status job and is likely to have an erratic work history and periods of unemployment. Deviant behavior tends to be versatile rather than specialized. That is, the typical offender not only commits property offenses, such as theft and

TABLE 10.2 **Risk Factors for Crime and Age at Which They Occur**

(a) Child problem behavior Troublesome 8–10 Dishonest 10 Lies frequently 12–14 Aggressive 12–14 Bullies 14	Low attainment 11 High delinquency in school 11 Frequently truant 12–14 Left school 15 No exams taken by 18
(b) Teenage antisocial behavior Heavy drinker 18 Heavy smoker 18 Drug user 18 Heavy gambler 18 High sexual activity 18	*(f) Family influences* Poor parental child-rearing 8 Poor parental supervision 8 Low parent interest in education 8 Separated from parents 10 Poor relation with parents 18
(c) Physical measures Small 8–10 Small 18 Tattooed 18	*(g) Antisocial influences* Convicted parent 10 Delinquent sibling 10 Sibling behavior problems 8 Delinquent friends 14
(d) Impulsivity Lacks concentration, is restless 8–10 High daring 8–10 Lacks concentration, is restless 12–14 High daring 12–14 High impulsivity 18	*(h) Socioeconomic factors* Low family income 8 Low socioeconomic-status family 8–10 Poor housing 8–10 Large family size 10 Unstable job record 18 Unskilled manual job 18
(e) School problems Low intelligence 8–10	

SOURCE: David Farrington, "Juvenile Delinquency," in J. Coleman, ed., *The School Years* (London: Routledge, 1992), p. 129.

burglary, but also engages in violence, vandalism, drug use, excessive drinking, drunk driving, smoking, reckless driving, and sexual promiscuity—evidence of a generalized problem behavior syndrome. Chronic offenders are more likely to live away from home and have conflict with their parents. They wear tattoos, go out most evenings, and enjoy hanging out with groups of their friends. They are much more likely than non-offenders to get involved in fights, to carry weapons, and to use them in violent encounters. The frequency of offending reaches a peak in the teenage years (about 17 or 18) and then declines in the twenties, when the offenders marry or live with a woman.

By the time he reaches his thirties, the former delinquent is likely to be separated or divorced from his wife and be an absent parent. His employment record remains spotty, and he moves often to rental units rather than owner-occupied housing. His life is still characterized by evenings out, heavy drinking and substance abuse, and more violent behavior than his contemporaries'. Because the typical offender provides the same kind of deprived and disrupted family life for his own children that he experienced, the social experiences and conditions that produce delinquency are carried on from one generation to the next.

Nonoffenders and Desisters

Farrington has also identified factors that predict the discontinuity of criminal offenses: people who exhibit these factors have a background that puts them at risk to crime but either are able to remain nonoffenders or begin a criminal career but later desist. The factors that "protected" high-risk youth from even beginning a criminal career included having a personality that rendered them somewhat shy, having few friends (at age eight), having a nondeviant family, and being highly regarded by their mother. Shy kids with few friends avoided damaging relationships with other adolescent boys, members of a high risk group, and were therefore able to avoid criminality.

What caused offenders to desist? Holding a relatively good job helped reduce criminal activity. Unemployment seems to be related to the escalation of theft offenses; violence and substance abuse were unaffected by unemployment. In a similar vein, getting married also helped diminish criminal activity. However, finding a spouse who was also involved in criminal activity and had a criminal record increased criminal involvement.

Physical relocation also helped some offenders desist. Leaving the city and going to a more rural or suburban area was linked to reductions in criminal activity. Relocation forced offenders to sever ties with co-offenders.

While employment, marriage, and relocation helped offenders desist, not all desisters found the key to success. At-risk youth who managed to avoid criminal convictions were unlikely to avoid other social problems. Rather than becoming prosperous homeowners with flourishing careers, they tended to live in unkempt homes and have large debts and low-paying jobs. Desisters were more likely to remain single and live alone: youths who experience social isolation at age eight also experience it at age 32.

Theoretical Modeling

Farrington has summarized these observations by proposing a theory of criminality based on his long-term data collections. Farrington's theoretical model is outlined below:

1. Childhood factors predict teenage antisocial behavior and adult dysfunction. There is continuity in criminal behavior.
2. Personal and social factors are associated with criminal propensity. Kids who suffer economic deprivation, poor parenting, and an antisocial family and have personalities marked by impulsivity, hyperactivity, and attention deficit disorder are the most likely to become delinquent.
3. Adolescents who have criminogenic tendencies are motivated or "energized" to offend by their desire for material goods, excitement, and status with peers. Boys from less affluent families are unable to achieve these goals through legitimate means so they tend to commit offenses.
4. Life events influence behavior. For example, family life is critical to a deviant career. Adolescents

exposed to effective child rearing, including consistent discipline and close supervision, tend to build up internal inhibitions against offending in a social learning process. In contrast, this same learning process causes kids raised in antisocial families to model their beliefs and behaviors in a dysfunctional manner.

5. The chance of offending *in any particular situation* depends on the perception of the costs and benefits of crime and noncrime alternatives. The more impulsive boys were more likely to offend because they were less likely to consider possible future consequences (as opposed to immediate benefits).
6. Factors that encourage criminality at one period during the life course may inhibit it in another. Being nervous and withdrawn and having few friends is negatively related to adolescent and teenage offending but positively related to adult social dysfunction.
7. Adult criminal behavior is predicted by external and internal behaviors. External behaviors include engaging in violence and getting arrested and convicted for crimes. Internalizing behaviors include psychiatric disorders, substance abuse, nervousness, and social isolation.

Farrington's theory suggests that experiences over the life course shape the direction and flow of behavior choices; people are not controlled by a single, unalterable latent trait. His work is included here as a life course theory because it is *age-graded:* though there may be continuity in offending, the factors that predict criminality at one point in the life course may not be the ones that predict criminality at another. While most adult criminals began their career in childhood, life events may help some children forgo criminality as they mature.

Interactional Theory

In an important work, Terence Thornberry has also proposed an age-graded view of crime that he calls **interactional theory** (see Figure 10.5).[64]

Thornberry agrees (with both Weis and Elliott) that the onset of crime can be traced to a deterioration of the social bond during adolescence, marked by a weakened attachment to parents, commitment to school, and belief in conventional values. Thornberry's view similarly recognizes the influence of social class position and other

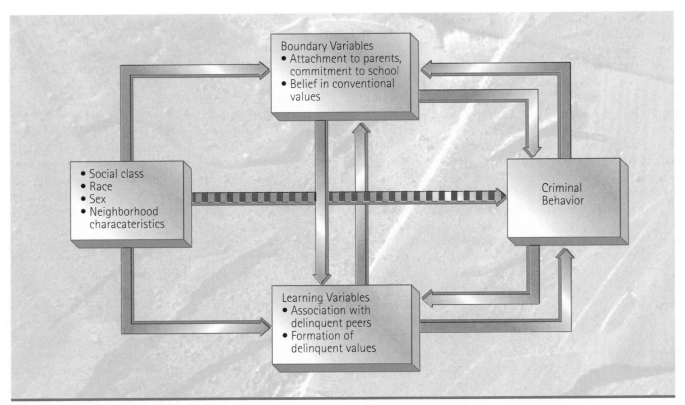

FIGURE 10.5   Overview of the Interactional Theory of Crime

SOURCE: Terence Thornberry, Margaret Farnworth, Alan Lizotte, and Susan Stern, "A Longitudinal Examination of the Causes and Correlates of Delinquency," working paper no. 1, Rochester Youth Development Study (Albany, N.Y.: Hindelang Criminal Justice Research Center, 1987), p. 11.

structural variables: youths growing up in social disorganized areas will also be the ones who stand the greatest risk of a weakened social bond and subsequent delinquency. The onset of a criminal career is supported by residence in a social setting in which deviant values and attitudes can be learned and reinforced by delinquent peers.

Interactional theory also holds that serious delinquent youth form belief systems that are consistent with their deviant life-style. They seek out the company of other kids who share their interests and who are likely to reinforce their beliefs about the world and support their delinquent behavior. According to interactional theory then, delinquents seek out a criminal peer group in the same fashion that chess buffs look for others who share their passion for the game; hanging out with other chess players helps improve their game. Similarly, deviant peers do not turn an otherwise "innocent" boy into a delinquent. They support and amplify the behavior of kids who have already accepted a delinquent way of life; they support and amplify offending patterns.

The key idea here is that causal influences are bidirectional. Weak bonds lead kids to develop deviant peers and get involved in high-rate delinquency. Frequent delinquency involvement further weakens bonds and makes it very difficult to reestablish conventional ones. Delinquency-promoting factors tend to reinforce one another and sustain a chronic criminal career.

Interactional theory is considered age-graded because it incorporates an element of the **cognitive perspective** in psychology: as people mature, they pass through different stages of reasoning and sophistication.[65] Thornberry applies this concept when he suggests that criminality is a developmental process that takes on different meaning and form as a person matures. As he puts it, "The causal process is a dynamic one that develops over a person's life." During early adolescence, attachment to the family is the single most important determinant of whether a youth will adjust to conventional society and be shielded from delinquency. By mid-adolescence, the influence of the family is replaced by the "world of friends, school and youth culture."[66] In adulthood, a person's behavioral choices are shaped by his or her place in conventional society and his or her own nuclear family.

Thornberry's model is in its early stages of development and is being tested with a panel of Rochester, New York, youth who will be followed through their offending careers.[67] Preliminary results support interactional theory hypothesis, including the deviance amplification powers of associating with a delinquent peer group.[68] In one analysis, Thornberry and his associates find that associating with delinquent peers does in fact increase delinquent involvement because the peer group reinforces antisocial behavior.[69] As delinquent behavior escalates, kids are more likely to seek out deviant friends. These friends reinforce delinquent beliefs (thinking it is OK to commit crimes). In contrast, con-

ventional youth seek out friends equally conforming who then reinforce their prosocial life-style.

The Rochester data also shows that life events can make even high-risk youth resilient to delinquency. Kids who grow up in indigent households, that experience unemployment, high mobility, and parental criminality and who are placed in the care of social service agencies can resist delinquent involvements if they sustain prosocial life experiences. Among those encounters developed in later adolescence that enable kids to resist delinquency are forming a commitment to school, developing an attachment to teachers, and establishing the goal of a college education; scoring high on reading and math tests is also associated with prosocial behaviors.[70]

In sum, interactional theory suggests that criminality is "part and parcel of a dynamic social process" and

A gang member works with kids in an urban center as part of a community outreach program. Exposing gang members to positive life events may help them resist crime-producing forces in their environment. According to interactional theory, people can avoid criminal careers if they are provided with prosocial life experiences.

According to Robert Sampson (left) and John Laub (right), turning points in the life course can help people desist from crime.

not simply an outcome of that process. Although crime is influenced by social forces, it also influences these processes and associations to create behavioral trajectories toward increasing law violations for some people.[71] In so doing, the interactional theory integrates elements of social disorganization, social control, social learning, and cognitive theory into a powerful model of the development of a criminal career.

≡ Laub and Sampson: Age-Graded Theory

If there are various pathways to crime and delinquency, are there trails back to conformity? In an important new work, *Crime in the Making*, Robert Sampson and John Laub, identify the **"turning points"** in a criminal career.[72] As devotees of the life course perspective, Sampson and Laub find that the stability of delinquent behavior can be effected by events that occur later in life, even after a chronic delinquent career has been undertaken. They agree with Hirschi and Gottfredson that formal and informal social controls restrict criminality and that the onset of crime begins early in life and continues over the life course; they disagree that once this course is set, nothing can impede its progress.

Laub and Sampson reanalyzed the data originally collected by the Gluecks more than 40 years ago. Using modern statistical analysis made possible by computers, a tool unavailable to the Gluecks, Laub and Sampson found evidence supportive of the life course view. They find that children who enter delinquent careers are those who have trouble at home and at school and maintain deviant friends—findings not dissimilar from earlier research on delinquent careers.

Turning Points and Social Capital

Laub and Sampson's most important contribution is identifying the life events that enable adult offenders to desist from crime (see Figure 10.6). Two critical turning points are marriage and career. When they achieve adulthood, even adolescents who had significant problems with the law are able to desist from crime if they can become attached to a spouse who supports and sustains them, even when the spouse knows they had "got in trouble when they were kids." They may encounter employers who are "willing to give them a chance" despite their record. People who cannot sustain secure marital relations or are failures in the labor market are less likely to desist from crime.

FIGURE 10.6 Age–Graded Theory

SOURCE: Robert Sampson and John Laub, *Crime in the Making*, Cambridge, Mass.: Harvard University Press (1993), pp. 244–45.

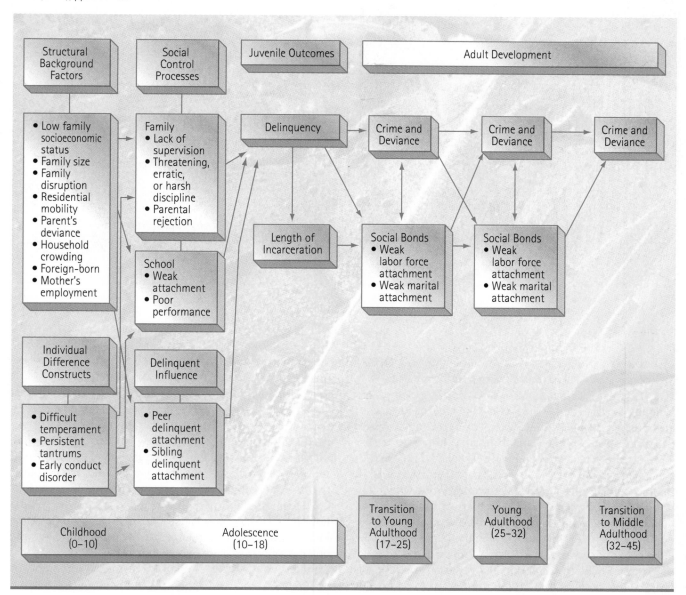

TABLE 10.3 **Integrated Theories**

Multifactor Theories

social development theory	Weak social controls produce crime. A person's place in the social structure influences his or her bond to society.	Combines elements of social structural and social process theories. Accounts for variations in the crime rate.
Elliott's integrated theory	Strained and weak social bonds lead youths to associate with and learn from deviant peers.	Combines elements of learning, strain, and control theories.
integrated structural theory	Delinquency is a function of family life, which is in turn controlled by the family's place in the economic system.	Explains the relationship between family problems and delinquency in terms of social and economic conditions.

Latent Trait Theories

general theory	Crime and criminality are separate concepts. People choose to commit crime when they lack self-control. People lacking in self-control will seize criminal opportunities.	Integrate choice and social control concepts. Identifies the difference between *crime* and *criminality*.
human nature theory	People choose to commit crime when they are biologically and psychologically impaired.	Shows how physical traits interact with social conditions to produce crime. Can account for noncriminal behavior in high-crime areas. Integrates choice and developmental theories.

Life Course Theories

Farrington's theory of delinquent development	Personal and social factors control the onset and stability of criminal careers.	Makes use of data collected over a twenty-year period to substantiate hypothesis.
interactional theory	Criminals go through life-style changes during their offending career.	Combines sociological and psychological theories.
age-graded theory	As people mature, the factors that influence their propensity to commit crime change. In childhood, family factors are critical; in adulthood, marital and job factors are key.	Shows how crime is a developmental process that shifts in direction over the life course.

According to Sampson and Laub, these life events help people build **social capital**—positive relations with individuals and institutions that are life-sustaining. Building social capital supports conventional behavior and inhibits deviant behavior. For example, a successful marriage creates social capital when it improves a person's stature, creates feelings of self-worth, and encourages people "to take a chance" on the individual. It inhibits crime by creating a stake in conformity; why commit crime when you are doing well at your job? The relationship is reciprocal: if people are chosen as an employee, they return the "favor" by doing the best job possible; if they are chosen as a spouse, they blossom into a devoted partner. Building social capital and strong social bonds reduces the likelihood of long-term deviance.

Sampson and Laub's research indicates that events that occur in later adolescence and adulthood do in fact influence the direction of delinquent and criminal careers. Life events can either help terminate or sustain deviant careers. For example, getting arrested and punished may have little direct effect on future criminality, but it can help sustain a criminal career because it reduces the chances of employment and job stability, two factors that are directly related to crime.[73]

Having established that change is possible, some important questions still need answering: Why do some kids change while others resist? Why do some people enter strong marriages while others fail? Why are some troubled youths able to conform to the requirements or a job or career while others cannot? To some extent, building social capital may be a matter of luck: being at the right place at the right time never hurts.

Summary

Recently, criminologists have been combining elements from a number of different theoretical models into integrated theories of crime, outlined in Table 10.3.

One approach is to use multiple factors derived from a number of different structural and process theories. Examples of this include Weis's social development theory and Elliott's integrated theory, which hold that social position controls life events. Weis finds that living in a disorganized area helps weaken social bonds; Elliott argues that strain leads to weakened bonds. Both theories find that weakened bonds lead to the development of deviant peer group associations. In another variation of integrated theory, Colvin and Pauly add conflict variables to structural and process factors.

Latent trait theories hold that some underlying condition present at birth or soon after controls behavior. Suspect traits include low IQ, impulsivity, and personality structure. This underlying trait explains the continuity of offending because once present, it remains with a person throughout his or her life. The latent trait theories developed by Gottfredson and Hirschi and Wilson and Herrnstein both integrate choice theory concepts: people with latent traits choose crime over noncrime. The opportunity for crime mediates their choice.

Life course theories argue that events that take place over the life course influence criminal choices. The cause of crime is constantly changing as people mature. At first, the nuclear family influences behavior; during adolescence, the peer group dominates; in adulthood, marriage and career are critical. There are a variety of pathways to crime: some kids are sneaky; others hostile; and still others defiant. Crime may be part of a garden variety of social problems, including health, physical, and interpersonal troubles.

Important life course theories have been formulated by Terence Thornberry, David Farrington, and John Laub and Robert Sampson.

KEY TERMS

multifactor theories	life course theory
integrated theory	integrated structural theory
developmental criminology	self-control
latent trait theory	impulsive
life cycle	authority conflict pathway
early onset	covert pathway
continuity of crime	overt pathway
developmental view	international theory
problem behavior	cognitive perspective
syndrome (PBS)	turning points
pathways	social capital

NOTES

1. Emilie Andersen Allan, "Theory Is Not a Zero-Sum Game: The Quest for an Integrated Theory" (Paper presented at the annual meeting of the American Society of Criminology, Phoenix, Arizona, November 1993).
2. David Rowe, D. Wayne Osgood, and W. Alan Nicewander, "A Latent Trait Approach to Unifying Criminal Careers," *Criminology* 28 (1990): 237–70.
3. G. R. Patterson, Barbara DeBaryshe, and Elizabeth Ramsey, "A Developmental Perspective on Antisocial Behavior," *American Psychologist* 44 (1989): 329–35.
4. Daniel Glazer, *Crime in Our Changing Society* (New York: Holt, Rinehart and Winston, 1978).
5. Ibid., p. 125.
6. Joseph Weis and J. David Hawkins, *Reports of the National Juvenile Assessment Centers, Preventing Delinquency* (Washington, D.C.: U.S. Department of Justice, 1981); Joseph Weis and John Sederstrom, *Reports of the National Juvenile Justice Assessment Centers, The Prevention of Serious Delinquency: What to Do* (Washington, D.C.: U.S. Department of Justice, 1981).
7. Delbert Elliott, David Huizinga, and Suzanne Ageton, *Explaining Delinquency and Drug Use* (Beverly Hills: Sage, 1985).
8. Mark Colvin and John Pauly, "A Critique of Criminology: Toward an Integrated Structural-Marxist Theory of Delinquency Production," *American Journal of Sociology* 89 (1983): 513–51.
9. Ibid., p. 542.
10. Steven Messner and Marvin Krohn, "Class, Compliance Structures, and Delinquency: Assessing Integrated Structural-Marxist Theory," *American Journal of Sociology* 96 (1990): 300–28.
11. Lee Ellis, "Neurohormonal Bases of Varying Tendencies to Learn Delinquent and Criminal Behavior," in *Behavioral Approaches to Crime and Delinquency*, ed. E. Morris and C. Braukmann (New York: Plenum, 1988), pp. 499–518.
12. James Q. Wilson and Richard Herrnstein, *Crime and Human Nature* (New York: Simon and Schuster, 1985).
13. Ibid., p. 44.
14. Ibid., p. 171.
15. Ibid.
16. Ibid., p. 528.
17. Michael Gottfredson and Travis Hirschi, *A General Theory of Crime* (Stanford, Calif.: Stanford Univsersity Press, 1990).

18. Ibid., p. 27.

19. Ibid., p. 90.

20. Ibid., p. 89.

21. Ibid.

22. Ibid.

23. Robert Agnew, "The Contribution of Social-Psychological Strain Theory to the Explanation of Crime and Delinquency," *Advances in Criminological Theory,* 6 (1994).

24. Travis Hirschi and Michael Gottfredson, "Rethinking the Juvenile Justice System," *Crime and Delinquency* 39 (1993): 262–71.

25. David Brownfield and Ann Marie Sorenson, "Self-Control and Juvenile Delinquency: Theoretical Issues and an Empirical Assessment of Selected Elements of a General Theory of Crime, *Deviant Behavior* 14 (1993): 243–64; Harold Grasmick, Charles Tittle, Robert Bursik, and Bruce Arneklev, "Testing the Core Empirical Implications of Gottfredson and Hirschi's General Theory of Crime," *Journal of Research in Crime and Delinquency* 30 (1993): 5–29; John Cochran, Peter Wood, and Bruce Arneklev, "Is the Religiosity-Delinquency Relationship Spurious? A Test of Arousal and Social Control Theories," *Journal of Research in Crime and Delinquency* 31 (1994): 92–123.

26. Carl Keane, Paul Maxim, and James Teevan, "Drinking and Driving, Self-Control, and Gender: Testing a General Theory of Crime," *Journal of Research in Crime and Delinquency* 30 (1993): 30–46.

27. Judith DeJong, Matti Virkkunen, and Marku Linnoila, "Factors Associated with Recidivism in a Criminal Population," *The Journal of Nervous and Mental Disease* 180 (1992): 543–50.

28. Grasmick et al., "Testing the Core Empirical Implications of Gottfredson and Hirschi's General Theory of Crime"; Daniel Nagin and Raymond Paternoster, "Enduring Individual Differences and Rational Choice Theories of Crime," *Law and Society Review* 27 (1993): 467–89.

29. Bruce Link, Elmer Streuning, Francis Cullen, Patrick Shrout, and Bruce Dohrenwend, "A Modified Labeling Theory Approach to Mental Disorders: An Empirical Assessment," *American Sociological Review* 54 (1989): 400–23.

30. Michael Benson and Elizabeth Moore, "Are White-Collar and Common Offenders the Same? An Empirical and Theoretical Critique of a Recently Proposed General Theory of Crime," *Journal of Research in Crime and Delinquency* 29 (1992): 251–72.

31. For a general review and critique, see Kenneth Polk's book review in *Crime and Delinquency* 37 (1991): 575–81.

32. Samuel Yochelson and Clifford Samenow, *The Criminal Personality* (New York: Jason Aronson, 1977).

33. Gottfredson and Hirschi, *A General Theory of Crime,* p. 153.

34. Ann Marie Sorenson and David Brownfield, "Normative Concepts in Social Control" (Paper presented at the annual meeting of the American Society of Criminology, Phoenix, Arizona, November 1993).

35. Scott Menard, Delbert Elliott, and Sharon Wofford, "Social Control Theories in Developmental Perspective," *Studies on Crime and Crime Prevention* 2 (1993): 69–87.

36. Delbert Elliott and Scott Menard, "Delinquent Friends and Delinquent Behavior: Temporal and Developmental Patterns," in *Current Theories of Crime and Deviance*, ed. J. David Hawkins (Cambridge: Cambridge University Press, in press).

37. Kevin Thompson, "Sexual Harassment and Low Self-Control: An Application of Gottfredson and Hirschi's General Theory of Crime" (Paper presented at the annual meeting of the American Society of Criminology, Phoenix, Arizona, November 1993).

38. R. E. Tremblay and L. C. Masse, "Cognitive Deficits, School Achievement, Disruptive Behavior and Juvenile Delinquency: A Longitudinal Look at Their Developmental Sequence" (Paper presented at the annual meeting of the American Society of Criminology, Phoenix, Arizona, November 1993).

39. David Nurco, Timothy Kinlock, and Mitchell Balter, "The Severity of Preaddiction Criminal Behavior among Urban, Male Narcotic Addicts and Two Nonaddicted Control Groups," *Journal of Research in Crime and Delinquency* 30 (1993): 293–316.

40. G. R. Patterson and Karen Yoerger, "Differentiating Outcomes and Histories for Early and Late Onset Arrests" (Paper presented at the annual meeting of the American Society of Criminology, Phoenix, Arizona, November 1993).

41. Robert Sampson and John Laub, "Crime and Deviance in the Life Course," *American Review of Sociology* 18 (1992): 63–84.

42. Joan McCord, "Family Relationships, Juvenile Delinquency, and Adult Criminality," *Criminology* 29 (1991): 397–417.

43. See, generally, Sheldon Glueck and Eleanor Glueck, *500 Criminal Careers* (New York: Knopf, 1930); idem, *One Thousand Juvenile Delinquents* (Cambridge: Harvard University Press, 1934); idem, *Predicting Delinquency and Crime* (Cambridge: Harvard University Press, 1967), pp. 82–83.

44. Sheldon Glueck and Eleanor Glueck, *Unraveling Juvenile Delinquency* (Cambridge: Harvard University Press, 1950).

45. See, generally, John Laub and Robert Sampson, "The Sutherland-Glueck Debate: On the Sociology of Criminological Knowledge," *American Journal of Sociology* 96 (1991): 1402–40; idem, "Unraveling Families and Delinquency: A Reanalysis of the Gluecks' Data," *Criminology* 26 (1988): 355–80.

46. Rolf Loeber and Marc LeBlanc, "Toward a Developmental Criminology," in *Crime and Justice,* vol. 12, ed. Norval Morris and Michael Tonry (Chicago: University of Chicago Press, 1990), pp. 375–473.

47. G. R. Patterson, L. Crosby, and S. Vuchinich, "Predicting Risk for Early Police Arrest," *Journal of Quantitative*

Criminology 8 (1992): 335–55.

48. Patterson, DeBaryshe, and Ramsey, "A Developmental Perspective on Antisocial Behavior," pp. 331–33.

49. Rolf Loeber, Magda Southamer-Loeber, Welmoet Van Kammen, and David Farrington, "Initiation, Escalation and Desistance in Juvenile Offending and Their Correlates," *Journal of Criminal Law and Criminology* 82 (1991): 36–82.

50. Richard Jessor, John Donovan, and Francis Costa, *Beyond Adolescence: Problem Behavior and Young Adult Development* (New York: Cambridge University Press, 1991).

51. D. Wayne Osgood, "The Covariation among Adolescent Problem Behaviors" (Paper presented at the annual meeting of the American Society of Criminology, Baltimore, November 1990).

52. Jeanne Hernandez, "The Concurrence of Eating Disorders with Histories of Child Abuse among Adolescents" (Paper presented at the annual meeting of the American Society of Criminology, Phoenix, Arizona, November 1993).

53. David Huizinga, Rolf Loeber, and Terence Thornberry, "Longitudinal Study of Delinquency, Drug Use, Sexual Activity, and Pregnancy among Children and Youth in Three Cities," *Public Health Reports* 108 (1993): 90–96.

54. Richard Jessor, "Risk Behavior in Adolescence: A Psychosocial Framework for Understanding and Action," in *Adolescents at Risk: Medical and Social Perspectives*, ed. D. E. Rogers and E. Ginzburg, (Boulder, Colo.: Westview, 1992).

55. Marianne Junger, "Accidents and Crime," in *The Generality of Deviance*, ed. T. Hirschi and M. Gottfredson (New Brunswick, N.J.: Transaction Press, 1993).

56. Helene Raskin White, "Early Problem Behavior and Later Drug Problems," *Journal of Research in Crime and Delinquency* 29 (1992): 412–29.

57. Helene Raskin White and Erich Labouvie, "Generality versus Specifity of Problem Behavior: Psychological and Functional Differences," *Journal of Drug Issues* 24 (1994): 55–74.

58. See, generally, Richard Dembo, Linda Williams, Werner Wothke, James Schmeidelr, Alan Getreu, Estrellita Berry, and Eric Wish, "The Generality of Deviance: Replication of a Structural Model among High-Risk Youths," *Journal of Research in Crime and Delinquency* 29 (1992): 200–16.

59. Rolf Loeber, Phen Wung, Kate Keenan, Bruce Giroux, Magda Stouthamer-Loeber, Wemoet Van Kammen, and Barbara Maughan, "Developmental Pathways in Disruptive Behavior," *Development and Psychopathology* (1993): 12–48.

60. See, for example, the Rochester Youth Development Study, Hindelang Criminal Justice Research Center, 135 Western Avenue, Albany, New York 12222.

61. David Farrington, "The Development of Offending and Antisocial Behavior from Childhood to Adulthood" (Paper presented at the Congress on Rethinking Delinquency, University of Minho, Braga, Portugal, July 1992).

62. See, generally, D. J. West and David P. Farrington, *The Delinquent Way of Life* (London: Hienemann, 1977).

63. The material in the following sections is summarized from Farrington, "The Development of Offending and Antisocial Behavior from Childhood to Adulthood"; idem, "Psychobiological Factors in the Explanation and Reduction of Delinquency," *Today's Delinquent* 7 (1988): 44–46; idem, "Childhood Origins of Teenage Antisocial Behaviour and Adult Social Dysfunction," *Journal of the Royal Society of Medicine* 86 (1993): 13–17; idem, "Psychosocial Influences on the Development of Antisocial Personality" (Paper presented at the annual meeting of the American Society of Criminology, Phoenix, Arizona, November 1993).

64. Terence Thornberry, "Toward an Interactional Theory of Delinquency," *Criminology* 25 (1987): 863–91.

65. See, for example, Jean Piaget, *The Grasp of Consciousness* (Cambridge: Harvard University Press, 1976).

66. Ibid., p. 386.

67. This research is known as the Rochester Youth Development Study. Thornberry's colleagues on the project include Alan Lizotte, Margaret Farnworth, Marvin Krohn, and Susan Stern.

68. Terence Thornberry, Alan Lizotte, Marvin Krohn, and Margaret Farnworth, "The Role of Delinquent Peers in the Initiation of Delinquent Behavior," working paper no. 6 (rev., Albany, N.Y.: Rochester Youth Development Study, Hindelang Criminal Justice Research Center, 1993).

69. Terence Thornberry, Alan Lizotte, Marvin Krohn, Margaret Farnworth, and Sung Joon Jang, "Delinquent Peers, Beliefs, and Delinquent Behavior: A Longitudinal Test of Interactional Theory," *Criminology* 32 (1994): 601–37.

70. Carolyn Smith, Alan Lizotte, Terence Thornberry, and Marvin Krohn, *Resilient Youth: Identifying Factors That Prevent High-Risk Youth from Engaging in Delinquency and Drug Use* (Albany, N.Y: Rochester Youth Development Study, 1994).

71. Thornberry et al., "Delinquent Peers, Beliefs, and Delinquent Behavior," pp. 628–29.

72. Robert Sampson and John Laub, *Crime in the Making: Pathways and Turning Points through Life* (Cambridge: Harvard University Press, 1993); John Laub and Robert Sampson, "Turning Points in the Life Course: Why Change Matters to the Study of Crime" (Paper presented at the annual meeting of the American Society of Criminology, New Orleans, November 1992).

73. Sampson and Laub, *Crime in the Making*, p. 249.

Crime

Typologies

Regardless of why people commit crime in the first place, their actions are defined by law as falling into particular crime categories, or *typologies*. Criminologists often seek to link individual criminal offenders or behaviors together so they may be more easily studied and understood. These are referred to as crime or offender typologies.

In this section, crime patterns are clustered into four typologies: violent crime (Chapter 11); economic crimes involving common theft offenses (Chapter 12); economic crimes involving criminal organizations (Chapter 13); and public-order crimes, such as prostitution and drug abuse (Chapter 14). This format groups criminal behaviors by their focuses and consequences: bringing physical harm to others; misappropriating other people's property; and violating laws designed to protect public morals.

Typologies can be useful in classifying large numbers of criminal offenses or offenders into easily understood categories. This text has grouped offenses and offenders on the basis of their (1) legal definitions and (2) collective goals, objectives, and consequences.

11 Violent Crime

≡ Introduction

In some 200 years of national sovereignty, Americans have been preoccupied repeatedly with trying to understand and control one form of violence or another.[1]

All across America, people are afraid of becoming crime victims and alter their life-style in an effort to remain safe. They are bombarded with TV news stories and newspaper articles featuring grisly accounts of mass murder, child abuse, and serial rape. These accounts may be an unfortunate reflection of the harsh realities of American life: violence rates in the United States far exceed those in any other industrialized nation.[2] Though per capita violent crime rates were actually higher in the 1930s and early 1980s, the larger population of today means that the *annual number* of violent incidents is at an *all-time high* (see Figure 11.1).

Many people have personally experienced violence or have a friend who has been victimized; almost everyone has heard about someone being robbed, beaten, or killed; riots and mass disturbances have ravaged urban areas; racial attacks plague schools and college campuses; assassination has claimed the lives of political, religious, and social leaders all over the world.[3] When asked if they worried about crime and violence, about 80 percent of U.S. high school seniors answer yes.[4]

The general public also believes that the government should take a "get tough" approach to violent crime. Public opinion polls indicate that about 70 percent of U.S. citizens favor the use of capital punishment for persons convicted of murder.[5] The U.S. Supreme Court has responded by making teenage criminals over the age of 16 eligible for the death penalty.[6] Despite all this attention and concern, we are still not sure of the causes of violence. Some experts suggest that the problem is created by a small number of inherently violence-prone individuals who may themselves have been the victims of physical or psychological abnormalities. Other social scientists consider violence and aggression inherently human traits that can affect any person at any time. Still another view is that there are violence-prone sub-cultures within society whose members value force, routinely carry weapons, and consider violence to have an acceptable place in social interaction.[7] This chapter will survey the nature and extent of violent crime. First, it will briefly review some hypothetical causes of violence. Then, it will turn its attention to specific types of interpersonal violence—rape, assault, homicide, robbery, and domestic violence. Finally, it will briefly examine political violence, state-sponsored violence, and terrorism.

≡ The Roots of Violence

What causes people to behave violently? There are a number of competing explanations for violent behavior.

FIGURE 11.1   Violent Crime from the Nation's Two Crime Measures

SOURCE: Marianne Zawitz, *Highlights from Twenty Years of Surveying Crime Victims* (Washington, D.C.: Bureau of Justice Statistics, 1993) p. 1.

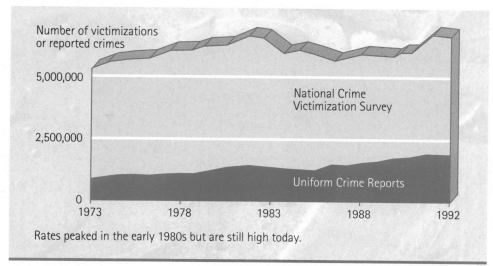

Number of victimizations or reported crimes

National Crime Victimization Survey

Uniform Crime Reports

1973   1978   1983   1988   1992

Rates peaked in the early 1980s but are still high today.

A few of the most prominent are discussed below and illustrated in Figure 11.2.

Personal Traits

On December 7, 1989, Marc Lapin, a deranged young Canadian, roamed through the hallways at the University of Montreal, shooting all the female students he encountered. Lapin took his own life after killing 14 women and injuring more than 12 others. The note he left on his body blamed his actions on his hatred of feminists, who, he claimed, were ruining his life.[8]

Bizarre outbursts such as Lapin's support a link between violence and personal traits. As you may recall from Chapter 6, biosocial theorists link violence to a number of biological irregularities, including but not limited to genetic influences and inheritance; the action of hormones, such as testosterone, on brain activity; the functioning of neurotransmitters, such as dopamine; brain structure, including abnormal temporal lobe structure; and diet, including excessive intake of sugar. Psychologists link violent behavior to a number of psychological influences, including observational learning from violent TV shows, traumatic childhood experiences, low intelligence, mental illness, impaired cognitive processes, and abnormal (psychopathic) personality structure.

More than 30 years ago, Laura Bender examined convicted juveniles who had killed their victims and concluded that they suffered from abnormal electroencephalogram readings, learning disabilities, and psychosis.[9] More recent research by Dorothy Lewis and her associates found that murderous youth suffered signs of major neurological impairment (such as abnormal EEGs,

FIGURE 11.2 **Sources of Violence**

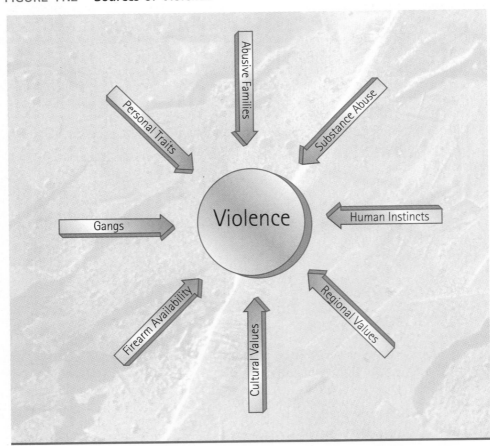

multiple psychomotor impairment, and severe seizures), low intelligence as measured on standard IQ tests, a psychotic close relative, and psychotic symptoms, such as paranoia, illogical thinking, and hallucinations.[10] While this evidence indicates that violent offenders are more prone to psychosis than other people, there is no single clinical diagnosis that can characterize their behavior.[11]

Abusive Families

Research indicates that habitually aggressive behavior is often learned in homes in which children are victimized and parents serve as aggressive role models; learned violence then persists into adulthood.[12]

A number of research studies have found that kids who were clinically diagnosed as abused later engaged in delinquent behaviors, including violence at a rate significantly greater than that of unabused children.[13]

One of the most outspoken critics of physical punishment of children is Murray Straus of the Family Research Laboratory at the University of New Hampshire. Straus has used survey and record data to show that children who are physically punished are the ones most likely to physically abuse a sibling and later engage in spouse abuse and other forms of criminal violence.[14] The relationship between deviant behavior and physical punishment is a constant across race, ethnic origin, and socioeconomic status.[15]

A number of research efforts focusing on early adolescent violence have found that samples of convicted young murderers contain a high percentage of seriously abused youth.[16] The abuse-violence association has been involved in a significant number of cases in which parents have been killed by their children; sexual abuse is also a constant factor in father (patricide) and mother (matricide) killings.[17]

Using actual case studies of violent criminals, Lonnie Athens found that antisocial careers are often created in a series of stages that begin with brutal episodes during early adolescence. The first stage involves the **brutalization process,** during which abusive parents or caretakers cause the young victim to develop a belligerent, angry demeanor. When confronted at home, school, or on the street, these belligerent youth respond with **violent performances** of angry, hostile behavior. The success of their violent confrontations provides them with a sense of power and achievement. In the **virulency** stage, the emerging criminals develop a violent identity that makes them feared; they enjoy intimidating others. To Athens, this process takes

now-violent youths full circle—from the victims of aggression to its initiators; they are now the same person they grew up despising, ready to begin the process with their own children.[18]

While a significant amount of evidence has shown the association between abuse and violent crime, it is also true that many offenders have not suffered abuse and that many abused youth do not grow up to become persistent adult offenders.[19]

Human Instinct

It is also possible that violent responses and emotions are actually inherent in all humans, needing only the right spark to trigger them. Sigmund Freud believed that human aggression and violence were produced by instinctual drives.[20] Freud maintained that humans possess two opposing instinctual drives that interact to control behavior: **eros,** the life instinct, which drives people to self-fulfillment and enjoyment; and **thanatos,** the death instinct, which produces self-destruction. Thanatos can be expressed externally (as violence and sadism) or internally (as suicide, alcoholism, or other self-destructive habits). Because aggression was instinctual, Freud saw little hope for its treatment.

A number of biologists and anthropologists have also speculated that instinctual violence-promoting traits may be common to the human species as a whole. One view is that aggression and violence are the results of instincts inborn in all animals, including human beings. A leading proponent of this view, Konrad Lorenz, developed this theory in his famous book, *On Aggression.*[21] Lorenz argued that aggressive energy is produced by inbred instincts that are independent of environmental forces. In the animal kingdom, aggression usually serves a productive purpose—for example, it leads members of grazing species to spread out over available territory to ensure an ample food supply and the survival of the fittest. Lorenz found that humans possess some of the same aggressive instincts as animals but without the inhibitions against fatal violence that members of lower species usually maintain. That is, among lower species, aggression is rarely fatal; when a conflict occurs, the winner is determined through a test of skill or endurance. This inhibition against killing members of their own species protects animals from self-extinction. Humans, lacking this inhibition against fatal violence, are thoroughly capable of killing their own kind; and as technology develops and more lethal weapons are produced, the extinction of the human species becomes a significant possibility.

Cultural Values

Explanations of the cause of violent behavior that focus on the individual offender fail to account for the patterns of violence in the United States. The various sources of crime statistics tell us that interpersonal violence is more common in large, urban, inner-city areas than in any other community.[22] It is unlikely that violent crime rates would be so high in these socially disorganized areas unless there were other *social forces* in operation that encouraged violent crime.[23]

To explain the existence of areas and groups within the social structure with disproportionately high violence rates, Marvin Wolfgang and Franco Ferracuti have suggested that a **subculture of violence** exists.[24] The subculture's norms are separate from society's central, dominant value system. In this subculture, a potent theme of violence influences life-styles, the socialization process, and interpersonal relationships. Even though the subculture's members share some of the values of the dominant culture, they expect that violence will be used to solve social conflicts and dilemmas. In some cultural subgroups, then, violence has become legitimized by custom and norms. It is considered appropriate behavior within culturally defined conflict situations in which an individual has been offended by a negative outcome in a dispute and seeks reparations through violent means **(disputatiousness).**[25]

Ganging. Empirical evidence shows that violence rates are highest in urban areas where subcultural values support teenage gangs whose members typically embrace the use of violence.[26] In a recent interview study of St. Louis gang boys, criminologist Scott Decker found that violence is a core value of gang membership; it helped boys define what a gang really was:

Int: Why do you call the group you belong to a gang?
Ans: Violence, I guess. There is more violence than a

Membership in the subculture of violence increases one's chances of both committing violent crime and becoming its victim. Here, a gang youth shows his wounded arm to a friend.

family. With a gang, it's like fighting all the time, killing, shooting.

Decker found that gang violence may be initiated for a variety of reasons. It enables new members to show toughness during initiation ceremonies; it can be used to retaliate against rivals for actual or perceived grievances; violence erupts when graffiti is defaced by rivals; it is used to protect turf from incursions by outsiders.[27]

Research conducted in Chicago by Carolyn Block indicates that the number of gang-related killings has increased significantly in recent years, a finding that implies that the proportion of urban violence that is a product of subcultural clashes has been growing.[28]

Regional Values

Some criminologists have suggested that *regional* values promote violence.[29] In well-known papers, Raymond Gastil found that a significant relationship existed between murder rates and residence in the South, that these differences predated the Civil War, and that outside the South, regional homicide rates are related to an influx of southern migration.[30] Gastil attributed high homicide rates to a southern culture that stresses a frontier mentality, mob violence, night riders, personal vengeance, and easily available firearms.

Not all criminologists have agreed with Gastil's conclusions.[31] For example, Colin Loftin and Robert Hill controlled for the effect of social class and economic variables on southern homicide rates and concluded that any argument pointing to a southern culture of lethal violence and murder was fallacious.[32] Gastil later replied to his critics by stating that they missed his real view—that southern culture promotes violence, not just the approval of violence.[33]

While the southern subculture view is still being debated, UCR data has been used to show that western states today have a higher overall violence rate than southern states.[34] According to research by Candice Nelsen, Jay Corzine, and Lin Huff-Corzine, this trend may be explained in part by relatively high homicide rates among the western region's Hispanic population.[35] Despite the fact that recent evidence refutes the "southern subculture of violence" theory, the stereotype of the violent southerner remains, unfortunately, an enduring myth.[36]

Substance Abuse

It has also become common to link violence to substance abuse. Drug abuse influences violence in three ways.[37] The relationship may be **psychopharmacological** when it is the direct consequence of ingesting mood-altering substances. Experimental evidence shows that acute doses of such drugs as PCP and amphetamines may produce violent and aggressive behaviors.[38] Alcohol abuse has long been associated with all forms of violence. A direct alcohol-violence link may be formed because drinking reduces cognitive ability, making miscommunication more likely while at the same time limiting the capacity for rational dialogue and compromise.[39]

Drug ingestion may result in **economic compulsive behavior** when drug users resort to violence to gain funds to support their habit. The federally sponsored Drug Use Forecasting (DUF) survey, which involves drug testing of all arrestees in major U.S. cities, consistently shows that those people who make up the criminal population are also heavily involved (more than 70 percent) in drug abuse; about 60 percent of all people arrested for violent crimes test positively for drugs.[40] Surveys of prison inmates also show a significant majority report being under the influence of drugs and alcohol at the time they committed their last criminal offense.[41]

A bond between violent crime and substance abuse is also forged by the activities of drug trafficking gangs whose members both sell and use drugs; this is referred to as a **systemic link.** Studies of gangs that engage in drug trafficking show that their violent activities may result in a significant proportion of all homicides in urban areas.[42]

In a series of studies, Paul Goldstein and his associates found that *more than half* of all homicides in New York City may be drug-related and 84 percent of these incidents involve cocaine (including crack) use and sales.[43] Most of the drug-related deaths are motivated by drug trafficking and interpersonal conflict brought on by drug abuse; relatively few people are killed by drug users trying to get drug money.[44]

Firearm Availability

While firearm availability is not a per se cause of violence, it is certainly a facilitating factor: a petty argument can escalate into a fatal encounter if one party or the other has a handgun. It may not be coincidence that the United States, which has a huge surplus of guns and in which most firearms (80 percent) used in crimes are stolen or obtained through illegal or unregulated transactions, also has one of the world's highest violence rates.[45] Disturbing new evidence indicates that more than 80 percent of inmates in juvenile correctional facilities owned a gun just prior to their confinement and 55 percent said they carried one almost all the time.[46]

The Uniform Crime Reports indicate that about half of all murders and a third of all robberies involve a firearm.[47] Handguns are the cause of death for two-thirds of all police killed in the line of duty. The presence of firearms in the home has been found to significantly increase the risk of suicide among adolescents, regardless of how carefully the guns were secured or stored.[48] Assaults and violence among family members and other intimates are *12 times more likely to result in death* if a handgun is used than if the attacks do not involve firearms.[49] It seems logical, then, that a ban on the sale and ownership of handguns might help reduce the violence rate.

≡ Violent Crimes

So far, we have reviewed a few of the various factors that are the suspected causes of violent crime. In the remainder of the chapter, we turn our attention to the individual acts that comprise violent crime in our society. When violence is directed toward strangers, it is said to be **instrumental**, designed to improve the financial or social position of the criminal, such as through an armed robbery. In contrast, **expressive** violence is designed to vent rage, anger, or frustration, for example, when a romantic triangle results in a murder.

Among the common-law violent crimes are included rape, murder, assault, and robbery. There are also newly recognized forms of violence that are directed at specific goals. Included within this category are workplace crimes and hate crimes. In addition, there are violent politically motivated crimes commonly referred to as terrorism. Some criminologists have also focused on "violent" business or corporate crimes, such as the release of toxic and fatal pollutants into the environment. Because these latter acts are linked to business organizations, they will be covered in the sections on corporate crime in Chapter 13.

≡ Forcible Rape

Rape (from the Latin *rapere,* to take by force) is defined by the common law as "the carnal knowledge of a female forcibly and against her will."[50] It is one of the most loathed, misunderstood, and frightening of crimes. Under traditional common-law definitions, rape involved nonconsensual sexual intercourse performed by a male against a female he was neither married to nor cohabitating with. Excluded from the crime of rape are sexual acts that are usually included in other crime categories; for example:

- Forced participation in fellatio, cunnilingus, and, in many states, anal intercourse; these are usually covered by sodomy statutes;

- Coerced participation of a male in intercourse or other sexual activity by a female or by another male or of a female by another female; and

- Coerced sexual intercourse induced by the threat of social, economic, or vocational harm, rather than of physical injury.[51]

Because of its content, rape was often viewed as a sexual offense in the traditional criminological literature; overcome by lust, a man forced his attentions on a woman. Even today, some men view rape as a sexual act, including one Tennessee judge who in 1994 released an accused rapist after stating that all he needed was a girlfriend and telling the public defender's office to arrange for a dating service; public outcry led to the release being rescinded.[52]

Criminologists now consider rape to be a violent, coercive act of aggression against women and not a forceful expression of sexuality. There has been a national campaign to alert the public to the seriousness of rape, initiate help for victims, and change legal definitions to facilitate the prosecution of rape offenders. Such efforts have been only marginally effective in reducing rape rates, but there has been significant change by overhauling rape laws and developing a vast social service network to aid victims.

History of Rape

Rape has been known throughout history. It has been the subject of art, literature, film, and theater. Paintings such as the "Rape of the Sabine Women," novels such as *Clarissa* by Samuel Richardson, poems such as "The Rape of Lucrece" by William Shakespeare, and films such as *The Accused* have as their central theme sexual violence.

In early civilization, rape was a common occurrence. Men staked a claim of ownership on women by forcibly abducting and raping them. This practice led to males' solidification of power and their historical domination of women.[53] In fact, in her often-cited book

Against Our Will, Susan Brownmiller charges that the criminalization of rape occurred only after the development of a monetary economy. Thereafter, the violation of a virgin caused an economic hardship on her family, who expected a significant dowry for her hand in marriage. According to Brownmiller, further proof of the sexist basis of rape law can be seen in Babylonian and Hebraic law. These ancient peoples considered the rape of a virgin to be a crime punishable by death. However, if the victim was a married woman, then both she and her attacker were considered equally to blame. Unless her husband chose to intervene, the victim and her attacker were put to death.

During the Middle Ages, it was a common practice for ambitious men to abduct and rape wealthy women in an effort to force them into marriage. The practice of "heiress stealing" illustrates how feudal law gave little thought or protection to women and equated them with property.[54] It was only in the late fifteenth century that forcible sex was outlawed and then only if the victim was of the nobility; peasant women and married women were not considered rape victims until well into the fifteenth century. The Christian condemnation of sex during this period was also a denunciation of women as evil, having lust in their hearts and redeemable only by motherhood. A woman who was raped was almost automatically suspected of contributing to her attack.

Rape and Warfare. Throughout recorded history, rape has also been associated with warfare. Soldiers of conquering armies have considered sexual possession of their enemies' women one of the spoils of war. Among the ancient Greeks, rape was socially acceptable and well within the rules of warfare. During the Crusades, even knights and pilgrims, ostensibly bound by vows of chivalry and Christian piety, took time off to rape as they marched toward Constantinople.

The belief that women are part of the spoils of war has continued through the ages, from the Crusades to the war in Vietnam. The systematic rape of Bosnian women by Serbian army officers during the civil war in the former Yugoslavia horrified the world. These crimes seemed even more atrocious because they seemed part of an official policy of genocide: rape was used as a means of impregnating Bosnian women with Serbian children. Reports out of Haiti also indicate that rape of politically involved women became a norm in the wake of the 1991 military coup that ousted President Jean Bertran-Aristede. Soldiers have attacked women in their homes and raped political prisoners.[55]

Incidence of Rape

How many rapes occur each year, and what is known about rape patterns? According to the most recent UCR data, about 109,000 rapes or attempted rapes were reported to police in 1992, a rate of over 84 per 100,000 females. The number of rapes reported to the police has risen dramatically: the reported rape rate increased 15 percent between 1988 and 1992; the rate has almost doubled since 1973 (84 versus 43). Geographical and ecological conditions influence the probability of a woman being raped. The West had the highest rape rate (91 per 100,000 females) followed closely by the South (90 per 100,000 females); the Northeast had the lowest rate (58 per 100,000 females). Population density also influenced the rape rate: metropolitan areas had a rape rate double that of rural areas. The police clear over half of all reported rape offenses by arrest. Of the offenders arrested, 44 percent were under 25 years of age, 55 percent were white, and 43 percent were black; the racial pattern of rape arrests has been fairly consistent for some time. Finally, rape is a warm-weather crime—most occur during July and August, with the lowest rates occurring during December, January, and February.

This data must be interpreted with caution, because according to NCVS data, rape is frequently underreported by victims (only about half of the incidents are reported). Official data may reflect reporting practices rather than crime trends: the UCR employs a common-law definition of rape (the carnal knowledge of a female forcibly and against her will) that may not jibe with current state definitions; the UCR includes in its computations assaults or attempts to commit rape whose interpretation may differ widely from state to state; and the acts committed by serial rapists make the relationship between the number of crimes and the number of offenders problematic.[56] NCVS data indicates that at last count (1992), about 140,000 attempted and completed rapes occur annually. Unlike the UCR, the NCVS provides little evidence that the rate or number of rapes has increased significantly during the past 20 years.

The NCVS findings must also be interpreted carefully. The NCVS may also have seriously undercounted rape because until 1993, it had never directly asked respondents whether they had been raped. During interviews, NCVS surveyors ask subjects if anyone tried to attack them "in some other way" or whether "anything else happened to them which they thought was a crime."[57] Because other victim surveys indicate that at least 20 percent of adult women, 15 percent of college-aged women, and 12 percent of adolescent girls have experienced sexual abuse or assault sometime during their lifetime, it is evident that the NCVS undercounts rape.[58] In response to this, a revised NCVS survey was used in 1993 that asked people directly if they had been raped. Preliminary analysis indicates that estimates of rape victimizations will increase by at least 300 percent.[59]

Types of Rape

Some rapes are planned, others are spontaneous; some focus on a particular victim, while others occur almost as an afterthought during the commission of another crime, such as a burglary.[60] Some rapists are one-time offenders, while others engage in multiple or serial rapes. Some attack their victims without warning ("blitz rapes"), others try to "capture" their victims by striking up a conversation or offering them a ride, and still others use a personal relationship to gain access to their target.[61] In all of these circumstances, rape involves a violent criminal offense in which a predatory criminal chooses to attack a victim.

In their studies, criminologists usually divide rapes into two broad categories: stranger-to-stranger rapes and acquaintance rapes. While the former involves people who had never met before the rape, the latter involves someone known to the victim, including family members and friends. Included within acquaintance rapes are the subcategories of **date rape,** which involves a sexual attack during a courting relationship, and marital rape, which is forcible sex between people who are legally married to each other.

It is difficult to estimate the ratio between rapes involving strangers and those in which victim and assailant were in some way acquainted because women may be more reluctant to report acts involving acquaintances. By some estimates, about 50 percent of rapes involve acquaintances.[62]

Stranger rapes are typically more violent than acquaintance rapes; attackers are more likely to carry a weapon, threaten the victim, and harm her physically. Stranger rapes are overrepresented in official statistics because victims who are more viciously harmed are the ones most likely to contact police.

Date Rape. Though official crime data indicate that most rapists and victims were strangers to one another, it is likely that acquaintance rapes constitute the bulk of sexual assaults. One disturbing trend of rape involves people who are in some form of courting relationship; this is referred to as *date rape.*

There is no single form of date rape. Some occur on first dates, others after a relationship has been developing, while still others occur after the couple have been involved for some time. In long-term or close relationships, the male partner may feel he has invested so much time and money in his partner that he is owed sexual relations or that sexual intimacy is an expression that the involvement is progressing. He may make comparisons to other couples who have dated for as long a period of time and are sexually active.[63]

Nor is date rape unique to the United States. A 1993 survey of Canadian college women found that while the overall crime rate of Canada is lower than the United States, the incidence of date rape is still extremely high. About one-third of the young women surveyed experienced an episode of physical, verbal, or psychological sexual coercion; 25 percent said they had sexual relations when they did not want to during the past year.[64]

Another disturbing phenomenon is campus gang rape, in which a group of men will attack a defenseless or inebriated victim. Well-publicized gang rapes have occurred at the University of New Hampshire, Duke University, Florida State University, Pennsylvania State University, and Bentley College in Massachusetts.[65]

Date rape is believed to occur frequently on college campuses. It has been estimated that 15 to 20 percent of all college women are victims of rape or attempted rape; one self-report survey conducted on a midwestern campus found that 100 percent of all rapists knew their victim beforehand.[66] The actual incidence of date rape may be even higher than surveys indicate because many victims blame themselves and do not recognize the incident as a rape, saying, for example, "I should have fought back harder," "I should have not gotten drunk."[67]

Despite their seriousness and prevalence, less than one in ten date rapes may be reported to police. Some victims do not report because they do not view their experiences as a "real rape," which they believe involves a strange man "jumping out of the bushes"; others are embarrassed and frightened. Coercive sexual encounters have become disturbingly common in our culture, prompting one commentator to state:

> the conclusion is inescapable that a very substantial minority of women on American college campuses have experienced an event which would fit most states' definitions of felony rape or sexual assault.[68]

To fight back, some campus women's groups have taken to writing on bathroom walls the names of men accused of date rape and sexual assault. Administration officials labeled it "libel and harassment" when a wall-writing campaign listed the names of 15 suspected rapists at Brown University. Brown women countered it was the only way to alert potential victims to the danger they faced from men who they might have considered trustworthy friends.[69]

Marital Rape.

In 1978, Greta Rideout filed rape charges against her husband, John. This Oregon case grabbed headlines because it was the first in which a husband was prosecuted for rape while domiciled with his wife. John was acquitted, and the couple briefly reconciled; later, continued violent episodes culminated in a divorce and a jail term for John.[70]

Traditionally, a legally married husband could not be charged with raping his wife; this was referred to as the **marital exemption.** The origin of this legal doctrine can be traced to the sixteenth-century pronouncement of Matthew Hale, England's chief justice, who wrote:

> But the husband cannot be guilty of rape committed by himself upon his lawful wife, for by their mutual matrimonial consent and contract the wife hath given up herself in this kind unto the husband which she cannot retract.[71]

However, research indicates that many women are raped each year by their husband as part of an overall pattern of spousal abuse, and they deserve the protection of the law. While there is a popular myth, illustrated by Rhett Butler overcoming the objections of his proper and reluctant bride Scarlett O'Hara in the classic film *Gone With the Wind*, that marital rapes are the result of "healthy male sexuality," the reality is quite the opposite. Research shows that many spousal rapes are accompanied by brutal and sadistic beatings and have little to do with normal sexual interests.[72]

Not surprisingly, the marital exemption is under attack. In 1980, only three states had laws against marital rape; as of 1992, marital rape is a crime if the couple were living together in all but two states.[73]

Piercing the marital exemption is not unique to U.S. courts; it has been abolished in Canada, Israel, Scotland, and New Zealand. In 1991, a London appeals court upheld the conviction of a 37-year-old man who had been found guilty of the rape of his estranged wife. In his opinion, the Lord Chief Justice Lane stated, "The idea that a wife by marriage consents in advance to her husband having sexual intercourse with her, whatever her state of health or however proper her objections, is no longer acceptable."[74]

The Cause of Rape

What factors predispose some men to commit rape? The answers formulated by criminologists to this question are almost as varied as the varieties of the crime of rape itself. However, most explanations can be grouped into a few consistent categories.

Evolutionary/Biological Factors.

One explanation for rape focuses on the evolutionary/biological aspects of the male sexual drive. It is suggested that rape may be instinctual, developed over the ages as a means of perpetuating the species. In more primitive times, forcible sexual contact may have served the purpose of spreading the gene pool and maximizing offspring. Some believe that these prehistoric drives remain in modern man. Males still have a natural sexual drive that encourages them to have intimate relations with as many women as possible.[75] The biosocial view is that the sexual urge is correlated with the unconscious need to preserve the species by spreading the gene pool as widely as possible. Rape is bound up with sexuality as well as violence because, according to Lee Ellis, the act involves the "drive to possess and control others to whom one is sexually attracted."[76]

Male Socialization.

In contrast to the biological view, some researchers argue that rape is a function of male socialization in modern society. In her book *The Politics of Rape,* Diana Russell suggests that rape is actually not a deviant act but one conforming to the qualities regarded as masculine in U.S. society.[77] From an early age, boys are taught to be aggressive, forceful, tough, and dominating. Men are taught to dominate at the same time that they are led to believe that women want to be dominated. Russell describes the virility mystique—the belief that males learn to separate their sexual feelings from needs for love, respect, and affection. She believes that men are socialized to be the aggressors and expect to be sexually active with many women; male virginity and sexual inexperience are marks of shame. Similarly, sexually aggressive women frighten some men and cause them to doubt their own masculinity. Sexual insecurity may lead some men to commit rape to bolster their self-image and masculine identity. Rape, argues Russell, helps keep women in their place.

Rape and Machismo.

If rape is an expression of male anger and devaluation of women and not an act motivated by sexual desire, it follows that men who hold so-called macho attitudes will be more likely to engage in sexual violence than men who scorn hypermasculinity. The more strongly some men are socialized into traditional sex role stereotypes, the more likely they are to be sexually aggressive. In fact, the sexually aggressive male may view the female as a legitimate victim of sexual violence.

To test the association between masculine attitudes and violent sexual behavior, psychologists Donald Mosher and Ronald Anderson surveyed 175 male college sophomores on their sexual attitudes and their history of sexual aggression.[78] They found that males who held callous sexual attitudes—for example, who agreed with the statement "Get a woman drunk, high or hot, and she'll let you do whatever you want"—were also the ones most likely to use sexually coercive behavior. Mosher and Anderson found that their subjects frequently used aggressive tactics: 75 percent admitted using drugs or alcohol to have sex with a date; 69 percent used verbal manipulation; 40 percent, anger; 13 percent threatened force; and 20 percent actually used force. Mosher and Anderson also had subjects listen to a taped account of a man describing his rape of a woman he had encountered on a country road. After asking the subjects to imagine themselves as the rapist, the researchers found that macho-oriented men experienced less intense negative emotions than nonmacho men and that subjects with a history of sexual aggressiveness reported more sexual arousal from the account.

Psychological Views.

Another view is that rapists are suffering from some type of personality disorder or mental illness. Paul Gebhard and his associates concluded that a significant percentage of incarcerated rapists exhibit psychotic tendencies, while many others have hostile and sadistic feelings toward women.[79] Similarly, Richard Rada found that many rapists were psychotics, others could be classified as sociopaths, and a large group suffered from a masculine identity crisis that made them oblivious to the sufferings of their victims.[80] One of the best-known attempts to classify the personality of rapists was made by psychologist A. Nicholas Groth. According to Groth, every rape encounter contains three elements: anger, power, and sexuality. Consequently, rapists can be classified according to one of these dimensions. Groth's views on rape are presented in the Close-Up entitled "Varieties of Rape."

Social Learning.

Another viewpoint is that men learn to commit rapes much as they learn any other behavior. Groth found that 40 percent of the rapists he studied were sexually victimized as adolescents.[81] A growing body of literature links personal sexual trauma with the desire to inflict sexual trauma on others. In a similar vein, evidence is mounting that some men are influenced by observing films and books with both violent and sexual content.[82] Watching violent or pornographic films featuring women who are beaten, raped, or tortured has been linked to sexually aggressive behavior in men.[83] In one startling case, a 12-year-old Providence, Rhode Island, boy sexually assaulted a 10-year-old girl on a pool table after watching on television trial coverage of a rape case in which a woman was similarly raped (the incident was made into a film, *The Accused,* starring actress Jodie Foster).[84] This view will be explored further in Chapter 14, when the issue of pornography and violence is analyzed in greater detail.

Sexual Motivation.

Most current views of rape hold that it is actually a violent act and not sexually motivated. Yet, as Richard Felson and Marvin Krohn point out, it might be premature to dismiss the sexual motive from all rapes.[85] They used NCVS data to show that rape victims tend to be young and that rapists prefer younger and presumably more attractive victims. Felson and Krohn also find an association between the age of rapists and their victims, indicating that men choose rape targets of approximately the same age as consensual sex partners. And, despite the fact that younger criminals are usually the most violent, older rapists tend to harm their victims more often than younger rapists. Felson and Krohn maintain that while older criminals may be raping for motives of power and control, younger offenders are seeking sexual gratification and are therefore less likely to harm their victims.

In sum, while criminologists are still at odds over the precise cause of rape, there is evidence that it is the product of a number of social, cultural, and psychological forces.[86] Though some experts view it as a normal response to an abnormal environment, others view it as the product of a disturbed mind and deviant life experiences.

Rape and the Law

Of all violent crimes, none has created such conflict in the legal system as rape. Women who are sexually assaulted are reluctant to report the crime to the police because of the discriminatory provisions built into rape laws; the sexist fashion in which rape victims are treated by police, prosecutors, and court personnel; and the legal technicalities that authorize invasion of women's privacy when a rape case is tried in court. Some state laws have made rape so difficult to prove that women believe that the slim chance their attacker will be convicted is not sufficient to warrant their participation in the prosecutorial process.

CLOSE-UP

Varieties of Rape

People have varied visions of the rapist: the psychopath who cannot control his sexual urges, the college student who gets drunk and forces his will on a classmate, the gang member who participates in rape to prove his manhood. A leading expert on the personality and behavior of rapists, A. Nicholas Groth, has disputed the idea that rapists are oversexed people or that rape is a sexual act. Groth maintains that rape is always a symptom of some psychological dysfunction, either temporary and transient or chronic and repetitive. Furthermore, it is usually a desperate act that results when an emotionally weak and insecure individual is unable to handle the stresses and demands of his life.

After observing 500 convicted rapists in his role as director of the sex offenders program for the Connecticut Department of Corrections, Groth found that in every act of rape, both aggression and sexuality were involved but that sexuality became the means of expressing the aggressive needs and feelings that underlay the assault. Groth identifies three patterns, or typologies, of rape offenders; these typologies help explain the hostility, control, and dominance associated with sexual assaults:

The *anger rape* occurs when sexuality becomes a means of expressing and discharging pent-up anger and rage. The rapist uses far more brutality than would have been necessary if his real objective had been simply to have sexual relations with his victim. His aim is to hurt his victim as much as possible; the sexual aspect of rape may have been an afterthought. Often the anger rapist acts on the spur of the moment after an upsetting incident has caused him conflict, irritation, or aggravation. Surprisingly, anger rapes are less psychologically traumatic for the victim than might be expected. Since a woman is usually physically beaten, she is more likely to receive sympathy from her peers, relatives, and the justice system and consequently be immune from any suggestion that she complied with the attack.

The *power rape* involves an attacker who does not want to harm his victim as much as he wants to possess her sexually. His goal is sexual conquest, and he uses only the amount of force necessary to achieve his objective. The power rapist wants to be in control, to be able to dominate women and have them at his mercy. Yet it is not sexual gratification that drives the power rapist; in fact, he often has consenting relationships with his wife or girlfriend. Rape is instead a way of putting personal insecurities to rest, asserting heterosexuality, and preserving a sense of manhood. The power rapist's victim usually is a woman equal in age to or younger than the rapist. The lack of physical violence may reduce the support given the victim by family and friends. Therefore, the victim's personal guilt over her rape experience is increased—perhaps, she thinks, she could have done something to get away.

The *sadistic rape* involves both sexuality and aggression. The sadistic rapist is bound up in ritual—he may torment his victim, bind her, torture her. Victims are usually related in the rapist's view to a personal characteristic that he wants to harm or destroy. The rape experience is intensely exciting to the sadist; he gets satisfaction from abusing, degrading, or humiliating his captive. This type of rape is particularly traumatic for the victim; Groth found that victims of such crimes need psychiatric care long after their physical wounds have healed.

In his treatment of rape offenders, Groth found that about 55 percent were of the power type; about 40 percent, the anger type; and about 5 percent, the sadistic type. Groth's major contribution has been his recognition that rape is generally a crime of violence and not a sexual act.

Discussion Questions

1. Can rape be motivated by sexual drive or by aggression?
2. What do you think is an appropriate penalty for rape?

SOURCE: A. Nicholas Groth and Jean Birnbaum, *Men Who Rape* (New York: Plenum Press, 1979).

Proving Rape. Proving guilt in a rape case is extremely challenging for prosecutors. First, some male psychiatrists and therapists still maintain that women fantasize rape and therefore may falsely accuse their alleged attackers. Some judges also fear that women may charge men with rape because of jealousy, false proposals of marriage, or pregnancy. While those concerned with protecting the rights of rape victims have campaigned for legal reforms, some well-publicized false accusations of rape have hindered change. In March 1985, Cathleen Webb, an alleged rape victim, stepped forward and claimed that Gary Dotson, convicted of raping her in Illinois, had been falsely accused.[87] Webb stated before a national audience that her fear of a teenage pregnancy led her to accuse Dotson of a crime that never occurred; Dotson was released after spending more than six years in prison. A 1990 case involving a false rape accusation prompted a Nebraska judge to order a young woman to take out newspaper and radio ads apologizing to a man she had identified to police as a rapist.[88] Such incidents make it more difficult for prosecutors to gain convictions in rape cases. The sexism that exists in U.S. society has resulted in a cultural suspiciousness of women, who are often seen as provocateurs in any sexual encounter with men. Consequently, the burden is shifted to the woman to prove she has not provoked or condoned the rape. Although the law does not recognize it, jurors are sometimes swayed by the insinuation that the rape was victim-precipitated; thus, the blame is shifted from rapist to victim. To get a conviction, it becomes essential for prosecutors to establish that the act was forced and violent and that no question of voluntary compliance exists. The legal consequences of rape often reflect archaic legal traditions along with inherent male prejudices and suspicions.

Consent. Rape represents a major legal challenge to the criminal justice system for a number of reasons.[89] One issue involves the concept of **consent.** It is essential to prove that the attack was forced and that the victim did not give voluntary consent to her attacker. In a sense, the burden of proof is on the victim to prove that her character is beyond question and that she in no way encouraged, enticed, or misled the accused rapist. Proving victim dissent is not a requirement in any other violent crime (robbery victims do not have to prove they did not entice their attacker by wearing expensive jewelry), yet it can still be introduced by the defense counsel in rape cases to create a reasonable doubt about the woman's credibility. It is a common defense tactic to introduce suspicion in the minds of the jury that the

woman may have consented to the sexual act and later regretted her decision. Conversely, it is difficult for a prosecuting attorney to establish that a woman's character is so impeccable that the absence of consent is a certainty. Such distinctions are important in rape cases, because male jurors may be sympathetic to the accused if the victim is portrayed as unchaste. Simply referring to the woman as sexually liberated may be enough to result in exoneration of the accused, even if violence and brutality were used in the attack. In one nationally publicized 1989 case, a Florida defendant was acquitted after jury members concluded his victim "asked for it by the way she was dressed." Steven Lord, the 26-year-old defendant, was freed after the jury was told his victim was wearing a lace miniskirt with nothing underneath and "was advertising for sex." The acquittal came despite the fact that other women were allowed to testify that Lord had also raped them.[90]

Efforts for reform include changing the language of statutes, dropping the condition that the victim resisted, and changing the requirement that the perpetrator used force to include "the threat of force or injury."[91] The need for change has not been lost on the public. Recent evidence can be found in a Texas case in which a rape defendant was found guilty despite the victim's request that he wear a condom. At trial, the victim testified that she made the request to protect herself from AIDS; the defense claimed that such a request was a form of consent.[92]

Reform. Because of the difficulty victims have in receiving justice in rape cases, the law of rape has been changing around the country. Most (48) states and the federal government have developed **shield laws,** which protect women from being questioned about their sexual history unless it is judged to have a direct bearing on the case. In some instances, these laws are quite restrictive, while in others, they grant the trial judge considerable discretion to admit prior sexual conduct in evidence if it is deemed relevant for the defense. In an important 1991 case, *Michigan v. Lucas*, the U.S. Supreme Court upheld the validity of shield laws and ruled that excluding evidence of a prior sexual relationship between the parties did not violate the defendant's right to a fair trial.[93]

In addition to requiring evidence that consent was not given, the common law of rape required **corroboration** that the crime of rape actually took place. This involved the need for independent or third-party evidence from police officers, physicians, and witnesses that the accused is actually the person who committed the crime, that sexual penetration took place, and that force was present and consent absent. This requirement shielded rapists from prosecution in cases where the victim delayed reporting the crime or in which physical evidence had been compromised or lost. Corroboration is no longer required except under extraordinary circumstances, such as when the victim was too young to understand the crime, had a previous sexual relationship with the defendant, or gives a version of events that is improbable and self-contradictory.[94]

The Limits of Reform.

Despite this reform effort, it is essential that the victim establish her intimate and detailed knowledge of the act for her testimony to be believed in court. This may include searching questions about her assailant's appearance, the location in which the crime took place, and the nature of the physical assault.

The federal government and states, including Nebraska and Michigan, have replaced rape laws with the more sexually neutral crimes of sexual assault.[95] Sexual assault laws outlaw any type of forcible sex, including homosexual rape.[96] Have these changes proved effective? A study by Susan Caringella-MacDonald compared the processing of sexual assault cases with nonsexual assault cases in Michigan. There was some similarity, but the credibility of sexual assault victims was more likely to be challenged in court; concomitantly, offenders were more likely to receive significant sentence reductions when they plea-bargained. Caringella-MacDonald concludes that "the historic difficulties in adjudicating sexual assault offenses cannot be erased by the stroke of a pen."[97] A nationwide review of rape law by Ronald Berger, Patricia Searles, and W. Lawrence Neuman finds that despite reform efforts, the efforts to revamp the legal processing of rape have fallen short of expectations. Judges, attorneys, and the public seem reluctant to embrace reforms, such as shield laws and the punishment of nonconsensual but unforced sex; significant reform of rape laws must remain a goal.[98]

≡ Murder and Homicide

Murder is defined in the common law as "the unlawful killing of a human being with malice aforethought."[99] It is the most serious of all common-law crimes and the only one that can still be punished by death. The fact that Western society abhors murderers is illustrated by the fact that there is no statute of limitations in murder

cases. While state laws usually limit prosecution of other crimes to a fixed period, usually seven to ten years, accused killers can be brought to justice years after their crime was committed. An example of the law's reach in murder cases was the murder conviction of George Franklin on January 29, 1991. Franklin's daughter Eileen Franklin-Lipsker had told legal authorities that while in recent psychotherapy sessions with her analyst, she had remembered how her father had sexually assaulted and killed her eight-year-old friend. The murder had taken place in 1969, more than 20 years earlier.[100]

To prove that a murder has taken place, most state jurisdictions require prosecutors to prove that the accused intentionally and with malice desired the death of the victim. Express or actual malice is the state of mind assumed to exist when someone kills another person in the absence of any apparent provocation. Implied or constructive malice is considered to exist when a death results from negligent or unthinking behavior; even though the perpetrator did not wish to kill the victim, the killing was the result of an inherently dangerous act and therefore is considered murder. An unusual example of this concept is the attempted murder conviction of Ignacio Perea, an AIDS-infected Miami man who kidnapped and raped an 11-year-old boy. Perea was sentenced to up to 25 years in prison when the jury agreed with the prosecutor's contention that the AIDS virus could be considered a deadly weapon.[101]

Degrees of Murder

There are different levels or degrees of homicide.[102] Murder in the first degree occurs when a person kills another after **premeditation** and deliberation. Premeditation means that the killing was considered beforehand and suggests that it was motivated by more than a simple desire to engage in an act of violence. Deliberation means the killing was planned and decided on after careful thought, rather than carried out on impulse. "To constitute a deliberate and premeditated killing, the slayer must weigh and consider the question of killing and the reasons for and against such a choice; having in mind the consequences, he decides to and does kill."[103] The planning implied by this definition need not be a long, drawn-out process but may be an almost instantaneous decision to take another's life. Also, a killing accompanying a felony, such as robbery or rape, usually constitutes first-degree murder (felony murder).

Second-degree murder requires the actor to have malice aforethought but not premeditation or deliberation.

A second-degree murder occurs when a person's wanton disregard for the victim's life and his or her desire to inflict serious bodily harm on the victim results in the loss of human life. An unlawful homicide without malice is called manslaughter and is usually punished by anywhere between one and 15 years in prison. Voluntary or nonnegligent manslaughter refers to a killing committed in the heat of passion or during a sudden quarrel considered to have provided sufficient provocation to produce violence; while intent may be present, malice is not. Involuntary or negligent manslaughter refers to a killing that occurs when a person's acts are negligent and without regard for the harm they may cause others. Most involuntary manslaughter cases involve motor vehicle deaths, for example, when a drunk driver causes the death of a pedestrian. However, one can be held criminally liable for the death of another in many unusual circumstances. For example, on February 16, 1990, Michael Patrick Berry, a man whose pit bull killed a child who had wandered into his yard, was sentenced to three years and eight months in prison; it was the nation's first case in which a person was convicted for manslaughter for the actions of a pet.[104] Ironically, six months later, a Florida man, Everston Eugene Smith, was given virtually the same sentence for killing a dog that had wandered into his yard.[105]

The Nature and Extent of Murder

It is possible to track murder rate trends from 1900 to the present with the aid of coroner's reports and UCR data. The murder rate reached a peak in 1933, a time of high unemployment and lawlessness, and then fell until 1958, when it began another upswing to a 1980 peak of 10.2 murders per 100,000 persons (a total of 23,000); it then declined until 1984, when the rate hit 8 per 100,000 (18,690); since then, it has slowly increased so that in 1992, the number of murders was about 23,600, a slight decrease from the year before.

What else do the official crime statistics tell us about murder today? Murder victims tend to be males (78 percent) and over 18 years of age (90 percent). There is a disturbing trend for African-Americans to become murder victims (55 percent), almost 90 percent male. Murder, like rape, tends to be an intraracial crime; about 90 percent of victims are slain by members of their own race. Similarly, people arrested for murder were generally young (45 percent were under 25) and male (90 percent), a pattern that has proven very consistent over time.[106] The UCR also collects information on the circumstances of murder. A number of important patterns stand out:

- Where it could be determined, most victims knew or were acquainted with their assailant; strangers committed only 14 percent of murders. Most commonly, victim and criminal were either acquaintances or relatives; of these, about 11 percent were members of the immediate family (husbands, wives, children, parents).

- Most murders involved firearms (69 percent), almost all of these being handguns; about 15 percent involved knives or cutting instruments. Some well-known weapons, such as poison, narcotics, and strangulation, are actually rarely used; there were only 13 known poisonings in 1992.

- When it could be determined, about 31 percent of murders occurred during commission of a felony, such as a robbery, while 68 percent were a result of an argument over money, love, or other passions. About 27 percent of all murder circumstances could not be determined. About 5 percent of convicted murderers receive a probation sentence (see Figure 11.3).

- The environmental pattern of murder is similar to that of rape. Murder rates are highest in large cities, in the South and West, and during the summer months and holiday seasons. In contrast, rural counties and midwestern states have relatively low murder rates. Some cities are extremely murder-prone. Nearly 25 percent of all murders in the United States usually occur in seven cities: New York, Los Angeles, Chicago, Houston, Detroit, Philadelphia, and Washington, D.C.

Today, few would deny that some relationship exists between social and ecological factors and murder. This section will explore some of the more important issues related to these factors.

Murderous Relations

One factor that has received a great deal of attention from criminologists is the relationship between the murderer and the victim.[107] Most criminologists generally agree that murders can be separated into those involving strangers, typically stemming from a felony attempt, such as a robbery or drug deal, and acquaintance homicides involving disputes between family, friends, and acquaintances.[108] Unlike most other crimes, the principals in homicide usually knew one another.[109] The UCR typically finds that in less than 15 percent of the murders in which the police were able to determine the relation-

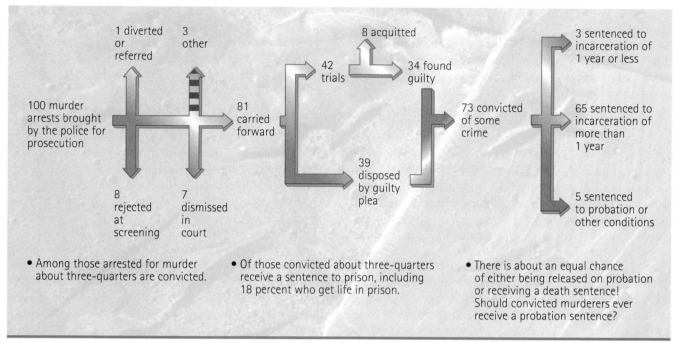

FIGURE 11.3 What Happens to Murder Suspects?

SOURCE: John Dawson, *Murder in Large Urban Counties, 1988* (Washington, D.C.: Bureau of Justice Statistics, 1993).

ship between criminal and victim were the actors classified strangers to one another.[110] In most instances, the victim and the criminal were either related (husband, wife, brother, son, or the like) or acquainted (friend, boyfriend, girlfriend, neighbor, and so on).[111] Using the records of murder cases in St. Louis, Scott Decker found that the quality of this relationship may determine the extent of violence; people were less likely to victimize people they considered close friends than those who were mere acquaintances.[112]

Have murderous relations changed? To address this question, Angela Browne and Kirk Williams looked at homicide trends over a 12-year period (1976–1987) and found a major shift in murder trends among people who shared an intimate relationship. The rate of homicide among married couples declined significantly, a finding they attribute to the shift away from marriage in modern society. However, Browne and Williams found significant gender differences in homicide trends among the unmarried: while the number of unmarried men killed by their partners *declined*, the rate of women killed by the men they lived with *increased* dramatically. They speculate that men kill their spouses either as a means of maintaining control or because they fear losing control and power. Since people who live together without

marriage have a legally and socially more "open" relationship, it is possible that males in such relationships are more likely to feel loss of control and exert their power with the use of violence.[113]

In contrast, research indicates that females who kill their mates do so after suffering repeated violent attacks.[114] It is possible that the number of males killed by their partners has declined because alternatives to abusive relationships, such as battered woman's shelters, are becoming more prevalent around the United States. Browne and Williams have shown that regions in which greater social support is provided for battered women and legislation has been passed to protect abuse victims also have lower rates of female-perpetrated homicide.[115]

Stranger Homicides

Not all murders involve friends, family, and acquaintances. Though the actual number is open to debate, Marc Reidel reports that somewhere between 14 percent and 29 percent of homicides are committed by strangers, and in some areas, the percentage of stranger murders is increasing.[116] However, other research efforts indicate that the rate of stranger homicides during the past two decades has remained relatively stable.[117] Under what circumstances do stranger homicides occur? In a study of homicide in nine U.S. cities, Margaret Zahn and Philip Sagi found that while 72 percent of murders involved family members or acquaintances, 28 percent were stranger homicides. Of this latter group, 16 percent involved felony murders, which occur during rapes, robberies, burglaries, and so on. In addition, about 12 percent consisted of those random acts of urban violence that fuel public fear: a homeowner tells a motorist to move his car because it is blocking the driveway, an argument ensues, and the owner gets a pistol and kills the motorist; a young boy kills a store manager because, he says, "something came into my head to hurt the lady."[118] Zahn and Sagi found important patterns in the stranger, nonfelony cases. For example, white victims were significantly older than their attackers, while there was little age differential between black and Hispanic victims and criminals. Zahn and Sagi attribute this difference to the fact that urban homicides occur in central city areas that white families with young children have left for suburbia, while older whites have remained on and become vulnerable to predatory crime.[119]

Murder Transactions

At one time, it was popular to view murderers as mentally unstable persons who killed because they were driven by psychotic personalities or were so deeply disturbed that they did not know what they were doing. Although it is true that some convicted murderers suffer from mental illnesses, such as schizophrenia or paranoia, it is also probably true that the incidence of psychosis among murderers is no greater than in the total population. Today, criminologists have revised their concepts of murder. Attempts have been made to classify criminal homicide by its cause and the relationship between the actors involved in it. For example, James Boudouris classifies murder interaction as follows: domestic relations (husband–wife); lovers' affairs; relations between friends and acquaintances; business relations (landlord–tenant, doctor–patient, employer–employee); criminal transactions (holdup man–store owner, drug user–pusher); noncriminal homicide (police officer– holdup man); cultural recreation–casual (bar fight, quarrel over a car accident); subcultural recreation–casual (two gamblers fight over a card game); psychiatric (murder by a mentally disturbed person); suicide–murder (the killer immediately kills himself or herself); incidental (a peacemaker in a fight is accidentally killed); and unknown cause. In a study of homicides occurring in Detroit between 1926 and 1968, Boudouris found that an overwhelming number were related to domestic and family quarrels and relatively few murders were caused by psychiatrically disturbed persons.[120]

David Luckenbill studied murder transactions to determine whether particular patterns of behavior are common to the transaction between killer and victim.[121] He found that many homicides take a sequential form: The victim made what the offender considered an offensive move; the offender typically retaliated in a verbal or physical manner; an agreement to end things violently was forged with the victim's response; the battle ensued, leaving the victim dead or dying; the offender's escape was shaped by his or her relationship to the victim or the reaction of the audience, if any. Thus, whereas some murders may be the result of wanton violence by a stranger, the typical homicide seems to involve a social interaction between two or more people who know each other and whose destructive social interaction leads to the death of one party.[122] If anything, this research seems to support Wolfgang's victim precipitation model.

Types of Murderers

There are other forms of stranger homicides that take a toll on society. **Thrill killing** involves impulsive violence motivated by the killer's decision to kill a stranger as an act of daring or recklessness. For example, children who throw a boulder over a highway overpass onto an oncoming car may be out for thrills or kicks.[123] While some thrill killings involve relatively stable youths who exhibit few prior symptoms of violence, others are committed by youngsters with long-standing mental or emotional problems.[124] **Gang killings** involve members of teenage gangs who make violence part of their group activity. Some of these gangs engage in warfare over territory or control of the drug trade; drive-by shootings, in which enemies are killed and strangers caught in the cross-fire, may account for thousands of killings each year.[125] Recent research on street gangs in Chicago by Carolyn Block and Richard Block shows that between 1987 and 1990, street gangs in Chicago committed more than 9,000 violent acts, including 288 homicides.[126]

Cult killings occur when members of religious cults, some of which are devoted to devil worship, satanism, and the "black mass," are ordered to kill by their leaders. On some occasions, the cult members are ordered to kill peers who are suspected of deviating from the leaders' teachings. Other crimes involve random violence against strangers either as a show of loyalty or because of the misguided belief that they are a threat to the cult's existence. Charles Ewing cites the case of three Missouri teenagers, all members of a self-styled satanic cult, who beat another boy to death with baseball bats and then stuffed his body down a well. For months before the killing, the boys planned the crime as a human sacrifice for Satan.[127] In April 1989, police in Matamoros, Mexico, uncovered the grave of a 21-year-old U.S. college student, Mark Kilroy, who had served as a human sacrifice for members of a Mexican drug ring that practiced *palo mayombe,* a form of black magic; killing the youth was believed to bring immunity from bullets and criminal prosecution.[128] Some murders blamed on the influence of Satan are not carried out by members of an organized group but rather are perpetrated by individuals who have visions of the Devil telling them to kill. In 1993, a 15-year-old Houston boy, Andrew Merritt, killed his mother after hearing the Devil tell him to "kill all the Christians"; law enforcement officials linked Andrew's passion for heavy metal music to the crime.[129]

While it is difficult to assess the numbers of stranger homicides that result from gang, cult, and thrill killings, it seems evident that they are becoming a disturbing element of U.S. violence.

Serial Murder

Donald Harvey is described as being neat, pleasant, outgoing, and remarkably normal by those who know him best. However, his co-workers in a Cincinnati-area hospital where he worked as a nurse's aide referred to Harvey as the "angel of death" because so many patients died in his ward. Their fears convinced a local TV station to conduct an investigation that resulted in Harvey's arrest and conviction on multiple murder charges. Harvey pleaded guilty to killing at least 21 patients and three other people, and he claims to have killed 28 others, though he cannot remember details of their deaths. Harvey claims that he was a mercy killer who "gained relief for the patients"; prosecutors described him as a thrill seeker whose behavior was triggered by his sexual ambivalence.[130] He was sentenced to life in prison with possibility of parole in 95 years. When all his activities come to light, Harvey may be known as the most prolific killer in U.S. history.

Donald Harvey's murderous actions fall within a frightening pattern referred to as **serial murder.** Some serial murderers, such as Theodore Bundy and the Australian race-car driver and photographer Christopher Wilder, roam the country killing at random.[131] Others terrorize a city, such as the Los Angeles-based Night Stalker; the Green River Killer, who is believed to have slain more than four dozen young women in Seattle; and the Hillside Stranglers, Kenneth Bianchi and Angelo Buono, who tortured and killed ten women in the Los Angeles area.[132] A third type of serial murderer, such as Donald Harvey and Milwaukee cannibal Jeffrey Dahmer, kills so cunningly that many victims are dispatched before the authorities even realize the deaths can be attributed to a single perpetrator.[133]

Serial killers operate over a long period of time and can be distinguished from the **mass murderer** who kills many victims in a single, violent outburst. For example, James Huberty killed 21 people in a McDonald's in San Ysidro, California. On occasion, mass murders even occur in usually nonviolent Great Britain.[134] On August 20, 1987, Michael Ryan, a 25-year-old British gun enthusiast, killed 14 people in a random shooting spree.[135] The Close-Up entitled "Mass Murder and Serial Killing" further discusses serial killers and multiple killers.

Types of Serial Murderers. Research shows that serial killers have long histories of violence, beginning in childhood, with the targeting of other children, siblings, and small animals.[136] They maintain superficial relationships with others, have trouble relating to the opposite sex, and maintain guilt feelings about their interest in sex. Despite these similarities, there is no single distinct type of serial killer. Some seem to be monsters—such as Edmund Kemper, who, in addition to killing six young female hitchhikers, killed his mother, cut off her head, and used it as a dart board. Others—such as Bianchi, Wilder, and Bundy—were suave ladies' men whose murderous actions surprised even close friends.

Consequently, the cause of serial murder eludes criminologists. Such widely disparate factors as mental illness, sexual frustration, neurological damage, child abuse and neglect, smothering relationships with mothers (David Berkowitz, the Son of Sam, slept in his parents' bed until he was ten), and childhood anxiety, have been suggested as possible causes. However, most experts view the serial killers as sociopaths who from early childhood demonstrated bizarre behavior, such as torturing animals; enjoyment in killing; immunity to their victims' suffering; and, when caught, basking in the media limelight. Wayne Henley, Jr., who along with Dean Corill killed 27 boys in Houston, offered to help prosecutors find the bodies of additional victims so he could break Chicago killer Wayne Gacy's record of 33 murders.[137] However, Philip Jenkin's study of serial murder in England identified one group of offenders who had no apparent personality problems until late in their lives, were married and respectable, and even had careers in the armed services and police.[138]

Ronald Holmes and James DeBurger have studied serial killers and found that they can be divided into at least four types:

Visionary killers—whose murders are committed in response to some inner voice or vision that demands that some person or category of persons be killed. This type of serial killer is almost always out of touch with reality and is usually considered psychotic.

Mission-oriented killers—whose murders are motivated to rid the world of a particular type of undesirable person, such as prostitutes. They are well aware of what they are doing and are in touch with reality. Joseph Paul Franklin, for example, killed as

CLOSE-UP

Mass Murder and Serial Killing

Criminologists Jack Levin and James Alan Fox have written extensively on two of the most frightening aspects of modern violence—mass murder and serial killing.

According to Levin and Fox, while it is difficult to estimate the number and extent of serial killings, a reasoned estimate is that up to 20 serial killers are active in a given year, accounting for up to 240 killings or about 1 percent of the total number of homicides.

There are different types of serial killers. Some wander the countryside killing at random; others stay in their hometown and lure victims to their death. Theodore Bundy, convicted killer of three young women and suspected killer of many others, roamed the country killing as he went, while Wayne Gacy killed over 30 boys and young men without leaving Chicago.

While they share many characteristics with the general population, one "special" trait stands out: serial killers are exceptionally skillful in their presentation of self so that they appear beyond suspicion. They kill for the "fun of it." They enjoy

James A. Fox and Jack Levin have conducted research on mass murder and serial killing.

the thrill, the sexual gratification, and the dominance they achieve over the lives of their victims. The serial killer rarely uses a gun to kill because this method is too quick and would deprive him of his greatest pleasure, "exalting in his victim's suffering." Serial killers are not "sick" or insane, but "more cruel than crazy."

Fox and Levin have their own typology of serial killers:

1. Thrill killers who strive for either sexual sadism or dominance. This is the most common form of serial murderer.

2. Mission killers who want to reform the world or have a vision that drives them to kill.

many as 12 young black males who were with white female companions.

Hedonistic killers—thrill-seeking murderers who get excitement and sometimes sexual pleasure from their acts.

Power/control-oriented killers—murderers who enjoy having complete control over their victims. If they rape or mutilate their victims, the violence is motivated not by sex but by the pleasure of having power over another human being.[139]

Other types of serial killers include the *mysoped*, or sadistic child killer, who gains sexual satisfaction from torturing and killing children.[140] The *psychopathic killer* is motivated by a character disorder that results in his or her being unable to experience feeling or shame, guilt,

---

3. Expedience killers who are out for profit or want to protect themselves from a perceived threat.

In contrast to serial killers, mass murderers engage in a single, uncontrollable outburst called simultaneous killing. Examples of simultaneous mass murderers include Charles Whitman, who killed 14 people and wounded 30 others from atop the 307-foot tower on the University of Texas campus on August 1, 1966; James Huberty, who killed 21 people in a McDonald's in San Ysidro, California, on July 18, 1984; and George Hennard, a deranged Texas man who, on October 16, 1991, smashed his truck through a plate glass window in a cafeteria in Killeen, Texas, got out and systematically killed 22 people before committing suicide as police closed in.

Fox and Levin find four types of mass murderers:

1. Revenge killers who seek to get even with individuals or society at large. Their typical target is an estranged wife and "her" children, an employer and "his" employees.
2. Love killers who are motivated by a warped sense of devotion. They are often despondent peo-

ple who commit suicide and take others, such as a wife and children, with them.
3. Profit killers are usually trying to cover up a crime, eliminate witnesses, and carry out a criminal conspiracy.
4. Terrorist killers are trying to send a message. Gang killings tell rivals to watch out; cult killers may actually leave a message behind to warn society about impending doom.

Levin and Fox dispute the notion that all mass murderers and serial killers have some form of biological or psychological problems, such as genetic anomalies or schizophrenia. Even the most sadistic serial murderers are not mentally ill or driven by delusions or hallucinations. Instead, they typically exhibit a sociopathic personality that deprives them of feelings of conscience or guilt to guide their behavior. Mass murderers are actually ordinary citizens driven to extreme acts. They experience long-term frustration, blame others for their problems, and then get "set off" by some catastrophic loss that they are unable to get help to deal with.

So far, police have been successful in capturing simultaneous killers whose outburst is directed at family

members or friends. The serial killer has proven a more elusive target. Today, the U.S. Justice Department is coordinating efforts to gather information on unsolved murders in different jurisdictions to find patterns linking the crimes. Unfortunately, when a serial murderer is caught, it is often the result of luck—or a snitch—and not investigative skill.

Discussion Questions

1. Can a mass murderer be legally sane?
2. Should there be a mandatory death sentence for all serial killers?

SOURCES: James Alan Fox and Jack Levin, *Overkill: Mass Murder and Serial Killing Exposed* (New York: Plenum, 1994); idem, "A Psycho-Social Analysis of Mass Murder," in *Serial and Mass Murder: Theory, Policy, and Research,* ed. Thomas O'Reilly-Fleming and Steven Egger (Toronto: University of Toronto Press, 1993); James Alan Fox and Jack Levin, "Serial Murder: A Survey," in *Serial and Mass Murder: Theory, Policy, and Research,* ed. Thomas O'Reilly-Fleming and Steven Egger (Toronto: University of Toronto Press, 1993); Jack Levin and James Alan Fox, *Mass Murder* (New York: Plenum Press, 1985).

sorrow, or other "normal" human emotions; these murderers are concerned solely with their own needs and passions. *Professional hit* killers assassinate complete strangers for economic, political, or ideological reasons; terrorists and organized crime figures fall within this category.[141]

When the Serial Killer Is a Woman.

An estimated 10 to 15 percent of serial killers are women. A recent study by Belea Keeney and Kathleen Heide investigated the characteristics of a sample of 14 female serial killers and found a pattern of distinct gender differences.[142]

Keeney and Heide found some striking differences between the way male and female killers carried out their crimes. Males were much more likely than females to use extreme violence and torture. While males used a "hands-on" approach, including beating, bludgeoning, and strangling their victims, females were more likely to poison or smother their victims. Men tracked or stalked their victims, while women were more likely to lure victims to their death.

There were also gender-based personality and behavior characteristics. Female killers, somewhat older than their male counterparts, were abusers of both alcohol and drugs; males were not likely to be substance abusers. Women were diagnosed as having histrionic, manic-depressive, borderline, dissociative, and antisocial personality disorders; men were more often diagnosed as having antisocial personalities.

The profile of the female serial killer that emerges is a person who smothers or poisons someone she knows. During childhood, she suffered from an abusive relationship in a disrupted family. Female killers' education levels are below average, and if they worked, it was in a low-status position.

Controlling Serial Killers.

Serial killers come from diverse backgrounds. So far, law enforcement officials have been at a loss to control random killers who leave few clues, constantly change their whereabouts, and have little connection to their victims. Catching serial killers is often a matter of luck. To help local law enforcement officials, the FBI has developed a profiling system to identify potential suspects. In addition, the Justice Department's Violent Criminal Apprehension Program (VICAP), a computerized information service, gathers information and matches offense characteristics on violent crimes around the country.[143] This way, crimes can be linked to determine if they are the product of a single culprit.

Efforts to control serial killers take on greater importance when the rate of increase of this crime is considered. Philip Jenkins has studied serial killing over the past 50 years and reports an upsurge since the 1960s. In addition, the number of victims per criminal and the ferocity and savagery of the killings also seem to be increasing. Jenkins attributes this increase to a variety of influences ranging from a permissive, drug-abusing culture to a mental health system so overcrowded that potentially dangerous people are released without supervision into an unsuspecting world.[144]

≡ Assault and Battery

Though many people mistakenly believe that "assault and battery" refers to a single act, they are actually two separate crimes. *Battery* requires an offensive touching, such as slapping, hitting, or punching a victim. *Assault* requires no actual touching but involves either attempted battery or intentionally frightening the victim by word or deed. While the common law originally intended these twin crimes to be misdemeanors, most jurisdictions now upgrade them to felonies when either a weapon is used or they occurred during the commission of a felony (for example, a person is assaulted during the course of a robbery). In the UCR, the FBI defines serious assault, or aggravated assault, as "an unlawful attack by one person upon another for the purpose of inflicting severe or aggravated bodily injury"; this definition is similar to the one used in most state jurisdictions.[145]

Under common law, battery required "bodily injury," such as broken limbs or wounds. However, under modern law, an assault and battery occurs if the victim suffers a temporarily painful blow, even if no injury results. A battery can also involve "offensive touching," for example, if a man kisses a woman against her will or puts his hands on her body.

Nature of Assault

The pattern of criminal assault is quite similar to that of homicide—one could say that the only difference between the two is that the victim survives. In 1992, the FBI recorded 1.1 million assaults, an increase of 3 percent from the preceding year. The official assault rate has risen significantly in the past few years, up 24 percent between 1988 and 1992.[146]

The pattern of assault is quite similar to that of both rape and murder. People arrested for assault and those identified by victims seem to be young, male, and white, though the arrest data contain disproportionate number of minority-group members (39 percent). Similarly, assault rates were highest in urban areas, during the summer months, and in southern regions. The most common weapons used in assaults were blunt instruments (31 percent), hands and feet (26 percent), firearms (25 percent), and knives (18 percent).

Assault in the Home

One of the most frightening aspects of assaultive behavior today is the incidence of violent attacks in the home. Criminologists are now aware that intrafamily violence is an enduring social problem in the United States. One area of intrafamily violence that has received a great deal of media attention is **child abuse.**[147] This term describes any physical or emotional trauma to a child for which no reasonable explanation, such as an accident or ordinary disciplinary practices, can be found.[148]

Child abuse can result from actual physical beatings administered to a child by hands, feet, weapons, belts, sticks, burning, and so on. Another form of abuse results from **neglect**—not providing a child with the care and shelter to which he or she is entitled. It is difficult to estimate the actual number of child abuse cases, since so many incidents are never reported to the police. Nonetheless, child abuse and neglect appears to be a serious social problem. National surveys conducted by Richard Gelles and Murray Straus found that over 1 million children in the United States are subject in a given year to physical abuse from their parents.[149] Physical abuse was found to be rarely a one-time event. The average number of assaults per year was 10.5; the median, 4.5. Children of all ages suffer abuse. In general, boys are more frequently abused than girls until age 12. Among teenagers, girls are more frequently the object of abuse. The American Human Society, which collects data on reported child abuse, also estimates that 1 million cases are discovered by authorities each year.[150]

Sexual Abuse

Another aspect of the abuse syndrome is **sexual abuse**—the exploitation of children through rape, incest, and molestation by parents or other adults. Though it is difficult to estimate the incidence of sexual abuse, numerous anecdotal incidents illustrate the seriousness of the problem. There have been many allegations of sexual impropriety made against religious figures. The Boy Scouts admitted having dismissed 1,800 scoutmasters suspected of molesting children between 1971 and 1991; some of those dismissed may have moved to other troops and continued their abuse.[151]

A number of attempts have been made to gauge the extent of the sexual abuse problem. One frequently cited study, Diana Russell's survey of women in the San Francisco area, found that 38 percent had experienced intra- or extrafamilial sexual abuse by the time they reached 18.[152] Jeanne Hernandez's more recent survey of Minnesota students in the sixth, ninth, and twelfth grades, found that about 2 percent of the males and 7 percent of the females experienced incest; 4 percent of the males and 13 percent of the females suffered extrafamilial sexual abuse. Though the percentage of abused females was smaller than found by Russell, research by Glenn Wolfner and Richard Gelles indicates that up to one in five girls suffers sexual abuse.[153]

While these results are disturbing, they most likely underestimate the incidence of sexual abuse. It is difficult to get people to answer about youthful sexual abuse, and many victims were too young to understand their abuse or have repressed their memory of the incidents. Children, the most common target, may be inhibited because parents are reluctant to admit abuse occurred. One study found that 57 percent of children referred to a clinic because they had sexually transmitted diseases claimed *not* to have been molested despite this irrefutable physical evidence. Parental response significantly influences reporting abuse: kids whose caretakers admitted the possibility of abuse were 3.5 times more likely to report abuse than those whose parents denied any possibility that their child was a victim.[154]

The growing incidence of sexual abuse is of particular concern when its long-term impact is considered. Abused kids experience a long list of symptoms, including fear, post-traumatic stress disorder, behavior problems, sexualized behavior, and poor self-esteem. The amount of force used, its duration, and its frequency are all related to the extent of the long-term effects and the length of time needed for recovery.[155]

Causes of Child Abuse

Why do parents physically assault their children? Such maltreatment is a highly complex problem with neither a single cause nor a readily available solution. It cuts across ethnic, religious, and socioeconomic lines. Abusive parents cannot be categorized by sex, age, or educational level; they come from all walks of life. Some general factors do seem to be present with some frequency in families in which abuse and neglect take place. Data from a national survey of child abuse patterns allowed sociologists Glenn Wolfner and Richard Gelles to create the profile of abusive families contained in Table 11.1.[156]

Another factor that has been associated with systematic child abuse is familial stress. Abusive parents are

TABLE 11.1 **Profile of Abuse**

Region: East
Number of children: five
Gender of caretaker: female
Age of caretaker: 18–27
Race: black
Income: below the poverty line
Education: some high school
Employment status: unemployed
Type of employment of father: blue-collar
Drug use: yes
Gender of child: male
Age of child: 3 to 6 years old

SOURCE: Glenn Wolfner and Richard Gelles, "A Profile of Violence Toward Children: A National Study," *Child Abuse and Neglect* 17 (1993): 197–212.

unable to cope with life crises—divorce, financial problems, alcohol and drug abuse, poor housing conditions. This inability leads them to maltreat their children. Statistics also show that a high rate of assault on children occurs among the lower economic classes. This has led to the misconception that lower-class parents are more abusive than those in the upper classes. However, two conditions may account for this discrepancy. First, low-income people are often subject to greater levels of environmental stress and have fewer resources to deal with it. Second, cases of abuse among poor families are more likely to be dealt with by public agencies and therefore are more frequently counted in official statistics.[157]

Two other factors have a direct correlation with abuse and neglect. First, parents who themselves suffered abuse as children tend to abuse their own children; second, isolated and alienated families tend to become abusive. A cyclical pattern of family violence seems to be perpetuated from one generation to another within families. Evidence indicates that a large number of abused and neglected children grow into adolescence and adulthood with a tendency to engage in violent behavior. The behavior of abusive parents can often be traced to negative experiences in their own childhood—physical abuse, lack of love, emotional neglect, incest, and so on. These parents become unable to separate their own childhood traumas from their relationships with their children. They also often have unrealistic perceptions of the appropriate stages of childhood

development. Thus, when their children are unable to act "appropriately"—when they cry, throw food, or strike their parents—the parents may react in an abusive manner. For parents such as these, "the axiom about not being able to love when you have not known love yourself is painfully borne out in their case histories. . . . They spend their days going around the house, ticking away like unexploded bombs. A fussy baby can be the lighted match."[158]

Parents also become abusive if they are isolated from friends, neighbors, or relatives who can provide a lifeline in times of crisis. Potentially or actually abusing parents live in states of alienation from society; they have carried the concept of the shrinking nuclear family to its most extreme form and are cut off from ties of kinship and contact with other people in the neighborhood.[159] Many abusive and neglectful parents describe themselves as highly alienated from their families and lacking close relationships with persons who could provide help and support in stressful situations.

Public concern about child abuse has led to the development of programs designed to prevent and deter it. The reporting of child abuse by doctors, social workers, and other such persons is mandated by law. Some states have created laws that bar abusive parents from the home even before guilt has been determined at trial. Courts have begun to recognize the rights of abused children to collect damages from parents even years after the abuse took place. In one 1990 case, a Colorado court awarded two sisters $2.4 million in damages from a sexually abusive parent more than 20 years after the abuse occurred.[160]

Spouse Abuse

On June 23, 1993, John Wayne Bobbitt returned home, and according to his wife, Lorena, committed a marital rape. Afterward, while he slept, Lorena used a 12-inch kitchen knife to slice off two-thirds of his penis. In a panic, she drove off and tossed the severed organ into a field. Police officers were able to recover it, and it was reattached in a nine and one-half-hour operation. The case drew reporters from around the United States; observers at the scene described the media as a "herd of buffaloes," backing into cars and falling in ditches.[161]

John was later tried and acquitted on charges of sexual assault stemming from the alleged rape. Claiming that her actions were a result of the rape and earlier abuse, Lorena was found not guilty on a charge of malicious wounding, by reason of insanity, on January 21, 1994. No longer considered a threat, she was released from Virginia's Central State Hospital on February 28, 1994.[162]

John Wayne Bobbitt is escorted out of Prince William Circuit court after the first day of his trial on charges of sexual assault in Manassas, Va., on Monday, November 8, 1993. A defense lawyer for John argued that Lorena Bobbitt, wife of John, cut off her husband's penis because she was upset over his insensitive lovemaking and only later claimed rape. Both John and Lorena were found not guilty as charged.

Though one of the most highly publicized cases of the decade, the Bobbit case is misleading: spouse abuse overwhelmingly involves a physical assault in which a wife is injured by a husband.[163] Though there are some cases of *husband battering,* they typically involve a defensive measure taken by a previously abused spouse. According to criminologists Martin Schwartz and Walter DeKeseredy, the presentation of women as violent helps maintain the dominance of men in marital relations.[164]

Spouse abuse has occurred throughout recorded history. During the Roman era, men had the legal right to beat their wives for minor acts, such as attending public games without permission, drinking wine, or walking outdoors with their faces uncovered.[165] More serious transgressions, such as adultery, were punishable by death. During the later stages of the Roman Empire, the practice of wife beating abated; and by the fourth century A.D., excessive violence on the part of husband or wife could be used as sufficient grounds for divorce.[166] Later, during the early Middle Ages, there was a separation of love and marriage.[167] The ideal woman was protected and cherished. The wife, with whom marriage

had been arranged by family ties, was guarded jealously and could be punished severely for violations of duty. A husband was expected to beat his wife for "misbehaviors" and might himself be punished by neighbors if he failed to do so.[168] Through the later Middle Ages and into modern times—that is, from 1400 to 1900—there was little objection within the community to a man using force against his wife as long as the assaults did not exceed certain limits, usually construed as death or disfigurement. By the mid-nineteenth century, severe wife beating fell into disfavor, and accused wife beaters were subject to public ridicule. Nonetheless, limited chastisement was still the rule. By the close of the nineteenth century, laws had been passed in England and the United States outlawing wife beating. Yet the long history of husbands' domination of their wives' lives made physical coercion hard to control. Until recent times, the subordinate position of women in the family was believed to give husbands the legal and moral obligation to manage their wives' behavior. Even after World War II, there is evidence of English courts finding domestic assault to be a reasonable punishment for a wife who had disobeyed her husband.[169] These ideas form the foundation of men's traditional physical control of women and have led to severe cases of spousal assault.

The Nature and Extent of Spouse Abuse. It is difficult to estimate how widespread spouse abuse is today; however, some statistics give indications of the extent of the problem. In their national survey of family violence, Gelles and Straus found that 16 percent of surveyed families had experienced husband-wife assaults. In police departments around the country, 60 to 70 percent of evening calls involve domestic disputes. Nor is violence restricted to the post-marital stage of domestic relations. In a national survey of college students, James Makepeace found that more than 20 percent of the females had experienced violence during their dating and courtship relationships.[170] What are the characteristics of the wife assaulter? The traits commonly found include:[171]

- *Presence of alcohol.* Excessive alcohol use may turn otherwise docile husbands into wife assaulters.

- *Hostility dependency.* Some husbands who appear docile and passive may resent their dependency on their wives and react with rage and violence; this factor has been linked to sexual inadequacy.

- *Excessive brooding.* Obsession with a wife's behavior, however trivial, can result in violent assaults.

- *Social approval.* Some husbands believe that society approves of wife assault and use these beliefs to justify their violent behavior.

- *Socioeconomic factors.* Men who fail as providers and are under economic stress may take their frustrations out on their wives.

- *Flash of anger.* Research shows that a significant amount of family violence resulted from a sudden burst of anger after a verbal dispute.

- *Military service.* Spouse abuse among men who have seen military service is extremely high. Similarly, those serving in the military are more likely to assault their wives than civilian husbands. The reasons for this phenomenon may be (a) the violence promoted by military training and (b) the close proximity of military families to one another.

- *Having been battered children.* Husbands who assault their wives were battered as children.

A growing amount of support is being given to battered women. Shelters for assaulted wives are springing up around the country, and laws are being passed to protect a wife's interests. It is essential that this problem be brought to public light and controlled.

☰ Robbery

The common-law definition of robbery, and the one used by the FBI, is "the taking or attempting to take anything of value from the care, custody or control of a person or persons by force or threat of force or violence and/or by putting the victim in fear."[172] A robbery is a crime of violence because it involves the use of force to obtain money or goods. Robbery is punished severely because the victim's life is put in jeopardy; the amount of force used and not the value of the items taken determines the level of punishment.

In 1992, 672,478 robberies were reported to police, a rate of 263 per 100,000 population, an increase of 24 percent since 1988. The ecological pattern for robbery is similar to that of other violent crimes, with one significant exception: northeastern states have by far the highest robbery rate (336 per 100,000).

NCVS data indicate that robbery is more of a problem than the FBI data show; according to the NCVS, about 1.2 million robberies are committed each year. However, victim data indicate that the overall robbery rate has actually declined since 1982. The two data

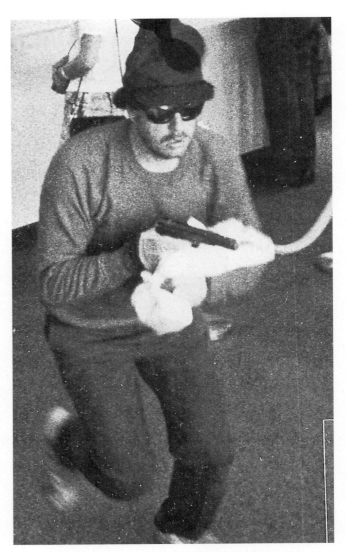

A gunman flees after an armed robbery. The NCVS indicates that 1.2 million robberies occur annually.

sources agree, however, on the age, race, and sexual makeup of the offenders: they are disproportionately young, male, and minority-group members.

The Nature of Robbery. Robbery is most often a street crime—that is, fewer robberies occur in the home than in public places, such as parks, streets, and alleys. For example, about 25 percent of rapes reported by victims to NCVS researchers occur in the home but only 14 percent of reported robberies; more than 50 percent of robberies occurred in streets or parking lots.[173] The Bureau of Justice Statistics analyzed over 14 million robbery victimizations to provide a more complete picture of the nature and extent of robbery. It found that about two-thirds of victims had property stolen, a third were injured, and a fourth suffered both personal injury and property loss.[174] The public nature of robbery has greatly influenced people's behavior. Most people believe that large cities suffer the most serious instances of violent crimes, such as robbery, and, not surprisingly, many people have moved out of inner-city areas into suburban communities for this reason.

Robber Typologies

Attempts have been made to classify and explain the nature and dynamics of robbery.[175] Among the patterns identified are:

1. Robbery of persons who, as part of their employment, are in charge of money or goods. This category includes robberies in jewelry stores, banks, offices, and other places in which money changes hands. In recent years, the rate of this category of robbery has dramatically increased. For example, robberies of convenience and grocery stores increased 28 percent, bank robbery was up 23 percent, and commercial robbery rose 23 percent between 1985 and 1990.
2. Robbery in an open area. These robberies include street offenses, muggings, purse snatchings, and other attacks. In urban areas, this type of robbery constitutes about 60 percent of reported totals; nationally, street robberies have increased 18 percent in the past four years. Street robbery is most closely associated with mugging or "yoking"—grabbing victims from behind and threatening them with a weapon.
3. Robbery on private premises. This type of robbery involves robbing people after breaking into homes. FBI records indicate that this type of robbery accounts for about 10 percent of all offenses.
4. Robbery after preliminary association of short duration. This type of robbery comes in the aftermath of a chance meeting—in a bar, at a party, or after a sexual encounter.
5. Robbery after previous association of some duration between the victim and offender.

Incidents in patterns 4 and 5 are substantially less common than stranger-to-stranger robberies, which account for more than 75 percent of the total.

Another well-known robber typology has been created by John Conklin. Instead of focusing on the nature of robbery incidents, Conklin categorizes robber types into the following specialties.[176]

Professional Robber. Professionals are those who "manifest a long-term commitment to crime as a source of livelihood, who plan and organize their crimes prior to committing them, and who seek money to support a particular life-style that may be called hedonistic." Some professionals are exclusively robbers, while others may engage in other types of crimes. Professionals are committed to robbing because it is direct, fast, and very profitable. They hold no other steady job and plan three or four "big scores" a year to support themselves. Planning and skill are the trademarks of the professional robber. Operating in groups in which assigned roles are the rule, professionals usually steal large amounts from commercial establishments. After a score, they may take a few weeks off until "things cool off."

Opportunist Robber. Opportunists steal to obtain small amounts of money when an accessible and vulnerable target presents itself. They are not committed to robbery but will steal from cab drivers, drunks, the elderly, and other such persons if they need some extra spending money for clothes or other elements of their life-style. Opportunists are usually young minority-group members who do not plan their crimes. Although they operate within the milieu of the juvenile gang, they are seldom organized and spend little time discussing weapon use, getaway plans, or other strategies.

Addict Robber. Addict robbers steal to support their drug habits. They have a low commitment to robbery because of its danger but a high commitment to theft because it supplies needed funds. The addict is less likely to plan crime or use weapons than the professional robber but is more cautious than the opportunist. Addicts choose targets that present a minimum of risk; however, when desperate for funds, they are sometimes careless in selecting the victim and executing the crime. They rarely think in terms of the big score; they only want enough money to get their next fix.

Alcoholic Robber. Many robbers steal for reasons related to their excessive consumption of alcohol. Alcoholic robbers steal (1) when, in a disoriented state, they attempt to get some money to buy liquor or (2) when their condition makes them unemployable and they need funds. Alcoholic robbers have no real commitment to robbery as a way of life. They plan their crimes randomly and give little thought to victim, circumstance, or escape; for that reason, they are the most likely to be caught.

As these typologies indicate, the typical armed robber is unlikely to be a professional who carefully studies targets while planning a crime. People walking along the street, convenience stores, and gas stations are much more likely to be the target of robberies than banks or other highly secure environments. Robbers, therefore, seem to be diverted by modest defensive measures, such as having more than one clerk in a store or locating stores in strip malls rather than stand-alone isolation.[177]

Evolving Forms of Violence

Assault, rape, robbery, and murder are traditional forms of interpersonal violence. As data becomes available, criminologists have recognized new categories within these crime types, such as serial murder and date rape. There are also new categories of interpersonal violence now receiving attention in the criminological literature, and the sections below describe two of these new forms of violent crime.

Hate Crimes

Hate crimes or **bias crimes** are now recognized as a new category of violent personal crimes.[178] These are violent acts directed toward a particular person or members of a group merely because the targets share a discernible racial, ethnic, religious, or gender characteristic. Hate crimes can include the desecration of a house of worship or cemetery, harassment of a minority-group family that has moved into a previously all-white neighborhood, or a racially motivated murder of an individual. For example, on August 23, 1989, Yusuf Hawkins, a black youth, was killed in the Bensonhurst section of Brooklyn, New York, because he had wandered into a racially charged white neighborhood.[179]

Hate crimes usually involve convenient and vulnerable targets who are incapable of fighting back. For example, there have been numerous reported incidences of teenagers attacking vagrants and the homeless in an effort to rid their town or neighborhood of people they consider undesirable.[180] Another group targeted for hate crimes are gay men and women. Gay bashing has become an all too common occurrence in U.S. cities. Racial and ethnic minorities have also been the targets of attack. Well-publicized hate crimes directed against racial minorities include the Howard Beach and Bensonhurst incidents in New York City, in which gangs of white youths chased and killed black youths who wandered into their neighborhoods. In California, whites have attacked and killed Mexican laborers, while in New Jersey, Indian immigrants have been the targets of racial hatred.[181] While hate crimes are often mindless attacks directed toward "traditional" minority victims, political and economic trends may cause violent attacks to be redirected. Asians have been the target of hate attacks from groups who resent the growing economic power of Japan and Korea as well as the commercial success of Asian-Americans. From October through December 1990, Asian students in Denver were the target of hate crimes ranging from vandalism to the assault on six Japanese youths by baseball-wielding attackers; Arab-Americans have been the target of hate crimes in the aftermath of the war against Iraq.[182]

The Roots of Hate

Why do people commit bias crimes? Research by sociologist Jack McDevitt finds that hate crimes are generally spontaneous incidents motivated by the victims' walking, driving, shopping, or socializing in an area in which their attacker believed they "did not belong."[183] Other reasons found for bias attacks were that the victim had moved into an ethnically distinct neighborhood or had dated a member of a different race or ethnic group. Though hate crimes are often unplanned, McDevitt finds that a majority of these crimes were serious incidents involving assaults and robberies.[184]

In their book *Hate Crimes*, McDevitt and Jack Levin find that while hate crimes do involve at least some planning, they are typically one of three types reflecting different motives:

Thrill-seeking hate crimes—In the same way some kids like to get together to "shoot hoops," hate mongers join forces to have fun by bashing minorities or destroying property. Inflicting pain on others gives them a sadistic thrill.

Reactive hate crimes—Perpetrators of these crimes rationalize their behavior as a defensive stand taken against "outsiders" who are threatening their community or way of life. A gang of teens who attack a new family in the neighborhood because they are the "wrong" race are committing a reactive hate crime.

Mission hate crimes—Some disturbed individuals see it as their duty to rid the world of evil. Those on a "mission" may seek to eliminate people who threaten their religious beliefs because they are members of a different faith or are a threat to racial purity because they are of a difference race.[185]

In a recent study of Boston Police Department records, Levin and McDevitt found that thrill crimes were the most common (58 percent) and most of these (70 percent) involved assaultive behavior. Reactive crimes (42 percent) also involved an assault on a stranger who happened to be in the "wrong place at the wrong time." While there was only one mission-type crime, it was the most violent incident and involved the beating of two supposedly gay males with baseball bats.[186]

Extent of Hate Crime

Information on the extent of hate crimes is just becoming available. The FBI now collects data on hate crimes as part of the Hate Crime Statistics Act of 1990. Preliminary data indicated that about 5,000 hate crimes occur each year. However, the FBI data is limited because law enforcement agents in relatively few reporting areas have been trained in identifying hate crimes.

Other indicators of hate crimes are collected by individuals and organizations concerned with this social problem. In one study, Daniel Bibel gathered information from states that collect bias crime data and estimates a national incidence rate of 12,362 per year.[187] The National Gay and Lesbian Task Force found that 1,898 antigay incidents, ranging from harassment to murder, were recorded in just four metropolitan areas (Boston, Chicago, Minneapolis/St. Paul, New York, and San Francisco) in 1992; this was an increase of 172 percent in five years![188] The Anti-Defamation League of the B'nai B'rith recorded 1,720 anti-Semitic incidents in 1992, an increase of 12 percent over the preceding year.[189] The Klanwatch program of the Southern Poverty Law Center found that there were 31 bias-motivated murders in 1992.[190]

Because of the extent and seriousness of the problem, a number of legal jurisdictions have made a special effort to control the spread of hate crimes. Boston maintains the Community Disorders Unit, while the New York City Police Department formed the Bias Incident Investigating Unit in 1980. When a crime anywhere in the city is suspected of being motivated by bias, the unit is notified and enters into the investigation. The unit also provides victim assistance and works with concerned organizations, such as the Commission on Human Rights and the Gay and Lesbian Task Force. These agencies deal with noncriminal bias incidents through mediation, education, and other forms of prevention.[191]

≡ Workplace Violence

Paul Calden, a former insurance company employee, walked into a Tampa cafeteria and opened fire on a table at which his former supervisors were dining. Calden shouted, "This is what you all get for firing me!", and began shooting. When he was finished, three were dead and two others wounded.[192]

It has become commonplace to read of irate employees or former employees attacking co-workers or sabotaging machinery and production lines. Workplace violence is now considered the third leading cause of occupational injury or death.[193]

Who engages in workplace violence? According to James A. Fox and Jack Levin, the typical offender is a middle-aged white male who faces termination in a worsening economy. The fear of economic ruin is especially strong in agencies such as the U.S. Postal Service where long-term employees fear job loss because of automation and reorganization. In contrast, when younger workers kill, it is usually while committing a robbery or other felony.

A number of factors precipitate workplace violence. According to sociologist John King, one may simply be the conflict caused by economic restructuring. As corporations cut their staffs, long-term employees who had never thought of themselves as the type who could lose a job are suddenly unemployed. There is often a connection between sudden and undeserved layoffs and violent reactions.[194]

Another trigger may be leadership styles. Some companies, including the U.S. Postal Service, have authoritarian management styles that demand performance above all else from employees. Managers who are unsympathetic and unsupportive may help trigger workplace violence.

Not all workplace violence is caused by an injustice triggered by management. There have been incidents in which co-workers have been killed because they refused a romantic relationship with the assailant or had reported them for sexual harassment; others have been killed because they got a job the assailant coveted. There have also been cases of irate clients and customers who kill because of poor service or perceived slights. In one Los Angeles incident, a former patient opened fire and critically wounded three doctors because his demands for painkillers had gone unheeded.[195]

There are also a variety of responses to workplace "provocations." Some attack supervisors to punish the company that dismissed them; a form of "murder by proxy."[196] Disgruntled employees may attack family members or friends, ignoring the actual cause of their rage and frustration. Others are content with sabotaging company equipment; computer data banks are particularly vulnerable to tampering. It is also possible that the aggrieved party does nothing to rectify the situation; this inaction is referred to as "sufferance." Over time, the unresolved conflict may be compounded by some other events that eventually cause an eruption.

Can workplace violence be controlled? King suggests the intervention of third parties in a dispute resolution capacity may help provide the control necessary to stave off the rising tide of workplace violence. Fox and Levin argue for a human resources approach with aggressive job retraining and continued medical coverage in case of layoffs and due process guarantees to thwart unfair terminations.[197]

Political Violence

In addition to interpersonal violence and street crime, violent behavior also involves acts that have a political motivation, including **terrorism.**

Political crime has been with us throughout history. It is virtually impossible to find a history book of any society that does not record the existence of political criminals, "those craftsmen of dreams who possess a gigantic reservoir of creative energy as well as destructive force."[198]

Political crime can be defined in various ways. Barton Ingraham suggests that it can be divided into two broad categories: (1) a betrayal of allegiance to principles or persons that bind the political order and (2) a challenge to or hindrance of political authority.[199]

It is often difficult to separate political from interpersonal crimes of violence. For example, if a group robs a bank to obtain funds for its revolutionary struggles, should the act be treated as a political crime or a common bank robbery? In this instance, the definition of a crime as political depends on the kind of legal response the act evokes from those in power.

To be a political crime, an act must carry with it the intent to disrupt and change the government and must not merely be a simple common-law crime committed for reasons of greed or egotism. Stephen Schafer refers to those who violate the law because they believe their actions will ultimately benefit society as **convictional criminals.** They are constantly caught in the dilemma of knowing their actions may be wrong and harmful but

believing these actions are necessary to create the changes they fervently desire. "A member of the Second World War Resistance," Schafer argues, "may have condemned violence, yet his own conviction overshadowed any sense of repugnance and induced him to engage in violent crimes in an effort to expel the invader from his Fatherland."[200]

Terrorism

One aspect of political violence that is of great concern to criminologists is terrorism.[201] Because of its complexity, an all-encompassing definition of terrorism is difficult to formulate, though most experts agree that it generally involves the illegal use of force against innocent people to achieve a political objective.[202] For example, according to one national commission, terrorism is "a tactic or technique by means of which a violent act or the threat thereof is used for the prime purpose of creating overwhelming fear for coercive purposes."[203]

Terrorism, then, is usually defined as a type of political crime that emphasizes violence as a mechanism to promote change. Whereas other political criminals may engage in such acts as demonstrating, counterfeiting, selling secrets, spying, and the like, terrorists make systematic use of murder and destruction or the threat of such violence to terrorize individuals, groups, communities, or governments into conceding to the terrorists' political demands.[204] However, it may be erroneous to equate terrorism with political goals, because not all terrorist actions are aimed at political change; some terrorists may desire economic or social reform, for example, by attacking women wearing fur coats or sabotaging property during a labor dispute. Terrorism must also be distinguished from conventional warfare because it requires secrecy and clandestine operations to exert social control over large populations.[205]

The term *terrorist* is often used interchangeably with *guerilla.* The latter term, meaning "little war," developed out of the Spanish rebellion against French troops after Napoleon's invasion of the Iberian peninsula in 1808.[206] Daniel Georges-Abeyie distinguishes between the two terms by suggesting that terrorists have an urban focus; that the objects of their attacks include the property and persons of civilians; and that they operate in small bands, or cadres, of three to five members.[207] Guerillas are located in rural areas; the objects of their attacks include the military, the police, and government officials; and their organization can grow quite large and eventually take the form of a conventional military force. However, guerillas can infiltrate urban areas in small bands, while terrorists can make forays into the countryside; consequently, the terms have come to be used interchangeably.[208]

Historical Perspective.

Acts of terrorism have been known throughout history. The assassination of Julius Caesar on March 15, 44 B.C., can be considered an act of terrorism. Terrorism became widespread at the end of the Middle Ages, when political leaders were subject to assassination by their enemies. The word *assassin* was derived from an Arabic term meaning "hashish eater"; it referred to members of a drug-using Moslem terrorist organization that carried out plots against prominent Christians and other religious enemies.[209] At a time when rulers were absolute despots, terrorist acts were viewed as one of the only means of gaining political rights. At times, European states encouraged terrorist acts against their enemies. For example, Queen Elizabeth I empowered her "sea dogs," John Hawkins and Francis Drake, to carry out attacks against the Spanish fleet. These privateers would have been considered pirates had they not operated with government approval. American privateers operated against the British during the Revolutionary War and the War of 1812. As you can see, history can turn terrorists into heroes, depending on which side wins. The term *terrorist* became popular during the French Revolution. From the fall of the Bastille on July 14, 1789, until July 1794, thousands suspected of counterrevolutionary activity went to their deaths on the guillotine. Here again, the relative nature of political crime is documented: while most victims of the French Reign of Terror were revolutionaries who had been denounced by rival factions, thousands of members of the hated nobility lived in relative tranquility. The end of the terror was signaled by the death of its prime mover, Maximilien Robespierre, on July 28, 1794, as the result of a successful plot to end his rule; he was executed on the same guillotine to which he sent almost 20,000 people to their deaths. In the hundred years after the French Revolution, terrorism continued around the world. The Hur Brotherhood in India was made up of religious fanatics who carried out terrorist acts.[210] In Eastern Europe, the Internal Macedonian Revolutionary Organization campaigned against the Turkish government, which controlled its homeland (Macedonia became part of the former Yugoslavia). Similarly, the protest of the Union of Death Society, or Black Hand, against the Austro-Hungarian empire's control of Serbia led to the group's assassination of Archduke Franz Ferdinand, an act that signaled the beginning of World War I. The Irish Republican Army developed around 1916 and kept up a steady battle with British forces from 1919 to 1923, culminating in the southern part of Ireland's gaining independence. Between the world wars, right-wing terrorism existed in Germany, Spain, and Italy. Russia was the scene of left-wing revolutionary activity leading to the death of the czar in 1917 and the rise of the Marxist state. During World War II, resistance to the Germans was common throughout Europe; these terrorists are now, of course, considered heroes. In Palestine, Jewish terrorist groups—the Haganah, Irgun, and Stern Gang, whose leaders included Menachim Begin, who later became prime minister—waged war against the British to force them to allow Jewish survivors of the Holocaust to settle in their traditional homeland. Today, of course, many of these alleged "terrorists" are considered "freedom fighters" who laid down their lives for a just cause.

Forms of Terrorism

Today, the term *terrorism* is used to describe many different behaviors and goals. Some of the more common forms are briefly described below.[211]

Revolutionary Terrorists.

Revolutionary terrorists use violence as a tool to invoke fear in those in power and their supporters. The ultimate goal is replacing the existing government with a regime that holds acceptable political views. Terrorist actions—kidnapping, assassination, bombing—are designed to draw repressive responses from governments trying to defend themselves. These responses help revolutionaries to expose, through the skilled use of media coverage, the governments' inhumane nature. The original reason for the governments' harsh response may be lost as the effect of counterterrorist activities is felt by uninvolved people.

In Europe, socialist- and Marxist-oriented groups have been pitted against capitalist governments for the past 30 years. During the 1980s, the Marxist Baader-Meinhoff group in Germany conducted a series of robberies, bombings, and kidnappings. With the reunification of Germany, terrorist actions were believed over. Yet, on April 1, 1991, the Red Army Faction, the successor to Baader-Meinhoff, claimed "credit" for assassinating Detlev Rohwedder, the head of the government agency charged with rebuilding the East German economy.[212] In Italy, the Red Brigade kidnapped and executed a former Italian president, Albert Moro, and abducted James Dozier, a U.S. general, who was later rescued by security forces.[213]

In the Middle East, terrorist activities have been linked to the Palestinians' desire to wrest a homeland from Israel. The leading group, the Palestinian Liberation Organization (PLO), has been active in directing terrorist activities against Israel. While the PLO has reached accommodation with Israel in preparation for Palestinian political control of the West Bank and the Gaza Strip, splinter groups have broken from the PLO, including the Abu Nidal group, the Popular Front for the Liberation of Palestine, and the Iranian-backed Hizballah group, to continue the conflict.

Though there have been numerous tragic incidents, two stand out because of the large loss of life: agents of the pro-Iranian Islamic Jihad used a truck bomb to blow up the U.S. Marine compound in Beirut, killing 241; and on Christmas Day, 1988, Pan Am Flight 103 was blown up over Lockerbie, Scotland, and 258 U.S. citizens died.[214] Though the target of Arab terrorism is presumably Israel and its Western allies, attacks are often directed at members of rival groups and factions. When the World Trade Center in New York City was bombed in 1993, the group responsible was demonstrating its hatred of U.S. policies in the Middle East.

Political Terrorism.

Political terrorism is directed at people or groups who oppose the terrorists' political ideology or whom the terrorists define as "outsiders" who must be destroyed. Political terrorists in the United States tend to be heavily armed groups organized around such themes as white supremacy, Nazism, militant tax resistance, and religious revisionism. Identified groups include the Aryan Nation, the Order, the Brotherhood, Posse Comitatus, Silent Brotherhood, and the White American Bastion, as well as the traditional Ku Klux Klan organizations.[215] Some of these groups have formed their own churches; for example, the Church of Jesus Christ Christian claims that Jesus was born an Aryan rather than a Jew and that white Anglo-Saxons are the true "chosen people."[216]

Nationalistic Terrorism.

Nationalistic terrorism is designed to promote the interests of a minority ethnic or religious groups who have been persecuted under majority rule. In India, Sikh radicals use violence for the purpose of recovering what they believe to be lost homelands. Sikh militants were responsible for assassinating Indian Prime Minister Indira Gandhi on November 6, 1984, in retaliation for the government's storming of their Golden Temple religious shrine (and revolutionary base) in June 1984.[217] In Egypt,

fundamentalist Moslems have attacked foreign tourists in an effort to wreck the tourist industry, topple the secular government, and turn Egypt into an Islamic state.[218]

The most well-known nationalistic terrorist group operating today is the Provisional Irish Republican Army (IRA), which is dedicated to unifying Northern Ireland with the Republic of Ireland under home rule.

Nonpolitical Terrorism.

Terrorist activity also involves groups that espouse a particular social or religious cause and use violence to address their grievances and not to topple governments. For example, antiabortion groups have sponsored demonstrations at abortion clinics and some members have gone so far as to attack clients, bomb offices, and kill doctors who perform abortions.

Animal rights organization members have harassed and thrown blood at people wearing fur coats. It has also become common for environmental groups to resort to terror tactics to sabotage their enemies' ability to harm the environment. One of the biggest targets is the livestock and research animal-producing industry. Members of such groups as the Animal Liberation Front (ALF) and Earth First! acknowledge making attacks against ranches and packing plants. At least four meatpacking plants have been destroyed by arson, numerous ranches attacked, and livestock-processing machinery destroyed. ALF members free animals; for example, raiding turkey farms before Thanksgiving and rabbit farms before Easter.[219]

State-Sponsored Terrorism.

State-sponsored terrorism occurs when a repressive governmental regime forces its citizens into obedience and stifles political dissent.[220] **Death squads** and the use of government troops to destroy political opposition parties are often associated with Latin American political terrorism.[221]

Some governments have been accused of using terrorist-type actions to control political dissidents. Much of what we know about state-sponsored terrorism comes from the efforts of the human rights group Amnesty International to document international incidents. In its latest report on political terrorism in 138 countries, this London-based group found that tens of thousands of people continue to become victims of security operations that result in disappearances and extrajudicial executions.[222] Political prisoners were tortured in about 100 countries, people disappeared or were held in secret detention in about 20 countries, and government-sponsored death squads operated in more than 35. Countries known for encouraging violent control of dissidents include Brazil, Colombia, Guatemala, Honduras, Peru, Iraq, and the Sudan.

Another form of state-sponsored terrorism, notes criminologist Ronald Kramer, is **structural violence,** which involves the physical harm caused by the unequal distribution of wealth. Structural violence involves a set of social conditions from which flows poverty, disease, hunger, malnutrition, poor sanitation, premature death, and high infant mortality.[223]

Who Is the Terrorist?

Terrorists engage in criminal activities, such as bombings, shootings, and kidnappings. What motivates these individuals to risk their lives and those of the innocent people? One view is that terrorists hold ideological beliefs that prompt their behavior. At first, they have heightened perceptions of oppressive conditions—relative deprivation.[224] Then potential terrorists begin to recognize that these conditions can be changed by an active governmental reform effort that has not been and will not be forthcoming. The terrorists conclude that they must resort to violence to encourage change. The violence need not be aimed at a specific goal. Rather, terror tactics must contribute to setting in motion a series of events that enlist others in the cause and lead to long-term change. "Successful" terrorists must accept the fact that their "self-sacrifice" outweighs the guilt created by committing a violent act that harms innocent people. Terrorism, therefore, requires violence without guilt. The cause justifies the need for violence.[225] According to Austin Turk, terrorists tend to come from upper- rather than lower-class backgrounds.[226] This may be because the upper classes can produce people who are more politically sensitive, articulate, and focused in their resentments. Since their position in the class structure gives them the feeling that they can influence or change society, upper-class citizens are more likely to seek confrontations with the authorities. Class differences are also manifested in different approaches to political violence. The violence of the lower class is more often associated with spontaneous expressions of dissatisfaction, manifested in collective riots and rampages and politically inconsequential acts. Higher-class violence tends to be more calculated and organized and uses elaborate strategies of resistance. Revolutionary cells; campaigns of terror and assassination; logistically complex and expensive assaults; and writing and disseminating formal critiques, manifestos, and theories are typically acts of the socially elite. Upper-class political

terrorism has been manifested in the death squads operating in Latin America and Asia. These vigilantes use violence to intimidate those opposing the ruling party. One graphic example of these terrorist activities occurred in Sri Lanka on October 5, 1989, when a death squad made up of members of the ruling parties' security forces beheaded 18 suspected members of the anti-government People's Liberation Front and placed their heads around a pond at a university campus.[227]

Responses to Terrorism

Governments have tried numerous responses to terrorism. Law enforcement agencies have infiltrated terrorist groups and turned members over to police.[228] Rewards have been given for information leading to the arrest of terrorists. "Democratic" elections have been held to discredit terrorists' complaints that the state is oppressive.

Counterterrorism laws have been passed to increase penalties and decrease political rights. In the United States, antiterrorist legislation includes acts providing jurisdiction over terrorist acts committed abroad against U.S. citizens and punishing the killing of foreign officials and politically protected persons.[229] Despite the existence of these and other antiterrorism statutes, most politically motivated acts are prosecuted as common-law crimes. Brent Smith and Gregory Orvis suggest that this underscores the government's effort to highlight the real motivation of domestic terrorism: personal profit.[230] Smith and Orvis found that politically motivated crimes are taken very seriously by U.S. prosecutors and defendants are usually charged with multiple criminal violations.

Although the United States has stated a policy prohibiting violence or assassination attempts against suspected terrorists, both federal law enforcement agencies and the U.S. military have specially trained antiterrorist squads. The military, for example, has created the renowned Delta Force, made up of members from the four service areas. Delta Force activities are generally secret, but it is known that the force saw action in Iran (1980), Honduras (1982), Sudan (1983), and during the Grenada invasion (1983) and was prepared to take action against the hijacking of the ship *Achille Lauro* (1985).

Despite the U.S. government's efforts to control terrorism, any attempts to meet force with force are fraught with danger. If the government's response is retaliation in kind, it could provoke increased terrorist activity—for revenge or to gain the release of captured comrades. Of course, a weak response may be interpreted as a license for terrorists to operate with impunity. The most impressive

U.S. antiterrorist action was the bombing of Libya on April 15, 1986, in an attempt to convince its leader, Colonel Muammar Quaddafi, to desist from sponsoring terrorist organizations. While the raid made a dramatic statement, preventing terrorism is a task that so far has stymied the governments of most nations.

Summary

People in the United States live in an extremely violent society. Among the various explanations for violent crimes, one postulates the existence of a subculture of violence that stresses violent solutions to interpersonal problems. Another view holds that humans may be instinctually violent. Still another claims that violence is related to economic inequality.

There are many types of interpersonal violent crime. Rape is defined as the carnal knowledge of a female forcibly and against her will. Rape has been known throughout history; at one time, it was believed that a woman was as guilty as her attacker for her rape. At present, it is estimated that close to 100,000 rapes are reported to police each year; the true number is probably much higher. Rape is an extremely difficult charge to prove in court. The victim's lack of consent must be proven; therefore, it almost seems that the victim is on trial. Consequently, changes are being made in rape law and procedure. Murder is the unlawful killing of a human being with malice aforethought. There are different degrees of murder, and punishments vary accordingly. One important characteristic of murder is that the victim and criminal often know each other. This has caused some criminologists to believe that murder is a victim-precipitated crime. Murder victims and offenders tend to be young, black, and male. Assault is another serious interpersonal violent crime. One important type of assault is that which occurs in the home, including child abuse and spouse abuse. It has been estimated that almost 1 million children are abused by their parents each year and that 16 percent of families report husband-wife violence. There also appears to be a trend toward violence between dating couples on college campuses. Robbery involves theft by force, usually in a public place. Types of offenders include professional, opportunist, addict, and alcoholic robbers. Political violence is another serious problem. Many terrorist groups exist, both at the national and international level. Hundreds of terrorist acts are reported each year in the United States alone.

Terrorists may be motivated by criminal gain, psychosis, grievance against the state, or ideology.

KEY TERMS

brutalization process	corroboration
violent performance	premeditation
virulency	thrill killing
eros	gang killings
thanatos	cult killings
subculture of violence	serial murder
disputatiousness	mass murderer
psychopharmacological	child abuse
economic compulsive	neglect
behavior	sexual abuse
systemic link	hate crimes
instrumental	bias crimes
expressive	terrorism
date rape	convictional criminals
marital exemption	death squads
consent	structural violence
shield laws	

NOTES

1. Albert Reiss and Jeffrey Roth, *Understanding and Preventing Violence* (Washington, D.C.: National Academy Press, 1993), p. ix. Herein cited as *Understanding Violence*.
2. *Understanding Violence*, p. 3.
3. Hans Toch, *Violent Men* (Chicago: Aldine, 1969), p. 1.
4. Lloyd Johnston, Jerald Bachman, and Patrick O'Malley, *Monitoring the Future, 1993* (Ann Arbor, Mich.: Institute for Social Research, 1994).
5. Timothy Flanagan and Kathleen Maguire, *Sourcebook of Criminal Justice Statistics, 1992* (Washington, D.C.: U.S. Government Printing Office, 1993), pp. 169–70.
6. *Stanford v. Kentucky,* 109 Supreme Court, 2969 (1989).
7. Robert Nash Parker and Catherine Colony, "Relationships, Homicides, and Weapons: A Detailed Analysis" (Paper presented at the annual meeting of the American Society of Criminology, Montreal, November 1987).
8. Sean Murphy, "Montreal Killer Laid Blame on Women for 'Ruining' Him," *Boston Globe,* 8 December 1989, p. 1.
9. Laura Bender, "Children and Adolescents Who Have Killed," *American Journal of Psychiatry* 116 (1959): 510–16.
10. Dorothy Otnow Lewis, Ernest Moy, Lori Jackson, Robert Aaronson, Nicholas Restifo, Susan Serra, and Alexander Simos, "Biopsychosocial Characteristics of Children Who Later Murder," *American Journal of Psychiatry* 142 (1985): 1161–67.

11. *Understanding Violence,* pp. 112–13.

12. For a thorough review, see Robin Malinosky-Rummell and David Hansen, "Long-Term Consequences of Childhood Physical Abuse," *Psychological Bulletin* 114 (1993): 68–79.

13. Robert Scudder, William Blount, Kathleen Heide, and Ira Silverman, "Important Links between Child Abuse, Neglect, and Delinquency," *International Journal of Offender Therapy* 37 (1993): 315–23.

14. Murray Straus, "Discipline and Deviance: Physical Punishment of Children and Violence and Other Crime in Adulthood," *Social Problems* 38 (1991): 133–54.

15. Murray Straus and Sean Lauer, "Corporal Punishment of Children, Substance Abuse, and Crime in Relation to Race, Culture, and Deterrence" (Paper presented at the annual meeting of the American Society of Criminology, New Orleans, November 1992).

16. Dorothy Lewis, et al., "Neuropsychiatric, Psychoeducational, and Family Characteristics of 14 Juveniles Condemned to Death in the United States," *American Journal of Psychiatry* 145 (1988): 584–88.

17. Charles Patrick Ewing, *When Children Kill* (Lexington, Mass: Lexington Books, 1990), p. 22.

18. Lonnie Athens, *The Creation of Dangerous Violent Criminals* (Urbana, Ill.: University of Illinois Press, 1992), pp. 27–80.

19. Cathy Spatz Widom, "Child Abuse, Neglect, and Violent Criminal Behavior," *Criminology* 27 (1989): 251–71; Beverly Rivera and Cathy Spatz Widom, "Childhood Victimization and Violent Offending," *Violence and Victims* 5 (1990): 19–34.

20. Sigmund Freud, *Beyond the Pleasure Principle* (London: Inter-Psychoanalytic Press, 1922).

21. Konrad Lorenz, *On Aggression* (New York: Harcourt Brace Jovanovich, 1966).

22. Paul Joubert and Craig Forsyth, "A Macro View of Two Decades of Violence in America," *American Journal of Criminal Justice* 13 (1988): 10–25.

23. M. Dwayne Smith and Victoria Brewer, "A Sex-Specific Analysis of Correlates of Homicide Victimization in United States Cities," *Violence and Victims* 7 (1992): 279–85.

24. Marvin Wolfgang and Franco Ferracuti, *The Subculture of Violence* (London: Tavistock, 1967).

25. David Luckenbill and Daniel Doyle, "Structural Position and Violence: Developing a Cultural Explanation," *Criminology* 27 (1989): 419–36.

26. Steven Messner, "Regional and Racial Effects on the Urban Homicide Rate: The Subculture of Violence Revisited," *American Journal of Sociology* 88 (1983): 997–1007; Steven Messner and Kenneth Tardiff, "Economic Inequality and Levels of Homicide: An Analysis of Urban Neighborhoods," *Criminology* 24 (1986): 297–317.

27. Scott Decker, "Gangs and Violence: The Expressive Character of Collective Involvement," (unpublished manuscript, University of Missouri–St. Louis, 1994).

28. Carolyn Rebecca Block, "Chicago Homicide from the Sixties to the Nineties: Have Patterns of Lethal Violence Changed?" (Paper presented at the annual meeting of the American Society of Criminology, Baltimore, November 1990).

29. See, generally, Kirk Williams and Robert Flewelling, "The Social Production of Criminal Homicide: A Comparative Study of Disaggregated Rates in American Cities," *American Sociological Review* 53 (1988): 421–31.

30. Raymond Gastil, "Homicide and the Regional Culture of Violence," *American Sociological Review* 36 (1971): 412–27.

31. Howard Erlanger, "Is There a Subculture of Violence in the South?" *Journal of Criminal Law and Criminology* 66 (1976): 483–90.

32. Colin Loftin and Robert Hill, "Regional Subculture of Violence: An Examination of the Gastil-Hackney Thesis," *American Sociological Review* 39 (1974): 714–24.

33. Raymond Gastil, "Comments," *Criminology* 16 (1975): 60–64.

34. Gregory Kowalski and Thomas Petee, "Sunbelt Effects on Homicide Rates," *Sociology and Social Research* 76 (1991): 73–79.

35. Candice Nelsen, Jay Corzine, and Lin Huff-Corzine, "The Violent West Reexamined: A Research Note on Regional Homicide Rates," *Criminology* 32 (1994): 149–61.

36. F. Frederick Hawley and Steven Messner, "The Southern Violence Construct: A Review of Arguments, Evidence, and the Normative Context," *Justice Quarterly* 6 (1989): 481–511.

37. Paul Goldstein, Henry Brownstein, and Patrick Ryan, "Drug-Related Homicide in New York: 1984–1988," *Crime and Delinquency* 38 (1992): 459–76.

38. *Understanding Violence,* pp. 193–94.

39. James Collins and Pamela Messerschmidt, "Epidemiology of Alcohol-Related Violence," *Alcohol Health and Research World* 17 (1993): 93–100.

40. Eric Wish, *Drug Use Forecasting 1992* (Washington, D.C.: National Institute of Justice, 1993).

41. Christopher Innes, *Profile of State Prison Inmates 1986* (Washington, D.C.: Bureau of Justice Statistics, 1988).

42. Paul Goldstein, Patricia Bellucci, Barry Spunt, and Thomas Miller, "Volume of Cocaine Use and Violence: A Comparison between Men and Women," *Journal of Drug Issues* 21 (1991): 345–67.

43. Paul Goldstein, Henry Brownstein, Patrick Ryan, and Patricia Bellucci, "Crack and Homicide in New York City, 1988: A Conceptually Based Event Analysis" (Unpublished paper, Narcotic and Drug Research, Inc., New York, 1989).

44. Goldstein, Brownstein, and Ryan, "Drug-Related Homicide in New York: 1984–1988," p. 473.

45. *Understanding Violence,* p. 19.

46. Joseph Sheley and James Wright, *Gun Acquisition and Possession in Selected Juvenile Samples* (Washington, D.C.: National Institute of Justice, 1993).

47. FBI, *Crime in the United States, 1992.*

48. David Brent, Joshua Perper, Christopher Allman, Grace Moritz, Mary Wartella, and Janice Zelenak, "The Presence and Accessibility of Firearms in the Home and Adolescent Suicides," *Journal of the American Medical Association* 266 (1991): 2989–95.

49. Linda Saltzman, James Mercy, Patrick O'Carroll, Mark Rosenberg, and Philip Rhodes, "Weapon Involvement and Injury Outcomes in Family and Intimate Assaults," *Journal of the American Medical Association* 267 (1992): 3043–47.

50. William Green, *Rape* (Lexington, Mass.: Lexington Books, 1988), p. 5.

51. Susan Randall and Vicki McNickle Rose, "Forcible Rape," in *Major Forms of Crime,* ed. Robert Meyer (Beverly Hills: Sage, 1984), p. 47.

52. Associated Press, "Judge Who Told Rape Suspect to Get a Girlfriend Orders Him into Custody," *Manchester Union Leader,* 19 February 1994, p. 2.

53. Susan Brownmiller, *Against Our Will: Men, Women and Rape* (New York: Simon & Schuster, 1975).

54. Green, *Rape,* p. 6.

55. Diego Ribadeneira, "In Haiti's Poorest Areas, Women Tell of Rape by Armed Men," *Boston Globe,* 29 August 1993, p. 6.

56. James LeBeau, "Some Problems with Measuring and Describing Rape Presented by the Serial Offender," *Justice Quarterly* 2 (1985): 385–98.

57. Helen Eigenberg, "The National Crime Survey and Rape: The Case of the Missing Question," *Justice Quarterly* 7 (1990): 655–73.

58. Angela Browne, "Violence against Women, Relevance for Medical Practitioners," *Journal of the American Medical Association* 267 (1992): 3184–89.

59. Personal communication with NCVS statisticians, March 22, 1994.

60. Mark Warr, "Rape, Burglary and Opportunity," *Journal of Quantitative Criminology* 4 (1988): 275–88.

61. James LeBeau, "Patterns of Stranger and Serial Rape Offending: Factors Distinguishing Apprehended and At-Large Offenders," *Journal of Criminal Law and Delinquency* 78 (1987): 309–26.

62. Julie Allison and Lawrence Wrightsman, *Rape: The Misunderstood Crime* (Newbury Park, Calif.: Sage, 1993), p. 51.

63. R. Lance Shotland, "A Model of the Causes of Date Rape in Developing and Close Relationships," in *Close Relationships,* ed. C. Hendrick (Newbury Park, Calif.: Sage, 1989), pp. 247–70.

64. Walter DeKeseredy, Martin Schwartz, and Karen Tait, "Sexual Assault and Stranger Aggression on a Canadian Campus," *Sex Roles* 28 (1993): 263–77.

65. Ibid.

66. Thomas Meyer, "Date Rape: A Serious Campus Problem That Few Talk about," *Chronicle of Higher Education* 29 (5 December 1984): 15.

67. Allison and Wrightsman, *Rape,* p. 64.

68. Martin Schwartz, "Humanist Sociology and Date Rape on the College Campus," *Humanity and Society* 15 (1991): 304–16.

69. Mark Starr, "The Writing on the Wall," *Newsweek,* 26 November 1990, p. 64.

70. Allison and Wrightsman, *Rape,* pp. 85–87.

71. Cited in Diana Russell, "Wife Rape," in *Acquaintance Rape: The Hidden Crime,* ed. A. Parrot and L. Bechhofer (New York: John Wiley, 1991), pp. 129–39 at 129.

72. David Finkelhor and K. Yllo, *License to Rape: Sexual Abuse of Wives* (New York: Holt, Rinehart and Winston, 1985).

73. Allison and Wrightsman, *Rape,* p. 89.

74. Associated Press, "British Court Rejects Precedent, Finds a Man Guilty of Raping Wife," *Boston Globe,* 15 March 1991, p. 68.

75. Donald Symons, *The Evolution of Human Sexuality* (Oxford: Oxford University Press, 1979).

76. Lee Ellis, "A Synthesized (Biosocial) Theory of Rape," *Journal of Consulting and Clinical Psychology* 39 (1991): 631–42.

77. Diana Russell, *The Politics of Rape* (New York: Stein and Day, 1975).

78. Donald Mosher and Ronald Anderson, "Macho Personality, Sexual Aggression and Reactions to Guided Imagery of Realistic Rape," *Journal of Research in Personality* 20 (1987): 77–94.

79. Paul Gebhard, John Gagnon, Wardell Pomeroy, and Cornelia Christenson, *Sex Offenders: An Analysis of Types* (New York: Harper & Row, 1965), pp. 198–205.

80. Richard Rada, ed., *Clinical Aspects of the Rapist* (New York: Grune & Stratton, 1978), pp. 122–30.

81. A. Nicholas Groth and Jean Birnbaum, *Men Who Rape* (New York: Plenum, 1979), p. 101.

82. See, generally, Edward Donnerstein, Daniel Linz, and Steven Penrod, *The Question of Pornography* (New York: Free Press, 1987); Diana Russell, *Sexual Exploitation* (Beverly Hills: Sage, 1985), pp. 115–16.

83. Neil Malamuth and John Briere, "Sexual Violence in the Media: Indirect Effects on Aggression against Women," *Journal of Social Issues* 42 (1986): 75–92.

84. Associated Press, "Trial on TV May Have Influenced Boy Facing Sexual-Assault Count," *Omaha World Herald,* 18 April 1984, p. 50.

85. Richard Felson and Marvin Krohn, "Motives for Rape," *Journal of Research in Crime and Delinquency* 27 (1990): 222–42.

86. Larry Baron and Murray Straus, "Four Theories of Rape: A Macrosociological Analysis," *Social Problems* 34 (1987): 467–89.

87. "Woman Urges Dotson's Release," *Omaha World Herald,*

25 April 1985, p. 3.

88. Associated Press, "Apology Is Aired for Lie about Rape," *Boston Globe*, 6 September 1990, p. 12.

89. Gerald Robin, "Forcible Rape: Institutionalized Sexism in the Criminal Justice System," *Crime and Delinquency* 23 (1977): 136–53.

90. Associated Press, "Jury Stirs Furor by Citing Dress in Rape Acquittal," *Boston Globe*, 6 October 1989, p. 12.

91. Susan Estrich, *Real Rape* (Cambridge: Harvard University Press, 1987), pp. 58–59.

92. Associated Press, "Man Convicted in Rape of Woman Who Asked Him to Wear Condom," *Boston Globe*, 14 May 1993, p. 3.

93. *Michigan v. Lucas* 90–149 (1991); Comment, "The Rape Shield Paradox: Complainant Protection amidst Oscillating Trends of State Judicial Interpretation," *Journal of Criminal Law and Criminology* 78 (1987): 644–98.

94. Andrew Karmen, *Crime Victims* (Pacific Grove, Calif.: Brooks/Cole, 1990), p. 252.

95. See, for example, Mich. Comp. Laws Ann. 750.5200-(1); Florida Statutes Annotated, Sec. 794.011. See, generally, Gary LaFree, "Official Reactions to Rape," *American Sociological Review* 45 (1980): 842–54.

96. Martin Schwartz and Todd Clear, "Toward a New Law on Rape," *Crime and Delinquency* 26 (1980): 129–51.

97. Susan Caringella-MacDonald, "The Comparability in Sexual and Nonsexual Assault Case Treatment: Did Statute Change Meet the Objective?" *Crime and Delinquency* 31 (1985): 206–23.

98. Ronald Berger, Patricia Searles, and W. Lawrence Neuman, "The Dimensions of Rape Reform Legislation," *Law and Society Review* 22 (1988): 328–49.

99. Donald Lunde, *Murder and Madness* (San Francisco: San Francisco Book, 1977), p. 3.

100. Amy Dockser Marcus, "Mists of Memory Cloud Some Legal Proceedings," *Wall Street Journal*, 3 December 1990, p. B1.

101. Lisa Baertlein, "HIV Ruled Deadly Weapon in Rape Case," *Boston Globe*, 2 March 1994, p. 3.

102. The legal principles here come from Wayne LaFave and Austin Scott, *Criminal Law* (St. Paul: West Publishing, 1986; updated, 1993). The definitions and discussion of legal principles used in this chapter lean heavily on this work.

103. Ibid.

104. Reuters, "California Man Gets 3 Years for Pit Bull's Attack on Toddler," *Boston Globe*, 17 February 1990, p. 3.

105. "Puppy Killing Brings Prison," *New York Times*, 2 August 1990, p. A11.

106. Marc Reidel and Margaret Zahn, *The Nature and Pattern of American Homicide* (Washington, D.C.: U.S. Government Printing Office, 1985).

107. See, generally, Reidel and Zahn, *The Nature and Pattern of American Homicide*.

108. James L. Williams, "A Discriminant Analysis of Urban Homicide Patterns" (Paper presented at the annual meeting of the American Society of Criminology, Baltimore, November 1990).

109. Scott Decker, Carolyn Phillips, and Susan Tyrey-Jefferson, "Victim-Offender Relationships in Homicide: Developing an Empirical Typology" (Paper presented at the annual meeting of the American Society of Criminology, Baltimore, November 1990).

110. FBI, *Crime in the United States, 1992*, p. 12.

111. Ibid., p. 252.

112. Scott Decker, "Exploring Victim-Offender Relationships in Homicide: The Role of Individual and Event Characteristics," *Justice Quarterly* 10 (1993): 585–613.

113. Angela Browne and Kirk Williams, "Gender, Intimacy, and Lethal Violence: Trends from 1976 through 1987," *Gender and Society* 7 (1993): 78–98.

114. Linda Saltzman and James Mercy, "Assaults between Intimates: The Range of Relationships Involved," in *Homicide, The Victim/Offender Connection*, ed. Anna Victoria Wilson (Cincinnati: Anderson Publishing, 1993) pp. 65–74.

115. Angela Browne and Kirk Williams, "Exploring the Effect of Resource Availability and the Likelihood of Female-Perpetrated Homicides," *Law and Society Review* 23 (1989): 75–94.

116. Marc Reidel, "Stranger Violence: Perspectives, Issues, and Problems," *Journal of Criminal Law and Criminology* 78 (1987): 223–58 at 229.

117. John Hewitt, "The Victim-Offender Relationship in Convicted Homicide Cases: 1960–1984," *Journal of Criminal Justice* 16 (1988): 25–33.

118. Margaret Zahn and Philip Sagi, "Stranger Homicides in Nine American Cities," *Journal of Criminal Law and Criminology* 78 (1987): 377–97.

119. Ibid., p. 396.

120. James Boudouris, "A Classification of Homicide," *Criminology* 11 (1974): 525–40.

121. David Luckenbill, "Criminal Homicide as a Situational Transaction," *Social Problems* 25 (1977): 176–86.

122. Michael Hazlett and Thomas Tomlinson, "Females Involved in Homicides: Victims and Offenders in Two Southern States" (Paper presented at the annual meeting of the American Society of Criminology, Montreal, November 1987; rev., 1988).

123. Associated Press, "Parents Forgive Teenager Convicted of Toddler's Death," *Boston Globe*, 22 January 1987.

124. Ewing, *When Children Kill*, p. 64.

125. Ibid.

126. Carolyn Rebecca Block and Richard Block, *Street Gang Crime in Chicago* (Washington, D.C.: National Institute of Justice, 1993), p. 2.

127. Cited in Ewing, *When Children Kill*, p. 71.

128. From Forward/Update to James A. Fox and Jack Levin, *Mass Murder*, 2d ed. (New York: Plenum Press, 1991).

129. Cindy Horswell, "Teen Held in Mom's Shooting Death: 'The Devil Made Me Do It,'" *Houston Chronicle,* 19 May 1993, p. 1.

130. Thomas Palmer, "A Doctor Smelled Arsenic, Leading to Arrest of Serial Killer," *Boston Globe,* 20 August 1987, p. 3.

131. "Police Suspect 'Something Snapped' to Ignite Wilder's Crime Spree," *Omaha World Herald,* 15 April 1984, p. 21A.

132. Mark Starr, "The Random Killers," *Newsweek,* 26 November 1984, pp. 100–106.

133. Thomas Palmer, "Ex-hospital Aide Admits Killing 24 in Cincinnati," *Boston Globe,* 19 August 1987, p. 3.

134. Philip Jenkins, "Serial Murder in England, 1940–1985," *Journal of Criminal Justice* 16 (1988): 1–15.

135. Associated Press, "Briton Kills 14 in Rampage," *Boston Globe,* 20 August 1987, p. 3.

136. Ronald Holmes and Stephen Homes, *Murder in America* (Thousand Oaks, Calif.: Sage, 1994), p. 6.

137. Ibid., p. 106.

138. Jenkins, "Serial Murder in England, 1940–1985," p. 9.

139. Ronald Holmes and James DeBurger, *Serial Murder* (Newbury Park, Calif.: Sage, 1988), pp. 58–59.

140. Holmes and Homes, *Murder in America,* 13–14.

141. Ibid., p. 17.

142. Belea Keeney and Kathleen Heide, "Gender Differences in Serial Murderers: A Preliminary Analysis," *Journal of Interpersonal Violence* 9 (1994, in press).

143. Jennifer Browdy, "VI-CAP System to Be Operational This Summer," *Law Enforcement News,* 21 May 1984, p. 1.

144. Philip Jenkins, "A Murder 'Wave'? Trends in American Serial Homicide 1940–1990," *Criminal Justice Review* 17 (1992): 1–18.

145. FBI, *Crime in the United States, 1992,* p. 21.

146. FBI, *Crime in the United States, 1992,* pp. 22–25.

147. See, generally, Joel Milner, ed., Special Issue: Physical Child Abuse, *Criminal Justice and Behavior* 18 (1991).

148. See, generally, Ruth S. Kempe and C. Henry Kempe, *Child Abuse* (Cambridge: Harvard University Press, 1978).

149. Richard Gelles and Murray Straus, "Violence in the American Family," *Journal of Social Issues* 35 (1979): 15–39.

150. The American Human Society, *Highlights of Official Child Neglect and Abuse Reporting* (Denver: 1984).

151. Steve Geissinger, "Boy Scouts Dismissed 1,800 Suspected Molesters from 1971–91," *Boston Globe,* 15 October 1993, p. 3.

152. Diana Russell, "The Incidence and Prevalence of Intrafamilial and Extrafamilial Sexual Abuse of Female Children," *Child Abuse and Neglect* 7 (1983): 133–46; see also David Finkelhor, *Sexually Victimized Children* (New York: Free Press, 1979), p. 88.

153. Jeanne Hernandez, "Eating Disorders and Sexual Abuse in Adolescents" (Paper presented at the annual meeting of the American Psychosomatic Society, Charleston, S.C., March, 1993); Glenn Wolfner and Richard Gelles, "A Profile of Violence toward Children: A National Study," *Child Abuse and Neglect* 17 (1993): 197–212.

154. Louanne Lawson and Mark Chaffin, "False Negatives in Sexual Abuse Disclosure Interviews," *Journal of Interpersonal Violence* 7 (1992): 532–42.

155. For a thorough review, see Kathleen Kendall-Tackett, Linda Meyer Williams, and David Finkelhor, "Impact of Sexual Abuse on Children: A Review and Synthesis of Recent Empirical Studies," *Psychological Bulletin* 133 (1993): 164–80.

156. Wolfner and Gelles, "A Profile of Violence toward Children."

157. Brandt Steele, "Violence within the Family," in *Child Abuse and Neglect: The Family and the Community,* ed. R. Helfer and C. H. Kempe (Cambridge, Mass.: Ballinger Publishing, 1976), p. 12.

158. Ruth Inglis, *Sins of the Fathers: A Study of the Physical and Emotional Abuse of Children* (New York: St. Martin's Press, 1978), p. 68.

159. Ibid., p. 53.

160. Alison Bass, "Daughter Wins Sex-Abuse Case against Father," *Boston Globe,* 18 May 1990, p. 17.

161. David Kaplan, "The Unkindest Cut," *Newsweek,* 16 August 1993, p. 56.

162. Associated Press, "Lorena Freed," *Manchester Union Leader,* 1 March 1994, p. 44.

163. Russell Dobash, R. Emerson Dobash, Margo Wilson, and Martin Daly, "The Myth of Sexual Symmetry in Marital Violence," *Social Problems* 39 (1992): 71–86; Martin Schwartz and Walter DeKeseredy, "The Return of the 'Battered Husband Syndrome' Typification of Women as Violent," *Crime, Law and Social Change* 8 (1993): 11–27.

164. Schwartz and DeKeseredy, "The Return of the 'Battered Husband Syndrome.'"

165. R. Emerson Dobash and Russell Dobash, *Violence against Wives* (New York: Free Press, 1979).

166. Julia O'Faolain and Laura Martines, eds., *Not in God's Image: Women in History* (Glasgow: Fontana/Collins, 1974).

167. Laurence Stone, "The Rise of the Nuclear Family in Modern England: The Patriarchal Stage," in *The Family in History,* ed. Charles Rosenberg (Philadelphia: University of Pennsylvania Press, 1975), p. 53.

168. Dobash and Dobash, *Violence against Wives,* p. 46.

169. John Braithwaite, "Inequality and Republican Criminology" (Paper presented at the annual meeting of the American Society of Criminology, San Francisco, November 1991), p. 20.

170. James Makepeace, "Social Factor and Victim-Offender Differences in Courtship Violence," *Family Relations* 33 (1987): 87–91.

171. Graeme Newman, *Understanding Violence* (New York: Lippincott, 1979), pp. 145–46.

172. FBI, *Crime in the United States, 1989,* p. 16.

173. Joan Johnson and Marshall DeBerry, Jr., *Criminal Victim-*

ization, 1988 (Washington, D.C.: Bureau of Justice Statistics, 1990), p. 61.

174. Caroline Wolf Harlow, *Robbery Victims* (Washington, D.C.: Bureau of Justice Statistics, 1989), pp. 1–5.

175. F. H. McClintock and Evelyn Gibson, *Robbery in London* (London: Macmillan, 1961), p. 15.

176. John Conklin, *Robbery and the Criminal Justice System* (New York: Lippincott, 1972), pp. 1–80.

177. James Calder and John Bauer, "Convenience Store Robberies: Security Measures and Store Robbery Incidents," *Journal of Criminal Justice* 20 (1992): 553–66.

178. James Garofalo, "Bias and Non-Bias Crimes in New York City: Preliminary Findings" (Paper presented at the annual meeting of the American Society of Criminology, Baltimore, November 1990).

179. Ronald Powers, "Bensonhurst Man Guilty," *Boston Globe,* 18 May 1990, p. 3.

180. "Boy Gets 18 Years in Fatal Park Beating of Transient," *Los Angeles Times,* 24 December 1987, p. 9B.

181. Ewing, *When Children Kill,* pp. 65–66.

182. Mike McPhee, "In Denver, Attacks Stir Fears of Racism," *Boston Globe,* 10 December 1990, p. 3.

183. Jack McDevitt, "The Study of the Character of Civil Rights Crimes in Massachusetts (1983–1987)" (Paper presented at the annual meeting of the American Society of Criminology, Reno, Nevada, November 1989).

184. Ibid., p. 8.

185. Jack Levin and Jack McDevitt, *Hate Crimes: The Rising Tide of Bigotry and Bloodshed* (New York: Plenum, 1993).

186. Jack Levin and Jack McDevitt, *Hate Crimes, A Study of Offenders' Motivations* (Boston, Mass.: Northeastern University, 1993).

187. Daniel Bibel, "Hate Crime Reporting in the United States, Preliminary Findings/Survey Results/Future Directions" (Center for Applied Social Research, Northeastern University, Boston, n.d.).

188. National Gay and Lesbian Task Force Policy Institute, *Anti-Gay/Lesbian Violence, Victimization and Defamation in 1992* (Washington, D.C.: National Gay and Lesbian Task Force, 1993), p. 3.

189. Ibid.

190. Ibid.

191. Garofalo, "Bias and Non-Bias Crimes in New York City," p. 3.

192. Carl Weiser, "This Is What You Get for Firing Me," *USA Today,* 28 January 1993, p. 3A.

193. James Alan Fox and Jack Levin, "Firing Back: The Growing Threat of Workplace Homicide," *Annals* (1994, in press).

194. John King, "Workplace Violence: A Conceptual Framework" (Paper presented at the annual meeting of the American Society of Criminology, Phoenix, Arizona, November 1993).

195. Associated Press, "Gunman Wounds 3 Doctors in L.A. Hospital," *Cleveland Plain Dealer,* 9 February 1993, p. 1B.

196. Fox and Levin, "Firing Back," p. 5.

197. Ibid., p. 20.

198. Stephen Schafer, *The Political Criminal* (New York: Free Press, 1974), p. 1.

199. Barton Ingraham, *Political Crime in Europe* (Berkeley: University of California Press, 1979), pp. vi–viii.

200. Schafer, *The Political Criminal,* p. 150.

201. Robert Friedlander, *Terrorism* (Dobbs Ferry, N.Y.: Oceana Publishers, 1979).

202. Walter Laquer, *The Age of Terrorism* (Boston: Little, Brown, 1987), p. 72.

203. National Advisory Commission on Criminal Justice Standards and Goals, *Report of the Task Force on Disorders and Terrorism* (Washington, D.C.: U.S. Government Printing Office, 1976), p. 3.

204. Paul Wilkinson, *Terrorism and the Liberal State* (New York: John Wiley, 1977), p. 49.

205. Jack Gibbs, "Conceptualization of Terrorism," *American Sociological Review* 54 (1989): 329–40, at 330.

206. Friedlander, *Terrorism,* p. 14.

207. Daniel Georges-Abeyie, "Political Crime and Terrorism," in *Crime and Deviance: A Comparative Perspective,* ed. Graeme Newman (Beverly Hills: Sage, 1980), pp. 313–33.

208. Ibid., p. 319.

209. This section relies heavily on Friedlander, *Terrorism,* pp. 8–20.

210. See Friedlander, *Terrorism,* p. 16.

211. For a general view, see Jonathan White, *Terrorism* (Pacific Grove, Calif.: Brooks/Cole, 1991).

212. Jonathan Kaufman, "Trauma of a German Slaying," *Boston Globe,* 3 April 1991, p. 2.

213. Claire Sterling, "Gen. Dozier and the International Terror Network," *Wall Street Journal,* 29 December 1981, p. 12.

214. Russell Watson, "An Explosion in the Sky," *Newsweek,* 2 January 1989, pp. 16–19.

215. Irwin Suall and David Lowe, "Special Report—The Hate Movement Today: A Chronicle of Violence and Disarray," *Terrorism* 10 (1987): 345–64.

216. Robert Zint, "Dreams of a Bigots' Revolution," *Time,* 18 February 1985, p. 42.

217. William Smith, "Libya's Ministry of Fear," *Time,* 30 April 1984, pp. 36–38.

218. Reuters, "Nile Tour Boat Is Attacked; Blast Hits Egyptian Resort," *Boston Globe,* 10 April 1993, p. 5.

219. Charles Hillsinger and Mark Stein, "Militant Vegetarians Tied to Attacks on Livestock Industry," *Boston Globe,* 23 November 1989, p. A34.

220. Ted Robert Gurr, "Political Terrorism in the United States: Historical Antecedents and Contemporary Trends," in *The Politics of Terrorism,* ed. Michael Stohl (New York: Dekker, 1988).

221. Martha Crenshaw, ed., *Terrorism, Legitimacy, and Power* (Middletown, Conn.: Wesleyan University Press, 1983), pp. 1–10.

222. Amnesty International, *Annual Report, 1992*

(Washington, D.C.), released July 1993.

223. Ronald Kramer, "Structural Violence and State Terrorism: Neglected Forms of Criminal Violence" (Paper presented at the annual meeting of the American Society of Criminology, Phoenix, Arizona, November 1993).

224. Theodore Gurr, *Why Men Rebel* (Princeton, N.J.: Princeton University Press, 1970).

225. M. Cherif Bassiouni, "Terrorism, Law Enforcement, and Mass Media: Perspectives, Problems and Proposals," *Journal of Criminal Law and Criminology* 72 (1981): 1–51 at 10.

226. Austin Turk, "Political Crime," in *Major Forms of Crime,* ed. R. Meier (Beverly Hills: Sage, 1984), pp. 119–35.

227. Reuters, "18 Beheaded in Sri Lanka; Revenge for Slaying Seen," *Boston Globe,* 6 October 1989, p. 13.

228. Kaplan, "The Unkindest Cut," p. 56.

229. 18 USC 113a; 18 USC 51, 1166.

230. Brent Smith and Gregory Orvis, "America's Response to Terrorism: An Empirical Analysis of Federal Intervention Strategies during the 1980's," *Justice Quarterly* 10 (1993): 660–81.

12 Economic Crimes: Street Crimes

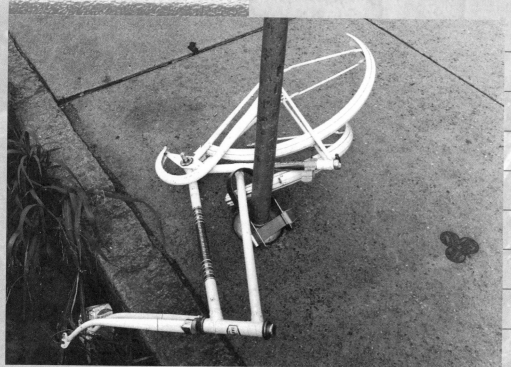

Introduction

As a group, economic crimes can be defined as acts in violation of the criminal law designed to bring financial reward to an offender. In U.S. society, the range and scope of criminal activity motivated by financial gain is tremendous: self-report studies show that property crime among the young of every social class is widespread; national surveys of criminal behavior indicate that more than 30 million personal and household thefts occur annually; corporate and other white-collar crimes are accepted as commonplace; and political scandals, such as ABSCAM, indicate that bribery and corruption reach even the highest levels of government. Though average citizens may be puzzled and enraged by violent crimes, believing them to be both senseless and cruel, they often view economic crimes with a great deal more ambivalence. While it is true that society generally disapproves of crimes involving theft and corruption, the public seems quite tolerant of the "gentleman bandit," even to the point of admiring such figures. They pop up as characters in popular myths and legends—Robin Hood, Jesse James, Bonnie and Clyde, D. B. Cooper. They are the semiheroic subjects of books and films, such as *48 Hours, Dirty Rotten Scoundrels, The Grifters,* and *The Getaway.*

How can such ambivalence toward criminality be explained? For one thing, national tolerance toward economic criminals may be prompted by the fact that if self-report surveys are accurate, almost every U.S. citizen has at some time been involved in economic crime. Even those among us who would never consider themselves criminals may have at one time engaged in petty theft, cheated on their income tax, stolen a textbook from a college bookstore, or pilfered from their place of employment. Consequently, it may be difficult for society to condemn economic criminals without feeling hypocritical.

People may also be somewhat more tolerant of economic crimes because they never seem to seriously hurt anyone—banks are insured, large businesses pass along losses to consumers, stolen cars can be easily replaced. The true pain of economic crime often goes unappreciated. Convicted offenders, especially businesspeople who commit white-collar crimes involving millions of dollars, often are punished rather lightly.

This chapter is the first of two that review the nature and extent of economic crime in the United States. It is divided into two principal sections. The first deals with the concept of professional crime and focuses on different types of professional criminals, including the **fence,** a buyer and seller of stolen merchandise. Then the chapter turns to a discussion of common theft-related offenses, often referred to by criminologists as **street crimes.** These crimes include the major forms of common theft: larceny, embezzlement, and theft by false pretenses. Included within these general offense categories are such common crimes as auto theft, shoplifting, and credit card fraud. Then the chapter discusses a more serious form of theft—**burglary**—that involves forcible entry into a person's home or place of work for the purpose of theft. Finally, the crime of arson is discussed briefly. In the following chapter, attention will be given to white-collar crimes and economic crimes that involve organizations devoted to criminal enterprise.

A Brief History of Theft

Theft offenses are frequent. Millions of auto thefts, shoplifting incidents, embezzlements, burglaries, and larcenies are recorded each year. National surveys indicate that almost 15 percent of the U.S. population are victims of theft offenses each year. Theft is not a phenomenon unique to modern times; the theft of personal property has been known throughout recorded history. The Crusades of the eleventh century inspired peasants and downtrodden noblemen to leave the shelter of their estates to prey upon passing pilgrims.[1] Not surprisingly, Crusaders felt it within their rights to appropriate the possessions of any infidels—Greeks, Jews, or Moslems—they happened to encounter during their travels. By the thirteenth century, returning pilgrims, not content to live as serfs on feudal estates, gathered in the forests of England and the Continent to poach on game that was the rightful property of their lord or king and, when possible, to steal from passing strangers. By the fourteenth century, many of such highwaymen and poachers were full-time livestock thieves, stealing great numbers of cattle and sheep.[2]

The fifteenth and sixteenth centuries brought hostilities between England and France in what has come to be known as the Hundred Years' War. Foreign mercenary troops fighting for both sides roamed the countryside; loot and pillage were viewed as a rightful part of their pay. Theft became more professional with the rise of the city and the establishment of a permanent class of propertyless urban poor.[3] By the eighteenth century, three separate groups of property criminals were active. In the larger cities, such as London and Paris, groups of skilled thieves, pickpockets, forgers, and counterfeiters operated freely. They congregated in **flash houses**— public meeting places, often taverns, that served as headquarters for gangs. Here, deals were made, crimes plotted, and the sale of stolen goods negotiated.[4] The second group of thieves were the smugglers, who moved freely in sparsely populated areas and transported goods without bothering to pay tax or duty. The third group were the poachers, who lived in the country and supplemented their diet and income with game that belonged to a landlord. By the eighteenth century, professional thieves in the larger cities had banded together into gangs to protect themselves, increase the scope of their activities, and help dispose of stolen goods. Jack Wild, perhaps London's most famous thief, perfected the process of buying and selling stolen goods and gave himself the title of "Thief-Taker General of Great Britain and Ireland." Before he was hanged, Wild controlled numerous gangs and dealt harshly with any thief who violated his strict code of conduct.[5] During this period, individual theft-related crimes began to be defined by the common law. The most important of these categories are still used today.

≡ Modern Thieves

Of the millions of property and theft-related crimes that occur each year, most are committed by **occasional criminals** who do not define themselves by a criminal role or view themselves as committed career criminals; other theft-offenders are in fact skilled, **professional criminals.** The following sections review these two orientations toward property crime.

Occasional Criminals

Though criminologists are not certain, they suspect that the great majority of **economic crimes** are the work of amateur criminals whose decision to steal is spontaneous and whose acts are unskilled, unplanned, and haphazard. Millions of theft-related crimes occur each year, and most are not reported to police agencies. Many of these theft offenses are committed by school-age youths who are unlikely to enter into a criminal career and whose behavior has been described as drifting between conventional and criminal behavior. Added to the pool of amateur thieves are the millions of adults whose behavior may occasionally violate the criminal law—shoplifters, pilferers, tax cheats—but whose main

source of income comes from conventional means and whose self-identity is noncriminal. Added together, their behaviors form the bulk of theft crimes.

According to John Hepburn, occasional property crime occurs when there is an opportunity or **situational inducement** to commit crime.[6] Opportunities are available to members of all classes, but members of the upper class have the opportunity to engage in the more lucrative business-related crimes of price-fixing, bribery, embezzlement, and so on, which are closed to the lower classes. Hence, lower-class individuals are overrepresented in street crime. Situational inducements are short-run influences on a person's behavior that increase risk-taking. These include psychological factors, such as financial problems, and social factors, such as peer pressure. According to Hepburn, opportunity and situational inducements are not the cause of crime; rather, they are the occasion for crime; hence, the term *occasional criminal.*

It seems evident that opportunity and inducements are not randomly situated. Consequently, the frequency of occasional property crime varies according to age, class, sex, and so on. Occasional offenders are not professional criminals, nor do they make crime their occupation. They do not rely on skills or knowledge to commit their crimes, they do not organize their daily activities around crime, and they are not committed to crime as a way of life. Occasional criminals have little group support for their acts. Unlike professionals, they do not receive informal, peer group support for their crimes. In fact, they will deny any connection to a criminal life-style and instead view their transgressions as being "out of character." They may see their crimes as being motivated by necessity. For example, they were only "borrowing" the car the police caught them with; they were going to pay back the store they stole merchandise from. Because of the lack of commitment, occasional offenders may be the most likely to respond to the general deterrent effect of the law.

Professional Criminals

In contrast, *professional criminals* make a significant portion of their income from crime. Professionals do not delude themselves with the belief that their acts are impulsive, one-time efforts, nor do they employ elaborate rationalizations to excuse the harmfulness of their action ("shoplifting doesn't really hurt anyone"). Consequently, professionals pursue their craft with vigor, attempting to learn from older, experienced criminals the techniques that will earn them the most money with the least risk.

Though their numbers are relatively few, professionals engage in crimes that produce the greater losses to society and perhaps cause the more significant social harm.

Professional theft traditionally refers to nonviolent forms of criminal behavior that are undertaken with a high degree of skill for monetary gain and that exploit interests tending to maximize financial opportunities and minimize the possibilities of apprehension. The most typical forms include pocket-picking, burglary, shoplifting, forgery and counterfeiting, extortion, sneak theft, and confidence swindling.[7]

Relatively little is known about the career patterns of professional thieves and criminals. From the literature on crime and delinquency, three patterns emerge: youths come under the influence of older, experienced criminals who teach them the trade; juvenile gang members continue their illegal activities at a time when most of their peers have "dropped out" to marry, raise families, and take conventional jobs; youths sent to prison for minor offenses learn the techniques of crime from more experienced thieves. For example, Harry King, a professional thief, relates this story about his entry into crime after being placed in a shelter-care home by his recently divorced mother:

> It was while I was at this parental school that I learned that some of the kids had been committed there by the court for stealing bikes. They taught me how to steal and where to steal them and where to sell them. Incidentally, some of the "nicer people" were the ones who bought bikes from the kids. They would dismantle the bike and use the parts: the wheels, chains, handlebars, and so forth.[8]

There is some debate in the criminological literature over who may be defined as a professional criminal. Some criminologists, such as Edwin Sutherland, use the term to refer only to thieves who do not use force or physical violence in their crimes and live solely by their wits and skill.[9] However, some criminologists use the term to refer to any criminal who identifies with a criminal subculture, who makes the bulk of his or her living from crime, and who possesses a degree of skill in his or her chosen trade.[10] Thus, one can become a professional safecracker, burglar, car thief, or fence. Some criminologists would not consider drug addicts who steal to support their habit as professionals; they lack skill and therefore are amateur opportunists, rather than professional technicians. However, professional criminals who take drugs might still be considered under the general pattern of professional crime. If the sole criteria for being judged a professional criminal is using crime as one's primary source of income, then many drug users would have to be placed in the professional category.

Sutherland's Professional Criminal

What we know about the lives of professional criminals has come to us through their journals, diaries, autobiographies, and the first-person accounts they have given to criminologists. The best-known account of professional theft is Edwin Sutherland's recording of the life of a professional thief or con man, Chic Conwell, in Sutherland's classic book, *The Professional Thief*.[11] Conwell and Sutherland's concept of professional theft has two critical dimensions. First, professional thieves engage in limited types of crime. They can be described by the following labels:

- Pickpocket (cannon)
- Sneak thief from stores, banks, and offices (heel)
- Shoplifter (booster)
- Jewel thief who substitutes fake gems for real ones (pennyweighter)
- Thief who steals from hotel rooms (hotel prowl)
- Confidence game artist
- Thief in rackets related to confidence games
- Forger
- Extortionist from those engaging in illegal acts (shakedown artist).[12]

Professionals depend solely on their wit and skill. Thieves who use force or commit crimes that require little expertise are not considered worthy of the title "professional." Their areas of activity include such "heavy rackets" as bank robbery, car theft, burglary, and safe-cracking. You can see that Conwell and Sutherland's criteria for professionalism are weighted heavily toward con games and trickery and give little attention to common street crimes. The second requirement to establish professionalism as a thief is the exclusive use of wits, front (a believable demeanor), and talking ability. Manual dexterity and physical force are of little importance. Professional thieves must acquire status in their profession. Status is based on their technical skill, financial standing, connections, power, dress, manners, and wide knowledge. In their world, "thief" is a title worn with pride. Conwell and Sutherland also argue that professional thieves share feelings, sentiments, and behaviors. Of these, none is more important than the code of honor of the underworld; even under threat of the most severe punishment, a professional thief must never inform (squeal) on his or her fellows. Sutherland and Conwell view professional theft as an occupation with much the same internal organization as that characterizing such legitimate professions as advertising, teaching, or police work. They conclude:

> A person can be a professional thief only if he is recognized and received as such by other professional thieves. Professional theft is a group way of life. One can get into the group and remain in it only by the consent of those previously in the group. Recognition as a professional thief by other professional thieves is the absolutely necessary, universal and definitive characteristic of the professional thief.[13]

Professional Criminals: The Fence

Some experts have argued that Sutherland's view of the professional thief may be outdated because modern thieves often work alone, are not part of a criminal subculture, and were not tutored early in their careers by other criminals.[14] However, some recent research efforts show that the principles set down by Sutherland still have value for understanding the behavior of one contemporary criminal—the professional fence, a person who earns his or her living solely by buying and reselling stolen merchandise.

Professional fences play an important role in the thief's working world. They act as middlemen who purchase stolen merchandise—ranging from diamonds to auto hubcaps—and then resell them to merchants who market them to legitimate customers.

The fence's critical role in criminal transactions has long been appreciated. As early as 1795, Patrick Colquhoun stated in his book, *A Treatise on the Police of the Metropolis:*

> In contemplating the characters of all these different classes of delinquents (that is, Thieves, Robbers, Cheats and Swindlers), there can be little hesitation in pronouncing the Receivers to be the most mischievous of the whole: inasmuch as without the aid they afford, in purchasing and concealing every species of property stolen or fraudulently obtained, Thieves, Robbers and Swindlers . . . must quit the trade, as unproductive and hazardous in the extreme. Nothing therefore can be more just than the old observation, "that if there were no Receivers there would be no Thieves."—Deprive a thief of a safe and ready market for his goods and he is undone.[15]

Fencing Professionally.   Much of what is known about fencing comes from three in-depth studies of individual fences by Carl Klockars, Darrell Steffensmeier, and Marilyn Walsh.[16]

Klockars examined the life and times of one successful fence who used the alias "Vincent Swaggi." Through 400 hours of listening to and observing Vincent, Klockars found that this highly professional criminal had developed techniques that made him almost immune to prosecution. During the course of a long and profitable career in crime, Vincent spent only four months in prison. He stayed in business in part because of his sophisticated knowledge of the law of stolen property: To convict someone of receiving stolen goods, the prosecution must prove that the accused was in possession of the goods and knew that they had been stolen. Vincent had the skills to make sure that these elements could never be proven. Also helping Vincent stay out of the law's grasp were the close working associations he maintained with society's upper classes, including influential members of the justice system. Vincent helped them purchase items at below-cost, bargain prices. He also helped authorities recover stolen goods and therefore remained in their good graces. Klockars's work strongly suggests that fences customarily cheat their thief-clients and at the same time cooperate with the law.

Sam Goodman, the fence studied by Darrell Steffensmeier, lived in a world similar to Vincent Swaggi's. He also purchased stolen goods from a wide variety of thieves and suppliers, including burglars, drug addicts, shoplifters, dockworkers, and truck drivers. According to Sam, to be successful, a fence must meet the following conditions:

1. *Upfront cash*—all deals are cash transactions, so an adequate supply of ready cash must always be on hand.
2. *Knowledge of dealing: learning the ropes*—the fence must be schooled in the knowledge of the trade, including developing a "larceny sense"; learning to "buy right" at acceptable prices; being able to "cover one's back" and not get caught; finding out how to make the right contacts; and knowing how to "wheel and deal" and create opportunities for profit.
3. *Connections with suppliers of stolen goods*—the successful fence is able to engage in long-term relationships with suppliers of high-value stolen goods who are relatively free of police interference. The warehouse worker who pilfers is a better supplier than the narcotics addict who is more likely to be apprehended and talk to the police.
4. *Connections with buyers*—the successful fence must have continuing access to buyers of stolen merchandise who are inaccessible to the common thief.

5. *Complicity with law enforcers*—the fence must work out a relationship with law enforcement officials who invariably find out about the fence's operations. Steffensmeier found that to stay in business, the fence must either bribe officials with good deals on merchandise and cash payments or act as an informer who helps police recover particularly important merchandise and arrest thieves. This latter role of informer differentiates Steffensmeier's description of the fence's role from that of Klockars.

Marilyn Walsh found that fences handle a tremendous number of products—televisions, cigarettes, stereo equipment, watches, autos, and cameras.[17] In dealing their merchandise, fences operate through many legitimate fronts, including art dealers, antique stores, furniture and appliance retailers, remodeling companies, salvage companies, trucking companies, and jewelry stores. When deciding what to pay the thief for goods, the fence uses a complex pricing policy: professional thieves who steal high-priced items are usually given the highest amounts—about 30 to 50 percent of the wholesale price. For example, furs valued at $5,000 may be bought for $1,200. However, the amateur thief or drug addict who is not in a good bargaining position may receive only ten cents on the dollar.

Fencing seems to contain many of the elements of professional theft as described by Sutherland: fences live by their wits, never engage in violence, depend on their skill in negotiating, maintain community standing based on connections and power, and share the sentiments and behaviors of their fellows. The only divergence between Sutherland's thief and the fence is the code of honor; it seems likely that the fence is much more willing to cooperate with authorities than most other professional criminals.

Occasional Criminals: The Nonprofessional Fence

Professional fences are the ones who have attracted the attention of criminologists. Yet like other forms of theft, fencing is not dominated by professional criminals alone; a significant portion of all fencing is performed by amateur or occasional criminals.

Using data collected in interviews with convicted thieves, fences, and people who bought stolen property, Paul Cromwell, James Olson, and D'Aunn Avary discovered that novice burglars, such as juveniles and drug addicts, often find it so difficult to establish relationships with professional fences they turn instead to nonprofessionals to unload their stolen goods.[18]

One type of occasional fence was the part-timer who, unlike professional fences, had other sources of income. Part-timers were often "legitimate" businesspeople who integrated the stolen merchandise into their regular stock. For example, the manager of a local video store buys stolen VCRs and tapes and rents them along with his legitimate merchandise. An added benefit is profit on these items is not reported for tax purposes.

Some merchants became actively involved in theft either by specifying the merchandise they want the burglars to steal or "fingering" victims. Some businessmen sold merchandise to people and then described the customers' homes and vacation plans to known burglars so that they could steal it back!

Some amateur fences bartered stolen goods for services rendered. These "associational fences" typically had legitimate professional dealings with known criminals and included bail bonds agents, police officers, and attorneys. One lawyer bragged of getting a $12,000 Rolex watch from one client in exchange for legal services. Bartering for stolen merchandise avoids taxes and becomes a transaction in the "underground economy."

"Neighborhood hustlers" buy and sell stolen property as but one of many ways they make a living; they keep some of the booty for themselves and sell the rest in the neighborhood. These deal makers are familiar figures to neighborhood burglars looking to get some quick cash.

"Amateur receivers" can be complete strangers approached in a public place by someone offering a great deal on valuable commodities. It is unlikely that anyone buying a $500 stereo for $200 cash would not suspect that it may have been stolen. Some amateur receivers make a habit of buying merchandise at reasonable prices from a "trusted friend."

The Cromwell, Olson, and Avary research indicates that the nonprofessional fence may account for a great deal of criminal receiving. It shows that both professional and amateur thieves have their own niche in the crime universe.

≡ Theft Categories

Criminologists and legal scholars recognize that common theft offenses fall into several categories linked together because they involve the intentional misappropriation of property for personal gain. In some cases, in fencing, it is bought from another who is in illegal possession of the goods. In the case of embezzlement, burglary, and larceny, the property is taken through stealth, while in others, such as bad checks, fraud, and false pretenses, it is obtained through deception. Some of the major categories of common theft offenses are discussed below in some detail.

Larceny/Theft

Larceny/theft was one of the earliest common-law crimes created by English judges to define acts in which one person took for his or her own use the property of another.[19] At common law, larceny was defined as "the trespassory taking and carrying away of the personal property of another with intent to steal."[20] Most state jurisdictions have incorporated the common-law crime of larceny in their legal codes. Today, definitions of larceny often include such familiar acts as shoplifting, passing bad checks, and other theft offenses that do not involve using force or threats on the victim or forcibly breaking into a person's home or place of work. (The former is robbery; the latter, burglary.)

As originally construed, larceny involved only taking property that was in the possession of the rightful owners. For example, it would have been considered larceny for someone to go secretly into a farmer's field and steal a cow. Thus, the original common-law definition required a "trespass in the taking"; this meant that for an act to be considered larceny, goods must have been taken from the physical possession of the rightful owner. In creating this definition of larceny, English judges were more concerned with disturbance of the peace than they were with thefts. They reasoned that if someone tried to steal property from another's possession, the act could eventually lead to a physical confrontation and possibly the death of one party or the other. Consequently, the original definition of larceny did not include crimes in which the thief had come into the possession of the stolen property by trickery or deceit. For example, if someone entrusted with another person's property decided to keep it, it was not considered larceny. The growth of manufacturing and the development of the free enterprise system required greater protection for private property. The pursuit of commercial enterprise often required that one person's legal property be entrusted to a second party; therefore, larceny evolved to include the theft of goods that had come into the thief's possession through legitimate means.

To get around the element of "trespass in the taking," English judges created the concept of **constructive possession**. This legal fiction applied to situations in which persons voluntarily and temporarily gave up custody of

their property but still believed that the property was legally theirs. For example, if a person gave a jeweler her watch for repair, she would still believe she owned the watch, although she had handed it over to the jeweler. Similarly, when a person misplaces his wallet and someone else finds it and keeps it—although identification of the owner can be plainly seen—the concept of constructive possession makes the person who has kept the wallet guilty of larceny.

Larceny Today

Most state jurisdictions have, as mentioned, incorporated larceny in their criminal codes. Larceny is usually separated by state statute into petit (or petty) larceny and grand larceny. The former involves small amounts of money or property; it is punished as a misdemeanor. Grand larceny, involving merchandise of greater value, is considered a felony and is punished by a sentence in the state prison. Each state sets its own boundary between grand larceny and petty larceny, but $50 to $100 is not unusual. This distinction often presents a serious problem for the justice system. Car thefts and other larcenies involving high-priced merchandise are easily classified, but it is often difficult to decide whether a particular theft should be considered petty or grand larceny. For example, if a ten-year-old watch that originally cost $500 is stolen, should its value be based on its original cost; on its current worth, say, $50; or on its replacement cost, say, $1,000? As most statutes are worded, the current market value of the property governs its worth. Thus, the theft of the watch would be considered petty larceny, since its worth today is only $50. However, if a painting originally bought for $25 has a current market value of $500, its theft would be considered grand larceny.

Larceny/theft is probably the most common criminal offense. Self-report studies, discussed in Chapter 4, indicate that a significant number of youths have engaged in theft-related activities. The FBI recorded over 7.9 million acts of larceny in 1992, a rate of over 3,100 per 100,000 persons; larceny rates have remained rather stable for the past five years.[21]

Shoplifting

Shoplifting is a common form of theft involving the taking of goods from retail stores. Usually, shoplifters try to snatch goods—jewelry, clothes, records, appliances—when store personnel are otherwise occupied and hide the goods on their person. The "five-finger discount" is an extremely common form of crime; losses from shoplifting are measured in the billions of dollars each year.[22] Retail security measures add to the already high cost of this crime, all of which is passed on to the consumer. Shoplifting incidents have increased dramatically in the past 20 years, and retailers now expect an annual increase of from 10 to 15 percent. Some studies estimate that about one in every nine shoppers steals from department stores. Moreover, the increasingly popular discount stores, such as K-Mart, Wal-Mart, and Target, have a minimum of sales help and depend on highly visible merchandise displays to attract purchasers, all of which makes them particularly vulnerable to shoplifters.

The Shoplifter.   The classic study of shoplifting was conducted by Mary Owen Cameron.[23] In her pioneering effort, Cameron found that about 10 percent of all shoplifters were professionals who derived the majority of their income from shoplifting. Sometimes called **boosters** or **heels,** professional shoplifters intend to resell stolen merchandise to pawnshops or fences, usually at half the original price.[24]

Cameron found that the majority of shoplifters are amateur pilferers, called **snitches** in thieves' argot. Snitches are usually respectable persons who do not conceive of themselves as thieves but are systematic shoplifters who steal merchandise for their own use. They are not simply taken by an uncontrollable urge to take something that attracts them; they come equipped to steal. Usually, snitches who are arrested have never been apprehended before. For the most part, they are people who lack the kinds of criminal experience that suggest extensive association with a criminal subculture.

Criminologists view shoplifters as people who are likely to reform if apprehended. Mary Owen Cameron reasoned that because snitches are not part of a criminal subculture and do not think of themselves as criminals, they are deterred by an initial contact with the law. Getting arrested has a traumatic effect on them, and they will not risk a second offense.[25] While this argument seems plausible, some criminologists argue that apprehension may have a labeling effect that inhibits deterrence and results in repeated offending. However, Lloyd Klemke found that youths who had been previously apprehended for shoplifting were unlikely to be deterred by official processing.[26]

Shoplifting continues to be a serious problem. FBI data indicate that shoplifting comprises about 16 percent of all larceny cases—over 1 million criminal acts; reported shoplifting has increased 30 percent since 1985. Many stores have installed elaborate security devices to combat shoplifting, but the growth of this type of larceny has continued.

Controlling Shoplifting.   One major problem associated with combating shoplifting is that many customers who observe pilferage are reluctant to report it to security agents. Store employees themselves are often reluctant to get involved in apprehending a shoplifter. For example, in a controlled experiment, Donald Hartmann and his associates found that customers observed only 28 percent of staged shoplifting incidents that had been designed to get their attention.[27] Furthermore, only 28 percent of people who said they had observed an incident reported it to store employees. In another controlled experiment using staged shoplifting incidents, Erhard Blankenburg found that less than 10 percent of shoplifting was detected by store employees and that customers appeared unwilling to report even serious cases.[28] Even in stores with an announced policy of full reporting and prosecution, only 70 percent of the shoplifting detected by employees was actually reported to managers, and only 5 percent was prosecuted. According to Blankenburg, foreigners, adults, and blue-collar workers were disproportionately represented among those officially punished. It is also likely that a store owner's decision to prosecute shoplifters will be based on the value of the goods stolen, the nature of the goods stolen, and the manner in which the theft was realized. For example, shoplifters who planned their crime by using a concealed apparatus, such as a bag pinned to the inside of their clothing, were more apt to be prosecuted than those who had impulsively put merchandise into their pockets.[29]

To aid in the arrest of shoplifters, a number of states have passed merchant privilege laws that are designed to protect retailers and their employers from litigation stemming from improper or false arrests of suspected shoplifters.[30] These laws protect but do not immunize merchants from lawsuits. They require that arrests be made on reasonable grounds or probable cause, detention be of short duration, and store employees or security guards conduct themselves in a reasonable fashion.

Private Justice.   Efforts to control the spread of shoplifting have prompted some commercial enterprises to establish highly sophisticated loss prevention units to combat would-be criminals. Melissa Davis, Richard Lundman, and Ramiro Martinez, Jr., investigated the loss prevention unit in a branch store of a large national retail chain.[31] They uncovered a private justice system that works parallel to but independent from the public justice system. Private security officers have many law enforcement powers also granted to municipal police officers, including arrest of suspects and search and seizure. A merchant's privilege statute immunized the store police from any criminal or civil liability charges stemming from false arrest.

Private police decision making seemed to be influenced by state law allowing stores to recover civil damages from shoplifters. In the 28 states that have implemented this type of legislation, shoplifters may be required to compensate store owners for the value of the goods they attempted to steal, costs incurred because of their illegal acts, and punitive damages. Davis, Lundman, and Martinez found that store detectives use the civil damage route to defray the costs of their operation. The researchers found that the availability of civil damages had important effects on decision making. Store owners go after the more affluent shoplifters for civil recovery and ship the poor to the public criminal justice system for criminal punishment.[32]

Bad Checks

Another form of theft is the cashing of a bank check, to obtain money or property, that is knowingly and intentionally drawn on a nonexistent or underfunded bank account. In general, for a person to be guilty of passing a bad check, the bank the check is drawn on must refuse payment, and the check casher must fail to make the check good within ten days after finding out the check was not honored.

The best-known study of check forgers was conducted by Edwin Lemert.[33] Lemert found that the majority of check forgers—he calls them **naive check forgers**—are amateurs who do not believe their actions will hurt anyone. Most naive check forgers come from middle-class backgrounds and have little identification with a criminal subculture. They cash bad checks because of a financial crisis that demands an immediate resolution—perhaps they have lost money at the horse track and have some pressing bills to pay. Lemert refers to this condition as **closure.** Naive check forgers are often socially isolated people who have been unsuccessful in their personal relationships. They are risk-prone when faced with a situation that is unusually stressful for them. The willingness of stores and other commercial establishments to cash checks with a minimum of fuss to promote business encourages the check forger to risk committing a criminal act.

Not all check forgers are amateurs. Lemert found that a few professionals—whom he calls **systematic forgers**—make a substantial living by passing bad checks. However, professionals constitute a relatively small segment of the total population of check forgers. It is difficult to estimate the number of check forgeries committed each year or the amounts involved. Stores and banks may choose not to press charges, since the effort to collect the money due them is often not worth their while. It is also difficult to separate the true check forger from the neglectful shopper.

Credit Card Theft

The use of stolen credit cards has become a major problem in U.S. society. It has been estimated that a billion-dollar loss through fraud has been experienced by credit card companies. In New York City alone, police officials estimate that 5,000 credit cards are stolen each month.[34]

Most credit card abuse is the work of amateurs who acquire stolen cards through theft or mugging and then use them for two or three days. However, professional credit card rings may be getting into the act. For example, in Los Angeles, members of a credit card gang got jobs as clerks in several stores, where they collected the names and credit card numbers of customers. Gang members bought plain plastic cards and had the names and numbers of the customers embossed on them. The gang created a fictitious wholesale jewelry company and applied for and received authorization to accept credit cards from the customers. The thieves then used the phony cards to charge nonexistent jewelry purchases on the accounts of the people whose names and card numbers they had collected. The banks that issued the original cards honored over $200,000 in payments before the thieves withdrew the money from their business account and left town.[35] To combat losses from credit card theft, Congress passed a law in 1971 limiting a person's liability to $50 per stolen card. Similarly, some states, such as California, have passed specific statutes making it a misdemeanor to obtain property or services by means of cards that have been stolen, forged, canceled, or revoked, or whose use is for any reason unauthorized.[36]

Auto Theft

Motor vehicle theft is another common larceny offense. Yet because of its frequency and seriousness it is treated as a separate category in the UCR. The FBI recorded 1.6 million auto thefts in 1992, accounting for a total loss of almost $8 billion; the number of auto thefts, which has increased sharply over the past decade, was up another 12 percent between 1988 and 1992.

UCR projections on auto theft are actually quite similar to the projections of the National Crime Victim Survey (1.9 million thefts in 1992). The similarity of data between these sources occurs because, since almost every state jurisdiction requires owners to insure their vehicles, auto theft is one of the most highly reported of all major crimes (75 percent of all auto thefts are reported to police).

Auto theft is usually considered the pastime of relatively affluent, white, middle-class teenagers looking for excitement through **joyriding.**[37] This belief is supported by the fact that 41 percent of people arrested for auto theft in 1992 were under 18 and about 60 percent were 21 or younger.

A number of attempts have been made to categorize the various forms of auto theft. Typically, distinctions are made between theft for temporary personal use, for resale, and for chopping or stripping cars for parts. One of the most detailed of these typologies was developed by Charles McCaghy and his associates after examining data from police and court files in several state jurisdictions.[38] The researchers uncovered five categories of auto theft transactions:

1. *Joyriding*—Many car thefts are motivated by teenagers' desire to acquire the power, prestige, sexual potency, and recognition associated with an automobile. Joyriders do not steal cars for profit or gain but to experience, even briefly, the benefits associated with owning an automobile.

2. *Short-term transportation*—Auto theft for short-term transportation is most similar to joyriding. It involves the theft of a car simply to go from one place to another. In more serious cases, the thief may drive to another city or state and then steal another car to continue the journey.

3. *Long-term transportation*—Thieves who steal cars for long-term transportation intend to keep the cars for their personal use. Usually older than joyriders and from a lower-class background, these auto thieves may repaint and otherwise disguise cars to avoid detection.

4. *Profit*—Auto theft for profit is, of course, motivated by hope for monetary gain. At one extreme

Arrest records show that most auto thieves are young white males.

are highly organized professionals who resell expensive cars after altering their identification numbers and falsifying their registration papers. At the other end of the scale are amateur auto strippers who steal batteries, tires, and wheel covers to sell them or reequip their own cars.

5. *Commission of another crime*—A small portion of auto thieves steal cars to use in other crimes, such as robberies and thefts. This type of auto thief desires both mobility and anonymity.

Carjacking.

You may have read about gunmen approaching a car and forcing the owner to give up the keys; in some cases, people have been killed when they reacted too slowly. This type of auto theft has become so common that it has its own name, **carjacking**.[39]

Carjacking is legally a type of robbery because it involves force to steal (see Chapter 11). It accounts for about 2 percent of all car thefts, or 35,000 per year.

Both the victims and offenders in carjackings tend to be young black men; about half of the carjackings were committed by gangs or groups. These crimes are most likely to occur in the evening, in the central city, in an open area or parking garage.

Because of carjacking's violent nature, about 24 percent of the victims suffered injuries, about 4 percent of which were considered serious (gun shots, knifings, internal injuries, broken bones and teeth). As Figure 12.1 shows, about 60 percent of the offenders in carjackings carried handguns.

Combating Auto Theft.

Because of its commonality and high loss potential, auto theft has been a target of situational crime prevention efforts.[40] In a thorough analysis, Ronald Clarke and Patricia Harris have outlined some of the methods being tried to combat auto theft. One approach has been to increase the risks of apprehension. Information hot lines offer rewards for information leading to the arrest of car thieves. A Michigan-based program, Operation HEAT (Help Eliminate Auto Theft), is credited with recovering over 900 vehicles with a value of $11 million and resulting in the arrest of 647 people. Another approach has been to place fluorescent decals on windows that indicate that the car is never used between 1 and 5 A.M.; if police spot a car with the decal being operated during this period, they know it is stolen. Cars have also been equipped with radio transmitters. The LOJACK system involves a tracking device installed in the car that gives off a signal enabling the police to pinpoint its location.

Other prevention efforts involve making it more difficult to steal cars. Publicity campaigns have been directed at encouraging people to lock their cars. Parking lots

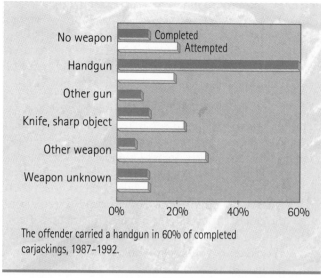

The offender carried a handgun in 60% of completed carjackings, 1987–1992.

FIGURE 12.1 **Use of Weapons in Carjackings, 1987–1992**

SOURCE: Michael Rand, *Carjacking* (Washington, D.C.: Bureau of Justice Statistics, 1994), p. 1.

have been equipped with theft-deterring closed-circuit TV cameras and barriers. Manufacturers have installed more sophisticated steering-column locking devices and other security systems that make theft harder.

So far, efforts to deter or prevent auto theft have suffered from a displacement effect: car protection devices have increased risks for other motorists. Considering the gravity of this offense, it is essential that further research be conducted to identify effective methods of auto theft prevention.

False Pretenses or Fraud

The crime of **false pretenses,** or **fraud,** involves a wrongdoer's misrepresenting a fact to cause a victim to willingly give his or her property to the wrongdoer, who keeps it.[41] The definition of false pretenses was created by the English Parliament in 1757 to cover an area of law left untouched by larceny statutes. The first false pretenses law punished people who "knowingly and designedly by false pretense or pretenses, [obtained] from any person or persons, money, goods, wares or merchandise with intent to cheat or defraud any person or persons of the same."[42] False pretenses differs from traditional larceny because the victims willingly give their possessions to the offender, and the crime does not, as does larceny, involve a "trespass in the taking." An example of false pretenses would be an unscrupulous merchant selling someone a chair by claiming it was an antique but knowing all the while that it was a cheap copy. Another example would be a phony healer selling a victim a bottle of colored sugar water as an "elixir" that would cure a disease. There are many different types of fraud, including confidence games.

Confidence Games.

Confidence games are run by swindlers whose goal is to separate a victim (or sucker) from his or her hard-earned money. These "con games" usually involve getting a "mark" interested in some get-rich-quick scheme, which may have illegal overtones. The criminal's hope is that when victims lose their money, they will either be too embarrassed or too afraid to call the police. There are hundreds of varieties of con games. The most common is called the **pigeon drop.**[43] Here, a package or wallet containing money is "found" by a con man or woman. A passing victim is stopped and asked for advice about what to do, since no identification can be found. Another "stranger," who is part of the con, approaches and enters the discussion. The three decide to split the money; but first, to make sure everything is legal, one of the swindlers goes off to consult a lawyer. Upon returning, he or she says that the lawyer claims the money can be split up; first, however, each party must prove he or she has the means to reimburse the original owner, should one show up. The victim then is asked to give some good-faith money for the lawyer to hold. When the victim goes to the lawyer's office to pick up a share of the loot, he or she finds the address bogus and the money gone.

With the growth of direct-mail marketing and "900" telephone numbers that charge callers over $2.50 per minute for conversations with what are promised to be beautiful and willing sex partners, a flood of new confidence games may be about to descend on the U.S. public. In all, about 424,000 people were arrested for fraud in 1992, most likely a very small percentage of all swindlers, scam artists, and frauds.

Embezzlement

The crime of embezzlement was observed in early Greek culture when, in his writings, Aristotle alluded to theft by road commissioners and other government officials.[44] It was first codified into the law by the English Parliament during the sixteenth century to fill a gap in the larceny law.[45] Until then, to be guilty of theft, a person had to take goods from the physical possession of another (trespass in the taking). However, as explained earlier, this definition did not cover instances in which one person trusted another and willfully gave that person temporary custody of his or her property. For exam-

ple, in everyday commerce, store clerks, bank tellers, brokers, and merchants gain lawful possession but not legal ownership of other people's money. Embezzlement occurs when someone who is so trusted with property fraudulently converts it—that is, keeps it for his or her own use or the use of others. It can be distinguished from fraud on the basis of when the criminal intent was formed.

Most U.S. courts require that a serious breach of trust must have occurred before a person can be convicted of embezzlement. The mere act of moving property without the owner's consent, or damaging it or using it, is not considered embezzlement. However, using it up, selling it, pledging it, giving it away, or holding it against the owner's will is held to be embezzlement.[46]

Although it is impossible to know how many embezzlement incidents occur annually, the FBI found that only 13,700 people were arrested for embezzlement in 1992—probably an extremely small percentage of all embezzlers. However, the number of people arrested for embezzlement has increased 52 percent since 1983, indicating that either (1) more employees are willing to steal from their employers, (2) more employers are willing to report instances of embezzlement, or (3) law enforcement officials are more willing to prosecute embezzlers.

≡ Burglary

At common law, the crime of burglary is defined as "the breaking and entering of a dwelling house of another in the nighttime with the intent to commit a felony within."[47] Burglary is considered a much more serious crime than larceny/theft, since it often involves entering another's home, a situation in which the threat of harm to occupants is great. Even though at the time of the burglary the home may be unoccupied, the potential for harm to the occupants is so significant that most state jurisdictions punish burglary as a felony. The legal definition of burglary has undergone considerable change since its common-law origins. When first created by English judges during the late Middle Ages, laws against burglary were designed to protect people whose home might be set upon by wandering criminals. Including the phrase "breaking and entering" in the definition protected people from unwarranted intrusions; if an invited guest stole something, it would not be considered a burglary. Similarly, the requirement that the crime be committed at nighttime was added because evening was considered the time when honest people might fall prey to criminals.[48] In more recent times, state jurisdictions have changed the legal requirements of burglary, and most have discarded the necessity of forced entry. Many now protect all structures and not just dwelling houses. A majority of states have removed the nighttime element from burglary definitions as well. It is quite common for states to enact laws creating different degrees of burglary. In this instance, the more serious and heavily punished crimes involve a nighttime forced entry into the home; the least serious involve a daytime entry into a nonresidential structure by an unarmed offender. Several gradations of the offense may be found between these extremes.

The Extent of Burglary

The FBI's definition of burglary is not restricted to burglary from a person's home; it includes any unlawful entry of a structure to commit theft or felony. Burglary is further categorized into three subclasses: forcible entry, unlawful entry where no force is used, and attempted forcible entry. According to the UCR, 2.9 million burglaries occurred in 1992. Burglary is one of the few crimes that has not increased substantially during the past ten years; the number of burglaries has dropped by almost 1 million since their peak in 1981. Most burglaries (66 percent) were of residences; the remainder were business-related. Burglary victims suffer annual losses of over $3.8 billion.

The NVCS reports that about 4.7 million burglaries occurred in 1992. The difference between the UCR and NCVS is explained by the fact that little more than half of all burglary victims reported the incident to police. However, similar to the trends found in the UCR, the number of households experiencing burglaries has declined from 7.4 percent in 1981 to about 4.2 percent today.

According to the NCVS, those most likely to be burglarized are relative poor Hispanic and African-American families (annual income under $7,500). Owner-occupied and single-family residences had lower burglary rates than renter-occupied and multiple dwellings.

Careers in Burglary

Great variety exists within the ranks of burglars. Many are crude thieves who, with little finesse, will smash a window and enter a vacant home or structure with minimal preparation. However, because it involves planning, risk, and skill, burglary has been a crime long associated with professional thieves. To become a skilled practitioner of burglary, the would-be burglar must learn the craft at the side of an experienced burglar. For example, Francis Hoheimer, an experienced professional burglar, has described his education in the craft of burglary by Oklahoma Smith when the two were serving time in the Illinois State Penitentiary. Among Smith's recommendations are:

> Never wear deodorant or shaving lotion; the strange scent might wake someone up. The more people there are in a house, the safer you are. If someone hears you moving around, they will think it's someone else. . . . If they call, answer in a muffled sleepy voice. . . . Never be afraid of dogs, they can sense fear. Most dogs are friendly, snap your finger, they come right to you. . . [49]

When he was released from prison, Hoheimer formed a criminal gang that specialized in burglary. Hoheimer and his associates would check into a motel near the home of their intended victim. Registering under assumed names and giving false addresses, they would correctly describe their cars but mix up license plate numbers. Checking out of the motel before the burglary, they would enter the victim's home between two and five o'clock in the morning. If the owners were present, they would be tied, hand and foot, with surgical tape. Hoheimer and his gang concentrated on taking jewelry, furs, and money. The victims would be asked for the location of wall safes and valuables. While on the job, Hoheimer carried a handgun as well as an attaché case containing such items as ski masks, work gloves, pen-type flashlights, a propane tank with a torch head, a pry bar, a screwdriver, a pair of lock pliers, a glass cutter, and six rolls of surgical tape. Despite his elaborate preparations, Hoheimer spent many years confined for his acts.

The Good Burglar. Neal Shover has studied the careers of professional burglars and uncovered the existence of a particularly successful type—the **good burglar**.[50] This is a characterization applied by professional burglars to colleagues who have distinguished themselves as burglars. Characteristics of the good burglar include: (1) technical competence, (2) maintenance of personal integrity, (3) specialization in burglary, (4) financial success at crime, and (5) ability to avoid prison sentences. Shover found that to receive recognition as good burglars, novices must develop four key requirements of the trade. First, they must learn the many skills needed to commit lucrative burglaries. This process may include learning such techniques as how to gain entry into homes and apartment houses, select targets with high potential payoffs, choose items with a high resale value, properly open safes without damaging their contents, and use the proper equipment, including cutting torches, electric saws, explosives, and metal bars. Second, the good burglar must be able to team up to form a criminal gang. Choosing trustworthy companions is essential if the obstacles to completing a successful

Most burglaries are committed by occasional criminals looking for a "quick score." Professional burglars, who commit fewer but more lucrative crimes, are more likely to use planning and stealth. A shopkeeper cleans up after his store had been ransacked and looted by a group of amateur burglars.

job—police, alarms, secure safes—are to be overcome. Third, the good burglar must have inside information. Without knowledge of what awaits them inside, burglars can spend a tremendous amount of time and effort on empty safes and jewelry boxes. Finally, the good burglar must cultivate fences or buyers for stolen wares. Once the burglar gains access to people who buy and sell stolen goods, he or she must also learn how to successfully sell these goods for a reasonable profit.

Shover finds that the process of becoming a professional burglar is similar to the process Sutherland described in his theory of differential association. According to Shover, a person becomes a good burglar through learning the techniques of the trade from older, more experienced burglars. During this process, the older burglar teaches the novice how to handle such requirements of the trade as dealing with defense attorneys, bail bond agents, and other agents of the justice system. Consequently, the opportunity to become a

good burglar is not open to everyone. Apprentices must be known to have the appropriate character before they are taken under the wing of the "old pro." Usually, the opportunity to learn burglary comes as a reward for being a highly respected juvenile gang member; from knowing someone in the neighborhood who has made a living at burglary; or, more often, from having built a reputation for being solid while serving time in prison.

The Burglary "Career Ladder"

Paul Cromwell, James Olson, and D'Aunn Wester Avary, who interviewed 30 active burglars in Texas, also found that burglars go through stages of career development. They begin as young novices who learn the trade from older more experienced burglars, frequently siblings or relatives. Novices will continue to get this tutoring as long as they can develop their own markets (fences) for stolen goods. After their education is over, novices enter the journeyman stage, characterized by forays in search of lucrative targets and careful planning; they develop reputations as experienced reliable criminals. Finally, they become professional burglars when they have developed advanced skills and organizational abilities that give them the highest esteem among their peers; they plan and execute their crimes after careful deliberation.

The Texas burglars also displayed evidence of rational decision making. Most seemed to carefully evaluate potential costs and benefits before deciding to commit crime. There is evidence that burglars follow this pattern in their choice of burglary sites. Burglars show preference for corner houses because they are easily observed and offer the maximum number of escape routes.[51] They look for houses that show evidence of long-term care and wealth. Though people may erect fences and other barriers to deter burglars, these devices may actually attract crime because they are viewed as protecting something worth stealing: if there was nothing valuable inside, why go through so much trouble to secure the premises?[52]

Cromwell, Olson, and Avary also found that many burglars had serious drug habits and that their criminal activity was in part aimed at supporting their substance abuse. The following Close-Up describes the activities of "professional" and "occasional" female burglars.

≡ Arson

Arson is the willful and malicious burning of a home, public building, vehicle, or commercial building. The

FBI found that 102,009 arsons were committed in 1992. Arson is a young man's crime. Of the 15,000 people arrested, about 42 percent were males 18 and under. The percentage of young teens arrested for the crime of arson was higher in 1992 than it was for any other Type I crime and most Type II crimes (except vandalism, running away, and curfew violations). Also, arson is primarily a white (74 percent), male (86 percent) crime.

The Cause of Arson

There are several motives for arson. Wayne Wooden studied juvenile arsonists and found that they can be classified in one of four categories:

1. *The "Playing with Matches" Fire Setter*—This is the youngest fire starter, usually between the ages of four and nine, who set fires because parents are careless with matches and lighters. Proper instruction on fire safety can help prevent fires set by these young children.
2. *The "Crying for Help" Fire Setter*—This type of fire setter is a seven- to thirteen-year-old who turns to fire to reduce stress. The source of the stress is family conflict, divorce, death, or abuse. These youngsters have difficulty expressing their feelings of sorrow, rage, or anger and turn to fire as a means of relieving stress or getting back at their antagonists.
3. *The "Delinquent" Fire Setter*—Some youths set fires to school property or surrounding areas to retaliate for some slight experienced at school. These kids may break into the school to vandalize property with friends and later set a fire to cover up their activities.
4. *The "Severely Disturbed" Fire Setter*—This youngster is obsessed with fires and often dreams about them in "vibrant colors." This is the most disturbed type of juvenile fire setter and the one most likely to set numerous fires with the potential for death and damage.[53]

Adult arson may also be a function of severe emotional turmoil. Some psychologists view fire starting as a function of a disturbed personality; arson, therefore, should be viewed as a mental health problem and not a criminal act.[54]

It is alleged that arsonists often experience sexual pleasure from starting fires and then observing their destructive effects. While some arsonists may be aroused sexually by their activities, there is little evidence that most arsonists are psychosexually motivated.[55] It is equally likely that fires are started by angry people looking for revenge against property owners or by teenagers out to vandalize property. Other arsons are set by "professional" arsonists who engage in **arson for profit.** Another form is **arson fraud,** which involves a business owner burning his or her property, or hiring someone to do it, to escape financial problems.[56] Over the years, investigators have found that businesspeople are willing to become involved in arson to collect fire insurance or for various other reasons, including but not limited to:

- Obtaining money during a period of financial crisis
- Getting rid of outdated or slow-moving inventory
- Destroying outmoded machines and technology
- Paying off legal and illegal debt
- Relocating or remodeling a business; for example, when a theme restaurant has not been accepted by customers
- Taking advantage of government funds available for redevelopment
- Applying for government building money, pocketing it without making repairs, and then claiming that fire destroyed the "rehabilitated" building
- Planning bankruptcies to eliminate debts, after the merchandise supposedly destroyed was secretly sold before the fire
- Eliminating business competition by burning out rivals
- Employing extortion schemes that demand that victims pay up or the rest of their holdings will be burned
- Solving labor-management problems; arson may be committed by a disgruntled employee
- Concealing another crime, such as embezzlement

Some recent technological advances may help prove that many alleged arsons were actually accidental fires. There is now evidence of an effect called **flashover** in which during the course of an ordinary fire, heat and gas at the ceiling of a room can reach 2,000 degrees. This causes clothes and furniture to burst into flame, duplicating the effects of arsonists' gasoline or explosives. It is possible that many suspected arsons are actually the result of flashover.[57]

The Female Burglar

Despite the interest shown in both the careers of residential burglars and with the female offender in general, relatively little is known about *female burglars*. Though most burglars apprehended by police are male, about 9 percent, or 33,000, are females.

To address this issue, Scott Decker, Richard Wright, Allison Redfern Rooney, and Dietrich Smith interviewed 18 females, ranging in age from 15 to 51, who were actively engaged in residential burglary. For comparison, 87 male burglars were also interviewed.

Decker and his associates found that female burglars had offending patterns quite similar to the males. In addition to burglary, both groups engaged in other thefts, such as shoplifting, and assault. The major difference was that male burglars also engaged in auto theft, while females shunned this form of larceny.

Another difference was that while females always worked with a partner, about 39 percent of the males said they seldom worked with others. Males also began their offending careers at an earlier age than females. About half of all females had been involved in less than 20 burglaries, while only 28 percent of males reported as few as 20 lifetime burglaries. Considering they start earlier and commit more

Dietrich Smith, Allison Redfern Rooney, Richard Wright, and Scott Decker conducted interviews with female burglars.

crimes, it is not surprising that males had a much greater chance of doing time (26 percent) than females (6 percent).

There were also many similarities between the two groups. A majority of both male and female burglars reported substance abuse problems, including cocaine, heroin, and marijuana use. About 47 percent of the females considered themselves addicts, and 72 percent said they drank alcohol before they committed crimes; males reported less addiction, drug use, and alcohol abuse than females.

Decker and his associates found that the female burglars could be divided into two groups, "accomplices" and "partners." Accomplices committed burglaries because they were caught up in circumstances beyond their control. They felt compelled or pressured to commit crimes because of a relationship with another, more dominant person, typically a boyfriend or husband. Accomplices got into crime because they lacked legitimate employment, were drug dependent, or had alcohol problems. Accomplices exercised little control over their crimes and relied on others for any planning and tactics. They commonly acted as a lookout or driver.

In contrast, partners, who made up two-thirds of the sample, were involved in the planning and carrying out of crimes because they enjoyed both the reward and the excitement of burglary. In planning their crimes, partners displayed many of the characteristics of the rational criminal: They helped spot targets and planned entries. As one female burglar stated:

That's one reason why we got so many youngsters in jail today. I see this, so let's go make a hit.

No, no, no. If they see this and it looks good, then it's going to be there for a while. So the point is, you have to case it and make sure you know everything. I want to know what time you go to work, the time the children go to school. I know there's no one coming home for lunch. So plan it with somebody else. We'll take the new dishwasher, washing machine, and this other stuff. We just put it in the truck. Do you know when people rent a truck, nobody ever pays that any attention? They think you're moving [but] only if you rent a truck. Now if you bring it out of there and put it in the car, that's a horse of another color.

Once the burglary began, partners carried out all forms of crime-related tasks, including gaining entry, searching the house, carrying loot outside, and disposing of the stolen merchandise.

In conclusion, most female burglars maintain roles and identities quite similar to their male colleagues. While some gender-based differences are evident (males more often work alone; women almost always had an accomplice), both male and female burglars actively plan crimes for many of the same reasons.

The Decker research is important because it shows that for the major-ity of both male and female burglars, criminal careers may be a function of economic need and role equality, a finding that supports a feminist view of crime. It also illustrates that repeat criminals use rational choice in planning their activities.

Discussion Questions

1. Does the fact that so many burglars, both male and female, drink and abuse drugs conflict with a rational choice approach to crime?

2. Why are male burglars more likely to be car thieves than females? Decker and his associates speculate that one reason may be a "strong cultural tradition linking masculinity to driving and car ownership." Can this be so?

SOURCE: Scott Decker, Richard Wright, Allison Redfern, and Dietrich Smith, "A Woman's Place Is in the Home: Females and Residential Burglary," *Justice Quarterly* 10 (1993): 143–63.

☰ Summary

Economic crimes are designed to bring financial reward to the offender. The majority of economic crimes are committed by opportunistic amateurs. However, economic crime has also attracted professional criminals. Professionals earn the bulk of their income from crime, view themselves as criminals, and possess skills that aid them in their law breaking. Edwin Sutherland's classic book *The Professional Thief* is perhaps the most famous portrayal of professional crime. According to Sutherland and his informant, Chic Conwell, professionals live by their wits and never resort to violence. A good example of the professional criminal is the fence who buys and sells stolen merchandise. There are also occasional thieves whose skill level and commitment fall below the professional level.

Common theft offenses include larceny, embezzlement, fraud, and burglary. These are common-law crimes, created by English judges to meet social needs. Larceny involves taking the legal possessions of another. Petty larceny is theft of amounts typically under $100; grand larceny, of amounts usually over $100. The crime of false pretenses, or fraud, is similar to larceny because it involves the theft of goods or money, but it differs because the criminal tricks victims into voluntarily giving up their possessions. Embezzlement is another larceny crime. It involves people taking something that was temporarily entrusted to them, such as bank tellers taking money out of the cash drawer and keeping it for themselves. Most states have codified these common-law crimes in their legal codes. New larceny crimes have also been defined to keep abreast of changing social conditions: passing bad checks, stealing or illegally using credit cards, shoplifting, stealing autos. Burglary, a more serious theft offense, was defined in the common law as the "breaking and entering of a dwelling house of another in the nighttime with the intent to commit a felony within."

Today, most states have modified their definitions of burglary to include theft from any structure at any time of day. Because burglary involves planning and risk, it attracts professional thieves. The most competent are known as good burglars. Good burglars have technical competence and personal integrity, specialize in burglary, are financially successful, and avoid prison sentences. Arson is another serious property crime. Though most arsonists are teenage vandals, there are professional arsonists who specialize in burning commercial buildings for profit.

☰ KEY TERMS

fence 592
street crimes 600
burglary 587
flash houses
occasional criminals
professional criminals
economic crimes 591
situational inducement
constructive possession 588
boosters
heels
snitches
naive check forgers

closure
systematic forgers
joyriding
carjacking
false pretenses 592
fraud 592
confidence games
pigeon drop
good burglar
arson for profit
arson fraud
flashover

☰ NOTES

1. Andrew McCall, *The Medieval Underworld* (London: Hamish Hamilton, 1979), p. 86.
2. Ibid., p. 104.
3. J. J. Tobias, *Crime and Police in England, 1700–1900* (London: Gill and Macmillan, 1979).
4. Ibid., p. 9.
5. Marilyn Walsh, *The Fence,* (Westport, Conn.: Greenwood Press, 1977), pp. 18–25.
6. John Hepburn, "Occasional Criminals," in *Major Forms of Crime,* ed. Robert Meier (Beverly Hills, Sage, 1984), pp. 73–94.
7. James Inciardi, "Professional Crime," in *Major Forms of Crime,* ed. Robert Meier (Beverly Hills: Sage, 1984), p. 223.
8. Harry King and William Chambliss, *Box Man: A Professional Thief's Journal* (New York: Harper & Row, 1972), p. 24.
9. Edwin Sutherland, "White-Collar Criminality," *American Sociological Review* 5 (1940): 2–10.
10. Gilbert Geis, "Avocational Crime," in *Handbook of Criminology,* ed. D. Glazer (Chicago: Rand McNally, 1974), p. 284.
11. Edwin Sutherland and Chic Conwell, *The Professional Thief* (Chicago: University of Chicago Press, 1937).
12. Ibid., pp. 197–98.
13. Ibid., p. 212.
14. See, for example, Edwin Lemert, "The Behavior of the Systematic Check Forger," *Social Problems* 6 (1958): 141–48.
15. Cited in Walsh, *The Fence,* p. 1.
16. Carl Klockars, *The Professional Fence* (New York: Free Press, 1976); Darrell Steffensmeier, *The Fence: In the Shadow of Two Worlds* (Totowa, N.J.: Rowman and Littlefield, 1986); Walsh, *The Fence,* pp. 25–28.
17. Walsh, *The Fence,* p. 34.
18. Paul Cromwell, James Olson, and D'Aunn Avary, "Who Buys Stolen Property? A New Look at Criminal Receiving,"

Journal of Crime and Justice 16 (1993): 75–95.

19. This section depends heavily on a classic book: Wayne La Fave and Austin Scott, *Handbook on Criminal Law* (St. Paul: West Publishing, 1972).

20. Ibid., p. 622.

21. FBI, *Crime in the United States, 1992* (Washington, D.C.: U.S. Government Printing Office, 1993), p. 45.

22. D. Hartmann, D. Gelfand, B. Page, and P. Walder, "Rates of Bystander Observation and Reporting of Contrived Shoplifting Incidents," *Criminology* 10 (1972): 248.

23. Mary Owen Cameron, *The Booster and the Snitch* (New York: Free Press, 1964).

24. Ibid., p. 57.

25. Lawrence Cohen and Rodney Stark, "Discriminatory Labeling and the Five-Finger Discount: An Empirical Analysis of Differential Shoplifting Dispositions," *Journal of Research on Crime and Delinquency* 11 (1974): 25–35.

26. Lloyd Klemke, "Does Apprehension for Shoplifting Amplify or Terminate Shoplifting Activity?" *Law and Society Review* 12 (1978): 390–403.

27. Hartmann, et al., "Rates of Bystander Observation and Reporting," p. 267.

28. Erhard Blankenburg, "The Selectivity of Legal Sanctions: An Empirical Investigation of Shoplifting," *Law and Society Review* 11 (1976): 109–29.

29. Michael Hindelang, "Decisions of Shoplifting Victims to Invoke the Criminal Justice Process," *Social Problems* 21 (1974): 580–95.

30. George Keckeisen, *Retail Security versus the Shoplifter* (Springfield, Ill.: Charles Thomas, 1993), pp. 31–32.

31. Melissa Davis, Richard Lundman, and Ramiro Martinez, "Private Corporate Justice: Store Police, Shoplifters, and Civil Recovery," *Social Problems* 38 (1991): 395–408.

32. Ibid., pp. 405–406.

33. Edwin Lemert, "An Isolation and Closure Theory of Naive Check Forgery," *Journal of Criminal Law, Criminology and Police Science* 44 (1953): 297–98.

34. "Credit Card Fraud Toll 1 Billion," *Omaha World Herald*, 16 March 1982, p. 1.

35. Ibid.

36. La Fave and Scott, *Handbook on Criminal Law*, p. 672.

37. Donald Gibbons, *Society, Crime and Criminal Careers* (Englewood Cliffs, N.J.: Prentice-Hall, 1977), p. 310.

38. Charles McCaghy, Peggy Giordano, and Trudy Knicely Henson, "Auto Theft," *Criminology* 15 (1977): 367–81.

39. Michael Rand, *Carjacking* (Washington, D.C.: Bureau of Justice Statistics, 1994), p. 1.

40. Ronald Clarke and Patricia Harris, "Auto Theft and Its Prevention," in *Crime and Justice, An Annual Review*, ed. N. Morris and M. Tonry (Chicago: Chicago University Press, in press).

41. La Fave and Scott, *Handbook on Criminal Law*, p. 655.

42. 30 Geo. III, C.24 (1975).

43. As described in Charles McCaghy, *Deviant Behavior* (New York: Macmillan, 1976), pp. 230–31.

44. Jerome Hall, *Theft, Law and Society* (Indianapolis: Bobbs-Merrill, 1952), p. 36.

45. La Fave and Scott, *Handbook on Criminal Law*, p. 644.

46. Ibid., p. 649.

47. La Fave and Scott, *Handbook on Criminal Law*, p. 708.

48. E. Blackstone, *Commentaries on the Laws of England* (London: 1769), p. 224.

49. Frank Hoheimer, *The Home Invaders: Confessions of a Cat Burglar* (Chicago: Chicago Review, 1975).

50. See, generally, Neal Shover, "Structures and Careers in Burglary," *Journal of Criminal Law, Criminology and Police Science* 63 (1972): 540–49.

51. Paul Cromwell, James Olson, and D'Aunn Wester Avary, *Breaking and Entering: An Ethnographic Analysis of Burglary* (Newbury Park, Calif.: Sage, 1991), pp. 48–51.

52. See, M. Taylor and C. Nee, "The Role of Cues in Simulated Residential Burglary: A Preliminary Investigation," *British Journal of Criminology* 28 (1988): 398–401; Julia MacDonald and Robert Gifford, "Territorial Cues and Defensible Space Theory: The Burglar's Point of View" *Journal of Environmental Psychology* 9 (1989): 193–205.

53. Wayne Wooden, "Juvenile Firesetters in Cross-Cultural Perspective: How Should Society Respond," in *Official Responses to Problem Juvenile: Some International Reflections*, ed. James Hackler (Onati, Spain: Onati Publications, 1991), pp. 339–48.

54. Nancy Webb, George Sakheim, Luz Towns-Miranda, and Charles Wagner, "Collaborative Treatment of Juvenile Firestarters: Assessment and Outreach," *American Journal of Orthopsychiatry* 60 (1990): 305–10.

55. Vernon Quinsey, Terry Chaplin, and Douglas Unfold, "Arsonists and Sexual Arousal to Fire Setting: Correlations Unsupported," *Journal of Behavior Therapy and Experimental Psychiatry* 20 (1989): 203–9.

56. Leigh Edward Somers, *Economic Crimes* (New York: Clark Boardman, 1984), pp. 158–68.

57. Michael Rogers, "The Fire Next Time," *Newsweek*, 26 November 1990, p. 63.

13

Organizational Criminality: White-Collar and Organized Crime

CHAPTER OUTLINE

≡ Introduction

The second component of economic crime involves illegal business activity. In this chapter, we divide these crimes of illicit **entrepreneurship** into two distinct categories: **white-collar crime** and **organized** crime. The former involves *illegal* activities of people and institutions whose acknowledged purpose is profit and gain through *legitimate* business transactions. The second category, organized crime, involves *illegal* activities of people and organizations whose acknowledged purpose is profit and gain through *illegitimate* business enterprise. Organized crime and white-collar crime are linked together here because, as criminologist Dwight Smith argues, **enterprise** and not crime is the governing characteristic of both phenomena:

> White-collar crime is not simply a dysfunctional aberration. Organized crime is not something ominously alien to the American economic system. Both are made criminal by laws declaring that certain ways of doing business, or certain products of business, are illegal. In other words, criminality is not an inherent characteristic either of certain persons or of certain business activities but rather, an externally imposed evaluation of alternative modes of behavior and action.[1]

According to Smith, business enterprise can be viewed as flowing through a spectrum of acts ranging from the most saintly to the most sinful.[2] Though "sinful" organizational practices may be desirable to many consumers (for example, the sale of narcotics) or an efficient way of doing business (such as the dumping of hazardous wastes), society has seen fit to regulate or outlaw these behaviors. Organized crime and the crimes of business are the results of a process by which "political, value-based constraints are based on economic activity."[3]

Are They Equivalent? Comparable? Similar?

White-collar and organized crime share some striking similarities. Mark Haller has coined the phrase *illegal enterprise crimes* to signify the sale of illegal goods and services to customers who know they are illegal. Haller's analysis also shows the overlap between criminal and business enterprise. For example, he compares the Mafia crime family to a chamber of commerce: it is an association of "businesspeople" who join to further their business careers. Joining a crime syndicate allows one to cultivate contacts and be in a position to take advantage of

"good deals" offered by more experienced players. The criminal group settles disputes between members, who, after all, cannot take their problems to court.[4]

Both these organizational crimes then taint and corrupt the free market system; they involve all phases of illegal entrepreneurial activity. Those commonly known as organized crime involve individuals or groups whose marketing techniques (threat, extortion, smuggling) and product lines (drugs, sex, gambling, loan-sharking) have been outlawed. White-collar crimes include the use of illegal business practices (embezzlement, price-fixing, bribery, and so on) to merchandise what are ordinarily legitimate commercial products.

Surprisingly to some, both forms of crime can involve violence. While the use of force and coercion by organized crime members has been popularized in the media and therefore comes as no shock, that white-collar crimes may result in the infliction of pain and suffering seems more astonishing. Yet experts claim that upwards of 200,000 occupational deaths occur each year and that "corporate violence" annually kills and injures more people than all street crimes combined.[5]

It is also possible to link organized and white-collar crime because some criminal enterprises involve both forms of activity. Nikos Passas and David Nelken find that organized criminals may seek out legitimate enterprises to launder money, diversify their source of income, increase their power and influence, and gain and enhance respectability.[6] Otherwise "legitimate" businesspeople may turn to organized criminals to help them with problems of an economic nature (such as breaking up a strike), stifle or threaten competition, and increase their influence. "The distinction," these researchers claim, "between organized crime and white-collar crime is hard to sustain on both theoretical and empirical grounds."[7]

Finally, as Kitty Calavita and Henry Pontell point out, some forms of white-collar crime may be more like organized crime than others. While some corporate executives "cheat" to improve their company's position in the business world, others are motivated purely for personal gain. It is this latter group, people who engage in ongoing criminal conspiracies for their own profit, that most resembles organized crime.[8]

≡ White-Collar Crime

In the late 1930s, the distinguished criminologist Edwin Sutherland first used the phrase *white-collar crime* to describe the criminal activities of the rich and powerful. He defined white-collar crime as "a crime committed by a person of respectability and high social status in the course of his occupation."[9]

As Sutherland saw it, white-collar crime involved conspiracies by members of the wealthy classes to use their position in commerce and industry for personal gain without regard to the law. All too often these actions were handled by civil courts, since injured parties were more concerned with getting back their losses than seeing the offenders punished criminally. Consequently, Sutherland believed that the great majority of white-collar criminals did not become the subject of criminological study. Yet their crimes were very costly: the financial cost of white-collar crime is probably several times as great as that of all the crimes that are customarily regarded as the "crime problem." The financial loss from white-collar crime, great as it is, seems less important than the damage to social relations. White-collar crimes violate trust and therefore create distrust, which lowers social morale and produces disorganization on a large scale. Other crimes produce relatively little effect on social institutions or social organization.[10]

Redefining White-Collar Crime

Though Sutherland's work is considered a milestone in criminological history, his focus was on corporate criminality. Today, some disagreement exists over the precise definition of white-collar crime. Sutherland's major concern was the crimes of the rich and powerful. Modern criminologists have broadened their definition of white-collar crime so that it includes a wide variety of situations.[11] For example, today's definition of white-collar criminals can encompass individuals who use the marketplace for the purpose of their criminal activity; they are middle-income Americans and not corporate titans.[12] This category of crime includes such acts as income tax evasion, credit card fraud, and bankruptcy fraud. Other white-collar criminals use their positions of trust in business or government to commit crimes. Their activities might include pilfering, soliciting bribes or kickbacks, and embezzlement. Some white-collar criminals set up business for the sole purpose of victimizing the general public. They engage in land swindles (for example, representing swamps as choice building sites), securities thefts, medical or health frauds, and so on. In addition to acting as individuals, some white-collar criminals become involved in criminal conspiracies designed to improve the market share or profitability of their corporations. This type of white-collar crime, which includes antitrust violations, price-fixing, and false advertising, is also known as corporate crime. It is evident that Sutherland's original concept of the upper-class, white-collar corporate criminal has been expanded by these later formulations.

Today, criminologists use the term *white-collar crime* to refer to almost any occupationally oriented law violation. Even Sutherland's core idea of corporate criminality has been expanded by Ronald Kramer and Raymond Michalowski in their concept of *state-corporate crime:* illegal or socially injurious actions resulting from cooperation between governmental and corporate institutions.[13] Kramer and Michalowski charge that the explosion of the Challenger space shuttle on January 28, 1986, was the result of a state-corporate crime involving the cooperative and criminally negligent actions of the National Aeronautics and Space Administration and Morton Thiokol, Inc., the shuttle builder. In sum, as criminologist Gilbert Geis claims: "White-collar crimes can be committed by persons in all social classes."[14]

The White-Collar Crime Problem

It is difficult to estimate the extent and influence of white-collar crime on victims because all too often, those who suffer the consequences of white-collar crime are ignored by victimologists.[15] Some experts place its total monetary value in the hundreds of billions of dollars, far outstripping the expense of any other type of crime. Beyond their monetary cost, white-collar crimes often involve damage to property and loss of human life. Violations of safety standards, pollution of the environment, and industrial accidents due to negligence can be classified as corporate violence. Laura Schrager and James Short suggest that corporate crime annually results in 20 million serious injuries, including 110,000 people who become permanently disabled and 30,000 deaths.[16] They say that "the potential impact ranges from acute environmental catastrophes such as the collapse of a dam to the chronic effects of diseases resulting from industrial pollution."[17] In a similar vein, sociologist Gilbert Geis charges that white-collar crime is actually likely to be much more serious than street crimes:

> It destroys confidence, saps the integrity of commercial life and has the potential for devastating destruction. Think of the possible results if nuclear regulatory rules are flouted or if toxic wastes are dumped into a community's drinking water supply.[18]

The public has begun to recognize the seriousness of white-collar crimes and demand that they be controlled. A national survey of crime seriousness found that people saw white-collar crimes—such as a county judge taking a bribe to give a light sentence, a doctor cheating on Medicare claims, and a factory owner knowingly getting rid of waste in a way that pollutes the water supply—as being more serious than a person stabbing another with a knife or stealing property worth $10,000 from outside a building.[19] Nonetheless, the prosecution of white-collar criminals remains a relatively rare event, and their imprisonment occurs even less often. Frequently, monetary fines and not prison sentences are the choice of judges and prosecutors who are loath to incarcerate offenders who do not fit the image of "common criminals."

International White-Collar Crime

White-collar crime is not a uniquely U.S. phenomenon. It occurs in other countries, as well, as in the form of corruption of office by government agents. For example, after studying the political process in Nigeria, sociologist Stephen Ekpenyong characterizes the nation as:

> . . . a society characterized by widening inequalities and looting of the public treasury by those who have access to it; where ostentatious display of ill-gotten wealth is applauded; where criminals, men in positions of power and trust, and law enforcement agents collude, and where the needs and aspirations of the majority are neglected.[20]

Ekpenyong suggests that the increase in the crime of armed robbery, punished in Nigeria by the death penalty, can be traced to the inequality in wealth produced by official corruption. In China, cases of corruption account for a high percentage of all cases of economic crime. Of the criminals committing corruption and bribery, most are state personnel, including some higher-ranking officials.[21] The conduct of corruption and bribery mainly occurs in the field of economic management and the practice of government management. State personnel have been playing a very important role in economic management, and some, taking advantage of the power in their hands, commit corruption and bribery in the fields of finance, management, commerce, civil and engineering construction, and international trade. The penalty in China for economic corruption has been death.

Nikos Passas and David Nelken have studied offenses perpetrated against the European Community (EC), an organization set up to bring regularity to the economic activities of its member states, which include England, France, Germany, and most other Western European nations.[22] Passas and Nelken group the crimes into four categories:[23]

1. *Corporate crime,* whereby legitimate companies or organizations, in the course of their usual business, occasionally cheat the EC. A strongly competitive environment may indirectly foster corporate irregularities. This environment may also be created by the illegal activities of competitors, thus creating pressure on those engaging presently only in legal operations to consider resorting to similar illegalities.

2. A second type of fraud can be termed *government crime.* This includes illegal acts committed by government officials or with their knowledge and support, as well as those that lead to cover-ups of other persons' crimes. This type is somehow between corporate crime and occupational crime: it is not perpetrated for one's (direct) personal benefit or monetary gain but for one's government and political party, the country, the national interest, or so on.

3. *Occupational crime*: this refers to people who come across an opportunity of making extra money by bending or breaking the rules. So while they may occasionally commit a fraud, their activities are mainly legal. Conditions under which they might be more likely to engage in such activities include financial straits or other business-related problems, which they try to solve by deviating from the rules.

4. *Organized/professional crime:* this involves people or groups of people whose primary source of income is illegal. They set out to commit frauds; they systematically look for possibilities of making money and profit illicitly. Since EC legislation provides such opportunities and loopholes, and control systems are less than uniform and efficient throughout the EC, there is no reason why criminal enterprises would not enter this market.

Passas and Nelken find that since each country has jurisdiction over cases originating in its territory, the response to white-collar frauds results in highly disparate treatment. It is evident from these research studies that white-collar crime and official corruption is a universal phenomenon.

Components of White-Collar Crime

As noted, white-collar crimes today represent a range of behaviors involving individuals acting alone and within the context of a business structure. The victims of white-collar crime can be the general public, the organization that employs the offender, or a competing organization. Numerous attempts have been made to create subcategories or typologies of white-collar criminality. One of the most well-known was presented by Marshall Clinard and Richard Quinney, who divide white-collar crime into occupational and corporate categories. The former involves offenses committed by individuals in the course of their occupation and by employees against their employers. The second category, corporate crime, is "the offenses committed by corporate officials for the corporation and the offenses of the corporation itself."[24] While this definition recognizes the dual nature of white-collar crime, it fails to take into account all of its many facets, for example, a public official selling undeserved privileges to the public. Several more recent efforts have attempted to account for this diversity. For example, Herbert Edelhertz divides white-collar criminality into four distinct categories:

1. *Ad-hoc violations.* Committed episodically for personal profit; for example, welfare fraud or tax cheating.
2. *Abuses of trust.* Committed by a person in a place of trust in an organization against the organization; for example, embezzlement, bribery, or taking kickbacks.
3. *Collateral business crimes.* Committed by organizations to further their business interests; for example, antitrust violations, the use of false weights and measures, or the concealment of environmental crimes.
4. *Con games.* Committed for the sole purpose of cheating clients; for example, fraudulent land sales, sales of bogus securities, or sales of questionable tax shelters.[25]

Edelhertz's typology captures the diverse nature of white-collar criminality and illustrates how both individuals and institutions can be the victims and offenders of a white-collar crime. In this text, a typology created by criminologist Mark Moore is adapted to organize the analysis of white-collar crime.[26] Moore's typology contains seven elements, ranging from an individual using a business enterprise to commit theft-related crimes, to an individual using his or her place within a business enterprise for illegal gain, to business enterprises collectively engaging in illegitimate activity. While no single typology may be sufficient to encompass the complex array of acts that the term usually denotes, the analysis of white-collar crime here is meant to be so broad and inclusive

that it contains the areas commonly considered important for criminological study.[27]

Stings and Swindles

The first category of white-collar crime involves stealing through deception by individuals who have no continuing institutional or business position and whose entire purpose is to bilk people out of their money. Offenses in this category range from frauds involving the door-to-door sale of faulty merchandise to the passing of millions of dollars in counterfeit stock certificates to an established brokerage firm. If caught, white-collar swindlers are usually charged with common-law crimes, such as embezzlement or fraud.

While swindlers are often considered petty thieves, swindles can run into millions of dollars. One of the largest to date involves the Equity Funding Corporation of America, whose officers bilked the public out of an estimated $2 billion in 1973. The directors of this firm, a life insurance company, claimed to have 90,000 policy holders. However, more than 60,000 of them existed as fictitious entries in the company's computer banks. Equity sold ownership and management of these bogus policies to reinsurance companies, and corporate officers pocketed the profit.[28]

The collapse of the Bank of Credit and Commerce International (BCCI) is another swindle that has cost depositors billions of dollars. BCCI was the world's seventh largest private bank, with assets of about $23 billion. Investigators believe that bank officials made billions in loans to confederates who had no intention of repaying them; BCCI officers also used false accounting methods to defraud depositors. Its officers helped clients, such as Colombian drug cartel leaders and dictators Saddam Hussein and Ferdinand Marcos, launder money, finance terrorist organizations, and smuggle illegal arms. BCCI officers aided drug deals and helped launder drug money so that it could be shifted to legitimate banks. U.S. Drug Enforcement Administration officials were able to compile a list of 379 cases in which BCCI laundered money for narcotics traffickers.[29]

Despite the notoriety of the Equity Funding and BCCI cases, investors continue to bite at bogus investment schemes promising quick riches. The North American Securities Administration Association estimates that U.S. investors lose more than $500 million each year in frauds involving overseas investments in foreign banks, currency speculation, and precious metals.[30]

Religious Swindles

One of the most cold-blooded swindles is an investment scam that uses religious affiliations to steal from trusting investors. In the most well-known case, TV evangelist Jim Bakker was convicted of defrauding followers of $3.7 million when he oversold lodging guarantees, called "lifetime partnerships," at his Heritage USA religious retreat. The jury found that Bakker had diverted ministry funds for personal use while knowing that his PTL ministry was in financial trouble. He bought vacation homes in California and Florida, a houseboat, expensive cars (including a Rolls-Royce), and unusual luxuries, such as an air-conditioned dog house. Bakker had sold hotel rooms to 153,000 people yet built only 258 rooms to accommodate them.[31] Bakker was sentenced to 45 years in prison, a harsh punishment that was later reduced on appeal.

The Bakker case is not unique. The North American Securities Administrators Association estimates that swindlers using fake religious identities bilk thousands of people out of $100 million per year.[32] Swindlers take in worshippers of all persuasions: Jews, Baptists, Lutherans, Catholics, Mormons, and Greek Orthodox have all fallen prey to religious swindles. How do religious swindlers operate? Many join close-knit churches and establish a position of trust that enables them to operate without the normal investor skepticism. Some use religious television and radio shows to sell their product. Others place verses from the scriptures on their promotional literature to comfort hesitant investors. Religious swindles are tough to guard against because they are promoted in the same manner as legitimate religious fund-raising efforts and rely on the faithfuls' trust in those who devote themselves to doing charitable work.

☰ Chiseling

Chiseling, the second category of white-collar crime, involves cheating consumers on a regular basis. Chiselers may be individuals looking to make quick profits in their own businesses or employees of large organizations who decide to cheat on obligations to customers or clients by doing something contrary to company policy. Chiseling can involve charging for bogus auto repairs, cheating customers on home repairs, or *short-weighting* (intentionally tampering with the accuracy of scales used to weigh products) in supermarkets or dairies, or fraudulently selling securities at inflated prices. It may even involve illegal use of information

about company policies, which have not been disclosed to the public. The secret information can be sold to speculators or used to make money in the stock market. Use of the information is in violation of the obligation to keep company policy secret.

Corporations can engage in large-scale chiseling when they misrepresent products or alter their content. The Beech-Nut Nutrition Corporation paid a $2 million fine for illegally selling a product labeled "apple juice" that was nothing more than sweetened water. Despite enforcement efforts, it is estimated that 10 percent of all fruit juices sold in the United States use illegal additives.[33]

It is not uncommon for professionals to use their positions to chisel clients. Pharmacists have been known to alter prescriptions or substitute low-cost generic drugs for more expensive name brands. One study found that pharmacists who were business-oriented—and therefore stressed merchandising, inventory turnover, and the pursuit of profit at the expense of professional ethics—were the ones most inclined to chisel customers.[34]

The legal profession has also come under fire because of the unscrupulous behavior of some of its members. The Watergate hearings, which revealed the unethical behavior of high-ranking government attorneys, prompted the American Bar Association to require that all law students take a course in legal ethics. This action is needed since lawyers chisel clients out of millions of dollars each year in such schemes as forging signatures on clients' compensation checks and tapping escrow accounts and other funds for personal investments; one New York lawyer went so far as to slip the name of an imaginary heiress into a client's will and then impersonate the heiress to collect the inheritance.[35] Special funds have been set up by state governments and bar associations to reimburse chiseled clients.[36]

Chiseling can also take place in the commodity and stock markets. For example, the **churning** of a client's account by an unscrupulous stockbroker involves repeated, excessive, and unnecessary buying and selling of stock. In 1989, the federal government's long-term probe of commodity futures trading on the Chicago Board of Trade resulted in many prominent brokers being indicted under racketeering and other statutes.[37] The brokers were alleged to have engaged in such practices as prearranged trading in which two or more brokers agree to buy and sell commodity futures among themselves without offering the orders to other brokers for competitive bidding; "front running," in which brokers place personal orders ahead of a large customer's order to profit from the market effects of the trade; and "bucketing," skimming customer trading profits.[38]

Securities Fraud

Another form of chiseling involves using one's position of trust to profit from inside business information. The information can then be used to buy and sell securities, giving the trader an unfair advantage over the general public, which lacks this inside information. Another twist on the exploitation of a business position involves using deceptive practices to buy and sell shares in publicly traded companies.

The federal securities laws that control trading in public companies can be found in a number of different statutes, but the two primary sources are the Securities Act of 1933 and the Securities Exchange Act of 1934. These acts prohibit the use of manipulative or deceptive devices, such as mail and wire fraud, making false statements in order to increase market share, conspiracy, and similar acts of unfair market practices. The federal watchdog agency, the Securities and Exchange Commission (SEC), has within its code Rule 10b-5, which articulates general antifraud provisions for securities trading:

> It shall be unlawful for any person directly or indirectly, by the use of any means or instrumentality of interstate commerce, or of the mails or of any facility of any national securities exchange,
>
> (a) To employ any device, scheme, or artifice to defraud,
>
> (b) To make any untrue statement of a material fact or to omit to state a material fact necessary in order to make the statements made, in light of the circumstances under which they were made, not misleading, or
>
> (c) To engage in any act, practice, or course of business which operates or would operate as a fraud or deceit upon any person, in connection with the purchase of sale of any security.[39]

Securities fraud can occur in a variety of situations. For example, as originally conceived, it was illegal for a corporate employee with direct knowledge of market-sensitive information to use that information for his or her own benefit. In recent years, the definition of **insider trading** has been expanded by federal courts to include employees of financial institutions, such as law or banking firms, who misappropriate confidential information on pending corporate actions to purchase stock or give the information to a third party so that party may buy shares in the company. Courts have ruled that such actions are deceptive and in violation of security trading codes.

Interpretations of what constitutes insider trading vary widely. To many, the "hot tip" is the bread and butter of stock market speculators, and the point when a tip becomes a criminal act is often fuzzy. For example, in one celebrated case, R. Foster Winans, the writer of the *Wall Street Journal's* influential "Heard on the Street" column, was convicted on misappropriation of information charges after he wrote favorably about stocks purchased previously by a co-conspirator and then sold for profits in which the writer shared. The U.S. Supreme Court upheld the conviction of Winans and his co-conspirators on the grounds that their actions fraudulently deprived Winan's employer (the *Wall Street Journal*) of its "property," the information contained in his column; their actions also amounted to a "scheme to defraud" under the Securities and Exchange Act.[40] Winans's case is important because it signifies that insider trading can occur even if the offender is neither an employee nor has a fiduciary interest (such as a company's outside accountants would have) in a company whose stock is traded; the Court also found that there need not be a "victim" who loses tangible property for the crime to take place.

Insider trading cases were also made against billionaires Ivan Boesky and Michael Milken, two of Wall

Michael Milken, the pioneer of the use of high-risk, high-yield junk bonds, is sworn in on Capitol Hill before a hearing of the House oversight and investment subcommittee. Milken invoked his constitutional right against self-incrimination three times during the hearing and was excused from testifying. Milken was later convicted on securities fraud and sent to prison.

Street's most prominent **arbitrage** experts. Arbitragers speculate on the stock of companies that are rumored to be takeover targets by other firms and hope to make profit on the difference between current stock prices and the price the acquiring company is willing to pay. Boesky used inside information on such deals as the merger negotiations between International Telephone and Telegraph and Sperry Corporation, Coastal Corporation's takeover of American Natural Resources, and the leveraged buyout of McGraw Edison. Possession of this information allowed Boesky to profit in the millions; he received a three-year prison sentence. Milken was indicted (with the help of information provided by Ivan Boesky) on 98 counts of security fraud, plead guilty to six relatively minor counts, and received a harsh ten-year prison sentence and a billion- dollar fine; Milken's sentence was later reduced because of his cooperation with authorities in other cases.[41]

Individual Exploitation of Institutional Position

Another type of white-collar crime involves individuals' exploiting their power or position in organizations to take advantage of other individuals who have an interest in how that power is used. For example, a fire inspector who demands that the owner of a restaurant pay him to be granted an operating license is abusing his institutional position. In most cases, this type of offense occurs when the victim has a clear right to expect a service and the offender threatens to withhold the service unless an additional payment or bribe is forthcoming.

Throughout U.S. history, various political and governmental figures have been accused of using their positions to profit from bribes and kickbacks.[42] As early as the 1830s, New York's political leaders used their position to control and profit from the city's police force. In the early nineteenth century, New York City's police chief, George Matsell, was the subject of numerous charges of bribe taking and profiteering. Though his wrongdoing was never proven in court, it was revealed five years after he retired in 1851 that he had "saved" enough on his modest salary to build a 20-room mansion on a 3,000-acre estate. During the Civil War, corruption increased proportionately with the amount of money being spent on the war effort. After the war, the nation's largest cities were controlled by political machines that used their offices to buy and sell political favors. The most notorious of the corrupt politicians was William Marcy "Boss" Tweed, who ruled New York City's Democratic Party (Tammany Hall) from 1857 to 1871.[43] Time and anticorruption campaigns eventually caught up with Tweed, and he died in jail.[44]

The use of political office for economic gain has not subsided. On the local and state level, it is common for scandals to emerge in which liquor license board members, food inspectors, and fire inspectors are named as exploiters. One survey of New York City workers who had contact with the building and construction trade found that all who responded to the survey had either been personally involved with corruption or heard of its existence.[45]

Exploitation can also occur in private industry. It is common for purchasing agents in large companies to demand a piece of the action for awarding contracts to suppliers and distributors. In one such case, a J.C. Penney employee received $1.4 million from a contractor who eventually did $23 million of business with the company.[46] In another case, a purchasing agent for the American Chiclets division of Warner-Lambert (maker of Dentyne, Chiclets, Trident, and Dynamints) received a $300,000 kickback from the makers of the wire racks on which the gum products are displayed in supermarkets. Recently, NYNEX fired or disciplined several managers for demanding kickbacks from contractors in return for granting building maintenance contracts.[47]

In some foreign countries, soliciting bribes to do business is a common, if not expected, practice. Not surprisingly, U.S. businesses have complained that stiff penalties for bribery give foreign competitors the edge over them. In European countries, such as Italy and France, giving bribes to secure contracts is perfectly legal; and in West Germany, corporate bribes are actually tax-deductible.[48] Some government officials will solicit bribes to allow American firms to do business in their countries. In one incident, the medical supply firm Baxter International is alleged to have bribed Arab officials to do business in Arab nations after it had been placed on a blacklist for owning a plant in Israel.[49]

Influence Peddling and Bribery

Sometimes individuals holding an important institutional position sell power, influence, and information to outsiders who have an interest in influencing or predicting the activities of the institution. Offenses within this category include government employees' taking of kickbacks from contractors in return for awarding them contracts they could not have won on merit or outsiders' bribing of government officials, such as those in the Securities and Exchange Commission, who might sell information about future government activities. Influence peddling may not be directed solely at personal enrichment and can also involve securing a favored position for one's political party or interest group. Political leaders have been convicted of securing bribes to obtain funds to rig elections and allow their party to control state politics.[50]

One major difference distinguishes influence peddling from the previously discussed exploitation of an institutional position. Exploitation involves forcing victims to pay for services to which they have a clear right. In contrast, influence peddlers and bribe takers use their institutional positions to grant favors and sell information to which their co-conspirators are not entitled. In sum, in crimes of institutional exploitation, the victim is the person forced to pay, whereas the victim of influence peddling is the organization compromised by its own employees for their own interests.

Influence Peddling in Government

The most widely publicized incident of government bribery in recent years was the ABSCAM case. In 1981, FBI agents, working with a convicted swindler, Melvin Weinberg, posed as wealthy Arabs looking for favorable treatment from high-ranking politicians. The pseudo-Arabs said they wished to obtain U.S. citizenship and receive favorable treatment in business ventures. Several office holders were indicted, including a U.S. senator from New Jersey, Harrison Williams.[51] Williams was convicted of accepting an interest in an Arab-backed mining venture in return for promising to use his influence to obtain government contracts. He also promised to use his influence to help the "Arab sheik" enter and stay in the United States. At Williams's trial, the prosecution played tapes showing Williams meeting with federal undercover agents, boasting of his influence in the government, and saying he could "with great pleasure talk to the president of the United States" about the business venture; a later tape showed the senator promising to seek immigration help for the bogus sheik and agreeing to take part in the mining operation.

The ABSCAM case is certainly not unique. Senior officials at the Pentagon were found to have received hundreds of thousands of dollars in bribes for ensuring the granting of contracts for military clothing to certain manufacturers. The corruption was so pervasive that the military found it difficult to locate sufficient replacement manufacturers who were not involved in the scandal. In another Pentagon scandal, senior officials were accused of accepting bribes from defense consultants and manufacturers in return for classified information, such as competitors' bids and designs, that would give the consultants and manufacturers an edge in securing government contracts. More than $1 billion worth of contracts were suspended. The scandal touched some of the largest defense contractors in the United States, including Raytheon, Litton Industries, and Lockheed.[52]

Even more shocking and disturbing to the U.S. public were the revelations that officials in the Department of Housing and Urban Development (HUD) channeled funds targeted for the poor into the hands of wealthy developers and consultants who were connected to the Reagan administration. One national magazine branded the conspirators as "poverty pimps" who got rich and powerful by subverting programs intended to help the poor.[53] Over a period of eight years, developers used political influence to drain billions of dollars into questionable enterprises. Former HUD officials, working as consultants and lobbyists, used their personal relationships to obtain cash for the profiteering builders. In the most important trial, Deborah Gore Dean, the executive assistant to the HUD director, was convicted of 12 felony counts of fraud, taking payoffs, and perjury. During the trial, former Kentucky Governor Louie Nunn testified how he had received $644,000 in consulting fees for very little work. He claimed that he paid $184,000 to former Attorney General John Mitchell, a convicted Watergate conspirator![54]

Federal officials are not the only ones to be accused of influence peddling. It has become all too common for legislators and other state officials to be forced to resign or even jailed for accepting bribes to use their influence. In West Virginia, two governors have been jailed on bribery charges since 1960. In Louisiana, the state insurance commissioner was convicted in 1991 on money laundering, conspiracy, and fraud charges connected to the collapse of the Champion Insurance Company, which cost policyholders $185 million; the commissioner took $2 million in bribes in return for regulatory favors.[55] And overseas, foreign businessmen and officials have been implicated in corruption. For example, in Italy, the former chairperson of the Montedison agricultural chemical firm admitted making illegal payments to political leaders to secure contracts.[56]

Corruption in the Criminal Justice System

Agents of the criminal justice system have also gotten caught up in official corruption, a circumstance that is particularly disturbing because society expects a higher standard of moral integrity from people empowered to uphold the law and judge their fellow citizens. When federal prosecutors mounted Operation Greylord to expose corruption in the Cook County, Illinois, court system, they uncovered examples of judges selling favors to corrupt attorneys for up to $50,000 in under-the-table payments; one culprit received a 15-year prison sentence. The credibility of the justice process is critically weakened when officials who hold power over other people's reputation, not to speak of their freedom and liberty, engage in criminal behavior.

Police officers have been particularly vulnerable to charges of corruption. More than 20 years ago, New York Mayor John Lindsay appointed a commission under the direction of Judge Whitman Knapp to investigate allegations of police corruption. The Knapp Commission found that police corruption was pervasive and widespread, ranging from patrol officers' accepting small gratuities from local businesspeople to senior officers receiving payoffs in the thousands of dollars from gamblers and narcotics violators.[57] The commission found that construction firms made payoffs to have police ignore violations of city ordinances, such as double parking, obstruction of sidewalks, and noise pollution. Bar owners paid police to allow them to operate after hours or to give free reign to the prostitutes, drug pushers, and gamblers operating on their premises. Drug dealers allowed police to keep money and narcotics confiscated during raids in return for their freedom.

The Knapp Commission report did not lay to rest police corruption. There have been noted scandals in many large cities. For example, 20 Philadelphia police officers were indicted on charges of extorting money from bar owners and video game vendors. James Martin, the former second-in-command of the Philadelphia Police Department, was sentenced to 18 years in prison in the case.[58] In Chicago, police officers conspired to sell relatively new police cars to other officers at cut-rate prices, forcing the department to purchase new cars unnecessarily. In Boston, a major scandal hit the police department in 1988 when a police captain was indicted in an exam-tampering and -selling scheme. Numerous officers bought promotion exams from the captain, while others had him lower the scores of rivals who were competing for the same job.[59]

In 1993, New York City empowered the **Mollen Commission** to investigate corruption among city police. The commission found that a relatively small number (compared to the pervasive corruption found earlier by the Knapp Commission) of rogue cops were immersed in a pattern of violence, coercion, theft, and drug dealing. Testifying before the commission to gain a reduced sentence on a narcotics charge, one officer told of "shaking down" drug dealers, brutalizing innocent citizens, and intimidating fellow officers to force their silence. Protected by the "blue curtain"—the police officer code of secrecy—rogue cops were able to purchase luxury homes and cars with the profits from their illegal thefts, extortion, and drug sales.[60]

How can police corruption be controlled? One approach is to strengthen the internal administrative review process within police departments. Some departments have adopted an *accountability system* that holds supervisors at each level directly responsible for the illegal behaviors of the officers under them; a commander can be forced to resign or be demoted if one of his or her command is found guilty of corruption. Outside review boards or special prosecutors have been formed to investigate reported incidents of corruption; outsiders, though, may face the problem of the "blue curtain," which is quickly raised when police officers feel their department is under scrutiny. Anticorruption training and education programs have been instituted for new recruits in the training academy.

A more realistic solution to police corruption might be to change the social context of policing. Police operations must be made more visible, and the public must be given freer access to police operations. It is also possible that some of the vice-related crimes the police now deal with might be decriminalized or referred to other agencies. Although decriminalization of vice cannot in itself end the problem, it could lower the pressure placed on individual police officers and help relieve their moral dilemmas, such as whether it is really wrong to take money from drug dealers or gamblers.

Influence Peddling in Business

Politicians and government officials are not the only ones accused of bribery; business has had its share of scandals. In the 1970s, revelations were made that multinational corporations regularly made payoffs to foreign officials and businesspeople to secure business contracts: Gulf Oil executives admitted paying $4 million to the South Korean ruling party; Burroughs Corporation admitted paying $1.5 million to foreign officials;

Lockheed Aircraft admitted paying $202 million. McDonnell-Douglas Aircraft Corporation was indicted for paying $1 million in bribes to officials of Pakistani International Airlines to secure orders.[61]

In response to these revelations, Congress in 1977 passed the Foreign Corrupt Practices Act (FCPA), which makes it a criminal offense to pay bribes to foreign officials or to make other questionable overseas payments. Violations of the FCPA draw strict penalties for both the defendant company and its officers.[62] Moreover, all fines imposed on corporate officers are paid by them and not absorbed by the company. For example, for violation of the antibribery provisions of the FCPA, a domestic corporation can be fined up to $1 million. Company officers, employees, or stockholders who are convicted of bribery may have to serve a prison sentence of up to five years and pay a $10,000 fine. Congressional dissatisfaction with the harshness and ambiguity of the bill has caused numerous revisions to be proposed. Despite the penalties imposed by the FCPA, corporations that deal in foreign trade have continued to give bribes to secure favorable trade agreements.[63]

≡ Embezzlement and Employee Fraud

The fourth type of white-collar crime involves individuals' use of their positions to embezzle company funds or appropriate company property for themselves. Here, the company or organization that employs the criminal, rather than an outsider, is the victim of white-collar crime.

Blue-Collar Fraud

Employee theft can reach all levels of the organizational structure. Blue-collar employees have been involved in systematic theft of company property, commonly called **pilferage.** The techniques of employee theft are quite varied. Charles McCaghy reports on different methods used to steal from employers:

- Piece workers zip up completed garments into their clothing and take them home.

- Cashiers ring up lower prices on single-item purchases and pocket the difference. Some will work with an accomplice and ring up [the lower] prices as [the accomplice goes] through the line.

- Clerks do not tag sale merchandise and then [they] sell it at its original cost, pocketing the difference.

- Receiving clerks obtain duplicate keys to storage facilities and then return after hours to steal.

- Truck drivers make fictitious purchases of fuel and repairs and then split the gains with truck stop owners. Truckers have been known to cooperate with the receiving staff of department stores to cheat employers. In one instance, truckers would keep 20 cases of goods out of every 100 delivered. The store receiving staff would sign a bill of lading for all 100, and the two groups split the profits after the stolen goods were sold to a fence.

- Some employees simply hide items in garbage pails [or] incinerators or under trash heaps until they can be retrieved later.[64]

John Clark and Richard Hollinger found that about 35 percent of employees they surveyed reported involvement in pilferage.[65] Clark and Hollinger's data indicate that employee theft is most accurately explained by factors relevant to the work setting, such as job dissatisfaction and the workers' belief they were being exploited by employers or supervisors; economic problems played a relatively small role in the decision to pilfer. So while employers attributed employee fraud to economic conditions and declining personal values, workers themselves say they steal because of strain and conflict. It is difficult to determine the value of goods taken by employees, but it has been estimated that pilferage accounted for 30 percent to 75 percent of all shrinkage and amounts to losses of up to $10 billion annually.[66]

Management Fraud

Blue-collar workers are not the only employees who commit corporate theft. Management-level fraud is also quite common. Such acts include: (1) converting company assets for personal benefit; (2) fraudulently receiving increases in compensation (such as raises or bonuses); (3) fraudulently increasing personal holdings of company stock; (4) retaining one's present position within the company by manipulating accounts; and (5) concealing unacceptable performance from stockholders.[67] There have been a number of well-publicized examples of management fraud. In one recent case, high- ranking employees of the Leslie Fay clothing com-

Savings and loan fraud cost American citizens billions of dollars. Here, hundreds of nervous depositors, some of whom arrived with beach chairs, wait to withdraw their money outside the Randallstown branch of the Old Court Savings and Loan Association, unswayed by assurances that their money was safe despite reported management problems at Maryland's second largest savings and loan.

pany were implicated in a fraudulent scheme to overstate company profits. In its accounting reports, inventories were overstated while the cost of making garments was understated to enhance profits; profits and revenues were also inflated. The false entries resulted in millions being paid executives because their bonuses were tied to company profits.[68]

Employee fraud seems widespread. A 1993 survey of 300 companies by the national accountant firm of KPMG Peat Marwick found that 75 percent reported having fallen prey to employee fraud during the past 12 months; the estimated total loss was $250 million.[69]

The most significant cases of management fraud in the nation's history occurred in the savings and loan industry. The Close-Up entitled "The Savings and Loan Case" discusses this scandal.

Computer Crime

Computer-related thefts are a new trend in employee theft and embezzlement. The widespread use of computers to record business transactions has encouraged some people to use them for illegal purposes. Computer crimes generally fall into one of four categories: (1) theft of services, in which the criminal uses the computer for unauthorized purposes or an unauthorized user penetrates the computer system; (2) use of data in a computer system for personal gain; (3) unauthorized use of computers employed for various types of financial processing to obtain assets; and (4) theft of property by computer for personal use or conversion to profit (see Table 13.1).[70] Several common techniques are used by computer criminals. In fact, computer theft has become

CLOSE-UP

The Savings and Loan Case

For ten or more years, the owners and managers of some of the nation's largest savings and loan (S&L) banks swindled investors, depositors, and the general public out of billions of dollars. It has been conservatively estimated that over the next 40 years, the cost of rectifying these savings and loan fraud cases could total $500 billion, a number almost too staggering to imagine. It is possible that 1,700 banks, about one-half of the industry, may eventually collapse. Government reports indicated that criminal activity was a central factor in 70 percent to 80 percent of all these cases.

How could crimes of this magnitude have been committed? In an impressive analysis, Kitty Calavita and Henry Pontell looked at the events that created the S&L crisis. At first, problems were created by the industry's efforts to remove federal regulations that had restricted its activities and way of doing business. In 1980, to help the industry recover from money-losing years, the federal government allowed the formerly conservative S&Ls to expand their business operations beyond residential housing loans. Savings banks could now get involved in high-risk commercial real estate lending and corporate or business loans. They were allowed to compete for deposits with commercial banks by offering high interest rates. The S&Ls made deals with brokerage firms to sell high-interest certificates of deposit,

encouraging investors around the nation to pour billions of dollars into banks they had never seen. Even more damaging ownership rules were relaxed so that almost anyone could own or operate an S&L. Yet the government insured all deposits. Even if crooked owners offered outlandish interest rates to attract deposits and then lent them to shady businesspeople, the federal government guaranteed that depositors could not lose money. Why ask questions about whom you were giving your money to and what it was being used for if the government *guaranteed* the principal?

Given this green light, the S&Ls made irresponsible and outright fraudulent loans. Losses began to mushroom. In the first six months of 1988, the industry lost an estimated $7.5 billion.

Calavita and Pontell find that the S&L violations fall into one of three categories. The first is making high-risk investments (unlawful risk-taking) in violation of law and regulation, including risky loans to commercial real estate developers. Sometimes kickbacks were made to encourage the loans.

The second criminal activity was collective embezzlement (looting). This involved robbing one's own bank by siphoning off funds for personal gain. For example, Erwin Hansen took over Centennial Savings and Loan of California in 1980 and threw a Christmas party that cost $148,000 for 500 friends and guests and included a ten-course, sit-down dinner, roving minstrels, court jesters, and pantomimes. Hansen and his

companion, Beverly Haines, traveled extensively around the world in the bank's private airplanes, purchased antique furniture at the S&L's expense, refurbished their home at a cost of over $1 million, and equipped it with a chef. Before it went bankrupt, the bank bought a fleet of luxury cars and an extensive art collection. Another case involved Don Dixon, owner of the Vernon Savings and Loan in Texas. Dixon transformed the small savings bank into one of the largest S&Ls in the state by advertising high interest rates. Dixon used company money for a $22,000 tour of Europe, to buy five airplanes, and to pay rent on a California home. The bank funded projects so shaky that when federal regulators took over, 96 percent of its loans were overdue. It has been estimated that the collapse of Vernon will eventually cost taxpayers $1.3 billion.

Other practices involved outright fraud. Land was sold or "flipped" between conspirators, driving up the assessed evaluation. The overpriced land could then be sold to or mortgaged by a friendly bank owned by a co-conspirator for far more than it was worth. One loan broker bought a piece of property in 1979 for $874,000, flipped it, and then sold it two years later to a S&L he had bought for $55 million. Another method was *reciprocal lending* in which bank insiders would lend each other money that was never paid back and then trade the bad loans back and forth to delay discovery of the fraud. Linked financing involved loans based on receipts of deposits in an equivalent amount; the loans were never repaid. Insiders received a "finder's fee" for attracting deposits, and bank operators got bonuses for increasing business. "S&L," some suggested, stood for squander and liquidate.

In the aftermath of these white-collar crimes, owners committed their final crime—covering up their crimes. Sometimes the cover-up was accomplished by shady accounting practices or fabricated income statements. The S&L crisis was allowed to develop because the conspirators were "respected" businesspeople who had lavish life-styles and political connections. For example, the collapse of Denver-based Silverado Banking Savings and Loan cost taxpayers $1 billion. While the sum was not extraordinary, the case was notable because President George Bush's son Neil was on Silverado's board of directors. The president was embarrassed when Neil Bush was called to testify before the House Banking Committee on his relationships with two developers who owed the bank considerable sums. One had given Bush $100,000 to invest with the condition that they share in the profits but not the losses. Even Neil Bush admitted, "I know it sounds a little fishy."

The crimes were also difficult to detect because they involved acts of business out of the public view. Bankers secretly dipped into depositors' money to fund parties, yachts, and tours of Europe, all ostensibly for business purposes. Much of the fraud revolved around seemingly innocent loans and mortgages made to associates for invest-ment purposes. Of course, the investments later turned out to be worthless, and the bank and its stockholders were left accountable. Because the government guarantees deposits, it was forced to take over the banks and reorganize their assets. Bank examiners were taken in because the S&L managers had made numerous cash contributions to politicians and used these connections to establish their legitimacy.

Another reason the S&L fraud went undetected for so long was the involvement of high-ranking government officials and Wall Street brokerage firms with first-class credentials. Drexel Burnham Lambert induced banks to purchase "junk bonds" (bonds issued in leveraged buyouts of corporations without sound backing). When these were devalued, the banks lost billions. Five U.S. senators, including Alan Cranston of California and John Glenn of Ohio, are alleged to have helped Charles Keating of the Lincoln Saving and Loan bypass federal regulators; they are now known as the *Keating Five.*"

Calavita and Pontell conclude that the S&L crisis was a result of the unregulated finance capitalism that dominated the U.S. economy in the 1980s. Because nothing is produced or sold, financial institutions are ripe for fraud. After all, their business is the manipulation of money; the line between smart business practices and white-collar crime is often thin. While white-collar criminals are all too often treated leniently, the savings and loan case will result in criminal prosecutions for many years. The wide national attention this case has gotten may result in unusually severe punishments. For example, Welda Lee "Bubba" Keetch, the ex-owner of First Savings and Loan of Burkburnett, Texas, was sentenced to 13 years in prison for pocketing $8 million in illicit proceeds. The sentencing of junk-bond financier Michael Milken to a ten-year prison sentence for relatively minor security trading offenses and the $6.8 billion fine being sought against the bankrupt Drexel Burnham Lambert junk bond firm, accused of using "bribery, coercion, extortion, fraud and other illegal means" to sell worthless bonds to S&Ls, illustrate the government's willingness to severely punish anyone connected to the S&L fiasco.

Discussion Questions

1. Should S&L criminals have their personal incomes and homes confiscated by the government?
2. What motivates already wealthy businesspeople to steal?
3. Are white-collar crime and organized crime really the same thing?

SOURCES: Kitty Calavita and Henry Pontell, "Savings and Loan Fraud as Organized Crime: Toward a Conceptual Typology of Corporate Illegality," *Criminology* 31 (1993): 519–48; idem, "'Heads I Win, Tails You Lose'": Deregulation, Crime, and Crisis in the Savings and Loan Industry," *Crime and Delinquency* 36 (1990): 309–41; Rich Thomas, "Sit Down Taxpayers," *Newsweek,* 4 June 1990, p. 60; John Gallagher, "Good Old Bad Boy," *Time,* 25 June 1990, pp. 42–43; L. Gordon Crovitz, "Milken's Tragedy: Oh, How the Mighty Fall before RICO," *Wall Street Journal,* 2 May 1990, p. A17.

so common that experts have created their own jargon to describe theft styles and methods:

- *The Trojan horse.* One computer is used to reprogram another for illicit purposes. In a recent incident, two high school-age computer users reprogrammed the computer at DePaul University, preventing that institution from using its own processing facilities. The youths were convicted of a misdemeanor.

- *The salami slice.* An employee sets up a dummy account in the company's computerized records. A small amount—even a few pennies—is subtracted from customers' accounts and added to the account of the thief. Even if they detect the loss, the customers don't complain, since a few cents is an insignificant amount to them. The pennies picked up here and there eventually amount to thousands of dollars in losses.

- *"Super-zapping."* Most computer programs used in business have built-in antitheft safeguards. However, employees can use a repair or maintenance program to supersede the antitheft program. Some tinkering with the program is required, but the "super-zapper" is soon able to order the system to issue checks to his or her private account.

- *The logic bomb.* A program is secretly attached to the company's computer system. The new program monitors the company's work and waits for a sign of error to appear, some illogic that was designed for the computer to follow. Illogic causes the logic bomb to kick into action and exploit the weakness. The way the thief exploits the situation depends on his or her original intent—theft of money or defense secrets, sabotage, and so on.

- *Impersonation.* An unauthorized person uses the identity of an authorized computer user to access the computer system.

- *Data leakage.* A person illegally obtains data from a computer system by leaking it out in small amounts.

A different type of computer crime involves the installation of a "virus" in a computer system. A **virus** is a program that disrupts or destroys existing programs and networks. All too often this high-tech vandalism is the work of "hackers," who consider their efforts to be "pranks." In one well-publicized case, a 25-year-old computer whiz named Robert Morris unleashed a program that wrecked a nationwide electronic mail network. His efforts netted him three years' probation, a $10,000 fine, and 400 hours of community service; some critics felt this punishment was too lenient to deter future virus creators.[71]

An accurate accounting of computer crime will probably never be made, since so many offenses go unreported. Sometimes company managers refuse to report the crime to police lest they display their incompetence to stockholders and competitors.[72] In other instances, computer crimes go unreported because they involve such "low visibility" acts as copying computer software in violation of copyright laws.[73]

It is likely that computer-related crime will blossom as business becomes more computer-dependent. For example, such recent advances as automatic bank teller machines have been a source of illegal gain. Bank employees have used returned or unused bank cards to

TABLE 13.1 **Categories of Computer Crime**

Internal computer crimes

- Trojan horses
- Logic bombs
- Trap doors
- Viruses

Telecommunications crimes

- Phone "phreaking"
- Hacking
- Illegal bulletin boards
- Misuse of telephone systems

Computer manipulation crimes

- Embezzlements
- Frauds

Support of criminal enterprises

- Data bases to support drug distributions
- Data bases to keep records of client transactions
- Money laundering

Hardware/software thefts

- Software piracy
- Thefts of computers
- Thefts of microprocessor chips
- Thefts of trade secrets

SOURCE: C. Conly & J. Thomas McEwan, "Computer Crime," *NIJ Reports* (January/February 1990): 3.

make withdrawals after electronically transferring funds to the nonexistent account. Similarly, computer culprits have benefited from the increased use of computerized phone networks, such as Sprint and MCI; in California, "hackers" ran up $60,000 worth of illegal charges on the Sprint account of a man whose access number they had obtained.[74]

As computer applications become more varied, so too will the use of computers for illegal purposes. The growth of computer-related crimes prompted Congress in 1984 to enact the Counterfeit Active Device and Computer Fraud and Abuse Act (amended 1986).[75] This statute makes it a felony for a person to use illegal entry to a computer to make a gain of $5,000, to cause another to incur a loss of $5,000, or to access data affecting the national interest. Violation of this act can bring up to ten years in prison and a $10,000 fine. Repeat offenders can receive 20-year prison sentences and $100,000 fines. Computer crime may also be controlled by other federal statutes, including the Electronic Communications Privacy Act of 1986, which prohibits unauthorized interception of computer communications and prohibits obtaining, altering or preventing authorized access to data through intentional unauthorized access to the stored data.[76] The act is designed to prevent hackers from intercepting computer communications and invading the privacy of computer users.[77]

≡ Client Frauds

A fifth component of white-collar crime is theft by an economic client from an organization that advances credit to its clients. Included in this category are insurance fraud, credit card fraud, fraud related to welfare and Medicare programs, and tax evasion. These offenses are linked together because they involve theft from organizations that have many individual clients who may take advantage of their positions of trust to steal from the organizations.

Client frauds may be common even among upper-income people. Some physicians have been caught cheating the federal government out of Medicare or Medicaid payments. Abusive practices include such techniques as "ping-ponging" (referring patients to other physicians in the same office), "gang visits" (billing for multiple services), and "steering" (directing patients to particular pharmacies). Doctors who abuse their Medicaid or Medicare patients in this way are liable to civil suit.[78] Of a more serious nature are fraudulent acts

designed to cheat both the government and the consumer. Such Medicaid frauds generally involve billing for services not actually rendered, billing in excessive amounts, setting up kickback schemes, and providing false identification on reimbursement forms. Doctors involved in these schemes are liable to criminal prosecution under federal and state law.[79] It has been estimated that between 10 percent and 25 percent of the $100 billion spent annually on federal health care is lost to fraudulent practices.[80] Despite the magnitude of this abuse, the state and federal governments have been reluctant to prosecute Medicaid fraud. A year-long study of enforcement practices in 18 states did not uncover a single conviction for Medicaid abuse, and the national average over a seven-year period was found to be 1.5 convictions per state per year. One trend has been to establish Medicaid fraud investigation units. The 30 states that have employed such measures have already disallowed $86.5 million in faulty Medicaid bills.[81]

At the other end of the income spectrum has been the accusation that some welfare recipients cheat the federal government on a regular basis. A government report released in 1994 claims that about $1 billion is lost through error and fraudulent claims.[82]

Tax Evasion

Another important aspect of client fraud is tax evasion. This is a particularly challenging area for criminological study, since (1) so many U.S. citizens regularly underreport their income, and (2) it is often difficult to separate honest error from deliberate tax evasion. The basic law on tax evasion is contained in the U.S. Internal Revenue Code, section 7201, which states:

> Any person who willfully attempts in any manner to evade or defeat any tax imposed by this title or the payment thereof shall, in addition to other penalties provided by law, be guilty of a felony and, upon conviction thereof, shall be fined not more than $100,000 or imprisoned not more than 5 years, or both, together with the costs of prosecution.

To prove tax fraud, the government must find that the taxpayer either underreported his or her income or did not report taxable income. No minimum dollar amount is stated before fraud exists, but the government can take legal action when there is a "substantial underpayment of tax." A second element of tax fraud is "willfulness" on the part of the tax evader. In the major case on this issue, willfulness was defined as a "voluntary, intentional violation of a known legal duty and not the careless disregard for the truth."[83] Finally, to prove tax fraud, the government must show that the taxpayer has purposely attempted to evade or defeat a tax payment. If the offender is guilty of passive neglect, the offense is a misdemeanor. Passive neglect simply means not paying taxes, not reporting income, or not paying taxes when due. On the other hand, affirmative tax evasion, such as keeping double books, making false entries, destroying books or records, concealing assets, or covering up sources of income, constitutes a felony.

Tax evasion is a difficult crime to prosecute. Since legal tax avoidance is a favorite U.S. pastime, it is often hard to prove the difference between the careless, unintentional nonreporting of income and willful fraud. The line between legal and fraudulent behavior is so fine that many people are willing to step over it. In fact, it has been estimated that the "underground economy" may amount to about 33 percent of the nation's pro-

duction; workers who provide services under the table and off the books range from moonlighting construction workers to "gypsy" cabdrivers (there are an estimated 21,000 gypsy cabs in New York City alone, twice the number of legal ones).[84] The Internal Revenue Service (IRS) estimates that more than $120 billion in taxes go uncollected each year because individuals fail to report all their income; nearly a third of that amount is from self-employed workers, including professionals, laborers, and door-to-door salespeople (see Figure 13.1).[85]

The IRS may be losing its battle against tax cheats. The number of audits it conducts is actually declining. In 1980, it audited about 8 percent of all people whose incomes exceeded $50,000; today, the number of audits has declined to 1.8 percent.[86] And despite some well-publicized cases involving the wealthy, such as a $16 million judgment against singer Willy Nelson and the prosecution and conviction of multimillionaire Leona

FIGURE 13.1 **Tax Evasion**

SOURCE: Internal Revenue Service, Tax Reporting Data, 1992 (Washington, D.C.: Internal Revenue Service, 1994).

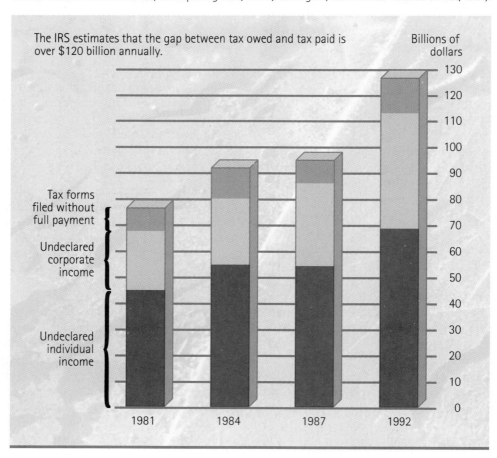

Helmsley, the IRS has been accused of targeting middle-income taxpayers and ignoring the upper classes and large corporations.

Corporate Crime

The final component of white-collar crime involves situations in which powerful institutions or their representatives willfully violate the laws that restrain these institutions from doing social harm or require them to do social good. This is also known as **corporate** or **organizational crime.**

Interest in corporate crime first emerged in the early 1900s, when a group of writers, known as the *muckrakers,* targeted the unscrupulous business practices of John D. Rockefeller, Andrew Carnegie, and J. P. Morgan and other corporate business leaders.[87] In a 1907 article, sociologist E. A. Ross described the "criminaloid," a business leader who while enjoying immunity from the law victimized an unsuspecting public.[88] It was Edwin Sutherland who focused theoretical attention on corporate crime when he began his research on the subject in the 1940s; corporate crime was probably what he had in mind when he coined the phrase "white-collar crime."[89]

Corporate crimes are socially injurious acts committed by people who control companies to further their business interests. The target of their crimes can be the general public, the environment, or even their company's workers. What makes these crimes unique is that the perpetrator is a legal fiction—a corporation—and not an individual. In reality, it is company employees or owners who commit corporate crimes and who ultimately benefit through career advancement or greater profits. Some of the acts included within the ambit of corporate crime are price-fixing and illegal restraint of trade, false advertising, and the use of company practices that violate environmental protection statutes. The variety of crimes contained within this category is great, and the damage they cause vast. The following subsections will examine some of the most important offenses.

Illegal Restraint of Trade and Price-Fixing

A restraint of trade involves a contract or conspiracy designed to stifle competition, create a monopoly, artificially maintain prices, or otherwise interfere with free market competition. The control of restraint of trade violations has its legal basis in the **Sherman Antitrust Act.** For violations of its provisions, this federal law created criminal penalties of up to three years' imprisonment and $100,000 in fines for individuals and $1 million in fines for corporations.[90] The act outlaws conspiracies between corporations designed to control the marketplace.

In most instances, the act leaves to the presiding court's judgment the determination of whether corporations have conspired to "unreasonably restrain competition." However, four types of market conditions are considered so inherently anticompetitive that federal courts, through the Sherman Antitrust Act, have defined them as illegal per se, without regard to the facts or circumstances of the case. The first is "division of markets"; here, firms divide a region into territories, and each firm agrees not to compete in the others' territories.[91] The second is the "tying arrangement" in which a corporation requires customers of one of its services to use other services it offers. For example, in the case of *Northern Pacific Railway Co. v. United States,* a federal court ruled that the railroad's requirement that all tenants of its land use the railroad to ship all goods produced on the land was an illegal restraint of trade.[92] A third type of absolute Sherman Act violation is "group boycotts," in which an organization or company boycotts retail stores that do not comply with its rules or desires. Finally, "price-fixing"—a conspiracy to set and control the price of a necessary commodity—is considered an absolute violation of the act.

Of all criminal violations associated with restraint of trade, none, perhaps, is as important as price-fixing. Michael Maltz and Stephen Pollack have described the four forms this act usually takes.[93] The first is *predation,* in which large firms agree among themselves to bid below market prices to drive out weaker firms. The goal is to reduce competition and permit the remaining firms to raise their prices with relative impunity. A second scheme is *identical bidding.* Here, all competitors agree to submit identical bids for each contract, although they may vary bids from contract to contract. The price is well above what would have been expected if collusion had not occurred. Purchasing agents use their discretion to choose among bidders. However, identical bidding usually ensures all vendors of getting a share of the market without losing any profitability. *Geographical market sharing* involves dividing the potential market into territories within which only one member of the conspiring group is permitted a low bid. The remaining conspirators either refrain from bidding or give artificially high bids. *Rotational bidding* involves a conspiracy in which the opportunity to submit a winning bid for a government or business contract is rotated among the institutional bidders. The conspirators meet in advance and determine who will give the low bid. The winning bid is, of course, higher than it should be, since the losers have all submitted abnormally high bids. Close coordination among the bidders is essential; therefore, these schemes usually involve only a few large firms. Despite enforcement efforts, restraint-of-trade conspiracies are quite common. The best-known case involved some of the largest members of the electrical equipment industry.[94] In 1961, 21 corporations, including industry leaders Westinghouse and General Electric, were successfully prosecuted; 45 executives were found guilty of criminal violations of the Sherman Antitrust Act. Company executives met secretly—they referred to their meetings as "choir practice"—and arranged the setting of prices on sales of equipment, the allocation of markets and territories, and the rigging of bids. At the sentencing, fines amounting to $1,924,500 were levied against the defendants, including $437,500 against General Electric and $372,500 against Westinghouse. Although these fines meant little to the giant corporations, subsequent civil suits cost General Electric $160 million. Even more significant was that seven defendants, all high-ranking executives, were sentenced to jail terms.

Not all price-fixing is done by billion-dollar corporations. In 1990, a federal grand jury indicted the Manischewitz Company for allegedly conspiring with its competitors, the Striet Company and Horowitz Margareten Company, to fix the price of matzos, the unleavened bread eaten by religious Jews during the Passover holiday.[95]

Deceptive Pricing.

It is common for even the largest U.S. corporations to use deceptive pricing schemes when they respond to contract solicitations. Deceptive pricing occurs when contractors provide the government or other corporations with incomplete or misleading information on how much it will actually cost to fulfill the contract they are bidding on or use mischarges once the contracts are signed.[96] For example, defense contractors have been prosecuted for charging the government for costs incurred on work they are doing for private firms or shifting the costs on fixed-price contracts to ones in which the government reimburses the contractor for all expenses ("cost-plus" contracts). One well-known example of deceptive pricing occurred when the Lockheed Corporation withheld information that its wage costs would be lower than expected on the C-5 cargo plane. The resulting overcharges were an estimated $150 million. Though the government was able to negotiate a cheaper price for future C-5 orders, it did not demand repayment on the earlier contract. The government prosecutes approxi-

mately 100 cases of deceptive pricing in defense work each year involving 59 percent of the nation's largest contractors.[97]

False Claims and Advertising

In 1991, the Food and Drug Administration seized all the Citrus Hill orange juice stored in a Minneapolis warehouse. It seems that the nation's third largest-selling breakfast drink had billed itself as "pure squeezed," "100% pure," and "fresh," despite the fact that it was made from concentrate. The federal agency also objected to the fact that Procter and Gamble, which sells Citrus Hill, claimed, "We pick our oranges at the peak of ripeness, then we hurry to squeeze them before they lose their freshness."[98]

Executives in even the largest corporations are sometimes caught in the position in which stockholders' expectations of ever-increasing company profits seem to demand that sales be increased at any cost. At times, executives respond to this challenge by making claims about their product that cannot be justified by its actual performance. However, the line between clever, aggressive sales techniques and fraudulent claims is a fine one. It is traditional to show a product in its best light, even if that involves resorting to fantasy. It is neither fraudulent to show a delivery service vehicle taking off into outer space nor to imply that taking one sip of iced tea will make people feel they have just jumped into a swimming pool. However, it is illegal to knowingly and purposely advertise a product as possessing qualities that the manufacturer realizes it does not have.

Charges stemming from false and misleading claims have been common in several U.S. industries. For example, the Federal Trade Commission reviewed and disallowed advertising by the three major U.S. car companies that alleged that new cars got higher gas mileage than buyers actually could expect. The Warner-Lambert drug company was prohibited from claiming that Listerine mouthwash could prevent or cure colds. Sterling Drug was prohibited from claiming that Lysol disinfectant killed germs associated with colds and flu. The A & P food company was sanctioned for mispricing and for advertising unavailable products. An administrative judge ruled that the American Home Products Company falsely advertised Anacin as a tension reliever. The list seems endless.[99]

In the pharmaceutical industry, false advertising has a long history.[100] It has been common for medicines to be advertised as cure-alls for previously incurable diseases. Such medicines include alleged cures for cancer and arthritis and drugs advertised to give energy and sexual potency. How can we explain the frequency of false advertising by drug manufacturers? Often the problem arises because several competing companies market similar products and the key to successful sales is believed to be convincing the public that one of these products is far superior to the rest. Sometimes the intense drive for profits leads to falsification of data and unethical and illegal sales promotions.[101]

It has been difficult for authorities to police such violations of the public trust. Often, the most serious consequence to the corporation is an order that it refrain from using the advertising or withdraw the advertising claims. Criminal penalties for false claims are rarely given. Recently, "900" telephone numbers have been used to advertise products involving sex and companionship with high fees charged for each phone call. The Federal Trade Commission filed charges against some companies that use these numbers for using deception in their ad campaigns by promising services they cannot deliver or for overcharging for information calls.[102]

Environmental Crimes

Much attention has been paid to the intentional or negligent environmental pollution caused by many large corporations. The numerous allegations in this area involve almost every aspect of U.S. business. There are many different types of environmental crimes. Some corporations have endangered the lives of their own workers by maintaining unsafe conditions in their plants and mines. It has been estimated that 21 million workers have been exposed to hazardous materials while on the job. The National Institute of Occupational Safety and Health estimated that it would cost about $40 million just to alert these workers to the danger of their exposure to hazardous waste and $54 billion to watch them and track whether they developed occupationally related disease.[103] Some industries have been particularly hard-hit by complaints and allegations. The asbestos industry was inundated with lawsuits after environmental scientists found a close association between exposure to asbestos and the development of cancer. Over 250,000 people have filed 12,000 lawsuits against 260 asbestos manufacturers. In all, some insurance company officials estimate, asbestos-related lawsuits could amount to as much as $150 billion. Similarly, some 100,000 cotton mill workers suffer from some form of respiratory disease linked to prolonged exposure to cotton dust. About one-third of the workers are seriously disabled by brown lung disease, an illness similar to emphysema.[104] The control of workers' safety has been the province of the Occupational Safety and Health Administration (OSHA).

OSHA sets industry standards for the proper use of such chemicals as benzene, arsenic, lead, and coke. Intentional violation of OSHA standards can result in criminal penalties.

Environmental Pollution. A second type of environmental crime committed by large corporations is the illegal pollution of the environment. Sometimes pollution involves individual acts caused by negligence on the part of the polluter. Two cases stand out. The first involved the leaking of methyl isocynate from a Union Carbide plant in Bhopal, India, on December 3, 1984. Estimates of the death toll range from 1,400 to 10,000 people; another 60,000 were injured. Union Carbide later reported that the plant had not been operating safely and should have been closed. The firm blamed the negligence, however, on local officials who were running the plant.[105] The second case occurred when the tanker *Exxon Valdez* ran aground on a reef off the coast of Alaska on March 24, 1989, dumping 11 million gallons of crude oil and fouling 700 miles of shoreline. On March 13, 1991, Exxon agreed to pay $1 billion in criminal and civil fines rather than face trial; this is the largest amount paid as a result of environmental pollution to date (a federal judge later refused to accept this amount, and the case is still being settled).[106]

Equally serious is the prolonged, intentional pollution of the environment. A case in point is the illegal dumping of polychlorinated biphenyl (PCB). This compound has been used since 1929 in power transformers, electric typewriters, and electrical capacitors. However,

Environmental pollution is a significant danger to the nation and is an important component of corporate crime. These barrels of hazardous waste were illegally dumped in central New York state.

scientists have recently linked PCB to cancer and birth defects in laboratory animals. In Japan, people who ate rice oil contaminated with PCB suffered a variety of health problems. Chemical companies have been ordered not to use PCB; however, disposing of the chemical presents a serious problem. The Environmental Protection Agency (EPA) estimates that 20 million pounds await disposal and that 750 million pounds must eventually be destroyed. Some chemical companies have dumped their PCB stocks along public highways and in remote, illegal dump sites. In some areas, illegally dumped PCB has proven extremely hazardous. When it has been carelessly dropped in landfills, pits, and lagoons, PCB has contaminated waters, fish, and wildlife. Because of PCB contamination, fishing has been restricted in rivers in New York, Connecticut, Michigan, and other states. The EPA has estimated that the cost of cleaning up the 1,500 to 2,500 hazardous waste dump sites scattered around the United States ranges from $7.6 billion to $22.7 billion; its best overall estimate is $11.7 billion. Although the cleanup is expected to be supported by taxes on petrochemicals that go into a "superfund," some experts believe that it is unrealistic to believe that private industry will pay even half the costs.

Controlling Environmental Pollution.

The nature and scope of environmental crimes have prompted the federal government to pass a series of control measures designed to outlaw the worst abuses.[107] These measures are described below:

- Clean Air Act provides sanctions for companies that do not comply with the air quality standards established by the EPA.[108] The act can impose penalties on any person or institution that, for example, knowingly violates EPA plan requirements or emission standards, tampers with EPA monitoring devices, or makes false statements to EPA officials. The Clean Air Act was amended in 1990 to toughen up standards for emissions of many air pollutants.

- Federal Water Pollution Control Act, more commonly called the Clean Water Act, punishes the knowing or negligent discharge of a pollutant into navigable waters.[109] According to the act, a pollutant is any "man-made or man-induced alteration of the chemical, physical, biological, and radiological integrity of the water."

- Rivers and Harbors Act of 1899 (Refuse Act) punishes any discharge of waste materials that damages natural water quality.[110]

- Resource Conservation and Recovery Act of 1976 provides criminal penalties for four acts involving the illegal treatment of solid wastes: (1) the knowing transportation of any hazardous waste to a facility that does not have a legal permit for solid waste disposal; (2) the knowing treatment, storage, or disposal of any hazardous waste without a government permit or in violation of the provision of the permit; (3) the deliberate making of any false statement or representation in a report filed in compliance with the act; and (4) the destruction or alteration of records required to be maintained by the act.[111]

- Toxic Substance Control Act addresses the manufacture, processing, or distributing of chemical mixtures or substances in a manner not in accordance with established testing or manufacturing requirements; commercial use of a chemical substance or mixture that the commercial user knew was manufactured, processed, or distributed in violation of the act's requirements; and noncompliance with the reporting and inspection requirements of the act.[112]

- Federal Insecticide, Fungicide and Rodenticide Act regulates the manufacture and distribution of toxic pesticides.[113]

- The Comprehensive Environmental Response, Compensation, and Liability Act, also referred to as the "Superfund," requires the cleanup of hazardous waste at contaminated sites.[114]

Considering the uncertainties of federal budget allocations, there is some question whether these acts can be enforced well enough to effectively deter environmental crime. It is possible that the solution to the environmental problem must be found on the local level.

The Cause of White-Collar Crime

When Ivan Boesky pled guilty to one count of security fraud, he agreed to pay a civil fine of $100 million, the largest at that time in SEC history. Boesky's fine was later superseded by Michael Milken's fine of more than $1 billion. How, people asked, can people with so much disposable wealth get involved in a risky scheme to produce even more? There probably are as many explanations for white-collar crime as there are white-collar crimes. Herbert Edelhertz, an expert on the white-collar crime phenomenon, suggests that many offenders feel free to engage in business crime because they can easily rationalize its effects. Some convince themselves that their actions are not really crimes, because the acts involved do not resemble street crimes. For example, a banker who uses his position of trust to lend his institution's assets to a company he secretly controls may see himself as a shrewd businessman, not as a criminal. Or a pharmacist who chisels customers on prescription drugs may rationalize her behavior by telling herself that it does not really hurt anyone. Further, some businesspeople feel justified in committing white-collar crimes because they believe that government regulators do not really understand the business world or the problems of competing in the free enterprise system. Even when caught, many white-collar criminals cannot see the error of their ways. For example, one offender who was convicted in the electrical industry price-fixing conspiracy discussed earlier categorically denied the illegality of his actions. "We did not fix prices," he said, "I am telling you that all we did was recover costs."[115] Some white-collar criminals believe that everyone violates business laws, so it is not so bad if they do so themselves. Rationalizing greed is a common trait of white-collar criminals.

Greedy or Needy?

Greed is not the only motivation for white-collar crime; need also plays an important role. Executives may tamper with company books because they feel the need to keep or improve their jobs, satisfy their egos, or support their children. Blue-collar workers may pilfer because they need to keep pace with inflation or buy a new car. Kathleen Daly's analysis of convictions in seven federal district courts indicated that many white-collar crimes involve relatively trivial amounts. Women convicted of white-collar crime typically work in lower-echelon positions, and their acts seem motivated more out of economic survival than greed and power.[116]

Even people in the upper echelons of the financial world, such as Ivan Boesky, may carry scars from an earlier needy period in their lives that can only be healed by accumulating ever greater amounts of money. As one of Boesky's associates put it:

> I don't know what his devils were. Maybe he's greedy beyond the wildest imaginings of mere mortals like you and me. And maybe part of what drives the guy is an inherent insecurity that was operative here even after he had arrived. Maybe he never arrived.[117]

A well-known study of embezzlers by Donald Cressey illustrates the important role need plays in white-collar crime.[118] According to Cressey, embezzlement is caused by what he calls a "nonshareable financial problem." This condition may be the result of offenders' living beyond their means, perhaps piling up gambling debts; offenders feel they cannot let anyone know about such financial problems without ruining their reputations. Cressey claims that the door to solving personal financial problems through criminal means is opened by the rationalizations society has developed for white-collar crime: "Some of our most respectable citizens got their start in life by using other people's money temporarily"; "in the real estate business, there is nothing wrong about using deposits before the deal is closed"; "all people steal when they get in a tight spot."[119] Offenders use these and other rationalizations to resolve the conflict they experience over engaging in illegal behavior. Rationalizations allow offenders' financial needs to be met without compromising their values.

There are a number of more formal theories of white-collar crime. In the sections below, two of the more prominent are described in detail.

Corporate Culture Theory

The corporate culture view is that some business organizations promote white-collar criminality in the same way that lower-class culture encourages the development of juvenile gangs and street crime. According to the corporate culture view, some business enterprises cause crime by placing excessive demands on employees while at the same time maintaining a business climate tolerant of employee deviance. New employees learn the attitudes and techniques needed to commit white-collar crime from their business peers in a learning process reminiscent of the way Edwin Sutherland described how gang boys learn the techniques of drug dealing and burglary from older youths through differential association.

A number of attempts have been made to use corporate culture and structure to explain white-collar crime. For example, Ronald Kramer argues that business organizations will encourage employee criminality if they encounter serious difficulties in attaining their goals, especially making profits. Some organizations will create cost-reduction policies that inspire lawbreaking and corner cutting to become a norm passed on to employees. When new employees balk at violating business laws, they are told informally, "This is the way things are done here, don't worry about it." Kramer finds that a business's organizational environment, including economic, political, cultural, legal, technological, and interorganizational factors, influences the level of white-collar crime. If market conditions are weak, competition intense, law enforcement lax, and managers willing to stress success at any cost, then conditions for corporate crime are maximized.[120]

Kramer's view is analogous to the cultural deviance approach that suggests that crime occurs when obedience to the cultural norms and values people are in immediate contact with causes them to break the rules of conventional society. However, cultural deviance theory was originally directed at lower-class slum boys, not business executives. Kramer's view is that the same crime-producing forces may be operating among both socioeconomic groups.

Australian sociologist John Braithwaite has promoted the corporate culture view in his writings on white-collar crime.[121] According to Braithwaite's model, businesspeople in any society may find themselves in a situation where their organization's stated goals cannot be achieved through conventional business practices; they perceive "blocked opportunities." In a capitalist society, up-and-coming young executives may find that their profit ratios are below par; in a socialist society, young bureaucrats panic when their production levels fall short of the five-year plan. Under such moments of stress, entrepreneurs may find that illegitimate opportunities are the only solution to their problem; their careers must be saved at all costs. So when a government official is willing to take a bribe to overlook costly safety violations, the bribe is gratefully offered. Or when insider trading can increase profits, the investment banker leaps at the chance to engage in it. But how can traditionally law-abiding people overcome the ties of conventional law and morality?

Braithwaite believes that organizational crime is a function of the corporate climate. Organizational crime flourishes in corporations that contain an ongoing employee subculture that resists government regulation and socializes new workers in the skills and attitudes necessary to violate the law. For example, junior executives may learn from their seniors how to meet clandestinely with their competitors to fix prices and how to rationalize this as a "good, necessary and inevitable thing." The existence of law-violating subcultures is enhanced when a hostile relationship exists between the organization and the governmental bodies that regulate it. When these agencies are viewed as uncooperative, untrustworthy, and resistant to change, corporations will be more likely to develop clandestine, law-violating subcultures. A positive working relationship with their governmental overseers will reduce the need for a secret, law-violating infrastructure to develop. Illegal corporate

behavior can only exist in secrecy; public scrutiny brings the "shame" of a criminal label to people whose social life and community standing rests upon their good name and character.

The shame of discovery has an important moderating influence on corporate crime. Its source may be external: the general community, professional or industry peers, or government regulatory agencies. The source of shame and disapproval can also be internal. Many corporations have stated policies that firmly admonish employees to obey the rule of law. For example, it is common for corporations to encourage whistle-blowing by co-workers and to sanction workers who violate the law and cause embarrassment. These organizations are "full of antennas" to pick up irregularities and make it widely known that certain individuals or subunits are responsible for law violations. In a sense, corporations that maintain an excess of definitions unfavorable to violating the law will be less likely to contain deviant subcultures and concomitantly less likely to violate business regulations. In contrast, corporate crime thrives in organizations that isolate people within spheres of responsibility, where lines of communication are blocked or stretched thin, and in which deviant subcultures are allowed to develop with impunity.

Those holding the corporate culture view, such as Braithwaite and Kramer, would view the savings and loan and insider trading scandals as prime examples of what happens when people work in organizations whose cultural values stress profit over fair play, in which government scrutiny is limited and regulators are viewed as the enemy, and in which senior members encourage newcomers to believe that "greed is good."

The Self-Control View

Not all criminologists agree with the corporate culture theory. Travis Hirschi and Michael Gottfredson take exception to the hypothesis that white-collar crime is a product of the corporate culture.[122] If that were true, there would be much more white-collar crime than actually exists, and white-collar criminals would not be embarrassed by their misdeeds, as most seem to be. Instead, Hirschi and Gottfredson maintain, the motives that produce white-collar crimes are the same as those that produce any other criminal behaviors; "the desire for relatively quick, relatively certain benefit, with minimal effort." As you may recall, Hirschi and Gottfredson's general theory of crime holds that criminals lack self-control; the motivation and pressure to commit white-collar crime is the same for any other form of crime.

White-collar criminals are people with low self-control who are inclined to follow momentary impulses without consideration of the long-term costs of such behavior.[123] They find that white-collar crime is relatively rare because, as a matter of course, business executives tend to hire people with self-control, thereby limiting the number of potential white-collar criminals. Hirschi and Gottfredson have collected data showing that the demographic distribution of white-collar crime is similar to other crimes. For example, gender, race, and age ratios are the same for such crimes as embezzlement and fraud as they are for street crimes, such as burglary and robbery.

Do White-Collar Criminals Lack Self-Control?

Business executives and corporate executives seem to be people who would have above, rather than below, average self-control. Can Gottfredson and Hirschi's view of white-collar crime be correct?[124] There is some independent evidence developed by David Weisburd, Ellen Chayet, and Elin Waring that white-collar criminals are often repeat offenders. They also share many characteristics with street criminals (such as being impulsive and egocentric), although they begin their careers later in life and offend at a slower pace.[125]

Even if the Gottfredson-Hirschi view is accurate, it is possible that white-collar offenders manifest a wide range of self-control. And, as Michael Benson and Elizabeth Moore suggest, the level of offenders' self-control may determine the path they take to crime. Benson and Moore find that some with low self-control impulsively commit fraud and other crimes to pursue their own self-interest; these are most like common criminals. Others with high self-control pursue "ego gratification in an aggressive and calculating fashion"; they are the products of the "greed is good" philosophy. In the middle are offenders who take advantage of criminal opportunities to satisfy an immediate personal need; in them, self-control becomes overwhelmed by special problems. Benson and Moore, then, view self-control as a variable and not a constant that interacts with need and opportunity to produce white-collar crimes.[126]

≡ Controlling White-Collar Crime

Conflict theorists argue that, unlike lower-class street criminals, white-collar criminals are rarely prosecuted and, when convicted, receive relatively light sentences. This claim is supported by studies of white-collar crimi-

nality that show it is rare for a corporate or white-collar criminal to receive a serious criminal penalty. [127] Paul Jesilow, Henry Pontell, and Gilbert Geis found that physicians who engage in Medicaid fraud are rarely prosecuted and when they are, judges are reluctant to severely punish them. As one official told them, "When we convicted a guy, I wanted to see him do hard time. But what the hell, seeing what's going on in prisons these days and things like that, I think to put one of these guys in prison for hard time doesn't make any sense. . . ."[128] Marshall Clinard and Peter Yeager's analysis of 477 corporations found that only one in ten serious and one in 20 moderate violations resulted in sanctions.[129] In a subsequent analysis, Yeager found that when white-collar statutes are enforced, there is a tendency to penalize small, powerless businesses while treating the market leaders more leniently.[130]

There are a number of reasons for the leniency afforded white-collar criminals. Though white-collar criminals may produce millions of dollars of losses and endanger human life, some judges believe they are not "real criminals" but businesspeople just trying to make a living.[131] As Clinard and Yeager report, businesspeople often seek legal advice and are well aware of the loopholes in the law. If caught, they can claim that they had sought legal advice and believed they were in compliance with the law.[132] White-collar criminals are often considered nondangerous offenders because they usually are respectable, older citizens who have families to support. These "pillars of the community" are not seen in the same light as a teenager who breaks into a drugstore to steal a few dollars. Their public humiliation at being caught is usually deemed punishment enough; a prison sentence seems unnecessarily cruel.

Judges and prosecutors may identify with the white-collar criminal based on shared background and world views; they may have engaged in similar types of illegal behavior themselves.[133] Still another factor complicating white-collar crime enforcement is that many legal business and governmental acts seem as morally tinged as those made illegal by government regulation. For example, the Air Force forced a general to step down and punished two others for mismanaging the C-17 cargo plane, which accrued $1.5 billion in cost overruns. Their alleged misconduct included funneling $450 million in payments to the contractor, McDonnell Douglas, that were "premature, improper and possibly illegal."[134] Despite their questionable morality and ethics, these acts were not treated as crimes. Yet when compared to other business practices made illegal by government regulation, such as price-fixing, the distinctions are hard to see. It may seem unfair to prosecutors and judges to penalize some government and business officials for actions not too dissimilar from those applauded in the *Wall Street Journal*.[135]

Finally, some corporate practices that result in death or disfigurement are treated as civil actions in which victims receive monetary damages. The most well-known case involves the A. H. Robins Company's Dalkon Shield intrauterine device, which caused massive trauma to hundreds of thousands of women, including pelvic disease, infertility, and septic abortions, and is suspected in 20 deaths. The outcome of the case was that the company went through bankruptcy and set up a multibillion-dollar trust for the survivors.[136] More recently, a number of drug companies, including Bristol Myers Squibb, set up a similar trust fund to compensate victims who suffered because their products used in breast implant surgery were defective and dangerous. Though these cases involve much more serious injury than, say, insider trading, they are not considered criminal matters.

White-Collar Law Enforcement Systems

On the federal level, detection of white-collar crime is primarily in the hands of administrative departments and agencies.[137] Usually, the decision to pursue criminal rather than civil violations is based on the seriousness of the case, the perpetrator's intent, actions to conceal the violation and prior record.

Any evidence of criminal activity is then sent to the Department of Justice or the FBI for investigation. Some other federal agencies, such as the Securities and Exchange Commission and the U.S. Postal Service, have their own investigative arms. Usually, enforcement is reactive (generated by complaints) rather than proactive (involving ongoing investigations or the monitoring of activities). Investigations are carried out by the various federal agencies and the FBI. The FBI has made enforcement of white-collar laws one of its three top priorities (along with combatting foreign counterintelligence and organized crime). If criminal prosecution is called for, the case will be handled by attorneys from the criminal, tax, antitrust, and civil rights divisions of the Justice Department. If insufficient evidence is available to warrant a criminal prosecution, the case will be handled civilly or administratively by some other federal agency. For example, the Federal Trade Commission can issue a cease and desist order in antitrust or merchandising fraud cases.

On the state and local level, enforcement of white-collar laws is often disorganized and inefficient. Confusion may exist over the jurisdiction of the state attorney general and local prosecutors. The technical expertise of the federal government is often lacking on the state level.

Local and state law enforcement officials have made progress in a number of areas, such as control of consumer fraud. The Environmental Crimes Strike Force in Los Angeles County, California, is considered a model for the control of illegal dumping and pollution.[138] The number of state-funded technical assistance offices to help local prosecutors has increased significantly; more than 40 states offer such services.

There is evidence that local prosecutors will pursue white-collar criminals more vigorously if they are part of a team effort involving a network of law enforcement agencies.[139] However, as Michael Benson, Francis Cullen, and William Maakestad found in their national survey, local prosecutors did not consider white-collar crimes particularly serious problems. They were more willing to prosecute cases if the offense causes substantial harm and other agencies fail to take action. Relatively few prosecutors participate in interagency task forces designed to investigate white-collar criminal activity.[140] Benson and his colleagues found that local prosecutors believe that the criminal law should be used against corporate offenders and that tougher criminal penalties would improve corporate compliance with the law.

The number of prosecutors who believe that upper-class criminals are not above the law is growing. While their findings were encouraging, Benson also found that the funds and staff needed for local white-collar prosecutions are often scarce. Crimes considered more serious, such as drug trafficking, usually take precedence over corporate violations. Coordination is uncommon, and there is relatively little resource sharing. It is likely that concern over the environment may encourage local prosecutors to take action against those who violate state pollution and antidumping laws.[141]

White-collar crime law enforcement is often left to business organizations themselves. Corporations spend hundreds of millions of dollars each year on internal audits that help unearth white-collar offenses. Local chambers of commerce, the insurance industry, and other elements of the business community have mounted campaigns against white-collar crime. Aiding the investigation of white-collar offenses is a movement toward protecting employees who "blow the whistle" on their firm's violations. Five states—Michigan, Connecticut, Maine, California, and New York—have passed laws protecting workers from being fired if they testify about violations.[142] Without such help, the hands of justice are tied.

The prevailing wisdom then is that many white-collar criminals avoid prosecution and those that are prosecuted receive lenient punishments. What efforts have been made to bring violators of the public trust to justice?

White-Collar Control Strategies: Compliance

White-collar enforcement typically involves two strategies designed to control organizational deviance: compliance and deterrence.[143]

Compliance strategies aim for law conformity without the necessity of detecting, processing, or penalizing individual violators. At a minimum, they ask for cooperation and self-policing among the business community. Compliance systems attempt to create conformity by providing economic incentives to companies to obey the law. They rely on administrative efforts to prevent unwanted conditions before they occur. Compliance systems depend on the threat of economic sanctions or civil penalties (referred to as *economism*) to control corporate violators.

One method of compliance is to set up administrative agencies to oversee business activity. For example, the Security and Exchange Commission regulates Wall Street activities, and the Food and Drug Administration regulates drugs, cosmetics, medical devices, meats, and other foods. The legislation creating these agencies usually spells out the penalties for violating regulatory standards. This approach has been used to control environmental crimes, for example, by levying heavy fines based on the quantity and quality of pollution released into the environment.[144] A recent case involved a lawsuit brought against the Sherwin-Williams paint company for a long pattern of dumping dangerous chemicals into the sewers on Chicago's Southside.[145]

A number of states, including New Jersey, Arkansas, California, and Ohio, have passed stringent laws making firms liable for cleaning up toxic sites; some prohibit the sale of companies or their assets unless environmental safety conditions have been met.[146]

In another form of economism, the federal government has instituted a policy of barring people and businesses from receiving government contracts if they are found to have engaged in fraudulent practices, such as bribing public officials. For example, in June 1993, the Computer Sciences Company was banned from bidding on government contracts because it made false claims in a contract; the ban was lifted one month later when the company paid $2.1 million in damages.[147]

While it is difficult to gauge the effectiveness of compliance, research indicates that strict enforcement of regulatory laws can reduce violations of illegal or dangerous business practices. For example, one study found that strict enforcement of penalties under the Occupational and Safety Health Act can significantly reduce workplace injuries.[148]

In sum, compliance strategies attempt to create a marketplace incentive to obey the law—for example, the more a company pollutes, the more costly and unprofitable that pollution becomes. They limit individual blame and punishment, a practice whose deterrent effect seems problematic. Compliance strategies also avoid stigmatizing and "shaming" businesspeople by focusing on the act, rather than the actor, in white-collar crime.[149]

The Limits of Compliance.

Compliance systems are not applauded by all criminologists. Some experts point out that economic sanctions have limited value in controlling white-collar crime because economic penalties are imposed only after crimes have occurred, require careful governmental regulation, and often amount to only a slap on the wrist.[150] Compliance is particularly difficult to achieve if the federal government adopts a pro-business, anti-regulation fiscal policy that encourages economic growth by removing controls over business.

It is also possible for corporations hit with fines and regulatory fees to pass the costs on to consumers in the form of higher prices or reduced services. Shareholders who had little to do with the crime may see their stock dividends cut or share prices fall.[151]

The fines and penalties involved in compliance strategies may be of little import for a company doing billions in annual business. When the Baxter International pharmaceutical company was banned from bidding on new federal contracts for one year because it deceived government purchasing agents, the punishment was a blow to its corporate reputation. Yet Baxter does $130 million in sales to federal agencies out of a total revenue of $8.5 billion annually! While humiliating, the ban affects a relatively small amount of the company's business.[152]

Because of these conditions, some criminologists maintain that the punishment of white-collar crimes should contain a retributive component similar to that used in common-law crimes. White-collar crimes, after all, are immoral activities that have harmed social values and deserve commensurate punishment.[153] Furthermore, as Raymond Michalowski and Ronald Kramer point out, corporations can get around economic sanctions by moving their rule-violating activities overseas, where legal controls over injurious corporate activities are lax or nonexistent.[154]

White-Collar Control Strategies: Deterrence

Deterrence strategies involve detection of criminal violations, determining who is responsible, and penalizing them to deter future violations.[155] Punishment serves as a warning to potential violators who might break rules if other violators had not already been penalized. Deterrence systems are oriented toward apprehending violators and punishing them rather than creating conditions that induce conformity to the law.

Deterrence strategies should—and have—worked, since white-collar crime by its nature is a rational act whose perpetrators are extremely sensitive to the threat of criminal sanctions. Gilbert Geis cites numerous instances in which prison sentences for corporate crimes have produced a significant decline in white-collar activity.[156] Similar reasearch by Steven Klepper and Daniel Nagin suggests perceptions of detection and punishment for white-collar crimes appear to be a powerful deterrent to future law violations.[157]

Punishing White-Collar Criminals

There have been dramatic examples of deterrence strategies used by federal and state justice systems to prevent white-collar crime. It is not extraordinary to hear of corporate officers receiving long prison sentences in conjunction with corporate crimes. Woody Lemons received a 30-year sentence for his role as chairman of the Vernon S&L.[158] Corporate executives have even been charged with murder because of the actions of their companies, as the Close-Up entitled "Can Corporations Commit Murder?" discusses.[159]

Are such stiff penalties the norm, or are they infrequent instances of governmental resolve? Two surveys conducted by the federal government's Bureau of Justice Statistics shed some light on this issue.[160] The first, a review of enforcement practices in nine states, found that (1) white-collar crimes account for about 6 percent of all arrest dispositions, (2) 88 percent of all those arrested for white-collar crimes were prosecuted, and (3) 74 percent subsequently were convicted in criminal court. The survey also showed that while 60 percent of white-collar criminals convicted in state courts were incarcerated (a number comparable to the punishment given most other offenders), relatively few white-collar offenders (18 percent) received a prison term of more than a year. The second survey followed white-collar cases prosecuted by the federal government between 1980 and 1985. Consistent with the government's "get

tough" policy on white-collar crime, convictions rose 18 percent between 1980 and 1985, and the conviction rate for white-collar offenders (85 percent) was higher than that for all other federal crimes (78 percent).

There are indications that deterrence policies may be aided now that the federal government has created sentencing guidelines that control punishment for convicted criminals. Prosecutors can now control the length and type of sentence through their handling of the charging process. The guidelines also create mandatory minimum prison sentences that must be served for some crimes; judicial clemency can no longer be counted on.[161]

This new "get tough" deterrence approach also appears to be affecting all classes of white-collar criminals. While the prevailing wisdom is that the affluent corporate executive usually avoids serious punishment, research by David Weisburd and his associates indicates that high-status offenders are more likely to be punished than previously believed.[162] The Weisburd research seems to indicate that public displeasure with such highly publicized white-collar crimes as the S&L scandal, the HUD fraud, and the BCCI case may be producing a backlash that is resulting in the more frequent use of prison sentences. Some commentators now argue that the government may actually be going overboard in its efforts to punish white-collar criminals, especially for crimes that are the result of negligent business practices rather than intentional criminal conspiracy.[163]

≡ Organized Crime

The second branch of organizational criminality involves **organized crime**—the ongoing criminal enterprise groups whose ultimate purpose is personal economic gain through illegitimate means. Here, a structured enterprise system is set up to supply consumers on a continuing basis with merchandise and services banned by the criminal law but for which a ready market exists: prostitution, pornography, gambling, and narcotics. The system may resemble a legitimate business run by an ambitious chief executive officer, his or her assistants, staff attorneys, and accountants, with highly thorough and efficient accounts receivable and complaint departments.[164]

Because of its secrecy, power, and fabulous wealth, a great mystique has grown up about organized crime. Its legendary leaders—Al Capone, Meyer Lansky, Lucky Luciano—have been the subjects of books and films. The famous *Godfather* films popularized and humanized organized crime figures; the media all too often glamorizes organized crime figures.[165] Most citizens believe that organized criminals are capable of taking over legitimate business enterprises if given the opportunity. Almost everyone is familiar with such terms as *mob, underworld, Mafia, wiseguys, syndicate,* or *La Cosa Nostra,* which refer to organized crime. Though most of us have neither met nor seen members of organized crime families, we feel sure that they exist, and most certainly, we fear them. This section will briefly define organized crime, review its history, and discuss its economic effect and control.

Characteristics of Organized Crime

A precise description of the characteristics of organized crime is difficult to formulate, but some of its general traits are:[166]

- Organized crime is a conspiratorial activity, involving the coordination of numerous persons in the planning and execution of illegal acts or in the pursuit of a legitimate objective by unlawful means (for example, threatening a legitimate business to get a stake in it). Organized crime involves continuous commitment by primary members, although individuals with specialized skills may be brought in as needed. Organized crime organizations are usually structured along hierarchical lines—a chieftain supported by close advisers, lower subordinates, and so on.

- Organized crime has economic gain as its primary goal, though achievement of power or status may also be motivating factors. Economic gain is achieved through maintenance of a near monopoly on illegal goods and services, including drugs, gambling, pornography, and prostitution.

- Organized crime activities are not limited to providing illicit services. They include such sophisticated activities as laundering illegal money through legitimate businesses, land fraud, and computer crimes.

- Organized crime employs predatory tactics, such as intimidation, violence, and corruption. It appeals to greed to accomplish its objectives and preserve its gains.

- By experience, custom, and practice, organized crime's conspiratorial groups are usually very quick and effective in controlling and disciplining their members, associates, and victims. The individuals involved know that any deviation from the rules of the organization will evoke a prompt response from the other participants. This response may range from a reduction in rank and responsibility to a death sentence.

- Organized crime is not synonymous with the Mafia (or La Cosa Nostra—"Our Thing"), the most experienced, most diversified, and possibly best-disciplined of these groups. The Mafia is actually a common stereotype of organized crime. Although several families in the organization called La Cosa Nostra are important components of organized crime activities, they do not hold a monopoly on underworld activities.

- Organized crime does not include terrorists dedicated to political change. Although violent acts are a major tactic of organized crime, the use of violence does not mean that a group is part of a confederacy of organized criminals.

Activities of Organized Crime

What are the main activities of organized crime? The traditional sources of income are derived from providing illicit materials and using force to enter into and maximize profits in legitimate businesses.[167] Annual gross income from criminal activity is at least $50 billion, more than 1 percent of the gross national product; some estimates put gross earnings as high as $90 billion, outranking most major industries in the United States.[168] Most organized crime income comes from narcotics distribution (over $30 billion annually), loan-sharking (lending money at illegal rates—$7 billion), and prostitution ($3 billion). However, additional billions come from gambling, theft rings, and other illegal enterprises. For example, the Attorney General's Commission on Pornography concluded that organized crime figures exert substantial influence and control over the pornography industry.[169] Organized criminals have infiltrated labor unions, taking control of their pension funds and dues. Alan Block has described mob control of the New York waterfront and its influence on the use of union funds to buy insurance, health care, and so on from mob-controlled companies.[170] Hijacking of shipments and cargo theft are other sources of income. One study found that the annual losses due to theft of air cargo amount to $400 million; rail cargo, $600 million; trucking, $1.2 billion; and maritime shipments, $300 million.[171] Underworld figures engage in the fencing of

CLOSE-UP

Can Corporations Commit Murder?

One of the most controversial issues surrounding the punishment of white-collar criminals involves the prosecution of corporate executives who work for companies that manufacture products believed to have caused the death of workers or consumers. Are the executives guilty of manslaughter or even murder?

The most famous case took place in the 1970s, when a local prosecutor failed in an attempt to convict Ford Motor Company executives on charges of homicide in crashes involving Pintos, as a result of deaths due to known dangers in the car's design. The Pinto had a gas tank that burst into flame when involved in a low-velocity, rear-end collision. Though the design defect could have been corrected for about $20 per car, the company failed to take prompt action. When three people were killed in crashes, an Indiana prosecutor brought murder charges against Ford executives. However, they were acquitted because the jury did not find sufficient evidence that they intended the deaths to occur.

The question of whether corporate executives could be successful-

ly prosecuted for murder was answered on June 16, 1985, when an Illinois judge found three officials of the Film Recovery Systems Corporation guilty of murder in the death of a worker. The employee died after inhaling cyanide poison under "totally unsafe" work conditions. During the trial, evidence was presented showing that employees were not warned that they were working with dangerous substances, that company officials ignored complaints of illness, and that safety precautions had been deliberately ignored. The murder convictions were later overturned on appeal.

The Pinto and Film Recovery cases opened the door for prosecuting corporate executives on violent crime charges stemming from unsafe products or working conditions. There is little question that corporate liability may be increasing. As Nancy Frank points out, a number of states have adopted the concept of unintended murder in their legal codes. This means that persons can be charged and convicted of murder if their acts, though essentially unintended, are imminently dangerous to another or have a strong probability of causing death or great bodily harm. This legal theory would include corpo-

rate executives who knew about the dangers of their products but chose to do nothing because either correction would lower profits or they simply did not care about consumers or workers.

A case illustrating this legal doctrine involved the fire on September 3, 1991, at Imperial Food Products, Inc., a North Carolina chicken processing plant. The fire, which claimed 25 lives, was deadly because the plant had no sprinkler system, windows, or escape routes. Company executives had *locked* exit doors to prevent employee pilferage. Emmett Roe, the firm's owner, was convicted of involuntary manslaughter and received a 19-year prison sentence. In this case and others around the country, local prosecutors are taking the initiative to prosecute corporate executives as violent criminals.

Discussion Questions

1. If the Ford executives knew they had a dangerous car, should they have been found guilty of murder, even though the deaths were the result of collisions?
2. Is it fair to blame a single executive for the activities of a company that has thousands of employees?

high-value items and maintain international sales territories. In recent years, they have branched into computer crime and other white-collar activities.

Organized Crime and Legitimate Enterprise

Outside of criminal enterprises, additional billions are earned by organized crime figures who force or buy

their way into legitimate businesses and use them both for profit and a means of siphoning off ("laundering") otherwise unaccountable profits. Merry Morash claims that mob control of legitimate enterprise today is influenced by market conditions. Businesses most likely to be affected are low-technology (such as garbage collection), have uniform products, and operate in rigid markets where increases in price will not result in reduced demand. In addition, industries most affected by labor

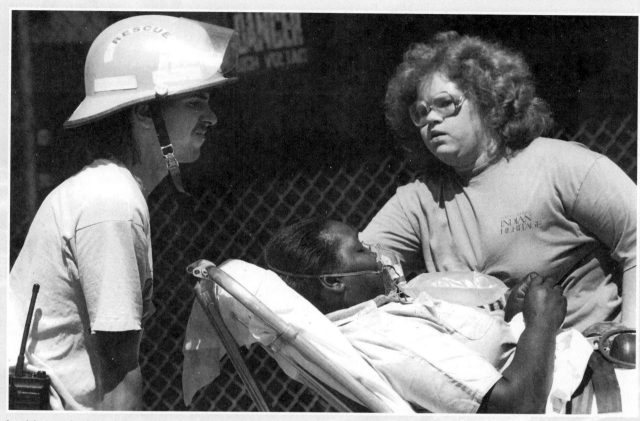

A stricken worker is carried out of the Imperial Food Processing plant. Twenty-four workers died in the fire because the exit doors were locked to prevent pilferage. The owner was later convicted of involuntary manslaughter and sent to prison.

SOURCES: John Wright, Francis Cullen, and Michael Blankenship, "The Social Construction of Corporate Violence: Media Coverage of the Imperial Food Products Fire" (Paper presented at the annual meeting of the American Society of Criminology, Phoenix, Arizona, November 1993); Nancy Frank, "Unintended Murder and Corporate Risk-taking: Defining the Concept of Justifiability," *Journal of Criminal Justice* 16 (1988): 17–24; Francis Cullen, William Maakestad, and Gary Cavender, "The Ford Pinto Case and Beyond: Corporate Crime, Moral Boundaries and the Criminal Sanction," in *Corporations as Criminals,* ed. Ellen Hochstedler (Beverly Hills: Sage, 1984), pp. 107–130.

pressure are highly susceptible to takeovers because a mob-controlled work stoppage would destroy a product or interfere with meeting deadlines. Morash lists five ways in which organized criminals today become involved in legitimate enterprise: (1) business activity that supports illegal enterprises—for example, providing a front; (2) predatory or parasitic exploitation—for example, demanding protection money; (3) organization of monopolies or cartels to limit competition; (4) unfair advantages gained by such practices as manipulation of labor unions and corruption of public officials; and (5) illegal manipulation of legal vehicles, particularly stocks and bonds.[172]

These traits show how organized crime is more like a business enterprise than a confederation of criminals seeking to merely enhance their power. Nowhere has this relationship been more visible than in the 1985 scandal that rocked the prestigious First National Bank of Boston. Federal prosecutors charged that the bank made unreported cash shipments of $1.2 million. It received $529,000 in small bills and sent $690,000 in bills of $100 or more. The bank was fined $500,000 for violating a law that requires that banks report any cash transaction of $10,000 or more. The bank's transaction came under scrutiny during an FBI investigation of the Angiulo crime family, which bought more than $41.7 million in cashier's checks from the bank.[173] The First National scandal illustrates that organized crime today involves a cooperative relationship between big business, politicians, and racketeers. The relationship is an expensive one: it has been estimated that organized crime activities stifle competition, resulting in the loss of 400,000 jobs and $18 billion in productivity; and since organized crime's profits go unreported, the rest of the population pays an extra $6.5 billion in taxes.[174]

≡ The Concept of Organized Crime

The term *organized crime* conjures up images of strong men in dark suits, machine-gun-toting bodyguards, rituals of allegiance to secret organizations, professional "gangland" killings, and meetings of "family" leaders who chart the course of crime much like the board members at General Motors decide on the country's transportation needs. These images have become part of what criminologists refer to as the alien conspiracy theory concept of organized crime. This is the belief, adhered to by the federal government and many respected criminologists, that organized crime is a direct offshoot of a criminal society—the Mafia—that first originated in Italy and Sicily and now controls racketeering in major U.S. cities. A major premise of the alien conspiracy theory is that the Mafia is centrally coordinated by a national committee that settles disputes, dictates policy, and assigns territory.[175] Not all criminologists believe in this narrow concept of organized crime, and many view the alien conspiracy theory as a figment of the media's imagination.[176] Their view depicts organized crime as a group of ethnically diverse gangs or groups who compete for profit in the sale of illegal goods and services or who use force and violence to extort money from legitimate enterprises. These groups are not bound by a central national organization but act independently on their own turf. We will now examine each of these two perspectives in some detail.

Alien Conspiracy Theory: La Cosa Nostra

According to the alien conspiracy theory, organized crime is really comprised of a national syndicate of 25 or so Italian-dominated crime families that call themselves La Cosa Nostra. The major families have a total membership of about 1,700 "made men," who have been inducted into organized crime families, and another 17,000 "associates," who are criminally involved with syndicate members.[177] The families control crime in distinct geographic areas. New York City, the most important organized crime area, alone contains five families—the Gambino, Columbo, Lucchese, Bonnano, and Genovese families—named after their founding "godfathers"; in contrast, Chicago contains a single mob organization called the "outfit," which also influences racketeering in such cities as Milwaukee, Kansas City, and Phoenix. The families are believed to be ruled by a "commission" made up of the heads of the five New York families and bosses from Detroit, Buffalo, Chicago, and Philadelphia, which settles personal problems and jurisdictional conflicts and enforces rules that allow members to gain huge profits through the manufacture and sale of illegal goods and services (see Figure 13.2).[178]

Development of a National Syndicate.
How did this concept of a national crime cartel develop? The first "organized" gangs were comprised of Irish immigrants who made their home in the slum districts of New York City.[179] The "Forty Thieves," considered the first New York gang with a definite, acknowledged leadership, were muggers, thieves, and pickpockets on the lower east side of Manhattan from the 1820s to just before the Civil War. Around 1890, Italian immigrants began forming gangs modeled after the Sicilian crime organization known as the Mafia; these gangs were called the "Black Hand." In 1900, Johnny Torrio, a leader of New York's "Five Points" gang, moved to Chicago and helped his uncle, Big Jim Colosimo, organize the dominant gang in the Chicago area. Other gangs also flourished in Chicago, including those of Hymie Weiss and "Bugs" Moran. A later leader was the infamous Al "Scarface" Capone. The turning point of organized crime was the onset of Prohibition and the Volstead Act. This created a multimillion-dollar bootlegging industry overnight. Gangs vied for a share of the business, and bloody wars for control of rackets and profits became common. However, the problems of supplying liquor to thousands of illegal drinking establishments (speakeasies) required organization and an end to open warfare.

In the late 1920s, several events helped create the structure of organized crime. First, Johnny Torrio became leader of the Unione Siciliano, an ethnic self-help group that had begun as a legitimate enterprise but had been taken over by racketeers. This helped bring together the Chicago and New York crime groups; and since Torrio was Italian, it also spurred the beginnings of détente between Italians and Sicilians, who had been at odds with one another. Also during the 1920s, more than 500 members of Sicilian gangs fled to the United States to avoid prosecution; these new arrivals included future gang leaders Carlo Gambino, Joseph Profaci, Stefano Maggadino, and Joseph Bonnano.[180]

In December 1925, gang leaders from across the nation met in Cleveland to discuss strategies for mediating their differences nonviolently and for maximizing profits. A similar meeting took place in Atlantic City in 1929 and was attended by 20 gang leaders, including

FIGURE 13.2 Traditional Organization of the Mafia "Family"

SOURCE: U.S. Senate, Permanent Subcommittee on Investigations, Committee on Governmental Affairs, *Hearings on Organized Crime and Use of Violence,* 96th Cong., 2d Sess., April 1980, p. 117.

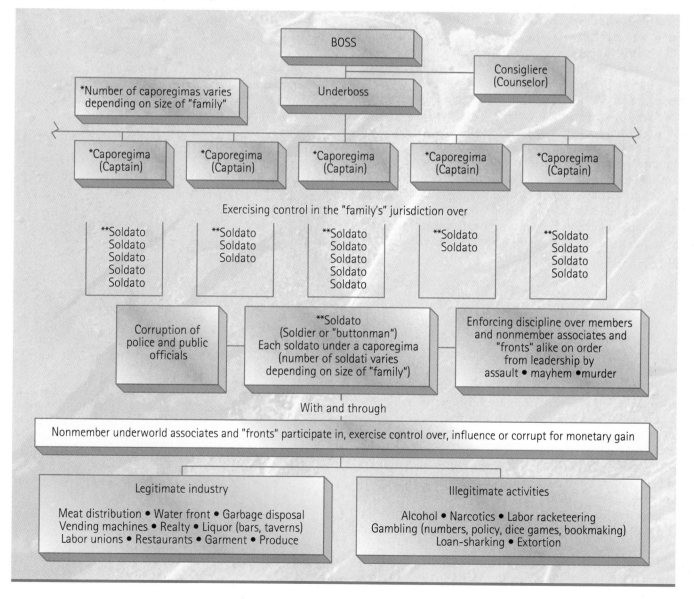

Lucky Luciano, Al Capone, and "Dutch" Schultz. Despite such efforts, however, gang wars continued into the 1930s. In 1934, according to some accounts, another meeting in New York, called by Johnny Torrio and Lucky Luciano, led to the formation of a national crime commission and acknowledged the territorial claims of 24 crime families around the country. This was considered the beginning of La Cosa Nostra.

Under the leadership of the national crime commission, organized crime began to expand more orderly. Benjamin "Bugsy" Siegel was dispatched to California to oversee West Coast operations. The end of Prohibition required a new source of profits, and narcotics sales became the mainstay of gangland business. Al Polizzi, a Cleveland crime boss, formed a news service that provided information on horse racing, thereby helping create a national network of gang-dominated bookmakers. After World War II, organized crime families began using their vast profits from liquor, gambling, and narcotics to buy into legitimate businesses, such as entertainment, legal gambling in Cuba and Las Vegas, hotel chains, jukebox concerns, restaurants, and taverns. By paying off politicians, police, and judges and by using blackmail and coercion, organized criminals became almost immune to prosecution. The machine-gun-toting gangster had given way to the businessman-racketeer. In the 1950s, cooperation among gangland figures reached its zenith. Gang control over unions became widespread, and many legitimate businesses made payoffs to promote labor peace. New gang organizations arose in Los Angeles, Kansas City, and Dallas.

Post-1950 Developments.

In 1950, the Senate Special Committee to Investigate Organized Crime in Interstate Commerce, better known as the Kefauver Committee (after its chairman), was formed to look into organized crime. It reported the existence of a national crime cartel whose members cooperated to make a profit and engaged in joint ventures to eliminate enemies. The Kefauver Committee also made public the syndicate's enforcement arm, Murder Inc., which, under the leadership of Albert Anastasia, disposed of enemies for a price. The committee also found that corruption and bribery of local political officials were widespread. This theme was revived by the Senate Subcommittee on Investigations, better known as the McClellan Committee, in its investigation of the role organized crime played in labor racketeering. The committee and its chief counsel, Robert Kennedy, uncovered a close relationship between gang activity and the Teamsters Union, then led by Jimmy Hoffa. Hoffa's disappearance

and assumed death has been linked to his gangland connections. Later investigations by the committee produced the testimony of Joseph Valachi, former underworld "soldier," who detailed the inner workings of La Cosa Nostra. The leaders of the national crime cartel at this time were Frank Costello, Vito Genovese, Carlo Gambino, Joseph Bonnano, and Joseph Profaci, all of New York; Sam Giancana of Chicago; and Angelo Bruno of Philadelphia.

During the next 15 years, gang activity expanded further into legitimate businesses. Nonetheless, gangland jealousy, competition, and questions of succession produced an occasional flare-up of violence. The most well-publicized conflict occurred between the Gallo brothers

Benjamin "Bugsy" Siegel (no relation to this author!) was a colorful crime figure who, before his shooting death, ran the first casino in Las Vegas. Here he is shown after being taken from his luxurious Holmby Hills home for questioning at Los Angeles police headquarters about the gangland slaying of Harry Schachter in Hollywood on Thanksgiving Day, 1940.

of Brooklyn—Albert, Larry, and Crazy Joe—and the Profaci crime family. The feud continued through the 1960s, uninterrupted by the death of Joseph Profaci and the new leadership of his group by Joe Colombo. Eventually, Colombo was severely injured by a Gallo hired assassin, and in return, Joey Gallo was killed in a New York restaurant, Umberto's Clam House. Gallo's death once again brought peace in the underworld. Emerging as the most powerful syndicate boss was Carlo Gambino, who held this position until his death by natural causes in 1976.

In sum, the alien conspiracy theory sees organized crime as being run by an ordered group of ethnocentric (primarily of Italian origin) criminal syndicates, maintaining unified leadership and shared values. These syndicates are in close communication with other groups and obey the decisions of a national commission charged with settling disputes and creating crime policy.

The Mafia Myth

Some scholars charge that this version of organized crime is fanciful. They argue that the alien conspiracy theory is too heavily influenced by media accounts and by the testimony of a single person, mobster Joseph Valachi, before the McClellan Committee. Valachi's description of La Cosa Nostra was relied upon by conspiracy theorists as an accurate portrayal of mob activities. Yet critics question its authenticity and direction. For example, criminologist Jay Albanese compared Valachi's statements to those of another mob informer, Jimmy Frantianno, and found major discrepancies with respect to the location and size of organized criminal activity.[181]

The challenges to the alien conspiracy theory have produced alternative views of organized crime. For example, Philip Jenkins and Gary Potter studied organized crime in Philadelphia and found little evidence that this supposed "Mafia stronghold" was controlled by an Italian-dominated crime family.[182] Sociologist Alan Block has argued that organized crime is both a loosely constructed social system and a social world that reflects the existing U.S. system, not a tightly organized national criminal syndicate. The system is composed of "relationships binding professional criminals, politicians, law enforcers, and various entrepreneurs."[183] In contrast, the social world of organized crime is often chaotic because of the constant power struggle between competing groups. Block rejects the idea that an all-powerful organized crime commission exists and instead views the world of professional criminals as one shaped by the political economy. He finds that independent crime organizations can be characterized as either enterprise syndicates or power syndicates. The former are involved in providing services and include madams, drug distributors, bookmakers, and so on. These are "workers in the world of illegal enterprise." They have set positions in an illegal enterprise system, with special tasks to perform if the enterprise is to function. In contrast, power syndicates perform no set task except to extort or terrorize. Their leaders can operate against legitimate business or against fellow criminals who operate enterprise syndicates. Through coercion, buyouts, and other similar means, power syndicates graft themselves onto enterprise systems, legal businesses, trade unions, and so on. Block's view of organized crime is revisionist since it portrays mob activity as a quasi-economic enterprise system swayed by social forces and not a tightly knit, unified cartel dominated by ethnic minorities carrying out European traditions. His world of organized crime is dominated by business leaders, politicians, and union leaders who work hand in hand with criminals. Moreover, the violent, chaotic social world of power syndicates does not lend itself to a tightly controlled syndicate.

≡ Organized Crime Groups

Even such devoted alien conspiracy advocates as the U.S. Justice Department now view organized crime as a loose confederation of ethnic and regional crime groups, bound together by a commonality of economic and political objectives.[184] Some of these groups are located in fixed geographical areas. For example, the so-called Dixie Mafia operates in the South. Chicano crime families are found in areas with significant Hispanic populations, such as California and Arizona. White-ethnic crime organizations are found across the nation. Some Italian and Cuban groups operate internationally. Some have preserved their past identity, while others are constantly changing organizations. One important recent change in organized crime is the interweaving of ethnic groups into the traditional structure. Black, Hispanic, and Asian racketeers now compete with the more traditional groups. In black or Hispanic areas, these newcomers oversee the distribution of drugs, prostitution, and gambling in a symbiotic relationship with old-line racketeers. As the traditional organized crime families drift into legitimate businesses, the distribution of contraband on the street is handled by newcomers, characterized by Francis Ianni as "urban social bandits."[185]

Have these newly emerging groups achieved the same level of control as traditional crime families? Some experts argue that minority gangs will have a tough time developing the network of organized corruption that involves working with government officials and unions, which traditional crime families enjoyed.[186]

As law enforcement pressure has been put on traditional organized crime figures, other groups have filled the vacuum. For example, the Hell's Angels motorcycle club is now believed to be one of the leading distributors of narcotics in the United States. Similarly, Chinese criminal gangs have taken over the dominant role in New York City's heroin market from the traditional Italian-run syndicates.[187]

In sum, most experts now agree that it is simplistic to view organized crime in the United States as a national syndicate that controls all illegitimate rackets in an orderly fashion. This view seems to ignore the variety of gangs and groups, their membership, and their relationship to the outside world.[188] Mafia-type groups may play a major role in organized crime, but they are by no means the only ones that can be considered organized criminals.[189]

Organized Crime Abroad

The United States is not the only country that confronts organized criminal gangs. The Cali and Medellin drug cartels in Colombia are world-famous for both their vast drug trafficking profits and their unflinching use of violence to achieve their objectives. When Pablo Escobar, the head of the Medellin cartel, was captured and killed by police and soldiers on December 2, 1993, experts predicted that drug smuggling would *increase* with the shift of the cocaine trade to the control of the smoother and more business-like Cali cartel.[190]

Drug-dealing gangs are not the only form of organized crime abroad. Japan has a long history of organized criminal activity by *Yakuza* gangs. In 1993, officials of the Kirin Brewery, Japan's largest beer maker resigned after allegations were made that they paid over 33 million yen in *sokaiya*—extortion money—to racketeers who threatened their business.[191] In China, organized gangs use violence to enforce contracts between companies, serving as an alternative to the legal system. They also help smuggle many of the 100,000 mainland Chinese who enter the United States each year. In June 1993, a Chinese ship foundered off the coast of New York and ten illegal immigrants drowned.[192]

Russia has been beset by organized crime activity since the breakup of the Soviet Union. As of 1993, an estimated 3,000 criminal gangs were active in Russia. Bloody shoot-outs have become common as gangs attempt to stake out territory and extort businesses. In one incident, an auto dealership was attacked and two security guards killed when the owners failed to pay "protection money."[193]

Computer and communications technology has fostered international cooperation among crime cartels. East European and Russian gangs sell arms seized from the former Soviet Army to members of the Sicilian Mafia; Japanese and Italian mob members have met in Paris; drug money from South America is laundered in Canada and England.[194]

Controlling Organized Crime

George Vold argued that the development of organized crime parallels early capitalist enterprises. Organized crime employs ruthless and monopolistic tactics to maximize profits; it is also secretive and protective of its operations and defensive against any outside intrusion.[195] Consequently, controlling its activities is extremely difficult.

The federal and state governments actually did little to combat organized crime until fairly recently. One of the first measures aimed directly at organized crime was the Interstate and Foreign Travel or Transportation in Aid of Racketeering Enterprises Act (Travel Act).[196] The Travel Act prohibits travel in interstate commerce or use of interstate facilities with the intent to promote, manage, establish, carry on, or facilitate an unlawful activity; it also prohibits the actual or attempted engagement in these activities. In 1970, Congress passed the Organized Crime Control Act (see the Close-Up on forfeiture for some of its provisions). Title IX of the act, probably its most effective measure, has been the **Racketeer Influenced and Corrupt Organization Act** (RICO).[197] RICO did not create new categories of crimes but rather new categories of offenses in racketeering activity, which it defined as involvement in two or more acts prohibited by 24 existing federal and eight state statutes. The offenses listed in RICO include state-defined crimes, such as murder, kidnapping, gambling, arson, robbery, bribery, extortion, and narcotic violations, and federally defined crimes, such as bribery, counterfeiting, transmission of gambling information, prostitution, and mail fraud. RICO is designed to limit patterns of organized criminal activity by prohibiting involvement in an act intended to:

- Derive income from racketeering or the unlawful collection of debts and to use or invest such income.

- Acquire through racketeering an interest in or control over any enterprise engaged in interstate or foreign commerce.

- Conduct business enterprises through a pattern of racketeering.

- Conspire to use racketeering as a means of making income, collecting loans, or conducting business.

An individual convicted under RICO is subject to 20 years in prison and a $25,000 fine. Additionally, the accused must forfeit to the U.S. government any interest in a business in violation of RICO. These penalties are much more potent than simple conviction and imprisonment. To enforce these policy initiatives, the federal government created the Strike Force Program. This program, operating in 18 cities, brings together various state and federal law enforcement officers and prosecutors to work as a team against racketeering. Several states,

John Gotti, the "Dapper Don," was the most powerful mob boss in the country before his arrest and conviction on murder charges in 1993.

CLOSE-UP

Forfeiture

Forfeiture is government seizure of property derived from or used in criminal activity. Its use as a sanction aims to strip racketeers and drug traffickers of their economic power because the traditional sanctions of imprisonment and fines have been found inadequate to deter or punish enormously profitable crimes. Seizure of assets aims not only to reduce the profitability of illegal activity but to curtail the financial ability of criminal organizations to continue illegal operations.

Two Types of Forfeiture: Civil and Criminal

Civil forfeiture is a proceeding against property used in criminal activity. Property subject to civil forfeiture often includes vehicles used to transport contraband, equipment used to manufacture illegal drugs,

cash used in illegal transactions, and property purchased with the proceeds of the crime. No finding of criminal guilt is required in such proceedings. The government is required to post notice of the proceedings so that any party who has an interest in the property may contest the forfeiture. The types of property that may be forfeited have been expanded since the 1970s to include assets; cash; securities; negotiable instruments; property, including houses or other real estate; and proceeds traceable directly or indirectly to violations of certain laws. Common provisions permit seizure of conveyances, such as airplanes, boats, or cars; raw materials, products, and equipment used in manufacturing, trafficking, or cultivation of illegal drugs; and drug paraphernalia.

Criminal forfeiture is a part of the criminal action taken against a defendant accused of racketeering

or drug trafficking. Forfeiture is a sanction imposed on conviction that requires the defendant to forfeit various property rights and interests related to the violation. In 1970, Congress revived this sanction that had been dormant in U.S. law since the Revolution. Over 100 federal forfeiture statutes are in force.

Use of Forfeiture

The federal government originally provided for criminal forfeiture in the Racketeer Influenced and Corrupt Organization statute and the Comprehensive Drug Abuse Prevention and Control Act (Controlled Substances Act), both enacted in 1970. Before that time, civil forfeiture had been provided in federal laws on some narcotics, customs, and revenue infractions. More recently, language on forfeiture has been included in the Comprehen-sive Crime Control Act of 1984, the Money Laundering Act of 1986, and the Anti-Drug

---

including New York, Illinois, New Jersey, and New Mexico, have created their own special investigative teams devoted to organized criminal activity.

These efforts began to pay off more than a decade ago when in April 1985, a New-York-based strike force successfully obtained indictments against members of the Lucchese, Genovese, and Bonnano families.[198] The investigation also uncovered evidence to support the national crime cartel concept. Similar sweeps were conducted in Boston, Chicago, and Miami during the remainder of the decade. From 1985 to 1987, many major organized crime figures were indicted, convicted, and imprisoned, including Gennaro Angiulo, second in command in New England, who received a 45-year sentence; Tony Salerno, Tony Corallo, Carmine Persico, and Gennaro Langella of the New York families each got 100 years in prison; and Nicodemo Scarfo of Philadelphia got 14 years for extortion. The arrest and imprisonment of John Gotti, the so-called "Dapper Don," was a firm illus-

tration of the decline of white-ethnic organized crime families and their replacement with emerging groups.

≡ The Future of Organized Crime

Indications exist that the traditional organized crime syndicates are in decline. Law enforcement officials in Philadelphia, New Jersey, New England, New Orleans, Kansas City, Detroit, and Milwaukee all report that years of federal and state interventions have severely eroded the Mafia organizations in their areas.[199] What has caused this alleged erosion of Mafia power? First, a number of the reigning family heads are quite old, in their 70s and 80s, prompting some law enforcement officials to dub them "the Geritol gang."[200] A younger generation

Abuse Act of 1986. Most state forfeiture procedures appear in controlled substances or RICO laws. A few states provide for forfeiture of property connected with the commission of any felony. Most state forfeiture provisions allow for civil rather than criminal forfeiture. One survey responded to by 44 states and territories found that under the controlled substances laws, most states provided only for civil forfeiture. Eight states (Arizona, Kentucky, Nevada, New Mexico, North Carolina, Utah, Vermont, and West Virginia), however, have criminal forfeiture provisions. Of the 19 states with RICO statutes, all but eight include the criminal forfeiture sanction.

What Happens to Forfeited Property?

In 1984, the federal government established the Department of Justice Assets Forfeiture Fund to collect proceeds from forfeitures and defray the costs of forfeitures under the Comprehensive Drug Abuse Prevention and Control Act, along with the Customs Forfeiture Fund for forfeitures under customs laws. These acts also require that the property and proceeds of forfeiture be shared equitably with state and local law enforcement agencies commensurate with their participation in the investigations leading to forfeiture.

Once property is legally forfeited, its disposition is a matter of governmental discretion. It may be sold and all profits retained by the government agency; seized property can also be used directly by the agency or awarded to a third party, such as an informant. Attempts by the defendant to transfer the property or sell it to an "innocent" third party can be overturned by the government.

All is not lost when the government seizes personal property. Defendants can recover their possessions by repurchasing them at appraised value, petitioning for their return from the agency that seized them, or filing a claim in a court of law.

Discussion Questions

1. Should a person's car be seized if police find a small amount of narcotics in the back seat?
2. Should *all* convicted criminals be stripped of their assets?

SOURCES: David Taube, "Civil Forfeiture," Eighth Survey of White Collar Crime, *American Criminal Law Review* 30 (1993): 1025–47, Bureau of Justice Statistics, *Report to the Nation on Crime and Justice*, 2d ed. (Washington, D.C.: National Institute of Justice, 1988), p. 93.

---

of mob leaders is stepping in to take control of the families, and there are indications that they lack the skill and leadership of the older bosses. In addition, active government enforcement policies have halved what the estimated made membership was 20 years ago; a number of the highest-ranking leaders have been imprisoned. Additional pressure comes from newly emerging ethnic gangs that want to "muscle in" on traditional syndicate activities, such as drug sales and gambling. For example, Chinese Triad gangs have been active in New York and California in the drug trade, loan-sharking, and labor racketeering. Other ethnic crime groups include black and Colombian drug cartels and the Sicilian Mafia, which operates independently of U.S. groups.

The Mafia has also been hurt by changing values in U.S. society. White, ethnic inner-city neighborhoods, which were the locus of Mafia power, have been reduced in size as families move to the suburbs. Organized crime groups have consequently lost their political and social base of operations. In addition, the "code of silence," which served to protect Mafia leaders, is now being broken regularly by younger members who turn informer rather than face prison terms. It is also possible that their success has hurt organized crime families; younger members are better educated than their forbearers and equipped to seek their fortunes through legitimate enterprise.[201]

Jay Albanese, a leading expert on organized crime, predicts that pressure by the federal government will encourage organized crime figures to engage in "safer" activities, such as credit card and airline ticket counterfeiting and illicit toxic waste disposal. Instead of running illegal enterprises, established families may be content with financing younger entrepreneurs and channeling or laundering profits through their legitimate business enterprises. There may be greater effort among organized criminals in the future to infiltrate legitimate business enterprises to obtain access to money for financing and the means to launder illicitly obtained cash. Labor unions and the construction industry have been favorite targets in the past.[202] While these actions are considered a major blow to Italian-dominated organized crime cartels, they are unlikely to stifle criminal entrepreneurship. As long as vast profits can be made from selling narcotics, producing pornography, or taking illegal bets, many groups stand ready to fill the gaps and reap the profits of providing illegal goods and services. It is likely that the New York and Chicago mobs, with a combined total of almost 1,500 made members, will continue to ply their trade.

≡ Summary

White-collar and organized criminals are similar because they both use ongoing illegal business enterprises to make personal profits. There are various types of white-collar crime. Stings and swindles involve the use of deception to bilk people out of their money. Chiseling customers, businesses, or the government on a regular basis is a second common type of white-collar crime. Surprisingly, many professionals engage in chiseling offenses. Other white-collar criminals use their positions in business and the marketplace to commit economic crimes. Their crimes include exploitation of position in a company or the government to secure illegal payments; embezzlement and employee pilferage and fraud; client fraud; and influence peddling and bribery. Further, corporate officers sometimes violate the law to improve the position and profitability of their businesses. Their crimes include price-fixing, false advertising, and environmental offenses.

So far, little has been done to combat white-collar crimes. Most offenders do not view themselves as criminals and therefore do not seem to be deterred by criminal statutes. Though thousands of white-collar criminals are prosecuted each year, their numbers are insignificant compared with the magnitude of the problem. The government has used various law enforcement strategies to combat white-collar crime. Some involve deterrence, which uses punishment to frighten potential abusers. Others involve economism or compliance strategies, which create economic incentives to obey the law.

The demand for illegal goods and services has produced a symbiotic relationship between the public and an organized criminal network. Though criminal gangs have existed since the early nineteenth century, their power and size were spurred by the Volstead Act and Prohibition in the 1920s. Organized crime supplies alcohol, gambling, drugs, prostitutes, and pornography to the public. It is immune from prosecution because of public apathy and because of its own strong political connections. Though organized criminals used to be white ethnics—Jews, Italians, and Irish—today, African Americans, Hispanics, and other groups have become included in organized crime activities. The old-line "families" are more likely to use their criminal wealth and power to buy into legitimate businesses. There is debate over the control of organized crime. Some experts believe there is a national crime cartel that controls all activities. Others view organized crime as a group of disorganized, competing gangs dedicated to extortion or to providing illegal goods and services. Efforts to control organized crime have been stepped up. The federal government has used antiracketeering statutes to arrest syndicate leaders. But as long as there are vast profits to be made, illegal enterprises should continue to flourish.

≡ KEY TERMS

entrepreneurship 591
white-collar crime
organized crime 602
enterprise 591
churning 587
insider trading 594
arbitrage 586
Mollen Commission 596
pilferage 599
virus
corporate crime 588

organizational crime 596
Sherman Antitrust Act
compliance 588
deterrence 590
organized crime 596
alien conspiracy theory 585
Mafia
La Cosa Nostra
Racketeer Influenced and Corrupt Organization Act 599
forfeiture 592

≡ NOTES

1. Dwight Smith, "White-Collar Crime, Organized Crime and the Business Establishment: Resolving a Crisis in Criminological Theory," in *White Collar and Economic Crime: A Multidisciplinary and Crossnational Perspective,* ed. P. Wickman and T. Dailey (Lexington, Mass.: Lexington Books, 1982), p. 53.
2. See, generally, Dwight Smith, Jr., "Organized Crime and Entrepreneurship," *International Journal of Criminology and Penology* 6 (1978): 161–77; Dwight C. Smith, Jr., "Paragons, Pariahs, and Pirates: A Spectrum-Based Theory of Enterprise," *Crime and Delinquency* 26 (1980): 358–86; Dwight C. Smith, Jr., and Richard S. Alba, "Organized Crime and American Life," *Society* 16 (1979): 32–38.
3. Smith, "White-Collar Crime, Organized Crime and the

Business Establishment," p. 33.

4. Mark Haller, "Illegal Enterprise: A Theoretical and Historical Intepretation," *Criminology* 28 (1990): 207–35.

5. Nancy Frank and Michael Lynch, *Corporate Crime, Corporate Violence* (Albany, N.Y.: Harrow and Heston, 1992), p. 7.

6. Nikos Passas and David Nelken, "The Thin Line between Legitimate and Criminal Enterprises: Subsidy Frauds in the European Community," *Crime, Law and Social Change* 19 (1993): 223–43.

7. Ibid., p. 238.

8. Kitty Calavita and Henry Pontell, "Savings and Loan Fraud as Organized Crime: Toward a Conceptual Typology of Corporate Illegality," *Criminology* 31 (1993): 519–48.

9. Edwin Sutherland, *White-Collar Crime: The Uncut Version* (New Haven: Yale University Press, 1983).

10. Edwin Sutherland, "White-Collar Criminality," *American Sociological Review* 5 (1940): 2–10.

11. See, generally, Herbert Edelhertz, *The Nature, Impact and Prosecution of White-Collar Crime* (Washington, D.C.: U.S. Government Printing Office, 1970), pp. 73–75.

12. David Weisburd and Kip Schlegel, "Returning to the Mainstream," in *White-Collar Crime Reconsidered,* ed. Kip Schlegel and David Weisburd, (Boston: Northeastern University Press, 1992), pp. 352–65.

13. Ronald Kramer and Raymond Michalowski, "State-Corporate Crime" (Paper presented at the annual meeting of the American Society of Criminology, Baltimore, November 1990).

14. Gilbert Geis, "Avocational Crime," in *Handbook of Criminology,* ed. Daniel Glazer (Chicago: Rand McNally, 1974), p. 284.

15. Elizabeth Moore and Michael Mills, "The Neglected Victims and Unexamined Costs of White-Collar Crime," *Crime and Delinquency* 36 (1990): 408–18.

16. Laura Schrager and James Short, "Toward a Sociology of Organizational Crime," *Social Problems* 25 (1978): 415–25.

17. Ibid., p. 415.

18. Gilbert Geis, "White-Collar and Corporate Crime," in *Major Forms of Crime,* ed. Robert Meier (Beverly Hills: Sage, 1984), p. 145.

19. Bureau of Justice Statistics, *The Severity of Crime* (Washington, D.C.: U.S. Government Printing Office, 1984).

20. Stephen Ekpenyong, "Social Inequalities, Collusion and Armed Robbery in Nigerian Cities," *British Journal of Criminology* 29 (1989): 21–34.

21. Xie Baogue, "The Function of the Chinese Procuratorial Organ in Combat against Corruption, *Police Studies* 11 (1988): 38–43.

22. Nikos Passas and Devid Nelkin, "The Fight against Fraud in the European Community: Cacophony Rather Than Harmony," *Corruption and Reform* 6 (1991): 237–66.

23. Passas and Nelkin, "The Fight against Economic Criminality in the European Community" (Paper presented at the annual meeting of the American Society of

Criminology, Baltimore, Md., November 1990), p. 3. See also Nikos Passas and David Nelkin, "The Thin Blue Line between Legitimate and Criminal Enterprises: Subsidy Fraud in the European Community," *Crime, Law and Social Change* 19 (1993): 223–43.

24. Marshall Clinard and Richard Quinney, *Criminal Behavior Systems: A Typology* (New York: Holt, Rinehart and Winston, 1973), p. 117.

25. Edelhertz, *The Nature, Impact and Prosecution of White-Collar Crime.*

26. Mark Moore, "Notes toward a National Strategy to Deal with White-Collar Crime," in *A National Strategy for Containing White-Collar Crime,* ed. Herbert Edelhertz and Charles Rogovin (Lexington, Mass.: Lexington Books, 1980), pp. 32–44.

27. For a general review, see John Braithwaite, "White Collar Crime," *Annual Review of Sociology* 11 (1985): 1–25.

28. Scott Paltrow, "Goldblum Now in Consulting and on Parole," *Wall Street Journal,* 22 March 1982, p. 25.

29. Nikos Passas, "Structural Sources of International Crime: Policy Lessons from the BCCI Affair," *Crime, Law and Social Change* (1994, in press).

30. North American Securities Administration Association, *Report to Congress, Subcommittee on Investment Fraud,* July 13, 1990.

31. Paul Nowell, "Bakker Convicted of Fraud," *Boston Globe,* 6 October 1989, p. 1.

32. Earl Gottschalk, "Churchgoers Are the Prey as Scams Rise," *Wall Street Journal,* 7 August 1989, p. C1.

33. Diana Henriques, "10 Percent of Fruit Juice Sold in U.S. Is Not All Juice, Regulators Say," *New York Times,* 31 October 1993, p. 1.

34. Richard Quinney, "Occupational Structure and Criminal Behavior: Prescription Violation of Retail Pharmacists," *Social Problems* 11 (1963): 179–85; see also John Braithwaite, *Corporate Crime in the Pharmaceutical Industry* (London: Routledge and Kegan Paul, 1984).

35. Amy Dockser Marcus, "Thievery by Lawyers Is on the Increase, with Duped Clients Losing Bigger Sums," *Wall Street Journal,* 26 November 1990, p. B1.

36. Ibid.

37. Robert Rose and Jeff Bailey, "Traders in CBOT Soybean Pit Indicted," *Wall Street Journal,* 3 August 1989, p. A4.

38. Scott McMurray, "Futures Pit Trader Goes to Trial," *Wall Street Journal,* 8 May 1990, p. C1; idem, "Chicago Pits' Dazzling Growth Permitted a Free-for-All Mecca," *Wall Street Journal,* 3 August 1989, p. A4.

39. Securities Act of 1933, 15 U.S.C. Sec. 77a to 77aa (1982); Securities Exchange Act of 1934 15 U.S.C. Sec. 78a to 78kk (1982); 17 C.F.R. 240.10b-5 (1987).

40. *Carpenter v. United States* 484 U.S. 19 (1987); also see, John Boland, "The SEC Trims the First Amendment," *Wall Street Journal,* 4 December 1986, p. 28.

41. Tim Metz and Michael Miller, "Boesky's Rise and Fall Illustrate a Compulsion to Profit by Getting Inside Track on Market," *Wall Street Journal,* 17 November 1986, p. 28;

Wade Lambert, "FDIC Receives Cooperation of Milken Aide," *Wall Street Journal,* 25 April 1991, p. A3.

42. This section depends heavily on Frank Browning and John Gerassi, *The American Way of Crime* (New York: Putnam, 1980), p. 151.

43. Ibid., p. 293.

44. Ibid.

45. Edward Ranzal, "City Report Finds Building Industry Infested by Graft," *New York Times,* 8 November 1974, p. 1.

46. Marshall Clinard and Peter Yeager, *Corporate Crime* (New York: Free Press, 1980), pp. 166–67.

47. Fraud Update, The White Paper (1991): 3–4.

48. Ibid., p. 67.

49. Ibid.

50. United Press International, "Minority Leader in N.Y. Senate Is Charged," *Boston Globe,* 17 September 1987, p. 20.

51. "Now Williams—Last, Not Least of ABSCAM Trials," *New York Times,* 5 April 1982, p. E7.

52. Edward Pound, "Honored Employee Is a Key in Huge Fraud in Defense Purchasing," *Wall Street Journal,* 2 March 1988, p. 1.

53. Steven Waldman, "The HUD Ripoff," *Newsweek,* 7 August 1989, pp. 16–22, quote at p. 16.

54. Harry Rosenthal, "Figure in Reagan-Era Housing Department Scandal Convicted of 12 Felony Counts," *Boston Globe,* 27 October 1993, p. 3.

55. Larry Tye, "A Tide of State Corruption Sweeps from Coast to Coast," *Boston Globe,* 25 March 1991, p. 1.

56. Maureen Kline, "Italian Magistrates Query Montedison Former Chairman," *Wall Street Journal,* 19 July 1993, p. A6.

57. *The Knapp Commission Report on Police Corruption* (New York: George Braziller, 1973), pp. 1–3, 170–82.

58. "Police Official Sentenced to 18 Years for Extortion," *Wall Street Journal,* 25 September 1984, p. 6.

59. Elizabeth Neuffer, "Seven Additional Detectives Linked to Extortion Scheme," *Boston Globe,* 25 October 1988; Kevin Cullen, "U.S. Probe Eyes Bookie Protection," *Boston Globe,* 25 October 1988; William Doherty, "Ex-Sergeant Says He Aided Bid to Sell Exam," *Boston Globe,* 26 February 1987, p. 61; Michael Johnston, *Political Corruption and Public Policy in America* (Monterey, Calif.: Brooks/Cole, 1982).

60. Michael Rezendes, "N.Y. Hears of Police Corrupted," *Boston Globe,* 10 October 1993, p. 1.

61. Cited in Hugh Barlow, *Introduction to Criminology,* 2d ed. (Boston: Little, Brown, 1984).

62. Pub. L. No. 95-213, 101-104, 91 Stat. 1494.

63. Thomas Burton, "The More Baxter Hides Its Israeli Boycott Role, the More Flak It Gets," *Wall Street Journal,* 25 April 1991, p. 1.

64. Charles McCaghy, *Deviant Behavior* (New York: Macmillan, 1976), p. 178.

65. John Clark and Richard Hollinger, *Theft by Employees in Work Organizations* (Washington, D.C.: U.S. Government Printing Office, 1983), pp. 2–3.

66. Business Fraud Prevails, May Worsen, Study Says," *Wall Street Journal,* 17 August 1993, p. A4.

67. J. Sorenson, H. Grove, and T. Sorenson, "Detecting Management Fraud: The Role of the Independent Auditor," in *White-Collar Crime, Theory and Research,* ed. G. Geis and E. Stotland (Beverly Hills: Sage, 1980), pp. 221–51.

68. Teri Agins, "Report Is Said to Show Pervasive Fraud at Leslie Fay," *Wall Street Journal,* 27 October 1993, p. B4.

69. "Business Fraud Prevails," p. A4.

70. M. Swanson and J. Terriot, "Computer Crime: Dimensions, Types, Causes and Investigations," *Journal of Political Science and Administration* 8 (1980): 305–306; see Donn Parker, "Computer-Related White-Collar Crime," in *White Collar Crime, Theory and Research,* ed. G. Geis and E. Stotland (Beverly Hills: Sage, 1980), pp. 199–220.

71. David Stipp, "Computer Virus Maker Is Given Probation, Fine," *Wall Street Journal,* 7 May 1990, p. B3.

72. Erik Larson, "Computers Turn out to Be Valuable Aid in Employee Crime," *Wall Street Journal,* 14 January 1985, p. 1.

73. John Hagan and Fiona Kay, "Gender and Delinquency in White-Collar Families: A Power-Control Perspective," *Crime and Delinquency* 36 (1990): 391–407.

74. "Computer Hackers Charge $60,000 to Sprint Number," *Omaha World Herald,* 6 February 1985, p. 1.

75. Comprehensive Crime Control Act of 1984, Pub. L. No. 98-473, 2101-03, 98 Stat. 1837, 2190 (1984) (adding 18 USC 1030 (1984). Amended by Pub. L. No. 99-474, 100 Stat. 1213 (1986) codified at 18 U.S.C. 1030 (Supp. V 1987).

76. 18 U.S.C. 2510-2520 (1988 and Supp. II 1990).

77. Project, Eighth Survey of White Collar Crime, *American Criminal Law Review,* 30 (1993): 501.

78. These sections lean on ibid.

79. Medicare and Medicaid Anti-Fraud and Abuse Amendment of 1977, Title XVIII, Pub. L. No. 95-142, 91 Stat. 1175.

80. Robert Pear, "Panel Says Most States Fail on Policing Medicaid Fraud," *New York Times,* 27 March 1982, p. 7.

81. Ibid.

82. Associated Press, "U.S. Reports $1 Billion in Welfare Overpayments in '91," *Boston Globe* 12 April 1994, p. 14.

83. *United States v. Bishop,* 412 U.S. 346 (1973).

84. Carl Hartman, "Study Says Underground Economy May Represent 33 Percent of Production," *Boston Globe,* 16 February 1988, p. 38.

85. Alan Murray, "IRS in Losing Battle against Tax Evaders Despite Its New Gear," *Wall Street Journal,* 10 April 1984, p. 1.

86. Paul Duke, "IRS Excels at Tracking the Average Earner but Not the Wealthy," *Wall Street Journal,* 15 April 1991, p. 1.

87. Frank and Lynch, *Corporate Crime, Corporate Violence,* pp. 12–13.

88. Ibid.

89. Sutherland, "White-Collar Criminality," pp. 2–10.

90. 15 U.S.C. 1–7 (1976).

91. See *United States v. Sealy, Inc.,* 383 U.S. 350.
92. *Northern Pacific Railways v. United States,* 356 U.S. 1 (1958).
93. M. Maltz and S. Pollack, "Suspected Collusion among Bidders," in *White Collar Crime, Theory and Research,* ed. G. Geis and E. Stotland (Beverly Hills: Sage, 1980), pp. 174–98.
94. Gilbert Geis, "White Collar Crime: The Heavy Electrical Equipment Antitrust Cases of 1961," in *Corporate and Governmental Deviance,* ed. M. Ermann and R. Lundman (New York: Oxford University Press, 1978), pp. 58–79.
95. Michael Selz, "How Three Companies Allegedly Conspired to Fix Matzo Prices," *Wall Street Journal,* 11 March 1991, p. 1.
96. Tim Carrington, "Federal Probes of Contractors Rise for Year," *Wall Street Journal,* 23 February 1987, p. 50.
97. Ibid.
98. Bruce Ingersoll and Alecia Swasy, "FDA Puts Squeeze on P&G over Citrus Hill Labeling," *Wall Street Journal,* 25 April 1991, p. B1.
99. Clinard and Yeager, *Corporate Crime.*
100. John Conklin, *Illegal But Not Criminal* (Englewood Cliffs, N.J.: Prentice-Hall, 1972), pp. 45–46.
101. For an analysis of false claims, see Jonathan Kaye and John Patrick Sullivan, "False Claims," in Eighth Survey of White Collar Crime, *American Criminal Law Review* 30 (1993): 643–57.
102. For an in-depth review see, American Criminal Law Review, *Ninth Survey of White Collar Crime,* 31 (1994): 703–721.
103. "Econotes," *Environmental Action* 13 (October 1981): 7.
104. "Econotes," *Environmental Action* 13 (September 1981): 5.
105. "Union Carbide Says Bhopal Plant Should Have Been Closed," *Wall Street Journal,* 21 March 1985, p. 18.
106. "Judge Rejects Exxon Alaska Spill Pact," *Wall Street Journal,* 25 April 1991, p. A3.
107. See, generally, Gary Green, *Occupational Crime* (Chicago: Nelson-Hall, 1990), pp. 136–38.
108. 42 U.S.C. Sec. 7401–7642 (1988), amended 1990, 104 Stat. 2399 (1990).
109. 33 U.S.C. 1251–1387 (1988).
110. 33 U.S.C. 407 (1988).
111. 42 U.S.C. 6901–92 (k) (1988).
112. 15 U.S.C. 2601–2629 (1988).
113. 7 U.S.C. 136 (1988).
114. 42 U.S.C. 9601–9675 (1988).
115. Herbert Edelhertz and Charles Rogovin, eds., *A National Strategy for Containing White-Collar Crime* (Lexington, Mass.: Lexington Books, 1980), Appendix A, pp. 122–23.
116. Kathleen Daly, "Gender and Varieties of White-Collar Crime," *Criminology* 27 (1989): 769–93.
117. Quoted in Metz and Miller, "Boesky's Rise and Fall Illustrate a Compulsion to Profit by Getting Inside Track on Market," p. 28.
118. Donald Cressey, *Other People's Money: A Study of the Social Psychology of Embezzlement* (Glencoe, Ill.: Free Press, 1973).
119. Ibid., p. 96.
120. Ronald Kramer, "Corporate Crime: An Organizational Perspective," in *White Collar and Economic Crime: A Multidisciplinary and Crossnational Perspective,* ed. P. Wickman and T. Dailey (Lexington, Mass.: Lexington Books, 1982), pp. 75–94.
121. John Braithwaite, "Toward a Theory of Organizational Crime" (Paper presented at the annual meeting of the American Society of Criminology, Montreal, November 1987).
122. Travis Hirschi and Michael Gottfredson, "Causes of White-Collar Crime," *Criminology* 25 (1987): 949–74.
123. Michael Gottfredson and Travis Hirschi, *A General Theory of Crime* (Stanford, Calif.: Stanford University Press, 1990), p. 191.
124. For an opposing view, see Darrell Steffensmeier, "On the Causes of 'White-Collar' Crime: An Assessment of Hirschi and Gottfredson's Claims," *Criminology* 27 (1989): 345–59.
125. David Weisburd, Ellen Chayet, and Elin Waring, "White-Collar and Criminal Careers: Some Preliminary Findings," *Crime and Delinquency* 36 (1990): 342–55.
126. Michael Benson and Elizabeth Moore, "Are White-Collar and Common Offenders the Same? An Empirical and Theoretical Critique of a Recently Proposed General Theory of Crime," *Journal of Research in Crime and Delinquency* 29 (1992): 251–72.
127. David Simon and D. Stanley Eitzen, *Elite Deviance* (Boston: Allyn and Bacon, 1982), p. 28.
128. Jesilow, Pontell, and Geis, "Physician Immunity from Prosecution and Punishment for Medical Program Fraud," p. 19.
129. Clinard and Yeager, *Corporate Crime,* p. 124.
130. Peter Yeager, "Structural Bias in Regulatory Law Enforcement: The Case of the U.S. Environmental Protection Agency," *Social Problems* 34 (1987): 330–44.
131. Geis, "Avocational Crime," p. 390.
132. Clinard and Yeager, *Corporate Crime,* p. 288.
133. See, generally, Stanton Wheeler, David Weisburd, Elin Waring, and Nancy Bode, "White-Collar Crimes and Criminals," *American Criminal Law Review* 25 (1988): 331–57.
134. Susanne Schafer, "One General Fired, Two Punished for Mismanaging C-17 Plane," *Boston Globe,* 1 May 1993, p. 3.
135. Paul Blustein, "Disputes Arise over Value of Laws on Insider Trading," *Wall Street Journal,* 17 November 1986, p. 28.
136. Paul Barrett, "For Many Dalkon Shield Claimants Settlement Won't End the Trauma," *Wall Street Journal,* 9 March 1988, p. 29.
137. This section relies heavily on Daniel Skoler, "White-Collar Crime and the Criminal Justice System: Problems and Challenges," in *A National Strategy for Containing White-Collar Crime,* ed. Herbert Edelhertz and Charles Rogovin (Lexington, Mass.: Lexington Books, 1980), pp. 57–76.

138. Theodore Hammett and Joel Epstein, *Prosecuting Environmental Crime: Los Angeles County* (Washington, D.C.: National Institute of Justice, 1993).

139. Michael Benson, Francis Cullen, and William Maakestad, "Local Prosecutors and Corporate Crime," *Crime and Delinquency* 36 (1990): 356–72.

140. Ibid., pp. 369–70.

141. Ibid., p. 371.

142. Alan Otten, "States Begin to Protect Employees Who Blow Whistle on Their Firms," *Wall Street Journal,* 31 December 1984, p. 11.

143. This section relies heavily on Albert Reiss, Jr., "Selecting Strategies of Social Control over Organizational Life," in *Enforcing Regulation,* ed. Keith Hawkins and John M. Thomas (Boston: Klowver Publications, 1984), pp. 25–37.

144. John Braithwaite, "The Limits of Economism in Controlling Harmful Corporate Conduct," *Law and Society Review* 16 (1981–1982): 481–504.

145. "EPA Sues Sherwin-Williams: Pattern of Pollution at Paint Factory Is Alleged," *Wall Street Journal,* 19 July 1993, p. 1.

146. "Making Firms Liable for Cleaning Toxic Sites," *Wall Street Journal,* 9 March 1988, p. 29.

147. Rhonda Rundle, "Computer Sciences Will Pay $2.1 Million to Settle Charges by U.S. Government," *Wall Street Journal,* 19 July 1993, p. B8.

148. Wayne Gray and John Scholz, "Does Regulatory Enforcement Work? A Panel Analysis of OSHA Enforcement," *Law and Society Review* 27 (1993): 177–91.

149. Michael Benson, "Emotions and Adjudication: Status Degradation among White-Collar Criminals," *Justice Quarterly* 7 (1990): 515–28; John Braithwaite, *Crime, Shame and Reintegration* (Sydney: Cambridge University Press, 1989).

150. John Braithwaite and Gilbert Geis, "On Theory and Action for Corporate Crime Control," *Crime and Delinquency* 28 (1982): 292–314.

151. Frank and Lynch, *Corporate Crime, Corporate Violence,* pp. 33–34.

152. James Miller, "U.S. Ban on Baxter International Bids Hurt Reputation More Than Business," *Wall Street Journal,* 16 August 1993, p. A3.

153. Kip Schlegel, "Desert, Retribution and Corporate Criminality," *Justice Quarterly* 5 (1988): 615–34.

154. Raymond Michalowski and Ronald Kramer, "The Space between Laws: The Problem of Corporate Crime in a Transnational Context," *Social Problems* 34 (1987): 34–53.

155. Ibid.

156. Geis, "White-Collar and Corporate Crime," p. 154.

157. Steven Klepper and Daniel Nagin, "The Deterrent Effect of Perceived Certainty and Severity of Punishment Revisited," *Criminology* 27 (1989): 721–46.

158. "The Follies Go on," *Time,* 15 April 1991, p. 45.

159. Bill Richards and Alex Kotlowitz, "Judge Finds Three Corporate Officials Guilty of Murder in Cyanide Death of Worker," *Wall Street Journal,* 17 June 1985, p. 2.

160. Donald Manson, *Tracking Offenders: White-Collar Crime* (Washington, D.C.: Bureau of Justice Statistics, 1986); Kenneth Carlson and Jan Chaiken, *White-Collar Crime* (Washington, D.C.: Bureau of Justice Statistics, 1987).

161. Robert Bennett, "Foreward," Eighth Survey of White Collar Crime, *American Criminal Law Review* 30 (1993).

162. David Weisburd, Elin Waring, and Stanton Wheeler, "Class, Status, and the Punishment of White-Collar Criminals," *Law and Social Inquiry* 15 (1990): 223–43.

163. Mark Cohen, "Environmental Crime and Punishment: Legal/Economic Theory and Empirical Evidence on Enforcement of Federal Environmental Statutes," *Journal of Criminal Law and Criminology* 82 (1992): 1054–1109.

164. See, generally, President's Commission on Organized Crime, Report to the President and the Attorney General, *The Impact: Organized Crime Today* (Washington, D.C.: U.S. Government Printing Office, 1986). Herein cited as *Organized Crime Today.*

165. Frederick Martens and Michele Cunningham-Niederer, "Media Magic, Mafia Mania," *Federal Probation* 49 (1985): 60–68.

166. *Organized Crime Today,* pp. 7–8.

167. Alan Block and William Chambliss, *Organizing Crime* (New York: Elsevier, 1981).

168. *Organized Crime Today,* p. 462.

169. Attorney General's Commission on Pornography, *Final Report* (Washington, D.C.: U.S. Government Printing Office, 1986), p. 1053.

170. Alan Block, *East Side/West Side* (New Brunswick, N.J.: Transaction Books, 1983), pp. VII, 10–11.

171. G. R. Blakey and M. Goldsmith, "Criminal Redistribution of Stolen Property: The Need for Law Reform," *Michigan Law Review* 81 (August 1976):45–46.

172. Merry Morash, "Organized Crime," in *Major Forms of Crime,* ed. Robert Meier (Beverly Hills: Sage, 1984), p. 198.

173. Stephen Koepp, "Dirty Cash and Tarnished Vaults," *Time,* 25 February 1985, p. 65.

174. Roy Rowan, "The 50 Biggest Mafia Bosses," *Fortune,* 10 November 1986, p. 24.

175. Donald Cressey, *Theft of the Nation* (New York: Harper and Row, 1969).

176. Dwight Smith, *The Mafia Mystique* (New York: Basic Books, 1975).

177. *Organized Crime Today,* p. 489.

178. Robert Rhodes, *Organized Crime, Crime Control versus Civil Liberties* (New York: Random House, 1984).

179. This section borrows heavily from Browning and Gerassi, *The American Way of Crime,* pp. 288–472; and August Bequai, *Organized Crime* (Lexington, Mass.: Lexington Books, 1979).

180. *Organized Crime Today,* p. 52.

181. Jay Albanese, "God and the Mafia Revisited: From Valachi to Frantianno" (Paper presented at the annual meeting of the American Society of Criminology, Toronto, 1982).

182. Philip Jenkins and Gary Potter, "The Politics and Mythology of Organized Crime: A Philadelphia Case Study," *Journal of Criminal Justice* 15 (1987): 473–84.

183. Block, *East Side/West Side.*

184. *Organized Crime Today,* p. 11.

185. Francis Ianni, *Black Mafia: Ethnic Succession in Organized Crime* (New York: Pocket Books, 1975).

186. Robert Kelly and Rufus Schatzberg, "Types of Minority Organized Crime: Some Considerations" (Paper presented at the annual meeting of the American Society of Criminology, Montreal, November 1987).

187. Peter Kerr, "Chinese Now Dominate New York Heroin Trade," *New York Times,* 9 August 1987, p. 1.

188. Jenkins and Potter, "The Politics and Mythology of Organized Crime."

189. William Chambliss, *On the Take* (Bloomington: Indiana University Press, 1978).

190. Russell Watson, "Death on the Spot," *Newsweek,* 13 December 1993, pp. 18–20.

191. Yumiko Ono, "Top Kirin Brewery Executives Resign Amid Reports of Paying off Racketeers," *Wall Street Journal,* 19 July 1993, p. A6.

192. Michael Elliott, "Global Mafia," *Newsweek,* 13 December 1993, pp. 22–29.

193. Associated Press, "Gangland Violence Rises and Startles in Moscow," *Boston Globe,* 22 July 1993, p. 44.

194. Ibid.

195. George Vold, *Theoretical Criminology,* 2d ed., rev. Thomas Bernard (New York: Oxford University Press, 1979).

196. 18 U.S.C. 1952 (1976).

197. Pub. L. No. 91-452, Title IX, 84 Stat. 922 (1970) (codified at 18 U.S.C. 1961–68, 1976).

198. Ed Magnuson, "Hard Days for the Mafia," *Time,* 4 March 1985.

199. Selwyn Raab, "A Battered and Ailing Mafia Is Losing Its Grip on America," *New York Times,* 22 October 1990, p. 1.

200. Ibid.

201. Ibid., p. B7.

202. Jay Albanese, *Organized Crime in America,* 2d ed. (Cinncinati: Anderson, 1989), p. 68.

14

Public Order Crime: Sex and Substance Abuse

☰ Introduction

In June 1993, police arrested 27-year-old Heidi Fleiss while she was taking the trash out of her $1.6 million Benedict Canyon home (previously owned by film star Michael Douglas). Fleiss was charged with allegedly running the most exclusive call-girl ring in Los Angeles. Fearing that she would "tell all" to the press, a number of prominent movie executives and entertainers issued unsolicited statements denying that they were patrons of Fleiss's ring; other well-known stars admitted to being her clients.

Fleiss had grown up a child of privilege; her father was a prominent physician and her mother a teacher. The young women whom she allegedly recruited were said to be models and college students hoping to break into the film business. When interviewed in *Newsweek* magazine, one of her former employees claimed that it was common to make $10,000 a month and that one month, she had actually earned $50,000.[1] Fleiss appeared on prominent talk shows and was interviewed by media personalities, such as Connie Chung and Howard Stern.

Many Americans probably think that Fleiss's arrest was not a top priority for the justice system. After all, her clients were people who *wanted* to hire call girls and *willingly* put up the money to purchase their services. It hardly seems possible that these clients could be considered crime victims. What of Fleiss's alleged employees? They *willingly* engaged in sexual activity for money, and their income was far higher than they would have earned in legitimate jobs. "Since no one was harmed," a critic might ask, "does Fleiss deserve to be punished?" Though they may be considered "immoral," should Fleiss, her employees, and her clients be considered criminals?

Despite what the more libertine members of the general public might think, it has long been the custom to ban or limit behaviors that are believed to run contrary to social norms, customs, and values. These behaviors are often referred to as **public order crimes** or **victimless crimes,** though this latter term can be misleading.[2] Public order crimes involve acts that interfere with the operations of society and the ability of people to function efficiently. Put another way, while such common-law crimes as rape or robbery are considered *mala in se*—evil unto themselves—inherently wrong and damaging, there are also *mala prohibitum* crimes—behaviors outlawed because they conflict with social policy, prevailing moral rules, and current public opinion. Statutes designed to uphold public order usually prohibit the manufacture and distribution of morally questionable goods and services—erotic material, commercial sex, mood-altering drugs. They may also ban acts which a few people holding political power consider morally tinged, such as homosexual contact. They are controversial in part because millions of otherwise law-abiding citizens—students, workers, professionals—often engage in these outlawed activities and consequently become involved in criminal activity. These statutes are also controversial because they represent the selective prohibition of desired goods, services, and behaviors; in other words, they outlaw sin and vice.

This chapter covers these public order crimes. It is divided into three main sections. The first briefly discusses the relationship between law and morality. The second deals with public order crimes of a sexual nature: pornography, prostitution, deviant sex, and homosexual acts. The third focuses on the abuse of drugs and alcohol.

☰ Law and Morality

Legislation of moral issues has been a continual source of frustration for lawmakers. There is little debate that the purpose of the criminal law is to protect society and reduce social harm. When a store is robbed or a child assaulted, it is relatively easy to see, and thereafter condemn, the social harm done the victim. It is, however, more difficult to sympathize with or even identify the victim of immoral acts, such as pornography or prostitution, where the parties involved may be willing participants; if there is no victim, can there be a crime? Should acts be made illegal merely because they violate prevailing moral standards? If so, who defines morality?

Is there actually a victim in so-called victimless crimes? Many participants in so-called "victimless crimes" may have been coerced or forced into their acts; they are therefore its "victims." Opponents of pornography, such as Andrea Dworkin, charge that women involved in "adult films" are far from being highly paid stars; they are "dehumanized—turned into objects and commodities."[3] Research on prostitution shows that many young runaways and abandoned children are coerced into a "life on the streets" where they are cruelly treated and held as virtual captives.[4]

Even if public order crimes do not actually harm their participants, then perhaps society as a whole should be considered the victim of these crimes. Is the community harmed when an adult book store opens or a brothel is established? Does this send out a message that a neighborhood is in decline? Does it help educate children that deviance is to be tolerated and profited from?

Debating Morality

Some scholars argue that acts such as pornography, prostitution, and drug use erode the moral fabric of society and therefore should be punished by law. They are crimes, according to the great legal scholar Morris Cohen, because "it is one of the functions of the criminal law to give expression to the collective feeling of revulsion toward certain acts, even when they are not very dangerous."[5] In his classic statement on the function of morality in the law, Sir Patrick Devlin states:

> Without shared ideas on politics, morals, and ethics no society can exist. . . . If men and women try to create a society in which there is no fundamental agreement about

good and evil, they will fail; if having based it on common agreement, the agreement goes, the society will disintegrate. For society is not something that is kept together physically; it is held by the invisible bonds of common thought. If the bonds were too far relaxed, the members would drift apart. A common morality is part of the bondage. The bondage is part of the price of society; and mankind, which needs society, must pay its price.[6]

According to this view then, so-called victimless crimes are prohibited because one of the functions of criminal law is to express public morality.[7]

Some argue that basing criminal definitions on moral beliefs is an impossible task: Who defines morality? Are we not punishing differences rather than social harm? Are photographs of nude children by famed photographer Robert Mapplethorpe art or obscenity? As U.S. Supreme Court Justice William O. Douglas so succinctly put it, "What may be trash to me may be prized by others."[8]

A Los Angeles area store serves as an outlet for adult books, magazines, tapes, and novelties. Are moral crusaders correct in their efforts to control sexually explicit material? Can we ever successfully legislate morality?

In the Puritan society of Salem, Massachusetts, were not women burned at the stake as witches because their behavior seemed strange or different? In Africa today, an estimated 100 million women have had their external genitalia removed. The surgery is done to ensure virginity, remove sexual sensation, and render them suitable for marriage. Critics of this practice, led by American author Alice Walker (who wrote *The Color Purple*), consider the procedure to be mutilation and torture; others argue that this ancient custom should be left to the discretion of the indigenous people who consider it part of their culture. "Torture," counters Walker, "is not culture." Can an outsider define the morality of another culture? [9]

Some influential legal scholars have questioned the propriety of legislating morals. H. L. A. Hart states:

> It is fatally easy to confuse the democratic principle that power should be in the hands of the majority with the utterly different claim that the majority, with power in their hands, need respect no limits. Certainly there is a special risk in a democracy that the majority may dictate how all should live.[10]

Joseph Gussfield argues that the purpose of outlawing acts because they are immoral is to show the moral superiority of those who condemn the acts over those who partake of them. The legislation of morality "enhances the social status of groups carrying the affirmed culture and degrades groups carrying that which is condemned as deviant."[11]

Criminal or Immoral?

It is possible that acts that most of us deem highly immoral are not criminal. There is no law against lust, gluttony, avarice, spite, or envy, though they are considered some of the "seven deadly sins." Nor is it a crime in most jurisdictions to ignore the pleas of a drowning person, even though such callous behavior is quite immoral.

Violations of conventional morality may also be tolerated because they serve a useful social function. For example, there is some evidence that watching sexually explicit films can provide excitement and release tension that might otherwise be satisfied in more harmful and violent acts.[12] Immoral behavior may be condoned because it provides ancillary benefits to legitimate enterprises: illegal betting on football games draws people to watch TV at the neighborhood bar; people go to legitimate massage parlors or hire escort services because they believe employees will engage in sex for profit on the side.[13]

Some acts also seem both well intentioned and moral but are still considered criminal: it is a crime (euthanasia) to kill a loved one who is suffering from an incurable disease to spare them further pain; stealing a rich man's money to feed a poor family is considered larceny; marrying many women (polygamy) is considered a crime (bigamy), though it may conform to religious beliefs.[14] As legal experts Wayne LaFave and Austin Scott, Jr., argue: "A good motive will not normally prevent what is otherwise criminal from being a crime."[15]

It might be possible to settle this argument by saying that immoral acts can be distinguished from crimes on the basis of the social harm they cause. Yet some acts that cause enormous amounts of social harm are perfectly legal: all of us are well aware of the illness and death associated with the consumption of tobacco and alcohol; manufacturers continue to sell sports cars and motorcycles that can accelerate to over 100 MPH, though the legal speed limit is at most 65. More people die each year from alcohol-, tobacco-, and auto-related deaths than from all drugs combined. Should drugs be legalized and fast cars outlawed?

Moral Crusaders

Americans are familiar with fictional superheroes who take it on themselves to enforce the law, battle evil, and personally deal with those who they consider immoral. From the Lone Ranger to Batman (the "Caped Crusader"), the righteous **vigilante** is an accepted part of the general culture. It is seldom questioned when these characters go on **moral crusades** without any authorization from legal authorities. Who called on Superman to battle for "truth, justice, and the American way"? The assumption that it is okay to violate the law if the cause is right and the target is "immoral" is not lost on the younger generation. It should come as no surprise that gang boys sometimes take on the "street" identity of "Batman" or "Superman" so that they can battle their rivals with impunity.

Fictional characters are not the only ones who take it upon themselves to fight for "moral decency"; members of special interest groups are often ready to do battle. For example, on March 21, 1993, Baylor University regents voted against allowing nude modeling in art classes after school administrators were swamped with phone calls objecting to "nudity in the classroom." Though many of the protesting calls were made by religious leaders, Bruce Presscot, minister of the Easthaven Baptist Church, claimed that those who objected to nudity in art classes would be "embarrassed living in the Garden of Eden."[16] The Baylor incident illustrates the pressure that can be placed on social institutions by moral crusaders.

Sociologist Daniel Claster suggests that an essential facet of the American culture is to divide people into "bad guys" and "good guys." This polarization of good and evil creates a climate where those categorized as "good" are deified, while the "bad" are demonized. Crime control policies influenced by exaggerated or one-sided moral judgments may be overly punitive and ineffective.[17] For example, the death penalty is justified if murderers are "bad guys"—unrepentant monsters who commit serial murders and mutilate their victims. If, instead, murderers were viewed as "good guys"—the disturbed victims of child abuse and neglect—then it would be out of the question to consider the death penalty.

Howard Becker has labeled people who wish to control the definition of morality, **moral entrepreneurs.** These rule creators, argues Becker, go on moral crusades to rid the world of evil. They operate with an absolute certainty that their way is right and that any means are justified to get their way; "the crusader is fervent and righteous, often self-righteous."[18]

Enforcement of morally tinged statutes then becomes a significant problem for law enforcement agencies. If laws governing morally tinged behavior are enforced too vigorously, local authorities are branded as reactionaries who waste time on petty issues. If, on the other hand, police agencies ignore public order crimes, they are accused of being soft on immorality and social degeneracy. "Society would be a lot better off," the argument goes, "if the cops cracked down on 'those people.'" Who "those people" are and what should be done about them is a matter of great public debate.

Let us now turn to specific examples of public order crimes.

≡ Illegal Sexuality

One type of public order crime relates to what conventional society considers to be deviant sexual practices. Among these outlawed practices are: homosexual acts, paraphilias, prostitution, and pornography. Laws controlling these behaviors have been the focus of much debate.

≡ Homosexuality

Homosexuality—the word derives from the Greek *homos,* meaning "same"—refers to erotic interest in members of one's own sex. However, to engage in homosexual behavior does not necessarily mean one is a homosexual. People may engage in homosexuality because heterosexual partners are unavailable (for example, in the armed services). Some may have sex forced on them by aggressive homosexuals, a condition common in prisons. Some adolescents may experiment with partners of the same sex, though their sexual affiliation is heterosexual. Albert Reiss has described the behavior of delinquent youths who engage in homosexual behavior for money but still regard themselves as heterosexuals and who discontinue all homosexual activities as adults.[19] Finally, it is possible to be a homosexual but not to engage in sexual conduct with members of the same sex. To avoid this confusion, it might be helpful to adopt the definition of a homosexual as one:

who is motivated in adult life by a definite preferential erotic attraction to members of the same sex and who usually (but not necessarily) engages in overt sexual relations with them.[20]

Homosexual behavior has existed in most societies. Records of it can be found in prehistoric art and hieroglyphics. In their review of the literature on 76 preliterate societies, C. S. Ford and F. A. Beach found that male homosexuality was viewed as normal in 49 of these societies and female homosexuality, in 17. Some cultures include homosexual experiences as part of their "manhood rituals."[21] Even when homosexuality was banned or sanctioned, it still persisted.[22]

In the United States, it has been estimated that 3 percent to 16 percent of the male population and 2 percent to 6 percent of the female population are exclusively homosexual, though many more may have had homosexual experiences sometime in their lives.[23] These numbers have been the subject of fierce debate, and the percentage of the population that is exclusively gay is still not known with certainty.

Attitudes toward Homosexuality

Throughout much of Western history, homosexuals have been subject to discrimination, sanction, and violence. The Bible implies that God destroyed the ancient cities of Sodom and Gommorah because of their residents' deviant behavior, presumably homosexuality; Sodom is the source of the term **sodomy** (deviant intercourse). The Bible expressly forbids homosexuality—in Leviticus in the Old Testament, Paul's Epistles, Romans, and Corinthians in the New Testament—and the prohibition has been the basis for repressing homosexual behavior.[24] Gays were brutalized and killed by the ancient Hebrews, a practice continued by the Christians who ruled Western Europe. Laws providing the death penalty for homosexuals existed until 1791 in France, until 1861 in England, and until 1889 in Scotland. Up until the Revolution, some American colonies punished homosexuality with death. In Hitler's Germany, 50,000 homosexuals were put in concentration camps; up to 400,000 more from occupied countries were killed.

Today, many reasons are given for an extremely negative overreaction to homosexuals referred to as *homophobia*.[25] Some religious leaders believe that the Bible condemns same-sex relations and that this behavior is therefore a sin. Others develop a deep-rooted hatred of gays because they are insecure about their own sexual identity. Some are ignorant about the life-style of gays and fear that homosexuality is a disease that can be caught or that homosexuals will seduce their children.[26] Cases involving homosexual violence, such as the gay serial killer Jeffrey Dahmer, help keep these views alive.

Surveys indicate that negative attitudes toward gays persist in our society. During the 1960s, 67 percent of people surveyed believed that homosexuality was obscene and vulgar. Fewer than 20 percent believed that laws banning homosexuality should be repealed.[27] Studies since the 1970s indicate that a majority of people still view gays as sick, sinful, or dangerous.[28] The Gallup Poll indicates that more than half of the general public neither considers homosexuality an acceptable life-style nor believes that gays should be allowed to hold teaching jobs, become members of the clergy, or serve as president.[29] As you may recall from Chapter 11, gay men and women are still subject to thousands of incidents of violence and other hate crimes each year.

Is it possible for antigay attitudes to change? There are some indications that antigay bias can be reversed. Harvard University now offers courses on gay life, and there is a gay studies major at the City University of New York and San Francisco State College.[30] Books are being published that explain their new family life to the estimated 7 million children living full- or part-time with gay and lesbian parents; titles include *Daddy's Roommate* and *Heather Has Two Mommies*.[31]

Homosexuality and the Law

Homosexuality, considered a legal and moral crime throughout most of Western history, is no longer a crime in the United States. In the case of *Robinson v. California*, the U.S. Supreme Court determined that people could not be criminally prosecuted because of their status (for example, drug addict or homosexual).[32] Despite this protection from criminal prosecution based on status, most states and the federal government criminalize the life-style and activities of homosexuals. No state or locality allows same sex marriages, and homosexuals cannot obtain a marriage license to legitimize their relationship. Lawsuits are pending to allow homosexual marriages.[33] Oral and anal sex and all other forms of nongenital heterosexual intercourse are banned in about half the states under statutes prohibiting sodomy, deviant sexuality, or buggery. Maximum penalties range from three years to life in prison, with ten years being the most common sentence.[34] In 1986, the Supreme Court in *Bowers v. Hardwick* upheld a Georgia statute making it a crime to engage in consensual sodomy, even within the confines of one's own home.[35] The Court disregarded Bowers's claims that homosexuals have a "fundamental right" to engage in sexual activity and that consensual, voluntary sex between adults in the home was a private matter that should not be controlled by the law. If all sex within the home were a private matter, Justice Byron White argued for the majority, then such crimes as incest and adultery could not be prosecuted. Citing the historical legal prohibitions against homosexual sodomy, the Court distinguished between the right of gay couples to engage in the sexual behavior of their choice and the sexual privacy the law affords married heterosexual couples. Ironically, the Georgia statute, which carries a 20-year prison sentence, is not directed solely toward homosexuals but refers to a "person" in its prohibition of sodomy.[36] Prestigious legal bodies, such as the American Law Institute (ALI), have called for the abolition of statutes prohibiting homosexual sex, unless force or coercion is used.[37] A number of states, including Illinois, Connecticut, and Nebraska, have adopted the ALI's Model Penal Code policy of legalizing any consensual sexual behavior between adults as long as it is conducted in private and is not forced; in all, about 20 states have decriminalized private, consensual sodomy between adult homosexuals.[38]

Homosexuals still suffer other legal restrictions. While 40 states have laws banning sexual discrimination, Miami repealed its gay rights ordinance in 1977, and in 1985, Houston voters rejected by a four-to-one margin a proposal to eliminate sexual preference in hiring, firing, and promoting city employees.[39] In 1992, major ballot initiatives in Colorado and Oregon were designed to restrict the civil liberties of gay men and women; the Oregon legislation failed, but the Colorado bill won a majority of votes.[40] As late as 1993, voters in Cincinnati repealed a city ordinance that banned discrimination in housing or employment based on sexual orientation.[41]

Though the U.S. Civil Service Commission found in 1975 that homosexuals could not be barred from federal employment, gays are still considered security risks and are not allowed to work in high-security jobs; it was not until December 1993 that the FBI lifted its ban on homosexuals.[42] The backlash over President Bill Clinton's attempt to make good on his campaign promise to allow gays in the military produced the first crisis of his presidency. The compromise (so far) has been a "don't ask, don't tell" policy.

Homosexuals may still be evicted from private housing at the landlord's discretion. Gays are prohibited from living together in public housing projects. In most areas, private employers may also discriminate against gay men and women. For example, a federal court upheld the right of an airline to fire a pilot who underwent a sex change operation.[43]

In sum, though it is not a crime to be a homosexual, homosexual acts are still illegal in most states. However, most police agencies enforce laws banning homosexual practices only if they are forced to do so, the acts occur in public places, or the acts are done for financial consideration.[44]

Paraphilias

Paraphilias (from the Greek *para,* "to the side of," and *philos,* "loving") are bizarre or abnormal sexual practices involving recurrent sexual urges focused on (1) nonhuman objects (underwear, shoes, leather), (2) humiliation or the experience of receiving or giving pain (sadomasochism, bondage), or (3) children or others who cannot grant consent.[45] Some paraphilias, such as wearing clothes normally worn by the opposite sex (transvestic fetishism), can be engaged in by adults in the privacy of their homes and do not involve a third party; these are usually out of the law's reach. Others, however, present a risk to society and are subject to criminal penalties. This group of outlawed sexual behavior includes:

Frotteurism—rubbing against or touching a nonconsenting person in a crowd, elevator, or other public area.

Voyeurism—obtaining sexual pleasure from spying upon a stranger while he or she disrobes or engages in sexual behavior with another.

Exhibitionism—deriving sexual pleasure from exposing the genitals to surprise or shock a stranger.

Sadomasochism—deriving pleasure from receiving pain or inflicting pain on another.

Pedophilia—attaining sexual pleasure through sexual activity with prepubescent children.

Paraphilias that involve unwilling or underage victims are subject to legal prosecution. Most state criminal codes carry specific laws banning indecent exposure and voyeurism. Others prosecute paraphilias under common-law assault and battery or sodomy statutes.

The Close-Up entitled "Autoerotic Asphyxia" describes one sometimes deadly paraphilia and its treatment in some detail.

Prostitution

Prostitution has been known for thousands of years. The term derives from the Latin *prostituere,* which means "to cause to stand in front of." By implication, the prostitute is viewed as publicly offering his or her body for sale. The earliest record of prostitution appears in ancient Mesopotamia, where priests engaged in sex to promote fertility in the community. All women were required to do temple duty, and passing strangers were expected to make donations to the temple after enjoying its services.[46]

Modern commercial sex appears to have its roots in ancient Greece, where Solon established licensed brothels in 500 B.C. The earnings of Greek prostitutes helped pay for the temple of Aphrodite. Famous men openly went to prostitutes to enjoy intellectual, aesthetic, and sexual stimulation; prostitutes, however, were prevented from marrying.[47]

Though some early Christian religious leaders, such as St. Augustine and St. Thomas Aquinas, were tolerant of prostitution as a necessary evil, this tolerance disappeared after the reformation. Martin Luther advocated the abolition of prostitution on moral grounds, and Lutheran doctrine depicted prostitutes as emissaries of the devil who were sent to destroy the faith.[48]

In more recent times, prostitution was tied to the rise of English brewery companies during the early nineteenth century. Saloons controlled by the companies employed prostitutes to attract patrons and encourage them to drink. This relationship was repeated in major U.S. cities, such as Chicago, until breweries were forbidden to own the outlets that distributed their product.

Today, there are many variations of prostitution, but in general, the term can be defined as the granting of nonmarital sexual access, established by mutual agreement of the prostitutes, their clients, and their employers, for remuneration. This definition is sexually neutral, since prostitutes can, of course, be straight or gay, male

CLOSE-UP

Autoerotic Asphyxia

On February 8, 1994, Britain was shocked to learn of the death of Stephen Milligan, a 45-year-old member of Parliament and a rising star in the Tory government. Milligan was found dead in his London apartment wearing women's stockings and garters, with a plastic bag over his head, tied around his neck with electric cable. Based on these findings, Milligan most likely died accidentally by strangulation while attempting to enhance sexual gratification with partial asphyxia.

According to the diagnostic and statistical manual of the American Psychiatric Association, sexual masochism is a paraphilia caused by an intense sexual urge or sexually arousing fantasies involving the real act of being humiliated, bound, or otherwise made to suffer. A subset of masochistic behavior is referred to as asphyxiophilia, hypoxyphilia, or autoerotic asphyxia, which by means of a noose, ligature, plastic bag, mask, volatile chemicals, or chest compression, a man or woman attempts partial asphyxia and oxygen deprivation to their brain to enhance sexual gratification; almost all cases of hypoxyphilia involve males.

Hypoxyphilia is rarely fatal, and there is always an "escape" mechanism planned. Though it is seldom associated with a partner, some hypoxyphiliacs will have a mate simulate choking them as part of sexual activity. The book and film *Rising Sun* concerned a hypoxyphiliac who dies as a result of strangulation during sexual activity. People who accidentally die from autoerotic asphyxia are usually reported to be well-adjusted before the revelation of their behavior. They usually have shown no evidence of psychiatric disturbance or previous aberrant sexual behavior; most are heterosexual.

Gender influences the nature of the disorder. Males engage in far more elaborate preparations. They use a significant amount of pornographic material; engage in a degree of cross-dressing; and use elaborate ligatures, bindings, or mechanisms to inflict pain, including at times electricity and heat. Frequently there are genital attachments. In all cases, the victim is usually found in a secluded area. In contrast, females use less elaborate preparations; they rarely employ pornographic material, sexual props, or costumes.

Hypoxyphilia is known universally. It has been suggested that the behavior be called "Kotzwarrism" after a Czech musician who died after convincing a prostitute to hang him for five minutes, after which she was unable to resuscitate him. The Marquis de Sade described asphyxiophilia in his erotic novels.

Fatal autoerotic asphyxia can often be confused with homicide or suicide. Forensic experts are now able to identify it, enabling law enforcement agencies to more easily make a correct determination of death. Death scenes usually involve evidence of repetitive activity, including wear marks from nooses or previous activities, either photographed or written about. Usually the door is locked from the inside, there is no suicide note, and the scene has sexual overtones.

The origin of this disorder is unclear. There are psychoanalytic, behavioral, and anatomical models. Frontal lobe disorders have also been suggested. Most likely, the disorder may stem from multiple factors, including biological, psychological, and social factors. Treatment is therefore difficult. One approach is behavior modification using aversion therapy. Occasionally, drug therapy has been helpful, including the use of Lithium and sex drive-reducing agents.

Hypoxyphilia remains an unusual and perplexing problem, but should it constitute a criminal act? Does the right to privacy extend to personal sexual behavior or should it be subject to government regulation?

Discussion Questions

1. Should hypoxyphilia be treated as a disease or a crime?
2. Should the government be allowed to order brain surgery if it could be proved that such treatment could eradicate a paraphilia?

SOURCE: This section was prepared by Dr. Wayne Goldner, M.D., Bedford, New Hampshire, March 1994.

This 1885 woodcut shows New York prostitutes, looking comfortably well-off, trying to entice customers by showing them suggestive photographs. In reality, prostitutes, both then and now, are more likely to be victims of abuse, violence, and maltreatment.

or female. A recent analysis has amplified the definition of prostitution by describing the conditions usually present in a commercial sexual transaction:

- Activity that has sexual significance for the customer. This includes the entire range of sexual behavior, from sexual intercourse to exhibitionism, sadomasochism, oral sex, and so on.

- Economic transaction. Something of economic value, not necessarily money, is exchanged for the activity.

- Emotional indifference. The sexual exchange is simply for economic consideration. Though the participants may know one another, their interaction has nothing to do with affection for one another.[49]

Incidence of Prostitution

It is difficult to assess the number of prostitutes operating in the United States. One estimate is 250,000 to 500,000 full- or part-time prostitutes—one in 200 to 500 women.[50] Fifty years ago, about two-thirds of noncollege-educated men, but only about one-fourth of college-educated men, had visited a prostitute; about 20 percent of college-educated men had been sexually initiated by prostitutes.[51] It is likely that the number of men who hire prostitutes has declined sharply, a trend punctuated by a 17 percent drop in the number of prostitutes arrested during the past decade.[52]

How can these changes be accounted for? Changing sexual mores, brought about by the so-called sexual revolution, have liberalized sexuality. Men are less likely to engage prostitutes because legitimate alternatives for sexuality are more open to them. In recent years, the prevalence of sexually transmitted diseases has changed sexual attitudes to the point where many men may avoid visiting prostitutes for fear of irreversible health hazards. Many prostitutes are intravenous drug takers. About 47 percent of males and 85 percent of females arrested for prostitution tested positively for drug abuse. Drug use increases their chances of contracting the AIDS virus and becoming carriers; a study conducted by the U.S. Centers for Disease Control of 1,305 prostitutes in eight U.S. cities found that almost 7 percent tested positively for the HTLV-I virus, which has been linked to leukemia and multiple sclerosis.[53]

Despite such supposed changes in sexual morality, the Uniform Crime Reports indicate that about 100,000 prostitution arrests are made annually, with the gender ratio being about two females to every male.[54] More alarming is the fact that about 1,000 arrests are of minors under 18. In 1992, about 165 recorded arrests were of children age 15 and under; a few (33 arrests) were kids under 12, including 14 who were under ten years of age. Arguing that the criminal law should not interfere with sexual transactions because no one is harmed is undermined by these disturbing statistics.

Types of Prostitution

Several different types of prostitutes operate in the United States.

Streetwalkers.

Prostitutes who work the streets in plain sight of police, citizens, and customers are referred to as hustlers, hookers, or streetwalkers. Though glamorized by the Julia Roberts character in the film *Pretty Woman* (who winds up with multimillionaire Richard Gere), streetwalkers are considered the least attractive, lowest paid, most vulnerable men and women in the profession. Streetwalkers wear bright clothing, makeup, and jewelry to attract customers; they take their customers to hotels. The term *hooker,* however, is not derived from the ability of streetwalkers to hook clients on their charms. It actually stems from the popular name given women who followed Union General "Fighting Joe" Hooker's army during the Civil War.[55] Because streetwalkers must openly display their occupation, they are very likely to be involved with the police. Studies indicate they are most likely to be members of ethnic or racial minorities who live in poverty. Many are young runaways who gravitate to major cities to find a new and

exciting life and escape from sexual and physical abuse at home.[56] Of all prostitutes, streetwalkers have the highest incidence of drug abuse and larceny arrests, and they are the toughest.[57]

Bar Girls.

B-girls, as they are also called, spend their time in bars, drinking and waiting to be picked up by customers. Though alcoholism may be a problem, B-girls usually work out an arrangement with the bartender so they are served diluted drinks or water colored with dye or tea, for which the customer is charged an exorbitant price. In some bars, the B-girl is given a credit for each drink she gets the customer to buy. It is common to find B-girls in towns with military bases and large transient populations, such as Boston and San Diego.[58]

Brothel Prostitutes.

In 1984, socialite Sydney Biddle Barrows was arrested by New York police for operating a $1-million-per-year prostitution ring out of a bordello on West Seventy-Fourth Street.[59] Descended from a socially prominent family who traced their line to the Mayflower, Barrows ranked her 20 women on looks and personality from A ($125 per hour) to C ($400 per hour) and kept 60 percent of their take. Her "black book" of clients was described by police as a mini *Who's Who.*

Also called bordellos, cathouses, sporting houses, and houses of ill repute, **brothels** flourished in the nineteenth and early twentieth centuries. They were large establishments, usually run by **madams,** that housed several prostitutes. A madam is a woman who employs prostitutes, supervises their behavior, and receives a fee for her services; her cut is usually 40 to 60 percent of the prostitutes' earnings. The madam's role may include recruiting women into prostitution and socializing them in the "trade."[60] The madam, often a retired prostitute, is the senior administrator and owner. She makes arrangements for opening the place, attracts prostitutes and customers, works out understandings with police authorities, and pacifies neighbors.[61] The madam is part psychologist, part parent figure, and part business entrepreneur.

Some brothels and their madams have received national notoriety. Polly Adler wrote a highly publicized autobiography of her life as a madam called *A House Is Not a Home.* Sally Stanford maintained a succession of luxuriously furnished brothels in San Francisco. Stanford never made a secret of her profession; she actually listed her phone number in the city directory. In 1962 and 1970, she ran for the San Francisco City Council.

Brothels declined in importance following World War II. The closing of the last brothel in Texas is chronicled in the play and movie *The Best Little Whorehouse in Texas.* Today, the most well-known brothels exist in Nevada, where prostitution is legal outside large population centers. Such houses as "Mustang Ranch," "Miss Kitty's," and "Pink Pussycat" service customers who drive out from Reno and Las Vegas.

Call Girls.

The aristocrats of prostitution are **call girls.** They charge customers up to $1,500 per night and may net over $100,000 per year. Some gain clients through employment in escort services, while others develop independent customer lists. Many call girls come from middle-class backgrounds and service upper-class customers. Attempting to dispel the notion that their service is simply sex for money, they concentrate on making their clients feel important and attractive. Working exclusively via telephone "dates," call girls get their clients by word of mouth or by making arrangements with bellhops, cab drivers, and so on. They either entertain clients in their own apartments or make "outcalls" to clients' hotels and apartments. Upon retiring from "the life," a call girl can sell her datebook listing client names and sexual preferences for thousands of dollars. Despite the lucrative nature of their business, call girls suffer considerable risk by being alone and unprotected with strangers. It is common for them to request the business cards of their clients to make sure they are dealing with "upstanding citizens."

Call Houses.

A relatively new phenomenon, call houses, combines elements of the brothel and call-girl rings. In this type of operation, a madam receives a call from a prospective customer, and if she finds the client acceptable, arranges a meeting between the caller and a prostitute in her service. The madam maintains a list of prostitutes who are on call rather than living together in a house. The call house insulates the madam from arrest because she never meets the client or receives direct payment.[62]

Circuit Travelers.

Prostitutes known as circuit travelers move around in groups of two or three to lumber, labor, and agricultural camps. They will ask the foremen for permission to ply their trade, service the whole crew in an evening, and then move on.

Rap Booth Prostitutes.

A phenomenon in commercial sex, rap booths are located in the adult entertainment zones of such cities as New York and San Francisco.[63] The prostitute and her customer occupy booths that are separated by a glass wall. They talk via telephone for as long as the customer is willing to pay. The more money he spends, the more she engages in sexual banter and disrobing. There is no actual touching, and sex is through masturbation, with the prostitute serving as a masturbation aid similar in function to a pornographic magazine.

Skeezers: Bartering Sex for Drugs.

With the prevalence of drug abuse and the introduction of "crack" cocaine to the street culture in the mid-1980s, a new form of prostitution, trading sex for drugs, became common. Surveys conducted in New York and Chicago have found that a significant portion of female prostitutes have substance abuse problems and more than half claim that prostitution is the method they use to support their drug habit; on the street, women who barter drugs for sex are called **skeezers.** Not all drug-addicted prostitutes barter sex for drugs, but those that do report more frequent drug abuse and sexual activity than other prostitutes.

There is some question of the impact bartering sex for drugs has on prostitutes. The prevailing wisdom is that those who engage in the practice are victims who are often the target of violent attacks and rapes. However, when interviewed by Paul Goldstein and his associates, barterers viewed themselves as being engaged in economic transactions in which they are treated fairly.[64] In opposition to widely held beliefs, these prostitutes are not drug slaves or victims who have no control over their lives. Many expressed the view that bartering gave them the "benefit" of the deal—valuable drugs for a few minutes of sexual service.

Other Varieties.

Some "working girls" are based in **massage parlors.** Though it is unusual for a masseuse to offer all the services of prostitution, oral sex and manual stimulation are common. Most localities have attempted to limit commercial sex in massage parlors by passing ordinances specifying that the masseuse keep certain parts of her body covered and limiting the areas of the body that can be massaged. Photography studios and model and escort services sometimes are covers for commercial sex. Some photo studios will allow customers to put body paint on models before the photo sessions start. Stag party girls will service all-male parties and groups by putting on shows and having sex with participants. In years past, many hotels had live-in prostitutes. Today's hotel prostitute makes a deal with the bell captain or manager to refer customers to her for a fee; some second-rate hotels still have resident prostitutes.

A male prostitute waits for his next client. About one third of all prostitute arrests involve males—many are homeless kids fleeing abusive homes.

Becoming a Prostitute

Why does someone turn to prostitution? Both male and female prostitutes often come from troubled homes marked by extreme conflict and hostility and from poor urban areas or rural communities. Divorce, separation, or death splits the family; most prostitutes grew up in homes with absent fathers.[65] Many prostitutes were initiated into sex by family members at as young as ten to 12 years of age; they have long histories of sexual exploitation and abuse.[66] The early experiences with sex help teach them that their bodies have value and that sexual encounters can be used to obtain affection, power, or money.

Lower-class girls who get into "the life" report conflict with school authorities, poor grades, and an overly regimented school experience.[67] Drug abuse, including heroin and cocaine addiction, are often factors in the prostitute's life.[68] Other personal characteristics found among samples of prostitutes include: grew up in a slum neighborhood; was born out of wedlock or into a broken home; dropped out of school; fantasizes about money and success; is a member of a "loose crowd"; saw prostitutes in the neighborhood; had unfortunate

experiences with a husband or boyfriend; had trouble keeping a job.[69] However, there is no actual evidence that people become prostitutes because of psychological problems or personality disturbances. Money, drugs, and survival seem to be greater motivations.

Research indicates that few girls were forced into the life by a pimp. Pimps may convince girls by flattery, support, promises, and affection, but relatively few kidnap or coerce kids into prostitution. There is more evidence that friends or relatives introduce kids into prostitution. Most report entering prostitution voluntarily because they disliked the discipline of conventional work.[70] Jennifer James claims that the primary cause of women becoming prostitutes is the supply-and-demand equation operating in society.[71] She contends that male clients are socialized to view sex as a commodity that can be purchased. The quantity of sex, rather than its quality, has the higher value for U.S. males. Women who are socialized to view themselves as sex objects may easily step over the line of propriety and accept money for their favors. These women view their bodies as salable commodities, and most prostitution does in fact pay better than other occupations available for women with limited education. Helping to push the women to take the final step into prostitution are the troubled personal circumstances described previously. James backs up her view with a research study that found that only 8 percent of prostitutes claim to have started because of dire economic necessity, while 57 percent were motivated by a desire for money and luxuries.

Pimps

A pimp derives part or all of his livelihood from the earnings of a prostitute. The pimp helps steer customers to the prostitute, stays on the alert for and deals with police, posts bail, and protects his prostitutes from unruly customers.[72] To the prostitute, the pimp is a surrogate father, husband, and lover. She may sell her body to customers, but she reserves her care and affection for her pimp. Pimps can pick up established "working girls" or they can "turn out" young girls who have never been in "the life." Occasionally, but not as often as the media would like us to believe, they pick up young runaways, buy them clothes and jewelry, and turn them into **"baby pros."**

What attracts men to the life of the pimp? One view is that many pimps originally worked on the fringes of prostitution as bellhops, elevator operators, or barmen and subsequently drifted into the profession. An opposing view is that pimps began as young men seduced by older prostitutes who taught them how to succeed in "the life," how to behave, and how to control women.[73]

The role of the pimp is undergoing change. The decline of the brothel, the development of independent prostitutes, and the control of prostitution by organized crime has decreased the number of full-time pimps.[74] Many prostitutes are drug-dependent, and in some areas, drug dealers have replaced pimps as the controlling force in prostitution. Even the cost of sex is drug-dependent, rather than being controlled by a pimp, with the going rate for sexual services geared to the cost of a rock of crack.[75] Even when a prostitute has a pimp, the relationship is often short-lived and unstable. Dorothy Bracey found that pimps are reluctant to work with younger prostitutes today because they face more severe legal penalties if caught running juveniles and also because they consider juveniles unstable and untrustworthy.[76]

Legalize Prostitution?

Prostitution is illegal in all states except Nevada (except in the counties in which Las Vegas and Reno are located). Typically, prostitution is considered a misdemeanor, punishable by a fine or a short jail sentence. The federal government's **Mann Act** (passed in 1925) prohibits bringing women into the country or transporting them across state lines for the purposes of prostitution. Often called the "white slave act," it carries with it a $5,000 fine, five years in prison, or both.

Feminists have staked out conflicting views of prostitution. One position is that women must become emancipated from male oppression and reach sexual equality. The *sexual equality* view considers the prostitute to be a victim of male dominance. In patriarchal societies like our own, male power is predicated on female subjugation, and prostitution is a clear example of this gender exploitation.[77]

In contrast, for some feminists, the fight for equality depends on controlling all attempts by men or women to impose their will on women. The free choice view is that prostitution is an expression of women's status as an equal; if freely chosen, it can be an expression of women's equality and not a symptom of subjugation.[78]

Advocates of both positions argue that the penalties for prostitution should be reduced (decriminalized); neither side advocates outright legalization. Decriminalization would relieve already desperate women of the additional burden of severe legal punishment. In contrast, legalization might be coupled with regulation by male-dominated justice agencies. For example, required medical examinations would mean increased male control over women's bodies. While both sides advocate change

in the criminal status of prostitution, few communities, save San Francisco, have openly debated or voted on its legalization.

☰ Pornography

The term **pornography** derives from the Greek *porne*, meaning "prostitute," and *graphein*, meaning "to write." In the heart of many major cities are stores devoted to the display and sale of books, magazines, and films that depict explicit sex acts of every imaginable kind. It has also become common for suburban video stores to rent and sell sexually explicit tapes, which make up to 15 percent of the home rental market. The purpose of this material is to provide sexual titillation and excitement for paying customers. Though material depicting nudity and sex is typically legal and protected by the First Amendment's provision limiting the governmental control of speech, most criminal codes contain provisions prohibiting the production, display, and sale of *obscene* material.

Obscenity, derived from the Latin *caenum* for "filth," is defined by Webster's dictionary as "deeply offensive to morality or decency . . . designed to incite to lust or depravity."[79] The problem of controlling pornography centers on this definition of obscenity. Police and law enforcement officials can legally seize only material that is judged obscene. "But who," critics ask, "is to judge what is obscene?" At one time, such novels as *Tropic of Cancer* by Henry Miller, *Ulysses* by James Joyce, and *Lady Chatterly's Lover* by D. H. Lawrence were prohibited because they were considered obscene. Today, they are considered works of great literary value. Thus, what is obscene today may be considered a work of art, or at least socially acceptable, at a future time. After all, *Playboy* and *Penthouse* magazines, sold openly on most college campuses, display nude models in all kinds of sexually explicit poses. Allowing individual judgments on what is obscene makes the Constitution's guarantee of free speech unworkable. Could not antiobscenity statutes also be used to control political and social dissent? The uncertainty surrounding this issue is illustrated by Supreme Court Justice Potter Stewart's famous 1964 statement on how he defined obscenity: "I know it when I see it."

The problems of controlling obscenity were heightened on June 8, 1990, when an undercover detective walked into a record shop in Fort Lauderdale, Florida, and bought a copy of "As Nasty as They Wanna Be," the hit album of the rap group 2 Live Crew. He and six of his fellow officers then arrested store owner Charles Freeman on the charge of distributing obscene material. This was the first arrest following a federal judge's decision that the group's songs (for example, "Me So Horny") contained lyrics having a sexual content that violated local community standards of decency and were therefore obscene.[80] To many, this incident represented an exercise of the criminal law that was a direct attack on the First Amendment's guarantee of free speech. Later, two members of 2 Live Crew were arrested for performing in a nightclub. It was the first case in which a music album was ruled obscene by a court.

The Dangers of Pornography

Dear Ann Landers,
 . . . several months ago, I caught my husband making calls to a 900-sex number. After a week of denial, he admitted that for several years he had been hooked on porn magazines, porn movies, peep shows, strippers and phone sex. This addiction can start early in life. With my husband it began at age 12, with just one simple, "harmless" magazine. By the time he was 19, it had become completely out of control. . . . For years my husband hated himself and it affected his entire life.[81]

Opponents of pornography argue that it degrades both the men and women who are photographed and members of the public who are sometimes forced to see obscene material. Pornographers exploit their models, who often include underage children. The Attorney General's Commission on Pornography, set up by the Reagan administration to review the sale and distribution of sexually explicit material, concluded that many performers and models are the victims of physical and psychological coercion.[82] The so-called kiddy porn industry is estimated to amount to over $1 billion of a total $2.5 billion spent annually on pornography. Each year, over a million children are believed to be used in pornography or prostitution, many of them runaways whose plight is exploited by adults.[83]

Child Pornography Rings.

How does child pornography get made and distributed? Many of the "hard-core" pictures that find their way into the hands of collectors are the work of pornographic groups or rings, adults who join together to exploit children and adolescents for sex. Ann Wolbert Burgess studied 55 child pornography rings and found that the typical one contained between three and 11 children, predominantly males, some of nursery school age. The adults who controlled the ring used a position of trust to recruit

the children and then continued to exploit them through a combination of material and psychological rewards. Burgess found that different types of child pornography rings exist. Solo sex rings involve several children involved with a single adult, usually male, who uses a position of trust (counselor, teacher, Boy Scout leader) to recruit children into sexual activity. Transition rings are impromptu groups set up to sell and trade photos and sex. Syndicated rings have well-structured organizations that recruit children and create extensive networks of customers who desire sexual services.[84] The sexual exploitation by these rings can have a devastating effect on the child victim. Burgess found that children suffered from physical problems ranging from headaches and loss of appetite to genital soreness, vomiting, and urinary infections. Psychological problems include mood swings, withdrawal, edginess, and nervousness. Exploited children were prone to such acting-out behavior as setting fires and becoming sexually focused in the use of language, dress, and mannerisms. In cases of extreme and prolonged victimization, children may lock onto the sex group's behavior and become prone to further victimization or even become victimizers themselves.

Does Pornography Cause Violence?

An issue critical to the debate over pornography is whether viewing it produces sexual violence or assaultive behavior against women. This debate was given added interest when serial killer Ted Bundy claimed his murderous rampage was fueled by reading pornography.

Some evidence exists that viewing sexually explicit material actually has little effect on behavior. In 1970, the National Commission on Obscenity and Pornography reviewed all available material on the effects of pornography and authorized independent research projects. The commission found no clear relationship between pornography and violence, and it recommended that federal, state, and local legislation should not interfere with the rights of adults who wish to read, obtain, or view explicit sexual materials.[85] Almost 20 years later, the highly controversial Attorney General's Commission on Pornography, sponsored by a conservative Reagan administration, called for legal attacks on hard-core pornography and condemnation of all sexually related material but also found little evidence that obscenity was a per se cause of antisocial behavior.[86]

How might we account for this surprisingly insignificant association? Some explanation may be found in Danish sociologist Berl Kutchinsky's widely cited research showing that the rate of sex offenses actually declined shortly after pornography was decriminalized in Denmark in 1967.[87] He attributed this trend to the fact that viewing erotic material may act as a safety valve for those whose impulses might otherwise lead them to violence. In a similar vein, Michael Goldstein found that convicted rapists and sex offenders report less exposure to pornography than a control group of nonoffenders.[88]

It is possible that viewing prurient material may have the unintended side effect of satisfying erotic impulses that otherwise might have resulted in more sexually aggressive behavior. This issue is far from settled. A number of criminologists believe that the positive relationship between pornography consumption and rape rates in various countries, including the United States, is evidence that obscenity may indeed have a powerful influence on criminality.[89] Nonetheless, the weight of the evidence shows little relationship between violence and pornography per se.

Violent Pornography, Violent Crime.

While there is little or no documentation of a correlation between pornography and violent crime, there is stronger evidence that people exposed to erotic literature that portrays violence and sadism and that indicates that women enjoy being raped and degraded are likely to be sexually aggressive toward female victims.[90] Even the Attorney General's Commission on Pornography concluded in 1986 that a causal link could be drawn between exposure to violent sexually explicit material and sexual violence. After reviewing the literature on the subject, the Commission found that while the behavioral effects of sexually nonviolent and nondegrading pornography were insignificant, exposure to sexually violent and degrading materials:

1. leads to a greater acceptance of rape myths and violence against women;
2. [has] more pronounced effects when the victim is shown enjoying the use of force or violence;
3. is arousing for rapists and for some males in the general population; and
4. has resulted in sexual aggression against women in controlled laboratory settings.[91]

Experimental laboratory studies by Edward Donnerstein, Seymour Fishbach, and Neil Malamuth, among others, have found that men exposed to violence in pornography are more likely to act aggressively toward women.[92]

The evidence suggests that violence and sexual aggression are not linked to erotic or pornographic films per se but that erotic films depicting violence, rape, bru-

tality, and aggression may evoke similar feelings in viewers. This finding is especially distressing because it is common for adult-only books and films to have sexually violent themes, such as rape, bondage, and mutilation.[93]

Pornography and the Law

The problems associated with legal control over obscene material were highlighted in 1990 by a controversy concerning a posthumous exhibition featuring the works of gay photographer Robert Mapplethorpe. The exhibition was heavily criticized by conservative politicians because it contained images of nude children and men in homoerotic poses and because it had received federal funding. When Cincinnati's Contemporary Arts Center mounted the show, obscenity charges were brought against its director; he was later found not guilty. The actions taken against the Mapplethorpe exhibit brought waves of protest from artists and performers, as well as civil libertarians, who fear governmental control over art, music, and theater. They also highlight the problems of enforcement when attempts at "serious" artistic expression contain sexual material that offends the standards of some segments of the public. Should free expression be controlled if it offends some people's sense of decency?

The First Amendment of the U.S. Constitution protects free speech and prohibits police agencies from limiting the public's right of free expression. However, the Supreme Court held in the twin cases of *Roth v. United States* and *Alberts v. California* that the First Amendment protects all "ideas with even the slightest redeeming social importance—unorthodox ideas, controversial ideas, even ideas hateful to the prevailing climate of opinion . . . but implicit in the history of the First Amendment is the rejection of obscenity as utterly without redeeming social importance."[94] In the 1966 case of *Memoirs v. Massachusetts,* the Supreme Court again required that for a work to be considered obscene, it must be shown to be "utterly without redeeming social value."[95] These decisions left unclear how obscenity is defined. If a highly erotic movie told a "moral tale," must it be judged legal even if 95 percent of its content was objectionable? A spate of movies made after the *Roth* decision alleged that they were educational or told a moral tale, so they could not be said to lack redeeming social importance. Many state obscenity cases were appealed to federal courts so judges could decide whether the films totally lacked redeeming social importance. To rectify the situation, the Supreme Court redefined its concept of obscenity in the case of *Miller v. California:*

The basic guidelines for the trier of fact must be (a) whether the average person applying contemporary community standards would find that the work taken as a whole appeals to the prurient interest; (b) whether the work depicts or describes, in a patently offensive way, sexual conduct specifically defined by the applicable state law, and (c) whether the work, taken as a whole, lacks serious literary, artistic, political or scientific value.[96]

To convict a person of obscenity under the *Miller* doctrine, the state or local jurisdiction must specifically define obscene conduct in its statute, and the pornographer must engage in that behavior. The Court gave some examples of what is considered obscene: "patently offensive representations or descriptions of masturbation, excretory functions and lewd exhibition of the genitals." In subsequent cases, the Court overruled convictions for "offensive" or "immoral" behavior; these are not considered obscene. The *Miller* doctrine has been criticized for not spelling out how community standards are to be determined.[97] Obviously, a plebiscite cannot be held to determine the community's attitude for every trial concerning the sale of pornography. Works that are considered obscene in Omaha might be considered routine in New York, but how can we be sure? To resolve this dilemma, the Supreme Court articulated in *Pope v. Illinois* a reasonableness doctrine: a work is obscene if a reasonable person applying objective (national) standards would find the material lacking in any social value.[98] While *Pope* should help clarify the legal definition of obscenity, the issue is far from settled. Justice John Paul Stevens in his dissent offered one interesting alternative: the First Amendment protects material "if some reasonable persons could (find) serious literary(,) artistic, political or scientific value" in it.[99] Stevens believes that if anyone could find merit in a work, it should be protected by law. Do you?

Controlling Sex for Profit

Sex for profit predates Western civilization. Considering its longevity, there seems to be little evidence that it can be controlled or eliminated by legal means alone. The Attorney General's Commission on Pornography advocated a strict law enforcement policy to control obscenity, urging that "the prosecution of obscene materials that portray sexual violence be treated as a matter of special urgency."[100] Since then, there has been a concerted effort by the federal government to prosecute adult movie distributors. Law enforcement has been so fervent that industry members have filed suit claiming they are the victims of a "moral crusade" by right-wing zealots.[101] While politically appealing, law enforcement crusades may not necessarily obtain the desired effect. A "get tough" policy could make sex-related goods and services a relatively scarce commodity, driving up prices and making their sale even more desirable and profitable. And going after national distributors may help decentralize the adult movie and photo business and encourage local rings to expand their activities, for example, by making and marketing videos as well as still photos or distributing them through on-line computer networks.

An alternate approach has been to control or restrict the sale of pornography within acceptable boundaries and areas. For example, municipal governments have tolerated or even established restricted adult entertainment zones in which obscene material can be openly sold. In the case of *Young v. American Mini Theaters,* the Supreme Court permitted a zoning ordinance that restricted theaters showing erotic movies to one area of the city, even though it did not find that any of the movies shown were obscene.[102] The state, therefore, has the right to regulate adult films as long as the public has the right to view them. Restricting the sale of sexually related material to a particular area can have unforeseen consequences. Skyrocketing real estate prices in the downtown areas of such cities as Boston and New York have made the running of sex clubs and stores in those areas relatively unprofitable. Land that was used for adult movie houses has been redeveloped into high-priced condominiums and office buildings. For example, the number of striptease clubs in Boston's Combat Zone shrank from 22 in 1977 to five in 1987 as the area was redeveloped.[103]

The threat of governmental regulation may also convince some participants in the sex-for-profit industry to police themselves. While some forms of sexually explicit material and activities will be tolerated by local law enforcement agencies, others will bring about prompt legal control. For example, child pornography usually spurs otherwise complacent governmental agencies to take swift action. Efforts to control this problem have been supported by the courts. The landmark *New York v. Ferber* case indicates the Supreme Court's willingness to allow the states to control child pornography.[104] In this case, Paul Ferber, a Manhattan bookstore owner, was sentenced to 45 days in jail for violating a New York statute banning material that portrays children engaged in sexually explicit, though not necessarily obscene, conduct. He challenged the law as a violation of free speech. By unanimously upholding Ferber's conviction, the

Supreme Court found that kiddy porn is damaging to the children it exploits and therefore can be legally banned. In his opinion, Justice Byron White said, "It has been found that sexually exploited children are unable to develop healthy affectionate relationships in later life, have sexual dysfunction and have a tendency to become sexual abusers as adults." The Court also found that the films were an invasion of the child's privacy that the child could not control. Fear of governmental control may already have had an influence on the content of nationally distributed adult magazines.

Criminologists have uncovered a correlation between rape rates and the circulation rates of national adult magazines.[105] The federal government has consequently asked the states to toughen their laws governing the distribution of sex-related material. Some mainstream sex magazines may have altered their content rather than risk provoking public officials.

Technology has also caused change in the sex-for-profit industry. Adult movie theaters are closing all over the nation as people are able to buy or rent tapes in their local video stores and play them in the privacy of their homes.[106] The government has moved to control the broadcast of obscene films via satellite and other technological innovations. On February 15, 1991, Home Dish Only Satellite Networks, Inc., was fined $150,000 for broadcasting pornographic movies to its 30,000 clients throughout the United States; it was the first case to involve prosecution for the illegal use of satellites to broadcast obscene films.[107]

A final modification may be brought about by the fear of AIDS and other sex-related diseases. The number of prostitutes and streetwalkers in downtown areas has decreased notably. Do these changes mean the end of criminal sex for profit in the United States? Hardly. The adult movie market has shifted its locale from downtown theaters to suburban video stores. And while inner-city streetwalkers may be declining in number, their place may be taken by suburban prostitution rings that operate under the guise of escort services or massage parlors.

≡ Substance Abuse

The problem of substance abuse stretches across the United States. Large urban areas are beset by drug-dealing gangs, drug users who engage in crime to support their habits, and alcohol-related violence. Even rural areas, argues criminologist Ralph Weisheit, have drug-related problems.[108] In addition to resident use, rural areas are important staging centers for the transshipment of drugs across the country and are often the site of the production of synthetic drugs and marijuana farming.

Another indication of the concern about drugs has been the increasing number of drug-related arrests from less than half a million in 1977 to more than 1 million in 1992! Similarly, the proportion of prison inmates incarcerated for drug offenses has increased by 300 percent since 1986.[109] Clearly, the justice system views drug abuse as a major problem and is taking what decision makers regard as decisive measures to control it.

Despite the scope of the drug problem, it is still viewed by some as another type of victimless public order crime. There is great debate over the legalization of drugs and the control of alcohol. Some consider drug use a private matter and drug control another example of government intrusion into people's private lives. Furthermore, legalization could reduce the profit of selling illegal substances and drive suppliers out of the market.[110] Others see these substances as dangerous, believing that the criminal activity of users makes the term *victimless* nonsensical. Still another position is that the possession and use of all drugs and alcohol should be legalized but that the sale and distribution of drugs should be heavily penalized. This would punish those profiting from drugs and would enable users to be helped without fear of criminal punishment.

When Did Drug Use Begin?

The use of chemical substances to change reality and provide stimulation, relief, or relaxation has gone on for thousands of years. Mesopotamian writings indicate that opium was used 4,000 years ago—it was known as the "plant of joy."[111] The ancient Greeks knew and understood the problem of drug use. At the time of the Crusades, the Arabs were using marijuana. In the Western Hemisphere, natives of Mexico and South America chewed coca leaves and used "magic mushrooms" in their religious ceremonies.[112] Drug use was also accepted in Europe well into the twentieth century. Recently uncovered pharmacy records circa 1900 to 1920 showed sales of cocaine and heroin solutions to members of the British royal family; records from 1912 show that Winston Churchill, then a member of Parliament, was sold a cocaine solution while staying in Scotland.[113]

In the early years of the United States, opium and its derivatives were easily obtained. Opium-based drugs were adopted for use in various patent medicine cure-alls. Morphine was used extensively to relieve the pain of wounded soldiers in the Civil War. By the turn of the century, an estimated 1 million U.S. citizens were opiate users.[114]

Several factors precipitated the stringent drug laws that are in force in the United States today. The rural religious creeds of the nineteenth century—for example, those of the Methodists, Presbyterians, and Baptists—emphasized individual human toil and self-sufficiency while designating the use of intoxicating substances as an unwholesome surrender to the evils of urban morality. Religious leaders were thoroughly opposed to the use and sale of narcotics. The medical literature of the late 1800s began to designate the use of morphine and opium as a vice, a habit, an appetite, and a disease. Nineteenth- and early twentieth-century police literature described drug users as habitual criminals. Moral crusaders in the nineteenth century defined drug use as evil and directed the actions of local and national rule creators to outlaw the sale and possession of drugs. Some well-publicized research efforts categorized drug use as highly dangerous.[115] Drug use was also associated with the foreign immigrants who were recruited to work in factories and mines and brought with them their national drug habits. Early antidrug legislation appears to be tied to prejudice against immigrating ethnic minorities.[116]

After the Spanish-American War of 1898, the United States inherited Spain's opium monopoly in the Philippines. Concern over this international situation, along with the domestic issues outlined above, led the U.S. government to participate in the First International Drug Conference, held in Shanghai in 1908, and a second one at The Hague in 1912. Participants in these two conferences were asked to strongly oppose free trade in drugs. The international pressure, coupled with a growing national concern, led to the passage of the antidrug laws discussed here.

Alcohol and Its Prohibition

The history of alcohol and the law in the United States has also been controversial and dramatic. At the turn of the century, a drive was mustered to prohibit the sale of alcohol. The **temperance movement** was fueled by the belief that the purity of the U.S. agrarian culture was being destroyed by the growth of the city. Urbanism was viewed as a threat to the life-style of the majority of the nation's population, then living on farms and in villages. The forces behind the temperance movement were such lobbying groups as the Anti-Saloon League led by Carrie Nation, the Women's Temperance Union, and the Protestant clergy of the Baptist, Methodist, and Congregationalist faiths.[117] They viewed the growing city, filled with newly arriving Irish, Italian, and Eastern

European immigrants, as centers of degradation and wickedness. The propensity of these ethnic people to drink heavily was viewed as the main force behind their degenerate life-style. The eventual prohibition of the sale of alcoholic beverages brought about by ratification of the Eighteenth Amendment in 1919 was viewed as a triumph of the morality of middle- and upper-class Americans over the threat posed to their culture by the "new Americans."[118]

Prohibition turned out to be a failure. It was enforced by the Volstead Act, which defined intoxicating beverages as those containing one-half of 1 percent, or more, alcohol.[119] What doomed Prohibition? One factor was the use of organized crime to supply illicit liquor. Also, the law made it illegal only to sell alcohol, not to purchase it; this factor cut into the law's deterrent capability. Finally, despite the work of Elliot Ness and his "Untouchables," law enforcement agencies were inadequate, and officials were more than likely to be corrupted by wealthy bootleggers.[120] Eventually, in 1933, the Twenty-First Amendment to the Constitution repealed Prohibition, signaling the end of the "noble experiment."

Commonly Abused Drugs

A wide variety of drugs are sold and used by drug abusers. Some are addicting, others not. Some provide hallucinations; others cause a depressing, relaxing stupor; and a few give an immediate, exhilarating uplift. This section will discuss some of the most widely used illegal drugs.[121] Common names for these drugs and other related terms are shown in Table 14.1.

Anesthetics. Anesthetic drugs are used as nervous system depressants. Local anesthetics block nervous system transmissions; general anesthetics act on the brain to produce a generalized loss of sensation, stupor, or unconsciousness (called narcosis). The most widely abused anesthetic drug is phencyclidine (PCP), known on the street as "angel dust." PCP can be sprayed on marijuana or other plant leaves and smoked, or it can be drunk or injected; the last two methods are extremely hazardous. Originally developed as an animal tranquilizer, PCP causes hallucinations and a spaced-out feeling. The effects of PCP can last up to two days; the danger of overdose is extremely high.

Volatile Liquids. Volatile liquids are liquids that are easily vaporized. Some substance abusers inhale vapors from lighter fluid, paint thinner, cleaning fluid, and model airplane glue to reach a drowsy, dizzy state sometimes accompanied by hallucinations. The

TABLE 14.1 Drug Terms

What do users call various forms of drug administration?

Inhaling Cocaine
Blow
Blow coke
Do a line
Geeze
Hitch up the reindeers
Pop
Sniff
Snort
Toot

Smoking Cocaine
Chase
Freebasing
Ghost busting

Smoking Marijuana
Blast
Blast a joint
Blast a roach
Blast a stick
Blow
Burn one
Do a joint
Dope smoke
Fire it up

Get a gage up
Hit
Hit the hay
Mow the grass
Poke
Puff the dragon
Tea party
Toke
Toke up
Up against the stem = addicted to
 smoking marijuana

Injecting an Opiate
Backjack
Backup = prepare vein for injection
Bang
Bingo
Blow a fix/blow a shot = injection miss
 es the vein and is wasted in the skin
Boot
Channel swimmer = one who injects
 heroin
Chipping = using only occasionally
Cooker
Cranking up

Cushion = the vein drug is injected
 into; also channel, gutter, pipe, sewer
Emergency gun = instrument used to
 inject other than syringe
Fix
Flag = appearance of blood in the vein
Fuete = hypodermic needle; also:
– gaffus
– glass
– glass gun
– hype stick
Geezer
Get off
Hit the main line
Hot load/hot shot=lethal injection of
 an opiate
Jolt
Joy pop
Main line
Shoot/shoot up
Skin popping
Slam
Spike

What are some trade names used to market marijuana?

Acapulco Gold = Southwestern Mexico
Acapulco Red
African Black
Angola Black
Black Gold= high potency
Black Gungi = India
Blue de Hue = Vietnam
Blue Sky Bond = high potency, Colombia
Cambodian Red/Cam Red = Cambodia
Culican= high potency, Mexico
Canadian Black
Citrol = high potency, Nepal

Colombian Black
Hawaiian = very high potency
Indian Boy
Indian Hay = marijuana from Indian
 hemp plant
Kentucky Blue
Indica = varieties of cannabis, found in
 hot climate, grows 3.5 to 4 feet
Manhattan Silver
Maui Wauie = Hawaii
Mexican Brown
Pakistani Black

Panama Gold
Panama Red
Sativa = varieties of cannabis, found in
 cool, damp climate, grows up to 18
 feet
Ruderalis = varieties of cannabis,
 found in Russia, grows 1 to 2.5 feet
Tex-Mex
Texas Tea
Texas Pot
Zacatecas Purple = Mexico

What are drug use combinations called?

Cocaine and Heroin
Dynamite
Goofball
Speedball

Cocaine, Heroin, and LSD
Frisco Special
Frisco Speedball

PCP and Marijuana
Wac
Zoom

PCP and Crack
Beam Me Up Scottie
Space Cadet
Tragic Magic

Others
Atom Bomb = heroin mixed with marijuana
Black Hash = opium mixed with hashish
C and M = cocaine and morphine
Cotton Brothers = cocaine, heroin, and morphine
Dusting = adding PCP, heroin, or another drug to marijuana
Fuel = marijuana mixed with insecticides
Herb and Al = marijuana and alcohol

SOURCE: Bureau of Justice Statistics, *Drugs, Crime, and the Justice System* (Washington, D.C.: Bureau of Justice Statistics, 1993), pp. 24–26.

psychological effect produced by inhaling these substances is a short-term sense of excitement and euphoria followed by a period of disorientation, slurred speech, and drowsiness. Amyl nitrate ("poppers") is a commonly used volatile liquid that is sold in capsules that are broken and inhaled. Poppers allegedly increase sensation and are sometimes used during sexual activity to prolong and intensify the experience.

Barbiturates. The hypnotic-sedative drugs—barbiturates—are able to depress the central nervous system into a sleep-like condition. On the illegal market, barbiturates are called "goofballs" or "downers" or are known by the color of the capsules—"reds" (Seconal), "blue dragons" (Amytal), and "rainbows" (Tuinal). Barbiturates can be prescribed by doctors as sleeping pills. In the illegal market, they are used to create relaxed, sociable, and good-humored feelings. However, if dosages get too high, users become irritable and obnoxious and finally slump off into sleep. Barbiturates are probably the major cause of drug overdose deaths.

Tranquilizers. Tranquilizers have the ability to relieve uncomfortable emotional feelings by reducing levels of anxiety. They ease tension and promote a state of relaxation. The major tranquilizers are used to control the behavior of the mentally ill who are suffering from psychoses, aggressiveness, and agitation. They are known by their brand names—Ampazine, Thorazine, Pacatal, Sparine, and so on. The minor tranquilizers are used by the average citizen to combat anxiety, tension, fast heart rate, and headaches. The most common are Valium, Librium, Miltown, and Equanil. These mild tranquilizers are easily obtained by prescription. However, increased dosages can lead to addiction, and withdrawal can be painful and hazardous.

Amphetamines. Amphetamines ("uppers," "beans," "pep pills") are synthetic drugs that stimulate action in the central nervous system. They produce an intense physical reaction: increased blood pressure, breathing rate, bodily activity, and elevation of mood. Amphetamines also produce psychological effects, such as increased confidence, euphoria, fearlessness, talkativeness, impulsive behavior, and loss of appetite. The commonly used amphetamines are Benzedrine ("bennies"), Dexedrine ("dex"), Dexamyl, Bephetamine ("whites"), and Methedrine ("meth," "speed," "crystal meth," "ice"). Methedrine is probably the most widely used and most dangerous amphetamine. Some people swallow it; heavy users inject it for a quick rush. Long-

term heavy use can result in exhaustion, anxiety, prolonged depression, and hallucinations.

Cannabis (Marijuana). Commonly called "pot," "grass," "ganja," "maryjane," "dope," and a variety of other names, marijuana is produced from the leaves of *Cannabis sativa,* a plant grown throughout the world. Hashish (hash) is a concentrated form of cannabis made from unadulterated resin from the female plant. Smoking large amounts of pot or hash can cause drastic distortion in auditory and visual perception, even producing hallucinatory effects. Small doses produce an early excitement ("high") that gives way to a sedated effect and drowsiness. Pot use is also related to decreased physical activity, overestimation in time and space, and increased food consumption ("the munchies"). When the user is alone, marijuana produces a quiet, dreamy state. In a group, it is common for users to become giddy and lose perspective. Though marijuana is nonaddicting, its long-term effects have been the subject of much debate.

Hallucinogens. Hallucinogens are drugs, either natural or synthetic, that produce vivid distortions of the senses without greatly disturbing the viewer's consciousness. Some produce hallucinations, and others cause psychotic behavior in otherwise normal people. One common hallucinogen is mescaline, named after the Mescalero Apaches, who first used it. Mescaline occurs naturally in the peyote, a small cactus that grows in Mexico and the southwestern United States. After initial discomfort, mescaline produces vivid hallucinations in all ranges of colors and geometric patterns, a feeling of depersonalization, and out-of-body sensations. A synthetic and highly dangerous form of mescaline used for a brief period in the 1960s was called STP. However, the danger of this drug made its use short-lived.

A second group of hallucinogens are alkaloid compounds. Alkaloids occur in nature or can be made in the laboratory. They include such familiar hallucinogens as DMT, morning glory seeds, and psilocybin. These compounds can be transformed into a D-lysergic acid diethylamide-25, commonly called LSD. This powerful substance (800 times more potent than mescaline) stimulates cerebral sensory centers to produce visual hallucinations in all ranges of colors, to intensify hearing, and to increase sensitivity. Users often report a scrambling of sensations; they may "hear colors" and "smell music." Users also report feeling euphoric and mentally superior, though to an observer, they appear disoriented and confused. Unfortunately, anxiety and panic (a "bad trip") may occur during the LSD experience, and overdoses can produce psychotic episodes, flashbacks, and even death.

Cocaine. Cocaine is an alkaloid derivative of the coca leaf first isolated in 1860 by Albert Niemann of Gottingen, Germany. When originally discovered, it was considered a medicinal breakthrough that could relieve fatigue, depression, and various other symptoms. Its discovery was embraced by no less a luminary than Sigmund Freud, who used it himself and prescribed it for his friends, patients, and relatives. It quickly became a staple of popular patent medicines. When pharmacist John Styth Pemberton first brewed his new soft drink in 1886, he added cocaine to act as a "brain tonic" and called the drink Coca-Cola; this secret ingredient was taken out in 1906.[122] When its addictive qualities and dangerous side effects became apparent, cocaine's use was controlled by the Pure Food and Drug Act of 1906. Until the 1970s, cocaine remained an underground drug—the property of artists, jazz musicians, beatniks, and sometimes even jet-setters.

Cocaine, or coke, is the most powerful natural stimulant. Its use produces euphoria, laughter, restlessness, and excitement. Overdoses can cause delirium, increased reflexes, violent manic behavior, and possible respiratory failure. Cocaine can be sniffed, or "snorted," into the nostrils or injected. The immediate feeling of euophoria ("rush") is short-lived, and heavy users may snort coke as often as every ten minutes. Mixing cocaine and heroin is called "speedballing"; it is a practice that is highly dangerous and is alleged to have killed comedian John Belushi.

Cocaine Derivatives: Freebase and Crack. A great deal of public attention has been focused on cocaine use and the popularity of new, more potent forms of cocaine, such as **freebase** and **crack.** Freebase is a chemical produced from street cocaine by treating it with a liquid to remove the hydrochloric acid with which pure cocaine is bonded during manufacture. The free cocaine, or cocaine base (hence, the term *freebase*) is then dissolved in a solvent, usually ether, that crystallizes the purified cocaine. The resulting crystals are crushed and smoked in a special glass pipe; the high produced is more immediate and powerful than snorting street-strength coke. Unfortunately for the user, freebase is dangerous to make since it involves highly flammable products, such as ether (you may recall the accident that seriously injured comedian Richard Pryor), it is an expensive habit, and it is highly addictive.

Despite the publicity, crack is not a new substance and has been on the street for more than 15 years. Crack, like freebase, is processed street cocaine. Its manufacture involves using ammonia or baking soda to remove the hydrochlorides and create a crystalline form of cocaine base that can then be smoked.[123] However, unlike freebase, crack is not a pure form of cocaine and contains both remnants of hydrochloride, along with additional residue from the baking soda (sodium bicarbonate). In fact, crack gets its name from the fact that the sodium bicarbonate often emits a crackling sound when the substance is smoked. Research by Thomas Mieczkowski indicates that today, smoking crack is the preferred method of cocaine ingestion among persistent users.[124] Also referred to as "rock," "gravel," and "roxanne," crack apparently was introduced and gained popularity on both coasts simultaneously. It is relatively reasonable in cost and can provide a powerful high; users rapidly become psychologically addicted to crack. An even more powerful form of the drug is "spacebase"—crack doused with LSD, heroin, or PCP. There are indications that the use of crack and other cocaine derivatives in the general population is less pervasive than previously believed.[125] However, there also is disturbing evidence that crack use, because of its relatively low cost and easy availability, is concentrated among the poor and the lower class, who are susceptible to this powerful and relatively inexpensive drug. One study of drug-using delinquents in Miami found that about 90 percent had used crack during their lifetime and about 30 percent report being daily users. So while crack may not be the national epidemic among the middle class as some thought it would turn into, its use has had a powerful effect in the inner city.[126]

Narcotics. Narcotic drugs have the ability to produce insensibility to pain (analgesia) and to free the mind of anxiety and emotion (sedation). Users experience a rush of euphoria, relief from fear and apprehension, release of tension, and elevation of spirits. After experiencing this uplifting mood for a short period, users become apathetic and drowsy and nod off. Narcotics can be injected under the skin or in a muscle. Experienced users inject the drugs directly into the bloodstream (mainlining), which provides an immediate "fix." The most common narcotics are derivatives of opium, a drug produced from the opium poppy flower. The Chinese popularized the habit of smoking or chewing opium extract to produce euphoric feelings. Morphine (from Morpheus, the Greek god of dreams), a derivative of opium, is about ten times as strong and is used legally by physicians to relieve pain. It was first popularized as a pain reliever during the Civil War, but its addictive qualities soon became evident. Heroin was first produced as a pain-killing alternative to morphine in 1875 because, though 25 times more powerful, it was considered nonaddicting by its creator Heinrich Dreser. (The drug's name derives from the fact it was considered a hero because of its painkilling ability when it was first isolated.)[127] Heroin is today the most commonly used narcotic in the United States. Due to its strength, dealers cut it with neutral substances, such as sugar (lactose); "street heroin" is often only 1 percent to 4 percent pure. Because users can rapidly build up a tolerance to the drug, they constantly need larger doses to feel an effect. They may also change the method of ingestion to get the desired kick. At first, heroin is usually sniffed or snorted; as tolerance builds, it is injected beneath the skin (skin-popped) and then shot directly into a vein (mainlined). Through the process, the user becomes an addict—a person with an overpowering physical and psychological need to continue taking a particular substance or drug by any means possible. If addicts cannot get a supply of heroin sufficient to meet their habit, they will suffer withdrawal symptoms. These include irritability, emotional depression, extreme nervousness, pain in the abdomen, and nausea. It is estimated that there are about 500,000 practicing heroin addicts and another 2 million to 3 million people who have tried heroin at least once in their lives.[128] Heroin abuse is generally considered a lower-class phenomenon, though a fair number of middle- and upper-class users exist. Even physicians are known to have serious narcotic-abuse problems.[129] Nonetheless, it is common to associate heroin addiction with minority youths in lower-class, inner-city neighborhoods. Other opium derivatives used by drug abusers include codeine, Dilaudid, Percodan, and Prinadol. It is also possible to create synthetic narcotics in the laboratory. Synthetics include Demerol, Methadone, Nalline, and Darvon. Though it is less likely that a user will become addicted to synthetic narcotics, it is still possible, and withdrawal symptoms are similar to those experienced by users of natural narcotics.

Steroids.

Anabolic steroids are used to gain muscle bulk and strength for athletics and body building. Black market sales of these drugs now approach $1 billion annually. While not physically addicting, steroid use can be almost an obsession among people who desire athletic success. Long-term users may spend up to $400 a week on steroids and may support their habit by dealing the drug.

Steroids are dangerous because of the significant health problems associated with long-term use: liver ailments; tumors; hepatitis; kidney problems; sexual dysfunction; hypertension; and mental problems, such as depression. Steroid use runs in cycles, and other drugs, such as Clomid, Teslac, and Halotestin, that carry their own dangerous side effects are used to curb the need for high dosages. Finally, steroid users often share needles, which puts them at high risk for contracting the AIDS virus.

Designer Drugs.

Designer drugs are chemical substances, made and distributed in relatively small batches, that induce mood-altering effects. Their chemical characteristics place them somewhere within the broad families of drugs described above. Because they are chemically unique, they escape federal regulation until their danger is recognized and they are added to the schedule of controlled substances. Popular today is MDMA or "ecstasy," which combines an amphetamine-like rush with hallucinogenic experiences; the hallucinogens DMT and 2c-B or "Nexus"; and steroid substitute GHB, which causes drowsiness.

Alcohol.

Though the purchase and sale of alcohol is legal today in most U.S. jurisdictions, excessive alcohol consumption is considered a major substance abuse problem. About 80 percent of high school seniors report using alcohol in the past year, and more than 90 percent say they have tried it sometime during their lifetime.[130] It is also estimated that upward of 20 million people in the United States are problem drinkers and at least half of these are alcoholics.

The cost of alcohol abuse is quite high. Alcohol may be a factor in nearly half of all U.S. murders, suicides, and accidental deaths.[131] Alcohol-related deaths number 100,000 a year, far more than that taken by all other illegal drugs combined; recent data suggest that after declining between 1979 and 1985, the number of alcohol-related deaths is on the rise.[132] The economic cost of the nation's drinking problem is equally staggering. An estimated $117 billion is lost each year, including $18 billion from premature deaths, $66 billion in reduced work effort, and $13 billion for treatment efforts.[133]

Considering these problems, why do so many people drink alcohol to excess? Drinkers report that alcohol reduces tension, diverts worries, enhances pleasure, improves social skills, and transforms experiences for the better.[134] While these reactions may follow the limited use of alcohol, higher doses act as a sedative and depressant. Long-term use has been linked with depression and numerous physical ailments ranging from heart disease to cirrhosis of the liver (though there is research linking moderate drinking to a reduction in the probability of heart attack).[135] And while many people think that drinking stirs their romantic urges, the weight of the scientific evidence indicates that alcohol decreases sexual response.[136]

The Extent of Substance Abuse

Though there has been a continuing effort to control it, the use of mood-altering substances persists in the United States. What is the extent of the substance-abuse problem today? Despite the media attention given to the incidence of drug abuse, there is actually significant controversy over the nature and extent of drug use. The prevailing wisdom is that drug use is a pervasive and growing menace that threatens to destroy the American way of life. This view is counterbalanced by national surveys that show that drug use has declined dramatically in recent years.

A number of important national surveys attempt to chart trends in drug abuse. The Household Survey on Drug Abuse is sponsored by the National Institute on Drug Abuse (NIDA), a branch of the U.S. Department of Health and Human Services.[137] Conducted with about 10,000 people aged 12 and older, this biannual survey shows that despite public perceptions to the contrary, a dramatic drop in drug use occurred between 1985 and 1992. Drug use among teenagers aged 12 to 17 declined by more than one-half between 1985 and 1992; the consumption trend in most drug and tobacco products is also downward. Still disturbing is the fact that millions of adolescents have tried drugs and hundreds of thousands are current users. More than 4 million are alcohol abusers (about 20 percent of the teenage population), another 11 percent are smokers, and 3 percent, about 600,000 kids, use smokeless tobacco.

The second national source of drug statistics is the annual self-report survey of drug abuse among high school seniors conducted by the Institute of Social Research (ISR) at the University of Michigan.[138] This survey is based on the responses of about 17,000 high school students, 15,500 tenth graders, and 18,800 eighth graders in hundreds of schools around the United States.

ISR survey results indicate that while adolescent drug use is still all too common, it has declined substantially during the past ten years. Figure 14.1 shows the prevalence or use rate among the high school seniors who responded to the annual nationwide survey. The lifetime use of all drugs has declined from their high point in the late 1970s and early '80s, when more than half of all students reported having used some drug during the past 12 months; in 1992, when 27 percent claimed to have used drugs during the past year, a drop of *50 percent*. Use of cocaine and crack, which had increased significantly during the mid-'80s, also declined by almost half.

While these results are encouraging, the 1993 survey indicates a slight uptick in drug use over the previous year. Kids in each grade report using more marijuana, LSD, and cocaine than in the prior year. Equally disturbing is that the 20-year decline in cigarette smoking has subsided and stabilized. Alcohol use, which is almost universal by 12th grade, is also common among eighth graders who may be only 14 years old. As Figure 14.1 shows, about 14 percent of eighth graders report having five or more drinks in the past two weeks; about 27 percent claimed to have gotten drunk at least once in their lives.

The recent upward trend in drug abuse among adolescents indicates that the drug problem has not gone away. Drug use remains a major social problem. Surveys of inmates and arrestees indicate a high level of drug use and that the frequency is higher today than in the past. More than 12 million U.S. citizens use illicit drugs every month, and if anything, this number most likely underreports the actual problem.

Are the Surveys Accurate?

While these two national surveys indicate that drug use has declined since its peak, their results must be interpreted with caution. Both surveys, while methodologically sophisticated, rely on self-report evidence that is subject to error. Drug users may boastfully overinflate the extent of their substance abuse, underreport out of fear, or simply be unaware or forgetful. Another problem is that both national surveys overlook important segments of the drug-using population. For example, the NIDA survey misses people who are homeless, in prison, in drug rehabilitation clinics, or in AIDS clinics and those (about 18 percent of the people contacted) who refuse to participate in the interview. The ISR survey omits kids who are institutionalized and those who have dropped out of school; research indicates that dropouts may, in fact, be the most frequent users of dangerous drugs.[139] These surveys also rely on accurate self-reporting by drug users, a group whose recall and dependability may both be questionable. As you may recall, a number of studies indicate that serious abusers underreport drug use in surveys.[140]

While these weaknesses are troubling, both surveys are administered yearly, in a consistent fashion, so that any sources of inaccuracy are consistent over time. That is, the effect of over- and underreporting and missing

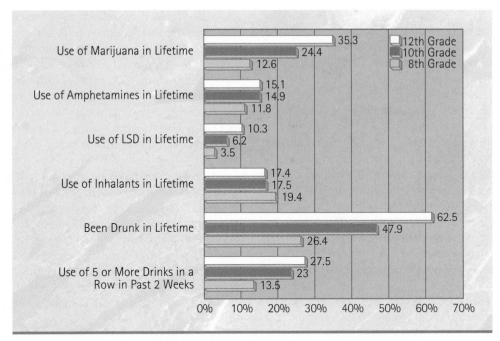

FIGURE 14.1 **Lifetime Use of Selected Drugs by Grade, 1993**

SOURCE: News Release, Institute for Social Research, Jan. 31, 1994, Ann Arbor, Mich.

subjects should have a consistent effect in every survey year. Consequently, while their validity is not beyond reproach, the ISR and NIDA surveys are probably *reliable* indicators of drug-use trends in the general population.

AIDS and Drug Use

If there is indeed an overall decline in the general drug-using population, it may be due to the threat of AIDS.[141] Middle-class drug users have been educated to the fact that intravenous drug users are the second largest risk group, after homosexual males, for HIV infection. (HIV is the AIDS-causing virus.) Since monitoring of the spread of AIDS began in 1981, about one-fourth of all adult AIDS cases reported to the Centers for Disease Control in Atlanta have occurred among intravenous (IV) drug users. It is now estimated that as many as one-third of all IV drug users are AIDS carriers.[142]

One reason for the AIDS-drug use relationship is the widespread habit of needle sharing among IV users. Since the AIDS infection is spread through blood transfer, the sharing of HIV-contaminated needles is the primary mechanism for the transmission of AIDS among the drug-using population. Needle sharing has been encouraged because a number of states, in an effort to control drugs, have outlawed the over-the-counter sale of hypodermic needles. Consequently, legal jurisdictions have developed outreach programs to help these drug users; others have made an effort to teach users how to clean their needles and syringes; a few states have gone so far as to provide addicts with sterile needles.[143]

Drug users also have a significant exposure to AIDS because they have multiple sex partners, some of whom may be engaging in prostitution to support a drug habit. Thus, members of the drug culture can be exposed to AIDS even if they do not inject drugs or share needles.[144]

While the threat of AIDS may be having an impact on the behavior of recreational and middle-class users, drug use may be still increasing among the poor, high school dropouts, and other disadvantaged groups. If that pattern is correct, then the recently observed decline in substance abuse may be restricted to one segment of the at-risk population, while another is continuing to use drugs at ever-increasing rates.

The Cause of Substance Abuse

What causes people to abuse substances? Though there are many different views on the cause of drug use, most can be characterized as seeing the onset of an addictive career as either an environmental or a personal matter.

Subcultural View. Those who view drug abuse as having an environmental basis concentrate on lower-class addiction. Because a disproportionate number of drug abusers are poor, then the onset of drug use can be tied to such factors as racial prejudice, "devalued identities," low self-esteem, poor socioeconomic status, and the high level of mistrust, negativism, and defiance found in lower socioeconomic areas.[145]

Residing in a deteriorated, inner-city slum area is often correlated with entry into a drug subculture. Youths living in these depressed areas, where feelings of alienation and hopelessness run high, often come in contact with established drug users who teach them that narcotics provide an answer to their feelings of personal inadequacy and stress.[146] Perhaps the youths will join with peers to learn the techniques of drug use and receive social support for their habit. Shared feelings and a sense of intimacy lead the youths to become fully enmeshed in what has been described as the "drug-use subculture."[147]

Those who can take advantage of educational or vocational opportunities can forego the drug culture and "make it" in the legitimate economic structure. Upward mobility is available to only a few because of the deterioration of the manufacturing economy. The indigent, especially among minority-group members, are much more likely to abuse substances than the upwardly mobile. This phenomenon takes on even greater importance considering the recent polarization of some minority communies into distinct groups of relatively affluent abstainers and desperately poor abusers.[148]

Psychodynamic View. Yet not all drug abusers reside in lower-class slum areas; the problem of middle-class substance abuse is very real. Consequently, some experts have linked substance abuse to personality disturbance and emotional problems that can strike people in any economic class. Psychodynamic explanations of substance abuse suggest that drugs help youths control or express unconscious needs and impulses. Drinking alcohol may reflect an oral fixation, which is associated with other nonfunctional behaviors, such as dependence and depression.[149] A young teen may resort to drug abuse to remain dependent on an overprotective mother, to reduce the emotional turmoil of adolescence, or to cope with troubling impulses.[150]

Research on the psychological characteristics of drug abusers does in fact reveal the presence of a significant degree of personal pathology. Studies have found that addicts suffer personality disorders characterized by a weak ego, low frustration tolerance, anxiety, and fantasies of omnipotence. Many addicts exhibit psychopathic or sociopathic behavior characteristics, form-

ing what is called an *addiction-prone personality*.[151] For example, alcoholism may reflect the need to remain dependent on an overprotective mother or an effort to reduce the emotional turmoil of adolescence or to cope with unconscious homosexual impulses. Research on the psychological characteristics of narcotics abusers reveals the presence of a significant degree of personal pathology. Personality testing of known users suggests that a significant percentage suffer from psychotic disorders, including various levels of schizophrenia.

These views have been substantiated by research involving a sample of over 20,291 people in five large U.S. cities. The results of this first large-scale study on the personality characteristics of abusers indicate a significant association between mental illness and drug abuse: about 53 percent of drug abusers and 37 percent of alcohol abusers have at least one serious mental illness. Conversely, 29 percent of the diagnosed mentally ill people in the survey have substance-abuse problems.[152]

Genetic Factors. It is also possible that substance abuse may have a genetic basis. Research has shown that the biological children of alcoholics reared by nonalcoholic adoptive parents more often develop alcohol problems than the biological children of the adoptive parents.[153] In a similar vein, a number of studies comparing alcoholism among identical twins and fraternal twins have found that the degree of concordance (both siblings behaving identically) is twice as high among the identical twin groups; however, these inferences are still at best inconclusive.

Social Learning. Social psychologists suggest that drug abuse patterns may also result from the observation of parental drug use. People who learn that drugs provide pleasurable sensations may be the most likely to experiment with illegal substances; a habit may develop if the user experiences lower anxiety, fear, and tension levels.[154] Having a history of family drug and alcohol abuse has been found to be a characteristic of violent teenage sexual abusers.[155] Heroin abusers report an unhappy childhood, which included harsh physical punishment and parental neglect and rejection.[156]

James Inciardi, Ruth Horowitz, and Anne Pottieger found a clear pattern of adult involvement in adolescent drug abuse. Kids on crack began their careers with early experimentation with alcohol at age seven, began getting drunk at age eight, having alcohol with an adult present by age nine, and becoming regular drinkers by the time they were eleven years old.[157] Drinking with an adult present, presumably a parent, was a significant precursor of future substance abuse and delinquency. "Adults who gave children alcohol," they argue, "were also giving them a head start in a delinquent career."[158]

Problem Behavior Syndrome.

For many people, substance abuse is just one of many problem behaviors. Longitudinal studies show that drug abusers are maladjusted, alienated, and emotionally distressed and that their drug use is one among many social problems.[159] Having a deviant life-style begins early in life and is punctuated with criminal relationships, family history of substance abuse, educational failure, and alienation. People who abuse drugs lack commitment to religious values, disdain education, and spend most of their time in peer activities.

Rational Choice.

Not all people who abuse drugs do so because of personal pathology. Some may choose to use drugs and alcohol because they want to enjoy their effects: get high, relax, improve creativity, escape reality, increase sexual responsiveness. Research indicates that adolescent alcohol abusers believe that getting high will make them powerful, increase their sexual performance and facilitate their social behavior; they care little about negative future consequences.[160] Substance abuse then may be a function of the rational, albeit mistaken, belief that substance abuse benefits the user.

In sum, there are many different views of why people take drugs, and no one theory has proven to be an adequate explanation of all forms of substance abuse. Recent research efforts show that drug users suffer a variety of family and socialization difficulties, have addiction-prone personalities, and are generally at risk for many other social problems; drug use seems to be part of a "problem behavior syndrome."[161] As James Inciardi points out:

> There are as many reasons people use drugs as there are individuals who use drugs. For some, it may be a function of family disorganization, or cultural learning, or maladjusted personality, or an "addiction-prone" personality. . . . For others, heroin use may be no more than a normal response to the world in which they live.[162]

Types of Drug Users

All too often, the general public groups all drug users together without recognizing there are many varieties, ranging from adolescent recreational drug users to adults who run large smuggling operations. Marcia Chaiken and Bruce Johnson have reviewed the literature on drug abuse to develop a typology of drug-involved offenders. The sections below discuss some of the most common drug-using life-styles.[163]

Adolescents Who Distribute Small Amounts of Drugs.

Many adolescents begin their involvement in the drug trade with the use and distribution of small amounts of drugs; they do not commit any other serious criminal acts. Kenneth Tunnell found in his interviews with low-level drug dealers that many started out as "stash dealers" who sold drugs to maintain a consistent access to drugs for their own consumption.[164]

Most of these petty dealers occasionally sell marijuana, crack, and PCP to support their own drug use. Their customers are almost always personal acquaintances, including friends and relatives. Deals are arranged over the phone, in school, or in public hangouts and meeting places; however, the actual distribution takes place in more private areas, such as at home or in cars. Petty dealers do not consider themselves seriously involved in drugs. They are insulated from the legal system because their activities rarely result in apprehension and sanction.

Adolescents Who Frequently Sell Drugs.

A small number of adolescents, most often multiple-drug users or heroin or cocaine users, are high-rate dealers who bridge the gap between adult drug distributors and the adolescent user. Though many are daily users, they are not "strung-out junkies" and maintain many normal adolescent roles, such as going to school and socializing with friends. Frequent dealers often have adults who "front" for them; that is, sell them drugs for cash. The teenagers then distribute the drugs to friends and acquaintances. They return most of the proceeds to the supplier while keeping a "commission" for themselves. They may also keep drugs for their own personal use, and in fact, some consider their drug dealing as a way of "getting high for free." Frequent dealers are more likely to sell drugs in public and can be seen in known drug-user hangouts in parks, schools, or other public places. Deals are irregular, so the chances of apprehension are slight.

Teenage Drug Dealers Who Commit Other Delinquent Acts.

A more serious type of drug-involved youth are those who use and distribute multiple substances and also commit both property and violent crimes. Though these youngsters make up about 2 percent of the teenage population, they commit 40 percent of the robberies and assaults and about 60 percent of all teenage felony thefts and drug sales. There is little gender or racial difference among these youths: girls are as likely as boys to become high-rate, persistent drug-involved offenders, white youths as likely as black youths, middle-class adolescents raised outside cities as likely as lower-class city children.

These youths are frequently hired by older dealers to act as street-level drug runners. Each member of a "crew" of three to 12 boys will handle small quantities of drugs, perhaps three bags of heroin, which are received on consignment and sold on the street; the supplier receives 50 percent to 70 percent of the drug's street value. The crew members also act as lookouts, recruiters, and guards. While they may be recreational drug users themselves, crew members refrain from using addictive drugs, such as heroin; some major suppliers will only hire "drug-free kids" to make street deals. Between drug sales, the young dealers commit robberies, burglaries, and other thefts.

Adolescents Who Cycle in and out of the Justice System.

Some drug-involved youth are failures at both dealing and crime. They do not have the savvy to join gangs or groups and instead begin committing unplanned, opportunistic crimes that increase their chances of arrest. They are heavy drug users, which both increases apprehension risk and decreases their value for organized drug-distribution networks. Drug-involved "losers" can earn a living steering customers to a seller in a "copping" area, "touting" drug availability for a dealer, or acting as a lookout. However, they are not considered trustworthy or deft enough to handle drugs or money. They may bungle other criminal acts, which solidifies their reputation as undesirable. Though these persistent offenders get involved in drugs at a very young age, they receive little attention from the justice system until they have developed an extensive arrest record. By then, they are approaching the end of their minority and will either spontaneously desist or become so deeply entrenched in the drug-crime subculture that little can be done to treat or deter their illegal activities.

Drug-Involved Youth Who Continue to Commit Crimes as Adults.

Though about two-thirds of substance-abusing youths continue to use drugs after they reach adulthood, about half desist from other criminal activities. Those who persist in both substance abuse and crime as adults have the following characteristics:

- They come from poor families;
- They have other criminals in the family;
- They do poorly in school;

- They started using drugs and committing other delinquent acts at a relatively young age;
- They used multiple types of drugs and committed crimes frequently; and
- They have few opportunities in late adolescence to participate in legitimate and rewarding adult activities.

Some evidence also exists that these drug-using persisters have low nonverbal IQs and poor physical coordination. Nonetheless, there is still little scientific evidence that indicates why some drug-abusing kids drop out of crime while others remain active into their adulthood.

Outwardly Respectable Adults Who Are Top-Level Dealers.

A few outwardly respectable adult dealers sell large quantities of drugs to support themselves in high-class life-styles. Outwardly respectable dealers often seem indistinguishable from other young professionals. However, they are rarely drawn from the highest professional circles, such as those of physicians or attorneys, nor are they likely to have worked their way up from lower-class origins. Upscale dealers seem to drift into dealing from many different walks of life. Most frequently, they are drawn from professions and occupations that are unstable, have irregular working hours, and accept drug abuse. Former graduate students, musicians, performing artists, and barkeepers are among those who are likely to fit the profile of the adult who begins drug dealing in his or her 20s. Some will use their business skills and drug profits to get into legitimate enterprise or illegal scams. Others will drop out of the drug trade because they are the victims of violent crime committed by competitors or disgruntled customers; a few wind up in jail or prison.

Smugglers.

Smugglers import drugs into the United States. What little is known about drug smugglers indicates they are generally men, middle-age or older, who have strong organizational skills, established connections, capital to invest, and a willingness to take large business risks. Smugglers are a loosely organized, competitive group of individual entrepreneurs. There is a constant flow in and out of the business as some sources become the target of law enforcement activities, new drug sources become available, older smugglers become dealers, and former dealers become smugglers.

Adult Predatory Drug Users Who Are Frequently Arrested.

Many users who begin abusing substances early in their adolescence will continue in drugs and crime in their adulthood. Getting arrested, doing time, using multiple drugs, and committing predatory crimes is a way of life for them. They have few skills, did poorly in school, and have a long criminal record. The threat of conviction and punishment has little effect on their criminal activities. These "losers" have friends and relatives involved in drugs and crime. They specialize in robberies, burglaries, thefts, and drug sales. They filter in and out of the justice system and will begin committing crimes as soon as they are released.

Adult Predatory Drug Users Who Are Rarely Arrested.

Some drug users are "winners." They commit hundreds of crimes each year but are rarely arrested. On the streets, they are known for their calculated violence. Their crimes are carefully planned and coordinated. They often work with partners and use lookouts to carry out the parts of their crimes that have the highest risk of apprehension. These "winners" are more likely to use recreational drugs, such as coke and pot, than the more addicting heroin or opiates. Some may become high-frequency users and risk apprehension and punishment. But for the lucky few, their criminal careers can stretch for up to 15 years without interruption by the justice system.

Less Predatory Drug-Involved Adult Offenders.

Most adult drug users are petty criminals who avoid violent crime. They are typically high school graduates and have regular employment that supports their drug use. They usually commit petty thefts or pass bad checks. They will stay on the periphery of the drug trade by engaging in such acts as helping addicts shoot up, bagging drugs for dealers, operating shooting galleries, renting needles and syringes, and selling small amounts of drugs. These petty criminal drug users do not have the stomach for a life of hard crime and drug dealing. They will violate the law in proportion to the amount and cost of the drugs they are using. Pot smokers will have a significantly lower frequency of theft violations than daily heroin users, whose habit is considerably more costly.

Women Who Are Drug-Involved Offenders.

Women who are drug-involved offenders constitute a separate type of substance abuser. Though women are far less likely than men to use addictive drugs, female offenders are just as likely to be involved in drugs as male offenders. Though not usually violent criminals, female drug users are involved in prostitution and low-level drug dealing; a few become top-level dealers. Female abusers are quite often mothers. Because they share needles, they are at high risk of contracting AIDS, and many pass the HIV virus to their newborn children. Female addicts are offered fewer services than men because treatment programs are geared toward males. Their children are often malnourished, mistreated, and exposed to a highly criminal population. Some are sold to pornographers and become involved in the sex-for-profit trade; others grow up to become criminals themselves.

Drugs and Crime

One of the main reasons for the criminalization of particular substances is the significant association believed to exist between drug abuse and crime. Research suggests that many criminal offenders have extensive experience with drug use and that drug users do in fact commit an enormous amount of crime. Arrestees who test positively for drugs are also more likely to recidivate than nonusers.[165]

While the drug-crime connection is powerful, it is still uncertain whether the relationship is causal because many users had a history of criminal activity *before* the onset of their substance abuse.[166] Nonetheless, if drug use is not a per se *cause* of crime, turning otherwise law-abiding citizens into criminals, it certainly amplifies the extent of their criminal activities.[167] And as addiction levels increase, so too does the frequency and seriousness of criminality.[168]

Two approaches have been used to study the relationship between drugs and crime. One has been to survey known addicts to assess the extent of their law violations; the other has been to survey known criminals to see if they were or are drug users. These are discussed separately below.

User Surveys.

Numerous studies have examined the criminal activity of drug users. As a group, they show that people who take drugs have extensive involvement in crime.[169] One often-cited study of this type was conducted by sociologist James Inciardi. After interviewing 356 addicts in Miami, Inciardi found that they reported 118,134 criminal offenses during a 12-month period; of these, 27,464 were index crimes.[170] If this behavior is typical, the country's estimated 500,000 heroin users could be responsible for a significant amount of all criminal behavior. In a more recent analysis, M. Douglas Anglin and George Speckart surveyed 671 known California addicts and found persuasive evidence of a link between drug use and property crime.[171] While their research also indicated that drug use is not an initiator of crime (since many users had committed crime before turning to drugs), there was strong evidence that the amount and value of crime increased proportionately with the frequency of the subjects' drug involvement. Interestingly, Anglin and Speckart found little evidence of an association between the frequency of drug use and violent crimes. The findings of these two surveys are typical of others measuring the criminality of narcotics users.[172]

Surveys of Known Criminals.

The second method used to link drugs and crime involves the testing of known criminals to determine the extent of their substance abuse. The most recent (1991) survey of prison inmates disclosed that many (80 percent) have engaged in a lifetime of drug and alcohol abuse. More than one-third claim to have been under the influence of drugs when they committed their last offense, including about 14 percent who were under the influence of crack and 6 percent who were using heroin. As Figure 14.2 shows, about 62 percent claimed to have used a major drug, such as heroin, cocaine, PCP, or LSD, on a regular basis before their arrest.[173] These data

FIGURE 14.2 Inmate Drug Use

SOURCE: Allen Beck, Darrell Gilliard, Lawrence Greenfeld, Caroline Harlow, Thomas Hester, Lewis Jankowski, Tracy Snell, James Stephen, and Danielle Morton, *Survey of State Prison Inmates, 1991* (Washington, D.C.: Bureau of Justice Statistics, 1993), p. 21.

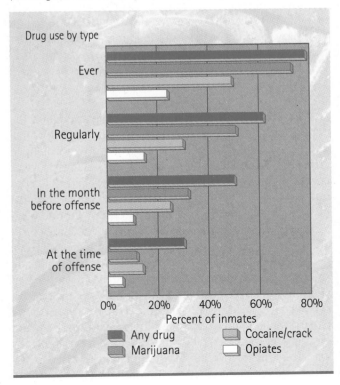

support the view that a strong association exists between substance abuse and serious crime (unless one believes that only substance-abusing criminals are caught and sent to prison).

Another important source of data on the drug abuse-crime connection is the federally sponsored Drug Use Forecasting (DUF) program. All arrestees in major cities around the country are tested for drug use. The results have been startling. In some cities, such as San Diego, New York, Philadelphia, and Washington, D.C., more than 70 percent of all arrestees test positively for some drug, and this association crosses both gender and racial boundaries.[174] As Figure 14.3 indicates, a significant portion of male and female arrestees test positively for drug use. In Houston, Chicago, Philadelphia, New York, Los Angeles, and other cities, more than 70 percent of young male arrestees are drug users; female offenders tested almost as high for drugs.

It is possible that most criminals are not actually drug users but that police are more likely to apprehend muddled-headed substance abusers than clear-thinking abstainers. A second, and probably more plausible, interpretation is that the DUF data is so powerful because most criminals are in fact substance abusers. Some may commit crime to support a drug habit. Others may become violent while under the influence of drugs or alcohol, which lower inhibitions and increase aggression levels. The drug-crime connection may also be a function of the violent world of drug distributors, who regularly use violence to do business.

In sum, research testing both the criminality of known narcotics users and the narcotics use of known criminals produces a very strong association between drug use and crime. Even if the crime rate of drug users were actually half of that reported in the research literature, users would be responsible for a significant portion of the total criminal activity in the United States.

The Cycle of Addiction

The drug-crime connection may also be mediated by the amount of drugs users require and their ability to support their habit through conventional means. During their interviews with drug users, Charles Faupel and Carl Klockars found that there are actually a variety of addict types.[175] Occasional users are people just beginning their addiction, who use small amounts of narcotics, and whose habit can be supported by income from conventional jobs; narcotics have relatively little influence on their life-styles. In contrast, "stabilized junkies" have learned the skills needed to purchase and process larger amounts of heroin. Their addiction enables them to

FIGURE 14.3   Drug Use by Male and Female Booked Arrestees

Note: Positive by urinalysis, January through December 1992. Drugs tested for include cocaine, opiates, PCP, marijuana, amphetamines, methadone, methaqualone, benzodiazepines, barbiturates, and propoxyphene.

SOURCE: National Institute of Justice, *Drug Use Forecasting, 1992* (Washington, D.C.: National Institute of Justice, 1994).

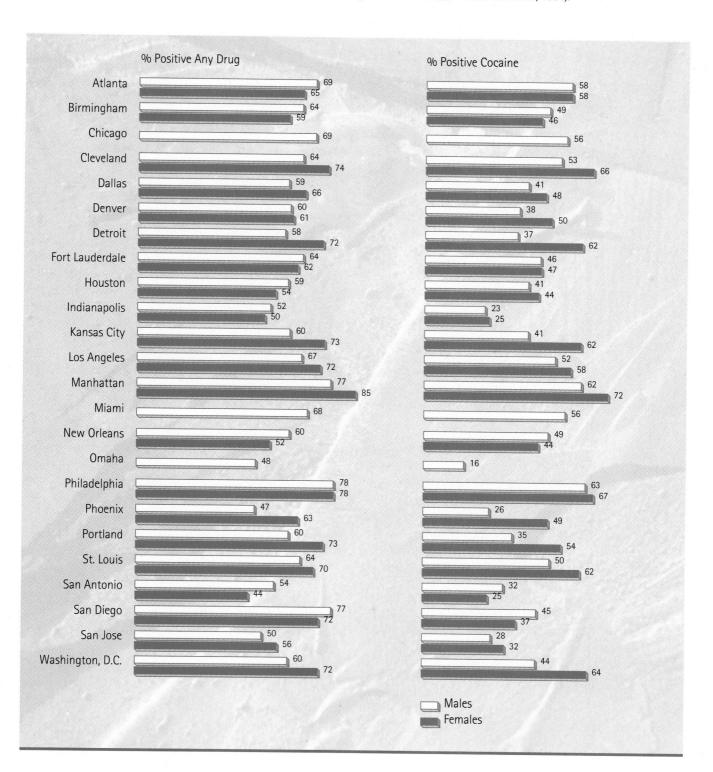

maintain their normal life-styles, though they may turn to drug dealing to create contacts with drug suppliers.

If stable users make a "big score," perhaps through a successful drug deal, they may significantly increase their drug use and become "free-wheelers." Their increased narcotics consumption then destabilizes their life-style, destroying family and career ties. When their finances dry up, free-wheelers may return to stabilized use or become "street junkies," whose habit cannot be satisfied through conventional means. Since their traditional life-style has been destroyed, street junkies turn to petty crime to maintain an adequate supply of drugs. Cut off from a stable source of quality heroin, not knowing from where his or her next fix or the money to pay for it will come, looking for any opportunity to make a buck, getting "sick" or "jonesing," being pathetically unkempt and unable to maintain even the most primitive routines of health or hygiene, the street junkie lives a very difficult, hand-to-mouth (or more precisely arm-to-arm) existence. Because they are unreliable and likely to become police informants, street junkies pay the highest prices for the poorest quality heroin; lack of availability increases their need to commit habit-supporting crimes.

Faupel and Klockars conclude that addiction is not a unidimensional process. There are various stages in the career of a hard-drug user, and criminal activity may vary according to one's drug life-style. Their view is that crime is a "drug facilitator," enabling addicts to increase their heroin consumption according to the success of their criminal careers.

Drugs and the Law

The federal government first initiated legal action to curtail the use of some drugs early in the twentieth century.[176] In 1906, the Pure Food and Drug Act required manufacturers to list the amounts of habit-forming drugs in products on the labels but did not restrict their use. However, the act prohibited the importation and sale of opiates except for medicinal purposes. In 1914, the Harrison Narcotics Act restricted the importation, manufacture, sale, and dispensing of narcotics. It defined narcotics as any drug that produces sleep and relieves pain, such as heroin, morphine, and opium. The act was revised in 1922 to allow the importation of opium and coca (cocaine) leaves for qualified medical practitioners. The Marijuana Tax Act of 1937 required registration and payment of a tax by all persons who imported, sold, or manufactured marijuana. Since marijuana was classified as a narcotic, those registering would also be subject to criminal penalty.

In later years, other federal laws were passed to clarify existing drug statutes and revise penalties. For example, the Boggs Act of 1951 provided mandatory sentences for violating federal drug laws. The Durham-Humphrey Act of 1951 made it illegal to dispense barbiturates and amphetamines without a prescription. The Narcotic Control Act of 1956 increased penalties for drug offenders. In 1965, the drug abuse control act set up stringent guidelines for the legal use and sale of mood-modifying drugs, such as barbiturates, amphetamines, LSD, and any other "dangerous drugs," except narcotics prescribed by doctors and pharmacists. Illegal possession was punished as a misdemeanor and manufacture or sale as a felony. Then, in 1970, the Comprehensive Drug Abuse Prevention and Control Act set up unified categories of illegal drugs and the penalties associated with their sale, manufacture, or possession. The law gave the U.S. attorney general discretion to decide in which category to place any new drug.

Since then, various federal laws have attempted to increase penalties imposed on drug smugglers and limit the manufacture and sale of newly developed substances. For example, the 1984 Controlled Substances Act set new, stringent penalties for drug dealers and created five categories of narcotic and nonnarcotic substances subject to federal laws.[177] The Anti-Drug Abuse Act of 1986 again set new standards for minimum and maximum sentences for drug offenders, increased penalties for most offenses, and created a new drug penalty classification for large-scale offenses (such as trafficking in more than one kilogram of heroin), for which the penalty for a first offense was ten years to life in prison.[178] With then President George Bush's endorsement, Congress passed the Anti-Drug Abuse Act of 1988, which created a coordinated national drug policy under a "drug czar," set treatment and prevention priorities, and, symbolizing the government's hard-line stance against drug dealing, imposed the death penalty for drug-related killings.[179] These statutes are set out in Table 14.2.

For the most part, state laws mirror federal statutes. Some, such as New York's, apply extremely heavy penalties for sale or distribution of dangerous drugs, involving long prison sentences of up to 25 years.

Alcohol Abuse

While drug control laws have been enacted on the federal and state levels, state legislatures have also acted to control alcohol-related crimes. One of the more serious problems of widespread drinking is the alarming number of highway fatalities linked to drunk driving. In an

TABLE 14.2 Four Major Federal Antidrug Bills Enacted in the Past Decade

The 1984 Crime Control Act

- expanded criminal and civil asset forfeiture laws
- amended the Bail Reform Act to target pretrial detention of defendants accused of serious drug offenses
- established a determinate sentencing system
- increased federal criminal penalties for drug offenses

The 1986 Anti-Drug Abuse Act

- budgeted money for prevention and treatment programs, giving the programs a larger share of federal drug control funds than previous laws
- restored mandatory prison sentences for large-scale distribution of marijuana
- imposed new sanctions on money laundering
- added controlled substances' analogs (designer drugs) to the drug schedule
- created a drug enforcement grant program to assist state and local efforts
- contained various provisions designed to strengthen international drug control efforts

The 1988 Anti-Drug Abuse Act

- increased penalties for offenses related to drug trafficking, created new federal offenses and regulatory requirements, and changed criminal procedures
- altered the organization and coordination of federal antidrug efforts
- increased treatment and prevention efforts aimed at reduction of drug demand
- endorsed the use of sanctions aimed at drug users to reduced the demand for drugs
- targeted for reduction drug production abroad and international trafficking in drugs

The Crime Control Act of 1990

- doubled the appropriations authorized for drug law enforcement grants to states and localities
- expanded drug control and education programs aimed at the nation's schools
- expanded specific drug enforcement assistance to rural states
- expanded regulation of precursor chemicals used in the manufacture of illegal drugs
- provided additional measures aimed at seizure and forfeiture of drug trafficker assets
- sanctioned anabolic steroids under the Controlled Substances Act
- included provisions on international money laundering, rural drug enforcement, drug-free school zones, drug paraphernalia, and drug enforcement grants

SOURCE: Bureau of Justice Statistics, *Drugs, Crime, and the Justice System* (Washington, D.C.: Bureau of Justice Statistics, 1993), p. 86.

average week, nearly 500 people die in alcohol-related accidents and 20,000 are injured. On a yearly basis, that amounts to 25,000 deaths, or about half of all auto fatalities. Spurred by such groups as Mothers Against Drunk Drivers, state legislatures are beginning to create more stringent penalties for drunk driving. For example, Florida has enacted legislation creating a minimum fine of $250, 50 hours of community service, and six months' loss of license for a first offense; a second offense brings a $500 fine and ten days in jail. In Quincy, Massachusetts, judges have agreed to put every drunk-driving offender in jail for three days.[180] In California, a drunk driver faces a maximum of six months in jail, a $500 fine, the suspension of his or her operator's license for six months, and impoundment of the vehicle. As a minimum penalty, a first offender could get four days in jail, a $375 fine, and a loss of license for six months or three years' probation, a $375 fine, and either two days in jail or restricted driving privileges for 90 days.[181] In New York, persons arrested for drunk driving now risk having their automobiles seized by the government under the state's new Civil Forfeiture Law. Originally designed to combat drug trafficking and racketeering, the new law will allow state prosecutors to confiscate cars involved in felony drunk-driving cases, sell them at auction, and give the proceeds to the victims of the crime; Texas enacted a similar law in 1984.[182] More than 30 jurisdictions have passed laws providing severe penalties for drunk drivers, including mandatory jail sentences.

A study conducted by the federal government's National Institute of Justice in such cities as Seattle, Minneapolis, and Cincinnati found that such measures significantly reduced traffic fatalities in the target areas studied.[183] However, there is a price to pay for get-tough policies. In California, arrest rates and court workload increased dramatically, and the use of plea bargaining, which first decreased, eventually rose and reduced the impact of legal reform.[184] Similarly, corrections facilities have become overloaded, prompting the building of expensive new ones to house exclusively drunk-driving offenders.

Alcoholics are a serious problem, because treatment efforts to help chronic sufferers have not proved successful.[185] Severe punishments have little effect on their future behavior.[186] In addition, chronic alcoholics are arrested over and over again for public drunkenness and are therefore a burden on the justice system. To remedy this situation, a federal court in 1966 ruled that chronic alcoholism may be used as a defense to crime.[187] However, in a subsequent case, *Powell v. Texas,* the Supreme Court ruled that a chronic alcoholic could be convicted under state public drunkenness laws.[188]

Nonetheless, the narrowness of the decision, 5 to 4, allowed those states desiring to excuse chronic alcoholics from criminal responsibility to do so. Thus, the trend has been to place arrested alcoholics in detoxification centers under a civil order rather than treat them as part of the justice system.

Drug Control Strategies

Substance abuse remains a major social problem in the United States. Politicians looking for a "safe" campaign issue can take advantage of the public's fear of drug addiction by calling for a "war on drugs." These "wars" have been declared even during periods when drug usage is stable or in decline.[189] Can these efforts pay off? Can illegal drug use be eliminated or controlled?

A number of different drug control strategies have been tried with varying degrees of success. Some are aimed at deterring drug use by stopping the flow of drugs into the country, apprehending and punishing dealers, and cracking down on street-level drug deals. Others focus on preventing drug use by educating potential users to the dangers of substance abuse (convincing them to "say no to drugs") and by organizing community groups to work with the at-risk population in their area. Still another approach is to treat known users so they can control their addictions. Some of the more important of these efforts are discussed below.

Source Control.

One approach to drug control is to deter the sale and importation of drugs through the systematic apprehension of large-volume drug dealers, coupled with the enforcement of strict drug laws that carry heavy penalties. This approach is designed to capture and punish known international drug dealers and deter those who are considering entering the drug trade.

A major effort has been made to cut off supplies of drugs by destroying overseas crops and arresting members of drug cartels in Central and South America, Asia, and the Middle East, where drugs are grown and manufactured. (See the Close-Up entitled "Where Do Drugs Come From?") This approach is known as source control. The federal government has been in the vanguard of encouraging exporting nations to step up efforts to destroy drug crops and prosecute dealers. Three South American nations, Peru, Bolivia, and Colombia, have agreed with the United States to coordinate control efforts. Translating words into deeds is a formidable task. Drug lords are willing and able to fight back through intimidation, violence, and corruption when necessary. The United States was forced to invade Panama with 20,000 troops in 1989 to stop its leader, General Manuel Noriega, from dealing cocaine. The Colombian drug cartels do not hesitate to use violence and assassination to protect their interests.

The amount of narcotics grown each year is so vast that even if three-quarters of the opium crop were destroyed, the U.S. market would still require only 10 percent of the remainder to sustain the drug trade. An estimated 24,000 tons of marijuana, 337,000 tons of coca leaf, and 3,400 tons of opium are produced annually.[190] Even if the amount of illegal drugs produced each year were radically reduced, it likely would have little effect on American consumption. Drug users in the United States are able and willing to pay more for drugs than anyone else in the world. Even if the supply were reduced, whatever drugs there were would find their way to the United States.

Adding to control problems is the fact that the drug trade is an important source of foreign revenue, and destroying the drug trade undermines the economies of Third World nations. An estimated 1 million people in Peru, Bolivia, and Colombia depend on the drug trade to earn their living. In Burma, Thailand, and Laos, hundreds of thousands of people are engaged in cultivating and processing heroin. The federal government estimates that U.S. citizens spend over $40 billion annually on illegal drugs, and much of this money is funneled overseas. And even if the government of one nation were willing to cooperate in vigorous drug suppression efforts, suppliers in other nations, eager to cash in on the seller's market, would be encouraged to turn more acreage over to coca or poppy production.

The difficulty of source control is illustrated by the pursuit, capture, and slaying of alleged billionaire drug lord Pablo Escobar on December 2, 1993.[191] His Medellin drug cartel at one time controlled 80 percent of the cocaine imported into the United States; *Forbes* magazine included him in its annual list of billionaires. While he was in hiding, his empire had been replaced by his competitors, the Cali cartel. More than 60 other drug-dealing groups, now supplying about 20 percent of the cocaine, wait in the wings if the Cali cartel folds.[192]

Interdiction Strategies.

Law enforcement efforts have also been directed at interdicting drug supplies as they enter the country. Border patrols and military personnel using sophisticated hardware have been involved in massive interdiction efforts; many impressive multimillion-dollar seizures have been made. Yet the U.S. borders are so vast and unprotected that meaningful interdiction is impossible. And even if all importation were shut down, home-grown marijuana and

Source control is now a significant drug suppression strategy. Jamaican military personnel burn a marijuana crop. Can such efforts destroy the drug trade or merely drive up prices and encourage people to grow drugs?

laboratory-made drugs, such as "ice," LSD, and PCP, could become the drugs of choice. Even now, their easy availability and relatively low cost are increasing their popularity among the at-risk population.

Law Enforcement Strategies. Local, state, and federal law enforcement agencies have been engaged in an active fight against drugs. One approach is to direct efforts at large-scale drug rings. The long-term consequence has been to decentralize drug dealing and encourage teenage gangs to become major suppliers. Ironically, it has proven easier for federal agents to infiltrate and prosecute traditional organized crime groups than to take on drug-dealing teen gangs. Consequently, some nontraditional groups have broken into the drug trade. For example, the Hell's Angels motorcycle club has become one of the primary distributors of cocaine and amphetamines in the United States.[193] Police can also target, intimidate, and arrest

street-level dealers and users in an effort to make drug use so much of a hassle that consumption is cut back and the crime rate reduced. Approaches that have been tried include "reverse stings" in which undercover agents pose as dealers to arrest users who approach them for a buy. Police have attacked fortified crack houses with heavy equipment to breach their defenses. They have used racketeering laws to seize the assets of known dealers. Special task forces of local and state police have used undercover operations and drug sweeps to discourage both dealers and users.[194]

While some street-level enforcement efforts have had success, others are considered failures. Drug sweeps have clogged courts and correctional facilities with petty offenders while proving a costly drain on police resources. There are also suspicions that a displacement effect occurs: stepped-up efforts to curb drug dealing in one area or city simply encourage dealers to seek out friendlier "business" territory.[195]

CLOSE-UP

Where Do Drugs Come From?

Illegal drugs begin as crops grown by independent peasant farmers in Asia, South and Latin America, and the Middle East. In some areas, the use of drugs is part of a culture that goes back centuries, while in others, such as Colombia and Mexico, production has been geared to supply illegal markets in the United States.

Heroin

Heroin is smuggled into the United States in west coast and northeastern states, and across the Mexican border. Southeast Asian heroin originates from Burma, Laos, and Thailand. It transits California for major markets there and is shipped to the eastern seaboard. Heroin smuggled directly to such markets as New York City and other east coast ports is produced in the Golden Triangle, the Middle East, or Southwest Asia. Mexican heroin is smuggled across the U.S.-Mexican border principally to markets in the Southwest. The drug is often transshipped across Africa and Europe. Nigeria, for example, has become a significant transshipment location.

Cocaine

Cocaine (see Figure A) enters the United States by land, sea, and air. Cocaine is:

- Transshipped overland from South America through Central America.
- Shipped directly to U.S. ports concealed in containers or packed with legitimate products through an extraordinary variety of concealment methods.
- Flown into the United States via couriers on commercial airlines or in private airplanes. Hundreds of air strips dot Mexico and Central America. Small planes can land on these strips and quickly off-load cocaine for transshipment to the United States.
- Air-dropped to waiting vessels in the Caribbean for shipment to U.S. markets.

Marijuana

Marijuana is smuggled in bulk, making it more difficult to conceal than cocaine or heroin. Marijuana produced overseas is smuggled into the United States by ocean-going vessels, small planes, and motor vehicles. Mexico is a principal source of the drug. Some marijuana also comes in from Colombia, Jamaica, and countries in Southeast Asia, such as Thailand.

Domestically, marijuana is grown in small plots and, increasingly, in greenhouses by individual growers. Outdoor plots are usually located in remote areas and have been found in some national parks and forests. Enforcement using aerial surveillance has driven many growers indoors.

Growers use modern technology to produce large quantities of more potent marijuana, often using special fertilizers and artificial lights in indoor operations. The Drug Enforcement Administration recently seized 14,547 plants in a single indoor production operation.

Discussion Questions

1. Would cutting off the supply coming from one nation encourage others to produce and export narcotics?
2. How could we convince nations with which we are not friendly, such as Libya or Iraq, to stop producing or distributing drugs?

SOURCE: Bureau of Justice Statistics, *Drugs, Crime, and the Justice System* (Washington, D.C.: Bureau of Justice Statistics, 1992), pp. 37–51.

FIGURE A   Cocaine Routes

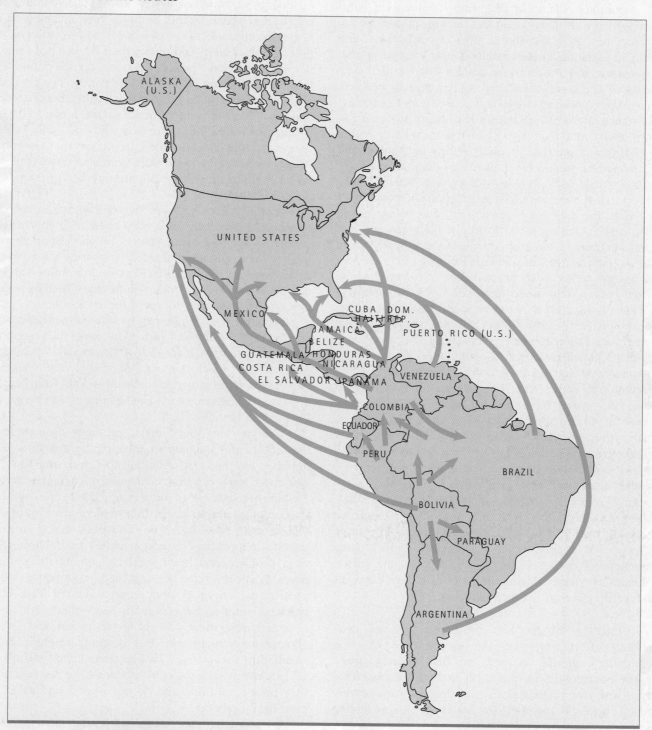

Punishment Strategies. Even if law enforcement efforts cannot produce a general deterrent effect, the courts may achieve the required result by severely punishing known drug dealers and traffickers. A number of initiatives have made the prosecution and punishment of drug offenders a top priority. State prosecutors have expanded their investigations into drug importation and distribution and created special prosecutors to focus on drug dealers. The fact that such drugs as crack are considered such a serious problem may have convinced judges and prosecutors to expedite substance abuse cases. One study of court processing in New York found that cases involving crack had a higher probability of pretrial detention, felony indictment, and incarceration sentences than other criminal cases.[196] Some states, such as New Jersey and Pennsylvania, report that these efforts have resulted in sharp increases in the number of convictions for drug-related offenses.[197] Once convicted, drug dealers can get very long sentences. Research by the federal government shows that the average sentence for drug offenders sent to federal prison is about six years.[198] However, these efforts often have their downside. Defense attorneys consider using delay tactics to be sound legal maneuvering in drug-related cases. Courts are so backlogged that prosecutors are anxious to plea-bargain. The consequence of this legal maneuvering is that about 25 percent of people convicted on federal drug charges are granted probation or some other form of community release.[199] Even so, prisons have become jammed with inmates, many of whom were involved in drug-related cases. Many drug offenders sent to prison do not serve their entire sentence because they are released in an effort to relieve prison overcrowding. The average prison stay is slightly more than one year, or about one-third of the original sentence. In fact, of all criminal types, drug offenders spend the least amount of their sentence behind bars.[200] It is unlikely that the public would approve of a drug control strategy in which large numbers of traffickers are locked up, forcing prison officials to release an equal number of violent criminals before they served out their sentence.

Community Strategies. Another type of drug control effort relies on the involvement of local community groups to lead the fight against drugs. Representatives of various local government agencies, churches, civic organizations, and similar institutions are being brought together to create drug prevention awareness programs.

Citizen-sponsored programs attempt to restore a sense of community in drug-infested areas, reduce fear, and promote conventional norms and values.[201] According to a survey by Saul Weingart, these efforts can be classified into one of four distinct categories.[202] The first involves law-enforcement type efforts, which may include block watches, cooperative police-community efforts, and citizen patrols. Some of these citizen groups are nonconfrontational, willing to simply observe or photograph dealers, take down their license plate number, and then notify police. On occasion, telephone hot lines have been set up to take anonymous tips on drug activity. Other groups engage in confrontational tactics that may even include citizens' arrests. Some of these community-based efforts are home-grown, while others attract outside organizations, such as the Guardian Angels or Black Muslims. Area residents have gone as far as contracting with private security firms to conduct neighborhood patrols.

Another tactic is to use the civil justice system to harass offenders. Landlords have been sued for owning properties that house drug dealers; neighborhood groups have formed and scrutinized drug houses for building code violations. Information acquired from these various sources is turned over to local authorities, such as police and housing agencies, for more formal action.

There are also community-based treatment efforts in which citizen volunteers participate in self-help support programs, such as Narcotics Anonymous or Cocaine Anonymous, which have more than 1,000 chapters nationally. Other programs provide youth with martial arts training, dancing, and social events as an alternative to the drug life.

Weingart also found that community drug prevention efforts are designed to enhance the quality of life, improve interpersonal relationships, and upgrade the neighborhood's physical environment. Activities might include the creation of drug-free school zones (which encourage police to keep drug dealers away from the vicinity of schools). Consciousness-raising efforts include demonstrations and marches to publicize the drug problem and build solidarity among the participants. Politicians have been lobbied to get better police protection or tougher laws passed: in New York City, residents went so far as sending bags filled with crack collected from street corners to the mayor and police commissioner to protest drug dealing. Residents have cleaned up streets, fixed broken street lights, and planted gardens in empty lots to broadcast the message that they have local pride and do not want drug dealers in their neighborhood.

While community crime prevention efforts seem appealing, there is little conclusive evidence that they are an effective drug control strategy. Some surveys indicate that most residents do not participate in programs. There is also evidence that community programs work better in stable, middle-income areas than in those that are crime-ridden and disorganized.[203] While these findings are discouraging, there have also been some studies that find the opposite, that deteriorated areas can sustain successful antidrug programs.[204] Future evaluations of community control efforts should determine whether they can work in the most economically depressed areas.

Drug Education and Prevention Strategies.

Prevention strategies are aimed at convincing youths not to get involved in drug abuse. Heavy reliance is placed on educational programs that teach kids to say no to drugs. One of the most familiar is the "McGruff, the Crime Dog" advertisements sponsored by the federal government's National Citizen's Crime Prevention Campaign. This friendly symbol, which is familiar to 99 percent of children between the ages of six and 12, has been used extensively in the media to teach kids how to protect themselves from crime and avoid the dangers of drug use. A multimedia drug prevention kit containing antidrug materials and videos has been distributed to almost every school district in the nation. A drug prevention curriculum featuring a McGruff puppet and audiocassette has been distributed to over 75,000 elementary classroom teachers, and millions of McGruff antidrug comic books have been given away to students. There is some indication that students in the program improve their antidrug attitudes, teachers like the program, and parents endorse the content and need for the program.[205]

Another familiar program is Drug Abuse Resistance Education, or DARE. This program is an elementary school course designed to give students the skills for

A police officer runs a drug education program in a local school. Can such efforts convince kids to "just say no" to drugs?

resisting peer pressure to experiment with tobacco, drugs, and alcohol. It is unique because it employs uniformed police officers to carry the antidrug message to the students before they enter junior high school. The program has five major focus areas:

- Providing accurate information about tobacco, alcohol, and drugs.

- Teaching students techniques to resist peer pressure.

- Teaching students respect for the law and law enforcers.

- Giving students ideas for alternatives to drug use.

- Building the self-esteem of students.

DARE is based on the concept that young students need specific analytical and social skills to resist peer pressure and say no to drugs. Instructors work with children to raise their self-esteem, provide them with decision-making tools, and help them identify positive alternatives to substance abuse. So far, police in more than 800 jurisdictions have received DARE training, and they have given the program to more than 3 million students.[206] A recent evaluation of the DARE program by Dennis Rosenbaum found no statistically significant effects on drug use or on attitudes and beliefs about drugs. Though this overall result is disappointing, the evaluation found that DARE may be effective with subsets of the population, such as female, urban, and Hispanic students.[207]

Drug education programs still hold promise as an effective means of reducing the onset of drug abuse. And while the DARE evaluation indicates less than hoped for success, there have been evaluations of other similar programs (Project Alert) that indicate that prevention strategies are capable of reducing the onset of drug use and cigarette smoking among students.[208]

Drug Testing Programs.
Drug testing of private employees, government workers, and criminal offenders is believed to have a deterrent effect on substance abuse.

In the workplace, employees are tested to enhance on the job safety and productivity. In some industries, such as mining and transportation, drug testing is considered essential because abuse can pose a threat to the public.[209] Business leaders have been enlisted in the fight against drugs. Mandatory drug-testing programs in government and industry are common. More than 40 percent of the country's largest companies, including IBM and AT&T, have drug-testing programs. The federal government requires employee testing in regulated industries, such as nuclear energy and defense contracting. About 4 million transportation workers will be subject to testing.

Drug testing is also quite common in government and criminal justice agencies. About 30 percent of local police departments test applicants, and 16 percent routinely test field officers. However, larger jurisdictions serving populations over 250,000 are much more likely to test applicants (84 percent) and field officers (75 percent). Drug testing is also part of the federal government's Drug Free Workplace Program, whose goal is to improve productivity and safety. Employees most likely to be tested include presidential appointees, law enforcement officers, and people in positions of national security.

Criminal defendants are now routinely tested at all stages of the justice system, from arrest to parole. The goal is to reduce criminal behavior by detecting current users and curbing their abuse. Can such programs reduce criminal activity? Two recent evaluations of pretrial drug-testing programs found little evidence that monitoring defendants' drug use influenced their behavior.[210]

Treatment Strategies.
A number of approaches are taken to treat known users, getting them clean of drugs and alcohol and thereby reducing the at-risk population. One approach rests on the assumption that users have low self-esteem and treatment efforts must focus on building a sense of self. One method has been to involve users in worthwhile programs of outdoor activities and wilderness training to create self-reliance and a sense of accomplishment.[211] More intensive efforts use group therapy approaches relying on group leaders who have been substance abusers. Through group sessions, users get the skills and support to help them reject the social pressure to use drugs. These programs are based on the Alcoholics Anonymous approach that holds that users must find within themselves the strength to stay clean and that peer support from those who understand their experiences can help them achieve a drug-free life.

There are also residential programs for the more heavily involved, and a large network of drug treatment centers has been developed. Some are detoxification units that use medical procedures to wean patients from the more addicting drugs to others, such as methadone, that can be more easily regulated. Methadone is a drug similar to heroin, and addicts can be treated at clinics where they receive methadone under controlled conditions. However, methadone programs have been undermined because some users sell their methadone in the black market, while others supplement their dosages with illegally obtained heroin.

Other therapeutic programs attempt to deal with the psychological causes of drug use. Hypnosis, aversion therapy (getting users to associate drugs with unpleasant sensations, such as nausea), counseling, biofeedback, and other techniques are often used.

Despite their good intentions, little evidence has been found that these treatment programs can efficiently terminate substance abuse. A stay in a residential program can help stigmatize people as "addicts," even though they never used hard drugs; while in treatment, they may be introduced to hard-core users who they will associate with upon release. Users do not often enter these programs voluntarily and have little motivation to change.[212] And even those who could be helped soon learn that there are simply more users who need treatment than there are beds in treatment facilities. Many facilities are restricted to users whose health insurance will pay for short-term residential care; when their insurance coverage ends, patients are often released, even though their treatment program is incomplete.

Legalization

Despite the massive effort to control drugs through prevention, deterrence, education, and treatment strategies, the fight against substance abuse has not proven successful. It is difficult to get people out of the drug culture because of the enormous profits involved in the drug trade: 500 kilos of coca leaves worth $4,000 to a grower yields about eight kilos of street cocaine valued at $500,000. A drug dealer who can move 100 pounds of coke into the United States can make $1.5 million in one shipment. An estimated 60 tons of cocaine are imported into the country each year with a street value of $17 billion.[213] It has also proven difficult to control drugs by convincing known users to quit; few treatment efforts have proven successful.

Considering these problems, some commentators have called for the legalization or decriminalization of restricted drugs. Legalization is warranted, according to Ethan Nadelmann, because the use of mood-altering substances is customary in almost all human societies; people have always wanted, and will find ways of obtaining, psychoactive drugs.[214] Banning drugs serves

to create networks of manufacturers and distributors many of whom use violence as part of their standard operating procedures. While some may charge that drug use is immoral, Nadelmann questions whether it is really any worse than the unrestricted use of alcohol and cigarettes, both of which are addicting and unhealthy. Far more people die each year because they abuse these legal substances than are killed in drug wars or from abusing illegal substances (since an estimated 100,000 people per year die from alcohol-related causes and another 320,000 from tobacco).[215]

Nadelmann also argues that just as Prohibition failed to stop the flow of alcohol in the 1920s while at the same time it increased the power of organized crime, the policy of prohibiting drugs is similarly doomed to failure. When drugs were legal and freely available earlier in this century, the proportion of Americans using drugs was not much greater than today; most users managed to lead normal lives, most likely because of the legal status of their drug use.[216]

If drugs were legalized, the argument goes, price and distribution could be controlled by the government. This would reduce addicts' cash requirements, thus crime rates would go down because users would no longer need the same cash flow to support their habit. Drug-related deaths would decline because government control would reduce needle sharing and the spread of AIDS. Legalization would also destroy the drug-importing cartels and gangs. Since drugs would be bought and sold openly, the government would reap a tax windfall from both taxes on the sale of drugs and the income taxes paid by drug dealers on profits that have been part of the hidden economy. Of course, drug distribution would be regulated, like alcohol, keeping it out of the hands of adolescents, public servants such as police and airline pilots, and known felons. Those who favor legalization point to the Netherlands as a country that has legalized drugs and remains relatively crime-free.[217]

The Consequences of Legalization. While this approach can have the short-term effect of reducing the association between drug use and crime, it may also have grave social consequences. According to David Courtwright, legalization would result in an increase in the nation's rate of drug usage, creating an even larger group of nonproductive, drug-dependent people who must be cared for by the rest of society.[218] If drugs were legalized and freely available, drug users might significantly increase their daily intake. In countries like Iran and Thailand, where drugs are cheap and readily available, the rate of narcotics use is quite high. Historically, the availability of cheap narcotics has preceded drug-use epidemics, as was the case when British and American merchants sold opium in nineteenth-century China.

Courtwright also finds that efforts to control legal use would backfire. If juveniles, criminals, and members of other at-risk groups were forbidden to buy drugs, who would be the customers? Noncriminal, nonabusing middle-aged adults? And would not those prohibited from legally buying drugs create an underground market almost as vast as the current one? If the government tried to raise money by taxing legal drugs, as it now does for liquor and cigarettes, might not that encourage drug smuggling to avoid tax payments; these "illegal" drugs might then fall into the hands of adolescents.

The problems of alcoholism should serve as a warning of what can happen when controlled substances are made readily available. For example, since women may be more disposed to becoming dependent on crack than men, the number of drug-dependent babies could begin to match or exceed the number who are delivered with fetal alcohol syndrome.[219] Drunk-driving fatalities, which today number about 25,000 per year, may be matched by deaths due to driving under the influence of pot or crack. And while distribution would be regulated, it is likely that adolescents would have the same opportunity to obtain potent drugs as they now have to obtain beer and hard liquor.

While decriminalization or legalization of controlled substances is unlikely in the near term, further study is warranted: What effect would a policy of partial decriminalization (for example, legalizing small amounts of marijuana) have on drug-use rates? Would a get-tough policy help to "widen the net" of the justice system and actually deepen some youths' involvement in substance abuse? Can society provide alternatives to drugs that will reduce teenage drug dependency?[220] The answers to these questions have proven elusive.

≡ Summary

Public order crimes are acts considered illegal because they conflict with social policy, accepted moral rules, and public opinion. There is usually great debate over public order crimes. Some charge that they are not really crimes at all and that it is foolish to legislate morality. Others view such morally tinged acts as prostitution, gambling, and drug abuse as harmful and therefore subject to public control. Many public order crimes are sex-related. Though homosexuality is not a crime per se, homosexual acts are subject to legal control. Some states still follow the archaic custom of legislating long prison terms for consensual homosexual sex.

Prostitution is another sex-related public order crime. Though prostitution has been practiced for thousands of years and is legal in some areas, most states outlaw commercial sex. There are a variety of prostitutes, including streetwalkers, B-girls, and call girls. Studies indicate that prostitutes came from poor, troubled families and have abusive parents. However, there is little evidence that prostitutes are emotionally disturbed, addicted to drugs, or sexually abnormal. Though prostitution is illegal, some cities have set up adult entertainment areas where commercial sex is tolerated by law enforcement agents.

Pornography involves the sale of sexually explicit material intended to sexually excite paying customers. The depiction of sex and nudity is not illegal, but it does violate the law when it is judged obscene. Obscene material is a legal term that today is defined as material offensive to community standards. Thus, each local jurisdiction must decide what pornographic material is obscene. A growing problem is in the exploitation of children in obscene materials—kiddy porn. The Supreme Court has ruled that local communities can pass statutes outlawing any sexually explicit material. There is no hard evidence that pornography is related to crime or aggression, but data suggest that sexual material with a violent theme is related to sexual violence by those who view it.

Substance abuse is another type of public order crime. There is great debate over the legalization of drugs, usually centering around such nonaddicting drugs as marijuana. However, most states and the federal government outlaw a wide variety of drugs they consider harmful, including narcotics, amphetamines, barbiturates, cocaine, hallucinogens, and marijuana. One of the main reasons for the continued ban on drugs is their relationship to crime. Numerous studies have found that drug addicts commit enormous amounts of property crime.

Alcohol is another commonly abused substance. Although alcohol is legal to possess, it too has been linked to crime. Drunk driving and deaths caused by drunk drivers are growing national problems. There are many different strategies to control substance abuse, ranging from source control to treatment. So far, no single method seems effective. While legalization is debated, both the fact that so many people already take drugs and that drug abuse is associated with crime makes legalization unlikely in the near term.

☰ KEY TERMS

public order crime	call girls
victimless crime	skeezers
vigilante	massage parlors
moral crusades	baby pros
moral entrepreneurs	Mann Act
homosexuality	pornography
sodomy	temperance movement
paraphilias	freebase
prostitution	crack
brothels	designer drugs
madams	

☰ NOTES

1. Charles Fleming and Michele Ingrassia, "The Heidi Chronicles," *Newsweek,* 16 August 1993, p. 51.
2. Edwin Schur, *Crimes without Victims* (Englewood Cliffs, N.J.: Prentice-Hall, 1965).
3. Andrea Dworkin, quoted in "Where Do We Stand on Pornography," *Ms,* January–February 1994, p. 34.
4. Jennifer Williard, *Juvenile Prostitution* (Washington, D.C.: National Victim Resource Center, 1991).
5. Morris Cohen, "Moral Aspects of the Criminal Law," *Yale Law Journal* 49 (1940): 1017.
6. Sir Patrick Devlin, *The Enforcement of Morals* (New York: Oxford University Press, 1959), p. 20.
7. See Joel Feinberg, *Social Philosophy* (Englewood Cliffs, N.J.: Prentice-Hall, 1973), chap. 2, 3.
8. *United States v. 12 200-ft Reels of Super 8mm Film,* 413 U.S. 123 (1973) at 137.
9. David Kaplan, "Is It Torture or Tradition?" *Newsweek,* 20 December 1993, p. 124.
10. H. L. A. Hart, "Immorality and Treason," *Listener* 62 (1959): 163.
11. Joseph Gussfield, "On Legislating Morals: The Symbolic Process of Designating Deviancy," *California Law Review* 56 (1968): 58–59.
12. E. Hatfield, S. Sprecher, and J. Traupman, "Men and Women's Reactions to Sexually Explicit Films: A Serendipitous Finding," *Archives of Sexual Behavior* 6 (1978): 583–92.
13. Henry Lesieur and Joseph Sheley, "Illegal Appended Enterprises: Selling the Lines," *Social Problems* 34 (1987): 249–60.
14. Wayne LaFave and Austin Scott, Jr., *Criminal Law* (St. Paul: West Publishing, 1986), p. 12.
15. Ibid.
16. "Baylor U. Cancels Art Class on Nudes," *Boston Globe,* 22 March 1993, p. 21.
17. Daniel Claster, *Bad Guys and Good Guys, Moral Polarization and Crime* (Westport, Conn: Greenwood Press, 1992), pp. 28–29.
18. Howard Becker, *Outsiders* (New York: Macmillan, 1963), pp. 13–14.
19. Albert Reiss, "The Social Integration of Queers and Peers," *Social Problems* 9 (1961): 102–20.
20. Judd Marmor, "The Multiple Roots of Homosexual Behavior," in *Homosexual Behavior,* ed. J. Marmor (New York: Basic Books, 1980), p. 5.
21. J. Money, "Sin, Sickness, or Status? Homosexual Gender Identity and Psychoneuroendocrinology," *American Psychologist* 42 (1987): 384–99.
22. C. S. Ford and F. A. Beach, *Patterns of Sexual Behavior* (New York: Harper & Bros., 1951).
23. A. Kinsey, W. Pomeroy, and C. Martin, *Sexual Behavior in the Human Male* (Philadelphia: W. B. Saunders, 1948); A. Kinsey, W. Pomeroy, and C. Martin, *Sexual Behavior in the Human Female* (Philadelphia: W. B. Saunders, 1953); Morton Hunt, *Sexual Behavior in the 1970's* (New York: Dell Books, 1974), p. 317.
24. J. McNeil, *The Church and the Homosexual* (Kansas City, Mo.: Sheed, Andrews, and McNeel, 1976).
25. Marmor, "The Multiple Roots of Homosexual Behavior," pp. 18–19.
26. Ibid., p. 19.
27. M. Weinberg and C. J. Williams, *Male Homosexuals: Problems and Adaptations* (New York: Oxford University Press, 1974).
28. Spencer Rathus, *Human Sexuality* (New York: Holt, Rinehart and Winston, 1983), p. 395.
29. "Homosexuality and Politics: A Newsweek Poll," *Newsweek,* 25 September 1989, p. 19.
30. Mark Muro, "Gay Studies Goes Mainstream," *Boston Globe,* 30 January 1991, p. 35.
31. "Daddy Is out of the Closet," *Newsweek,* 7 January 1991, p. 60.
32. 376 U.S. 660; 82 S.Ct. 1417; 8 L.Ed.2d 758 (1962).
33. Richard Keil, "Gay Couple Sues D.C. over Marriage License," *Boston Globe,* 27 November 1990, p. 5.
34. F. Inbau, J. Thompson, and J. Zagel, *Criminal Law and Its Administration* (Mineola, N.Y.: Foundation Press, 1974), p. 287.
35. *Bowers v. Hardwick,* 106 S.Ct. 2841 (1986); reh. den. 107 S.Ct. 29 (1986).
36. Georgia Code Ann. 16–6–2 (1984).
37. American Law Institute, Model Penal Code, Section 207.5.
38. Gary Caplan, "Fourteenth Amendment—The Supreme Court Limits the Right to Privacy," *Journal of Criminal Law and Criminology* 77 (1986): 894–930.

39. Associated Press, "Voters in Houston Defeat 'Sexual Orientations' Issues," *Omaha World Herald,* 20 January 1985, p. 1.

40. Christopher Boyd, "Gay Rights Coming of Age," *Boston Globe,* 7 December 1992, p. 3.

41. Andy Mead and Gail Gibson, "Private Life Stirs a Public Furor," *Boston Globe,* 9 November 1993, p. 3.

42. Carolyn Skorneck, "Reno Orders FBI to End Hiring Bias against Gays," *Boston Globe,* 4 December 1993, p. 3.

43. Associated Press, "Court Rules against Transsexual Pilot," *Omaha World Herald,* 31 August 1984, p. 3.

44. For the classic study of homosexual encounters, see Laud Humphreys, *Tearoom Trade: Impersonal Sex in Public Places* (Chicago: Aldine, 1970).

45. See, generally, Spencer Rathus and Jeffery Nevid, *Abnormal Psychology* (Englewood Cliffs, N.J.: Prentice-Hall, 1991), pp. 373–411.

46. See, generally, V. Bullogh, *Sexual Variance in Society and History* (Chicago: University of Chicago Press, 1958), pp. 143–44.

47. Rathus, *Human Sexuality,* p. 463.

48. Annette Jolin, "On the Backs of Working Prostitutes: Feminist Theory and Prostitution Policy," *Crime and Delinquency* 40 (1994): 60–83.

49. Charles McCaghy, *Deviant Behavior* (New York: Macmillan, 1976), pp. 348–49.

50. Rathus, *Human Sexuality,* p. 463.

51. Cited in Ibid.

52. FBI, *Crime in the United States, 1992,* p. 221.

53. Michael Waldholz, "HTLV-I Virus Found in Blood of Prostitutes," *Wall Street Journal,* 5 January 1990, p. B2.

54. FBI, *Crime in the United States, 1992,* p. 172.

55. Charles Winick and Paul Kinsie, *The Lively Commerce,* (Chicago: Quadrangle Books, 1971), p. 58.

56. Mark-David Janus, Barbara Scanlon, and Virginia Price, "Youth Prostitution," in *Child Pornography and Sex Rings,* ed. Ann Wolbert Burgess (Lexington, Mass.: Lexington Books, 1989), pp. 127–46.

57. Jennifer James, "Prostitutes and Prostitution," in *Deviants: Voluntary Action in a Hostile World,* ed. E. Sagarin and F. Montanino (New York: Scott, Foresman, 1977), p. 384.

58. Winick and Kinsie, *The Lively Commerce,* pp. 172–73.

59. Alessandra Stanley, "Case of the Classy Madam," *Time,* 29 October 1984, p. 39.

60. Paul Goldstein, "Occupational Mobility in the World of Prostitution: Becoming a Madam," *Deviant Behavior* 4 (1983): 267–79.

61. Ibid., p. 267.

62. Goldstein, "Occupational Mobility in the World of Prostitution," (1983): 267–70.

63. Described in Rathus, *Human Sexuality,* p. 468.

64. Paul Goldstein, Lawrence Ouellet, and Michael Fendrich, "From Bag Brides to Skeezers: A Historical Perspective on Sex-for-Drugs Behavior," *Journal of Psychoactive Drugs* 24 (1992): 349–61.

65. D. Kelly Weisberg, *Children of the Night: A Study of Adolescent Prostitution* (Lexington, Mass.: Lexington Books, 1985), pp. 44–55.

66. Gerald Hotaling and David Finkelhor, *The Sexual Exploitation of Missing Children* (Washington, D.C.: U.S. Department of Justice, 1988).

67. N. Jackman, Richard O'Toole, and Gilbert Geis, "The Self-Image of the Prostitute," in *Sexual Deviance,* ed. J. Gagnon and W. Simon (New York: Harper and Row, 1967), pp. 152–53.

68. Weisberg, *Children of the Night,* p. 98.

69. Winick and Kinsie, *The Lively Commerce,* p. 51.

70. Paul Gebhard, "Misconceptions about Female Prostitutes," *Medical Aspects of Human Sexuality* 3 (July 1969): 28–30.

71. James, "Prostitutes and Prostitution," pp. 388–89.

72. Winick and Kinsie, *The Lively Commerce,* p. 109.

73. James, "Prostitutes and Prostitution," p. 419.

74. Winick and Kinsie, *The Lively Commerce,* p. 120.

75. Goldstein, Ouellet, and Fendrich, "From Bag Brides to Skeezers," p. 359.

76. Dorothy Bracey, *"Baby Pros": Preliminary Profiles of Juvenile Prostitutes* (New York: JohnJay Press, 1979).

77. Andrea Dworkin, *Pornography* (New York: Dutton, 1989).

78. Jolin, "On the Backs of Working Prostitutes," pp. 76–77.

79. *Merriam-Webster Dictionary* (New York: Pocket Books, 1974), p. 484.

80. Tracy Fields, "Florida Vendor Booked for Rap Record Sale," *Boston Globe,* 9 June 1990, p. 1; Richard Lacayo, "The Rap against a Rap Group," *Time,* 25 June 1990, p. 18.

81. Ann Landers, "Pornography Can Be an Addiction," *Boston Globe,* 19 July 1993, p. 36.

82. Attorney General's Commission Report on Pornography, Final Report (Washington, D.C.: U.S. Government Printing Office, 1986), pp. 837–901. Hereinafter cited as Pornography Commission.

83. John Hurst, "Children—A Big Profit Item for the Smut Peddlers," *Los Angeles Times,* 26 May 1977, cited in *Take Back the Night,* ed. Laura Lederer (New York: William Morrow, 1980), pp. 77–78.

84. Albert Belanger, et al. "Typology of Sex Rings Exploiting Children," in *Child Pornography and Sex Rings,* ed. Ann Wolbert Burgess (Lexington, Mass.: Lexington Books, 1984), pp. 51–81.

85. *The Report of the Commission on Obscenity and Pornography* (Washington, D.C.: U.S. Government Printing Office, 1970).

86. Pornography Commission, pp. 837–902.

87. Berl Kutchinsky, "The Effect of Easy Availability of Pornography on the Incidence of Sex Crimes," *Journal of Social Issues* 29 (1973): 95–112.

88. Michael Goldstein, "Exposure to Erotic Stimuli and Sexual Deviance," *Journal of Social Issues* 29 (1973): 197–219.

89. John Court, "Sex and Violence: A Ripple Effect," *Pornography and Aggression,* ed. Neal Malamuth and Edward Donnerstein (Orlando, Fla.: Academic Press, 1984).

90. See Edward Donnerstein, Daniel Linz, and Steven Penrod, *The Question of Pornography* (New York: Free Press, 1987).

91. Pornography Commission, pp. 901–1037.

92. Edward Donnerstein, "Pornography and Violence against Women," *Annals of the New York Academy of Science* 347 (1980): 277–88; E. Donnerstein and J. Hallam, "Facilitating Effects of Erotica on Aggression against Women," *Journal of Personality and Social Psychology* 36 (1977): 1270–77; Seymour Fishbach and Neil Malamuth, "Sex and Aggression: Proving the Link," *Psychology Today* 12 (1978): 111–22.

93. Don Smith, "Sexual Aggression in American Pornography: The Stereotype of Rape" (Paper presented at the annual meeting of the American Sociological Association, 1976).

94. 354 U.S. 476; 77 S.Ct. 1304 (1957).

95. 383 U.S. 413 (1966).

96. 413 U.S. 15 (1973).

97. R. George Wright, "Defining Obscenity: The Criterion of Value," *New England Law Review* 22 (1987): 315–41.

98. *Pope v. Illinois,* 107 S.Ct. 1918 (1987).

99. Ibid. at 1927 (Stevens, J. dissenting).

100. Pornography Commission, pp. 376–77.

101. Bob Cohn, "The Trials of Adam and Eve," *Newsweek,* 7 January 1991, p. 48.

102. 427 U.S. 50 (1976).

103. Kevin Cullen, "The Bad Old Days Are Over," *Boston Globe,* 23 December 1987, p. 33.

104. 50 L.W. 5077 (1982).

105. Joseph Scott, "Violence and Erotic Material—The Relationship between Adult Entertainment and Rape?" (Paper presented at the annual meeting of the American Association for the Advancement of Science, Los Angeles, 1985).

106. Ibid.

107. Associated Press, "N.Y. Firm Fined for Broadcasting Pornographic Films by Satellite," *Boston Globe,* 16 February 1991, p. 12.

108. Ralph Weisheit, "Studying Drugs in Rural Areas: Notes from the Field," *Journal of Research in Crime and Delinquency* 30 (1993): 213–32.

109. See, generally, Marianne Zawitz, ed., *Drugs, Crime and the Justice System* (Washington, D.C.: U.S. Government Printing Office, 1992). Herein cited as *Drugs.*

110. Arnold Trebach, *The Heroin Solution* (New Haven: Yale University Press, 1982).

111. James Inciardi, *The War on Drugs* (Palo Alto, Calif.: Mayfield, 1986), p. 2.

112. See, generally, David Pittman, "Drug Addiction and Crime," in *Handbook of Criminology,* ed. D. Glazer (Chicago: Rand McNally, 1974), pp. 209–32; Board of Directors, National Council on Crime and Delinquency, "Drug Addiction: A Medical, Not a Law Enforcement, Problem," *Crime and Delinquency* 20 (1974): 4–9.

113. Associated Press, "Records Detail Royals' Turn-of-Century Drug Use," *Boston Globe,* 29 August 1993, p. 13.

114. See Edwin Brecher, *Licit and Illicit Drugs* (Boston: Little, Brown, 1972).

115. James Inciardi, *Reflections on Crime* (New York: Holt, Rinehart and Winston, 1978), p. 15.

116. William Bates and Betty Crowther, "Drug Abuse," in *Deviants: Voluntary Actors in a Hostile World,* ed. E. Sagarin and F. Montanino (New York: Foresman and Co., 1977), p. 269.

117. Inciardi, *Reflections on Crime,* pp. 8–10. See also A. Greeley, William McCready, and Gary Theisen, *Ethnic Drinking Subcultures* (New York: Praeger, 1980).

118. Joseph Gusfield, *Symbolic Crusade* (Urbana: University of Illinois Press, 1963), chap. 3.

119. McCaghy, *Deviant Behavior,* p. 280.

120. Ibid.

121. This section relies heavily on the descriptions in Kenneth Jones, Louis Shainberg, and Curtin Byer, *Drugs and Alcohol* (New York: Harper & Row, 1979), pp. 57–114.

122. Rathus and Nevid, *Abnormal Psychology,* p. 344.

123. Jeffrey Fagan and Ko-Lin Chin, "Initiation into Crack and Powdered Cocaine: A Tale of Two Epidemics," *Contemporary Drug Problems* 16 (1989): 579–617.

124. Thomas Mieczkowski, "The Damage Done: Cocaine Methods in Detroit," *International Journal of Comparative and Applied Criminal Justice* 12 (1988): 261–67.

125. News release, Institute of Social Research, University of Michigan, Ann Arbor, 31 January 1994.

126. John Hagedorn, "Homeboys, Dope Fiends, Legits, and New Jacks," *Criminology* 32 (1994): 197–220.

127. Rathus and Nevid, *Abnormal Psychology,* p. 342.

128. These numbers are open to debate. See Inciardi, *The War on Drugs,* pp. 70–71; Jerome Platt and Christina Platt, *Heroin Addiction* (New York: Wiley, 1976), p. 324.

129. Charles Winick, "Physician Narcotics Addicts," *Social Problems* 9 (1961): 174–86.

130. News release, Institute for Social Research, University of Michigan, Ann Arbor, 27 January 1994, table 4.

131. Ibid.

132. Associated Press, "Alcohol Deaths Stopped Declining," *Boston Globe,* 27 January 1991, p. 8.

133. Ibid.

134. D. J. Rohsenow, "Drinking Habits and Expectancies about Alcohol's Effects for Self versus Others," *Journal of Consulting and Clinical Psychology* 51 (1983): 752–56.

135. G. Kolata, "Study Backs Heart Benefits in Light Drinking," *New York Times,* 3 August 1988, p. A24.

136. Spencer Rathus, *Psychology,* 4th ed. (New York: Holt, Rinehart and Winston, 1990), p. 161.

137. Data in this section comes from *The Household Survey on Drug Abuse, 1990* (Washington, D.C.: U.S. Department of Health and Human Services, 1990).

138. News release, University of Michigan, Ann Arbor, 31 January, 1994. The annual survey is conducted by Lloyd Johnston, Jerald Bachman, and Patrick O'Malley of the

Institute of Social Research.

139. Eric Wish, *Drug Use Forecasting Program, Annual Report 1990* (Washington, D.C.: National Institute of Justice, 1990).

140. Thomas Gray and Eric Wish, *Maryland Youth at Risk: A Study of Drug Use in Juvenile Detainees* (College Park, Md.: Center for Substance Abuse Research, 1993); Eric Wish and Christina Polsenberg, "Arrestee Urine Tests and Self-Reports of Drug Use: Which Is More Related to Rearrest?" (Paper presented at the annual meeting of the American Society of Criminology, Phoenix, Arizona, November 1993).

141. See, generally, Mark Blumberg, ed., *AIDS, The Impact on the Criminal Justice System* (Columbus, Ohio: Merrill Publishing, 1990).

142. Scott Decker and Richard Rosenfeld, "Intravenous Drug Use and the AIDS Epidemic: Findings for a Twenty-City Sample of Arrestees" (Paper presented at the annual meeting of the American Society of Criminology, Baltimore, November 1990).

143. Mark Blumberg, "AIDS and the Criminal Justice System: An Overview," in *AIDS, The Impact on the Criminal Justice System,* ed. Mark Blumberg (Columbus Ohio: Merrill Publishing, 1990), p. 11.

144. Ibid., pp. 2–3.

145. G. E. Vallant, "Parent-Child Disparity and Drug Addiction," *Journal of Nervous and Mental Disease* 142 (1966): 534–39; Charles Winick, "Epidemiology of Narcotics Use," in *Narcotics,* ed. D. Wilner and G. Kassenbaum (New York: McGraw-Hill, 1965), pp. 3–18.

146. C. Bowden, "Determinants of Initial Use of Opiods," *Comprehensive Psychiatry* 12 (1971): 136–40.

147. R. Cloward and L. Ohlin, *Delinquency and Opportunity: A Theory of Delinquent Gangs* (Glencoe, Ill.: Free Press, 1960).

148. Kellie Barr, Michael Farrell, Grace Barnes and John Welte, "Race, Class, and Gender Differences in Substance Abuse: Evidence of Middle-Class/Underclass Polarization among Black Males," *Social Problems* 40 (1993): 314–26.

149. Rathus and Nevid, *Abnormal Psychology,* p. 361.

150. Rathus, *Psychology,* p. 158.

151. Platt and Platt, *Heroin Addiction,* p. 127.

152. Alison Bass, "Mental Ills, Drug Abuse Linked," *Boston Globe,* 21 November 1990, p. 3.

153. D. W. Goodwin, "Alcoholism and Genetics," *Archives of General Psychiatry* 42 (1985): 171–74.

154. Denise Kandel and Mark Davies, "Friendship Networks, Intimacy and Illicit Drug Use in Young Adulthood: A Comparsion of Two Competing Theories," *Criminology* 29 (1991): 441–71.

155. J. S. Mio, G. Nanjundappa, D. E. Verlur, and M. D. DeRios, "Drug Abuse and the Adolescent Sex Offender: A Preliminary Analysis," *Journal of Psychoactive Drugs* 18 (1986): 65–72.

156. D. Baer and J. Corrado, "Heroin Addict Relationships with Parents during Childhood and Early Adolescent Years," *Journal of Genetic Psychology* 124 (1974): 99–103.

157. James Inciardi, Ruth Horowitz, and Anne Pottieger, *Street Kids, Street Drugs, Street Crime: An Examination of Drug Use and Serious Delinquency in Miami* (Belmont, Calif.: Wadsworth, 1993), p. 43.

158. Ibid.

159. John Wallace and Jerald Bachman, "Explaining Racial/Ethnic Differences in Adolescent Drug Use: The Impact of Background and Lifestyle," *Social Problems* 38 (1991): 333–57.

160. A. Christiansen, G. T. Smith, P. V. Roehling, and M. S. Goldman, "Using Alcohol Expectancies to Predict Adolescent Drinking Behavior after One Year," *Journal of Counseling and Clinical Psychology* 57 (1989): 93–99.

161. Judith Brook, Martin Whiteman, Elinor Balka, and Beatrix Hamburg, "African-American and Puerto Rican Drug Use: Personality, Familial, and Other Environmental Risk Factors," *Genetic, Social, and General Psychology Monographs* 118 (1992): 419–38.

162. Inciardi, *The War on Drugs,* p. 60.

163. These life-styles are described in Marcia Chaiken and Bruce Johnson, *Characteristics of Different Types of Drug-Involved Offenders* (Washington, D.C.: National Institute of Justice, 1988).

164. Kenneth Tunnell, "Inside the Drug Trade: Trafficking from the Dealer's Perspective," *Qualitative Sociology* 16 (1993): 361–81.

165. Douglas Smith and Christina Polsenberg, "Specifying the Relationship between Arrestee Drug Test Results and Recidivism," *Journal of Criminal Law and Criminology* 83 (1992): 364–77.

166. George Speckart and M. Douglas Anglin, "Narcotics Use and Crime: An Overview of Recent Research Advances," *Contemporary Drug Problems* 13 (1986): 741–69; Charles Faupel and Carl Klockars, "Drugs-Crime Connections: Elaborations from the Life Histories of Hard-Core Heroin Addicts," *Social Problems* 34 (1987): 54–68.

167. M. Douglas Anglin, Elizabeth Piper Deschenes, and George Speckart, "The Effect of Legal Supervision on Narcotic Addiction and Criminal Behavior" (Paper presented at the annual meeting of the American Society of Criminology, Montreal, November 1987), p. 2.

168. Speckart and Anglin, "Narcotics Use and Crime: An Overview of Recent Research Advances," p. 752.

169. Ibid.

170. James Inciardi, "Heroin Use and Street Crime," *Crime and Delinquency* 25 (1979): 335–46. See also W. McGlothlin, M. Anglin, and B. Wilson, "Narcotic Addiction and Crime," *Criminology* 16 (1978): 293–311.

171. M. Douglas Anglin and George Speckart, "Narcotics Use and Crime: A Multisample, Multimethod Analysis," *Criminology* 26 (1988): 197–235.

172. David Nurco, Ira Cisin, and John Ball, "Crime as a Source of Income for Narcotics Addicts," *Journal of Substance Abuse Treatment* 2 (1985): 113–15.

173. Allen Beck, Darrell Gilliard, Lawrence Greenfeld, Caroline Harlow, Thomas Hester, Lewis Jankowski, Tracy Snell, James Stephen, and Danielle Morton, *Survey of*

State Prison Inmates, 1991 (Washington, D.C.: Bureau of Justice Statistics, 1993). The survey of prison inmates is conducted by the Bureau of Justice Statistics every five to seven years.

174. National Institute of Justice, *Drug Use Forecasting, 1992* (Washington, D.C.: National Institute of Justice, 1993).

175. Faupel and Klockars, "Drugs-Crime Connections."

176. See Jones, Shainberg, and Byer, *Drugs and Alcohol,* pp. 137–46.

177. Controlled Substance Act, 21 U.S.C. 848 (1984).

178. Anti-Drug Abuse Act of 1986, Pub. L. No. 99-570, U.S.C. 841 (1986).

179. Anti-Drug Abuse Act of 1988, Pub. L. No. 100-690; 21 U.S.C. 1501; Subtitle A-Death Penalty, Sec. 7001, Amending the Controlled Substances Abuse Act, 21 U.S.C. 848.

180. Bennett Beach, "Is the Party Finally Over?" *Time,* 26 April 1982, p. 58.

181. "New Drunken Driver Law Shows Results in California," *Omaha World Herald,* 26 May 1982, p. 34.

182. Faye Silas, "Gimme the Keys," *ABA Journal* 71 (1985): 36.

183. Fred Heinzelmann, *Jailing Drunk Drivers* (Washington, D.C.: National Institute of Justice, 1984).

184. Rodney Kingsworth and Michael Jungsten, "Driving under the Influence: The Impact of Legislative Reform on Court Sentencing Practices," *Crime and Delinquency* 34 (1988): 3–28.

185. Jones, Shainberg, and Byer, *Drugs and Alcohol,* pp. 190–93.

186. Gerald Wheeler and Rodney Hissong, "Effects of Criminal Sanctions on Drunk Drivers: Beyond Incarceration," *Crime and Delinquency* 34 (1988): 29–42.

187. *Easter v. District of Columbia,* 361 F.2d 50 (D.C. Cir. 1966).

188. 392 U.S. 514 (1968).

189. Eric Jensen, Jurg Gerber, and Ginna Babcock, "The New War on Drugs: Grass Roots Movement or Political Construction?" *Journal of Drug Issues* 21 (1991): 651–67.

190. *Drugs,* p. 36.

191. Diego Ribadneira, "In Escobar Death, No Curb in Drugs Seen," *Boston Globe,* 4 December 1993, p. 2.

192. Ibid.

193. Walter Shapiro, "Going after the Hell's Angels," *Newsweek,* 13 May 1985, p. 41.

194. David Hayeslip, "Local-Level Drug Enforcement: New Strategies," *NIJ Reports,* March/April 1989.

195. Mark Moore, *Drug Trafficking* (Washington, D.C.: National Institute of Justice, 1988).

196. Steven Belenko, Jeffrey Fagan, and Ko-Lin Chin, "Criminal Justice Responses to Crack," *Journal of Research in Crime and Delinquency* 28 (1991): 55–74.

197. *FY 1988 Report on Drug Control* (Washington, D.C.: National Institute of Justice, 1989), p. 103.

198. Carol Kaplan, *Sentencing and Time Served* (Washington, D.C.: Bureau of Justice Statistics, 1987).

199. Ibid., p. 2.

200. *Time Served in Prison and on Parole* (Washington, D.C.: Bureau of Justice Statistics, 1988).

201. Robert Davis, Arthur Lurigio, and Dennis Rosenbaum, eds., *Drugs and the Community* (Springfield, Ill.: Charles Thomas, 1993), pp. xii–xv.

202. Saul Weingart, "A Typology of Community Responses to Drugs," in *Drugs and the Community,* ed. Robert Davis, Arthur Lurigio, and Dennis Rosenbaum (Springfield, Ill.: Charles Thomas, 1993), pp. 85–105.

203. Davis, Lurigio, and Rosenbaum, *Drugs and the Community,* pp. xii–xiii.

204. Bureau of Justice Statistics, *Drugs, Crime and the Justice System* (Washington, D.C.: Bureau of Justice Statistics, 1992), pp. 109–112.

205. *FY 1988 Report on Drug Control* (Washington, D.C.: National Institute of Justice, 1989), p. 50.

206. Ibid.

207. Dennis Rosenbaum, Robert Flewelling, Susan Bailey, Chris Ringwalt, and Deanna Wilkinson, "Cops in the Classroom: A Longitudinal Evaluation of Drug Abuse Resistance Education (DARE)," *Journal of Research in Crime and Delinquency* 31 (1994): 3–31.

208. Phyllis Ellickson and Robert Bell, "Challenges to Social Experiments: A Drug Prevention Example," *Journal of Research in Crime and Delinquency* 29 (1992): 79–101; idem, "Drug Prevention in Junior High: A Multi-Site Longitudinal Test," *Science* 247 (1990): 1299–1305.

209. *Drugs,* pp. 115–112.

210. John Goldkamp and Peter Jones, "Pretrial Drug-Testing Experiments in Milwaukee and Prince George's County: The Context of Implementation," *Journal of Research in Crime and Delinquency* 29 (1992): 430–65; Chester Britt, Michael Gottfredson, and John Goldkamp, "Drug Testing and Pretrial Misconduct: An Experiment on the Specific Deterrent Effects of Drug Monitoring Defendants on Pretrial Release," *Journal of Research in Crime and Delinquency* 29 (1992): 62–78.

211. See, generally, Peter Greenwood and Franklin Zimring, *One More Chance* (Santa Monica, Calif.: Rand Corporation, 1985).

212. Eli Ginzberg, Howard Berliner, and Miriam Ostrow, *Young People at Risk, Is Prevention Possible?* (Boulder, Colo.: Westview Press, 1988), p. 99.

213. Robert Taylor and Gary Cohen, "War against Narcotics by U.S. Government Isn't Slowing Influx," *Wall Street Journal,* 27 November 1984, p. 1.

214. Ethan Nadelmann, "America's Drug Problem," *Bulletin of the American Academy of Arts and Sciences* 65 (1991): 24–40.

215. Ibid., p. 24.

216. Ethan Nadelmann, "Should We Legalize Drugs? History Answers Yes," *American Heritage* (February/March 1993): 41–56.

217. See, generally, Ralph Weisheit, *Drugs, Crime and the Criminal Justice System* (Cincinnati: Anderson, 1990).

218. David Courtwright, "Should We Legalize Drugs? History Answers No," *American Heritage* (February/March 1993): 43–56.

219. James Inciardi and Duane McBride, "Legalizing Drugs: A Gormless, Naive Idea," *Criminologist* 15 (1990): 1–4.

220. Kathryn Ann Farr, "Revitalizing the Drug Decriminalization Debate," *Crime and Delinquency* 36 (1990): 223–37.

The
Criminal
Justice
System

The text's final section reviews the agencies and the process of justice designed to exert social control over criminal offenders. Chapter 15 provides an overview of the justice system and describes its major institutions and processes; Chapter 16 looks at the police; Chapter 17 and 18 analyze the court and correctional systems.

This vast array of people and institutions is beset by conflicting goals and values. Some view it as a mammoth agency of social control; others see it as a great social service dispensing therapy to those who cannot fit within the boundaries of society.

Consequently, a major goal of justice system policy makers is to formulate and disseminate effective models of crime prevention and control. Efforts are now being undertaken at all levels of the justice system to improve information flow, experiment with new program concepts, and evaluate current operating procedures.

There are many important links within the system, so the agencies of justice can be studied on a cross-national level. For example, all agencies must obey the rule of law, and most use a common framework of operations in such everyday events as arrest, detention, bail, and trial. However, the system fails to communicate effectively on what works, what doesn't, and why.

These chapters provide a good foundation for studying the justice system and its links to criminological thought.

Overview of the Criminal Justice System

☰ Introduction

In 1994, the media reported that Michael Fay, an American teenager living in the island nation of Singapore, had pleaded guilty to throwing eggs and spray-painting cars. His punishment was a fine, four months in jail, and a severe flogging with a rattan cane. Surprisingly, his sentence drew approval from many Americans. Public opinion polls at the time indicated about 40 percent of the general public, fed up with crime in the streets, approved of the sentence, though the beating would cause severe pain, profuse bleeding, and permanent scars.[1] "Just the thing we need in America to reduce crime," argued some people; "a barbaric display of savagery," countered others; famed historian David Rothman called the punishment "torture."[2]

The Fay case illustrates the kind of dilemmas faced daily by the criminal justice system: Who is to be punished? How? Can the correct form of punishment reduce crime? President Bill Clinton, who asked the ruler of Singapore to grant mercy to Michael Fay, is himself an advocate of the death penalty. How can Americans complain about the severity of punishment in Singapore when there are more than 2,000 people on death row in the United States and more than 70 percent of Americans, including the president, approve of capital punishment?

After more than 30 years of study, questions are still being asked about the general direction the justice system should take, how the problem of crime control should be approached, and what is the most effective method of dealing with known criminal offenders. It is clear that criminal justice is far from a unified field. Practitioners, academics, and commentators alike have expressed irreconcilable differences concerning its goals, purpose, and direction. This lack of consensus is particularly vexing when the multitude of problems facing the justice system is considered. The agencies of justice must attempt to eradicate such seemingly diverse social problems as substance abuse, gang violence, and environmental pollution, while at the same time respecting individual liberties and civil rights. It is also assumed that the justice system's agencies can efficiently carry out a multiplicity of diverse tasks and that its representatives possess a wide range of knowledge of law, psychology, and social welfare.

Because it is charged with enforcing the wide spectrum of criminal laws, the justice system must be able to respond as effectively to multibillion-dollar criminal frauds as it does to neighborhood gangs. Its component agencies—police, courts, and corrections—are charged

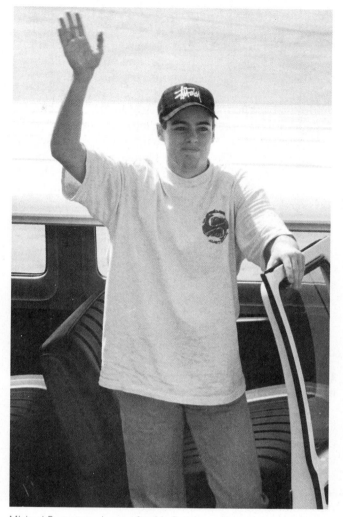

Michael Fay returns home after his flogging and imprisonment for vandalism in Singapore. Was his sentence too harsh and brutal, or could such tough punishments reduce crime rates in the United States?

by law with dispensing fair and equal justice to all Americans. In carrying out this task, the justice system must face the overwhelming reality of its burden—maintaining the rule of law in a society beset by racial and social injustice and conflict.

In the midst of these swirling debates and controversies is the criminal justice system. **Criminal justice** refers to both the formal process and the component agencies that have been established to apprehend, adjudicate, sanction, and treat criminal offenders. In recent years, it has become popular to refer to the components of justice as a system—"the criminal justice system." This term implies that the major segments of justice—the various police, court, and correctional agencies—operate as a unified whole. Change in one area of the system should automatically produce a corresponding change in the others. In addition, the systems approach to criminal justice suggests that the planning and coordination of justice-related agencies would best be served by creating unified rules, policies, and procedures that would uniformly benefit the agencies within the justice network and the people who come into contact with them. Unfortunately, there is little actual "system" to justice in the United States. The various elements of the criminal justice system—police, courts, and corrections—are all related, but they are influenced by each other's policies and practices only to a degree. Greater coordination and cooperation is a goal for the future.

In this chapter, the various components and processes of criminal justice will be reviewed. Then the legal constraints on criminal justice agencies will be discussed. Some of the philosophical concepts that dominate the system will be mentioned and explained.

≡ The Concept of Criminal Justice

Criminal justice refers to the agencies of government charged with the enforcement of law, the adjudication of crime, and the correction of criminal conduct. The study of criminal justice involves analysis of how these institutions influence human behavior and how they are in turn influenced by law and society.

The criminal justice system is essentially an instrument of **social control:** society considers some behaviors so dangerous and destructive that it chooses to either strictly control their occurrence or outlaw them outright. It is the job of the agencies of justice to prevent these behaviors by apprehending and punishing transgressors or deterring their future occurrence. While society maintains other forms of social control, such as the family, school, and church, they are designed to deal with moral and not legal misbehavior. Only the criminal justice system maintains the power to control crime and punish criminals.

Until fairly recently, there was little recognition that the agencies of criminal justice worked in concert or formed a "system."[3] Before the nineteenth century, there was little formal justice, and each legal jurisdiction developed its own methods to deal with criminal offenses. Such familiar institutions as local police departments and state prisons only began to develop in the nineteenth century. Though firmly entrenched in our culture, common criminal justice agencies have only existed for 150 years or so. At first, these institutions operated independently, with little recognition that their functions could be coordinated or have common ground.

In fact, it was not until 1919 that a unified criminal justice system received recognition. In that year, the **Chicago Crime Commission,** a professional association funded by private contributions, was created. This organization acted as a citizens' advocacy group and kept track of the ongoing activities of local justice agencies. The commission still carries out its work today.

The pioneering work of the Chicago group was soon copied in a number of other jurisdictions. In 1922, the Cleveland Crime Commission provided a detailed analysis of local criminal justice policy and uncovered the widespread use of discretion, plea bargaining, and other practices unknown to the public. Some commentators view the Cleveland survey as the first that treats criminal justice as a people-processing system, a view still widely held today. Similar projects were conducted by the Missouri Crime Survey (1926) and the Illinois Crime Survey (1929).

In 1931, President Herbert Hoover appointed the National Commission of Law Observance and Enforcement, commonly known today as the **Wickersham Commission.** This national study group analyzed the American justice system in detail and helped usher in the era of treatment and rehabilitation in

Prior to the liberal reforms of the twentieth century, treatment in the criminal justice system was often harsh and brutal. This nineteenth-century woodcut shows a prisoner at hard labor wearing a "collar cap" for punishment.

THE PUNISHMENT OF THE COLLAR CAP.

the U.S. correctional system. It showed in great detail the complex rules and regulations that govern the system and exposed how difficult it was for justice personnel to keep track of its legal and administrative complexity.

The Modern Era

The modern era of criminal justice study began with a series of explorations of the criminal justice process conducted under the auspices of the American Bar Foundation. These research studies produced field data that were later incorporated into classic books, including *Arrest* by Wayne LaFave and *Conviction* by Donald Newman, which focused on the decision-making process in criminal justice.[4] As a group, the Bar Foundation studies brought to light some of the hidden or "low visibility" processes that were at the heart of justice system operations. They showed how informal decision making and the use of personal discretion were essential ingredients of the justice process.

Another milestone occurred in 1967, when the President's Commission on Law Enforcement and the Administration of Justice (the Crime Commission), which had been appointed by President Lyndon Johnson, published its final report, entitled *The Challenge of Crime in a Free Society*.[5] This group of practitioners, educators, and attorneys had been charged with creating a comprehensive view of the criminal justice process and offering recommendations for its reform. Concomitantly, Congress passed the Safe Streets and Crime Control Act of 1968, providing for the expenditure of federal funds for state and local crime control efforts. This act helped launch a massive campaign to restructure the justice system by funding the Law Enforcement Assistance Administration (LEAA), an agency that provided hundreds of millions of dollars in aid to local and state justice agencies. Federal intervention through the LEAA ushered in a new era in research and development in criminal justice and established once and for all the concept that its component agencies actually make up a system.[6] Since that time, other national groups and agencies, including the American Bar Association and the National Advisory Commission on Criminal Justice Standards and Goals, have also explored the American criminal justice system in depth, reinforcing the systems concept.[7]

As a result of these efforts, the concept of a unified system of criminal justice is now generally recognized. Nearly every federal, state, and local crime control program began to use the term "criminal justice system" in one way or another. Rather than viewing police, court, and correctional agencies as thousands of independent institutions, it has become common to view them as components in a large, integrated, people-processing system that manages law violators from the time of their arrest, through trial, punishment, and release.

≡ Components of Criminal Justice

The basic components of the criminal justice system are the various police, court, and correctional agencies organized on the local, state, and federal levels of government. Together, they are a large and diverse collection of approximately 55,000 separate agencies. The overwhelming majority (81 percent) are part of local government structures, and the remainder are funded by state and federal jurisdictions.

Police

Approximately 17,000 law enforcement agencies are operating in the United States. Most are municipal, general-purpose police forces, numbering about 12,000 in all. In addition, local jurisdictions maintain over 1,000 special police units, including park rangers, harbor police, transit police, and campus security agencies at local universities. At the county level, there are approximately 3,000 **sheriff's departments,** which, depending on the jurisdiction, provide police protection in the unincorporated areas of the county; perform judicial functions, such as serving subpoenas; and maintain the county jail and detention facilities. Every state except Hawaii maintains a state police force. The federal government has its own law enforcement agencies, including the FBI and the Secret Service. All told, approximately 900,000 people work in federal, state, county, and local law enforcement agencies.[8]

Since their origin in early nineteenth-century Britain, law enforcement agencies have been charged with peacekeeping, deterring potential criminals, and apprehending law violators.[9] The traditional police role involved maintaining order through the patrol of public streets and highways, responding to calls for assistance, investigating crimes, and identifying criminal suspects. The police role has gradually expanded to include a variety of human service functions, including: preventing youth crime and diverting juvenile offenders from the criminal justice system, resolving family conflicts, facilitating the movement of people and vehicles, preserving civil order during emergencies, providing emergency medical care, and improving police-community relations.[10]

Police are charged with deterring crime, apprehending criminals, and maintaining the peace. Can these goals be better accomplished by bringing police closer to the community and having them work closely with neighborhood groups?

By the nature of their functions and roles, police are the most visible agents of the justice process. Their reactions to victims and offenders are carefully scrutinized in the news media. On numerous occasions, the police have been criticized for being too harsh or too lenient, too violent or too passive. Police control of such groups as minority citizens, youths, political dissidents, protesters, and union workers has been the topic of serious public debate. Compounding the problem is the tremendous discretion afforded police officers. The officer has the power to determine when a domestic dispute becomes disorderly conduct or criminal assault, whether it is appropriate to arrest juveniles or refer them to a social agency, and when to assume that probable cause exists to arrest a suspect for a crime.[11] At the same time, police agencies have been criticized for such problems

as internal corruption, inefficiency, lack of effectiveness, brutality, and discriminatory hiring.[12] Widely publicized cases of police brutality, such as the Rodney King beating in Los Angeles, have prompted calls for the investigation and prosecution of police officers. Consequently, at all levels of government, the police have traditionally been defensive toward and suspicious of the public, resistant to change, and secretive in their activities.

Courts

There are approximately 25,000 court-related agencies in the United States. These include more than 16,000 criminal courts, of which about 13,000 try misdemeanor cases, 3,235 are felony courts, and 207 are appellate courts. There are also slightly over 8,000 federal, state, and local prosecutors' offices, which represent the government in criminal and civil trials and appeals. Over half of these offices are municipal, about one-third are county, and the remainder are state and federally affiliated. In addition, some 1,000 public defender offices, which dispense free legal aid to indigent defendants, are operating around the country. About 320,000 people work in the various courts and prosecutors' and public defenders' offices in the United States.

The **criminal court** is considered by many to be the core element in the administration of criminal justice. In the purest sense of justice, the court is responsible for determining the criminal liability of criminal defendants. Ideally, it is expected to convict and sentence those found guilty of crimes while ensuring that the innocent are freed without any consequence or burden. The courts are formally required to seek the truth, obtain justice, and maintain the integrity of the government's rule of law.

Once the truth has been determined, and in the event the defendant is found guilty, the criminal court is responsible for sentencing the offender. Whatever sentence is ordered by the court may serve not only to rehabilitate the offender but also to deter others from crime. Once sentencing is accomplished, the corrections component of criminal justice begins to function.

Hypothetically, the entire criminal court process is undertaken with the recognition that the rights of the individual should be protected at all times. These rights, determined by federal and state constitutional mandates, statutes, and case law, form the foundation for protection of the accused. They include such basic concepts as the right to an attorney, the right to a jury trial, and the right to a speedy trial. Under the Fifth and Fourteenth Amendments of the U.S. Constitution, the defendant also has the right to **due process,** or the right to be treated with **fundamental fairness.** Under the protective umbrella of due process are included the right to be present at trial, to be notified of the charges, to have an opportunity to confront hostile witnesses, and to have favorable witnesses appear. Such practices are an integral part of a system and process that seek to balance the interests of the individual and the state.

Unfortunately, the ideal conditions of objectivity, fairness, and equal rights under which the nation's courts should operate are rarely achieved in actual practice or procedure. While some well-publicized defendants, such as O. J. Simpson and Michael Milken, receive their full share of rights and privileges, a significant number are herded through the court system with a minimum of interest or care. Court dockets are too crowded and funds are too scarce to grant each defendant the full share of justice. Consequently, a system known as **plea bargaining** has developed; in it, defendants are asked to plead guilty as charged in return for consideration of leniency or mercy.[13] Such "bargain justice" is estimated to occur in more than 90 percent of all criminal trials. Although the criminal court system is founded on the concept of equality before the law, there are unquestionably differences in the treatment that poor and wealthy citizens receive when they are accused of crimes.

Corrections

About 9,000 agencies are devoted to the correction and treatment of convicted offenders. Approximately 3,500 are adult and juvenile probation and parole agencies supervising offenders in the community. There are also about 5,700 residential correctional facilities, divided into 3,500 jails, 800 prisons, and 1,100 juvenile institutions. Close to 5 million Americans are under some form of correction, including about 950,000 in prison and 500,000 in jail.[14] Almost 500,000 people are employed by the nation's correctional systems.[15]

Following a criminal trial that results in conviction and sentencing, the offender enters this correctional system. Correctional agencies are charged with administering the postjudicatory care given to offenders, which, depending on the seriousness of the crime and the individual needs of offenders, can range from casual monitoring in the community to solitary confinement in a maximum security prison.

The most common correctional treatment, probation, is a legal disposition that allows the convicted offender to remain in the community, subject to conditions imposed by court order under the supervision of a probation officer. This lets the offender continue working and avoid the crippling effects of incarceration. Today, about 3 million people are on probation, and more than 25 percent of felony offenders receive a probation sentence.

A person given a sentence involving incarceration ordinarily is confined to a correctional institution for a specified period of time. Different types of institutions are used to hold offenders. Jails or houses of correction hold offenders convicted of misdemeanors and those awaiting trial or involved in other proceedings, such as grand jury deliberations, arraignments, or preliminary hearings. Many of these institutions for short-term detention are administered by county governments, and consequently, little is done in the way of treating inmates, principally because the personnel and institutions lack the qualifications, services, and resources.

State and federally operated facilities that receive felony offenders sentenced by the criminal courts are called prisons or **penitentiaries.** They may be minimum-, medium-, and maximum-security institutions. Prison facilities vary throughout the country. Some have high walls, cells, and large, heterogeneous inmate populations; others offer much freedom, good correctional programs, and small, homogeneous populations.

Most new inmates are first sent to a reception and classification center, where they are given diagnostic evaluations and assigned to institutions that meet their individual needs as much as possible within the system's resources. The diagnostic process in the reception center may range from a physical examination and a single interview to an extensive series of psychiatric tests, orientation sessions, and numerous personal interviews. Classification is a way of evaluating inmates and assigning them to appropriate placements and activities within the state institutional system.

Since the gap between what correctional programs promise to deliver and their actual performance is often significant, many jurisdictions have instituted a fourth type of confinement—community-based correctional facilities. Theses programs emphasize the use of small, neighborhood residential centers, halfway houses, prerelease centers, and work-release and home-furlough programs. This movement results from the experts' belief that only a small percentage of prison inmates require maximum security and that most can be more effectively rehabilitated in community-based facilities. Rather than totally confining offenders in an impersonal and harsh prison, such programs offer them the opportunity to maintain normal family and social relationships while providing rehabilitative services and resources at lower cost to taxpayers.

The last segment of the corrections system, **parole,** is a process whereby an inmate is selected for early release and serves the remainder of the sentence in the community under the supervision of a parole officer. The main purpose of parole is to help the ex-inmate bridge the gap between institutional confinement and a positive adjustment within the community. All parolees must adhere to a set of rules of behavior while they are "on the outside." If these rules are violated, the parole privilege can be terminated (revoked), and the parolee will be sent back to the institution to serve the remainder of the sentence.

Other ways an offender may be released from an institution include mandatory release upon completion of the sentence, and the pardon, a form of executive clemency.

Costs of Justice

The complex array of criminal justice agencies handles upward of 2 million offenders a year and employs more than 1.6 million people: about 900,000 in law enforcement agencies, 325,000 in the courts, and 500,000 in correctional agencies.

The costs of maintaining this system are vast: It costs about $30,000 annually to keep one juvenile in an institution; a prison cell costs about $100,000 to construct. The monetary burden on each American for the justice system is $248 annually, almost as much as the per capita costs for transportation and hospital and health care.[16] The estimated cost of operating the system is almost $75 billion annually. Criminal justice has become "big business," with many private companies vying to supply a variety of goods and services ranging from police communications gear to building the prison cells for which the system seems to have developed an insatiable appetite.[17] In addition to this vast enterprise, there is also an independent juvenile justice which handles minors who violate the law. This system is described in the following Close-Up entitled "Juvenile Justice."

≡ The Process of Justice

In addition to viewing the criminal justice system as a collection of agencies, it is possible to see it as a series of decision points through which offenders flow. This process, illustrated in Figure 15.1, begins with an initial contact with police and ends with the offender's reentry into society. At any point in the process, the accused may be no longer considered to be an offender and allowed back into society without further penalty for such reasons as: (1) the case is considered unimportant or trivial; (2) legally admissible evidence is unavailable; (3) the accused is considered not to need further treatment, punishment, or attention; or (4) for personal reasons (discretion), those in power decide not to take further action in the case.

Herbert Packer has described this process as follows:

The image that comes to mind is an assembly line conveyor belt down which moves an endless stream of cases, never stopping, carrying them to workers who stand at fixed stations and who perform on each case as it comes by the same small but essential operation that brings it one step closer to being a finished product, or to exchange the metaphor for the reality, a closed file. The criminal process is seen as a screening process in which each successive stage—pre-arrest investigation, arrest, post-arrest investigation, preparation for trial, or entry of plea, conviction, disposition—involves a series of routinized operations whose success is gauged primarily by their tendency to pass the case along to a successful conclusion.[18]

Though each jurisdiction is somewhat different, a comprehensive view of the processing of a felony offender would probably contain the following decision points:

- *Initial contact.* The initial contact an offender has with the justice system is usually with police. Police officers may observe a criminal act during their patrol of city streets, parks, or highways. They may also find out about a crime through a citizen or victim complaint. Similarly, an informer can alert them about criminal activity in return for financial or other consideration. Sometimes political officials, such as the mayor or city council, will ask police to look into an ongoing criminal activity, such as gambling, and during their subsequent investigations, police officers will encounter an illegal act.

- *Investigation.* Regardless whether the police observe, hear of, or receive a complaint about a crime, they may choose to conduct an investigation. The purpose of this procedure is to gather sufficient facts, or evidence, to identify the perpetrator, justify an arrest, and bring the offender to trial. An investigation may take a few minutes, as when police officers see a burglary in progress and apprehend the burglar at the scene of the crime. It may take months and involve hundreds of investigators, as was the case with

FIGURE 15.1   The Critical Stages in the Justice Process

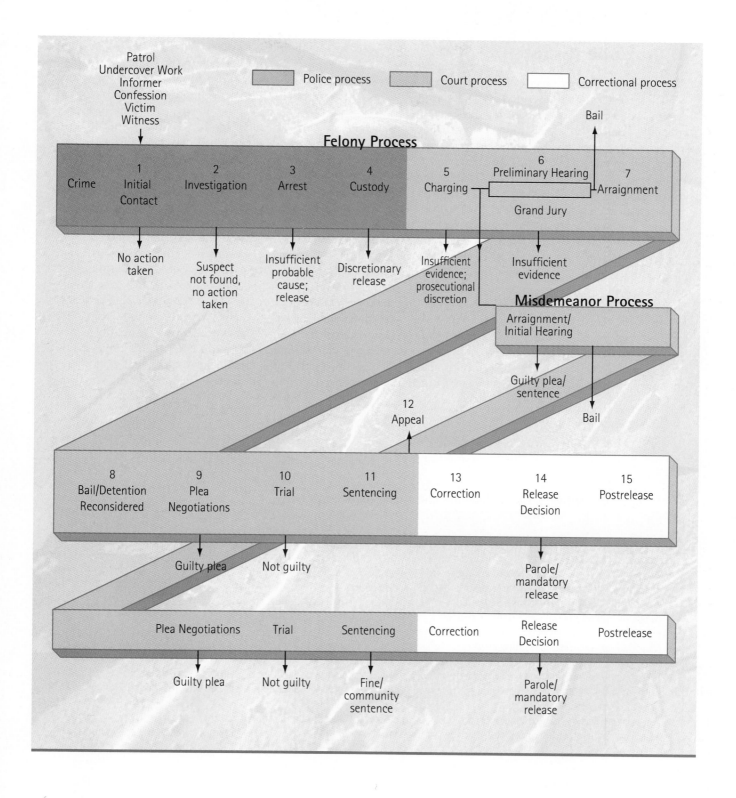

CLOSE-UP

Juvenile Justice

Independent of but interrelated with the adult criminal justice system, the juvenile justice system is primarily responsible for dealing with juveniles who commit crimes (*delinquents*) and those who are incorrigible, truants, runaways, or unmanageable (*status offenders*).

The notion that juveniles who commit criminal acts should be treated separately from adults is a relatively new one. Until the late nineteenth century, youthful criminals were tried in adult courts and punished in adult institutions. However, in the 1890s, reformers, today known as "child savers," lobbied to separate young offenders from serious adult criminals. Their efforts were rewarded when the first separate juvenile court was set up in Chicago in 1899. Over the next 20 years, most other states created separate juvenile court and correctional systems.

At first, the juvenile system was based on the philosophy of *parens patriae*. This meant that the state was acting in the best interests of children in trouble who could not care for themselves. Under the parens patriae doctrine, delinquents and status offenders (sometimes called "wayward minors" or "children in need of supervision") were adjudicated in an informal juvenile court hearing without the benefit of counsel or other procedural rights. The juvenile correctional system, designed for treatment rather than punishment, was usually located in small institutions referred to as schools or camps. (The first juvenile reform school was opened in 1847 in Massachusetts.) However, after the separate juvenile justice system was developed, almost all incarcerated youths were maintained in separate juvenile institutions that stressed individualized treatment, education, and counseling.

In the 1960s, the Supreme Court revolutionized the juvenile justice system when, in a series of cases—the most important being *In Re Gault*—it granted procedural and due process rights, such as the right to legal counsel, to juveniles at trial. The Court recognized that many youths were receiving long sentences without the benefit of counsel and other Fifth and Sixth Amendment rights and that many institutions did not carry out their

TABLE A   Similarities between Juvenile and Adult Justice Systems

- Police officers, judges, and correctional personnel use discretion in decision making in both adult and juvenile systems.
- The right to receive *Miranda* warnings applies to juveniles as well as to adults.
- Procedural safeguards similar to those of adults protect juveniles when they admit guilt.
- Prosecutors and defense attorneys play equally critical roles in juvenile and adult advocacy.
- Juveniles and adults have the right to counsel at most crucial stages of the court process.
- Pretrial motions are available in juvenile and criminal court proceedings.
- Negotiations and plea bargaining exist for juvenile and adult offenders.
- Both juveniles and adults have a right to a hearing and an appeal.
- The standard of evidence in juvenile delinquency adjudications, as in adult criminal trials, is proof beyond a reasonable doubt.
- Both juveniles and adults can be kept in preventive pretrial detention without bail if they are considered dangerous or a risk to themselves or society.
- Juveniles and adults can be placed on probation by the court, or placed in community treatment programs.
- Juveniles can be placed in prison and even receive the death penalty if their case is transferred or waived to the adult court.

treatment role. Consequently, the juvenile justice process became more similar to the adult process.

In the 1970s, the nonintervention movement once again changed juvenile justice. Every effort was made to divert youths from the official justice process and place them in alternative, community-based treatment programs. One state, Massachusetts, went so far as to close its secure correctional facilities and place all youths, no matter how serious their crimes, in community programs.

Today, concern over juvenile violence has caused some critics to question the juvenile justice system's treatment philosophy. Some states, such as New York, have liberalized their procedures for trying serious juvenile offenders in the adult system, consequently making them eligible for incarceration in adult prisons. The general trend has been to remove as many nonviolent and status offenders as possible from secure placements in juvenile institutions and at the same time to lengthen the sentences of serious

offenders or to move such offenders to the adult system.

Some of the similarities between the adult and juvenile systems are listed in Table A. Some of the differences are listed in Table B.

Discussion Questions
1. Should serious juvenile offenders be treated like adults and tried in adult courts?
2. Should incorrigible and truant youths be given the same treatment as delinquents (criminal youths)?

TABLE B   **Differences between Juvenile and Adult Justice Systems**

- The primary purpose of juvenile procedures is protection and treatment; with adults, the aim is punishment of the guilty.
- Age determines the jurisdiction of the juvenile court; in the adult system, jurisdiction is determined by the nature of the offense.
- Juveniles can be apprehended for acts that would not be criminal if they were committed by an adult (status offenses), such as truancy or running away from home.
- Juvenile proceedings are not considered criminal; adult proceedings are.
- Juvenile court procedures are generally informal and private; those of adult courts are more formal and are open to the public.
- Courts cannot release identifying information concerning a juvenile to the media but must release information about an adult.
- Parents are highly involved in the juvenile process but not in the adult process.
- The standard of arrest is more stringent for adults than for juveniles.
- Juveniles are released into parental custody, while adults are generally given the opportunity for bail.
- Juveniles have no constitutional right to a jury trial; adults have this right.
- Juveniles have the right to treatment under the Fourteenth Amendment; adult offenders have no such recognized right.
- A juvenile's record is sealed when the age of majority is reached; an adult's record is permanent.
- Juveniles under the age of 16 cannot be given the death penalty.
- A juvenile court cannot sentence juveniles to county jails or state prisons, which are reserved for adults.
- Juveniles can be searched under circumstances in which adults would be immune. For example, teachers can search students without probable cause that a crime has been committed.

SOURCE: Tables A and B are adapted from Larry Siegel and Joseph Senna, *Juvenile Delinquency,* 5th ed. (St. Paul: West Publishing, 1994), p. 340.

the Atlanta child murders investigation, which lasted from 1980 through 1981, until a suspect, Wayne Williams, was identified.

- *Arrest.* An **arrest** occurs when the police take a person into custody and deprive the person of freedom for allegedly committing a criminal act. An arrest is legal when all of the following conditions exist: (a) the police officer believes there is sufficient evidence (probable cause) that a crime is being or has been committed and that the suspect committed the crime; (b) the police officer deprives the individual of freedom; and (c) the suspect believes that he or she is in the custody of a police officer and cannot voluntarily leave. The police officer is not required to use the word *arrest* or any similar word to initiate an arrest; nor does the officer first have to bring the suspect to the police station. For all practical purposes, a person who has been deprived of liberty is under arrest. Arrests can be made at the scene of a crime or upon a warrant being issued by a magistrate.

- *Custody.* After arrest, the suspect remains in police custody. The person may be taken to the police station to be fingerprinted and photographed and to have personal information recorded—a procedure popularly referred to as booking. Witnesses may be brought in to view the suspect (in a **lineup**), and further evidence may be gathered on the case. Suspects may be interrogated by police officers to get their side of the story, they may be asked to sign a confession of guilt, or they may be asked to identify others involved in the crime. The law allows suspects to have their lawyers present when police conduct in-custody interrogations.

- *Complaint.* After police turn the evidence in a case over to the prosecutor, who is entrusted with representing the state at any criminal proceedings, a decision will be made whether to file a complaint, **information,** or bill of indictment with the court having jurisdiction over the case. Complaints are used in misdemeanors; information and indictment are employed in felonies. Each is a charging document asking the court to bring a case forward to be tried. The decision of whether to charge an offender with a criminal offense is a complex one that will be discussed further in Chapter 17.

- *Preliminary hearing—grand jury.* Since it is a tremendous personal and financial burden to stand trial for a serious felony crime, the U.S. Constitution provides that the state must first prove to an impartial hearing board that there is **probable cause** that the accused committed the crime and, therefore, that there is sufficient reason to try the person as charged. In about half the states and in the federal system, the decision whether to bring a suspect to trial (indictment) is made by a group of citizens brought together to form a **grand jury.** The grand jury considers the case in a closed hearing, in which only the prosecutor presents evidence. In the remaining states, an information is filed before an impartial lower-court judge, who decides whether the case should go forward. This is known as a *preliminary hearing* or probable cause hearing. The defendant may appear at a preliminary hearing and dispute the prosecutor's charges. During either procedure, if the prosecution's evidence is accepted as factual and sufficient, the suspect will be called to stand trial for the crime. These procedures are not used for misdemeanors because of their lesser importance and seriousness.

- *Arraignment.* An arraignment brings the accused before the court that will actually try the case. There, defendants are apprised of the formal charges and informed of their constitutional rights (such as the right to legal counsel), have their bail considered, and have the trial date set.

- *Bail or detention.* If the bail decision has not been considered previously, it will be evaluated at arraignment. Bail is a money bond, the amount of which is set by judicial authority; it is intended to ensure the presence of suspects at trial while allowing them their freedom until that time. Suspects who do not show up for trial forfeit their bail. Suspects who cannot afford bail or whose cases are so serious that a judge refuses them bail (usually restricted to capital cases) must remain in detention until trial. In most instances, this means an extended stay in the county jail. In many jurisdictions, programs have been developed to allow defendants awaiting trial to be released on their own recognizance, without bail, if they are stable members of the community.

- *Plea bargaining.* After arraignment, it is common for the prosecutor to meet with the defendant and his or her attorney to discuss a possible guilty plea arrangement. If a bargain can be struck, the accused will plead guilty as charged, thus ending the criminal trial process. In return for the plea, the prosecutor may reduce charges, request a lenient sentence, or grant the defendant some other consideration.

- *Adjudication.* If a plea bargain cannot be arranged, a criminal trial will take place. This involves a full-scale inquiry into the facts of the case before a judge, a jury, or both. The defendant can be found guilty or not guilty, or the jury can fail to reach a decision (hung jury), thereby leaving the case unresolved and open for a possible retrial.

- *Disposition.* After a criminal trial, a defendant who is found guilty as charged will be sentenced by the presiding judge. Disposition usually involves either a fine, a term of community supervision (probation), a period of incarceration in a penal institution, or some combination of the above. In the most serious capital cases, it is possible to sentence the offender to death. Dispositions are usually made after a presentencing investigation is conducted by the court's probation staff. After disposition, the defendant may appeal the conviction to a higher court.

- *Correctional treatment.* Offenders who are found guilty and are formally sentenced come under the jurisdiction of correctional authorities. They may serve a term of community supervision under control of the county probation department, they may have a term in a community correctional center, or they may be incarcerated in a large penal institution.

Most criminal cases are resolved by plea bargains. Even some famous criminals such as skater Tonya Harding are allowed to plea bargain to escape harsher penalties.

- *Release*. At the end of the correctional sentence, the offender is released into the community. Most incarcerated offenders are granted parole before the expiration of the maximum term given them by the court and therefore finish their prison sentences in the community under supervision of the parole department. Offenders sentenced to community supervision, if successful, simply finish their terms and resume their lives unsupervised by court authorities.

At every stage of the process then, a decision is made whether to send the case farther down the line or "kick it" from the system. Decision making and discretion mark each stage of the system.

≡ The "Wedding Cake" Model

The traditional model of the criminal justice process described above depicts it as a uniform series of decision points through which cases flow, each characterized by uniform procedures and rights. Yet many experts view this model as fanciful; they argue that the justice system is a political entity that actually works much more subjectively. While some cases receive the full attention of the law, the great majority are settled with a minimum of legal and procedural due process.

Samuel Walker, a justice historian, suggests that the criminal justice process is best conceived as a four-layer cake, depicted in Figure 15.2.[19]

The relatively small first layer of Walker's model is made up of the celebrated cases involving the famous, wealthy, or powerful, such as Mike Tyson, Ivan Boesky, William Kennedy Smith, or the not-so-powerful who victimize a famous person, such as Sirhan Sirhan (Robert Kennedy's assassin) or John Hinckley (President Ronald Reagan's would-be assassin). Also included within this category are unknown criminals whose case becomes celebrated either because it is brought before the Supreme Court because of some procedural irregularity, such as that of Ernesto Miranda or Clarence Gideon, or because it involves a media event, such as the Charles Manson or Heidi Fleiss case.

People in the first layer of the criminal justice wedding cake receive a great deal of public attention, and their case usually involves the full panoply of criminal justice procedures, including famous defense attorneys,

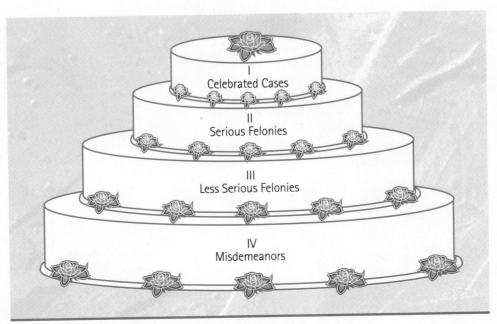

FIGURE 15.2 **The Criminal Justice "Wedding Cake"**

SOURCE: Based on Samuel Walker, *Sense and Nonsense about Crime* (Belmont, Calif.: Wadsworth Publishers, 1985).

jury trials, and elaborate appeals. Because the public hears so much about these cases, they believe them to be a norm, but in reality, they do not represent how the system really operates.

The second and third layers of the cake are made up of serious felonies encountered daily in urban jurisdictions around the United States, such as robberies, burglaries, rapes, and homicides. Those that fall in the second layer do so by virtue of their seriousness, the prior record of the defendant, and the defendant's relationship to the victim. For example, police treat a burglary in which thousands of dollars are stolen quite differently than a simple break-in that netted the criminal a stereo.[20] Similarly, a gang rape of an investment banker is perceived by criminal justice decision makers as being more serious than the rape of a female acquaintance during a fraternity beer party. The more serious second-layer crimes are likely to be prosecuted to the fullest extent of the law, and if convicted, these offenders will receive lengthy prison sentences. In contrast, felonies relegated to the third layer because the amount of money taken is relatively small or the damage done trivial will usually be dealt with an outright dismissal, a plea bargain, a reduction in charges, and a probationary sentence.

The fourth layer of the cake is made up of the millions of misdemeanors, such as disorderly conduct, shoplifting, public drunkenness, passing bad checks, and minor assault. These are handled by the lower criminal courts in assembly-line fashion. Few defendants insist on exercising their constitutional rights because the delay would cost them valuable time and money. Since the typical penalty is a small fine, everyone wants to get the case over with and move on to other matters. Malcolm Feeley's study of the lower court in New Haven, Connecticut, found that in a sense, the experience of going to court is the real punishment in a misdemeanor case; few (4.9 percent) of the cases involved any jail time.[21]

Is There a Criminal Justice Wedding Cake?

The wedding cake model is an intriguing alternative to the traditional criminal justice flow chart. According to Walker's view, the outcome of cases in the criminal justice system is a function of how they are evaluated by decision makers. Within each layer, there is a high degree of consistency; regardless of the size of the jurisdiction, high-profile cases will get serious treatment that differs markedly from the attention and time given to run-of-the-mill felonies.

Support for the wedding cake model comes from research that shows that the criminal justice system acts like a funnel in which a great majority of cases are screened out before trial. As Figure 15.3 shows, at each stage of the system, cases are dismissed and relatively few reach the trial stage. Those that do are more likely to be handled with a plea bargain than a criminal trial. The funnel indicates that the justice system does not treat all felonies alike; it is only the relatively few and most likely serious cases that make it through to the end of the formal process.[22]

The Walker model is useful because it helps us realize that all too often, public opinion about criminal justice is formed on the basis of what happened in a few celebrated cases. In fact, criminal justice experts commonly view the process as being dominated by judges, prosecutors, and defense counsels who work in concert to get cases processed; this spirit of cooperation is referred to as the *courtroom work group*. The tired assistant district attorney, irritable judge, and overworked public defender who get together to settle cases involving lower-class victims and offenders are now common characters in TV shows, films, and books. In contrast are the celebrated cases, such as that of the Menendez brothers, which inspire movies and TV miniseries and attract top criminal lawyers.

≡ Criminal Justice and the Rule of Law

For many years, U.S. courts exercised little control over the operations of criminal justice agencies, believing that their actions were not an area of judicial concern. This policy is referred to as the *hands-off doctrine*. However, in the 1960s, under the guidance of Chief Justice Earl Warren, the U.S. Supreme Court became more active in the affairs of the justice system, thereby lifting the hands-off doctrine. Today, each component of the justice system is closely supervised by state and federal courts. In this section, we will review the influence of the rule of law on criminal justice agencies and discuss how it affects daily operations and decision making.

Procedural Laws

The law of criminal procedure guarantees citizens certain rights and privileges when they are accused of crime. Procedural laws control the action of the agencies

FIGURE 15.3   **The Criminal Justice Funnel**

SOURCE: Edward Lisefski and Donald Manson, *Tracking Offenders, 1984* (Washington, D.C.: Bureau of Justice Statistics, 1988): Patrick Langan, *Felony Sentences in State Courts, 1986* (Washington, D.C.: Bureau of Justice Statistics, 1989).

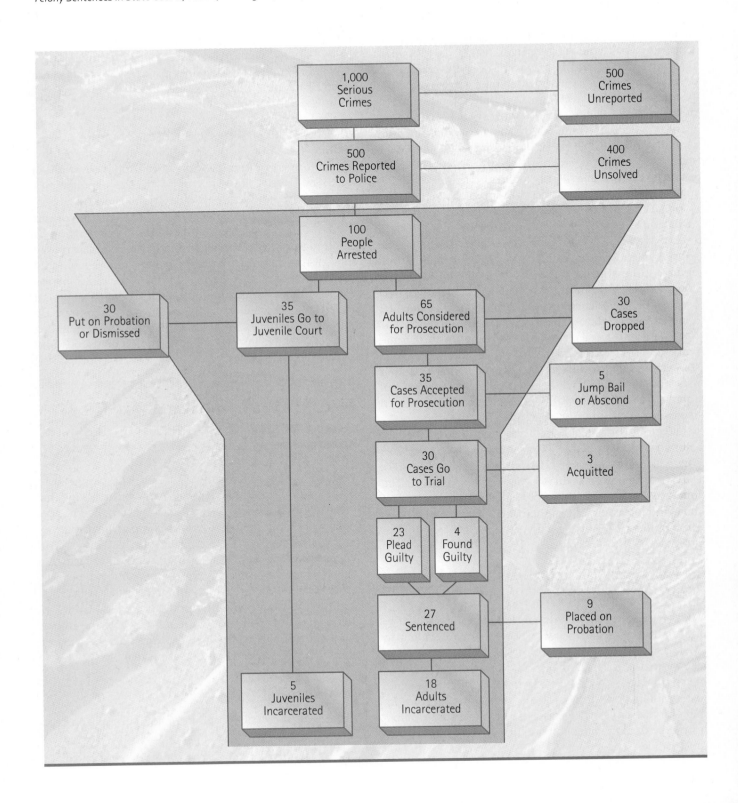

of justice and define the rights of criminal defendants. They first come into play when people are suspected of committing crimes and the police wish to investigate them, search their property, interrogate them, and so on. Here, the law answers such questions as: Can the police search my home if I don't want them to? Do I have to answer their questions even if I don't want to? If a formal charge is filed, procedural laws guide pretrial and trial activities. For example, they determine when and if people can obtain state-financed attorneys or when they can be released on bail. If, after a trial, a person is found guilty of committing a criminal offense, procedural laws guide the posttrial and correctional process. For example, they determine when a conviction can be appealed.

Procedural laws have several different sources. Most important are the first ten amendments of the U.S. Constitution, ratified in 1791 and generally called the **Bill of Rights.** The original Constitution, ratified in 1788, set up the structure of government and set out the rights and duties of its executive, legislative, and judicial branches. However, aware of the abuses people had been subjected to by royal decree in England and its colonies, the framers of the Constitution wanted to ensure that the national government could not usurp the personal rights of citizens. Therefore, the Bill of Rights guaranteed, among other things, the right of the people to practice the religion of their choice, have freedom of speech and press, be secure in their homes from unwarranted intrusion by government agents, and be protected against cruel punishments, such as torture.

The guarantees of freedom contained in the Bill of Rights initially applied only to the federal government and did not affect the individual states. Then, in 1868, the Fourteenth Amendment made the first ten amendments to the Constitution binding on the state governments. However, it has remained the duty of state and federal court systems to interpret constitutional law and develop a body of case law that spells out the exact procedural rights to which a person is entitled. For example, the Sixth Amendment states that a person has the right to be represented by legal counsel at a criminal trial. This right once had little meaning, because many criminal defendants were indigent and could not afford to pay for their legal defense. Then, in 1963, the U.S. Supreme Court interpreted the Sixth Amendment to mean that all people accused of felonies had the right to counsel; if they could not afford an attorney, the state had to provide the funds to hire one for them. Thus, it is the U.S. Supreme Court that interprets the Constitution and sets out the procedural laws that must be followed by the lower federal and state courts. If the Supreme Court has not ruled on a procedural issue, then the lower courts are free to interpret the Constitution as they see fit.

Court Decision Making

Until the passage of the Fourteenth Amendment, the rights and privileges made binding on the federal government by the first ten amendments did not apply to the states. However, ratification of the Fourteenth Amendment did not mean that the granting of rights and liberties was an automatic process. Instead, each right was decided on when cases dealing with the particular issue came before the Supreme Court. Determining how to incorporate the rights into state criminal procedures became a topic of some debate. In the late 1930s, the Supreme Court developed the concept of fundamental fairness and used it to guide its own decision making. Under this concept, if the Supreme Court decided that a particular guarantee in the Bill of Rights was fundamental to and implicit in the U.S. system of justice, it would hold that guarantee applicable to the states. This became the method by which states could be held to the same standards of criminal due process as the federal government.

With this formula, the provisions of the Bill of Rights were incorporated by the states, case by case. In 1953, Earl Warren became the Chief Justice of the U.S. Supreme Court; under his leadership, the due process movement reached its peak. Numerous landmark cases focusing on the rights of the accused were decided, and a revolution in constitutional criminal procedure resulted. The Warren Court granted many new rights to those accused of crimes and went so far as to impose specific guidelines on the policies of police, courts, and correctional services to ensure that due process of law would be maintained. Under Warren's replacements, first Warren Berger and current Chief Justice William Rehnquist, the Court has moved somewhat more cautiously in granting additional rights; and in some areas, such as capital punishment and prisoners' rights, the Court has reversed the trend toward liberalism established by the Warren Court.

Because the makeup of the Supreme Court has changed under the Clinton administration and procedural laws are subject to different interpretations, Court decision making remains fluid. The Constitution and Bill of Rights are fairly abstract documents; hence, there is much leeway as to the direction and content of procedural laws—what is law today may not be tomorrow.

Of the criminal justice issues the courts deal with, few are as important and have as much influence on the justice system as the concept of *due process* and the *exclusionary rule*. Therefore, these legal issues will be reviewed here in some detail.

Due Process

The concept of *due process* is mentioned in the Fifth (where it is applied to the federal government) and Fourteenth Amendments (where it is applied to the states) of the U.S. Constitution. It is usually divided into substantive and procedural areas. The substantive aspects are generally used to determine whether a statute is fair, reasonable, and appropriate use of the legal power of the legislature. The concept of substantive due process was used extensively in the 1930s and 1940s to invalidate minimum-wage standards, price-fixing, and employment restriction statutes. Today, it is used more sparingly; for example, it may be employed to hold that criminal statutes dealing with disorderly conduct, capital punishment, or a ban on pornography may be unconstitutional because they are arbitrary, vague, or unreasonable.

Much more important today are the procedural aspects of due process. In seeking to define the term, most legal experts indicate that it refers to the essential elements of fairness under law. An elaborate and complex definition of *due process* is found in *Black's Law Dictionary:*

> Due process of law in each particular case means such an exercise of the powers of government as the settled maxims of law permit and sanction, and under such safeguards for the protection of individual rights as those maxims prescribe for the class of cases to which the one in question belongs.[23]

This definition refers to the need for rules and procedures in the legal system to protect individual rights. The objectives of due process help define the term even more explicitly. Due process seeks to ensure that no person will be deprived of life, liberty, or property without notice of charges, assistance from legal counsel, a hearing, and an opportunity to confront accusers. Basically, due process is intended to guarantee that functional fairness exists in each individual case. This doctrine of fairness as expressed in due process of the law is guaranteed under both the Fifth and Fourteenth Amendments.

Abstract definitions are only one aspect of due process. Much more significant are the procedures that give meaning to due process in the everyday practices of the criminal justice system. In this regard, due process provides numerous procedural safeguards for the offender, including:

- Notice of charges
- A formal hearing
- The right to counsel or some other representation
- The opportunity to respond to charges
- The opportunity to confront and cross-examine witnesses and accusers
- The privilege to be free from self-incrimination
- The opportunity to present one's own witnesses
- A decision made on the basis of substantial evidence and facts produced at the hearing
- A written statement of the reasons for the decision
- An appellate review procedure

Exactly what constitutes due process in a specific case depends on the facts of the case, the federal and state constitutional and statutory provisions, previous court decisions, and the ideas and principles that society considers important at a given time and in a given place.[24] Justice Felix Frankfurter emphasized this point in *Rochin v. California* (1952), when he wrote:

> Due process of law requires an evaluation based on a disinterested inquiry, pursued in the spirit of science on a balanced order or facts, exactly and clearly stated, on the detached consideration of conflicting claims . . . on a judgement not ad hoc and episodic but duly mindful of reconciling the needs both of continuity and of change in a progressive society.[25]

Both the elements and the definition of due process seem to be flexible and constantly changing. For example, due process at one time did not require a formal hearing for parole revocation, but today it does. Before 1968, juvenile offenders did not have the right to an attorney at their adjudication; counsel is now required in the juvenile court system. Thus, the interpretations of due process of law reflect what society deems fair and just at a particular time and in a particular place. The degree of loss suffered by the individual (victim or offender) balanced against the state's interest also determines which and how many due process requirements are ordinarily applied. When the accused person's freedom is at stake in the criminal justice system, all applicable due process rights are usually granted; in other cases, due process may be modified.

Changing Concepts of Due Process

In recent years, the concept of due process as applied by the courts seems to be changing. The balance of fairness is shifting away from the criminal, and emphasis instead is being placed more squarely on the needs of the states to protect their citizens. The rights of both those accused of crime and those convicted of crime have been curtailed. For example, police have been given a freer hand in questioning suspects, searching for evidence, and obtaining search warrants. For example, in a 1991 case, *Arizona v. Fulminate,* the Court ruled that convictions would not be automatically overturned even if it is shown that police officers used coercion to obtain confessions. The Court ruled that it is possible that a coerced confession could be "harmless error" if there were other evidence sufficient to convict the suspect.[26] Similarly, the Court has allowed the resumption of the death penalty with fewer judicial restraints. In *McClesky v. Zant,* the Court limited the ability of death row inmates to appeal their cases to federal courts, paving the way for faster turnover in capital punishment cases.[27]

These and similar cases give weight to the charge that the Supreme Court has shifted the balance of due process away from the criminal offender and embraced a crime control emphasis. The Court may be responding to recent victim surveys, which indicate that more than half of all Americans believe the justice system favors defendant's rights over the rights of crime victims.[28]

While such policy shifts are not uncommon, the basic concept of due process has a secure place in our legal system. Freedom from self-incrimination, the right to legal representation at all stages of the justice system, a fair hearing and trial, and sentencing review are rights that are immutable. And while courts continue to redefine rights, they do so in the spirit of granting fairness to the criminal defendant without sacrificing the public interest.

In this context, the focus has turned to the exclusionary rule, considered by some to be a cornerstone of individual freedom and by others to be a serious impediment to public safety.

The Exclusionary Rule

If constitutional rights are to be anything more than pious pronouncements, then some measurable consequence must be attached to their violation. It would be intolerable if the guarantee against unreasonable search and seizure could be violated without practical consequences.[29]

The foundation of the **exclusionary rule** is contained in the Fourth Amendment of the Constitution, which states:

The right of the people to be secure in their persons, houses, papers, and effects, against unreasonable searches and seizures, shall not be violated and no warrant shall issue, but upon probable cause, supported by Oath or affirmation, and particularly describing the place to be searched, and the persons or things to be seized.

The primary function of the Fourth Amendment is to protect the individual against an illegal arrest and prevent illegal searches and seizures of a person's possessions. This means that police must follow certain guidelines in searching for and seizing evidence. As a rule, they must have a properly drawn-up search warrant that is obtained from a court officer after evidence is presented that a crime has occurred and there is probable cause to believe that the person or place to be searched is involved in it; the police cannot act arbitrarily.

Over the years, the Court has articulated exceptions to the search warrant rule. In other words, there are times, such as when a suspect volunteers to be searched, that a warrant need not be obtained. The standard as stated in the Fourth Amendment is that of reasonableness, and the Supreme Court has gone to great lengths to explain and interpret what this means. In doing so, the Court has balanced the individual's right to privacy, protected by the Fourth Amendment, with the right of the public to be protected against crime. Consequently, there exists a large body of case law describing how searches are to be conducted, when police can seize evidence, when search warrants are needed, and so on.

The Fourth Amendment clearly states that an individual's right against unreasonable searches and seizures is to be protected. However, for many years, evidence obtained in violation of the Fourth Amendment was admitted in criminal trials, even though it should have been considered illegal. In 1914, the Supreme Court rectified this injustice in the case of *Weeks v. United States.*[30] The defendant, Weeks, was accused of the federal violation of using the mails for illegal purposes. The evidence on which he was convicted was acquired through a search of his room without a valid search warrant. The Supreme Court ruled that in a federal criminal trial, evidence acquired through an unreasonable search and seizure must be excluded; it could neither be mentioned nor used at trial. Thus, the exclusionary rule was established.

The ruling in *Weeks* applied only to the federal government. The states were still free to admit evidence obtained by unreasonable searches and seizures. It was not until 1961, in the case of *Mapp v. Ohio,* that the Supreme Court made the exclusionary rule applicable to the states.[31] Thus, for the first time, the Supreme Court required that state law enforcement employees follow federal constitutional standards.

The exclusionary rule has been one of the most controversial aspects of justice system legal control. Its opponents argue that it permits the guilty to go free if the police err in the handling of a case. The rights of honest citizens and society as a whole are threatened because of arbitrary court rulings. The rule weakens the power of the justice system to deter crime because victims and witnesses are reluctant to come forward for fear that an obviously guilty defendant will be released on a technicality.

Those who favor the exclusionary rule find that it is one of the cornerstones of our freedom and that it protects us from becoming a police state in which law enforcement agents have a free hand to use any means at their disposal to investigate crime. Without the exclusionary rule, houses could be broken into, phones tapped, people searched, and cars stopped—with impunity. The exclusionary rule separates our society from those "evil" totalitarian regimes that we read about in the newspapers.

In sum, the exclusionary rule means that evidence judged to be improperly obtained by police through illegal interrogation of suspects or searches of their person and property cannot be used (or even mentioned) against them in a court of law. It is as if the evidence did not exist.

The Future of the Exclusionary Rule

The exclusionary rule is under legal attack. For example, in *Illinois v. Gates,* the Supreme Court allowed the use of a search warrant that had been obtained upon consideration of information contained in an anonymous letter to police; prior to *Gates,* warrants had to based on verifiable information.[32] Then in two cases, *United States v. Leon*[33] and *Massachusetts v. Sheppard,*[34] the Supreme Court spelled out what is known as the **good faith exception** to the rule. The Court said that if police officers acted in what they believed to be a proper manner in obtaining

evidence and it was discovered later that they or a magistrate had made an unintentional legal or administrative error invalidating the search warrant, the evidence might still be admitted in a court of law. In other cases, the Court has allowed police to use overflights to spy on drug growers without the use of a warrant.[35]

Critics believe that these and similar cases foretell a new era of a weakened exclusionary rule.[36] There seems little doubt that the nation's courts are now granting the police and other agencies of justice greater leeway in conducting their business, even if it means restricting the rights of criminal suspects. But how much will these measures actually affect the justice system? Studies indicate that exclusionary rule violations occur rather infrequently.[37] Research evidence suggests that only 1 to 2 percent of all criminal cases are rejected because police made a technical legal error resulting in the invocation of the exclusionary rule. Only in narcotics-related offenses were a significant number of cases terminated because of exclusionary rule violations, and there again, the percentages were smaller than might be expected—under 3 percent in the jurisdictions surveyed. Police appear more apt to illegally seize evidence in narcotics cases because there is usually no victim or complaining party to help them obtain proper search warrants.

In an important analysis, Craig Uchida and Timothy Bynum studied "lost cases" in which evidence was suppressed even though police had obtained a search warrant. Less than 1 percent of the cases they evaluated (15 of 1,748) involved evidence suppressed because of exclusionary rule violations. Uchida and Bynum conclude that when obtaining warrants, police officers do in fact make an effort to obey the dictates of the Fourth Amendment, and that consequently, the legal "cost" of the exclusionary rule is slight.[38]

Though abolishing or severely limiting the exclusionary rule might have relatively little effect on the justice system, the rule itself is of great symbolic value. It stands for the right to privacy and the primacy of the individual over the state. Even if relatively few cases are thrown out of court on exclusionary rule violations, knowing of its existence places law enforcement agents on notice: obey constitutional limitations, respect the individual's right to privacy, or pay the consequences in court. The exclusionary rule must be evaluated not by those few cases that come under public scrutiny but by the millions of others in which police power is limited by the rule's influence.

In the following chapters, the effect of the law on the individual components of the justice system will be reviewed in greater detail. Table 15.1 summarizes some of the more important constitutional cases that define procedural law.

≡ Concepts of Justice

Many justice system operations are controlled by the rule of law, but they are also influenced by the various philosophies or viewpoints held by its practitioners and policy makers. These, in turn, have been influenced by criminological theory and research. Knowledge about crime, its causes, and its control has significantly affected perceptions of how criminal justice should be managed.

Not surprisingly, many competing views of justice exist simultaneously in our culture. Those in favor of one position or another try to win public opinion to their side, hoping to influence legislative, judicial, or administrative decision making. Over the years, different philosophical viewpoints tend to predominate, only to fall into disfavor as programs based on their principles fail to prove effective.

Below, the most important concepts of criminal justice are briefly discussed.

Crime Control Model

Those espousing the crime control model believe that the overriding purpose of the justice system is protection of the public, deterrence of criminal behavior, and incapacitation of known criminals. Those who embrace its principles view the justice system as a barrier between destructive criminal elements and conventional society. Speedy and efficient justice, unencumbered by legal red tape and followed by punishment designed to fit the crime, is the goal of advocates of the crime control model. Its disciples promote such policies as increasing the size of police forces, maximizing the use of discretion, building more prisons, using the death penalty, and reducing legal controls on the justice system.

The crime control model has its roots in classical theory. Fear of criminal sanctions is viewed as the primary deterrent to crime. Since criminals are rational and choose to commit crime, it stands to reason that their activities can be controlled if the costs of crime become too high. Swift, sure, and efficient justice are considered essential elements of an orderly society.

The crime control philosophy emphasizes the protection of society and the compensation of victims. The criminal is someone who is responsible for his or her actions, who has broken faith with society and chosen to violate the law for reasons of anger, greed, revenge, and so forth. Therefore, money spent should be directed not at making criminals more comfortable but on increasing the efficiency of police to apprehend them and the courts to effectively try them. As David Garland suggests, criminal punishments have only a limited ability to change the wicked. Instead, they can enforce cultural values and express the conviction that crime will not be tolerated. Punishments are symbolic of the legitimate social order and the power societies have to regulate behavior and punish those who break social rules.[39]

The crime control philosophy has become a dominant force in American justice. Fear of crime in the 1960s and 1970s was coupled with a growing skepticism about the effectiveness of rehabilitation efforts. A number of important reviews claimed that treatment and rehabilitation efforts directed at known criminals just did not work.[40] For example, in an impressive review, Kathleen Maguire and her associates found that inmates in New York correctional institutions who participated in a prison work program were as likely to recidivate upon release as nonparticipants.[41] The Maguire research is similar to other efforts that find little clear evidence that correctional treatment programs are effective.[42]

The lack of clear-cut evidence that criminals can be successfully treated has produced a climate in which conservative, hard-line solutions to the crime problem are being sought. The results of this swing can be seen in such phenomena as the resumption of the death penalty, erosion of the exclusionary rule, prison overcrowding, and attacks on the insanity defense.

Justice Model

> Principled and fair punishment for wrongdoing treats individuals as persons and as human beings rather than as objects. Punishment is an affirmation of the autonomy, responsibility, and dignity of the individual; paternalistic rehabilitative treatment is a denial of all three.[43]

One of the newer models of criminal justice is known as the justice model.[44] First articulated by corrections expert David Fogel, the justice model contains elements of both liberal and conservative philosophies. Put another way, it is an essentially conservative view that is palatable to liberals because of its emphasis on fairness and due process.

Essentially, the justice model holds that it is futile to rehabilitate criminals because treatment programs are

TABLE 15.1 Some Leading Constitutional Cases and Their Findings

The Police Process

Mapp v. Ohio,
367 U.S. 643 (1961)

When evidence is obtained in violation of the Fourth Amendment's right against unreasonable searches and seizures, it is not admissible in a state trial. This case made the exclusionary rule applicable to the states through the due process clause of the Fourteenth Amendment.

Miranda v. Arizona,
384 U.S. 436 (1966)

The police have a duty to warn a suspect in custody of the basic Fifth Amendment right against self-incrimination. If the warning is not given, any statement made by the defendant must be excluded from the evidence.

Katz v. United States,
389 U.S. 347 (1967)

The Fourth Amendment protects a person's right to privacy at all times and is not limited to certain places or property. A search occurs whenever police activity violates a person's privacy.

Bumper v. North Carolina,
391 U.S. 543 (1968)

For a consent search to be effective, the consent must be voluntary; threat or compulsion will invalidate the search.

Terry v. Ohio,
392 U.S. 1 (1968)

Even though there is no probable cause to arrest, the police have the power to stop an individual and conduct a pat-down search of outer clothing for weapons, if an officer has reasonable belief that a threat to safety exists.

Chimel v. California,
395 U.S. 752 (1969)

In a search incident to an arrest, the police are allowed to search only the defendant and the surroundings that are under the defendant's immediate control.

Steagald v. United States,
451 U.S. 204 (1981)

The Fourth Amendment privacy principle applies not only when searching a home for property but also when searching a home for a person.

New York v. Belton,
453 U.S. 454 (1981)

The passenger compartment of a car is within the scope of a search when an arrest takes place after the car is stopped for a speeding violation.

United States v. Ross,
72 L.Ed.2d 572 (1982)

Opening and searching without a warrant the closed opaque containers found in a car is legal if the officers have probable cause to believe that contraband is concealed somewhere in the car.

Illinois v. Gates,
103 S.Ct. 2317 (1983)

A judge may issue a search warrant based on the "totality of the circumstances" of the case.

New York v. Quarles,
104 S.Ct. 2626 (1984)

A suspect's statements made without benefit of the Miranda warning are admissible if "public safety" is at risk.

Nix v. Williams,
104 S.Ct. 2501 (1984)

Evidence can be seized without a warrant if it would have been "inevitably discovered by police officers."

United States v. Leon,
104 S.Ct. 3405 (1984)

Evidence may be admitted to trial even if a search warrant was faulty but the police officers acted on "good faith."

Moran v. Burbine,
106 S.Ct. 1135 (1986)

Police need not tell suspects in custody about a call from their attorney.

Colorado v. Connelly,
107 S.Ct. 515 (1986)

Mentally impaired defendants can waive their Miranda rights.

Arizona v. Hicks,
107 S.Ct. 1149 (1987)

Probable cause is required to invoke the plain view doctrine.

Colorado v. Spring
107 S.Ct. 851 (1987)

A suspect need not be aware of all the topics of questioning for the Miranda waiver to be valid.

California v. Greenwood,
105 S.Ct. 1625 (1988)

Police do not need a warrant to search trash left at the curbside.

Maryland v. Buie,
110 S.Ct. 1093 (1990)

Police may make a "protective sweep" of the premises while enforcing an arrest warrant.

Arizona v. Fulminate
(1991)

A confession may be used at trial even if police used coercion when it was acquired.

The Trial Stage

Powell v. Alabama,
287 U.S. 45 (1932)

The state must provide counsel to an indigent defendant who is prosecuted for a capital offense.

Gideon v. Wainwright, 372 U.S. 335 (1963)	An indigent defendant subjected to a felony prosecution must have counsel provided by the state. This Sixth Amendment right was made applicable to the states through the due process clause of the Fourteenth Amendment.
Klopfer v. North Carolina 387 U.S. 213 (1967)	The Sixth Amendment right to a speedy trial is applicable to the states through the due process clause of the Fourteenth Amendment.
Duncan v. Louisiana, 391 U.S. 145 (1968)	The Sixth Amendment right to a jury trial when the defendant is accused of a serious offense is applicable to the states through the due process clause of the Fourteenth Amendment.
North Carolina v. Pearce, 395 U.S. 711 (1969)	A judge who imposes a more severe sentence upon reconviction must state the reasons for the more severe sentence on the record.
Benton v. Maryland, 395 U.S. 784 (1969)	The Fifth Amendment protection against double jeopardy is applicable to the states through the due process clause of the Fourteenth Amendment.
Baldwin v. New York, 399 U.S. 66 (1970)	A defendant has a constitutional right to a jury trial under the Sixth and Fourteenth Amendments when the penalty is imprisonment for six months or more.
Williams v. Florida, 399 U.S. 78 (1970)	A six-person jury fulfills a defendant's Sixth Amendment right to a jury trial.
Argersinger v. Hamlin, 407 U.S. 25 (1972)	The state must provide an indigent defendant with counsel in any case in which the sentence results in imprisonment, regardless of whether the crime is classified as a misdemeanor or a felony.
Apodica v. Oregon, 406 U.S. 404 (1972)	A criminal conviction by less than a unanimous jury verdict in a non–first-degree murder case is constitutional under the Sixth and Fourteenth Amendments when a 12-person jury is used.
Barker v. Wingo, 407 U.S. 514 (1972)	Four factors must be considered when determining whether a defendant's right to a speedy trial has been violated: (1) length of the delay; (2) reason for the delay; (3) defendant's assertion of the right; and (4) prejudice to the defendant.
Strunk v. United States, 412 U.S. 434 (1973)	When a person's right to a speedy trial is violated, the charges against the person must be dismissed.
Richmond Newspapers v. Virginia, 448 U.S. 555 (1980)	The press has the right to attend and report on trials.
Strickland v. Washington 104 S.Ct. 2052 (1984)	Defendants have a right to effective, competent counsel in criminal cases.
United States v. Salerno, 107 S.Ct. 2095 (1987)	A dangerous person may be held in pretrial detention without bail.

Sentencing and Corrections

Gagnon v. Scarpelli, 411 U.S. 778 (1973)	Probationers and parolees are entitled to limited representation of counsel at revocation hearings.
Wolff v. McDonnell, 418 U.S. 539 (1974)	Prisoners who may face sanctions because of disciplinary problems are entitled to a hearing to defend their behavior.
Gregg v. Georgia, 482 U.S. 153 (1976)	The death penalty may be applied when aggravating circumstances exist in a murder case, such as murder for profit.
Estelle v. Gamble, 429 U.S. 97 (1976)	An inmate is entitled to proper medical care.
Rhodes v. Chapman, 452 U.S. 337 (1981)	Prisoners may be forced to share a cell if prison overcrowding exists.
McClesky v. Kemp, 107 S.Ct. 1756 (1987)	The death penalty is not unconstitutional, even if it can be shown that black offenders in general have a greater chance of receiving it in a particular jurisdiction.
McClesky v. Zant (1991)	The use of habeas corpus to appeal death sentences is limited, barring error.

The jury listens as defending counsel questions a witness during a murder trial in Orange County Superior Court, Santa Ana, California. The Due Process Model's stress on legal fairness and procedural regularity requires a guarantee that such trials be held in a fair manner before an impartial jury.

ineffective. Moreover, rehabilitation models, which include individualized treatment and discretion, are basically an unfair violation of the constitutional right to equal protection. If two people commit the same crime but receive different sentences because one is receptive to treatment and the other not, the consequence is a sense of injustice in the criminal justice system and inmate anger at those who placed them in an institution. Beyond these problems, justice advocates find fault with both crime control and rehabilitation models because they depend on predicting what offenders will do in the future when deciding what to do with them in the present.

As an alternative, the justice model calls for fairness in criminal procedure. This would mean *determinate sentencing,* in which all offenders in a particular crime category would receive the same sentence. Furthermore, prisons would be viewed as places of just and even-handed punishment and not rehabilitation. Parole would be abolished to avoid the discretionary unfairness associated with that mechanism of early release.

The justice model has had an important influence on criminal justice policy making. Some states have adopted flat sentencing statutes and have limited the use of parole. There is a trend toward giving prison sentences because people deserve punishment rather than because the sentences will deter or rehabilitate them.

Due Process Model

In *The Limits of the Criminal Sanction,* Herbert Packer contrasted the crime control model with an opposing view that he referred to as the due process model.[45] According to Packer, the *due process model* combines elements of liberal/positivist criminology with the legal concept of procedural fairness for the accused. Those who adhere to due process principles believe in individualized justice, treatment, and rehabilitation of the offender. If discretion exists in the criminal justice system, it should be used to evaluate the treatment needs of the offender. Most important, the civil rights of the accused should be protected at all costs. This means such practices as strict scrutiny of police search and interrogation procedures, review of sentencing policies, and development of prisoners' rights.

Advocates of the due process model have demanded that competent defense counsel, jury trials, and other procedural safeguards be offered to every criminal defendant. They have also called for establishing procedures to make public the operations of the justice system and placing controls over their discretionary power.

For obvious reasons, proponents of the due process philosophy are usually members of the legal profession who see themselves as protectors of civil rights. They view overzealous cops as violators of the basic constitutional rights that make our country great. Similarly, they are skeptical about the intentions of meddling social workers, whose treatments often entail greater confinement and penalties than punishment ever did. Due process is there to protect citizens—both from those who wish to punish them and those who wish to treat them without regard for legal and civil rights.

Advocates of the due process orientation are quick to point out that the justice system remains an adversary process that pits the forces of an all-powerful state against those of a solitary individual accused of crime. If an overwhelming concern for justice and fairness did not exist, the defendant who lacked resources could easily be overwhelmed. They point to miscarriages of justice, such as the Gary Dotson case, as examples of what could happen if our vigilance is let down for a moment. As you may recall, Dotson was the young man imprisoned for rape only to be released years later when his accuser recanted her testimony. Since such mistakes can happen, all criminal defendants deserve the fullest protection of the law.

The due process orientation has not fared well in recent years. The movement to grant greater civil rights protections to criminal defendants has been undermined by Supreme Court decisions expanding the police officer's ability to search and seize evidence and to question suspects. Similarly, the movement between 1960 and 1980 to grant prison inmates an ever-increasing share of constitutional protections has been curtailed. There is growing evidence that the desire to protect the public has overshadowed concerns for the rights of criminal defendants. And while most of the most important legal rights won by criminal defendants in the 1960s and 1970s remain untouched (for example, the right to have a fair and impartial jury of one's peers), there was little urgency to increase the scope of civil rights in the more conservative 1990s.

Rehabilitation Model

The rehabilitation model embraces the notion that given the proper care and treatment, criminals can be changed into productive, law-abiding citizens. Influenced by positivist criminology, the rehabilitation school suggests that people commit crimes through no fault of their own. Instead, criminals themselves are the victims of social injustice, poverty, and racism; and their acts are a response to a society that has betrayed them. And, because of their disturbed and impoverished upbringing, they may

be suffering psychological problems and personality disturbances that further enhance their crime-committing capabilities. While the general public wants protection from crime, the argument goes, it also favors programs designed to help unfortunate people who commit crime because of emotional and or social problems.[46]

To deal effectively with crime, its root causes must be attacked. First, funds must be devoted to equalize access to conventional means of success. This means supporting such programs as Aid to Dependent Children, educational opportunity, and job training. If individuals run afoul of the law, efforts should be made to treat and not punish them. This means emphasizing counseling and psychological care in community-based treatment programs. Whenever possible, offenders should be placed on probation in halfway houses or in other rehabilitation-oriented programs.

This view of the justice system portrays it as a method for dispensing "treatment" to needy "patients." Also known as the "medical model," it portrays offenders as people who, because they have failed to exercise self-control, need the help of the state. The medical model rejects the crime control philosophy on the ground that it ignores the needs of offenders, who are people whom society has failed to help. The popularity of the medical model reached its zenith in the 1950s and 1960s; enthusiasm for it waned in the conservative, crime control-oriented 1970s, 1980s, and into the 1990s.

Yet rehabilitation still retains its enthusiasts. In contradistinction to literature reviews that find that treatment has little or no effect on known offenders, competing analyses find that a number of programs can have an important influence on offenders.[47] Paul Gendreau and Robert Ross reviewed evaluations of rehabilitation programs and concluded that ". . . it is downright ridiculous to say 'Nothing works' . . . offender rehabilitation has been, can be and will be achieved."[48]

Nonintervention Model

In the late 1960s and 1970s, both the rehabilitation ideal and the due process movement were viewed suspiciously by experts concerned with the stigmatization of offenders. Regardless of the purpose, the more the government intervenes in the lives of people, the greater the harm done to their future behavior patterns.

Noninterventionist philosophy was influenced by Edwin Lemert's call for *judicious nonintervention*[49] and Edwin Schur's 1973 book, *Radical Nonintervention.*[50] These called for limiting government intrusion into the

CLOSE-UP

Criminal Justice Versus Civil Liberties

An area of the justice system that concerns civil libertarians is the use of the new technology to monitor suspected and convicted criminals. Does high tech pose a threat to civil liberties?

The new surveillance techniques operate on a number of levels. Computers are now used with extensive data retrieval systems to cross-reference people and activities. Personal and financial information available on national and local data bases (including credit ratings, bank holdings, stock transfers, medical information, and outstanding loans) can be accessed by law enforcement agencies.

Computer networks also contain criminal justice system information. The most well-known network is the National Crime Information Center operated by the Justice Department, which houses an extensive collection of arrest records, allowing local police departments to instantly determine whether a suspect has a record.

Technology has also been improved in visual and audio surveillance. The FBI has made national headlines filming and taping drug deals and organized crime meetings. Federal agents in New England were able to tape a Mafia induction ceremony involving members of the Patriarca family, complete with blood oaths and secret incantations. Hundreds of new devices make listening and watching more extensive and virtually self-sufficient. For example, audio listening devices that use lasers permit eavesdropping without having to enter a home or secure a warrant. Airborne cameras can monitor human movement from 30,000 feet and help spot fields of marijuana and other illegal drugs.

Also in use is electronic equipment that monitors offenders in the community. Instead of a prison or jail sentence, convicted offenders are placed under "house arrest" and kept under surveillance by a central computer. A government agency, most typically the probation department, keeps track of the offenders by requiring them to wear a nonremovable ankle or neck device that signals a computer if they move from their home without permission. The dangers represented by the new electronic surveillance are the subject of an important book by sociologist Gary Marx. He cites the following characteristics of the new surveillance techniques that set them apart from traditional methods of social control:

1. The new surveillance transcends distance, darkness, and physical barriers.
2. It transcends time; its records can be stored, retrieved, combined, analyzed, and communicated.
3. It has low visibility or is invisible.
4. It is often involuntary.

---

lives of people, especially minors, who run afoul of the law. They advocated *deinstitutionalization* of nonserious offenders, *diversion* from formal court processes into informal treatment programs, and *decriminalization* of nonserious offenses, such as the possession of small amounts of marijuana. Under this concept, the justice system should interact as little as possible with offenders. Police, courts, and correctional agencies would concentrate their efforts on diverting law violators out of the formal justice system, thereby helping them avoid the stigma of formal labels, such as "delinquent" or "ex-con." Programs instituted under this model include mediation (instead of trial), diversion (instead of formal processing), and community-based corrections (instead of secure corrections).

The popularity of the noninterventionist philosophy has cooled. There has been little evidence that alternative programs actually reduce recidivism rates. Similarly, critics charge that alternative programs result in *widening the net*.[51] This refers to the process by which efforts to remove people from the justice system actually enmesh them further within it by ordering them to spend more time in treatment than they would have had to spend in the formal legal process.

Despite such criticism, the nonintervention philosophy is alive and well. For example, the juvenile justice system has made a major effort to remove youths from adult jails and reduce the use of pretrial detention. Mediation programs have proven successful alternatives to formal trial process.[52] In the adult system, pretrial release programs (alternatives to bail) are now the norm instead of an experimental innovation. And, though the prison population is rising, probation remains the modal correctional treatment. New forms of probation featuring house arrest

5. Prevention of crime is a major emphasis.
6. It is capital- rather than labor-intensive.
7. It involves decentralized self-policing.
8. It triggers a shift from targeting a specific suspect to categorical suspicion of everyone.
9. It is more intensive.
10. It is more extensive.

According to Marx, the use of electronic eavesdropping and other modern surveillance methods has changed the relationship between police and the public. New techniques have overcome the physical limitations that existed when surveillance was a function of human labor. Today's electronic devices never rest, are undetectable, and can store information forever. People now may be required to aid in their own monitoring by wearing devices that keep them under scrutiny; electronic devices can follow suspects everywhere, can gather extensive information on them, and can include thousands in the information net. As Marx puts it:

Between the camera, tape recorder, the identity card, the metal detector, the tax form, and the computer, everyone becomes a reasonable target.

Marx warns that the dangers of the new surveillance include a redefinition of the concept of "invasion of privacy" in which almost any personal information is open to scrutiny, "fishing expeditions" in which the government can do a general check on a citizen without a court order, and the possiblity that machine error will destroy the lives of innocent people. He cautions us:

The first task of a society that would have liberty and privacy is to guard against the misuse of physical coercion on the part of the state and private parties. The second task is to guard against "softer" forms of secret and manipulative control. Because these are often subtle, indirect, invisible, diffuse, deceptive, and shrouded in benign justifications, this is clearly the more difficult task.

It seems evident that agents of the justice system must confront the issue of privacy: How much control is needed? What are its most important targets? What are the most effective and efficient social control strategies? How can the need for control be balanced with concern for civil rights and personal liberty?

Discussion Questions
1. Should all evidence be admissible in criminal trials, even if obtaining it involved an invasion of the suspect's privacy?
2. Should law enforcement agencies be allowed to access bank, financial, and educational records without notifying the suspect?

SOURCE: Gary Marx, *Undercover, Police Surveillance in America* (Berkeley: University of California Press, 1988); quotes from pp. 217–219, 233.

---

and the electronic monitoring of offenders by computers may be the next major form of corrections (more on this in Chapter 18).

In the future, the nonintervention philosophy will be aided by the rising cost of justice. Though low-impact, nonintrusive programs may work no better than prison, they are certainly cheaper! At a time of high state and federal budget deficits, program costs may take greater consideration over program effectiveness.

Radical Model

There is also a radical/conflict view of the justice system. Radicals reject the due process-crime control dichotomy. Instead, they view the justice system as a "state-initiated and state-supported effort to rationalize mechanisms of social control."[53] The criminologist's role is to expose the aspects of the justice system that are designed to specifically control or exploit the laboring classes. Conflict criminologists call this *praxis,* the bringing about through writings, discussion, or social action a transformation of the current arrangements and relationships in society.

Radical thinkers argue that current crime control-oriented programs are counterproductive; they may actually help produce crime by undermining the lower classes, for example, by severely punishing already at-risk kids.[54] Some radical thinkers have called for a return to "War on Poverty" type programs popular in the 1960s, including the creation of better education opportunities, full employment, and national service; these ideas are not dissimilar from prevailing liberal social welfare policies.[55]

Some radical thinkers have called for peacemaking concepts to be introduced into the justice system. They believe that correctional programs should be instituted that help law violators heal emotionally.[56] Conceptualization of behavior should be expanded in a more spiritual direction so that a more complete understanding of human action can be developed.[57] "The funds that have been allocated to crime have gone to fighting those who suffer from the harms of a mean-spirited capitalist economy," argues Richard Quinney. "A criminology that can end suffering and thereby reduce crime requires criminologists of sound mind and gentle heart, peacemakers of the world."[58]

Criminal Justice Today

The various philosophies of justice compete today for dominance in the criminal justice system (see Figure 15.4). Each has supporters who lobby diligently for their positions. At the time of this writing, it seems that the crime control and justice models have captured the support of legislators and the general public. There is a growing emphasis on protection of the public, supplemented with attempts to create fair and equal punish-

ments. These issues are addressed in the above Close-Up entitled "Criminal Justice versus Civil Liberties."

But this is not to say that the other views of justice have been abandoned. Police, courts, and correctional agencies still supply a wide range of treatment alternatives to criminal offenders at all stages of the justice system. Whenever possible, offenders are given the least restrictive alternative, a reflection of the noninterventionist view.

Similarly, the radical viewpoint has helped shift public focus onto corrupt practices and unfair procedures in the justice system. Are police too harsh in dealing with the underprivileged? Is there a disproportionate number of minorities in prison and on death row? Has the justice system been zealous enough in prosecuting white-collar offenders? These views fit well with due process advocates, who are also determined to root out injustice in the justice system.

Another theme that has begun to dominate justice policy is the need to create and emphasize nontraditional methods of punishment and correction. As the cost of justice skyrockets and the correctional system becomes

FIGURE 15.4 Perspectives on Justice: Key Concerns and Concepts

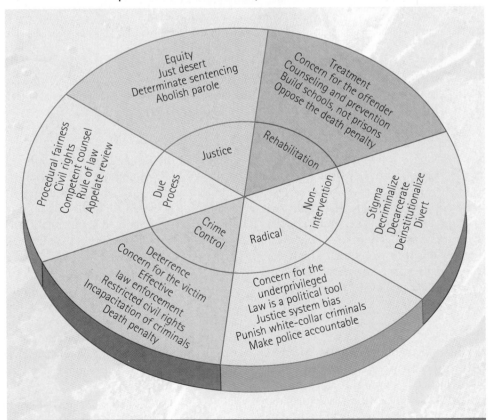

increasingly overcrowded, such alternatives as house arrest, electronic monitoring, intensive probation supervision, and other cost-effective programs have come to the forefront. So while there has been demand for punitive treatment for serious, chronic offenders, necessity has opened the door for greater reliance on treatment and limited intervention for nonviolent, nonchronic offenders. Consequently, the number of noninterventionist programs may actually increase in the years ahead.

In sum, there are a number of competing views on the core values of criminal justice. These have influenced everyday policy in the justice system.

☰ Summary

Criminal justice refers to the formal processes and institutions that have been established to apprehend, try, punish, and treat law violators. The major components of the criminal justice system are the police, courts, and correctional agencies. Police maintain public order, deter crime, and apprehend law violators. The courts are charged with determining the criminal liability of accused offenders brought before them and dispensing fair and effective sanctions to those found guilty of crime. Corrections agencies provide postjudicatory care to offenders who are sentenced by the courts to confinement or community supervision. Dissatisfaction with traditional forms of corrections has spurred the development of community-based facilities and work-release and work-furlough programs. There are about 55,000 justice-related agencies in the United States. About 20,000 of them are police-related, 25,000 are court-related and 9,000 are correctional agencies. They employ over 1 million people and cost taxpayers about $75 billion per year.

Justice can also be conceived of as a process through which offenders flow. The justice process begins with an initial contact by a police agency and proceeds through investigation and custody, trial stages, and correctional system processing. At any stage of the process, the offender can be excused because a lack of evidence exists, the case is trivial, or a decision maker simply decides to discontinue interest in the case.

Procedures, policies, and practices employed within the criminal justice system are scrutinized by the courts to make sure they do not violate the guidelines set down in the first ten amendments to the Constitution. If a violation occurs, the defendant can appeal the case and seek to overturn the conviction. Among the rights that must be honored are freedom from illegal searches and seizures and treatment with overall fairness and due process.

Several different philosophies or perspectives dominate the justice process. One is the crime control model, which asserts that the goals of justice are the protection of the public and incapacitation of known offenders. In contrast, the due process model emphasizes liberal principles, such as legal rights and procedural fairness for the offender. The rehabilitation model views the justice system as a wise and caring parent; the interactionist perspective calls for a minimum of interference in offenders' lives; the radical approach tries to expose the capitalist tendencies of the justice system; and the justice model calls for fair, equal treatment for all offenders.

☰ KEY TERMS

criminal justice	penitentiaries
social control	parole
Chicago Crime Commission	arrest
	lineup
Wickersham Commission	information
sheriff's departments	probable cause
criminal court	grand jury
due process	Bill of Rights
fundamental fairness	exclusionary rule
plea bargaining	good faith exception

☰ NOTES

1. Michael Elliott, "Crime and Punishment," *Newsweek,* 18 April 1994, pp. 18–22.
2. Ibid.
3. This section leans heavily on Samuel Walker, *Popular Justice* (New York: Oxford University Press, 1980).
4. For a detailed analysis of this work, see Samuel Walker, "Origins of the Contemporary Criminal Justice Paradigm: The American Bar Foundation Survey, 1953–1969," *Justice Quarterly* 9 (1992): 47–76.
5. President's Commision of Law Enforcement and the Administration of Justice, *Challenge of Crime in a Free Society* (Washington, D.C.: U.S. Government Printing Office, 1967).
6. See Public Law 90-351, Title I—Omnibus Crime Control Safe Streets Act of 1968, 90th Congress, June 19, 1968.
7. American Bar Association, *Project on Standards for Criminal Justice* (New York: Institute of Judicial Administration, 1968–1973); National Advisory Commission

on Criminal Justice Standards and Goals, *A National Strategy to Reduce Crime* (Washington, D.C.: U.S. Government Printing Office, 1973).

8. Brian Reaves, *Census of State and Local Law Enforcement Agencies, 1992* (Washington, D.C.: Bureau of Justice Statistics, 1993); Sue Lindgren, *Justice Expenditure and Employment* (Washington, D.C.: Bureau of Justice Statistics, 1990).

9. See Albert Reiss, *Police and the Public* (New Haven: Yale University Press, 1972).

10. American Bar Association, *Standards Relating to the Urban Police Function* (New York: Institute of Judicial Administration, 1973), Standard 2.2, p. 9.

11. Kenneth L. Davis, *Police Discretion* (St. Paul: West Publishing, 1975).

12. See Peter Manning and John Van Mannen, eds., *Policing: A View from the Streets* (Santa Monica, Calif.: Goodyear Publishing, 1978).

13. See Donald Newman, *Conviction: The Determination of Guilty or Innocence without Trial* (Boston: Little, Brown, 1966).

14. Allen Beck, Thomas Bonczar, and Darrell Gilliard, *Jail Inmates, 1992* (Washington, D.C.: Bureau of Justice Statistics, 1993); Darrell Gilliard, *Prisoners in 1992* (Washington, D.C.: Bureau of Justice Statistics, 1993).

15. Sue Lindgren, *Justice Expenditure and Employment, 1990* (Washington, D.C.: Bureau of Justice Statisitics, 1992).

16. Ibid., p. 2.

17. J. Robert Lilly and Paul Knepper, "The Corrections-Commercial Complex," *Crime and Delinquency* 39 (1993): 150–66.

18. Herbert L. Packer, *The Limits of the Criminal Sanction* (Stanford, Calif.: Stanford University Press, 1968), p. 159.

19. Samuel Walker, *Sense and Nonsense about Crime and Drugs,* 3d ed. (Belmont, Calif.: Wadsworth Publishers, 1994).

20. Steven Brandl, "The Impact of Case Characteristics on Detectives' Decision Making," *Justice Quarterly* 10 (1993): 395–415.

21. Malcolm Feeley, *The Process Is the Punishment* (New York: Russell Sage Foundation, 1979).

22. Barbara Boland, Catherine Conly, Paul Mahanna, Lynn Warner, and Ronald Sones, *The Prosecution of Felony Arrests, 1987* (Washington, D.C.: Bureau of Justice Statistics, 1990), p. 3.

23. *Black's Law Dictionary,* 4th ed. rev. (St. Paul: West Publishing, 1967), p. 590.

24. See Joseph J. Senna, "Changes in Due Process of Law," *Social Work* 19 (1974): 319.

25. *Rochin v. California,* 342 U.S. 165 (1952).

26. *Arizona v. Fulminate,* 48 Cr.L. 2105 (1991).

27. *McClesky v. Zant,* 49 Cr.L. 2029 (1991).

28. "Survey: Americans Think System Favors Defendants over Victims," *Criminal Justice Newsletter* 22 (1991): 5.

29. D. H. Oaks, "Studying the Exclusionary Rule in Search and Seizure," *University of Chicago Law Review* 37 (1970): 756.

30. *Weeks v. United States,* 323 U.S. 383 (1914).

31. *Mapp v. Ohio,* 367 U.S. 643 (1961).

32. *Illinois v. Gates,* 462 U.S. 213 (1983).

33. *United States v. Leon,* 104 S.Ct. 3405 (1984).

34. *Massachusetts v. Sheppard,* 104 S.Ct. 2424 (1984).

35. *California v. Ciraolo,* 106 S.Ct. 1809 (1986).

36. Robert Misner, "Limiting *Leon:* A Mistake of Law Analogy," *Journal of Criminal Law and Criminology* 77 (1986): 507–45.

37. Walker, *Sense and Nonsense about Crime and Drugs,* pp. 126–28.

38. Craig Uchida and Timothy Bynum, "Search Warrants, Motions to Suppress and 'Lost Cases': The Effects of the Exclusionary Rule in Seven Jurisdictions," *Journal of Criminal Law and Criminology* 81 (1991): 1034–66.

39. David Garland, *Punishment and Modern Society* (Chicago: University of Chicago Press, 1990).

40. The most often-cited of these is Douglas Lipton, Robert Martinson, and Judith Wilks, *The Effectiveness of Correctional Treatment: A Survey of Treatment Evaluation Studies* (New York: Praeger, 1975).

41. Kathleen Maguire, Timothy Flanagan, and Terence Thornberry, "Prison Labor and Recidivism," *Journal of Quantitative Criminology* 4 (1988): 3–18.

42. Steven Lab and John Whitehead," An Analysis of Juvenile Correctional Treatment," *Crime and Delinquency* 34 (1988): 60–83 at 60.

43. Charles Logan and Gerald Gaes, "Meta-Analysis and the Rehabilitation of Punishment," *Justice Quarterly* 10 (1993): 245–63.

44. David Fogel, . . . *We Are the Living Proof* (Cincinnati: Anderson, 1975). See also idem, *Justice as Fairness* (Cincinnati: Anderson, 1980).

45. Packer, *Limits of the Criminal Sanction.*

46. Richard McCorkle, "Research Note: Punish and Rehabilitate? Public Attitudes toward Six Common Crimes," *Crime and Delinquency* 39 (1993): 240–52.

47. For example, see D. A. Andrews, Ivan Zinger, R. D. Hoge, James Bonta, Paul Gendreau, and Francis Cullen, "Does Correctional Treatment Work? A Clinically-Relevant and Pyschologically-Informed Meta-Aanalysis," *Criminology* 28 (1990): 369–404; Carol Garrett, "Effects of Residential Treatment on Adjudicated Delinquents: A Meta-Analysis," *Journal of Research in Crime and Delinquency* 22 (1985): 287–308.

48. Paul Gendreau and Robert Ross, "Revivification of Rehabilitation: Evidence from the 1980's," *Justice Quarterly* 4 (1987): 349–407.

49. Edwin M. Lemert, "The Juvenile Court—Quest and Realities," in President's Commission on Law Enforcement and the Administration of Justice, *Task Force Report: Juvenile Delinquency and Youth Crime* (Washington, D.C.: U.S. Government Printing Office, 1967).

50. Edwin Schur, *Radical Nonintervention* (Englewood Cliffs, N.J.: Prentice-Hall, 1973).

51. James Austin and Barry Krisberg, "The Unmet Promise of

Alternatives to Incarceration," *Crime and Delinquency* 28 (1982): 3–19; for an alternative view, see Arnold Binder and Gilbert Geis, "Ad Populum Argumentation in Criminology: Juvenile Diversion as Rhetoric," *Criminology* 30 (1984): 309–33.

52. Mark Umbreit and Robert Coates, "Cross-Site Analysis of Victim-Offender Mediation in Four States," *Crime and Delinquency* 39 (1993): 565–85.

53. I. Taylor, P. Walton, and J. Young, *Critical Criminology* (London: Routledge and Kegan Paul, 1975), p. 24.

54. Herman Schwendinger and Julia Schwendinger, "Giving Crime Prevention Top Priority," *Crime and Delinquency* 39 (1993): 425–46.

55. Mark Colvin, "Crime and Reproduction: A Response to the Call for 'Outrageous Proposals'," *Crime and Delinquency* 37 (1991): 436–48.

56. Clemens Bartollas and Michael Braswell, "Correctional Treatment, Peacemaking and the New Age Movement," *Journal of Crime and Justice* 16 (1993): 43–48.

57. Randy Martin, "Transpersonal Psychology and Criminological Theory: Rethinking the Paradigm," *Journal of Crime and Justice* 16 (1993): 11–16.

58. Richard Quinney, "A Life of Crime: Criminology and Public Policy as Peacemaking," *Journal of Crime and Justice* 16 (1993): 3–9.

☰ Introduction

In March 1991, the nation was shaken by media coverage of a home video showing a large group of Los Angeles cops brutally beating a handcuffed black man later identified as Rodney King. The beating, which had taken place on the night of March 3, 1991, involved punches, kicks, clubbing, and the use of an electric shock device. King suffered nine skull fractures and a shattered eye socket, among other injuries. The police involved were heard joking about the incident on their car radios. The fact that King was African-American and the officers white sadly illustrated the current of racial conflict that still runs between the police and the black community in many urban areas. The officers involved were charged with assault. When they were acquitted after their first trial, Los Angeles broke out in rioting in which more than 50 people died. Two of the officers were later convicted in federal court of violating King's civil rights and sentenced to prison. On April 19, 1994, a Los Angeles jury awarded King $3.8 million in damages stemming from his arrest and beating.[1]

The King case underscores the critical role police play in the justice system and the need for developing a professional, competent police force. The police are the **gatekeepers** of the criminal justice process. They initiate contact with law violators and decide whether to formally arrest them and start their journey through the criminal justice system, settle the issue in an informal way (such as by issuing a warning), or simply take no action at all. The strategic position of law enforcement officers, their visibility and contact with the public, and their use of weapons and arrest power have kept them in the forefront of public thought for most of the twentieth century.

In the late 1960s and early 1970s, great issue was taken with the political and social roles of the police. Critics viewed police agencies as biased organizations that harassed minority citizens, controlled political dissidents, and generally seemed out of touch with the changing times. The major issues appeared to be controlling the abuse of police power and making police agencies more responsible to public control.

During this period, major efforts were undertaken in the nation's largest cities to curb police power. The work of the **Knapp Commission**, which investigated police corruption in New York, was discussed in Chapter 13. Police review boards designed to allow community members to oversee police policies and operations and investigate citizen complaints were set up in such cities as Philadelphia, New York, and Detroit.

Since the mid-1970s, the relationship between police and the public has changed. Police departments have become more sensitive to their public image. Programs have been created to improve relations between police and community, to help police officers on the beat to be more sensitive to the needs of the public, and to cope more effectively with the stress of their jobs.[2]

Nonetheless, as the Los Angeles beating illustrates, city police departments continue to be the subject of public scrutiny. There is continuing concern over police use of force and treatment of citizens. The recent **Mollen Commission** and other police investigations showed that corruption was still rampant in New York City and the rogue cops of the 1990s are even more brazen and violent than the corrupt cops found by the Knapp Commission 20 years earlier. Even in smaller cities, police procedures have been questioned because there may be overenforcement in minority communities. For example, John Klofas found that aggressive drug enforcement policies in Rochester, New York, were applied in minority neighborhoods but not in more affluent suburban areas.[3]

While critical of the police, people are more concerned than ever with increasing their effectiveness—the public wants its police agencies to control the law-violating members of society. The role of the police is being reconsidered. Are they strictly crime fighters, or are they multifaceted social service agencies that include law enforcement as only one part of their daily activities?

This chapter reviews the function and role of police in U.S. society. First, the history of police will be briefly discussed. Then, the role and structure of police agencies will be reviewed. Finally, some of the critical issues facing the police in society will be analyzed.

☰ History of Police

As with the criminal law, the origin of U.S. police agencies can be traced back to early English society.[4]

Before the Norman Conquest, there was no regular English police force. Every man living in the villages scattered throughout the countryside was responsible for aiding his neighbors and protecting the settlement from thieves and marauders. This was known as the **pledge system.** As reviewed in Chapter 2, people were grouped into a collective of ten families called a *tithing* and entrusted with policing their own minor problems. Ten tithings were grouped into a *hundred,* whose affairs were supervised by a *constable* appointed by the local nobleman. The constable, who might be considered the first real police officer, dealt with more serious breaches of the law.[5]

Later, the hundreds were grouped into *shires* resembling the counties of today. The *shire reeve* was appointed by the crown to supervise a certain territory and assure the local nobleman that order would be kept. The shire reeve, forerunner of today's sheriff, soon began to pursue and apprehend law violators as part of his duties.

In the thirteenth century, during the reign of King Edward I, the **watch system** was created to help protect property in England's larger cities and towns. Watchmen patrolled at night and helped protect against robberies, fires, and disturbances. They reported to the area constable, who became the primary metropolitan law enforcement agent. In larger cities such as London, the watchmen were organized within church parishes; those applying for the job were usually members of the parish they protected.

In 1326, the office of **justice of the peace** was created to assist the shire reeve in controlling the county. Eventually, the justices took on judicial functions in addition to their primary duty as peacekeeper. A system developed in which the local constable became the operational assistant to the justice of the peace, supervising the night watchmen, investigating offenses, serving summonses, executing warrants, and securing prisoners. This working format helped delineate the relationship between police and the judiciary that endured intact for 500 years.

At first, the position of constable was an honorary one given to a respected person in the village or parish for a one-year period. Often, these men were wealthy merchants who had little time for their duties. It was common for them to hire assistants to help them fulfill their obligations, thereby creating another element of a paid police force. Thus, by the seventeenth century, the justice of the peace, the constable, his assistants, and the night watch formed the nucleus of the local metropolitan justice system. (The sheriff's duties lay outside the cities and towns.).

The London Police

At the end of the eighteenth century, the Industrial Revolution lured thousands from the English countryside to work in the larger factory towns. The swelling population of urban poor, whose minuscule wages could hardly sustain them, heightened the need for police protection. In response to pressure from established citizens, the government passed statutes creating new police offices in London. These offices employed three justices of the peace who were each authorized to hire six paid constables. Law enforcement began to be more centralized and professional. However, many parishes still maintained their own foot patrols, horse patrols, and private investigators.

In 1829, **Sir Robert Peel,** England's home secretary, guided through Parliament an "Act for Improving the Police In and Near the Metropolis." The act established the first organized police force in London. Composed of over a thousand men, the London police force was structured along military lines. Its members wore a distinctive uniform and were led by two magistrates, who were later given the title of commissioner. However, the ultimate responsibility for the police fell to the home secretary and consequently the Parliament.

The London experiment proved so successful that the metropolitan police soon began helping outlying areas that requested law enforcement assistance. Another act of Parliament allowed justices of the peace to establish local police forces; by 1856, every borough and county in England was required to form its own police force.

The American Colonial Experience

Law enforcement in colonial America paralleled the British model. In the colonies, the county sheriff became the most important law enforcement agent.[6] In addition to peacekeeping and crime fighting, these sheriffs collected taxes, supervised elections, and handled a great deal of other legal business.

The colonial sheriff did not patrol or seek out crime. Instead, he reacted to citizens' complaints and investigated crimes that had already occurred. His salary was related to his effectiveness. Sheriffs were paid by the fee system. They were given a fixed amount for every arrest made, subpoena served, or court appearance made. Unfortunately, their tax collecting chores were more lucrative than crime fighting, so law enforcement was not one of their primary concerns.

In the cities, law enforcement was the province of the town marshal, who was aided, often unwillingly, by a variety of constables, night watchmen, police justices, and city council members. However, local governments had little power of administration, and enforcement of the criminal law was largely an individual or community responsibility. Individual initiative was encouraged by the practice of offering rewards for the capture of felons.[7] If trouble arose, citizens might be called on to form a posse to chase offenders or break up an angry mob.

As the size of cities grew, it became exceedingly difficult for local leaders to organize citizens' groups. Moreover, the early nineteenth century was an era of widespread urban unrest and mob violence. Local leaders began to realize that a more structured police function was needed to control demonstrators and keep the peace.

Early American Police Agencies

The modern police department was born out of urban mob violence, which wracked the nation's cities in the nineteenth century. Boston created the nation's first formal police department in 1838. New York formed its police department in 1844; Philadelphia, in 1854. The new police departments replaced the night watch system and relegated constables and sheriffs to serving court orders and running the jail.

At first, the urban police departments inherited the functions of the older institutions they replaced. For example, Boston police were charged with maintaining public health until 1853; in New York, the police were responsible for street sweeping until 1881.

Politics dominated the departments and determined the recruitment of new officers and promotion of supervisors. An individual with the right connections could be hired despite a lack of qualifications. "In addition to the pervasive brutality and corruption," writes one justice historian, Samuel Walker, "the police did little to effectively prevent crime or provide public services. Officers were primarily tools of local politicians; they were not impartial and professional public servants."[8]

At mid-nineteenth century, the detective bureau was set up as part of the Boston police. Until then, "thief-taking" had been the province of amateur bounty hunters, who hired themselves out to victims for a price. When professional police departments replaced bounty hunters, the close working relationships that developed between police detectives and their underworld informants produced many scandals and, consequently, high personnel turnover.

Police during the nineteenth century were generally incompetent, corrupt, and disliked by the people they served. The police role was only minimally directed at law enforcement. Its primary function was serving as the enforcement arm of the reigning political power, protecting private property, and keeping control of the ever-rising numbers of foreign immigrants.

Reform Movements

Police agencies evolved slowly through the latter half of the nineteenth century. Uniforms were introduced in 1853 in New York. Technological innovations, such as linking precincts to central headquarters by telegraph, appeared in the late 1850s; somewhat later, call boxes allowed patrolmen on the beat to communicate with their commanders. Nonpolice functions, such as care of the streets, began to be abandoned after the Civil War.

Despite any steps they may have made toward improvement, big-city police were neither respected by the public, successful in their role as crime stoppers, nor involved in progressive activities. The control of police departments by local politicians impeded effective law enforcement and fostered graft and corruption.

In an effort to prevent police corruption, civil leaders in some jurisdictions created police administrative boards to reduce the control over police exercised by local officials. These tribunals were given the responsibility for appointing police administrators and controlling police affairs. In many instances, these measures failed because the private citizens appointed to the review boards lacked expertise in the intricacies of police work.

Another reform movement was the takeover of some big-city police agencies by state legislators. Though police budgets were paid through local taxes, control of police was usurped by rural politicians in the state capitals. It was not until the first decades of the twentieth century that cities regained control of their police forces.

The Boston police strike of 1914 heightened interest in police reform. The strike was brought about by dissatisfaction with the status of police officers in society. While other professions were unionizing and increasing their standard of living, police salaries lagged behind. The Boston police officers' organization, the Boston Social Club, voted to become a union affiliated with the American Federation of Labor. The officers struck on September 9, 1914. Rioting and looting broke out, resulting in Governor Calvin Coolidge's mobilization of the state militia to take over the city. Public support turned against the police, and the strike was broken. Eventually, all the striking officers were fired and replaced by new recruits. The Boston police strike ended police unionism for decades and solidified power in the hands of a reactionary, autocratic police administration.

In the aftermath of the strike, local, state, and national crime commissions began to investigate the extent of crime and the ability of the justice system to effectively deal with it. The **Wickersham Commission** was created by President Herbert Hoover to study police issues on a national scale. In its 1931 report, the commission identified many of the problems of policing, including a weak command structure and overly complex job requirements.[9]

With the onset of the Great Depression, justice reform became a less important issue than economic revival, and for many years, there was little change in the nature of policing.

The Advent of Professionalism

The onset of police professionalism might be traced to the 1920s and the influence of **August Vollmer.**[10] While serving as police chief of Berkeley, California, Vollmer instituted university training as an important part of his development of young officers. He also helped develop the School of Criminology at the University of California at Berkeley, which became the model of justice-related programs around the country.

Vollmer's disciples included O. W. Wilson, who pioneered the use of advanced training for officers when he took over and reformed the Wichita, Kansas, police department in 1923. Wilson also was instrumental in applying modern management and administrative techniques to policing. His text, *Police Administration,* became the single most influential work on the subject. Wilson eventually became dean of the Criminology School at Berkeley and ended his career in Chicago, where Mayor Richard J. Daley asked him to take over and reform the Chicago police department in 1960.

One important aspect of professionalism was the technological breakthroughs that significantly increased and expanded the scope of police operations. The first innovation came in the area of communications, when telegraph police boxes were installed in 1867; an officer could turn a key in a box and his location and number would automatically register at headquarters. The Detroit police department outfitted some of its patrol officers with bicycles in 1897. By 1913, the motorcycle was being employed by departments in the eastern part of the country. The first police car was used in Akron, Ohio, in 1910; the police wagon became popular in Cincinnati in 1912.

Through the 1960s, police professionalism was interpreted as being a tough, highly trained, rule-oriented law enforcement department organized along militaristic lines. The urban unrest of the late 1960s changed the course of police department development. Efforts were made to promote understanding between police and the community, reduce police brutality, and recognize the stresses of police work. Efforts also were made, usually under court order, to add members of minority groups and women to police departments. The federal government's Law Enforcement Education Program encouraged officers to get college training. As rank-and-file patrol officers became dissatisfied with administration

from the top down, local police unions were formed. With increasing professionalism, the ideal police officer came to be viewed as a product of the computer age, skilled in using the most advanced techniques to fight crime. A majority of funds went toward developing police hardware; in some quarters, technological advances were seen as the answer to the crime problem.[11]

Despite technological and professional achievements, the effectiveness of the police is still questioned, and their ability to control crime is still considered problematic. Critics argue that plans to increase police professionalism place too much emphasis on hardware and not enough on police-citizen cooperation.

≡ Law Enforcement Agencies

Law enforcement duties are distributed across local, county, state, and federal jurisdictions. This section discusses the role of federal, state, and county agencies. The remainder of the chapter will focus more directly on local police.

Federal Law Enforcement

The federal government maintains about 50 organizations that are involved in law enforcement. Some of the most important of these are discussed below.

The Federal Bureau of Investigation.
In 1870, the U.S. Department of Justice became involved in actual policing when the attorney general hired investigators to enforce the Mann Act (which prohibited prostitution across state lines). In 1908, this group of investigators was formally made a distinct branch of the government, the Bureau of Investigation; in the 1930s, the agency was reorganized into the Federal Bureau of Investigation under the direction of J. Edgar Hoover.

Today's FBI is not a police agency but an investigative agency, with jurisdiction over all matters in which the United States is, or may be, an interested party. It limits its jurisdiction to federal laws, including all federal statutes not specifically assigned to other agencies.[12] These include statutes dealing with espionage, sabotage, treason, civil rights violations, the murder and assault of federal officers, mail fraud, robbery and burglary of federally insured banks, kidnapping, and interstate transportation of stolen vehicles and property.

The FBI offers important services to local law enforcement agencies. Its identification division, established in 1924, collects and maintains a vast fingerprint file that can be used by local police agencies. Its sophisticated crime laboratory, established in 1932, aids local police in testing and identifying evidence, such as hairs, fibers, blood, tire tracks, and drugs.

The Uniform Crime Report is another service of the FBI. Finally, the FBI's National Crime Information Center is a computerized network linked to local police departments by terminals. Through it, information on stolen vehicles, wanted persons, stolen guns, and so on is made readily available to local law enforcement agencies.

For many years, the FBI was considered by many to be the elite U.S. law enforcement agency. Its agents were considered incorruptible, highly trained, and professional. FBI agents always got their man, whether it was gangsters of the 1930s, such as John Dillinger; Nazi saboteurs during World War II; or Soviet agents during the Cold War. However, during the era of political suspicion that followed the Watergate break-ins, information came to light that tarnished the agency's image. J. Edgar Hoover was portrayed as placing undue emphasis on controlling radical groups and harassing black civil rights leaders. One famous incident was the bugging of Martin Luther King's hotel rooms. The FBI's COINTELPRO (counterintelligence program) used wiretaps, opened mail, and burglarized the offices of radical political groups.[13] After a period of turmoil and internal unrest, the FBI seems to have successfully restricted its activities and is now directed toward pursuing organized crime figures and enforcing white-collar crime statutes.

Other Federal Agencies.
The U.S. government's interest in drug trafficking can be traced back to 1914, when the Harrison Act established federal jurisdiction over the supply and use of narcotics. Several drug enforcement units, including the Bureau of Narcotics and Dangerous Drugs, were originally charged with enforcing drug laws. However, in 1973, these agencies were combined to form the Drug Enforcement Administration (DEA). Agents of the DEA assist local and state authorities in their investigation of illegal drug use and carry out independent surveillance and enforcement activities to control the importation of narcotics.

Federal law enforcement agencies under the direction of the Justice Department include the U.S. marshals, the Immigration and Naturalization Service, and the Organized Crime and Racketeering Unit. The U.S. marshals are court officers who help implement federal court rulings, transport prisoners, and enforce court orders. The Immigration and Naturalization Service is responsible for the administration of immigration laws, the deportation of illegal aliens, and the naturalization of

aliens lawfully present in the United States. This service also maintains border patrols to prevent aliens from entering the United States illegally.

The Treasury Department maintains the Alcohol, Tobacco, and Firearms Bureau, which has jurisdiction over the sales and distribution of firearms, explosives, alcohol, and tobacco products. The Bureau made national headlines with its tragic confrontation and shootout with the Branch Davidian cult in Waco, Texas, in 1993. Fighting started when ATF agents attempted to serve a warrant issued because cult members were believed to be in possession of illegal automatic weapons.

The Internal Revenue Service, established in 1862, enforces violations of income, excise, stamp, and other tax laws. Its intelligence division actively pursues gamblers, narcotics dealers, and other violators who do not report their illegal financial gains as taxable income.

The Customs Bureau guards points of entry into the United States and prevents smuggling of contraband into (or out of) the country.

The Secret Service, an arm of the Treasury Department, was originally charged with enforcing laws against counterfeiting. Today, it also protects the president and vice-president and their families, presidential candidates, and former presidents.

County Law Enforcement

The county police department is an independent agency whose senior officer, the **sheriff,** is usually an elected political official. The county sheriff's role has evolved from that of the early English **shire reeve,** whose main duty was to assist the royal judges in trying prisoners and enforcing the law outside of cities. From the time of U.S. westward expansion until municipal departments were developed, the sheriff often was the sole legal authority in vast territories.

Today, there are about 136,000 full-time officers and 89,000 other employees in about 3,000 sheriff's departments in the United States.[14] Their duties vary according to the size and degree of development of the county. Officials within the department may serve as coroners, tax assessors, tax collectors, overseers of highways and bridges, custodians of the county treasury, keepers of the county jail, court attendants, and executors of criminal and civil processes; in years past, sheriff's offices also conducted executions. Many of the sheriff's law enforcement functions today are carried out only in incorporated areas within a county or in response to city departments' requests for aid in such matters as patrol or investigation.

Probably the most extensive sheriff's department is located in Los Angeles County, which services over 30 cities.[15] It maintains a modern communications system and a police laboratory, in addition to performing standard enforcement functions.

State Police

The Texas Rangers, organized in 1835, are considered the first state police force. However, the Rangers were more a quasi-military force that supported the Texas state militia than a true law enforcement body. The first true state police forces emerged at the turn of the twentieth century, with Pennsylvania's leading the way.

The impetus for creating state police agencies can be traced both to the low regard of the public for the crime-fighting ability of local police agencies and the increasingly greater mobility of law violators. Using automobiles, thieves could strike at will and be out of the jurisdiction of local police before an investigation could be mounted. Therefore, a law enforcement agency with statewide jurisdiction was needed. Also, state police gave governors a powerful enforcement arm that was under their personal control and not that of city politicians.

Today, there are about 53,000 full-time state police officers and 26,000 other full-time employees in 49 departments (Hawaii has no state police).[16] The major role of state police is controlling traffic on the highway system, helping trace stolen automobiles, and aiding in disturbances and crowd control. In states with large and powerful county sheriff's departments, the state police function is usually restricted to highway patrol. In others, where the county sheriff's law enforcement role is limited, state police usually maintain a more active investigative and enforcement role.

Metropolitan Police

Metropolitan police agencies make up the vast majority of the law enforcement community's members. There are approximately 375,000 local police officers and 103,000 other full-time employees in 12,000 departments. They range in size from New York's, which employs around 35,750 people including 28,800 sworn officers, and Chicago's, with more than 12,000 officers, to the single police officer who is a small town's only staff.[17] In all, about 37 departments have more than 1,000 officers, and 1,600 departments have only one.

Most larger urban departments are independent agencies operating without specific administrative control from any higher governmental authority. They are organized at the executive level of government. It is therefore common for the city mayor (or the equivalent) to control the hiring and firing of the police chief and, consequently, determine departmental policies.

Most municipal departments are organized in a military way, often using military terms to designate seniority (sergeant, lieutenant, captain).

The organization of a typical metropolitan police department is illustrated in Figure 16.1. This complex structure is a function of the multiplicity of roles that police are entrusted with. Among the daily activities of police agencies are:

- Identifying criminal suspects.

- Investigating crimes.

- Apprehending offenders and participating in their trials.

- Deterring crime through patrol.

- Aiding individuals in danger or in need of assistance; providing emergency services.

- Resolving conflict and keeping the peace.

- Maintaining a sense of community security.

- Keeping vehicular and pedestrian movement efficient.

- Promoting civil order.

- Operating and administering the police department.

The remainder of this chapter will be devoted to the nature of local policing.

Police Role

If you watch fictional police officers played by Mel Gibson and Danny Glover in *Lethal Weapon* or Steven Segal in *Out to Kill* get involved in shoot-outs with automatic weapons, it is easy to see why many people believe that the major police role is law enforcement. In reality, relatively little of a police officer's time is spent on "crime-fighting duties."[18] Instead, the great bulk of effort is devoted to what has been described as *order maintenance,* or *peacekeeping.*[19] James Q. Wilson's pioneering work, *Varieties of Police Behavior,* viewed the major police role to be "handling the situation."[20] Wilson found that police encounter many troubling incidents that need some sort of "fixing up." Enforcing the law

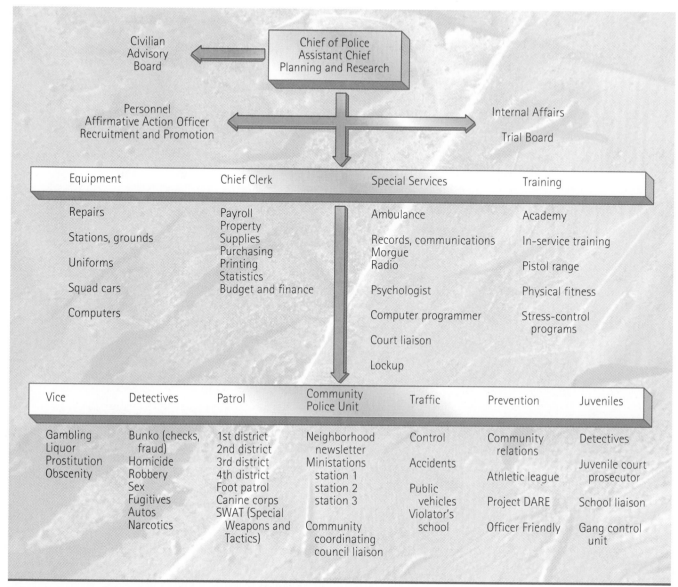

FIGURE 16.1 **Organization of a Metropolitan Police Department**

might be one tool a police officer uses; threat, coercion, sympathy, understanding, and apathy might be others. Most important is "keeping things under control so that there are no complaints that he is doing nothing or that he is doing too much."

The peacekeeping role of the police has been documented by several different studies that find that the police function essentially as order-keeping, dispute-settling agents of public health and safety.[21] Just being there to handle the situation is the officers' main task; the better they are at it, the less likely they are to resort to violence. Unfortunately, police have a tendency to

dominate actions and sometimes disregard the feelings of those who need their aid.

Today, the police officer's role is becoming more multidimensional. Police officers are required to be peacekeepers, crime investigators, emergency medical technicians, traffic controllers, and symbols of public morality and stability. They are asked to spend a considerable amount of time helping people with special needs, such as the homeless and mentally ill, whose problems are quite difficult to solve and create a great deal of frustration.[22] And while police spend a lot of time on service activities, they are also devoting considerable

While the media implies that police officers spend a great deal of time in shoot-outs with drug dealers, they actually spend most of their time on order maintenance and peacekeeping. Here, an officer uses a radar gun to check for speeding bicyclists on the beach.

time to crime-related activities that are relatively new phenomena: gang control, antidrug campaigns, and the control of domestic violence. Two police experts, Jack Greene and Carl Klockars, indicate that crime fighting may now take up to half of a police officer's time, considerably more than previously believed.[23] As crime rates expand, so too do stressful, crime-related police activities.

The burdens of police work have helped set law enforcement officers outside the mainstream of society and encouraged the development of a police subculture marked by insulation from the outside world and a code of secrecy.[24]

Community Policing

In a highly regarded article, "Broken Windows: The Police and Neighborhood Safety," criminologists James Q. Wilson and George Kelling called for a return to a nineteenth-century style of policing in which police maintained a presence in the community, walked beats, got to know citizens, and inspired feelings of public safety.[25] Wilson and Kelling asked police administrators to get their officers out of depersonalizing patrol cars. Instead of deploying police on the basis of crime rates or in areas where citizens make the most calls for help, police administrators should station their officers where they can do the most to promote public confidence and elicit citizen cooperation. Community preservation, public safety, and order maintenance—not crime fighting—should become the primary focus of police. Implied in the Wilson and Kelling model was a *proactive* police role. Instead of merely responding to calls for help (known as *reactive* policing), police should play an active role in the community, identify neighborhood problems and needs, and set a course of action for an effective response. They conclude:

Just as physicians now recognize the importance of fostering health rather than simply treating illness, so the police—and the rest of us—ought to recognize the importance of maintaining intact communities without broken windows.[26]

The "broken windows" article had an important impact on policing, and since its publication, there has been a continuing reanalysis of the police role.

Implementing Community Policing

A form of community policing was first implemented in the 1970s, when **team policing** was instituted around the United States.[27] This concept brought together a group of junior officers and a supervisor who were given jurisdiction over a designated neighborhood area on a 24-hour-a-day basis. The supervisor had complete responsibility for the team area, and the team could patrol the area in the manner it believed would be the most effective. The team determined its own deployment, working hours, assignments, and methods within broad policy guidelines established by the department. The purpose of the team was to create strong ties between the police officers and the community they served and to involve the neighborhood in police operation.[28] When team policing proved less effective than imagined and federal funds dried up, programs were terminated.

The current community policing "movement" began when **foot patrols** were reintroduced in a limited number of jurisdictions. Foot patrol was believed to be an effective device that could help police monitor community concerns and control drug dealers, vandals, and other petty criminals associated with community decline. Officers on foot are more easily approachable and offer a comforting presence to citizens. And with today's mobile communication gear, the foot patrol officer is not isolated on the street. In many cities, they carry the same communications gear that is used in patrol cars.

The Police Foundation, a private nonprofit study group, evaluated several of these programs in New Jersey and found that while foot patrols had little effect on community crime rates, they did help to improve citizen attitudes toward the police.[29]

The success of these early experiments encouraged other cities to sponsor foot patrols, so that today, hundreds of jurisdictions have implemented some form of community policing involving foot patrol strategies. Other community policing strategies include Neighborhood Watch and other programs in which police organize local citizens to aid them in crime prevention efforts, decentralized command structures in which police operate out of neighborhood mini-stations, newsletters, and other devices that bring the police and the community in closer contact.[30]

Community Policing in Action. Some community policing programs assign officers to neighborhoods, organize training programs for community leaders, and feature a bottom-up approach to deal with community problems: decision making involves the officer on the scene and not a directive from central headquarters. The police in Newark went so far as to set up a neighborhood clean-up program for juveniles who might ordinarily have little interest in civic affairs. In one neighborhood, police officers were given time to visit 500 businesses and homes to see if there were any problems the police should know about. While not all the programs work, the overall impression was that patrol officers can reduce the level of fear in the community.[31]

To achieve the goals of community policing, some agencies have tried to decentralize, an approach sometimes referred to as **neighborhood policing.** Problem solving is best done at the neighborhood level where issues originate, not at a far off central headquarters. Because each neighborhood has its own particular needs, police decision making must be flexible and adaptive.

Community policing also stresses sharing power with local groups and individuals. Citizens actively participate with police to fight crime, for example, by providing information in area crime investigations or helping police reach out to troubled area youths. Police in Houston adopted the Positive Interaction Program in which captains in each of the city's nine (decentralized) substations were required to meet monthly with area business leaders and prominent residents to discuss neighborhood problems. Substation captains were then charged with using available resources to resolve the problems.[32]

Problem-Oriented Policing

Another community policing strategy involves the development of **problem-oriented policing.** According to originator Herman Goldstein, police departments have been too concerned with internal efficiency and have therefore given insufficient attention to substantive problems in the work environment.[33] Police have been reactive, responding to calls for help. Instead, they should play an active role in identifying particular community problems—street-level drug dealers, prostitution rings, gang hangouts—and developing strategies to counteract them. Problems are better defined narrowly; the focus would be on reducing larceny from the mall on weekends and not a general reduction in the crime rate. Solutions can be achieved by drawing on the creative and innovative talents found in two important resources: the community and the line officers who are familiar with community problems. Rather than stifle or control creativity, problem-oriented policing encourages new solutions to old problems.

Problem-oriented policing techniques are being used in a number of police departments. An evaluation of this approach instituted by police in Newport News, Virginia, found that it was effective in reducing theft from cars, problems associated with prostitution, and household burglaries.[34]

Problem-oriented policing strategies are also aimed at reducing community fear levels. Fear reduction is viewed both as an important element of police services to the community and also as a means of increasing citizen cooperation with police officers.[35]

Crackdowns and Hot Spots.   One strategy of crime-specific policing is the **crackdown,** in which particular problem areas are the target of increased police resources. As you may recall from Chapter 5, Lawrence Sherman found that crackdowns work effectively as a short-term crime reduction strategy, perhaps because they have a shock effect on the local criminal population. In the long term, however, their effect on crime control decays. Sherman finds that this form of problem-oriented policing might be best instituted for short periods of time and rotated among different problem areas.[36]

Sherman, with Patrick Gartin and Michael Buerger, also found that a significant portion of all police calls emanate from a relatively few locations: bars, malls, the bus depot, hotels, certain apartment buildings.[37] By implication, concentrating police resources on these **hot spots** could appreciably reduce crime.[38]

An elaborate problem-oriented police program that illustrates both the crackdown and hot spot concepts was Operation Pressure Point, a massive police initiative in which an additional 240 officers (the crackdown) were dispatched to a high-drug area in the Lower East Side of New York (the hot spot). The program combined aggressive law enforcement tactics, including the arrest and detention of all suspects, and undercover surveillance work. Enforcement strategies were combined with community organization programs designed to strengthen neighborhood structure and increase resident support for police operations. Lynn Zimmer reviewed the outcome of Operation Pressure Point and found that it successfully reduced drug trafficking in the area, while at the same time it revived community spirit.[39] But, as Zimmer warns, the success of such street-level problem solving may be tempered by the effects of displacement and extinction: the targeted crime problem will be displaced to other "safer" areas of the city, and the criminals will return shortly after the program is called a success and the additional police forces pulled from the area.[40]

Does Community Policing Work?

Although many police experts and administrators have embraced the community and problem-oriented policing concept as a revolutionary revision of the basic police role, it is not without its critics. Not all criminologists agree that a return to the police officer of yesteryear is the panacea it is thought to be by Wilson and Kelling. For example, Samuel Walker has criticized the "broken windows" concept on the grounds that it misinterprets and romanticizes police history: old-style police were neither liked nor respected.[41] Police expert Jack Greene has argued that community policing strategies fail to accurately define the concept of community. Greene finds that in most community policing projects, the concept of community is defined in terms of administrative areas traditionally used by police departments to allocate patrols. Police departments rarely define community in terms of an ecological area defined by common norms, shared values, and interpersonal bonds.[42] Recent research by Roger Dunham and Geoffrey Alpert does in fact show that residents of different neighborhoods have distinct views of the police role and that no single approach to community policing can possibly be correct for all areas.[43]

It may also be difficult to retrain and reorient police from their traditional roles into more of a social service orientation. Most police officers do not have the social service skills required of effective community agents. A national survey of police departments by David Carter and Allen Sapp found that only 14 percent have a policy requiring some college education for employment and 75 percent did not require college course work for promotion. Even those departments that did encourage officers to take courses did not mandate that they be part of a degree program.[44]

While these criticisms may have validity, a number of research evaluations indicate that community policing programs improve community relations, upgrade the image of local police, and reduce levels of community fear.[45] There is also evidence that local police departments can implement community programs without straining or sacrificing their ability to provide emergency services.[46]

Little question exists that community and problem-oriented policing will continue to find support. They fit well with efforts to reduce crime among high-risk populations.[47] They offer the benefit of less dependence on the criminal justice system to fight crime and more emphasis on new problem-solving methods that use awareness of community problems as a basis for designing more effective police responses.[48]

≡ Police Functions

What do local police actually do? What are their major functions, and how well do they perform them? This section will discuss a few of the most critical ones.

Patrol Function

Patrol entails police officers' visible presence on the streets and public places of their jurisdiction. The purpose of patrol is to deter crime, maintain order, enforce laws, and aid in service functions, such as emergency medical care. There is a large variety of patrol techniques. In early police forces, foot patrol was almost exclusively used. Each officer had a particular area, or *beat,* to walk; the police officer was the symbol of state authority in that area. The beat officer dispensed "street justice," and some became infamous for their use of clubs or nightsticks.

When the old-style beat officer needed assistance, he would pound the pavement with his stick to summon his colleagues from nearby areas. Later, call boxes were introduced so the officer could communicate more easily with headquarters. Today, the introduction of patrol cars as well as motorcycles, helicopters, and other types of mechanized transportation has all but ended *walking the beat.* Though the patrol car allows the police to supervise more territory with fewer officers, it has removed and isolated patrol officers from the communities they serve. Some experts argue that this impersonal style of enforcement has worsened relations between police and community. In some communities, **aggressive preventive patrol,** designed to deter crime, has heightened tensions between the police and minorities.

Considerable tension is involved in patrolling, especially in high-crime areas where police feel they are open targets. The patrol officer must learn to work the street, taking whatever action is necessary to control the situation and no more.

When patrol officers take inappropriate action or when their behavior results in violence or death, they are subject to intense scrutiny by public agencies and may be subject to disciplinary measures from the police department's **internal affairs division.** Patrol officers, then, are expected to make mature and reasoned decisions while facing a constant flow of people in emotional crisis.

A patrol officer's job is extremely demanding and often is unrewarding and unappreciated. It is not surprising that the attitudes of police officers toward the public have been characterized by ambivalence, cynicism, and tension.[49]

How Effective Is Patrol?

In most police departments, the majority of officers are assigned to patrol work; it can be stated that the patrol officer is the backbone of policing. Yet the question remains, "Does police patrol deter crime?" Put another way, should police spend so much time and resources keeping a visible presence on the street if their efforts do little to control crime?

As you may recall from Chapter 5, the most comprehensive effort to evaluate the patrol function, the *Kansas City study,* found that police patrol had little effect on the crime patterns. The presence or absence of patrol did not seem to affect residential or business burglaries, auto thefts, larcenies involving auto accessories, robberies, vandalism, or other criminal behavior.[50]

One reason may be that patrol officers rarely invoke the criminal law. Albert Reiss found that the typical tour of duty does not involve a single arrest.[51] Egon Bittner concluded that patrol officers average about ten arrests per month and only three index crime arrests per year.[52] Although arrests alone cannot be equated with effectiveness, they do give some indication of the relative value of patrol work.

While the mere presence of police may not be sufficient to deter crime, the manner in which they approach their task may make a difference. In a classic study, James Q. Wilson and Barbara Boland found that a proactive, aggressive law enforcement style may help reduce crime rates. Jurisdictions that encourage patrol officers to stop motor vehicles to issue citations and to aggressively arrest and detain suspicious persons also experience lower crime rates than jurisdictions that do not follow such proactive policies.[53] In a more recent analysis of police activities in 171 American cities, Robert Sampson and Jacqueline Cohen also found that departments that more actively enforced public order crimes, such as disorderly conduct, and traffic laws experience lower robbery rates. [54]

Like Wilson and Boland before them, Sampson and Cohen find it difficult to determine why proactive policing works so effectively. It may have a direct deterrent effect: aggressive policing increases community perception that police arrest a lot of criminals and that most violators get caught. Its effect may be indirect: aggressive police arrest more suspects, and their subsequent conviction gets them off the street; fewer criminals produce lower crime rates.

Before a general policy of vigorous police work can be adopted, the downside of aggressive tactics must be considered. Proactive police strategies breed resentment in minority areas where citizens believe they are the target of police suspicion and reaction.[55] Evidence exists that such aggressive police tactics as random stop and frisks and rousting teenagers who congregate on street corners are the seeds from which racial conflict grows.[56]

In sum, while the Kansas City study questioned the value of police patrol as a crime deterrent, later research efforts raise the possibility that it may be a more effective, albeit socially costly, crime suppression mechanism than earlier thought possible.

Investigation Function

The second prominent police role is investigation and crime detection. The detective has been a figure of great romantic appeal since the first independent bureau was established by the London Metropolitan Police in 1841. The detective has been portrayed as the elite of the police force in such films and television shows as *Dirty Harry,* "Kojak," and *Lethal Weapon,* to name but a few.

Detective branches are organized on the individual precinct level or out of a central headquarters and perform various functions. Some jurisdictions maintain morals or vice squads, which are usually staffed by plainclothes officers or detectives specializing in victimless crimes, such as prostitution or gambling. Vice squad officers may set themselves up as customers for illicit activities to make arrests. For example, undercover detectives may frequent public men's rooms and make advances toward men; those who respond are arrested for homosexual soliciting. In other instances, female police officers may pose as prostitutes. These covert police activities have often been criticized as violating the personal rights of citizens, and their appropriateness and fairness have been questioned.

Investigators must often enter a case after it has been reported to police and attempt to accumulate enough evidence to identify the perpetrator.[57] Detectives use various investigatory techniques. Sometimes they obtain fingerprints from the scene of a crime and match them with those on file. Other cases demand the aid of informers to help identify perpetrators. In some instances, victims or witnesses are asked to identify offenders by viewing their pictures, or **mug shots,** or by pulling them out of lineups. It is also possible for detectives to solve a crime by being familiar with the working methods of particular offenders—their *modus operandi,* or MO. The detective identifies the criminal by matching the facts of the crime with the criminal's peculiar habits or actions. In some cases, stolen property is located, and then the case is cleared. Either the suspect is arrested on another matter and subsequently found to be in possession of stolen merchandise, or during routine questioning, a person confesses to criminal acts the police did not suspect him or her of in the first place.

Finally, detectives can use their own initiative to take special action in solving a case. For example, the *sting* type of operation has received widespread publicity.[58] Here, detectives pose as fences and conduct property transactions with thieves interested in selling stolen merchandise. Transactions are videotaped to provide prosecutors with extremely strong cases.

Sting-type undercover operations are controversial since they involve a police officer's becoming involved in illegal activity and encouraging offenders to break the law. It is possible that stings encourage crime when area residents realize that there is a new group offering cash for stolen goods.[59] The ethics of these operations have been questioned, especially when the police actively recruit criminals. Nonetheless, the sting operation seems to have found a permanent place in the law enforcement repertoire.

Are Investigations Effective?

Although detectives in the movies and on television always capture the villain, research evidence indicates that real detectives are much less successful. The Rand Corporation, in a classic 1975 study of 153 detective bureaus, found that a great deal of detectives' time was spent in nonproductive work and that investigative expertise did little to help them solve cases.[60] In more than half of the cases cleared, simple, routine actions solved the case; there was little need for scientific, highly trained investigators. The Rand researchers estimated that half of all detectives could be removed without negatively influencing crime clearance rates.

The Rand findings have been replicated by Mark Willman and John Snortum, who tracked 5,336 reported crimes and spent thousands of hours monitoring detective work in a suburban U.S. police department.[61] They found that when a suspect was identified, it usually occurred *before* the case was assigned to a detective. Initial identification usually took place at the scene of the crime or through routine follow-up procedures. Similarly, the Police Executive Research Forum found that a great majority of solved cases involved data gathered at the crime scene by patrol officers; detectives dropped 75 percent of cases after one day and spent an average of four hours on each case.[62]

Efforts have been made to revamp investigation procedures. One practice has been for patrol officers to be given greater responsibilities in conducting preliminary investigations at the scene of the crime. In addition, the precinct detective is being replaced by specialized units, such as homicide or burglary squads, which operate over larger areas and can bring specific expertise to bear on a particular case.

Another trend has been the development of regional squads of local, state, and federal officers (called regional strike forces) that concentrate on major crimes, such as narcotics offenses, and organized crime activities and use their wider jurisdiction and expertise to provide services beyond the capabilities of a metropolitan police department. Another common operation is to focus on the investigation and arrest of hard-core career criminals.[63]

Other Police Functions

Another important public-contact police task is traffic control. This involves such activities as intersection control (directing traffic), traffic law enforcement, radar operations, parking law enforcement, and accident investigation.[64]

Traffic control is a complex daily task involving thousands, even millions, of motor vehicles within a single police jurisdiction. Consequently, police departments use selective enforcement in maintaining traffic laws. Police departments neither expect nor wish to punish all traffic violators. A department may set up traffic control units only at particular intersections, although its traffic coordinators know that violations are occurring in many other areas of the city. Officers may be allocated to the traffic division based on prediction of accident or violation expectancy rates, determined by statistical analysis of previous patterns and incidents.

As the model of the typical police department in Figure 16.1 (see above) indicates, various other roles are carried out by police agencies. For example, most departments are responsible for administering and controlling their budgets. This task involves purchasing equipment and services, planning for future expenditures, and managing the department's resources.

Many departments maintain separate units that keep records on offenders. Modern data management systems have been used to provide easy access to records for case investigations. Similarly, most larger departments have sophisticated communications networks that process citizen complaints and police calls for assistance and dispatch vehicles to respond to them as efficiently as possible.

To promote citizen cooperation, many police departments have specialized community relations officers. Community relations teams perform such tasks as working with citizen groups, lecturing students on traffic safety, and creating neighborhood programs to prevent crime.

Some police agencies maintain (or have access to) forensic laboratories that enable them to identify substances to be used as evidence, classify fingerprints, and augment investigations in other ways.

Another function often found in larger departments is planning and research. The planning and research division designs new programs to increase police efficiency and develops strategies to test their effectiveness. Police planners monitor recent technological developments and institute programs to adapt them to ongoing police services.

Police and the Rule of Law

Like other areas of criminal justice, police behavior is carefully controlled by court action. On the one hand, police want a free hand to enforce the law as they see fit. On the other hand, the courts must balance the needs of efficient law enforcement with the rights of citizens under the U.S. Constitution. Some important legal issues have emerged from this conflict, the most critical being citizen rights during a police interrogation and the right to be free from illegal searches and seizures by police officers.

Custodial Interrogation

The Fifth Amendment guarantees people the right to be free from self-incrimination. This has been interpreted as meaning that law enforcement agents cannot use physical or psychological coercion while interrogating suspects under their control to get them to confess or give information.

The federal government has long held that a confession must be made voluntarily if it is to be admissible as evidence in a criminal trial. Confessions obtained from defendants through coercion, force, trickery, or promises of leniency are inadmissible because their trustworthiness is questionable. The rule of voluntariness applies to confessions obtained at any time, whether the defendant was in police custody or not. In the past, one of the major drawbacks to determining the voluntariness of confessions was that the decision was subjective and made case by case.

In 1966, the Supreme Court, in the case of *Miranda v. Arizona,* created objective standards for questioning by police after a defendant has been taken into custody.[65] Custody occurs when a person is not free to walk away, as when an individual is arrested. The Court maintained that before the police can question a person who has been arrested or is in custody, they must inform the individual of the Fifth Amendment right to be free from self-incrimination. This is accomplished by the police issuing what is known as the *Miranda warning.* The warning informs the suspect that:

1. He or she has the right to remain silent.
2. If he or she makes a statement, it can be used against him or her in court.
3. He or she has the right to consult an attorney and to have the attorney present at the time of the interrogation.
4. If he or she cannot afford an attorney, one will be appointed by the state.

If the defendant is not given the Miranda warning before the investigation, the evidence obtained from the interrogation cannot be admitted at the trial. Finally, the accused can waive his or her Miranda rights at any time. However, for the waiver to be effective, the state must first show that the defendant was aware of all the Miranda rights and must then prove that the waiver was made with the full knowledge of constitutional rights.

The Miranda Rule Today

The Supreme Court has used case law to define the boundaries of the Miranda warning since its inception. Important Court rulings on the Miranda warning have created the following guidelines:

1. Evidence obtained in violation of the Miranda warning can be used by the government to impeach a defendant's testimony during trial.[66]
2. At trial, the testimony of a witness is permissible even though his or her identity was revealed by the defendant in violation of the Miranda rule.[67]

3. It is permissible to renew questioning of suspects who had invoked their Miranda right to remain silent if the warning is restated by police.
4. The Miranda warning applies only to the right to have an attorney present; the suspect cannot demand to speak to a priest, probation officer, or any other officials.[68]
5. Information provided by a suspect that leads to the seizure of incriminating evidence is permissible if the evidence would have been obtained anyway by other means or sources; this is now referred to as the **inevitable discovery rule.**[69]
6. A suspect can be questioned in the field without a Miranda warning if the information the police seek is needed to protect *public safety;* for example, in an emergency, suspects can be asked where they hid their weapon.[70]
7. Initial errors by police in getting statements do not make subsequent statements inadmissible; a subsequent Miranda warning that is properly given can "cure the condition" that made the initial statements inadmissible.[71]
8. Suspects need not be aware of all the possible outcomes of waiving their rights for the Miranda warning to be considered properly given.[72]
9. The admissions of mentally impaired defendants can be admitted in evidence as long as the police acted properly and there is a "preponderance of the evidence" that they understood the meaning of Miranda.[73]
10. An attorney's request to see the defendant does not affect the validity of the defendant's waiver of the right to counsel; police misinformation to an attorney does not affect waiver of Miranda rights. [74]
11. People who are mentally ill due to clinically diagnosed schizophrenia may voluntarily confess and waive their Miranda rights.[75]
12. Once a criminal suspect has invoked his or her Miranda rights, police officials cannot reinitiate interrogation in the absence of counsel even if the accused has consulted with an attorney in the meantime.[76]
13. The erroneous admission of a coerced confession at trial can be ruled a "harmless error" that would not automatically result in overturning a conviction.[77]

While it appears that recent case law has narrowed the scope of Miranda and given police greater leeway in their actions, the rule still serves to protect criminal defendants who are being interrogated by police.

Search and Seizure

As you may recall from Chapter 15, the Fourth Amendment protects against unreasonable searches and seizures by police officers. This means that, with some exceptions, police officers must have a **search warrant** issued by a magistrate to search a person and his or her possessions.

Most often when the police try to obtain search warrants, they rely on the word of informers. In the case of *Illinois v. Gates*, the Court created what is known as the *totality of the circumstances* test for obtaining a search warrant.[78] Loosely interpreted, if judges are presented with sufficient, knowledgeable evidence for issuing a warrant, they may do so even if the source of the information is anonymous or unknown. The *Gates* doctrine makes it significantly easier for police to obtain valid search warrants.

To make it easier for police to conduct investigations and to protect public safety, the Court has ruled that under certain circumstances, a valid search may be conducted without a search warrant. The six major exceptions are: (1) search incident to a valid arrest, (2) threshold inquiry (stop and frisk), (3) automobile search, (4) consent search, (5) plain-sight search, and (6) seizure of nonphysical evidence.

1. *Search Incident to an Arrest.* A warrantless search is valid if it is made incident to a lawful arrest. The reason for this exception is that the arresting officer must have the power to disarm the accused, protect him- or herself, preserve the evidence of the crime, and prevent the accused's escape from custody. Since the search is lawful, the officer retains what he or she finds if it is connected with a crime. The officer is permitted to search only the defendant's person and the areas in the defendant's immediate physical surroundings that are under his or her control.[79]

2. *Threshold Inquiry (Stop and Frisk).* Threshold inquiry deals with the situation in which, although the officer does not have probable cause to arrest, his or her suspicions are raised concerning the behavior of an individual. In such a case, the officer has a right to stop and question the individual; if the officer has reason to believe that the person is carrying a concealed weapon, he or she may frisk the suspect. Unlike searching, frisking is a limited procedure; it is a patdown of the outer clothing for the purpose of finding a concealed weapon. If no weapon is found, the search must stop. However, if an illegal weapon is found, then an arrest can be made and a search incident to the arrest performed.[80] In a threshold inquiry situation, a police officer is permitted to conduct a limited search—that is, one confined to determining whether a suspect is armed.

3. *Automobile Search.* An automobile may be searched without a warrant if there is probable cause to believe that the car was involved in a crime.[81] The rationale for allowing a search of an automobile involves the mobility of automobiles, which creates a significant chance that the evidence will be lost if the search is not conducted immediately, and the fact that people should not expect as much privacy in their cars as in their homes.[82] Police officers who have legitimately stopped an automobile and who have probable cause to believe that contraband is concealed somewhere within it may conduct a warrantless search of the vehicle that is as thorough as a magistrate could authorize by warrant.

4. *Consent Search.* In a consent search, individuals waive their constitutional rights; therefore, neither a warrant nor probable cause need exist. However, for the search to be legal, the consent must be given voluntarily; threat or compulsion invalidates the search.[83] Although it has been held that a voluntary consent is required, it has also been maintained that the police are under no obligation to inform individuals of their right to refuse the search.

5. *Plain View.* Even when an object is in a house or other areas involving an expectation of privacy, the object can be freely inspected if it can be seen by the general public. For example, if a police officer looks through a fence and sees marijuana growing in the suspect's fields, then no search warrant is needed for the property to be seized. The articles are considered to be in plain view, and therefore, a search warrant need not be obtained to seize them.[84]

6. *Seizure of Nonphysical Evidence.* Police can seize nonphysical evidence, such as a conversation, if the suspects had no reason to expect privacy; for example, if police overhear and record a conversation in which two people conspire to kill a third party. In *Katz v. United States*, the Supreme Court addressed the issue that the Fourth Amendment protects people and not property.[85] In *Katz*, the FBI attached an electronic listening and recording device to a public telephone booth for the purpose of obtaining evidence that the defendant was transmitting wagering information

in violation of a federal statute. The Court held that the FBI's action constituted an unreasonable search and seizure. The Court maintained that a search occurs whenever police activity violates a person's privacy. In this case, it was reasonable for the defendant to expect that he would have privacy in a phone booth.

In recent years, the Court has given police greater latitude to search for and seize evidence and eased restrictions on how they conduct their operations. The Court's policy has reflected the legal orientation of its more conservative members. The exclusionary rule discussed in Chapter 15, once a powerful control on police evidence-gathering procedures, has been substantially weakened.

≡ Issues in Policing

A number of important issues face police departments today. Though an all-encompassing discussion of each is beyond the scope of this text, a few of the more important aspects of policing are discussed below.

Police Personality and Subculture

It has become commonplace to argue that a majority of U.S. police officers maintain a unique set of personality traits that place them apart from the "average" citizen. The typical police personality is thought to include authoritarianism, suspicion, racism, hostility, insecurity, conservatism, and *cynicism*.[86] Maintenance of these negative values and attitudes is believed to cause police officers to be secretive and isolated from the rest of society, producing what has been described by William Westly as the **blue curtain** subculture.[87] Isolation and conflict may also contribute to the extreme stress that is an occupational hazard of police work.[88] Isolation and stress have also been linked to burnout and suicide.[89]

There are two opposing viewpoints on the cause of this phenomenon: one position holds that police departments attract recruits who are by nature cynical, authoritarian, secretive, and so on; other experts maintain that socialization and experience on the police force cause these character traits to develop in police officers.[90] Since research evidence supportive of both viewpoints has been produced, neither position dominates on the issue of how the police personality develops; it is not even certain that such a personality actually exists.

Research studies have attempted to describe the development of the police personality. In a classic study, social psychologist Milton Rokeach found that the values of police officers in Lansing, Michigan, differed from those of the general public. Police officers seemed more oriented toward self-control and obedience than the average citizen; in addition, police were more interested in personal goals, such as "an exciting life," and less interested in social goals, such as "a world at peace."[91] When comparing the values of veteran officers with those of recruits, Rokeach and his associates found evidence that police officers' on-the-job experience had not significantly influenced their personalities and that most police officers probably had a unique value orientation and personality when they first embarked upon their careers in the force.

In contrast, more than 40 years ago, police expert William Westly argued that most police officers develop into cynics because of their daily duties.[92] Westly maintained that police officers learn to mistrust the citizens they protect because they are constantly faced with keeping people in line and come to believe that most people are out to break the law or harm a police officer. Arthur Niederhoffer's famous book *Behind the Shield* tested Westly's view by surveying the attitudes and values of 220 New York City police officers.[93] Among his most important findings were that cynicism did increase with length of service, that patrol officers with college educations became quite cynical if they were denied promotion, and that militarylike police academy training caused new recruits to quickly become cynical about themselves, the department, and the community. For example, Niederhoffer found that nearly 80 percent of recruits on their first day believed that the police department was an "efficient, smoothly operating organization"; two months later, less than a third professed that belief. Similarly, half the new recruits believed that a police superior was "very interested in the welfare of his subordinates"; two months later, that number declined to 13 percent.[94]

It has been charged that the unique police personality causes most officers to band together in a police subculture characterized by clannishness, secrecy, and insulation from others in society. Police officers tend to socialize with each other and believe their occupation cuts them off from relationships with civilians. Joining the police subculture means having to support fellow officers against outsiders; maintaining a tough, macho exterior personality; and mistrusting the motives and behavior of outsiders.[95] Strong myths develop about police work that, after becoming institutionalized, help shape the structure and activities of police departments themselves.[96]

The most serious consequences of the police subculture are police officers' resistance to change and mistrust of the public they serve. Opening the police to change will be a prime task of police officials who seek professionalism and progress in their department.

Developing the Police Personality.
The police personality seems to be developed through doing police work. At first, police recruits become socialized into their roles in the police academy. Their field training officer teaches them the ins and outs of police work, helping them through the *rites de passage* of becoming a "real cop."[97] The folklore, tales, myths, and legends surrounding the department are communicated to recruits. Soon, they begin to understand the rules of police work. John Van Maanen suggests that "the adjustment of a newcomer in police departments is one which follows the line of least resistance."[98]

By becoming similar in sentiments and behavior to their peers, recruits avoid censure by their department, their supervisor, and, most important, their colleagues. Thus, young officers adapt their personality to that of the "ideal cop." An esprit de corps soon develops in police work because of the dangerous and unpleasant tasks police officers are required to do and the support they get from their fellow officers. Police solidarity and a "one for all, and all for one" attitude are two of the most cherished aspects of the police occupation.[99]

While most experts agree that police develop an insulated subculture, evidence also shows that police roles and job views vary considerably within and between departments. Within a department, the more experienced officers may be the most cynical and suspicious as they approach the end of their careers.[100] Police officers' orientations also differ. Some officers are service-oriented, while others take a much more active law enforcement role; some are more concerned about their advancement through the ranks, while others enjoy the action of the streets.[101] Departments themselves differ in their orientation toward police activities; some take a more active role in arresting felons, while others exhibit a less legalistic orientation.[102] The various styles of policing are illustrated in Figure 16.2.

While disagreement exists over the exact nature and definition of the police working personality, research by William Walsh has shown that police officers who define themselves as "active" are much more likely to make arrests than their peers who are looking merely to retire and who already hold outside jobs.[103] Consequently,

understanding the nature and direction of the police personality and its effect on role definition and job performance is an essential task of police administrators and reformers.

Discretion

In one of the most important papers on a justice-related issue, Joseph Goldstein argued in 1960 that the law enforcement function of police is not merely a matter of enforcing the rule of law but also involves an enormous amount of personal *discretion* as to whether to invoke the power of arrest.[104] Since then, police discretion has been recognized as a crucial force in all law enforcement decision making.[105]

Police discretion involves the **selective enforcement** of the law by duly authorized police agents. However, unlike members of almost every other criminal justice agency, police officers are neither regulated in their daily procedures by administrative scrutiny nor subjected to judicial review (except when their behavior clearly violates an offender's constitutional rights). As a result, the exercise of discretion by police may sometimes deteriorate into discrimination, violence, and other abusive practices.[106]

Various factors have been associated with the exercise of police discretion. Some relate to the officers' working environment, the size of the department, and the officers' view of their professional worth.[107] Community attitudes and beliefs certainly influence the enforcement or nonenforcement of certain laws (for example, obscenity statutes), as do the policies, practices, and customs of the police department. An individual supervisor, such as a sergeant or lieutenant, can influence subordinates' decisions by making well known his or her personal preferences and attitudes.

Peer pressure also influences decision making. Fellow police officers dictate acceptable responses to street-level problems by displaying or withholding approval in squad room discussions. The officer who takes the job seriously and desires the respect and friendship of others will take their advice, abide by their norms, and seek out the most experienced and most influential patrol officers on the force and follow their behavior models.

A final environmental factor affecting the police officer's performance is his or her perception of community alternatives to police intervention or processing. A police officer may exercise discretion and arrest an individual in a particular circumstance if it seems that nothing else can be done, even if the officer does not believe

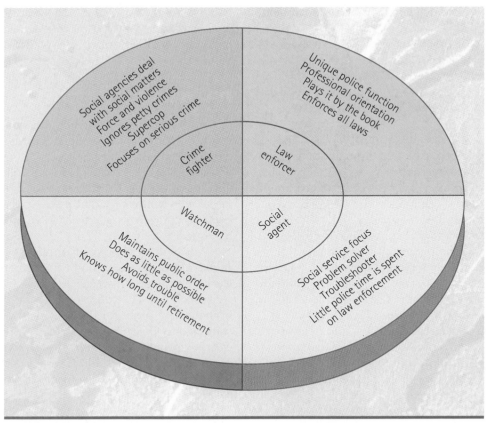

FIGURE 16.2   Police Styles

that an arrest is the best possible example of good police work. In an environment with a proliferation of social agencies—detoxification units, drug control centers, and child care services, for example—a police officer has more alternatives from which to choose in the decision-making process. In fact, referring cases to these alternative agencies saves the officer both time and effort—no records need be made out and court appearances can be avoided. Thus, social agencies provide for greater latitude in police decision making.

Another discretionary influence is the way that a crime or situation is encountered. If, for example, a police officer stumbles on an altercation or a break-in, the discretionary response may be quite different than if the officer had been summoned by police radio. If official police recognition has been given to an act, action must be taken or an explanation made as to why it was not taken. If a matter is brought to an officer's attention by a citizen observer, the officer can ignore the request and risk a complaint or take discretionary action. When an officer chooses to become involved in a situation

without benefit of a summons or complaint, maximum discretion can be used. Even in this circumstance, however, the presence of a crowd or witnesses may contribute to the officer's decision.

And, of course, the officer who acts alone is affected by personal matters—physical condition, mental state, whether there are other duties to perform, and so on.

Finally, the race, age, and gender of the offender may be considered when police officers decide to invoke their arrest powers. While this issue is far from settled, empirical studies indicate that police discretion works against the young, the poor, and members of minority groups and may often favor the wealthy, the politically well connected, and members of the majority group.[108]

Limiting Police Discretion.   Numerous efforts have been made to limit police discretion. Police administrators have attempted to establish guidelines for police officers' operating behavior.[109] Most departments have created rules to guide police officers in their daily

Police officers maintain the discretion to arrest people or take informal action to settle a dispute.

activities. Some departments have established special units to oversee patrol activities; others have created boundaries of police behavior and suggested that any conduct in excess of these limits would not be tolerated.[110]

Despite some success, limiting police discretion has proven to be a difficult task.[111] Advocates of specialized units, policy statements, legal mandates, and other approaches can only assume that the officer in the field will comply with the intent and spirit of the administrator's desire. Little information is available concerning what the specific influence of any particular legal or administrative measure on police discretion will be, whether it will affect all officers equally, or why some officers will respond in one way and others in an opposite way. It is not known what police officers are really like, how they differ from or resemble one another, or how they react to pressures from above.

It is possible that limiting police discretion can only be carried out by outside review. One approach is to develop civilian review boards that monitor police behavior and tactics and investigate civilian complaints. While no two models are alike, a national study of the 50 largest police departments by Samuel Walker indicates that the review board model is gaining acceptance. About 30 departments have adopted some form of civilian board, most since 1986.[112]

Do Social Factors Influence Discretion?

One important issue in the study of police discretion is whether police discriminate on the basis of sex, race, ethnic origin, or class. Some research studies found that the police did in fact discriminate against the poor and racial minorities.[113] Efforts to improve police sensitivity to minority rights may have helped reduce discrimination because some recent studies indicate that police may be less biased than before. For example, Marvin Krohn and his associates examined almost 20,000 cases in a north-central American city and found that gender bias was a relatively insignificant problem.[114] While Douglas Smith and Jodie Klein failed to discover racial bias in their study of the police use of discretion, they did find that gender and class influenced police decision making: police tended to disregard nonviolent disputes involving female complainants in lower-class neighborhoods.[115]

Similarly, Richard Hollinger studied the use of police discretion in arresting drunk drivers in Georgia.[116] He found that police bias was often a function of the socioeconomic status of the culprit and not his or her racial background. If African-Americans were overrepresented in the arrested group, it was because of their overrepresentation in the lower economic classes.

Research indicates that police discretion may also be influenced by the characteristics of crime victims. In one such study, Douglas Smith and his associates uncovered little evidence of racial bias in police decision making.[117] However, Smith did find that police are more likely to take action if the victim of crime was white rather than black. The victim's gender and race may be a more important determinant of arrest decision making than the race and sex of the suspect.

While there is little conclusive evidence of widespread personal bias in police decision making, organizational behavior may play an important role in the way police deal with different groups in society. Police departments may routinely patrol particular areas of the city while leaving others relatively unattended. Consequently, some residents have a greater chance of experiencing detection and arrest. Though racial bias in arrest decisions violates constitutional rights, courts have upheld the use of race as a personal identifying factor that helps narrow police searches for suspects. Police manuals also suggest that officers be aware of race when on the lookout for suspicious characters (for example, questioning those who do not "belong" on their beat). Similarly, courts have upheld the government's use of race as a condition of determining probable cause in searches for illegal aliens and in drug courier profiles.[118]

In sum, research indicates that the effect of offenders' class, race, and gender characteristics may be diminishing in magnitude, but it continues to influence police discretion.

Women and Minority Police Officers

For the past decade, U.S. police departments have made a concerted effort to attract women and minority police officers. The latter group includes African-Americans, Asians, Hispanics, Native Americans, and members of other racial minorities. The reasons for recruiting minority and female officers are varied. Viewed in its most positive light, such recruitment reflects police departments' desire to field a more balanced force that truly represents the community it serves. A culturally diverse police force can be instrumental in gaining the public's confidence by helping to dispel the view that police departments are generally bigoted or biased organizations.

Another important reason for recruiting female and minority police officers is the need to comply with various federal guidelines on hiring.[119] A series of legal actions brought by minority representatives have resulted in local, state, and federal courts ordering police departments to either create hiring quotas to increase minority representation or rewrite entrance exams and requirements to encourage the employment of women and minorities. In one important case, *United States v. Paradise,* the Supreme Court upheld the use of racial quotas as a measure to counter the effects of past discrimination. The decision upheld a lower court ruling that ordered the Alabama Department of Public Safety to promote one black trooper for every white candidate elevated in rank as long as qualified black candidates were available, until 25 percent of each rank was filled by minorities; this would represent the actual racial makeup of the labor market.[120] Several such lawsuits have resulted in either court-ordered hiring judgments or voluntary compliance.

Despite court orders, women and minorities are still underrepresented in many police departments. The problem is even more significant among senior officers and departmental executives. A national survey of African-American and Hispanic officers by Samuel Walker revealed a mixed bag of progress. While some cities, such as Detroit, Dallas, Jacksonville, New Orleans, and Seattle, have substantially increased the number of minority officers, many have departments in which minorities and women are still significantly underrepresented and have reported less than successful efforts to recruit these groups.[121] A national survey conducted by the Bureau of Justice Statistics substantiates Walker's conclusions.[122] The bureau's survey found that about 7.5 percent of police officers were women, 8 percent black males, and another 4 percent Hispanic males.

Minority representation is highest in the nation's largest police departments, reflecting both the population of their locale and their sensitivity to affirmative action issues. Many cities, such as Los Angeles, have had, or now have, African-American police chiefs and a few, most notably Houston, have promoted women to command positions, including chief.

Minority Officers. African-Americans have served on police forces since the mid-nineteenth century. A Republican mayor appointed the first black police officer in Chicago in 1972; and by 1984, there were 23 African-American officers serving in that city.[123] While black officers are still underrepresented on the nation's police forces, legal and social pressure has been mounted to increase their numbers. The reduction in local operating funds experienced in recent years has not helped alleviate this problem.

The life of the African-American officer can be difficult. In a classic work published more than 25 years ago, Nicholas Alex found that black police officers sufferd "double marginality."[124] On the one hand, African-American officers must deal with the expectation that they will give members of their own race "a break." On the other hand, they often experience overt racism from police colleagues.

Alex found that black officers' treatment of other blacks ranged from denying that African-Americans should be treated differently from whites to treating black offenders more harshly than white offenders to prove lack of bias. Alex offered various reasons why some black police officers are tougher on black offenders: they desire acceptance from their white colleagues; they are particularly sensitive to any disrespect shown them by black teenagers; they view themselves as the protectors of the black community.[125]

The problems of black officers can also be exacerbated by the cool reception they are given by their white colleagues, who see them as potential competitors for promotions and special assignments. As James Jacobs and Jay Cohen point out, white police officers view affirmative action hiring and promotion programs as a threat to their job security.[126] They note that in Chicago, white officers intervened on the side of the city when a black police officers' organization filed suit to change the criteria for promotion.[127]

As a greater number of minorities join U.S. police forces, it is likely that they will experience the same problems encountered by white officers. For example, Stephen Leinen interviewed black police officers in New York City and found that their attitudes toward policing were similar to those of white police officers.[128] They were dissatisfied that people in the black community still expressed mistrust and contempt for police, even though an increasing number of black officers had been assigned to these areas. They believed that black cops would be better able to deal with problems in minority communities than whites. Nonetheless, their job perception seemed to mirror the cynicism and apathy that have plagued white police officers.

Female Police Officers.

The first female police officers were appointed in New York as early as 1845, but they were designated as "matrons," and their duties were restricted to handling females in jail custody.[129] In 1893, Chicago hired policewomen but again restricted their activities to making court visitations and assisting male detectives with cases involving women and children. In 1910, Alice Stebbins Wells of the Los Angeles Police Department became the first woman to hold the title of police officer and have full arrest powers. It was not until the passage of the final version of Title VII of the Civil Rights Act in 1972 that police departments around the nation began to hire females and assign them to regular patrol duties. Today, slightly less than 10 percent of all police officers are women.

In general, evaluations of policewomen show them to be equal or superior to male officers in most areas of police work. In one highly regarded study of policewomen, Catherine Milton found that female officers in Washington, D.C., responded to similar types of calls as their male colleagues and that the arrests they made were as likely to result in conviction.[130] Women were more likely to receive support from the community and less likely to be charged with police misconduct. On the

For the past decade, police departments have made a concerted effort to attract women and minority police recruits.

negative side, policewomen made fewer felony and misdemeanor arrests and received lower supervisory ratings than male officers. The generally favorable results obtained by Milton have also been found in other studies assessing policewomen's performance.[131]

Despite their relative proficiency, female police officers have not received general support from their colleagues or the public. One study found that male officers perceive the public to be less cooperative toward them if females are on patrol and report that they receive more insults and threats when patrolling with female partners.[132] Consequently, surveys have shown a relatively low acceptance rate for females in police functions, especially those involving hazardous duties.[133] Some male police officers believe that female officers are more likely to use deadly force than males because their smaller stature prevents them from using unarmed techniques to subdue suspects. Research shows, however, that female officers are actually less likely to use firearms than male officers and that when male and female officers are partners, it is the male who is more likely to use a firearm.[134] Some jurisdictions still assign female officers to secretarial and clerical posts; and in some cities, when budget cutbacks require layoffs, women officers are released in disproportionate numbers.[135]

There is evidence that both male and female officers share many personality traits. Both had a high degree of self-confidence and idealism on entering police work, but their self-perceptions diminished significantly after their police academy training.[136] Sex-role conflicts produced disillusionment with police work, accompanied by denial, self-doubt, repressed anger, and confusion. It is not surprising then that there seems to be few gender differences in the perception of job stress.[137]

It is likely that as the number of women on police forces increases, so too will their job satisfaction and work experiences. Research by Joanne Belknap and Jill Kastens Shelley shows that women who work in departments with a large proportion of female officers report that they are viewed as more professionally competent and also perceive greater acceptance by fellow officers and police administrators.[138]

≡ The Police and Violence

Police officers are empowered to use force and violence in pursuit of their daily task. Some scholars argued that this is the core of the police role:

The role of the police is best understood as a mechanism for the distribution of non-negotiable coercive force employed in accordance with the dictates of an intuitive group of situational exigencies.[139]

Police violence first became a major topic for discussion in the 1940s, when rioting provoked serious police backlash. Thurgood Marshall, then of the National Association for the Advancement of Colored People, referred to the Detroit police as a "gestapo" after a 1943 race riot left 34 people dead.[140] Twenty-five years later, excessive police force was again an issue when television cameras captured police violence against protestors at the Democratic National Convention in Chicago. However, general day-to-day police brutality against individual citizens seems to be diminishing. In 1967, the President's Commission on Criminal Justice concluded:

The Commission believes that physical abuse is not as serious a problem as it was in the past. The few statistics which do exist suggest small numbers of cases involving excessive use of force. Although the relatively small number of reported complaints cannot be considered an accurate measurement of the total problem, most persons, including civil rights leaders, believe that verbal abuse and harassment, not excessive use of force, is the major police-community relations problem today.[141]

Similarly, a study by Albert Reiss found that police abuse was verbal and coercive rather than physically violent. Reiss found little difference in the way police treated blacks and whites; when force was used, it was used selectively—against those who showed disrespect or disregard for police authority once they had been arrested.[142] Thus, while not perfect, as the Rodney King beating and similar incidents show, police officers do seem to have improved their relationships with citizens of all races.

A more recent area of concern has been the use of deadly force in apprehending fleeing or violent offenders. As commonly used, **deadly force** refers to the actions of a police officer who shoots and kills a suspect who is either fleeing from arrest, assaulting a victim, or attacking the officer.[143]

The justification for the use of deadly force can be traced to English common law, in which almost every criminal offense merited a felony status and subsequent death penalty. Thus, execution effected during the arrest of a felon was considered expedient, saving the state from the burden of trial. It is estimated that somewhere between 250 and 1,000 citizens are killed by police each year, though these figures are highly speculative.[144] The numbers of shooting incidents have been declining, reflecting efforts to control police use of deadly force (discussed later in this section).

Research studies indicate that the following factors have been related to police violence:[145]

- *Exposure to threat and stress.* Areas with an unusually high incidence of violent crime are likely to experience shootings by police.

- *Police workload.* Violence corresponds with the number of police officers on the street, the number of calls for service, the number and nature of police dispatches, and the number of arrests made in a given jurisdiction.

- *Firearm availability.* Cities that have a large number of crimes committed with firearms are also likely to have high police violence rates. For example, Houston, which ranks first in firearm availability, has many more police shootings per 1,000 arrests than San Francisco, which ranks tenth.

- *Population type and density.* Jurisdictions swollen by large numbers and varied types of transients and nonresidents also experience a disproportionate amount of police shootings. Research findings suggest that many individuals shot by

The police role often involves potentially violent confrontations. The police must learn to deal effectively with violent situations and use minimal amounts of force while making an arrest.

police are nonresidents caught at or near the scenes of robberies or burglaries of commercial establishments.

- *Race and class discrimination.* It is alleged that blacks and other racial minorities are killed at a significantly higher rate than whites. Betty Jenkins and Adrienne Faison found that 52 percent of those killed by police from 1970 to 1973 were black and 21 percent Hispanic. It is common to focus on the racial factor as the primary predictive factor in police violence.[146] The poorest areas with high degrees of income inequality and a large percentage of minority citizens experienced the highest levels of police shootings.[147]

Despite the evidence indicating that police shootings are motivated by racial bias, research indicates that police officers were most likely to shoot suspects when they were attacked by armed suspects, that many shootings stemmed from incidents in which police officers were injured or killed, and that minorities were more likely to be involved in weapon assaults on police officers than whites (37 percent of events involving white citizens were gun incidents, while the rates for blacks and Hispanics were 58 and 56 percent respectively).[148]

Research also indicates that minority police officers are responsible for a disproportionate number of police shootings and that they are more likely to shoot other minorities than white officers. James Fyfe found that minority officers were often assigned to inner-city ghetto areas in which violence against police was common; it is therefore not surprising that minority officers' use of violence was relatively more frequent. However, in an analysis of police shootings in Memphis, Tennessee, Fyfe found that white police were more likely to shoot black citizens than white and that "police there did differentiate racially with their trigger fingers, by shooting blacks in circumstances less threatening than those in which they shot whites."[149] Thus, the charge that police "have one trigger finger for whites and another for blacks" may have more validity in some areas than in others.

Not all research suggests that personal factors account for police shooting. Some points to the nature of the criminal interaction itself. Peter Scharf and Arnold Binder found that police shootings are influenced by the nature of the opponent the officers faced; whether the officers were on duty or off duty; the number of officers present; and the nature of the physical environment.[150] Rather than being purely spontaneous, Binder and Scharf found, the shootings actually can be described as following a five-step model involving anticipation, confrontation, dialogue, shooting, and aftermath stages in which information is processed and acted on.

Police departments might control the use of deadly force by developing policies that stress containment of armed offenders while specially trained backup teams are sent to take charge of the situation. Training might also emphasize the outcome choices available in situations involving violence and conflict. Lorie Fridell and Arnold Binder found that deadly force situations often involve ambiguity and surprise.[151] Officers trained to take advantage of what little information is available to make quick yet accurate decisions may be the most likely to avoid a potentially fatal confrontation.

Controlling Deadly Force

In 1985, the Supreme Court moved to restrict police use of deadly force when, in *Tennessee v. Garner,* it banned the shooting of unarmed or nondangerous fleeing felons.[152] The Court based its decision on the premise that shooting an unarmed, nondangerous suspect was an illegal seizure of his or her body under the Fourth Amendment. According to the ruling, police could not justifiably use force unless it was "necessary to prevent the escape, and the officer has probable cause to believe that the suspect poses a significant threat of death or serious physical injury to the officers or others," for example, if the suspect threatens the officer or the officer has probable cause to believe that the suspect has committed a crime involving serious physical harm. Before *Garner,* the policy of shooting unarmed fleeing felons had still been used in 17 states.

There are other methods of controlling police shootings. One is through training and counseling sessions that teach police to use less violence. Another is through internal review and policy making by police departments. For example, in New York City, the police department established a new firearms policy based on the American Law Institute's Model Penal Code. The policy stated:

> a. In all cases, only the minimum amount of force will be used which is consistent with the accomplishment of a mission. Every other reasonable means will be utilized for arresting, preventing or terminating a felony or for the defense of oneself or another before a police officer resorts to the use of his firearms.
>
> b. A firearm shall not be discharged under circumstances where lives of innocent persons may be endangered.
>
> c. The firing of a warning shot is prohibited.

> d. The discharging of a firearm to summon assistance is prohibited, except where the police officer's safety is endangered.
>
> e. Discharging a firearm at or from a moving vehicle is prohibited unless the occupants of the other vehicle are using deadly force against the officer or another, by means other than the vehicle.[153]

The New York police department also created the Firearm Discharge Review Board to evaluate shooting incidents. In an examination of the effects of this policy, James Fyfe found that a considerable reduction in the frequency of police shootings followed the policy change.[154]

Change in law and policy may not always work to change police behavior. William Waegel studied police shootings in Philadephia before (1970 to 1972) and after (1974 to 1978) the "fleeing felon" rule was abandoned. He found that after the state had restricted the police use of deadly force, about 20 percent of all shootings violated the new shooting code. In the five-year period after the rule change, police continued to violate shooting rules, and few officers were punished for their transgressions. Waegel found that shooting restrictions clash with the informal rules of the police culture. Unless police departments actively counteract informal proviolence attitudes, changes in law and policy may be ineffective.[155]

While police use of force continues to be an important issue, there is little question that control measures seem to be working. Lawrence Sherman found that the number of civilians killed by police has dropped in half from a high of 353 in 1971.[156] Similarly, the number of law enforcement officers killed on duty has also declined from 104 in 1980 to less than 70 per year today.[157] In 1992, 62 officers were feloniously killed in the line of duty, most while answering disturbance calls and making arrests.

≡ Improving Police Effectiveness

What can police agencies do to become more effective crime fighters and peacekeepers? Over the past 25 years, a number of approaches have been tried and the results have been a mixed bag.

One approach has been to increase the number of sworn officers on the theory that more police will provide greater public protection, deter crime, and so on. Research has not shown this to be the case. In one study, David Greenberg and his associates examined the relationship between police employment levels and crime in over 500 jurisdictions.[158] They concluded that although cities responded to violent crime rate increases by hiring more police, little evidence exists that police employment levels are related to crime rate reductions. Similarly, Craig Uchida and Robert Goldberg found in a study of 88 American cities that jurisdictions with the highest crime rates were also ones that spent the most on police services; between 1960 and 1980, cities with the highest crime rates tripled their expenditures on police services.[159]

Another approach has been to improve police response time through improved communications (911 systems). This approach has potential only if it encourages citizens to report crime frequently and promptly. Research shows a significant relationship between the time it takes to report a crime and the probability of making an arrest. The Police Executive Research Forum found that if a crime is reported while in progress, there is a 33 percent chance of making an arrest; the arrest probability declines to 10 percent if the crime is reported one minute later and to about 5 percent if 15 minutes have elapsed.[160]

The Effect of Technology

Technology is also being used to improve police effectiveness.[161] The growth of technology has been explosive. In 1964, for example, only one city, St. Louis, had a police computer system; by 1968, ten states and 50 cities had state-level criminal justice information systems; today, almost every city of more than 50,000 has some sort of computer support services.[162]

Computers now link neighboring agencies so that they can share information on cases, suspects, and warrants. For example, the Homicide Investigation and Tracking System in Washington serves as a statewide data base for information on murders, attempted murders, predatory sex offenses, and cases involving missing people in which foul play is suspected.[163]

Computers are also being used to expedite the analysis of evidence taken from witnesses and gathered at the crime scene. Los Angeles police can cross-reference data bases (for example, compare the files on suspects who own brown Fords with those who have facial scars) without having to go over the cases manually.[164]

Some police departments are using computerized imaging systems to replace mug books. A vast library of facial features enable witnesses to scan through thousands of noses, eyes, and lips until they find those that match the suspect. Eyeglasses, mustaches, and beards can be added; skin tones can be altered. When the composite is created, an attached camera makes a hard-copy image for distribution.[165] Figure 16.3 illustrates one of these imaging systems.

The use of computer-based automated fingerprint systems is growing around the United States. Using mathematical models, automated fingerprint identification systems can classify fingerprints and identify up to 250 characteristics (minutiae) of the print. These automated systems use high-speed silicon chips to plot each point of minutiae and count the number of ridge lines between each point and its four nearest neighbors, which substantially improves its speed and accuracy over earlier systems.[166]

Another area of high-tech suspect identification is the use of new forensic methods of identification and analysis. The most prominent approach is *DNA fingerprinting*. This technique allows suspects to be identified

The automatic fingerprint information system by Digital Biometrics, Inc. enables investigators to match a suspect's prints with those already on file. An image display monitor lets operators view each fingerprint as it is being rolled. Immediate quality checks notify the operator if the print is too light or too dark, ensuring the highest quality fingerprint image possible with full card preview as a standard feature.

CLOSE-UP

Private Police Systems

Since it is now understood that police forces alone can have only a limited influence on controlling the crime rate and protecting victims, alternative methods of policing have been developed. In the next decade, the presence of private security forces should significantly affect law enforcement.

The emergence of the private security industry has been dramatic, increasing at a much greater pace than public policing. In fact, as Figure A shows, it is now estimated that more money is spent on private protection than on state-sponsored law enforcement agencies; by the year 2000, over $100 billion will be spent on private security. Today, more than 1.5 million people work in the private security area, a number that far exceeds the total number of sworn police officers.

Much of what is known about the national trends in the study of private policing comes from a national survey referred to as the *Hallcrest report* found that the use of private security can be categorized into two major groups. *Proprietary security* is undertaken by an organization's own employees and includes both plainclothes and uniformed agents directed by the organization's head of security. The second type of private security is *contractual services,* such as guards, investigators, armored cars, and so on, which are provided by private companies, such as Wackenhut and Pinkerton. Also included within the category of contractual security must be included the wide variety of security products, such as safes, electronic access control devices, and closed-circuit television.

Private security forces take on responsibilities that are also within the domain of local police agencies. These include responding to burglar alarms, investigating misdemeanors, and providing parking enforcement and court security. Despite this overlap, there was customarily little contact or cooperation between private and public policing. In the 1980s, the International Association of Chiefs of Police, the National Sheriff's Association, and the American Society for Industrial Security began joint meetings to improve relations between the public and private sectors. In 1986, the Joint Council on Law Enforcement and Private Security Associations was formed.

One reason public-private cooperation is essential is the movement to privatize services that have been within the jurisdiction of public police agencies. Candidates for privatization include public building security, parking enforcement, park patrol, animal control, special-event security (such as rock concerts), funeral escorts, prisoner escort, and public housing security. About 18 states already have instituted some form of privatization. In some small towns, private police may even replace the town police force. Reminderville, Ohio, experimented with an all-private police force and found that it resulted in great cost savings without any decline in service.

One area that may be ideal for privatization is responding to private security systems. There has been a rapid expansion in the number of private security systems and a corresponding increase in the number of false alarms. In some jurisdictions, 30 percent of calls for police service

are false alarms. This problem will intensify because the number of residences with alarm systems should double by the year 2000 (about 20 percent of all homes). One approach has been to fine or charge home owners for repeat false alarm calls. It is also likely that private firms may be contracted to handle alarm calls and screen out false alarms before notifying police.

The Future of Private Security

The Hallcrest report estimates that by the year 2000, there will be 750,000 contract guards and 410,000 proprietary security forces. The technology that supports the field will grow rapidly, bringing, more sophisticated alarm systems, access control, and closed-circuit television.

The expanded role of private security is not without its perils. Many law enforcement executives are critical of the quality of private security and believe it has little value as a crime control mechanism. One complaint heard by the Hallcrest researchers was the lack of training and standards in the profession. Still another source of contention between private security and local police agencies is the increasing number of police calls that are generated by private security measures, such as alarms.

The Hallcrest report recommends a number of strategies to improve the quality of private security in this country: upgrade employee quality; create statewide regulatory bodies and statutes for controlling security firms; create mandatory training; increase police knowledge of private security; expand interaction between police and private security, such as

Close-Up text continued on page 500

FIGURE A   The Growth of Private Security

SOURCE: William Cunningham, John Strauchs, and Clifford Van Meter, *Private Security: Patterns and Trends* (Washington, D.C.: National Institute of Justice, 1991), p. 3.

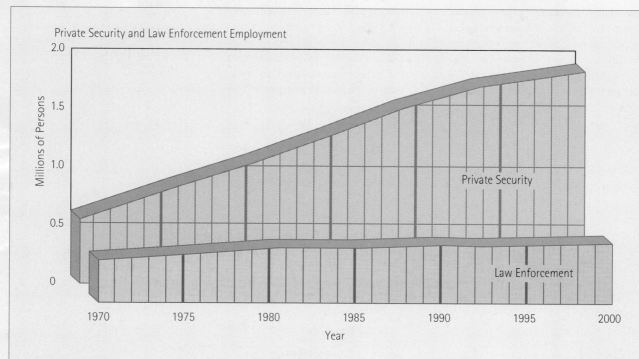

Private Security and Law Enforcement Employment

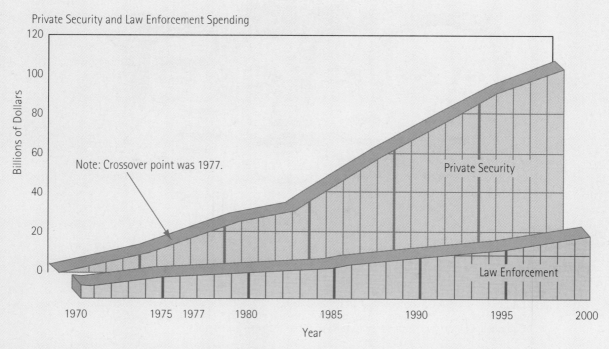

Private Security and Law Enforcement Spending

CLOSE-UP   continued

sharing information; and transfer some police functions, such as burglar alarm checking, to the private sector. The report recommends that the industry create its own standards similar to those adapted by the British Security Industry Association and use them in an effort to professionalize the trade.

Discussion Questions

1. Should private security officers have similar law enforcement powers as local police?
2. Is it fair for police officers trained at state expense to work for private police agencies? Can this create a conflict of interest?

SOURCES: William Cunningham, John Strauchs, and Clifford Van Meter, *The*

Hallcrest Report I: Private Security and Police in America (Stoneham, Mass.: Butterworth-Heineman, 1985); idem, *The Hallcrest Report II: Private Security Trends 1970–2000* (Stoneham, Mass.: Butterworth-Heineman, 1990); idem, *Private Security: Patterns and Trends* (Washington, D.C.: National Institute of Justice, 1991).

FIGURE 16.3   Computer-Generated Composites for Identifying Suspects

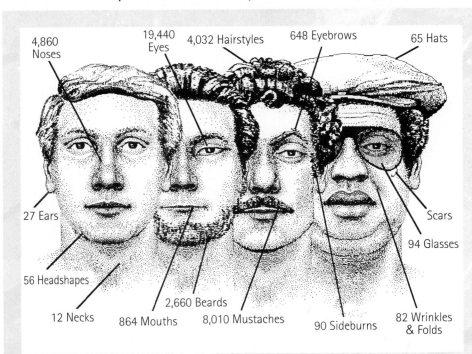

Computer-generated composites can be used to help a witness create a precise sketch of criminal suspects. The Compusketch program developed by the Visatex Corporation of Campbell, California, contains thousands of facial features and details.

on the basis of the genetic material found in hair, blood, and other bodily tissues and fluids. When DNA is used as evidence in a rape trial, DNA segments are taken from the victim, the suspect, and blood and semen found on the victim. A DNA match indicates there is a 4 billion-to-one chance the suspect is the offender.[167]

Technological improvements have also come in police communications. Some departments are using cellular phones in their police cars to facilitate communications with victims and witnesses. Departments that cover wide geographical areas and maintain independent precincts and substations are experimenting with *teleconferencing* systems that provide audio and video linkages. Police agencies may use advanced communications gear to track stolen vehicles. Car owners will be able to buy transmitters that give off a signal beamed to a satellite or other listening device that can then be monitored and tracked by the specially equipped patrol cars.

Many other efforts have been made to improve police performance through training, education, technological advances, and so on. However, the overwhelming load on police has limited their effectiveness in bringing down the crime rate. Consequently, some alternative systems have been created, the most prominent being private security and police agencies, as discussed in the Close-Up entitled "Private Police Systems."

≡ Summary

Police officers are the gatekeepers of the criminal justice process. They use their power to arrest to initiate the justice process.

U.S. police agencies are modeled after their British counterparts. Early in British history, law enforcement was a personal matter. Later, constables were appointed to keep peace among groups of a hundred families. This rudimentary beginning was the seed of today's police departments. In 1838, the first true U.S. police department was developed in Boston.

The first U.S. departments were created because of the need to control mob violence, which was common during the nineteenth century. The police were viewed as being dominated by political bosses who controlled their hiring practices and policies.

Reform movements begun during the 1920s culminated in the concept of professionalism in the 1950s and 1960s. Police professionalism was interpreted to mean tough, rule-oriented police work featuring advanced technology and hardware. However, the view that these measures would quickly reduce crime proved incorrect.

There are several major law enforcement agencies. On the federal level, the FBI is the premier law enforcement organization. Other agencies include the Drug Enforcement Administration, the U.S. marshals, and the Secret Service. County-level law enforcement is provided by sheriff's departments, and most states maintain state police agencies. However, the great bulk of law enforcement activities are carried out by local police agencies.

The police role is multilevel. Police officers fight crime, keep the peace, and provide community services. The conflicts and burdens involved in their work insulate them from the community and create great stress which has been linked to burnout and suicide. There is some question whether police patrol is actually effective. One important study conducted in Kansas City found that the extent of patrol had little effect on the crime rate or citizens' satisfaction.

The second prominent police role is investigation. Detectives collect evidence to identify perpetrators. Although detectives use various techniques, including sting operations, studies have shown that detective work is generally ineffective.

Other police functions include traffic control, departmental administration and maintenance, and improvement of relations between police and community.

In recent years, many police operations have been controlled by court decisions. Most important, the courts have set limits on the extent of police interrogations and search and seizure of evidence.

Police departments face crucial issues today. One involves understanding the police personality and its effect on performance. Another involves police officers' use of discretion and how it can be controlled. Women and minority officers probably will become more prevalent on police departments, and their worth must be more fully appreciated by rank-and-file patrol officers. Police violence has received much attention. There is some debate over whether police officers kill members of minority groups more frequently than white citizens; recent evidence indicates that that may be the case in some cities.

≡ KEY TERMS

gatekeepers	pledge system
Knapp Commission	watch system
Mollen Commission	justice of the peace

Sir Robert Peel

Wickersham Commission

August Vollmer

sheriff

shire reeve

team policing

foot patrols

neighborhood policing

problem-oriented policing

crackdown

hot spots

aggressive preventive
patrol

internal affairs division

mug shots

inevitable discovery rule

search warrant

blue curtain

selective enforcement

deadly force

≡ NOTES

1. Associated Press, "Jury Awards Rodney King $3.8 Million in Damages," *Boston Globe,* 20 April 1994, p. 1.

2. Bernie Patterson, "Job Experience and Perceived Job Stress among Police, Correctional and Probation/Parole Officers," *Criminal Justice and Behavior* 19 (1992): 260–85.

3. John Klofas, "Drugs and Justice: The Impact of Drugs on Criminal Justice in a Metropolitan Community," *Crime and Delinquency* 39 (1993): 204–24.

4. This section relies heavily on Daniel Devlin, *Police Procedure, Administration and Organization* (London: Butterworth, 1966); Robert Fogelson, *Big City Police* (Cambridge: Harvard University Press, 1977); Roger Lane, *Policing the City, Boston 1822–1885* (Cambridge: Harvard University Press, 1967); Roger Lane, "Urban Police and Crime in Nineteenth Century America," in *Crime and Justice,* vol. 2, ed. N. Morris and M. Torrey (Chicago: University of Chicago Press, 1980), pp. 1–45; J. J. Tobias, *Crime and Industrial Society in the Nineteenth Century* (New York: Schoken Books, 1967); Samuel Walker, *A Critical History of Police Reform: The Emergence of Professionalism* (Lexington, Mass.: Lexington Books, 1977); Samuel Walker, *Popular Justice* (New York: Oxford University Press, 1980); President's Commission on Law Enforcement and the Administration of Justice, *Task Force Report: The Police* (Washington, D.C.: Government Printing Office, 1967), pp. 1–9.

5. Devlin, *Police Procedure, Administration and Organization,* p. 3.

6. Walker, *Popular Justice,* p. 18.

7. Lane, "Urban Police and Crime in Nineteenth Century America," p. 5.

8. Walker, *Popular Justice,* p. 61.

9. Preston William Slossom, *A History of American Life,* 12 vols., *The Great Crusade and After, 1914–1929,* vol. 12, ed. Arthur M. Schlesinger and Dixon Ryan Fox, (New York: Macmillan, 1931), p. 102.

10. See, generally, Walker, *A Critical History of Police Reform.*

11. This section was adapted from Law Enforcement Assistance Administration, *Two Hundred Years of American Criminal Justice* (Washington, D.C.: Government Printing Office, 1976).

12. Thomas Adams, *Law Enforcement* (Englewood Cliffs, N.J.: Prentice-Hall, 1968), p. 99.

13. Walker, *Popular Justice,* p. 238.

14. Brian Reaves, *Census of State and Local Law Enforcement Agencies, 1992* (Washington, D.C.: Bureau of Justice Statistics, 1993), pp. 3, 9.

15. John Sullivan, *Introduction to Police Science* (New York: McGraw-Hill, 1968), p. 24.

16. Reaves, *Census of State and Local Law Enforcement Agencies, 1992.*

17. Ibid., p. 8.

18. See Clarence Schrag, *Crime and Justice: American Style* (Washington, D.C.: U.S. Government Printing Office, 1970), p. 47.

19. Egon Bittner, *The Functions of Police in Modern Society* (Cambridge, Mass.: Delgeschlager, Gunn and Hain, 1980), p. 149.

20. J. Q. Wilson, *Varieties of Police Behavior: The Management of Law and Order in Eight Communities* (Cambridge: Harvard University Press, 1968).

21. Richard Sykes and Edward Brent, *Policing: A Social Behaviorist Perspective* (New Brunswick, N.J.: Rutgers University Press, 1983).

22. David Carter and Allen Sapp, "Police Experiences and Responses to the Homeless," *Journal of Crime and Justice* 16 (1993): 87–97.

23. Jack Greene and Carl Klockars, "What Police Do," in *Thinking about Police,* ed. Carl Klockars and Stephen Mastrofski (New York: McGraw-Hill, 1991), pp. 273–85.

24. Bittner, *The Functions of Police in Modern Society,* pp. 63–72.

25. James Q. Wilson and George Kelling, "Broken Windows: The Police and Neighborhood Safety," *Atlantic Monthly,* March 1982, pp. 29–38.

26. Ibid., p. 37.

27. See, generally, Lawrence Sherman, *Team Policing—Seven Case Studies* (Washington, D.C.: Police Foundation, 1973).

28. John Angell, "The Democratic Model Needs a Fair Trial: Angell's Response," *Criminology* 12 (1975): 379–84.

29. "Many Cities Experimenting with Foot Patrol," *Criminal Justice Newsletter* 16 (15 May 1985): 1–2.

30. Jerome Skolnick and David Bayley, "Theme and Variation in Community Policing," in *Crime and Justice, A Review of Research,* vol. 12, ed. Michael Tonry and Norval Morris (Chicago: University of Chicago Press, 1988), pp. 1–38.

31. Police Foundation, "The Effects of Police Fear Reduction Strategies: A Summary of Findings from Houston and Newark" (Washington, D.C.: Police Foundation, 1986).

32. Lee Brown, "Neighborhood-Oriented Policing," *American Journal of Police* 9 (1990): 197–207.

33. Herman Goldstein, *Problem-Oriented Policing* (New York: McGraw-Hill, 1990).

34. Mark Moore and Robert Trojanowicz, *Policing and the Fear of Crime* (Washington, D.C: National Institute of

Justice, 1988), p. 5.

35. George Kelling, *What Works—Research and the Police* (Washington, D.C.: National Institute of Justice, 1988), p. 3.

36. Lawrence Sherman, "Police Crackdowns: Initial and Residual Deterrence," in *Crime and Justice, A Review of Research,* vol. 12, ed. Michael Tonry and Norval Morris (Chicago: University of Chicago Press, 1990), pp. 1–48.

37. Lawrence Sherman, Patrick Gartin, and Michael Buerger, "Hot Spots of Predatory Crime: Routine Activities and the Criminology of Place," *Criminology* 27 (1989): 27–55.

38. Dennis Roncek and Pamela Maier, "Bars, Blocks, and Crimes Revisited: Linking the Theory of Routine Activities to the Empiricism of 'Hot Spots'," *Criminology* 29 (1991): 725–53.

39. Lynn Zimmer, "Proactive Policing against Street-Level Drug Trafficking," *American Journal of Police* 9 (1990): 43–65.

40. Ibid., pp. 64–65.

41. Samuel Walker, "Broken Windows and Fractured History: The Use and Misuse of History in Recent Police Patrol Analysis," *Justice Quarterly* 1 (1984): 75–90.

42. Jack R. Greene, "The Effects of Community Policing on American Law Enforcement: A Look at the Evidence" (Paper presented at the International Congress on Criminology, Hamburg, Germany, September 1988), p. 19.

43. Roger Dunham and Geoffrey Alpert, "Neighborhood Differences in Attitudes toward Policing: Evidence for a Mixed-Strategy Model of Policing in a Multi-Ethnic Setting," *Journal of Criminal Law and Criminology* 79 (1988): 504–22.

44. David Carter and Allen Sapp, *The State of Police Education: Critical Findings* (Washington, D.C: Police Executive Research Forum, 1988).

45. Quint Thurman, Andrew Giacomazzi, and Phil Bogen, "Research Note: Cops, Kids, and Community Policing— An Assessment of a Community Policing Demonstration Project," *Crime and Delinquency* 39 (1993): 554–664; Bonnie Fisher, "What Works: Block Watch Meetings or Crime Prevention Seminars," *Journal of Crime and Justice* 16 (1993): 1–20.

46. David Kessler, "Integrating Calls for Services with Community- and Problem-Oriented Policing: A Case Study," *Crime and Delinquency* 39 (1993) 485–508.

47. Susan Guarino-Ghezzi, "Reintegrative Police Surveillance of Juvenile Offenders: Forging an Urban Model," *Crime and Delinquency* 40 (1994): 131–53.

48. Herman Goldstein, "Toward Community-Oriented Policing: Potential, Basic Requirements, and Threshold Questions," *Crime and Delinquency* 33(1987): 6–30, at 27–28.

49. See Harlan Hahn, "A Profile of Urban Police," in *The Ambivalent Force,* ed. A. Niederhoffer and A. Blumberg (Hinsdale, Ill.: Dryden Press, 1967), p. 59.

50. George Kelling, Tony Pate, Duane Dieckman, and

Charles Brown, *The Kansas City Preventive Patrol Experiment: A Summary Report* (Washington, D.C.: Police Foundation, 1974).

51. Albert J. Reiss, *The Police and the Public* (New Haven: Yale University Press, 1971), p. 19.

52. Bittner, *The Functions of Police in Modern Society,* p. 127.

53. James Q. Wilson and Barbara Boland, "The Effect of Police on Crime," *Law and Society Review* 12 (1978): 367–84.

54. Robert Sampson and Jacqueline Cohen, "Deterrent Effects of the Police on Crime: A Replication and Theoretical Extension," *Law and Society Review* 22 (1988): 163–91.

55. Lawrence Sherman, "Policing Communities: What Works," in *Crime and Justice,* vol. 8, ed. Al Reiss and Michael Tonry (Chicago: University of Chicago Press, 1986), pp. 366–79.

56. Ibid., p. 368.

57. See, generally, Peter Greenwood and Joan Petersilia, *The Criminal Investigation Process, Vol. 1: Summary and Policy Implications* (Santa Monica, Calif.: Rand Corporation, 1975); P. Greenwood, J. Chaiken, J. Petersilia, and L. Prusoff, *The Criminal Investigation Process, Vol. 3: Observations and Analysis* (Santa Monica, Calif.: Rand Corporation, 1975).

58. C. Cotter and J. Burrows, *Property Crime Program, a Special Report: Overview of the STING Program and Project Summaries* (Washington, D.C.: Criminal Conspiracies Division, Office of Criminal Justice Programs, Law Enforcement Assistance Administration, U.S. Department of Justice, 1981).

59. Robert Langworthy, "Stings: A Crime Control Tool," (Paper presented at the American Society of Criminology, Atlanta, November 1986).

60. Greenwood and Petersilia, *The Criminal Investigation Process.*

61. Mark T. Willman and John R. Snortum, "Detective Work: The Criminal Investigation Process in a Medium-Size Police Department," *Criminal Justice Review* 9 (1984): 33–39.

62. John Eck, *Solving Crimes: The Investigation of Burglary and Robbery* (Washington, D.C.: Police Executive Research Forum, 1984).

63. See, for example, Susan Martin, "Policing Career Criminals: An Examination of an Innovative Crime Control Program," *Journal of Criminal Law and Criminology* 77 (1986): 1159–82.

64. See, generally, Robert Sheehan and Gary Cordner, *Introduction to Police Administration* (Reading, Mass.: Addison-Wesley, 1979).

65. *Miranda v. Arizona,* 384 U.S. 436 (1966).

66. *Harris v. New York,* 401 U.S. 222 (1971).

67. *Michigan v. Tucker,* 417 U.S. 433 (1974).

68. *Moran v. Burbine,* 106 S.Ct. 1135 (1986); *Michigan v. Mosley,* 423 U.S. 96 (1975); *Fare v. Michael C.,* 442 U.S. 23 (1979).

69. *Nix v. Williams,* 104 S.Ct. 2501 (1984).

70. *New York v. Quarles,* 104 S.Ct. 2626 (1984).

71. *Oregon v. Elstad,* 105 S.Ct. 1285 (1985).

72. *Colorado v. Spring,* 107 S.Ct. 851 (1987).

73. *Colorado v. Connelly,* 107 S.Ct. 515 (1986).

74. *Moran v. Burbine,* 106 S.Ct. 1135 (1986).

75. *Colorado v. Connelly,* 107 S.Ct. 515 (1986).

76. *Minnick v. Miss.,* 48 Cr.L. 2051 (1990).

77. *Arizona v. Fulminante,* 48 Cr.L. 2105 (1991).

78. *Illinois v. Gates,* 104 S.Ct. 2626 (1984).

79. *Chimel v. California,* 395 U.S. 752 (1969).

80. *Terry v. Ohio,* 392 U.S. 1 (1968).

81. *Carroll v. United States,* 267 U.S. 132 (1925).

82. *United States v. Ross,* 102 S.Ct. 2147 (1982).

83. *Bumper v. North Carolina,* 391 U.S. 543 (1960).

84. Limitations on the plain view doctrine have been defined in *Arizona v. Hicks,* 107 S.Ct. 1149 (1987) (the recording of serial numbers from stereo components in a suspect's apartment could not be justified as being in plain view).

85. *Katz v. United States,* 389 U.S. 347 (1967).

86. Richard Lundman, *Police and Policing* (New York: Holt, Rinehart and Winston, 1980); see also Jerome Skolnick, *Justice without Trial* (New York: Wiley, 1966).

87. Cited in Authur Neiderhoffer, *Behind the Shield: The Police in Urban Society* (Garden City, N.Y.: Doubleday, 1967), p. 65.

88. For an impressive review, see Richard Farmer, "Clinical and Managerial Implication of Stress Research on the Police," *Journal of Police Science and Administration* 17 (1990): 205–17; see also Harvey McMurray, "Attitudes of Assaulted Police Officers and Their Policy Implications," *Journal of Police Science and Administration* 17 (1990): 44–48.

89. Rose Lee Josephson and Martin Reiser, "Officer Suicide in the Los Angeles Police Department: A Twelve-Year Follow Up," *Journal of Police Science and Administration* 17 (1990): 227–30; Vivian Lord, Denis Gray, and Samuel Pond, "The Police Stress Inventory: Does It Measure Stress?" *Journal of Criminal Justice* 19 (1991): 139–49.

90. See, for example, Richard Bennett and Theodore Greenstein, "The Police Personality: A Test of the Predispositional Model," *Journal of Police Science and Administration* 3 (1975): 439–45.

91. Milton Rokeach, Martin Miller, and John Snyder, "The Value Gap between Police and Policed," *Journal of Social Issues* 27 (1971): 155–71; for a similar view, see James Teevan and Bernard Dolnick, "The Values of the Police: A Reconsideration and Interpretation," *Journal of Police Science and Administration* 1 (1973): 366–69.

92. William Westly, *Violence and the Police: A Sociological Study of Law, Custom and Morality* (Cambridge: MIT Press, 1970); W. Westly, "Violence and the Police," *American Journal of Sociology* 49 (1953): 34–41.

93. Niederhoffer, *Behind the Shield.*

94. Ibid., pp. 216–20.

95. See, for example, Richard Harris, *The Police Academy: An Inside View* (New York: John Wiley, 1973); John Van Maanen, "Observations on the Making of Policemen," *Human Organization* 32 (1973): 407–18; Jonathan Rubenstein, *City Police* (New York: Ballantine, 1973); John Broderick, *Police in a Time of Change* (Morristown, N.J.: General Learning Press, 1977).

96. John Crank and Robert Langworthy, "An Institutional Perspective of Policing," *Journal of Criminal Law and Criminology* 83 (1992): 338–457.

97. John Van Maanen, "Observations on the Making of Policemen," in *Order under Law,* ed. R. Culbertson and M. Tezak (Prospect Heights, Ill.: Waveland Press, 1981), p. 59.

98. Ibid., p. 66.

99. Bittner, *The Function of Police in Modern Society,* p. 63.

100. Barry Evans, Greg Coman, and Robb Stanley, "The Police Personality : Type A Behavior and Trait Anxiety," *Journal of Criminal Justice* 20 (1992): 429–41.

101. Michael Brown, *Working the Street: Police Discretion and the Dilemmas of Reform* (New York: Russell Sage Foundation, 1981); William Muir, *Police: Streetcorner Politicians* (Chicago: University of Chicago Press, 1977).

102. John Crank, "Police Style and Legally Serious Crime: A Contextual Analysis of Municipal Police Departments," *Journal of Criminal Justice* 20 (1992): 401–12.

103. William Walsh, "Patrol Officer Arrest Rates: A Study of the Social Organization of Police Work," *Justice Quarterly* 2 (1986): 271–90.

104. Joseph Goldstein, "Police Discretion Not to Invoke the Criminal Process," *Yale Law Journal* 69 (1960): 543–94.

105. Richard C. Donnelly, "Police Authority and Practices," *Annals of the American Academy of Political and Social Science* 339 (January 1962): 91–92.

106. See, generally, Kenneth C. Davis, *Discretionary Justice— A Preliminary Inquiry* (Baton Rouge: Louisiana State University Press, 1969).

107. Stephen Mastrofski, R. Richard Ritti, and Debra Hoffmaster, "Organizational Determinants of Police Discretion: The Case of Drinking and Driving," *Journal of Criminal Justice* 15 (1987): 387–402.

108. See, for example, Nathan Goldman, *The Differential Selection of Juvenile Offenders for Court Appearance* (New York: National Council on Crime and Delinquency, 1963); Aaron Cicourel, *The Social Organization of Juvenile Justice* (New York: John Wiley, 1968); Irving Piliavin and Scott Briar, "Police Encounters with Juveniles," *American Journal of Sociology* 70 (1964): 206.

109. Jerome Skolnick and J. Richard Woodworth, "Bureaucracy, Information and Social Control: A Study of a Morals Detail," in *The Police, Six Sociological Essays,* ed. David Bordua (New York: John Wiley, 1960).

110. John Gardiner, *Traffic and the Police: Variations in Law Enforcement Policy* (Cambridge: Harvard University Press, 1969).

111. One notable exception is control of deadly force, which will be discussed later in this chapter.

112. Samuel Walker, *Civilian Review of the Police: A National*

Survey of the 50 Largest Cities, 1991 (Omaha: University of Nebraska, Department of Criminal Justice, 1991).

113. Gregory Howard Williams, *The Law and Politics of Police Discretion* (Westport, Conn: Greenwood Press, 1984); Dennis Powell, "Race, Rank, and Police Discretion," *Journal of Police Science and Administration* 9 (1981): 383–89; Douglas Smith and Jody Klein, "Police Control of Interpersonal Disputes," *Social Problems* 31 (1984): 468–81; Goldman, *The Differential Selection of Juvenile Offenders for Court Appearance;* Dale Dannefer and Russell Schutt, "Race and Juvenile Justice Processing in Court and Police Agencies," *American Journal of Sociology* 87 (1982): 1113–32.

114. Marvin Krohn, James Curry, and Shirley Nelson-Kilger, "Is Chivalry Dead? An Analysis of Changes in Police Dispositions of Males and Females," *Criminology* 21 (1983): 417–37.

115. Douglas Smith and Jody Klein, "Police Control of Interpersonal Disputes," *Social Problems* 31 (1984): 468–81.

116. Richard C. Hollinger, "Race, Occupational Status and Pro-Active Police Arrest for Drinking and Driving," *Journal of Criminal Justice* 12 (1984): 173–83.

117. Douglas A. Smith, Christy A. Visher, and Laura A. Davidson, "Equity and Discretionary Justice: The Influence of Race on Police Arrest Decisions," *Journal of Criminal Law and Criminology* 75 (1984): 234–49.

118. Sherri Lynn Johnson, "Race and the Decision to Detain a Suspect," *Yale Law Journal* 93 (1983): 214–58.

119. Most important is the Equal Employment Opportunity Act of 1972, amending Title VII of the Civil Rights Act of 1964.

120. *United States v. Paradise,* 55 L.W. 4211 (1987).

121. Samuel Walker, *Employment of Black and Hispanic Police Officers, 1983–1988: A Follow-Up Study* (Omaha: Center for Applied Urban Research, University of Nebraska, 1989).

122. Brian Reaves, *Profile of State and Local Law Enforcement Agencies, 1987* (Washington, D.C.: Bureau of Justice Statistics, 1989).

123. Walker, *Popular Justice,* p. 61.

124. Nicholas Alex, *Black in Blue: A Study of the Negro Policeman* (New York: Appleton Century Crofts, 1969).

125. Ibid., p. 154.

126. James Jacobs and Jay Cohen, "The Impact of Racial Integration on the Police," *Journal of Police Science and Administration* 6 (1978): 182.

127. See *Afro-American Patrolmen's League v. Duck,* 366 F.Supp. 1095 (1973); 503 F.2d 294 (6th Cir., 1974); 538 F.2d 328 (6th Cir., 1976).

128. Stephen Leinen, *Black Police, White Society* (New York: New York University Press, 1984).

129. See, generally, David J. Bell, "Policewomen: Myths and Reality," *Journal of Police Science and Administration* 10 (1982): 112–20.

130. Catherine Milton, *Women in Policing* (Washington, D.C.: Police Foundation, 1972).

131. See, generally, A. Bouza, "Women in Policing," *FBI Law Enforcement Bulletin* 44 (1975): 2–7; Joyce Sichel, Lucy Friedman, Janet Quint, and Micall Smith, *Women on Patrol, A Pilot Study of Police Performance in New York City* (Washington, D.C.: National Criminal Justice Reference Service, 1978); William Weldy, "Women in Policing: A Positive Step toward Increased Police Enthusiasm," *Police Chief* 43 (1976): 47.

132. Patricia Marshall, "Policewomen on Patrol," *Manpower* 5 (1973): 14–20.

133. R. Hindman, "A Survey Related to Use of Female Law Enforcement Officers," *Police Chief* 42 (1975): 58–60.

134. Sean Grennan, "Findings on the Role of Officer Gender in Violent Encounters with Citizens," *Journal of Police Science and Administration* 15 (1987): 79–85.

135. Bell, "Policewomen: Myths and Realities," p. 114.

136. Sally Gross, "Women Becoming Cops: Developmental Issues and Solutions," *Police Chief* 51 (1984): 32–35.

137. Curt Bartol, George Bergen, Julie Seager Volckens, and Kathleen Knoras, "Women in Small-Town Policing," *Criminal Justice and Behavior* 19 (1992): 240–59.

138. Joanne Belknap and Jill Kastens Shelley, "The New Lone Ranger: Policewomen on Patrol," *American Journal of Police* 12 (1993): 47–75.

139. Bittner, *The Functions of Police in Modern Society,* p. 46.

140. Walker, *Popular Justice,* p. 197.

141. President's Commission on Law Enforcement and the Administration of Justice, *Task Force Report: The Police,* pp. 181–82.

142. Reiss, *The Police and the Public.*

143. For a comprehensive view of this issue, see William Geller and Michael Scott, "Deadly Force: What We Know," in *Thinking about Police,* ed. Carl Klockars and Stephen Mastrofski (New York: McGraw-Hill, 1991), pp. 446–77; James Fyfe, "Police Use of Deadly Force: Research and Reform," *Justice Quarterly* 5 (1988): 165–205.

144. Fyfe, "Police Use of Deadly Force: Research and Reform," p. 178; Kenneth Mattulla, *A Balance of Forces* (Washington, D.C.: U.S. Government Printing Office, 1982), p. 17.

145. This discussion is adapted from James Fyfe, "Toward a Typology of Police Shootings" (Paper presented at the annual meeting of the Academy of Criminal Justice Sciences, Oklahoma City, March 1980).

146. Betty Jenkins and Adrienne Faison, *An Analysis of 248 Persons Killed by New York City Policemen* (New York: Metropolitan Applied Research Center, 1974).

147. Jonathan Sorensen, James Marquart, and Deon Brock, "Factors Related to Killings of Felons by Police Officers: A Test of the Community Violence and Conflict Hypotheses," *Justice Quarterly,* 10 (1993): 417–40.

148. James Fyfe, "Race and Extreme Police-Citizen Violence," in *Race, Crime and Criminal Justice,* ed. R. L. McNeely and Carl Pope (Beverly Hills: Sage, 1981).

149. James Fyfe, "Blind Justice? Police Shooting in Memphis"

(Paper prepared for the annual meeting of the Academy of Criminal Justice Science, Philadelphia, March 1981), p. 18.

150. Peter Scharf and Arnold Binder, *The Badge and the Bullet: Police Use of Deadly Force* (New York: Praeger, 1983).

151. Lorie Fridell and Arnold Binder, "Police Officer Decisionmaking in Potentially Violent Confrontations," *Journal of Criminal Justice* 20 (1992): 385–99.

152. *Tennessee v. Garner,* 105 S.Ct. 1694 (1985).

153. New York City Police Department, *Temporary Operating Procedure 237,* p. 1.

154. James Fyfe, "Administrative Interventions on Police Shooting Discretion: An Empirical Examination," *Journal of Criminal Justice* 7 (1979): 309–23.

155. William Waegel, "The Use of Lethal Force by Police: The Effect of Statutory Change," *Crime and Delinquency* 30 (1984): 121–40.

156. Estimate based on Geller and Scott, "Deadly Force: What We Know," p. 452.

157. Ibid.

158. David Greenberg, Ronald Kessler, and Colin Loftin, "The Effect of Police Employment on Crime," *Criminology* 21 (1983): 375–94.

159. Craig Uchida and Robert Goldberg, *Police Employment and Expenditure Trends* (Washington, D.C.: Bureau of Justice Statistics, 1986); see also Colin Loftin and David McDowall, "The Police, Crime, and Economic Theory: An Assessment," *American Sociological Review* 47 (1982): 393–401.

160. Police Executive Research Forum, *Calling the Police: Citizen Reporting of Serious Crime* (Washington, D.C.: PERF, 1981).

161. For a general review, see Malcolm Sparrow, *Information Systems and the Development of Policing* (Washington, D.C.: National Institute of Justice, 1993).

162. Ibid.

163. Robert Keppel and Joseph Weis, *Improving the Investigation of Violent Crime: The Homicide Investigation and Tracking System* (Washington, D.C.: National Institute of Justice, 1993).

164. Kristen Olson, "LAPD's Newest Investigative Tool," *Police Chief* 55 (1988): 30.

165. Judith Blair Schmitt, "Computerized ID Systems," *Police Chief* 59 (1992): 33–45.

166. Richard Rau, "Forensic Science and Criminal Justice Technology: High-Tech Tools for the 90's," *NIJ Reports,* June 1991, pp. 6–10.

167. Ibid., pp. 6–9.

17

The Judicatory Process

☰ Introduction

The judicatory process is designed to provide an open and impartial forum for deciding the justice of a conflict between two or more parties. The conflict may be between criminal and victim, law enforcement agents and violators of the law, parent and child, federal government and violators of governmental regulations, and so on. Regardless of the parties or issues involved, their presence in a courtroom should guarantee them that they will have a hearing conducted under regulated rules of procedure in an atmosphere of fair play and objectivity and that the outcome of the hearing will be clear. If a defendant believes that the ground rules have been violated, he or she may take the case to a higher court, where the procedures of the original trial will be examined. If it finds that a violation of legal rights has occurred, the appellate court may deem the findings of the original trial improper and either order a new hearing or hold that some other measure must be carried out; for example, the court may dismiss the charge outright.

The court is a complex social agency with many independent but interrelated subsystems—police, prosecutor, defense attorney, judge, and probation department—each having a role in the court's operation. It is also the scene of many important elements of criminal justice decision making—detention, jury selection, trial, and sentencing.

Ideally, the judicatory process operates under a cloak of absolute fairness and equality. The entire process—from the filing of the initial complaint to final sentencing of the defendant—is governed by precise rules of law designed to ensure fairness. No defendant being tried before a U.S. court should suffer or benefit because of his or her personal characteristics, beliefs, or affiliations.

However, U.S. criminal justice can be a very selective process. Decision makers' discretion accompanies defendants through every step of the process of justice, determining what will happen to them and how their case will be resolved. Sometimes the direction justice takes is difficult to understand. While most people convicted of homicide receive a prison sentence, about 5 percent receive probation as a sole sentence; more murderers get probation than the death penalty. About 14 percent of convicted rapists are given probation only, although their offenses may at first seem indistinguishable from the offenses of those who are imprisoned.[1] Of adults convicted on violent felony charges, about 20 percent get probation only, while 59 percent get sent to a state prison and 21 percent to a county jail. Why should one violent offender receive a long prison sentence and another be released on probation? Although the judicatory process should be impartial and fair, very often it is marked by the same informal, low-visibility decision making that characterizes the law enforcement process.[2]

This chapter will review some of the institutions and processes involved in adjudication and trial. First, the chapter will briefly describe the court structure. Then, the actors in the process—prosecution, defense, judges, and juries—will be discussed. The pretrial stage of the justice process will next be the focus of attention as such issues as bail and plea bargaining are described. The criminal trial will then be discussed in some detail; and finally, sentencing formats will be explained.

☰ Court Structure

The criminal adjudication process is played out within the court system. The nation's 16,000 courts are organized on the municipal, county, state, and federal levels.

State Courts

The typical state court structure is illustrated in Figure 17.1. Most states employ a three- or four-tiered court structure. Lower courts try misdemeanors and conduct the preliminary processing of felony offenses. Superior trial courts have jurisdiction over the trying of felony cases. Appellate courts review the criminal procedures of trial courts to determine whether the offenders were treated fairly. Superior appellate courts or state supreme courts, used in about half the states, review lower appellate court decisions.

Federal Courts

The federal court system has three tiers, as shown in Figure 17.2. The **U. S. district courts** are the trial courts of the system; they maintain jurisdiction over cases involving violations of federal law, such as interstate transportation of stolen vehicles and racketeering.

Appeals from the district court are heard in one of the intermediate **federal courts of appeal.** However, the highest federal appeals court is the **U.S. Supreme Court.** It is the court of last resort for all cases tried in the various federal and state courts.

The Supreme Court is composed of nine members, appointed for lifetime terms by the president with the approval of Congress. In general, the Court has discretion as to which cases it will consider and may choose

FIGURE 17.1 State Judicial System

*Courts of special jurisidiction, such as probate, family, or juvenile courts, and the so-called inferior courts, such as common pleas or municipal courts, may be separate courts or part of the trial court of general jurisdiction.
**Justices of the peace do not exist in all states. Where they do exist, their jurisdictions vary greatly from state to state.

SOURCE: American Bar Association, *Law and the Courts* (Chicago: American Bar Association, 1974), p. 20. Updated information provided by West Publishing Company, St. Paul, Minnesota.

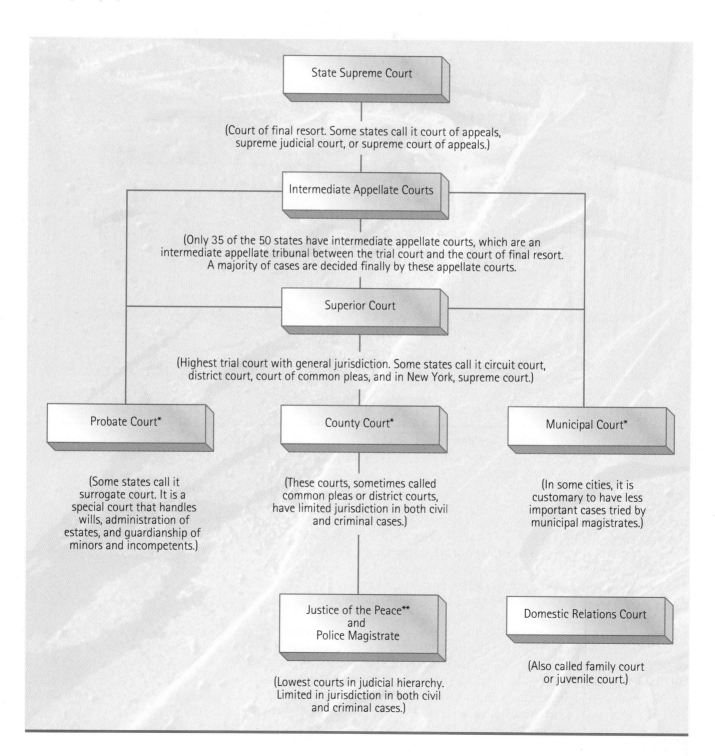

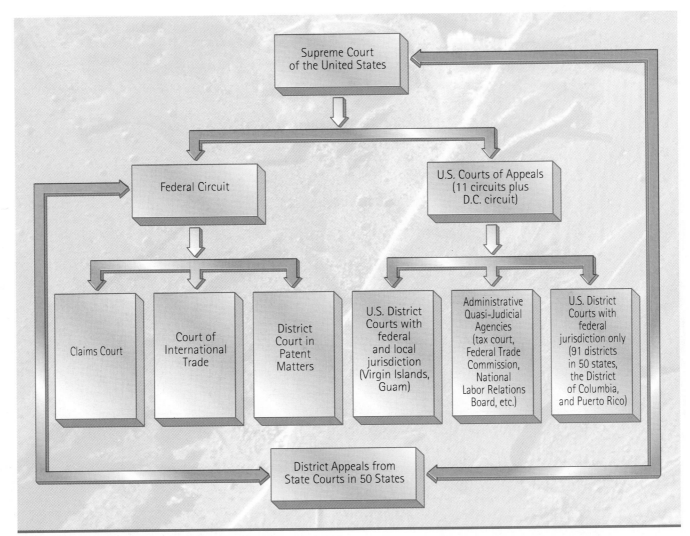

FIGURE 17.2 **Federal Judicial System**

SOURCE: American Bar Association, *Law and the Courts* (Chicago: American Bar Association, 1974), p. 21. Updated information provided by the Federal Courts Improvement Act of 1982 and West Publishing Company, St. Paul, Minnesota.

to hear only those it deems important, appropriate, and worthy of its attention. When the Court decides to hear a case, it usually grants a **writ of certiorari,** requesting a transcript of the proceedings of the case for review.

The Supreme Court can word a decision so that it becomes a precedent that must be honored by all lower courts. For example, if the Court grants a particular litigant the right to counsel at a police lineup, then all people in similar situations must be given the same right. This type of ruling is usually referred to as a **landmark decision.** The use of precedent in the legal system gives the Supreme Court power to influence and mold the everyday operating procedures of police agencies, trial courts, and corrections institutions. This influence was

quite pronounced during the tenure of Chief Justice Earl Warren, who, during the 1960s, greatly amplified and extended the power of the Court to affect criminal justice policies.

Court Caseloads

The American court system is a vast enterprise. Each year more than 90 million new cases of all kinds and 250,000 appeals are brought before the courts of the 50 states and the District of Columbia.[3]

These statistics can be misleading, since about 60 percent of all cases are traffic violations handled by municipal or traffic court. Nonetheless, about 13 million cases

A morning in a lower court. A woman seeks the court's protection by asking for a restraining order against her husband.

involving criminal actions are handled by the courts each year, including more than 1 million felony cases in which approximately 800,000 people are convicted.[4]

The number of felony cases filed in the nation's courts has trended upwards since the mid-1980s, a movement explained in part by the increases in violent crimes and drug offenses. The extent of this caseload has placed great pressure on the major actors in the pretrial, trial, and sentencing process: the prosecutor; the defense attorney; and the judge.

≡ Prosecutor

The major role of the **prosecution** is to represent the state in criminal matters that come before the courts. Among prosecutors' major duties are:

- *Conducting investigations of law violations.* Prosecutors are empowered to conduct their own

investigations into alleged violations of the law. In some jurisdictions, they maintain a staff of detectives and investigators; in others they rely on local or state police. In jurisdictions with grand jury systems, the prosecutor can convene the grand jury to act as a fact-finding body to collect information and interview witnesses for the purpose of accumulating enough evidence to indict suspects in criminal conspiracies.

- *Cooperating with police.* The prosecutor's office usually maintains a close working relationship with police agencies. Police prepare the investigation report of a crime according to the format desired by the prosecutor's office. Prosecutors also advise police agents about the legal issues in a given case. For example, they supervise the drawing up of requests **(affidavits)** for search warrants and then make sure that the police understand the limitations presented by the warrant. Some prosecutor's offices help train police officers, making them aware of the legal issues involved in securing a warrant or a legal arrest, interrogating a suspect, and so on.

- *Determining charges.* The prosecutor makes the final determination of the charges to be brought against the suspect. The charge on which defendants are brought to trial may have little resemblance to the original reasons they were arrested. For example, a suspect picked up for disorderly conduct may later be identified at a police lineup as the perpetrator of a string of liquor store robberies. The disorderly conduct charge may then be dropped in favor of prosecution on the more serious robbery charges.

- *Representing the government in pretrial hearings and motions.* The prosecutor is charged with bringing the case to trial. Prosecutors make contact with witnesses and prepare them to testify, secure physical evidence, and discuss the victim's testimony. If the defendant attempts to have evidence suppressed at a pretrial hearing (for example, because of violations of the exclusionary rule), the prosecutor represents the state's position on the matter.

- *Plea bargaining.* The prosecutor is empowered to negotiate a guilty plea with the defendant, thereby ending the formal trial process.

- *Trying criminal cases.* The prosecutor acts as the state's attorney at criminal trials. Consequently, another name for the prosecutor is *people's attorney.*

- *Sentencing.* The prosecutor recommends dispositions at the completion of the trial. Usually, the type of sentence recommended is influenced by plea bargaining cooperation, public opinion, the seriousness of the crime, the offender's prior record, and other factors related to the case.

- *Representing the government at appeals.* If the defendant is found guilty as charged, he or she may appeal the conviction before a higher court. The prosecutor represents the government at these hearings.

- *Conducting special investigations.* Some jurisdictions empower special prosecutors to seek indictments for serious crimes considered important to the public interest. This practice became well known during the Watergate investigation, when first Archibald Cox and then Leon Jaworski was appointed special prosecutor to investigate the break-ins and subsequent cover-up.

Types of Prosecutors

In the federal system, the chief prosecuting officer is the U.S. attorney general, and her assistant prosecutors are known as U.S. attorneys and are appointed by the president. They are responsible for representing the government in federal district courts. The chief prosecutor is usually an administrator; assistants normally handle the actual preparation and trial work. Federal prosecutors are professional civil service employees with reasonable salaries and job security.

At the state level, the chief prosecuting officer is the attorney general; at the county level, the district attorney. Both are elected officials. Again, the bulk of criminal prosecution and staff work is performed by scores of full-time and part-time attorneys, police investigators, and clerical personnel. Most attorneys who work for prosecutors at state and county levels are political appointees who earn low salaries, handle many cases, and in some jurisdictions, maintain private law practices. Many young lawyers serve in this capacity to gain trial experience, then leave for better-paying positions. In some state, county, and municipal jurisdictions, however, the office of the prosecutor can be described as meeting the highest standards of professional skill, personal integrity, and working conditions.

In urban settings, the structure of the district attorney's office is often specialized, with separate divisions for felonies, misdemeanors, and trial and appeal assignments. In rural offices, chief prosecutors handle many of the criminal cases themselves. Where assistant prosecutors are employed, they often work part-time, have limited professional opportunities, and depend on the political patronage of chief prosecutors for their positions.

Prosecutorial Discretion

Prosecutors maintain broad discretion in the exercise of their duties. In fact, for more than 60 years, it has been well documented that full enforcement of the law is so rare that it is assumed that prosecutors will pick and choose the cases they decide to bring to court.[5]

Prosecutors exercise their discretion in a variety of circumstances. One major decision involves the choice of acting on the information brought by police or deciding not to file for an indictment. The prosecutor can also attempt to prosecute and then decide to drop the case; this is known as a *nolle prosequi.*

Figure 17.3 shows the pattern of prosecutor decision making found by Barbara Boland, Paul Mahanna, and Ronald Sones in their study of case processing in 30 urban jurisdictions.[6] About half of all arrests result in dismissal before they reach the trial stage: some are divert-

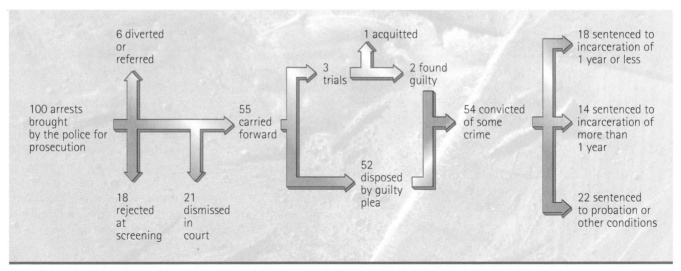

FIGURE 17.3   Typical Outcome of 100 Felony Arrests Brought by the Police for Prosecution

SOURCE: Barbara Boland, Paul Mahanna, and Ronald Sones, *The Prosecution of Felony Arrests, 1988* (Washington, D.C.: Bureau of Justice Statistics, 1993), p. 3.

ed into treatment programs; others are rejected after being screened by the prosecutor; and another group are dealt with in lower court either by a dismissal or misdemeanor conviction. Of those carried forward to trial, the great majority end with a plea bargain.

The Boland research illustrates the significant influence prosecutors have over the criminal process. By effectively screening out cases in which conviction could not reasonably be expected, cases inappropriate for criminal action (such as minor thefts by first offenders), and cases involving offenders with special needs (such as the emotionally disturbed or mentally retarded), the prosecutor can concentrate on bringing to trial those who commit more serious criminal offenses. The relatively few cases that do get to trial are most often settled through plea negotiations conducted by the prosecutor's office.[7]

Factors Influencing Decision Making

Research indicates that a wide variety of factors influence prosecutorial discretion in invoking the criminal sanction, including the characteristics of the crime, the criminal, and the victim. A defendant who is a known drug user, who has a long history of criminal offending, and who causes the victim extensive physical injuries will more likely be prosecuted than one who is a first offender, does not use drugs, and does not seriously injure a victim.[8]

Numerous attempts have been made to examine the charging decision. Best known is the classic work

Prosecution: The Decision to Charge a Subject by Frank Miller.[9] In his incisive analysis, Miller pinpoints the factors influencing prosecutorial discretion, including (1) the attitude of the victim; (2) the cost of prosecution to the criminal justice system; (3) the possibility of undue harm to the suspect; (4) the availability of alternative procedures; (5) the availability of civil sanctions; and (6) the willingness of the suspect to cooperate with law enforcement authorities.

In another classic work, Wayne LaFave also identified factors related to the decision to invoke prosecutorial discretion.[10] According to LaFave, when acts have been *overcriminalized*—such as when laws provide stiff sentences for possessing small quantities of recreational drugs—they are not prosecuted. Limited resources force the prosecutor to select only the most serious cases. Finally, alternatives to prosecution are used whenever possible to spare the offenders the stigma of a criminal conviction.

In some instances, LaFave found that the prosecutor may decide to take no action; this occurs when the victim expresses the desire not to prosecute, the cost would be excessive, the harm of prosecution outweighs the benefits, or the harm done by the offender can be corrected without a criminal trial. LaFave also points out that prosecutors have tools at their disposal to invoke obscure statutes to punish unrepenting offenders or refuse leniency to defendants who will not cooperate with them. Thus, to LaFave, prosecutorial discretion is a two-edged sword.

The following also have been identified as influencing prosecutorial discretion:

- *Evidence problems* that result from a failure to find sufficient physical evidence linking the defendant to the offense

- *Witness problems* that arise, for example, when a witness fails to appear, gives unclear or inconsistent statements, is reluctant to testify, or is unsure of the identity of the offender

- *Office policy,* wherein the prosecutor decides not to prosecute certain types of offenses, particularly those that violate the letter but not the spirit of the law (for example, offenses involving insignificant amounts of property damage)

- *Due process problems* that involve violations of the constitutional requirements for seizing evidence and questioning the accused

- *Combination with other cases,* for example, when the accused is charged in several cases and the prosecutor prosecutes all of the charges in a single case

- *Pretrial diversion* that occurs when the prosecutor and the court agree to drop charges when the accused successfully meets the conditions for diversion, such as completion of a treatment program[11]

Case pressure is also considered an important influence on prosecutorial discretion. While some criminologists dispute whether prosecutor's decision making is based on their work schedule, others view the prosecutor who is deluged by serious cases as the one most likely to not prosecute or to offer a plea bargain. One study found that prosecutors in large counties (with over 600,000 population) are less likely to bring felons to trial (28 percent) than those in smaller, less crime-ridden counties (38 percent). While these data are not conclusive proof of the effect of case pressure (an alternative explanation is that police work is sloppier in urban areas, forcing prosecutors to drop cases), they show that jurisdictions in which prosecutors are forced to deal with more serious and violent felonies are also the ones in which the most selectivity is used.[12]

Is prosecutorial discretion inherently harmful? Not necessarily, argues Judge Charles Breitel, who, in a famous statement, asserted that prosecutorial discretion is indispensable to ensure efficiency in the criminal justice system.

> If every policeman, every prosecutor, every court, and every post-sentence agency performed his or its responsibility in strict accordance with rules of law, precisely and narrowly laid down, the criminal law would be ordered but intolerable. Living would be a sterile compliance with soul-killing rules and taboos. By comparison, a primitive tribal society would seem free, indeed.[13]

Although eliminating prosecutorial discretion may not always be desirable, efforts have been made to control its content and direction. For example, national commissions have established guidelines for the exercise of appropriate prosecutorial actions.[14] Other methods of controlling prosecutorial decision making include: (1) identification of the reasons for charging decision; (2) publication of prosecution office policies; (3) review by nonprosecutorial groups; (4) charging conferences; and (5) evaluation of charging policies and decisions and development of screening, diversion, and plea negotiation procedures.[15]

Defense Attorney

The *defense* counsel performs many functions while representing the accused in the criminal process. They include, but are not limited to, the following:

- Investigating the incident

- Interviewing the client, police officers, and other witnesses

- Discussing the matter with the prosecutor

- Representing the defendant at the various prejudicial procedures, such as arrest, interrogation, lineup, and arraignment

- Entering into plea negotiations

- Preparing the case for trial, including developing the tactics and strategy to be used

- Filing and arguing legal motions with the court

- Representing the defendant at trial

- Providing assistance at sentencing

- Determining the appropriate basis for appeal

Although prominent criminal defense lawyers are numerous in the United States, the majority of criminal defendants are indigents who cannot afford legal counsel. The Supreme Court has interpreted the Sixth Amendment of the Constitution to mean that people facing trial for offenses that can be punished by incarceration have the right to legal counsel.[16] If they cannot afford counsel, the state must provide an attorney free of charge. Consequently, three systems have been developed to provide legal counsel to the indigent:

1. Assigning private attorneys to represent indigent clients on a case-by-case basis (sometimes referred to as an attorney list system), with the state paying their fees.
2. Contracting with a law firm or group of private attorneys to regularly provide defense services to indigents.
3. Creating a publicly funded defender's office.

These three systems can be used independently or in combination. In general, the **attorney list/assigned counsel system** is used in less populated areas, where case flow is minimal and a full-time public defender is not needed. **Public defenders** are usually found in larger urban areas with high case flow rates. So while a proportionately larger area of the country is served by the assigned counsel system, a significant proportion of criminal defendants receive public defenders. Public defenders can be part of a statewide agency, county government, the judiciary, or an independent nonprofit organization or other institution.

A government survey found that of the more than 3,000 counties that had indigent defendant services, 60 percent had assigned counsel systems, 1,100 or (37 percent) had public defenders, and 330 (11 percent) had contract attorneys. Some jurisdictions employ more than one system; for example, counties with public defenders may assign counsel if there is a conflict of interest or simply a case overload.[17] Public defenders were found in the most populous counties, containing 68 percent of the U.S. population (see Figure 17.4). Since crime rates are also higher in larger metropolitan areas, public defenders serve a majority of all criminal defendants.

Conflicts of Defense

Because of the way the U.S. system of justice operates today, criminal defense attorneys face many role conflicts. They are viewed as prime movers in what is essentially an **adversarial process:** the prosecution and the defense engage in conflict over the facts of the case at hand, with the prosecutor arguing the case for the state and the defense counsel using all the means at his or her disposal to aid the client.

FIGURE 17.4 **Indigent Criminal Defense Systems in the United States**

SOURCE: Carla Gaskins, *Criminal Defense for the Poor—1986* (Washington, D.C.: Bureau of Justice Statistics, 1988).

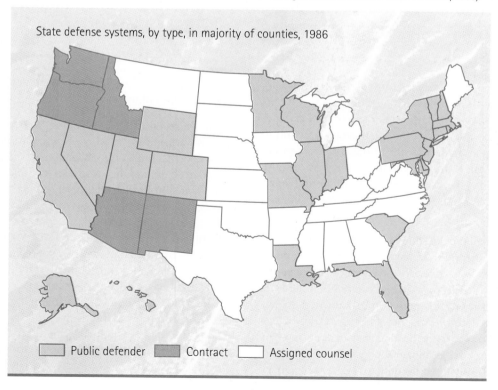

State defense systems, by type, in majority of counties, 1986

Public defender　　Contract　　Assigned counsel

The role of the judge was shaped in the common law courts of England.

However, as members of the legal profession, defense counsels must be aware of their role as officers of the court. As an attorney, the defense counsel is obligated to uphold the integrity of the legal profession and to observe the requirements of the *Code of Professional Responsibility* of the American Bar Association in the defense of a client. The code makes the following statement regarding the duties of the lawyer in the adversary system of justice:

> Our legal system provides for the adjudication of disputes governed by the rules of substantive, evidentiary, and procedural law. An adversary presentation counters the natural human tendency to judge too swiftly in terms of the familiar that which is not yet fully known; the advocate, by his zealous preparation of facts and law, enables the tribunal to come to the hearing with an open and neutral mind and to render impartial judgements. The duty of a lawyer to his client and his duty to the legal system are

the same: To present his client zealously within the boundaries of the law.[18]

In this dual capacity of being both a defensive advocate and an officer of the court, the attorney is often confronted with conflicting obligations to client and profession. These issues are often so complex that even the Supreme Court has had difficulty setting standards of proper behavior. However, in *Nix v. Whiteside,* the Court went so far as to sustain an attorney's right to refuse to represent a client whom he suspected would commit perjury. The Court also ruled that an attorney's threat to withdraw from the case and tell the court of the perjury did not violate the client's right to competent assistance of counsel.[19]

Beyond their ethical problems, criminal defense attorneys often find themselves at the bottom of the legal profession's financial hierarchy. In prestigious urban law firms, attorneys begin at about $75,000, average $140,000 by their seventh year, and make between

$250,000 and $600,000 when they become partner. In contrast, a public defender averages between $20,000 and $30,000. Consequently, talented criminal attorneys feel pressure to leave the field and enter more lucrative areas of the law.[20]

Judge

The third major participant in the criminal trial is the **judge**—the senior officer in a court of criminal law. Judges' duties are quite varied and are far more extensive than the average citizen might suspect. During trials, the judge rules on the appropriateness of conduct, settles questions of evidence and procedure, and guides the questioning of witnesses. When a jury trial occurs, the judge must instruct jury members on which evidence it is proper to examine and which should be ignored. The judge also formally charges the jury by instructing its members on what points of law and evidence they must consider before reaching a decision of guilty or innocent. When a jury trial is waived, the judge must decide whether to hold for the complainant or the defendant. Finally, in the event that a defendant is found guilty, the judge has the authority to decide on the sentence (in some cases, the sentence is legislatively determined). This duty includes choosing the type of sentence, its length, and—in the case of probation—the conditions under which it may be revoked. Obviously, this decision has a significant effect on an offender's future.[21]

Beyond these stated duties, the trial judge has extensive control and influence over the other service agencies of the court: probation agencies, court clerks, police agencies, and the district attorney's office. Probation and the clerk may be under the judge's explicit control. In some courts, the operations, philosophy, and procedures of these agencies are within the magistrate's administrative domain. In other courts—for example, where a state agency controls the probation department—the attitudes of the county or district court judge still have a great deal of influence on how a probation department is run and how its decisions are made.

Judicial Selection

Several methods are used to select state court judges.[22] In some jurisdictions, the governor simply appoints judges. In others, judicial recommendations must be confirmed by either (1) the state senate, (2) the governor's council, (3) a special confirmation committee, (4) an executive council elected by the state assembly, or (5) an elected review board. Some states employ screening bodies that submit names to the governor for approval.

Another form of judicial selection is through popular election, either partisan or nonpartisan. This practice is used in a majority of states.

About 16 states have adopted what is known as the **Missouri Plan** to select judges. This three-part approach consists of: (1) a judicial nominating commission to nominate candidates for the bench, (2) an elected official (usually from the executive branch) to make appointments from the list submitted by the commission, and (3) subsequent nonpartisan and noncompetitive elections in which incumbent judges run on their records. Some states, such as New York and Texas, use different methods to select judges on the appellate and trial level. In New York, appellate court judges are appointed by the governor, trial court judges are elected, and criminal court and family court judges in New York City are appointed by the mayor.[23]

Judicial Overload

There has been great concern about stress being placed upon judges because of case pressure. In most states, people appointed to the bench have had little or no training in the role of judge. Others may have held administrative posts and may not have appeared before a court in years. Once they are appointed to the bench, judges are given an overwhelming amount of work that has risen dramatically over the years. The number of civil and criminal filings per state court judge has increased significantly since 1985; federal judges handle fewer cases and the number of civil cases in federal court has actually declined. There are 1,412 civil and criminal case filings per state court judge and 430 per federal judge. While state court judges deal with far more cases, it is possible that federal cases are more complex and demand more judicial time. In any event, the number of civil and criminal cases, especially in state courts, seems to be outstripping the ability of states to create new judgeships (see Figure 17.5).

Several agencies have been created to improve the quality of the judiciary. The National Conference of State Court Judges and the National College of Juvenile Justice both operate judicial training seminars and publish manuals and guides on state-of-the-art judicial techniques. Their ongoing efforts are designed to improve the quality of the nation's judges.

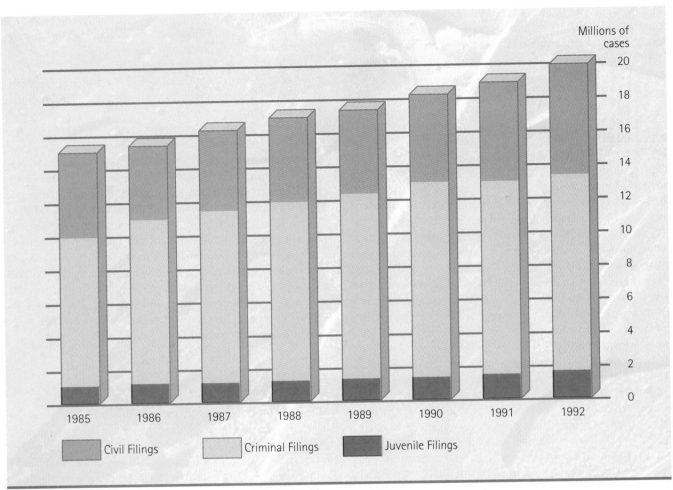

FIGURE 17.5 Total Case Filings by Major Category, 1985–1992

SOURCE: State Court Caseload Statistics, 1992 (Williamsburg, Va.: National Center for State Courts, 1994), p. 5.

Now that the actors in the judicatory process have been introduced and the structure within which they work defined, our attention will turn to the three main stages of the process itself: pretrial procedures, the trial, and sentencing.

☰ Pretrial Procedures

After arrest, or if an arrest warrant has been served, a criminal charge is drawn up by the appropriate prosecutor's office. The charge is a formal written document identifying the criminal activity, the facts of the case, and the circumstances of the arrest. If the crime is a felony, the charge is called a **bill of indictment,** if it is to be considered by a grand jury, or an **information,** if that

particular jurisdiction uses the preliminary hearing system; misdemeanants are charged with a **complaint.**

After an indictment or information in a felony offense is filed, the accused is brought before the trial court for arraignment, at which time the judge informs the defendant of the charge, ensures that the accused is properly represented by counsel, and determines whether the person should be released on bail or some alternative plan pending a hearing or trial.

The defendant who is arraigned on an indictment or information can ordinarily plead guilty, not guilty, or *nolo contendere,* which is equivalent to a guilty plea but which cannot be used as evidence in subsequent cases. When a guilty plea is entered, the defendant admits to all the elements of the crime, and the court begins to review the person's background for sentencing purposes. A plea of not guilty sets the stage for a trial on the merits of the case or for negotiations between the prosecutor and the defense attorney with the aim of reaching a guilty plea arrangement.

This section will review in more detail three important issues related to pretrial procedures: bail, plea bargaining, and noncriminal alternatives to prosecution.

☰ Bail

Bail represents money or some other security provided to the court to ensure the appearance of the defendant at trial. The amount of bail is set by a magistrate who reviews the facts of the case and the history of the defendant. Defendants who cannot afford or are denied bail are kept in secure detention, usually in a county jail or lockup until their trial date. Those who make bail are free to pursue their defense before trial.

The bail system goes back to Great Britain and the English common law. At one time, the legal relationship existing in the contract law of bailment even permitted the trying and sentencing of the bailor (the person who posted bail) if the bailee did not appear for trial.[24]

Under the U.S. system of justice, the right to bail comes from the Eighth Amendment of the Constitution. However, the Eighth Amendment does not guarantee bail; rather, it states that people can expect to be released on *reasonable* bail in all but capital cases. Thus, in most cases, accused persons have the right to be released on reasonable bail to prepare their defense and continue their life in the community.

Bail Today

Today, about two-thirds of all criminal defendants are released on bail, and research studies indicate that the great majority return for their trial.[25] Nonetheless, there is still concern over the criminal behavior of bailees awaiting trial. Some defendants are detained because they cannot afford to make bail, while others are denied bail because of the danger they present to the community, a practice called **preventive detention.**

The likelihood of making bail is directly related to the criminal charge: drug and public order offenders are the most likely to be bailed; violent offenders, the more likely to be detained. A prior history of absconding before trial is also related to a lower probability of release. And as might be expected, the lower the bail, the most likely the defendant is to be released.[26]

Most offenders are released before trial, including those arrested for such violent crimes as murder and robbery. Relatively few offenders are denied bail outright: 6 percent in state courts and 29 percent in federal. About 42 percent of people released on bail in state courts were either rearrested (18 percent) or absconded (24 percent). The failure rate in federal courts is considerably lower: 3 percent were rearrested and another 3 percent failed to appear at trial. It is possible that federal bail is more successful because fewer defendants are violent criminals (6 percent versus 26 percent in state courts) and those who are violent are more likely to be denied bail (29 percent versus 6 percent in state courts). Those rearrested tend to (1) be males under age 21; (2) have a serious prior record; and (3) be drug abusers.

People detained before trial get convicted more often and, when convicted, receive significantly longer sentences than those granted pretrial release. About 66 percent of defendants who were released until case disposition were convicted, as opposed to 79 percent who were detained; 50 percent of released offenders were incarcerated, while 83 percent of the detainees were sentenced to prison or jail.

The Problems of Bail

Bail is quite controversial because it penalizes the indigent offender who does not have the means to pay the bond. Of concern is the fact that detention centers are dreary, dangerous places and those who are held in them can be victims of the justice system though they are innocent of all charges. Caleb Foote, one of the nation's leading experts on bail, stated:

> The basic problem—poor people and those being locked up before trial—remains. I still think pretrial detention is the most pervasive denial of equal protection and equal rights in American law.[27]

The bail system is also costly because the state must pay for the detention of offenders who are unable to raise bail and who might otherwise remain in the community. The significance of bail is further amplified because both the amount of bail ordered and the length of stay in pretrial detention for those who cannot raise bail are associated with a greater likelihood of conviction and a longer prison sentence after conviction.[28]

Another problem of the bail system is the institution of the professional bail **bonding agent.** Normally, the bail bonding agent puts up 90 percent of a bond fee and the defendant the remaining 10 percent (this is called surety bond). When the defendant appears at trial, the bail is returned and the bonding agent keeps the entire amount, the defendant's 10 percent serving as the bonding agent's commission. If the defendant does not show up for trial, the bonding agent must pay the entire bail. Usually, bonding agents expect defendants, their friends, or their relatives to put up further collateral (such as the deed to their house) to cover the risk; they may also purchase insurance to reduce their risk. If collateral is unavailable or the bonding agent believes the offender presents too great a risk, the bonding agent will refuse to lend bail money, relegating the defendant to a jail stay until the trial date.

Bail bonding agents have often been accused of unscrupulous practices, such as bribing police and court personnel to secure referrals. Some judges have been accused of refusing to collect forfeited bail owed from bonding agents.[29]

Because it is so critical, a bail reform movement has been ongoing for more than 40 years.

Bail Reform

The bail reform movement was started in 1961 to help alleviate the problems presented by the bail process. In New York, the Vera Foundation, set up by the philanthropist Louis Schweitzer and later supported by the Ford Foundation, pioneered the concept of **release on recognizance** (ROR).[30] This project found that if the court had sufficient background information about the defendant, it could make a reasonably good judgment about whether the accused would return to court.

The project proved to be a great success. A significant majority of clients returned for trial when released on their own recognizance. The success of ROR in New York prompted its adoption in many other large cities around the country. The Federal Bail Reform Act of 1984 has made release on recognizance an assumption unless the need for greater control can be shown in court. It is disappointing that 27 percent of defendants receiving ROR fail to appear for trial, compared to 20 percent who used surety bail and 26 percent who paid full cash bail.[31]

Abuses by bail bonding agents have prompted a number of jurisdictions, including Wisconsin, Nebraska, Kentucky, Oregon, and Illinois, to set up systems that allow defendants to post a percentage of their bond (usually 10 percent) with the court; the full amount is required only if the defendant fails to show for trial. This **deposit bail** system is designed to replace the bonding agents. The major forms of bail are set out in Table 17.1.

Bail reform has been considered one of the great successes in criminal justice reform, but some research efforts indicate great disparity in the way judges handle bail decisions. They also show that racial and socioeconomic disparity might be a factor in decision making.[32] If this is so, then the original purposes of creating bail

TABLE 17.1 Innovative Bail Systems

Nonfinancial Release

(1) **Release on recognizance**—The defendant is released on a promise to appear, without any requirement of money bond. This form of release is unconditional; that is, without imposition of special conditions, supervision, or specially provided services. The defendant must simply appear in court for all scheduled hearings.

(2) **Conditional release**—The defendant is released on a promise to fulfill some stated requirements that go beyond those associated with release on recognizance. Four types of conditions are placed on defendants, all of which share the common aims of increasing the defendant's likelihood of returning to court and/or maintaining community safety: (1) status quo conditions such as requiring that the defendant maintain residence or employment status; (2) restrictive conditions, such as requiring that the defendant remain in the jurisdiction, stay away from the complainant, or maintain a curfew; (3) contact conditions, such as requiring that the defendant report by telephone or in person to the release program or a third party at various intervals; and (4) problem-oriented conditions, such as requiring that the defendant participate in drug or alcohol treatment programs.

Financial Release

(3) **Unsecured bail**—The defendant is released with no immediate requirement of payment. However, if the defendant fails to appear, he or she is liable for the full amount.

(4) **Privately secured bail**—A private organization or individual posts the bail amount, which is returned when the defendant appears in court. In effect, the organization provides services akin to those of a professional bonding agent, but without cost to the defendant.

(5) **Property bail**—The defendant may post evidence of real property in lieu of money.

(6) **Deposit bail**—The defendant deposits a percentage of the bail amount, typically 10 percent, with the court. When the defendant appears in court, the deposit is returned, sometimes minus an administrative fee. If the defendant fails to appear, he or she is liable for the full amount of the bail.

(7) **Surety bail**—The defendant pays a percentage of the bond, usually 10 percent, to a bonding agent who posts the full bail. The fee paid to the bonding agent is not returned to the defendant if he or she appears in court. The bonding agent is liable for the full amount of the bond should the defendant fail to appear. Bonding agents often require posting of collateral to cover the full bail amount.

(8) **Cash bail**—The defendant pays the entire amount of bail set by the judge to secure release. The bail is returned to the defendant when he or she appears in court.

SOURCE: Adapted from Andy Hall, *Pretrial Release Program Options* (Washington, D.C.: National Institute of Justice, 1984), pp. 32–33.

reform would be negated by bias in the justice system. One approach to limit disparity is the use of **bail guidelines,** which set standard bail amounts based on such factors as criminal history and the current charge.[33]

In sum, bail reform movements have encouraged the use of pretrial release. Studies show that most defendants return for trial and most bailees do not commit more crime while in the community.

Preventive Detention

While only about 20 percent of bailees are rearrested before trial, the threat they present to the public is disturbing. After all, if 1.5 million people receive bail each year, that means that about 300,000 crimes are committed by bailees who could have remained in pretrial detention. And assuming a five-to-one ratio of crimes to arrests, bailees may be responsible for 1.5 million serious crimes each year.

Because of the concern over defendant misconduct while on bail, about 30 states have limited bail for certain offenses and offenders, such as those who previously absconded, are recidivists, or have violent histories. Similarly, the federal Bail Reform Act of 1984 provides that federal offenders may be detained without bail if "no condition or combination of conditions (of bail) will reasonably assure . . . the safety of any other person and the community. . . ."[34]

The issue of preventive detention is particularly vexing since it means that a person who has not been convicted of any crime will be incarcerated for an extended period of time without the chance to participate in his or her own defense. Those supporting preventive detention argue that it will help control witness intimidation and reduce avoidable criminal acts.

In a landmark decision, *United States v. Salerno,* the Supreme Court upheld the Bail Reform Act's preventive detention provision on the grounds that its purpose was public safety, that it was not excessive for its stated purpose, and that it contained no punitive intent but was designed to regulate the behavior of accused criminals in a legally permissible way.[35] Similarly, in the case of *Schall v. Martin,* the court upheld a New York law providing for the preventive detention of a juvenile offender if the judicial authority believes the offender will be a danger to community safety.[36]

An analysis of the federal Bail Reform Act shows that it did increase the number of people being held before trial. Before the act took effect, about 24 percent of all defendants were detained or did not make bail; after the act took effect, the number went up to 29 percent; 19 percent of the detainees did not qualify for bail consideration under the new guidelines.[37] Most of those held without bail were involved in the use of firearms, were drug offenders, or had violated immigration laws.

Despite years of reform efforts, bail remains a troubling aspect of the criminal process. It is one of the few areas in which people are seriously penalized because of their economic circumstances. While some defendants are kept in jail for lack of a few hundred dollars, others are released because they can afford bail in the millions. And those who cannot make bail face a greater chance of conviction and a harsher penalty if convicted.

≡ Plea Bargaining

The majority of defendants in criminal trials are convicted by their own pleas of guilty; plea bargains are also common in juvenile court.[38] About 90 percent of all those charged with felonies plead guilty; if misdemeanors are included, the percentage jumps to 98 percent.[39]

The **plea bargaining** process usually occurs between arraignment (or initial appearance, in the case of a misdemeanor) and the onset of trial. There are a number of ways a bargain can be struck in exchange for a guilty plea, including:

1. The initial charges may be reduced to those of a lesser offense, thus automatically reducing the sentence imposed. A first-degree murder charge is reduced to second-degree, eliminating the threat of the death penalty.

2. The charge is reduced from a felony to a misdemeanor. For example, a felony burglary charge is reduced to breaking and entering, a misdemeanor for which time can be served in the local jail.

3. In cases where there are multiple offenses or counts (multiple charges for the same crime, for example, three rape accusations), only a single charge will be filed. A person is accused of raping five women. By his pleading guilty on one charge, the other four are dropped. People convicted of a single crime are less likely to be given a long sentence than those convicted of four or five. A defendant who commits armed robbery may plead guilty to unarmed robbery. Possessing a gun during a robbery adds an automatic three years to the sentence, which the defendant can avoid with his plea.

4. The prosecutor may promise to recommend a lenient sentence, such as probation or a short prison term, in exchange for a plea.

5. When the charge imposed has a negative label attached (for example, child molester), the

prosecutor may alter the charge to a less damaging one (for example, assault) in exchange for a plea of guilty.

6. Prosecutors may promise to get a defendant into a specific treatment program in exchange for his or her plea. For example, a substance abuser is promised admission into the state's detoxification unit in exchange for a guilty plea.

There are a number of different motivations for plea bargaining. Defendants, aware of the prosecutor's strong case, plea-bargain to minimize their sentence and avoid the negative labels and harmful effects of a criminal conviction. Some may agree to negotiate a guilty plea to protect accomplices or confederates by "taking the rap" themselves.[40] It is also possible that some innocent defendants will plead to a reduced charge because they fear that they will be convicted on a much more serious charge.

The defense attorney may seek a bargain to limit his or her own involvement in the case. In some instances, defense counsels may wish to increase their operating profits by minimizing the effort they put forth for an obviously guilty client.[41] In other instances, they may simply wish to adapt to the bureaucratic structure favorable to plea bargaining that exists in most U.S. criminal courts.[42] Defense attorneys may wish to secure noncriminal dispositions for their clients, such as placement in a treatment program, and may advise them to plead guilty in exchange for this consideration.

The prosecution also can benefit from a plea bargain. The prosecutor's case may be weaker than hoped for, convincing her that a trial is too risky. A prosecutor may also believe that the arresting officers made a serious procedural error in securing evidence that would be brought out during pretrial motions. When a defendant pleads guilty, it voids all prior constitutional errors made in that case. And, of course, no matter how strong the state's case, there is always the chance that a jury will render an unfavorable decision. Prosecutors also bargain to gain the cooperation of informers and codefendants.

Plea Bargaining Issues

Those who favor plea bargaining argue that it actually benefits both the state and the defendant in the following ways: (1) the overall financial costs of criminal prosecution are reduced; (2) the administrative efficiency of the courts is greatly improved; (3) the prosecution is able to devote more time to cases of greater seriousness and importance; and (4) the defendant avoids possible detention and extended trial and may receive a reduced

sentence.[43] Thus, those who favor plea bargaining believe it is appropriate to enter into plea discussions where the effective administration of justice will be served. Whether a plea bargain actually "pays" is discussed in the Close-Up, "Does Plea Bargaining Pay?"

It has been argued, however, that plea bargaining is basically objectionable because it encourages defendants to waive their constitutional right to a trial. In addition, some experts suggest that sentences tend to be less severe in guilty plea situations than as a result of trials and that plea bargains result in even greater sentencing disparity. Particularly in the eyes of the general public, this allows the defendant to beat the system and further tarnishes the criminal justice process. Plea bargaining also raises the danger that an innocent person will be convicted of a crime if the individual is convinced that the lighter treatment resulting from a guilty plea is preferable to the possible risk of a harsher sentence following a formal trial. Some suggest that plea bargaining allows dangerous offenders to get off lightly and therefore weakens the deterrent effect of the criminal law.[44] It may also undermine public confidence in the law.[45]

Control of Plea Bargaining

It is unlikely that plea negotiations will be eliminated or severely curtailed in the near future. Those who support their total abolition are in the minority. As a result of abuses, however, efforts are being made to improve plea bargaining operations. Such reforms include (1) the development of uniform plea practices, (2) the presence of counsel during plea negotiations, and (3) the establishment of time limits on plea negotiations.[46]

In recent years, some efforts have been made to convert plea bargaining into a more visible, understandable, and fair dispositional process. Safeguards and guidelines have been developed in many jurisdictions to prevent violations of due process and to ensure that innocent defendants do not plead guilty under coercion. Such safeguards include: (1) the judge questions the defendant about the facts of the guilty plea before accepting the plea; (2) the defense counsel is present and able to advise the defendant of his or her rights; (3) open discussions about the plea occur between the prosecutor and the defense attorney; and (4) full and frank information regarding the offender and the offense is made available at this stage of the process. In addition, judicial supervision is an effective mechanism to ensure that plea bargaining is undertaken fairly.

The most extreme method of reforming plea bargaining has been to abolish it completely. A ban on plea

CLOSE-UP

Does Plea Bargaining Pay?

Plea bargains are controversial because the general public believes they let criminals "get away with murder." How accurate is this perception? Do many criminals "beat the rap"?

To answer this question, the federal government has sponsored a number of surveys of felony plea negotiations. One that evaluated plea negotiations in 14 jurisdictions found wide disparity in the use of pleas: some jurisdictions averaged four pleas for every trial, while in others, the ratio was 20 to one; overall, pleas were used in 80 percent of felony cases. The survey found that, surprisingly, 60 percent of the pleas were to the top charge filed. This implies that most plea negotiations are directed at sentence reduction, for example, pleading guilty in exchange for the dropping of lesser included charges that could add to the sentence (such as possession of a firearm), rather than at lowering the most serious charge

filed against the defendant. Even in jurisdictions where prosecutors are reluctant to reduce charges or engage in bargaining, a majority of defendants still enter a guilty plea.

Guilty pleas are usually inversely related to crime seriousness: murder suspects are much less likely to plead guilty than those charged with larceny. Murder suspects who did plead guilty were able to escape both life sentences and the death penalty more frequently than those who asked for a trial: 40 percent of murder suspects who went to trial received a life sentence, while only 15 percent who pleaded guilty were similarly punished; 5 percent of murder suspects who had a trial got the death sentence, compared to less than 0.5 percent of those who pleaded guilty.

What happens to those who plead guilty? In addition to murder suspects, most defendants who demand jury trials are much more likely to be sent to prison than those who plead guilty and, if incarcerated, receive longer sentences. For every crime category, convicted

defendants were much better off pleading guilty than risking a jury trial. Interestingly, the outcome of bench trials (held before a judge alone) compare favorably with plea outcomes.

Does plea bargaining pay? While defendants are assured a conviction, they will most likely receive a much more favorable sentence by plea-bargaining than by going to trial.

Discussion Questions

1. Should felony plea negotiations be eliminated or strictly controlled?
2. How could plea negotiations convince an innocent person to plead guilty?

SOURCES: Patrick Langan and Richard Solari, *National Judicial Reporting Program, 1990* (Washington, D.C.: Bureau of Justice Statistics, 1993); Patrick Langan and John Dawson, *Felony Sentences in State Courts, 1988* (Washington, D.C.: Bureau of Justice Statistics, 1990); Mark Cuniff, *Sentencing Outcomes in 28 Felony Courts, 1985* (Washington, D.C.: Bureau of Justice Statistics, 1987).

bargaining has been tried in numerous jurisdictions throughout the country. Alaska eliminated the practice in 1975. In Honolulu, Hawaii, efforts were made to abolish plea bargaining. Jurisdictions in other states, including Iowa, Arizona, and Delaware, along with the District of Columbia, have also sought to limit the use of plea bargaining.[47] These jurisdictions would give no consideration or concessions to the defendant in exchange for a guilty plea.

Efforts to control plea bargaining have met with mixed results. Evaluation of the Alaska experiment found that the number of pleas did not change significantly after plea bargaining was eliminated, nor did it increase the prison sentences given to the most serious

offenders.[48] This and other similar efforts indicate that attempts to eliminate plea bargaining will most likely move prosecutorial discretion farther up in the system. For example, eliminating felony plea bargaining may cause prosecutors to automatically charge offenders with a misdemeanor, so they can retain the option of offering them a "deal" in exchange for their cooperation before trial.

Legal Issues in Plea Bargaining

The U.S. Supreme Court has reviewed the propriety of plea bargaining in several court decisions, particularly in regard to the voluntariness of guilty pleas. In *Boykin v.*

Alabama, the Court held that an effort must be made in open court to question the defendant on the voluntariness of the admission of guilt before a trial judge may accept a guilty plea.[49] This is essential, since a guilty plea constitutes a waiver of the defendant's Fifth Amendment right to avoid self-incrimination and Sixth Amendment right to a jury trial. After the *Boykin* case, the Court ruled, in the case of *Brady v. United States,* that a guilty plea is not invalid merely because it is entered to avoid the possibility of the death penalty.[50] And in *Santobello v. New York,* which involved a guilty plea made after plea bargaining, the Court held that the promise of the prosecutor must be kept and that the breaking of a plea bargaining agreement by the prosecutor required a reversal for the defendant.[51] The Court ruled in the 1978 case of *Bordenkircher v. Hayes* that a defendant's due process rights are not violated when a prosecutor threatens to reindict the accused on more serious charges if he or she does not plead guilty to the original offense.[52]

The problem of controlling plea bargaining remains. Despite calls for its abolishment, it flourishes in U.S. trial practice. As Donald Newman states:

> There are, at present, no good answers to all of the unresolved bargaining issues. One thing, however, is abundantly clear; plea bargaining is with us and is probably here to stay in most jurisdictions throughout the country.[53]

≡ Alternatives to Prosecution: Diversion

In the past 20 years, great effort has been made to remove as many people as possible from the formal criminal justice process and to deal with them in an informal, treatment-oriented fashion.

Several reasons underlie this movement. On the one hand, advocates of the labeling perspective forcefully argue that the stigma of criminal conviction serves only to reinvolve the offender in crime. Thus, noncriminal alternatives can, in the long run, help reduce criminal activity.

From another viewpoint, it is alleged that pretrial alternatives to prosecution are usually cheaper than full trials and, more important, they free the justice system to concentrate on more serious offenders. Alternatives to prosecution can reduce the need for plea bargaining by reducing caseload pressure to settle cases.

In most instances, pretrial programs are designed to treat offenders rather than punish them. Some pretrial programs are organized around a particular type of rehabilitation effort. For example, a judge may allow a case to continue indefinitely without a hearing if the offender voluntarily enrolls in a residential alcohol or drug treatment program.

More common today are formalized **diversion** programs operating out of the local police, prosecutor's office, or probation department. Involvement with the diversion program usually begins after the arrest and arraignment of the individual but before trial. The individual is released on a continuance to the diversion program—that is, the trial is postponed—if the relevant court personnel (judge, probation officer, assistant district attorney, defense lawyer, arresting officer) and the program representative (usually called a screener) agree on the potential suitability of the accused for the program. Most diversion programs then provide some mix of job counseling, placement, drug rehab, and family intervention.

Despite the prevalence of diversion, critics have claimed that the practice is no more successful than the formal justice system. In some cases, it entangles the offender in social services more intensely than if he or she had gone to trial; this effect is known as **widening the net.** While this claim is persuasive, there are also indications that, when used properly, diversion programs can be an effective method of reducing the stigma of punishment without "widening the net" of justice.[54]

≡ The Criminal Trial

Although the jury trial is a relatively rare occurrence, it is still one of the cornerstones of the criminal justice process. Although most criminal prosecutions result in a plea bargain and do not involve the adversary determination of guilty or innocence, the trial process remains a matter of vital importance to the criminal justice system. The opportunity to go to trial provides a valuable safeguard against abuse of informal processing and a basis for encouraging faith in the criminal justice system.[55] Because of its importance, jury trial stages, critical issues, and associated legal rights are discussed below, while the Close-Up entitled "Adversary Justice v. the Court Room Work Group" considers the courtroom work group.

Jury Selection

The first stage of the trial process involves jury selection. Jurors are selected randomly in both civil and criminal cases usually from voter registration lists within each

CLOSE-UP

Adversary Justice Versus The Court Room Work Group

The hard-fought criminal trial is a popular topic for literature and the media. Every defendant has a fair chance if he or she can retain Perry Mason, Matlock, or the "LA Law" firm. Films such as the *Jagged Edge* hinge on glib lawyers convincing the jury of their client's innocence. But does it really work that way? Of course not. On TV and in the movies, defendants are typically attractive and wealthy, and while this type of defendant actually exists (O. J. Simpson, Tonya Harding, and Heidi Fleiss come to mind), we know that most defendants are urban, lower-class teenagers who are heavy users of drugs or alcohol when they are arrested. If they could have afforded the "LA Law" firm of McKenzie, Brackman, Chaney and Becker, they probably would not have committed the crime in the first place.

As you may recall, most criminal defendants retain public defenders. Because of their career conflicts, case pressure, and ambivalent feelings toward their clients, public defenders and other attorneys for the indigent have been accused of caring more about their reputation in court and their relationships with prosecutors and judges than their clients. Private attorneys who are criminal court regulars are seen as businesspeople for whom profit and not justice is the major motivating force.

Beyond these issues, the overwhelming number of cases in the criminal dockets, many of them involving acquaintances and family members, has created a situation in which "settling the matter" and cutting legal corners has supplanted the adversary system of justice. Rather than opposing each other in court, the prosecution and the defense, sometimes aided by the magistrate, form a relationship that has been described as a **courtroom work group.** This group functions to streamline the process of justice through the extensive use of plea bargaining and other alternatives rather than to provide a spirited defense or prosecution. In most criminal cases, cooperation rather than conflict between prosecution and defense appears to be the norm. It is only in the widely publicized "heavy" criminal cases involving rape or murder (the top layer of the criminal justice "wedding cake") that the adversarial process is called into play. Consequently, upwards of 90 percent of all felony cases and over 90 percent of misdemeanors are settled without trial.

A system has developed in which criminal court experiences can be viewed as a training ground for young attorneys looking for seasoning and practice, a means for newly established lawyers to receive government compensation for cases taken to get their practice going, or an arena in which established firms can place their new associates for seasoning before they are assigned to paying clients. The fact that defense lawyers receive their livelihood from a court dominated by prosecutors and the judiciary shapes their judgments. Prosecutors may be looking forward to a political career or to joining a high-paying firm.

Informal kinship and friendship ties to other attorneys also influence decision making. Where does loyalty lay—with an indigent client, a vengeful victim, or a peer whom they may have known since law school days?

While the courtroom work group limits the constitutional rights of defendants, it may be essential for keeping our overburdened justice system afloat. Moreover, while informal justice exists, it is not absolutely certain that it is inherently unfair to either the victim or the offender. The research evidence shows that the defendants who benefit the most from informal court procedures commit the least serious crimes, while the more chronic offenders gain relatively little.

Discussion Questions

1. Which kind of cases do you think are most likely to be handled informally?
2. Does the courtroom work group ethic erode our faith in the fairness of the law and legal system?

SOURCES: Roy Flemming, Peter Nardulli, and James Eisenstein, *The Craft of Justice: Politics and Work in Criminal Court Communities* (Philadelphia: University of Pennsylvania Press, 1992); James Eisenstein and Herbert Jacob, *Felony Justice* (Boston: Little, Brown, 1977); Peter Nardulli, *The Courtroom Elite* (Cambridge, Mass.: Ballinger, 1978); Paul Wice, *Chaos in the Courthouse* (New York: Praeger, 1985); Marcia Lipetz, *Routine Justice: Processing Cases in Women's Court* (New Brunswick, N.J.: Transaction Books, 1983).

court's jurisdiction. The initial list of persons chosen, which is called a **venire**, or jury array, provides the state with a group of potentially capable citizens able to serve on a jury. Many states, by rule of law, review the venire to eliminate unqualified persons and to exempt those who by reason of their professions are not allowed to be jurors; this latter group may include, but is not limited to, physicians, the clergy, and government officials. The actual jury selection process begins with those remaining on the list.

The court clerk, who handles the administrative affairs of the trial—including the processing of the complaint, the evidence, and other documents—randomly selects enough names (sometimes from a box) to fill the required number of places on the jury. In most cases, the jury in a criminal trial consists of 12 persons, with two alternate jurors standing by to serve should one of the regular jurors be unable to complete the trial. Once the prospective jurors have been chosen, the process of *voir dire* is begun; all persons selected are questioned by both the prosecution and the defense to determine their appropriateness to sit on the jury. They are examined under oath by the government, the defense, and sometimes the judge about their backgrounds, occupations, residences, and possible knowledge or interest in the case. A juror who acknowledges any bias for or prejudice against the defendant—a juror who is a friend or relative of the defendant, for example, or who has already formed an opinion about the case—is removed for *cause* and replaced with another. Thus, any prospective juror who reveals an inability to be impartial and render a verdict solely on the basis of the evidence to be presented at the trial may be removed by either the prosecution or the defense. Because normally no limit is placed on the number of challenges for cause that can be offered, it often takes considerable time to select a jury for controversial and highly publicized criminal cases.

In addition to challenges for cause, both the prosecution and the defense are allowed **peremptory challenges,** through which they can excuse jurors for no particular or an undisclosed reason. For example, a prosecutor might not want a bartender as a juror in a drunken driving case, believing that a person in that occupation might be sympathetic to the accused. Or a defense attorney might excuse a male prospective juror to try to obtain a predominantly female jury for the client. The number of peremptory challenges permitted is limited by state statute and often varies by case and jurisdiction.

The peremptory challenge has long been criticized by legal experts who question the fairness and propriety

with which it has been employed.[56] Of particular concern was the challenging of African-American jurors in interracial crimes that resulted in the trying of African-American defendants by all-white juries. In a significant case, *Batson v. Kentucky,* the Supreme Court ruled that the use of peremptory challenge to dismiss all black jurors was a violation of the defendant's right to equal protection of the law.[57] Later, in *Powers v. Ohio,* the Court ruled that a defendant can challenge jury exclusion based on race regardless of whether the defendant and the excluded jurors are of the same race. In *Powers,* a white defendant successfully appealed his conviction because seven of the prosecutor's ten peremptory challenges were used to strike African-American jurors; the practice was judged to violate the right of ordinary citizens to participate in the administration of justice.[58] The latest blow to the peremptory challenge occurred in the 1994 case of *J.E.B. V. Alabama,* in which the Court barred the dismissal of jurors based on gender.[59] The *J.E.B.* ruling will prevent prosecutors from creating all-female or -male juries in gender-sensitive cases, such as rape, harassment, or paternity.

Impartial Juries

The Sixth Amendment to the Constitution provides for the right to a speedy and public trial by an impartial jury. Throughout the 1960s and 1970s, the Supreme Court sought to ensure compliance with this constitutional mandate of impartiality through decisions eliminating racial discrimination in jury selection. For instance, in *Ham v. South Carolina* in 1973, the Court held that the defense counsel of an African-American civil rights leader was entitled to question each juror on the issue of racial prejudice.[60] In *Turner v. Murray,* the Court ruled that African-American defendants accused of murdering whites are entitled to have jurors questioned about their racial bias.[61] In *Taylor v. Louisiana,* the Court overturned the conviction of a man by an all-male jury because a Louisiana statute allowed women but not men to exempt themselves from jury duty.[62]

These similar decisions have had the effect of providing safeguards against jury bias. However, in many instances, potential jury bias is not part of the trial process. For example, while the Supreme Court in *Ham* ruled that bias was a consideration in a trial involving a civil rights worker, it ruled in another case that in "ordinary crimes"—noncapital cases, such as a robbery—defense counsel may not question the racial bias of jurors even if the crime is interracial.[63]

Trial Process

The trial of a criminal case is a formal process conducted in a specific and orderly fashion in accordance with rules of criminal law, procedure, and evidence (see Figure 17.6).

Unlike trials in popular television programs, where witnesses are often asked leading and prejudicial questions and where judges go far beyond their supervisory role, the modern criminal trial is a complicated and often time-consuming technical affair. It is a structured adversary proceeding in which both the prosecution and the defense follow specific procedures and argue the merits of their cases before the judge and the jury. Each side seeks to present its case in the most favorable light. Where possible, the prosecutor and the defense attorney object to evidence they consider damaging to their individual points of view. The prosecutor uses direct testimony, physical evidence, and a confession, if available, to convince the jury that the accused is guilty beyond a reasonable doubt. The defense attorney rebuts the government's case with his or her own evidence, makes certain that the rights of the criminal defendant under the federal and state constitutions are considered during all phases of the trial, and determines whether an appeal is appropriate if the client is found guilty. From the beginning of the process to its completion, the judge promotes an orderly and fair administration of the criminal trial.

Although each administration in the United States differs in its trial procedures, all conduct criminal trials in a generally similar fashion. The basic steps of the criminal trial proceed in the following established order.

1. *Opening statements.* As the trial begins, both prosecution and defense address the jury and present their cases. They alert the jury to what they will attempt to prove and what the major facts of the case are. They introduce the witnesses, prepare the jury for their testimony, and tell them what information to be sure to listen for. The defense begins to emphasize that any doubts about the guilt of the accused must be translated into an acquittal; the prosecution dwells on civic duty and responsibility.

FIGURE 17.6 The Steps of a Jury Trial

SOURCE: Marvin Zalman and Larry Siegel, *Criminal Procedure: Constitution and Society* (St. Paul: West Publishing, 1991), p. 655.

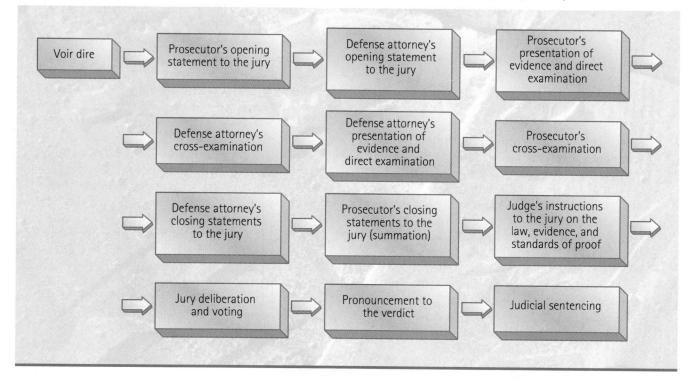

2. *The prosecution's case.* Following the opening statement, the government begins its case by presenting evidence to the court through its witnesses. Those called as witnesses—such as police officers, victims, or expert witnesses—provide testimony via **direct examination,** during which the prosecutor questions the witness to reveal the facts believed pertinent to the government case. Testimony involves what the witness actually saw, heard, or touched; it does not include opinions. However, a witness's opinion can be given in certain situations, such as in describing the motion of a vehicle or indicating whether a defendant appeared to act intoxicated or insane. Witnesses may also qualify to give their opinions because they are experts on a particular subject relevant to the case; for example, a psychiatrist may testify as to a defendant's mental capacity at the time of the crime.

After the prosecutor finishes questioning a witness, the defense cross-examines the same witness by asking questions in an attempt to clarify the defendant's role in the crime. The prosecutor may seek a redirect examination after the defense attorney has completed **cross-examination;** this allows the prosecutor to ask additional questions about information brought out during cross-examination. Finally, the defense attorney may question or cross-examine the witness once again. All witnesses for the trial are sworn in and questioned in the same basic manner.

3. *The defense's case.* At the close of the prosecution's case, the defense may ask the presiding judge to rule on a *motion for a directed verdict.* If this motion is sustained, the judge will direct the jury to acquit the defendant, thereby ending the trial. A directed verdict means that the prosecution did not present enough evidence to prove all the elements of the alleged crime. If the judge fails to sustain the motion, the defense will present its case. Witnesses are called to testify in the same manner used by the prosecution.

After the defense concludes its case, the government may present *rebuttal evidence.* This normally involves bringing evidence forward that was not used when the prosecution initially presented its case. The defense may examine the rebuttal witnesses and introduce new witnesses in a process called *surrebuttal.* After all the evidence has been presented to the court, the defense attorney may again submit a motion for a directed verdict. If the motion is denied, both the prosecution and the defense prepare to make closing arguments; and the case on the evidence is ready for consideration by the jury.

4. *Closing arguments.* Closing arguments are used by the attorneys to review the facts and evidence of the case in a manner favorable to their positions. At this stage of the trial, both prosecution and defense are permitted to draw reasonable inferences and show how the facts prove or refute the defendant's guilt. Often, both attorneys have a free hand in arguing about facts, issues, and evidence, including the applicable law. They cannot comment, however, on matters not in evidence, nor, where applicable, can they comment on the defendant's failure to testify. Normally, the defense attorney makes a closing statement first, followed by the prosecutor. Either party can elect to forgo the right to make a final summation to the jury.

5. *Instructions to the jury.* In a criminal trial, the judge instructs, or charges, the jury on the principles of law that ought to guide and control the decision on the defendant's innocence or guilt. Included in the charge is information about the elements of the alleged offense, the type of evidence needed to prove each element, and the burden of proof required to obtain a guilty verdict. Although the judge commonly provides the instructions, he or she may ask the prosecutor and the defense attorney to submit instructions for consideration; the judge then uses discretion in determining whether to use any of their instructions. The instructions that cover the law applicable to the case are extremely important, since they may serve as the basis for a subsequent appeal.

One important aspect of instructing the jury is explaining the level of proof needed to find the person guilty of a crime. As mentioned, the U.S. system of justice requires guilt to be proved *beyond a reasonable doubt.* The judge must inform the jurors that if they have even the slightest suspicion that the defendant is not guilty, then they cannot find for the prosecution. Also, the judge must explain how, in criminal cases, the burden of proof is on the prosecution to prove the defendant guilty; the accused does not have to prove his or her innocence.

6. *Verdict.* Once the charge has been given to the jury, the jurors retire to deliberate on a verdict. As previously mentioned, the verdict in a criminal case—regardless of whether the trial involves a

six- or 12-person jury—is usually required to be unanimous. A review of the case by the jury may take hours or even days. The jurors are always sequestered during their deliberations; and in some lengthy, highly publicized cases, they are kept overnight in a hotel until the verdict is reached. In less sensational cases, the jurors may be allowed to go home but are often cautioned not to discuss the case with anyone. If a verdict cannot be reached, the trial may result in a hung jury; in this case, the prosecutor has to bring the defendant to trial again if the prosecution desires a conviction.

7. *Sentence.* If found not guilty, the defendant is released. If the defendant is convicted, the judge normally orders a presentence investigation by the probation department preparatory to imposing a sentence. Before sentencing, the defense attorney often submits a motion for a new trial, alleging that legal errors occurred in the trial proceedings. The judge may deny the motion and impose a sentence immediately, a practice quite common in most misdemeanor offenses. In felony cases, however, the judge sets a date for sentencing, and the defendant is either placed on bail or held in custody until that time. Sentencing usually occurs a short time after trial. At the sentencing hearing, the judge may consider evidence that is relevant to the case, including *victim impact statements* in which victims get to be heard on how the crime affected their lives.[64] In most jurisdictions, the typical criminal penalties include fines, community supervision, incarceration, and the death penalty.

8. *Appeal.* After sentencing, defendants have the right to appeal the case, charging either that the law under which they were tried was unconstitutional (for example, discriminatory or vague) or

If a verdict cannot be reached there is a "hung jury." The state can decide to prosecute the case again. The first trial of Eric and Lyle Menendez, charged with the shotgun slaying of their parents, resulted in a hung jury and a new trial.

that the procedures used by agents of the justice system violated their constitutional rights (for example, police did not give them a proper Miranda warning or improperly obtained evidence was used at trial). If the appeal is granted, a new trial may be ordered. If the appeal is not sustained, the convicted offender will begin serving the sentence imposed, thus marking the end of the judicatory process.

Trials and the Rule of Law

Every trial has its constitutional issues, complex legal procedures, rules of court, and interpretations of statutes, all designed to ensure that the accused will have a fair trial. This section discusses the most important constitutional rights of the accused at the trial stage of the criminal justice system and reviews the legal nature of the trial process.

Right to a Speedy and Public Trial.
The Sixth Amendment guarantees a defendant the right to a speedy trial. This means that an accused is entitled to be tried within a reasonable period of time. If a person's right to a speedy trial is violated, then a complete dismissal of the charges against him or her is required, according to *Strunk v. United States*.[65] The right to a speedy trial was made applicable to state courts through the Due Process Clause of the Fourteenth Amendment in the case of *Klopfer v. North Carolina*.[66] It should be noted, however, that a defendant can waive the right to a speedy trial. A waiver of the right is implied when defendants cause the delay or when they do not assert their right when the trial takes too long to get under way.

In determining whether a violation of a defendant's right to speedy trial has occurred, several factors are considered; length of the delay alone is not enough to constitute a violation. The Supreme Court, in the case of *Barker v. Wingo*, enumerated the factors that should be considered in determining whether the speedy trial requirement has been complied with: (1) the length of the delay, (2) the reason for the delay, (3) the timeliness of the defendant's assertion of his or her right to a speedy trial, and (4) the prejudice to the defendant.[67]

How speedy does a speedy trial have to be? There is no set standard, but the Federal Speedy Trial Act of 1974 mandates 30 days from arrest to indictment and 70 days from indictment to trial. However, the states vary widely in their definitions of a speedy trial. For example, in Louisiana, the limit is 730 days (two years) in a non-capital case and 1,095 days (three years) in capital cases; in New York, the time limit is 180 days.[68]

Right to a Jury Trial.
Because a jury trial is considered a fundamental right, the Supreme Court, in the case of *Duncan v. Louisiana*, made the guarantee applicable to the states through the Fourteenth Amendment.[69] However, the question arises as to whether this right extends to all defendants—those charged with misdemeanors as well as felonies. The Supreme Court addressed this issue in the case of *Baldwin v. New York*, in which it decided that defendants are entitled to a jury trial only if they face the possibility of a prison sentence of *more than six months*.[70] Later, in *Blanton v. City of North Las Vegas*, the Court upheld the six month-plus jail sentence requirement for a jury trial, but did not rule out that a lesser term accompanied by the possibility of other punishments, such as a large fine or loss of a driver's license for a year, might warrant a jury trial.[71]

Although most people think of a jury as having 12 members and, historically, most have had 12, the Sixth Amendment does not specify that that size is required. In fact, in the case of *Williams v. Florida*, the Supreme Court held that a six-person jury fulfilled a defendant's right to a trial by jury.[72] However, a unanimous verdict is required when a six-person jury is used. When a 12-person jury is used, the Supreme Court has maintained that the Sixth Amendment does not require a unanimous verdict, except in first-degree murder cases. In *Apodica v. Oregon*, the Court found constitutional an Oregon statute that required a finding of guilty by ten out of 12 jurors in cases dealing with assault with a deadly weapon, burglary, and larceny.[73] However, it should be noted that the majority of states and the federal courts still require a unanimous verdict.

Right to Be Free from Double Jeopardy.
The Fifth Amendment provides that no person shall "be subject for the same offense to be twice put in jeopardy of life or limb." This means that a defendant cannot be prosecuted by a jurisdiction more than once for a single offense. For example, if a defendant is tried and convicted of murder in Texas, he cannot be tried again for the same murder in Texas. The right to be protected from double jeopardy was made applicable to the states through the Fourteenth Amendment in the case of *Benton v. Maryland*.[74] However, a person tried in federal court can be tried in state court, and vice versa.[75] And in 1985, the Court ruled in *Heath v. Alabama* that if a single act violates the laws of two states, the offender may be punished for each offense under the *dual sovereignty doctrine*: legal jurisdictions have the right to enforce their own laws and a single act can violate the laws of two separate jurisdictions.[76]

Right to Legal Counsel. Regardless of the legal rights citizens command at trial, without legal counsel to aid them, they would be rendered defenseless before the law. Consequently, the Sixth Amendment provides the right to be represented by an attorney in criminal trials. However, the vast majority of criminal defendants are indigents who cannot afford private legal services. In a series of cases beginning in the 1930s, the U.S. Supreme Court established the defendant's right to be represented by an attorney and, in the event he or she cannot pay for representation, to have the state provide free legal services. First, in *Powell v. Alabama,* the Court held that an attorney was essential in capital cases where the defendant's life was at stake.[77] Then, in the critically important case of *Gideon v. Wainwright,* the Court granted the absolute right to counsel in all felony cases.[78] Finally, in *Argersinger v. Hamlin,* the defendant's right to counsel in misdemeanor cases was established.[79] Today, most defendants are represented by attorneys from the time they are in police custody until their final sentencing and appeal.

Right to Competent Legal Representation. In the 1984 case of *Strickland v. Washington,* the Supreme Court found that defendants also have the right to *reasonably effective assistance* of counsel. The Court enumerated the qualities characterizing competent representation:

> Representation of a criminal defendant entails certain basic duties. Counsel's function is to assist the defendant, and hence counsel owes the client a duty of loyalty, a duty to avoid conflicts of interest. From counsel's function as assistant to the defendant derive the overarching duty to advocate the defendant's cause and the more particular duties to consult with the defendant on important decisions and to keep the defendant informed of important developments in the course of the prosecution. Counsel also has a duty to bring to bear such skill and knowledge as will render the trial a reliable adversarial testing process.[80]

If convicted, defendants can have their sentence overturned if they can prove that (1) counsel's performance was so deficient that he or she was not functioning as the counsel guaranteed by the Sixth Amendment and (2) the deficient performance prejudiced the case and deprived them of a fair trial.

Right to Confront Witnesses. The accused has the right to confront witnesses to challenge their assertions and perceptions: Did they really hear what they thought they did? Or see what they think they saw? Are they biased? Honest? Trustworthy?

One recent issue involving confrontation is the role of child witnesses in sex abuse cases. Sometimes, a court appearance is so traumatic to children that they are unable to give accurate information in court. A number of devices have been used to make the experience less difficult. In one recent case, the Supreme Court overturned the conviction of an alleged sex criminal after the trial judge allowed his two teenage victims to testify behind a screen so as to avoid eye-to-eye contact.[81] Then in an important case, *Maryland v. Craig,* the Court ruled that child witnesses could testify via closed-circuit television as long as safeguards were set up to protect the defendant's rights.[82] Protections included the defendant being able to view the witness and being in communication with the witness's attorney at all times.

In a 1992 case, *White v. Illinois,* the Court again restricted the confrontation clause by ruling that the state's attorney is neither required to produce victims in child abuse cases nor demonstrate the reason they were unavailable to serve as witnesses.[83] *White* involved the use as testimony of statements given by a child to the child's baby-sitter, mother, doctor, nurse, and a police officer concerning the facts and identity of the alleged assailant in a sexual assault case. The prosecutor twice tried to call the child to testify, but both times, the four-year-old experienced emotional difficulty and was unavailable to appear in court. The case outcome then hinged solely on the testimony of the five witnesses who repeated in court the statements made to them by the child. By allowing the use of *hearsay* evidence (second-party statements) in this case, the *White* decision negates the requirement that defendants be allowed to confront their accusers in open court. In both *Craig* and *White,* the Court gave clear indication that it is willing to compromise defendant's rights of confrontation to achieve a social objective—the prosecution of child abuse.[84]

☰ Sentencing

After a defendant has been found guilty of a criminal offense or has entered a plea of guilty, he or she is brought before the court for imposition of a criminal penalty—sentencing.

Historically, a full range of punishments has been meted out to criminal offenders: corporal punishments, such as whipping or mutilation; fines; banishment;

incarceration; death. The evolution of punishment as a means of correction will be discussed in Chapter 18.

In U.S. society, incarceration in a federal, state, or local institution is generally the most serious penalty meted out to offenders. In addition, the *death penalty* remains on the statute books of most jurisdictions and has been used at an increasing rate in recent years.

Purposes of Sentencing

A multiplicity of goals lies behind the imposition of a criminal sentence.[85] It is safe to say that no single philosophy of justice holds sway when a sentencing decision is made. Each jurisdiction employs its own sentencing philosophies, and each individual decision maker views the purpose of sentencing differently. A 23-year-old college student arrested for selling cocaine might be seen as essentially harmless by one judge and granted probation; another judge might see the young drug dealer as a threat to the moral fabric of society and deserving of a prison term. One of the great flaws then of the U.S. system of justice has been the extraordinary amount of *disparity* in the way criminal punishment has been meted out.[86]

In general, four goals—deterrence, incapacitation, rehabilitation, and desert/retribution—are associated with imposition of a sentence.[87]

1. *Deterrence.* By imposing a sentence on the convicted criminal, the court hopes to deter others from committing similar crimes. The validity of deterrence rests on the premise that punishing one offender will convince other potential criminals to abstain from criminal activity.
2. *Incapacitation.* Incapacitation is directed at controlling the behavior of offenders considered a menace to society. At least for the period of time the offenders are under correctional control, they will not be able to repeat their criminal behavior. In some instances, incapacitation involves supervising offenders while they remain in the community. In others, it calls for confining them in an institution. Incapacitation involves prediction of behavior patterns: offenders are confined not for what they have done but for what it is feared they might do in the future.
3. *Rehabilitation.* Correctional rehabilitation is another goal of sentencing. Its purpose is to reduce future criminality by administering some type of treatment under supervision of correctional agents. Rehabilitation efforts focus on emotional stress, vocational training, education, or substance abuse. Rehabilitation also involves prediction of future behavior: unless the offenders receive treatment, they will commit future crimes; treatment will reduce the likelihood of their reoffending.
4. *Desert/Retribution.* Another goal of sentencing is to punish offenders for their misdeeds. Whereas the goals of deterrence, incapacitation, and rehabilitation are based on what might happen or what the offender might do, desert focuses on the event that led to conviction. Since the criminals benefited from their misdeeds, they must now pay society back to make things even. For example, it is only fair that criminals who have committed the worst crime, murder, receive the most severe penalty, death. For example, those who benefit from illegal business transactions should pay large fines to return their illegal gains.

Each of these goals is in operation when a person is sentenced. Sometimes, one policy or goal becomes popular in public opinion and for a while dominates sentencing considerations. In the 1960s and 1970s, rehabilitation became the prime goal of sentencing, and innovative treatment methods were stressed. Today, rising violence rates, the supposed failure of rehabilitation, and a generally conservative outlook make desert, deterrence, and incapacitation the primary sentencing goals.

Sentencing Dispositions

Generally, five kinds of sentences or dispositions are available to the court:

1. Fines
2. Probation
3. Alternate or intermediate sanctions
4. Incarceration
5. Capital punishment

A fine is usually exacted for a minor crime and may also be combined with other sentencing alternatives, such as probation or confinement.[88] Probation allows the offender to live in the community subject to compliance with legally imposed conditions. Alternative sanctions involve probation plus some other sanction, such as house arrest, electronic monitoring, or forfeiture of property. The sentence of total confinement, or incarceration, is imposed when it has been decided that the general public needs to be protected from further criminal activity by the defendant. Capital punishment or the death penalty is reserved for people who commit first-degree murder under aggravated circumstances, such as with extreme cruelty, violence, or torture.

Imposing the Sentence

The sentence itself is generally imposed by the judge, and sentencing is one of the most crucial functions of judgeship. Sentencing authority may also be exercised by the jury, an administrative body, or a group of judges, or it may be mandated by statute.

In most felony cases, save for where the law provides for **mandatory prison terms,** sentencing is usually based on a variety of information available to the judge. Some jurisdictions allow victims to make impact statements that are considered at sentencing hearings. Edna Erez and Pamela Tontodonato found that these often have little impact on sentencing outcomes, though other victim-related factors, such as having the victims show an interest in the case and be present in the courtroom, influence judicial decision making.[89] Most judges consider a *presentence investigation report* by the probation department. This report, which is a social and personal history as well as an evaluation of the defendant, is used by the judge in making a sentencing decision.[90] Some judges heavily weigh the presentence investigation report; others may dismiss it completely or rely only on certain portions.

When an accused is convicted of two or more charges, he or she must be sentenced on each charge. If the sentences are **concurrent,** they begin the same day, and the sentence has been completed after the longest term has been served. For example, a defendant is sentenced to three years' imprisonment on a charge of assault and ten years for burglary, the sentences to be served concurrently. After the offender serves ten years in prison, the sentences would be completed. Conversely, a **consecutive sentence** means that upon completion of one sentence, the other term of incarceration begins. For example, a defendant is sentenced to three years' imprisonment on a charge of assault and ten years for burglary, the sentences to be served consecutively. After three years are served on the assault charge, the offender begins serving the burglary sentence. Therefore, the total term on the two charges would be 13 years. In most instances, sentences are given concurrently.

The following sections discuss incarceration sentences and the death penalty. For purposes of organization, community sentences, such as probation and fines, are discussed in Chapter 18.

Sentencing Structures

When a convicted offender is sentenced to prison, the statutes of the jurisdiction in which the crime was committed determine the penalties that may be imposed by the court. Over the years, a variety of sentencing structures have been used in the United States. They include determinate sentences, indeterminate sentences, and mandatory sentences.

The Indeterminate Sentence

The first prison sentences used in the United States were for a fixed period of years that the offender was forced to serve before release. Harsh prison conditions and rules enforced by physical punishment left inmates with little incentive for rehabilitation or self-improvement. The prevailing concept was "let the punishment fit the crime."

By 1870, penal reformers in Australia (Alexander Maconochie) and Ireland (Sir Walter Crofton) had instituted plans in which inmates could earn early release by exhibiting a positive attitude and work habits. In 1870, at a meeting of the National Congress on Penitentiary and Reformatory Discipline in Cincinnati, progressive prison reformers, such as Enoch Wines and Zebulon Brockway, called for sentencing reform that would allow inmates to be released from prison once they were reformed. *Progressives* were firmly convinced that the state, using scientific methods, could achieve social reform. They believed that prison sentences should be tailored to fit individual needs and that offenders should only be placed in confinement until they were rehabilitated. Brockway called for the development of **indeterminate sentences,** which require that criminals serve a short minimum stay in prison during which they would be encouraged to work on self-improvement. Once the offenders were reformed, prison administrators would be empowered to release them back into the community on parole. Rather than the "punishment fitting the crime," reformers believed the "treatment should fit the offender."

Reform did not come at once. By 1900, five states had adopted the indeterminate sentencing model; during the following 20 years, another 32 states adopted indeterminacy.[91] The indeterminate sentence became the most widely used type of sentence in the United States. Some states went so far to develop true *indefinite sentences* with very brief minimums and very long maximums, allowing inmates to be released as soon as a parole board concluded they were "rehabilitated."

The indeterminate sentence is still used in a majority of states. Under most sentencing models, convicted offenders who are not eligible for community supervision are given a short minimum sentence that must be served and a lengthy maximum sentence that is the outer boundary of the time that can possibly be served.

For example, the legislature might set a sentence of a minimum of one year and a maximum of 20 years for burglary.

Under this scheme, the actual length of time served by the inmate is controlled by the corrections agency. The inmate can be paroled from confinement after serving the minimum sentence whenever the institution and parole personnel believe that he or she is ready to live in the community. The minimum (or maximum) might also be reduced by inmates earning "time off for good behavior" or for participating in counseling and vocational training programs. In many instances, sentencing reduction programs allow inmates to serve only a fraction of their minimum sentence.

The underlying purpose of the indeterminate sentencing approach is to individualize each sentence in the interests of rehabilitating the offender. This type of sentencing allows for flexibility not only in the type of sentence to be imposed but also in the length of time to be served.

There are a number of possible variations on the indeterminate sentence. One approach is for the judge to set both the maximum and the minimum sentence within guidelines established by the legislature. For example, the minimum and maximum sentence for burglary is one to 20 years. Offender A gets one to 20; offender B, four to ten; offender C, three to six. The maximum the judge sets cannot exceed 20 years; the minimum cannot be less than one. Another variation on this model is to have the maximum set by the judge within an upper limit, with the minimum determined by the legislature. For example, all sentenced burglars do at least one year in prison but no more than 20. Offender A receives one to ten; offender B, one to 20; offender C, one to five.

Today, about 40 states still use indeterminate sentencing. Most of these have statutes that specify minimum and maximum terms but allow judges discretion to fix the actual sentence within those limits. The typical minimum sentence is at least one year; a few state jurisdictions require at least a two-year minimum sentence for felons.[92]

The indeterminate sentence is the predominant form of sentence used in the criminal process. It is the heart of the rehabilitation model of justice because offenders may be released after a relatively short prison stay if they convince correctional authorities that they can forgo a criminal career. Yet because many policymakers believe that the rehabilitation of offenders has generally failed, alternative sentencing schemes are being given more consideration.

The Determinate Sentence

Determinate sentences were actually the first kind used in the United States. As originally constructed, the judge could impose a sentence, based on his or her personal and professional judgments, that fell within limits set by statute. For example, a state criminal code could set the sentence for burglary at up to 20 years in prison. After evaluating each case, the judge could impose a sentence of five years on a first-time defendant, ten on a more experienced criminal, and the full 20 on a third who may have been a repeater and carried a weapon to the crime scene. Unlike the indeterminate models in which release dates are controlled by correctional authorities, a *determinate sentence* is one in which the duration of the offender's prison stay is determined by the judiciary at the time the sentence is imposed.

When the original determinate sentencing statutes were replaced by indeterminate sentences early in the twentieth century, judicial discretion remained quite broad. Both determinate and indeterminate sentences allowed judges to place one defendant on probation while sentencing another to a lengthy prison term for what was essentially the same crime. Such unbridled discretion left the door open to disparity and unfairness in the sentencing process. In addition, there was dramatic evidence that indeterminate sentences gave correctional authorities quasi-judicial power, allowing them to decide when an inmate was to be returned to society. Correctional discretion could then be used to control the inmate population.

In 1969, Kenneth Culp Davis published *Discretionary Justice,* which was followed in 1972 by Judge Marvin Frankel's landmark study *Criminal Sentences—Law without Order.*[93] These works exposed the disparity that existed in the justice process and called for reform of the criminal law. Frankel stated, "The almost wholly unchecked and sweeping powers we give to judges in the fashioning of sentences are terrifying and intolerable for a society that professes devotion to the rule to law."[94]

The focus of concern was the degree to which *disparity* existed in the sentencing process. Widely disparate sentences were often given to offenders who were convicted of similar offenses and who had identical criminal records.

In response to these concerns, a number of jurisdictions replaced the indeterminate sentence and discretionary parole with a system of determinate sentencing that featured a single term of years without discretionary parole. Earned good time can reduce sentences, in some cases, by up to one-half. These modern versions of determinate sentencing reflect an orientation toward desert, deterrence, and equality at the expense of treatment and rehabilitations. Most have attempted to structure and control judicial decision making by suggesting appropriate prison terms for particular crimes. A variety of methods are being used to structure sentencing, but the most important are efforts to create **guideline sentences,** which are discussed below in greater detail.

Guideline Sentencing

Guidelines are usually based on the seriousness of a crime and the background of an offender: the more serious the crime and the more extensive the offender's background, the longer the prison term recommended by the guidelines. For example, guidelines might require that all people convicted of robbery who had no prior offense record and who did not use excessive force or violence be given an average of a five-year sentence; those who used force and had a prior record will have three years added on their sentence.

In some states, including Delaware and Maryland, *descriptive guidelines* were devised by analyzing how similar offenders were treated in the past; judges were then asked to voluntarily comply with suggested sentences. In contrast, *prescriptive guidelines,* used in such states as Michigan, Washington, Oregon, Pennsylvania, and Minnesota and by the U.S. government, are created by appointed sentencing commissions. The commission members determine what an "ideal" sentence would be for a particular crime and offender. Prescriptive guidelines are generally mandatory and receive a much higher rate of judicial compliance than the voluntary guideline models.

Sentencing guidelines can be computed for a variety of offense and offender types. Table 17.2 shows the guidelines used in Minnesota. Each case is evaluated on the basis of offense seriousness and offender's prior record to determine where it fits in the guideline grid. Those that fall above the incarceration line give the judge the opportunity to choose probation or sentence the offender to up to 12 months in jail.[95] In more serious cases that fall below the incarceration line, judges may impose the guideline sentence but are granted discretion to increase or decrease the sentence based on mitigating or aggravating circumstances. The range of sentences in the Minnesota guideline grid has been altered over the years with some penalties being increased and others decreased. In 1989, the Minnesota legislature adopted get-tough policies, including mandatory minimum prison terms for certain drug crimes and

life without parole for certain first-degree murderers. In the original guidelines, a first-level offense with a criminal history score of six was eligible for a probation sentence, while today, offenders falling in that category get 19 months in prison.

The Federal System. When a defendant appears in federal court for sentencing, his or her fate is determined by a very complex set of rules set down by the seven-member U.S. Sentencing Commission.[96] The guidelines themselves are quite extensive and detailed. To determine the actual sentence, a magistrate must first determine the *base penalty* that a particular charge is given in the guidelines. For example, robbery has a base offense level of 18. The base level can be adjusted upward if the case was particularly serious or violent. For example, seven points could be added to the robbery base if a firearm was discharged during the crime and five points if it was just "possessed" by the offender. Similarly, points can be added to a robbery if a large amount of money was taken, a victim was injured, a person was abducted or restrained to facilitate an escape, or the object of the robbery was to steal weapons or drugs. Upward adjustments can also be made if defendants were ringleaders in the crime, obstructed justice, or used a professional skill or position of trust (such as doctor, lawyer, or politician) to commit crime. Offenders designated as "career criminals" by a court can likewise receive longer sentences. Once the base score is computed, judges determine the sentence by consulting a *sentencing table* that converts scores into months to be served.

Future of Structured Sentencing

There seems little question that structured sentencing will continue to be considered in other jurisdictions now that the federal government has adopted them and the Supreme Court has upheld their use.[97] A number of states have been or are considering guidelines.[98]

Despite the widespread acceptance of guidelines, some nagging problems remain. Research indicates that judges diverge from sentences established by the guidelines.[99] Others suggest that race and economic status continue to influence sentencing.[100] For example, Michael Tonry found that the Minnesota guidelines helped conserve state resources, were resistant to political pressures, and increased overall fairness in the sentencing system.[101] Yet he also found evidence that the federal guidelines have never been accepted by the judiciary and are often circumvented and or breached;

TABLE 17.2 Minnesota Guideline Grid, Presumptive Sentence Lengths in Months

Severity Levels of Conviction Offense		Criminal History Score						
		0	1	2	3	4	5	6 or more
Sale of a Simulated Controlled Substance	I	12*	12*	12*	13	15	17	19 18–20
Theft Related Crimes ($2,500 or less) Check Forgery ($200–$2500)	II	12*	12*	13	15	17	19	21 20–22
Theft Crimes ($2,500 or less)	III	12*	13	15	17	19 18–20	22 21–23	25 24–26
Nonresidential Burglary Theft Crimes (over $2,500)	IV	12*	15	18	21	25 24–26	32 30–34	41 37–45
Residential Burglary Simple Robbery	V	18	23	27	30 29–31	38 36–40	46 43–49	54 50–58
Criminal Sexual Conduct 2nd Degree (a) & (b)	VI	21	26	30	34 33–35	44 42–46	54 50–58	65 60–70
Aggravated Robbery	VII	48 44–52	58 54–62	68 64–72	78 74–82	88 84–92	98 94–102	108 104–112
Criminal Sexual Conduct, 1st Degree Assault, 1st Degree	VIII	86 81–91	98 93–103	110 105–115	122 117–127	134 129–139	146 141–151	158 153–163
Murder, 3rd Degree Murder, 2nd Degree (felony murder)	IX	150 144–156	165 159–171	180 174–186	195 189–201	210 204–216	225 219–231	240 234–246
Murder, 2nd Degree (with intent)	X	306 299–313	326 319–333	346 339–353	366 359–373	386 379–393	406 399–413	426 419–433

First-degree murder is excluded from the guidelines by law and continues to have a mandatory life sentence.
*One year and one day.
Italicized numbers within the grid denote the range within which a judge may sentence without the sentence being deemed a departure.
Offenders with nonimprisonment felony sentences are subject to jail time according to law.
■ At the discretion of the judge, up to a year in jail and/or other nonjail sanctions can be imposed as conditions of probation.
□ Presumptive commitment to state imprisonment.

SOURCE: Minnesota Sentencing Guideline Commission, 1990.

he calls them "the most controversial and disliked sentencing reform initiative in United States history."[102]

Some defense attorneys oppose the use of guidelines because they result in longer prison terms, prevent judges from considering mitigating circumstances, and reduce the use of probation.[103]

Mandatory Sentences

Another effort to limit judicial discretion has been the development of mandatory (minimum) sentences that require the incarceration of all offenders convicted of specific crimes. Some states, for example, exclude offenders convicted of certain offenses, such as drug trafficking or handgun crimes, from even the possibility of being placed on probation; some exclude recidivists; and others bar certain offenders from being considered for parole. Mandatory sentencing generally limits the judge's discretionary power to impose any disposition but that authorized by the legislature; it is in opposition to the idea of the individualized sentence.

Mandatory sentencing legislation may be imposed as a supplement to an indeterminate sentencing structure or as a feature of structured sentencing. For example, in Massachussetts, which uses indeterminate sentencing, conviction for possession of an unregistered handgun brings with it a mandatory prison term.[104] In contrast, the federal government, which uses guidelines, creates mandatory sentences for some crimes by giving them a base score so high that a prison term is required. The Federal Drug Control Acts of 1986 and 1988 mandate long minimum sentences for drug trafficking and double these sentences in the event of a prior conviction; these terms are then built into the guidelines.[105]

It is difficult to say if depriving the judiciary of discretion and placing all sentencing power in the hands of the legislature or a sentencing commission will have a deterrent effect on the commission of these offenses. The use of mandatory minimum sentences can lead to an increase in plea bargaining as offenders seek avenues to escape harsh sentences and prosecutors use the threat of mandatory sentences to force guilty pleas to lesser offenses.[106] Michael Tonry argues that lawyers and judges will take steps to avoid application of laws they consider unduly harsh; that dismissal rates typically increase at early stages of the criminal justice process after mandatory laws are implemented as practitioners attempt to shield some defendants from the laws' reach; that defendants whose case is not dismissed or diverted make more vigorous efforts to avoid conviction and delay sentencing; that defendants who are convicted of the target offense are often sentenced more severely than they would be in the absence of the mandatory law; and that because declines in conviction rates for those arrested tend to offset increases in imprisonment rates for those convicted, the overall probability that defendants will be incarcerated remains about the same after enactment of a mandatory sentencing law.[107]

So while some of the desired effects of mandatory sentencing have been achieved (serious criminals do get longer sentences), they are counterbalanced by the efforts of justice system personnel to shield some offenders from the more punitive aspects of mandatory sentencing.

Sentencing Disparity and Control

Sentencing disparity has long been a problem in the justice system. Simply put, it is common for people to be convicted of similar criminal acts but to receive widely different sentences. For example, one person convicted of burglary receives a three-year prison sentence, while another is granted probation. As Figure 17.7 shows, few defendants actually serve their entire sentence, causing even greater disparity. Such differences make it seem a violation of the constitutional right to due process and equal protection to maintain a sentencing system that results in wide variations in punishment. State sentencing codes usually include various factors that can legitimately influence the length of prison sentences, including:

- How severe the offense is
- The offender's prior criminal record
- Whether the offender used violence
- Whether the offender used weapons
- Whether the crime was committed for money

Research studies do in fact show a strong correlation between these legal variables and the type and length of sentence received.

The suspicion remains, however, that race, gender, and economic status influence sentencing outcomes. These extralegal factors appear to influence sentencing because the inmate population is disproportionately male, African-American, and lower class. Although this phenomenon may be a result of discrimination, it could also be simply a function of existing crime patterns—males, minorities, and members of the lower class commit the crimes that are most likely to result in a prison sentence (homicide, rape, armed robbery, and so on).

Numerous research studies have been conducted to determine the cause of sentencing disparity in the United States.[108] Some have found a pattern of racial discrimination in sentencing, while others indicate that class bias exists.[109] There is also considerable evidence being assembled that the race and class of the *victim* and not the offender may be the most important factor in sentencing decisions. Crimes involving a white victim seem to be more heavily punished than those in which a minority-group member is the target.[110]

While considerable effort has been expended to gather evidence of race and class bias in criminal sentencing, the actual impact of extralegal factors is often hard to determine.[111] Nonetheless, an extensive analysis of sentencing in 300 jurisdictions conducted by the

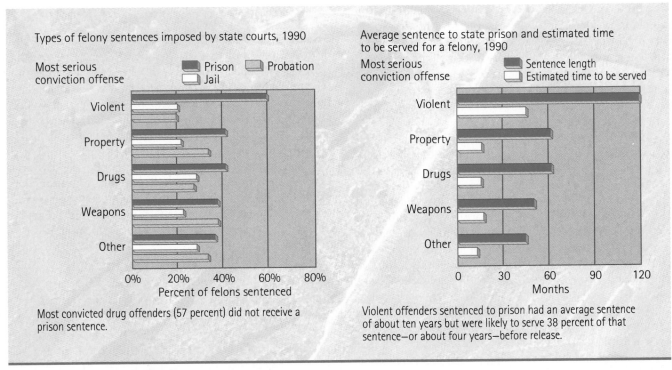

FIGURE 17.7 Sentences and Time Served

SOURCE: Patrick Langan and Richard Solari, *National Judicial Reporting Program, 1990* (Washington, D.C.: Bureau of Justice Statistics, 1993), p. 4.

Bureau of Justice Statistics indicates that more African-Americans are sent to prison (54 percent) than whites (42 percent). As Figure 17.8 indicates, blacks have a greater chance than whites of being incarcerated for violent, property, and drug crimes, while whites have the edge for weapon-related offenses.[112]

While these data are persuasive, it is also possible that disparity in the incarceration rate is a function of factors unrelated to judicial bias and discrimination. For example, the greatest percentage of the African-American population lives in the South, where prison sentences tend to be highest for all races.[113] There is also evidence that the association between race and legal factors, such as plea bargaining, crime seriousness, prior record, and use of a weapon all help to explain interracial sentencing disparity.[114] Stephen Klein, Joan Petersilia, and Susan Turner found that after relevant legal factors were considered, race had little effect on sentencing outcomes in California.[115] This data is especially important because California uses a determinate sentencing model and the Klein finding might indicate that legislative control over judicial discretion might help reduce disparity.

Other studies show that defendants who can afford bail receive more lenient sentences than those who remain in pretrial detention.[116] There is also evidence that sentencing outcome is indirectly affected by the defendant's ability to afford a private attorney, though research does not always support this contention.[117] And while considerations of prior record may be legitimate in forming sentencing decisions, there is evidence that blacks and poor whites are more likely to have prior records because of organizational and individual bias on the part of police.[118]

In sum, the evidence seems to show that whereas judicial bias may have been an important factor in the past, its *direct* influence on sentencing may be decreasing today.[119] However, other correlates of race and class within the criminal justice system may indirectly influence sentencing outcome. Defendants who cannot afford to make bail, obtain proper legal representation, take advantage of plea bargaining, or whose background fails to impress the probation department, will receive the most severe criminal sentences; all too often, these are the poor and minority-group members. And in the all-important area of capital punishment, racial bias in sentencing may be a function of the victim's and not the criminal's race.

Because of the lingering problem of racial and class bias in the sentencing process, one primary goal of the

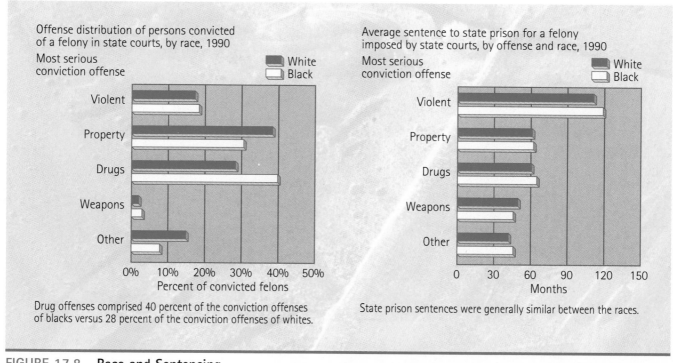

FIGURE 17.8   Race and Sentencing

SOURCE: Patrick Langan and Richard Solari, *National Judicial Reporting Program, 1993* (Washington, D.C.: Bureau of Justice Statistics, 1993), p. 14.

criminal justice system in the 1990s is to reduce disparity by creating new forms of criminal sentences that limit judicial discretion and are aimed at uniformity and fairness.

The Death Penalty

Though the execution of convicted criminals has been common throughout human history, it is a topic that has long perplexed social thinkers. Today, the death penalty for murder is used in 36 states and by the federal government with the approval of about 75 percent of the population. Capital punishment has become a fairly commonplace event in American culture: about 2,600 people are on death row, and more than 180 have been executed since 1976.[120] States without the death penalty tend to be located in the Northeast and Midwest (areas with the lowest violence rates), while states in the South are the most likely to conduct executions. The most common method of execution today is lethal injection, followed by electrocution and lethal gas. The typical death row inmate is a white male (only 25 death row inmates are female), under 35 years of age, who was an unmarried, school dropout.

Death Penalty Debate

The death penalty has long been one of the most controversial aspects of the justice system, and it likely will continue to be a source of significant debate.[121]

Arguments for the Death Penalty. Various arguments have been offered in support of the death penalty. Among these rationales are that executions have always been used, that it is inherent in human nature to punish the wicked, and that the death penalty is favored by most Americans and used in three-quarters of the nations of the world, including Japan, which has an extremely low murder rate.[122] The Bible describes methods of executing criminals. Many moral philosophers and religious leaders, such as Thomas More, John Locke, and Immanuel Kant, did not oppose the death penalty; neither did the framers of the U.S. Constitution.

The death penalty also seems to be in keeping with the current mode of dispensing punishment. The criminal law exacts proportionately harsher penalties for crimes based on their seriousness; logic says that this practice is testimony to a retributionist philosophy.

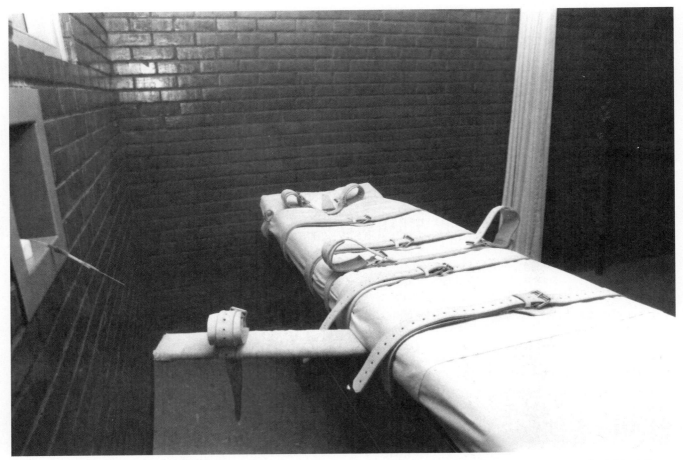

A gurney used for carrying out death by lethal injection. Note the restraints at the top of the gurney and the intravenous needle visible at the observation window at the left.

Therefore, the harshest penalty for the most severe crime represents a logical step in the process.

Some also argue that the death penalty is sometimes the only real threat available to deter crime. For example, prison inmates serving life sentences can be controlled only if they are aware that further transgressions can lead to death. Or a person committing a crime that carries with it a long prison sentence might be more likely to kill witnesses if the threat of death did not exist.

Death is the ultimate incapacitation. Some offenders are so dangerous that they can never be safely let out in society. The death penalty is a sure way of preventing these people from ever harming others; it simply may be the only alternative available. *More than 200* inmates on death row today had prior homicide convictions; if they had been executed for their first offense, close to 200 innocent people would still be alive.

Finally, the death penalty is believed to be cost-effective. Considering the crowded state of the nation's prison system and the expense of keeping an inmate locked up for many years, an execution makes financial sense.

In summary, supporters view capital punishment as the ultimate deterrent to crime. They believe that so serious a sanction prevents many potential criminals from taking the lives of innocent victims. The justification for the death penalty, therefore, relies on the premise that sacrificing the life of a few evil people is a cost effective way to save the lives of many innocent ones.

Arguments against the Death Penalty.

Even if the general public voices approval of the death penalty, abolitionists argue that "social vengeance by death is a primitive way of revenge which stands in the way of moral progress."[123] Its inherent brutality places it in violation of the Eighth Amendment of the U.S. Constitution, which prohibits "cruel and unusual punishment." And while the public may approve of capital punishment in principle, it does not find it an acceptable punishment for all the varieties of acts that qualify for the death penalty today, such as being an accessory to a fatal crime but not actually killing anyone.[124]

Opponents also object to the finality of the death penalty. It, of course, precludes any possibility of rehabilitation. Studies indicate that death row inmates released because of legal changes rarely recidivate and present little threat to the community.[125]

It is also quite possible for an innocent person to be convicted of crime; once the person is executed, the mistake can never be rectified.[126] "It is better that a thousand guilty go free than one innocent man be executed" is a statement abolitionists often make. This point has been convincingly made by Michael Radelet and Hugo Bedau, who claim that there have been about 350 wrongful convictions this century, of which 23 led to executions. They estimate that about three death sentences are returned every two years in cases where the defendant has been falsely accused. More than half the errors stem from perjured testimony, false identifications, coerced confessions, and suppression of evidence. In addition to the 23 who were executed, 128 of the falsely convicted served more than six years in prison; 39 served more than 16 years, and eight died while serving their sentence![127] It is their view that even though the system attempts to be especially cautious in capital cases, it is evident that unacceptable mistakes can occur.

The discretionary nature of the death penalty also draws criticism from its opponents. Legal scholar Charles Black argues that "arbitrary discretion pervades every road to the chair."[128] The beliefs and personal background of judges, including their age and political affiliation, can determine whether they uphold the death penalty (not surprisingly, younger Democrats seem more liberal than older Republicans).[129] Because discretion and personal beliefs influence decision making, the death penalty can be employed in a discriminatory fashion. Between 1930 and 1967, 3,859 alleged criminals were executed in the United States. Of those executed, 53.5 percent were African-American and 45.4 percent were white. This trend has not changed; in 1993, about half of all prisoners on death row were black, Hispanic, or Native American.[130]

Research indicates that white defendants convicted of murder actually have a greater probability of receiving the death penalty than African-Americans.[131] One reason is that the *victim's race* controls death penalty decision making, not the offender's.[132] People who kill whites are significantly more likely to be sentenced to death than people who kill blacks.[133] Since murder is essentially intraracial, whites are more likely to receive capital sentences because their victims are most often white. Nonetheless, the likelihood of receiving the death penalty is greatest in the relatively infrequent instance where a African-American criminal kills a white victim.[134]

Abolitionists claim that capital punishment has never proven to be a deterrent, any more than has life in prison. As you may recall from Chapter 5, there is little hard evidence that the threat of capital punishment is related to murder rates or incidents. In fact, capital punishment may encourage murder, since it sets an example of violence and brutality.[135]

Abolitionists also point out that such nations as Denmark and Sweden have long abandoned the death penalty and that 40 percent of the countries with a death penalty have active abolitionist movements.[136]

The death penalty is also capricious; receiving death is similar to losing a lottery.[137] Each year, about 10,000 people are convicted of murder; more receive probation as a sole sentence than get the death penalty. Is it fair to release one person who has taken a life into the community and execute another?

Legality of the Death Penalty

For most of this country's history, capital punishment was used in a discretionary, haphazard manner without strict legal controls. As a result, its application was marked by extreme racial disparity; more than half the executions conducted in America involved African Americans. Then, in 1972, the United States Supreme Court, in its *Furman v. Georgia* decision, ruled that the discretionary imposition of the death penalty was cruel and unusual punishment under the Eighth and Fourteenth Amendments of the Constitution.[138] The Court did not rule out the use of capital punishment as a penalty; rather, it objected to the arbitrary and capricious manner in which it was imposed. After *Furman,* many states changed statutes that had allowed juries discretion in imposing the death penalty. In some states, this was accomplished by enacting statutory guidelines for jury decisions that spelled out specific conditions of aggravation that must be met for the death penalty to be considered.

Despite these changes in statutory law, no further executions were carried out while the Supreme Court pondered additional cases concerning the death penalty. In July 1976, the Supreme Court ruled on the constitutionality of five states' death penalty statutes. In the first case, *Gregg v. Georgia,* the Court found valid the Georgia statute that held that a jury must find at least one "aggravating circumstance" out of ten before the death penalty can be imposed in murder cases.[139] In the *Gregg* case, for example, the jury imposed the death penalty after establishing beyond a reasonable doubt the presence of two aggravating circumstances:

1. The murder was committed while the offender was engaged in the commission of two other capital felonies.
2. The offender committed the murder for the purpose of receiving money and other financial gains (an automobile).

The Court also upheld the constitutionality of a Texas statute on capital punishment in *Jurek v. Texas*[140] and of a Florida statute in *Proffitt v. Florida*.[141] These statutes are similar to Georgia's in that they limit sentencing discretion not only by specifying the crimes for which capital punishment can be handed down but also by stipulating criteria concerning the circumstances surrounding the crimes. However, the Supreme Court declared that mandatory death sentences were unconstitutional.

In the late 1970s and early 1980s, a more conservative Supreme Court eased the way for executions by lifting some of the legal roadblocks to capital punishment, such as allowing the removal of jurors who are opposed to the death penalty.[142] In a 1987 case, *Tison v. Arizona,* the Court permitted executions of people who were major participants in a murder case and displayed reckless indifference to human life but did not actually kill anybody.[143]

In what may have been the last major challenge to the death penalty, *McKlesky v. Kemp,* the Supreme Court upheld the capital sentence of an African-American man in Georgia despite social science evidence that an African-American criminal who kills a white victim has a much greater chance of receiving the death penalty than a white criminal who kills a black victim.[144] Many observers felt that this case was the last legal obstacle the death penalty had to overcome to become a standard mode of punishment in the American justice system. To punctuate its hardline stance, the Court subsequently upheld the state's right to use the death penalty on youthful offenders who killed after reaching their sixteenth birthday.[145] Ironically, when McKlesky reappealed his case on other procedural grounds, the Court used it as a vehicle to limit the access of death row inmates to the appeal process; Warren McKlesky was executed in 1993.[146]

☰ Summary

The judicatory process is designed to provide an important forum for deciding the justice of a conflict between two or more parties. Unfortunately, discretion and personal decision making interfere with the equality that should be built into the law.

The judicatory process is played out in the nation's court system. State courts usually involve a three- or four-tiered system—lower trial courts, superior trial courts, appellate courts, and supreme court. The federal system is similar; it contains trial courts, appellate courts, and the Supreme Court. The U.S. Supreme Court is the final court of appeals for all cases on both state and federal levels.

There are three main actors in the judicatory process. The prosecutor brings charges against the offender and then represents the state in all criminal matters. The defense attorney represents the accused at all stages of the judicatory process. Some defendants can afford to hire private attorneys for their defense, but the majority are represented by defense counsel appointed and paid for by the state. The judge controls the trial, rules on issues of evidence, charges the jury, and in some cases can choose the type and length of sentence.

The pretrial stage of the justice process involves such issues as bail, plea bargaining, and alternatives to prosecution. Bail is a money bond the defendant puts up to secure freedom before trial. It is controversial, since those who cannot make bail must spend their time in detention. Critics charge that bail discriminates against the poor, who can neither afford bond nor borrow it from bonding agents. Consequently, reform programs, such as release on recognizance, have been started.

Plea bargaining involves the prosecutor's allowing defendants to plead guilty as charged in return for some consideration—for example, a reduced sentence or dropped charges. Plea bargaining has been criticized, since it represents the unchecked use of discretion by prosecutors. Often, serious criminals can receive light sentences by bargaining, while some people may be coerced into pleading guilty because they fear a harsh sentence if they go to trial. An effort has been made to control plea bargains, but they are still frequently used.

One way of influencing plea bargains is through noncriminal alternatives to prosecution. These include diversion and other types of treatment-oriented programs.

The second stage of the judicatory process is the criminal trial. The trial has a number of distinct stages, including jury selection, opening statements, presentation of evidence by prosecution and defense, closing arguments, instructions to the jury, verdict, sentence, and appeal. The rule of law also affects criminal trials. The Supreme Court has required that trials be speedy, public, and fair and has ruled that people have a right to be free from double jeopardy and to be represented by competent counsel.

After a conviction, sentencing occurs. Each state, as well as federal, government has its own type of sentences and punishments. Fines, suspended sentences, community supervision, and prison are the most common forms of punishment. Prison sentences are divided into determinate and indeterminate types. There are also mandatory sentences that must be served upon conviction and carry no hope of probation. Efforts to control sentencing disparity include the use of sentencing councils and sentencing guidelines, as well as determinate and mandatory, sentences.

≡ KEY TERMS

U.S. district courts	release on recognizance
federal courts of appeal	deposit bail
U.S. Supreme Court	bail guidelines
writ of certiorari	plea bargaining
landmark decision	diversion
prosecution	widening the net
affidavits	courtroom work group
attorney list/assigned	venire
council system	peremptory challenge
public defenders	direct examination
adversarial process	cross-examination
judge	mandatory prison term
Missouri Plan	concurrent sentence
bill of indictment	consecutive sentence
information	indeterminate sentence
complaint	determinate sentence
bail	guideline sentences
preventive detention	sentencing disparity
bonding agents	

≡ NOTES

1. Patrick Langan and Richard Solari, *National Judicial Reporting Program, 1990* (Washington, D.C.: Bureau of Justice Statistics, 1993).
2. See, generally, Jerome Skolnick, *Justice without Trial* (New York: John Wiley, 1966).
3. National Center for State Courts, *State Court Caseload Statistics: Annual Report 1991* (Williamsburg, Va.: National Center for State Courts, 1993), p. xi.
4. Langan and Solari, *National Judicial Reporting Program, 1990,* p. 4.
5. Newman Baker, "The Prosecutor Initiation of Prosecution," *Journal of Criminal Law, Criminology and Police Science* 23 (1933): 770–71.
6. Barbara Boland, Paul Mahanna, and Ronald Sones, *The Prosecution of Felony Arrests, 1988* (Washington, D.C.: Bureau of Justice Statistics, 1993), p. 3.
7. Edward Lisefski and Donald Manson, *Tracking Offenders, 1984* (Washington, D.C.: Bureau of Justice Statistics, 1988), p. 1.
8. Janell Schmidt and Ellen Hochstedler Steury, "Prosecutorial Discretion in Filing Charges in Domestic Violence Cases," *Criminology* 27 (1989): 487–510.
9. Frank W. Miller, *Prosecution: The Decision to Charge a Suspect with a Crime* (Boston: Little, Brown, 1970).
10. Wayne LaFave, "The Prosecutor's Discretion in the United States," *American Journal of Comparative Law* 18 (1970): 532–48.
11. Bureau of Justice Statistics, *Report to the Nation on Crime and Justice* (Washington, D.C.: U.S. Department of Justice, 1983), p. 56.
12. Patrick Langan, *State Felony Courts and Felony Laws,* (Washington, D.C.: Bureau of Justice Statistics, 1987), pp. 1–3.
13. Charles Breitel, "Controls in Criminal Law Enforcement," *University of Chicago Law Review* 27 (1960): 427–35.
14. See, generally, "A Symposium on Prosecutorial Discretion," *American Criminal Law Review* (1976): 379–99.
15. George Cole, "The Decision to Prosecute," *Law and Society Review* 4 (1970): 331–43.
16. *Gideon v. Wainwright,* 372 U.S. 335 (1963); *Argersinger v. Hamlin,* 407 U.S. 25 (1972).
17. Carla Gaskins, *Criminal Defense for the Poor* (Washington, D.C.: Bureau of Justice Statistics, 1988).
18. See American Bar Association, Special Committee on Evaluation of Ethical Standards, *Code of Professional Responsibility* (Chicago: American Bar Association 1968), p. 81.
19. *Nix v. Whiteside,* 106 S.Ct. 988 (1986).
20. James Eisenstein and Jacob Herbert, *Felony Justice* (Boston: Little, Brown, 1977). See, generally, Malcolm Feeley, *The Process Is the Punishment* (New York: Russell Sage Foundation, 1979).
21. William Lineberry, ed., *Justice in America: Law, Order and the Courts* (New York: H. W. Wilson, 1972).
22. Sari Escovitz, with Fred Kurland and Nan Gold, *Judicial Selection and Tenure* (Chicago: American Judicature Society, 1974), pp. 3–16.
23. Conference of State Court Administrators and National Center for State Courts, *State Court Organization 1987* (Williamsburg, Va.: National Center for State Courts, 1988).
24. M. Ozanne, R. Wilson, and D. Gedney, Jr., "Toward a Theory of Bail Risk," *Criminology* 18 (1980): 149.
25. Brian Reaves, *Pretrial Release of Federal Felony Defendants* (Washington, D.C.: Bureau of Justice Statistics, 1994).
26. Ibid.
27. Caleb Foote, "A Study of the Administration of Bail in New York," *University of Pennsylvania Law Review* 106 (1960): 693–730; William Rhodes, *Pretrial Release and Misconduct* (Washington, D.C.: Bureau of Justice Statistics, 1985).
28. John Goldkamp, *Two Classes of Accused* (Cambridge, Mass.: Ballinger, 1979).

29. Ibid.

30. Vera Institute of Justice, *Programs in Criminal Justice* (New York: Vera Institute, 1972).

31. Reaves, *Pretrial Release of Felony Defendants*, p. 5.

32. Malcolm Feeley, *Court Reform on Trial* (New York: Basic Books, 1983); John Goldkamp, "Judicial Reform of Bail Practices: The Philadelphia Experiment," *Court Management Journal* (1983): 16–20.

33. John Goldkamp and Michael Gottfredson, *Judicial Decision Guidelines for Bail: The Philadelphia Experiment* (Washington, D.C.: National Institute of Justice, 1983).

34. 18 U.S.C. Sec. 3142 (e) (1985).

35. *United States v. Salerno,* 107 S.Ct. 2095 (1987).

36. *Schall v. Martin,* 104 S.Ct. 2403 (1984).

37. Stephen Kennedy and Kenneth Carlson, *Pretrial Release and Detention: The Bail Reform Act of 1984* (Washington, D.C.: Bureau of Justice Statistics, 1988).

38. Joseph Sanborn, "Philosophical, Legal, and Systemic Aspects of Juvenile Court Plea Bargaining," *Crime and Delinquency* 39 (1993): 509–27.

39. Carla Gaskins, *Felony Case Processing in State Courts, 1986* (Washington, D.C.: Bureau of Justice Statistics, 1990), p. 1. See also Donald Newman, "Making a Deal," in *Legal Process and Corrections,* ed. N. Johnston and L. Savitz (New York: John Wiley, 1982), p. 93.

40. Ibid., pp. 96–97.

41. These sentiments are similar to those expressed by Abraham Blumberg in "The Practice of Law as a Confidence Game: Organizational Co-optation of a Profession," *Law and Society Review* 1 (1967): 15–39.

42. Again, these thoughts are similar to Blumberg's views as expressed in "The Practice of Law as a Confidence Game."

43. National Advisory Commission on Criminal Justice Standards and Goals, *Courts* (Washington, D.C.: U.S. Government Printing Office, 1976).

44. Richard Kuh, "Plea Copping," *Bar Bulletin* 24 (1966–1967): 160.

45. Alan Alschuler, "The Defense Counsel's Role in Plea Bargaining," *Yale Law Journal* 84 (1975): 1179.

46. See, generally, Milton Heumann, "A Note on Plea Bargaining and Case Pressure," *Law and Society Review* 9 (1975): 515.

47. National Institute of Law Enforcement and Criminal Justice, *Plea Bargaining in the United States* (Washington, D.C.: Georgetown University, 1978), p. 8.

48. Michael Rubenstein, Stevens Clarke, and Teresa White, *Alaska Bans Plea Bargaining* (Washington, D.C.: U.S. Department of Justice, 1980).

49. *Boykin v. Alabama,* 395 U.S. 238, 89 S.Ct. 1709, 23 L.Ed.2d 274 (1969).

50. *Brady v. United States,* 297 U.S. 742, 90 S.Ct. 1463, 25 L.Ed.2d 747 (1970).

51. *Santobello v. New York,* 404 U.S. 257, 92 S.Ct. 495, 30 L.Ed.2d 427 (1971).

52. *Bordenkircher v. Hayes,* 434 U.S. 357 (1978).

53. Newman, "Making a Deal," p. 102.

54. John Fuller and William Norton, "Juvenile Diversion: the Impact of Program Philosophy on Net Widening," *Journal of Crime and Justice* 16 (1993): 29–41.

55. National Advisory Commission on Criminal Justice Standards and Goals, *Courts,* p. 66.

56. See, for example, "Limiting the Peremptory Challenge: Representation of Groups on Petit Juries," *Yale Law Journal* 86 (1977): 1715.

57. *Batson v. Kentucky,* 476 U.S. 79 (1986).

58. *Powers v. Ohio,* 49 Cr.L. 2003 (1991).

59. *J.E.B. v. Alabama,* 92.1239 (1994).

60. *Ham v. South Carolina,* 409 U.S. 524, 93 S.Ct. 848, 35 L.Ed.2d 46 (1973).

61. *Turner v. Murray,* 106 S.Ct. 1683 (1986).

62. *Taylor v. Louisiana,* 419 U.S. 522, 42 L.Ed.2d 690, 95 S.Ct. 692 (1975).

63. In *Ristaino v. Ross,* [424 U.S. 589 (1976)] the Court said questioning the jury on racial issues was not automatic in all interracial crimes.

64. Edna Erez, "Victim Participation in Sentencing: Rhetoric and Reality," *Journal of Criminal Justice* 18 (1990): 19–31.

65. *Strunk v. United States,* 412 U.S. 434 (1973).

66. *Klopfer v. North Carolina,* 38 U.S. 213 (1967).

67. *Barker v. Wingo,* 404 U.S. 307 (1971).

68. Bureau of Justice Statistics, *Report to the Nation on Crime and Justice,* p. 66.

69. *Duncan v. Louisiana,* 391 U.S. 145 (1968).

70. *Baldwin v. New York,* 399 U.S. 66 (1970).

71. *Blanton v. City of North Las Vegas,* 489 U.S. 538, 109 S.Ct. 1289, 103 L.Ed.2d 550 (1989).

72. *Williams v. Florida,* 399 U.S. 78 (1970).

73. *Apodica v. Oregon,* 406 U.S. 404 (1972).

74. *Benton v. Maryland,* 395 U.S. 784 (1969).

75. *United States v. Lanza,* 260 U.S. 377 (1922); *Bartkus v. Illinois,* 359 U.S. 121 (1959); *Abbate v. U.S.,* 359 U.S. 187 (1959).

76. *Heath v. Alabama,* 106 S.Ct. 433 (1985).

77. *Powell v. Alabama,* 287 U.S. 45 (1932).

78. *Gideon v. Wainwright,* 372 U.S. 335 (1963).

79. *Argersinger v. Hamlin,* 407 U.S. 25 (1972).

80. *Strickland v. Washington,* 104 S.Ct. 2052 (1984).

81. *Coy v. Iowa,* 48 U.S. 1012, 108 S.Ct. 2798, 101 L.Ed.2d. 857 (1988).

82. *Maryland v. Craig,* 110 S.Ct. 3157, 111 L.Ed.2d 666 (1990).

83. *White v. Illinois,* 112 S.Ct. 736 (1992).

84. Myrna Raeder, "*White's* Effect on Right to Confront One's Accuser," *Criminal Justice* (Winter 1993): 2–7.

85. See Marvin E. Frankel, *Criminal Sentences—Law without Order* (New York: Hill & Wang, 1973).

86. See, generally, Norval Morris, *Equal Justice under the Law* (Washington, D.C.: U.S. Government Printing Office, 1977).

87. See V. O'Leary, M. Gottfredson, and A. Gelman,

"Contemporary Sentencing Proposals," *Criminal Law Bulletin* 11 (1975): 558–60.

88. Sally Hillsman, Barry Mahoney, George Cole, and Bernard Auchter, *Fines as Criminal Sanctions* (Washington, D.C.: National Institute of Justice, 1987).

89. Edna Erez and Pamela Tontodonato, "The Effect of Victim Participation in Sentencing on Sentencing Outcome," *Criminology* 28 (1990): 451–74.

90. Kriss Drass and J. William Spencer, "Accounting for Presentencing Recommendations: Typologies and Probation Officers' Theory of Office," *Social Problems* 34 (1987): 277–93.

91. David Rothman, *Incarceration and Its Alternatives in 20th Century America* (Washington, D.C.: U.S. Government Printing Office, 1979).

92. Langan, *State Felony Courts and Felony Laws,* p. 6.

93. Kenneth Culp Davis, *Discretionary Justice, A Preliminary Inquiry* (Baton Rouge: Louisiana State University Press, 1969).

94. See Frankel, *Criminal Sentences—Law without Order,* p. 5.

95. John Kramer, Robin Lubitz, and Cynthia Kempinen, "Sentencing Guidelines: A Quantitative Comparison of Sentencing Policies in Minnesota, Pennsylvania, and Washington," *Justice Quarterly* 6 (1989): 565–87.

96. U.S. Sentencing Commission, Special Report to the Congress, *Mandatory Minimum Penalties in the Federal Criminal Justice System* (Washington, D.C.: U.S. Government Printing Office, 1991); Jim Beck and Elaine Wolf, "Departures for Substantial Assistance under the Federal Sentencing Guidelines" (Paper presented at the annual meeting of the American Society of Criminology, San Francisco, November 1991); Stefan Cassella, "A Step-by-Step Guide to the New Federal Sentencing Guidelines," *Practical Lawyer* 34 (1988): 13–23.

97. *Mistretta v. United States,* 44 Cr.L. 3061 (January 15, 1989).

98. Kay Knapp, "Structured Sentencing: Building on Experience," *Judicature* 72 (1988): 47–52.

99. David Griswold, "Deviation from Sentencing Guidelines: The Issue of Unwarranted Disparity," *Journal of Criminal Justice* 16 (1988): 317–29; Minnesota Sentencing Guidelines Commission, *The Impact of the Minnesota Sentencing Guidlines: Three-Year Evaluation* (St. Paul: Minnesota Sentencing Guidelines Commission, 1984), p. 162.

100. Terance Miethe and Charles Moore, "Socioeconomic Disparities under Determinate Sentencing Systems: A Comparison of Preguideline and Postguidline Practices in Minnesota," *Criminology* 23 (1985): 337–63; Richard Frase, "Implementing Commission-Based Sentencing Guidelines: The Lessons of the First Ten Years in Minnesota" (Paper presented at the annual meeting of the American Society of Criminology, San Francisco, November 1991), p. 5.

101. Michael Tonry, "The Politics and Process of Sentencing Commissions," *Crime and Delinquency* 37 (1991): 307–29.

102. Michael Tonry, "The Failure of the U.S. Sentencing Commission's Guidelines," *Crime and Delinquency* 39 (1993): 131–49 at 131.

103. Chris Eskridge, "Sentencing Guidelines: To Be or Not to Be," *Federal Probation* 50 (1986): 70–76.

104. Michael Tonry, *Sentencing Reform Impacts* (Washington, D.C.: U.S. Government Printing Office, 1987), pp. 26–27.

105. Timothy Bynum, "Prosecutorial Discretion and the Implementation of a Legislative Mandate," in *Implementing Criminal Justice Policies,* ed. Merry Morash (Beverly Hills: Sage, 1982).

106. Alan Dershowitz, *Fair and Certain Punishment: Report of the Twentieth Century Task Force on Criminal Sentencing* (New York: Twentieth Century Fund, 1976).

107. Tonry, *Sentencing Reform Impacts,* pp. 26–30.

108. For a general review of this issue, see Florence Ferguson, "Sentencing Guidelines: Are (Black) Offenders Given Just Treatment?" (Paper presented at the American Society of Criminology meeting, Montreal, November 1987).

109. Alfred Blumstein, "On the Racial Disproportionality of the United States Prison Population," *Journal of Criminal Law and Criminology* 73 (1982): 1259–81; Darnell Hawkins, "Race, Crime Type and Imprisonment," *Justice Quarterly* 3 (1986): 251–69; Martha Myers, "Offended Parties and Official Reactions: Victims and the Sentencing of Criminal Defendants," *Sociological Quarterly* 20 (1979): 529–40.

110. Raymond Paternoster, "Race of the Victim and Location of the Crime: The Decision to Seek the Death Penalty in South Carolina," *Journal of Criminal Law and Criminology* 74 (1983): 754–85.

111. Cassia Spohn and Susan Welch, "The Effect of Prior Record in Sentencing Research: An Examination of the Assumption That Any Measure Is Adequate," *Justice Quarterly* 4 (1987): 286–302.

112. Patrick Langan and Richard Scolari, *National Judicial Reporting Program* (Washington, D.C.: Bureau of Justice Statistics, 1993), p. 15.

113. Ibid.

114. Alan Lizotte, "Extra-Legal Factors in Chicago's Criminal Courts: Testing the Conflict Model of Criminal Justice," *Social Problems* 25 (1978): 564–80; P. Burke and A. Turk, "Factors Affecting Post-Arrest Dispositions: A Model for Analysis," *Social Problems* 22 (1975): 313–32; and Terence Thornberry, "Race, Socioeconomic Status and Sentencing in the Juvenile Justice System," *Journal of Criminal Law and Criminology* 64 (1973): 90–98.

115. Stephen Klein, Joan Petersilia, and Susan Turner, "Race and Imprisonment Decisions in California," *Science* 247 (1990): 812–16.

116. William Rhodes, *Pretrial Release and Misconduct* (Washington, D.C.: U.S. Government Printing Office, 1985).

117. David Willison, "The Effects of Counsel on the Severity of Criminal Sentences: A Statistical Assessment," *Justice System Journal* 9 (1984): 87–101.

118. Dale Dannefer and Russell Schutt, "Race and Juvenile Justice Processing in Court and Police Agencies,"

American Journal of Sociology 87 (1982): 1113–32; Douglas Smith and Christy Visher, "Street-Level Justice: Situational Determinants of Police Arrest Decisions," *Social Problems* 29 (1981): 267–77.

119. Charles R. Pruitt and James Q. Wilson, "A Longitudinal Study of the Effect of Race on Sentencing," *Law and Society Review* 17 (1983): 613–35; Candace Kruttschnitt, "Sex and Criminal Court Dispositions," *Journal of Research in Crime and Delinquency* 21 (1984): 213–32; Cynthia Kempinen, "Changes in the Sentencing Patterns of Male and Female Defendants," *Prison Journal* 63 (1983): 3–11.

120. Lawrence Greenfeld and James Stephan, *Capital Punishment, 1992* (Washington, D.C.: Bureau of Justice Statistics, 1993).

121. For two impressive views on the death penalty, see Robert Bohm, "Humanism and the Death Penalty with Special Emphasis on the Post-*Furman* Experience," *Justice Quarterly* 6 (1989): 173–96; and David Friedrichs, "Comment-Humanism and the Death Penalty: An Alternative Perspective," *Justice Quarterly* 6 (1989): 197–211.

122. Dennis Wiechman, Jerry Kendall, and Ronald Bae, "International Use of the Death Penalty," *International Journal of Comparative and Applied Criminal Justice* 14 (1990): 239–59.

123. See, for example, Ernest Van Den Haag, *Punishing Criminals: Concerning a Very Old and Painful Question* (New York: Basic Books, 1975), pp. 209–11; Walter Berns, "Defending the Death Penalty," *Crime and Delinquency* 26 (1980): 503–11.

124. Norman Finkel and Stefanie Smith, "Principals and Accessories in Capital Felony-Murder: The Proportionality Principle Reigns Supreme," *Law and Society Review* 27 (1993): 129–46.

125. James Marquart and Jonathan Sorensen, "Institutional and Postrelease Behavior of *Furman*-Commuted Inmates in Texas," *Justice Quarterly* 26 (1988): 677–93.

126. Kilman Shin, *Death Penalty and Crime* (Fairfax, Va.: George Mason University, 1978), p. 1.

127. Michael Radelet and Hugo Bedeau, "Miscarriages of Justice in Potentially Capital Cases," *Stanford Law Review* 40 (1987): 21–181. For an opposing view, see Stephen Markman and Paul Cassell, "Protecting the Innocent: A Response to the Bedeau-Radelet Study," *Stanford Law Review* 41 (1988): 121–70; for their response, see Hugo Adam Bedeau and Michael Radelet, "The Myth of Infallibility: A Reply to Markman and Cassell," *Stanford Law Review* 42 (1988): 161–70.

128. Charles Black, "Objections to S. 1382, a Bill to Establish Rational Criteria for the Imposition of Capital Punishment," *Crime and Delinquency* 26 (1980): 441–53.

129. Melinda Gann Hall and Paul Brace, "The Vicissitudes of Death by Decree: Forces Influencing Capital Punishment Decision Making in State Supreme Courts," *Social Science Quarterly* 75 (1994): 138–48.

130. Greenfeld and Stephan, *Capital Punishment, 1992,* p. 5.

131. Ibid.

132. Thomas Keil and Gennaro Vito, "Race, Homicide Severity, and Application of the Death Penalty: A Consideration of the Barnett Scale," *Criminology* 27 (1989): 511–31; idem, "Capital Sentencing in Kentucky: An Analysis of Factors Influencing Decision Making in the Post-*Gregg* Period," *Journal of Criminal Law and Criminology* 79 (1988): 483–503.

133. David Baldus, C. Pulaski, and G. Woodworth, "Comparative Review of Death Sentences: An Empirical Study of the Georgia Experience," *Journal of Criminal Law and Criminology* 74 (1983): 661–93.

134. D. Dwayne Smith, "Patterns of Discrimination in Assessments of the Death Penalty: The Case of Louisiana," *Journal of Criminal Justice* 15 (1987): 279–86; S. Gross and R. Mauro, "Patterns of Death: An Analysis of Racial Disparities in Capital Sentencing and Homicide Victimization," *Stanford Law Review* 37 (1984): 27–153.

135. William Bowers and Glenn Pierce, "Deterrence or Brutalization: What Is the Effect of Executions?" *Crime and Delinquency* 26 (1980): 453–84.

136. Joseph Schumacher, "An International Look at the Death Penalty," *International Journal of Comparative and Applied Criminal Justice* 14 (1990): 307–15.

137. Richard Berk, Robert Weiss, and Jack Boger, "Chance and the Death Penalty," *Law and Society Review* 27 (1993): 89–108. For an opposing view, see Raymond Paternoster, "Assessing Capriciousness in Capital Cases," *Law and Society Review* 27 (1993): 111–22.

138. *Furman v. Georgia,* 408 U.S. 238, 92 S.Ct. 2726, 33 L.Ed.2d 346 (1972).

139. *Gregg v. Georgia,* 428 U.S. 153, 96 S.Ct. 2909, 49 L.Ed.2d 859 (1976).

140. *Jurek v. Texas,* 428 U.S. 262, 96 S.Ct. 2950, 49 L.Ed.2d 929 (1976).

141. *Proffitt v. Florida,* 428 U.S. 325, 96 S.Ct. 3001, 49 L.Ed.2d 944 (1976).

142. *Witherspoon v. Illinois,* 391 U.S. 510 (1968); *Wainwright v. Witt,* 469 U.S. 412 (1985).

143. *Tison v. Arizona,* 481 U.S. 137 (1987).

144. *McKlesky v. Kemp,* 106 S.Ct. 1331 (1986).

145. *Stanford v. Kentucky* and *Wilkins v. Missouri,* 109 S.Ct. 2969 (1989).

146. *McKlesky v. Zant,* 49 Cr.L. 2031 (1991).

18 Corrections

≡ Introduction

When a person is convicted for a criminal offense, society exercises the right to punish or *correct* his or her behavior. Equating crime and punishment is certainly not a new practice. Criminal offenders have been subjected to punishment by governmental authority throughout recorded history. Over the centuries, there has been significant debate as to why people should be punished and what type of punishment is most appropriate to correct, treat, or deter criminal offenders. The style and purpose of criminal correction have gone through many stages and have featured a variety of penal sanctions.

The correctional system provides a great number of services in programs differentiated by level of security and intrusiveness. The least secure and intrusive programs involve community supervision by probation officers. Some offenders who need more secure treatment or control are placed under house arrest or held in community correctional centers. Those who require the most secure settings are placed in an incarceration facility. Felons are usually incarcerated in a state or federal *prison;* misdemeanants are housed in county *jails* or reformatories.

The entire correctional system has been a source of great controversy. Probation is viewed as a slap on the wrist for people convicted of serious crimes. Jails have been the scene of suicides and rapes. Prisons have been viewed as warehouses that, far from helping rehabilitate inmates, are places of violence and degradation. There is evidence that prison populations are highest in states with large minority populations, reinforcing the conflict theory's charge that the justice system is biased.[1] Some critics call for tearing down prisons, while others argue that new ones should be built and sentences lengthened. The basic debate, argues William Selke, is how will society treat its least fortunate members, "with compassion and opportunity or with scorn and punishment."[2]

This chapter considers some of the basic elements of correctional treatment in U.S. society. First, the history of corrections will be reviewed to show how our current system evolved over time and the social trends that influenced its development. Then, modern correctional institutions will be explored. Such issues as penal institutions, the prisoner's social world, correctional treatment, and prisoners' rights will be discussed.

≡ History of Punishment and Corrections

Throughout history, punishment, in its *severest physical forms,* has been present in all major institutions.[3]

The *punishment* of criminals has undergone many noteworthy changes, reflecting custom, economic conditions, and religious and political ideals.[4]

In ancient times, the most common state-administered punishment was banishment or exile. Only slaves were commonly subject to harsh physical punishment for their misdeeds. In Rome, for example, the only crime for which capital punishment could be administered was *furtum manifestum*—a thief caught in the act was executed on the spot. More common were economic sanctions and fines, levied for such crimes as assault on a slave, arson, or housebreaking.

In both ancient Greece and Rome, interpersonal violence, even when it resulted in death, was viewed as a private matter. Neither Greek nor Roman (until quite late in its history) state laws provided for the punishment of a violent crime. Execution of an offender was looked upon as the prerogative of the deceased's family.

The Middle Ages

As noted in Chapter 2, little law or governmental control existed during the early Middle Ages (fifth century to eleventh century A.D.). Offenses were settled by blood feuds carried out by the families of the injured parties. When possible, the Roman custom of settling disputes by fine or an exchange of property was adopted as a means of resolving interpersonal conflicts with a minimum of bloodshed.

After the eleventh century, during the feudal period, forfeiture of land and property was common punishment for people who violated law and customs or who failed in the feudal obligations to their lord. The word *felony* comes from the twelfth century, when the term *felonia* referred to a breach of faith with one's feudal lord.

During this period, the main emphasis on criminal law and punishment lay in maintaining public order.[5] If in the heat of passion or in a state of intoxication, a person severely injured or killed his or her neighbor, free men in the area would gather to pronounce a judgment and make the culprit do penance or pay a fine called *wergild* (see Chapter 2). The purpose of the fine was to pacify the injured party and ensure that the conflict would not develop into a blood feud and anarchy. The inability of lower-class offenders to pay a fine led to the development of corporal punishment, such as whipping or branding, as a substitute penalty.

By the fifteenth century, changing social conditions influenced the relationship between crime and punishment. First, the population of England and Europe began to increase after a century of being decimated by constant warfare and plague. At the same time, the developing commercial system caused large tracts of agricultural fields to be converted to grazing lands. Soon, unemployed peasants and landless noblemen began flocking to newly developing urban centers, such as London and Paris, or taking to the roads as highwaymen, beggars, or vagabonds.

The later Middle Ages also saw the rise of strong monarchs, such as Henry VIII and Elizabeth I of England, who were determined to keep a powerful grip on their realm. The administration of the "King's Peace" under the shire reeve and constable became stronger.

These developments led to the increased use of **capital** and **corporal punishment** to control the criminal poor. While the wealthy could buy their way out of punishment and into exile, the poor were executed and mutilated at ever-increasing rates. It is estimated that 72,000 thieves were hanged during the reign of Henry VIII alone.[6] Execution, banishment, mutilation, branding, and flogging were used on a wide range of offenders, from murderers and robbers to vagrants and gypsies. Punishments became unmatched in their cruelty, featuring a gruesome variety of physical tortures. Also during this period, punishment became a public spectacle, presumably so the sadistic sanctions would act as a deterrent. But the variety and imagination of the tortures inflicted on even minor criminals before their death suggests that sadism and spectacle were more important than any presumed deterrent effect.

While criminologists generally view the rise of the prison as an eighteenth-century phenomenon, Marvin Wolfgang has written about Le Stinche, a prison in Florence, Italy, which was used to punish offenders as early as 1301. Prisoners were enclosed in separate cells and classified on the basis of gender, age, mental state, and crime seriousness. Furloughs and conditional release were permitted, and perhaps for the first time, a period of incarceration replaced corporal punishment for some offenses. Though Le Stinche existed for 500 years, relatively little is known about its administration or whether this early example of incarceration is unique to Florence or can be discovered in other areas.[7]

Punishment in the Seventeenth and Eighteenth Centuries

By the end of the sixteenth century, the rise of the city and overseas colonization provided tremendous markets for manufactured goods. In England and France, population growth was checked by constant warfare and internal disturbances. Labor was scarce in many manufacturing areas of England, Germany, and Holland. The Thirty Years War in Germany and the constant warfare among England, France, and Spain helped drain the population.

The punishment of criminals changed to meet the demands created by these social conditions. Instead of the wholesale use of capital and corporal punishment, many offenders were made to do forced labor for their crimes. **Poor laws** developed in the early seventeenth century required that the poor, vagrants, and vagabonds be put to work in public or private enterprise. Houses of correction were developed to make it convenient for petty law violators to be assigned to work details. Many convicted offenders were pressed into sea duty as galley slaves, a fate considered so loathsome that many convicts mutilated themselves rather than submit to it.

The constant shortage of labor in the colonies also prompted the authorities to transport convicts overseas. In England, the Vagrancy Act of 1597 legalized deportation for the first time. An Order in Council of 1617 granted a reprieve and stay of execution to people convicted of robbery and other felonies who were strong enough to be employed overseas. Similar measures were used in France and Italy to recruit galley slaves and workers.

Transportation to the colonies became popular; it supplied labor, cost little, and was actually profitable for the government, since manufacturers and plantation owners paid for convicts' services. The Old Bailey Court in London supplied at least 10,000 convicts between 1717 and 1775.[8] Convicts would serve a period as workers and then become free again.

Transportation to the colonies waned as a method of punishment with the increase in colonial population, the further development of the land, and the increasing importation of African slaves in the eighteenth century. The American Revolution ended transportation of felons to North America; the remaining areas used were Australia, New Zealand, and African colonies.

Corrections in the Late Eighteenth and Nineteenth Centuries

Between the American Revolution in 1776 and the first decades of the nineteenth century, the population of Europe and America increased rapidly. The gulf between poor workers and wealthy landowners and merchants widened. The crime rate rose significantly, prompting a return to physical punishment and the increased use of the death penalty. During the last part of the eighteenth century, 350 types of crime in England were punishable by death.[9] Although many people sentenced to death for trivial offenses were spared the gallows, there is little question that the use of capital punishment rose significantly between 1750 and 1800.[10] Prompted by these excesses, legal philosophers, such as Jeremy Bentham and Cesare Beccaria (see Chapter 5), argued that physical punishment should be replaced by periods of confinement and incapacitation in prison.

Correctional reform in the United States was first instituted in Pennsylvania under the leadership of William Penn.[11] At the end of the seventeenth century, Penn revised Pennsylvania's criminal code to forbid torture and the capricious use of mutilation and physical punishment. These devices were replaced by the penalties of imprisonment at hard labor, moderate flogging, fines, and forfeiture of property. All lands and goods belonging to felons were to be used to make restitution to the victims of crimes, with restitution being limited to twice the value of the damages. Felons who owned no property were required by law to labor in the prison workhouse until the victim was compensated.

Penn ordered that a new type of institution be built to replace the widely used public forms of punishment—stocks, pillories, the gallows, and the branding iron. Each county was instructed to build a house of corrections similar to today's jails. These measures remained in effect until Penn's death in 1718, when the criminal penal code reverted to its earlier emphasis on open public punishment and harsh brutality.

In 1776, postrevolutionary Pennsylvania again adopted William Penn's code, and in 1787, a group of Quakers led by Dr. Benjamin Rush formed the Philadelphia Society for Alleviating the Miseries of Public Prisons. The aim of the society was to bring some degree of humane and orderly treatment to the growing penal system. The Quakers' influence on the legislature resulted in limiting the use of the death penalty to cases involving treason, murder, rape, and arson.

Under pressure from the Quakers, the Pennsylvania Legislature in 1790 called for the renovation of the prison system. The ultimate result was the creation of Philadelphia's **Walnut Street Prison.** At this institution, most prisoners were placed in solitary cells, where they remained in isolation and did not have the right to work.[12] Quarters that contained the solitary or separate cells were called the *penitentiary house,* as was already the custom in England.

The new Pennsylvania prison system took credit for a rapid decrease in the crime rate—from 131 convictions in 1789 to 45 in 1793.[13] The prison became known as a school for reform. The Walnut Street Prison's equitable conditions were credited with reducing escapes to none in the first four years of its existence (except for 14 on opening day).

However, the Walnut Street Prison was not a total success. Overcrowding undermined the goal of solitary confinement of serious offenders, and soon more than one inmate was placed in each cell. Despite these difficulties, similar institutions were erected in New York (Newgate in 1791), New Jersey (Trenton in 1798), Virginia (1800), Massachusetts (Castle Island in 1785) and Kentucky (1800). In a recent paper, Alexis Durham III has described the Newgate prison of Connecticut, which was constructed in an old copper mine. Durham considers Newgate, built in 1773, the first "prison" in America.[14]

The Auburn System

In the early 1800s, both the Pennsylvania and New York prison systems were experiencing difficulties maintaining the ever-increasing numbers of convicted criminals. Initially, administrators dealt with the problem by increasing the use of pardons, relaxing prison discipline, and limiting supervision.

In 1816, New York built a new prison at Auburn, hoping to alleviate some of the overcrowding at Newgate. The Auburn Prison design became known as the *tier system,* because cells were built vertically on five floors of the structure. It was sometimes also referred to as the *congregate system,* since most prisoners ate and worked in groups. Later, in 1819, construction was started on a wing of solitary cells to house unruly prisoners. Three classes of prisoners were then created: one group remained continually in solitary confinement as a result of breaches of prison discipline; the second group was allowed labor as an occasional form of recreation; and the third and largest class worked and ate together during the days and only went into seclusion at night.

The philosophy of the **Auburn system** was crime prevention through fear of punishment and silent confinement. The worst felons were to be cut off from all contact with other prisoners; and although they were treated and fed relatively well, they had no hope of pardon to relieve their isolation. For a time, some of the worst convicts were forced to remain totally alone and silent during the entire day; this practice caused many prisoners to have mental breakdowns, resulting in many suicides and self-mutilations. This practice was abolished in 1823.[15]

The combination of silence and solitude as a method of punishment was not abandoned easily. Prison officials sought to overcome the side effects of total isolation while maintaining the penitentiary system. The solution Auburn adopted was to keep convicts in separate cells at night but allow them to work together during the day under enforced silence. Hard work and silence became the foundation of the Auburn system wherever it was adopted. Silence was the key to prison discipline; it prevented the formulation of escape plans, averted plots and riots, and allowed prisoners to contemplate their infractions.

When discipline was breached in the Auburn system, punishment was applied in the form of a rawhide whip on the inmate's back. Immediate and effective, Auburn discipline was so successful that when a hundred inmates were chosen to build the famous Sing-Sing prison in 1825, not one dared escape, although they were housed in an open field with only minimal supervision.[16]

The New Pennsylvania System

In 1818, Pennsylvania took the radical step of establishing a prison that placed each inmate in a single cell with no work to do. Classifications were abolished, because each cell was intended as a miniature prison that would prevent the inmates from contaminating one another.

The new Pennsylvania prison, called the Western Penitentiary, had an unusual architectural design. It was built in a semicircle, with the cells positioned along its circumference. Built back-to-back, some cells faced the boundary wall while others faced the internal area of the circle. Its inmates were kept in solitary confinement almost constantly, being allowed about an hour a day for exercise. In 1820, a second, similar penitentiary using the isolate system was built in Philadelphia and called the Eastern Penitentiary.

The supporters of the Pennsylvania system believed that the penitentiary was truly a place to do penance. By advocating totally removing the sinner from society and allowing the prisoner a period of isolation in which to reflect alone upon the evils of crime, the supporters of the Pennsylvania system reflected the influence of religion and religious philosophy on corrections. In fact, its advocates believed that solitary confinement (with in-cell labor as a recreation) would eventually make working so attractive that upon release, the inmate would be well suited to resume a productive existence in society. The Pennsylvania system eliminated the need for large numbers of guards or disciplinary measures. Isolated from each other, inmates could not plan escapes or collectively break rules. When discipline was a problem, the whip and the iron gag were used.

The congregate system eventually prevailed, however, and spread throughout the United States; many of its features are still used today. Its innovations included congregate working conditions, the use of solitary confinement to punish unruly inmates, military regimentation, and discipline. In Auburn-like institutions, prisoners were marched from place to place; their time was regulated by bells telling them to wake up, sleep, and work. The system was so like the military that many of its early administrators were recruited from the armed services.

Although the prison was viewed as an improvement over capital and corporal punishment, it quickly became the scene of depressed conditions; inmates were treated harshly, and routinely whipped and tortured. As one historian, Samuel Walker, notes:

> Prison brutality flourished. It was ironic that the prison had been devised as a more humane alternative to corporal and capital punishment. Instead, it simply moved corporal punishments indoors where, hidden from public view, it became even more savage.[17]

Post-Civil War Developments

The prison of the late nineteenth century was remarkably similar to that of today. The congregate system was adapted in all states except Pennsylvania. Prisons experienced overcrowding, and the single-cell principle was often ignored. The prison, like the police department, became the scene of political intrigue and efforts by political administrators to control the hiring of personnel and dispensing of patronage.

Prison industry developed and became the predominant theme around which institutions were organized. Some prisons used the **contract system,** in which officials sold the labor of inmates to private businesses. Sometimes, the contractor supervised the inmates inside the prison itself. Under the **convict-lease system,** the state leased its prisoners to a business for a fixed annual fee and gave up supervision and control. Finally, the **state account system** had prisoners produce goods in prison for state use.[18]

The development of prison industry quickly led to abuse of inmates, who were forced to work for almost no wages, and to profiteering by dishonest administrators and businessmen. During the Civil War era, prisons were major manufacturers of clothes, shoes, boots, furniture, and the like. During the 1880s, opposition by trade unions sparked restrictions on interstate commerce in prison goods and ended their profitability.

There were also reforms in prison operations. **Z. R. Brockway,** warden at the Elmira Reformatory in New York, advocated individualized treatment, the indeterminate sentence, and parole. The reformatory program initiated by Brockway included elementary education for illiterates, designated library hours, lectures by faculty members of the local Elmira College, and a group of vocational training shops. The cost to the state of the institution's operations was to be held to a minimum. Although Brockway proclaimed Elmira to be an ideal reformatory, his actual achievements were limited. The

Prisoners in typical striped attire sit with the warden in front of the old Utah Penitentiary. The iron rule of the nineteenth-century warden has been replaced by the chaos of overcrowded, gang-controlled prisons.

greatest significance of his contribution was the injection of a degree of humanitarianism into the industrial prisons of that day. Although many institutions were constructed across the country and labeled reformatories as a result of the Elmira model, most of them continued to be industrially oriented.[19]

The Progressive Era and Beyond

The early twentieth century was a time of contrasts in the prison system of the United States.[20] At one extreme were those who advocated reform, such as the Mutual Welfare League, led by Thomas Mott Osborne. Prison reform groups proposed better treatment for inmates, an end to harsh corporal punishment, and the creation of meaningful prison industries and educational programs. Reformers argued that prisoners should not be isolated from society, but that the best elements of society—education, religion, meaningful work, self-governance—should be brought to the prison. Osborne went so far as to spend one week in New York's notorious Sing-Sing Prison to learn about its conditions firsthand.

Opposed to the reformers were conservative prison administrators and state officials, who believed that stern disciplinary measures were needed to control dangerous prison inmates. They continued the time-honored system of regimentation and discipline. Although the whip and the lash were eventually abolished, solitary confinement in dark, bare cells became a common penal practice.

In time, some of the more rigid prison rules gave way to liberal reform. By the mid-1930s, few prisons required inmates to wear the red-and-white-striped convict suit and substituted nondescript gray uniforms. The code of silence ended, as did the lockstep shuffle. Prisoners were allowed "the freedom of the yard" to mingle and exercise an hour or two each day.[21] Movies and radio appeared in the prisons in the 1930s. Visiting policies and mail privileges were liberalized.

A more important trend was the development of specialized prisons designed to treat particular types of offenders. For example, in New York, the prisons at Clinton and Auburn were viewed as industrial facilities for hard-core inmates, Great Meadow as an agricultural center to house nondangerous offenders, and Dannemora as a facility for the criminally insane. In California, San Quentin housed inmates considered salvageable by correctional authorities, while Folsom was reserved for hard-core offenders.[22]

Prison industry also evolved. Opposition by organized labor helped put an end to the convict-lease system and forced inmate labor. Although some vestiges of private prison industry existed into the 1920s, most convict labor was devoted to state-use items, such as license plates and laundry.

Despite these changes and reforms, the prison in the mid-twentieth century remained a destructive total institution. Although some aspects of inmate life improved, severe discipline, harsh rules, and solitary confinement were the way of life in prison.

The Modern Era

In the modern era, we have witnessed a period of change and turmoil in the nation's correctional system. Three trends stand out. First, between 1960 and 1980, a great deal of litigation was brought by inmates seeking greater rights and privileges. State and federal court rulings gave inmates rights to freedom of religion and speech, medical care, due process, and proper living conditions. Since 1980, the "prisoners' rights" movement has slowed as judicial activism waned during the Reagan-Bush era.

Second, violence within the correctional system became a national scandal. Well-publicized riots at New York's Attica Prison and the New Mexico State Penitentiary have drawn attention to the potential for death and destruction that lurks in every prison. One reaction has been to improve conditions and provide innovative programs that give inmates a voice in running the institution. Another has been to tighten discipline and call for the building of maximum-security prisons to control dangerous offenders.

Third, the alleged failure of correctional rehabilitation has prompted many *penologists* to reconsider the purpose of incapacitating criminals. Today, it is more common to view the correctional system as a mechanism for control and punishment than as a device for rehabilitation and reform.

The alleged failure of correctional treatment has prompted the development of alternatives to incarceration, including diversion, restitution, and community-based corrections. The nation's correctional policy seems to be to keep as many nonthreatening offenders out of the correctional system as possible by means of community-based programs and, conversely, to incarcerate dangerous, violent offenders for long periods of time.[23] Unfortunately, despite the development of alternatives to incarceration, the number of people under lock and key has skyrocketed.

The following section reviews the most prominent types of correctional facilities used today.

Corrections Today

Correctional treatment can be divided into community-based programs and secure confinement. Community-based corrections include **probation,** which involves supervision under the control of the sentencing court, and an array of **intermediate sanctions,** which are programs that provide greater supervision and treatment than traditional probation but are less intrusive than incarceration.

Treatment in the community is viewed as a viable alternative to traditional correctional practices.[24] First, it is significantly less expensive to supervise inmates in the community than to house them in secure institutional facilities. Second, community-based corrections are necessary if the prison system is not to be overwhelmed by an influx of offenders. Third, community-based treatment is designed so that first-time or nonserious offenders can avoid the stigma and pains of imprisonment and be rehabilitated in the community.

The second element of corrections involves secure confinement. The jail houses misdemeanants (and some felons) serving their sentences, as well as felons and misdemeanants awaiting trial who have not been released on bail. State and federal prisons are used to incarcerate felons for extended periods of time. Finally, parole and aftercare agencies supervise prisoners who have been given early release from their sentences. Though parolees are actually in the community, parole is usually considered both organizationally and philosophically part of the secure correctional system.

These institutions are discussed in the sections below.

Probation

Probation usually involves the suspension of the offender's sentence in return for the promise of good behavior in the community under the supervision of the probation department. It usually replaces a term in an institution, although minors can be placed on probation without the threat of detention. In some cases, the offender is first sentenced to a prison term, and then the sentence is suspended and the defendant placed on probation. In others, the imposition of a prison sentence is delayed or suspended while the offender is put on probation.

As practiced in all 50 states and by the federal government, probation implies a contract between the court and the offender in which the former promises to hold a prison term in abeyance while the latter promises to adhere to a set of rules or conditions required by the court. If the rules are violated, and especially if the probationer commits another criminal offense, probation may also be **revoked;** this means that the contract is terminated and the original sentence enforced. If an offender on probation commits a second offense that is more severe than the first, he or she may also be indicted, tried, and sentenced on that second offense. Probation may also be revoked simply because the rules and conditions of probation have not been met, even if the offender has not committed another crime.

Each probationary sentence is for a fixed period of time, depending on the seriousness of the offense and the statutory law of the jurisdiction. Probation is considered served when the offender fulfills the conditions set by the court for that period of time; after that, he or she can live without interference from the state.

Probationary Sentences.

Probationary sentences may be granted by state and federal district courts and state superior (felony) courts. Probation has become an accepted and widely used sentence for adult felons and misdemeanants and juvenile delinquents.

In most jurisdictions, juries can recommend probation, but the judge has the final say in the matter and can grant probation at his or her discretion. In nonjury trials, probation is granted solely by judicial mandate. Except where state law expressly prohibits a community supervision option, almost all offenders are eligible for probation, even those convicted of violent felonies, such as rape and homicide. Only mandatory sentencing laws that require that convicted offenders be incarcerated for such crimes as drug trafficking and use of handguns preclude the probation option.

The term of the probationary sentence may extend to the limit of the suspended prison term, or the court may set a time limit that reflects the sentencing period. For misdemeanors, probation usually extends for the entire period of the jail sentence. For felonies, probationary periods are likely to be shorter and more limited than the prison sentences would have been.

Probation Organizations

About 2,000 agencies nationwide list adult probation as their major function; they supervise in excess of 2.6 million adult probationers.[25] During any given year, about 1.5 million people are placed on probation and the same number complete their probationary sentence. In all, almost two-thirds of the correctional population is on probation.

Most probation agencies are state-level agencies; the remainder are organized at the county or municipal levels. About 30 states combine probation and parole supervision into a single state agency.[26]

There are arguments for both placing probation services under the supervision of individual courts and creating statewide agencies. Local supervision makes probation more responsive to court discretion and helps judges get better information on the effectiveness of their decisions. Since the bulk of the probation department's work is in the local courts, it seems appropriate that the agencies should be organized at the county level.

Those who advocate large state probation agencies argue that probation is a correctional service and therefore should be part of the executive level of government.[27] Larger agencies can facilitate coordination of programs and staff, establishment of training programs, and distribution of budget. However, as of this writing, no one position prevails; probation remains organized at both the state and the local level.

Probation Services

After a person is convicted of a crime, the probation department investigates the case to determine the factors related to the criminality of the offender. Based on this presentence investigation, the department recommends to the sentencing judge whether the offender should be given eligibility for community release. In the event the offender is placed on probation, the investigation findings will be used as the basis for treatment and supervision.

If the offender is placed on probation, the department makes a diagnosis of his or her personality and treatment needs. Based on this evaluation, those offenders classified as minimum risks will be given little supervision, perhaps a monthly phone call or visit, while others classified as high risks will receive close supervision and intensive care and treatment. Developing accurate risk classification methods is a major goal of probation.[28]

At one time, probation officers commonly participated in treatment supervision. Today, it is more common to place clients in community mental health, substance abuse, and family counseling clinics. Based on concepts of psychology, social work, or counseling and on the diagnosis of the offender, the probation officer will plan a treatment schedule that, it is hoped, will allow the probationer to fulfill the probation contract and make a reasonable adjustment to the community. There is evidence that probationers who are able to complete their treatment plans are less likely to recidivate than offenders who fail at treatment.[29]

The treatment function is a product of both the investigative and the diagnostic aspect of probation. It is based on the probation officer's perceptions of the probationer, including family problems, peer relationships, and employment background. For example, a probation officer who discovers that a client has a drinking problem may help to find a detoxification center willing to accept the case, while a chronically underemployed offender may be placed with a job counseling center. Or, in the case of juvenile delinquency, a probation officer may work with teachers and other school officials to help a young offender stay in school. Of course, most cases do not (or cannot) receive such individualized treatment; some treatment mechanisms merely involve a yearly phone call to determine whether the offender is maintaining a job or attending school.[30]

Probation also has a law enforcement function. Probation officers supervise clients, and if further law violations occur, they notify police. While some probation officers view their role as social work-oriented, others consider themselves law enforcement officers.[31]

Probation Rules and Revocation. Each offender granted probation is given a set of rules to guide his or her behavior. Most jurisdictions have a standard set of rules, which include: (1) maintaining steady employment; (2) making restitution for loss or damage; (3) cooperating with the probation officer; (4) obeying all laws; and (5) meeting family responsibilities. Sometimes an individual probationer is given specific rules that relate to his or her particular circumstances, such as the requirement to enroll in a drug treatment program.

If rules are violated, a person's probation may be *revoked* by the court, and the person either begins serving the sentence or, if he or she has not yet been sentenced, receives a prison sentence from the court. Revocation for violation of probation rules is called a **technical violation;** probation also can be revoked if the offender commits another offense.

In a series of cases, most importantly *Gagnon v. Scarpelli,*[32] the Supreme Court has ruled that before pro-

bation can be revoked, the offender (1) must be given a hearing before the sentencing court and (2) must be provided with counsel if there is a substantial reason for him or her to require the assistance of an attorney.

Success of Probation

How successful is probation? How often do probationers commit new crimes while they are under supervision? In an often-cited study, Joan Petersilia and her colleagues at the Rand Corporation followed the careers of 1,672 California men granted probation for felony offenses.[33] They found that 1,087 (65 percent) were rearrested, 853 (51 percent) were convicted, and 568 (34 percent) were incarcerated. The researchers uncovered the disturbing fact that 75 percent of the new arrests were for serious crimes, including larceny, burglary, and robbery; and that 18 percent of the probationers were convicted on serious violent crime charges. They also found that about 25 percent of felons granted probation had personal and legal characteristics indistinguishable from people put in prison for the same original charge. The Petersilia research was an early indication that felons often qualified for and later failed on probation.

A more broadly based study of felony probation by Patrick Langan and Mark Cuniff also found that community supervision orders routinely fail.[34] About 62 percent of their sample of 79,000 probationers in 17 states had either a disciplinary hearing for violating a condition of probation or were arrested for another serious criminal offense within three years of their release. Within that time, almost half of the probationers had either been sent to prison or jail or had absconded from the jurisdiction. This pattern is illustrated in Figure 18.1. As the figure shows, about 43 percent of the sample, or 34,000 felony probationers, were rearrested within three years. They accounted for a total of *64,000 felony charges* during the follow-up period. Though murderers and rapists were the least likely to recidivate, they were the most likely to commit new murders and rapes while on probation. Langan and Cuniff found that probationers who were frequent drug abusers were arrested at a far higher rate (55 percent) than nonabusers (36 percent); drug treatment and testing efforts did not seem to lower recidivism rates.

While the recidivism rate of probationers seems high, it is still somewhat lower than the recidivism rate of prison inmates.[35] And relatively few of all criminal offenses are committed by probationers; even if all had been placed in prisons, the effect on the crime rate would have been negligible.[36]

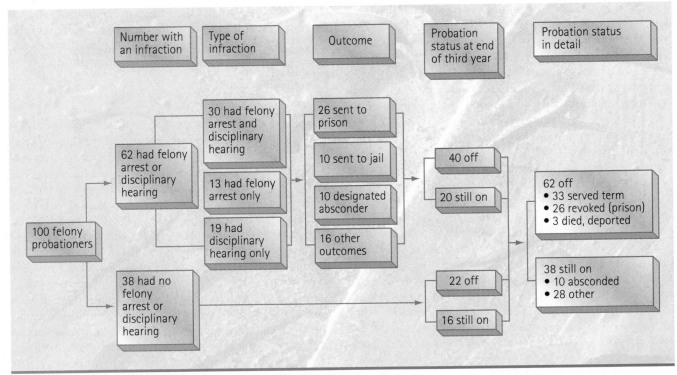

FIGURE 18.1 **Probation Outcomes of One Hundred Felons**

SOURCE: Patrick Langan and Mark Cuniff, *Recidivism of Felons on Probation, 1986–1989* (Washington, D.C.: Bureau of Justice Statistics, 1992).

Probation remains the sentence of choice in almost half of all felony cases, including 6 percent of murder cases, 20 percent of rapes, and 54 percent of felony drug cases. Because it costs far less to maintain an offender in the community than in prison and prison overcrowding continues, there is constant economic pressure to grant probation to serious felony offenders. Even if probation is no more successful than prison, it costs less, and that is extremely attractive to policy-makers during a time of fiscal austerity.

Intermediate Sanctions

Following conviction, disposition to non-institutional community correctional alternatives must become a right rather than a privilege for the nonviolent offender.[37]

At a time when overcrowding has produced a crisis in the nation's prison system, alternative sanctions are viewed as a new form of corrections that fall somewhere between probation and incarceration.[38] Alternative sanc-tions include fines, forfeiture, home confinement, electronic monitoring, intensive probation supervision, restitution, community corrections, and boot camps.

The development of these intermediate sanctions can be tied to a number of different sources. Primary is the need to develop alternatives to prisons, which have proved to be both ineffective and injurious. Research indicates that about half of all prison inmates are likely to be rearrested and returned to prison, many within a short period after their release from an institution.[39] Little evidence exists that incapacitation is either a deterrent to crime or a specific deterrent against future criminality. Nonetheless, prisons remain overused, overcrowded, and very expensive to operate.

Intermediate sanctions also meet the need to develop punishments that are fair, equitable, and proportional. It seems unfair to treat both a rapist and a shoplifter with the same type of sentence, considering the differences in their criminal acts. Intermediate sanctions can provide the successive steps for a meaningful "ladder" of scaled punishments outside of prison (see Figure 18.2), thereby restoring fairness and equity to nonincarceration sentences.[40] For example, a forger may be ordered to

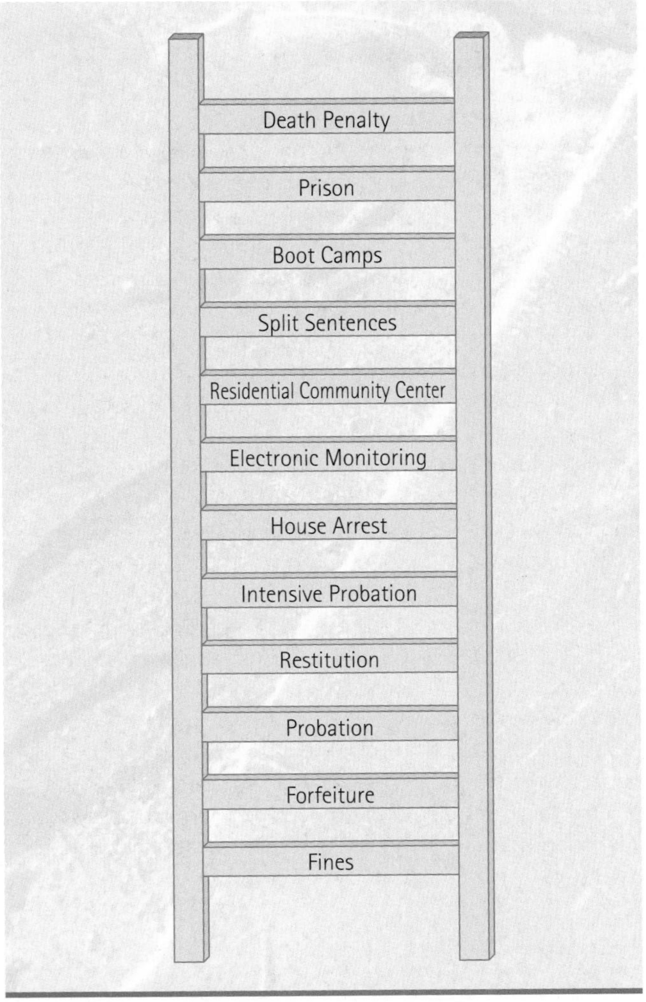
Death Penalty
Prison
Boot Camps
Split Sentences
Residential Community Center
Electronic Monitoring
House Arrest
Intensive Probation
Restitution
Probation
Forfeiture
Fines

FIGURE 18.2 **The Punishment Ladder**

make restitution to the victim, and an abusive husband can be ordered to reside in a community correctional center, while a rapist is sent to state prison. This feature of intermediate sanctions allows judges to fit the punishment to the crime without resorting to a prison sentence. Intermediate sanctions can be designed to be punitive by *increasing* punishments for people whose serious and/or repeat crimes make a straight probation sentence inappropriate yet for whom a prison sentence would be unduly harsh and dysfunctional.[41] In fact, the punitive nature of intermediate sanctions is not lost on offenders, some of whom prefer prison to the new, tougher forms of probation.[42]

The most likely candidates are convicted criminals who would normally be sent to prison but are either at a low risk of recidivating or are of little threat to society (such as nonviolent property offenders). Used in this sense, intermediate sanctions are a viable solution to the critical problem of prison overcrowding.

In the following sections, the forms of intermediate sanctions in use will be more thoroughly discussed.

Fines

Fines are monetary payments imposed on an offender as an intermediate punishment for criminal acts. They are a direct offshoot of the early common-law practice requiring compensation be paid to the victim and the state (wergild) for criminal acts.

While fines are most commonly used in misdemeanors, they are also frequently employed in felonies where the offender benefited financially. Investor Ivan Boesky paid over $100 million in fines for violating insider stock trading rules; the firm of Drexel, Burnham Lambert paid $650 million in 1988 for securities violations.[43]

Fines may be used as a sole sanction or combined with other punishments, such as probation or confinement. Quite commonly, judges levy other monetary sanctions along with fines, such as court costs, public defender fees, probation and treatment fees, and victim restitution, to increase the force of the financial punishment.[44] Some jurisdictions, such as New York City, are experimenting with **day fines,** a concept originated in Europe that gears fines to an offender's net daily income in an effort to make them more equitable and fairly distributed (see the Close-Up entitled "Day Fines").[45]

Though it is far from certain that fines are an effective sanction, either alone or in combination with other penalties, they remain one of the most commonly used criminal penalties. Research sponsored by the federal government found that lower-court judges impose fines alone or in tandem with other penalties in 86 percent of their cases, while superior court judges imposed fines in 42 percent of their cases.[46]

Forfeiture

Another alternative sanction that has a financial basis and is therefore similar to a fine is criminal (in personam) and civil (in rem) **forfeiture.** Both involve the seizure of goods and instrumentalities related to the commission or outcome of a criminal act. For example, federal law provides that after arresting drug traffickers, the government may seize the boat they used to import the narcotics, the car they used to carry it overland, the warehouse in which it was stored, and the home paid for with drug money; upon conviction, the drug dealers lose permanent ownership of these "instrumentalities" of crime.

CLOSE-UP

Day Fines

An intriguing new approach to exacting financial penalties is the day fine, which is based on the offender's earning capacity. The National Institute of Justice (NIJ), one of the research and development arms of the U.S. Justice Department, has helped fund several day-fine projects.

In contrast to the traditional fixed-sum fining system, in which the fine amount is governed principally by the nature of the crime, the day-fine approach tailors the fine amount to the defendant's ability to pay. Thus, for a given crime, the day-fine amount is larger for a high-income offender than for an irregularly employed or low-paid offender. The impact of the fine on each should be approximately equal. Under the traditional approach, a given fine amount could be relatively severe for a low-income offender but trivial for a person of substantial means.

Judges first establish how severe an offender's punishment should be, with severity of punishment expressed in terms of punishment units. For example, a Staten Island court participating in the NIJ-sponsored research set the maximum number of misdemeanor punishment units at 120 (for sexual misconduct) and the minimum at 5 (for trespass or disorderly conduct). Between those extremes are 35 to 60 units for possession of a weapon, 10 to 45 for attempted assault, 25 for resisting arrest, and 15 for harassment.

To then relate the amount of the fine to the ability to pay, the court multiplied the number of punishment units by the amount that the offender normally earns in one day, which is adjusted downward depending on personal needs and family support responsibilities.

Advocates of day fines, which are common in Europe, foresee the system's use across a broader spectrum of crimes and criminals than is the case for the flat-sum approach. But that does not mean that day fines are to be used when stronger punishment is warranted. Advocates also point out that day fines, unlike some other sanctions, permit retention of the offender's ties to family and community. Day fines constitute an important revenue source and can be implemented without the resources of additional administrative agencies.

Staten Island Project

In 1987, NIJ funded the Vera Institute of Justice, a private criminal justice-oriented foundation, located

---

Forfeiture is not a new sanction. During the Middle Ages, "forfeiture of estate" was a mandatory result of most felony convictions. The Crown could seize all of a felon's real and personal property. Forfeiture derived from the common-law concept of "corruption of blood" or "attaint," which prohibited a felon's family from inheriting or receiving his or her property or estate. The common law mandated that descendants could not inherit property from a relative who may have attained the property illegally: "(T)he Corruption of Blood stops the Course of Regular Descent, as to Estates, over which the Criminal could have no Power, because he never enjoyed them."[47]

The use of forfeiture has been reintroduced to American law with the passage of the Racketeer Influenced and Corrupt Organizations (RICO) and the Continuing Criminal Enterprises acts, both of which are designed to allow the seizure of any property derived from illegal enterprises or conspiracies. While these acts were designed to apply to ongoing criminal conspiracies, such as drug or pornography rings, they now are being applied to a far-ranging series of criminal acts, including white-collar crimes. Though law enforcement officials at first applauded the use of forfeiture as a hard-hitting way of seizing the illegal profits of drug law violators, the practice has been criticized because the government has often been overzealous in its application. For example, million-dollar yachts have been seized because someone aboard possessed a small amount of marijuana; this confiscatory practice is referred to as *zero tolerance*. The Supreme Court restricted such confiscatory practices in two recent cases, *Austin v. U.S.* (92-6073, 1993) and *Alexander v. U.S.* (91-1526, 1993), in which they held that the seizure of property must be *proportional* to the seriousness of the crime in both civil and criminal forfeitures. In the *Alexander* case, the government seized an entire chain of adult bookstores and ordered the destruction of the entire inventory of 100,000 items after the owner had been convicted of selling *seven obscene items*. *Austin* involved the civil seizure of the defendant's home and

in New York, to develop, with the Staten Island Criminal Court, the first day-fine system in the United States. Vera Institute's subsequent NIJ-sponsored evaluation concluded that between 1988 and 1990, the one-year pilot project in Staten Island's Richmond County was successful. This day-fine experiment evolved from earlier NIJ-supported research by the Vera Institute, which assessed the use of the fine as a criminal sanction.

Researchers selected Staten Island for the project as a representative middle-sized suburban American community. The social setting was stable and the economic base sound, but Staten Island had a substantial crime problem and a sizable amount of poverty and unemployment.

The pilot project demonstrated that a rather typical American court of limited jurisdiction could implement the day-fine concept successfully, substituting day for fixed fines. Judges found the mechanics of computing a day fine simple once they were trained to use the day-fine workbook they had helped develop. No conflicts of principle arose from prosecutors or from either the private or the public defense bar.

The researchers also found that:

- The total dollar amount of fines imposed by the court increased by 14 percent during the pilot project (to $93,856 from $82,060). Absent statutory caps on fines, fines collected during the project would have been almost 50 percent more (rising to $137,660 from $93,856) than those actually imposed.

- Despite significantly larger average fines and longer collection periods, day fines were collected in full as frequently as the lower, fixed fines.
- The introduction of the day fine did not greatly affect the types of offenses that typically drew a fine.

The success of the Staten Island pilot project has encouraged continued adaptation of the day-fine concept in jurisdictions outside New York.

Discussion Questions
1. Is it fair to punish offenders more harshly because they earn more money?
2. Are day fines a form of indentured servitude?

SOURCE: Adapted from Voncile Gowdy, *Intermediate Sanctions* (Washington, D.C.: National Institute of Justice, 1993).

---

business after he was convicted of possessing two grams of cocaine. Despite this setback, it is likely that forfeiture will continue to be used as an alternative sanction against such selective targets as drug dealers and white-collar criminals.

Restitution

Another popular intermediate sanction is restitution, which can take the form of requiring convicted defendants to either pay back the victims of crime **(monetary restitution)** or serve the community to compensate for their criminal acts **(community service restitution)**.[48]

Ordinarily, restitution programs require offenders to pay back victims of crime (or serve the community) as a condition of probation. The process offers the convicted offender a chance to avoid a jail or prison sentence or a more lengthy probationary period. Restitution may also be used as a diversionary device and offer some offenders the chance to avoid a criminal record altogether. In this instance, a judge will continue the case "without a finding" while the defendant completes the restitution order; after the probation department determines that restitution has been made, the case is dismissed.[49]

Because restitution appears to have benefits for the victim of crime, the offender, the criminal justice system, and society as a whole, national interest in the concept has been tremendous. Restitution is inexpensive, avoids stigma, and helps compensate victims of crime. Offenders doing community service work have been placed in schools, hospitals, and nursing homes. Helping them avoid a jail sentence can mean saving the public thousands of dollars that would have gone to maintaining them in a secure institution, frees up needed resources, and gives the community the feeling that equity has been returned to the justice system.

Does restitution work? Most reviews give it a qualified success rating. It is estimated that almost 90 percent of the eligible offenders successfully complete their restitution orders and that restitutioners have equal or lower recidivism rates when compared to control groups of various kinds.[50]

Shock Probation and Split Sentencing

Split sentences and shock probation are alternative sanctions designed to allow judges to grant offenders community release only after they have sampled prison life. These sanctions are based on the premise that if offenders are given a taste of incarceration sufficient to "shock" them into law-abiding behavior, they will be reluctant to violate the rules of probation or commit another criminal act.

In a number of states and in the federal criminal code, a jail term can actually be a condition of probation, known as **split sentencing.** Under current federal practices, about 25 percent of all convicted federal offenders receive some form of split sentence, including both prison and jail as a condition of probation.[51]

Another approach, known as **shock probation,** involves the resentencing of an offender after a short prison stay. The shock comes because the offender originally receives a long maximum sentence but is then eligible for release to community supervision at the discretion of the judge (usually within 90 days of incarceration). About one-third of all probationers in the 14 states that use the program, including Ohio, Kentucky, Idaho, New Jersey, Tennessee, Utah, and Vermont, receive a period of confinement.[52] Evaluations of shock probation have indicated that it is between 78 percent and 91 percent effective.[53]

Shock probation has been praised as a program that limits prison time and provides offenders with a chance to be quickly integrated into the community, a mechanism that can maintain family ties, and a way of reducing prison populations and the costs of corrections.[54]

Intensive Probation Supervision

Intensive probation supervision (IPS) programs are another important form of intermediate sanction. IPS programs, which have been implemented in some form in about 45 states, involve small caseloads of 15 to 40 clients who are kept under close watch by probation officers.[55] The primary goal of IPS is *diversion:* without intensive supervision, clients would normally have been sent to already overcrowded prisons or jails.[56] The second goal is *control:* high-risk offenders can be maintained in the community under much closer security than traditional probation efforts can provide. A third

goal is *reintegration:* offenders can maintain community ties and be reoriented toward a more productive life while avoiding the pains of imprisonment.

Who is eligible for IPS? Most programs have set up admissions criteria based on the nature of the offense and the offender's criminal background. Some programs, such as New Jersey's, exclude violent offenders; others will not consider substance abusers. In contrast, some jurisdictions, such as Massachusetts, do not exclude offenders based on their prior criminal history. About 60 percent of IPS programs exclude offenders who have already violated probation orders or otherwise failed on probation.

The form and structure of IPS programs vary a great deal. The typical model requires clients to meet with their supervisors almost every day. However, a national survey discovered significant variations between programs.[57] While 16 percent demanded almost daily contacts, 13 percent required only one to four contacts with clients per month. There is also significant differences in the length and types of contacts. For example, most IPS programs are divided into treatment phases, with the number of contacts diminishing as the client progresses between program stages. In some programs, the most intensive stage in which clients are seen daily lasts almost six months, while in others, daily contact is terminated after 90 days. Some programs demand face-to-face contacts at home, work, or in the office, while others rely on telephone contacts, curfew checks, or collateral contacts (with family, friends or employers); most employ routine drug testing.[58]

There are indications that despite its promise, the failure rate in IPS caseloads is quite high. Michael Agopian evaluated IPS programs in California and found that the failure rate in IPS caseloads was 50 percent.[59] Research conducted by Peter Jones in Kansas found that while IPS was successful in diverting inmates from the correctional system, failure rates were 45 percent within two years, compared to 32 percent for traditional probationers.[60] And Langan and Cuniff's 17-state survey found that IPS clients had a higher rearrest rate than traditional probationers.[61] It is possible that closer supervision "produces" failures because supervisors are better able to detect technical and legal violations. Continuous drug testing alone should produce a higher failure rate among IPS clients than traditional probationers.

While these failure rates seem high, IPS is designed for clients who have more serious prior records and histories of drug abuse than regular probationers. However, in an important analysis of IPS in three California counties, Joan Petersilia and Susan Turner found that IPS clients were actually *less dangerous* than those sent to prison and just as likely to recidivate as clients in traditional probation caseloads.[62] IPS is a waste of taxpayers' money if it works no better than traditional probation while serving a similar clientele.

Home Confinement

A number of states, including Florida, Oklahoma, Oregon, Kentucky, and California, have developed **home confinement** (HC) programs (also called house arrest or home detention) as an intermediate sanction. The HC concept requires convicted offenders to spend extended periods of time in their own home as an alternative to an incarceration sentence. For example, an individual convicted on a drunk-driving charge might be sentenced to spend the period between 6 P.M. Friday and 8 A.M. Monday and every weekday after 5:30 P.M. in their home for the next six months. Current estimates indicate that as many as 10,000 people are placed under HC yearly.[63]

Like IPS programs, there is a great deal of variation in HC initiatives: some are administered by probation departments, while others are simply judicial sentences monitored by *surveillance officers;* some check clients ten or more times a month, while others make only a few curfew checks; some use 24-hour confinement, while others allow offenders to attend work or school. Regardless of the model used, house arrest programs are designed to be more punitive than IPS and are considered a "last chance" before prison: if you are caught violating a house arrest order, the next logical stop is a secure correctional facility.[64]

As yet, there is no definitive data indicating that HC is an effective crime deterrent, nor is there sufficient evidence to conclude that it is useful in lowering the recidivism rate. Nonetheless, considering its advantages in cost and the overcrowded status of prisons and jails, it is evident that house arrest will continue to grow in the 1990s.

Electronic Monitoring

For house arrest to work, sentencing authorities must be assured that arrestees are actually at home during their assigned times. Random calls and visits are one way to check on compliance with house arrest orders. However, a more advanced method of control has been the introduction of **electronic monitoring** (EM) devices to manage offender obedience to home confinement orders.

Electronically monitored offenders wear devices attached to their ankles, wrists, or around their necks that send signals back to a control office. Two basic types of systems are used: active and passive. Active systems constantly monitor the offender by continuously sending a signal back to the central office. If the offender leaves his or her home at an unauthorized time, the signal is broken and the "failure" recorded. In some cases, the control officer is automatically notified electronically through a beeper.

In contrast, passive systems usually involve random phone calls generated by computers to which the offender has to respond within a particular time (such as 30 seconds). Some passive systems require the offender to place the monitoring device into a verifier box, which then sends a signal back to the control computer; another approach is to have the arrestee repeat words that are analyzed by a voice verifier. While most electronic surveillance systems use telephone lines, some employ radio transmitters that receive a signal from a device worn by the offender and relay it back to a computer monitoring system.

Growth in the number of electronically monitored offenders has been explosive. In 1986, the daily count was 95 people; by 1988, the number had jumped to 2,277; in 1989, 39 jurisdictions were monitoring 6,490 offenders; by 1991, 14,000 people were being monitored.[65] Up to 1 million people may eventually be monitored electronically in the United States![66]

EM is being hailed as one of the most important developments in correctional policy.[67] It has the benefits of relatively low cost and high security, while at the same time helping offenders avoid the pains of imprisonment in overcrowded, dangerous state facilities. Electronic monitoring is capital- rather than labor-intensive. Since offenders are monitored by computers, an initial investment in hardware rules out the need for hiring many more supervisory officers to handle large numbers of clients. It can also be used at many stages of the justice process, including at the front end as a condition of pretrial bail release and at the back end as part of parole (see Figure 18.3).

A general review of EM programs indicates that recidivism rates are lower than recorded for comparable groups of probationers or parolees.[68] There are variations in the success rates of programs, and EM may be more effective with some offenders than others and at certain stages of the justice process than at others. For example, one evaluation by Terry Baumer, Michael Maxfield, and Robert Mendelsohn found that EM works much more efficiently with convicted offenders than as a pretrial detention; juveniles responded better than adults.[69] EM may be an effective method of reducing recidivism among targeted groups of nonviolent

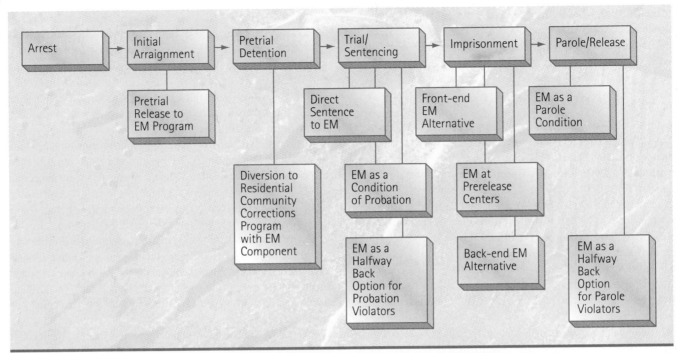

FIGURE 18.3   Key Decision Points Where Electronic Monitoring Programs Are Being Used

SOURCE: James Byrne, Arthur Lurigio, and Christopher Baird, *The Effectiveness of the New Intensive Supervision Programs,* Research in Corrections Series, vol. 2, no. 2 (preliminary unpublished draft; Washington, D.C.: National Institute of Corrections, 1989).

offenders, especially drunk drivers, whose incarceration helps clog the correctional system.[70]

While EM holds the promise of being a low-cost, less painful alternative to incarceration, to some it presents the potential for excessive government intrusion in the lives of American citizens.[71]

Residential Community Corrections

A more secure intermediate sanction is a sentence to a residential community corrections (RCC) program. These programs have been defined by the National Institute of Corrections as:

> a freestanding nonsecure building that is not part of a prison or jail and houses pre-trial and adjudicated adults. The residents regularly depart to work, to attend school, and/or participate in community corrections activities and programs.[72]

The traditional role of community corrections was to provide a nonsecure "halfway house" environment designed to reintegrate soon-to-be-paroled prison inmates back into the community. Inmates spend the last few months in the halfway house acquiring suitable employment, building up cash reserves, obtaining an apartment, and developing a job-related wardrobe. These facilities often look like residential homes, since many were originally private residences. In urban centers, small apartment buildings have been used to house clients. Usually, these facilities have a central treatment theme—such as group therapy or reality therapy—for rehabilitating and reintegrating clients. Another popular approach in community-based corrections is the use of ex-offenders as staff members. These individuals have experienced making the transition between the closed institution and society and can be invaluable in helping residents overcome the many hurdles to proper readjustment. Clients learn how to reestablish family and friendship ties, and the shock of sudden reentry into society is considerably reduced.

The traditional concept of community corrections has expanded recently. Today, the community correctional facility serves as a vehicle to provide intermediate sanctions as well as a prerelease center for those about to be paroled from the prison system. For example, RCC has been used as a direct sentencing option for judges who believe particular offenders need a correctional alternative halfway between traditional probation and a stay in prison. Placement in a RCC center can be used as a condition of probation for offenders who need a nonsecure community facility that provides a more structured treatment environment than traditional probation.

Probation departments and other correctional authorities have been charged with running RCC centers that serve as a preprison sentencing alternative. In addition, some RCC programs are operated by private, nonprofit groups that receive referrals from county or district courts.

In addition to being a sole sentence and a halfway house, RCC programs have also been used as a residential pretrial release center for offenders who are in immediate need of social services before their trial and as a halfway-back alternative for both parole and probation violators who might otherwise have to be imprisoned. In this capacity, RCC programs serve as a base from which offenders can be placed in outpatient psychiatric facilities, drug and alcohol treatment programs, job training, and so on.

Boot Camps/Shock Incarceration

Another intermediate sanction gaining popularity around the United States is **shock incarceration** (SI) or **boot camps.** These programs typically include youthful, first-time offenders and feature military discipline and physical training. The concept is that short periods (90 to 180 days) of high-intensity exercise and work will shock young criminals into going straight. Tough physical training is designed to promote responsibility and improve decision-making skills, build self-confidence, and teach socialization skills. Inmates are treated with rough intensity by drill masters, who may call them names and punish the entire group for the failure of one of its members. Most state programs also include educational and training components, counseling sessions, and treatment for special-needs populations. Examples of SI programs

Female boot campers in New York have exactly eight minutes to eat and must line up in formation to empty their trays. Everything they do is under constant surveillance by military-style guards.

include the Regimented Inmate Discipline Programs in Mississippi, the About Face Program in Louisiana, and the shock incarceration program in Georgia. The U.S. Army has created a shock program, Specialized Treatment and Rehabilitation in Army Corrections, at its prison in Fort Riley, Kansas. At least four states now have boot camp programs for female inmates—Oklahoma, Mississippi, South Carolina, and Louisiana.

Is shock incarceration a correctional panacea or another fad doomed to failure? The results so far are mixed. The costs of boot camps are no lower than those of traditional prisons, but since sentences are shorter, they do provide long-term savings. Some programs suffer high failure-to-complete rates, which makes program evaluations difficult (even if "graduates" are successful, it is possible that success is achieved because troublesome cases drop out and are placed in the general inmate population). What evaluations exist indicate that the recidivism rates of inmates who attend shock programs are in some cases no lower than those released from traditional prisons.[73] One study by Doris Layton Mackenzie and James Shaw found that while boot camp inmates may have lower recidivism rates than probationers and parolees, they had higher rates of technical violations and revocations.[74] While these results are disappointing, Mackenzie reports that both staff and inmates seem excited by the programs, and even those who fail on parole report they felt SI was a valuable experience.[75] She also finds, with Alex Piquero, that carefully managed boot camp programs can make a major dent in prison overcrowding.[76]

Can Alternatives Work?

As a group, there is little evidence that alternative sanctions can prevent crime, reduce recidivism, or work much better than traditional probation or prison. Those who favor this approach argue that even if there is little conclusive evidence that alternative sanctions are better than prison, they are certainly cheaper. Yet this rationale is valid only if the client population served would have been placed in more restrictive and costly secure confinements absent the opportunity for alternative sentencing. If, as some critics contend, placement is restricted to people who would have ordinarily been granted probation, then alternative sanctions are actually a more expensive method to achieve about the same result.

In a careful analysis of alternative sanctions, Frank Cullen finds that while they often produce some "small victories," they "have not shown the general ability to defeat the powerful forces fueling the [corrections] crisis."[77] Cullen finds that the "deteriorating fabric and

social misery" of the nation's cities create high rates of predatory crime. Alternative sanctions can do little to stem the tide of misery and despair.

Jails

The jail is a secure institution used to (1) detain offenders before trial if they cannot afford or are not eligible for bail and (2) house misdemeanants sentenced to terms of one year or less, as well as some nonserious felons. In some jurisdictions, such as Massachussetts, jails are used strictly to hold detainees, while sentenced offenders are placed in the county house of corrections.

The jail originated in Europe in the sixteenth century and was used to house those awaiting trial and punishment. Jails were not used to house sentenced criminals, since at that time, punishment was either by fine, exile, corporal punishment, or death.

Throughout their history, jails have been considered hell holes of pestilence and cruelty. In early English history, they were used to house offenders awaiting trial, as well as vagabonds, debtors, the mentally ill, and assorted others.[78] The early colonists adopted the European custom of detaining prisoners in jail. As noted previously, William Penn instituted the first jails to house convicted offenders while they worked off their sentence. The Walnut Street Prison, built in 1790, is considered the first modern jail.

Jail Populations

As you may recall, there has been a national effort to remove as many people from local jails as possible through the adoption of both bail reform measures and pretrial diversion. Nonetheless, jail populations have been steadily increasing, due in part to the increased use of mandatory jail sentences for such common crimes as drunk driving and the use of local jails to house inmates for whom there is no room in state prisons.

There are approximately 440,000 jail inmates today, split almost equally between sentenced offenders and detainees.[79] Whereas the number of jails has declined from a high of 4,037 in 1970 to about 3,500 today, the number of inmates increased about 150 percent (from 160,683); there is a trend toward fewer but larger jails. Figure 18.4 shows the explosive growth of the jail population. On an annual basis, close to 10 million people are admitted to jail. In 1970, there were 79 inmates per 100,000 population; today, there are 174 per 100,000, an increase of 120 percent.

While the removal of juveniles from adult jails has long been a national priority, it is likely that more than 50,000 youths are admitted to adult jails each year. On any given day, 2,800 juveniles are held in adult jail.

Equally disturbing is the fact that minorities are disproportionately represented in the jail population; about 44 percent of jail inmates are black and 14 percent Hispanic. Figure 18.4 shows that while the number of white jail inmates per 100,000 population has remained stable, the number of African-American inmates has increased dramatically during the past decade.

Jail Conditions

Jail conditions have become a national scandal. Throughout the United States, jails are marked by violence, overcrowding, deteriorated physical conditions, and lack of treatment or rehabilitation efforts. Suicides are common, as are fires and other natural calamities.[80] Another problem is the housing together of convicted offenders and detainees. And, despite government efforts to end the practice, many juvenile offenders occupy cells in adult jail facilities. About one-quarter of jails with large populations were under court order to improve. The most common grievances are overcrowding, inadequate recreational facilities and services, insufficient libraries, and deficient medical services and facilities.[81]

Some effort has been made to ameliorate jail conditions. The American Correctional Association has set up the Commission on Accreditation for Corrections, which has defined standards for health care, treatment, and visitations. A multistate pilot project has helped local facilities improve conditions so they may be accredited by the commission.[82]

In a similar vein, a number of states have passed minimum standard acts to force counties to improve their jail conditions. State funding is made available to counties that cannot comply with conditions because of budgetary problems.[83] When state efforts have not been sufficient, national agencies have sometimes helped.

FIGURE 18.4   **Jail Populations: Racial Inequality Continues**

SOURCE: Allen Beck, Thomas Bonczar, and Darrell Gilliard, *Jail Inmates 1992* (Washington, D.C.: Bureau of Justice Statistics, 1993), p. 1.

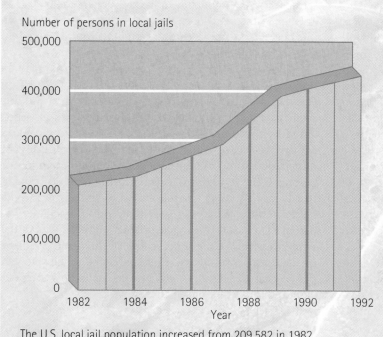

The U.S. local jail population increased from 209,582 in 1982 to 444,584 in 1992.

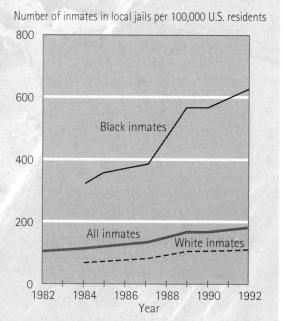

The number of local jail inmates per 100,000 U.S. residents increased from 90 in 1982 to 174 in 1992. In 1992, the rates were 109 white inmates per 100,000 white residents and 619 black inmates per 100,000 black residents.

The National Institute of Corrections has established a national jail center in Boulder, Colorado, to develop training materials and hold workshops for jail personnel.

The Prison

State and federal governments maintain closed correctional facilities to house convicted felons. Usually called prisons or penitentiaries, these institutions have become familiar to most people as harsh, frightening places filled with dangerous men and women. San Quentin (California), Attica (New York), Joliet (Illinois), and Marion (Illinois) are but a few of the large state and federal prisons made well known by films, books, or the media.

This section will discuss types of correctional institutions, life and treatment in prison, and the prisoners' rights movement.

Types of Institutions

Of the more than 500 adult prisons operating in this country, the overwhelming majority are state institutions.[84] These prisons are usually categorized according to their level of security and inmate populations as maximum-, medium-, and minimum-security institutions. Large maximum-security prisons are surrounded by high walls and have elaborate security measures and armed guards. They house inmates classified as potentially dangerous. Some jurisidictions are developing so-called maxi-maxi institutions modeled after the federal prison in Marion, Illinois. These house the most dangerous offenders in virtually permanent solitary confinement.

Medium-security prisons have similar protective measures but usually contain less violent inmates. Consequently, they are more likely to offer a variety of treatment and educational programs to their residents. Minimum-security prisons operate without armed guards or walls; usually, they are constructed in compounds surrounded by a metal mesh fence.

Minimum-security prisons usually house the least violent offenders; white-collar criminals may be their most common occupants. Work furloughs and educational releases are encouraged, and vocational training is of the highest level. Dress codes are lax.

Minimum-security facilities may have dormitories or small private rooms for inmates. Prisoners are allowed much discretion in keeping with them personal possessions that might be deemed dangerous in a maximum-security prison. The major security measure in minimum-security institutions is the threat that an escape will lead to transfer to a more secure facility.

Private Prisons

A current development in corrections is the increased use of privately run correctional institutions.[85] The federal government has used private companies to run detention centers for aliens who are being held for trial or deportation. One firm, the Corrections Corporation of America, runs a federal halfway house, two detention centers, and a 370-bed jail in Bay County, Florida. On January 6, 1986, the U.S. Corrections Corporation opened the first privately run state prison in Marion, Kentucky—a 300-bed minimum-security facility for inmates who are within three years of parole. Today, more than 20 companies are trying to enter the private prison market, five states are contracting with private companies to operate facilities, and more than ten others are considering doing so.

Though privately run institutions have been around for a few years, their increased use may present a number of problems. For example, will private providers be able to effectively evaluate programs knowing that a negative evaluation might cause them to lose their contract? Will they skimp on services and programs to reduce costs? Might they not skim off the "easy" cases and leave the hard-core inmate for state care? And will the need to keep business booming require "widening the net" to fill empty cells?

The notion of running prisons for profit may be unpalatable to large segments of the population. However, is this very much different from a private hospital or college, both of which offer services also provided by the state? The issues that determine the future of private corrections may be efficiency and cost-effectiveness and not fairness and morality. In an important analysis by Charles Logan and Bill McGriff, privately run correctional institutions were found to provide better services at lower cost than public facilities.[86] A recent evaluation of private prisons in Texas shows that while they may experience some of the same problems of state-run institutions, there is little conclusive evidence that they cannot operate as or even more efficiently than traditional institutions.[87]

Prisoners in the United States

One of the most significant problems in the criminal justice system has been the meteoric rise in the prison population; today, there are more than 950,000 people in prisons.[88] This number represents a dramatic increase of

168 percent since 1980, when 329,000 were incarcerated in state prisons. Because of this influx of offenders, many of the nation's prisons are operating at over 100 percent of capacity, even though thousands of prisoners were being held in local jails because of overcrowding.

Why has the prison population skyrocketed? One reason is that there are more crimes today than ever before; even if rates have stabilized, the population has grown larger. In addition, the violent crime rate has increased, and violent criminals are more liable to be incarcerated than property offenders. Another reason is that a conservative, "get-tough" judicial attitude, supplemented by mandatory sentences, has resulted in more people going to prison per criminal offense committed. In 1977, about 121 people per 1,000 arrested were sent to prison; today, the number is 143 per 1,000. Considering there are about 3 million felony arrests, the increased incarceration rate alone adds 60,000 people per year to the prison population. The major influence has been the explosive growth of drug arrests and the increased use of prison for drug offenders. As you may recall from Chapter 14, between 1977 and 1990, the number of drug-related arrest offenses doubled (to about 1 million), and the number of drug offenders sentenced to prison rose from 27 per 1,000 arrests to 103 per 1,000! As Figure 18.5 shows, the number and percent of drug offenders being committed to prison have risen steeply.

Recognizing the dangers associated with overcrowding, courts have ordered a number of state jurisdictions to reduce their inmate populations. To address the situation, various state correctional authorities have adopted plans to reduce the inmate population and a number of jurisdictions are operating under court order to reduce overcrowding. Others have called for the removal of less dangerous older inmates from secure facilities to less expensive community alternatives.[89] Some states, such as Texas, have undertaken a prison expansion campaign that calls for the building of thousands of more cells in the coming decade.

Profile of Prison Inmates

What are the personal characteristics of U.S. prison inmates? As expected, prisoners reflect the same qualities that are found in samples of arrestees. Inmates of state prisons are predominantly poor, young adult males with less than a high school education.[90] Prison is not a new experience for them; more than 60 percent had been incarcerated before. About 80 percent of all inmates had prior sentences to either probation or incarceration; about 5 percent had 100 or more priors!

In years past, most inmates were doing time for robbery or burglary. Today, drug trafficking has risen to the number two spot (13 percent) behind robbery (15 percent) and just ahead of burglary (12 percent).

The profile of inmates reinforces the presumed association between criminal behavior and social problems. Many inmates (43 percent) grew up in a single-parent household; 37 percent had at least one other family member who had been incarcerated. More than a quarter said their parents had abused drugs or alcohol; the great majority (80 percent) had been substance abusers themselves; more than 60 percent were regular drug users.

Minorities were overrepresented in the prison population; only 35 percent of the population was white. In contrast, African-Americans made up 46 percent of the population and Hispanics 17 percent.

Inmates were educational and vocational underachievers. Only one-third had graduated from high school, and about one-half had full-time employment before their incarceration. It is therefore no surprise that 53 percent earned under $10,000 per year, and 22 percent earned less than $3,000. Only 18 percent were married, far below the standard rate for adult Americans.

The profile of the prison inmate supports the reality of a problem-behavior syndrome. From birth, the path that led the inmate to prison was littered with insurmountable family, economic, and social problems. It seems likely that neither the benevolent effect of treatment nor the deterrent effect of punishment can have much impact on a life shaped by such damaging social forces. It should come as no surprise, then, that recidivism rates are so high.

Prison Life: Males

Inmates in large, inaccessible prisons find themselves physically cut off from families, friends, and former associates. Those who are fathers may become depressed because they are anxious about their kids.[91] Their families and friends may find it difficult to travel great distances to visit them; mail is censored and sometimes destroyed. The prison is a "total institution," regulating dress, work, sleep, and eating habits.[92]

Inmates soon find themselves in a totally new world with its own logic, behavior, rules, and language. They must learn to live with the stress of prison life. According to Gresham Sykes, the major losses are goods and services, liberty, heterosexual relationships, autonomy, and security.[93] Prisoners find they have no privacy; even when locked in their own cells, they are surrounded and observed by others.

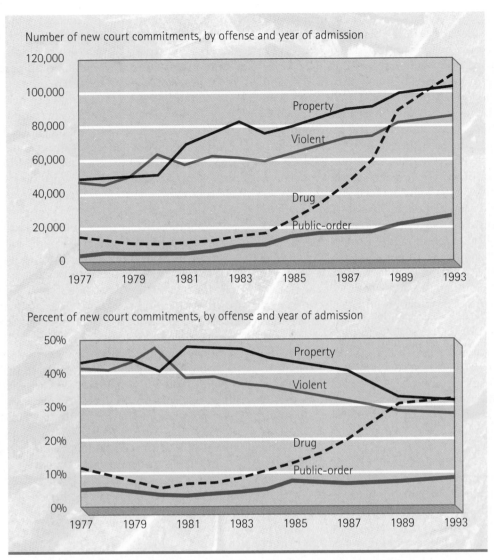

Number of new court commitments, by offense and year of admission

Percent of new court commitments, by offense and year of admission

FIGURE 18.5 **The Changing Composition of the Inmate Population**

SOURCE: D. Gilliard and A. Beck, *Prisoners, 1993* (Washington, D.C.: Bureau of Justice Statistics, 1994).

Inmates must adjust to the incentives prison administrators have created to promote security and control behavior.[94] One type of incentive involves the level of comfort provided the inmate. Those obeying rules are given choice work assignments, privileges, and educational opportunities. Those who flout prison rules may be segregated, locked in their cells, or put in solitary confinement **(the hole).**

Administrators can also control the amount of time spent in prison. Furloughs can be dispensed to allow prisoners the opportunity to work or visit outside the prison walls. Good-time credit can be extended to lessen the minimum sentence. Parole decisions can be influenced by reports on inmates' behavior.

The inmate must learn to deal with sexual exploitation and violence in the prison. One position says that this phenomenon is a function of racial conflict; another holds that inmates who become victims are physically weaker and less likely to form cohesive defensive groups.[95] In one study, Daniel Lockwood found that inmate aggressors come from a street culture that stresses violence and continue to behave violently while in prison.[96] Young males may be raped and kept as sexual slaves by older, more aggressive inmates. When these

Overcrowding is the single greatest problem faced by the correctional system today.

"slave holders" are released, they often sell their "prison wives" to other inmates.[97]

To cope with sexual aggression, some inmates fight back to prove they are not people who can be taken advantage of. While some kill their attackers and get even longer sentences, others can join cliques and gangs that provide protection and the ability to acquire power within the institution. Gangs are powerful in the larger prison systems, especially in California. Some seek transfers to a different cell block or prison, ask for protective custody, or simply remain in their cells all the time.

Part of inmates' early adjustment involves their becoming familiar with and perhaps participating in the hidden, black-market economy of the prison—the *hustle*. Hustling provides inmates with a source of steady income and the satisfaction of believing they are beating the system.[98]

Hustling involves the sale of such illegal commodities as drugs (uppers, downers, pot), alcohol, weapons, and illegally obtained food and supplies. When prison officials crack down on hustled goods, it merely serves to drive the price up—giving hustlers a greater incentive to promote their black-market activities.[99]

Inmates must also learn to deal with the racial conflict that is a daily fact of life. Prisoners tend to segregate themselves and, if peace is to reign in the institution, stay out of each other's way. Often, racial groupings are quite exact; for example, Hispanics may separate themselves according to their national origin (Mexicans, Puerto Ricans, Colombians, and so on). In large California prisons, segregation and power struggles create even narrower divisions. For example, Hispanic gangs are now organized by area of origin: northern California (Nortenos), southern California (Surenos), and Mexican-born (Border Brothers).[100] Prisons represent one area in which minorities often hold power; as sociologist James B. Jacobs observed, "Prison may be the one institution in American society that blacks control."[101]

Prisoners must learn to deal with their frustrations over getting a "rotten deal." They may find that some other inmates received far lower sentences for similar crimes. They may be turned down for parole and then observe that others with similar records are granted early release. There is some evidence that perceived discrimination in the distribution of rewards and treatment may contribute to dissatisfaction, maladjustment, and prison violence.[102]

Finally, as the inmate's sentence winds down and his parole date nears, he must learn to cope with the anxiety of being released into the outside world. During this period, inmates may question their ability to make it in an environment in which they have failed before. Have their families stood by them? Are they outcasts?

Thus, adapting to prison requires coping with a whole series of new conditions and personal crises. Failure to cope can lead to mental breakdown and suicide.

Inmate Society. A significant element of the inmate's adjustment to prison is the encounter with what was commonly known as the **inmate subculture.**[103] One major aspect of the inmate subculture was a unique **social code,** unwritten guidelines that expressed the values, attitudes, and types of behavior that the older inmates demanded of younger inmates. Passed on from one generation of inmates to another, the inmate social code represented the values of interpersonal relations within the prison.

National attention was first drawn to the inmate social code and subculture by Donald Clemmer. In *The Prison Community,* Clemmer set out to present a detailed sociological study of life in a maximum-security prison.[104] Referring to thousands of conversations and interviews, as well as to inmate essays and biographies, Clemmer was able to identify a unique language *(argot)* of prisoners. In addition, Clemmer found that prisoners tend to group themselves into cliques on the basis of such personal criteria as sexual preference, political beliefs, and offense history. He found that there were complex sexual relationships in prison and concluded that many heterosexual men will turn to homosexual relationships when faced with long sentences and the loneliness of prison life.

Clemmer's most important contribution may have been his identification of the **prisonization** process. This he defined as the inmate's assimilation into the prison culture through acceptance of its language, sexual code, and norms of behavior. Those who become the most "prisonized" will be the least likely to reform on the outside.

Using Clemmer's work as a jumping-off point, some prominent sociologists set out to explore more fully the various roles in the prison community. For example, in one important analysis entitled *The Society of Captives,* Gresham Sykes further defined prison argot and argued that prison roles exist because of the deprivations presented by the prison.[105] Later, writing with Sheldon Messinger, Sykes identified the following as the most important principles of the prison community:

- *Don't interfere with inmates' interests.* Within this area of the code are maxims concerning the serving of the least amount of time in the greatest possible comfort. For example, inmates are warned . . . never [to betray another] inmate to authorities; . . . [in other words,] grievances must be handled personally. Other aspects of the noninterference doctrine include "Don't be nosy," "Don't have a loose lip," "Keep off [the other inmates' backs]," and "Don't put [another inmate] on the spot."

- *Don't lose your head.* Inmates are also cautioned to refrain from arguing, [quarreling, or engaging in] other emotional displays with fellow inmates. The novice may hear such warnings as "Play it cool" and "Do your own time."

- *Don't exploit inmates.* Prisoners are warned not to take advantage of one another—"Don't steal from cons," "Don't welsh on a debt," "Be right."

- *Inmates are cautioned to be tough and not lose their dignity.* While rule 2 forbids conflict, once it starts an inmate must be prepared to deal with it effectively and [thoroughly]. Maxims include "Don't cop out," "Don't weaken," "Be tough; be a man."

- *Don't be a sucker.* Inmates are cautioned not to make fools . . . of themselves and support the guards or prison administration over the interest of the inmates—"Be sharp."[106]

Not all prison experts believe that the prison culture is a function of the harsh conditions existing in a total institution. In 1962, John Irwin and Donald Cressey published a paper in which they conceded that a prison culture exists but claimed that its principles are actually imported from the outside world.[107] In their **importation model,** Irwin and Cressey conclude that the inmate culture is affected by the values of newcomers: Many inmates come to any given prison with a record of many terms in correctional institutions. These men, some of whom have institutional records dating back to early childhood, bring with them a ready-made set of patterns, which they apply to the new situation, and take control of the prison culture's content.

The New Inmate Culture.

While the "old" inmate subculture may have been harmful because its norms and values insulated the inmate from change efforts, it also helped create order within the institution and prevented violence among the inmates. People who violated the code and victimized others were sanctioned by their peers. An understanding developed between guards and inmate leaders: the guards would let the inmates have things their own way, and the inmates would not let things get out of hand and draw the attention of the administration.

The old system may be dying or already dead in most institutions. The change seems to have been precipitated by the black power movement in the 1960s and 1970s. Black inmates were no longer content to fill a subservient role and challenged the power of established white inmates. As the black power movement gained prominence, racial tension in prisons created divisions that severely altered the inmate subculture. Older, respected inmates could no longer cross racial lines to mediate disputes. Predatory inmates could victimize others without fear of retaliation.[108] Consequently, more inmates than ever are assigned for their safety to protective custody.

Sociologist James B. Jacobs is perhaps the most influential expert on the changing inmate subculture. His research has helped him to conclude that the development of "black (and Latino) power" in the 1960s, spurred by the Black Muslim movement, significantly influenced the nature of prison life.[109]

According to Jacobs, black and Latin inmates are much more cohesively organized than whites. Their groups are sometimes rooted in religious and political affiliations, such as the Black Muslims; created specifically to combat discrimination in prison, such as the Latin group *La Familia;* or reformations of street gangs, such as the Vice Lords, Disciples, or Blackstone Rangers in the Illinois prison system and the Crips in California. Only in California have white inmates successfully organized, and there it is in the form of neo-Nazi groups, such as the *Aryan Brotherhood*. Racially homogeneous gangs are so cohesive and powerful that they are able to supplant the original inmate code with one of their own. Consider the oath taken by new members of *Nuestra Familia* (Our Family), a Latin gang operating in California prisons: "If I go forward, follow me. If I hesi-

tate, push me. If they kill me, avenge me. If I am a traitor, kill me."

Racial conflict prompted Jacobs to suggest that it may be humane and appropriate to segregate inmates along racial lines to maintain order and protect individual rights. Jacobs believes that in some prisons, administrators use integration as a threat to keep inmates in line; to be transferred to a racially mixed setting may mean beatings or death.

While the portrait Jacobs paints of the new prison culture is one of danger and chaos, there is evidence that in some areas, prison life has become even more disorganized, with new gangs forming and engaging in ever-increasing violent confrontations. The new breed of inmate is younger, more dangerous, and disdainful of older gang members.[110] As the prison population expands, the violence and danger of the streets will be imported into the prison culture.

Prison Life: Females

Women make up about 5 percent of the adult prison population. Usually, they are housed in minimum-security institutions more likely to resemble college dormitories than high-security male prisons.

Women in prison tend to be of three basic types, described by Esther Heffernan as: "the square," who is basically a noncriminal but who, in a fit of rage, may have shot or stabbed a husband or boyfriend; "the life," who is a repeat offender—shoplifter, prostitute, drug user, or pusher; and "the cool," who is part of the sophisticated criminal underworld. The square usually espouses conventional values and wants to follow the rules; the life rejects prison authority and is a rebel; the cool is aloof, manipulates the environment, and does not participate in prison life.[111]

Like men, female inmates must adjust to the prison experience. Female inmates first go through a period in which they deny the reality of their situation. Then comes a period of anger over the circumstances that led to their incarceration; during this phase, they begin to accept the circumstances of their imprisonment. A third stage finds female inmates greatly depressed because they can no longer deny that they are in prison to stay. Many female inmates eventually find reason to hope that their lives will improve.[112]

Daily life in the women's prison community is also somewhat different from that in male institutions. For one thing, women usually do not present the immediate physical danger to staff and fellow inmates that many male prisoners do. For another, the rigid, antiauthority

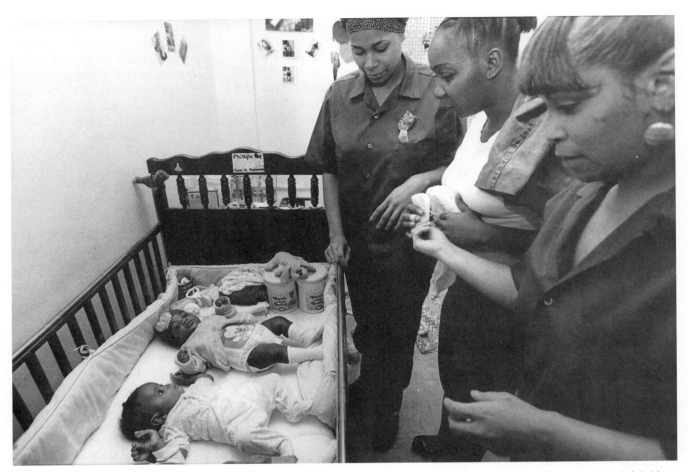

Female inmates in a New York prison are allowed to raise their infants in a special maternity ward. Inmates are now allowed to keep their babies for only twelve months. Should this privilege be expanded to the entire sentence?

inmate social code found in many male institutions does not exist in female prisons. Despite the fact that they present less threat, female inmates are more often controlled with mood-altering drugs than male inmates.[113]

Confinement for women, however, may produce severe anxiety and anger because they are separated from families and loved ones and unable to function in normal female roles. Low self-esteem is a major problem among female inmates.[114] Unlike men, who direct their anger outward, female prisoners may revert to more self-destructive acts to cope with their problems. Female inmates are perhaps more likely than males to mutilate their own bodies and attempt suicide. It is not surprising, considering these circumstances, that female inmates are more likely to be treated with mood-altering drugs and placed in psychiatric care, while male inmates' adjustment difficulties are viewed as disciplinary problems.[115]

One common form of adaptation to prison employed by women is the surrogate family. This group contains masculine and feminine figures acting as fathers and mothers; some even act as children and take on the role of either brother or sister. Formalized marriages and divorces may be conducted. Sometimes, multiple roles are held by one inmate, so that a "sister" in one family may "marry" and become the "wife" in another.[116]

The special needs of female inmates must be addressed by correctional authorities. Many institutions have inadequate facilities to care for women who are pregnant when they enter prison or become pregnant during their prison stay.[117] Surveys also indicate that the prison experience does little to prepare women to re-enter the work force after their sentence has been completed. Gender stereotypes still shape vocational opportunities. Female inmates are trained for "women's roles," such as child rearing, and not given the programming to make successful adjustments in the community.[118]

Correctional Treatment

Correctional treatment has been an integral part of prison life since Z. R. Brockway introduced it as part of the daily regime at the Elmira Reformatory.

Today, more than 90 percent of all prison inmates participate in some form of program or activity after admission.[119] There are many approaches to treatment. Some, based on a medical model, rely heavily on counseling and clinical therapy. Others attempt to prepare inmates for reintegration into the community; they rely on work release, vocational training, and educational opportunities. Others stress self-help through 12-step or Alcoholics Anonymous programs. The most popular programs have a religious theme and involve Bible clubs and other pious activities. Although it is beyond the scope of this book to describe the vast number of correctional treatment programs, a few important types will be discussed.

Therapy and Counseling.

The most traditional type of treatment in prison involves psychological counseling and therapy. Counseling programs exist in almost every major institution. Some stress individual treatment with psychotherapy or other techniques. However, because of lack of resources, it is more common for group methods to be used. Some groups are led by trained social workers, counselors, or therapists; others rely on lay personnel as leaders.

Group counseling in prison usually tries to stimulate inmates' self-awareness and their ability to deal with everyday problems.[120] A wide variety of innovative psychological treatment approaches have been used in the prison system: *behavior therapy* uses tokens to reward conformity and help develop positive behavior traits; *reality therapy* is meant to help satisfy individuals' needs to feel worthwhile to themselves and others; *transactional analysis* encourages inmates to identify the different aspects of their personalities and to be their own therapists; *milieu therapy* uses the social structure and processes of the institution to influence the behavior patterns of offenders.[121]

Educational Programs.

The first prison treatment programs were educational. A prison school was opened at the Walnut Street Prison in 1784. Elementary courses were offered in New York's prison system in 1801 and in Pennsylvania's in 1844. An actual school system was established in Detroit's House of Corrections in 1870, and Elmira Reformatory opened a vocational trade school in 1876.

Today, most institutions provide some type of educational program. At some prisons, inmates are given the opportunity to obtain a high school diploma through equivalency exams or general educational development (GED) certificates. Some prisons provide college courses, usually staffed by teachers who work at nearby institutions. Nearly one-half of all inmates have received some form of academic education, and about one-third have had vocational training since entering prison.[122]

Vocational Rehabilitation.

Most prisons operate numerous vocational training programs designed to help inmates develop skills for securing employment on their release. In the past, the traditional prison industries of laundry and license plate manufacture failed to provide these skills. Today, programs stress such marketable skills as dental laboratory work, computer programming, auto repair, and radio and television work.

Unfortunately, prisons often have difficulty obtaining the necessary equipment to run meaningful programs. Therefore, many have adopted *work furlough* programs that allow inmates to work in the community during the day and return to the institution at night.

Several state correctional departments also have instituted prerelease and postrelease employment services. Employment program staff members assess inmates' backgrounds to determine their abilities, interests, goals, and capabilities. They also help them create job plans (which are essential to their receiving early release, or parole) and help them obtain placements in sheltered environments to help inmates bridge the gap between institutions and the outside world; services include job placement, skill development, family counseling, and legal and medical attention.

Private Industry in Prisons.

A new version of vocational rehabilitation is the development of private industry in prison. This can take many different forms, including private citizens sitting on prison industry boards, private vendors marketing goods from prison industry, inmates manufacturing and marketing their own goods, private management of state-owned prison industry, franchising within the prison system in which manufactured goods are marketed under license from a private firm and privately owned industries on prison grounds employing inmate labor.

Another approach is the **free-venture programs** developed in the 1980s in Minnesota, Kansas, and other areas with the aid of the federal government.[123] The programs involve businesses set up by private entrepreneurs off prison grounds that contract with state officials to hire inmates at free-market wages and produce goods that are competitively marketed. Inmates can be fired by being sent back to the general prison population.

On paper, private industry in prison is quite attractive. It teaches inmates skills in usually desirable commercial areas, such as data processing. It increases employment opportunities on the outside in areas where the ex-offender can earn enough to forgo a life of crime. Various evaluations of the programs have given them high marks. However, private industry programs have so far used relatively few inmates. It is questionable whether they could be applied to the general prison population, which contains many people with educational deficiencies and a history of substance abuse. Yet a policy of "full employment" in prison may be one way of reducing future recidivism.[124]

Does Rehabilitation Work?

Despite the variety and number of treatment programs in operation, some question remains about their effectiveness. In their often-cited research, Robert Martinson and his associates found that a majority of treatment programs were failures.[125] Martinson found in a national study that, with few exceptions, rehabilitative efforts seemed to have no appreciable effect on recidivism.

Martinson's work was followed by efforts that found, embarrassingly, that some high-risk offenders were more likely to commit crimes after they had been placed in treatment programs than before the onset of rehabilitation efforts.[126] Even California's highly touted community treatment program, which matched youthful offenders and counselors on the basis of their psychological profiles, was found by Paul Lerman to exert negligible influence on its clients.[127] Recent analysis of correctional treatment programs have reaffirmed the inadequacy of correctional treatment efforts.[128]

These less-than-enthusiastic reviews of correctional rehabilitation helped develop a more conservative view of corrections, which, according to such advocates as Charles Logan, means that prisons are viewed as places of incapacitation and confinement; their purpose is punishment and not treatment.[129] Current social policy stresses eliminating the nonserious offender from the correctional system while increasing the sentences of serious, violent offenders. The development of lengthy mandatory and determinate sentences to punish serious offenders and the simultaneous evolution of alternative sanctions to limit the nonserious offender's interface with the system are demonstrable manifestations of this view.

Some criminologists continue to challenge the "nothing works" philosophy.[130] For example, D. A. Andrews and his associates have suggested that treatment can be effective if treatment modalities are matched with the needs of inmates.[131] So while the concept of correctional treatment is often questioned, many criminologists still believe that it is possible that some inmates can be helped within prison walls.

Prison Violence

One of the more significant problems facing prison administrators is the constant fear of interpersonal and collective violence. Hans Toch, an expert on violence, has said:

> Jails and prisons . . . have a climate of violence which has no free-world counterpart. Inmates are terrorized by other inmates and spend years in fear of harm. Some inmates request segregation, others lock themselves in and some are hermits by choice. Many inmates injure themselves.[132]

What are the causes of prison violence? Though there is no single explanation for either collective or individual violence, theories abound. One position holds that inmates are often violence-prone individuals who have always used force to get their own way. In the crowded, dehumanizing world of the prison, it is not surprising that they resort to force to exert their dominance over others.[133]

A second view is that prisons convert people to violence by their inhumane conditions, including overcrowding, depersonalization, and threats of homosexual rape. One social scientist, Charles Silberman, suggests that even in the most humane prisons, life is a constant put-down and prison conditions threaten the inmates' sense of self-worth; that violence is a consequence of these conditions is not surprising.[134]

Still another view is that prison violence stems from mismanagement, lack of strong security, and inadequate control by prison officials.[135] This view has contributed to the escalated use of solitary confinement in recent years as a means of control. Also contributing to prison violence is the changing prison population. Younger, more violent inmates, who often have been members of teenage gangs, now dominate prison life. The old code of "do your own time" and "be a right guy" may be giving way to a prison culture dominated by gangs, whose very nature breeds violence.

Prison violence may also be associated with the overcrowding caused by rapid increases in the prison population. Data from Texas indicate that a large increase in the inmate population, unmatched by creation of new space, was associated with increases in suicide, violent death, and disciplinary action rates. The largest prisons in Texas (with populations of over 1,600) demonstrated violence rates higher than the smaller prisons (800 or less).[136]

Prison Riots.

Sometimes prison violence takes the form of large-scale rioting. The American Correctional Association gives these reasons for such prison flare-ups: (1) unnatural institutional environment; (2) antisocial characteristics of inmates; (3) inept management; (4) inadequate personnel practices; (5) inadequate facilities; (6) insufficient constructive, meaningful activity; (7) insufficient legitimate rewards; (8) basic social values and unrest in the larger community; (9) inadequate finances; and (10) inequities and complexities in the criminal justice system.[137] In a more recent analysis, Randy Martin and Sherwood Zimmerman have identified the following causes of prison riots:

1. Environmental conditions—Poor physical conditions make the prison a "time bomb" waiting to go off.
2. Spontaneity—Some spark, a fight between gangs, escalates into a general prison disturbance.
3. Conflict—A repressive administration denies inmate rights, which leads to violence.
4. Collective behavior and social control—Informal social control mechanisms, such as inmate leaders and councils, break down and violence escalates.
5. Power vacuum—A conflict between guards and the administration creates an anomic condition exploited by the inmates.
6. Rising expectations—Inmates expect increased freedom and better conditions. When these are not met, their frustration leads to collective violence.[138]

Each of these conditions can trigger collective prison disturbances. In an analysis of the similarities between the two worst prison riots of recent times, Attica in 1971 and New Mexico State in 1980, the following phenomena were observed and seem typical of the conditions that produce prison disturbances:

- Prisoners felt they were not being treated like human beings.
- Line officers were unprepared; they were not informed of plans and regulations at the prison.
- Administrators lacked consistency. Their policies lacked stability.
- Legislators were insensitive to the needs of the penal system.

- The public and media were unconcerned about the corrections system.[139]

Corrections and the Rule of Law

For many years, the nation's courts did not interfere in the operation of prisons, maintaining what is called the **hands-off doctrine.** The judiciary's reluctance to interfere in prison matters was based on (1) the belief that it lacked technical competence in prison administration, (2) society's general apathy toward the prison, and (3) the belief that prisoners' complaints involved privileges rather than rights.[140] Consequently, prisoners had no legal rights and were "slaves of the state."

The hands-off doctrine was lifted in the 1960s. General concern with civil and human rights, an increasing militancy in the prison population, and the reformist nature of the Warren Court created a climate conducive to reform.

The first area of change came in the First Amendment right of freedom of religion. The Black Muslims, a politically active religious organization led by Elijah Muhammed of Chicago, recruited many members in the prison system (including Malcolm X). Using their legal and financial clout, the Muslims litigated claims that their followers were being denied the right to worship according to their faith. A series of Supreme Court cases upheld the Muslims' freedom of religion and opened the door to other issues of inmates' rights.[141]

Today, most litigation is brought under the federal Civil Rights Act (28 U.S.C. 1982), which states:

> Every person who, under color of any statute, ordinance, regulation, custom, or usage of any State or Territory subjects, or causes to be subjected, any citizen of the United States or other person within the jurisdiction thereof to the deprivation of any rights, privileges, or immunities secured by the Constitution and laws shall be liable to the party injured in an action at law, suit in equity or other proper proceeding for redress.

Although the Supreme Court has recently limited the methods by which inmates can seek release or redress, it has consistently upheld the rights of inmates to seek legal remedies. Some of the more important areas of prisoners' rights will be briefly discussed.

Freedom of Press and Speech.

The courts have ruled that inmates retain freedom of speech and press unless correctional authorities can show that it interferes with or threatens institutional freedom. For example, in *Procunier v. Martinez,* a court ruled that an inmate's mail could be censored only if there existed substantial belief that its contents would threaten security. However, in *Saxbe v. Washington Post*, the right of an inmate to grant press interviews was limited, since the Supreme Court argued that such interviews would enhance the reputations of particular inmates and jeopardize the authorities' desire to treat everyone equally.[143]

Medical Rights. After many years of indifference, inmates have only recently been given the right to secure proper medical attention. To gain their medical rights, prisoners have generally resorted to class action suits to ask courts to require adequate medical care.[144]

In 1976, after reviewing the legal principles established over the preceding 20 years, the Supreme Court, in *Estelle v. Gamble,* clearly stated the inmate's right to have medical care:[145]

> Deliberate indifference to serious medical needs of prisoners constitutes the "unnecessary and wanton infliction of pain," . . . proscribed by the Eighth Amendment. This is true whether the indifference is manifested by prison doctors in their response to the prisoner's needs or by prison guards in intentionally denying or delaying access to medical care or intentionally interfering with the treatment once prescribed. [146]

Lower courts will now decide, case by case, whether "deliberate indifference" actually occurred.

Cruel and Unusual Punishment and Overall Conditions. Prisoners have long suffered severe physical punishments in prison, ranging from whipping to extended periods of solitary confinement. The courts have held that such treatment is unconstitutional when it:

- Degrades the dignity of human beings.[147]

- Is more severe than the offense for which it has been given.[148]

- Shocks the general conscience and is fundamentally unfair.[149]

The courts have also ruled on the necessity for maintaining the general prison system in a humane manner. For example, in 1970, the entire prison system in Arkansas was declared unconstitutional because its practices of overt physical punishment were ruled to be in violation of the Eighth Amendment.[150]

In *Rhodes v. Chapman,*[151] the Supreme Court upheld the practice of double-bunking two or more inmates in a small cell (50 square feet). "Conditions of confinement," the court argued, "must not involve the wanton and unnecessary infliction of pain nor may they be grossly disproportionate to the severity of the crime warranting imprisonment," but "conditions that cannot be said to be cruel and unusual under contemporary standards are not unconstitutional. To the extent that such conditions are restrictive and even harsh, they are part of the penalty that criminal offenders pay for their offenses against society."[152]

While *Rhodes* limited inmates' rights to better living conditions, a number of state cases, especially *Estelle v. Ruiz,* have put corrections departments on notice that overcrowding will not be tolerated and no new inmates can be admitted to prison unless the number of inmates is reduced.[153]

☰ Parole

Parole is the planned release and community supervision of incarcerated offenders before the expiration of their prison sentences. It is usually considered to be a way of completing a prison sentence in the community and is not the same as a pardon; the paroled offender can be legally recalled to serve the remainder of his or her sentence in an institution if the parole authorities deem the offender's adjustment inadequate or if the offender commits another crime while on parole.

The decision to parole is determined by statutory requirement and usually involves the completion of a minimum sentence. Parole is granted by a state *parole board,* a body of men and women who review cases and determine whether an offender has been rehabilitated sufficiently to deal with the outside world. The board also dictates the specific parole rules a parolee must obey. Some states with determinate sentencing statutes, such as Indiana and California, do not use parole boards but release inmates at the conclusion of their maximum term less accumulated good time. This is referred to as *mandatory* parole release.

In states where discretionary parole is used, the decision is made at a **parole grant hearing.** There, the full board or a subcommittee reviews information, may meet with the offender, and then decides whether the parole applicant has a reasonable chance of succeeding outside of prison. Candidates for parole may be chosen by statutory eligibility on the basis of time served in relation to their sentences. In most jurisdictions, good time reduces the minimum sentence and therefore hastens eligibility for parole. In making its decision, the board will consider the inmate's offense, time served, evidence of adjustment, and opportunities on the outside.

To help these parole decision makers, parole prediction tables have been developed.[154] These tables correlate personal information on inmates who were released in the past with their rates of rearrest. The best known predictive device is the Salient Factor Score Index. The salient factor score includes age, type of offense, prior parole revocations, history of heroin use, and employment background.[155]

The Parolee in the Community

Once community release has begun, the offender is supervised by a trained staff of parole officers who help the offender adjust to the community and search for employment as they monitor behavior and activities to ensure that the offender conforms to the conditions of parole.

Parolees are subject to a strict standardized or personalized set of rules that guide their behavior and set limits on their activities. If at any time these rules are violated, the offender can be returned to the institution to serve the remainder of the sentence; this is known as a technical parole violation. Inmates released in determinate sentencing states can have part or all of their good time revoked if they violate the conditions of their release.

Parole can also be revoked if the offender commits a second offense; the offender may also be tried and sentenced for this crime. The Supreme Court has granted parolees due process rights similar to those of probationers at revocation hearings.

Parole is viewed as an act of grace on the part of the criminal justice system. It is a manifestation of the policy of returning the offender to the community. There are two conflicting sides to parole, however; on one hand, the paroled offender is given a break and allowed to serve part of the sentence in the community; on the other hand, the sentiment exists that parole is a privilege and not a right and that the parolee is in reality a dangerous criminal who must be carefully watched and supervised. The conflict between the treatment and enforcement aspects of parole has not been reconciled by the criminal justice system, and the parole process still contains elements of both orientations.

About half a million people are on parole in the United States, and the number has been rising along with the prison population.[156]

How Effective Is Parole?

Conservative thinkers criticize parole because it allows possibly dangerous offenders into the community before the completion of their sentence. Since parole decision making relies on human judgment, it is quite possible that dangerous offenders, who should actually have remained inside a secure facility, are released into society while others who would probably make a good adjustment to the community are denied release.

The evaluation of parole effectiveness has produced some disturbing results. A federal study of 16,000 men and women released in 11 states in 1983 found that within three years, 63 percent had been rearrested for a felony or serious misdemeanor, 47 percent had been convicted of a new crime, and 41 percent had been sent back to prison.[157] The inmates most likely to fail on parole have extensive prior arrests; the study found that 5 percent of the inmates released on parole had 45 or more prior arrests! The inmates most likely to be rearrested shared the following characteristics: released at age 24 or younger; more than seven prior arrests; prior escape attempt; prior parole revocation; committed robbery, burglary, or property offenses; first arrested at a relatively young age; prior drug and violent crime arrest.

The specter of recidivism is especially frustrating to the American public: it is so difficult to apprehend and successfully prosecute criminal offenders that it seems foolish to grant them early release so they can prey on more victims. This problem is exacerbated when the parolee is a chronic offender who has engaged in frequent and repeat criminal acts.

Technical Violations.   Do many parolees return to prison because they violated the rules of parole, such as failing to stay in the jurisdiction or keep a job? A study conducted by the National Center on Institutions and Alternatives in ten states, including California, Florida, and Ohio, found that 15,400 people were incarcerated for technical parole violations, which amounted to 7 percent of their prison population; in some states, technical parole violators made up 20 percent of the prison population.[158]

In sum, many parolees are in fact returned to prison for technical violations. It is therefore likely that one of the reasons for prison overcrowding is the large number of technical parole violators who are returned within three years of their release. If overcrowding is to be successfully dealt with, a more realistic parole violation policy may have to be developed in areas where the correctional system is under stress.

Should Parole Be Abolished?

There have been many attacks on early release via parole and calls to eliminate the practice. The criticism leveled against parole is threefold:

1. The procedures that control the decision to grant parole are vague and have not been controlled by due process considerations. Consequently, some inmates may be subject to the unfair denial of parole, while some who are undeserving may benefit.

2. It is beyond the capacity of parole authorities to either predict who will make a successful adjustment on parole or accurately monitor parolees' behavior in the community.

3. It is unjust to decide whether to release an individual from prison based on what we expect that person to do in the future. After all, we have no way of determining that accurately.[159]

Beyond these considerations, the parole process has been criticized as heightening the inmate's sense of injustice and powerlessness in the face of an omnipotent prison administration that has absolute control over the release date. As one prison expert, David Fogel, suggests:

> Parole board decisions are also non-reviewable and are not hammered out in an adversary clash; rather they are five to fifteen minute sessions with members frequently using a combination of whim, caprice, and arbitrariness.[160]

Some states—Illinois, Maine, Indiana, and New Mexico—have abolished discretionary parole completely. Others, such as California, have retained parole but use it as a postrelease supervisory authority for inmates who have completed their prison sentences. Monitored by the community release board, inmates can have their good time revoked for behavioral indiscretions and can therefore be returned to prison. Because of these changes, the percentage of inmates leaving prison on parole has declined dramatically; in 1977, 72 percent received discretionary parole, a figure that dropped to about 40 percent in 1990.

The abolition of parole likely will shift the burden of discretion from the prison authorities to the district attorney (who charges the defendants and conducts plea bargains), the judge (who sentences), and the prison authorities, who control the awarding of good time. Of course, the inmate's sense of frustration might still remain, and sentencing disparity could still occur. Abolishing parole can hurt prison discipline and increase overcrowding. Despite these factors, the anti-parole movement probably will continue in the years ahead, especially now that the federal government's new criminal code replaces parole with determinate sentences.

≡ Summary

Corrections involve the punishment, treatment, and incapacitation of convicted criminal offenders. Methods of punishing offenders have undergone many changes through history. At first, fines were levied to compensate the victims and their families for losses. Then, cruel corporal and capital punishments were developed. The mercantile system and the development of overseas colonies created the need for labor, so slavery and forced labor began to replace physical punishments. In the late eighteenth century, the death penalty began to be used once again.

Reformers pushed for alternatives to harsh, brutal, physical punishment. The prison developed as an alternative that promised to reform and rehabilitate offenders. However, early institutions were brutal places featuring silence, corporal punishment, work details, and warehousing of prisoners. Around the turn of the century, reformers began to introduce such measures as educational training and counseling for inmates.

Today, corrections can be divided into four components—community-based corrections, jails, prisons, and parole programs.

Many convicted offenders are treated in the community. Some are put on probation under the supervision of local probation departments. If they obey the rules of probation, they are allowed to serve their sentences in the community. A new development is intermediate sanctions, including fines, forfeiture, intensive probation supervision, house arrest, electronic monitoring, and community-based correction facilities. These programs fall somewhere between placement in a closed correctional institution and the freedom of probation. Despite their promise, the effectiveness of alternative corrections methods has not been adequately tested.

The jail is the second element of corrections. It houses misdemeanant offenders serving their sentences and both felons and misdemeanants awaiting trial. The jail is a sore spot in the criminal justice system, because jails are usually old and dilapidated and lack rehabilitation programs.

Prisons are used to house convicted felony offenders. Recently, shifts in criminal justice philosophy and the passage of laws requiring mandatory sentences have caused a large increase in the U.S. prison population and consequent overcrowding.

Prisons are total institutions. Inmates must adjust to a new regime that controls every aspect of their lives. Prison is a violent, stressful place with its own unique subculture and language.

Various rehabilitation devices are used in the prison system, including counseling, educational programs, and vocational training. However, critics charge that these methods do not seem to work. Consequently, the most recent philosophy to dominate the justice system holds that prisons are places of punishment and incapacitation and not treatment.

In the past 20 years, prisoners have been awarded some legal rights by the nation's courts, including rights to medical treatment, freedom of religion, procedural due process, and correspondence with the media.

The fourth component of corrections is aftercare or parole. Parole officers supervise inmates in the community while they complete their sentences. Recently, parole has been under attack; four states have abolished the practice. Flat and mandatory sentences without parole are viewed as promoting fairness and ending sentencing disparity.

≡ KEY TERMS

capital punishment	split sentencing
corporal punishment	shock probation
poor laws	intensive probation
Walnut Street Prison	supervision
Auburn system	home confinement
contract system	electronic monitoring
convict-lease system	shock incarceration
state account system	boot camps
Z. R. Brockway	the hole
probation	inmate subculture
intermediate sanction	social code
technical violation	prisonization
day fines	importation model
forfeiture	free-venture programs
monetary restitution	hands-off doctrine
community service	parole
restitution	parole grant hearing

≡ NOTES

1. Edmund McGarrell, "Institutional Theory and the Stability of a Conflict Model of Incarceration Rate," *Justice Quarterly* 10 (1993): 7–28.

2. William Selke, *Prisons in Crisis* (Bloomington: Indiana University Press, 1993), p. 139.

3. Graeme Newman, *The Punishment Response* (Philadelphia: J. B. Lippincott, 1978), p. 13.

4. Among the most helpful sources for this section are Benedict Alper, *Prisons Inside-Out* (Cambridge, Mass.: Ballinger, 1974); Gustave de Beaumont and Alexis de Tocqueville, *On the Penitentiary System in the United States and Its Application in France* (Carbondale: Southern Illinois University Press, 1964); Orlando Lewis, *The Development of American Prisons and Prison Customs 1776–1845* (Montclair, N.J.: Patterson-Smith, 1967); Leonard Orland, ed., *Justice, Punishment and Treatment* (New York: Free Press, 1973); J. Goebel, *Felony and Misdemeanor* (Philadelphia: University of Pennsylvania Press, 1976); Georg Rusche and Otto Kircheimer, *Punishment and Social Structure* (New York: Russell and Russell, 1939); Samuel Walker, *Popular Justice* (New York: Oxford University Press, 1980); Newman, *The Punishment Response.*

5. Rusche and Kircheimer, *Punishment and Social Structure,* p. 9.

6. Ibid., p. 19.

7. Marvin Wolfgang, "Crime and Punishment in Renaissance Florence," *Journal of Criminal Law and Criminology* 81 (1990): 567–84.

8. G. Ives, *A History of Penal Methods* (Montclair, N.J.: Patterson-Smith, 1970).

9. Leon Radzinowicz, *A History of English Criminal Law,* vol. 1 (London: Stevens, 1943), p. 5.

10. Newman, *The Punishment Response,* p. 139.

11. Walker, *Popular Justice,* p. 34.

12. Lewis, *Development of American Prisons and Prison Customs,* p. 17.

13. Ibid., p. 29.

14. Alexis Durham III, "Social Control and Imprisonment during the American Revolution: Newgate of Connecticut," *Justice Quarterly* 7 (1990): 293–324.

15. Beaumont and de Tocqueville, *On the Penitentiary System in the United States,* p. 49.

16. Orland, *Justice, Punishment and Treatment,* p. 143.

17. Walker, *Popular Justice,* p. 70.

18. Ibid., p. 71.

19. See Z. R. Brockway, "The Ideal of a True Prison System for a State," in *Transactions of the National Congress on Penitentiary and Reformatory Discipline,* reprint ed. (Washington, D.C.: American Correctional Association, 1970), pp. 38–65.

20. This section relies heavily on David Rothman, *Conscience and Convenience* (Boston: Little, Brown, 1980). See also David Rothman, *The Discovery of the Asylum* (Boston: Little, Brown, 1970).

21. Ibid., p. 23.

22. Ibid., p. 133.

23. See, generally, Jameson Doig, *Criminal Corrections: Ideals and Realities* (Lexington, Mass.: Lexington Books,

1983).

24. See, generally, Chris Eskridge, Richard Seiter, and Eric Carlson, "Community Based Corrections: From the Community to the Community," in *Critical Issues in Corrections,* ed. V. Webb and R. Roberg (St. Paul: West Publishing, 1981), pp. 171–203.

25. Louis Jankowski, *Probation and Parole, 1989* (Washington, D.C.: Bureau of Justice Statistics, 1990).

26. H. Allen, E. Carlson, and E. Parks, *Critical Issues in Adult Probation* (Washington, D.C.: U.S. Government Printing Office, 1979), p. 47.

27. Ibid.

28. Patricia Harris, "Client Managment Classification and Prediction of Probation Outcomes," *Crime and Delinquency* 40 (1994): 154–74.

29. Kit Van Stelle, Elizabeth Mauser, and D. Paul Moberg, "Recidivism to the Criminal Justice System of Substance-Abusing Offenders Diverted into Treatment," *Crime and Delinquency* 40 (1994): 175–96.

30. See, generally, Patrick McAnany, Doug Thomson, and David Fogel, *Probation and Justice: Reconsideration of Mission* (Cambridge, Mass.: Oelgeschlager, Gunn and Hain, 1984).

31. Todd Clear and Edward Latessa, "Probation Officers' Roles in Intensive Supervision: Surveillance versus Treatment," *Justice Quarterly* 10 (1993): 440–62.

32. *Gagnon v. Scarpelli,* 411 U.S. 778, 93 S.Ct. 1756, 36 L.Ed.2d 655 (1973).

33. Joan Petersilia, Susan Turner, James Kahan, and Joyce Peterson, *Granting Felons Probation: Public Risks and Alternatives* (Santa Monica, Calif.: Rand Corporation, 1985).

34. Patrick Langan and Mark Cuniff, *Recidivism of Felons on Probation, 1986–1989* (Washington, D.C.: Bureau of Justice Statistics, 1992).

35. Ibid.

36. Michael Geerken and Hennessey Hayes, "Probation and Parole: Public Risk and the Future of Incarceration Alternatives," *Criminology* 31 (1993): 549–64.

37. Selke, *Prisons in Crisis,* p. 17.

38. For a thorough review, see James Byrne, Arthur Lurigio, and Joan Petersilia, eds., *Smart Sentencing: The Emergence of Intermediate Sanctions* (Newbury Park, Calif.: Sage, 1992).

39. Allen Beck, *Recidivism of Prisoners Released in 1983* (Washington, D.C.: Bureau of Justice Statistics, 1989).

40. Michael Tonry and Richard Will, *Intermediate Sanctions,* Preliminary Report to the National Institute of Justice (Washington, D.C.: National Institute of Justice, 1988), p. 6.

41. Ibid., p. 8.

42. Ben Crouch, "Is Incarceration Really Worse? Analysis of Offenders' Preferences for Prison over Probation," *Justice Quarterly* 10 (1993): 67–88.

43. David Pauly and Carolyn Friday, "Drexel's Crumbling Defense," *Newsweek,* 19 December 1988, p. 44.

44. George Cole, Barry Mahoney, Marlene Thorton, and Roger Hanson, *The Practices and Attitudes of Trial Court Judges Regarding Fines as a Criminal Sanction* (Washington, D.C.: U.S. Government Printing Office, 1987).

45. "'Day Fines' Being Tested in a New York City Court," *Criminal Justice Newsletter,* 1 September 1988, pp. 4–5.

46. Cole, Mahoney, Thorton, and Hanson, *The Practices and Attitudes of Trial Court Judges Regarding Fines as a Criminal Sanction.*

47. C. Yorke, *Some Consideration on the Law of Forfeiture for High Treason* 26 (2d ed. 1746), cited in David Freid, "Rationalizing Criminal Forfeiture," *Journal of Criminal Law and Criminology* 79 (1988): 328–436 at 329.

48. For a general review, see Robert Carter, Jay Cocks, and Daniel Glazer, "Community Service: A Review of the Basic Issues, *Federal Probation* 51 (1987): 4–11.

49. For a further analysis of restitution, see Larry Siegel, "Court Ordered Victim-Restitution: An Overview of Theory and Action," *New England Journal of Prison Law* 5 (1979): 135–50.

50. Peter Schneider, Anne Schneider, and William Griffith, *Two-Year Report on the National Evaluation of the Juvenile Restitution Initiative: An Overview of Program Performance* (Eugene, Ore.: Institute of Policy Analysis, 1982); Anne Schneider, "Restitution and Recidivism Rates of Juvenile Offenders: Four Experimental Studies," *Criminology* 24 (1936): 533–52.

51. Michael Block and William Rhodes, *The Impact of Federal Sentencing Guidelines* (Washington, D.C.: National Institute of Justice, 1987).

52. Lawrence Greenfeld, *Probation and Parole 1984* (Washington, D.C.: Bureau of Justice Statistics, 1985), p. 2.

53. Harry Allen, Chris Eskridge, Edward Latessa, and Gennaro Vito, *Probation and Parole in America* (New York: Free Press, 1985), p. 88.

54. Sue Mahan, "An 'Orgy of Brutality' at Attica and the 'Killing Crowd' at Santa Fe: A Comparison of Prison Riots," in *Coping with Imprisonment,* ed., Nicolette Parisi (Beverly Hills: Sage, 1982), p. 75.

55. James Byrne, Arthur Lurigio, and Christopher Baird, *The Effectiveness of the New Intensive Supervision Programs,* Research in Corrections Series, vol. 2, No. 2 (preliminary unpublished draft; Washington, D.C.: National Institute of Corrections, 1989), p. 16.

56. Stephen Gettinger, "Intensive Supervision, Can It Rehabilitate Probation?" *Corrections* 9 (April 1983): 7–18.

57. James Byrne, "The Control Controversy: A Preliminary Examination of Intensive Probation Supervision Programs in the United States," *Federal Probation* 50 (1986): 4–16.

58. Billie Erwin and Lawrence Bennett, *New Dimensions in Probation: Georgia's Experience with Intensive Probation Supervision (IPS)* (Washington, D.C: National Institute of Justice, 1987).

59. Michael Agopian, "The Impact of Intensive Supervision Probation on Gang-Drug Offenders," *Criminal Justice Policy Review* 4 (1990): 214–22.

60. Peter Jones, "Expanding the Use of Non-Custodial Sentencing Options: An Evaluation of the Kansas Community Corrections Act," *Howard Journal* 29 (1990): 114–29.

61. Langan and Cuniff, *Recidivism of Felons on Probation, 1986–1989,* pp. 1–4.

62. Joan Petersilia, "An Evaluation of Intensive Probation in California," *Journal of Criminal Law and Criminology* 82 (1992): 610–58; idem, "Comparing Intensive and Regular Supervision for High-Risk Probationers: Early Results from an Experiment in California," *Crime and Delinquency* 36 (1990): 87–111; see also, Joan Petersilia, "Conditions That Permit Intensive Supervision Programs to Survive," *Crime and Delinquency* 36 (1990): 126–45.

63. Joan Petersilia, *Expanding Options for Criminal Sentencing* (Santa Monica, Calif.: Rand Corporation, 1987), p. 32.

64. Ibid., p. 28.

65. Marc Renzema and David Skelton, "Use of Electronic Monitoring in the United States: 1989 Update," *NIJ Reports,* November/December 1990, pp. 9–13.

66. Ibid., p. 13.

67. Kenneth Moran and Charles Lindner, "Probation and the Hi-Technology Revolution: Is Reconceptualization of the Traditional Probation Officer Role Model Inevitable?" *Criminal Justice Review* 3 (1987): 25–32.

68. For an extensive review, see Frank Cullen, "Control in the Community: The Limits of Reform" (Paper presented at the annual meeting of the International Association of Residential and Community Alternatives, Philadelphia, 1993).

69. Terry Baumer, Michael Maxfield, and Robert Mendelsohn, "A Comparative Analysis of Three Electronically Monitored Home Detention Programs," *Justice Quarterly* 10 (1993): 121–42.

70. J. Robert Lilly, Richard Ball, G. David Curry, and John McMullen, "Electronic Monitoring of the Drunk Driver: A Seven-Year Study of the Home Confinement Alternative," *Crime and Delinquency* 39 (1993): 462–84.

71. Alexander Esteves, "Electronic Incarceration in Massachusetts: A Critical Analyis," *Social Justice* 17 (1991): 76–90.

72. James Byrne and Linda Kelly, *Restructuring Probation as an Intermediate Sanction: An Evaluation of the Massachussetts Intensive Probation Supervision Program* (Final Report to the National Institute of Justice, Research Program on the Punishment and Control of Offenders, 1989), p. 33.

73. See, for example, Dale Sechrest, "Prison 'Boot Camps' Do Not Measure Up," *Federal Probation* 53 (1989): 15–20.

74. Doris Layton Mackenzie and James Shaw, "The Impact of Shock Incarceration on Technical Violations and New Criminal Activities," *Justice Quarterly* 10 (1993): 463–87.

75. Doris Layton Mackenzie, "Boot Camp Prisons: Components, Evaluations, and Empirical Issues," *Federal Probation* 54 (1990): 44–52.

76. Doris Layton MacKenzie and Alex Piquero, "The Impact of Shock Incarceration Programs on Prison Crowding," *Crime and Delinquency* 40 (1994): 222–49.

77. Cullen, "Control in the Community: the Limits of Reform," p. 28.

78. Margaret Wilson, *The Crime of Punishment,* Life and Letter Series no. 64 (London: Jonathan Cape Ltd., 1934), p. 186.

79. Allen Beck, Thomas Bonczar, and Darrell Gilliard, *Jail Inmates 1992* (Washington, D.C.: Bureau of Justice Statistics, 1993).

80. See, generally, Daniel Kennedy, "A Theory of Suicide While in Police Custody," *Journal of Police Science and Administration* 12 (1984): 191–200.

81. Beck, Bonczar, and Gilliard, *Jail Inmates 1992,* p. 3.

82. Note, *Jail Administration Digest* 3 (1980): 4.

83. See Note, *Jail Administration Digest* 2 (1979): 6.

84. Bureau of Justice Statistics, *Prisons and Prisoners* (Washington, D.C.: U.S. Government Printing Office, 1982).

85. John DiIulio, *Private Prisons* (Washington, D.C.: U.S. Government Printing Office, 1988); Joan Mullen, *Corrections and the Private Sector* (Washington, D.C.: National Institute of Justice, 1984).

86. Charles Logan and Bill McGriff, "Comparing Costs of Public and Private Prisons: A Case Study," *NIJ Reports,* September/October 1989, pp. 2–8.

87. Philip Ethridge and James Marquart, "Private Prisons in Texas: The New Penology for Profit," *Justice Quarterly* 10 (1993): 29–48.

88. The data cited in this section is from Darrell Gilliard and Allen Beck, *Prisoners in 1993* (Washington, D.C.: Bureau of Justice Statistics, 1994).

89. Julia G. Hall, "Why Not Free Older Prisoners?," *Philadelphia Inquirer,* 11 January 1991, p. 19A.

90. Data here is taken from Allen Beck, Darrell Gilliard, Lawrence Greenfeld, Caroline Harlow, Thomas Hester, Louis Jankowski, Tracy Snell, James Stephan, and Danielle Morton, *Survey of State Prison Inmates, 1991* (Washington, D.C.: Bureau of Justice Statistics, 1993).

91. C. S. Lanier, "Affective States of Fathers in Prison," *Justice Quarterly* 10 (1993): 48–65.

92. See E. Goffman, "Characteristics of Total Institutions," in *Justice, Punishment and Treatment,* ed. Leonard Orland (New York: Free Press, 1973), pp. 153–58.

93. Gresham Sykes, *The Society of Captives* (Princeton, N.J.: Princeton University Press, 1958), pp. 79–82.

94. Nicolette Parisi, "The Prisoner's Pressures and Responses," in *Coping with Imprisonment,* ed. N. Parisi (Beverly Hills: Sage, 1982), pp. 9–16.

95. Daniel Lockwood, "The Contribution of Sexual Harassment to Stress and Coping in Confinement," in *Coping with Imprisonment,* ed. N. Parisi (Beverly Hills: Sage, 1982), p. 47.

96. Ibid.

97. Wilbert Rideau and Ron Wikberg, *Life Sentences: Rage and Survival Behind Bars* (New York: Times Books,

1992), pp. 78–80.

98. Sandra Gleason, "Hustling: The 'Inside' Economy of a Prison," *Federal Probation* 42 (1978): 32–39.

99. Ibid., p. 39.

100. Geoffrey Hunt, Stephanie Riegel, Tomas Morales, and Dan Waldorf, "Changes in Prison Culture: Prison Gangs and the Case of the 'Pepsi Generation'," *Social Problems* 40 (1993): 398–407.

101. James B. Jacobs, "The Killing Ground," *Newsweek*, 18 February 1980, p. 75.

102. Parisi, "The Prisoner's Pressures and Responses."

103. John Irwin, "Adaptation to Being Corrected: Corrections from the Convict's Perspective," in *Handbook of Criminology*, ed. Daniel Glazer (Chicago: Rand McNally, 1974), pp. 971–93.

104. Donald Clemmer, *The Prison Community* (New York: Holt, Rinehart & Winston, 1958).

105. Gresham Sykes, *The Society of Captives* (Princeton, N.J.: Princeton University Press, 1958), pp. 79–82.

106. Gresham Sykes and Sheldon Messinger, "The Inmate Social Code," in *The Sociology of Punishment and Corrections*, ed. Norman Johnston, Leonard Savitz, and Marvin Wolfgang (New York: John Wiley & Sons, 1970), pp. 401–408.

107. John Irwin and Donald Cressey, "Thieves, Convicts, and the Inmate Culture," *Social Problems* 10 (1962): 142–55.

108. Paul Gendreau, Marie-Claude Tellier, and J. Stephen Wormith, "Protective Custody: The Emerging Crisis within Our Prisons," *Federal Probation* 69 (1985): 55–64.

109. James B. Jacobs, *New Perspectives on Prisons and Imprisonment* (Ithaca, N.Y.: Cornell University Press, 1983); idem, "Street Gangs Behind Bars," *Social Problems* 21 (1974): 395–409; idem, "Race Relations and the Prison Subculture," in *Crime and Justice*, ed. N. Morris and M. Tonry (Chicago: University of Chicago Press, 1979), pp. 1–28.

110. Hunt, Riegel, Morales, and Waldorf, "Changes in Prison Culture," pp. 405–408.

111. Esther Hefferman, *Making It in Prison: The Square, the Cool and the Life* (New York: John Wiley, 1972).

112. Christina Jose-Kampfner, "Coming to Terms with Existential Death: An Analysis of Women's Adaptation to Life in Prison," *Social Justice* 17 (1991): 110–20.

113. Merry Morash, Robin Harr, and Lila Rucker, "A Comparison of Programming for Women and Men in U.S. Prison in the 1980's," *Crime and Delinquency* 40 (1994): 197–221.

114. Beverly Fletcher, Lynda Dixon Shaver, and Dreama Moon, *Women Prisoners: A Forgotten Population* (Westport, Conn.: Greenwood Press, 1993), chap. 3.

115. Ira Sommers and Deborah Baskin, "The Prescription of Psychiatric Medications in Prison: Psychiatric versus Labeling Perspectives," *Justice Quarterly* 7 (1990): 739–55.

116. Rose Giallombardo, *Society of Women: A Study of a Women's Prison* (New York: John Wiley, 1966), pp.

165–89.

117. John Woodredge and Kimberly Masters, "Confronting Problems Faced by Pregnant Inmates in State Prisons," *Crime and Delinquency* 39 (1993): 195–203.

118. Morash, Harr, and Rucker, "A Comparsion of Programming for Women and Men in U.S. Prison in the 1980's," pp. 214–17.

119. Beck, *Survey of State Prison Inmates, 1991*, p. 27.

120. See, generally, G. Kassebaum, D. Ward, and D. Wilner, "Group Counseling," in *Legal Process and Corrections*, ed. N. Johnston and L. Savitz (New York: John Wiley, 1982), pp. 255–70.

121. See William Glasser, *Reality Therapy* (New York: Harper & Row, 1965).

122. Beck, *Survey of State Prison Inmates*, p. 27.

123. See, generally, Michael Fedo, "Free Enterprise Goes to Prison," *Corrections* 7 (1981): 11–18.

124. Timothy Flanagan and Kathleen Maguire, "A Full Employment Policy for Prisons in the United States: Some Arguments, Estimates and Implications," *Journal of Criminal Justice* 21 (1993): 117–30.

125. D. Lipton, R. Martinson, and J. Wilks, *The Effectiveness of Correctional Treatment: A Survey of Treatment Evaluation Studies* (New York: Praeger, 1975).

126. Charles Murray and Louis Cox, *Beyond Probation: Juvenile Corrections and the Chronic Delinquent* (Beverly Hills: Sage, 1979).

127. Paul Lerman, *Community Treatment and Social Control* (Chicago: University of Chicago Press, 1975).

128. John Whitehead and Steven Lab, "A Meta-Analysis of Juvenile Correctional Treatment," *Journal of Research in Crime and Delinquency* 26 (1989): 276–95.

129. Charles Logan, *Well Kept: Comparing the Quality of Confinement in a Public and Private Prison* (Washington, D.C.: National Institute of Justice, 1991).

130. Francis Cullen and Karen Gilbert, *Reaffirming Rehabilitation* (Cincinnati: Anderson Publications, 1982).

131. D. A. Andrews, Ivan Zinger, Robert Hoge, James Bonta, Paul Gendreau, and Francis Cullen, "Does Correctional Treatment Work? A Clinically Relevant and Psychologically Informed Meta-Analysis," *Criminology* 28 (1990): 369–405; for an alternative view, see Steven Lab and John Whitehead, "From Nothing Works to the Appropriate Works: The Latest Stop on the Search for the Secular Grail," *Criminology* 28 (1990): 405–19.

132. Hans Toch, *Police, Prisons and the Problems of Violence* (Washington, D.C.: U.S. Government Printing Office, 1977), p. 53.

133. For a series of papers on the position, see A. Cohen, G. Cole, and R. Baily, eds., *Prison Violence* (Lexington, Mass.: Lexington Books, 1976).

134. Charles Silberman, *Criminal Violence, Criminal Justice* (New York: Vintage Books, 1978).

135. See Hans Toch, "Social Climate and Prison Violence," *Federal Probation* 42 (1978): 21–23.

136. Cited in G. McCain, V. Cox, and P. Paulus, *The Effect of*

Prison Crowding on Inmate Behavior (Washington, D.C.: U.S. Government Printing Office, 1981), p. vi.

137. American Correctional Association, *Riots and Disturbances in Correctional Institutions* (Washington, D.C.: American Correctional Association, 1970), p. 1.

138. Randy Martin and Sherwood Zimmerman, "A Typology of the Causes of Prison Riots and an Analytical Extension to the 1986 West Virginia Riot," *Justice Quarterly* 7 (1990): 711–37.

139. Sue Mahan, "An 'Orgy of Brutality' at Attica and the 'Killing Ground' at Santa Fe," in *Prison Violence in America,* ed. M. Braswell, S. Dillingham, and R. Montgomery (Cincinnati: Anderson, 1985), pp. 73–78.

140. National Advisory Commission on Criminal Justice Standards and Goals, *Volume on Corrections* (Washington, D.C.: U.S. Government Printing Office, 1973), p. 18.

141. See, for example, *Cooper v. Pate,* 378 U.S. 546 (1964).

142. *Procunier v. Martinez,* 416 U.S. 396 (1974).

143. *Saxbe v. Washington Post,* 41 L.Ed.2d 514 (1974).

144. *Newman v. Alabama,* 349 F.Supp. 278 (M.D.Ala., 1974).

145. *Estelle v. Gamble,* 429 U.S. 97 (1976).

146. 97 S.Ct. 291 (1976).

147. See, for example, *Trop v. Dulles,* 356 U.S. 86, 78 S.Ct. 590 (1958); see also *Furman v. Georgia,* 408 U.S. 238, 92 S.Ct. 2726, 33 L.Ed.2d 346 (1972).

148. See, for example, *Weems v. United States,* 217 U.S. 349, 30 S.Ct. 544, 54 L.Ed. 793 (1910).

149. See, for example, *Lee v. Tahash,* 352 F.2d 970 (8th Cir., 1965).

150. 309 F. Supp. 362 (E.D. Ark. 1970); aff'd 442 F.2d 304 (Ninth Cir., 1971).

151. *Rhodes v. Chapman,* 452 U.S. 337 (1981).

152. Ibid., 337.

153. *Estelle v. Ruiz,* 74-329 (E.D. Texas, 1980).

154. See Peter Hoffman and Lucille DeGostin, "Parole Decision–Making: Structuring Discretion," *Federal Probation* 38 (1974): 19–21.

155. Peter Hoffman and Barbara Stone-Meierhoefer, "Post-Release Arrest Experiences of Federal Prisoners: A Six Year Follow-Up," *Journal of Criminal Justice* 7 (1979): 193–216.

156. Jankowski, *Probation and Parole, 1989,* p. 3.

157. Allen Beck and Bernard Shipley, *Recidivism of Prisoners Released in 1983* (Washington, D.C.: Bureau of Justice Statistics, 1989).

158. "Study Finds Many in Prison for Technical Parole Violation," *Criminal Justice Newsletter,* 16 January 1986, p. 5.

159. Listed in Andrew Von Hirsch and Kathleen Hanrahan, *Abolish Parole?* (Washington, D.C.: U.S. Government Printing Office, 1978).

160. David Fogel, . . . *We are the Living Proof . . .: The Justice Model for Corrections* (Cincinnati: Anderson, 1979), p. 197.

Glossary

absolute deterrent A legal control measure designed to totally eliminate a particular criminal act.

Academy of Criminal Justice Sciences The society that serves to further the development of the criminal justice profession; its membership includes academics and practitioners involved in criminal justice.

access control A crime prevention technique that stresses target hardening through security measures, such as alarm systems, that make it more difficult for criminals to attack a target.

accountability system A way of dealing with police corruption by making superiors responsible for the behavior of their subordinates.

actus reus An illegal act. The *actus reus* can be an affirmative act, such as taking money or shooting someone, or a failure to act, such as failing to take proper precautions while driving a car.

adjudication The determination of guilt or innocence; a judgment concerning criminal charges. Most offenders plead guilty as charged. The remainder are adjudicated by a judge and a jury, some by a judge without a jury, and others are dismissed.

adversary system The procedure used to determine truth in the adjudication of guilt or innocence in which the defense (advocate for the accused) is pitted against the prosecution (advocate for the state), with the judge acting as arbiter of the legal rules. Under the adversary system, the burden is on the state to prove the charges beyond a reasonable doubt. This system of having the two parties publicly debate has proved to be the most effective method of achieving the truth regarding a set of circumstances. (Under the accusatory, or inquisitorial, system, which is used in continental Europe, the charge is evidence of guilt that the accused must disprove; the judge takes an active part in the proceedings.)

aging out The process in which the crime rate declines with the perpetrators' age.

aggressive preventive patrol A patrol technique designed to suppress crime before it occurs.

alien conspiracy theory The view that organized crime was imported by Europeans and that crime cartels restrict their membership to people of their own ethnic background.

alternative sanctions The group of punishments falling between probation and prison; "probation plus." Community-based sanctions, including house arrest and intensive supervision, serve as alternatives to incarceration.

American Society of Criminology The professional society of criminology that is devoted to enhancing the status of the discipline.

androgens Male sex hormones.

anger rape A rape motivated by the rapist's desire to release pent-up anger and rage.

anomie A condition produced by normlessness. Because of rapidly shifting moral values, a person has few guides to what is socially acceptable behavior.

antisocial personality Synonymous with psychopath, the antisocial personality is characterized by lack of normal responses to life situations, the inability to learn from punishment, and violent reactions to non-threatening events.

appeal A review of lower-court proceedings by a higher court. Appellate courts do not retry the case under review. Rather, the transcript of the lower-court case is read by the appellate judges, who determine the legality of lower-court proceedings. When appellate courts reverse lower-court judgments, it is usually because of "prejudicial error" (deprivation of rights), and the case is remanded for retrial.

appellate courts Courts that reconsider a case that has already been tried to determine whether the measures used complied with accepted rules of criminal procedure and were in line with constitutional doctrines.

arbitrage The practice of buying large blocks of stock in companies that are believed to be the target of corporate buy-outs or takeovers.

argot The unique language that influences the prison culture.

arraignment The step at which the accused are read the charges against them, asked how they plead, and advised of their rights. Possible pleas are guilty, not guilty, *nolo contendere,* and not guilty by reason of insanity.

arrest The taking of a person into the custody of the law, the legal purpose of which is to restrain the accused until he or she can be held accountable for the offense at court proceedings. The legal requirement for an arrest is probable cause. Arrests for investigation, suspicion, or harassment are improper and of doubtful legality. The police have the responsibility to use only the reasonable physical force necessary to make an arrest. The summons has been used as a substitute for arrest.

Aryan Brotherhood A white supremacist prison gang.

assembly-line justice The view that the justice process resembles an endless production line that handles most cases in a routine and perfunctory fashion.

atavistic traits According to Lombroso, the physical characteristics that distinguish born criminals from the general population and are throwbacks to animals or primitive people.

attainder The loss of all civil rights due to a conviction for a felony offense.

attorney general The senior federal prosecutor and cabinet member who heads the Justice Department.

Auburn system The prison system developed in New York during the nineteenth century that stressed congregate working conditions.

Augustus, John The individual credited with pioneering the concept of probation.

authoritarian A person whose personality revolves around blind obedience to authority.

authority conflict pathway The path to a criminal career that begins with early stubborn behavior and defiance of parents.

bail The monetary amount for or condition of pretrial release, normally set by a judge at the initial appearance. The purpose of bail is to ensure the return of the accused at subsequent proceedings. If the accused is unable to make bail, he or she is detained in jail. The Eighth Amendment provides that excessive bail shall not be required.

bail bonding The business of providing bail to needy offenders, usually at an exorbitant rate of interest.

Bail Reform Act of 1984 Federal legislation that provides for both greater emphasis on release on recognizance for nondangerous offenders and preventive detention for those who present a menace to the community.

base penalty The model sentence in a structured sentencing state, which can be enhanced or diminished to reflect aggravating or mitigating circumstances.

Beccaria, Cesare An eighteenth-century Italian philosopher who argued that crime could be controlled by punishments only severe enough to counterbalance the pleasure obtained from them.

behaviorism The branch of psychology concerned with the study of observable behavior rather than unconscious motives. It focuses on the relationship between the particular stimuli and people's responses to them.

bill of indictment A document submitted to a grand jury by the prosecutor asking it to take action and indict a suspect.

Bill of Rights The first ten amendments to the U.S. Constitution.

blameworthiness The amount of culpability or guilt a person maintains for participating in a particular criminal offense.

blue curtain According to William Westly, the secretive, insulated police culture that isolates the officer from the rest of society.

booking The administrative record of an arrest listing the offender's name, address, physical description, date of birth, employer, the time of arrest, offense, and name of arresting officer. Photographing and fingerprinting of the offender are also part of booking.

boot camp A short-term militaristic correctional facility in which inmates undergo intensive physical conditioning and discipline.

bot Under Anglo-Saxon law, the restitution paid for killing someone in an open fight.

bourgeoisie In Marxist theory, the owners of the means of production; the capitalist ruling class.

broken windows The term used to describe the role of the police as maintainers of community order and safety.

brothel A house of prostitution, typically run by a madam who sets prices and handles "business" arrangements.

brutalization effect The belief that capital punishment creates an atmosphere of brutality that enhances rather than deters the level of violence in society. The death penalty reinforces the view that violence is an appropriate response to provocations.

brutalization process According to Athens, the first stage in a violent career during which parents victimize children, causing them to develop a belligerent, angry demeanor.

burglary Breaking into and entering a home or structure for the purposes of committing a felony.

call girls Prostitutes who make dates via the phone and then service customers in hotel rooms or apartments. Call girls typically have a steady clientele who are repeat customers.

capital punishment The use of the death penalty to punish transgressors.

career criminal A person who repeatedly violates the law and organizes his or her life-style around criminality.

Carriers case A fifteenth-century case that defined the law of theft and reformulated the concept of taking the possessions of another.

challenge for cause Removing a juror because he or she is biased, has prior knowledge about a case, or for other reasons that demonstrate the individual's inability to render a fair and impartial judgment in a case.

chancery court A court created in fifteenth-century England to oversee the lives of high-born minors who were orphaned or otherwise could not care for themselves.

charge In a criminal case, the specific crime the defendant is accused of committing.

Chicago Crime Commission A citizen action group set up in Chicago to investigate problems in the criminal justice system and explore avenues for positive change; the forerunner of many such groups around the country.

child abuse Any physical, emotional, or sexual trauma to a child for which no reasonable explanation, such as an accident, can be found. Child abuse can also be a function of neglecting to give proper care and attention to a young child.

chronic offender According to Wolfgang, a delinquent offender who is arrested five or more times before he or she is 18 and who stands a good chance of becoming an adult criminal; these offenders are responsible for more than half of all serious crimes.

Christopher Commission An investigatory group led by Warren Christopher that investigated the Los Angeles Police Department in the wake of the Rodney King beating.

churning A white-collar crime in which a stockbroker makes repeated trades to fraudulently increase his or her commissions.

civil death The custom of terminating the civil rights of convicted felons; for example, forbidding them the right to vote or marry. No state uses civil death today.

civil law All law that is not criminal, including torts (personal wrongs), contract, property, maritime, and commercial law.

Civil Rights Division That part of the U.S. Justice Department that handles cases involving violations of civil rights guaranteed by the Constitution and federal law.

classification The procedure in which prisoners are categorized on the basis of their personal characteristics and criminal history and then assigned to an appropriate institution.

classical theory The theoretical perspective suggesting that: (1) people have free will to choose criminal or conventional behaviors; (2) people choose to commit crime for reasons of greed or personal need; and (3) crime can be controlled only by the fear of criminal sanctions.

Code of Hammurabi The first written criminal code developed in Babylonia about 2000 B.C.

coeducational prison An institution that houses both male and female inmates who share work and recreational facilities.

cognitive theory The study of the perception of reality; the mental processes required to understand the world we live in.

cohort study A study using a sample of subjects whose behavior is followed over a period of time.

common law Early English law, developed by judges, that incorporated Anglo-Saxon tribal custom, feudal rules and practices, and the everyday rules of behavior of local villages. Common law became the standardized law of the land in England and eventually formed the basis of the criminal law in the United States.

community policing A police strategy that emphasizes fear reduction, community organization, and order maintenance rather than crime fighting.

community service restitution An alternative sanction that requires an offender to work in the community at such tasks as cleaning public parks or helping handicapped children in lieu of an incarceration sentence.

community treatment The actions of correctional agencies that attempt to maintain the convicted offender in the community, instead of a secure facility; includes probation, parole, and residential programs.

compensation Financial aid awarded to the victims of crime to repay them for their loss and injuries.

complaint A sworn allegation made in writing to a court or judge that an individual is guilty of some designated (complained of) offense. This is often the first legal document filed regarding a criminal offense. The complaint can be "taken out" by the victim, the police officer, the district attorney, or other interested party. Although the complaint charges an offense, an indictment or information may be the formal charging document.

compliance A white-collar enforcement strategy that encourages law-abiding behavior through both the threat of economic sanctions and the promise of rewards for conformity.

concurrent sentences Prison sentences for two or more criminal acts that are served simultaneously.

conduct norms Behaviors expected of social group members. If group norms conflict with those of the general culture, members of the group may find themselves described as outcasts or criminals.

conflict view The view that human behavior is shaped by interpersonal conflict and that those who maintain social power will use it to further their own needs.

conjugal visit A prison program that allows inmates to receive private visits from their spouses for the purpose of maintaining normal interpersonal relationships.

consecutive sentences Prison sentences for two or more criminal acts that are served one after the other.

consensus view of crime The belief that the majority of citizens in a society share common ideals and work toward a common good and that crimes are acts that are outlawed because they conflict with the rules of the majority and are harmful to society.

constable The peacekeeper in early English towns. The constable organized citizens to protect his territory and supervised the night watch.

constructive intent The finding of criminal liability for an unintentional act that is the result of negligence or recklessness.

constructive possession In the crime of larceny, willingly giving up temporary physical possession of property but retaining legal ownership.

continuance A judicial order to continue a case without a finding to gather more information or allow the defendant to begin a community-based treatment program.

continuity of crime The view that crime begins early in life and continues throughout the life course. The best predictor of future criminality is past criminality.

contract system (attorney) Providing counsel to indigent offenders by having attorneys under contract to the county to handle all (or some) such cases.

contract system (convict) The system used earlier in the century in which inmates were leased out to private industry to work.

convict subculture The separate culture in the prison that has its own set of rewards and behaviors. The traditional culture is now being replaced by a violent gang culture.

conviction A judgment of guilt; a verdict by a jury, a plea by a defendant, or a judgment by a court that the accused is guilty as charged.

corporal punishment The use of physical chastisement, such as whipping or electroshock, to punish criminals.

corporate crime White-collar crime involving a legal violation by a corporate entity, such as price-fixing, restraint of trade, or hazardous waste dumping.

corpus delicti The body of the crime made up of the *actus reus* and *mens rea*.

corrections The agencies of justice that take custody

of offenders after their conviction and are entrusted with their treatment and control.

court administrator The individual who controls the operations of the courts system in a particular jurisdiction; he or she may be in charge of scheduling, juries, judicial assignment, and so on.

court of last resort A court that handles the final appeal on a matter. The U.S. Supreme Court is the official court of last resort for criminal matters.

courtroom work group The phrase used to denote that all parties in the adversary process work together to settle cases with the least amount of effort and conflict.

courts of limited jurisdiction Courts that handle misdemeanors and minor civil complaints.

covert pathway A path to a criminal career that begins with minor underhanded behavior and progresses to fire starting and theft.

crack A smokable form of purified cocaine that provides an immediate and powerful high.

crackdown The concentration of police resources on a particular problem area, such as street-level drug dealing, to eradicate or displace criminal activity.

crime A violation of societal rules of behavior as interpreted and expressed by a criminal legal code created by people holding social and political power. Individuals who violate these rules are subject to sanctions by state authority, social stigma, and loss of status.

crime control A model of criminal justice that emphasizes the control of dangerous offenders and the protection of society. Its advocates call for harsh punishments as a deterrent to crime, such as the death penalty.

crime displacement An effect of crime prevention efforts in which efforts to control crime in one area shift illegal activities to another.

crime fighter The police style that stresses dealing with hard crimes and arresting dangerous criminals.

Criminal Division The branch of the U.S. Justice Department that prosecutes federal criminal violations.

criminal justice process The decision-making points from the initial investigation or arrest by police to the eventual release of the offender and his or her reentry into society; the various sequential criminal justice stages through which the offender passes.

criminal law The body of rules that define crimes, set out their punishments, and mandate the procedures in carrying out the criminal justice process.

criminal sanction The right of the state to punish people if they violate the rules set down in the criminal code; the punishment connected to commission of a specific crime.

criminology The scientific study of the nature, extent, cause, and control of criminal behavior.

cross-examination The process in which the defense and the prosecution interrogate witnesses during a trial.

cruel and unusual punishment Physical punishment that is far in excess of that given to people under similar circumstances and is therefore banned by the Eighth Amendment. The death penalty has so far not been considered cruel and unusual if it is administered in a fair and nondiscriminatory fashion.

cultural transmission The concept that conduct norms are passed down from one generation to the next so that they become stable within the boundaries of a culture. Cultural transmission guarantees that group life-style and behavior are stable and predictable.

culture conflict According to Sellin, a condition brought about when the rules and norms of an individual's subcultural affiliation conflict with the role demands of conventional society.

culture of poverty The view that people in the lower class of society form a separate culture with its own values and norms that are in conflict with conventional society; the culture is self-maintaining and ongoing.

curtilage The fields attached to a house.

custodial convenience The principle of giving jailed inmates the minimum comforts required by law to contain the costs of incarceration.

cynicism The belief that most peoples' actions are motivated solely by personal needs and selfishness.

DARE The acronym for Drug Abuse Resistance Education, a school-based antidrug program initiated by the Los Angeles police and now adopted around the United States.

day fines Fines geared to the average daily income of the convicted offender in an effort to bring equity to the sentencing process.

day reporting centers Nonresidential, community-based treatment programs.

deadly force The ability of the police to kill suspects if they resist arrest or present a danger to an officer or the community. The police cannot use deadly force against an unarmed fleeing felon.

decriminalize To reduce the penalty for a criminal act but not actually legalize it.

defeminization The process by which policewomen become enculturated into the police profession at the expense of their feminine identity.

defendant The accused in criminal proceedings; he or she has the right to be present at each stage of the criminal justice process, except grand jury proceedings.

defense attorney The counsel for the defendant in a criminal trial who represents the individual from arrest to final appeal.

defensible space The principle that crime prevention can be achieved through modifying the physical environment to reduce the opportunity criminals have to commit crime.

degenerate anomalies According to Lombroso, the primitive physical characteristics that make criminals animalistic and savage.

deinstitutionalization The movement to remove as many offenders as possible from secure confinement and treat them in the community.

demeanor The way in which a person outwardly manifests his or her personality.

demystify The process by which Marxists unmask the true purpose of the capitalist system's rules and laws.

desert-based sentences Sentences in which the length is based on the seriousness of the criminal act and not the personal characteristics of the defendant or the deterrent impact of the law; punishment is based on what people have done and not on what they or others may do in the future.

desistance The process in which crime rate declines with the perpetrator's age; synonymous with the aging-out process.

detective The police agency assigned to investigate crimes after they have been reported, gather evidence, and identify the perpetrator.

detention Holding an offender in secure confinement before trial.

determinate sentences Fixed terms of incarceration, such as three years' imprisonment. Determinate sentences are felt by many to be too restrictive for rehabilitative purposes; the advantage is that offenders know how much time they have to serve, that is, when they will be released.

deterrence The act of preventing crime before it occurs by means of the threat of criminal sanctions.

developmental criminology A branch of criminology that examines change in a criminal career over the life course. Developmental factors include biological, social, and psychological change. Among the topics of developmental criminology are desistance, resistance, escalation, and specialization.

deviance Behavior that departs from the social norm.

differential association According to Sutherland, the principle that criminal acts are related to a person's exposure to an excess amount of antisocial attitudes and values.

diffusion of benefits An effect that occurs when an effort to control one type of crime has the unexpected benefit of reducing the incidence of another.

direct examination The questioning of one's own (prosecution or defense) witness during a trial.

directed verdict The right of a judge to direct a jury to acquit a defendant because the state has not proven the elements of the crime or otherwise has not established guilt according to law.

discouragement An effect that occurs when an effort made to eliminate one type of crime also controls others because it reduces the value of criminal activity by limiting access to desirable targets.

discretion The use of personal decision making and choice in carrying out operations in the criminal justice system. For example, police discretion can involve the decision to make an arrest, while prosecutorial discretion can involve the decision to accept a plea bargain.

disposition For juvenile offenders, the equivalent of sentencing for adult offenders. The theory is that disposition is more rehabilitative than retributive. Possible dispositions may be to dismiss the case, release the youth to the custody of his or her parents, place the offender on probation, or send him or her to an institution or state correctional institution.

disputatiousness In the subculture of violence, it is considered appropriate behavior for a person who has been offended to seek satisfaction through violent means.

district attorney The county prosecutor who is charged with bringing offenders to justice and enforcing the laws of the state.

diversion An alternative to criminal trial usually featuring counseling, job training, and educational opportunities.

DNA profiling The identification of criminal suspects by matching DNA samples taken from them with specimens found at crime scenes.

double bunking The practice of holding two or more inmates in a single cell because of prison overcrowding; upheld in *Rhodes v. Chapman*.

double marginality According to Alex, the social burden African-American police officers carry by being both minority-group members and law enforcement officers.

drift According to Matza, the view that youths move in and out of delinquency and that their life-styles can embrace both conventional and deviant values.

drug courier profile A way of identifying drug runners based on their personal characteristics; police may stop and question individuals based on the way they fit the characteristics contained in the profile.

Drug Enforcement Administration (DEA) The federal agency that enforces federal drug control laws.

due process The constitutional principle based on the concept of the primacy of the individual and the complementary concept of limitation on governmental power; a safeguard against arbitrary and unfair state procedures in judicial or administrative proceedings. Embodied in the due process concept are the basic rights of a defendant in criminal proceedings and the requisites for a fair trial.

Durham rule A definition of insanity used in New Hampshire that required that the crime be excused if it was a product of a mental illness.

early onset A term that refers to the assumption that a criminal career begins early in life and that people who are deviant at a very young age are the ones most likely to persist in crime.

economic compulsive behavior Behavior that occurs when drug users resort to violence to gain funds to support their habit.

economic crime An act in violation of the criminal law that is designed to bring financial gain to the offender.

economism The policy of controlling white-collar crime through monetary incentives and sanctions.

electroencephalogram (EEG) A device that can record the electronic impulses given off by the brain, commonly called brain waves.

embezzlement A type of larceny that involves taking the possessions of another (fraudulent conversion) that have been placed in the thief's lawful possession for safekeeping; for example, a bank teller misappropriating deposits or a stockbroker making off with a customer's account.

enterprise syndicate An organized crime group that profits from the sale of illegal goods and services, such as narcotics, pornography, and prostitution.

entrapment A criminal defense that maintains the police originated the criminal idea or initiated the criminal action.

entrepreneur One willing to take risks for profit in the marketplace.

equity The action or practice of awarding each his or her just due; sanctions based on equity seek to compensate individual victims and the general society for their losses due to crime.

exceptional circumstances doctrine Under this policy, courts would hear only those cases brought by inmates in which the circumstances indicated a total disregard for human dignity, while denying hearings to less serious crimes. Cases allowed access to the courts usually involved a situation of total denial of medical care.

exclusionary rule The principle that prohibits using evidence illegally obtained in a trial. Based on the Fourth Amendment "right of the people to be secure in their persons, houses, papers, and effects, against unreasonable searches and seizures," the rule is not a bar to prosecution, as legally obtained evidence may be available that may be used in a trial.

excuse A defense to a criminal charge in which the accused maintains he or she lacked the intent to commit the crime (*mens rea*).

ex post facto laws Laws that make criminal an act after it was committed or retroactively increase the penalty for a crime; for example, an *ex post facto* law could change shoplifting from a misdemeanor to a felony and penalize people with a prison term, even though they had been apprehended six months before. Such laws are unconstitutional.

expressive crime A crime that has no purpose except to accomplish the behavior at hand; for example, shooting someone, as opposed to creating monetary gain.

expressive violence Violence that is designed not for profit or gain but to vent rage, anger, or frustration.

extinction The condition in which a crime prevention effort has an immediate impact that then dissipates as criminals adjust to new conditions.

false pretenses Illegally obtaining money, goods, or merchandise from another by fraud or misprestentation.

Federal Bureau of Investigation (FBI) The arm of the U.S. Justice Department that investigates violations of federal law, gathers crime statistics, runs a comprehensive crime laboratory, and helps train local law enforcement officers.

felony A more serious offense that carries a penalty of incarceration in a state prison, usually for one year or more. Persons convicted of felony offenses lose such rights as the right to vote, to hold elective office, or to maintain certain licenses.

fence A buyer and seller of stolen merchandise.

field training officer A senior police officer who trains recruits in the field.

fixed time rule A policy in which people must be tried within a stated period after their arrest; overruled in *Barker v. Wingo,* which created a balancing test.

flat or fixed sentencing A sentencing model that mandates that all people who are convicted of a specific offense and who are sent to prison must receive the same length of incarceration.

focal concerns According to Miller, the value orientations of lower-class cultures whose features include the need for excitement, trouble, smartness, fate, and personal autonomy.

folkways Generally followed customs that do not have moral values attached to them, such as not interrupting people when they are speaking.

foot patrols Police patrols that take officers out of cars and put them on a walking beat to strengthen ties with the community.

forfeiture The seizure of personal property by the state as a civil or criminal penalty.

fraud The taking of the possessions of another through deception or cheating, such as selling a person a desk that is represented as an antique but is known to be a copy.

free venture Privately run industries in a prison setting in which the inmates work for wages and the goods are sold for profit.

functionalism The sociological perspective that suggests that each part of society makes a contribution to the maintenance of the whole. Functionalism stresses social cooperation and consensus of values and beliefs among a majority of society's members.

furlough A correctional policy that allows inmates to leave the institution for vocational or educational training, for employment, or to maintain family ties.

general deterrence A crime-control policy that depends on the fear of criminal penalties. General deterrence measures, such as long prison sentences for violent crimes, are aimed at convincing the potential law violator that the pains associated with crime outweigh its benefits.

general intent Actions that on their face indicate a criminal purpose; for example, breaking into a locked building or trespassing on someone's property.

gentrification A process of reclaiming and reconditioning deteriorated neighborhoods by refurbishing depressed real estate and then renting or selling the properties to upper-middle-class professionals.

good faith exception The principle of law that holds that evidence may be used in a criminal trial even though the search warrant used to obtain it is technically faulty, if the police acted in good faith and to the best of their ability when they sought to obtain it from a judge.

good-time credit Time taken off a prison sentence in exchange for good behavior within the institution; for example, ten days per month. The device is used to limit disciplinary problems within the prison.

grand jury A group (usually comprised of 23 citizens) chosen to hear testimony in secret and to issue formal criminal accusations (indictments). It also serves an investigatory function.

grass eaters A term used for police officers who accept payoffs when their everyday duties place them in a position to be solicited by the public.

greenmail The process by which an arbitrager buys

large blocks of a company's stock and threatens to take over the company and replace the management. To ward off the threat to their positions, members of management use company funds to repurchase the shares at a much higher price, creating huge profits for the corporate raiders.

guardian *ad litem* A court-appointed attorney who protects the interests of a child in cases involving the child's welfare.

habeas corpus See **writ of habeas corpus.**

habitual criminal statutes Laws that require long-term or life sentences for offenders who have multiple felony convictions.

halfway house A community-based correctional facility that houses inmates before their outright release so that they can become gradually acclimated to conventional society.

Hallcrest Report A government-sponsored national survey of the private security industry conducted by the Hallcrest Corporation.

hands-off doctrine The judicial policy of not interfering in the administrative affairs of a prison.

hate crimes Acts of violence or intimidation designed to terrorize or frighten people considered undesirable because of their race, religion, ethnic origin, or sexual orientation.

hearsay evidence Testimony that is not firsthand but relates information told by a second party.

hot spots of crime According to Sherman, a significant portion of all police calls originate from only a few locations. These hot spots include taverns and housing projects.

house of correction A county correctional institution generally used for the incarceration of more serious misdemeanants, whose sentences are usually less than one year.

Howard, John An eighteenth-century British penal reformer who wrote *The State of Prisons.*

hue and cry In medieval England, the policy of self-help used in villages demanded that everyone respond if a citizen raised a hue and cry to get their aid.

hulks Mothballed ships that were used to house prisoners in eighteenth-century England.

hundred In medieval England, a group of one hundred families that were responsible for maintaining the order and trying minor offenses.

hustle The underground prison economy.

importation model The view that the violent prison culture reflects the criminal culture of the outside world and is neither developed in nor unique to prisons.

impulsivity According to Gottfredson and Hirschi's general theory, the trait that produces criminal behavior. Impulsive people lack self-control.

incapacitation The policy of keeping dangerous criminals in confinement to eliminate the risk of their repeating their offense in society.

indentured servant Prior to the eighteenth century, a debtor or convicted offender who would work off his or her debt by being assigned a term of servitude to a master who purchased the services from the state.

indeterminate sentence A term of incarceration with a stated minimum and maximum length; for example, a sentence to prison for a period of from three to ten years. The prisoner would be eligible for parole after the minimum sentence had been served. Based on the belief that sentences should fit the criminal, indeterminate sentences allow individualized sentences and provide for sentencing flexibility. Judges can set a high minimum to override the purpose of the indeterminate sentence.

index crimes The eight crimes that, because of their seriousness and frequency, the FBI reports the incidence of in the annual Uniform Crime Reports. Index crimes include murder, rape, assault, robbery, burglary, arson, larceny, and motor vehicle theft.

indictment A written accusation returned by a grand jury charging an individual with a specified crime after determination of probable cause; the prosecutor presents enough evidence (a *prima facie* case) to establish probable cause.

inevitable discovery A rule of law that states that evidence that almost assuredly would be independently discovered can be used in a court of law, even though it was obtained in violation of legal rules and practices.

information Like the indictment, a formal charging document. The prosecuting attorney makes out the information and files it in court. Probable cause is determined at the preliminary hearing, which, unlike grand jury proceedings, is public and attended by the accused and his or her attorney.

initial appearance   The stage in the justice process during which the suspect is brought before a magistrate for consideration of bail. The suspect must be taken for initial appearance within a "reasonable time" after arrest. For petty offenses, this step often serves as the final criminal proceeding, either through adjudication by a judge or the offering of a guilty plea.

inmate social code   The informal set of rules that govern inmates.

inmate subculture   The loosely defined culture that pervades prisons and has its own norms, rules, and language.

insanity   A legal defense that maintains that a defendant was incapable of forming criminal intent because he or she suffered from a defect of reason or mental illness.

insider trading   The illegal buying of stock in a company based on information provided by another who has a fiduciary interest in the company, such as an employee or an attorney or accountant retained by the firm. Federal laws and the rules of the Security and Exchange Commission require that all profits from such trading be returned and provide for both fines and a prison sentence.

instrumental Marxist theory   The view that capitalist institutions, such as the criminal justice system, have as their main purpose the control of the poor to maintain the hegemony of the wealthy.

instrumental violence   Violence that is designed to improve the financial or social position of the criminal.

intensive probation supervision   A type of intermediate sanction involving small probation caseloads and strict daily or weekly monitoring.

interactional theory   According to Thornberry, interaction with institutions and events during the life course determines criminal behavior patterns. Crimogenic influences evolve over time.

interactionist perspective   The view that one's perception of reality is significantly influenced by one's interpretations of the reactions of others to similar events and stimuli.

interrogation   The method of accumulating evidence in the form of information or confessions from suspects by police; questioning that has been restricted because of concern about the use of brutal and coercive methods and to protect against self-incrimination.

investigation   An inquiry concerning suspected criminal behavior for the purpose of identifying offenders or gathering further evidence to assist the prosecution of apprehended offenders.

jail   A place to detain people awaiting trial, hold drunks and disorderly individuals, and confine convicted misdemeanants serving sentences of less than one year.

jail house lawyer   An inmate trained in law or otherwise educated who helps other inmates prepare legal briefs and appeals.

just desert   The philosophy of justice that asserts that those who violate the rights of others deserve to be punished. The severity of punishment should be commensurate with the seriousness of the crime.

justice model   A philosophy of corrections that stresses determinant sentences, abolition of parole, and the view that prisons are places of punishment and not rehabilitation.

justification   A defense to a criminal charge in which the accused maintains that his or her actions were justified by the circumstances and therefore he or she should not be held criminally liable.

juvenile delinquency   Participation in illegal behavior by a minor who falls under a statutory age limit.

juvenile justice process   Court proceedings for youths within the juvenile age group that differ from the adult criminal process. Originally, under the paternal (*parens patriae*) philosophy, juvenile procedures are informal and nonadversary, invoked *for* the juvenile offender rather than against him or her; a petition instead of a complaint is filed; courts make findings of involvement or adjudication of delinquency instead of convictions; and juvenile offenders receive dispositions instead of sentences. Court decisions (*In re Kent* and *In re Gault*) have increased the adversary nature of juvenile court proceedings. However, the philosophy remains one of diminishing the stigma of delinquency and providing for the youth's well-being and rehabilitation rather than seeking retribution.

Kansas City study   An experimental program that evaluated the effectiveness of patrol. The Kansas City study found that the presence of patrol officers had little deterrent effect.

Knapp Commission   A public body that led an investigation into police corruption in New York and uncovered a widespread network of payoffs and bribes.

labeling   The process by which a person becomes fixed with a negative identity, such as "criminal" or "ex-con," and is forced to suffer the consequences of outcast status.

landmark decision A decision handed down by the Supreme Court that becomes the law of the land and serves as precedence for similar legal issues.

latent trait A stable feature, characteristic, property, or condition, present at birth or soon after, that makes some people crime-prone over the life course.

left realism A branch of conflict theory that holds that crime is a "real" social problem experienced by the lower classes. Lower-class concerns about crime must be addressed by radical scholars.

legalization The removal of all criminal penalties from a previously outlawed act.

life course The study of changes in criminal offending patterns over a person's entire life. Are there conditions or events that occur later in life that influence the way people behave, or is behavior predetermined by social or personal conditions at birth?

life history A research method that uses the experiences of an individual as the unit of analysis; for example, using the life experience of an individual gang member to understand the natural history of gang membership.

longitudinal cohort study Research that tracks the development of a group of subjects over time.

lower courts A generic term referring to those courts that have jurisdiction over misdemeanors and conduct preliminary investigations of felony charges.

make-believe families Peer units formed by women in prison to compensate for the loss of family and loved ones that contain mother and father figures.

Mala in se **crimes** Acts that are outlawed because they violate basic moral values, such as rape, murder, assault, and robbery.

Mala prohibitum **crimes** Acts that are outlawed because they clash with current norms and public opinion, such as tax, traffic, and drug laws.

mandamus See **writ of mandamus.**

mandatory sentence A statutory requirement that a certain penalty shall be set and carried out in all cases on conviction for a specified offense or series of offenses.

Manhattan Bail Project The innovative experiment in bail reform that introduced and successfully tested the concept of release on recognizance.

Mann Act Federal legislation that made it a crime to transport women across state lines for the purpose of prostitution.

marital exemption The practice in some states of prohibiting the prosecution of husbands for the rape of their wives.

masculinity hypothesis The view that women who commit crimes have biological and psychological traits similar to those of men.

mass murder The killing of a large number of people in a single incident by an offender who typically does not seek concealment or escape.

matricide The murder of a mother by her son or daughter.

maxi-maxi prisons High-security prisons, based on the federal prison in Marion, Illinois, that house the most dangerous inmates in around-the-clock solitary confinement.

maximum security prisons Correctional institutions that house dangerous felons and maintain strict security measures, high walls, and limited contact with the outside world.

meat eaters A term used to describe police officers who actively solicit bribes and vigorously engage in corrupt practices.

medical model A view of corrections that holds that convicted offenders are victims of their environment who need care and treatment to be transformed into valuable members of society.

medium-security prisons Less secure institutions that house nonviolent offenders and provide more opportunities for contact with the outside world.

mens rea Guilty mind. The mental element of a crime or the intent to commit a criminal act.

methadone A synthetic narcotic that is used as a substitute for heroin in drug-control efforts.

middle-class measuring rods According to Cohen, the standards by which teachers and other representatives of state authority evaluate lower-class youths. Because they cannot live up to middle-class standards, lower-class youths are bound for failure, which gives rise to frustration and anger at conventional society.

minimum-security prisons The least secure institutions that house white-collar and nonviolent offenders, maintain a few security measures, and have liberal furlough and visitation policies.

Miranda warning The result of two U.S. Supreme Court decisions (*Escobedo v. Illinois* [378 U.S. 478] and *Miranda v. Arizona* [384 U.S. 436]) that require police officers to inform individuals under arrest of their constitutional right to remain silent and to know that their statements can later be used against them in court, that they can have an attorney present to help them, and that the state will pay for an attorney if they cannot afford to hire one. Although aimed at protecting an individual during in-custody interrogation, the warning must also be given when the investigation shifts from the investigatory to the accusatory stage, that is, when suspicion begins to focus on an individual.

misdemeanor A minor crime usually punished by less than one year's imprisonment in a local institution, such as a county jail.

Missouri Plan A way of picking judges through nonpartisan elections as a means of ensuring judicial performance standards.

Mollen Commission An investigative unit set up to inquire into police corruption in New York in the 1990s.

monetary restitution A sanction that requires that convicted offenders compensate crime victims by reimbursing them for out-of-pocket losses caused by the crime. Losses can include property damage, lost wages, and medical costs.

moonlighting The practice of police officers holding after-hours jobs in private security or other related professions.

moral crusades Efforts by interest-group members to stamp out behavior that they find objectionable. Typically, moral crusades are directed at public order crimes, such as drug abuse or pornography.

moral entrepreneurs People who use their influence to shape the legal process in ways they see fit.

motion An oral or written request asking the court to make a specified finding, decision, or order.

murder transaction The concept that murder is usually a result of behavior interactions between the victim and the offender.

National Crime Survey The ongoing victimization study conducted jointly by the Justice Department and the U.S. Census Bureau that surveys victims about their experiences with law violation.

neighborhood policing A style of police management that emphasizes community-level crime-fighting programs and initiatives.

neurotics People who fear that their primitive id impulses will dominate their personality.

niche A way of adapting to the prison community that stresses finding one's place in the system rather than fighting for one's individual rights.

no bill A decision by a grand jury not to indict a criminal suspect.

nolle prosequi The term used when a prosecutor decides to drop a case after a complaint has been formally made. Reasons for a *nolle prosequi* include evidence insufficiency, reluctance of witnesses to testify, police error, and office policy.

nolo contendere No contest. An admission of guilt in a criminal case with the condition that the finding cannot be used against the defendant in any subsequent civil cases.

nonintervention A justice philosophy that emphasizes the least intrusive treatment possible. Among its central policies are decarceration, diversion, and decriminalization. Less is better.

obscenity According to current legal theory, sexually explicit material that lacks a serious purpose and appeals solely to the prurient interest of the viewer. While nudity per se is not usually considered obscene, open sexual behavior, masturbation, and exhibition of the genitals is banned in many communities.

official crime Criminal behavior that has been recorded by the police.

opportunist robber Someone who steals small amounts when a vulnerable target presents itself.

organizational crime Crimes that involve large corporations and their efforts to control the marketplace and earn huge profits through unlawful bidding, unfair advertising, monopolistic practices, and other illegal means.

paraphilias Bizarre or abnormal sexual practices that may involve recurrent sexual urges focused on objects, humiliation, or children.

parole The early release of a prisoner from imprisonment subject to conditions set by a parole board. Depending on the jurisdiction, inmates must serve a certain proportion of their sentences before becoming eligible for parole. If an inmate is granted parole, the conditions of which may require him or her to report regularly to a parole officer, refrain from criminal conduct, maintain and support his or her family, avoid contact with other convicted criminals, abstain from using alcohol and drugs, remain within the jurisdiction, and so on. Violations of the conditions of parole may result in revocation of parole, in which case the individual will be returned to prison. The concept behind parole is to allow the release of the offender to community supervision, where rehabilitation and readjustment will be facilitated.

parricide The killing of a close relative by a child.

partial deterrent A legal measure designed to restrict or control rather than eliminate an undesirable act.

particularity The requirement that a search warrant state precisely where the search is to take place and what items are to be seized.

paternalism Male domination. A paternalistic family, for instance, is one in which the father is the dominant authority figure.

pathways A term that refers to the view that a life of crime may have more than one entry point or origin.

patriarchy A male-dominated system. The patriarchal family is one dominated by the father.

patricide The murder of a father by his son or daughter.

peacemaking A branch of conflict theory that stresses humanism, mediation, and conflict resolution as a means to end crime.

Peel, Sir Robert The British home secretary who in 1829 organized the London Metropolitan Police, the first local police force.

Pennsylvania system The prison system developed in Pennsylvania during the nineteenth century that stressed total isolation and individual penitence as a means of reform.

peremptory challenge The dismissal of a potential juror by either the prosecution or the defense for unexplained, discretionary reasons.

persisters Those criminals who do not age out of crime; chronic delinquents who continue offending into their adulthood.

pilferage Theft by employees through stealth or deception.

plain view Evidence that is in plain view to police officers may be seized without a search warrant.

plea An answer to formal charges by an accused. Possible pleas are guilty, not guilty, *nolo contendere,* and not guilty by reason of insanity. A guilty plea is a confession of the offense as charged. A not guilty plea is a denial of the charge and places the burden on the prosecution to prove the elements of the offense.

plea bargaining The discussion between the defense counsel and the prosecution by which the accused agrees to plead guilty for certain considerations. The advantage to the defendant may be a reduction of the charges, a lenient sentence, or (in the case of multiple charges) dropped charges. The advantage to the prosecution is that a conviction is obtained without the time and expense of lengthy trial proceedings.

pledge system An early method of law enforcement that relied on self-help and mutual aid.

police discretion The ability of police officers to enforce the law selectively. Police officers in the field have great latitude to use their discretion in deciding whether to invoke their arrest powers.

police officer style The belief that the bulk of police officers can be classified into ideal personality types. Popular style types include: supercops, who desire to enforce only serious crimes, such as robbery and rape; professionals, who use a broad definition of police work; service-oriented officers, who see their job as a helping profession; the avoiders, who do as little as possible. The actual existence of ideal police officer types has been much debated.

poor laws Seventeenth-century laws that bound out vagrants and abandoned children to masters as indentured servants.

population All people who share a particular personal characteristic, for example, all high school students or all police officers.

positivism The branch of social science that uses the scientific method of the natural sciences and suggests that human behavior is a product of social, biological, psychological, or economic forces.

power groups Criminal organizations that do not provide services or illegal goods but trade exclusively in violence and extortion.

power rape A rape motivated by the need for sexual conquest.

power syndicates Organized crime groups that use force and violence to extort money from legitimate businesses and other criminal groups engaged in illegal business enterprises.

praxis The application of theory in action; in Marxist criminology, applying theory to promote revolution.

preliminary hearings The step at which criminal charges initiated by an information are tested for probable cause; the prosecution presents enough evidence to establish probable cause, that is, a *prima facie* case. The hearing is public and may be attended by the accused and his or her attorney.

preponderance of the evidence The level of proof in civil cases; more than half the evidence supports the allegations of one side.

presentence report An investigation performed by a probation officer attached to a trial court after the conviction of a defendant. The report contains information about the defendant's background, education, previous employment, and family; his or her own statement concerning the offense; prior criminal record; interviews with neighbors or acquaintances; and his or her mental and physical condition (that is, information that would not be made record in the case of a guilty plea or that would be inadmissible as evidence at a trial but could be influential and important at the sentencing stage). After conviction, a judge sets a date for sentencing (usually ten days to two weeks from the date of conviction), during which time the presentence report is made. The report is required in felony cases in federal courts and in many states, is optional with the judge in some states, and in others is mandatory before convicted offenders can be placed on probation. In the case of juvenile offenders, the presentence report is also known as a social history report.

presumptive sentences Sentencing structures that provide an average sentence that should be served along with the option of extending or decreasing the punishment because of aggravating or mitigating circumstances.

preventive detention The practice of holding dangerous suspects before trial without bail.

prison A state or federal correctional institution for incarceration of felony offenders for terms of one year or more.

probability sample A randomly drawn sample in which each member of the population being tapped has an equal chance of being selected.

probable cause The evidentiary criterion necessary to sustain an arrest or the issuance of an arrest or search warrant; less than absolute certainty or "beyond a reasonable doubt" but greater than mere suspicion or "hunch." A set of facts, information, circumstances, or conditions that would lead a reasonable person to believe that an offense was committed and that the accused committed that offense. An arrest made without probable cause may be susceptible to prosecution as an illegal arrest under "false imprisonment" statutes.

probation A sentence entailing the conditional release of a convicted offender into the community under the supervision of the court (in the form of a probation officer), subject to certain conditions for a specified time. The conditions are usually similar to those of parole. (Probation is a sentence, an alternative to incarceration; parole is administrative release from incarceration.) Violation of the conditions of probation may result in revocation of probation.

problem-oriented policing A style of police management that stresses proactive problem solving rather than reactive crime fighting.

pro bono The practice by private attorneys of taking without fee the cases of indigent offenders as a service to the profession and the community.

procedural law The rules that define the operation of criminal proceedings. Procedural law describes the methods that must be followed in obtaining warrants, investigating offenses, affecting lawful arrests, using force, conducting trials, introducing evidence, sentencing convicted offenders, and reviewing cases by appellate courts (in general, legislatures have ignored post-sentencing procedures). While the substantive law defines criminal offenses, procedural law delineates how the substantive offenses are to be enforced.

progressives Early twentieth-century reformers who believed that state action could relieve human ills.

proof beyond a reasonable doubt The standard of proof needed to convict in a criminal case. The evidence offered in court does not have to amount to absolute certainty, but it should leave no reasonable doubt that the defendant committed the alleged crime.

property in service The eighteenth-century practice of selling control of inmates to shipmasters who would then transport them to colonies for sale as indentured servants.

proximity hypothesis The view that people become crime victims because they live or work in areas with large criminal populations.

psychopath A person whose personality is characterized by a lack of warmth and feeling, inappropriate behavior responses, and an inability to learn from experience. While some psychologists view psychopathy as a result of childhood trauma, others see it as a result of biological abnormality.

psychotics People whose id has broken free and now dominates their personality. Psychotics suffer from delusions and experience hallucinations and sudden mood shifts.

Racketeer Influenced and Corrupt Organizations Act (RICO) Federal legislation that enables prosecutors to bring additional criminal or civil charges against people whose multiple criminal acts constitute a conspiracy. RICO features monetary penalties that allow the government to confiscate all profits derived from criminal activities. Originally intended to be used against organized criminals, RICO also has been employed against white-collar criminals.

random sample A sample selected on the basis of chance so that each person in the population has an equal opportunity to be selected.

rational choice The view that crime is a function of a decision-making process in which the potential offender weighs the potential costs and benefits of an illegal act.

reaction formation According to Cohen, rejecting goals and standards that seem impossible to achieve. Because a boy cannot hope to get into college, for example, he considers higher education a waste of time.

reasonable competence The standard by which legal representation is judged: did the defendant receive a reasonable level of legal aid?

reasonable doubt A jury cannot find the defendant guilty if a reasonable doubt exists that he or she committed the crime. The level of proof needed to convict in a criminal trial is "beyond a reasonable doubt."

recoupment Forcing indigents to repay the state for at least part of their legal costs.

reintegration The correctional philosophy that stresses reintroducing the inmate into the community.

reintegrative shaming A method of correction that encourages offenders to confront their misdeeds, experience shame because of the harm they caused, and then be reincluded in society.

relative deprivation The condition that exists when people of wealth and poverty live in close proximity to one another. Some criminologists attribute crime-rate differentials to relative deprivation.

release on recognizance A nonmonetary condition for the pretrial release of an accused individual; an alternative to monetary bail that is granted after the court determines that the accused has ties in the community, has no prior record of default, and is likely to appear at subsequent proceedings.

restitution A condition of probation in which the offender repays society or the victim of crime for the trouble the offender caused. Monetary restitution involves a direct payment to the victim as a form of compensation. Community-service restitution may be used in victimless crimes and involves work in the community in lieu of more severe criminal penalties.

routine activities The view that crime is a "normal" function of the routine activities of modern living. Offenses can be expected if there is a suitable target that is not protected by capable guardians.

sadistic rape A rape motivated by the offender's desire to torment and abuse the victim.

sample A limited number of people selected for study from a population.

schizophrenia A type of psychosis often marked by bizarre behavior, hallucinations, loss of thought control, and inappropriate emotional responses. There are different types of schizophrenia: catatonic, which characteristically involves impairment of motor activity; paranoid, which is characterized by delusions of persecution; and hebephrenic, which is characterized by immature behavior and giddiness.

search and seizure The legal term, contained in the Fourth Amendment to the U.S. Constitution, that refers to the searching for and carrying away of evidence by police during a criminal investigation.

secondary deviance According to Lemert, the accepting of deviant labels as a personal identity.

seductions of crime According to Katz, the visceral and emotional appeal that the situation of crime has for those who engage in illegal acts.

selective incapacitation The policy of creating enhanced prison sentences for the relatively small group of dangerous chronic offenders.

self-report study A research approach that requires subjects to reveal their own participation in delinquent or criminal acts.

sentence The criminal sanction imposed by the court on a convicted defendant, usually in the form of a fine, incarceration, or probation. Sentencing may be carried out by a judge, jury, or sentencing council (panel or judges), depending on the statutes of the jurisdiction.

sequester The insulation of jurors from the outside world so that their decision making cannot be influenced or affected by extralegal events.

serial murder The killing of a large number of people over time by an offender who seeks to escape detection.

sheriff The chief law enforcement officer in a county.

shield laws Laws designed to protect rape victims by prohibiting the defense attorney from inquiring about their previous sexual relationships.

shire reeve In early England, the senior law enforcement figure in a county, the forerunner of today's sheriff.

shock incarceration A short prison sentence served in boot camp-type facilities.

shock probation A sentence in which offenders serve a short prison term to impress them with the pains of imprisonment before they begin probation.

short-run hedonism According to Cohen, the desire of lower-class gang youths to engage in behavior that will give them immediate gratification and excitement but in the long run will be dysfunctional and negativistic.

situational crime prevention A method of crime prevention that stresses tactics and strategies to eliminate or reduce particular crimes in narrow settings; for example, reducing burglaries in a housing project by increasing lighting and installing security alarms.

skeezers Prostitutes who trade sex for drugs, usually crack.

social capital Positive relations with individuals and institutions that are life-sustaining.

social control The ability of society and its institutions to control, manage, restrain, or direct human behavior.

social disorganization A neighborhood or area marked by culture conflict, lack of cohesiveness, transient population, insufficient social organizations, and anomie.

sodomy Illegal sexual intercourse. Sodomy has no single definition, and acts included within its scope are usually defined by state statute.

special (specific) deterrence A crime control policy that suggests that punishment should be severe enough to convince convicted offenders never to repeat their criminal activity.

specific intent The intent to accomplish a specific purpose as an element of crime; for example, breaking into someone's house for the express purpose of stealing jewels.

stare decisis To stand by decided cases. The legal principle by which the decision or holding in an earlier case becomes the standard by which subsequent similar cases are judged.

statutory law Laws created by legislative bodies to meet changing social conditions, public opinion, and custom.

stigma An enduring label that taints a person's identity and changes him or her in the eyes of others.

sting An undercover police operation in which police pose as criminals to trap law violators.

stoopers Petty criminals who earn their living by retrieving winning tickets that are accidentally discarded by racetrack patrons.

stop and frisk The situation where police officers who are suspicious of an individual run their hands lightly over the suspect's outer garments to determine if the person is carrying a concealed weapon. Also called a "patdown" or "threshold inquiry," a stop and frisk is intended to stop short of any activity that could be considered a violation of Fourth Amendment rights.

stradom formations According to the Schwendingers, adolescent social networks whose members have distinct dress, grooming, and linguistic behaviors.

strain The emotional turmoil and conflict caused when people believe they cannot achieve their desires and goals through legitimate means.

street crime Illegal acts designed to prey on the public through theft, damage, and violence.

strict-liability crimes Illegal acts whose elements do not contain the need for intent, or *mens rea;* usually acts that endanger the public welfare, such as illegal dumping of toxic wastes.

structural Marxist theory The view that the law and the justice system are designed to maintain the capitalist system and that members of both the owner and worker classes whose behavior threatens the stability of the system will be sanctioned.

subculture A group that is loosely part of the dominant culture but maintains a unique set of values, beliefs, and traditions.

subpoena A court order requiring the recipient to appear in court on an indicated time and date.

substantive criminal laws A body of specific rules that declare what conduct is criminal and prescribe the punishment to be imposed for such conduct.

suitable targets According to routine activities theory, a target for crime that is relatively valuable, easily transportable, and not capably guarded.

summons An alternative to arrest usually used for petty or traffic offenses; a written order notifying an individual that he or she has been charged with an offense. A summons directs the person to appear in court to answer the charge. It is used primarily in instances of low risk, where the person will not be required to appear at a later date. The summons is advantageous to police officers in that they are freed from having to spend time on arrest and booking procedures; it is advantageous to the accused in that he or she is spared time in jail.

sureties During the Middle Ages, people who made themselves responsible for the behavior of offenders released in their care.

surplus value The Marxist view that the laboring classes produce wealth that far exceeds their wages and goes to the capitalist class as profits.

surrebuttal Introducing witnesses during a criminal trial to disprove damaging testimony by other witnesses.

suspended sentence A prison term that is delayed while the defendant undergoes a period of community treatment. If the treatment is successful, the prison sentence is terminated.

symbolic interaction The sociological view that people communicate through symbols. People interpret symbolic communication and incorporate it within their personality. A person's view of reality, then, depends on his or her interpretation of symbolic gestures.

systemic link Violent behavior that results from the conflict inherent in the drug trade.

team policing An experimental police technique in which groups of officers are assigned to a particular area of the city on a 24-hour basis.

technical parole violation Revocation of parole because conditions set by correctional authorities have been violated.

technique of neutralization According to neutralization theory, the ability of delinquent youth to neutralize moral constraints so they may drift into criminal acts.

temperance movement An effort to prohibit the sale of liquor in the United States that resulted in the passage of the Eighteenth Amendment to the Constitution in 1919, which prohibited the sale of alcoholic beverages.

thanatos According to Freud, the instinctual drive toward aggression and violence.

threshold inquiry A term used to describe a stop and frisk.

tort The law of personal wrongs and damage. Tort-type actions include negligence, libel, slander, assault, and trespass.

totality of the circumstances A legal doctrine that mandates that a decision maker consider all the issues and circumstances of a case before judging the outcome. For example, before concluding whether a suspect understood a *Miranda* warning, a judge must consider the totality of the circumstances under which the warning was given. The suspect's age, intelligence, and competency may influence his or her understanding and judgment.

transferred intent If an illegal yet unintended act results from the intent to commit a crime, that act is also considered illegal.

transitional neighborhood An area undergoing a shift in population and structure, usually from middle-class residential to lower-class mixed use.

turning points According to Laub and Sampson, the life events that alter the development of a criminal career.

type I offenses Another term for index crimes.

type II offenses All crimes other than index and minor traffic offenses. The FBI records annual arrest information for Type II offenses.

venire The group called for jury duty from which jury panels are selected.

vice squad Police officers assigned to enforce morally tinged laws, such as those on prostitution, gambling, and pornography.

victimization survey A crime-measurement technique that surveys citizens to measure their experiences as victims of crime.

victimology The study of the victim's role in criminal transactions.

victim-precipitated A description of a crime in which the victim's behavior was the spark that ignited the subsequent offense; for example, the victim abused the offender verbally or physically.

virulency According to Athens, a stage in a violent career in which criminals develop a violent identity that makes them feared. They consequently enjoy hurting others.

voir dire The process in which a potential jury panel is questioned by the prosecution and the defense to select jurors who are unbiased and objective.

waiver The act of voluntarily relinquishing a right or advantage; often used in the context of waiving one's right to counsel (for example, the *Miranda* warning) or waiving certain steps in the criminal justice process (such as the preliminary hearing). Essential to waiver is the voluntary consent of the individual.

warrant A written court order issued by a magistrate authorizing and directing that an individual be taken into custody to answer criminal charges.

watch system During the Middle Ages in England, men were organized in church parishes to guard at night against disturbances and breaches of the peace under the direction of the local constable.

watchman A style of policing that stresses reacting to calls for service rather than aggressively pursuing crime.

wergild Under medieval law, the money paid by the offender to compensate the victim and the state for a criminal offense.

white-collar crime Illegal acts that capitalize on a person's place in the marketplace. White-collar crimes can involve theft, embezzlement, fraud, market manipulation, restraint of trade, and false advertising.

Wickersham Commission Created in 1931 by President Herbert Hoover to investigate the state of the nation's police forces, the commission found that police training was inadequate and that the average officer was incapable of effectively carrying out his duties.

widen the net The charge that programs designed to divert offenders from the justice system actually enmesh them further in the process by substituting more intrusive treatment programs for less intrusive punishment-oriented outcomes.

wite The portion of the wergild that went to the victim's family.

work furlough A prison treatment program that allows inmates to be released during the day to work in the community and returned to prison at night.

writ of certiorari An order of a superior court requesting that the record of an inferior court (or administrative body) be brought forward for review or inspection.

writ of habeas corpus A judicial order requesting that a person detaining another produce the body of the prisoner and give reasons for his or her capture and detention. Habeas corpus is a legal device used to request that a judicial body review the reasons for a person's confinement and the conditions of confinement. Habeas corpus is known as "the great writ."

writ of mandamus An order of a superior court commanding that a lower court, administrative body, or executive body perform a specific function. It is commonly used to restore rights and privileges lost to a defendant through illegal means.

Subject Index

Name Index

Table of Cases